ANNALS AND ANTIQUITIES OF RAJASTHAN

ANNALS AND ANTIQUITIES
OF
RAJASTHAN

OR THE CENTRAL AND WESTERN RAJPUT STATES OF INDIA

BY

LIEUT.-COL. JAMES TOD
LATE POLITICAL AGENT TO THE WESTERN RAJPUT STATES

EDITED WITH AN INTRODUCTION AND NOTES BY

WILLIAM CROOKE, C.I.E.
HON, D.SC. OXON., B.A., F.R.A.I.,
LATE OF THE INDIAN CIVIL SERVICE

IN THREE VOLUMES

VOL. I

GYAN

Published by

Gyan Publishing House
5, Ansari Road
Daryaganj, New Delhi-110002
Phone: 011-47034999, 9811692060
E-mail: books@gyanbooks.com

Distribution Network
gyanbooks.com
India, USA, Canada, UK, Australia, France

ISBN : 978-81-212-3130-5 (Set)
ISBN : 978-81-212-4823-5 (HB)
First Published, London, 1920

2nd Impression 2020

Printed at: Gyan Press, Delhi.

Annals and Antiquities of Rajasthan Vol. I
Author: Lt. Col. James Tod

ANNALS AND ANTIQUITIES
OF
RAJASTHAN

OR THE CENTRAL AND WESTERN RAJPUT STATES OF INDIA

BY

LIEUT.-COL. JAMES TOD
LATE POLITICAL AGENT TO THE WESTERN RAJPUT STATES

EDITED WITH AN INTRODUCTION AND NOTES BY

WILLIAM CROOKE, C.I.E.
HON. D.SC. OXON., B.A., F.R.A.I.
LATE OF THE INDIAN CIVIL SERVICE

IN THREE VOLUMES

VOL. I

HUMPHREY MILFORD
OXFORD UNIVERSITY PRESS
LONDON EDINBURGH GLASGOW NEW YORK
TORONTO MELBOURNE BOMBAY
1920

[*Original Dedication of the First Volume.*]

TO

HIS MOST GRACIOUS MAJESTY

GEORGE THE FOURTH

SIRE,

The gracious permission accorded me, to lay at the foot of the Throne the fruit of my labours, allows me to propitiate Your Majesty's consideration towards the object of this work, the prosecution of which I have made a paramount duty.

The Rajput princes, happily rescued, by the triumph of the British arms, from the yoke of lawless oppression, are now the most remote tributaries to Your Majesty's extensive empire; and their admirer and annalist may, perhaps, be permitted to hope that the sighs of this ancient and interesting race for the restoration of their former independence, which it would suit our wisest policy to grant, may be deemed not undeserving Your Majesty's regard.

With entire loyalty and devotion, I subscribe myself,

YOUR MAJESTY'S

Most faithful subject and servant,

JAMES TOD.

BIRD HURST, CROYDON,
June 20, 1829.

[*Original Dedication of the Second Volume.*]

TO

HIS MOST GRACIOUS MAJESTY

WILLIAM THE FOURTH

SIRE,

YOUR MAJESTY has graciously sanctioned the presentation of the Second Volume of the *Annals of Rajputana* to the Public under the auspices of Your Majesty's name.

In completing this work, it has been my endeavour to draw a faithful picture of States, the ruling principle of which is the paternity of the Sovereign. That this patriarchal form is the best suited to the genius of the people may be presumed from its durability, which war, famine, and anarchy have failed to destroy. The throne has always been the watchword and rallying-point of the Rajputs. My prayer is, that it may continue so, and that neither the love of conquest, nor false views of policy, may tempt us to subvert the independence of these States, some of which have braved the storms of more than ten centuries.

It will not, I trust, be deemed presumptuous in the Annalist of these gallant and long-oppressed races thus to solicit for them a full measure of Your Majesty's gracious patronage; in return for which, the Rajputs, making Your Majesty's enemies their own, would glory in assuming the "saffron robe," emblematic of death or victory, under the banner of that chivalry of which Your Majesty is the head.

That Your Majesty's throne may ever be surrounded by chiefs who will act up to the principles of fealty maintained at all hazards by the Rajput, is the heartfelt aspiration of,

SIRE,

YOUR MAJESTY'S

Devoted subject and servant,

JAMES TOD.

PREFACE

No one can undertake with a light heart the preparation of a new edition of Colonel Tod's great work, *The Annals and Antiquities of Rajasthan*. But the leading part which the Rājputs have taken in the Great War, the summoning of one of their princes to a seat at the Imperial Conference, the certainty that as the result of the present cataclysm they will be entitled to a larger share in the administration of India, have contributed to the desire that this classical account of their history and sociology should be presented in a shape adapted to the use of the modern scholar and student of Indian history and antiquities.

In the Introduction which follows I have endeavoured to estimate the merits and defects of Colonel Tod's work. Here it is necessary only to state that though the book has been several times reprinted in India and once in this country, the obvious difficulties of such an undertaking have hitherto prevented any writer better qualified than myself from attempting to prepare an annotated edition. Irrespectively of the fact that this work was published a century ago, when the study of the history, antiquities, sociology, and geography of India had only recently started, the Author's method led him to formulate theories on a wide range of subjects not directly connected with the Rājputs. In the light of our present knowledge some of these speculations have become obsolete, and it might have been possible, without impairing the value of the work as a Chronicle of the Rājputs, to have discarded from the text and notes much which no longer possesses value. But the work is a classic, and it deserves to be treated as such, and it was decided that any mutilation of the original text and notes would be inconsistent with the object of this series of reprints of classical works on Indian subjects. The only alternative course was to correct in notes, clearly distinguished from those of the Author, such facts and theories as are no longer accepted by scholars.

It is needless to say that during the last century much advance has been made in our knowledge of Indian history, antiquities, philology, and sociology. We are now in a position to use improved translations of many authorities which were quoted by the Author from inadequate or incorrect versions. The translation of *Ferishta's History* by A. Dow and Jonathan Scott has been superseded by that of General J. Briggs, that of the *Āīn-i-Akbarī* of F. Gladwin by the version by Professor H. Blochmann and Colonel H. S. Jarrett. For the *Memoirs of Jahāngīr*, the Author relied on the imperfect version by Major David Price, which has been replaced by a new translation of the text in its more complete form by Messrs. A. Rogers and H. Beveridge. For the *Laws of Manu* we have the translation by Dr. G. Bühler. The passages in classical literature relating to India have been collected, translated, and annotated by the late Mr. J. W. McCrindle. Much information not available for the Author's use has been provided by *The History of India as told by its own Historians*, by Sir H. M. Elliot and Professor J. Dowson, and by Mr. W. Irvine's translation, with elaborate notes, of N. Manucci's *Storia do Magor*. Among original works useful for the present edition the following may be mentioned: J. Grant Duff's *History of the Mahrattas*; Dr. Vincent A. Smith's *Early History of India*, *History of Fine Art in India and Ceylon*, *Asoka, the Buddhist Emperor of India*, and *Akbar, the Great Mogul*; Professor Jadunath Sarkar's *History of Aurangzib*, of which only three volumes have been published; Mr. W. Irvine's *Army of the Indian Moghuls*; Sir W. Lee-Warner's *Protected Princes of India*.

Much historical, geographical, and ethnological information has been collected in the new edition of the *Imperial Gazetteer of India* the *Bombay Gazetteer* edited by Sir J. M. Campbell, and, more particularly, in the revised *Gazetteer of Rajputana*, including that of Mewār and the Western States Residency and Bīkaner Agency by Lieutenant-Colonel K. D. Erskine, and that of Ajmer by Mr. C. C. Watson. Lieutenant-Colonel Erskine's work, based on the best local information, has been of special value, and it is much to be regretted that this officer, after serving as Consul-

General at Baghdad, was invalided and died in England in 1914, leaving that part of the *Gazetteer* dealing with the Eastern States, Jaipur, Kotah, and Būndi, unrevised. For botany, agriculture, and natural productions I have used Sir G. Watt's *Dictionary of the Economic Products of India*, and his *Commercial Products of India*; for architecture and antiquities, J. Fergusson's *History of Indian and Eastern Architecture*, edited by Dr. J. Burgess, and *The Cave Temples of India* by the same writers. In ethnology I have consulted the publications of the Ethnological Survey of India, of which Mr. H. A. Rose's *Glossary of the Tribes and Castes of the Punjab and North-West Frontier Province*, Mr. Bhimbhai Kirparam's account of the Hindus and Khān Bahādur Fazalullah Lutfullah's of the Musalmāns of Gujarāt, published in the *Bombay Gazetteer*, vol. ix. Parts i. ii., have been specially valuable. Besides the general works to which reference has been made, many articles on Rajputana and the Rājputs will be found in the *Journal of the Royal Asiatic Society* and its Bombay branch, in the *Journal of the Asiatic Society of Bengal*, and in the *Indian Antiquary*, and other periodicals. The Reports of the Archaeological Survey of India conducted by Sir A. Cunningham, Dr. J. Burgess, and Sir J. H. Marshall, are of great importance.

I cannot pretend to have exhausted the great mass of new information available in the works to which I have referred, and in others named in the Bibliography; and it was not my object to overload the notes which are already voluminous. To the general reader the system of annotation which I have attempted to carry out may appear meticulous; but no other course seemed possible if the work was to be made more useful to the historian and to the scholar. The editor of a work of this class is forced to undertake the somewhat invidious duty of calling attention to oversights or errors either in fact or theory. But this does not detract from the real value of the work. In some cases I have been content with adding a note of interrogation to warn the reader that certain statements must be received with caution. As regards geography, I have in many cases indicated briefly the position of the more important places, so far as they can be traced in the maps with which I was provided. The Author was so intimately acquainted with the ground, that he assumed in the general reader a degree of knowledge which he does not possess.

The text and notes, with the exception of a few obvious oversights, have been reprinted as they stood in the first edition, and as the latter is often quoted in books of authority, I have added its pagination for facility of reference. It was decided, after much consideration, to correct the transliteration of personal and place names and other vernacular terms according to the system now adopted in official gazetteers, maps, and reports. This change might have been unnecessary if the transliteration of these words, according to the system in use at the time when the book was written, had been uniformly correct. But this is not the case. At the same time I have preserved the original readings of those names which have become established in popular usage, such as "Mogul," "Mahratta," "Deccan," in place of "Mughal," "Marhāta," "Dakkhin." Following the Author's example, I have not thought it necessary to overload the text by the use of accents and diacritical marks, which are useless to the scholar and only embarrass the general reader. But in the Index I have accentuated the personal and place names so far as I believed I could do so with safety. Some of these I have been unable to trace in later authorities, and I fear that I may have failed to secure complete uniformity of method.

The scheme of the book, which attempts to give parallel accounts of each State, naturally causes difficulty to the reader. A like embarrassment is felt by any historian who endeavours to combine in a single narrative the fortunes of the Mughal Empire with those of the kingdoms in Bengal, the Deccan, or southern India; by the historian of Greece, where the centre of activity shifts from Athens to Sparta, Thebes, or Macedonia; by the historian of Germany before the minor kingdoms were more or less fully absorbed by the Hohenzollerns. I have endeavoured to assist the reader in dealing with these independent annals by largely extending the original Index, and by the use of page headings and paragraph summaries.

In the dates recorded in the summaries I have generally followed Lieutenant-Colonel Erskine's guidance, so far as his work was available. In view of the inconsistencies between some dates in the text and those recorded in the summaries, it must be remembered that it was the Author's habit in adapting the dates of the Samvat to those of the Christian era, to deduct 56, not 57 from the former, contrary to the practice of modern historians.

I am indebted to many friends for assistance. Captain C. D. M'K. Blunt has kindly given me much help in the record of Colonel Tod's life, and has supplied a photograph of the charming miniature of the Author as a young officer and of a bust which have been reproduced in the frontispieces. Mr. R. E. Enthoven, C.I.E., has given me the photograph of the Author engaged in his studies with his Jain Guru.[1] The fragments of local ballads scattered through the text were unfortunately copied from very incorrect texts. Dr. L. P. Tessitori, an Italian scholar, who, until the outbreak of the War, was engaged in collecting the local ballads of the Rājputs, has given a correct version of these ballads; and in improving the text of them I have been assisted by Colonel C. E. Luard, his Pandit, and Sir G. Grierson, K.C.I.E. Since the greater part of the following pages was in type, I have received copies of three reports by Dr. L. P. Tessitori, "A Scheme for the Bardic and Historical Survey of Rājputāna," and two Progress Reports for the years 1915 and 1916, published in the *Journal of the Asiatic Society of Bengal* (New Series, vol. x. No. 10; xii. No. 3; xiii. No. 4). These contain information regarding the MSS. copies of some ballads and inscriptions, which throw light on the traditions and antiquities of the Rājputs. I regret that I was unable to use these papers, which, however, do not supply much information on questions connected with *The Annals*. Among other friends who have helped me in various ways I may name the late Sir G. Birdwood; Mr. W. Foster, C.I.E.; Professor A. Keith, F.R.S.; Lieutenant-Colonel Sir D. Prain, F.R.S.; and Dr. Vincent A. Smith, C.I.E.

W. CROOKE.

[1] This picture, supposed to be the work of Ghāsi, the Author's artist, was recently discovered in Rājputāna.

CONTENTS

BOOK I

GEOGRAPHY OF RAJASTHAN OR RAJPUTANA

BOOK II

HISTORY OF THE RAJPUT TRIBES

CHAPTER 1

CHAPTER 2

CHAPTER 3

CHAPTER 4

CHAPTER 5

CHAPTER 6

CHAPTER 7

CHAPTER 8

BOOK III

SKETCH OF A FEUDAL SYSTEM IN RAJASTHAN

CHAPTER 1

CHAPTER 2

CHAPTER 3

CHAPTER 4

CHAPTER 5

BOOK IV

ANNALS OF MEWAR

CHAPTER 1

CHAPTER 2

CHAPTER 3

CHAPTER 4

CHAPTER 5

CHAPTER 6

CHAPTER 7

CHAPTER 8

CHAPTER 9

CHAPTER 10

CHAPTER 11

CHAPTER 12

CHAPTER 13

CHAPTER 14

CHAPTER 15

CHAPTER 16

CHAPTER 17

CHAPTER 18

ILLUSTRATIONS

INTRODUCTION

James Tod, the Author of this work, son of James Tod and Mary Heatly, was born at Islington on March 20, 1782. His father, James Tod the first, eldest son of Henry Tod of Bo'ness and Janet Monteath, was born on October 26, 1745. In 1780 he married in New York Mary, daughter of Andrew Heatly, a member of a family originally settled at Mellerston, Co. Berwick, where they had held a landed estate for some four centuries. Andrew Heatly emigrated to Rhode Island, where he died at the age of thirty-six in 1761. He had married Mary, daughter of Sueton Grant, of the family of Gartinbeg, really of Balvaddon, who left Inverness for Newport, Rhode Island, in 1725, and Temperance Talmage or Tollemache, granddaughter of one of the first and principal settlers at Easthampton, Rhode Island. He had been forced to emigrate to America during the Protectorate, owing to his loyalty to King Charles I. James Tod, the first, left America, and in partnership with his brother John, became an indigo-planter at Mirzapur, in the United Provinces of Agra and Oudh.

James Tod, the second, was thus through his father and his uncles Patrick and S. Heatly, both members of the Civil Service of the East India Company, closely connected with India, and in 1798, being then sixteen years old, he obtained through the influence of his uncle, Patrick Heatly, a cadetship in the service of the East India Company. On his arrival at Calcutta he was attached to the 2nd European Regiment. In 1800 he was transferred, with the rank of Lieutenant, to the 14th Native Infantry, from which he passed in 1807, with the same rank, to the 25th Native Infantry. In 1805 he was appointed to the command of the escort of his friend Mr. Graeme Mercer, then Government Agent at the Camp of Daulat Rao Sindhia, who had been defeated two years before at the battle of Assaye by Sir Arthur Wellesley. In more than one passage in *The Annals* Tod speaks of Mr. Graeme Mercer with respect and affection, and by him he was introduced to official life and Rājput and Mahratta politics. His tastes for geographical inquiries led him to undertake surveys in Rājputāna and Central India between 1812 and 1817, and he employed several native surveyors to traverse the then little-known region between Central India and the valley of the Indus.

At this period the Government of India was engaged in a project for suppressing the Pindāris, a body of lawless free-booters, of no single race, the débris of the adventurers who gained power during the decay of the Mughal Empire, and who had not been incorporated in the armies of the local powers which rose from its ruins. In 1817, to effect their suppression, the Governor-General, the Marquess of Hastings, collected the strongest British force which up to that time had been assembled in India. Two armies, acting in co-operation from north and south, converged on the banditti, and met with rapid success. Sindhia, whose power depended on the demoralized condition of Rājputāna, was overawed; Holkar was defeated; the Rāja of Nāgpur was captured; the Mahratta Peshwa became a fugitive; the Pindāris were dispersed. One of their leaders, Amīr Khān, who is frequently mentioned in Tod's narrative, disbanded his forces, and received as his share of the spoils the Principality of Tonk, still ruled by his descendants.

In the course of this campaign Tod performed valuable services. At the beginning of the operations he supplied the British Staff with a rough map of the seat of war, and in other ways his local knowledge was utilized by the Generals in charge of the operations. In 1813 he had been promoted to the rank of Captain in command of the escort of the Resident, Mr. Richard Strachey, who nominated him to the post of his Second Assistant. In 1818 he was appointed Political Agent of Western Rājputāna, a post which he held till his retirement in June 1822. The work which he carried out in Rājputāna during this period is fully described in *The Annals* and in his "Personal Narrative." Owing to Mahratta oppression and the ravages of the Pindāris, the condition of the country, political, social, and economical, was deplorable. To remedy this prevailing anarchy the States were gradually brought under British control, and their relations with the paramount power were embodied in a series of treaties. In this work of reform, reconstruction, and conciliation, Tod played an active part, and the confidence and respect with which he was regarded by the Princes, Chiefs, and peasantry enabled him to interfere with good effect in tribal quarrels, to rearrange the fiefs of the minor Chiefs, and to act as arbitrator between the Rāna of Mewār and his subjects.

Tod was convinced that the miserable state of the country was chiefly due to the hesitation of the Indian Government in interfering for the re-establishment of order; and on this ground he does not hesitate to condemn the cautious policy of Lord Cornwallis during his second term of office as Governor-General. Few people at the present day would be disposed to defend the policy of non-intervention. "This policy has been condemned by historians and commentators, as well as by statesmen, soldiers, and diplomatists; by Mill and his editor, H. H. Wilson, and by Thornton; by Lord Lake and Sir John Malcolm. The mischief was done and the loss of influence was not regained for a decade. It was not till the conclusion of an expensive and protracted campaign, that the Indian Government was replaced in the position where it had been left by Wellesley. The blame for this weak and unfortunate policy must be divided between Cornwallis and Barlow, between the Court of Directors and the Board of Control." But it was carried out in pursuance of orders from the Home Government. "The Court of Directors for some time past had been alarmed at Lord Wellesley's vigorous foreign policy. Castlereagh at the Board of Control had taken fright, and even Pitt was carried away and committed himself to a hasty opinion that the Governor-General had acted imprudently and illegally."[1]

Tod tells us little of his relations with the Supreme Government during his four years' service as Political Agent. He was notoriously a partisan of the Rājput princes, particularly those of Mewār and Mārwār; he is never tired of abusing the policy of the Emperor Aurangzeb, and, fortunately for the success of his work, Muhammadans form only a slight minority in the population of Rājputāna. This attitude naturally exposed him to criticism. Writing in 1824, Bishop Heber,[2] while he recognizes that he was

[1] W. S. Seton Carr, *The Marquess Cornwallis*, 180, 189 f.

[2] *Narrative of a Journey through the Upper Provinces*, ed. 1861, ii. 54.

held in affection and respect by "all the upper and middling classes of society," goes on to say: "His misfortune was that, in consequenee of his favouring the native princes so much, the Government of Calcutta were led to suspect him of corruption, and consequently to narrow his powers and associate other officers with him in his trust till he was disgusted and resigned his plaee. They are now, I believe, well satisfied that their suspicions were groundless. Captain Todd (*sic*) is strenuously vindicated from the charge by all the officers with whom I have conversed, and some of whom had abundant means of knowing what the natives themselves thought of him." The Bishop's widow, in a later issue of the *Diary* of her husband, adds that "she is anxious to remove any unfavourable impressions which may exist on the subject by stating, that she has now the authority of a gentleman, who at the time was a member of the Supreme Council, to say, that no such imputation was ever fixed on Colonel Todd's (*sic*) character."

Whatever may have been the real reason for the premature termination of his official career at the age of forty, ill-health was put forward as the ostensible cause of his retirement. He had served for about twenty-four years in the Indian plains without any leave; he had long suffered from malaria; and, though he hardly suspected it at the time, an attempt had been made by one of his servants to poison him with Datura; he had met with a serious accident when, by chance or design, his elephant-driver dashed his howdah against the gate of Begūn fort in eastern Mewār. In spite of all this, he retained sufficient health to make, on the eve of his departure from India, the extensive tour recorded in his *Travels in Western India*. Neither on his retirement, nor at any subsequent period, were his services, official and literary, rewarded by any distinction.

During his seventeen years' service in Central India and Rājputāna he showed indefatigable industry in the collection of the materials which were partially used in his great work. His taste for the study of history and antiquities, ethnology, popular religion, and superstitions was stimulated by the pioneer work of Sir W. Jones and other writers in the *Asiatic Researches*. He was not a trained philologist, and he gained much of his information from his Guru, the Jain Yati Gyānchandra, and the Brāhman Pandits whom he employed to make inquiries on his behalf. They, too, were not trained scholars in the modern sense of the term, and many of his mistakes are due to his rashness in following their guidance.

His life was prolonged for thirteen years after he left India. In 1824 he attained the rank of Major, and in 1826 that of Lieutenant-Colonel. Much of his time in England was spent in arranging his materials and compiling the works upon which his reputation depends: *The Annals*, published between 1829 and 1832; and his *Travels in Western India*, published after his death, in 1839. He was in close relations with the Royal Asiatic Society, of which he acted for a time as Librarian. In this fine collection of books and manuscripts he gained much of that discursive learning which appears in *The Annals*. He presented to the Society numerous manuscripts, inscriptions, and coins. The fine series of drawings made to illustrate his works by Captain P. T. Waugh and a native artist named Ghāsi, have recently been rearranged and catalogued in the Library of the Society. They well deserve inspection by any one interested in Indian art. He also made frequent tours on the Continent, and on one occasion visited the great soldier, Count Benoit de Boigne, who died in 1830, leaving a fortune of twenty millions of francs.

On November 16, 1826, Tod married Julia, daughter of Dr. Henry Clutterbuck, an eminent London surgeon, by whom he had two sons and a daughter. In 1835 he settled in a house in Regent's Park; and on November 17 of the same year he died suddenly while transacting business at the office of his bankers, Messrs. Robarts of Lombard Street. The names of his descendants will appear from the pedigree appended to this Introduction.

The Annals of Rajasthan, the two volumes of which were, by permission, dedicated to Kings George IV. and William IV. respectively, was received with considerable favour. A contemporary critic deals with it in the following terms: [1] "Colonel Tod deserves the praise of a most delightful and industrious collector of materials for history, and his own narrative style in many places displays great freedom, vigour, and perspicuity. Though not always correct, and occasionally stiff and formal, it is not seldom highly animated and picturesque. The faults of his work are inseparable from its nature; it would have been almost impossible to mould up into one continuous history the

[1] *Quarterly Review*, vol. xlviii. Oct.–Dec. 1832, pp. 38 f.

distinct and separate annals of the various Rajput races. The patience of the reader is thus unavoidably put to a severe trial, in having to reascend to the origin, and again to trace downwards the parallel annals of some new tribe—sometimes interwoven with, sometimes entirely distinct from, those which have gone before. But, on the whole, as no one but Colonel Tod could have gathered the materials for such a work, there are not many who could have used them so well. No candid reader can arise from its perusal without a very high sense of the character of the Author—no scholar, more certainly, without respect for his attainments, and gratitude for the service which he has rendered to a branch of literature, if far from popular, by no means to be estimated, as to its real importance, by the extent to which it may command the favour of an age of duodecimos."

In estimating the value of the local authorities on which the history is based, Tod reposed undue confidence in the epics and ballads composed by the poet Chānd and other tribal bards. It is believed that more than one of these poems have disappeared since his time, and these materials have been only in part edited and translated. The value to be placed on bardic literature is a question not free from difficulty. "On the faith of ancient songs, the uncertain but the only memorials of barbarism," says Gibbon, "they [Cassiodorus and Jornandes] deduced the first origin of the Goths."[1] The poet may occasionally record facts of value, but in his zeal for the honour of the tribe which he represents, he is tempted to exaggerate victories, to minimize defeats. This is a danger to which Indian poets are particularly exposed. Their trade is one of fulsome adulation, and in a state of society like that of the Rājputs, where tribal and personal rivalries flourish, the temptation to give a false colouring to history is great. In fact, bardic literature is often useful, not as evidence of occurrences in antiquity, but as an indication of the habits and beliefs current in the age of the writer. It exhibits the facts, not as they really occurred, but as the writer and his contemporaries supposed that they occurred. The mind of the poet, with all its prejudices, projects itself into the distant past. Good examples of the methods of the bards will appear in the attempt to connect the Rāthors with the dynasty of Kanauj, or to represent the Chauhāns as the founders of an empire in the Deccan.

[1] *Decline and Fall*, ed. W. Smith, i. 375.

Recent investigation has thrown much new light on the origin of the Rājputs. A wide gulf lies between the Vedic Kshatriya and the Rājput of medieval times which it is now impossible to bridge. Some clans, with the help of an accommodating bard, may be able to trace their lineage to the Kshatriyas of Buddhist times, who were recognized as one of the leading elements in Hindu society, and, in their own estimation, stood even higher than the Brāhmans.[1] But it is now certain that the origin of many clans dates from the Saka or Kushān invasion, which began about the middle of the second century B.C., or more certainly, from that of the White Huns who destroyed the Gupta empire about A.D. 480. The Gurjara tribe connected with the latter people adopted Hinduism, and their leaders formed the main stock from which the higher Rājput families sprang. When these new claimants to princely honours accepted the faith and institutions of Brahmanism, the attempt would naturally be made to affiliate themselves to the mythical heroes whose exploits are recorded in the Mahābhārata and Rāmāyana. Hence arose the body of legend recorded in *The Annals* by which a fabulous origin from the Sun or Moon is ascribed to two great Rājput branches, a genealogy claimed by other princely families, like the Incas of Peru or the Mikado of Japan. Or, as in the case of the Rāthors of Mārwār, an equally fabulous story was invented to link them with the royal house of Kanauj, one of the genuine old Hindu ruling families. The same feeling lies at the root of the *Aeneid* of Virgil, the court poet of the new empire. The clan of the emperor Augustus, the Iulii, a patrician family of Alban origin, was represented as the heirs of Iulus, the supposed son of Aeneas and founder of Alba Longa, thus linking the new Augustan house with the heroes of the *Iliad*.

One of the merits of Tod's work is that, though his knowledge of ethnology was imperfect, and he was unable to reject the local chronicles of the Rājputs, he advocated, in anticipation of the conclusions of later scholars, the so-called "Scythic" origin of the race. To make up for the lack of direct evidence of Scythian manners and sociology to support this position, he was forced to rely on certain superficial resemblances of custom and belief, not between Rājputs, Scythians and Huns, but between Rājputs,

[1] V. A. Smith, *Early History of India*, 3rd ed. 408; Rhys Davids, *Buddhist India*, 60 f.

Getae or Thracians, or the Germans of Tacitus. In the same way a supposed identity of name led him to identify the Jāts of northern India with the Getae or with the Goths, and finally to bring them with the Jutes into Kent.

A similar process of groping in semi-darkness induced him to make constant references to serpent worship, which, as Sir E. Tylor remarked, "years ago fell into the hands of speculative writers who mixed it up with occult philosophies, druidical mysteries, and that portentous nonsense called the 'Arkite symbolism,' till now sober students hear the very name of ophiolatry with a shudder."[1] He repeatedly speaks of a people whom he calls the "Takshaks," apparently one of the Scythian tribes. There is, however, no reason to believe that serpent worship formed an important element in the beliefs of the Scythians, or to suppose that the cult, as we observe it in India, is of other than indigenous origin.

The more recent views of the origin of the Rājputs may be briefly illustrated in connexion with some of the leading septs. Dr. Vincent A. Smith holds that the term Kshatriya was not an ethnical but an occupational designation. Rājaputra, 'son of a Rāja,' seems to have been a name applied to the cadets of ruling houses who, according to the ancient custom of tribal society, were in the habit of seeking their fortunes abroad, winning by some act of valour the hand of the princess whose land they visited, and with it the succession to the kingdom vested in her under the system of Mother Right. Sir James Frazer has described various forms of this mode of succession in the case of the Kings of Rome, Ashanti, Uganda, in certain Greek States, and other places.[2] Dr. Smith goes on to say: "The term Kshatriya was, I believe, always one of very vague meaning, simply denoting the Hindu ruling classes which did not claim Brahmanical descent. Occasionally a rājā might be a Brahman by caste, but the Brahman's place at court was that of a minister rather than that of king."[3] This office in Rajputana, as we learn from numerous instances in *The Annals*, was often taken by members of the Bania or mercantile class, because the Brāhmans of the Desert, by their laxity of

[1] *Primitive Culture*, 2nd ed. ii. 239.

[2] *Lectures on the Early History of the Kingship*, 231 ff.; *The Golden Bough*, 3rd ed.; *The Magic Art*, ii. 269 ff.

[3] *Early History of India*, 408.

practice, had acquired an equivocal reputation, and were generally illiterate. The Rājput has always, until recent times, favoured the Bhāt or bard more than the Brāhman.

The group denoted by the name Kshatriya or Rājput thus depended on status rather than on descent, and it was therefore possible for foreigners to be introduced into the tribes without any violation of the prejudices of caste, which was then only partially developed. In later times, under Brāhman guidance, the rules of endogamy, exogamy, and *confarreatio* have been definitely formulated. But as the power of the priesthood increased, it was necessary to disguise this admission of foreigners under a convenient fiction. Hence arose the legend, told in two different forms in *The Annals*, which describes how, by a solemn act of purification or initiation, under the superintendence of one of the ancient Vedic Rishis or inspired saints, the "fire-born" septs were created to help the Brāhmans in repressing Buddhism, Jainism, or other heresies, and in establishing the ancient traditional Hindu social policy, the temporary downfall of which, under the stress of foreign invasions, is carefully concealed in the Hindu sacred literature. This privilege was, we are told, confined to four septs, known as Agnikula, or 'fire-born'—the Pramār, Parihār, Chālukya or Solanki, and the Chauhān. But there is good reason to believe that the Pramār was the only sept which laid claim to this distinction before the time of the poet Chānd, who flourished in the twelfth century of our era.[1] The local tradition in Rājputāna was so vague that in one version of the story Vasishtha, in the other Visvāmitra, is said to have been the officiating priest.

In the case of the Sesodias of Mewār, Mr. D. R. Bhandarkar has given reasons to believe that Gehlot or Guhilot means simply 'son of Guhila,' an abbreviation of Guhadatta, the name of its founder.[2] He is said to have belonged to the Gurjara stock, kinsmen or allies of the Huns who entered India about the sixth century of our era, and founded a kingdom in Rājputāna with its capital at Bhilmāl or Srīmāl, about fifty miles from Mount Ābu,

[1] *Journal Royal Asiatic Society*, 1905, 1 ff. The tradition seems to have started earlier in Southern India, S. Krishnaswami Aiyangar, *Ancient India*, 1911, 390 ff.

[2] *Journal Asiatic Society Bengal*, 1909, 167 ff. The criticism by Pandit Mohanlal Vishnulal Pandia (*ibid.*, 1912, 63 ff.) is extremely feeble.

the scene of the regeneration of the Rājputs. This branch, which took the name of Maitrika, is said to be closely connected with the Mer tribe, which gave its name to Merwāra, and is fully described in *The Annals.* The actual conqueror of Chitor, Bāpa or Bappa, is said in inscriptions to have belonged to the branch known as Nāgar, or 'City' Brāhmans which has its present headquarters at the town of Vadnagar in the Baroda State. This conversion of a Brāhman into a Rājput is at first sight startling, but the fact implies that the institution of caste, as we observe it, was then only imperfectly established, and there was no difficulty in believing that a Brāhman could be ancestor of a princely house which now claims descent from the Sun. As will appear later on, Bāpa seems to be a historical personage. These facts help us to understand the strange story in *The Annals,* which tells how Gohāditya received inauguration as chief by having his forehead smeared with blood drawn from the finger of a Bhīl, a form of the blood covenant which appears among many savage tribes.[1] In those days no definite line was drawn between the Bhīls, now a wild forest tribe, and the Rājputs. The Bhīls were the free lords of the jungle, original owners of the soil, and though they practised rites and followed customs repulsive to orthodox Hindus, they did not share in the impurity which attached to foul outcastes like the Dom or the Chandāla.. As the Bhīls were believed to be autochthonous, and thus understood the methods of controlling or conciliating the local spirits, by this form of inauguration they passed on their knowledge to the Rājputs whom they accepted as their lords. The relations of the Mīnas, another jungle tribe of the same class, with the Kachhwāhas of Jaipur were of the same kind.

According to the bardic legend given in *The Annals,* the Rāthors, the second great Rājput clan, owed their origin to a migration of a body of its members to the western Desert when the territory of Kanauj was conquered by Shihābu-d-dīn in A.D. 1193. But it is now certain that the ruling dynasty of Kanauj belonged, not to the Rāthor, but to the Gaharwār clan, and that the first Rāthor settlement in Rājputāna must have occurred anterior to the conquest of Kanauj by the Musalmāns. An inscription, dated A.D. 997, found in the ruins of the ancient town of Hathūndi or Hastikūndi in the Bali Hakūmat of the Jodhpur

[1] E. S. Hartland, *Primitive Paternity,* i. 258 ff.

State, names four Rāthor Rājas who reigned there in the tenth century.[1] The local legend is an attempt to connect the line of Rāthor princes with the Kanauj dynasty. It has been suggested that the Deccan dynasty of the Rāshtrakūtas which, in name at least, is identical with Rāthor, reigning at Nāsik or Malkhed from A.D. 753 to 973, was connected with the Reddis or Raddis, a caste of cultivators which seem to have migrated from Madras into the Deccan at an early period. But any racial connexion between the Deccan Reddis and the Rāthors of Rājputāna is very doubtful.[2]

The Chandel clan, ranked in *The Annals* among the Thirty-six Royal Races, is believed to be closely connected with the Bhars and Gonds, forest tribes of Bundelkhand and the Central Provinces. Mr. R. V. Russell prefers to connect them with the Bhars alone, on the ground that the Gonds, according to the best traditions, entered the Central Provinces from the south, and made no effective settlement in Bundelkhand, the headquarters of the Chandels.[3] But there was a Gond settlement in the Hamīrpur District of Bundelkhand, and the close connexion between the Gonds and the Chandels began in what is now the Chhatarpur State.

The results of recent investigations into Rājput ethnology are thus of great importance, and enable us to correct the bardic legends on which the genealogies recorded in *The Annals* were founded. Much remains to be done before the question can be finally settled. The local Rājput traditions and the ballads of the bards must be collected and edited; the ancient sites in Rājputāna must be excavated; physical measurements, now somewhat discredited as a test of racial affinities, must be made in larger numbers and by more scientific methods. But the general thesis that some of the nobler Rājput septs are descended from Gurjaras or other foreigners, while others are closely connected with the autochthonous races, may be regarded as definitely proved.

One of the most valuable parts of *The Annals* is the chapter

[1] K. D. Erskine, *Gazetteer Western Rajput States and Bikaner Agency*, A. i. 177.

[2] *Bombay Gazetteer*, I. Part i. 385; *Bombay Census Report*, 1911, i. 279; Smith, *Early History*, 413.

[3] *Tribes and Castes of the Central Provinces*, iv. 441.

describing the popular religion of Mewār, the festival and rites in honour of Gauri, the Mother goddess. There are also many incidental notices of cults and superstitions scattered through the work. A race of warriors like the Rājputs naturally favours the worship of Siva who, as the successor of Rudra, the Vedic storm-god, was originally a terror-inspiring deity, a side of his character only imperfectly veiled by his euphemistic title of Siva, 'the blessed or auspicious One.' In his phallic manifestation his chief shrine is at Eklingji, 'the single or notable phallus,' about fourteen miles north of Udaipur city. The Rānas hold the office of priest-kings, Dīwāns or prime-ministers of the god. Their association with this deity has been explained by an inscription recently found in the temple of Nātha, 'the Lord,' now used as a storeroom of the Eklingji temple.[1] The inscription, dated A.D. 971, is in form of a dedication to Lakulīsa, a form of Siva represented as bearing a club, and refers to the Saiva sect known as Lakulīsa-Pāsapatas. It records the name of a king named Srī-Bappaka, 'the moon among the princes of the Guhila dynasty,' who reigned at a place called Nāgahvada, identified with Nāgda, an ancient town several times mentioned in *The Annals*, the ruins of which exist at the foot of the hill on which the temple of Eklingji stands. Srī-Bappaka is certainly Bāpa or Bappa, the traditional founder of the Mewār dynasty, which had at that time its capital at Nāgda. From this inscription it is clear that the Eklingji temple was in existence before A.D. 971, and, as Mr. Bhandarkar remarks, "it shows that the old tradition about Nāgendra and Bappa Rāwal's infancy given by Tod had some historical foundation, and it is intelligible how the Rānas of Udaipur could have come to have such an intimate connexion with the temple as that of high priests, in which capacity they still officiate." This office vested in them is a good example of one of those dynasties of priest-kings of which Sir James Frazer has given an elaborate account.[2]

The milder side of the Rājput character is represented in the cult of Krishna at Nāthdwāra. The Mahant or Abbot of the temple, situated at the old village of Siārh, twenty-two miles

[1] D. R. Bhandarkar, *Journal Bombay Branch Royal Asiatic Society*, 1916, Art. xii.

[2] *The Golden Bough*, 3rd ed.; *The Magic Art*, i. 44 ff.; *Adonis, Attis, Osiris*, i. 42 f., 143 ff.

from the city of Udaipur, enjoys semi-royal state. In anticipation of the raid by Aurangzeb on Mathura, A.D. 1669–70, the ancient image of Kesavadeva, a form of Krishna, 'He of the flowing locks,' was removed out of reach of danger by Rāna Rāj Singh of Mewār. When the cart bearing the image arrived at Siārh, the god, by stopping the cart, is said to have expressed his intention of remaining there. This was the origin of the famous temple, still visited by crowds of pilgrims, and one of the leading seats of the Vallabhāchārya sect, 'the Epicureans of the East,' whose practices, as disclosed in the famous Mahārāja libel case, tried at Bombay in 1861, gave rise to grievous scandal.[1] The ill-feeling against this sect, aroused by these revelations, was so intense that the Mahārāja of Jaipur ordered that the two famous images of Krishna worshipped in his State, which originally came from Gokul, near Mathura, should be removed from his territories into those of the Bharatpur State.

Tod bears witness to the humanizing effect on the Rājputs of the worship of this god, whom he calls "the Apollo of Braj," the holy land of Krishna near Mathura. He also asserts that the Emperor Akbar favoured the worship of Krishna, a feeling shared by his successors Jahāngīr and Shāh Jahān. Akbar, in his search for a new faith to supersede Islām, of which he was *parcus cultor et infrequens*, dallied with Hindu Pandits, Parsi priests, and Christian missionaries, and he was doubtless well informed about the sensuous ritual of the temple of Nāthdwāra.[2]

The character of the Rājputs is discussed in many passages in *The Annals*. The Author expresses marked sympathy with the people among whom his official life was spent, and he expresses gratitude for the courtesy and confidence which they bestowed upon him. This applies specially to the Sesodias of Mewār and the Rāthors of Mārwār, with whom he lived in the closest intimacy. He shows, on the other hand, a decided prejudice against the Kachhwāhas of Jaipur, of whose diplomacy he disapproved. This feeling, we may suspect, was due in part to their hesitation in accepting the British alliance, a policy in which he was deeply interested.

[1] Karsandas Mulji, *History of the Sect of the Mahārājas or Vallabhāchāryas*, London, 1865; *Report of the Mahārāj Libel Case*, Bombay, 1862; F. S. Growse, *Mathura*, 3rd ed. 283 f.

[2] V. A. Smith, *Akbar, The Great Mogul*, 162 ff.

The virtues of the Rājput lie on the surface—their loyalty, devotion, and gallantry; their chivalry towards women; their regard for their national customs. Their weaknesses—though Tod does not enumerate them in detail—are obvious from a study of their history—their instability of character, their liability to sudden outbreaks of passion, their tendency to yield to panic on the battlefield, their inability, as a result of their tribal system, to form a permanent combination against a public enemy, their occasional faithlessness to their chiefs and allies, their excessive use of opium. These defects they share with most orientals, but, on the whole, they compare favourably with other races in the Indian Empire. There is much in their character and institutions which reminds us of the Gauls as pictured by Mommsen in a striking passage.[1] Rājput women are described as virtuous, affectionate, and devoted, taking part in the control of the family, sharing with their husbands the dangers of war and sport, contemptuous of the coward, and exercising a salutary influence in public and domestic affairs.

Strangely enough, Tod omits to give us a detailed account of their marriage regulations and ceremonies. According to Mr. E. H. Kealy,[2] while male children under one year old exceed the females, "the excess is not sufficiently great to justify the conclusion that female babies are murdered, nor is the theory that female infants lost their lives by neglect supported by the statistics. Unhappily the returns show that a high proportion of married women is combined with a very low percentage of females as compared with males between the ages of ten and fourteen, the early stage of married life, and this defect is largely due to premature cohabitation, lack of medical attendance, and of sanitary precautions." No one can read without horror the many narratives of the Johar, the final sacrifice by which women in the hour of defeat gave their lives to save their honour, and of the numerous cases of Sati. Both these customs are now only a matter of history, but so late as 1879 General Hervey was able to count at the Bikaner palace the handmarks of at least thirty-seven widows who ascended the pyre with their lords.[3]

Much space in *The Annals* is occupied by a review of the

[1] *History of Rome*, ed. 1866, iv. 209 ff.

[2] *Census Report, Rājputāna*, 1911, i. 132.

[3] *Some Records of Crime*, ii. 217 f.

so-called 'Feudal' system in Rājputāna. Tod was naturally attracted in the course of his discursive reading by Henry Hallam's *View of the State of Europe during the Middle Ages*, which first appeared in 1818, four years before Tod resigned his Indian appointment. Hallam himself was careful to point out that "it is of great importance to be on our guard against seeming analogies which vanish away when they are closely observed."[1] This warning Tod unguardedly overlooked. Hallam recognized that Feudalism was an institution the ultimate origin of which is still, to some extent, obscure. It possibly began with the desire for protection, the *rakhwāli* of the Rājputs, but it seems to have been ultimately based on the private law of Rome, while the influence of the Church, interested in securing its endowments, was a factor in its evolution. In its completed form it represented the final stage of a process which began under the Frankish conquerors of Gaul. At any rate, it was of European origin, and though it absorbed much that was common to the types of tribal organization found in other parts of the world, it was moulded by the political, social, and economical environment amidst which it was developed. Hence, while it is possible to trace, as Tod has done, certain analogies between the tribal institutions of the Rājputs and the social organization of medieval Europe—analogies of feudal incidents connected with Reliefs, Fines upon alienation, Escheats, Aids, Wardship, and Marriage — these analogies, when more closely examined, are found to be in the main superficial. If we desire to undertake a comparative study of the Rājput tribal system, it is unnecessary to travel to medieval Europe, while we have close at hand the social organization of more or less kindred tribes on the Indian borderland, Pathāns, Afghāns, or Baloch; or, in a more primitive stage, those of the Kandhs, Gonds, Mūndas, or Orāons. It is of little service to compare two systems of which only the nucleus is common to both, and to place side by side institutions which present only a factitious similitude, because the social development of each has progressed on different lines.

The Author's excursions into philology are the diversions of a clever man, not of a trained scholar, but interested in the subject as an amateur. In his time the new learning on oriental subjects had only recently begun to attract the attention of

[1] *View of the State of Europe during the Middle Ages*, 12th ed. 1868, i. 186.

scholars, of which Sir W. Jones was the prophet. Tod was a diligent student of *The Asiatic Researches*, the publication of which began at Calcutta in 1788. While much material of value is to be found in these volumes, many papers of Captain Francis Wilford and others are full of rash speculations which have not survived later criticism. Tod is not to blame because he followed the guidance of scholars who contributed articles to the leading Indian review of his time ; because he was ignorant of the laws of Grimm or Verner; because, like his contemporaries, he believed that the mythology of Egypt or Palestine influenced the beliefs of the Indian people. It was his fate that many of his guesses were quoted with approval by writers like T. Maurice in his *Indian Antiquities*, and by N. Pococke in his *India in Greece*. It is also well to remember that many of the derivations of the names of Indian deities, confidently proposed by Kuhn and Max Müller a few years ago, are no longer accepted. Tod, at any rate, published his views on Feudalism and Philology without any pretence of dogmatism.

One special question deserves examination—the constant references to the cult of Bāl-Siva, a form of the Sun god. A learned Indian scholar, Pandit Gaurishankar Ojha, who is now engaged on an annotated edition of *The Annals* in Hindi, states that no temple or image dedicated to this god is known in Rājputāna. It is, of course, not unlikely that Siva, as a deity of fertility, should be associated with Sun worship, but there is no evidence of the cult on which Tod lays special stress. It is almost useless to speculate on the source of his error. It may be based on a reference in the *Āīn-i-Akbarī*[1] to a certain Bālnāth, Jogi, who occupied a cell in a place in the Sindh Sāgar Duāb of the Panjāb. At the same time, like many of the writers of his day, he may have had the Semitic Baal in his mind.

It was largely due to imperfect information received from his assistants that he shared with other writers of the time the confusion between Buddhism and Jainism, and supposed that the former religion was introduced into India from Central Asia. His elaborate attempt to extract history and a trustworthy scheme of chronology from the Purānas must be pronounced to be a failure. Recently a learned scholar, Mr. F. E. Pargiter, has

[1] ii. 315.

shown how far an examination of these authorities can be conducted with any approach to probability.[1]

The questions which have been discussed do not, to any important extent, detract from the real value of the work. Even in those points which are most open to criticism, *The Annals* possesses importance because it represents a phase in the study of Indian religions, ethnology, and sociology. No one can examine it without increasing pleasure and admiration for a writer who, immersed in arduous official work, was able to indulge his tastes for research. His was the first real attempt to investigate the beliefs of the peasantry as contrasted with the official Brahmanism, a study which in recent years has revolutionized the current conceptions of Hinduism. Even if his versions of the inscriptions which he collected fail to satisfy the requirements of more recent scholars, he deserves credit for rescuing from neglect and almost certain destruction epigraphical material for the use of his successors. The same may be said of the drawings of buildings, some of which have fallen into decay, or have been mutilated by their careless guardians. When he deals with facts which came under his personal observation, his accounts of beliefs, folk-lore, social life, customs, and manners possess permanent value.

He observed the Rājputs when they were in a stage of transition. Isolated by the inaccessibility of their country, they were the last guardians of Hindu beliefs, institutions, and manners against the rising tide of the Muhammadan invasions; without their protection much that is important for the study of the Hindus must have disappeared. To avoid anarchy and the ultimate destruction of these States, it was necessary for them to accept a closer union with the British as the paramount power. By this they lost something, but they gained much. The new connexion involved new duties and responsibilities in adapting their primitive system of government to modern requirements. Tod thus stood at the parting of the ways. With the introduction of the railway and the post-office, the disappearance of the caravan as a means of transport, the increase of trade, the growth of new wants and possibilities of development in association with the

[1] "Ancient Indian Genealogies and Chronology," "Earliest Indian Traditional History," *Journal Royal Asiatic Society*, January 1910, April 1914.

Empire, the period of Rājput isolation came to a close. To some it may be a matter of regret that the personal rule of the Chief over a people strongly influenced by what they term *swāmīdharma*, the reciprocal loyalty of subject to prince and of prince to people, should be replaced by a government of a more popular type. But this change was, in the nature of things, inevitable. As an example of this, a statement made by the Mahārāja of Bīkaner, when he was summoned to attend the Imperial Conference in 1917, may be quoted. "In my own territories we inaugurated some years ago the beginnings of a representative assembly. It now consists of elected, as well as nominated, non-official members, and their legislative powers follow the lines of those laid down for the Legislatures of British India in the 1909 reforms. In respect to the Budget they have the same powers as those conferred on the Supreme and Provincial Legislatures in British India by the Lansdowne reforms in force from 1893 to 1909. When announcing my intention of creating this representative body, I intimated that as the people showed their fitness they would be entrusted with more powers. Accordingly, at the end of the first triennial term, when the elections will take place, we are revising the rules of business in the direction of greater liberality and of removing unnecessary restrictions." It remains to be seen how far this policy will prove to be successful.

It was a happy accident that before the period of transition had begun in earnest, such a competent and sympathetic observer should have been able to examine and record one of the most interesting surviving phases of the ancient Hindu polity.

A soldier and a sportsman, Tod learned to understand the romantic, adventurous side of the Rājput character, and he recorded with full appreciation the fine stories of manly valour, of the self-sacrifice of women, the tragedies of the sieges of Chitor, the heroism of Rānas Sanga and Partāb Singh, or of Durgādās. Many of these tales recall the age of medieval chivalry, and Tod is at his best in recording them. No one can read without admiration his account of the attack of the Saktāwats and Chondāwats on Untāla; of Sūja and the tiger; the tragedy of Krishna Kunwāri; of the queen of Ganor; of Sanjogta of Kanauj; of Gūga Chauhān and Alu Hāra. In many of these tales the Rājput displays the loyalty and valour, the punctilious regard for his personal honour which in the case of the Spanish grandee have passed into a proverb.

While the Rājput is courteous in his intercourse with those who are prepared to take him as he is, when he meets an English officer he resents any hint of patronage, he is jealous of any intrusion on the secluded folk behind the curtain, and he is often rather an acquaintance than a friend, inclined to shelter himself behind a dignified reserve, unwilling to open his mind to any one who does not accept his traditional attitude towards men of a different race and of a different faith. When he makes a ceremonial visit to a European officer, his conversation is often confined to conventional compliments, or chat about the weather and the state of the crops.

To remove these difficulties which obstruct friendly and confidential intercourse, the young officer in India may be advised to study the methods illustrated in this work. But he will do well to avoid Tod's openly expressed partisanship. He owed the affection and respect bestowed upon him by prince and peasant, and even by the jealously guarded ladies of the zenanah, to his kindliness and sympathy, his readiness to converse freely with men of all classes, his patience in listening to grievances, even those which he had no power to redress, his impartiality as an arbitrator between the Rāna of Mewār and his people or between individuals or sects unfriendly to each other. He studied the national traditions and usages; he knew enough of religious beliefs and of social customs to save him from giving offence by word or deed; he could converse with the people in their own patois, and could give point to a remark by an apt quotation of a proverb or a scrap of an old ballad.

When, if ever, a new history of the Rājputs comes to be written, it must be largely based on Tod's collections, supplemented by wider historical, antiquarian, and epigraphical research. The history of the last century cannot be compiled until the recent administration reports, now treated as confidential, and the muniment rooms of Calcutta and London are open to the student. But it is unlikely that, for the present at least, any writer will enjoy, as Tod did, access to the records and correspondence stored in the palaces of the Chiefs.

For the Rājput himself and for natives of India interested in the history of their country, the work will long retain its value.

It preserves a record of tribal rights and privileges, of claims based on ancient tradition, of feuds and their settlement, of genealogies and family history which, but for Tod's careful record, might have been forgotten or misinterpreted even by the Rājputs themselves. In the original English text which many Rājputs are now able to study they will find a picture of tribal society, now rapidly disappearing, drawn by a competent and friendly hand. Its interest will not be diminished by the fact that while the writer displays a hearty admiration for the Rājput character, he is not blind to its defects. At any rate, the Rājput will enjoy the satisfaction that his race has been selected to furnish the materials for the most comprehensive monograph ever compiled by a British officer describing one of the leading peoples of India.

PEDIGREE OF THE TOD FAMILY

James Tod, Merchant, Bo'ness. = Helen Moir.

James Tod, Shipmaster, Bo'ness, *b.* 1672. = Elizabeth Monteath.

Henry Tod. *b.* 1717. = Janet Monteath.

James Tod, Indigo Planter. = Mary Heatly.

Suetonius Henry Tod, General. = Mary Macdonald, Sleat, Skye. | JAMES TOD = Julia Clutterbuck, of a Dutch family that came to England in sixteenth century.

Suetonius Macdonald Tod. | Ewen Monteath Tod.

Grant Heatly Tod-Heatly. ob.s.p. | Edward H. M. Tod. ob.s.p. | Mary Augusta Tod = Charles Harris Blunt, Major-General, C.B., Bengal Horse Artillery.

Edward Walter Blunt-Mackenzie, Lt.-Col., R.A. = Sibell Lilian, Countess of Cromartie. | Charles David Mackinnon. unm. | Janet Heatly. unm.

Roderick Grant Francis, Viscount Tarbat. | Walter Blunt Mackenzie. | Isobel.

BIBLIOGRAPHY

WITH SOME ABBREVIATED TITLES OF WORKS QUOTED IN THE NOTES

ABULGHAZI. General History of the Turks, Moguls, and Tartars. 2 vols. London, 1729–30.

ĀIN. Abu-l Fazl, Allāmi. The Āin-i-Akbari, translated and edited by H. Blochmann and H. S. Jarrett. 3 vols. Calcutta, 1873–94.

AITKEN, E. H. Gazetteer of Sind. Karachi, 1907.

Akbarnāma. The Akbarnāma of Abu-l Fazl, Allāmi, trans. H. Beveridge. Calcutta. Vol. i., 1907; vol. ii., 1912; vol. iii., in the press.

Asiatic Researches. 20 vols. Calcutta, 1788–1836.

ASR. Archaeological Survey Reports, India, ed. Sir A. Cunningham, Sir J. H. Marshall, J. Burgess. Calcutta, 1871–

BADAONI. Muntakhabat-tawārīkh, ed. G. S. A. Ranking, W. H. Lowe, E. B. Cowell. 2 vols. Calcutta, 1884–98.

BADEN-POWELL, B. H. The Indian Village Community. London, 1892.

BALFOUR, E. Cyclopaedia of India. 3rd ed. 3 vols. London, 1885.

BARNETT, L. D. The Antiquities of India. London, 1914.

BAYLEY, Sir E. C. The Local Muhammadan Dynasties of Gujarat. London, 1886.

BEAL, S. SI-YU-KI. Buddhist Annals of the Western World, translated from the Chinese of Hiuen Tsiang. 2 vols. London, 1884.

BERNIER, F. Travels in the Mogul Empire, ed. A. Constable, V. A. Smith. Oxford, 1914.

BG. Gazetteer of the Bombay Presidency, ed. Sir J. Campbell. 27 vols. Bombay, 1874–1904.

BILGRAMI, SYED HOSSAIN; WILMOTT, C. Historical and Descriptive Sketch of H.H. The Nizam's Dominions. 2 vols. Bombay, 1883.

BOILEAU, Lieutenant A. H. E. Narrative of a Tour through Rajwara in 1835. Calcutta, 1837.

BROUGHTON, T. D. Letters written in a Mahratta Camp. Westminster, 1892.

BUCKLAND, C. Dictionary of Indian Biography. London, 1906.

BÜHLER, J. G.; BURGESS, J. The Indian Sect of the Jainas. London, 1875.

BURTON, Sir R. The Book of a Thousand Nights and a Night. 12 vols. London, 1893.

CARDEW, F. G. Sketch of the Services of the Bengal Army to 1895. Calcutta, 1903.

Census Reports. India, 1891, London, 1893; 1901, Calcutta, 1903; 1911, Calcutta, 1913; Baluchistan, 1901, Bombay, 1902; Baroda, 1901, Bombay, 1902; Bombay, 1911, Bombay, 1912; Marwar, 1891, Jodhpore, 1894; Rajputana and Ajmer-Merwara, 1901, Lucknow, 1902; 1911, Ajmer, 1913.

CHEVERS, N. Manual of Medical Jurisprudence for India. Calcutta, 1870.

COLEBROOKE, H. T. Essays on the Religion and Philosophy of the Hindus. London, 1858.

COMPTON, H. A Particular Account of the European Military Adventurers of Hindostan. London, n.d.; original edition, 1892.

COOK, A. B. Zeus: a Study in Ancient Religion. Vol. i. Cambridge, 1914.

Cosmas Indicopleustes, ed. J. W. McCrindle. London, 1897.

CROOKE, W. Tribes and Castes of the North-Western Provinces and Oudh. 4 vols. Calcutta, 1896.

Popular Religion and Folklore of Northern India. 2 vols. Westminster, 1896.

Things Indian. London, 1906.

ÇUNNINGHAM, Sir A. The Ancient Geography of India; the Buddhist Period. London, 1871.

Dabistan, or School of Manners, trans. D. Shea, A. Troyer, Paris. 3 vols., 1843.

DAVIDS, T. W. RHYS. Buddhist India. London, 1893.

DOW, A. The History of Hindostan, translated from the Persian. 3 vols. London, 1812.

DOWSON, J. A Classical Dictionary of Hindu Mythology and Religion, Geography, History, and Literature. London, 1879.

DUFF, C. M. The Chronology of India to the Beginning of the Sixteenth Century. London, 1899.

EGERTON, Hon. W. An Illustrated Handbook of Indian Arms. London, 1880.

ELLIOT-DOWSON. The History of India as told by its own Historians, ed. by Sir H. M. Elliot, J. Dowson, 8 vols. London, 1867–77.

ELPHINSTONE, M. The History of India; the Hindu and Mahomedan Period. 6th ed. London, 1874.

An Account of the Kingdom of Caubul and its Dependencies. 2nd ed. 2 vols. London, 1842.

Encyclopaedia Biblica, ed. T. K. Cheyne, J. S. Black. 4 vols. London, 1901.

EB. Encyclopaedia Britannica. 11th ed. 28 vols. Cambridge, 1910.

ENTHOVEN, R. E. The Ethnographic Survey of Bombay, 1904. Folklore Notes, i. Gujarat; ii. Konkan. 2 vols. Bombay, 1914–15.

ERMAN, A. Life in Ancient Egypt. London, 1894.

ERSKINE, Major K. D. Rajputana Gazetteers; ii. A., ii. B. The Mewar Residency. Ajmer, 1908; iii. A., iii. B. The Western Rajput States and Bikaner Agency. Allahabad, 1908–9.

ERSKINE, W. The History of India under Baber and Humayun. 2 vols. London, 1854.

FANSHAWE, H. C. Delhi Past and Present. London, 1902.

FERGUSSON, J. The History of Indian and Eastern Architecture. 2 vols. London, 1910.

and J. BURGESS. The Cave Temples of India. London, 1880.

FERISHTA. The History of the Mahomedan Power in India till the Year A.D. 1612, translated from the original Persian of Mahomed Kasim Ferishta, by J. Briggs. 4 vols. Calcutta, 1908.

FORBES, A. See Rasmala.

FRANCKLIN, W. History of the Reign of Shah-Aulum. London, 1798.

Military Memoirs of Mr. George Thomas. Calcutta, 1803.

FRAZER, Sir J. G. The Golden Bough. 3rd ed. 12 vols. London, 1907–12.

Lectures on the Early History of the Kingship. London, 1905.

Totemism and Exogamy. 4 vols. London, 1910.

FRAZER, R. W. A Literary History of India. London, 1898.

FRYER, J. A New Account of India and Persia, ed. W. Crooke. 3 vols., Hakluyt Society. London, 1909–13.

FÜHRER, A. The Monumental Antiquities and Inscriptions of the North-West Provinces and Oudh. Allahabad, 1891.

GRANT, C. Gazetteer of the Central Provinces of India. Nagpur, 1870.

GREAVES, E. Kashi, the Illustrious, or Benares. Allahabad, 1909.

GRIERSON, G. A. The Modern Vernacular Literature of Hindustan. Calcutta, 1889.

GRIMM, J. Teutonic Mythology, trans. J. E. Stallybrass. 4 vols. London, 1880–88.

GROWSE, F. S. Mathura, a District Memoir. 3rd ed. Allahabad, 1883.

HALL, H. R. H. The Oldest Civilization in Greece; Studies of the Mycenaean Age. London, 1901.

HALLAM, H. A View of the State of Europe during the Middle Ages. 2 vols. London, 1818.

HARRISON, J. E. Prolegomena to the Study of Greek Religion. Cambridge, 1903.

HARTLAND, E. S. Primitive Paternity. 2 vols. London, 1910.

Ritual and Belief; Studies in the History of Religion. London, 1914.

HASTINGS, J. Encyclopaedia of Religion and Ethics. 8 vols. Edinburgh, 1908–

HEBER, R. Narrative of a Journey through the Upper Provinces of India. 2 vols. London, 1861.

HEHN, V. The Wanderings of Plants and Animals from their First Home. London, 1885.

Herodotus, ed. G. Rawlinson. 3rd ed. 4 vols. London, 1875.

HERVEY, Colonel C. R. W. Some Records of Crime, the Diary of an Officer of Thuggee and Dacoitee Police. 2 vols. London, 1892.

HOWORTH, Sir H. H. A History of the Mongols. 3 vols. London, 1876–88.

HÜGEL, C. A. A. Travels in Kashmir and the Panjab. London, 1845.

IA. The Indian Antiquary. Bombay, 1872–

IBBETSON, D. C. J. Punjab Ethnography. Calcutta, 1883.

IBN BATUTA. Travels, ed. S. Lee. London, 1829.

IGI. The Imperial Gazetteer of India. 26 vols. with Atlas. Oxford, 1907.

JASB. Journal of the Asiatic Society of Bengal. Calcutta, 1834–

JRAS. Journal of the Royal Asiatic Society. London, 1834–

JADUNATH SARKAR. History of Aurangzib, mainly based on Persian Sources. 3 vols. Calcutta, 1912–16.

JAFFUR SHUREEF. Qanoon-e-Islam, or Customs of the Mussulmans of India. 2nd ed. Madras, 1863.

JAHANGIR. Memoirs, trans. Major D. Price. London, 1829.

Tuzuk-i-Jahangiri, or Memoirs of Jahangir, trans. A. Rogers, H. Beveridge. 2 vols. London, 1909–14.

JATAKA. Stories of the Buddha's Former Births. 7 vols. Cambridge, 1895–1914.

KALHANA. Rajatarangini, a Chronicle of the Kings of Kashmir, ed. and trans. M. A. Stein. 2 vols. London, 1900.

KAYE, Sir J. W. Life and Correspondence of Lord Metcalfe. 2 vols. London, 1854.

KEENE, H. G. The Turks in India. London, 1879.

Sketch of the History of Hindustan. London, 1885.

Madhava Rao Sindhia. Oxford, 1891.

The Fall of the Moghul Empire of Hindustan. London, 1887.

KENNEDY, M. Notes on the Criminal Classes of the Bombay Presidency. Bombay, 1908.

KERN, H. A Manual of Indian Buddhism. Strassburg, 1896.

LANE, E. An Account of the Manners and Customs of the Modern Egyptians. 5th ed. 2 vols. London, 1871.

LUARD, Major C. E. Ethnographic Survey of Central India. Bombay, 1909.

MACDONELL, A. A. A History of Sanskrit Literature. London, 1900; and A. Keith, A Vedic Index of Names and Subjects. 2 vols. London, 1912.

MALCOLM, Sir J. History of Persia. 2nd ed. 2 vols. London, 1829. Memoir of Central India. 2nd ed. 2 vols. London, 1824.

MALIK MUHAMMAD DIN. Gazetteer of the Bahawalpur State. Lahore, 1908.

MALLESON, G. B. Historical Sketch of the Native States of India. London, 1875.

MANU. The Laws, trans. G. Bühler. Oxford, 1886.

MANUCCI, N. Storia do Magor, ed. W. Irvine. 4 vols. London, 1907.

MARCO POLO. The Book of. Ed. Sir H. Yule. 2 vols. London, 1871.

McCRINDLE, ALEXANDER. The Invasion of India by Alexander the Great, ed. J. W. McCrindle. Westminster, 1893.

PTOLEMY, Ancient India as described by Ptolemy. London, 1885.

ANCIENT INDIA, Ancient India as described in Classical Literature. Westminster, 1901.

MEGASTHENES, Ancient India as described by Megasthenes and Arrian. Calcutta, 1877.

PERIPLUS, The Commerce and Navigation of the Erythraean Sea. Calcutta, 1879.

MINN, E. H. Scythians and Greeks. Cambridge, 1913.

MONIER-WILLIAMS, Sir M. Brāhmanism and Hinduism. 4th ed. London, 1891.

MUIR, J. Original Sanskrit Texts on the Origin and History of the People of India. 5 vols. London, 1858–72.

MÜLLER, F. MAX. India, what can it teach us? London, 1905.

OPPERT, G. The Original Inhabitants of Bharatavarsa or India. Westminster, 1893.

[ORME, R.] Historical Fragments of the Mogul Empire, of the Morattoes, and of the English Concern in Indostan. London, 1782.

[PARKS, F.] Wanderings of a Pilgrim in Search of the Picturesque. 2 vols. London, 1850.

PRINSEP, J. Useful Tables. Calcutta, 1834.

RAJENDRALA MITRA. The Indo-Aryans; Contributions towards their Ancient and Mediaeval History. 2 vols. London, 1881.

Rajputana Gazetteer. 3 vols. Simla, 1879–80.

Rāsmālā, or Hindoo Annals of the Province of Goozerat in Western India, by A. K. Forbes. London, 1878.

RAWLINSON, G. The Seventh Great Oriental Monarchy: the Sassanians or New Persian Empire. London, 1876.

RHYS, Sir J. Celtic Britain. 3rd ed. London, 1904.

RICE, B. L. Mysore Gazetteer, revised ed. 2 vols. Westminster, 1897.

Mysore and Coorg from the Inscriptions. London, 1909.

RISLEY, Sir H. H. The People of India. 2nd ed. London, 1915.

Tribes and Castes of Bengal. 2 vols. Calcutta, 1891.

ROSE, H. A. A Glossary of the Tribes and Castes of the Punjab and North-West Frontier Province. 2 vols. Lahore, 1911–14.

RUSSELL, R. V. The Tribes and Castes of the Central Provinces of India. 4 vols. London, 1916.

SHERRING, C. R. Western Tibet and the British Borderland. London, 1906.

SHERRING, M. A. The Sacred City of the Hindus. London, 1868.

SKRINE, F. H. D.; ROSS, E. D. The Heart of Asia. London, 1899.

SLEEMAN, W. H. Rambles and Recollections of an Indian Official, ed. V. A. Smith. 2nd ed. Oxford, 1915.

SMITH, VINCENT A. EHI. The Early History of India from 600 B.C. to the Muhammadan Conquest, including the Invasions of Alexander the Great. 3rd ed. Oxford, 1914.

HFA. A History of Fine Art in India and Ceylon from the Earliest Period to the Present Day. Oxford, 1911.

Asoka, The Buddhist Emperor of India. 2nd ed. Oxford, 1909.

Akbar, the Great Mogul. Oxford, 1917.

SMITH, W. R. The Religion of the Semites. 2nd ed. London, 1894.

SYAD MUHAMMAD LATIF. Agra Historical and Descriptive. Calcutta, 1896.

SYKES, Lieut.-Colonel P. M. The History of Persia. 2 vols. London, 1915.

Tarikh-i-Rashidi: A History of the Moghuls of Central Asia, trans. N. E. Elias, E. D. Ross. London, 1898.

TAVERNIER, J. B. Travels in India, ed. V. Ball. 2 vols. London, 1889.

TEMPLE, Sir R. C. The Legends of the Panjab. 3 vols. Bombay, 1884.

TERRY, E. A Voyage to East-India. London, 1777.

THOMAS, E. The Chronicles of the Pathan Kings of Delhi. London, 1871.

THURSTON, E. Castes and Tribes of Southern India. 7 vols. Madras, 1909.

Tod, J. Annals and Antiquities of Rajasthan, or the Central and Western Rajpoot States. 2 vols. London, 1829–32. Reprinted, Madras, 1873; Calcutta, 1884, 1898; London, 1914.

Travels in Western India. London, 1839.

Vishnu Purana, trans. H. H. Wilson. London, 1840.

Watson, C. C. Rajputana Gazetteer. I. A. Ajmer-Merwara. Ajmer, 1914.

Watt. Econ. Dict.: A Dictionary of the Economic Products of India, by Sir G. Watt. 6 vols. Calcutta, 1889–93.

Com. Prod. The Commercial Products of India. London, 1908.

Webb, W. W. The Currencies of the Hindu States of Rajputana. Westminster, 1893.

Wilberforce-Bell, Captain H. The History of Kathiawar from the Earliest Times. London, 1916.

Wilson, C. R. The Early Annals of the English in Bengal. 3 vols. Calcutta, 1895–1911.

Wilson, H. H. Sketch of the Religious Sects of the Hindus. 2 vols. London, 1861.

The History of British India from 1805 to 1835. 3 vols. London, 1845.

Wilson, J. Indian Caste. 2 vols. Bombay, 1877.

Yule, Sir H.; Burnell, A. C. Hobson-Jobson: A Glossary of Colloquial Anglo-Indian Words and Phrases. 2nd ed. London, 1903.

AUTHOR'S INTRODUCTION TO THE FIRST VOLUME OF THE ORIGINAL EDITION

MUCH disappointment has been felt in Europe at the sterility of the historic muse of Hindustan. When Sir William Jones first began to explore the vast mines of Sanskrit literature, great hopes were entertained that the history of the world would acquire considerable accessions from this source. The sanguine expectations that were then formed have not been realized; and, as it usually happens, excitement has been succeeded by apathy and indifference. It is now generally regarded as an axiom, that India possesses no national history; to which we may oppose the remark of a French Orientalist, who ingeniously asks, whence Abu-l Fazl obtained the materials for his outlines of ancient Hindu history?[1] Mr. Wilson has, indeed, done much to obviate this prejudice, by his translation of the *Raja Tarangini*, or History of Kashmir,[2] which clearly demonstrates that regular historical composition was an art not unknown in Hindustan, and affords satisfactory ground for concluding that these productions were once less rare than at present, and that further exertion may bring more relics to light. Although the labours of Colebrooke, Wilkins, Wilson, and others of our own countrymen, emulated by

[1] M. Abel Rémusat, in his *Mélanges Asiatiques*, makes many apposite and forcible remarks on this subject, which, without intention, convey a just reproof to the lukewarmness of our countrymen. The institution of the Royal Asiatic Society, especially that branch of it devoted to Oriental translations, may yet redeem this reproach.

[2] *Asiatic Researches*, vol. xv. [The *Rājatarangini* of Kalhana has been translated by M. A. Stein, 2 vols., London, 1910.]

many learned men in France [viii] and Germany,[1] have revealed to Europe some of the hidden lore of India; still it is not pretended that we have done much more than pass the threshold of Indian science; and we are consequently not competent to speak decisively of its extent or its character. Immense libraries, in various parts of India, are still intact, which have survived the devastations of the Islamite. The collections of Jaisalmer and Patan, for example, escaped the scrutiny of even the lynx-eyed Alau-d-din who conquered both these kingdoms, and who would have shown as little mercy to those literary treasures, as Omar displayed towards the Alexandrine library. Many other minor collections, consisting of thousands of volumes each, exist in Central and Western India, some of which are the private property of princes, and others belong to the Jain communities.[2]

If we consider the political changes and convulsions which have happened in Hindustan since Mahmud's invasion, and the intolerant bigotry of many of his successors, we shall be able to account for the paucity of its national works on history, without being driven to the improbable conclusion, that the Hindus were

[1] When the genius and erudition of such men as Schlegel are added to the zeal which characterizes that celebrated writer, what revelations may we not yet expect from the cultivation of oriental literature?

[2] Some copies of these Jain MSS. from Jaisalmer, which were written from five to eight centuries back, I presented to the Royal Asiatic Society. Of the vast numbers of these MS. books in the libraries of Patan and Jaisalmer, many are of the most remote antiquity, and in a character no longer understood by their possessors, or only by the supreme pontiff and his initiated librarians. There is one volume held so sacred for its magical contents, that it is suspended by a chain in the temple of Chintaman, at the last-named capital in the desert, and is only taken down to have its covering renewed, or at the inauguration of a pontiff. Tradition assigns its authorship to Somaditya Suru Acharya, a pontiff of past days, before the Islamite had crossed the waters of the Indus, and whose diocese extended far beyond that stream. His magic mantle is also here preserved, and used on every new installation. The character is, doubtless, the nail-headed Pali; and could we introduce the ingenious, indefatigable, and modest Mons. E. Burnouf, with his able coadjutor Dr. Lassen, into the temple, we might learn something of this Sibylline volume, without their incurring the risk of loss of sight, which befel the last individual, a female Yati of the Jains, who sacrilegiously endeavoured to acquire its contents. [For the temple library at Jaisalmer see *IA*, iv. 81 ff; for those at Udaipur, *ibid.* xiii. 31. J. Burgess visited the Pātan library, described by the Author (*WI*, 232 ff.), and found a collection of palm-leaf MSS., carefully wrapped in cloth and deposited in large chests (*BG*, vii. 598).]

ignorant of an art which has been cultivated in other countries from almost the earliest ages. Is it to be imagined that a nation so highly civilized as the Hindus, amongst whom the exact sciences flourished in perfection, by whom the fine arts [ix], architecture, sculpture, poetry, music, were not only cultivated, but taught and defined by the nicest and most elaborate rules, were totally unacquainted with the simple art of recording the events of their history, the characters of their princes, and the acts of their reigns? Where such traces of *mind* exist, we can hardly believe that there was a want of competent recorders of events, which synchronical authorities tell us were worthy of commemoration. The cities of Hastinapur and Indraprastha, of Anhilwara and Somanatha, the triumphal columns of Delhi and Chitor, the shrines of Abu and Girnar, the cave-temples of Elephanta and Ellora, are so many attestations of the same fact; nor can we imagine that the age in which these works were erected was without an historian. Yet from the Mahabharata or Great War, to Alexander's invasion, and from that grand event to the era of Mahmud of Ghazni, scarcely a paragraph of pure native Hindu history (except as before stated) has hitherto been revealed to the curiosity of Western scholars. In the heroic history of Prithiraj, the last of the Hindu sovereigns of Delhi, written by his bard Chand, we find notices which authorize the inference that works similar to his own were then extant, relating to the period between Mahmud and Shihabu-d-din (A.D. 1000–1193); but these have disappeared.

After eight centuries of galling subjection to conquerors totally ignorant of the classical language of the Hindus; after almost every capital city had been repeatedly stormed and sacked by barbarous, bigoted, and exasperated foes; it is too much to expect that the literature of the country should not have sustained, in common with other important interests, irretrievable losses. My own animadversions upon the defective condition of the annals of Rajwara have more than once been checked by a very just remark: "when our princes were in exile, driven from hold to hold, and compelled to dwell in the clefts of the mountains, often doubtful whether they would not be forced to [x] abandon the very meal preparing for them, was that a time to think of historical records?"

Those who expect from a people like the Hindus a species of

composition of precisely the same character as the historical works of Greece and Rome, commit the very egregious error of overlooking the peculiarities which distinguish the natives of India from all other races, and which strongly discriminate their intellectual productions of every kind from those of the West. Their philosophy, their poetry, their architecture, are marked with traits of originality; and the same may be expected to pervade their history, which, like the arts enumerated, took a character from its intimate association with the religion of the people. It must be recollected, moreover, that until a more correct taste was imparted to the literature of England and of France, by the study of classical models, the chronicles of both these countries, and indeed of all the polished nations of Europe, were, at a much more recent date, as crude, as wild, and as barren as those of the early Rajputs.

In the absence of regular and legitimate historical records, there are, however, other native works (they may, indeed, be said to abound), which, in the hands of a skilful and patient investigator, would afford no despicable materials for the history of India. The first of these are the Puranas and genealogical legends of the princes, which, obscured as they are by mythological details, allegory, and improbable circumstances, contain many facts that serve as beacons to direct the research of the historian. What Hume remarks of the annals and annalists of the Saxon Heptarchy, may be applied with equal truth to those of the Rajput Seven States:[1] "they abound in names, but are extremely barren of events; or they are related so much without circumstances and causes, that the most profound and eloquent writer must despair [xi] of rendering them either instructive or entertaining to the reader. The monks" (for which we may read "Brahmans"), "who lived remote from public affairs, considered the civil transactions as subservient to the ecclesiastical, and were strongly affected with credulity, with the love of wonder, and with a propensity to imposture."

The heroic poems of India constitute another resource for history. Bards may be regarded as the primitive historians of mankind. Before fiction began to engross the attention of poets, or rather, before the province of history was dignified by a class of writers who made it a distinct department of literature, the

[1] Mewar, Marwar, Amber, Bikaner, Jaisalmer, Kotah, and Bundi.

functions of the bard were doubtless employed in recording real events and in commemorating real personages. In India Calliope has been worshipped by the bards from the days of Vyasa, the contemporary of Job, to the time of Benidasa, the present chronicler of Mewar. The poets are the chief, though not the sole, historians of Western India; neither is there any deficiency of them, though they speak in a peculiar tongue, which requires to be translated into the sober language of probability. To compensate for their magniloquence and obscurity, their pen is free: the despotism of the Rajput princes does not extend to the poet's lay, which flows unconfined except by the shackles of the *chand bhujanga*, or 'serpentine stanza'; no slight restraint, it must be confessed, upon the freedom of the historic muse. On the other hand, there is a sort of compact or understanding between the bard and the prince, a barter of "solid pudding against empty praise," whereby the fidelity of the poetic chronicle is somewhat impaired. This sale of "fame," as the bards term it, by the court-laureates and historiographers of Rajasthan, will continue until there shall arise in the community a class sufficiently enlightened and independent, to look for no other recompense for literary labour than public distinction.

Still, however, these chroniclers dare utter truths, sometimes most [xii] unpalatable to their masters. When offended, or actuated by a virtuous indignation against immorality, they are fearless of consequences; and woe to the individual who provokes them! Many a resolution has sunk under the lash of their satire, which has condemned to eternal ridicule names that might otherwise have escaped notoriety. The *vish*, or poison of the bard, is more dreaded by the Rajput than the steel of the foe.

The absence of all mystery or reserve with regard to public affairs in the Rajput principalities, in which every individual takes an interest, from the noble to the porter at the city-gates, is of great advantage to the chronicler of events. When matters of moment in the disorganized state of the country rendered it imperative to observe secrecy, the Rana of Mewar, being applied to on the necessity of concealing them, rejoined as follows: "this is Chaumukha-raj;[1] Eklinga the sovereign, I his vicegerent; in him I trust, and I have no secrets from my children." To this

[1] 'Government of *four mouths*,' alluding to the quadriform image of the tutelary divinity.

publicity may be partly ascribed the inefficiency of every general alliance against common foes; but it gives a kind of patriarchal character to the government, and inspires, if not loyalty and patriotism in their most exalted sense, feelings at least much akin to them.

A material drawback upon the value of these bardic histories is, that they are confined almost exclusively to the martial exploits of their heroes, and to the *rang-ran-bhum*, or 'field of slaughter.' Writing for the amusement of a warlike race, the authors disregard civil matters and the arts and pursuits of peaceful life; love and war are their favourite themes. Chand, the last of the great bards of India, tells us, indeed, in his preface, "that he will give rules for governing empires; the laws of grammar and composition; lessons in diplomacy, home and foreign, etc.": and he fulfils his promise, by interspersing precepts on these points in various episodes throughout his work [xiii].

Again: the bard, although he is admitted to the knowledge of all the secret springs which direct each measure of the government, enters too deeply into the intrigues, as well as the levities, of the court, to be qualified to pronounce a sober judgment upon its acts.

Nevertheless, although open to all these objections, the works of the native bards afford many valuable data, in facts, incidents, religious opinions, and traits of manners; many of which, being carelessly introduced, are thence to be regarded as the least suspicious kind of historical evidence In the heroic history of Prithiraj, by Chand, there occur many geographical as well as historical details, in the description of his sovereign's wars, of which the bard was an eye-witness, having been his friend, his herald, his ambassador, and finally discharging the melancholy office of accessory to his death, that he might save him from dishonour. The poetical histories of Chand were collected by the great Amra Singh of Mewar, a patron of literature, as well as a warrior and a legislator.[1]

Another species of historical records is found in the accounts given by the Brahmans of the endowments of the temples, their dilapidation and repairs, which furnish occasions for the introduction of historical and chronological details. In the legends,

[1] [Only portions of the *Chand-rāesa* or *Prithirāj Rāesa* have been translated (Smith, *EHI*, 387, note; *IA*, i. 269 ff., iii. 17 ff., xxxii. 167 f.]

respecting places of pilgrimage and religious resort, profane events are blended with superstitious rites and ordinances, local ceremonies and customs. The controversies of the Jains furnish, also, much historical information, especially with reference to Gujarat and Nahrwala, during the Chaulukya dynasty. From a close and attentive examination of the Jain records, which embody all that those ancient sectarians knew of science, many chasms in Hindu history might be filled up. The party-spirit of the rival sects of India was, doubtless, adverse to the purity of history; and the very ground upon which the Brahmans built their ascendency was the ignorance of the people. There appears to have been in India [xiv], as well as in Egypt in early times, a coalition between the hierarchy and the state, with the view of keeping the mass of the nation in darkness and subjugation.

These different records, works of a mixed historical and geographical character which I know to exist; *raesas* or poetical legends of princes, which are common; local Puranas, religious comments, and traditionary couplets;[1] with authorities of a less dubious character, namely, inscriptions 'cut on the rock,' coins, copper-plate grants, containing charters of immunities, and expressing many singular features of civil government, constitute, as I have already observed, no despicable materials for the historian, who would, moreover, be assisted by the synchronisms which are capable of being established with ancient Pagan and later Muhammadan writers.

From the earliest period of my official connexion with this interesting country, I applied myself to collect and explore its early historical records, with a view of throwing some light upon a people scarcely yet known in Europe and whose political connexion with England appeared to me to be capable of undergoing a material change, with benefit to both parties. It would be wearisome to the reader to be minutely informed of the process I adopted, to collect the scattered relics of Rajput history into the form and substance in which he now sees them. I began with the sacred genealogy from the Puranas; examined the Mahabharata,

[1] Some of these preserve the names of princes who invaded India between the time of Mahmud of Ghazni and Shihabu-d-din, who are not mentioned by Ferishta, the Muhammadan historian. The invasion of Ajmer and the capture of Bayana, the seat of the Yadu princes, were made known to us by this means.

and the poems of Chand (a complete chronicle of his times); the voluminous historical poems of Jaisalmer, Marwar, and Mewar;[1] the histories of the Khichis, and those of the Hara princes [xv] of Kotah and Bundi, etc., by their respective bards. A portion of the materials compiled by Jai Singh of Amber or Jaipur (one of the greatest patrons of science amongst the modern Hindu princes), to illustrate the history of his race, fell into my hands. I have reason to believe that there existed more copious materials, which his profligate descendant, the late prince, in his division of the empire with a prostitute, may have disposed of on the partition of the library of the State, which was the finest collection in Rajasthan. Like some of the renowned princes of Timur's dynasty, Jai Singh kept a diary, termed *Kalpadruma*, in which he noted every event: a work written by such a man and at such an interesting juncture, would be a valuable acquisition to history. From the Datia prince I obtained a transcript of the journal of his ancestor, who served with such *éclat* amongst the great feudatories of Aurangzeb's army, and from which Scott made many extracts in his history of the Deccan.

For a period of ten years I was employed, with the aid of a learned Jain, in ransacking every work which could contribute any facts or incidents to the history of the Rajputs, or diffuse any light upon their manners and character. Extracts and versions of all such passages were made by my Jain assistant into the more familiar dialects (which are formed from the Sanskrit) of these tribes, in whose language my long residence amongst them enabled me to converse with facility. At much expense, and during many wearisome hours, to support which required no ordinary degree of enthusiasm, I endeavoured to possess myself not merely of their history, but of their religious notions, their familiar opinions, and their characteristic manners, by

[1] Of Marwar, there were the *Vijaya Vilas*, the *Surya Prakas*, and *Khyat*, or legends, besides detached fragments of reigns. Of Mewar, there was the *Khuman Raesa*, a modern work formed from old materials which are lost, and commencing with the attack of Chitor by Mahmud, supposed to be the son of Kasim of Sind, in the very earliest ages of Muhammadanism: also the *Jagat Vilas*, the *Raj-prakas*, and the *Jaya Vilas*, all poems composed in the reigns of the princes whose names they bear, but generally introducing succinctly the early parts of history. Besides these, there were fragments of the Jaipur family, from their archives; and the *Man Charitra*, or history of Raja Man.

associating with their chiefs and bardic chroniclers, and by listening to their traditionary tales and allegorical poems. I might ultimately, as the circle of my [xvi] inquiries enlarged, have materially augmented my knowledge of these subjects ; but ill-health compelled me to relinquish this pleasing though toilsome pursuit, and forced me to revisit my native land just as I had obtained permission to look across the threshold of the Hindu Minerva ; whence, however, I brought some relics, the examination of which I now consign to other hands. The large collection of ancient Sanskrit and Bhakha MSS., which I conveyed to England, have been presented to the Royal Asiatic Society, in whose library they are deposited. The contents of many, still unexamined, may throw additional light on the history of ancient India. I claim only the merit of having brought them to the knowledge of European scholars ; but I may hope that this will furnish a stimulus to others to make similar exertions.

The little exact knowledge that Europe has hitherto acquired of the Rajput States, has probably originated a false idea of the comparative importance of this portion of Hindustan. The splendour of the Rajput courts, however, at an early period of the history of that country, making every allowance for the exaggeration of the bards, must have been great. Northern India was rich from the earliest times ; that portion of it, situated on either side the Indus, formed the richest satrapy of Darius. It has abounded in the more striking events which constitute the materials for history ; there is not a petty State in Rajasthan that has not had its Thermopylae, and scarcely a city that has not produced its Leonidas. But the mantle of ages has shrouded from view what the magic pen of the historian might have consecrated to endless admiration : Somnath might have rivalled Delphos ; the spoils of Hind might have vied with the wealth of the Libyan king ; and compared with the array of the Pandus, the army of Xerxes would have dwindled into insignificance. But the Hindus either never had, or have unfortunately lost, their Herodotus and Xenophon.

If "the moral effect of history depend on the sympathy it excites" [xvii], the annals of these States possess commanding interest. The struggles of a brave people for independence during a series of ages, sacrificing whatever was dear to them for the maintenance of the religion of their forefathers, and sturdily defending to death, and in spite of every temptation, their rights and national liberty, form a picture which it is difficult to contemplate without emotion. Could I impart to the reader but a small portion of the enthusiastic delight with which I have listened to the tales of times that are past, amid scenes where their events occurred, I should not despair of triumphing over the apathy which dooms to neglect almost every effort to enlighten my native country on the subject of India; nor should I apprehend any ill effect from the sound of names, which, musical and expressive as they are to a Hindu, are dissonant and unmeaning to a European ear: for it should be remembered that almost every Eastern name is significant of some quality, personal or mental. Seated amidst the ruins of ancient cities, I have listened to the traditions respecting their fall; or have heard the exploits of their illustrious defenders related by their descendants near the altars erected to their memory. I have, whilst in the train of the southern Goths (the Mahrattas), as they carried desolation over the land, encamped on or traversed many a field of battle, of civil strife or foreign aggression, to read in the rude memorials on the tumuli of the slain their names and history. Such anecdotes and records afford data of history as well as of manners. Even the couplet recording the erection of a 'column of victory,' or of a temple or its repairs, contributes something to our stock of knowledge of the past.

As far as regards the antiquity of the dynasties now ruling in Central and Western India, there are but two the origin of which is not perfectly within the limits of historical probability; the rest having owed their present establishments to the progress of the Muslim arms, their annals are confirmed by those of their conquerors. All the existing [xviii] families, indeed, have attained their present settlements subsequently to the Muhammadan invasions, except Mewar, Jaisalmer, and some smaller principalities in the desert; whilst others of the first magnitude, such as the Pramara and Solanki, who ruled at Dhar and Anhilwara, have for centuries ceased to exist.

I have been so hardy as to affirm and endeavour to prove the common origin of the martial tribes of Rajasthan and those of ancient Europe. I have expatiated at some length upon the evidence in favour of the existence of a feudal system in India, similar to that which prevailed in the early ages on the European continent, and of which relics still remain in the laws of our own nation. Hypotheses of this kind are, I am aware, viewed with suspicion, and sometimes assailed with ridicule. With regard to the notions which I have developed on these questions, and the frequent allusions to them in the pages of this volume, I entertain no obstinate prepossessions or prejudices in their favour. The world is too enlightened at the present day to be in danger of being misled by any hypothetical writer, let him be ever so skilful; but the probability is, that we have been induced, by the multitude of false theories which time has exposed, to fall into the opposite error, and that we have become too sceptical with regard to the common origin of the people of the east and west. However, I submit my proofs to the candid judgment of the world; the analogies, if not conclusive on the questions, are still sufficiently curious and remarkable to repay the trouble of perusal and to provoke further investigation; and they may, it is hoped, vindicate the author for endeavouring to elucidate the subject, "by steering through the dark channels of antiquity by the feeble lights of forgotten chronicles and imperfect records."

I am conscious that there is much in this work which demands the indulgence of the public; and I trust it will not be necessary for me to assign a more powerful argument in plea than that which I have already [xix] adverted to, namely, the state of my health, which has rendered it a matter of considerable difficulty, indeed I may say of risk, to bring my bulky materials even into their present imperfect form. I should observe, that it never was my intention to treat the subject in the severe style of history, which would have excluded many details useful to the politician as well as to the curious student. I offer this work as a copious collection of materials for the future historian; and am far less concerned at the idea of giving too much, than at the apprehension of suppressing what might possibly be useful.

I cannot close these remarks without expressing my obligations to my friend and kinsman, Major Waugh, to the genius of whose pencil the world is indebted for the preservation and transmission of the splendid monuments of art which adorn this work.

AUTHOR'S INTRODUCTION TO THE SECOND VOLUME OF THE ORIGINAL EDITION

In placing before the public the concluding volume of the *Annals of Rajputana* I have fulfilled what I considered to be a sacred obligation to the races amongst whom I have passed the better portion of my life; and although no man can more highly appreciate public approbation, I am far less eager to court that approbation than to awaken a sympathy for the objects of my work, the interesting people of Rajputana.

I need add nothing to what was urged in the Introduction to the First Volume on the subject of Indian History; and trust that, however slight the analogy between the chronicles of the Hindus and those of Europe, as historical works, they will serve to banish the reproach, which India has so long laboured under, of possessing no records of past events: my only fear now is, that they may be thought redundant.

I think I may confidently affirm, that whoever, without being alarmed at their bulk, has the patience attentively to peruse these Annals, cannot fail to become well acquainted with all the peculiar features of Hindu society, and will be enabled to trace the foundation and progress of each State in Rajputana, as well as to form a just notion of the character of a people, upon whom, at a future period, our existence in India may depend.

Whatever novelty the inquirer into the origin of nations may find in these [viii] pages, I am ambitious to claim for them a higher title than a mass of mere archaeological data. To see humanity under every aspect, and to observe the influence of different creeds upon man in his social capacity, must ever be one of the highest sources of mental enjoyment ; and I may hope that the personal qualities herein delineated, will allow the labourer in this vast field of philosophy to enlarge his sphere of acquaintance with human varieties. In the present circumstances of our alliance with these States, every trait of national character, and even every traditional incident, which, by leading us to understand and respect their peculiarities, may enable us to secure their friendship and esteem, become of infinite importance. The more we study their history, the better shall we comprehend the causes of their international quarrels, the origin of their tributary engagements, the secret principles of their mutual repulsion, and the sources of their strength and their weakness as an aggregate body : without which knowledge it is impossible we can arbitrate with justice in their national disputes ; and, as respects ourselves, we may convert a means of defence into a source of bitter hostility.

It has been my aim to diversify as much as possible the details of this volume. In the Annals of Marwar I have traced the conquest and peopling of an immense region by a handful of strangers ; and have dwelt, perhaps, with tedious minuteness on the long reign of Raja Ajit Singh and the Thirty Years' War ; to show what the energy of one of these petty States, impelled by a sense of oppression, effected against the colossal power of its enemies. It is a portion of their history which should be deeply studied by those who have succeeded to the paramount power ; for Aurangzeb had less reason to distrust the stability of his dominion than we have : yet what is now the house of Timur ? The resources of Marwar were reduced to as low an ebb at the close of Aurangzeb's reign, as they are at the present time ; yet did that [ix] State surmount all its difficulties, and bring armies into the field that annihilated the forces of the empire. Let us not, then, mistake the supineness engendered by long oppression, for want of feeling, nor mete out to these high-spirited people the same measure of contumely, with which we have treated the subjects of our earlier conquests.

The Annals of the Bhattis may be considered as the link connecting the tribes of India Proper with the ancient races west of the Indus, or Indo-Scythia ; and although they will but slightly interest the general reader, the antiquary may find in them many new topics for investigation, as well as in the Sketch of the Desert, which has preserved the relics of names that once promised immortality.

The patriarchal simplicity of the Jat communities, upon whose ruins the State of Bikaner was founded, affords a picture, however imperfect, of petty republics—a form of government little known to eastern despotism, and proving the tenacity of the ancient Gete's attachment to liberty.

Amber, and its scion Shaikhavati, possess a still greater interest from their contiguity to our frontier. A multitude of singular privileges is attached to the Shaikhavati federation, which it behoves the paramount power thoroughly to understand, lest it should be led by false views to pursue a policy detrimental to them as well as to ourselves. To this extensive community belong the Larkhanis, so utterly unknown to us, that a recent internal tumult of that tribe was at first mistaken for an irruption of our old enemies, the Pindaris.

Haraoti may claim our regard from the high bearing of its gallant race, the Haras; and the singular character of the individual with whose biography its history closes, and which cannot fail to impart juster notions of the genius of Asiatics [x].

So much for the matter of this volume—with regard to the manner, as the Rajputs abhor all pleas *ad misericordiam*, so likewise does their annalist, who begs to repeat, in order to deprecate a standard of criticism inapplicable to this performance, that it professes *not* to be constructed on exact historical principles: *Non historia, sed particulae historiae.*

In conclusion, I adopt the peroration of the ingenuous, pious, and liberal Abu-l Fazl, when completing his History of the Provinces of India; "Praise be unto God, that by the assistance of his Divine Grace, I have completed the History of the Rajputs. The account cost me a great deal of trouble in collecting, and I found such difficulty in ascertaining dates, and in reconciling the contradictions in the several histories of the Princes of Rajputana, that I had nearly resolved to relinquish the task altogether: but who can resist the decrees of Fate? I trust that those, who have been able to obtain better information, will not dwell upon my errors; but that upon the whole I may meet with approbation." [1]

[1] [*Āīn*, ii. 418.]

York Place, Portman Square,
March 10, 1832.

ANNALS AND ANTIQUITIES OF RAJASTHAN

BOOK I

GEOGRAPHY OF RAJASTHAN OR RAJPUTANA

Boundaries of Rajputana.—Rajasthan is the collective and classical denomination of that portion of India which is 'the abode[1] of (Rajput) princes.' In the familiar dialect of these countries it is termed Rajwara, but by the more refined Raethana, corrupted to Rajputana, the common designation amongst the British to denote the Rajput principalities.

What might have been the nominal extent of Rajasthan prior to the Muhammadan conqueror Shihabu-d-din (when it probably reached beyond the Jumna and Ganges, even to the base of the Himalaya) cannot now be known. At present we may adhere to its restrictive definition, still comprehending a wide space and a variety of interesting races.

Previous to the erection of the minor Muhammadan monarchies of Mandu and Ahmadabad (the capitals of Malwa and Gujarat), on the ruins of Dhar and Anhilwara Patan, the term Rajasthan would have been appropriated to the space comprehended in the map prefixed to this work: the valley of the Indus on the west, and Bundelkhand[2] on the east; to the north, the sandy tracts (south of the Sutlej) termed Jangaldes; and the Vindhya mountains to the south.

[1] Or 'regal (*rāj*) dwelling (*thān*).'

[2] It is rather singular that the Sind River will mark this eastern boundary, as does the Indus (or great Sind) that to the west. East of this minor Sind the Hindu princes are not of pure blood, and are excluded from Rajasthan or Rajwara.

This space comprehends nearly 8° of latitude and 9° of longitude, being from 22° to 30° north latitude, and 69° to 78° east longitude, embracing a superficial area of 350,000 square miles[1] [2].

Although it is proposed to touch upon the annals of all the States in this extensive tract, with their past and present condition, those in the centre will claim the most prominent regard; especially Mewar, which, copiously treated of, will afford a specimen, obviating the necessity of like details of the rest.

The States of Rājputāna.—The order in which these States will be reviewed is as follows:

1. Mewar, or Udaipur.
2. Marwar, or Jodhpur.
3. Bikaner and Kishangarh.
4. Kotah } or Haraoti.
5. Bundi }
6. Amber, or Jaipur, with its branches, dependent and independent.
7. Jaisalmer.
8. The Indian desert to the valley of the Indus.

History of Geographical Surveys.—The basis of this work is the geography of the country, the historical and statistical portion being consequent and subordinate thereto. It was, indeed, originally designed to be essentially geographical; but circumstances have rendered it impossible to execute the intended details, or even to make the map[2] so perfect as the superabundant material at the command of the author might have enabled him to do; a matter of regret to himself rather than of loss to the general reader, to whom geographic details, however important, are usually dry and uninteresting.

It was also intended to institute a comparison between the map and such remains of ancient geography as can be extracted from the Puranas and other Hindu authorities; which, however, must be deferred to a future period, when the deficiency of the

[1] [Rājputāna, as now officially defined, lies between lat. 23° 3′ and 30° 12′ N., and long. 69° 30′ and 78° 17′ E., the total area, according to the Census Report, 1911, including Ajmer-Merwāra, being 131,698 square miles.]

[2] Engraved by that meritorious artist Mr. Walker, engraver to the East India Company, who, I trust, will be able to make a fuller use of my materials hereafter. [This has been replaced by a modern map.]

present rapid and general sketch may be supplied, should the author be enabled to resume his labours.

The laborious research, in the course of which these data were accumulated, commenced in 1806, when the author was attached to the embassy sent, at the close of the Mahratta wars, to the court of Sindhia. This chieftain's army was then in Mewar, at that period almost a *terra incognita*, the position of whose two capitals, Udaipur and Chitor, in the best existing maps, was precisely reversed [3]; that is, Chitor was inserted S.E. of Udaipur instead of E.N.E., a proof of the scanty knowledge possessed at that period.

In other respects there was almost a total blank. In the maps prior to 1806 nearly all the western and central States of Rajasthan will be found wanting. It had been imagined, but a little time before, that the rivers had a southerly course into the Nerbudda; a notion corrected by the father of Indian geography, the distinguished Rennell.[1]

This blank the author filled up; and in 1815, for the first time, the geography of Rajasthan was put into combined form and presented to the Marquess of Hastings, on the eve of a general war, when the labour of ten years was amply rewarded by its becoming in part the foundation of that illustrious commander's plans of the campaign. It is a duty owing to himself to state that every map, without exception, printed since this period has its foundation, as regards Central and Western India, in the labours of the author.[2]

[1] [James Rennell, 1742–1830.]

[2] When the war of 1817 broke out, copies of my map on a reduced scale were sent to all the divisions of the armies in the field, and came into possession of many of the staff. Transcripts were made which were brought to Europe, and portions introduced into every recent map of India. One map has, indeed, been given, in a manner to induce a supposition that the furnisher of the materials was the author of them. It has fulfilled a prediction of the Marquess of Hastings, who, foreseeing the impossibility of such materials remaining private property, "and the danger of their being appropriated by others," and desirous that the author should derive the full advantage of his labours, had it signified that the claims for recompense, on the records of successive governments, should not be deferred. It will not be inferred the author is surprised at what he remarks. While he claims priority for himself, he is the last person to wish to see a halt in science—

"For emulation has a thousand sons."

The Author's Surveys.—The route of the embassy was from Agra, through the southern frontier of Jaipur to Udaipur. A portion of this had been surveyed and points laid down from celestial observation, by Dr. W. Hunter, which I adopted as the basis of my enterprise. The Resident Envoy[1] to the court of Sindhia was possessed of the valuable sketch of the route of Colonel Palmer's embassy in 1791, as laid down by Dr. Hunter, the foundation of my subsequent surveys, as it merited from its importance and general accuracy. It embraced all the extreme points of Central India: Agra, Narwar, Datia, Jhansi, Bhopal, Sarangpur, Ujjain, and on return from this, the first meridian of the Hindus, by Kotah, Bundi, Rampura (Tonk), Bayana, to Agra. The position of all these places was more or less accurately fixed, according to the time which could be bestowed, by astronomical observation [4].

At Rampura Hunter ceased to be my guide: and from this point commenced the new survey of Udaipur, where we arrived in June 1806. The position then assigned to it, with most inadequate instruments, has been changed only 1′ of longitude, though the latitude amounted to about 5′.

From Udaipur the subsequent march of the army with which we moved led past the celebrated Chitor, and through the centre of Malwa, crossing in detail all the grand streams flowing from the Vindhya, till we halted for a season on the Bundelkhand frontier at Khimlasa. In this journey of seven hundred miles I twice crossed the lines of route of the former embassy, and was gratified to find my first attempts generally coincide with their established points.

In 1807, the army having undertaken the siege of Rahatgarh, I determined to avail myself of the time which Mahrattas waste in such a process, and to pursue my favourite project. With a small guard I determined to push through untrodden fields, by the banks of the Betwa to Chanderi, and in its latitude proceed in a westerly direction towards Kotah, trace the course once more of all those streams from the south, and the points of junction of the most important (the Kali Sind, Parbati, and Banas) with the Chambal; and having effected this, continue my journey to Agra. This I accomplished in times very different from the

[1] My esteemed friend, Graeme Mercer, Esq. (of Maevisbank), who stimulated my exertions with his approbation.

present, being often obliged to strike my tents and march at midnight, and more than once the object of plunder.[1] The chief points in this route were Khimlasa, Rajwara, Kotra on the Betwa, Kanyadana,[2] Buradungar,[3] Shahabad, Barah,[4] Puleta,[5] Baroda, Sheopur, Pali,[6] Ranthambhor, Karauli, Sri Mathura, and Agra.

On my return to the Mahratta camp I resolved further to increase the sphere, and proceeded westward by Bharatpur, Katumbar, Sentri, to Jaipur, Tonk, Indargarh, Gugal Chhapra, Raghugarh, Aron, Kurwai, Borasa, to Sagar: a journey of more than one thousand miles. I found the camp nearly where I left it.

With this ambulatory court I moved everywhere within this region, constantly employed in surveying till 1812, when Sindhia's court became stationary. It was then I formed my plans for obtaining a knowledge of those countries into which I could not personally penetrate [5].

Survey Parties.—In 1810–11 I had despatched two parties, one to the Indus, the other to the desert south of the Sutlej. The first party, under Shaikh Abu-l Barakat, journeyed westward, by Udaipur, through Gujarat, Saurashtra and Cutch, Lakhpat and Hyderabad (the capital of the Sindi government); crossed the Indus to Tatta, proceeded up the right bank to Sehwan; recrossed, and continued on the left bank as far as Khairpur, the residence of one of the triumvirate governors of Sind, and having reached the insulated Bakhar[7] (the capital of the Sogdoi of Alexander), returned by the desert of Umrasumra to Jaisalmer, Marwar, and Jaipur, and joined me in camp at Narwar. It was

[1] Many incidents in these journeys would require no aid of imagination to touch on the romantic, but they can have no place here.

[2] Eastern tableland.

[3] Sind River.

[4] Parbati River.

[5] Kali Sind River.

[6] Passage of the Chambal and junction of the Par.

[7] The Shaikh brought me specimens of the rock, which is siliceous; and also a piece of brick of the very ancient fortress of Sehwan, and some of the grain from its pits, charred and alleged by tradition to have lain there since the period of Raja Bhartarihari, the brother of Vikramaditya. It is not impossible that it might be owing to Alexander's terrific progress, and to their supplies being destroyed by fire. Sehwan is conjectured by Captain Pottinger to be the capital of Musicanus. [The capital of the Sogdoi has been identified with Alor or Aror; but Cunningham places it between Alor and Uchh. The capital of Mousikanos was possibly Alor, and Sehwān the Sindimana of the Greeks. But, owing to changes in the course of the Lower Indus, it is very difficult to identify ancient sites (McCrindle, *Alexander*, 157, 354 f.).]

a perilous undertaking; but the Shaikh was a fearless and enterprising character, and moreover a man with some tincture of learning. His journals contained many hints and directions for future research in the geography, statistics, and manners of the various races amongst whom he travelled.

The other party was conducted by a most valuable man, Madari Lal, who became a perfect adept in these expeditions of geographical discovery, and other knowledge resulting therefrom. There is not a district of any consequence in the wide space before the reader which was not traversed by this spirited individual, whose qualifications for such complicated and hazardous journeys were never excelled. Ardent, persevering, prepossessing, and generally well-informed, he made his way when others might have perished.[1]

From these remote regions the best-informed native inhabitants were, by persuasion and recompense, conducted to me; and I could at all times, in the Mahratta camp at Gwalior, from 1812 to 1817, have provided a native of the valley of the Indus, the deserts of Dhat, Umrasumra, or any of the States of Rajasthan.

The precision with which Kasids and other public conveyers of letters, in countries where posts are little used, can detail the peculiarities of a long line of route, and the accuracy of their distances would scarcely be credited in Europe. I have no hesitation in asserting that if a correct estimate were obtained of the measured [6] coss of a country, a line might be laid down upon a flat surface with great exactitude. I have heard it affirmed that it was the custom of the old Hindu governments to have measurements made of the roads from town to town, and that the *Abu Mahatma*[2] contains a notice of an instrument for that purpose. Indeed, the singular coincidence between lines measured by the perambulator and the estimated distances of the natives is the best proof that the latter are deduced from some more certain method than mere computation.

I never rested satisfied with the result of one set of my parties,

[1] His health was worn out at length, and he became the victim of depressed spirits. He died suddenly: I believe poisoned. Fateh, almost as zealous as Madari, also died in the pursuit. Geography has been destructive to all who have pursued it with ardour in the East.

[2] A valuable and ancient work, which I presented to the Royal Asiatic Society.

with the single exception of Madari's, always making the information of one a basis for the instruction of another, who went over the same ground; but with additional views and advantages, and with the aid of the natives brought successively by each, till I exhausted every field.

Thus, in a few years, I had filled several volumes with lines of route throughout this space; and having many frontier and intermediate points, the positions of which were fixed, a general outline of the result was constructed, wherein all this information was laid down. I speak more particularly of the western States, as the central portion, or that watered by the Chambal and its tributary streams, whether from the elevated Aravalli on the west, or from the Vindhya mountains on the south, has been personally surveyed and measured in every direction, with an accuracy sufficient for every political or military purpose, until the grand trigonometrical survey from the peninsula shall be extended throughout India. These countries form an extended plain to the Sutlej north, and west to the Indus, rendering the amalgamation of geographical materials much less difficult than where mountainous regions intervene.

After having laid down these varied lines in the outline described, I determined to check and confirm its accuracy by recommencing the survey on a new plan, viz. trigonometrically.

My parties were again despatched to resume their labours over fields now familiar to them. They commenced from points whose positions were fixed (and my knowledge enabled me to give a series of such), from each of which, as a centre, they collected every radiating route to every town within the distance of twenty miles. The points selected were generally such as to approach equilateral [7] triangles; and although to digest the information became a severe toil, the method will appear, even to the casual observer, one which must throw out its own errors; for these lines crossed in every direction, and consequently corrected each other. By such means did I work my way in those unknown tracts, and the result is in part before the reader. I say, in part; for my health compels me reluctantly to leave out much which could be combined from ten folios of journeys extending throughout these regions.

The Author's Map.—In 1815, as before stated, an outline map containing all the information thus obtained, and which the subsequent crisis rendered of essential importance, was presented by me to the Governor-General of India. Upon the very eve of the war I constructed and presented another, of the greater portion of Malwa, to which it appeared expedient to confine the operations against the Pindaris. The material feature in this small map was the general position of the Vindhya mountains, the sources and course of every river originating thence, and the passes in this chain, an object of primary importance. The boundaries of the various countries in this tract were likewise defined, and it became essentially useful in the subsequent dismemberment of the Peshwa's dominions.

In the construction of this map I had many fixed points, both of Dr. Hunter's and my own, to work from; and it is gratifying to observe that though several measured lines have since been run through this space, not only the general, but often the identical features of mine have been preserved in the maps since given to the world. As considerable improvement has been made by several measured lines through this tract, and many positions affixed by a scientific and zealous geographer, I have had no hesitation in incorporating a small portion of this improved geography in the map now presented.[1]

Many surveyed lines were made by me from 1817 to 1822; and here I express my obligations to my kinsman,[2] to whom alone I owe any aid for improving this portion of my geographical labours. This officer made a circuitous survey, which comprehended nearly the extreme points of Mewar, from the capital, by Chitor, Mandalgarh, Jahazpur, Rajmahall, and in return by Banai, Badnor, Deogarh [8], to the point of outset. From these extreme points he was enabled to place many intermediate ones, for which Mewar is so favourable, by reason of its isolated hills.

In 1820 I made an important journey across the Aravalli, by Kumbhalmer, Pali, to Jodhpur, the capital of Marwar, and thence by Merta, tracing the course of the Luni to its source at Ajmer; and from this celebrated residence of the Chauhan

[1] It is, however, limited to Malwa, whose geography was greatly improved and enlarged by the labours of Captain Dangerfield; and though my materials could fill up the whole of this province, I merely insert the chief points to connect it with Rajasthan.

[2] Captain P. T. Waugh, 10th Regiment Light Cavalry, Bengal.

kings and Mogul emperors; returning through the central lands of Mewar, by Banai and Bancra, to the capital.

I had the peculiar satisfaction to find that my position of Jodhpur, which has been used as a capital point in fixing the geography west and north, was only 3′ of space out in latitude, and little more in longitude ; which accounted for the coincidence of my position of Bikaner with that assigned by Mr. Elphinstone in his account of the embassy to Kabul.

Besides Udaipur, Jodhpur, Ajmer, etc., whose positions I had fixed by observations, and the points laid down by Hunter, I availed myself of a few positions given to me by that enterprising traveller, the author of the journey into Khorasan,[1] who marched from Delhi, by Nagor and Jodhpur, to Udaipur.

The outline of the countries of Gujarat,[2] the Saurashtra peninsula, and Cutch, inserted chiefly by way of connexion, is entirely taken from the labours of that distinguished geographer, the late General Reynolds. We had both gone over a great portion of the same field, and my testimony is due to the value of his researches in countries into which he never personally penetrated, evincing what may be done by industry, and the use of such materials as I have described.

Physiography of Rājputāna.—I shall conclude with a rapid sketch of the physiognomy of these regions ; minute and local descriptions will appear more appropriately in the respective historical portions

Rajasthan presents a great variety of feature. Let me place the reader on the highest peak of the insulated Abu, 'the saint's pinnacle,'[3] as it is termed, and guide his eye in a survey over this wide expanse, from the 'blue waters' of the Indus west to the 'withy-covered'[4] Betwa on the east. From this, the most [9] elevated spot in Hindustan, overlooking by fifteen hundred feet the Aravalli mountains, his eye descends to the plains of Medpat[5]

[1] Mr. J. B. Fraser [whose book was published in 1825].

[2] My last journey, in 1822–23, was from Udaipur, through these countries towards the Delta of the Indus, but more with a view to historical and antiquarian than geographical research. It proved the most fruitful of all my many journeys. [The results are recorded in *Travels in Western India*, published in 1839, after the author's death.]

[3] Guru Sikhar.

[4] Its classic name is *Vetravati*, *Vetra* being the common willow [or reed] in Sanskrit ; said by Wilford to be the same in Welsh.

[5] Literally 'the central (*madhya*) flat.' [It means 'Land of the Med tribe.']

(the classic term for Mewar), whose chief streams, flowing from the base of the Aravalli, join the Berach and Banas, and are prevented from uniting with the Chambal only by the Patar[1] or plateau of Central India.

Ascending this plateau near the celebrated Chitor, let the eye deviate slightly from the direct eastern line, and pursue the only practicable path by Ratangarh, and Singoli, to Kotah, and he will observe its three successive steppes, the miniature representation of those of Russian Tartary. Let the observer here glance across the Chambal and traverse Haraoti to its eastern frontier, guarded by the fortress of Shahabad: thence abruptly descend the plateau to the level of the Sind, still proceeding eastward, until the table-mountain, the western limit of Bundelkhand. affords a resting-point.

To render this more distinct, I present a profile of the tract described from Abu to Kotra on the Betwa:[2] from Abu to the Chambal, the result of barometrical measurement, and from the latter to the Betwa from my general observations[3] of the irregularities of surface. The result is, that the Betwa at Kotra is one thousand feet above the sea-level, and one thousand lower than the city and valley of Udaipur, which again is on the same level with the base of Abu, two thousand feet above the sea. This line, the general direction of which is but a short distance from the tropic, is about six geographic degrees in length: yet is this small space highly diversified, both in its inhabitants and the production of the soil, whether hidden or revealed.

[1] Meaning 'table (*pat*) mountain (*ar*).'—Although *ar* may not be found in any Sanskrit dictionary with the signification 'mountain,' yet it appears to be a primitive root possessing such meaning—instance, Ar-buddha, 'hill of Buddha'; Aravalli, 'hill of strength.' *Ar* is Hebrew for 'mountain' (qu. Ararat ?) Ὄρος in Greek ? The common word for a mountain in Sanskrit, *gir*, is equally so in Hebrew. [These derivations are out of date. The origin of the word *patār* is obscure. Sir G. Grierson, to whom the question was referred, suggests a connexion with Marāthi *pathār*, 'a tableland,' or Gujarati *pathār* (Skr. *prastara*, 'expanse, extent'). The word is probably not connected with Hindi *pāt*, 'a board.']

[2] The Betwa River runs under the tableland just alluded to, on the east.

[3] I am familiar with these regions, and confidently predict that when a similar measurement shall be made from the Betwa to Kotah, these results will little err, and the error will be in having made Kotah somewhat too elevated, and the bed of the Betwa a little too low. [Udaipur city is 1950 feet above sea-level.]

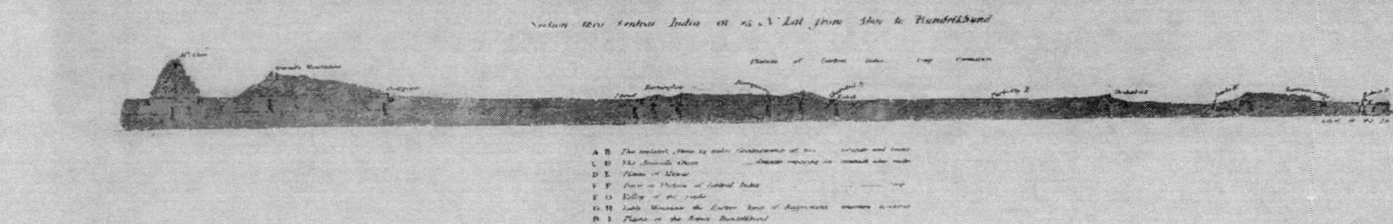

SECTION OF THE COUNTRY FROM ĀBU TO THE BETWA.

To face page 10.

Let us now from our elevated station (still turned to the east) carry the eye both south and north of the line described, which nearly bisects Madhyadesa,[1] 'the central land' of Rajasthan; best defined by the course of the Chambal and [10] its tributary streams, to its confluence with the Jumna: while the regions west of the transalpine Aravalli,[2] may as justly be defined Western Rajasthan.

Looking to the south, the eye rests on the long-extended and strongly-defined line of the Vindhya mountains, the proper bounds of Hindustan and the Deccan. Though, from our elevated stand on 'the Saint's Pinnacle' of Abu, we look down on the Vindhya as a range of diminished importance, it is that our position is the least favourable to viewing its grandeur, which would be most apparent from the south; though throughout this skirt of descent, irregular elevations attain a height of many hundred feet above such points of its abrupt descent.

The Aravalli itself may be said to connect with the Vindhya, and the point of junction to be towards Champaner; though it might be as correct to say the Aravalli thence rose upon and stretched from the Vindhya. Whilst it is much less elevated than more to the north, it presents bold features throughout,[3] south by Lunawara, Dungarpur, and Idar, to Amba Bhawani and Udaipur.

Still looking from Abu over the tableland of Malwa, we observe her plains of black loam furrowed by the numerous streams from the highest points of the Vindhya, pursuing their northerly course; some meandering through valleys or falling over precipices; others bearing down all opposition, and actually forcing an exit through the central plateau to join the Chambal.

The Aravalli Range.—Having thus glanced at the south, let us cast the eye north of this line, and pause on the alpine Aravalli.[4]

[1] Central India, a term which I first applied as the title of the map presented to the Marquess of Hastings, in 1815, 'of Central and Western India,' and since become familiar. [Usually applied to the Ganges-Jumna Duāb.]

[2] Let it be remembered that the Aravalli, though it loses its tabular form, sends its branches north, terminating at Delhi.

[3] Those who have marched from Baroda towards Malwa and marked the irregularities of surface will admit this chain of connexion of the Vindhya and Aravalli.

[4] 'The refuge of strength' [?], a title justly merited, from its affording protection to the most ancient sovereign race which holds dominion, whether

Let us take a section of it, from the capital, Udaipur, the line of our station on Abu, passing through Oghna Panarwa, and Mirpur, to the western descent near Sirohi, a space of nearly sixty miles in a direct line, where "hills o'er hills and alps on alps arise," from the ascent at Udaipur, to the descent to Marwar. All this space to the Sirohi frontier is inhabited by communities of the aboriginal races, living in a state of primeval and almost savage independence, owning no paramount power, paying no tribute, but with all the simplicity of republics; their leaders, with the title of Rawat, being hereditary. Thus the Rawat of the Oghna commune can assemble five thousand bows, and several others [11] can on occasion muster considerable numbers. Their habitations are dispersed through the valleys in small rude hamlets, near their pastures or places of defence.[1]

Let me now transport the reader to the citadel pinnacle of Kumbhalmer,[2] thence surveying the range running north to Ajmer, where, shortly after, it loses its tabular form, and breaking into lofty ridges, sends numerous branches through the Shaikhavati federation, and Alwar, till in low heights it terminates at Delhi.

From Kumbhalmer to Ajmer the whole space is termed Merwāra, and is inhabited by the mountain race of Mer or Mair, the habits and history of which singular class will be hereafter related. The range averages from six to fifteen miles in breadth,

in the east or west—the ancient stock of the Suryavans, the Heliadai of India, our 'children of the sun,' the princes of Mewar. [Ārāvalli probably means 'Corner Line.']

[1] It was my intention to have penetrated through their singular abodes; and I had negotiated, and obtained of these 'forest lords' a promise of hospitable passport, of which I have never allowed myself to doubt, as the virtues of pledged faith and hospitality are ever to be found in stronger keeping in the inverse ratio of civilization. Many years ago one of my parties was permitted to range through this tract. In one of the passes of their lengthened valleys 'The Lord of the Mountain' was dead: the men were all abroad, and his widow alone in the hut. Madari told his story, and claimed her surety and passport; which the Bhilni delivered from the quiver of her late lord; and the arrow carried in his hand was as well recognised as the cumbrous roll with all its seals and appendages of a traveller in Europe.

[2] *Meru* signifies 'a hill' in Sanskrit, hence Komal, or properly Kūmbhalmer, is 'the hill' or 'mountain of Kūmbha,' a prince whose exploits are narrated. Likewise Ajmer is the 'hill of Ajaya,' the 'Invincible' hill. *Mer* is with the long é, like *Mère* in French, in classical orthography. [Ajmer, 'hill of Aja, Chauhān.']

having upwards of one hundred and fifty villages and hamlets scattered over its valleys and rocks, abundantly watered, not deficient in pasture, and with cultivation enough for all internal wants, though it is raised with infinite labour on terraces, as the vine is cultivated in Switzerland and on the Rhine.

In vain does the eye search for any trace of wheel-carriage across this compound range from Idar to Ajmer; and it consequently well merits its appellation *ara*, 'the barrier,' for the strongest arm of modern warfare, artillery, would have to turn the chain by the north to avoid the impracticable descent to the west.[1]

Views from the Aravalli Hills.—Guiding the eye along the chain, several fortresses are observed on pinnacles guarding the passes on either side, while numerous rills descend, pouring over the declivities, seeking their devious exit between the projecting ribs of the mountain. The Berach, the Banas, the Kothari, the Khari, the Dahi all unite with the Banas to the east, while to the west the still more numerous streams which fertilize the rich province of Godwar, unite to 'the Salt River,' the Luni, and mark the true line of the desert. Of these the chief are the Sukri and the [12] Bandi; while others which are not perennial, and depend on atmospheric causes for their supply, receive the general denomination of *rela*, indicative of rapid mountain torrents, carrying in their descent a vast volume of alluvial deposit, to enrich the siliceous soil below.

However grand the view of the chaotic mass of rock from this elevated site of Kumbhalmer, it is from the plains of Marwar that its majesty is most apparent; where its 'splintered pinnacles' are seen rising over each other in varied form, or frowning over the dark indented recesses of its forest-covered and rugged declivities.

On reflection, I am led to pronounce the Aravalli a connexion of the 'Apennines of India'; the Ghats on the Malabar coast of

[1] At the point of my descent this was characteristically illustrated by my Rajput friend of Semar, whose domain had been invaded and cow-pens emptied, but a few days before, by the mountain bandit of Sirohi. With their booty they took the shortest and not most practicable road: but though their alpine kine are pretty well accustomed to leaping in such abodes, it would appear they had hesitated here. The difficulty was soon got over by one of the Minas, who with his dagger transfixed one and rolled him over the height, his carcase serving at once as a precedent and a *stepping-stone* for his horned kindred.

the peninsula: nor does the passage of the Nerbudda or the Tapti, through its diminished centre, militate against the hypothesis, which might be better substantiated by the comparison of their intrinsic character and structure.

Geology of the Aravallis.—The general character of the Aravalli is its primitive formation:[1] granite, reposing in variety of angle (the general dip is to the east) on massive, compact, dark blue slate, the latter rarely appearing much above the surface or base of the superincumbent granite. The internal valleys abound in variegated quartz and a variety of schistous slate of every hue, which gives a most singular appearance to the roofs of the houses and temples when the sun shines upon them. Rocks of gneiss and of syenite appear in the intervals; and in the diverging ridges west of Ajmer the summits are quite dazzling with the enormous masses of vitreous rose-coloured quartz.

The Aravalli and its subordinate hills are rich in both mineral and metallic products; and, as stated in the annals of Mewar, to the latter alone can be attributed the resources which enabled this family so long to struggle against superior power, and to raise those magnificent structures which would do honour to the most potent kingdoms of the west.

The mines are royalties; their produce a monopoly, increasing the personal revenue of their prince. *An-Dan-Khan* is a triple figurative expression, which comprehends the sum of sovereign rights in Rajasthan, being *allegiance, commercial duties, mines.* The tin-mines of Mewar were once very productive, and yielded, it is asserted, no inconsiderable portion of silver: but the caste of miners is extinct, and political reasons, during the Mogul domination, led to the [13] concealment of such sources of wealth. Copper of a very fine description is likewise abundant, and supplies the currency; and the chief of Salumbar even coins by sufferance from the mines on his own estate. *Surma*, or the oxide of anti-

[1] [" Oldest of all the physical features which intersect the continent is the range of mountains known as the Arāvallis, which strikes across the Peninsula from north-east to south-west, overlooking the sandy wastes of Rājputāna. The Arāvallis are but the depressed and degraded relics of a far more prominent mountain system, which stood, in Palaeozoic times, on the edge of the Rājputāna Sea. The disintegrated rocks which once formed part of the Arāvallis are now spread out in wide red-stone plains to the east" (*IGI*, i. 1).]

mony, is found on the western frontier. The garnet, amethystine quartz, rock crystal, the chrysolite, and inferior kinds of the emerald family are all to be found within Mewar; and though I have seen no specimens decidedly valuable, the Rana has often told me that, according to tradition, his native hills contained every species of mineral wealth.

The Patār Plateau.—Let us now quit our alpine station on the Aravalli, and make a tour of the *Patar*, or plateau of Central India, not the least important feature of this interesting region. It possesses a most decided character, and is distinct from the Vindhya to the south and the Aravalli to the west, being of the secondary formation, or trap, of the most regular horizontal stratification.

The circumference of the plateau is best explained in the map, though its surface is most unequally detailed, and is continually alternating its character between the tabular form and clustering ridges.

Commencing the tour of Mandalgarh, let us proceed south, skirting Chitor (both on insulated rocks detached from the plateau), thence by Jawad, Dantoli, Rampura,[1] Bhanpura, the Mukunddarra Pass,[2] to Gagraun (where the Kali Sind forces an entrance through its table-barrier to Eklera)[3] and Margwas (where the Parbati, taking advantage of the diminished elevation, passes from Malwa to Haraoti), and by Raghugarh, Shahabad, Ghazigarh, Gaswani, to Jadonwati, where the plateau terminates on the Chambal, east; while from the same point of outset, Mandalgarh, soon losing much of its table form, it stretches away in bold ranges, occasionally tabular, as in the Bundi fortress, by Dablana, Indargarh,[4] and Lakheri,[4] to Ranthambhor and Karauli, terminating at Dholpur Bari

The elevation and inequalities of this plateau are best seen by crossing it from west to east, from the plains to the level of the Chambal, where, with the exception of the short flat between Kotah and Pali ferry, this noble stream is seen rushing through the rocky barrier.

At Ranthambhor the plateau breaks into lofty ranges, their

[1] Near this the Chambal first breaks into the Patar.
[2] Here is the celebrated pass through the mountains.
[3] Here the Niwaz breaks the chain.
[4] Both celebrated passes, where the ranges are very complicated.

white summits [14] sparkling in the sun ; cragged but not peaked, and preserving the characteristic formation, though disunited from the mass. Here there are no less than seven distinct ranges (*Satpara*), through all of which the Banas has to force a passage to unite with the Chambal. Beyond Ranthambhor, and the whole way from Karauli to the river, is an irregular tableland, on the edge of whose summit are the fortresses of Utgir, Mandrel, and that more celebrated of Thun. But east of the eastern side there is still another steppe of descent, which may be said to originate near the fountain of the Sind at Latoti, and passing by Chanderi, Kanyadana, Narwar, and Gwalior, terminates at Deogarh, in the plains of Gohad. The descent from this second steppe is into Bundelkhand and the valley of the Betwa.

Distinguished as is this elevated region of the surface of Central India, its summit is but little higher than the general elevation of the crest of the Vindhya, and upon a level with the valley of Udaipur and base of the Aravalli. The slope or descent, therefore, from both these ranges to the skirts of the plateau is great and abrupt, of which the most intelligible and simple proof appears in the course of these streams. Few portions of the globe attest more powerfully the force exerted by the action of waters to subdue every obstacle, than a view of the rock-bound channels of these streams in this adamantine barrier. Four streams—one of which, the Chambal, would rank with the Rhine and almost with the Rhone—have here forced their way, laying bare the stratification from the water's level to the summit, from three to six hundred feet in perpendicular height, the rock appearing as if chiselled by the hand of man. Here the geologist may read the book of nature in distinct character ; few tracts (from Rampura to Kotah) will be found more interesting to him, to the antiquarian, or to the lover of nature in her most rugged attire.

The surface of this extensive plateau is greatly diversified. At Kotah the bare protruding rock in some places presents not a trace of vegetation ; but where it bevels off to the banks of the Par it is one of the richest and most productive soils in India, and better cultivated than any spot even of British India. In its indented sides are glens of the most romantic description (as the fountain of 'the snake King' near Hinglaj), and deep dells, the source of small streams, where many treasures of art,[1]

[1] I have rescued a few of these from oblivion to present to my countrymen.

in temples and ancient dwellings, yet remain to reward the traveller [15].

This central elevation, as before described, is of the secondary formation, called trap. Its prevailing colour, where laid bare by the Chambal, is milk-white: it is compact and close-grained, and though perhaps the mineral offering the greatest resistance to the chisel, the sculptures at the celebrated Barolli evince its utility to the artist. White is also the prevailing colour to the westward. About Kotah it is often mixed white and porphyritic, and about Shahabad of a mixed red and brown tint. When exposed to the action of the atmosphere in its eastern declivity the decomposed and rough surface would almost cause it to be mistaken for gritstone.

This formation is not favourable to mineral wealth. The only metals are lead and iron; but their ores, especially the latter, are abundant. There are mines, said to be of value, of sulphuret of lead (*galena*) in the Gwalior province, from which I have had specimens, but these also are closed. The natives fear to extract their mineral wealth; and though abounding in lead, tin, and copper, they are indebted almost entirely to Europe even for the materials of their culinary utensils.

Without attempting a delineation of inferior ranges, I will only further direct the reader's attention to an important deduction from this superficial review of the physiognomy of Rajwara.

The Mountain System of Central India.—There are two distinctly marked declivities or slopes in Central India: the chief is that from west to east, from the great rampart, the Aravalli (interposed to prevent the drifting of the sands into the central plains, bisected by the Chambal and his hundred arms) to the Betwa; the other slope is from south to north, from the Vindhya, the southern buttress of Central India, to the Jumna.

Extending our definition, we may pronounce the course of the Jumna to indicate the central fall of that immense vale which has its northern slope from the base of the Himalaya, and the southern from that of the Vindhya mountains.

It is not in contemplation to delineate the varied course of the magnificent Nerbudda, though I have abundant means; for the moment we ascend the summit of the tropical [1] Vindhya, to

[1] Hence its name, *Vindhya*, 'the barrier,' to the further progress of the sun in his northern declination. [Skr. root, *bind*, *bid*, 'to divide.']

descend into the valley of the Nerbudda, we abandon Rajasthan and the Rajputs for the aboriginal races, the first proprietors of the land. These I shall leave to others, and commence and end with the Chambal, the paramount lord of the floods of Central India [16].

The Chambal River.—The Chambal has his fountains in a very elevated point of the Vindhya, amidst a cluster of hills on which is bestowed the local appellation of Janapao. It has three co-equal sources from the same cluster, the Chambal, Chambela, and Gambhir; while no less than nine other streams have their origin on the south side, and pour their waters into the Nerbudda. The Sipra from Pipalda, the little Sind [1] from Dewas, and other minor streams passing Ujjain, all unite with the Chambal in different stages before he breaks through the plateau.

The Kali Sind, from Bagri, and its petty branch, the Sodwia, from Raghugarh; the Niwaz (or Jamniri), from Morsukri and Magarda; the Parbati, from the pass of Amlakhera, with its more eastern arm from Daulatpur, uniting at Pharhar, are all points in the crest of the Vindhya range, whence they pursue their course through the plateau, rolling over precipices,[2] till engulfed in the Chambal at the ferries of Nunera and Pali. All these unite on the right bank.

On the left bank his flood is increased by the Banas, fed by the perennial streams from the Aravalli, and the Berach from the lakes of Udaipur; and after watering Mewar, the southern frontier of Jaipur, and the highlands of Karauli, the river turns south to unite at the holy Sangam,[3] Rameswar. Minor streams contribute (unworthy, however, of separate notice), and after a thousand involutions he reaches the Jumna, at the holy Triveni,[4] or 'triple-allied' stream, between Etawa and Kalpi.

[1] This is the fourth Sind of India. We have, first, the Sind or Indus; this little Sind; then the Kali Sind, or 'black river'; and again the Sind rising at Latoti, on the plateau west and above Sironj. *Sin* is a Scythic word for river (now unused), so applied by the Hindus. [Skr. *Sindhu*, probably from the root *syand*, 'to flow.']

[2] The falls of the Kali Sind through the rocks at Gagraun and the Parbati at Chapra (Gugal) are well worthy of a visit. The latter, though I encamped twice at Chapra, from which it was reputed five miles, I did not see.

[3] *Sangam* is the point of confluence of two or more rivers, always sacred to Mahadeva.

[4] The Jumna, Chambal, and Sind [*triveni*, 'triple braid'].

The course of the Chambal, not reckoning the minor sinuosities, is upwards of five hundred miles ;[1] and along its banks specimens of nearly every race now existing in India may be found : Sondis, Chandarawats, Sesodias, Haras, Gaur, Jadon, Sakarwal, Gujar, Jat,[2] Tuar, Chauhan, Bhadauria, Kachhwaha, Sengar, Bundela ; each in associations of various magnitudes, from the substantive state of the little republic communes between the Chambal and Kuwari[3] [17].

The Western Desert.—Having thus sketched the central portion of Rajasthan, or that eastward of the Aravalli, I shall give a rapid general[4] view of that to the west, conducting the reader over the 'Thal ka Tiba,' or 'sand hills' of the desert, to the valley of the Indus.

The Luni River.—Let the reader again take post on Abu, by which he may be saved a painful journey over the Thal.[5] The most interesting object in this arid 'region of death' is the 'salt river,' the Luni, with its many arms falling from the Aravalli to enrich the best portion of the principality of Jodhpur, and distinctly marking the line of that extensive plain of ever-shifting sand, termed in Hindu geography Marusthali, corrupted to Marwar.

The Luni, from its sources, the sacred lakes of Pushkar and Ajmer, and the more remote arm from Parbatsar to its embouchure in the great western salt marsh, the Rann, has a course of more than three hundred miles.

In the term Eirinon of the historians of Alexander, we have the corruption of the word Ran or Rann,[6] still used to describe that extensive fen formed by the deposits of the Luni, and the equally saturated saline streams from the southern desert of Dhat. It is one hundred and fifty miles in length ; and where broadest, from Bhuj to Baliari, about seventy :[7] in which direc-

[1] [650 miles.]

[2] The only tribes not of Rajput blood.

[3] The 'virgin' stream.

[4] I do not repeat the names of towns forming the arrondissements of the various States; they are distinctly laid down in the boundary lines of each.

[5] Thal is the general term for the sand ridges of the desert. [Skr. *sthala*, 'firm ground.']

[6] Most probably a corruption of *aranya*, or desert ; [or *irina*, *īrina*, 'desert, salt soil '], so that the Greek mode of writing it is more correct than the present.

[7] [The area of the Rann is about 9000 square miles : its length 150, breadth, 60 miles. Bhuj lies inland, not on the banks of the Rann.]

tion the caravans cross, having as a place of halt an insulated oasis in this mediterranean salt marsh. In the dry season, nothing meets the eye but an extensive and glaring sheet of salt, spread over its insidious surface, full of dangerous quicksands: and in the rains it is a dirty saline solution, up to the camels' girths in many places. The little oasis, the Khari Kaba, furnishes pasture for this useful animal and rest for the traveller pursuing his journey to either bank.

The Mirage.—It is on the desiccated borders [1] of this vast salt marsh that the illusory phenomenon, the mirage, presents its fantastic appearance, pleasing to all but the wearied traveller, who sees a haven of rest in the embattled towers, the peaceful hamlet,[2] [18] or shady grove, to which he hastens in vain; receding as he advances, till "the sun in his might," dissipating these "cloud-capp'd towers," reveals the vanity of his pursuit.

Such phenomena are common to the desert, more particularly where these extensive saline depositions exist, but varying from certain causes. In most cases, this powerfully magnifying and reflecting medium is a vertical stratum; at first dense and opaque, it gradually attenuates with increased temperature, till the maximum of heat, which it can no longer resist, drives it off in an ethereal vapour. This optical deception, well known to the Rajputs, is called *sikot*, or 'winter castles,' because chiefly visible in the cold season: hence, possibly, originated the equally illusory and delightful 'Chateau en Espagne,' so well known in the west.[3]

[1] It is here the wild ass (*gorkhar*) roams at large, untamable as in the day of the Arabian Patriarch of Uz, "whose house I have made the wilderness, the barren land (or, according to the Hebrew, *salt places*), his dwelling. He scorneth the multitude of the city, neither regardeth he the crying of the driver" (Job xxxix. 6, 7).

[2] Purwa.

[3] I have beheld it from the top of the ruined fortress of Hissar with unlimited range of vision, no object to diverge its ray, save the miniature forests; the entire circle of the horizon a chain of more than fancy could form of palaces, towers, and these airy 'pillars of heaven' terminating in turn their ephemeral existence. But in the deserts of Dhat and Umrasumra, where the shepherds pasture their flocks, and especially where the alkaline plant is produced, the stratification is more horizontal, and produces more of the watery deception. It is this illusion to which the inspired writer refers, when he says, "the mock pool of the desert shall become real water" [Isaiah xxv. 7]. The inhabitants of the desert term it *Chitram*, literally 'the picture,' by no means an unhappy designation.

The Desert.—From the north bank of the Luni to the south, and the Shaikhavat frontier to the east, the sandy region commences. Bikaner, Jodhpur, Jaisalmer are all sandy plains, increasing in volume as you proceed westward. All this portion of territory is incumbent on a sandstone formation: soundings of all the new wells made from Jodhpur to Ajmer yielded the same result: sand, concrete siliceous deposits, and chalk.

Jaisalmer is everywhere encircled by desert; and that portion round the capital might not be improperly termed an oasis, in which wheat, barley, and even rice are produced. The fortress is erected on the extremity of a range of some hundred feet in elevation, which can be traced beyond its southern confines to the ruins of the ancient Chhotan erected upon them, and which tradition has preserved as the capital of a tribe, or prince, termed Hapa, of whom no other trace exists. It is not unlikely that this ridge may be connected with that which runs through the rich province of Jalor; consequently an offset from the base of Abu.

Though all these regions collectively bear the term Marusthali, or 'region of death' (the emphatic and figurative phrase for the desert), the restrictive definition applies to a part only, that under the dominion of the Rathor race [19].

From Balotra on the Luni, throughout the whole of Dhat and Umrasumra, the western portion of Jaisalmer, and a broad strip between the southern limits of Daudputra and Bikaner, there is real solitude and desolation. But from the Sutlej to the Rann, a space of five hundred miles of longitudinal distance, and varying in breadth from fifty to one hundred miles, numerous oases are found, where the shepherds from the valley of the Indus and the Thal pasture their flocks. The springs of water in these places have various appellations, *tar, par, rar, dar,* all expressive of the element, round which assemble the Rajars, Sodhas, Mangalias, and Sahariyas,[1] inhabiting the desert.

[1] *Sehraie* [in the text], from *sahra,* 'desert.' Hence Sarrazin, or Saracen, is a corruption from *sahra,* 'desert,' and *zadan,* 'to strike,' contracted. *Rāhzani,* 'to strike on the road' (*rāh*). *Rāhbar,* '*on* the road,' corrupted by the Pindaris to *labar,* the designation of their forays. [The true name is Sahariya, which has been connected with that of the Savara, a tribe in Eastern India. Saracen comes to us from the late Latin *Saraceni,* of which the origin is unknown; it cannot be derived from the Arabic *Sharqi,* 'eastern' (see *New English Dictionary, s.v.*).]

I will not touch on the salt lakes or natron beds, or the other products of the desert, vegetable or mineral; though the latter might soon be described, being confined to the jasper rock near Jaisalmer, which has been much used in the beautiful arabesques of that fairy fabric, at Agra, the mausoleum of Shah Jahan's queen.

Neither shall I describe the valley of the Indus, or that portion eastward of the stream, the termination of the sand ridges of the desert. I will merely remark, that the small stream which breaks from the Indus at Dara, seven miles north of the insulated Bakhar, and falls into the ocean at Lakhpat, shows the breadth of this eastern portion of the valley, which forms the western boundary of the desert. A traveller proceeding from the Khichi or flats of Sind to the east, sees the line of the desert distinctly marked, with its elevated *tibas* or sand ridges under which flows the Sankra, which is generally dry except at periodical inundations. These sand-hills are of considerable elevation, and may be considered the limit of the inundation of the 'sweet river,' the Mitha Maran, a Scythic or Tatar name for river, and by which alone the Indus is known, from the Panjnad [1] to the ocean [20].

[1] The confluent arms or sources of the Indus.

BOOK II

HISTORY OF THE RĀJPUT TRIBES

CHAPTER 1

The Purānas.—Being desirous of epitomizing the chronicles of the martial races of Central and Western India, it was essential to ascertain the sources whence they draw, or claim to draw, their lineage. For this purpose I obtained from the library of the Rana of Udaipur their sacred volumes, the Puranas, and laid them before a body of pandits, over whom presided the learned Jati Gyanchandra. From these extracts were made of all the genealogies of the great races of Surya and Chandra, and of facts historical and geographical.

Most of the Puranas [1] contain portions of historical as well as geographical knowledge; but the Bhagavat, the Skanda, the Agni, and the Bhavishya are the chief guides. It is rather fortunate than to be regretted that their chronologies do not perfectly agree. The number of princes in each line varies, and names are transposed; but we recognize distinctly the principal features in each, affording the conclusion that they are the productions of various writers, borrowing from some common original source [21].

[1] "Every Purana," says the first authority existing in Sanskrit lore, "treats of five subjects: the creation of the universe; its progress, and the renovation of the world; the genealogy of gods and heroes; chronology, according to a fabulous system; and heroic history, containing the achievements of demi-gods and heroes. Since each purana contains a cosmogony, both mythological and heroic history, the works which bear that title may not unaptly be compared to the Grecian theogonies" ('Essay on the Sanskrit and Pracrit Languages,' by H. T. Colebrooke, Esq.; *As. Res.* vol. vii. p. 202). [On the age of the Purānas see Smith, *EHI*, 21 ff.]

Deluge Legend.—The Genesis[1] of India commences with an event described in the history of almost all nations, the deluge, which, though treated with the fancy peculiar to the orientals, is not the less entitled to attention. The essence of the extract from the Agni Purana is this: "When ocean quitted his bounds and caused universal destruction by Brahma's command, Vaivaswata[2] Manu (Noah), who dwelt near the Himalaya[3] mountains was giving water to the gods in the Kritamala river, when a small fish fell into his hand. A voice commanded him to preserve it. The fish expanded to an enormous size. Manu, with his sons and their wives, and the sages, with the seed of every living thing, entered into a vessel which was fastened to a horn on the head of the fish, and thus they were preserved."

Here, then, the grand northern chain is given to which the abode of the great patriarch of mankind approximated. In the Bhavishya it is stated, that "Vaivaswata (sun-born) Manu ruled at the mountain Sumeru. Of his seed was Kakutstha Raja, who obtained sovereignty at Ayodhya,[4] and his descendants filled the land and spread over the earth."

I am aware of the meaning given to Sumeru, that thus the Hindus designated the north pole of the earth. But they had also a mountain with this same appellation of pre-eminence of Meru, 'the hill,' with the prefix Su, 'good, sacred': the Sacred Hill.

Meru, Sumeru.—In the geography of the Agni Purana, the term is used as a substantial geographical limit;[5] and some of

[1] Resolvable into Sanskrit, *janam*, 'birth,' and *is* and *iswar*, 'lords' [γένω, γίγνομαι, Skr. root *jan*, 'to generate'].

[2] Son of the sun.

[3] The snowy Caucasus. Sir William Jones, in an extract from a work entitled *Essence of the Pooranas*, says that this event took place at Dravira in the Deccan.

[4] The present Ajodhya, capital of one of the twenty-two satrapies constituting the Mogul Empire, and for some generations held by the titular Vizir, who has recently assumed the regal title. [Ghāziu-d-dīn Haidar in 1819.]

[5] "To the south of Sumeru are the mountains Himavan, Hemakūta, and Nishadha; to the north are the countries Nīl, Sveta, and Sringi. Between Homāchal and the ocean the land is Bhāratkhand, called Kukarma Bhūmi (*land of vice*, opposed to Āryāvarta, or *land of virtue*), in which the seven grand ranges are Mahendra, Malaya, Sahya, Suktimat, Riksha, Vindhya, and Paripatra" (*Agni Purana*).

the rivers flowing from the mountainous ranges, whose relative position with Sumeru are there defined, still retain their ancient appellations. Let us not darken the subject, by supposing only allegorical meanings attached to explicit points. In the distribution of their seven dwipas, or continents, though they interpose seas of curds, milk, or wine, we should not reject strong and evident facts, because subsequent ignorant interpolators filled up the page with puerilitics [22].

This sacred mountain (Sumeru) is claimed by the Brahmans as the abode of Mahadeva,[1] Adiswar,[2] or Baghes[3]; by the Jains, as the abode of Adinath,[4] the first Jiniswara, or Jain lord. Here they say he taught mankind the arts of agriculture and civilized life. The Greeks claimed it as the abode of Bacchus; and hence the Grecian fable of this god being taken from the thigh of Jupiter, confounding *meros* (thigh) with the *meru* (hill) of this Indian deity. In this vicinity the followers of Alexander had their Saturnalia, drank to excess of the wine from its indigenous vines, and bound their brows with ivy (*vela*)[5] sacred to the Baghes of the east and west, whose votaries alike indulge in 'strong drink.'

These traditions appear to point to one spot, and to one individual, in the early history of mankind, when the Hindu and the Greek approach a common focus; for there is little doubt that Adinath, Adiswara, Osiris, Baghes, Bacchus, Manu, Menes designate the patriarch of mankind, Noah.

The Hindus can at this time give only a very general idea of the site of Meru; but they appear to localize it in a space of which Bamian, Kabul, and Ghazni would be the exterior points. The former of these cities is known to possess remains of the

[1] The Creator, literally 'the Great God.

[2] The 'first lord.'

[3] Baghes, 'the tiger lord. He wears a tiger's or panther's hide; which he places beneath him. So Bacchus did. The phallus is the emblem of each. Baghes has several temples in Mewar. [In identifying Bacchus with a Hindu tiger god the author depended on *Asiatic Researches*, i. 258, viii. 51. For the Greek story in the text see Quintus Curtius viii. 10; Diodorus iii. 63; Arrian, *Anabasis*, vii.]

[4] First lord.

[5] Vela is the general term for a climber, sacred to the Indian Bacchus (Baghes, Adiswara, or Mahadeva), whose priests, following his example, are fond of intoxicating beverages, or drugs. The amarbel, or immortal vela, is a noble climber.

religion of Buddha, in its caves and colossal statues.[1] The Paropamisan Alexandria is near Bamian; but the Meru and Nyssa[2] of Alexander are placed more to the eastward by the Greek writers, and according to the cautious Arrian between the Cophas and Indus. Authority localizes it between Peshawar and Jalalabad, and calls it Merkoh, or Markoh,[3] "a bare rock 2000 feet high [23] with caves to the westward, termed Bedaulat by the Emperor Humayun from its dismal appearance."[4] This

[1] ["In the Tūmān of Zohāk and Bāmiān, the fortress of Zohāk is a monument of great antiquity, and in good preservation, but the fort of Bāmiān is in ruins. In the mountain-side caves have been excavated and ornamented with plaster and paintings. Of these there are 12,000 which are called Sumaj, and in former times were used by the people as winter retreats. Three colossal figures are here: one is the statue of a man, 80 yards in height; another that of a woman, 50 yards high, and the third that of a child measuring 15 yards. Strange to relate, in one of the caves is placed a coffin containing the body of one who reposes in his last sleep. The oldest and most learned of antiquarians can give no account of its origin, but suppose it to be of great antiquity. In days of old the ancients prepared a medicament with which they anointed corpses and consigned them to earth in a hard soil. The simple, deceived by this art, attribute their preservation to a miracle" (*Āīn*, ii. 409 f., with Jarrett's notes). For Bāmiān see *EB*, iii. 304 f.]

[2] Nishadha is mentioned in the Purana as a mountain. If in the genitive case (which the final syllable marks), it would be a local term given from the city of Nissa. [Nysa has no connexion with Nishadha. It probably lay near Jalalabad or Koh-i Mor (Smith, *EHI*, 53).]

[3] *Meru*, Sanskrit, and *Koh*, Persian, for a 'hill.'

[4] *Asiatic Researches*, vol. vi. p. 497. Wilford appears to have borrowed largely from that ancient store-house (as the Hindu would call it) of learning, Sir Walter Raleigh's *History of the World*. He combines, however, much of what that great man had so singularly acquired and condensed, with what he himself collected, and with the aid of imagination has formed a curious mosaic. But when he took a peep into "the chorographical description of the Terrestrial Paradise," I am surprised he did not separate the nurseries of mankind before and after the flood. There is one passage, also, of Sir Walter Raleigh which would have aided his hypothesis, that Eden was in Higher Asia, between the common sources of the Jihun and other grand rivers: the abundance of the *Ficus Indica*, or bar-tree, sacred to the first lord, Adnath or Mahadeva.

"Now for the tree of knowledge of good and evil, some men have presumed further; especially Gorapius Bocanus, who giveth himself the honour to have found out the kind of this tree, which none of the writers of former times could ever guess at, whereat Gorapius much marvelleth."

—"Both together went
Into the thickest wood; there soon they chose

designation, however, of Dasht-i Bedaulat, or 'unhappy plain,' was given to the tract between the cities beforementioned [24].

The only scope of these remarks on Sumeru is to show that

The fig tree; not that kind for fruit renowned,
But such as at this day, to Indians known
In Malabar or Decan, spreads her arms
Branching so broad and long, that in the ground
The bended twigs take root, and daughters grow
About the mother tree, a pillar'd shade
High overarched, and echoing walks between.
There oft the Indian herdsman, shunning heat,
Shelters in cool and tends his pasturing herds."
——"Those leaves
They gathered, broad as Amazonian targe."
Paradise Lost, Book ix. 1100 ff.

Sir Walter strongly supports the Hindu hypothesis regarding the locality of the nursery for rearing mankind, and that "India was the first planted and peopled countrie after the flood" (p. 99). His first argument is, that it was a place where the vine and olive were indigenous, as amongst the Sakai Scythai (and as they still are, together with oats, between Kabul and Bamian); and that Ararat could not be in Armenia, because the Gordian mountains on which the ark rested were in longitude 75°, and the Valley of Shinar 79° to 80°, which would be reversing the tide of migration. "As they journeyed *from the East*, they found a plain, in the land of Shinar, and they dwelt there" (Genesis, chap. xi. ver. 2). He adds, "Ararat, named by Moses, is not any one hill, but a general term for the great Caucasian range; therefore we must blow up this mountain Ararat, or dig it down and carry it out of Armenia, or find it elsewhere in a warmer country, and east from Shinar." He therefore places it in Indo-Scythia, in 140° of longitude and 35° to 37° of latitude, "where the mountains do build themselves exceeding high": and concludes, "It was in the plentiful warm East where Noah rested, where he planted the vine, where he tilled the ground and lived thereon. Placuit vero Noacho agriculturæ studium in qua tractanda ipse omnium peritissimus esse dicitur; ob eamque rem, sua ipsius lingua, *Ish-Adamath*: * hoc est, *Telluris Vir*, appellatur, celebratusque est. The study of husbandry pleased Noah (says the excellent learned man, Arius Montanus) in the order and knowledge of which it is said that Noah excelled all men, and therefore was he called in his own language, *a man exercised in the earth.*" The title, character, and abode exactly suit the description

---

* In Sanskrit, *Īsh*, 'Lord,' *ādi*, 'the first,' *matti*, 'Earth.' [The derivation is absurd: *matti*, 'clay,' is modern Hindi.] Here the Sanskrit and Hebrew have the same meaning, 'first lord of the earth.' In these remote Rajput regions, where early manners and language remain, the strongest phrase to denote a man or human being is literally 'earth.' A chief describing a fray between his own followers and borderers whence death ensued, says, *Meri matti māri*, 'My earth has been struck': a phrase requiring no comment, and denoting that he must have blood in return.

the Hindus themselves do not make India within the Indus the cradle of their race, but west, amidst the hills of Caucasus,[1] whence the sons of Vaivaswata, or the 'sun-born,' migrated eastward to the Indus and Ganges, and founded their first establishment in Kosala, the capital, Ayodhya, or Oudh.

Most nations have indulged the desire of fixing the source whence they issued, and few spots possess more interest than this elevated Madhya-Bhumi, or 'central region' of Asia, where the Amu, Oxus, or Jihun, and other rivers, have their rise, and in which both the Surya and Indu[2] races (*Sakha*) claim the hill,[3]

---

the Jains give of their first Jiniswara, Adinath, the first lordly man, who taught them agriculture, even to "muzzling the bull in treading out the corn."

Had Sir Walter been aware that the Hindu sacred books styled their country Aryavarta,* and of which the great Imaus is the northern boundary, he would doubtless have seized it for his Ararat. [Needless to say, these speculations are obsolete.]

[1] Hindu, or Indu-kush or koh, is the local appellation; 'mountain of the moon.' [Hindu-kush is said to mean 'Hindu-slayer' or 'Indian Caucasus.']

[2] Solar and lunar.

[3] Meru, 'the hill,' is used distinctively, as in Jaisalmer (the capital of the Bhatti tribe in the Western Desert), 'the hill of Jaisal'; Merwara, or the 'mountainous region'; and its inhabitants Meras, or 'mountaineers.' Thus, also, in the grand epic the Ramayana (Book i. p. 236), Mena is the mountain-nymph, the daughter of Meru and spouse of Himavat; from whom sprung two daughters, the river goddess Ganga and the mountain-nymph Parbati. She is, in the Mahabharata, also termed Saila, the daughter of Sail, another designation of the snowy chain; and hence mountain streams are called in Sanskrit *silletee* [?]. Saila bears the same attributes with the Phrygian Cybele, who was also the daughter of a mountain of the same name; the one is carried, the other drawn, by lions. Thus the Greeks also metamorphosed *Parbat Pamer*, or 'the mountain Pamer,' into Paropamisan, applied to the Hindu Koh west of Bamian: but the *Parbat put Pamer*, or 'Pamer chief of hills,' is mentioned by the bard Chand as being far east of that tract, and under it resided Hamira, one of the great feudatories of Prithwiraja of Delhi. Had it been Paropanisan (as some authorities write it), it would better accord with the locality where it takes up the name, being near to Nyssa and Meru, of which Parbat or Pahar would be a version, and form Paronisan, 'the Mountain of Nyssa,' the range Nishadha of the Puranas. [The true form is Paropanisos: the suggested derivation is impossible.]

---

* *Āryāvarta*, or the land of promise or virtue, cannot extend to the flat plains of India south of the Himavat; for this is styled in the *Purānas* the very reverse, *kukarma des*, or land of vice. [Āryāvarta is the land bounded by the Himalaya and Vindhya, from the eastern to the western seas (Manu, *Laws*, ii. 22).]

sacred to a great patriarchal ancestor, whence they migrated eastward.

The Rajput tribes could scarcely have acquired some of their still existing Scythic habits and warlike superstitions on the burning plains of Ind It was too hot to hail with fervent adoration the return of the sun from his southern course to enliven the northern hemisphere. This should be the religion of a colder clime, brought from their first haunts, the sources of the Jihun and Jaxartes. The grand solstitial festival, the Aswamedha, or sacrifice of the horse (the type of the sun), practised by the children of Vaivaswata, the 'sun-born,' was most probably simultaneously introduced from Scythia into the plains of Ind, and west, by the sons of Odin, Woden, or Budha, into Scandinavia, where it became the Hi-el or Hi-ul,[1] the festival of the winter solstice; the grand jubilee of northern nations, and in the first ages of Christianity, being so near the epoch of its rise, gladly used by the first fathers of the church to perpetuate that event[2] [25].

CHAPTER 2

Puranic Genealogies.—The chronicles of the Bhagavat and Agni, containing the genealogies of the Surya (*sun*) and Indu (*moon*) races, shall now be examined. The first of these, by calculation, brings down the chain to a period six centuries subsequent to Vikramaditya (A.D. 650), so that these books may have been remodelled or commented on about this period: their fabrication cannot be supposed.

Although portions of these genealogies by Sir William Jones, Mr. Bentley, and Colonel Wilford, have appeared in the volumes of the *Asiatic Researches*, yet no one should rest satisfied with the inquiries of others, if by any process he can reach the fountain-head himself.

If, after all, these are fabricated genealogies of the aneient

[1] *Haya* or *Hi*, in Sanskrit, 'horse'—*El*, 'sun': whence ἵππος and ἥλιος. Ηλ appears to have been a term of Scythian origin for the sun; and Hari, the Indian Apollo, is addressed as the sun. Hiul, or Jul, of northern nations (qu. *Noel* of France ?), is the Hindu Sankrānti, of which more will be said hereafter. [The feast was known as Hvil, Jul, or Yule, and the suggested derivation is impossible.]

[2] Mallet's *Northern Antiquities*.

families of India, the fabrication is of ancient date, and they are all they know themselves upon the subject. The step next in importance to obtaining a perfect acquaintance with the genuine early history of nations, is to learn what those nations repute to be such.

Doubtless the original Puranas contained much valuable historical matter; but, at present, it is difficult to separate a little pure metal from the base alloy of ignorant expounders and interpolators. I have but skimmed the surface: research, to the capable, may yet be rewarded by many isolated facts and important transactions, now hid under the veil of ignorance and allegory.

Neglect of History by the Hindus.—The Hindus, with the decrease of intellectual power, their possession of which is evinced by their architectural remains, where just proportion and elegant mythological device are still visible, lost the relish for the beauty of truth, and adopted the monstrous in their writings as well as their edifices. But for detection and shame, matters of history would be hideously distorted even in civilized Europe; but in the East, in the moral decrepitude of ancient Asia, with no judge to condemn, no public to praise, each priestly expounder may revel in an unfettered imagination, and reckon his admirers in proportion to the mixture of the marvellous[1] [26]. Plain historical truths have long ceased to interest this artificially fed people.

If at such a comparatively modern period as the third century before Christ, the Babylonian historian Berosus composed his fictions, which assigned to that monarchy such incredible antiquity, it became capable of refutation from the many historians of repute who preceded him. But on the fabulist of India we have no such check. If Vyasa himself penned these legends as now existing, then is the stream of knowledge corrupt from the fountain-head. If such the source, the stream, filtering through ages of ignorance, has only been increased by fresh impurities. It is difficult to conceive how the arts and sciences could advance,

[1] The celebrated Goguet remarks on the madness of most nations pretending to trace their origin to infinity. The Babylonians, the Egyptians, and the Scythians, particularly, piqued themselves on their high antiquity, and the first assimilate with the Hindus in boasting they had observed the course of the stars 473,000 years. Each heaped ages on ages; but the foundations of this pretended antiquity are not supported by probability, and are even of modern invention (*Origin of Laws*).

when it is held impious to doubt the truth of whatever has been handed down, and still more to suppose that the degenerate could improve thereon. The highest ambition of the present learned priesthood, generation after generation, is to be able to comprehend what has thus reached them, and to form commentaries upon past wisdom; which commentaries are commented on *ad infinitum*. Whoever dare now aspire to improve thereon must keep the secret in his own breast. They are but the expounders of the olden oracles; were they more they would be infidels. But this could not always have been the case.

With the Hindus, as with other nations, the progress to the heights of science they attained must have been gradual; unless we take from them the merit of original invention, and set them down as borrowers of a system. These slavish fetters of the mind must have been forged at a later period, and it is fair to infer that the monopoly of science and religion was simultaneous. What must be the effect of such monopoly on the impulses and operations of the understanding? Where such exists, knowledge could not long remain stationary; it must perforce retrograde. Could we but discover the period when religion [1] ceased to be a *profession* [27] and became hereditary (and that such there was these very genealogies bear evidence), we might approximate the era when science attained its height.

The Priestly Office.—In the early ages of these Solar and Lunar dynasties, the priestly office was not hereditary in families; it was a profession; and the genealogies exhibit frequent instances of branches of these races terminating their martial career in the

[1] It has been said that the Brahmanical religion was foreign to India; but as to the period of importation we have but loose assertion. We can easily give credit to various creeds and tenets of faith being from time to time incorporated, ere the present books were composed, and that previously the sons of royalty alone possessed the office. Authorities of weight inform us of these grafts; for instance, Mr. Colebrooke gives a passage in his *Indian Classes*: "A chief of the twice-born tribe was brought by Vishnu's eagle from Saca Dwipa; hence Saca Dwipa Brahmins were known in Jambu Dwipa." By Saka Dwipa, Scythia is understood, of which more will be said hereafter. Ferishta also, translating from ancient authorities, says, to the same effect, that "in the reign of Mahraje, King of Canouj, a Brahmin came from Persia, who introduced magic, idolatry, and the worship of the stars"; so that there is no want of authority for the introduction of new tenets of faith. [The passage, inaccurately quoted, is taken from Dow i. 16. See Briggs's translation, i. Introd. lxviii.]

commencement of a religious sect, or *gotra*, and of their descendants reassuming their warlike occupations. Thus, of the ten sons of Ikshwaku,[1] three are represented as abandoning worldly affairs and taking to religion; and one of these, Kanina, is said to be the first who made an *agnihotra*, or pyreum, and worshipped fire, while another son embraced commerce. Of the Lunar line and the six sons of Pururavas, the name of the fourth was Raya; "from him the fifteenth generation was Harita, who with his eight brothers took to the office of religion, and established the Kausika Gotra, or tribe of Brahmans."

From the twenty-fourth prince in lineal descent from Yayati, by name Bharadwaja, originated a celebrated sect, who still bear his name, and are the spiritual teachers of several Rajput tribes.

Of the twenty-sixth prince, Manava, two sons devoted themselves to religion, and established celebrated sects, viz. Mahavira, whose descendants were the Pushkar Brahmans; and Sankriti, whose issue were learned in the Vedas From the line of Ajamidha these ministers of religion were continually branching off.

In the very early periods, the princes of the Solar line, like the Egyptians and Romans, combined the offices of the priesthood with kingly power, and this whether Brahmanical or Buddhist.[2] Many of the royal line, before and subsequent to Rama, passed great part of their lives as ascetics; and in ancient sculpture and drawings the head is as often adorned with the braided lock of the ascetic as with the diadem of royalty.[3]

The greatest monarchs bestowed their daughters on these royal hermits and sages [28]. Ahalya, the daughter of the powerful Panchala,[4] became the wife of the ascetic Gautama. The sage Jamadagni espoused the daughter of Sahasra [5] Arjuna, of

[1] See Table I. [now obsolete, not reprinted].

[2] Some of the earlier of the twenty-four *Tirthakaras*, or Jain hierarchs, trace their origin from the solar race of princes. [As usual, Buddhism confused with Jainism.]

[3] Even now the Rana of Mewar mingles spiritual duties with those of royalty, and when he attends the temple of the tutelary deity of his race, he performs himself all the offices of the high priest for the day. In this point a strong resemblance exists to many of the races of antiquity.

[4] Prince of the country of Panjab, or five streams east of the Indus. [Panchāla was in the Ganges-Jumna Duāb and its neighbourhood.]

[5] The legend of this monarch stealing his son-in-law's, the hermit's, cow (of which the Ramayana gives another version), the incarnation of Para-

Mahishmat,[1] king of the Haihaya tribe, a great branch of the Yadu race.

Among the Egyptians, according to Herodotus [ii. 37, 141], the priests succeeded to sovereignty, as they and the military class alone could hold lands; and Sethos, the priest of Vulcan, caused a revolution, by depriving the military of their estates.

We have various instances in India of the Brahmans from Jamadagni to the Mahratta Peshwa, contesting for sovereignty; power [2] and homage being still their great aim, as in the days of Vishvamitra [3] and Vasishtha, the royal sages [29] whom "Janaka

---

suram, son of Jamadagni, and his exploits, appear purely allegorical, signifying the violence and oppression of royalty over the earth (*prithivi*), personified by the sacred *gao*, or cow; and that the Brahmans were enabled to wrest royalty from the martial tribe, shows how they had multiplied.

On the derivatives from the word *gao*, I venture an etymology for others to pursue:

ΓΑΐΑ, γέα, γῆ (*Dor.* γᾶ), that which produces all things (from γάω, *genero*); the earth.—*Jones's Dictionary*.

ΓΆΛΑ, Milk. *Gaola*, Herdsman, in Sanskrit. Γαλατικοί, Κέλτοι, Galatians, or Gauls, and Celts (allowed to be the same) would be the shepherd races, the pastoral invaders of Europe [?].

[1] Maheswar, on the Nerbudda River.

[2] Hindustan abounds with Brahmans, who make excellent soldiers, as far as bravery is a virtue; but our officers are cautious, from experience, of admitting too many into a troop or company, for they still retain their intriguing habits. I have seen nearly as many of the Brahmans as of military in some companies; a dangerous error [realized in the Great Mutiny].

[3] The Brahman Vasishtha possessed a cow named Savala, so fruitful that with her assistance he could accomplish whatever he desired. By her aid he entertained King Vishvamitra and his army. It is evident that this cow denotes some tract of country which the priest held (bearing in mind that *gao*, *prithivi*, signify 'the earth,' as well as 'cow'): a grant, beyond doubt, by some of Vishvamitra's unwise ancestors, and which he wished to resume. From her were supplied "the oblations to the gods and the *pitrideva* (father-gods, or ancestors), the perpetual sacrificial fire, the burnt-offerings and sacrifices." This was "the fountain of devotional acts"; this was the Savala for which the king offered "a hundred thousand cows"; this was "the jewel of which a king only should be proprietor."—The subjects of the Brahman appeared not to relish such transfer, and by "the lowing of the cow Savala" obtained numerous foreign auxiliaries, which enabled the Brahman to set his sovereign at defiance. Of these "the Pahlavi (Persian) kings, the dreadful Sakas (Sakai), and Yavanas (Greeks), with scymitars and gold armour, the Kambojas," etc., were each in turn created by the all-producing cow. The armies of the Pahlavi kings were cut to pieces by Vishvamitra; who at last, by continual reinforcements, was overpowered

sovereign of Mithila, addressed with folded hands in token of superiority."

Relations of Rajputs with Brahmans.—But this deference for the Brahmans is certainly, with many Rajput classes, very weak. In obedience to prejudice, they show them outward civility; but, unless when their fears or wishes interfere, they are less esteemed than the bards.

The story of the King Vishvamitra of Gadhipura[1] and the Brahman Vasishtha, which fills so many sections of the first book of the Ramayana,[2] exemplifies, under the veil of allegory, the

---

by the Brahman's levies. These reinforcements would appear to have been the ancient Persians, the Sacae, the Greeks, the inhabitants of Assam and Southern India, and various races out of the pale of the Hindu religion; all classed under the term *Mlechchha*, equivalent to the 'barbarian' of the Greeks and Romans.

The King Vishvamitra, defeated and disgraced by this powerful priest, "like a serpent with his teeth broken, like the sun robbed by the eclipse of its splendour, was filled with perturbation. Deprived of his sons and array, stripped of his pride and confidence, he was left without resource as a bird bereft of his wings." He abandoned his kingdom to his son, and like all Hindu princes in distress, determined, by penitential rites and austerities, "to obtain Brahmanhood." He took up his abode at the sacred Pushkar, living on fruits and roots, and fixing his mind, said, "I will become a Brahman." By these penances he attained such spiritual power that he was enabled to usurp the Brahman's office. The theocrats caution Vishvamitra, thus determined to become a Brahman by austerity, that "the divine books are to be observed with care only by those acquainted with their evidence; nor does it become thee (Vishvamitra) to subvert the order of things established by the ancients." The history of his wanderings, austerities, and the temptations thrown in his way is related. The celestial fair were commissioned to break in upon his meditations. The mother of love herself descended; while Indra, joining the cause of the Brahmans, took the shape of the kokila, and added the melody of his notes to the allurements of Rambha, and the perfumed zephyrs which assailed the royal saint in the wilderness. He was proof against all temptation, and condemned the fair to become a pillar of stone. He persevered "till every passion was subdued," till "not a tincture of sin appeared in him," and gave such alarm to the whole priesthood, that they dreaded lest his excessive sanctity should be fatal to them: they feared "mankind would become atheists." "The gods and Brahma at their head were obliged to grant his desire of Brahmanhood; and Vashishtha, conciliated by the gods, acquiesced in their wish, and formed a friendship with Vishvamitra" [Muir, *Original Sanskrit Texts*, Part i. (1858), 75 ff.].

[1] Kanauj, the ancient capital of the present race of Marwar. [This is a myth.]

[2] See translation of this epic, by Messrs. Carey and Marshman [in verse, by R. T. H. Griffith].

contests for power between the Brahmanical and military classes, and will serve to indicate the probable period when the castes became immutable. Stripped of its allegory, the legend appears to point to a time when the division of the classes was yet imperfect: though we may infer, from the violence of the struggle. that it was the last in which Brahmanhood could be obtained by the military.

Vishvamitra was the son of Gadhi (of the race of Kausika), King of Gadhipura, and contemporary of Ambarisha, King of Ayodhya or Oudh, the fortieth prince from Ikshwaku; consequently about two hundred years anterior to Rama. This event therefore, whence we infer that the system of castes was approaching perfection, was probably about one thousand four hundred years before Christ.

Dates of the Genealogies.—If proof can be given that these genealogies existed in the days of Alexander, the fact would be interesting. The legend in the Puranas, of the origin of the Lunar race, appears to afford this testimony.

Vyasa, the author of the grand epic the Mahabharata, was son of Santanu (of the race of Hari),[1] sovereign of Delhi, by Yojanagandha, a fisherman's daughter,[2] [30] consequently illegitimate. He became the spiritual father, or preceptor, of his nieces, the daughters of Vichitravirya, the son and successor of Santanu.

The Herakles Legend.—Vichitravirya had no male offspring. Of his three daughters, one was named Pandaia[3]; and Vyasa,

[1] Hari-Kula.

[2] It is a very curious circumstance that Hindu legend gives to two of their most celebrated authors, whom they have invested with a sacred character, a descent from the aboriginal and impure tribes of India: Vyasa from a fisherman, and Valmiki, the author of the other grand epic the Ramayana, from a Baddhik or robber, an associate of the Bhil tribe at Abu. The conversion of Valmiki (said to have been miraculous, when in the act of robbing the shrine of the deity) is worked into a story of considerable effect, in the works of Chand, from olden authority.

[3] The reason for this name is thus given. One of these daughters being by a slave, it was necessary to ascertain which: a difficult matter, from the seclusion in which they were kept. It was therefore left to Vyasa to discover the pure of birth, who determined that nobility of blood would show itself, and commanded that the princesses should walk uncovered before him. The elder, from shame, closed her eyes, and from her was born the blind Dhritarashtra, sovereign of Hastinapura; the second, from the same feeling, covered herself with yellow ochre, called *pandu*, and henceforth she bore the name of Pandya, and her son was called Pandu; while the third stepped forth unabashed. She was adjudged not of gentle blood, and her issue was Vidura.

being the sole remaining male branch of the house of Santanu, took his niece, and spiritual daughter, Pandaia, to wife, and became the father of Pandu, afterwards sovereign of Indraprastha.

Arrian gives the story thus: "It is further said that he [Herakles] [1] had a very numerous progeny of children born to

[1] A generic term for the sovereigns of the race of Hari, used by Arrian as a proper name [?]. A section of the Mahabharata is devoted to the history of the Harikula, of which race was Vyasa.

Arrian notices the similarity of the Theban and the Hindu Hercules, and cites as authority the ambassador of Seleucus, Megasthenes, who says: "This Herakles is held in special honour by the Sourasenoi, an Indian tribe who possess two large cities, Methôra and Cleisobora. . . . But the dress which this Herakles wore, Megasthenes tells us, resembled that of the Theban Herakles, as the Indians themselves admit." [Arrian, *Indika*, viii., Methora is Mathura; Growse (*Mathura*, 3rd ed. 279) suggests that Cleisobora is Krishnapura, 'city of Krishna.']

Diodorus has the same legend, with some variety. He says: "Hercules was born amongst the Indians, and like the Greeks they furnish him with a club and lion's hide. In strength (*bala*) he excelled all men, and cleared the sea and land of monsters and wild beasts. He had many sons, but only one daughter. It is said that he built Palibothra, and divided his kingdom amongst his sons (the Balika-putras, sons of Bali). They never colonized; but in time most of the cities assumed a democratical form of government (though some were monarchical) till Alexander's time." The combats of Hercules, to which Diodorus alludes, are those in the legendary haunts of the Harikulas, during their twelve years' exile from the seats of their forefathers.

How invaluable such remnants of the ancient race of Harikula! How refreshing to the mind yet to discover, amidst the ruins on the Yamuna, Hercules (Baldeva, god of strength) retaining his club and lion's hide, standing on his pedestal at Baldeo, and yet worshipped by the Suraseni! This name was given to a large tract of country round Mathura, or rather round Surpura, the ancient capital founded by Surasena, the grandfather of the Indian brother-deities, Krishna and Baldeva, Apollo and Hercules. The title would apply to either; though Baldeva has the attributes of the 'god of strength.' Both are *es* (lords) of the race (*kula*) of Hari (Hari-kul-es), of which the Greeks might have made the compound Hercules. Might not a colony after the Great War have migrated westward? The period of the return of the Heraclidae, the descendants of Atreus (Atri is progenitor of the Harikula), would answer: it was about half a century after the Great War. [These speculations are worthless.]

It is unfortunate that Alexander's historians were unable to penetrate into the arcana of the Hindus, as Herodotus appears to have done with those of the Egyptians. The shortness of Alexander's stay, the unknown language in which their science and religion were hid, presented an insuperable difficulty. They could have made very little progress in the study of the language without discovering its analogy to their own.

him in India . . . [31] but that he had only one daughter.[1] The name of this child was Pandaia, and the land in which she was born, and with the sovereignty of which Herakles entrusted her, was called after her name Pandaia" (*Indika*, viii.).

This is the very legend contained in the Puranas, of Vyasa (who was Hari-kul-es, or chief of the race of Hari) and his spiritual daughter Pandaia, from whom the grand race the Pandavas, and from whom Delhi and its dependencies were designated the Pandava sovereignty.

Her issue ruled for thirty-one generations in direct descents, or from 1120 to 610 before Christ; when the military minister,[2] connected by blood, was chosen by the chiefs who rebelled against the last Pandu king, represented as "neglectful of all the cares of government," and whose deposition and death introduced a new dynasty.

Two other dynasties succeeded in like manner by the usurpation of these military ministers, until Vikramaditya, when the Pandava sovereignty and era of Yudhishthira were both overturned.

[1] Arrian generally exercises his judgment in these matters, and is the reverse of credulous. On this point he says, "Now to me it seems that even if Herakles could have done a thing so marvellous, he could have made himself longer-lived, in order to have intercourse with his daughter when she was of mature age" [*Indika*, ix.].

Sandrocottus is mentioned by Arrian to be of this line; and we can have no hesitation, therefore, in giving him a place in the dynasty of Puru, the second son of Yayati, whence the patronymic used by the race now extinct, as was Yadu, the elder brother of Puru. Hence Sandrocottus, if not a Puru himself, is connected with the chain of which the links are Jarasandha (a hero of the Bharat), Ripunjaya, the twenty-third in descent, when a new race, headed by Sanaka and Sheshnag, about six hundred years before Christ, usurped the seat of the lineal descendants of Puru; in which line of usurpation is Chandragupta, of the tribe Maurya, the Sandrocottus of Alexander, a branch of this Sheshnag, Takshak, or Snake race, a race which, stripped of its allegory, will afford room for subsequent dissertation. The Prasioi of Arrian would be the stock of Puru; Prayag is claimed in the annals yet existing as the cradle of their race. This is the modern Allahabad; and the Eranaboas must be the Jumna, and the point of junction with the Ganges, where we must place the capital of the Prasioi. [For Sandrokottos or Chandragupta Maurya see Smith, *EHI*, 42 ff. He certainly did not belong to the 'Snake Race.' The Erannoboas (Skr. Hiranyavaha, 'gold-bearing') is the river Son. The Prasioi (Skr. Prāchyās, dwellers in the east') had their capital at Pātaliputra, the modern Patna (McCrindle, *Alexander*, 365 f.).]

[2] Analogous to the *maire du palais* of the first races of the Franks.

Indraprastha remained without a sovereign, supreme power being removed from the north to the southern parts of India, till the fourth, or, according to some authorities, the eighth century after Vikrama, when the throne of Yudhishthira was once more occupied by the Tuar tribe of Rajputs, claiming descents from the Pandus. To this ancient capital, thus refounded, the new appellation of Delhi was given; and the dynasty of the founder, Anangpal, lasted to the twelfth century, when he abdicated in favour of his grandson,[1] Prithiviraja, the last imperial Rajput sovereign of India, whose defeat and death introduced the Muhammadans.

This line has also closed with the pageant of a prince, and a colony returned from the extreme west is now the sole arbiter of the thrones of Pandu and Timur.

Britain has become heir to the monuments of Indraprastha raised by the descendants of Budha and Ila; to the iron pillar of the Pandavas, "whose pedestal[2] [32] is fixed in hell"; to the columns reared to victory, inscribed with characters yet unknown; to the massive ruins of its ancient continuous cities, encompassing a space still larger than the largest city in the world, whose mouldering domes and sites of fortresses,[3] the very names of which are

[1] His daughter's son. This is not the first or only instance of the Salic law of India being set aside. There are two in the history of the sovereigns of Anhilwara Patan. In all adoptions of this nature, when the child 'binds round his head the turban' of his adopted father, he is finally severed from the stock whence he had his birth. [For the early history of Delhi see Smith, *EHI*, 386 ff.]

[2] The khil, or iron pillar of the Pandus, is mentioned in the poems of Chand. An infidel Tuar prince wished to prove the truth of the tradition of its depth of foundation: "blood gushed up from the earth's centre, the pillar became loose (*dhili*)," as did the fortune of the house from such impiety. This is the origin of *Delhi*. [The inscription on the pillar proves the falsity of the legend, and the name Delhi is older than the Tuar dynasty (*IGI*, xi. 233).]

[3] I doubt if Shahpur is yet known. I traced its extent from the remains of a tower between Humayun's tomb and the grand column, the Kutb. In 1809 I resided four months at the mausoleum of Safdar Jang, the ancestor of the present [late] King of Oudh, amidst the ruins of Indraprastha, several miles from inhabited Delhi, but with which these ruins forms detached links of connexion. I went to that retirement with a friend now no more, Lieutenant Macartney, a name well known and honoured. We had both been employed in surveying the canals which had their sources in common from the head of the Jumna, where this river leaves its rocky barriers, the Siwalik chain, and issues into the plains of Hindustan. These canals on

lost, present a noble field for speculation on the ephemeral nature of power and glory. What monument would Britain bequeath to distant posterity of her succession to this dominion? Not one: except it be that of a still less perishable nature, the monument of national benefit. Much is in our power: much has been given, and posterity will demand the result.

CHAPTER 3

Princes of the Solar Line.—Vyasa gives but fifty-seven princes of the Solar line, from Vaivaswata Manu to Rama; and no list which has come under my observation exhibits more than fifty-eight, for the same period, of the Lunar race. How different from the Egyptian priesthood, who, according to Herodotus, gave a list up to that period of three hundred and thirty[1] sovereigns from their first prince, also the 'sun-born[2] Menes!'

Ikshwaku was the son of Manu, and the first who moved to the eastward, and founded Ayodhya.

Budha (Mercury) founded the Lunar line; but we are not told who established their first capital, Prayag,[3] though we are authorized to infer that it was founded by Puru, the sixth in descent from Budha [33].

A succession of fifty-seven princes occupied Ayodhya from Ikshwaku to Rama. From Yäyati's sons the Lunar races descend

each side, fed by the parent stream, returned the waters again into it; one through the city of Delhi, the other on the opposite side. [Cunningham (*ASR*, i. 207 ff.) proved that the true site of the ancient city, Siri, was the old ruined fort to the north-east of Rāī Pithora's stronghold, which is at present called Shāhpur. This identification has been disputed by C. J. Campbell (*JASB*, 1866, p. 206). But Cunningham gives good reasons for maintaining his opinion. The place took its name from Sher Shāh and his son Islām or Salīm Shāh. See also Carr Stephens, *Archaeological and Monumental Remains of Delhi* (1876), pp. 87 f., 190.]

[1] Herodotus ii. 99, 100.

[2] The Egyptians claim the sun, also, as the first founder of the kingdom of Egypt.

[3] The Jaisalmer annals give in succession Prayag, Mathura, Kusasthala, Dwaraka, as capitals of the Indu or Lunar race, in the ages preceding the Bharat or Great War. Hastinapur was founded twenty generations after these, by Hastin, from whom ramified the three grand Sakha, viz. Ajamidha, Vimidha, and Purumidha, which diversified the Yadu race.

in unequal lengths. The lines from Yadu,[1] concluding with Krishna and his cousin Kansa, exhibit fifty-seven and fifty-nine descents from Yayati; while Yudhishthira,[2] Salya,[3] Jarasandha,[4] and Vahurita,[5] all contemporaries of Krishna and Kansa, are fifty-one, forty-six, and forty-seven generations respectively, from the common ancestor Yayati.

Solar and Lunar Genealogies.—There is a wide difference between the Solar and the Yadu branches of the Lunar lines; yet is that now given fuller than any I have met with. Sir William Jones's lists of the Solar line give fifty-six, and of the Lunar (Budha to Yudhishthira) forty-six, being one less in each than in the tables now presented; nor has he given the important branch terminating with Krishna. So close an affinity between lists, derived from such different authorities as this distinguished character and myself had access to, shows that there was some general source entitled to credit.

Mr. Bentley's [6] lists agree with Sir William Jones's, exhibiting fifty-six and forty-six respectively for the last-mentioned Solar and Lunar races. But, on a close comparison, he has either copied them or taken from the same original source; afterwards transposing names which, though aiding a likely hypothesis, will not accord with their historical belief.

Colonel Wilford's [7] Solar list is of no use; but his two dynasties of Puru and Yadu of the Lunar race are excellent, that part of the line of Puru, from Jarasandha to Chandragupta, being the only correct one in print.

It is surprising Wilford did not make use of Sir William Jones's Solar chronology; but he appears to have dreaded bringing down Rama to the period of Krishna, as he is known to have preceded by four generations 'the Great War' of the Yadu races.

It is evident that the Lunar line has reached us defective. It is supposed so by their genealogists; and Wilford would have

1 See Table I. [not reprinted].

2 Of Delhi—Indraprastha.

3 Salya, the founder of Aror on the Indus, a capital I had the good fortune to discover. Salya is the Siharas of Abu-l Fazl. [*Āīn*, ii. 343.]

4 Jarasandha of Bihar.

5 Vahoorita, unknown yet. [? Bahuratha.]

6 *Asiatic Researches*, vol. v. p. 341.

7 *Ibid.* vol. v. p. 241.

increased the error by taking it as the standard, and reducing the Solar to conform thereto.

Mr. Bentley's method is therefore preferable; namely, to suppose eleven princes omitted in the Lunar between Janmejaya and Prachinvat. But as there is no [84] authority for this, the Lunar princes are distributed in the tables collaterally with the Solar, preserving contemporaneous affinity where synchronisms will authorise. By this means all hypothesis will be avoided, and the genealogies will speak for themselves.

There is very little difference between Sir William Jones's and Colonel Wilford's lists, in that main branch of the Lunar race, of which Puru, Hastin, Ajamidha, Kuru, Santanu, and Yudhishthira are the most distinguished links. The coincidence is so near as to warrant a supposition of identity of source; but close inspection shows Wilford to have had a fuller supply, for he produces new branches, both of Hastin's and Kuru's progeny. He has also one name (Bhimasena) towards the close, which is in my lists, but not in Sir William Jones's; and immediately following Bhimasena, both these lists exhibit Dilipa, wanting in my copy of the Bhagavat, though contained in the Agni Purana: proofs of the diversity of the sources of supply, and highly gratifying when the remoteness of those sources is considered. There is also in my lists Tansu, the nineteenth from Budha, who is not in the lists either of Sir William Jones or Wilford. Again; Wilford has a Suhotra preceding Hastin, who is not in Sir William Jones's genealogies.[1]

Again; Jahnu is made the successor to Kuru; whereas the Purana (whence my extracts) makes Parikshit the successor, who adopts the son of Jahnu. This son is Viduratha, who has a place in all three. Other variations are merely orthographical.

A comparison of Sir William Jones's Solar genealogies with my tables will yield nearly the same satisfactory result as to original authenticity. I say Sir William Jones's list, because there is no other efficient one. We first differ at the fourth from Ikshwaku. In my list this is Am-Prithu, of which he makes two names, Anenas and Prithu. Thence to Purukutsa, the eighteenth, the difference is only in orthography. To Irisuaka, the twenty-third in mine, the twenty-sixth in Sir William Jones's list, one name is above accounted for; but here are two wanting in mine, Trasa-

[1] I find them, however, in the Agni Purana.

dasyu and Haryaswa. There is, also, considerable difference in the orthography of those names which we have in common. Again; we differ as to the successors of Champa, the twenty-seventh, the founder of Champapur in Bihar. In Sir William's, Sadeva succeeds, and he is followed by Vijaya; but my authorities state these both to be sons of Champa, and that Vijaya, the [35] younger, was his successor, as the elder, Sadeva, took to religious austerity. The thirty-third and thirty-sixth, Kesi and Dilipa, are not noticed by Sir William Jones; but there is a much more important person than either of these omitted, who is a grand link of connexion, and affording a good synchronism of the earliest history. This is Ambarisha, the fortieth, the contemporary of Gadhi, who was the founder of Gadhipura or Kanauj. Nala, Sarura, and Dilipa (Nos. 44, 45, 54 of my lists) are all omitted by Sir William Jones.

This comparative analysis of the chronologies of both these grand races cannot fail to be satisfactory. Those which I furnish are from the sacred genealogies in the library of a prince who claims common origin with them, and are less liable to interpolation. There is scarcely a chief of character for knowledge who cannot repeat the genealogy of his line. The Prince of Mewar has a peculiarly retentive memory in this way. The professed genealogists, the Bhats, must have them graven on their memory, and the Charanas (the encomiasts) ought to be well versed therein.

The first table exhibits two dynasties of the Solar race of Princes of Ayodhya and Mithila Des, or Tirhut, which latter I have seen nowhere else. It also exhibits four great and three lesser dynasties of the Lunar race; and an eighth line is added, of the race of Yadu, from the annals of the Bhatti tribe at Jaisalmer.

Ere quitting this halting-place in the genealogical history of the ancient races, where the celebrated names of Rama, Krishna, and Yudhishthira close the brazen age of India, and whose issue introduce the present iron age, or Kali Yuga, I shall shortly refer to the few synchronic points which the various authorities admit.

Of periods so remote, approximations to truth are the utmost to be looked for; and it is from the Ramayana and the Puranas these synchronisms are hazarded.

Harischandra.—The first commences with a celebrated name of the Solar line, Harischandra, son of Trisanku, still proverbial for his humility.[1] He is the twenty-fourth,[2] and declared contemporary of Parasurama, who slew the celebrated Sahasra-Arjuna [3] of [36] the Haihaya (Lunar) race, Prince of Mahishmati on the Nerbudda. This is confirmed by the Ramayana, which details the destruction of the military class and assumption of political power by the Brahmans, under their chief Parasurama, marking the period when the military class 'lost the umbrella of royalty,' and, as the Brahmans ridiculously assert, their purity of blood. This last, however, their own books sufficiently contradict, as the next synchronism will show.

Sagara.—This synchronism we have in Sagara, the thirty-second prince of the Solar line, the contemporary of Talajangha, of the Lunar line, the sixth in descent from Sahasra Arjuna, who had five sons preserved from the general slaughter of the military class by Parasurama, whose names are given in the Bhavishya Purana.

Wars were constantly carried on between these great rival races, Surya and Indu, recorded in the Puranas and Ramayana. The Bhavishya describes that between Sagara and Talajangha

[1] [The tragical story of Harischandra is told by J. Muir, *Original Sanskrit Texts*, i. 88 ff.]

[2] Sahyadri Khanda of the Skanda Purana.

[3] In the Bhavishya Purana this prince, Sahasra-Arjuna, is termed a Chakravartin, or paramount sovereign. It is said that he conquered Karkotaka of the Takshak, Turushka, or Snake race, and brought with him the population of Mahishmati, and founded Hemanagara in the north of India, on his expulsion from his dominions on the Nerbudda. Traditionary legends yet remain of this prince on the Nerbudda, where he is styled Sahasrabahu, or 'with a thousand arms,' figurative of his numerous progeny. The Takshak, or Snake race, here alluded to, will hereafter engage our attention. The names of animals in early times, planets, and things inanimate, all furnished symbolic appellations for the various races. In Scripture we have the fly, the bee, the ram to describe the princes of Egypt, Assyria, and Macedonia; here we have the snake, horse, monkey, etc. The Snake or Takshak race was one of the most extensive and earliest of Higher Asia, and celebrated in all its extent, and to which I shall have to recur hereafter. [By the Takshak race, so often referred to, the author seems to mean a body of Scythian snake-worshippers. There are instances of a serpent barrow, and of the use of the snake as a form of ornament among the Scythians; but beyond this the evidence of worship of the serpent is scanty (E. H. Minns, *Scythians and Greeks*, 328 f., 66 note, 294, 318, 323, etc.). It was really the Takka, a Panjāb tribe (Beal, *Si-yu-ki*, i. 165 ff.; Cunningham, *Ancient Geography of India*, 148 ff.; Stein, *Rājatarangini*, i. 204 f.).]

In the Ramayana it is stated that the sacrificial horse was stolen by "a serpent (Takshak) assuming the form of Ananta."

"to resemble that of their ancestors, in which the Haihayas suffered as severely as before." But that they had recovered all their power since Parasurama is evident from their having completely retaliated on the Suryas, and expelled the father[1] of Sagara from his capital of Ayodhya. Sagara and Talajangha appear to have been contemporary with Hastin of Hastinapura, and with Anga, descended from Budha, the founder of Angadesa,[2] or Ongdesa, and the Anga race.

Ambarisha.—The Ramayana affords another synchronism; namely, that Ambarisha of Ayodhya, the fortieth prince of the Solar line, was the contemporary of Gadhi, the founder of Kanauj, and of Lomapada the Prince of Angadesa.

Krishna.—The last synchronism is that of Krishna and Yudhishthira, which terminates the [37] brazen, and introduces the Kali Yuga or iron age. But this is in the Lunar line; nor have we any guide by which the difference can be adjusted between the appearance of Rama of the Solar and Krishna of the Lunar races.

Thus of the race of Krostu we have Kansa, Prince of Mathura, the fifty-ninth, and his cousin Krishna, the fifty-eighth from Budha; while of the line of Puru, descending through Ajamidha and Dvimidha, we have Salya, Jarasandha, and Yudhishthira, the fifty-first, fifty-third, and fifty-fourth respectively.

The race of Anga gives Prithusena as one of the actors and survivors of the Mahabharata, and the fifty-third from Budha.

Thus, taking an average of the whole, we may consider fifty-five princes to be the number of descents from Budha to Krishna

[1] "Asita, the father of Sagara, expelled by hostile kings of the Haihayas, the Talajanghas, and the Sasa-vindus, fled to the Himavat mountains, where he died, leaving his wives pregnant, and from one of these Sagara was born" (Ramayana, i. 41). It was to preserve the Solar race from the destruction which threatened it from the prolific Lunar race, that the Brahman Parasurama armed: evidently proving that the Brahmanical faith was held by the Solar race; while the religion of Budha, the great progenitor of the Lunar, still governed his descendants. This strengthened the opposition of the sages of the Solar line to Vishvamitra's (of Budha's or the Lunar line) obtaining Brahmanhood. That Krishna, of Lunar stock, prior to founding a new sect, worshipped Budha, is susceptible of proof.

[2] Angdes, Ongdes, or Undes adjoins Tibet. The inhabitants call themselves Hungias, and appear to be the Hong-niu of the Chinese authors, the Huns (Hūns) of Europe and India, which prove this Tartar race to be Lunar, and of Budha. [Anga, the modern Bhāgalpur, is confounded with Hundes or Tibet.]

and Yudhishthira; and, admitting an average of twenty years for each reign, a period of eleven hundred years; which being added to a like period calculated from thence to Vikramaditya, who reigned fifty-six years before Christ, I venture to place the establishment in India Proper of these two grand races, distinctively called those of Surya and Chandra, at about 2256 years before the Christian era; at which period, though somewhat later, the Egyptian, Chinese, and Assyrian monarchies are generally stated to have been established,[1] and about a century and a half after that great event, the Flood.

Though a passage in the Agni Purana indicates that the line of Surya, of which Ikshwaku was the head, was the first colony which entered India from Central Asia, yet we are compelled to place the patriarch Budha as his contemporary, he being stated to have come from a distant region, and married to Ila, the sister of Ikshwaku.

Ere we proceed to make any remarks on the descendants of Krishna and Arjuna, who carry on the Lunar line, or of the Kushites and Lavites, from Kusa and Lava, the sons of Rama, who carry on that of the Sun, a few observations on the chief kingdoms established by their progenitors on the continent of India will be hazarded in the ensuing Chapter [38].

CHAPTER 4

Ayodhya.—Ayodhya[2] was the first city founded by the race of Surya. Like other capitals, its importance must have risen by

[1] Egyptian, under Misraim, 2188 B.C.; Assyrian, 2059; Chinese, 2207. [The first Egyptian dynasty is now dated 5500 B.C.; Chinese, 2852 B.C.; Babylonian, 2300 B.C. Any attempt to establish an Indian chronology from the materials used by the Author does not promise to be successful.]

[2] The picture drawn by Valmiki of the capital of the Solar race is so highly coloured that Ayodhya might stand for Utopia, and it would be difficult to find such a catalogue of metropolitan embellishments in this, the iron age of Oudh. "On the banks of the Surayu is a large country called Kosala, in which is Ayodhya, built by Manu, twelve yojans (forty-eight miles) in extent, with streets regular and well watered. It was filled with merchants, beautified by gardens, ornamented with stately gates and high-arched porticoes, furnished with arms, crowded with chariots, elephants, and horses, and with ambassadors from foreign lands; embellished with palaces whose domes resembled the mountain tops, dwellings of equal height, resounding with the delightful music of the tabor, the flute, and the harp.

slow degrees; yet, making every allowance for exaggeration, it must have attained great splendour long anterior to Rama. Its site is well known at this day under the contracted name of Oudh, which also designates the country appertaining to the titular wazir of the Mogul empire; which country, twenty-five years ago, nearly marked the limits of Kosala, the pristine kingdom of the Surya race. Overgrown greatness characterized all the ancient Asiatic capitals, and that of Ayodhya was immense. Lucknow, the present capital, is traditionally asserted to have been one of the suburbs of ancient Oudh, and so named by Rama, in compliment to his brother Lakshman.

Mithila.—Nearly coeval in point of time with Ayodhya was Mithila,[1] the capital of a country of the same name, founded by Mithila, the grandson of Ikshwaku.

The name of Janaka,[2] son of Mithila, eclipsed that of the founder and became the patronymic of this branch of the Solar race.

Other Kingdoms.—These are the two chief capitals of the kingdoms of the Solar line described in [39] this early age: though there were others of a minor order, such as Rohtas, Champapura,[3] etc., all founded previously to Rama.

By the numerous dynasties of the Lunar race of Budha many kingdoms were founded. Much has been said of the antiquity of Prayag; yet the first capital of the Indu or Lunar race appears

It was surrounded by an impassable moat, and guarded by archers. Dasaratha was its king, a mighty charioteer. There were no atheists. The affections of the men were in their consorts. The women were chaste and obedient to their lords, endowed with beauty, wit, sweetness, prudence, and industry, with bright ornaments and fair apparel; the men devoted to truth and hospitality, regardful of their superiors, their ancestors, and their gods.

"There were eight councillors; two chosen priests profound in the law, besides another inferior council of six. Of subdued appetites, disinterested, forbearing, pleasant, patient; not avaricious; well acquainted with their duties and popular customs; attentive to the army, the treasury; impartially awarding punishment even on their own sons; never oppressing even an enemy; not arrogant; comely in dress; never confident about doubtful matters; devoted to the sovereign."

[1] Mithila, the modern Tirhut in Bengal [including the modern districts of Darbhanga, Champāran, and Muzaffarpur].

[2] Kusadhwaja, father of Sita (spouse of Rama), is also called Janaka; a name common in this line, and borne by the third prince in succession after Suvarna Roma, the 'golden-haired' chief Mithila.

[3] [Rohtās in the modern Shāhābād district; Champapura in Bhāgalpur.]

to have been founded by Sahasra Arjuna, of the Haihaya tribe. This was Mahishmati on the Nerbudda, still existing in Maheswar.[1] The rivalry between the Lunar race and that of the Suryas of Ayodhya, in whose aid the priesthood armed, and expelled Sahasra Arjuna from Mahishmati, has been mentioned. A small branch of these ancient Haihayas[2] yet exist in the line of the Nerbudda, near the very top of the valley at Sohagpur, in Baghelkhand, aware of their ancient lineage; and, though few in number, are still celebrated for their valour.[3]

Dwarka.—Kusasthali Dwarka, the capital of Krishna, was founded prior to Prayag, to Surpur, or Mathura. The Bhagavat attributes the foundation of the city to Anrita, the brother of Ikshwaku, of the Solar race, but states not how or when the Yadus became possessed thereof.

The ancient annals of the Jaisalmer family of the Yadu stock give the priority of foundation to Prayag, next to Mathura, and last to Dwarka. All these cities are too well known to require description; especially Prayag, at the confluence of the Yamuna and Ganges. The Prasioi were the descendants of Puru[4] of Prayag, visited by Megasthenes, ambassador of Seleucus, and the principal city of the Yadus, ere it sent forth the four branches from Satwata. At Prayag resided the celebrated Bharat, the son of Sakuntala.

In the Ramayana the Sasavindus[5] (another Yadu race) are inscribed as allied with the Haihayas in the wars with the race of Surya; and of this race was Sisupal[6] (the founder of Chedi[7]), one of the foes of Krishna [40].

[1] Familiarly designated as Sahasra Bahu ki Basti, or 'the town of the thousand-armed.' [In Indore State (*IGI*, xvii. 8).]

[2] The Haihaya race, of the line of Budha, may claim affinity with the Chinese race which first gave monarchs to China [?].

[3] Of this I have heard the most romantic proofs in very recent times.

[4] Puru became the patronymic of this branch of the Lunar race. Of this Alexander's historians made Porus. The Suraseni of Methoras (descendants of the Sursen of Mathura) were all Purus, the Prasioi of Megasthenes [see p. 37, n.]. Allahabad yet retains its Hindu name of Prayag, pronounced Prag.

[5] The Hares. Sesodia is said to have the same derivation. [From Sesoda in Mewâr.]

[6] The princes of Ranthambhor, expelled by Prithwiraja of Delhi, were of this race.

[7] The modern Chanderi [in the Gwalior State, *IGI*, x. 163 f.] is said to be

Surpur.—We are assured by Alexander's historians that the country and people round Mathura, when he invaded India, were termed Surasenoi. There are two princes of the name of Sursen in the immediate ancestry of Krishna; one his grandfather, the other eight generations anterior Which of these founded the capital Surpur,[1] whence the country and inhabitants had their appellation, we cannot say Mathura and Cleisobara are mentioned by the historians of Alexander as the chief cities of the Surasenoi. Though the Greeks sadly disfigure names, we cannot trace any affinity between Cleisobara and Surpur.

---

this capital, and one of the few to which no Englishman has obtained entrance, though I tried hard in 1807. Doubtless it would afford food for curiosity; for, being out of the path of armies in the days of conquest and revolution, it may, and I believe does, retain much worthy of research. [The capital of the Chedi or Kalachuri dynasty was Tripura or Karanbel, near Jabalpur (*IGI*, x. 12).]

[1] I had the pleasure, in 1814, of discovering a remnant of this city, which the Yamuna has overwhelmed. [The ancient Sūryapura was near Batesar, 40 miles south-east of Agra city. Sir H. Elliot (*Supplemental Glossary*, 187) remarks that it is strange that the Author so often claims the credit of discovery when its position is fixed in a set of familiar verses. For Sūryapura see A. Führer, *Monumental Antiquities and Inscriptions*, 69.] The sacred place of pilgrimage, Batesar, stands on part of it. My discovery of it was doubly gratifying, for while I found out the Surasenoi of the Greeks, I obtained a medal of the little known Apollodotus, who carried his arms to the mouths of the Indus, and possibly to the centre of the land of the Yadus. He is not included by Bayer in his lists of the kings of Bactria, but we have only an imperfect knowledge of the extent of that dynasty. The Bhagavat Purana asserts thirteen Yavan or Ionian princes to have ruled in Balichdes [?] or Bactria, in which they mention Pushpamitra Dvimitra. We are justified in asserting this to be Demetrius, the son of Euthydemus, but who did not succeed his father, as Menander intervened. Of this last conqueror I also possess a medal, obtained amongst the Surasenoi, and struck in commemoration of victory, as the winged messenger of heavenly peace extends the palm branch from her hand. These two will fill up a chasm in the Bactrian annals, for Menander is well known to them. Apollodotus would have perished but for Arrian, who wrote the Periplus of the Erythraean Sea in the second century, while commercial agent at Broach, or classically Brigukachchha, the Barugaza of the Greeks. [The Periplus of the Erythraean Sea was written by an unknown Greek merchant of first century A.D. (McCrindle, *Commerce and Navigation*, Introd. p. 1).]

Without the notice this writer has afforded us, my Apollodotus would have lost half its value. Since my arrival in Europe I have also been made acquainted with the existence of a medal of Demetrius, discovered in Bokhara, and on which an essay has been written by a *savant* at St. Petersburg.

Hastinapura.—The city of Hastinapura was built by Hastin a name celebrated in the Lunar dynasties. The name of this city is still preserved on the Ganges, about forty miles south of Hardwar,[1] where the Ganges breaks through the Siwalik mountains and enters the plains of India. This mighty stream, rolling its masses of waters from the glaciers of the Himalaya, and joined by many auxiliary streams, frequently carries destruction before it. In one night a column of thirty feet in perpendicular height has been known to bear away all within its sweep, and to such an occurrence the capital of Hastin is said to have owed its ruin.[2] As it existed, however, long after the Mahabharata, it is surprising it is not mentioned by the historians of Alexander, who invaded India probably about eight centuries after that event. In this abode of the sons of Puru resided Porus, one of the two princes of that name, opponents of Alexander, and probably Bindusara the son of Chandragupta, surmised to be the Abisares[3] and Sandrakottos of Grecian authorities. Of the two princes named Porus mentioned by Alexander's [41] historians, one resided in the very cradle of the Puru dynasties; the abode of the other bordered on the Panjab: warranting an assertion that the Pori of Alexander were of the Lunar race, and destroying all the claims various authors[4] have advanced on behalf of the princes of Mewar.[5]

Hastin sent forth three grand branches, Ajamidha, Dvimidha, and Purumidha. Of the two last we lose sight altogether; but Ajamidha's progeny spread over all the northern parts of India, in the Panjab and across the Indus. The period, probably one thousand six hundred years before Christ.

[1] The portal of Hari or Hara, whose trisula or trident is there.

[2] Wilford says this event is mentioned in two Puranas as occurring in the sixth or eighth generation of the Great War. Those who have travelled in the Duab must have remarked where both the Ganges and Jumna have shifted their beds.

[3] [Abisares is Abhisāra in the modern Kashmīr State (Smith, *EHI*, 59).]

[4] Sir Thomas Roe; Sir Thomas Herbert; the Holstein ambassador (by Olearius); Della Valle; Churchill, in his collection: and borrowing from these, D'Anville, Bayer, Orme, Rennell, etc.

[5] The ignorance of the family of Mewar of the fact would by no means be a conclusive argument against it, could it be otherwise substantiated; but the race of Surya was completely eclipsed at that period by the Lunar and new races which soon poured in from the west of the Indus, and in time displaced them all.

From Ajamidha,[1] in the fourth generation, was Bajaswa, who obtained possessions towards the Indus, and whose five sons gave their name, Panchala, to the Panjab, or space watered by the five rivers. The capital founded by the younger brother, Kampila, was named Kampilnagara.[2]

The descendants of Ajamidha by his second wife, Kesini, founded another kingdom and dynasty, celebrated in the heroic history of Northern India. This is the Kausika dynasty.

Kanauj.—Kusa had four sons, two of whom, Kusanabha and Kusamba, are well known to traditional history, and by the still surviving cities founded by them. Kusanabha founded the city of Mahodaya on the Ganges, afterwards changed to Kanyakubja, or Kanauj, which maintained its celebrity until the Muhammadan invasion of Shihabu-d-din (A.D. 1193), when this overgrown city was laid prostrate for ever. It was not unfrequently called Gadhipura, or the 'city of Gadhi.' This practice of multiplying names of cities in the east is very destructive to history. Abu-l Fazl has taken from Hindu authorities an account of Kanauj; and could we admit the authority of a poet on such subjects, Chand, the bard of Prithwiraja,[3] would afford materials. Ferishta states it in the early ages to have been twenty-five coss [42] (thirty-five miles) in circumference, and that there were thirty thousand shops for the sale of the areca or beetle-nut only;[4] and this in the sixth century, at which period the Rathor dynasty, which terminated with Jaichand, in the twelfth, had been in possession from the end of the fifth century.

Kusamba also founded a city, called after his own name

[1] Ajamidha, by his wife Nila, had five sons, who spread their branches (Sakha) on both sides the Indus. Regarding three the Puranas are silent, which implies their migration to distant regions. Is it possible they might be the origin of the Medes? These Medes are descendants of Yayati, third son of the patriarch Manu; and Madai, founder of the Medes, was of Japhet's line. Ajamidha, the patronymic of the branch of Bajaswa, is from *Aja*, 'a goat.' The Assyrian Mede, in Scripture, is typified by the goat. [These speculations are worthless.]

[2] Of this house was Draupadi, the wife, in common, of the five Pandava brothers: manners peculiar to Scythia.

[3] King of Delhi.

[4] [Briggs i. 57. The accounts of the size of the city are extravagant (Elphinstone, *HI*, 332 note; Cunningham, *ASR*, i. 279 ff.).]

Kausambi.[1] The name was in existence in the eleventh century; and ruins might yet exist, if search were made on the shores of the Ganges, from Kanauj southward.

The other sons built two capitals, Dharmaranya and Vasumati; but of neither have we any correct knowledge.

Kuru had two sons, Sudhanush and Parikhshita. The descendants of the former terminated with Jarasandha, whose capital was Rajagriha (the modern Rajmahal) on the Ganges, in the province of Bihar.[2] From Parikhshita descended the monarchs Santanu and Balaka: the first producing the rivals of the Great War, Yudhishthira and Duryodhana; the other the Balakaputras.

Duryodhana, the successor to the throne of Kuru, resided at the ancient capital, Hastinapura; while the junior branch, Yudhishthira, founded Indraprastha, on the Yamuna or Jumna, which name in the eighth century was changed to Delhi.

The sons of Balaka founded two kingdoms: Palibothra, on the lower Ganges; and Aror,[3] on the eastern bank of the Indus, founded by Sahl [43].

[1] An inscription was discovered at Kara on the Ganges, in which Yaspal is mentioned as prince of the realm of Kausambi (*As. Res.* vol. ix. p. 440). Wilford, in his Essay on the Geography of the Purans, says "Causambi, near Alluhabad" (*As. Res.* vol. xiv.). [The site is uncertain (Smith, *EHI*, 293, note).]

[2] [Rājgīr in Patna District.]

[3] Aror, or Alor, was the capital of Sind in remote antiquity: a bridge over the stream which branched from the Indus, near Dara, is almost the sole vestige of this capital of the Sogdoi of Alexander. On its site the shepherds of the desert have established an extensive hamlet; it is placed on a ridge of siliceous rock, seven miles east of the insular Bakhar, and free from the inundations of the Indus. The Sodha tribe, a powerful branch of the Pramara race, has ruled in these countries from remote antiquity, and to a very late period they were lords of Umarkot and Umrasumra, in which divisions was Aror. Sahl and his capital were known to Abu-l Fazl, though he was ignorant of its position, which he transferred to Debal, or Dewal, the modern Tatta. This indefatigable historian thus describes it: "In ancient times there lived a raja named Siharas (Sahl), whose capital was Alor, and his dominions extended north to Kashmīr and south to the ocean" [*Āīn*, ii. 343]. Sahl, or Sahr, became a titular appellation of the country, its princes, and its inhabitants, the Sehraes. [See p. 21 above.] Alor appears to have been the capital of the kingdom of Sigerdis, conquered by Menander of Bactria. Ibn Haukal, the Arabian geographer, mentions it; but a superfluous point in writing has changed Aror into Azor, or Azour, as translated by Sir W. Ouseley. The illustrious D'Anville mentions it; but, in ignorance of its position, quoting Abulfeda, says, in grandeur "Azour est presque comparable à Mooltan." I have to claim the discovery of

One great arm of the tree of Yayati remains unnoticed, that of Uru or Urvasu, written by others Turvasu. Uru was the father of a line of kings who founded several empires. Virupa, the eighth prince from Uru, had eight sons, two of whom are particularly mentioned as sending forth two grand shoots, Druhyu and Bhabru. From Druhyu a dynasty was established in the north. Aradwat, with his son Gandhara, is stated to have founded a State: Prachetas is said to have become king of Mlecchhades, or the barbarous regions. This line terminated with Dushyanta, the husband of the celebrated Sakuntala, father of Bharat, and who, labouring under the displeasure of some offended deity, is said by the Hindus to have been the cause of all the woes which subsequently befell the race. The four grandsons of Dushyanta, Kalanjar, Keral, Pand, and Chaul, gave their names to countries.

Kalanjar.—Kalanjar is the celebrated fortress in Bundelkhand, so well known for its antiquities, which have claimed considerable notice.

Kerala.—Of the second, Kerala, it is only known that in the list of the thirty-six royal races in the twelfth century, the Kerala makes one, but the capital is unknown.[1]

---

several ancient capital cities in the north of India: Surpur, on the Jumna, the capital of the Yadus; Alor, on the Indus, the capital of the Sodhas; Mandodri, capital of the Pariharas; Chandravati, at the foot of the Aravalli mountains; and Valabhipura, in Gujarat, capital of the Balaka-raes, the Balharas of Arab travellers. The Bala Rajput of Saurashtra may have given the name to Valabhipura, as descendants of Balaka, from Sahl of Aror. The blessing of the bard to them is yet, Tatta Multān ka Rāo ('lord of Tatta and Multān,' the seats of the Balaka-putras): nor is it improbable that a branch of these under the Indian Hercules, Balaram, who left India after the Great War, may have founded Balich, or Balkh, emphatically called the 'mother of cities.' The Jaisalmer annals assert that the Yadu and Balaka branches of the Indu race ruled Khorasan after the Great War, the Indo-Scythic races of Grecian authors. Besides the Balakas, and the numerous branches of the Indo-Medes, many of the sons of Kuru dispersed over these regions: amongst whom we may place Uttara Kuru (*Northern Kurus*) of the Puranas, the Ottorokorrhai of the Greek authors. Both the Indu and Surya races were eternally sending their superfluous population to those distant regions, when probably the same primeval religion governed the races east and west of the Indus. [Much of this is incorrect.]

[1] [The Chera or Kerala kingdom comprised the Southern Konkans or Malabar coast, the present Malabar district with Travancore and Cochin, the dynasty being in existence early in the Christian era (Smith, *EHI*, 447; *IGI*, x. 192 f.).]

Pandya.—The kingdom founded by Pand may be that on the coast of Malabar, the Pandu-Mandal of the Hindus, the Regia Pandiona of the geographers of the west, and of which, probably, Tanjore is the modern capital.[1]

Chaul.—Chaul [2] is in the Saurashtra peninsula, and on the coast, towards Jagat Khunt, 'the world's end,' and still retains its appellation.

Anga.—The other shoot from Bhabru became celebrated. The thirty-fourth prince, Anga, founded the kingdom of Angadesa, of which Champapuri [3] was the [44] capital, established about the same time with Kanauj, probably fifteen hundred years before Christ. With him the patronymic was changed, and the Anga race became famous in ancient Hindu history; and to this day Un-des still designates the Alpine regions of Tibet bordering on Chinese Tartary.

Prithusena terminates the line of Anga; and as he survived the disasters of the Great War, his race probably multiplied in those regions, where caste appears never to have been introduced.

Recapitulation.—Thus have we rapidly reviewed the dynasties of Surya and Chandra, from Manu and Budha to Rama, Krishna, Yudhishthira, and Jarasandha; establishing, it is hoped, some new points, and perhaps adding to the credibility of the whole.

The wrecks of almost all the vast cities founded by them are yet to be traced in ruins. The city of Ikshwaku and Rama, on the Sarju; Indraprastha, Mathura, Surpura, Prayag on the Yamuna; Hastinapura, Kanyakubja, Rajagriha on the Ganges; Maheswar on the Nerbudda; Aror on the Indus; and Kusasthali

[1] [The Pāndya kingdom included the Madura and Tinnevelly districts, with parts of Trichinopoly, and sometimes Travancore, its capitals being Madura, or Kūdal, and Korkai (Smith, *op. cit.* 449 f.; *IGI*, xix. 394 f.).]

[2] From Chaul on the coast, in journeying towards Junagarh, and about seven miles from the former, are the remains of an ancient city.

[3] From the description in the Ramayana of King Dasaratha proceeding to Champamalina, the capital of Lomapada, king of Anga (sixth in descent from the founder), it is evident that it was a very mountainous region, and the deep forests and large rivers presented serious obstructions to his journey. From this I should imagine it impossible that Angadesa should apply to a portion of Bengal, in which there is a Champamalina, described by Colonel Francklin in his Essay on Palibothra. [The Anga kingdom, with its capital at Champapuri, near Bhāgalpur, corresponded to the modern districts of North Monghyr, North Bhāgalpur, and Purnea west of the Mahananda river (*IGI*, v. 373).]

Dwarka on the shore of the Indian Ocean. Each has left some memorial of former grandeur: research may discover others.

There is yet an unexplored region in Panchala; Kampilanagara its capital, and those cities established west of the Indus by the sons of Bajaswa.

Traces of the early Indo-Scythic nations may possibly reward the search of some adventurous traveller who may penetrate into Transoxiana, on the sites of Cyropolis, and the most northern Alexandria; in Balkh, and amidst the caves of Bamian.

The plains of India retain yet many ancient cities, from whose ruins somewhat may be gleaned to add a mite to knowledge; and where inscriptions may be found in a character which, though yet unintelligible, will not always remain so in this age of discovery. For such let the search be general, and when once a key is obtained, they will enlighten each other. Wherever the races of Kuru, Uru, and Yadu have swayed, have been found ancient and yet undeciphered characters.

Much would reward him who would make a better digest of the historical and geographical matter in the Puranas. But we must discard the idea that the history of Rama, the Mahabharata of Krishna and the five Pandava [1] brothers, are [45] mere allegory: an idea supported by some, although their races, their cities, and their coins still exist. Let us master the characters on the columns of Indraprastha, of Prayag and Mewar, on the rocks of Junagarh,[2] at Bijolli, on the Aravalli, and in the Jain

[1] The history and exploits of the Pandavas and Harikulas are best known in the most remote parts of India: amidst the forest-covered mountains of Saurashtra, the deep woods and caves of Hidimba and Virat (still the shelter of the savage Bhil and Koli), or on the craggy banks of the Charmanvati (Chambal). In each, tradition has localized the shelter of these heroes when exiled from the Yamuna; and colossal figures cut from the mountain, ancient temples and caves inscribed with characters yet unknown, attributed to the Pandavas, confirm the legendary tale.

[2] The 'ancient city,' *par eminence*, is the only name this old capital, at the foot of, and guarding, the sacred mount Girnar, is known by. Abu-l Fazl says it had long remained desolate and unknown, and was discovered by mere accident. [*Āīn*, ii. 245. For a description of the place see *BG*, viii. 487; E. C. Bayley, *Local Muhammadan Dynasties*, *Gujarāt*, 182 ff.] Tradition even being silent, they gave it the emphatic appellation of Juna (old) Garh (fortress). I have little doubt that it is the Asaldurga, or Asalgarh, of the Guhilot annals; where it is said that prince Āsal raised a fortress, called after him, near to Girnar, by the consent of the Dabhi prince, his uncle.

temples scattered over India, and then we shall be able to arrive at just and satisfactory conclusions.

CHAPTER 5

HAVING investigated the line from Ikshwaku to Rama, and that from Budha (the parent and first emigrant of the Indu [1] race, from Saka Dwipa, or Scythia, to Hindustan) to Krishna and Yudhishthira, a period of twelve hundred years, we proceed to the second division and second table of the genealogies.

The Suryavansa or Solar Line.—From Rama all the tribes termed Suryavansa, or 'Race of the Sun,' claim descent, as the present princes of Mewar, Jaipur, Marwar, Bikaner, and their numerous clans; while from the Lunar (Indu) line of Budha and Krishna, the families of Jaisalmer and Cutch (the Bhatti [2] and Jareja races), extending throughout the Indian desert from the Sutlej to the ocean, deduce their pedigrees.

Rama preceded Krishna: but as their historians, Valmiki and Vyasa, who wrote the events they witnessed, were contemporaries, it could not have been by many years [46].

The present table contains the dynasties which succeeded these great beacons of the Solar and Lunar races, and are three in number.[3]

1. The Suryavansa, descendants of Rama
2. The Induvansa, descendants of Pandu through Yudhishthira.
3. The Induvansa, descendants of Jarasandha, monarch of Rajagriha.

The Bhagavat and Agni Puranas are the authorities for the

[1] Indu, Som, Chandra, in Sanskrit 'the moon'; hence the Lunar race is termed the Chandravansa, Somvansa, or Induvansa, most probably the root of *Hindu*. [Pers. *hindū*, Skr. *sindhu*.]

[2] The isolated and now dependent chieftainship of Dhat, of which Umarkot is the capital, separates the Bhattis from the Jarejas. Dhat is now amalgamated with Sind; its prince, of Pramara race and Sodha tribe, ancient lords of all Sind.

[3] A fourth and fifth might have been given, but imperfect. First the descendants of Kusa, second son of Rama, from whence the princes of Narwar and Amber: secondly, the descendants of Krishna, from whom the princes of Jaisalmer.

lines from Rama and Jarasandha ; while that of Pandu is from the Raja Tarangini and Rajavali.

The existing Rajput tribes of the Solar race claim descent from Lava and Kusa, the two elder sons of Rama ; nor do I believe any existing tribes trace their ancestry to his other children, or to his brothers.

From the eldest son, Lava, the Ranas of Mewar claim descent : so do the Bargujar tribe, formerly powerful within the confines of the present Amber, whose representative now dwells at Anupshahr on the Ganges.

From Kusa descend the Kachhwaha[1] princes of Narwar and Amber, and their numerous clans. Amber, though the first in power, is but a scion of Narwar, transplanted about one thousand years back, whose chief, the representative of the celebrated Prince Nala, enjoys but a sorry district[2] of all his ancient possessions.

The house of Marwar also claims descent from this stem, which appears to originate in an error of the genealogists, confounding the race of Kusa with the Kausika of Kanauj and Kausambi. Nor do the Solar genealogists admit this assumed pedigree.

The Amber prince in his genealogies traces the descent of the Mewar[3] family from Rama to Sumitra, through Lava, the eldest brother, and not through Kusa,[4] as in some copies of the Puranas, and in that whence Sir William Jones had his lists [47].

Mr. Bentley, taking this genealogy from the same authority as Sir William Jones, has mutilated it by a transposition, for

[1] In modern times always written and pronounced *Kutchwāha.*

[2] It is in the plateau of Central India, near Shahabad.

[3] Whatever dignity attaches to this pedigree, whether true or false, every prince, and every Hindu of learning, admit the claims of the princes of Mewar as heir to 'the chair of Rama' ; and a degree of reverence has consequently attached, not only to his person, but to the seat of his power. When Mahadaji Sindhia was called by the Rana to reduce a traitorous noble in Chitor, such was the reverence which actuated that (in other respects) little scrupulous chieftain, that he could not be prevailed on to point his cannon on the walls within which consent established 'the throne of Rama.' The Rana himself, then a youth, had to break the ice, and fired a cannon against his own ancient abode.

[4] Bryant, in his *Analysis*, mentions that the children of the Cushite Ham used his name in salutation as a mark of recognition. 'Ram, Ram,' is the common salutation in these Hindu countries ; the respondent often joining Sita's name with that of her consort Rama, 'Sīta Ram.'

which his reasons are insufficient, and militate against every opinion of the Hindus. Finding the names Vrihadbala and Vridasura, declared to be princes contemporary with Yudhishthira, he transposes the whole ten princes of his list intervening between Takshak [1] and Bahuman.[2]

Bahuman,[3] or 'the man with arms' (Darazdasht or Longimanus) is the thirty-fourth prince from Rama; and his reign must be placed nearly intermediate between Rama and Sumitra, or his contemporary Vikrama, and in the sixth century from either.

Sumitra concludes the line of Surya or Rama from the Bhagavat Purana. Thence it is connected with the present line of Mewar, by Jai Singh's authorities; which list has been compared with various others, chiefly Jain, as will be related in the annals of Mewar.

It will be seen that the line of Surya exhibits fifty-six princes, from Lava, the son of Rama, to Sumitra, the last prince given in the Puranas. Sir William Jones exhibits fifty-seven.

To these fifty-six reigns I should be willing to allow the average of twenty years, which would give 1120 from Rama to Sumitra, who preceded by a short period Vikramaditya; and as 1100 have been already calculated to have preceded the era of Rama and Yudhishthira, the inference is, that 2200 years elapsed from Ikshwaku, the founder of the Solar line, to Sumitra.

Chandravansa or the Lunar Line.—From the Raja Tarangini and Rajavali the Induvansa family (descendants of Pandu through Yudhishthira) is supplied. These works, celebrated in Rajwara as collections of genealogies and historical facts, by the

[1] Twenty-eighth prince from Rama in Mr. Bentley's list, and twenty-fifth in mine.

[2] Thirty-seventh in Mr. Bentley's list and thirty-fourth in mine; but the intervening names being made to follow Rama, Bahuman (written by him *Banumat*) follows Takshak.

[3] The period of time, also, would allow of their grafting the son of Artaxerxes and father of Darius, the worshipper of Mithras, on the stem of the adorers of Surya, while a curious notice of the Raja Jai Singh's on a subsequent name on this list which he calls Naushirwan, strengthens the coincidence. Bahuman (see article 'Bahaman,' D'Herbelot's *Bibl. Orient.*) actually carried his arms into India, and invaded the kingdoms of the Solar race of Mithila and Magadha. The time is appropriate to the first Darius and his father; and Herodotus [iii. 94] tells us that the richest and best of the satrapies of his empire was the Hindu.

Pandits Vidyadhara and Raghunath, were compiled under the eye of the most learned prince of his period, Sawai Jai Singh of Amber, and give the various dynasties which ruled at Indraprastha, or Delhi, from Yudhishthira to Vikramaditya; and although barren of events, may be considered of value in filling up a period of entire darkness [48].

The Tarangini commences with Adinath[1] or Rishabhdeva,[2] being the Jain[3] theogony. Rapidly noticing the leading princes of the dynasties discussed, they pass to the birth of the kings Dhritarashtra and Pandu, and their offspring, detailing the causes of their civil strife, to that conflict termed the Mahabharata or Great War.

The Pandava Family.—The origin of every family, whether of east or west, is involved in fable. That of the Pandu[4] is entitled to as much credence as the birth of Romulus, or other founders of a race.

Such traditions[5] were probably invented to cover some great disgrace in the Pandu family, and have relation to the story already related of Vyasa, and the debasement of this branch of the Harikulas. Accordingly, on the death of Pandu, Duryodhana, nephew of Pandu (son of Dhritarashtra, who from blindness could not inherit), asserted their illegitimacy before the assembled kin at Hastinapura. With the aid, however, of the priesthood, and the blind Dhritarashtra, his nephew, Yudhishthira, elder son of Pandu, was invested by him with the seal of royalty, in the capital, Hastinapura.

Duryodhana's plots against the Pandu and his partisans were

[1] First lord. [2] Lord of the Bull.

[3] Vidhyadhar was a Jain.

[4] Pandu not being blessed with progeny, his queen made use of a charm by which she enticed the deities from their spheres. To Dharma Raj (Minos) she bore Yudhishthira; by Pavan (Aeolus) she had Bhima; by Indra (Jupiter Coelus) she had Arjuna, who was taught by his sire the use of the bow, so fatal in the Great War; and Nakula and Sahadeva owed their birth to Aswini Kumar (Aesculapius) the physician of the gods.

[5] We must not disregard the intellect of the Amber prince, who allowed these ancient traditions to be incorporated with the genealogy compiled under his eye. The prince who obtained De Silva from Emmanuel III. of Portugal, who combined the astronomical tables of Europe and Asia, and raised these monuments of his scientific genius in his favourite pursuit (astronomy) in all the capital cities of India, while engrossed in war and politics, requires neither eulogy nor defence.

so numerous that the five brothers determined to leave for a while their ancestral abodes on the Ganges. They sought shelter in foreign countries about the Indus, and were first protected by Drupada, king of Panchala, at whose capital, Kampilanagara, the surrounding princes had arrived as suitors for the hand of his daughter, Draupadi.[1] But the prize was destined for the exiled Pandu, and the skill of Arjuna in archery obtained him the fair, who " threw round his neck the (barmala) garland of marriage." The disappointed princes indulged their resentment against the exile ; but by Arjuna's bow they suffered the fate of Penelope's suitors, and the Pandu brought home his bride, who became the wife in common of the five brothers : manners[2] decisively Scythic [49].

The deeds of the brothers abroad were bruited in Hastinapura and the blind Dhritarashtra's influence effected their recall. To stop, however, their intestine feuds, he partitioned the Pandu sovereignty ; and while his son, Duryodhana, retained Hastinapura, Yudhishthira founded the new capital of Indraprastha ; but shortly after the Mahabharata he abdicated in favour of his grand-nephew, Parikshita, introducing a new era, called after himself, which existed for eleven hundred years, when it was overturned, and Indraprastha was conquered by Vikramaditya Tuar of Ujjain, of the same race, who established an era of his own.

On the division of the Pandu sovereignty, the new kingdom of Indraprastha eclipsed that of Hastinapura. The brothers reduced to obedience the surrounding[3] nations, and compelled their princes to sign tributary engagements (*paenama*).[4]

Yudhishthira, firmly seated on his throne, determined to

[1] Drupada was of the Aswa race, being descended from Bajaswa (or Hyaswa) of the line of Ajamidha.

[2] This marriage, so inconsistent with Hindu delicacy, is glossed over. Admitting the polyandry, but in ignorance of its being a national custom, puerile reasons are interpolated. In the early annals of the same race, predecessors of the Jaisalmer family, the younger son is made to succeed : also Scythic or Tatar. The manners of the Scythae described by Herodotus are found still to exist among their descendants : " a pair of slippers at the wife's door " is a signal well understood by all Eimauk husbands (Elphinstone's *Caubul*, vol. ii. p. 251).

[3] *Tarangini.*

[4] *Paenama* is a [Persian] word peculiarly expressive of subserviency to paramount authority, whether the engagement be in money or service : from *pae*, ' the foot.'

signalize his reign and paramount sovereignty, by the imposing and solemn rites of Asvamedha [1] and Rajasuya.

The Asvamedha.—In these magnificent ceremonies, in which princes alone officiate, every duty, down to that of porter, is performed by royalty.

The 'Steed of Sacrifice' was liberated under Arjuna's care, having wandered whither he listed for twelve months; and none daring to accept this challenge of supremacy, he was reconducted to Indraprastha, where, in the meanwhile, the hall of sacrifice was prepared, and all the princes of the land were summoned to attend.

The hearts of the Kurus [2] burned with envy at the assumption of supremacy by the Pandus, for the Prince of Hastinapura's office was to serve out the sacred food [50].

The rivalry between the races burst forth afresh; but Duryodhana, who so often failed in his schemes against the safety of his antagonists, determined to make the virtue of Yudhishthira the instrument of his success. He availed himself of the national propensity for play, in which the Rajput continues to preserve his Scythic [3] resemblance. Yudhishthira fell into the snare prepared for him. He lost his kingdom, his wife, and even his personal liberty and that of his brothers, for twelve years, and became an exile from the plains of the Yamuna.

The traditional history of these wanderers during the term of probation, their many lurking places now sacred, the return to their ancestral abodes, and the grand battle (Mahabharata) which ensued, form highly interesting episodes in the legends of Hindu antiquity.

To decide this civil strife, every tribe and chief of fame, from the Caucasus to the ocean, assembled on Kurukshetra, the field

[1] Sacrifice of the horse to the sun, of which a full description is given hereafter.

[2] Duryodhana, as the elder branch, retained his title as head of the Kurus; while the junior, Yudhishthira, on the separation of authority, adopted his father's name, Pandu, as the patronymic of his new dynasty. The site of the great conflict (or Mahabharata) between these rival clans, is called Kurukshetra, or 'Field of the Kurus.'

[3] Herodotus describes the ruinous passion for play amongst the Scythic hordes, and which may have been carried west by Odin into Scandinavia and Germany. Tacitus tells us that the Germans, like the Pandus, staked even personal liberty, and were sold as slaves by the winner [*Germania*, 24].

on which the empire of India has since more than once been contested [1] and lost.

This combat was fatal to the dominant influence of the "fifty-six tribes of Yadu." On each of its eighteen days' combat, myriads were slain; for "the father knew not the son, nor the disciple his preceptor."

Victory brought no happiness to Yudhishthira. The slaughter of his friends disgusted him with the world, and he determined to withdraw from it; previously performing, at Hastinapura, funeral rites for Duryodhana (slain by the hands of Bhima), whose ambition and bad faith had originated this exterminating war. "Having regained his kingdom, he proclaimed a new era, and placing on the throne of Indraprastha, Parikshita, grandson to Arjuna, retired to Dwarka with Krishna and Baldeva: and since the war to the period of writing, 4636 years have elapsed." [2]

Yudhishthira, Baldeva, and Krishna, having retired with the wreck of this ill-fated struggle to Dwarka, the two former had soon to lament the death of Krishna, slain by one of the aboriginal tribes of Bhils; against whom, from their shattered condition, they were unable to contend. After this event, Yudhishthira, with [51] Baldeva and a few followers, entirely withdrew from India, and emigrating northwards, by Sind, to the Himalayan mountains, are there abandoned by Hindu traditional history, and are supposed to have perished in the snows.[3]

[1] On it the last Hindu monarch, Prithwiraja, lost his kingdom, his liberty, and life.

[2] Rajatarangini. The period of writing was A.D. 1740.

[3] Having ventured to surmise analogies between the Hercules of the east and west, I shall carry them a point further. Amidst the snows of Caucasus, Hindu legend abandons the Harikulas, under their leaders Yudhishthira and Baldeva: yet if Alexander established his altars in Panchala, amongst the sons of Puru and the Harikulas, what physical impossibility exists that a colony of them, under Yudhishthira and Baldeva, eight centuries anterior, should have penetrated to Greece? Comparatively far advanced in science and arms, the conquest would have been easy. When Alexander attacked the 'free cities' of Panchala, the Purus and Harikulas who opposed him evinced the recollections of their ancestor, in carrying the figure of Hercules as their standard. Comparison proves a common origin to Hindu and Grecian mythology; and Plato says the Greeks had theirs from Egypt and the East. May not this colony of the Harikulas be the Heraclidae, who penetrated into the Peloponnesus (according to Volney) 1078 years before Christ, sufficiently near our calculated period of the Great War? The Heraclidae claimed from Atreus: the Harikulas claim from Atri. Eurysthenes was

From Parikshita, who succeeded Yudhishthira, to Vikramaditya, four [1] dynasties are given in a continuous chain, exhibiting sixty-six princes to Rajpal, who, invading Kumaon, was slain by Sukwanti. The Kumaun conqueror seized upon Delhi, but was soon dispossessed by Vikramaditya, who transferred the seat of imperial power from Indraprastha to Avanti, or Ujjain, from which time it became the first meridian of the Hindu astronomy.

Indraprastha ceased to be a regal abode for eight centuries, when it was re-established by Anangpal,[2] the founder of the Tuar race, claiming descent from the Pandus. Then the name of Delhi superseded that of Indraprastha.

---

the first king of the Heraclidae: Yudhishthira has sufficient affinity in name to the first Spartan king not to startle the etymologist, the *d* and *r* being always permutable in Sanskrit. The Greeks or Ionians are descended from Yavan, or Javan, the seventh from Japhet. The Harikulas are also Yavans claiming from Javan or Yavan, the thirteenth in descent from Yayati, the third son of the primeval patriarch. The ancient Heraclidae of Greece asserted they were as old as the sun, and older than the moon. May not this boast conceal the fact that the Heliadae (or *Suryavansa*) of Greece had settled there anterior to the colony of the Indu (Lunar) race of Harikula? In all that relates to the mythological history of the Indian demi-gods, Baldeva (Hercules), Krishna or Kanhaiya (Apollo), and Budha (Mercury), a powerful and almost perfect resemblance can be traced between those of Hindu legend, Greece, and Egypt. Baldeva (the god of strength) Harikula, is still worshipped as in the days of Alexander; his shrine at Baldeo in Vraj (the Surasenoi of the Greeks), his club a ploughshare, and a lion's skin his covering. A Hindu intaglio of rare value represents Hercules exactly as described by Arrian, with a monogram consisting of two ancient characters now unknown, but which I have found wherever tradition assigns a spot to the Harikulas; especially in Saurashtra, where they were long concealed on their exile from Delhi. This we may at once decide to be the exact figure of Hercules which Arrian describes his descendants to have carried as their standard, when Porus opposed Alexander. The intaglio will appear in the *Trans. R.A.S.* [The speculations in this note have no authority.]

[1] The twenty-eighth prince, Khemraj, was the last in lineal descent from Parikshita, the grand-nephew of Yudhishthira. The first dynasty lasted 1864 years. The second dynasty was of Visarwa, and consisted of fourteen princes; this lasted five hundred years. The third dynasty was headed by Mahraj, and terminated by Antinai, the fifteenth prince. The fourth dynasty was headed by Dudhsen, and terminated by Rajpal, the ninth and last king (Rajatarangini).

[2] The Rajatarangini gives the date A.V. 848, or A.D. 792, for this; and adds: "Princes from Siwalik, or northern hills, held it during this time, and it long continued desolate until the Tuars."

"Sukwanti, a prince from the northern mountains of Kumaun, ruled fourteen [52] years, when he was slain by Vikramaditya;[1] and from the Bharat to this period 2915 years have elapsed."[2]

Such a period asserted to have elapsed while sixty-six princes occupied the throne, gives an average of forty-four years to each; which is incredible, if not absolutely impossible.

In another passage the compiler says: "I have read many books (shastras), and all agreed to make one hundred princes, all of Khatri[3] race, occupy the throne of Delhi from Yudhishthira to Prithwiraja, a period of 4100 years,[4] after which the Ravad[5] race succeeded."

It is fortunate for these remnants of historical data that they have only extended the duration of reigns, and not added more heads. Sixty-six links are quite sufficient to connect Yudhishthira and Vikramaditya.

We cannot object to the "one hundred princes" who fill the space assigned from Yudhishthira to Prithwiraja, though there is no proportion between the number which precedes and that which follows Vikramaditya, the former being sixty-six, the latter only thirty-four princes, although the period cannot differ half a century.

Let us apply a test to these one hundred kings, from Yudhishthira to Prithwiraja: the result will be 2250 years.

This test is derived from the average rate of reigns of the chief dynasties of Rajasthan, during a period of 633[6] to 663[7] years, or from Prithwiraja to the present date.

[1] 56 B.C. [Cunningham remarks that the defeat of Rāja Pāl of Delhi by Sukwanti, Sukdati, or Sukāditya, Rāja of Kumaun, must be assigned to A.D. 79: but he has little confidence in such traditions, unless supported by independent evidence (*ASR*, i. 138).]

[2] Raghunath.

[3] Rājput, or Kshatriya.

[4] This period of 4100 years may have been arrived at by the compiler taking for granted the number of years mentioned by Raghunath as having elapsed from the Mahabharata to Vikramaditya, namely 2915, and adding thereto the well-authenticated period of Prithwiraja, who was born in Samvat 1215: for if 2915 be subtracted from 4100, it leaves 1185, the period within thirty years of the birth of Prithwiraja, according to the Chauhan chronicles.

[5] Solar.

[6] From S. 1250, or A.D. 1194, captivity and dethronement of Prithwiraja.

[7] From S. 1212, A.D. 1516, the founding of Jaisalmer by Jaisal, to the accession of Gaj Singh, the present prince, in S. 1876, or A.D. 1820.

Of Mewar . .	34[1] princes, or 19 years to each reign.	
Of Marwar . .	28 princes, or 23¼	„ „
Of Amber . .	29 princes, or 22½	„ „
Of Jaisalmer . .	28 princes, or 23¼	„ „

giving an average of twenty-two years for each reign [53].

It would not be proper to ascribe a longer period to each reign, and it were perhaps better to give the minimum, nineteen, to extended dynasties; and to the sixty-six princes from Yudhishthira and Vikramaditya not even so much, four revolutions[2] and usurpations marking this period.

Jarasandha.—The remaining line, that of Jarasandha, taken from the Bhagavat, is of considerable importance, and will afford scope for further speculation.

Jarasandha was the monarch of Rajagriha,[3] or Bihar, whose son Sahadeva, and grandson Marjari, are declared to have been contemporaries of the Mahabharata, and consequently coeval with Parikshita, the Delhi sovereign.

The direct line of Jarasandha terminates in twenty-three descents with Ripunjaya, who was slain, and his throne assumed by his minister, Sanaka, whose dynasty terminated in the fifth generation with Nandivardandhana. Sanaka derived no personal advantage from his usurpation, as he immediately placed his son, Pradyota, on the throne. To these five princes one hundred and thirty-eight years are assigned.

A new race entered Hindustan, led by a conqueror termed Sheshnag, from Sheshnagdesa,[4] who ascended the Pandu throne,

[1] Many of its early princes were killed in battle; and the present prince's father succeeded his own nephew, which was retrograding.

[2] The historians sanction the propriety of these changes, in their remarks, that the deposed were "deficient in [capacity for] the cares and duties of government."

[3] Rajagriha, or Rajmahal, capital of Magadhades, or Bihar. [In Patna district, *IGI*, xxi. 72.]

[4] Figuratively, the country of the 'head of the Snakes'; *Nag, Tak*, or *Takshak*, being synonymous: and which I conclude to be the abode of the ancient Scythic *Tachari* of Strabo, the *Tak-i-uks* of the Chinese, the *Tajiks* of the present day of Turkistan. This race appears to be the same with that of the Turushka (of the Puranas), who ruled on the Arvarma (the Araxes), in Sakadwipa, or Scythia. [This is a confused reference to the Saisunāga dynasty, which took its name from its founder, Sisunāga, and comprised roughly the present Patna and Gaya districts, its capital being

and whose line terminates in ten descents with Mahanandin, of spurious birth. This last prince, who was also named Baikyat, carried on an exterminating warfare against the ancient Rajput princes of pure blood, the Puranas declaring that since the dynasty of Sheshnag the princes were Sudras. Three hundred and sixty years are allotted to these ten princes.

Chandragupta Maurya.—A fourth dynasty commenced with Chandragupta Maurya, of the same Takshak race.[1] The Maurya dynasty consisted of ten princes, who are stated to have passed away in one hundred and thirty-seven years. [322–185 B.C.]

Sunga, Kanva Dynasties.—The fifth dynasty of eight princes were from Sringides, and are said to have ruled one hundred and twelve years, when a prince of Kanvades deprived the last of life and kingdom. Of these eight princes, four were of pure blood, when Kistna, by a Sudra woman, succeeded. The dynasty of Kanvades terminates in twenty-three generations with Susarman[2] [54].

Recapitulation.—Thus from the Great War six successive dynasties are given, presenting a continuous chain of eighty-two princes, reckoning from Sahadeva, the successor of Jarasandha, to Susarman.

To some of the short dynasties periods are assigned of moderate length: but as the first and last are without such data, the test

---

Rājagriha; the modern Rājgīr-Sisunāga means 'a young elephant,' and has no connexion with Sheshnāg, the serpent king (*Vishnu Purana*, 466 f.; Smith, *EHI*, 31).]

[1] [Chandragupta Maurya was certainly not a "Takshak": he was probably "an illegitimate scion of the Nanda family" (Smith, *EHI*, 42).]

[2] Mr. Bentley ('On the Hindu System of Astronomy,' *As. Res.* vol. viii. pp. 236-7) states that the astronomer, Brahmagupta, flourished about A.D. 527, or of Vikrama 583, shortly preceding the reign of Susarman; that he was the founder of the system called the Kalpa of Brahma, on which the present Hindu chronology is founded, and to which Mr. Bentley says their historical data was transferred. This would strengthen my calculations; but the weight of Mr. Bentley's authority has been much weakened by his unwarrantable attack on Mr. Colebrooke, whose extent of knowledge is of double value from his entire aversion to hypothesis. [The Sunga dynasty, founded by Pushyamitra, about 185 B.C., lasted till about 73 B.C., when the tenth king, Devabhūti, was slain by his Brāhman minister, Vasudeva, who founded the Kānva dynasty. He was followed by three kings, and the dynasty lasted only forty-five years, the last member of it being slain, about 28 B.C., by a king of the Andhra or Sātāvahana dynasty, then reigning in the Deccan. For the scanty details see Smith, *EHI*, 198 ff.]

already decided on must be applied; which will yield 1704 years, being six hundred and four after Vikramaditya, whose contemporary will thus be Basdeva, the fifty-fifth prince from Sahadeva of the sixth dynasty, said to be a conqueror from the country of Katehr [or Rohilkhand]. If these calculations possess any value, the genealogies of the Bhagavat are brought down to the close of the fifth century following Vikramaditya. As we cannot admit the gift of prophecy to the compilers of these books, we may infer that they remodelled their ancient chronicles during the reign of Susarman, about the year of Vikrama 600, or A.D. 546.

With regard to calculations already adduced, as to the average number of years for the reigns of the foregoing dynasties, a comparison with those which history affords of other parts of the world will supply the best criterion of the correctness of the assumed data.

From the revolt of the ten tribes against Rehoboam [1] to the capture of Jerusalem, a period of three hundred and eighty-seven years, twenty kings sat on the throne of Judah, making each reign nineteen and a half years; but if we include the three anterior reigns of Saul, David, and Solomon, prior to the revolt, the result will be twenty-six and a half years each.

From the dismemberment of the Assyrian [2] empire under Sardanapalus, nearly nine hundred years before Christ, the three consequent confluent dynasties of Babylonia, Assyria, and Media afford very different results for comparison.

The Assyrian preserves the medium, while the Babylonish and Median run into extremes. Of the nine princes who swayed Babylon, from the period of its separation from, till its reunion to Assyria, a space of fifty-two years, Darius, who ruled Media sixty [thirty-six] years [55], outlived the whole. Of the line of Darius there were but six princes, from the separation of the kingdoms to their reunion under Cyrus, a period of one hundred and seventy-four years, or twenty-nine to each reign.

The Assyrian reigns form a juster medium. From Nebuchadnezzar to Sardanapalus we have twenty-two years to a reign; but from thence to the extinction of this dynasty, eighteen.

The first eleven kings, the Heraclidae of Lacedaemon, com-

[1] 987 years before Christ.

[2] For these and the following dates I am indebted to Goguet's chronological tables in his *Origin of Laws*.

mencing with Eurysthenes (1078 before Christ), average thirty-two years; while in republican Athens, nearly contemporary, from the first perpetual archon until the office became decennial in the seventh Olympiad, the reigns of the twelve chief magistrates average twenty-eight years and a half.

Thus we have three periods, Jewish, Spartan, and Athenian, each commencing about eleven hundred years before Christ, not half a century remote from the Mahabharata; with those of Babylonia, Assyria, and Media, commencing where we quit the Grecian, in the eighth century before the Christian era, the Jewish ending in the sixth century.

However short, compared with our Solar and Lunar dynasties, yet these, combined with the average reigns of existing Hindu dynasties, will aid the judgment in estimating the periods to be assigned to the lines thus afforded, instead of following the improbable value attached by the Brahmans.

From such data, longevity appears in unison with climate and simplicity of life: the Spartan yielding the maximum of thirty-two to a reign, while the more luxurious Athens gives twenty-eight and a half. The Jews, from Saul to their exile "to the waters of Babylon," twenty-six and a half. The Medes equal the Lacedaemonians, and in all history can only be paralleled by the princes of Anhilwara, one of whom, Chawand, almost equalled Darius.[1]

Of the separated ten tribes, from the revolt to the captivity, twenty kings of Israel passed away in two centuries, or ten years each.

The Spartan and Assyrian present the extremes of thirty-two and eighteen, giving a medium of twenty-five years to a reign.

The average result of our four Hindu dynasties, in a period of nearly seven hundred years, is twenty-two years.

From all which data, I would presume to assign from twenty to twenty-two years to each reign in lines of fifty princes [56].

If the value thus obtained be satisfactory, and the lines of dynasties derived from so many authorities correct, we shall arrive at the same conclusion with Mr. Bentley; who, by the more philosophical process of astronomical and genealogical

[1] [It is not clear to whom the author refers: Chāmunda Chāvada (A.D. 880–908): or Chāmunda Chaulukya (A.D. 997–1010), (*EG*, i. Part i. 154, 162).]

combination, places Yudhishthira's era in the year 2825 of the world; which being taken from 4004 (the world's age at the birth of Christ) will leave 1179 before Christ for Yudhishthira's era, or 1123 before Vikramaditya.[1]

CHAPTER 6

Rajputs and Mongols.—Having thus brought down the genealogical history of the ancient martial races of India, from the earliest period to Yudhishthira and Krishna, and thence to Vikramaditya and the present day, a few observations on the races invading India during that time, and now ranked amongst the thirty-six royal races of Rajasthan, affording scope for some curious analogies, may not be inopportune.

The tribes here alluded to are the Haihaya or Aswa, the Takshak, and the Jat or Getae; the similitude of whose theogony, names in their early genealogies, and many other points, with the Chinese, Tatar, Mogul, Hindu, and Scythic races, would appear to warrant the assertion of one common origin.

Though the periods of the passage of these tribes into India cannot be stated with exactitude, the regions whence they migrated may more easily be ascertained.

Mongol Origin.—Let us compare the origin of the Tatars and Moguls, as given by their historian, Abulghazi, with the races we have been treating of from the Puranas.

Mogol was the name of the Tatarian patriarch. His son was Aghuz,[2] the founder of all the races of those northern regions, called Tatars and Mogol [57]. Aghuz had six sons.[3] First, Kun,[4] 'the sun,' the Surya of the Puranas; secondly, Ai,[5] 'the moon,'

[1] [The evidence quoted in this chapter by which the author endeavours to frame a chronology for this early period, is untrustworthy. Mr. Pargiter tentatively dates the great Bhārata battle about 1000 B.C., but the evidence is very uncertain (*JRAS*, January 1910, p. 56; April 1914, p. 294).]

[2] Query, if from Mogol and Aghuz, compounded, we have not the Magog, son of Japhet, of Scripture?

[3] The other four sons are the remaining elements, personified: whence the six races of Tatars. The Hindus had long but two races, till the four Agnikula made them also six, and now thirty-six!

[4] In Tatar, according to Abulghazi, the sun and moon.

[5] De Guignes.

the Indu of the Puranas. In the latter, Ai, we have even the same name [Ayus] as in the Puranas for the Lunar ancestor. The Tatars all claim from Ai, 'the moon,' the Indus of the Puranas. Hence with them, as with the German tribes, the moon was always a male deity. The Tatar Ai had a son, Yulduz. His son was Hyu, from whom [1] came the first race of the kings of China. The Puranic Ayus had a son, Yadu (pronounced Jadon); from whose third son, Haya, the Hindu genealogist deduces no line, and from whom the Chinese may claim their Indu [1] origin. Il Khan (ninth from Ai) had two sons: first, Kian; and secondly, Nagas; whose descendants peopled all Tatary. From Kian, Jenghiz Khan claimed descent.[2] Nagas was probably the founder of the Takshak, or Snake race [3] of the Puranas and Tatar genealogists, the Tak-i-uk Moguls of De Guignes.

Such are the comparative genealogical origins of the three races. Let us compare their theogony, the fabulous birth assigned by each for the founder of the Indu race.

Mongol and Hindu Traditions.—1. The Puranic. "Ila (*the earth*), daughter of the sun-born Ikshwaku, while wandering in the forests was encountered by Budha (*Mercury*), and from the rape of Ila sprung the Indu race."

2. The Chinese account of the birth of Yu (Ayu), their first monarch. "A star [4] (Mercury or Fo) struck his mother while journeying. She conceived, and gave to the world Yu, the founder of the first dynasty which reigned in China. Yu divided China into nine provinces, and began to reign 2207 [5] years before Christ" [58].

Thus the Ai of the Tatars, the Yu of the Chinese, and the Ayus

[1] Sir W. Jones says the Chinese assert their Hindu origin; but a comparison proves both these Indu races to be of Scythic origin. [Yadu was son of Yayāti, and Haya was Yadu's grandson, not son. The comparison of Mongol with Hindu tradition is of no value.]

[2] [For the Mongol genealogy see Howorth, *History of the Mongols*, Part i. 35. Abu-l Fazl (*Akbarnāma*, trans. H. Beveridge, i. 171 f.) gives the names as follows: Aghūz Khān, whose sons were—Kūn (Sun); Ai (Moon); Yūlduz (Star); Kok or Gok (Sky); Tāgh (Mountain); Tangiz (Sky)].

[3] Naga and Takshak are Sanskrit names for a snake or serpent, the emblem of Budha or Mercury. The Naga race, so well known to India, the Takshaks or Takiuks of Scythia, invaded India about six centuries before Christ.

[4] De Guignes, *Sur les Dynasties des Huns*, vol. i. p. 7.

[5] Nearly the calculated period from the Puranas.

of the Puranas, evidently indicate the great Indu (Lunar) progenitor of the three races. Budha (Mercury), the son of Indu (the moon), became the patriarchal and spiritual leader; as Fo, in China; Woden and Teutates,[1] of the tribes migrating to Europe. Hence it follows that the religion of Buddha must be coeval with the existence of these nations; that it was brought into India Proper by them, and guided them until the schism of Krishna and the Suryas, worshippers of Bal, in time depressed them, when the Buddha religion was modified into its present mild form, the Jain.[2]

Scythian Traditions.—Let us contrast with these the origin of the Scythic nations, as related by Diodorus;[3] when it will be observed the same legends were known to him which have been handed down by the Puranas and Abulghazi.

"The Scythians had their first abodes on the Araxes.[4] Their origin was from a virgin born of the earth[5] of the shape of a woman from the waist upwards, and below a serpent (symbol of Budha or Mercury); that Jupiter had a son by her, named Scythes,[6] whose name the nation adopted. Scythes had two sons, Palas and Napas (*qu.* the Nagas, or Snake race, of the Tatar genealogy ?), who were celebrated for their great actions, and who divided the countries; and the nations were called after them, the Palians (*qu.* Pali ?)[7] and Napians. They led their forces as far as the Nile on Egypt, and subdued many nations. They enlarged the empire of the Scythians as far as the Eastern ocean,

[1] *Tauth*, 'father' in Sanskrit [? tāta]. *Qu.* Teuths, and Toth, the Mercury of Egypt ?

[2] [The author seems to confuse Budha (Mercury) with Gautama Buddha, the teacher. Buddhism arose in India, not in Central Asia, and Jainism was not a milder form of it, but an independent, and probably earlier, religion.]

[3] Diodorus Siculus book ii.

[4] The Arvarma of the Puranas; the Jaxartes or Sihun. The Puranas thus describe Sakadwipa or Scythia. Diodorus (lib. ii.) makes the Hemodus the boundary between Saka-Scythia and India Proper.

[5] Ila, the mother of the Lunar race, is the earth personified. Ertha of the Saxons; *ἔρα* of the Greeks; *ard* in Hebrew [?].

[6] Scythes, from *Sakatai*, 'Sakadwipa,' and *is*, 'Lord': Lord of Sakatai, or Scythia [?].

[7] *Qu.* Whether the Scythic Pali may not be the shepherd invaders of Egypt [?]. The Pali character yet exists, and appears the same as ancient fragments of the Buddha inscriptions in my possession: many letters assimilate with the Coptic.

and to the Caspian and lake Moeotis. The nation had many kings, from whom the Sacans (*Sakae*), the Massagetae (*Getae* or *Jats*), the Ari-aspians (*Aswas* of Aria), and many other races. They overran Assyria and Media [1] [59], overturning the empire, and transplanting the inhabitants to the Araxes under the name of Sauro-Matians." [2]

As the Sakae, Getae, Aswa, and Takshak are names which have crept in amongst our thirty-six royal races, common with others also to early civilization in Europe, let us seek further ancient authority on the original abodes.

Strabo [3] says: "All the tribes east of the Caspian are called Scythic. The Dahae [4] next the sea, the Massagetae (*great* Gete) and Sakae more eastward; but every tribe has a particular name. All are nomadic: but of these nomads the best-known are the Asii,[5] the Pasiani, Tochari, Sacarauli, who took Bactria from the Greeks. The Sakae [6] ('races') have made in Asia irruptions similar to those of the Cimmerians; thus they have been seen to possess themselves of Bactria, and the best district of Armenia, called after them Sakasenae." [7]

Which of the tribes of Rajasthan are the offspring of the Aswa and Medes, of Indu race, returned under new appellations, we

[1] The three great branches of the Indu (Lunar) Aswa bore the epithet of *Midia* (pronounced *Mede*), viz. Urumidha, Ajamidha, and Dvimidha. *Qu.* The Aswa invaders of Assyria and Media, the sons of Bajaswa, expressly stated to have multiplied in the countries west of the Indus, emigrating from their paternal seats in Panchalaka? [*Midha* means 'pouring out seed, prolific,' and has no connexion with Mede, the Madai of Genesis x. 2; the Assyrian Mada.]

[2] Sun-worshippers, the Suryavansa.

[3] Strabo lib. xi. p. 511.

[4] Dahya (one of the thirty-six tribes), now extinct.

[5] The Asii and Tochari, the Aswa and Takshak, or Turushka races, of the Puranas, of Sakadwipa [?]. "C'est vraisemblablement d'après le nom de Tachari, que M. D'Anville aura cru devoir placer les tribus ainsi dénommées dans le territoire qui s'appelle aujourdhui Tokarist'han, situé, dit ce grand géographe, entre les montagnes et le Gihon ou Amou" (Note 3, liv. xi. p. 254, Strabon).

[6] Once more I may state *Sakha* in Sanskrit has the aspirate: literally, the 'branches' or 'races.' [*Saka* and *Sākha* have no connexion; see Smith, *EHI*, 226.]

[7] "La Sacasene étoit une contrée de l'Arménie sur les confins de l'Albanie ou du Shirvan" (Note 4, tome i. p. 191, Strabon). "The Sacasenae were the ancestors of the Saxons" (Turner's *History of the Anglo-Saxons*).

shall not now stop to inquire, limiting our hypothesis to the fact of invasions, and adducing some evidence of such being simultaneous with migrations of the same bands into Europe. Hence the inference of a common origin between the Rajput and early races of Europe; to support which, a similar mythology, martial manners and poetry, language, and even music and architectural ornaments, may be adduced.[1]

Of the first migrations of the Indu-Scythic Getae, Takshak, and Asii, into India, that of Sheshnag (Takshak), from Sheshnagdes (Tocharistan ?) or Sheshnag, six centuries, by calculation, before Christ, is the first noticed by the Puranas.[2] About this period a grand irruption of the same races conquered Asia Minor, and [60] eventually Scandinavia; and not long after the Asii and Tochari overturned the Greek kingdom of Bactria, the Romans felt the power of the Asi,[3] the Chatti, and Cimbri, from the Baltic shore.

"If we can show the Germans to have been originally Scythae or Goths (Getes or Jits), a wide field of curiosity and inquiry is open to the origin of government, manners, etc.; all the antiquities of Europe will assume a new appearance, and, instead of being traced to the bands of Germany, as Montesquieu and the greatest writers have hitherto done, may be followed through long descriptions of the manners of the Scythians, etc., as given by Herodotus. Scandinavia was occupied by the Scythae five hundred years before Christ. These Scythians worshipped Mercury (Budha), Woden or Odin, and believed themselves his progeny. The Gothic mythology, by parallel, might be shown

[1] Herodotus (iv. 12) says: "The Cimmerians, expelled by the Massagetae, migrated to the Crimea." Here were the Thyssagetae, or western Getae [the lesser Getae, Herodotus iv. 22]; and thence both the Getae and Cimbri found their way to the Baltic. Rubruquis the Jesuit, describing the monuments of the Comani in the Dasht-i Kipchak, whence these tribes, says: "Their monuments and circles of stones are like our Celtic or Druidical remains" (Bell's *Collection*). The Khumān are a branch of the Kāthi tribe of Saurashtra, whose paliyas, or funeral monumental pillars, are seen in groups at every town and village. The Chatti were one of the early German tribes. [Needless to say, the German Chatti had no connexion with the Kāthi of Gujarāt.]

[2] [The reference, again, is to the Saisunāga dynasty, p. 64 above.]

[3] Asi was the term applied to the Getes, Yeuts, or Juts, when they invaded Scandinavia and founded Yeutland or Jutland (see '*Edda*,' Mallet's Introduction).

to be Grecian, whose gods were the progeny of Coelus and Terra (Budha and Ella).[1] Dryads, satyrs, fairies, and all the Greek and Roman superstition, may be found in the Scandinavian creed. The Goths consulted the heart of victims, had oracles, had sibyls, had a Venus in Freya, and Parcae in the Valkyrie."[2]

The Scythian Descent of the Rajputs.—Ere we proceed to trace these mythological resemblances, let us adduce further opinions in proof of the position assumed of a common origin of the tribes of early Europe and the Scythic Rajput.

The translator of Abulghazi, in his preface, observes: "Our contempt for the Tatars would lessen did we consider how nearly we stand related to them, and that our ancestors originally came from the north of Asia, and that our customs, laws, and way of living were formerly the same as theirs. In short, that we are no other than a colony of Tatars.

"It was from Tatary those people came, who, under the successive names of Cymbrians,[3] Kelts, and Gauls, possessed all the northern part of Europe. What were the Goths, Huns, Alans, Swedes, Vandals, Franks, but swarms of the same hive? The Swedish chronicles bring the Swedes[4] from Cashgar, and [61] the affinity between the Saxon language and Kipchak is great; and the Keltick language still subsisting in Britany and Wales is a demonstration that the inhabitants are descended from Tatar nations."

[1] Mercury and earth.

[2] Pinkerton, *On the Goths*, vol. ii. p. 94. [All this is obsolete.]

[3] Camari was one of the eight sons of Japhet, says Abulghazi: whence the Camari, Cimmerii, or Cimbri. Kamari is one of the tribes of Saurashtra. [Kymry = fellow-countrymen (Rhys, *Celtic Britain*, 116).]

[4] The Suiones, Suevi, or Su. Now the Su, Yueh-chi, or Yuti, are Getes, according to De Guignes. Marco Polo calls Cashgar, where he was in the sixth century, the birthplace of the Swedes; and De la Croix adds, that in 1691 Sparvenfeldt, the Swedish ambassador at Paris, told him he had read in Swedish chronicles that Cashgar was their country. When the Huns were chased from the north of China, the greater part retired into the southern countries adjoining Europe. The rest passed directly to the Oxus and Jaxartes; thence they spread to the Caspian and Persian frontiers. In Mawaru-l-nahr (Transoxiana) they mixed with the Su, the Yueh-chi, or Getes, who were particularly powerful, and extended into Europe. One would be tempted to regard them as the ancestors of those Getes who were known in Europe. Some bands of Su might equally pass into the north of Europe, known as the Suevi. [The meaning of Suevi is uncertain, but the word has no connexion with that of any Central Asian tribe.]

From between the parallels of 30° and 50° of north latitude, and from 75° to 95° of east longitude, the highlands of Central Asia, alike removed from the fires of the equator and the cold of the arctic circle, migrated the races which passed into Europe and within the Indus. We must therefore voyage up the Indus, cross the Paropanisos, to the Oxus or Jihun, to Sakatai [1] or Sakadwipa, and from thence and the Dasht-i Kipchak conduct the Takshaks, the Getae, the Kamari, the Chatti, and the Huns, into the plains of Hindustan.

We have much to learn in these unexplored regions, the abode of ancient civilisation, and which, so late as Jenghiz Khan's invasion, abounded with large cities. It is an error to suppose that the nations of Higher Asia were merely pastoral; and De Guignes, from original authorities, informs us that when the Su invaded the Yueh-chi or Jats, they found upwards of a hundred cities containing the merchandise of India, and with the currency bearing the effigies of the prince.

Such was the state of Central Asia long before the Christian era, though now depopulated and rendered desert by desolating wars, which have raged in these countries, and to which Europe can exhibit no parallel. Timur's wars, in more modern times, against the Getic nation, will illustrate the paths of his ambitious predecessors in the career of destruction.

If we examine the political limits of the great Getic nation in the time of Cyrus, six centuries before Christ, we shall find them little circumscribed in power on the rise of Timur, though twenty centuries had elapsed [62].

Jāts and Getae.—At this period (A.D. 1330), under the last prince of Getic race, Tughlak Timur Khan, the kingdom of Chagatai [2] was bounded on the west by the Dasht-i Kipchak, and

[1] Mr. Pinkerton's research had discovered Sakatai, though he does not give his authority (D'Anville) for the Sakadwipa of the Puranas! "Sakitai, a region at the fountains of the Oxus and Jaxartes, styled Sakita from the Sacae" (D'Anville, *Anc. Geog.*). The Yadus of Jaisalmer, who ruled Zabulistan and founded Ghazni, claim the Chagatais as of their own Indu stock: a claim which, without deep reflection, appeared inadmissible; but which I now deem worthy of credit.

[2] Chagatai, or Sakatai, the Sakadwipa of the Puranas (corrupted by the Greeks to Scythia), "whose inhabitants worship the sun and whence is the river Arvarma." [For the Chagatai Mongols see Elias-Ross, *History of the Moghuls of Central Asia*, Introd. 28 ff.]

on the south by the Jihun, on which river the Getic Khan, like Tomyris, had his capital. Kokhand, Tashkent, Utrar,[1] Cyropolis, and the most northern of the Alexandrias, were within the bounds of Chagatai.

The Getae, Jut, or Jat, and Takshak races, which occupy places amongst the thirty-six royal races of India, are all from the region of Sakatai. Regarding their earliest migrations, we shall endeavour to make the Puranas contribute; but of their invasions in more modern times the histories of Mahmud of Ghazni, and Timur abundantly acquaint us.

From the mountains of Jud [2] to the shores of Makran,[3] and along the Ganges, the Jat is widely spread; while the Takshak name is now confined to inscriptions or old writings.

Inquiries in their original haunts, and among tribes now under different names, might doubtless bring to light their original designation, now best known within the Indus; while the Takshak or Takiuk may probably be discovered in the Tajik, still in his ancient haunts, the Transoxiana and Chorasmia of classic authors; the Mawaru-n-nahr of the Persians; the Turan, Turkistan, or Tocharistan of native geography; the abode of the Tochari, Takshak, or Turushka invaders of India, described in the Puranas and existing inscriptions.

The Getae had long maintained their independence when Tomyris defended their liberty against Cyrus. Driven in successive wars across the Sutlej, we shall elsewhere show them preserving their ancient habits, as desultory cavaliers, under the Jat leader of Lahore, in pastoral communities in Bikaner, the Indian

[1] Utrar, probably the Uttarakuru of ancient geography: the uttara (northern) kuru (race); a branch of Indu stock.

[2] Jadu ka dang, the Joudes of Rennell's map; the Yadu hills high up in the Panjab, where a colony of the Yadu race dwelt when expelled Saurashtra. [The Salt Range in the Jhelum, Shāhpur, and Miānwāli districts of the Panjāb, was known to ancient historians as Koh-i-Jūd, or 'the hills of Jūd,' the name being applied by the Muhammadans to this range on account of its resemblance to Mount Al-Jūdi, or Ararat. The author constantly refers to it, and suggests that the name was connected with the Indian Yadu, or Yādava tribe (*IGI*, xxi. 412; Abu-l Fazl, *Akbarnāma*, i. 237; Elliot-Dowson, ii. 235, v. 561; *Āīn*, ii. 405; *ASR*, ii. 17; Hughes, *Dict. of Islām*, 23).]

[3] The Numri, or Lumri (foxes) of Baluchistan, are Jats [?]. These are the Nomardies of Rennell. [They are believed to be aborigines (*IGI*, xvi. 146; *Census Report, Baluchistan*, 1911, i. 17).]

desert and elsewhere, though they have lost sight of their early history. The transition from pastoral to agricultural pursuits is but short, and the descendant of the nomadic Getae of Transoxiana is now the best husbandman on the plains of Hindustan [1] [63].

The invasion of these Indu-Scythic tribes, Getae, Takshaks, Asii, Chatti, Rajpali,[2] Huns, Kamari, introduced the worship of Budha, the founder of the Indu or Lunar race.

Herodotus says the Getae were theists,[3] and held the tenets of the soul's immortality; so with the Buddhists.

Before, however, touching on points of religious resemblance between the Asii, Getae, or Jut of Scandinavia (who gave his name to the Cimbric Chersonese) and the Getae of Scythia and India, let us make a few remarks on the Asii or Aswa.

The Aswa.—To the Indu race of Aswa (the descendants of Dvimidha and Bajaswa), spread over the countries on both sides the Indus, do we probably owe the distinctive appellation of Asia. Herodotus [4] says the Greeks denominated Asia from the wife of Prometheus; while others deduce it from a grandson of Manes, indicating the Aswa descendants of the patriarch Manu. Asa,[5] Sakambhari,[6] Mata,[7] is the divinity Hope, 'mother-protectress of the Sakha,' or races. Every Rajput adores Asapurna, 'the fulfiller of desire'; or, as Sakambhari Devi (goddess protectress), she is invoked previous to any undertaking.

The Aswas were chiefly of the Indu race; yet a branch of the Suryas also bore this designation. It appears to indicate their celebrity as horsemen.[8] All of them worshipped the horse, which they sacrificed to the sun. This grand rite, the Asvamedha, on

[1] [There is no evidence, beyond resemblance of name, to connect the Jats with the Getae.]

[2] Royal pastors [?].

[3] [iv. 59.] The sun was their 'great deity,' though they had in Xamolxis a lord of terror, with affinity to Yama, or the Hindu Pluto. "The chief divinity of the Fenns, a Scythic race, was Yammalu" (Pinkerton's *Hist. of the Goths*, vol. ii. p. 215).

[4] iv. 45 [Asia probably means 'land of the rising sun.']

[5] Āsa, 'hope.'

[6] Sakambhari: from *sakham*, the plural of *sakha*, 'branch or race,' and *ambhar*, 'covering, protecting.' [The word means 'herb nourishing.']

[7] Mata, 'mother.'

[8] *Aswa* and *haya* are synonymous Sanskrit terms for 'horse'; *asp* in Persian; and as applied by the prophet Ezekiel [xxxviii. 6] to the Getic invasion of Scythia, A.C. 600: "the sons of Togarmah riding on horses"; described by Diodorus, the period the same as the Takshak invasion of India.

the festival of the winter solstice, would alone go far to exemplify their common Scythic origin with the Getic Saka, authorising the inference of Pinkerton, "that a grand Scythic nation extended from the Caspian to the Ganges."

The Asvamedha.—The Asvamedha was practised on the Ganges and Sarju by the Solar princes [64], twelve hundred years before Christ, as by the Getae in the time of Cyrus; "deeming it right," says Herodotus [i. 216] "to offer the swiftest of created to the chief of uncreated beings": and this worship and sacrifice of the horse has been handed down to the Rajput of the present day. A description of this grand ceremony shall close these analogies.

The Getic Asii carried this veneration for the steed, symbolic of their chief deity the sun, into Scandinavia: equally so of all the early German tribes, the Su, Suevi, Chatti, Sucimbri, Getae, in the forests of Germany, and on the banks of the Elbe and Weser. The milk-white steed was supposed to be the organ of the gods, from whose neighing they calculated future events; notions possessed also by the Aswa, sons of Budha (Woden), on the Yamuna and Ganges, when the rocks of Scandinavia and the shores of the Baltic were yet untrod by man. It was this omen which gave Darius Hystaspes [1] (*hinsna*, 'to neigh,' *aspa*, 'a horse') a crown. The bard Chand makes it the omen of death to his principal heroes. The steed of the Scandinavian god of battle was kept in the temple of Upsala, and always "found foaming and sweating after battle." "Money," says Tacitus, "was only acceptable to the German when bearing the effigies of the horse." [2]

In the Edda we are informed that the Getae, or Jats, who entered Scandinavia, were termed Asi, and their first settlement As-gard.[3]

Pinkerton rejects the authority of the Edda and follows Torfaeus, who "from Icelandic chronicles and genealogies concludes Odin to have come into Scandinavia in the time of Darius Hystaspes, five hundred years before Christ."

[1] [Hystaspes is from old Persian, Vishtāspa, 'possessor of horses.' The author derives it from a modern Hindi word *hīnsna*, 'to neigh,' possibly from recollection of the story in Herodotus iii. 85.]

[2] [He possibly refers to the statement (*Germania*, v.), that their coins bore the impress of a two-horse chariot.]

[3] Asirgarh, 'fortress of the Asi' [*IGI*, vi. 12].

This is the period of the last Buddha, or Mahavira, whose era is four hundred and seventy-seven years before Vikrama, or five hundred and thirty-three before Christ.

The successor of Odin in Scandinavia was Gotama; and Gautama was the successor of the last Buddha, Mahavira,[1] who as Gotama, or Gaudama, is still adored from the Straits of Malacca to the Caspian Sea.

"Other antiquaries," says Pinkerton, "assert another Odin, who was put as the supreme deity one thousand years before Christ" [65].

Mallet admits two Odins, but Mr. Pinkerton wishes he had abided by that of Torfaeus, in 500 A.C.

It is a singular fact that the periods of both the Scandinavian Odins should assimilate with the twenty-second Buddha [Jain Tirthakara], Neminath, and twenty-fourth and last, Mahavira; the first the contemporary of Krishna, about 1000 or 1100 years, the last 533, before Christ. The Asii, Getae, etc., of Europe worshipped Mercury as founder of their line, as did the Eastern Asi, Takshaks, and Getae. The Chinese and Tatar historians also say Buddha, or Fo, appeared 1027 years before Christ. "The Yuchi, established in Bactria and along the Jihun, eventually bore the name of Jeta or Yetan,[2] that is to say, Getae. Their empire subsisted a long time in this part of Asia, and extended even into India. These are the people whom the Greeks knew under the name of Indo-Scythes. Their manners are the same as those of the Turks.[3] Revolutions occurred in the very heart of the East, whose consequences were felt afar." [4]

The period allowed by all these authorities for the migration of these Scythic hordes into Europe is also that for their entry into India.

The sixth century is that calculated for the Takshak from Sheshnagdesa; and it is on this event and reign that the Puranas declare, that from this period "no prince of pure blood would be

[1] The great (*maha*) warrior (*vir*). [Buddha lived 567–487 B.C.: Mahāvīra, founder of Jainism, died about 527 B.C.]

[2] Yeutland was the name given to the whole Cimbric Chersonese, or Jutland (Pinkerton, *On the Goths*).

[3] Turk, Turushka, Takshak, or 'Taunak, fils de Turc' (Abulghazi, *History of the Tatars*).

[4] *Histoire des Huns*, vol. i. p. 42.

found, but that the Sudra, the Turushka, and the Yavan, would prevail."

All these Indu-Scythic invaders held the religion of Buddha: and hence the conformity of manners and mythology between the Scandinavian or German tribes and the Rajputs increased by comparing their martial poetry.

Similarity of religious manners affords stronger proofs of original identity than language. Language is eternally changing —so are manners; but an exploded custom or rite traced to its source, and maintained in opposition to climate, is a testimony not to be rejected.

Personal Habits, Dress.—When Tacitus informs us that the first act of a German on rising was ablution, it will be conceded this habit was not acquired in [66] the cold climate of Germany, but must have been of eastern [1] origin; as were "the loose flowing robe; the long and braided hair, tied in a knot at the top of the head"; with many other customs, personal habits, and superstitions of the Scythic Cimbri, Juts, Chatti, Suevi, analogous to the Getic nations of the same name, as described by Herodotus, Justin, and Strabo, and which yet obtain amongst the Rajput Sakhae of the present day.

Let us contrast what history affords of resemblance in religion or manners. First, as to religion.

Theogony.—Tuisto (Mercury) and Ertha (the earth) were the chief divinities of the early German tribes. Tuisto [2] was born of the Earth (Ila) and Manus (Manu). He is often confounded with Odin, or Woden, the Budha of the eastern tribes, though they are the Mars and Mercury of these nations.

[1] Though Tacitus calls the German tribes indigenous, it is evident he knew their claim to Asiatic origin, when he asks, "Who would leave the softer abodes of Asia for Germany, where Nature yields nothing but deformity?"

[2] In an inscription of the Geta or Jat Prince of Salindrapur (Salpur) of the fifth century, he is styled "of the race of Tusta" (*qu.* Tuisto ?). It is in that ancient nail-headed character used by the ancient Buddhists of India, and still the sacred character of the Tatar Lamas: in short, the Pali. All the ancient inscriptions I possess of the branches of the Agnikulas, as the Chauhan, Pramara, Solanki, and Parihara, are in this character. That of the Jat prince styles him "Jat Kathida" (*qu.* of (da) Cathay ?). From Tuisto and Woden we have our Tuesday and Wednesday. In India, Wednesday is Budhwar (Dies Mercurii), and Tuesday Mangalwar (Dies Martis), the Mardi of the French.

Religious Rites.—The Suiones or Suevi, the most powerful Getic nation of Scandinavia, were divided into many tribes, one of whom, the Su (Yueh-chi or Jat), made human sacrifices in their consecrated groves [1] to Ertha (Ila), whom all worshipped, and whose chariot was drawn by a cow.[2] The Suevi worshipped Isis (Isa, Gauri, the Isis and Ceres of Rajasthan), in whose rites the figure of a ship is introduced; "symbolic," observes Tacitus, "of its foreign origin." [3] The festival of Isa, or Gauri, wife of Iswara, at Udaipur, is performed on the lake, and appears to be exactly that of Isis and Osiris in Egypt, as described by Herodotus. On this occasion Iswara (Osiris), who is secondary to his wife, has a stalk of the onion in blossom in his hand; a root detested by the Hindus generally, though adored by the Egyptians.

Customs of War.—They sung hymns in praise of Hercules, as well as Tuisto or Odin, whose banners and images they carried to the field; and fought in clans, using the feram or javelin, both in close and distant combat. In all maintaining [67] the resemblance to the Harikula, descendants of Budha, and the Aswa, offspring of Bajaswa, who peopled those regions west of the Indus, and whose redundant population spread both east and west.

The Suevi, or Suiones, erected the celebrated temple of Upsala, in which they placed the statues of Thor, Woden, and Freya, the triple divinity of the Scandinavian Asii, the Trimurti of the Solar and Lunar races. The first (Thor, the thunderer, or god of war) is Hara, or Mahadeva, the destroyer; the second (Woden) is Budha,[4] the preserver; and the third (Freya) is Uma, the creative power.

The grand festival to Freya was in spring, when all nature revived; then boars were offered to her by the Scandinavians, and even boars of paste were made and swallowed by the peasantry.

As Vasanti, or spring personified, the consort of Hara is worshipped by the Rajput, who opens the season with a grand

[1] Tacitus, *Germania*, xxxviii.

[2] The gau, or cow, symbolic of Prithivi, the earth. On this see note, p. 33.

[3] [*Germania*, ix.]

[4] Krishna is the preserving deity of the Hindu triad. Krishna is of the Indu line of Budha, whom he worshipped prior to his own deification.

hunt,[1] led by the prince and his vassal chiefs, when they chase, slay, and eat the boar. Personal danger is disregarded on this day, as want of success is ominous that the Great Mother will refuse all petitions throughout the year.

Pinkerton, quoting Ptolemy (who was fifty years after Tacitus), says there were six nations in Yeutland or Jutland, the country of the Juts, of whom were the Sablingii (Suevi,[2] or Suiones), the Chatti and Hermandri, who extended to the estuary of the Elbe and Weser. There they erected the pillar Irmansul to "the god of war," regarding which Sammes[3] observes: "some will have it to be Mars his pillar, others Hermes Saul, or the pillar of Hermes or Mercury"; and he naturally asks, "how did the Saxons come to be acquainted with the Greek name of Mercury?"

Sacrificial pillars are termed *Sula* in Sanskrit; which, conjoined with Hara,[4] the Indian god of war, would be Harsula. The Rajput warrior invokes Hara with his trident (trisula) to help him in battle, while his battle-shout is 'mar! mar!' The Cimbri, one of the most celebrated of the six tribes of Yeutland, derive their name from their fame as warriors [68].[5]

Kumara[6] is the Rajput god of war. He is represented with seven heads in the Hindu mythology: the Saxon god of war has six.[7] The six-headed Mars of the Cimbri Chersonese, to whom was raised the Irmansul on the Weser, was worshipped by the Sakasenae, the Chatti, the Siebi or Suevi, the Jotae or Getae, and the Cimbri, evincing in name, as in religious rites, a common origin with the martial warriors of Hindustan.

Rajput Religion.—The religion of the martial Rajput, and the rites of Hara, the god of battle, are little analogous to those of

1 'Mahurat ka shikar.'

2 The Siebi of Tacitus.

3 Sammes's *Saxon Antiquities*.

4 Hara is the Thor of Scandinavia; Hari is Budha, Hermes, or Mercury.

5 Mallet derives it from *kempfer*, 'to fight.' [The name is said to mean 'comrades' (Rhys, *Celtic Britain*, 116). Irmansūl means 'a colossus,' and has no connexion with Skr. *sūla* (Grimm, *Teutonic Mythology*, i. 115).]

6 *Ku* is a mere prefix, meaning 'evil'; 'the evil striker (*Mar*).' Hence, probably, the Mars of Rome. The birth of Kumar, the general of the army of the gods, with the Hindus, is exactly that of the Grecians, born of the goddess Jahnavi (Juno) without sexual intercourse. Kumāra is always accompanied by the peacock, the bird of Juno. [Kumāra probably means 'easily dying'; there is no connexion with Mars, originally a deity of vegetation.]

7 For a drawing of the Scandinavian god of battle see Sammes.

the meek Hindus, the followers of the pastoral divinity, the worshippers of kine, and feeders on fruits, herbs, and water. The Rajput delights in blood: his offerings to the god of battle are sanguinary, blood and wine. The cup (kharpara) of libation is the human skull. He loves them because they are emblematic of the deity he worships; and he is taught to believe that Hara loves them, who in war is represented with the skull to drink the foeman's blood, and in peace is the patron of wine and women. With Parbati on his knee, his eyes rolling from the juice of the phul (ardent spirits) and opium, such is this Bacchanalian divinity of war. Is this Hinduism, acquired on the burning plains of India? Is it not rather a perfect picture of the manners of the Scandinavian heroes?

The Rajput slays buffaloes, hunts and eats the boar and deer, and shoots ducks and wild fowl (*kukkut*); he worships his horse, his sword, and the sun, and attends more to the martial song of the bard than to the litany of the Brahman. In the martial mythology and warlike poetry of the Scandinavians a wide field exists for assimilation, and a comparison of the poetical remains of the Asi of the east and west would alone suffice to suggest a common origin.

Bards.—In the sacred Bardai of the Rajput we have the bard of our Saxon ancestry; those reciters of warlike poetry, of whom Tacitus says, "with their barbarous strains, they influence their minds in the day of battle with a chorus of military virtue."

A comparison, in so extensive a field, would include the whole of their manners and religious opinions, and must be reserved for a distinct work.[1] The Valkyrie [69], or fatal sisters of the Suevi or Siebi, would be the twin sisters of the Apsaras, who summon the Rajput warrior from the field of battle, and bear him to "the mansion of the sun," equally the object of attainment with the children of Odin in Scandinavia, and of Budha and Surya in the

[1] I have in contemplation to give to the public a few of the sixty-nine books of the poems of Chand, the last great bard of the last Hindu emperor of India, Prithwiraja. They are entirely heroic: each book a relation of one of the exploits of this prince, the first warrior of his time. They will aid a comparison between the Rajput and Scandinavian bards, and show how far the Provençal Troubadour, the Neustrienne Trouveur, and Minnesinger of Germany, have anything in common with the Rajput Bardai. [For Rajput bards on horseback, drunk with opium, singing songs to arouse warriors' courage, see Manucci ii. 437 f.]

plains of Scythia and on the Ganges, like the Elysium[1] of the Heliadae of Greece.

In the day of battle we should see in each the same excitements to glory and contempt of death, and the *dramatis personae* of the field, both celestial and terrestrial, move and act alike. We should see Thor, the thunderer, leading the Siebi, and Hara (Siva) the Indian Jove, his own worshippers (Sivseva); in which Freya, or Bhavani, and even the preserver (Krishna) himself, not unfrequently mingle.

War Chariots.—The war chariot is peculiar to the Indu-Scythic nations, from Dasaratha,[2] and the heroes of the Mahabharata, to the conquest of Hindustan by the Muhammadans, when it was laid aside. On the plains of Kurukshetra, Krishna became charioteer to his friend Arjun; and the Getic hordes of the Jaxartes, when they aided Xerxes in Greece, and Darius on the plains of Arbela,[3] had their chief strength in the war chariot.

The war chariot continued to be used later in the south-west of India than elsewhere, and the Kathi,[4] Khuman, Kumari of

[1] Ἡλύσιος, from Ἥλιος, 'the sun'; also a title of Apollo, the Hari of India. [The two words, from the accentuation, can have no connexion.]

[2] This title of the father of Rama denotes a 'charioteer' ['having ten chariots.' Harsha (A.D. 612–647) discarded the chariot (Smith, *EHI*, 339)].

[3] The Indian satrapy of Darius, says Herodotus [iii. 94], was the richest of all the Persian provinces, and yielded six hundred talents of gold. Arrian informs us that his Indo-Scythic subjects, in his wars with Alexander, were the élite of his army. Besides the Sakasenae, we find tribes in name similar to those included in the thirty-six Rajkula; especially the Dahae (Dahya, one of the thirty-six races). The Indo-Scythic contingent was two hundred war chariots and fifteen elephants, which were marshalled with the Parthii on the right, and also near Darius's person. By this disposition they were opposed to the cohort commanded by Alexander in person. The chariots commenced the action, and prevented a manœuvre of Alexander to turn the left flank of the Persians. Of their horse, also, the most honourable mention is made; they penetrated into the division where Parmenio commanded, to whom Alexander was compelled to send reinforcements. The Grecian historian dwells with pleasure on Indo-Scythic valour: "there were no equestrian feats, no distant fighting with darts, but each fought as if victory depended on his sole arm." They fought the Greeks hand to hand [Arrian, *Anabasis*, iii. 15].

But the loss of empire was decreed at Arbela, and the Sakae and Indo Scythae had the honour of being slaughtered by the Yavans of Greece, far from their native land, in the aid of the king of kings.

[4] The Kathi are celebrated in Alexander's wars. The Kathiawar Kathi can be traced from Multan (*the ancient abode*) [*mūlasthāna*, 'principal place'].

Saurashtra have to recent times retained their Scythic habits, as their monumental stones testify, expressing their being slain from their cars [70].

Position of Women.—In no point does resemblance more attach between the ancient German and Scandinavian tribes, and the martial Rajput or ancient Getae, than in their delicacy towards females.

"The Germans," says Tacitus [*Germania*, viii.], "deemed the advice of a woman in periods of exigence oracular." So does the Rajput, as the bard Chand often exemplifies; and hence they append to her name the epithet *Devi* (or contracted *De*), 'god-like.' "To a German mind," says Tacitus, "the idea of a woman led into captivity is insupportable"; and to prevent this the Rajput raises the poignard against the heart which beats only for him, though never to survive the dire necessity. It is then they perform the sacrifice 'johar,' when every sakha (branch) is cut off: and hence the Rajput glories in the title of *Sakha-band*, from having performed the sakha; an awful rite, and with every appearance of being the *sacaea* of the Scythic Getae, as described by Strabo.[1]

The Dahya (Dahae), Johya (the latter Hunnish), and Kathi are amongst the thirty-six races. All dwelt, six centuries ago, within the five streams and in the deserts south of the Ghara. The two last have left but a name.

[1] The Sakae had invaded the inhabitants on the borders of the Pontic Sea: whilst engaged in dividing the booty, the Persian generals surprised them at night, and exterminated them. To eternize the remembrance of this event, the Persians heaped up the earth round a rock in the plain where the battle was fought, on which they erected two temples, one to the goddess Anaïtis, the other to the divinities Omanus and Anandate, and then founded the annual festival called *Sacaea*, still celebrated by the possessors of Zela. Such is the account by some authors of the origin of *Sacaea*. According to others it dates from the reign of Cyrus only. This prince, they say, having carried the war into the country of the Sakae (Massagetae of Herodotus) lost a battle. Compelled to fall back on his magazines, abundantly stored with provisions, but especially wine, and having halted some time to refresh his army, he departed before the enemy, feigning a flight, and leaving his camp standing full of provisions. The Sakae, who pursued, reaching the abandoned camp stored with provisions, gave themselves up to debauch. Cyrus returned and surprised the inebriated and senseless barbarians. Some, buried in profound sleep, were easily massacred; others occupied in drinking and dancing, without defence, fell into the hands of armed foes: so that all perished. The conqueror, attributing his success to divine protection, consecrated this day to the goddess honoured in his country, and decreed it should be called 'the day of the *Sacaea*.' This is the battle

Gaming.—In passion for play at games of chance, its extent and dire consequences, the Rajput, from the earliest times, has evinced a predilection, and will stand comparison with the Scythian and his German offspring. The German staked his personal liberty, became a slave, and was sold as the property of the winner. To this vice the Pandavas owed the loss of their sovereignty and personal liberty, involving at last the destruction of all the Indu [71] races; nor has the passion abated. Religion even consecrates the viee; and once a year, on 'the Festival of Lamps' (*Diwali*), all propitiate the goddess of wealth and fortune (Lakshmi) by offering at her shrine.

Destitute of mental pursuits, the martial Rajput is often slothful or attached to sensual pleasures, and when roused, reckless on what he may wreak a fit of energy. Yet when order and discipline prevail in a wealthy chieftainship, there is much of that patriarchal mode of life, with its amusements, alike suited to the Rajput, the Getae of the Jihun, or Scandinavian.

Omens, Auguries.—Divination by lots, auguries, and omens by flights of birds, as practised by the Getic nations described by Herodotus, and amongst the Germans by Tacitus, will be found amongst the Rajputs, from whose works [1] on this subject might have been supplied the whole of the Augurs and Aruspices, German or Roman.

Love of Strong Drink.—Love of liquor, and indulgence in it to excess, were deep-rooted in the Scandinavian Asi and German tribes, and in which they showed their Getic origin; nor is the

---

related by Herodotus, to which Strabo alludes, between the Persian monarch and Tomyris, queen of the Getae. Amongst the Rajput Sakha, all grand battles attended with fatal results are termed *sakha*. When besieged, without hope of relief, in the last effort of despair, the females are immolated, and the warriors, decorated in saffron robes, rush on inevitable destruction. This is to perform *sakha*, where every branch (sakha) is cut off. Chitor has to boast of having thrice (and a half) suffered sakha. *Chitor sakha ka pap*, 'by the sin of the sack of Chitor,' the most solemn adjuration of the Guhilot Rajput. If such the origin of the festival from the slaughter of the Sakae of Tomyris, it will be allowed to strengthen the analogy contended for between the Sakae east and west the Indus. [For the Sacaea festival see Sir J. Frazer, *The Golden Bough, The Dying God*, 113 ff. It has no connexion with the Rajput Sākha, 'a fight,' which, again, is a different word from Sākha, 'a branch, clan.']

[1] I presented a work on this subject to the Royal Asiatic Society, as well as another on Palmistry, etc.

Rajput behind his brethren either of Scythia or Europe. It is the free use of this and similar indulgences, prohibited by ordinances which govern the ordinary Hindu, that first induced me to believe that these warlike races were little indebted to India.

The Rajput welcomes his guest with the *munawwar piyala*, or 'cup of request,' in which they drown ancient enmities. The heroes of Odin never relished a cup of mead more than the Rajput his *madhu*;[1] and the bards of Scandinavia and Rajwara are alike eloquent in the praise of the bowl, on which the Bardai exhausts every metaphor, and calls it ambrosial, immortal.[2] "The bard, as he sipped the ambrosia, in which sparkled the ruby seed of the pomegranate, rehearsed the glory of the race of the fearless.[3] May the king live for ever, alike bounteous in gifts to the bard and the foe!" Even in the heaven of Indra, the Hindu warrior's paradise, akin to Valhalla [72], the Rajput has his cup, which is served by the Apsaras, the twin sister of the celestial Hebe of Scania. "I shall quaff full goblets amongst the gods," says the dying Getic warrior;[4] "I die laughing": sentiments which would be appreciated by a Rajput.

A Rajput inebriated is a rare sight: but a more destructive and recent vice has usurped much of the honours of the 'invitation cup,' which has been degraded from the pure 'flower'[5] to an infusion of the poppy, destructive of every quality. Of this pernicious habit we may use the words which the historian of German manners applies to the tribes of the Weser and Elbe, in respect to their love of strong drink: "Indulge it, and you need not employ the terror of your arms; their own vices will subdue them."

[1] *Madhu* is intoxicating drink, from *madhu*, 'a bee,' in Sanskrit [madhu, 'anything sweet']. It is well known that mead is from honey. It would be curious if the German mead was from the Indian madhu (bee): then both cup (*kharpara*) and beverage would be borrowed. [*Madhu* does not mean 'a bee' in Sanskrit.]

[2] *Amrita* (immortal), from the initial privative and *mrit*, 'death.' Thus the *Immurthal*, or 'vale of immortality,' at Neufchatel, is as good Sanskrit as German [?].

[3] Abhai Singh, 'the fearless lion,' prince of Marwar, whose bard makes this speech at the festal board, when the prince presented with his own hand the cup to the bard.

[4] Regner Lodbrog, in his dying ode, when the destinies summon him.

[5] Phūl, the flower of the mahua tree, the favourite drink of a Rajput. Classically, in Sanskrit it is *madhūka*, of the class Polyandria Monogynia [*Bassia latifolia*] (see *As. Res.* vol. i. p. 300).

The cup of the Scandinavian worshippers of Thor, the god of battle, was a human skull, that of the foe, in which they showed their thirst of blood; also borrowed from the chief of the Hindu Triad, Hara, the god of battle, who leads his heroes in the 'red field of slaughter' with the *khopra* [1] in his hand, with which he gorges on the blood of the slain.

Hara is the patron of all who love war and strong drink, and is especially the object of the Rajput warrior's devotion: accordingly blood and wine form the chief oblations to the great god of the Indus. The Gosains,[2] the peculiar priests of Hara, or Bal, the sun, all indulge in intoxicating drugs, herbs, and drinks. Seated on their lion, leopard, or deer skins, their bodies covered with ashes, their hair matted and braided, with iron tongs to feed the penitential fires, their savage appearance makes them fit organs for the commands of the blood and slaughter. Contrary, likewise, to general practice, the minister of Hara, the god of war, at his death is committed to the earth, and a circular tumulus is raised over him; and with some classes of Gosains, small tumuli, whose form is the frustrum of a cone, with lateral steps, the apex crowned with a cylindrical stone [73].[3]

Funeral Ceremonies.—In the last rites for the dead, comparison will yield proofs of original similarity. The funeral ceremonies of Scandinavia have distinguished the national eras, and the 'age of fire' and 'the age of hills,' [4] designated the periods when the warrior was committed to mother earth or consumed on the pyre.

Odin (Budha) introduced the latter custom, and the raising of tumuli over the ashes when the body was burned; as also the practice of the wife burning with her deceased lord. These

[1] A human skull; in the dialects pronounced *khopar*: *Qu. cup* in Saxon? [Cup, in Low Latin *cuppa.*]

[2] The Kanphara [or Kanphata] Jogis, or Gosains, are in great bodies, often in many thousands, and are sought as allies, especially in defensive warfare. In the grand military festivals at Udaipur to the god of war, the scymitar, symbolic of Mars, worshipped by the Guhilots, is entrusted to them [*IA*, vii. 47 ff.; *BG*, ix. part i. 543].

[3] An entire cemetery of these, besides many detached, I have seen, and also the sacred rites to their manes by the disciples occupying these abodes of austerity, when the flowers of the *ak* [*Calatropis gigantea*] and leaves of evergreen were strewed on the grave, and sprinkled with the pure element.

[4] Mallet's *Northern Antiquities*, chap. xii.

manners were carried from Sakadwipa, or Saka Scythia, "where the Geta," says Herodotus [v. 5], "was consumed on the pyre or burned alive with her lord." With the Getae, the Siebi or Suevi of Scandinavia, if the deceased had more than one wife, the elder claimed the privilege of burning.[1] Thus, "Nanna was consumed in the same fire with the body of her husband, Balder, one of Odin's companions." But the Scandinavians were anxious to forget this mark of their Asiatic origin, and were not always willing to burn, or to make "so cruel and absurd a sacrifice to the manes of their husbands, the idea of which had been picked up by their Scythian ancestors, when they inhabited the warmer climates of Asia, where they had their first abodes."[2]

"The Scythic Geta," says Herodotus [iv. 71], "had his horse sacrificed on his funeral pyre; and the Scandinavian Geta had his horse and arms buried with him, as they could not approach Odin on foot."[3] The Rajput warrior is carried to his final abode armed at all points as when alive, his shield on his back and brand in hand; while his steed, though not sacrificed, is often presented to the deity, and becomes a perquisite of the priest.

Sati.—The burning of the dead warrior, and female immolation, or *Sati*, are well-known rites, though the magnificent cenotaphs raised on the spot of sacrifice are little known or visited by Europeans; than which there are no better memorials of the rise and decline of the States of the Rajput heptarchy. It is the son who raises the mausoleum to the memory of his father; which last token of respect, or laudable vanity, is only limited by the means of the treasury. It is commemorative [74] of the splendour of his reign that the dome of his father should eclipse that of his predecessor. In every principality of Rajwara, the remark is applicable to chieftains as well as princes.

Each sacred spot, termed 'the place of great sacrifice' (Mahasati), is the haunted ground of legendary lore. Amongst the altars on which have burned the beauteous and the brave, the harpy[4] takes up her abode, and stalks forth to devour the hearts

[1] Mallet chap. xii. vol. i. p. 289.

[2] Edda.

[3] Mallet's *Northern Antiquities*, chap. xii. The Celtic Franks had the same custom. The arms of Chilperic, and the bones of the horse on which he was to be presented to Odin, were found in his tomb.

[4] The Dakini (the Jigarkhor of Sindh) is the genuine vampire [*Āīn*, ii. 338 f.]. Captain Waugh, after a long chase in the valley of Udaipur, speared

of her victims. The Rajput never enters these places of silence but to perform stated rites, or anniversary offerings of flowers and water to the manes (pitri-deva [1]) of his ancestors.

Odin [2] guarded his warriors' final abode from rapine by means of "wandering fires which played around the tombs"; and the tenth chapter of the Salic law is on punishments against "carrying off the boards or carpets of the tombs." Fire and water are interdicted to such sacrilegious spoliators.

The shihaba,[3] or wandering meteoric fires, on fields of battle and in the places of 'great sacrifice,' produce a pleasing yet melancholy effect; and are the source of superstitious dread and reverence to the Hindu, having their origin in the same natural cause as the 'wandering fires of Odin'; the phosphorescent salts produced from animal decomposition.

The Scandinavian reared the tumulus over the ashes of the dead; so did the Geta of the Jaxartes, and the officiating priests of Hara, the Hindu god of battle.

The noble picture drawn by Gibbon of the sepulture of the Getic Alaric is paralleled by that of the great Jenghiz Khan. When the lofty mound was raised, extensive forests were planted, to exclude for ever the footsteps of man from his remains.

The tumulus, the cairn, or the pillar, still rises over the Rajput who falls in [75] battle; and throughout Rajwara these sacrificial monuments are found, where are seen carved in relief the warrior on his steed, armed at all points; his faithful wife (*Sati*)

---

a hyena, whose abode was the tombs, and well known as the steed on which the witch of Ar sallied forth at night. Evil was predicted: and a dangerous fall, subsequently, in chasing an elk, was attributed to his sacrilegious slaughter of the weird sister's steed.

[1] Pitri-deva, 'Father-lords.'

[2] Mallet chap. xii.

[3] At Gwalior, on the east side of that famed fortress, where myriads of warriors have fattened the soil, these phosphorescent lights often present a singular appearance. I have, with friends whose eyes this will meet, marked the procession of these lambent night-fires, becoming extinguished at one place and rising at another, which, aided by the unequal *locale*, have been frequently mistaken for the Mahratta prince returning with his numerous torch-bearers from a distant day's sport. I have dared as bold a Rajput as ever lived to approach them; whose sense of the levity of my desire was strongly depicted, both in speech and mien: "men he would encounter, but not the spirits of those erst slain in battle." It was generally about the conclusion of the rains that these lights were observed, when evaporation took place from these marshy grounds impregnated with salts.

beside him, denoting a sacrifice, and the sun and moon on either side, emblematic of never-dying fame.

Cairns, Pillars.—In Saurashtra, amidst the Kathi, Khuman, Bala, and others of Scythic descent, the Paliya, or Jujhar (sacrificial pillars), are conspicuous under the walls of every town, in lines, irregular groups, and circles. On each is displayed in rude relief the warrior, with the manner of his death, lance in hand, generally on horseback, though sometimes in his car; and on the coast 'the pirates of Budha'[1] are depicted boarding from the shrouds. Amidst the Khuman of Tatary the Jesuits found stone circles, similar to those met with wherever the Celtic rites prevailed; and it would require no great ingenuity to prove an analogy, if not a common origin, between Druidic circles and the Indo-Scythic monumental remains. The trilithon, or seat, in the centre of the judicial circle, is formed by a number sacred to Hara, Bal, or the sun, whose priest expounds the law.

Worship of Arms. The Sword.—The devotion of the Rajput is still paid to his arms, as to his horse. He swears 'by the steel,' and prostrates himself before his defensive buckler, his lance, his sword, or his dagger.

The worship of the sword (*asi*) may divide with that of the horse (*aswa*) the honour of giving a name to the continent of Asia. It prevailed amongst the Scythic Getae, and is described exactly by Herodotus [iv. 62]. To Dacia and Thrace it was carried by Getic colonies from the Jaxartes, and fostered by these lovers of liberty when their hordes overran Europe.

The worship of the sword in the Acropolis of Athens by the Getic Attila, with all the accompaniments of pomp and place, forms an admirable episode in the history of the decline and fall of Rome; and had Gibbon witnessed the worship of the double-edged sword (*khanda*) by the prince of Mewar and all his chivalry, he might even have embellished his animated account of the adoration of the scymitar, the symbol of Mars.

Initiation to Arms.—Initiation to military fame was the same with the [76] German as with the Rajput, when the youthful candidate was presented with the lance, or buckled with the sword; a ceremony which will be noticed when their feudal

[1] At Dwarka, the god of thieves is called Budha Trivikrama, or of triple energy: the Hermes Triplex, or three-headed Mercury of the Egyptians. [No such cult is mentioned in the account of Dwārka, *BG*, viii. 601.]

manners are described; many other traits of character will then be depicted. It would be easy to swell the list of analogous customs, which even to the objects of dislike in food[1] would furnish comparison between the ancient Celt and Rajput; but they shall close with the detail of the most ancient of rites.

Asvamedha, the Horse Sacrifice.—There are some things, animate and inanimate, which have been common objects of adoration amongst the nations of the earth, the sun, the moon, and all the host of heaven; the sword; reptiles, as the serpent; animals, as the noblest, the horse. This last was not worshipped as an abstract object of devotion, but as a type of that glorious orb which has had reverence from every child of nature. The plains of Tatary, the sands of Libya, the rocks of Persia, the valley of the Ganges, and the wilds of Orinoco, have each yielded votaries alike ardent in devotion to his effulgence:

Of this great world both eye and soul.

His symbolic worship and offerings varied with clime and habit; and while the altars of Bal in Asia, of Belenus among the Celts of Gaul and Britain, smoked with human sacrifices, the bull[2] bled to Mithras in Babylon, and the steed was the victim to Surya on the Jaxartes and Ganges.

The father of history says that the great Getae of Central Asia deemed it right to offer the swiftest of created to the swiftest of non-created beings. It is fair to infer that the sun's festival with the Getae and Aswa nations of the Jaxartes, as with those of Scandinavia, was the winter solstice, the Sankrant of the Rajput

[1] Caesar informs us that the Celts of Britain would not eat the hare, goose, or domestic fowl. The Rajput will hunt the first, but neither eats it, nor the goose, sacred to the god of battle (Hara). The Rajput of Mewar eats the jungle fowl, but rarely the domestic.

[2] As he did also to Balnath (the god Bal) in the ancient times of India. The *baldan*, or gift of the bull to the sun, is well recorded. [*Baldān, balidāna* does not mean the offering of a bull: it is the daily presentation of a portion of the meat to Earth and other deities.] There are numerous temples in Rajasthan of Baalim [?]; and Balpur (Mahadeo) has several in Saurashtra. All represent the sun—

Peor his other name, when he enticed
Israel in Sittim, on their march from Nile.

Paradise Lost, book i. 412 f. [77].

The temple of Solomon was to Bal, and all the idolaters of that day seem to have held to the grosser tenets of Hinduism.

and Hindu in general. *Hi, Haya, Hywor, Aswa* denote the steed in Sanskrit and its dialects. In Gothic, *hyrsa* ; Teutonic, *hors* ; Saxon, *horse*. The grand festival of the German tribes of the Baltic was the *Hiul*, or *Hiel* (already commented on), the Asvamedha [1] of the children of Surya, on the Ganges.

The Asvamedha Ceremonies.—The ceremonies of the Asvamedha are too expensive, and attended with too great risk, to be attempted by modern princes. Of its fatal results we have many historical records, from the first dawn of Indian history to the last of its princes, Prithwiraja. The Ramayana, the Mahabharata, and the poems of Chand all illustrate this imposing rite and its effects.[2]

The Ramayana affords a magnificent picture of the Asvamedha. Dasaratha, monarch of Ayodhya, father of Rama, is represented as commanding the rite: "Let the sacrifice be prepared, and the horse [3] liberated from the north bank of the Sarju!" [4] A year being ended, and the horse having returned from his wanderings,[5] the sacrificial ground was prepared on the spot of liberation.

[1] In *Aswa* (*medha* signifies 'to kill') we have the derivation of the ancient races, sons of Bajaswa, who peopled the countries on both sides the Indus, and the probable etymon of *Asia* [?]. The Assakenoi, the Ariaspai of Alexander's historians, and Aspasianae, to whom Arsaces fled from Seleucus, and whom Strabo terms a Getic race, have the same origin ; hence Asigarh, 'the fortress of the Asi' (erroneously termed Hansi), and Asgard were the first settlements of the Getic Asi in Scandinavia. Alexander received the homage of all these Getic races at 'the mother of cities,' Balkh, 'seat of Cathaian Khan' (the Jat Kathida of my inscription), according to Marco Polo, from whom Milton took his geography.

[2] The last was undertaken by the celebrated Sawai Jai Singh of Amber ; but the milk-white steed of the sun, I believe, was not turned out, or assuredly the Rathors would have accepted the challenge.

[3] A milk-white steed is selected with peculiar marks. On liberation, properly guarded, he wanders where he listeth. It is a virtual challenge. Arjuna guarded the steed liberated by Yudhishthira ; but that sent round by Parikshita, his grandson, "was seized by the Takshak of the north." The same fate occurred to Sagara, father of Dasaratha, which involved the loss of his kingdom.

[4] The Sarju, or Gandak, from the Kumaun mountains, passes through Kosalades, the dominion of Dasaratha.

[5] The horse's return after a year evidently indicates an astronomical revolution, or the sun's return to the same point in the ecliptic. This return from his southern declination must have been always a day of rejoicing to the Scythic and Scandinavian nations, who could not, says Gibbon, fancy a worse hell than a large abode open to the cold wind of the north. To the south they looked for the deity ; and hence, with the Rajputs, a religious law forbids their doors being to the north.

Invitations were sent to all surrounding monarchs to repair to Ayodhya: King Kaikeya,[1] the king of Kasi,[2] Lomapada of Angadesa,[3] Kosala of Magadhadesa,[4] with the kings of Sindhu,[5] Sauvira,[6] and Saurashtra [78].[7]

When the sacrificial pillars are erected, the rites commence. This portion of the ceremony, termed *Yupochchraya*, is thus minutely detailed: "There were twenty-one yupas, or pillars,[8] of octagonal shape, each twenty-one feet in height and four feet in diameter, the capitals bearing the figure of a man, an elephant, or a bull. They were of the various sorts of wood appropriated to holy rites, overlaid with plates of gold and ornamented cloth, and adorned with festoons of flowers. While the yupas were erecting, the Adhvaryu, receiving his instructions from the Hotri, or sacrificing priest, recited aloud the incantations.

[1] Kaikeya is supposed by the translator, Dr. Carey, to be a king of Persia, the Kaivansa preceding Darius. The epithet *Kai* not unfrequently occurs in Hindu traditional couplets. One, which I remember, is connected with the ancient ruins of Abhaner in Jaipur, recording the marriage of one of its princes with a daughter of Kaikamb.

Tu beti Kaikamb *ki, nam Parmala ho*, etc. 'Thou art the daughter of *Kaikamb*: thy name Fairy Garland.' *Kai* was the epithet of one of the Persian dynasties. *Qu. Kam-bakhsh*, the Cambyses of the Greeks? [Cambyses, Kābuzīya or Kambūzīya, possibly 'a bard' (Rawlinson, *Herodotus*, iii. 543).]

[2] Benares.

[3] Tibet or Ava [N. Bengal].

[4] Bihar.

[5] Sind valley.

[6] Unknown to me [W. and S. Panjab and its vicinity].

[7] Peninsula of Kathiawar.

[8] I have seen several of these sacrificial pillars of stone of very ancient date. Many years ago, when all the Rajput States were suffering from the thraldom of the Mahrattas, a most worthy and wealthy banker of Surat, known by the family name of Trivedi, who felt acutely for the woes inflicted by incessant predatory foes on the sons of Rama and Krishna, told me, with tears in his eyes, that the evils which afflicted Jaipur were to be attributed to the sacrilege of the prince, Jagat Singh, who had dared to abstract the gold plates of the sacrificial pillars, and send them to his treasury: worse than Rehoboam, who, when he took away from the temple "the shields of gold Solomon had made," had the grace to substitute others of brass. Whether, when turned into currency, it went as a war contribution to the Mahrattas, or was applied to the less worthy use of his concubine queen, 'the essence of camphor,' it was of a piece with the rest of this prince's unwise conduct. Jai Singh, who erected the pillars, did honour to his country, of which he was a second founder, and under whom it attained the height from which it has now fallen. [Some sacrificial pillars (yūpa) were recently found in the bed of the Jumna near Mathura, with inscriptions dated in the twenty-fourth year of Kanishka's reign, about A.D. 102.]

"The sacrificial pits were in triple rows, eighteen in number, and arranged in the form of the eagle. Here were placed the victims for immolation; birds, aquatic animals, and the horse.

"Thrice was the steed of King Dasaratha led round the sacred fire by Kosala, and as the priests pronounced the incantations he was immolated [1] amidst shouts of joy.

"The king and queen, placed by the high priest near the horse, sat up all night watching the birds; and the officiating priest, having taken out the hearts, dressed them agreeably to the holy books. The sovereign of men smelled the smoke of the offered hearts, acknowledging his transgressions in the order in which they were committed.

"The sixteen sacrificing priests then placed (as commanded in the ordinances) on the fire the parts of the horse. The oblation of all the animals was made on wood, except that of the horse, which was on cane.

"The rite concluded with gifts of land to the sacrificing priests and augurs; but the holy men preferring gold, ten millions of jambunada [2] were bestowed on them" [79].

Such is the circumstantial account of the Asvamedha, the most imposing and the earliest heathen rite on record. It were superfluous to point out the analogy between it and similar rites of various nations, from the chosen people to the Auspex of Rome and the confessional rite of the Catholic church.

The Sankrant,[3] or Sivaratri (night of Siva), is the winter solstice. On it the horse bled to the sun, or Balnath.

[1] On the Nauroz, or festival of the new year, the Great Mogul slays a camel with his own hand, which is distributed, and eaten by the court favourites. [A camel is sacrificed at the Īdu-l-azha festival (Hughes, *Dict. Islām*, 192 ff.).]

[2] This was native gold, of a peculiarly dark and brilliant hue, which was compared to the fruit jambu (not unlike a damson). Everything forms an allegory with the Hindus; and the production of this metal is appropriated to the period of gestation of Jahnavi, the river-goddess (Ganges), when by Agni, or fire, she produced Kumara, the god of war, the commander of the army of the gods. This was when she left the place of her birth, the Himalaya mountain (the great storehouse of metallic substances), whose daughter she is: and doubtless this is in allusion to some very remote period, when, bursting her rock-bound bed, Ganga exposed from 'her side' veins of this precious metal.

[3] Little bags of brocade, filled with seeds of the sesamum or cakes of the

The Scandinavians termed the longest night the 'mother night,'[1] on which they held that the world was born. Hence the Beltane, the fires of Bal or Belenus; the Hiul of northern nations, the sacrificial fires on the Asvamedha, or worship of the sun, by the Suryas on the Ganges, and the Syrians (Σύροι) and Sauromatae on the shores of the Mediterranean.

The altars of the Phoenician Heliopolis, Balbec[2] or Tadmor,[3] were sacred to the same divinity as on the banks of Sarju, or Balpur, in Saurashtra, where "the horses of the sun ascended from his fountain (*Surya-kund*)," to carry its princes to conquest.

From Syria came the instructors of the Celtic Druids, who made human sacrifices, and set up the pillar of Belenus on the hills of Cambria and Caledonia.

When "Judah did evil in the sight of the Lord, and built them high places, and images, and groves, on every high hill and under every tree," the object was Bal, and the pillar (the lingam) was his symbol. It was on his altar they burned incense, and "sacrificed unto the calf on the fifteenth[4] day of the month" (the sacred Amavas of the Hindus). The calf of Israel is the bull (*nandi*) of Balkesar or Iswara; the Apis of the Egyptian Osiris [80].

Sacred Trees.—The ash was sacred to the sun-god in the west. The asvattha (or pipal)[5] is the 'chief of trees,' say the books

same, are distributed by the chiefs to friends on this occasion. While the author writes, he has before him two of these, sent to him by the young Mahratta prince, Holkar.

[1] Sivaratri would be 'father night' [?]. Siva-Iswara is the 'universal father.'

[2] Ferishta, the compiler of the imperial history of India, gives us a Persian or Arabic derivation of this, from *Bal*, 'the sun,' and *bec*, 'an idol.' [This has not been traced in Dow or Briggs.]

[3] Corrupted to Palmyra, the etymon of which, I believe, has never been given, which is a version of Tadmor. In Sanskrit, *tal*, or *tar*, is the 'date-tree'; *mor* signifies 'chief.' We have more than one 'city of palms' (*Talpur*) in India; and the tribe ruling in Haidarabad, on the Indus, is called *Talpuri*, from the place whence they originated. [Tadmor is Semitic, probably meaning 'abounding in palms.' The suggested derivation is impossible.]

[4] 1 Kings xiv. 23.

[5] *Ficus religiosa*. It presents a perfect resemblance to the popul (poplar) of Germany and Italy, a species of which is the aspen. [They belong to different orders.] So similar is it, that the specimen of the pipal from Carolina is called, in the Isola Bella of the Lago Maggiore, *Populus angulata*;

sacred to Bal in the East: and death, or loss of limb, is incurred by the sacrilegious mutilator of his consecrated groves,[1] where a pillar is raised bearing the inhibitory edict.

We shall here conclude the analogy between the Indo-Scythic Rajput races and those of early Europe. Much more might be adduced; the old Runic characters of Scandinavia, the Celtic, and the Osci or Etruscan, might, by comparison with those found in the cave temples and rocks in Rajasthan and Saurashtra, yield yet more important evidence of original similarity; and the very

---

and another, in the Jardin des Plantes at Toulon, is termed the *Ficus populifolia, ou figuier à feuilles de peuplier*. The aspen, or ash, held sacred by the Celtic priests, is said to be the mountain-ash. 'The calf of Bal' is generally placed under the pipal; and Hindu tradition sanctifies a never-dying stem, which marks the spot where the Hindu Apollo, Hari (the sun), was slain by the savage Bhil on the shores of Saurashtra. [This is known as the Prāchi Pīpal, and death rites are performed close to it (*BG*, viii. 271, note 2).]

[1] The religious feelings of the Rajput, though outraged for centuries by Moguls and mercenary Pathans, will not permit him to see the axe applied to the noble pipal or umbrageous bar (*Ficus indica*), without execrating the destroyer. Unhappy the constitution of mind which knowingly wounds religious prejudices of such ancient date! Yet is it thus with our countrymen in the East, who treat all foreign prejudices with contempt, shoot the bird sacred to the Indian Mars, slay the calves of Bal, and fell the noble pipal before the eyes of the native without remorse. He is unphilosophic and unwise who treats such prejudices with contumely: prejudices beyond the reach of reason. He is uncharitable who does not respect them; impolitic, who does not use every means to prevent such offence by ignorance or levity. It is an abuse of our strength, and an ungenerous advantage over their weakness. Let us recollect who are the guardians of these fanes of Bal, his pipal, and sacred bird (the peacock); the children of Surya and Chandra, and the descendants of the sages of yore, they who fill the ranks of our army, and are attentive, though silent, observers of all our actions: the most attached, the most faithful, and the most obedient of mankind! Let us maintain them in duty, obedience, and attachment, by respecting their prejudices and conciliating their pride. On the fulfilment of this depends the maintenance of our sovereignty in India: but the last fifteen years have assuredly not increased their devotion to us. Let the question be put to the unprejudiced, whether their welfare has advanced in proportion to the dominion they have conquered for us, or if it has not been in the inverse ratio of this prosperity? Have not their allowances and comforts decreased? Does the same relative standard between the currency and conveniences of life exist as twenty years ago? Has not the first depreciated twenty-five per cent, as half-batta stations and duties have increased? For the good of ruler and servant, let these be rectified. With the utmost solemnity, I aver, I have but the welfare of all at heart in these observations. I loved the service, I loved the native soldier. I have

name of German (from wer, *bellum*)[1] might be found to be derived from the *feud (vair)* and *foe-man (vairi)* of the Rajput.

If these coincidences are merely accidental, then has too much been already said; if not, authorities are here recorded, and hypotheses founded, for the assistance of others [81].

CHAPTER 7

HAVING discussed the ancient genealogies of the martial races of Rajasthan, as well as the chief points in their character and religion analogous to those of early Europe, we proceed to the catalogue of the Chhattis Rajkula, or 'thirty-six royal races.'[2]

The table before the reader presents, at one view, the authorities on which this list is given: they are as good as abundant. The first is from a detached leaf of an ancient work, obtained from a Yati of a Jain temple at the old city of Nadol, in Marwar. The second is from the poems of Chand,[3] the bard of the last Hindu king of Delhi. The third is from an estimable work

proved what he will do, where devoted, when, in 1817, thirty-two firelocks of my guard attacked, defeated, and dispersed a camp of fifteen hundred men, slaying thrice their numbers.* Having quitted the scene for ever, I submit my opinion dispassionately for the welfare of the one, and with it the stability or reverse of the other.

[1] D'Anville's derivation of German, from *wer* (bellum) and *manus*. [Possibly O. Irish, *gair*, 'neighbour,' or *gairm*, 'battle-cry' (*New Eng. Dict.* *s.v.*).]

[2] [This catalogue is now of historical or traditional, rather than of ethnographical value. It includes some which are admittedly extinct: others which are proved to be derived from Gurjara and other foreign tribes, while it omits many clans which are most influential at the present day, and some of those included in the list are now represented by scattered groups outside Rājputāna.]

[3] Of his works I possess the most complete copy existing.

* What says the Thermopylae of India, Corygaum? Five hundred firelocks against twenty thousand men! Do the annals of Napoleon record a more brilliant exploit? Has a column been reared to the manes of the brave, European and native, of this memorable day, to excite to future achievement? What order decks the breast of the gallant Fitzgerald, for the exploit on the field of Nagpur? At another time and place his words, "At my peril be it! *Charge!*" would have crowned his crest! These things call for remedy! [Korēgāon in Poona District, where Captain Staunton defeated a large force of Mahrattas on January 1, 1818 (Wilson-Mill, *Hist. of India*, ii. (1846), 303 ff.).]

contemporary with Chand's, the Kumarpal Charitra[1] or "History of the Monarchy of Anhilwara Patan." The fourth list is from the Khichi bard.[2] The fifth, from a bard of Saurashtra.

From every one of the bardic profession, from all the collectors and collections of Rajasthan, lists have been received, from which the catalogue No. 6 has been formed, admitted by the genealogists to be more perfect than any existing document. From it, therefore, in succession, each race shall have its history rapidly sketched; though, as a text, a single name is sufficient to fill many pages.

The first list is headed by an invocation to Mata Sakambhari Devi, or mother-goddess, protectress of the races (sakha) [the mother of vegetation].

Each race (sakha) has its Gotracharya,[3] a genealogical creed, describing [82] the essential peculiarities, religious tenets, and pristine locale of the clan. Every Rajput should be able to repeat this; though it is now confined to the family priest or the genealogist. Many chiefs, in these degenerate days, would be astonished if asked to repeat their gotracharya, and would refer to the bard. It is a touchstone of affinities, and guardian of the laws of intermarriage. When the inhibited degrees of propinquity have been broken, it has been known to rectify the mistake, where, however, "ignorance was bliss."[4]

1 Presented to the Royal Asiatic Society.

2 Moghji, one of the most intelligent bards of the present day; but, heartbroken, he has now but the woes of his race to sing. Yet has he forgot them for a moment to rehearse the deeds of Parsanga, who sealed his fidelity by his death on the Ghaggar. Then the invisible mantle of Bhavani was wrapt around him; and with the birad (*furor poeticus*) flowing freely of their deeds of yore, their present degradation, time, and place were all forgot. But the time is fast approaching when he may sing with the Cambrian bard:

> "Ye lost companions of my tuneful art,
> Where are ye fled?"

3 One or two specimens shall be given in the proper place.

4 A prince of Bundi had married a Rajputni of the Malani tribe, a name now unknown: but a bard repeating the 'gotracharya,' it was discovered to have been about eight centuries before a ramification (sakha) of the Chauhan, to which the Hara of Bundi belonged—divorce and expiatory rites, with great unhappiness, were the consequences. What a contrast to the unhallowed doctrines of polyandry, as mentioned amongst the Pandavas, the Scythic nations, the inhabitants of Sirmor of the present day, and pertaining even to Britain in the days of Caesar!—"Uxores habent deni

LIST OF THE THIRTY-SIX ROYAL RACES OF RAJASTHAN[1] — SAKAMBHARI MATA

ANCIENT MSS.

Ikshwaku.
Surya.
Soma or Chandra.
Yadu.[4]
5 Chahuman (Chauhan).
Pramara.
Chalukya or Solanki.
Parihara.
Chawura.
10 Dorla.
Rathor.
Gehlot.
Ushla.
Makwahana.
15 Norka.
Aswaria.
Sailar or Silara.
Sinla.
Sepat.
20 Hun or Hun.
Kirjal.
Hondra.
Rajpali.
Dhanpali.
25 Agnipali.
Bala.
Jhala.
Bhagdola.
Moldan.
30 Mohor.
Kagnir.
Karieo.
Chadila.
Takara.
Nikumbha.
36 Salala.

CHAND BARDAI.[2]

Ravya or Surya.
Sashu or Soma.
Yadu
Kakustha
5 Pramara
Chauhan
Chalukya.
Chandak
Silar
10 Abhira
Makwahana.
Gohil
Chapotkat
Parihara.
15 Rathor.
Deora.
Tak.
Sindhu
Ananga
20 Patak
Pratihara
Dadhich
Karitpal
Kutpala.
25 Hul.
Gaur
Nikumbha.
Rajpalika.
Kaci.
30 Kalchurak or Kurkara.

KUMAR PAL CHARITRA.[3]

[illegible]

Ikshwaku.
Soma
Yadu
Pramara
5 Chauhan
Chalukya
Chandak.
Silar (Raj Tilak)
Chapotkat
10 Pratihara
Sakeonka
Kurpala.
Chandal.
Gohil
15 Palaka.
Maurya.
Makwahana
Dhanpala
Rajpalaka.
20 Dahia
Turandalika
Nikumbha.
Hun
Bala
25 Gurial
Mokar
Pakara.

[illegible]

Gohelwar Gohil
Asl Gohil.
Kathi.
Kaser.
5 Nikumbha.
Hadhota
Bhawariya.
Mora
Makwahana
10 Dahima
Dodia.
Itch.
Bagdol
Yadu
15 Jethwa.
Jareja.
Jat
Solanki
Pramara.
20 Kaba
Chawara
Chandrasima.
Khant
Khyera
25 Rawali
Mewada
Palani
Bala
Jhala.
30 Daharia.
Daharia
Surwyea "Chhatirya (is bar"
Parihara
Chauhan

KHICHI BARD.[4]

Gohil.
Pramara
Chauhan
Solanki
5 Rathor
Dor
Baregujar
Parihara.
Jhala
10 Yadu
Kachhwaha
Gaur

[illegible]

Sulanir
Bala
15 Kharwar
Chawara
Dahima
Johya
Bais
20 Gaharwal
Nikumbha
Dewal.
Johya
Sikarwal
25 Dahiha.
Dodu
Maurya.
Mohara.
Abhira
30 Kalchurak (Hun race)
Agnipala
Aswaria or Surja.
Hul
Munstnal.
Malla
36 Chahil

CORRECTED LIST BY THE AUTHOR.

Ikshwaku, Kakutstha, or Surya
Awasi, Indu, Soma, or Chandra
Grahilot or Gahilot . 24 Sakha.
Yadu . 8
5 Tuar . 17
Rathor . 13
Kachhwaha or Kachhwaha
Pramara . 35
Chahuman or Chauhan . 26
10 Chalukya or Solanki . 16
Parihara . 12
Chawara . Single
Tak, Tāk, or Takshak
Jat or Geta.
15 Hun or Hūn.
Kathi.
Bala
Jhala . [illegible]
Jethwa or Kamari
20 Gohil
Sarwya
Silar
Dabhi.
Gaur . [illegible]
25 Dodo or Dor
Gaharwal
Baregujar . 3
Sengar . Single
Sikarwal . do
30 Bais . do
Dahia
Johya
Mohil
Nikumbha
Rajpali.
36 Dahima . do.

Extra.
Hul.
Daharya.

[1] The author, after the invocation to "the mother protectress," says, "I write the names of the thirty-six royal tribes."
[2] The bard Chand says, "of the thirty-six races, the four Agnipalas are the greatest—the rest are born of women, but these from fire."
[3] As the work is chiefly filled with the exploits of Kumarpal, who was of Chauhan tribe, the author reserves it for a peroration to the last "of all the mightiest is the Chauhan."
[4] By name Moghji.

Most of the kula (races) are divided into numerous branches [1] (sakha), and these sakha subdivided into innumerable clans (gotra),[2] the most important of which shall be given. A few of the kula never ramified: these are termed *eka*, or 'single'; and nearly one-third are *eka*.

A table of the 'eighty-four' mercantile tribes, chiefly of Rajput origin, shall also be furnished, in which the remembrance of some races are preserved which would have perished. Lists of the aboriginal, the agricultural and the pastoral tribes are also given to complete the subject.

Solar and Lunar Races.—In the earlier ages there were but two races, Surya and Chandra, to which were added the four Agnikulas [3]; in all six. The others are subdivisions of Surya and Chandra, or the sakha of Indo-Scythic origin, who found no difficulty in obtaining a place (though a low one), before the Muhammadan era, amongst the thirty-six regal races of Rajasthan. The former we may not unaptly consider as to the time, as the Celtic, the latter as the Gothic, races of India. On the generic terms Surya and Chandra, I need add nothing [83].

Grahilot or Guhilot.—*Pedigree* [4] *of the Suryavansi Rana, of royal race, Lord of Chitor, the ornament of the thirty-six royal races.*

By universal consent, as well as by the gotra of this race, its princes are admitted to be the direct descendants of Rama, of the Solar line. The pedigree is deduced from him, and connected

---

duodenique inter se communes," says that accurate writer, speaking of the natives of this island; "et maximè fratres cum fratribus, parentesque cum liberis: sed si qui sint ex his nati, eorum habentur liberi, quo primum virgo quaeque deducta est." A strange medley of polyandry and polygamy!

[1] *Aparam sakham*, 'of innumerable branches,' is inscribed on an ancient tablet of the Guhilot race.

[2] *Got*, *khanp*, denote a clan; its subdivisions have the patronymic terminating with the syllable '*ot*,' '*awat*,' '*sot*,' in the use of which euphony alone is their guide: thus, *Saktawat*, 'sons of Sakta'; *Kurmasot*, 'of Kurma'; *Mairawat*, or *mairot*, mountaineers, 'sons of the mountains.' Such is the Greek *Mainote*, from *maina*, a mountain, in the ancient Albanian dialect, of eastern origin.

[3] From *agni* (*qu. ignis?*) 'fire,' the sons of Vulcan, as the others of Sol and Luna, or Lunus, to change the sex of the parent of the Indu (moon) race.

[4] *Vansavali, Suryavansi Rajkuli Rana Chitor ka Dhani, Chhattis Kuli Sengar.*—MSS. from the Rana's library, entitled *Khuman Raesa.*

with Sumitra, the last prince mentioned in the genealogy of the Puranas.

As the origin and progressive history of this family will be fully discussed in the "Annals of Mewar," we shall here only notice the changes which have marked the patronymic, as well as the regions which have been under their sway, from Kanaksen, who, in the second century, abandoned his native kingdom, Kosala, and established the race of Surya in Saurashtra.

On the site of Vairat, the celebrated abode of the Pandavas during exile, the descendant of Ikshwaku established his line, and his descendant Vijaya, in a few generations, built Vijayapur.[1]

They became sovereigns, if not founders, of Valabhi, which had a separate era of its own, called the Valabhi Samvat, according with S. Vikrama 375.[2] Hence they became the Balakaraes, or kings of Valabhi; a title maintained by successive dynasties of Saurashtra for a thousand years after this period, as can be satisfactorily proved by genuine history and inscriptions.

Gajni, or Gaini, was another capital, whence the last prince, Siladitya (who was slain), and his family, were expelled by Parthian invaders in the sixth century.

A posthumous son, called Grahaditya, obtained a petty sovereignty at Idar. The change was marked by his name becoming the patronymic, and Grahilot, *vulgo* Guhilot, designated the Suryavansa of Rama.

With reverses and migration from the wilds of Idar to Ahar,[3] the Guhilot was changed to Aharya, by which title the race continued to be designated till the twelfth century, when the elder brother, Rahup, abandoned his claim to "the [84] throne of Chitor," obtained [4] by force of arms from the Mori,[5] and settled at Dungar-

[1] Always conjoined with Vairat—'Vijayapur Vairatgarh.' [Vairāt forty-one miles north of Jaipur city. The reference in the text is merely a bardic fable, there being no connexion between Vijaya and this place (*ASR*, ii. 249).]

[2] A.D. 319. The inscription recording this, as well as others relating to Valabhi and this era, I discovered in Saurashtra, as well as the site of this ancient capital, occupying the position of 'Byzantium' in Ptolemy's geography of India. They will be given in the *Transactions* of the Royal Asiatic Society. [The Valabhi agrees with the Gupta era (Smith, *EHI*, 20).]

[3] Anandpur Ahar, or 'Ahar the city of repose.' By the tide of events, the family was destined to fix their last capital, Udaipur, near Ahar.

[4] The middle of the eighth century.

[5] [Or Maurya], a Pramara prince.

pur, which he yet holds, as well as the title Aharya; while the younger, Mahup, established the seat of power at Sesoda, whence Sesodia set aside both Aharya and Guhilot.

Sesodia is now the common title of the race; but being only a subdivision, the Guhilot holds its rank in the kula.

The Guhilot kula is subdivided into twenty-four sakha,[1] or ramifications, few of which exist:

Sakha	
1. Aharya	At Dungarpur.
2. Mangalia	In the Deserts.
3. Sesodia	Mewar.
4. Pipara	In Marwar.
5. Kalam	
6. Gahor	
7. Dhornia	
8. Goda	
9. Magrasa	
10. Bhimla	In few numbers, and mostly now unknown. (5–16)
11. Kāmkotak	
12. Kotecha	
13. Sora	
14. Uhar	
15. Useba	
16. Nirrup	
17. Nadoria	
18. Nadhota	
19. Ojakra	
20. Kuehhra	Almost extinct. (17–24)
21. Dosadh	
22. Betwara	
23. Paha	
24. Purot	[85]

Yadu, Yādava.—The Yadu was the most illustrious of all the tribes of Ind, and became the patronymic of the descendants of Budha, progenitor of the Lunar (Indu) race. Yudhishthira and Baladeva, on the death of Krishna and their expulsion from Delhi and Dwaraka, the last stronghold of their power, retired by Multan across the Indus. The two first are abandoned by

[1] [For a different list, see *Census Report, Rajputana*, 1911, i. 256.]

tradition; but the sons of Krishna, who accompanied them after an intermediate halt in the further Duab[1] of the five rivers, eventually left the Indus behind, and passed into Zabulistan,[2] founded Gajni, and peopled these countries even to Samarkand.

The annals of Jaisalmer, which give this early history of their founder, mix up in a confused manner[3] the cause of their being again driven back into India; so that it is impossible to say whether it was owing to the Greek princes who ruled all these countries for a century after Alexander, or to the rise of Islamism.

Driven back on the Indus, they obtained possession of the Panjab and founded Salivahanpur. Thence expelled, they retired across the Sutlej and Ghara into the Indian deserts; whence expelling the Langahas, the Johyas, Mohilas, etc., they founded successively Tanot, Derawar, and Jaisalmer,[4] in S. 1212,[5] the present capital of the Bhattis, the lineal successors of Krishna.

Bhatti was the exile from Zabulistan, and as usual with the Rajput races on any such event in their annals, his name set aside the more ancient patronymic, Yadu. The Bhattis subdued all the tracts south of the Ghara; but their power has been greatly circumscribed since the arrival of the Rathors. The Map defines their existing limits, and their annals will detail their past history.

Jāreja, Jādeja is the most important tribe of Yadu race next to the Bhatti. Its history is similar. Descended from Krishna, and migrating simultaneously with the remains of the Harikulas, there is the strongest ground for believing that their range was not so wide as that of the elder branch, but that they settled themselves in the valley of the Indus, more especially on the west shore in Seistan; and in nominal and armorial distinctions, even in Alexander's time, they retained the marks of their ancestry [86].

Sambos, who brought on him the arms of the Grecians, was in

[1] The place where they found refuge was in the cluster of hills still called *Yadu ka dang*, 'the Yadu hills':—the *Joudes* of Rennell's geography [see p. 75 above].

[2] [Zabulistan, with its capital, Ghazni, in Afghanistan.]

[3] The date assigned long prior to the Christian era, agrees with the Grecian, but the names and manners are Muhammadan.

[4] Lodorwa Patan, whence they expelled an ancient race, was their capital before Jaisalmer. There is much to learn of these regions.

[5] A.D. 1155.

all likelihood a Harikula; and the Minnagara of Greek historians Samanagara ('city of Sama'), his capital.[1]

The most common epithet of Krishna, or Hari, was Shama or Syama, from his dark complexion. Hence the Jareja bore it as a patronymic, and the whole race were Samaputras (children of Sama), whence the titular name Sambos of its princes.[2]

The modern Jareja, who, from circumstances has so mixed with the Muhammadans of Sind as to have forfeited all pretensions to purity of blood, partly in ignorance and partly to cover disgrace, says that his origin is from Sham, or Syria, and of the stock of the Persian Jamshid: consequently, Sam has been converted into Jam[3]; which epithet designates one of the Jareja petty governments, the Jam Raj.

These are the most conspicuous of the Yadu race; but there are others who still bear the original title, of which the head is the prince of the petty State of Karauli on the Chambal.

This portion of the Yadu stock would appear never to have strayed far beyond the ancient limits of the Suraseni,[4] their ancestral abodes. They held the celebrated Bayana; whence expelled, they established Karauli west, and Sabalgarh east, of the Chambal. The tract under the latter, called Yaduvati, has been wrested from the family by Sindhia. Sri Mathura[5] is an independent fief of Karauli, held by a junior branch.

The Yadus, or as pronounced in the dialects Jadon, are scattered over India, and many chiefs of consequence amongst the Mahrattas are of this tribe.

There are eight sakha of the Yadu race:

1. Yadu . . . Chief Karauli.
2. Bhatti . . . Chief Jaisalmer.
3. Jareja . . . Chief Cutch Bhuj.
4. Samecha . . . Muhammadans in Sind.

[1] [The capital of Sambos was Sindimana, perhaps the modern Sihwān (Smith, *EHI*, 101).]

[2] [This is very doubtful.]

[3] They have an infinitely better etymology for this, in being descendants of Jambuvati, one of Hari's eight wives. [The origin of the term Jām is very doubtful: see Yule, *Hobson-Jobson*, s.v.]

[4] The Suraseni of Vraj, the tract so named, thirty miles around Mathura.

[5] Its chief, Rao Manohar Singh, was well known to me, and was, I may say, my friend. For years letters passed between us, and he had made for me a transcript of a valuable copy of the Mahabharata.

5. Madecha . .	Unknown [87].
6. Bidman . .	
7. Badda . .	
8. Soha . . .	

Tuar, Tonwar, Tomara.—The Tuar, though acknowledged as a subdivision of the Yadu, is placed by the best genealogists as one of the 'thirty-six,' a rank to which its celebrity justly entitles it.

We have in almost every case the etymon of each celebrated race. For the Tuar we have none; and we must rest satisfied in delivering the dictum of the Bardai, who declares it of Pandu origin.

If it had to boast only of Vikramaditya, the paramount lord of India, whose era, established fifty-six years before the Christian, still serves as the grand beacon of Hindu chronology, this alone would entitle the Tuar to the highest rank. But it has other claims to respect. Delhi, the ancient Indraprastha, founded by Yudhishthira, and which tradition says lay desolate for eight centuries, was rebuilt and peopled by Anangpal Tuar, in S. 848 (A.D. 792), who was followed by a dynasty of twenty princes, which concluded with the name of the founder, Anangpal, in S. 1220 (A.D. 1164),[1] when, contrary to the Salic law of the Rajputs, he abdicated (having no issue) in favour of his grandchild, the Chauhan Prithviraja.

The Tuar must now rest on his ancient fame; for not an independent possession remains to the race[2] which traces its lineage to the Pandavas, boasts of Vikrama, and which furnished the last dynasty, emperors of Hindustan.

It would be a fact unparalleled in the history of the world, could we establish to conviction that the last Anangpal Tuar was the lineal descendant of the founder of Indraprastha; that the issue of Yudhishthira sat on the throne which he erected, after a lapse of 2250 years Universal consent admits it, and the fact is

[1] [Vigraha-rāja, known as Visaladeva, Bisal Deo, in the middle of the twelfth century, is alleged to have conquered Delhi from a chief of the Tomara clan. That chief was a descendant of Ānangapāla, who, a century before, had built the Red Fort (Smith, *EHI*, 386).]

[2] Several Mahratta chieftains deduce their origin from the Tuar race, as Ram Rao Phalkia, a very gallant leader of horse in Sindhia's State.

as well established as most others of a historic nature of such a distant period : nor can any dynasty or family of Europe produce evidence so strong as the Tuar, even to a much less remote antiquity.

The chief possessions left to the Tuars are the district of Tuargarh, on the right bank of the Chambal towards its junction with the Jumna, and the small [88] chieftainship of Patan Tuarvati in the Jaipur State, and whose head claims affinity with the ancient kings of Indraprastha.

Rāthor.—A doubt hangs on the origin of this justly celebrated race. The Rathor genealogies trace their pedigree to Kusa, the second son of Rama ; consequently they would be Suryavansa. But by the bards of this race they are denied this honour ; and although Kushite, they are held to be the descendants of Kasyapa, of the Solar race, by the daughter of a Daitya (Titan). The progeny of Hiranyakasipu is accordingly stigmatized as being of demoniac origin. It is rather singular that they should have succeeded to the Lunar race of Kusanabha, descendants of Ajamidha, the founders of Kanauj. Indeed, some genealogists maintain the Rathors to be of Kusika race.

The pristine locale of the Rathors is Gadhipura, or Kanauj, where they are found enthroned in the fifth century ; and though beyond that period they connect their line with the princes of Kosala or Ayodhya, the fact rests on assertion only.

From the fifth century their history is cleared from the mist of ages, which envelops them all prior to this time ; and in the period approaching the Tatar conquest of India, we find them contesting with the last Tuar and Chauhan kings of Delhi, and the Balakaraes of Anhilwara, the right to paramount importance amidst the princes of Ind. The combats for this phantom supremacy destroyed them all. Weakened by internal strife, the Chauhan of Delhi fell, and his death exposed the north-west frontier. Kanauj followed ; and while its last prince, Jaichand, found a grave in the Ganges, his son sought an asylum in Marusthali, 'the regions of death.'[1] Siahji was this son ; the founder of the Rathor dynasty in Marwar, on the ruins of the Pariharas of Mandor. Here they brought their ancient martial spirit, and a more valiant being exists not than can be found amongst the sons of Siahji. The Mogul emperors were indebted for half their

[1] [This is a pure myth (Smith, *EHI*, 385, 413).]

conquests to the *Lakh Tarwar Rathoran*, ' the 100,000 swords of the Rathors ' ; for it is beyond a doubt that 50,000 of the blood of Siahji have been embodied at once. But enough of the noble Rathors for the present.

The Rathor has twenty-four sakha : Dhandal, Bhadel, Chachkit, Duharia, Khokra, Badara, Chajira, Ramdeva, Kabria, Hatundia, Malavat, Sunda, Katecha, Maholi, Gogadeva, Mahecha, Jaisingha, Mursia, Jobsia, Jora, etc., etc.[1] [89].

Rathor Gotracharya.—Gotama [2] Gotra (race),—Mardawandani Sakha (branch),—Sukracharya Guru (Regent of the planet Venus, Preceptor),—Garupata Agni,[3]—Pankhani Devi (tutelary goddess, winged).[4]

Kachhwāha.—The Kachhwaha race [5] is descended from Kusa, the second son of Rama. They are the Kushites [6] as the Rajputs of Mewar are the Lavites of India. Two branches migrated from Kosala : one founded Rohtas on the Son, the other established a colony amidst the ravines of the Kuwari, at Lahar.[7] In the course of time they erected the celebrated fortress of Narwar, or Nirwar, the abode of the celebrated Raja Nala, whose descendants continued to hold possession throughout all the vicissitudes of the Tatar and Mogul domination, when they were deprived of

1 [For a fuller list, see *Census Report, Rajputana*, 1911, i. 255 f.]

2 From this I should be inclined to pronounce the Rathors descendants of a race (probably Scythic) professing the Buddhist faith, of which Gotama was the last great teacher, and disciple of the last Buddha Mahivira, in S. 477 (A.D. 533). [Buddhism and Jainism are, as usual, confused.]

3 Enigmatical—' Clay formation by fire ' (*agni*).

4 [The Kuldevi, or family goddess, of the Rāthors in Nāgnaichiān, whose original title was Rājeswari or Ratheswari, her present name being taken from the village of Nāgāna in Pachbhadra ; and she has a temple in the Jodhpur fort, with shrines under the *nīm* tree (*Azadirachta Indica*) which is held sacred in all Rathor settlements (*Census Report, Marwar*, 1891, ii. 25).]

5 Erroneously written and pronounced Kutchwaha.

6 The resemblance between the Kushite Ramesa of Ayodhya and the Rameses of Egypt is strong. Each was attended by his army of satyrs, Anubis and Cynocephalus, which last is a Greek misnomer, for the animal bearing this title is of the Simian family, as his images (in the Turin museum) disclose, and the brother of the faithful Hanuman. The comparison between the deities within the Indus (called *Nilab*, ' blue waters ') and those of the Nile in Egypt, is a point well worth discussion. [These speculations are untenable.]

7 A name in compliment, probably, to the elder branch of their race, Lava.

it by the Mahrattas, and the abode of Nala is now a dependency of Sindhia.

In the tenth century a branch emigrated and founded Amber, dispossessing the aborigines, the Minas, and adding from the Rajput tribe Bargujar, who held Rajor and large possessions around. But even in the twelfth century the Kachhwahas were but principal vassals to the Chauhan king of Delhi; and they have to date their greatness, as the other families (especially the Ranas of Mewar) of Rajasthan their decline, from the ascent of the house of Timur to the throne of Delhi. The map shows the limits of the sway of the Kachhwahas, including their branches, the independent Narukas of Macheri, and the tributary confederated Shaikhavats. The Kachhwaha subdivisions have been mislaid;[1] but the present partition into Kothris (chambers), of which there are twelve, shall be given in their annals.

Agnikulas, Pramāra.—1st *Pramara.* There are four races to whom the Hindu genealogists have given Agni, or the element of fire, as progenitor. The Agnikulas are therefore the sons of Vulcan, as the others are of Sol,[2] Mercurius, and Terra [90].

The Agnikulas are the Pramara, the Parihara, the Chalukya or Solanki, and the Chauhan.[3]

That these races, the sons of Agni, were but regenerated, and converted by the Brahmans to fight their battles, the clearest interpretations of their allegorical history will disclose; and,

[1] [See a list in *Census Report, Rajputana*, 1911, i. 255.]

[2] There is a captivating elegance thrown around the theogonies of Greece and Rome, which we fail to impart to the Hindu; though that elegant scholar, Sir William Jones, could make even Sanskrit literature fascinating; and that it merits the attempt intrinsically, we may infer from the charm it possesses to the learned chieftain of Rajasthan. That it is perfectly analogous to the Greek and Roman, we have but to translate the names to show. For instance:—

Solar.		Lunar.
Maricha . . .	(Lux) .	. Atri.
Kasyapa . . .	(Uranus)	. Samudra (Oceanus).
Vaivaswata or Surya	(Sol) .	. Soma, or Ind (Luna; *qu.* Lunus ?).
Vaivaswa Manu .	(Filius Solis)	Brihaspati (Jupiter).
Ila	(Terra)	. Budha (Mercurius).

[3] [Hoernle (*JRAS*, 1905, p. 20) believes that the Parihāras were the only sept which claimed fire-origin before Chand (*flor.* A.D. 1191). But a legend of the kind was current in South India in the second century A.D. (*IA*, xxxiv. 263).]

as the most ancient of their inscriptions are in the Pali character, discovered wherever the Buddhist religion prevailed, their being declared of the race of Tasta or Takshak,[1] warrants our asserting the Agnikulas to be of this same race, which invaded India about two centuries before Christ. It was about this period that Parsvanatha the twenty-third Buddha,[2] appeared in India; his symbol, the serpent. The legend of the snake (Takshak) escaping with the celebrated work Pingala, which was recovered by Garuda, the eagle of Krishna, is purely allegorical; and descriptive of the contentions between the followers of Parswanatha, figured under his emblem, the snake, and those of Krishna, depicted under his sign, the eagle.

The worshippers of Surya probably recovered their power on the exterminating civil wars of the Lunar races, but the creation of the Agnikulas is expressly stated to be for the preservation of the altars of Bal, or Iswara, against the Daityas, or Atheists.

The celebrated Abu, or Arbuda, the Olympus of Rajasthan, was the scene of contention between the ministers of Surya and these Titans, and their relation might, with the aid of imagination, be equally amusing with the Titanic war of the ancient poets of the west [91]. The Buddhists claim it for Adinath, their first Buddha; the Brahmans for Iswara, or, as the local divinity styled Achaleswara.[3] The Agnikunda is still shown on the summit of Abu, where the four races were created by the Brahmans to fight the battles of Achaleswara and polytheism, against the monotheistic Buddhists, represented as the serpents or Takshaks. The probable period of this conversion has been hinted at; but of the

[1] Figuratively, 'the serpent.'

[2] To me it appears that there were four distinguished Buddhas or wise men, teachers of monotheism in India, which they brought from Central Asia, with their science and its written character, the arrow or nail-headed, which I have discovered wherever they have been,—in the deserts of Jaisalmer, in the heart of Rajasthan, and the shores of Saurashtra; which were their nurseries.

The first Budha is the parent of the Lunar race, A.C. 2250.
The second (twenty-second of the Jains), Nemnath, A.C. 1120.
The third (twenty-third do.), Parsawanath, A.C. 650.
The fourth (twenty-fourth do.), Mahivira, A.C. 533.

[The author confuses Budha, Mercury, with Buddha, the Teacher, and mixes up Buddhists with Jains.]

[3] *Achal*, 'immovable,' *eswara*, 'lord.'

dynasties issuing from the Agnikulas, many of the princes professed the Buddhist or Jain faith, to periods so late as the Muhammadan invasion.

The Pramara, though not, as his name implies, the 'chief warrior,' was the most potent of the Agnikulas. He sent forth thirty-five sakha, or branches, several of whom enjoyed extensive sovereignties. 'The world is the Pramar's,' is an ancient saying, denoting their extensive sway; and the Naukot [1] Marusthali signified the nine divisions into which the country, from the Sutlej to the ocean, was partitioned amongst them.

Maheswar, Dhar, Mandu, Ujjain, Chandrabhaga, Chitor, Abu, Chandravati, Mhau Maidana, Parmavati, Umarkot, Bakhar, Lodorva, and Patan are the most conspicuous of the capitals they conquered or founded.

Though the Pramara family never equalled in wealth the famed Solanki princes of Anhilwara, or shone with such lustre as the Chauhan, it attained a wider range and an earlier consolidation of dominion than either, and far excelled in all, the Parihara, the last and least of the Agnikulas, which it long held tributary.

Maheswar, the ancient seat of the Haihaya kings, appears to have been the first seat of government of the Pramaras. They subsequently founded Dharanagar, and Mandu on the crest of the Vindhya hills; and to them is even attributed the city of Ujjain, the first meridian of the Hindus, and the seat of Vikrama.

There are numerous records of the family, fixing eras in their history of more modern times; and it is to be hoped that the interpretation of yet undeciphered inscriptions may carry us back beyond the seventh century.

The era [2] of Bhoj, the son of Munja, has been satisfactorily settled; and an [92] inscription [3] in the nail-headed character, carries it back a step further,[4] and elicits an historical fact of infinite value, giving the date of the last prince of the Pramaras of Chitor, and the consequent accession of the Guhilots.

[1] It extended from the Indus almost to the Jumna, occupying all the sandy regions, Naukot, Arbuda or Abu, Dhat, Mandodri, Kheralu, Parkar, Lodorva, and Pugal.

[2] See *Transactions of the Royal Asiatic Society*, vol. i. p. 227. [Rāja Munja of Mālwa reigned A.D. 974–995. The famous Bhoja, his nephew, not his son, 1018–60 (Smith, *EHI*, 395).]

[3] Which will be given in the *Transactions of the Royal Asiatic Society*.

[4] S. 770, or A.D. 714.

The Nerbudda was no limit to the power of the Pramaras About the very period of the foregoing inscription, Ram Pramar held his court in Telingana, and is invested by the Chauhan Bard, Chand, with the dignity of paramount sovereign of India, and head of a splendid feudal[1] association, whose members became independent on his death. The Bard makes this a voluntary act of the Pramaras ; but coupled with the Guhilots' violent acquisition of Chitor, we may suppose the successor of Ram was unable to maintain such supremacy.

While Hindu literature survives the name of Bhoj Pramara and 'the nine gems' of his court cannot perish ; though it is difficult to say which of the three[2] princes of this name is particularly alluded to, as they all appear to have been patrons of science

Chandragupta, the supposed opponent of Alexander, was a Maurya, and in the sacred genealogies is declared of the race of Takshak. The ancient inscriptions of the Pramars, of which the Maurya is a principal branch, declare it of the race of Tasta and Takshak, as does that now given from the seat of their power, Chitor.[3]

Salivahana, the conqueror of Vikramaditya, was a Takshak, and his era set aside that of the Tuar in the Deccan.

Not one remnant of independence exists to mark the greatness of the Pramaras : ruins are the sole records of their power. The

[1] "When the Pramar of Tilang took sanctuary with Har, to the thirty-six tribes he made gifts of land. To Kehar he gave Katehr, to Rae Pahar the coast of Sind, to the heroes of the shell the forest lands. Ram Pramar of Tilang, the Chakravartin lord of Ujjain, made the gift. He bestowed Delhi on the Tuars, and Patan on the Chawaras ; Sambhar on the Chauhans, and Kanauj on the Kamdhuj ; Mardes on the Parihar, Sorath on the Jadon, the Deccan on Jawala, and Cutch on the Charan" (*Poems of Chand*). [This is an invention of the courtly bard.]

[2] The inscription gives S. 1100 (A.D. 1044) for the third Bhoj : and this date agrees with the period assigned to this prince in an ancient Chronogrammatic Catalogue of reigns embracing all the Princes of the name of Bhoj, which may therefore be considered authentic. This authority assigns S. 631 and 721 (or A.D. 575 and 665) to the first and second Bhoj.

[3] Herbert has a curious story of Chitor being called Taxila ; thence the story of the Ranas being sons of Porus. I have an inscription from a temple on the Chambal, within the ancient limits of Mewar, which mentions Takshasilanagara, 'the stone fort of the Tak,' but I cannot apply it. The city of Toda (Tonk, or properly Tanka) is called in the Chauhan chronicles, Takatpur. [Takshasila, the Taxila of the Greeks, the name meaning 'the hewn rock,' or more probably, 'the rock of Taksha,' the Nāga king, is the modern Shāhderi in the Rāwalpindi District, Panjāb (*IGI*, xxii. 200 f.).]

prince of Dhat,[1] in the Indian [93] desert, is the last phantom of royalty of the race; and the descendant of the prince who protected Humayun, when driven from the throne of Timur, in whose capital, Umarkot, the great Akbar was born, is at the foot of fortune's ladder; his throne in the desert, the footstool of the Baloch, on whose bounty he is dependent for support.

Among the thirty-five sakha of the Pramaras the Vihal was eminent, the princes of which line appear to have been lords of Chandravati, at the foot of the Aravalli. The Rao of Bijolia, one of the sixteen superior nobles of the Rana's court, is a Pramara of the ancient stock of Dhar, and perhaps its most respectable representative.

Thirty-Five Sakha of the Pramaras

Mori [or *Maurya*].—Of which was Chandragupta, and the princes of Chitor prior to the Guhilot.

Sodha.—Sogdoi of Alexander, the princes of Dhat in the Indian desert.

Sankhla.—Chiefs of Pugal, and in Marwar.

Khair.—Capital Khairalu.

Umra and Sumra.—Anciently in the desert, now Muhammadans.

Vihal, or Bihal.—Princes of Chandravati.

Mepawat.—Present chief of Bijolia in Mewar.

Balhar.—Northern desert.

Kaba.—Celebrated in Saurashtra in ancient times, a few yet in Sirohi.

Umata.—The princes of Umatwara in Malwa, there established for twelve generations. Umatwara is the largest tract left to the Pramaras. Since the war in 1817, being under the British interference, they cannot be called independent.

Rehar . . . }
Dhunda . . . } Girasia petty chiefs in Malwa.
Sorathia . . . }
Harer[2] . . . }

[1] Of the Sodha tribe, a grand division of the Pramaras, and who held all the desert regions in remote times. Their subdivisions, Umra and Sumra, gave the names to Umarkot and Umrasumra, in which was the insular Bakhar, on the Indus: so that we do not misapply etymology, when we say in Sodha we have the Sogdoi of Alexander.

[2] [For a different list see *Census Report Rajputana*, 1911, i. 255.]

Besides others unknown ; as Chaonda, Khejar, Sagra, Barkota, Puni, Sampal, Bhiba, Kalpusar, Kalmoh, Kohila, Papa, Kahoria, Dhand, Deba, Barhar, Jipra, Posra, Dhunta, Rikamva, and Taika. Many of these are proselytes to Islamism, and several beyond the Indus [94].

Chahuman or Chauhan.—On this race so much has been said elsewhere,[1] that it would be superfluous to give more than a rapid sketch of them here.

This is the most valiant of the Agnikulas, and it may be asserted not of them only, but of the whole Rajput race. Actions may be recorded of the greater part of each of the Chhattis-kula, which would yield to none in the ample and varied pages of history ; and though the 'Talwar Rathoran' would be ready to contest the point, impartial decision, with a knowledge of their respective merits, must assign to the Chauhan the van in the long career of arms.

Its branches (sakha) have maintained all the vigour of the original stem ; and the Haras, the Khichis, the Deoras, the Sonigiras, and others of the twenty-four, have their names immortalised in the song of the bard.

The derivation of Chauhan is coeval with his fabulous birth : 'the four-handed warrior' (*Chatur-bhuja Chatur-bahu Vira*). All failed when sent against the demons, but the Chauhan, the last creation of the Brahmans to fight their battles against infidelity.

A short extract may be acceptable from the original respecting the birth of the Chauhan, to guard the rites of our Indian Jove on this Olympus, the sacred Abu : " the Guru of mountains, like Sumer or Kailas, which Achaleswara made his abode. Fast but one day on its summit, and your sins will be forgiven ; reside there for a year, and you may become the preceptor of mankind."

The Agnikunda Fire-pit.—Notwithstanding the sanctity of Abu, and the little temptation to disturb the anchorites of Bal, " the Munis, who passed their time in devotion, whom desire never approached, who drew support from the cow, from roots, fruits, and flowers," yet did the Daityas, envying their felicity, render the sacrifice impure, and stop in transit the share of the gods. " The Brahmans dug the pit for burnt-sacrifice to the

[1] See *Transactions of the Royal Asiatic Society*, vol. i. p. 133, 'Comments on a Sanskrit Inscription.'

south-west (nairrit); but the demons[1] raised storms which darkened the air and filled it with clouds of sand, showering ordure, blood, bones and flesh, with every impurity, on their rites. Their penance was of no avail."

Again they kindled the sacred fire; and the priests, assembling round the Agnikunda,[2] prayed for aid to Mahadeo [95]. "From the fire-fountain a figure issued forth, but he had not a warrior's mien. The Brahmans placed him as guardian of the gate, and thence his name, Prithivi-dwara.[3] A second issued forth, and being formed in the palm (*challu*) of the hand was named Chalukya. A third appeared and was named Pramara.[4] He had the blessing of the Rishis, and with the others went against the demons, but they did not prevail. Again Vasishtha,[5] seated on the lotus, prepared incantations; again he called the gods to aid: and, as he poured forth the libation, a figure arose, lofty in stature, of elevated front, hair like jet, eyes rolling, breast expanded, fierce, terrific, clad in armour, quiver filled, a bow in one hand and a brand in the other, quadriform (*Chaturanga*),[6] whence his name, *Chauhan*.

"Vasishtha prayed that his hope[7] might be at length fulfilled, as the Chauhan was despatched against the demons. Sakti-devi[8] on her lion, armed with the trident, descended, and bestowed her blessing on the Chauhan, and as Asapurna, or Kalika, promised always to hear his prayer. He went against the demons; their leaders he slew. The rest fled, nor halted till they reached the depths of hell. Anhal slew the demons. The Brahmans were made happy; and of his race was Prithwiraja."[9]

[1] Asura-Daitya, which Titans were either the aboriginal Bhils or the Scythic hordes.

[2] I have visited this classic spot in Hindu mythology. An image of Adipal (the 'first-created'), in marble, still adorns its embankment, and is a piece of very fine sculpture. It was too sacred a relic to remove.

[3] 'Portal or door (*dwar*) of the earth'; contracted to Prithihara and Parihara.

[4] 'The first striker.'

[5] [In the Hāra version of the legend the presiding priest is Visvāmitra.]

[6] *Chatur*; *anga*, 'body' [*chaturbāhu*].

[7] *Asa*, 'hope,' *purna*, to 'fulfil'; whence the tutelary goddess of the Chauhan race, Asapurna.

[8] The goddess of energy (*Sakti*).

[9] [Cunningham points out that in the original story only the Chauhān was created from the fire-pit, the reference to other clans being a later addition (*ASR*, ii. 255).]

The genealogical tree of the Chauhans exhibits thirty-nine princes, from Anhal, the first created Chauhan, to Prithwiraja, the last of the Hindu emperors of India.[1] But whether the chain is entire we cannot say. The inference is decidedly against its being so; for this creation or regeneration is assigned to an age centuries anterior to Vikramaditya: and we may safely state these converts to be of the Takshak race, invaders of India at a very early period.

Ajaipal is a name celebrated in the Chauhan chronicles, as the founder of the fortress of Ajmer, one of the earliest establishments of Chauhan power.[2]

Sambhar,[3] on the banks of the extensive salt lake of the same name, was probably anterior to Ajmer, and yielded an epithet to the princes of this race, who [96] were styled Sambhari Rao. These continued to be the most important places of Chauhan power, until the translation of Prithwiraja to the imperial throne of Delhi threw a parting halo of splendour over the last of its independent kings. There were several princes whose actions emblazon the history of the Chauhans. Of these was Manika Rae, who first opposed the progress of the Muhammadan arms. Even the history of the conquerors records that the most obstinate opposition which the arms of Mahmud of Ghazni encountered was from the prince of Ajmer,[4] who forced him to retreat, foiled and disgraced, from this celebrated stronghold, in his destructive route to Saurashtra.

The attack on Manika Rae appears to have been by Kasim, the general of Walid, on the close of the first century of the Hegira.[5] The second attack was at the end of the fourth century. A third was during the reign of Bisaladeva, who headed a grand con-

[1] Born in S. 1215, or A.D. 1159. [Anhala or Agnipāla is here the head of the Chauhān line; but a different list appears in the *Hammīra Mahākāvya* of Nayachhandra Sūri (*IA*, viii. 55 ff.).]

[2] [Ajmer is commonly said to have been founded by Rāja Aja, A.D. 145. It was founded by Ajayadeva Chauhān about A.D. 1100 (*IA*, xxv. 162 f.).]

[3] A name derived from the goddess Sakambhari, the tutelary divinity of the tribes, whose statue is in the middle of the lake.

[4] Dharma Dhiraj, father of Bisaladeva, must have been the defender on this occasion.

[5] [Muhammad bin Kāsim seems to have marched along the Indus valley, not in the direction of Ajmer (Malik Muhammad Din, *Bahawalpur Gazetteer*, i. 28).]

federacy of the Rajput princes against the foes of their religion. The celebrated Udayaditya Pramar is enumerated amongst the chiefs acting in subserviency to the Chauhan prince on this occasion, and as his death has been fixed by unerring records in A.D. 1096, this combination must have been against the Islamite king Maudud, the fourth from Mahmud ; and to this victory is the allusion in the inscription on the ancient pillar of Delhi.[1] But these irruptions continued to the captivity and death of the last of the Chauhans, whose reign exhibits a splendid picture of feudal manners.

The Chauhans sent forth twenty-four branches, of whom the most celebrated are the existing families of Bundi and Kotah, in the division termed Haravati. They have well maintained the Chauhan reputation for valour. Six princely brothers shed their blood in one field, in the support of the aged Shah Jahan against his rebellious son Aurangzeb, and of the six but one survived his wounds.

The Khichis [2] of Gagraun and Raghugarh, the Deoras of Sirohi, the Sonigiras of Jalor, the Chauhans of Sui Bah and Sanchor, and the Pawechas of Pawagarh, have all immortalized themselves by the most heroic and devoted deeds. Most of these families yet exist, brave as in the days of Prithwiraja.

Many chiefs of the Chauhan race abandoned their faith to preserve their lands, the Kaimkhani,[3] the Sarwanis, the Lowanis, the Kararwanis, and the Bedwanas [97], chiefly residing in Shaikhavati, are the most conspicuous. No less than twelve petty princes thus deserted their faith : which, however, is not contrary to the Rajput creed ; for even Manu says, they may part with wife to preserve their land. Isaridas, nephew of Prithwiraja, was the first who set this example.

Twenty-four Sakha of the Chauhans.—Chauhan, Hara, Khichi, Sonigira, Deora, Pabia, Sanchora, Goelwal, Bhadauria, Nirwan, Malani, Purbia, Sura, Madrecha, Sankrecha, Bhurecha, Balecha, Tasera, Chachera, Rosia, Chanda, Nikumbha, Bhawar, and Bankat.[4]

[1] [This is doubtful. Maudūd seems to have not come further south than Siālkot (Al Badaoni, *Muntakhabu-t-tawārīkh*, i. 49 ; Elliot-Dowson ii. 273, iv. 139 f., 199 f., v. 160 f.).]

[2] [The author has barely noticed the Khīchis ; for an account of them see *ASR*, ii. 249 ff.]

[3] About Fatehpur Jhunjhunu.

[4] [For a different list see *Rajputana Census Report*, 1911, i. 255.]

Chalukya or Solanki.—Though we cannot trace the history of this branch of the Agnikulas to such periods of antiquity as the Pramara or Chauhan, it is from the deficiency of materials, rather than any want of celebrity, that we are unable to place it, in this respect, on a level with them. The tradition of the bard makes the Solankis important as princes of Sura on the Ganges, ere the Rathors obtained Kanauj.[1] The genealogical test[2] claims Lohkot, said to be the ancient Lahore, as a residence, which makes them of the same Sakha (Madhwani) as the Chauhans. Certain it is, that in the eighth century we find the Langahas[3] and Togras inhabiting Multan and the surrounding country, the chief opponents of the Bhattis on their establishment in the desert. They were princes of Kalyan, on the Malabar coast,[4] which city still exhibits vestiges of ancient grandeur. It was from Kalyan that a scion of the Solanki tree was taken, and engrafted on the royal stem of the Chawaras of Anhilwara Patan.

It was in S. 987 (A.D. 931) that Bhojraj, the last of the Chawaras, and the Salic law of India were both set aside, to make way for the young Solanki, Mulraj,[5] who ruled Anhilwara for the space of fifty-eight years. During the reign of his son and successor, Chamund Rae,[6] Mahmud of Ghazni carried his desolating arms into the kingdom of Anhilwara. With its wealth he raised those [98] magnificent trophies of his conquest, among which the 'Celestial

[1] [The Chalukya is a Gurjara tribe, the name being the Sanskritized form of the old dynastic title, Chalkya, of the Deccan dynasty (A.D. 552–973); and of this Solanki is a dialectical variant (*IA*, xi. 24; *BG*, i. Part i. 156, Part ii. 336).]

[2] Solanki Gotracharya is thus: "Madhwani Sakha — Bharadwaja Gotra—Garh Lohkot nikas—Sarasvati Nadi (river)—Sama Veda—Kapaliswar Deva—Karduman Rikheswar—Tin Parwar Zunar (zone of three threads) —Keonj Devi—Mahipal Putra (one of the Penates)." [Lohkot is Lohara in Kashmīr (Stein, *Rājatarangini*, i. Introd. 108, ii. 293 ff.).]

[3] Called Malkhani, being the sons of Mal Khan, the first apostate from his faith to Islamism. Whether these branches of the Solankis were compelled to quit their religion, or did it voluntarily, we know not.

[4] Near Bombay. [In Thana District, not Malabar coast.]

[5] Son of Jai Singh Solanki, the emigrant prince of Kalyan, who married the daughter of Bhojraj. These particulars are taken from a valuable little geographical and historical treatise, incomplete and without title. [Mūlarāja Chaulukya, A.D. 961–96, was son of Bhūbhata: Chāmunda, A.D. 997–1010; it was in the reign of Bhīma I. (1022–64) that Mahmūd's invasion in A.D. 1024 occurred (*BG*, i. Part i. 156 ff. 164).]

[6] Called Chamund by Muhammadan historians.

Bride' might have vied with anything ever erected by man as a monument of folly.[1] The wealth abstracted, as reported in the history of the conquerors, by this scourge of India, though deemed incredible, would obtain belief, if the commercial riches of Anhilwara could be appreciated. It was to India what Venice was to Europe, the entrepôt of the products of both the eastern and western hemispheres. It fully recovered the shock given by Mahmud and the desultory wars of his successors; and we find Siddharaja Jayasingha,[2] the seventh from the founder, at the head of the richest, if not the most warlike, kingdom of India. Two-and-twenty principalities at one time owned his power, from the Carnatic to the base of the Himalaya Mountains; but his unwise successor drew upon himself the vengeance of the Chauhan, Prithwiraja, a slip of which race was engrafted, in the person of Kumarapala, on the genealogical tree of the Solankis;[3] and it is a curious fact that this dynasty of the Balakaraes alone gives us two examples of the Salic law of India being violated. Kumarapala, installed on the throne of Anhilwara, 'tied round his head the turban of the Solanki.' He became of the tribe into which he was adopted. Kumarapala, as well as Siddharaja, was the patron of Buddhism;[4] and the monuments erected under them and their successors claim our admiration, from their magnificence and the perfection of the arts; for at no period were they more cultivated than at the courts of Anhilwara.

The lieutenants of Shihābu-d-din disturbed the close of Kumarapal's reign; and his successor, Balo Muldeo, closed this dynasty in S. 1284 (A.D. 1228), when a new dynasty, called the Vaghela (descendants of Siddharaja) under Bīsaldeo, succeeded.[5] The dilapidations from religious persecution were repaired; Somnath, renowned as Delphos of old, rose from its ruins, and the kingdom

[1] [Ferishta i. 61.]

[2] He ruled from S. 1150 to 1201 [A.D. 1094–1143]. It was his court that was visited by El Edrisi, commonly called the Nubian geographer, who particularly describes this prince as following the tenets of Buddha. [He was probably not a Jain (*BG*, i. Part i. 179).]

[3] [The Gujarāt account of the campaign is different (*BG*, i. Part i. 184 f.).]

[4] [Kumārapāla made many benefactions to the Jains (*Ibid.* i. Part i. 190 f.).]

[5] [Ajayapāla succeeded Kumārapāla. Bhima II. (A.D. 1179–1242), called Bholo, 'the simpleton,' was the last of the Chaulukya dynasty, which was succeeded by that of the Vāghelas (1219–1304). Vīsaladeva reigned A.D. 1243–61. See a full account, *Ibid.* 194 ff.]

of the Balakaraes was attaining its pristine magnificence, when, under the fourth prince, Karandeva, the angel of destruction appeared in the shape of Alau-d-din, and the kingdom of Anhilwara was annihilated. The lieutenants of the Tatar despot of Delhi let loose the spirit of intolerance and avarice on the rich cities and fertile plains of Gujarat and Saurashtra. In contempt of their faith, the altar of an Islamite Darvesh was placed in contact with the shrine of Adinath, on the [99] most accessible of their sacred mounts:[1] the statues of Buddha [the Jain Tirthankaras] were thrown down, and the books containing the mysteries of their faith suffered the same fate as the Alexandrian library. The walls of Anhilwara were demolished; its foundations excavated, and again filled up with the fragments of their ancient temples.[2]

The remnants of the Solanki dynasty were scattered over the land, and this portion of India remained for upwards of a century without any paramount head, until, by a singular dispensation of Providence, its splendour was renovated, and its foundations rebuilt, by an adventurer of the same race from which the Agnikulas were originally converts, though Saharan the Tak hid his name and his tribe under his new epithet of Zafar Khan, and as Muzaffar ascended the throne of Gujarat, which he left to his son. This son was Ahmad, who founded Ahmadabad, whose most splendid edifices were built from the ancient cities around it.[3]

Bāghels.—Though the stem of the Solankis was thus uprooted, yet was it not before many of its branches (Sakha), like their own indigenous bar-tree, had fixed themselves in other soils. The most conspicuous of these is the Baghela[4] family, which gave its

[1] Satranjaya. [*IGI*, xix. 361 ff.]

[2] In 1822 I made a journey to explore the remains of antiquity in Saurashtra. I discovered a ruined suburb of the ancient Patan still bearing the name of *Anhilwara*, the *Nahrwara*, which D'Anville had "fort à cœur de retrouver." I meditate a separate account of this kingdom, and the dynasties which governed it.

[3] [Zafar Khān, son of Sahāran of the Tānk tribe of Rājputs, embraced Islam, and became viceroy of Gujarāt. According to Ferishta, he threw off his allegiance to Delhi in 1396, or rather maintained a nominal allegiance till 1403. Ahmad was grandson, not son, of Muzaffar. (Ferishta iv. 2 f.; Bayley, *Dynasties of Gujarat*, 67 ff.; *BG*, i. Part i. 232 f.).]

[4] The name of this subdivision is from Bagh Rao, the son of Siddharāja; though the bards have another tradition for its origin. [They take their name from the village Vaghela near Anhilwāra (*BG*, i. Part i. 198).]

name to an entire division of Hindustan; and Baghelkhand has now been ruled for many centuries by the descendants of Siddharaja.

Besides Bandhugarh, there are minor chieftainships still in Gujarat of the Baghela tribe. Of these, Pethapur and Tharad are the most conspicuous. One of the chieftains of the second class in Mewar is a Solanki, and traces his line immediately from Siddharaja: this is the chief of Rupnagar,[1] whose stronghold commands one of the passes leading to Marwar, and whose family annals would furnish a fine picture of the state of border-feuds. Few of them, till of late years, have died natural deaths.

The Solanki is divided into sixteen branches [100].

1. Baghela—Raja of Baghelkhand (capital Bandhugarh), Raos of Pitapur, Tharad, and Adalaj, etc.
2. Birpura—Rao of Lunawara.
3. Bahala—Kalyanpur in Mewar, styled Rao, but serving the chief of Salumbar.
4. Bhurta[2]
5. Kalacha[2] } In Baru, Tekra, and Chahir, in Jaisalmer.
6. Langaha—Muslims about Multan.
7. Togra—Muslims in the Panjnad.
8. Brika— " "
9. Surki—In Deccan.
10. Sarwaria[3]—Girnar in Saurashtra.
11. Raka—Toda in Jaipur.
12. Ranakia—Desuri in Mewar.
13. Kharara—Alota and Jawara, in Malwa.
14. Tantia—Chandbhar Sakanbari.[4]
15. Ahmecha—No land.
16. Kalamor—Gujarat.[5]

Pratihāra or Parihāra.—Of this, the last and least of the

[1] I knew this chieftain well, and a very good specimen he is of the race. He is in possession of the famous war-shell of Jai Singh, which is an heirloom.

[2] Famous robbers in the deserts, known as the Malduts.

[3] Celebrated in traditional history.

[4] Desperate robbers. I saw this place fired and levelled in 1807, when the noted Karim Pindari was made prisoner by Sindhia. It afterwards cost some British blood in 1817.

[5] [For another list see *Census Report, Rajputana*, 1911, i. 256.]

Agnikulas, we have not much to say. The Pariharas never acted a conspicuous part in the history of Rajasthan. They are always discovered in a subordinate capacity, acting in feudal subjection to the Tuars of Delhi or the Chauhans of Ajmer; and the brightest page of their history is the record of an abortive attempt of Nahar Rao to maintain his independence against Prithwiraja. Though a failure, it has immortalized his name, and given to the scene of action,[1] one of the passes of the Aravalli, a merited celebrity. Mandor [1] (classically Maḍdodara) was the capital of the Parihars, and was the chief city of Marwar which owned the sway of this tribe prior to the invasion and settlement of the Rathors. It is placed five miles northward of the modern [101] Jodhpur, and preserves some specimens of the ancient Pali character, fragments of sculpture and Jain temples.

The Rathor emigrant princes of Kanauj found an asylum with the Parihars. They repaid it by treachery, and Chonda, a name celebrated in the Rathor annals, dispossessed the last of the Parihars, and pitched the flag of the Rathors on the battlements of Mandor. The power of the Parihars had, however, been much reduced previously by the princes of Mewar, who not only abstracted much territory from them, but assumed the title of its princes—Rana.[2]

The Parihara is scattered over Rajasthan, but I am unaware of the existence of any independent chieftainship there. At the confluence of the Kuhari, the Sind, and the Chambal, there is a colony of this race, which has given its name to a commune of twenty-four villages, besides hamlets, situated amidst the ravines of these streams. They were nominally subjects of Sindhia; but it was deemed requisite for the line of defence along the Chambal that it should be included within the British demarcation, by which we incorporated with our rule the most notorious body of thieves in the annals of Thug history.

The Parihars had twelve subdivisions, of which the chief were

[1] Though now desolate, the walls of this fortress attest its antiquity, and it is a work that could not be undertaken in this degenerate age. The remains of it bring to mind those of Volterra or Cortona, and other ancient cities of Tuscany: enormous squared masses of stone without any cement. [For a full account of Mandor, see Erskine iii. *A.* 196 ff.]

[2] This was in the thirteenth century [A.D. 1381], when Mandor was captured, and its prince slain, by the Rawal of Chitor.

the Indha and Sindhal: a few of both are still to be found about the banks of the Luni.[1]

Chāwara or Chaura.—This tribe was once renowned in the history of India, though its name is now scarcely known, or only in the chronicles of the bard. Of its origin we are in ignorance. It belongs neither to the Solar nor Lunar race, and consequently we may presume it to be of Scythic origin.[2] The name is unknown in Hindustan, and is confined, with many others originating from beyond the Indus, to the peninsula of Saurashtra. If foreign to India proper, its establishment must have been at a remote period, as we find individuals of it intermarrying with the Suryavansa ancestry of the present princes of Mewar, when this family were the lords of Valabhi.

The capital of the Chawaras was the insular Deobandar, on the coast of Saurashtra, and the celebrated temple of Somnath, with many others on this coast, dedieated to Balnath, or the sun, is attributed to this tribe of the Sauras,[3] or [102] worshippers of the sun; most probably the generic name of the tribe as well as of the peninsula.[4]

By a natural catastrophe, or as the Hindu superstitious chroniclers will have it, as a punishment for the piracies of the prince of Deo, the element whose privilege he abused rose and overwhelmed his capital. As all this coast is very low, such an occurrence is not improbable; though the abandonment of Deo might have been compelled by the irruptions of the Arabians, who at this period carried on a trade with these parts, and the plunder of some of their vessels may have brought this punishment on the Chawaras. That it was owing to some such political

[1] [Six sub-clans are named in *Census Report, Rajputana*, 1911, i. 255.]

[2] [They have been supposed to be a branch of the Pramārs, but they are certainly of Gurjara origin (*IA*, iv. 145 f.; *BG*, ix. Part i. 124, 488 f.; i. Part i. 149 ff.). According to Wilberforce-Bell, the word Chaura in Gujarāt means 'robber' (*History of Kathiawad*, 51).]

[3] The Σύροι of the Greek writers on Bactria, the boundary of the Bactrian kingdom under Apollodotus. On this see the paper on Grecian medals in the *Transactions of the Royal Asiatic Society*, vol. i.

[4] Many of the inhabitants of the south and west of India cannot pronounce the *ch*, and invariably substitute the *s*. Thus the noted Pindari leader Chitu was always called Situ by the Deccanis. Again, with many of the tribes of the desert, the *s* is alike a stumbling-block, which causes many singular mistakes, when Jaisalmer, the 'hill of Jaisal,' becomes Jahlmer, 'the hill of fools.'

catastrophe, we have additional grounds for belief from the annals of Mewar, which state that its princes inducted the Chawaras into the seats of the power they abandoned on the continent and peninsula of Saurashtra.

At all events, the prince of Deo laid the foundation of Anhilwara Patan in S. 802 (A.D. 746), which henceforth became the capital city of this portion of India, in lieu of Valabhipura, which gave the title of Balakaraes to its princes, the Balhara of the earlier Arabian travellers, and following them, the geographers of Europe.[1]

Vana Raja (or, in the dialects, Banraj) was this founder, and his dynasty ruled for one hundred and eighty-four years, when, as related in the sketch of the Solanki tribe, Bhojraj, the seventh from the founder, was deposed by his nephew.[2] It was during this dynasty that the Arabian travellers[3] visited this court, of which they have left but a confused picture. We are not, however, altogether in darkness regarding the Chawara race, as in the Khuman Raesa, one of the chronicles of Mewar, mention is made of the auxiliaries under a leader named Chatansi, in the defence of Chitor against the first attack on record of the Muhammadans.

When Mahmud of Ghazni invaded Saurashtra and captured its capital, Anhilwara, he deposed its prince, and placed upon the throne, according to Ferishta, a prince of the former dynasty, renowned for his ancient line and purity of blood, and who is styled Dabichalima; a name which has puzzled all European commentators. Now the Dabhi was a celebrated tribe, said by some to be a branch of the [103] Chawara, and this therefore may be a compound of Dabhi Chawara, or the Chaurasima, by some called a branch of the ancient Yadus.[4]

[1] [The Balhara of Arab travellers of the tenth century were the Rashtrakūta dynasty of Mālkhed, Balhara being a corruption of Vallabharāja, Vallabha being the royal title (*BG*, i. Part ii. 209).]

[2] [Vanarāja reigned from A.D. 765 to 780, and the dynasty is said to have lasted 196 years, but the evidence is still incomplete. The name of Bhojrāj does not appear in the most recent lists (*BG*, i. Part i. 152 ff.).]

[3] *Rélations anciennes des Voyageurs*, par Renaudot.

[4] [The true form of this puzzling term seems to be Dābshalīm, whose story is told in Elliot-Dowson (ii. 500 ff., iv. 183). Much of the account is mere tradition, but it has been plausibly suggested that when Bhīma I., the Chaulukya king of Anhilwāra was defeated by Mahmūd of Ghazni in A.D.

This ancient connexion between the Suryavansi chiefs and the Chawaras, or Sauras, of Saurashtra, is still maintained after a lapse of more than one thousand years ; for although an alliance with the Rana's family is deemed the highest honour that a Hindu prince can obtain, as being the first in rank in Rajasthan, yet is the humble Chawara sought out, even at the foot of fortune's ladder, whence to carry on the blood of Rama. The present heir-apparent of a line of 'one hundred kings,' the prince Jawān Singh [1828–38], is the offspring of a Chawara mother, the daughter of a petty chieftain of Gujarat.

It were vain to give any account of the present state of the families bearing this name. They must depend upon the fame of past days; to this we leave them.

Tāk or Takshak.—Takshak appears to be the generic term of the race from which the various Scythic tribes, the early invaders of India, branched off. It appears of more ancient application than Getae, which was the parent of innumerable sakha. It might not be judicious to separate them, though it would be speculative to say which was the primitive title of the races called Scythic, after their country, Sakatai or Sakadwipa, the land of the great Getae.

Abulghazi makes Taunak[1] the son of Turk or Targetai, who appears to be the Turushka of the Puranas, the Tukyuks of the Chinese historians, the nomadic Tokhari of Strabo, who aided to overturn the Greek kingdom of Bactria, and gave their name to

---

1024, the latter may have appointed Durlabha, uncle of Bhīma, to keep order in Gujarāt, and that the two Dābshalīms may be identified with Durlabha and his son (*BG*, i. Part i. 168). Also see Ferishta i. 76 ; Bayley, *Muhammadan Dynasties of Gujarāt*, 32 ff.]

[1] Abulghazi [*Hist. of the Turks, Moguls, and Tartars*, 1730, i. 5 f.] says, when Noah left the ark he divided the earth amongst his three sons : Shem had Iran : Japhet, the country of 'Kuttup Shamach,' the name of the regions between the Caspian Sea and India. There he lived two hundred and fifty years. He left eight sons, of whom Turk was the elder and the seventh Camari, supposed the Gomer of Scripture. Turk had four sons ; the eldest of whom was Taunak, the fourth from whom was Mogul, a corruption of Mongol, signifying *sad*, whose successors made the Jaxartes their winter abode. [The word means 'brave' (Howorth, *Hist. of the Mongols*, i. 27).] Under his reign no trace of the true religion remained : idolatry reigned everywhere. Aghuz Khan succeeded. The ancient Cimbri, who went west with Odin's horde of Jats, Chattis, and Su, were probably the tribes descended from Camari, the son of Turk.

the grand division of Asia, Tokharistan [1] or Turkistan : and there is every appearance of that singular race, the Tajik,[2] still scattered over these [104] regions, and whose history appears a mystery, being the descendants of the Takshak.

It has been already observed, that ancient inscriptions in the Pali or Buddhist character have been discovered in various parts of Rajasthan, of the race called Tasta, Takshak, and Tak, relating to the tribes, the Mori [or Maurya], Pramara, their descendants. Naga and Takshak are synonymous appellations in Sanskrit for the snake, and the Takshak is the celebrated Nagvansa of the early heroic history of India. The Mahabharata describes, in its usual allegorical style, the wars between the Pandavas of Indraprastha and the Takshaks of the north. The assassination of Parikshita by the Takshak, and the exterminating warfare carried on against them by his son and successor, Janamejaya, who at last compelled them to sign tributary engagements, divested of its allegory,[3] is plain historical fact.

[1] Tacash continued to be a proper name with the great Khans of Khārizm (Chorasmia) until they adopted the faith of Muhammad. The father of Jalal, the foe of Jenghiz Khan, was named Tacash. Tashkent on the Jaxartes, the capital of Turkistan, may be derived from the name of the race. Bayer says, "Tocharistan was the region of the Tochari, who were the ancient Τόχαροι (Tochari), or Τάχαροι (Tacharoi)." Ammianus Marcellinus says, "many nations obey the Bactrians, whom the Tochari surpass" (*Hist. Reg. Bact.* p. 7).

[2] This singular race, the Tajiks, are repeatedly mentioned by Mr. Elphinstone in his admirable account of the kingdom of Kabul. They are also particularly noticed as monopolising the commercial transactions of the kingdom of Bokhara, in that interesting work, *Voyage d'Orenbourg à Bokhara*, the map accompanying which, for the first time, lays down authentically the sources and course of the Oxus and Jaxartes. [The term Tājik means the settled population, as opposed to the Turks or tent-dwellers. It is the same word as Tāzi, 'Arab,' still surviving in the name of the Persian greyhound, which was apparently introduced by the Arabs. Sykes (*Hist. of Persia*, ii. 153, note) and Skrine-Ross (*The Heart of Asia*, 3, 364 note) state that the Tājiks represent the Iranian branch of the Aryans.]

[3] The Mahabharata describes this warfare against the snakes literally : of which, in one attack, he seized and made a burnt-offering (hom) of twenty thousand. It is surprising that the Hindu will accept these things literally. It might be said he had but a choice of difficulties, and that it would be as impossible for any human being to make the barbarous sacrifice of twenty thousand of his species, as it would be difficult to find twenty thousand snakes for the purpose. The author's knowledge of what barbarity will inflict leaves the fact of the human sacrifice, though not perhaps to this extent, not even improbable. In 1811 his duties called him to a survey

When Alexander invaded India, he found the Paraitakai, the mountain (*pahar*) Tak, inhabiting the Paropamisos range; nor is it by any means unlikely that Taxiles,[1] the ally of the Macedonian king, was the chief (*es*) of the Taks; and in the early history of the Bhatti princes of Jaisalmer, when driven from Zabulistan, they dispossessed the Taks on the Indus, and established themselves in their land, the capital of which was called Salivahanpura; and as the date of this event is given as 3008 of the Yudhishthira era, it is by no means unlikely that Salivahana, or Salbhan (who was a Takshak), the conqueror of the Tuar Vikrama, was of the very family dispossessed by the Bhattis, who compelled them to migrate to the south.

The calculated period of the invasion of the Takshaks, or Nagvansa, under Sheshnag, is about six or seven centuries before the Christian era, at which very [105] period the Scythic invasion of Egypt and Syria, "by the sons of Togarmah riding on horses" (the Aswas, or Asi), is alike recorded by the prophet Ezekiel and Diodorus. The Abu Mahatma calls the Takshaks "the sons of Himachal," all evincing Scythic descent; and it was only eight reigns anterior to this change in the Lunar dynasties of India, that Parsvanath, the twenty-third Buddha [Jain Tirthankara], introduced his tenets into India, and fixed his abode in the holy mount Sarnet.[2]

---

amidst the ravines of the Chambal, the tract called Gujargarh, a district inhabited by the Gujar tribe. Turbulent and independent, like the sons of Esau, their hand against every man and every man's hand against them, their nominal prince, Surajmall, the Jāt chief of Bharatpur, pursued exactly the same plan towards the population of these villages, whom they captured in a night attack, that Janamejaya did to the Takshaks: he threw them into pits with combustibles, and actually thus consumed them! This occurred not three-quarters of a century ago.

[1] Arrian says that his name was Omphis [Āmbhi], and that his father dying at this time, he did homage to Alexander, who invested him with the title and estates of his father Taxiles. Hence, perhaps (from *Tak*), the name of the Indus, *Attak*; [?] not *Atak*, or 'forbidden,' according to modern signification, and which has only been given since the Muhammadan religion for a time made it the boundary between the two faiths. [All these speculations are valueless.]

[2] In Bihar, during the reign of Pradyota, the successor of Ripunjaya. Parsva's symbol is the serpent of Takshak. His doctrines spread to the remotest parts of India, and the princes of Valabhipura of Mandor and Anhilwara all held to the tenets of Buddha. [As usual, Jains are confounded with Buddhists. There is no reason to believe that the Nāgas, a serpent-worshipping tribe, were not indigenous in India.]

Enough of the ancient history of the Tak; we will now descend to more modern times, on which we shall be brief. We have already mentioned the Takshak Mori [or Maurya] as being lords of Chitor from a very early period; and but a few generations after the Guhilots supplanted the Moris, this palladium of Hindu liberty was assailed by the arms of Islam. We find amongst the numerous defenders who appear to have considered the cause of Chitor their own, "the Tak from Asirgarh."[1] This race appears to have retained possession of Asir for at least two centuries after this event, as its chieftain was one of the most conspicuous leaders in the array of Prithwiraja. In the poems of Chand he is called the "standard-bearer, Tak of Asir."[2]

This ancient race, the foe of Janamejaya and the friend of Alexander, closed its career in a blaze of splendour. The celebrity of the kings of Gujarat will make amends for the obscurity of the Taks of modern times, of whom a dynasty of fourteen kings followed each other in succession, commencing and ending with the proud title of Muzaffar. It was in the reign of Muhammad,[3] son of the first Tughlak, that an accident to his nephew Firoz proved the dawn of the fortunes of the Tak; purchased, however, with the change of name and religion. Saharan the Tak was the first apostate of his line, who, under the name of Wajihu-l-mulk, concealed both his origin and tribe. His son, Zafar Khan, was raised by his patron Firoz to the government of Gujarat, about the period when Timur invaded India. Zafar availed himself of the weakness of his master and the distraction of the times, and mounted the throne of Gujarat under the name of [106] Muzaffar.[4] He was assassinated by the hand of his grandson, Ahmad, who changed the ancient capital, Anhilwara, for the city founded by himself, and called Ahmadabad, one of the most splendid in the east. With the apostasy of the Tak,[5] the name appears to have

[1] This is the celebrated fortress in Khandesh, now in the possession of the British.

[2] In the list of the wounded at the battle of Kanauj he is mentioned by name, as "Chatto the Tak."

[3] He reigned from A.D. 1324 to 1351.

[4] 'The victorious' [see p. 118 above].

[5] The *Mirātu-l-Sikandari* gives the ancestry of the apostate for twenty-three generations; the last of whom was Sesh, the same which introduced the Nagvansa, seven centuries before the Christian era, into India. The author of the work gives the origin of the name of Tak, or Tank, from *tarka*, 'expulsion,' from his caste, which he styles Khatri, evincing his ignorance of this ancient race.

been obliterated from the tribes of Rajasthan; nor has my search ever discovered one of this name now existing.

Jat, Jāt.—In all the ancient catalogues of the thirty-six royal races of India the Jat has a place, though by none is he ever styled 'Rajput'; nor am I aware of any instance of a Rajput's intermarriage with a Jat.[1] It is a name widely disseminated over India, though it does not now occupy a very elevated place amongst the inhabitants, belonging chiefly to the agricultural classes.

In the Panjab they still retain their ancient name of Jat. On the Jumna and Ganges they are styled Jāts, of whom the chief of Bharatpur is the most conspicuous. On the Indus and in Saurashtra they are termed Jats. The greater portion of the husbandmen in Rajasthan are Jats; and there are numerous tribes beyond the Indus, now proselytes to the Muhammadan religion, who derive their origin from this class.

Of its ancient history sufficient has been already said. We will merely add, that the kingdom of the great Getae, whose capital was on the Jaxartes, preserved its integrity and name from the period of Cyrus to the fourteenth century, when it was converted from idolatry to the faith of Islam. Herodotus [iv. 93-4] informs us that the Getae were theists and held the tenet of the soul's immortality; and De Guignes,[2] from Chinese authorities, asserts that at a very early period they had embraced the religion of Fo or Buddha.

The traditions of the Jats claim the regions west of the Indus as the cradle of the race, and make them of Yadu extraction; thus corroborating the annals of the Yadus, which state their migration from Zabulistan, and almost inducing us to [107] dispense with the descent of this tribe from Krishna, and to pro-

[1] [Though apparently there is no legal connubium between Jāts and Rājputs, the two tribes are closely connected, and it has been suggested that both had their origin in invaders from Central Asia, the leaders becoming Rājputs, the lower orders Jāt peasants. The author, at the close of Vol. II., gives an inscription recording the marriage of a Jāt with a Yādava princess.]

[2] "The superiority of the Chinese over the Turks caused the great Khan to turn his arms against the Nomadic Getae of Mawaru-l-nahr (Transoxiana), descended from the Yueh-chi, and bred on the Jihun or Oxus, whence they had extended themselves along the Indus and even Ganges, and are there yet found. These Getae had embraced the religion of Fo" (*Hist. Gén. des Huns*, tom. i. p. 375).

nounce it an important colony of the Yueh-chi, Yuti, or Jats. Of the first migration from Central Asia of this race within the Indus we have no record; it might have been simultaneous with the Takshak, from the wars of Cyrus or his ancestors.

It has been already remarked that the Jat divided with the Takshak the claim of being the parent name of the various tribes called Scythic, invaders of India; and there is now before the author an inscription of the fifth century applying both epithets to the same prince,[1] who is invested moreover with the Scythic quality of worshipping the sun. It states, likewise, that the mother of this Jat prince was of Yadu race: strengthening their claims to a niche amongst the thirty-six Rajkulas, as well as their Yadu descent.

The fifth century of the Christian era, to which this inscription belongs, is a period of interest in Jat history. De Guignes, from original authorities, states the Yuch-chi or Jats to have established themselves in the Panjab in the fifth and sixth centuries, and the inscription now quoted applies to a prince whose capital is styled Salindrapura in these regions; and doubtless the Salivahanpur[2] where the Yadu Bhattis established themselves on the expulsion of the Tak.

[1] "To my foe, salutation! This foe how shall I describe? Of the race of *Jat Kathida,* whose ancestor, the warrior Takshak, formed the garland on the neck of Mahadeva." Though this is a figurative allusion to the snake necklace of the father of creation, yet it evidently pointed to the Jat's descent from the Takshak. But enough has been said elsewhere of the snake race, the parent of the Scythic tribes, which the divine Milton seems to have taken from Diodorus's account of the mother of the Scythae:

"Woman to the waist, and fair;
But ended foul in many a scaly fold!"

Paradise Lost, Book ii. 650 f.

Whether the *Jat Kathida* is the Jat or Getae of Cathay (*da* being the mark of the genitive case) we will leave to conjecture [?]. [Ney Elias (*History of the Moghuls of Central Asia,* 75) suggests that the theory of the connexion between Jāts and Getae was largely based on an error regarding the term *jatah,* 'rascal,' applied as a mark of reproach to the Moguls by the Chagatai.]

[2] This place existed in the twelfth century as a capital; since an inscription of Kamarpal, prince of Anhilwara, declares that this monarch carried his conquests "even to Salpur." There is Sialkot in Rennell's geography, and Wilford mentions "Sangala, a famous city in ruins, sixty miles west by north of Lahore, situated in a forest, and said to be built by Puru.'

How much earlier than this the Jat penetrated into Rajasthan must be left to more ancient inscriptions to determine: suffice it that in A.D. 440 we find him in power.[1]

When the Yadu was expelled from Salivahanpura, and forced to seek refuge [108] across the Sutlej among the Dahia and Johya Rajputs of the Indian desert, where they founded their first capital, Derawar, many from compulsion embraced the Muhammadan faith; on which occasion they assumed the name of Jat,[2] of which at least twenty different offsets are enumerated in the Yadu chronicles.

That the Jats continued as a powerful community on the east bank of the Indus and in the Panjab, fully five centuries after the period our inscription and their annals illustrate, we have the most interesting records in the history of Mahmud, the conqueror of India, whose progress they checked in a manner unprecedented in the annals of continental warfare. It was in 416 of the Hegira (A.D. 1026) that Mahmud marched an army against the Jats, who had harassed and insulted him on the return from his last expedition against Saurashtra. The interest of the account authorizes its being given from the original.

"The Jats inhabited the country on the borders of Multan, along the river that runs by the mountains of Jud.[3] When Mahmud reached Multan, finding the Jat country defended by great rivers, he built fifteen hundred boats,[4] each armed with six iron spikes projecting from their prows, to prevent their being

[1] At this time (A.D. 449) the Jut brothers, Hengist and Horsa, led a colony from Jutland and founded the kingdom of Kent (*qu. Kantha*, 'a coast,' in Sanskrit, as in Gothic *Kontu* ?). The laws they there introduced, more especially the still prevailing one of gavelkind, where all the sons share equally, except the youngest who has a double portion, are purely Scythic, and brought by the original Goth from the Jaxartes. Alaric had finished his career, and Theodoric and Genseric (*ric*, 'king,' in Sanskrit [?]) were carrying their arms into Spain and Africa. [These speculations are valueless.]

[2] Why should these proselytes, if originally Yadu, assume the name of Jat or Jāt ? It must be either that the Yadus were themselves the Scythic Yuti or Yueh-chi, or that the branches intermarried with the Jats, and consequently became degraded as Yadus, and the mixed issue bore the name of the mother.

[3] The Jadu ka Dang, 'or hills of Yadu,' mentioned in the sketch of this race as one of their intermediate points of halt when they were driven from India after the Mahabharata.

[4] Near the spot where Alexander built his fleet, which navigated to Babylon thirteen hundred years before.

boarded by the enemy, expert in this kind of warfare. In each boat he placed twenty archers, and some with fire-balls of naphtha to burn the Jat fleet. The monarch having determined on their extirpation, awaited the result at Multan. The Jats sent their wives, children, and effects to Sind Sagar,[1] and launched four thousand, or, as others say, eight thousand boats well armed to meet the Ghaznians. A terrible conflict ensued, but the projecting spikes sunk the Jat boats while others were set on fire. Few escaped from this scene of terror; and those who did, met with the more severe fate of captivity."[2]

Many doubtless did escape; and it is most probable that the Jat communities, on whose overthrow the State of Bikaner was founded, were remnants of this very warfare [109].

Not long after this event the original empire of the Getae was overturned, when many fugitives found a refuge in India. In 1360 Togultash Timur was the great Khan of the Getae nation; idolaters even to this period. He had conquered Khorasan, invaded Transoxiana (whose prince fled, but whose nephew, Amir Timur, averted its subjugation), gained the friendship of Togultash, and commanded a hundred thousand Getae warriors. In 1369, when the Getic Khan died, such was the ascendancy obtained by Timur over his subjects, that the Kuriltai, or general assembly, transferred the title of Grand Khan from the Getic to the Chagatai Timur. In 1370 he married a Getic princess, and added Khokhand and Samarkand to his patrimony, Transoxiana. Rebellions and massacres almost depopulated this nursery of mankind, ere the Getae abandoned their independence; nor was it till 1388, after six invasions, in which he burnt their towns, brought away their wealth, and almost annihilated the nation, that he felt himself secure.[3]

[1] Translated by Dow, 'an island.' Sind Sagar is one of the Duabas of the Panjab. I have compared Dow's translation of the earlier portion of the history of Ferishta with the original, and it is infinitely more faithful than the world gives him credit for. His errors are most considerable in numerals and in weights and measures; and it is owing to this that he has made the captured wealth of India appear so incredible.

[2] Ferishta vol. i. [The translation in the text is an abstract of that of Dow (i. 72). That of Briggs (i. 81 f.) is more accurate. In neither version is there any mention of the Sind Sāgar. Rose (*Glossary*, ii. 359) discredits the account of this naval engagement, and expresses a doubt whether the Jats at this period occupied Jūd or the Salt Ranges.]

[3] [By the 'Getae' of the text the author apparently means Mongols.]

In his expedition into India, having overrun great part of Europe, "taken Moscow, and slain the soldiers of the barbarous Urus," he encountered his old foes "the Getae, who inhabited the plains of Tohim, where he put two thousand to the sword, pursuing them into the desert and slaughtering many more near the Ghaggar."[1]

Still the Jat maintained himself in the Panjab, and the most powerful and independent prince of India at this day is the Jat prince of Lahore, holding dominion over the identical regions where the Yueh-chi colonized in the fifth century, and where the Yadus, driven from Ghazni, established themselves on the ruins of the Taks. The Jat cavalier retains a portion of his Scythic manners, and preserves the use of the chakra or discus, the weapon of the Yadu Krishna in the remote age of the Bharat.

Hun or Hūn.—Amongst the Scythic tribes who have secured for themselves a niche with the thirty-six races of India, is the Hun. At what period this race, so well known by its ravages and settlement in Europe, invaded India, we know not.[2] Doubtless it was in the society of many others yet found in the peninsula of [110] Saurashtra, as the Kathi, the Bala, the Makwana, etc. It is, however, confined to the genealogies of that peninsula; for although we have mention of the Hun in the chronicles and inscriptions of India at a very early period, he failed to obtain a place in the catalogue of the northern bards.

The earliest notice of the tribe is in an inscription[3] recording the power of a prince of Bihar, who, amidst his other conquests, "humbled the pride of the Hūns." In the annals of the early history of Mewar, in the catalogue of princes who made common cause with this the chief of all the Rajputs, when Chitor was assailed in the first irruption of the Muhammadans, was Angatsi,

[1] Abulghazi vol. ii. chap. 16. After his battle with Sultan Mahmud of Delhi, Timur gave orders, to use the word of his historian, "for the slaughter of a hundred thousand infidel slaves. The great mosque was fired, and the souls of the infidels were sent to the abyss of hell. Towers were erected of their heads, and their bodies were thrown as food to the beasts and birds of prey. At Mairta the infidel Guebres were flayed alive." This was by order of Tamerlane, to whom the dramatic historians of Europe assign every great and good quality!

[2] [The first Hun invasion occurred in 455 A.D., and about 500 they overthrew the Gupta Empire (Smith, *EHI*, 309, 316).]

[3] *Asiatic Researches*, vol. i. p. 136.

lord of the Huns, who led his quota on this occasion. De Guignes [1] describes Angat as being the name of a considerable horde of Huns or Moguls; and Abulghazi says that the Tartar tribe who guarded the great wall of China were termed Angatti, who had a distinct prince with high pay and honour. The countries inhabited by the Hiong-nou and the Ou-huon, the Turks and Moguls, called 'Tatar' from Tatan,[2] the name of the country from the banks of the Irtish along the mountains of Altai to the shores of the Yellow Sea, are described at large by the historian of the Huns; following whom and other original sources, the historian of the Fall of Rome has given great interest to his narrative of their march into Europe. But those who are desirous to learn all that relates to the past history and manners of this people, must consult that monument of erudition and research, the Geography of Malte-Brun.[3]

D'Anville,[4] quoting Cosmas the traveller, informs us that the White Huns (λευκοὶ Οὔννοι) [5] occupied the north of India; and it is most probable a colony of these found their way into Saurashtra and Mewar.

It is on the eastern bank of the Chambal, at the ancient Barolli, that tradition assigns a residence to the Hun; and one of the celebrated temples at that place, called the Singar Chaori, is the marriage hall of the Hun prince, who is also declared to have been possessed of a lordship on the opposite bank, occupying the [111] site of the present town of Bhainsror. In the twelfth century the Hun must have possessed consequence, to occupy the place he holds in the chronicle of the princes of Gujarat. The race is not extinct. One of the most intelligent of the living bards of India assured the author of their existence; and in a tour where he accompanied him, redeemed his pledge, by pointing out the

[1] *Hist. Gén. des Huns*, tom. iii. p. 238.

[2] [The name Tatar is derived from that of the Ta-ta Mongols (*EB*, xxvi. 448).]

[3] *Précis de Géographie universelle.* Malte-Brun traces a connexion between the Hungarians and the Scandinavians, from similarity of language: "A ces siècles primitifs où les Huns, les Goths, les Jotes, les Ases, et bien d'autres peuples étaient réunis autour des anciens autels d'Odin." Several of the words which he affords us are Sanskrit in origin. Vol. vi. p. 370.

[4] *Eclaircissemens Géographiques sur la Carte de l'Inde*, p. 43 [Smith, *EHI*, 315 ff.].

[5] An orthography which more assimilates with the Hindu pronunciation of the name Huon, or Oun, than Hun.

residence of some in a village on the estuary of the Mahi, though degraded and mixed with other classes.[1]

We may infer that few convulsions occurred in Central Asia, which drove forth these hordes of redundant population to seek subsistence in Europe, without India participating in such overflow. The only singular circumstance is, by what means they came to be recognized as Hindus, even though of the lowest class. Sudra we cannot term them; for although the Kathi and the Bala cannot be regarded as, or classed with Rajputs, they would scorn the rank of Sudra.

Kāthi.—Of the ancient notices of this people much has been already said, and all the genealogists, both of Rajasthan and Saurashtra, concur in assigning it a place amongst the royal races of India. It is one of the most important tribes of the western peninsula, and which has effected the change of the name from Saurashtra to Kathiawar.

Of all its inhabitants the Kathi retains most originality: his religion, his manners, and his looks, all are decidedly Scythic. He occupied, in the time of Alexander, that nook of the Panjab near the confluent five streams. It was against these Alexander marched in person, when he nearly lost his life, and where he left such a signal memorial of his vengeance. The Kathi can be traced from these scenes to his present haunts. In the earlier portion of the Annals of Jaisalmer mention is made of their conflicts with the Kathi; and their own traditions [2] fix their settlement in the peninsula from the south-eastern part of the valley of the Indus, about the eighth century.

In the twelfth century the Kathi were conspicuous in the wars with Prithwiraja, there being several leaders of the tribe attached

[1] The same bard says that there are three or four houses of these Huns at Trisawi, three coss from Baroda; and the Khichi bard, Moghji, says their traditions record the existence of many powerful Hun princes in India. [On the Huns in W. India see *BG*, i. Part i. 122 ff. The difficulty in the text is now removed by the proof that many of them became Rājputs.]

[2] The late Captain Macmurdo, whose death was a loss to the service and to literature, gives an animated account of the habits of the Kathi. His opinions coincide entirely with my own regarding this race. See vol. i. p. 270, *Trans. Soc. of Bombay*. [For accounts of the Kāthi see *BG*, ix. Part i. 252 ff., viii. 122 ff. Under the Mahrattas Kāthiāwār, the name of the Kāthi tract, was extended to the whole of Saurāshtra (Wilberforce-Bell, *Hist. of Kathiawad*, 132 f.).]

to his army, as well as to that of [112] his rival, the monarch of Kanauj.[1] Though on this occasion they acted in some degree of subservience to the monarch of Anhilwara, it would seem that this was more voluntary than forced.

The Kathi still adores the sun,[2] scorns the peaceful arts, and is much less contented with the tranquil subsistence of industry than the precarious earnings of his former predatory pursuits. The Kathi was never happy but on horseback, collecting his blackmail, lance in hand, from friend and foe.

We will conclude this brief sketch with Captain Macmurdo's character of this race. "The Kathi differs in some respects from the Rajput. He is more cruel in his disposition, but far exceeds him in the virtue of bravery;[3] and a character possessed of more energy than a Kathi does not exist. His size is considerably larger than common, often exceeding six feet. He is sometimes seen with light hair and blue-coloured eyes. His frame is athletic and bony, and particularly well adapted to his mode of life. His countenance is expressive, but of the worst kind, being harsh, and often destitute of a single mild feature."[4]

Bāla.—All the genealogists, ancient and modern, insert the Bala tribe amongst the Rajkulas. The birad, or 'blessing,' of the bard is *Tatta Multan ka rao*,[5] indicative of their original abodes on the Indus. They lay claim, however, to descent from the Suryavansi, and maintain that their great ancestor, Bala or Bapa, was the offspring of Lava, the eldest son of Rama; that their first settlement in Saurashtra was at the ancient Dhank, in more remote periods called Mungi Paithan; and that, in conquering the country adjacent, they termed it Balakshetra (their capital Valabhipura), and assumed the title of Balarae. Here they claim identity with the Guhilot race of Mewar: nor is it impos-

[1] It is needless to particularise them here. In the poems of Chand, some books of which I have translated and purpose giving to the public, the important part the Kathi had assigned to them will appear.

[2] [In the form of a symbol like a spider, the rays forming the legs (*BG*, ix. Part i. 257).]

[3] It is the Rajput of Kathiawar, not of Rajasthan, to whom Captain Macmurdo alludes.

[4] Of their personal appearance, and the blue eye indicative of their Gothic or Getic origin, the author will have occasion to speak more particularly in his personal narrative.

[5] 'Princes of Tatta and Multan.'

sible that they may be a branch of this family, which long held power in Saurashtra.[1] Before the Guhilots adopted the worship of Mahadeo, which period is indicated in their annals, the chief object of their adoration was the sun, giving them that Scythic resemblance to which the Balas have every appearance of claim [113].

The Balas on the continent of Saurashtra, on the contrary, assert their origin to be Induvansa, and that they are the Balakaputras who were the ancient lords of Aror on the Indus. It would be presumption to decide between these claims; but I would venture to surmise that they might be the offspring of Salya, one of the princes of the Mahabharata, who founded Aror.

The Kathis claim descent from the Balas: an additional proof of northern origin, and strengthening their right to the epithet of the bards, 'Lords of Multan and Tatta.' The Balas were of sufficient consequence in the thirteenth century to make incursions on Mewar, and the first exploit of the celebrated Rana Hamir was his killing the Bala chieftain of Chotila.[2] The present chief of Dhank is a Bala, and the tribe yet preserves importance in the peninsula.

Jhāla Makwāna.—This tribe also inhabits the Saurashtra peninsula. It is styled Rajput, though neither classed with the Solar, Lunar, nor Agnikula races; but though we cannot directly prove it, we have every right to assign to it a northern origin. It is a tribe little known in Hindustan or even Rajasthan, into which latter country it was introduced entirely through the medium of the ancient lords of Saurashtra, the present family of Mewar; a sanction which covers every defect. A splendid act of self-devotion of the Jhala chief, when Rana Partap was oppressed with the whole weight of Akbar's power, obtained, with the gratitude of this prince, the highest honours he could confer,—his daughter in marriage, and a seat on his right hand. That it was the act, and not his rank in the scale of the thirty-six tribes, which gained him this distinction, we have decided proof in later times, when it was deemed a mark of great condescension that the present Rana should sanction a remote branch of his own

[1] [The origin of the Bālas is not certain: they were probably Gurjaras (*Ibid.* 495 f.).]

[2] [Chotila in Kāthiāwār (*BG*, viii. 407).]

family bestowing a daughter in marriage on the Jhala ruler of Kotah.[1] This tribe has given its name to one of the largest divisions of Saurashtra, Jhalawar, which possesses several towns of importance. Of these Bankaner, Halwad, and Dhrangadra are the principal.

Regarding the period of the settlement of the Jhalas tradition is silent, as also on their early history: but the aid of its quota was given to the Rana against the [114] first attacks of the Muhammadans; and in the heroic history of Prithwiraja we have ample and repeated mention of the Jhala chieftains who distinguished themselves in his service, as well as in that of his antagonist, and the name of one of these, as recorded by the bard Chand, I have seen inscribed on the granite rock of the sacred Girnar, near their primitive abodes, where we leave them. There are several subdivisions of the Jhala, of which the Makwana is the principal.

Jethwa, Jaithwa, Kamāri.—This is an ancient tribe, and by all authorities styled Rajput; though, like the Jhala, little known out of Saurashtra, to one of the divisions of which it has given its name, Jethwar. Its present possessions are on the western coast of the peninsula: the residence of its prince, who is styled Rana, is Porbandar.

In remote times their capital was Ghumli, whose ruins attest considerable power, and afford singular scope for analogy, in architectural device, with the style termed Saxon of Europe.[2] The bards of the Jethwas run through a long list of one hundred and thirty crowned heads, and in the eighth century have chronicled the marriage of their prince with the Tuar refounder of Delhi. At this period the Jethwa bore the name of Kamar; and Sahl Kamar is reported to be the prince who was driven from Ghumli, in the twelfth century, by invaders from the north. With this change the name of Kamar was sunk, and that of Jethwa assumed,

[1] His son, Madho Singh, the present administrator, is the offspring of the celebrated Zalim and a Ranawat chieftain's daughter, which has entitled his (Madho Singh's) issue to marry far above their scale in rank. So much does superiority of blood rise above all worldly considerations with a Rajput, that although Zalim Singh held the reins of the richest and best ordered State of Rajasthan, he deemed his family honoured by his obtaining to wife for his grandson the daughter of a Kachhwaha minor chieftain.

[2] [Ghumli in the Barda hills, about 40 miles east of Porbandar (Wilberforce-Bell, *Hist. of Kathiawad*, 49 f.; *BG*, viii. 440).]

which has induced the author to style them Kamari ; [1] and as they, with the other inhabitants of this peninsula, have all the appearance of Scythic descent, urging no pretensions to connexion with the ancient races of India, they may be a branch of that celebrated race, the Cimmerii of higher Asia, and the Cimbri of Europe.

Their legends are as fabulous as fanciful. They trace their descent from the monkey-god Hanuman, and confirm it by alleging the elongation of the spine of their princes, who bear the epithet of Puncharia, or the 'long-tailed,' Ranas of Saurashtra. But the manners and traditions of this race will appear more fully in the narrative of the author's travels amongst them.

Gohil.[2]—This was a distinguished race : it claims to be Suryavansi, and with some pretension. The first residence of the Gohils was Juna Khergarh, near the bend of the Luni in Marwar.[3] How long they had been established here we know not. They took it from one of the aboriginal Bhil chiefs named Kherwa, and had been in possession of it for twenty generations when expelled by the [115] Rathors at the end of the twelfth century. Thence migrating to Saurashtra, they fixed at Piramgarh ; [4] which being destroyed, one branch settled at Bhagwa, and the chief marrying the daughter of Nandanagar or Nandod,[5] he usurped or obtained his father-in-law's estates ; and twenty-seven generations are enumerated, from Sompal to Narsingh, the present Raja of Nandod. Another branch fixed at Sihor, and thence founded Bhaunagar and Gogha. The former town, on the gulf of the Mahi, is the residence of the Gohils, who have given their name, Gohilwar, to the eastern portion of the peninsula of Saurashtra. The present chief addicts himself to commerce, and possesses ships which trade to the gold coast of Sofala.

Sarwaiya or Sariaspa.—Of this race tradition has left us only the knowledge that it once was famous ; for although, in the catalogues of the bard, it is introduced as the "essence of the Khatri race," [6] we have only a few legends regarding its present

[1] [The terms Kamār and Kamāri seem to have disappeared.]

[2] A compound word from goh, 'strength' ; Ila, 'the earth.' [This is out of the question : cf. Guhilot.]

[3] [For Kher, 'the cradle of the Rāthors,' see Erskine iii. A. 199.]

[4] [For the island of Piram in Ahmadabad district see *IGI*, xx. 149 f., and for the tradition Wilberforce-Bell, *op. cit.* 71 f. ; *BG*, iv. 348, viii. 114.]

[5] [The ancient Nandapadra in Rājpīpla, Bombay (*IGI*, xviii. 361 ; *BG*, i. Part ii. 314).]

[6] *Sarwaiya Khatri tain sar.*

degradation. Its name, as well as this epithet of the bard, induces a belief that it is a branch of the Aswas, with the prefix of *sar*, denoting 'essence,' or priority. But it is useless to speculate on a name.

Silār or Salār.—Like the former, we have here but the shade of a name; though one which, in all probability, originated the epithet Larike, by which the Saurashtra peninsula was known to Ptolemy and the geographers of early Europe. The tribe of Lar was once famous in Saurashtra, and in the annals of Anhilwara mention is made of Siddharaja Jayasingha having extirpated them throughout his dominions. Salar, or Silar, would therefore be distinctively *the* Lar.[1] Indeed, the author of the Kumarpal Charitra styles it Rajtilak, or 'regal prince'; but the name only now exists amongst the mercantile classes professing the faith of Buddha [Jainism]: it is inserted as one of the eighty-four. The greater portion of these are of Rajput origin.

Dabhi.—Little can be said of this tribe but that it was once celebrated in Saurashtra. By some it is called the branch of the Yadu, though all the genealogists give it distinct importance. It now possesses neither territory nor numbers.[2]

Gaur.—The Gaur tribe was once respected in Rajasthan, though it never there attained to any considerable eminence. The ancient kings of Bengal were of this race, and gave their name to the capital, Lakhnauti [116].

We have every reason to believe that they were possessors of the land afterwards occupied by the Chauhans, as they are styled in all the old chronicles the 'Gaur of Ajmer.' Repeated mention is made of them in the wars of Prithwiraja, as leaders of considerable renown, one of whom formed a small State in the centre of India, which survived through seven centuries of Mogul domination, till it at length fell a prey indirectly to the successes of the British over the Mahrattas, when Sindhia in 1809 annihilated the power of the Gaur and took possession of his capital, Sheopur.[3] A

[1] *Su*, as before observed, is a distinctive prefix, meaning 'excellent.' [The derivation is impossible. Lāta was S. Gujarāt.]

[2] [For the Dābhi tribe, see *IA*, iii. 69 ff., 193 f.; Forbes, *Rāsmāla*, 237 f.]

[3] In 1807 the author passed through this territory, in a solitary ramble to explore these parts, then little known; and though but a young *Sub.*, was courteously received and entertained both at Baroda and Sheopur. In 1809 he again entered the country under very different circumstances, in the suite of the British envoy with Sindhia's court, and had the grief to

petty district, yielding about £5000 annually, is all this rapacious head of a predatory government has left to the Gaur, out of about twelve lacs of annual revenue. The Gaur has five sakha: Untahar, Silhala, Tur, Dusena, and Budana.[1]

Dor or Doda.—We have little to say of this race. Though occupying a place in all the genealogies, time has destroyed all knowledge of the past history of a tribe, to gain a victory over whom was deemed by Prithwiraja worthy of a tablet.[2]

Gaharwār.—The Gaharwar Rajput is scarcely known to his brethren in Rajasthan, who will not admit his contaminated blood to mix with theirs; though, as a brave warrior, he is entitled to their fellowship. The original country of the Gaharwar is in the ancient kingdom of Kasi.[3] Their great ancestor was Khortaj Deva, from whom Jasaunda, the seventh in descent, in consequence of some grand sacrificial rites performed at Vindhyavasi, gave the title of Bundela to his issue. Bundela has now usurped the name of Gaharwar, and become the appellation of the immense tract which its various branches inhabit in Bundelkhand, on the ruins of the Chandelas, whose chief cities, Kalanjar, Mohini, and Mahoba, they took possession of.[4]

Chandel.—The Chandela, classed by some of the genealogists amongst the thirty-six tribes, were powerful in the twelfth century, possessing the whole of the regions between [117] the Jumna and Nerbudda, now occupied by the Bundelas and Baghelas.

---

witness the operations against Sheopur, and its fall, unable to aid his friends. The Gaur prince had laid aside the martial virtues. He became a zealot in the worship of Vishnu, left off animal food, was continually dancing before the image of the god, and was far more conversant in the mystical poetry of Krishna and his beloved Radha than in the martial song of the bard. His name was Radhikadas, 'the slave of Radha'; and, as far as he is personally concerned, we might cease to lament that he was the last of his race.

[1] [Only two sub-clans are named in *Rajputana Census Report*, 1911, i. 255. Gaur Rājputs are numerous in the United Provinces, and the Gaur Brāhmans of Jaipur represent a foreign tribe merged into Hindu society (*IA*, xi. 22). They can have no connexion with the Pāla or Sena dynasty of Bengal (Smith, *EHI*, 397 ff.).]

[2] See *Transactions of Royal Asiatic Society*, vol. i. p. 133. [They are found in the Upper Ganges-Jumna Duab, and are Musalmāns.]

[3] Benares.

[4] [For the Gaharwār, see Crooke, *Tribes and Castes N.W.P. and Oudh*. ii. 32 ff., and for the Gaharwār dynasty of Kanauj (Smith, *EHI*, 384 ff.).]

Their wars with Prithwiraja, forming one of the most interesting of his exploits, ended in the humiliation of the Chandela, and prepared the way for their conquest by the Gaharwars; the date of the supremacy of the Bundela Manvira was about A.D. 1200. Madhukar Sah, the thirteenth in descent from him, founded Orchha on the Betwa, by whose son, Birsingh Deva, considerable power was attained. Orchha became the chief of the numerous Bundela principalities; but its founder drew upon himself everlasting infamy, by putting to death the wise Abu-l Fazl,[1] the historian and friend of the magnanimous Akbar, and the encomiast and advocate of the Hindu race.

From the period of Akbar the Bundelas bore a distinguished part in all the grand conflicts, to the very close of the monarchy: nor, amongst all the brave chiefs of Rajasthan, did any perform more gallant or faithful services than the Bundela chieftains of Orchha and Datia. Bhagwan of Orchha commanded the advanced guard of the army of Shah Jahan. His son, Subhkarana, was Aurangzeb's most distinguished leader in the Deccan, and Dalpat fell in the war of succession on the plains of Jajau.[2] His descendants have not degenerated; nor is there anything finer in the annals of the chivalry of the West, than the dignified and heroic conduct of the father of the present chief.[3] The Bundela is now a numerous race, while the name Gaharwar remains in their original haunts.

Bargūjar.—This race is Suryavansi, and the only one, with the exception of the Guhilot, which claims from Lava, the elder son

[1] Slain at the instigation of Prince Salim, son of Akbar, afterwards the emperor Jahangir. See this incident stated in the emperor's own *Commentaries* [*Āīn*, i. Introd. xxiv. ff.].

[2] [For Subhkaran Singh, see Manucci (i. 270, 272). Dalpat was one of his patients (*Ibid.* ii. 298).]

[3] On the death of Mahadaji Sindhia, the females of his family, in apprehension of his successor (Daulat Rao), sought refuge and protection with the Raja of Datia. An army was sent to demand their surrender, and hostility was proclaimed as the consequence of refusal. This brave man would not even await the attack, but at the head of a devoted band of three hundred horse, with their lances, carried destruction amongst their assailants, neither giving nor receiving quarter: and thus he fell in defence of the laws of sanctuary and honour. Even when grievously wounded, he would accept no aid, and refused to leave the field, but disdaining all compromise awaited his fate. The author has passed upon the spot where this gallant deed was performed; and from his son, the present Raja, had the annals of his house.

of Rama. The Bargujar held considerable possessions in Dhundhar,[1] and their capital was the hill fortress of Rajor[2] in the principality of Macheri. Rajgarh and Alwar were also their [118] possessions. The Bargujars were expelled these abodes by the Kachhwahas. A colony found refuge and a new residence at Anupshahr on the Ganges.

Sengar.—Of this tribe little is known, nor does it appear ever to have obtained great celebrity. The sole chieftainship of the Sengars is Jagmohanpur on the Jumna.[3]

Sakarwāl.—This tribe, like the former, never appears to have claimed much notice amidst the princes of Rajasthan; nor is there a single independent chieftain now remaining, although there is a small district called after them, Sakarwar, on the right bank of the Chambal, adjoining Jaduvati, and like it now incorporated in the province of Gwalior, in Sindhia's dominions. The Sakarwal is therefore reduced to subsist by cultivation, or the more precarious employment of his lance, either as a follower of others, or as a common depredator. They have their name from the town of Sikri (Fatehpur), which was formerly an independent principality.[4]

Bais.—The Bais has obtained a place amongst the thirty-six races, though the author believes it but a subdivision of the Suryavansi, as it is neither to be met with in the lists of Chand, nor in those of the Kumarpal Charitra. It is now numerous, and has given its name to an extensive district, Baiswara in the Duab, or the land between the Ganges and Jumna.[5]

Dahia.—This is an ancient tribe, whose residence was the banks of the Indus, near its confluence with the Sutlej; and although they retain a place amongst the thirty-six royal races, we have not the knowledge of any as now existing. They are

[1] Amber or Jaipur, as well as Macheri, were comprehended in Dhundhar, the ancient geographical designation [said to be derived from an ancient sacrificial mound (*dhūndh*), on the western frontier of the State, or from a demon-king, Dhūndhu (*IGI*, xiii. 385).]

[2] The ruins of Rajor are about fifteen miles west of Rajgarh. A person sent there by the author reported the existence of inscriptions in the temple of Nilkantha Mahadeo.

[3] [They are numerous in the United Provinces, but their origin and traditions are uncertain.]

[4] [See Crooke, *Tribes and Castes N.W.P. and Oudh*, iv. 263 ff.]

[5] [They are almost certainly of mixed origin (Crooke, *op. cit.* i. 118 ff.).]

mentioned in the annals of the Bhattis of Jaisalmer, and from name as well as from locale, we may infer that they were the Dahae of Alexander.[1]

Joiya, Johya.—This race possessed the same haunts as the Dahia, and are always coupled with them. They, however, extended across the Ghara into the northern desert of India, and in ancient chronicles are entitled 'Lords of Jangaldesa,' a tract which comprehended Hariana, Bhatner, and Nagor. The author possesses a work relative to this tribe, like the Dahia, now extinct.[2]

Mohil.—We have no mode of judging of the pretensions of this race to the place it is allowed to occupy by the genealogists. All that can be learned of its past history is, that it inhabited a considerable tract so late as the foundation of the present State of Bikaner, the Rathor founders of which expelled, if not extirpated, the Mohil. With the Malan, Malani, and Mallia, also extinct, it may [119] claim the honour of descent from the ancient Malloi, the foes of Alexander, whose abode was Multan. (*Qu.* Mohilthan ?)[3]

Nikumbha.—Of this race, to which celebrity attaches in all the genealogies, we can only discover that they were proprietors of the district of Mandalgarh prior to the Guhilots.[4]

Rājpāli.—It is difficult to discover anything regarding this race, which, under the names of Rajpali, Rajpalaka, or simply Pala, are mentioned by all the genealogists ; especially those of Saurashtra, to which in all probability it was confined. This tends to make it Scythic in origin ; the conclusion is strengthened by the derivation of the name, meaning 'royal shepherd' : it was probably a branch of the ancient Pali.[5]

Dahariya.—The Kumarpal Charitra is our sole authority for

[1] [They lived east of the Caspian Sea, and can have no connexion with the Indian Dahia (Sykes, *Hist. of Persia*, i. 330).]

[2] [Their origin is very uncertain ; in Bahāwalpur they now repudiate Rājput descent, and claim to be descendants of the Prophet (Rose, *Glossary*, ii. 410 ff. ; Malik Muhammad Din, *Gazetteer Bahawalpur*, i. 23, 133 ff.).]

[3] [The Malloi (Skt. Mālava) occupied the present Montgomery District, and parts of Jhang. They had no connexion with Multan (Skt. Mūlasthānapura), (Smith, *EHI*, 96 ; McCrindle, *Alexander*, 350 ff.).]

[4] [They are a mixed race, early settlers in Alwar (Crooke, *Tribes and Castes N.W.P. and Oudh*, iv. 86 ff.).]

[5] The final syllable *ka* is a mark of the genitive case [?].

classing this race with the thirty-six. Of its history we know nothing. Amongst the princes who came to the aid of Chitor, when first assailed by the arms of Islam, was 'the lord of Debal, Dahir, Despati.'[1] From the ignorance of the transcriber of the Guhilot annals, *Delhi* is written instead of *Debal*; but we not only have the whole of the names of the Tuar race, but Delhi was not in existence at this time. Slight as is the mention of this prince in the Chitor annals, it is nevertheless of high value, as stamping them with authenticity; for this Dahir was actually the despot of Sind, whose tragical end in his capital Debal is related by Abu-l Fazl. It was in the ninety-ninth year of the Hegira that he was attacked by Muhammad bin Kasim, the lieutenant of the Caliph of Bagdad, and treated with the greatest barbarity.[2] Whether this prince used Dahir as a proper name, or as that of his tribe, must be left to conjecture.

Dahima.—The Dahima has left but the wreck of a great name.[3] Seven centuries have swept away all recollection of a tribe who once afforded one of the proudest themes for the song of the bard. The Dahima was the lord of Bayana, and one of the most powerful vassals of the Chauhan emperor, Prithwiraja. Three brothers of this house held the highest offices under this monarch, and the period during which the elder, Kaimas, was his minister, was the brightest in the history of the Chauhan: but he fell a victim to a blind jealousy. Pundir, the second brother [120], commanded the frontier at Lahore. The third, Chawand Rae, was the principal leader in the last battle, where Prithwiraja fell, with the whole of his chivalry, on the banks of the Ghaggar. Even the historians of Shihabu-d-din have preserved the name of the gallant Dahima, Chawand Rae, whom they style Khandirai; and to whose valour, they relate, Shihabu-d-din himself nearly fell a sacrifice. With the Chauhan, the race seems to have been extinguished. Rainsi, his only son, was by this sister of Chawand Rae, but he did not survive the capture of Delhi. This marriage

[1] 'Chief of a country,' from *des*, 'country,' and *pati*, 'chief.' (*Qu.* δεσπότης ?)

[2] [*Āīn*, ii. 344 f. Dāhir was killed in action: the real tragedy was the death of Muhammad bin Kāsim in consequence of a false accusation (Elliot-Dowson i. 292).]

[3] [Elliot (*Supplemental Glossary*, 262) writes the name Dhāhima, and says they are found in Meerut District.]

forms the subject of one of the books of the bard, who never was more eloquent than in the praise of the Dahima.[1]

Aboriginal Races[2]

Bagri, Mer, Kaba, Mina, Bhil, Sahariya, Thori, Khangar, Gond, Bhar, Janwar, and Sarad.

Agricultural and Pastoral Tribes

Abhira or Ahir, Goala, Kurmi or Kulumbi, Gujar, and Jat

Rajput Tribes to which no Sakha is assigned

Jalia, Peshani, Sohagni, Chahira, Ran, Simala, Botila, Gotchar, Malan, Uhir, Hul, Bachak, Batar, Kerach, Kotak, Busa, and Bargota.

Catalogue of the Eighty-Four Mercantile Tribes

Sri Sri Mal, Srimal, Oswal, Bagherwal, Dindu, Pushkarwal, Mertawal, Harsora, Surawal, Piliwal, Bhambu, Kandhelwal, Dohalwal, Kederwal, Desawal, Gujarwal, Sohorwal, Agarwal, Jaelwal, Manatwal, Kajotiwal, Kortawal, Chçhtrawal, Soni, Sojatwal, Nagar, Mad, Jalhera, Lar, Kapol, Khareta, Barari, Dasora, Bambarwal, Nagadra, Karbera, Battewara, Mewara, Narsinghpura, Khaterwal, Panchamwal, Hanerwal, Sirkera, Bais, Stukhi, Kambowal, Jiranwal, Baghelwal, Orchitwal, Bamanwal, Srigur, Thakurwal, Balmiwal, Tepora, Tilota, Atbargi,

[1] Chand, the bard, thus describes Bayana, and the marriage of Prithwiraja with the Dahimi: "On the summit of the hills of Druinadahar, whose awful load oppressed the head of Sheshnag, was placed the castle of Bayana, resembling Kailas. The Dahima had three sons and two fair daughters: may his name be perpetuated throughout this iron age! One daughter was married to the Lord of Mewat, the other to the Chauhan. With her he gave in dower eight beauteous damsels and sixty-three female slaves, one hundred chosen horses of the breed of Irak, two elephants, and ten shields, a pallet of silver for the bride, one hundred wooden images, one hundred chariots, and one thousand pieces of gold." The bard, on taking leave, says: "the Dahima lavished his gold, and filled his coffers with the praises of mankind. The Dahimi produced a jewel, a gem without price, the Prince Rainsi."

The author here gives a fragment of the ruins of Bayana, the ancient abode of the Dahima.

[2] [Many names in the following list are not capable of identification, and their correct form is uncertain. Those of the mercantile tribes are largely groups confined to Rājputāna.]

Ladisakha, Badnora, Khicha, Gasora, Bahaohar, Jemo, Padmora, Maharia, Dhakarwal, Mangora, Goelwal, Mohorwal, Chitora, Kakalia, Bhareja, Andora, Sachora, Bhungrawal, Mandahala, Bramania, Bagria, Dindoria, Borwal, Sorbia, Orwal, Nuphag, and Nagora. (One wanting.)

CHAPTER 8

Having thus taken a review of the tribes which at various times inhabited and still inhabit Hindustan, the subject must be concluded.

In so extensive a field it was impossible to introduce all that could have been advanced on the distinctive marks in religion and manners; but this deficiency will be remedied in the annals of the most prominent races yet ruling, by which we shall prevent repetition.

The same religion governing the institutions of all these tribes operates to counteract that dissimilarity in manners, which would naturally be expected amidst so great a variety, from situation or climate; although such causes do produce a material difference in external habit. Cross but the elevated range which divides upland Mewar from the low sandy region of Marwar, and the difference of costume and manners will strike the most casual observer. But these changes are only exterior and personal; the mental character is less changed, because the same creed, the same religion (the principal former and reformer of manners), guides them all.

Distinctions between the Rājput States.—We have the same mythology, the same theogony, the same festivals, though commemorated with peculiar distinctions. There are niceties in thought, as in dress, which if possible to communicate would excite but little interest; when the tie of a turban and the fold of a robe are, like Masonic symbols, distinguishing badges of tribes. But it is in their domestic circle that manners are best seen [122]; where restraint is thrown aside, and no authority controls the freedom of expression. But does the European seek access to this sanctum of nationality ere he gives his debtor and creditor account of character, his balanced catalogue of virtues and vices? He may, however, with the Rajput, whose independence of mind places him above restraint, and whose hospitality and love of character will always afford free communication to those who respect his opinions and his prejudices, and who are devoid of that overweening opinion of self, which imagines that nothing can be learned from such friendly intercourse. The personal dissimilarity accordingly arises from locale ; the mental similarity results from a grand fixed principle, which, whatever its intrinsic moral effect, whatever its incompatibility with the elevated notions we entertain, has preserved to these races, as nations, the enjoyment of their ancient habits to this distant period. May our boasted superiority in all that exalts man above his fellows, ensure to our Eastern empire like duration ; and may these notions of our own peculiarly favoured destiny operate to prevent us from laying prostrate, in our periodical ambitious visitations, these the most ancient relics of civilization on the face of the earth. For the dread of their amalgamation with our empire will prevail, though such a result would be opposed not only to their happiness, but to our own stability.

Alliances with the British.—With our present system of alliances, so pregnant with evil from their origin, this fatal consequence (far from desired by the legislative authorities at home) must inevitably ensue. If the wit of man had been taxed to devise a series of treaties with a view to an ultimate rupture, these would be entitled to applause as specimens of diplomacy.

There is a perpetual variation between the spirit and the letter of every treaty ; and while the internal independence of each State is the groundwork, it is frittered away and nullified by successive stipulations, and these positive and negative qualities continue mutually repelling each other, until it is apparent that independence cannot exist under such conditions. Where discipline is lax, as with these feudal associations, and where each subordinate vassal is master of his own retainers, the article of military contingents alone would prove a source of contention. By leading to interference with each individual chieftain, it would render such aid worse than useless. But this is a minor consideration to the tributary pecuniary stipulation which, unsettled and undetermined, leaves a door open to a [123] system of espionage into their revenue accounts—a system not only disgusting, but contrary to treaty, which leaves 'internal administration' sacred. These openings to dispute, and the general laxity of their governments coming in contact with our regular system, present dangerous handles for ambition : and who so blind as not to know that ambition to be distinguished must influence every viceregent in the East ? While deeds in arms and acquisition of territory outweigh the meek éclat of civil virtue, the periodical visitations to these kingdoms will ever be like the comet's,

> Foreboding change to princes.

Our position in the East has been, and continues to be, one in which conquest forces herself upon us. We have yet the power, however late, to halt, and not anticipate her further orders to march. A contest for a mud-bank has carried our arms to the Aurea Chersonesus, the limit of Ptolemy's geography. With the Indus on the left, the Brahmaputra to the right, the Himalayan barrier towering like a giant to guard the Tatarian ascent, the ocean and our ships at our back, such is our colossal attitude ! But if misdirected ambition halts not at the Brahmaputra, but plunges in to gather laurels from the teak forest of Arakan, what surety have we for these Hindu States placed by treaty within the grasp of our control ?

But the hope is cherished, that the same generosity which formed those ties that snatched the Rajputs from degradation and impending destruction, will maintain the pledge given in the fever of success, " that their independence should be sacred " ; that it will palliate faults we may not overlook, and perpetuate this oasis of ancient rule, in the desert of destructive revolution, of races whose virtues are their own, and whose vices are the grafts of tyranny, conquest, and religious intolerance.[1]

To make them known is one step to obtain for them, at least, the boon of sympathy ; for with the ephemeral power of our governors and the agents of government, is it to be expected that the rod will more softly fall when ignorance of their history prevails, and no kind association springs from a knowledge of their martial achievements and yet proud bearing, their generosity, courtesy, and extended hospitality ? These are Rajput virtues yet extant amidst all their revolutions, and which have survived ages of Muhammadan bigotry and power ; though to the honour of the virtuous and magnanimous few among the crowned heads

[1] [The present relations of the States to the Government of India justify these expectations.]

of eight centuries, both Tatar and Mogul, there were some great souls [124]; men of high worth, who appeared at intervals to redeem the oppression of a whole preceding dynasty.

The high ground we assumed, and the lofty sentiments with which we introduced ourselves amongst the Rajputs, arrogating motives of purity, of disinterested benevolence, scarcely belonging to humanity, and to which their sacred writings alone yielded a parallel, gave such exalted notions of our right of exerting the attributes of divinity, justice, and mercy, that they expected little less than almighty wisdom in our acts; but circumstances have throughout occurred in each individual State, to show we were mere mortals, and that the poet's moral:

> 'Tis distance lends enchantment to the view,

was true in politics. Sorrow and distrust were the consequences —anger succeeded; but the sense of obligation is still too powerful to operate a stronger and less generous sentiment. These errors may yet be redeemed, and our Rajput allies yet be retained as useful friends: though they can only be so while in the enjoyment of perfect internal independence, and their ancient institutions.

"No political institution can endure," observes the eloquent historian of the Middle Ages, "which does not rivet itself to the heart of men by ancient prejudices or acknowledged merit. The feudal compact had much of this character. In fulfilling the obligations of mutual assistance and fidelity by military service, the energies of friendship were awakened, and the ties of moral sympathy superadded to those of positive compact."

We shall throw out one of the assumed causes which give stability to political institutions; 'acknowledged merit,' which never belonged to the loose feudal compact of Rajwara; but the absence of this strengthens the necessary substitute, 'ancient prejudices,' which supply many defects.

Our anomalous and inconsistent interference in some cases, and our non-interference in others, operate alike to augment the dislocation induced by long predatory oppression in the various orders of society, instead of restoring that harmony and continuity which had previously existed. The great danger, nay, the inevitable consequence of perseverance in this line of conduct, will be their reduction to the same degradation with our other allies, and their ultimate incorporation with our already too extended dominion [125].

It may be contended, that the scope and tenor of these alliances were not altogether unfitted for the period when they were formed, and our circumscribed knowledge; but was it too late, when this knowledge was extended, to purify them from the dross which deteriorated the two grand principles of mutual benefit, on which all were grounded, viz. 'perfect internal independence' to them, and 'acknowledged supremacy' to the protecting power? It will be said, that even these corner-stones of the grand political fabric are far from possessing those durable qualities which the contracting parties define, but that, on the contrary, they are the Ormuzd and Ahrimanes, the good and evil principles of contention. But when we have superadded pecuniary engagements of indefinite extent, increasing in the ratio of their prosperity, and armed quotas or contingents of their troops, whose loose habits and discipline would ensure constant complaint, we may certainly take credit for having established a system which must compel that direct interference, which the broad principle of each treaty professes to check.

The inevitable consequence is the perpetuation of that denationalising principle, so well understood by the Mahrattas, '*divide et impera*.' We are few; to use an Oriental metaphor, our agents must 'use the eyes and ears of others.' That mutual dependence, which would again have arisen, our interference will completely nullify. Princes will find they can oppress their chiefs, chiefs will find channels by which their sovereign's commands may be rendered nugatory, and irresponsible ministers must have our support to raise these undefined tributary supplies; and unanimity, confidence, and all the sentiments of gratitude which they owe, and acknowledge to be our due, will gradually fade with the national degradation. That our alliances have this tendency cannot be disputed. By their very nature they transfer the respect of every class of subjects from their immediate sovereign to the paramount authority and its subordinate agents. Who will dare to urge that a government, which cannot support its internal rule without restriction, can be national? that without power unshackled and unrestrained by exterior council or espionage, it can maintain self-respect, the corner-stone of every virtue with States as with individuals? This first of feelings these treaties utterly annihilate. Can we suppose such denationalised allies are to be depended upon in emergencies ? or, if allowed to retain a spark of their ancient moral inheritance, that it [126] will not be kindled into a flame against us when opportunity offers, instead of lighting up the powerful feeling of gratitude which yet exists towards us in these warlike communities ?

Like us they were the natural foes of that predatory system which so long disturbed our power, and our preservation and theirs were alike consulted in its destruction. When we sought their alliance, we spoke in the captivating accents of philanthropy ; we courted them to disunite from this Ahrimanes of political convulsion. The benevolent motives of the great mover of these alliances we dare not call in question, and his policy coincided with the soundest wisdom. But the treaties might have been revised, and the obnoxious parts which led to discord, abrogated, at the expense of a few paltry lacs of tribute and a portion of sovereign homage. It is not yet too late. True policy would enfranchise them altogether from our alliance ; but till then let them not feel their shackles in the galling restraint on each internal operation. Remove that millstone to national prosperity, the poignant feeling that every increased bushel of corn raised in their long-deserted fields must send its tithe to the British granaries. Let the national mind recover its wonted elasticity, and they will again attain their former celebrity. We have the power to advance this greatness, and make it and its result our own ; or, by a system unworthy of Britain, to retard and even quench it altogether.[1]

Never were their national characteristics so much endangered as in the seducing calm which followed the tempestuous agitations in which they had so long floated ; doubtful, to use their own figurative expression, whether 'the gift of our friendship,

[1] If Lord Hastings' philanthropy, which rejoiced in snatching these ancient States from the degradation of predatory warfare, expected that in four short years order should rise out of the chaos of a century, and "was prepared to visit with displeasure all symptoms of internal neglect, arising from supineness, indifference, or concealed ill-will" ; if *he* signified that "government would take upon itself the task of restoring order," and that "all changes" on this score "would be demanded and rigidly exacted" : in fine, that "such arrangements would be made as would deprive them of the power of longer abusing the spirit of liberal forbearance, the motives of which they were incapable of understanding or appreciating" ; what have they to hope from those without his sympathies ?

or our arms,' were fraught with greater evil. The latter they could not withstand ; though it must never be lost sight of, that, like ancient Rome when her glory was fading, we use 'the arms of the barbarians' to defend our conquests against them ! Is the mind ever stationary ? are virtue and high notions to be acquired from contact and example ? Is there no mind above the level of £10 monthly pay in all the native legions of the three presidencies of India ? no Odoacer, no Sivaji, [127] again to revive ? Is the book of knowledge and of truth, which we hold up, only to teach them submission and perpetuate their weakness ? Can we without fresh claims expect eternal gratitude, and must we not rationally look for reaction in some grand impulse, which, by furnishing a signal instance of the mutability of power, may afford a lesson for the benefit of posterity ?

Is the mantle of protection, which we have thrown over these warlike races, likely to avert such a result ? It might certainly, if imbued with all those philanthropic feelings for which we took credit, act with soporific influence, and extinguish the embers of international animosity. 'The lion and the lamb were to drink from the same fountain' ; they were led to expect the holy Satya Yug, when each man reposed under his own fig-tree, which neither strife nor envy dared approach.

When so many nations are called upon, in a period of great calamity and danger, to make over to a foreigner, their opposite in everything, their superior in most, the control of their forces in time of war, the adjudication of their disputes in time of peace, and a share in the fruits of their renovating prosperity, what must be the result ; when each Rajput may hang up his lance in the hall, convert his sword to a ploughshare, and make a basket of his buckler ? What but the prostration of every virtue ? It commences with the basis of the Rajput's—the martial virtues ; extinguish these and they will soon cease to respect themselves. Sloth, low cunning and meanness will follow. What nation ever maintained its character that devolved on the stranger the power of protection ! To be great, to be independent, its martial spirit must be cherished ; happy if within the bounds of moderation. Led away by enthusiasm, the author experienced the danger of interference, when observing but one side of the picture —the brilliant lights which shone on their long days of darkness, not calculating the shade which would follow the sudden glare.

On our cessation from every species of interference alone depends their independence or their amalgamation—a crisis fraught with danger to our overgrown rule.

Let Alexander's speech to his veterans, tired of conquest and refusing to cross the Hyphasis, be applied, and let us not reckon too strongly on our empire of opinion: "Fame never represents matters truly as they are, but on the contrary magnifies everything. This is evident; for our own reputation and glory, though founded on solid truth, is yet more obliged to rumour than reality." [1]

We may conclude with the Macedonian conqueror's reasons for showing the [128] Persians and his other foreign allies so much favour: "The possession of what we got by the sword is not very durable, but the obligation of good offices is eternal. If we have a mind to keep Asia, and not simply pass through it, our clemency must extend to them also, and their fidelity will make our empire everlasting. As for ourselves, we have more than we know what to do with, and it must be an insatiable, avaricious temper which desires to continue to fill what already runs over." [2] [129]

[1] Quintus Curtius, lib. ix. [ii. 6].
[2] *Ibid.* lib. viii. [viii. 27].

BOOK III

SKETCH OF A FEUDAL SYSTEM IN RĀJASTHĀN

CHAPTER 1

Feudalism in Rājasthān.—It is more than doubtful whether any code of civil or criminal jurisprudence ever existed in any of these principalities; though it is certain that none is at this day discoverable in their archives. But there is a martial system peculiar to these Rajput States, so extensive in its operation as to embrace every object of society. This is so analogous to the ancient feudal system of Europe, that I have not hesitated to hazard a comparison between them, with reference to a period when the latter was yet imperfect. Long and attentive observation enables me to give this outline of a system, of which there exists little written evidence. Curiosity originally, and subsequently a sense of public duty (lest I might be a party to injustice), co-operated in inducing me to make myself fully acquainted with the minutiae of this traditionary theory of government; and incidents, apparently trivial in themselves, exposed parts of a widely-extended system, which, though now disjointed, still continue to regulate the actions of extensive communities, and lead to the inference, that at one period it must have attained a certain degree of perfection.

Many years have elapsed since I first entertained these opinions, long before any connexion existed between these States and the British Government; when their geography was little known to us, and their history still less so. At that period I frequently travelled amongst them for amusement, making these objects subservient thereto, and laying the result freely before my Government. I had [130] abundant sources of intelligence to guide me in forming my analogies; Montesquieu, Hume, Millar, Gibbon[1]: but I sought only general resemblances and lineaments similar to those before me. A more perfect, because more familiar picture, has since appeared by an author,[2] who has drawn aside the veil of mystery which covered the subject, owing to its being till then but imperfectly understood. I compared the features of Rajput society with the finished picture of this eloquent writer, and shall be satisfied with having substantiated the claim of these tribes to participation in a system, hitherto deemed to belong exclusively to Europe. I am aware of the danger of hypothesis, and shall advance nothing that I do not accompany by incontestable proofs.

The Tribal System.—The leading features of government amongst semi-barbarous hordes or civilized independent tribes must have a considerable resemblance to each other. In the same stages of society, the wants of men must everywhere be similar, and will produce the analogies which are observed to regulate Tatar hordes or German tribes, Caledonian clans, the Rajput Kula (race), or Jareja Bhayyad (brotherhood). All the countries of Europe participated in the system we denominate feudal; and we can observe it, in various degrees of perfection or deterioration, from the mountains of Caucasus to the Indian Ocean. But it requires a persevering toil, and more discriminating judgement than I possess, to recover all these relics of civilization: yet though time, and still more oppression, have veiled the ancient institutions of Mewar, the mystery may be penetrated, and will discover parts of a system worthy of being rescued from oblivion.

Influence of Muhammadans and Mahrattas.—Mahratta cunning, engrafted on Muhammadan intolerance, had greatly obscured these institutions. The nation itself was passing rapidly away: the remnant which was left had become a matter of calculation, and their records and their laws partook of this general decay. The nation may recover; the physical frame may be renewed; but the *morale* of the society must be recast. In this chaos a casual observer sees nothing to attract notice; the theory of government appears, without any of the dignity which now marks our regular system. Whatever does exist is attributed

[1] *Miscellaneous Works*, vol. iii. [2] Hallam's *Middle Ages*.

to fortuitous causes—to nothing systematic: no fixed principle is discerned, and none is admitted; it is deemed a mechanism without a plan. This opinion is hasty. Attention to distinctions, though often merely nominal [131], will aid us in discovering the outlines of a picture which must at some period have been more finished; when real power, unrestrained by foreign influence, upheld a system, the plan of which was original. It is in these remote regions, so little known to the Western world, and where original manners lie hidden under those of the conquerors, that we may search for the germs of the constitutions of European States.[1] A contempt for all that is Asiatic too often marks our countrymen in the East: though at one period on record the taunt might have been reversed.

In remarking the curious coincidence between the habits, notions, and governments of Europe in the Middle Ages, and those of Rajasthan, it is not absolutely necessary we should conclude that one system was borrowed from the other; each may, in truth, be said to have the patriarchal form for its basis. I have sometimes been inclined to agree with the definition of Gibbon, who styles the system of our ancestors the offspring of chance and barbarism. "Le système féodal, assemblage monstrueux de tant de parties que le tems et l'hazard ont réunies, nous offre un objet très compliqué: pour l'étudier il faut le décomposer."[2] This I shall attempt.

The form, as before remarked, is truly patriarchal in these

[1] It is a high gratification to be supported by such authority as M. St. Martin, who, in his *Discours sur l'Origine et l'Histoire des Arsacides*, thus speaks of the system of government termed feudal, which I contend exists amongst the Rajputs: "On pense assez généralement que cette sorte de gouvernement qui dominait il y a quelques siècles, et qu'on appelle *système féodal*, était particulière à l'Europe, et que c'est dans les forêts de la Germanie qu'il faut en chercher l'origine. Cependant, si au lieu d'admettre les faits sans les discuter, comme il arrive trop souvent, on examinait un peu cette opinion, elle disparaîtrait devant la critique, ou du moins elle se modifierait singulièrement; et l'on verrait que, si c'est des forêts de la Germanie que nous avons tiré le gouvernement féodal, il n'en est certainement pas originaire. Si l'on veut comparer l'Europe, telle qu'elle était au xiie siècle, avec la monarchie fondée en Asie par les Arsacides trois siècles avant notre ère, partout on verra des institutions et des usages pareils. On y trouvera les mêmes dignités, et jusqu'aux mêmes titres, etc., etc. Boire, chasser, combattre, faire et défaire des rois, c'étaient là les nobles occupations d'un Parthe" (*Journal Asiatique*, vol. i. p. 65). It is nearly so with the Rajput.

[2] Gibbon, *Miscell.* vol. iii. Du gouvernement féodal.

States, where the greater portion of the vassal chiefs, from the highest of the sixteen peers to the holders of a *charsa*[1] of land, claim affinity in blood to the sovereign.[2]

The natural seeds are implanted in every soil, but the tree did not gain [132] maturity except in a favoured aspect. The perfection of the system in England is due to the Normans, who brought it from Scandinavia, whither it was probably conveyed by Odin and the Sacasenae, or by anterior migrations, from Asia; which would coincide with Richardson's hypothesis, who contends that it was introduced from Tatary. Although speculative reasoning forms no part of my plan, yet when I observe analogy on the subject in the customs of the ancient German tribes, the Franks or Gothic races, I shall venture to note them. Of one thing there is no doubt—knowledge must have accompanied the tide of migration from the east: and from higher Asia emerged in the Asi, the Chatti, and the Cimbric Lombard, who spread the system in Scandinavia, Friesland, and Italy.

Origin of Feuds.—"It has been very common," says the enlightened historian of the Feudal System in the Middle Ages, "to seek for the origin of feuds, or at least for analogies to them, in the history of various countries; but though it is of great importance to trace the similarity of customs in different parts of the world, we should guard against seeming analogies, which vanish away when they are closely observed. It is easy to find partial resemblances to the feudal system. The relation of patron and client in the republic of Rome has been deemed to resemble it, as well as the barbarians and veterans who held frontier lands on the tenure of defending them and the frontier; but they were

[1] A 'skin or hyde.' Millar (chap. v. p. 85) defines a 'hyde of land,' the quantity which can be cultivated by a single plough. A *charsa*, 'skin or hyde' of land, is as much as one man can water; and what one can water is equal to what one plough can cultivate. If irrigation ever had existence by the founders of the system, we may suppose this the meaning of the term which designated a *knight's fee*. It may have gone westward with emigration. [The English 'hide': "the amount considered adequate for the support of one free family with its dependants: at an early date defined as being as much land as could be tilled by one plough in a year," has no connexion with 'hide,' 'a skin.' It is O.E. *hīd*, from *hiw*, *hig*, 'household." 'Hide,' 'a skin,' is O.E. *hýd* (*New English Dict. ssv.*).]

[2] *Bapji*, 'sire,' is the appellation of royalty, and, strange enough, whether to male or female; while its offsets, which form a numerous branch of vassals, are called *babus*, 'the infants.'

bound not to an individual, but to the state. Such a resemblance of fiefs may be found in the Zamindars of Hindustan and the Timariots of Turkey. The clans of the Highlanders and Irish followed their chieftain into the field: but their tie was that of imagined kindred and birth, not the spontaneous compact of vassalage."[1]

I give this at length to show, that if I still persist in deeming the Rajput system a pure relation of feuds, I have before my eyes the danger of seeming resemblances. But grants, deeds, charters, and traditions, copies of all of which will be found in the Appendix, will establish my opinions. I hope to prove that the tribes in the northern regions of Hindustan did possess the system, and that it was handed down, and still obtains, notwithstanding seven centuries of paramount sway of the Mogul and Pathan dynasties, altogether opposed to them except in this feature of government where there was an original similarity. In some of these States —those least affected by conquest—the system remained freer from innovation. It is, however, from Mewar chiefly that I shall deduce my examples, as its internal [133] rule was less influenced by foreign policy, even to the period at which the imperial power of Delhi was on the decline.

Evidence from Mewar.—As in Europe, for a length of time, traditionary custom was the only regulator of the rights and tenures of this system, varying in each State, and not unfrequently (in its minor details) in the different provinces of one State, according to their mode of acquisition and the description of occupants when required. It is from such circumstances that the variety of tenure and customary law proceeds. To account for this variety, a knowledge of them is requisite; nor is it until every part of the system is developed that it can be fully understood. The most trifling cause is discovered to be the parent of some important result. If ever these were embodied into a code (and we are justified in assuming such to have been the case), the varied revolutions which have swept away almost all relics of their history were not likely to spare these. Mention is made of several princes of the house of Mewar who legislated for their country; but precedents for every occurring case lie scattered in formulas, grants, and traditionary sayings. The inscriptions still existing on stone would alone, if collected, form a body of

[1] Hallam's *Middle Ages*, vol. i. p. 200.

laws sufficient for an infant community; and these were always first committed to writing, and registered ere the column was raised. The seven centuries of turmoil and disaster, during which these States were in continual strife with the foe, produced many princes of high intellect as well as valour. Sanga Rana, and his antagonist, Sultan Babur, were revived in their no less celebrated grandsons, the great Akbar and Rana Partap: the son of the latter, Amra, the foe of Jahangir, was a character of whom the proudest nation might be vain.

Evidence from Inscriptions.—The pen has recorded, and tradition handed down, many isolated fragments of the genius of these Rajput princes, as statesmen and warriors, touching the political division, regulations of the aristocracy, and commercial and agricultural bodies. Sumptuary laws, even, which append to a feudal system, are to be traced in these inscriptions: the annulling of monopolies and exorbitant taxes; the regulation of transit duties; prohibition of profaning sacred days by labour; immunities, privileges, and charters to trades, corporations, and towns; such as would, in climes more favourable to liberty, have matured into a league, or obtained for these branches a voice in the councils of the State. My search for less perishable documents than parchment when I found the cabinet of the prince contained them not, was unceasing; but though the bigoted Muhammadan destroyed [134] most of the traces of civilization within his reach, perseverance was rewarded with a considerable number. They are at least matter of curiosity. They will evince that monopolies and restraints on commerce were well understood in Rajwara, though the doctrines of political economy never gained footing there. The setting up of these engraved tablets or pillars, called Seoras,[1] is of the highest antiquity. Every subject commences with invoking the sun and moon as witnesses, and concludes with a denunciation of the severest penalties on those who break the spirit of the imperishable bond. Tablets of an historical nature I have of twelve and fourteen hundred years' antiquity, but of grants of land or privileges about one thousand years is the oldest. Time has destroyed many, but man more. They became more numerous during the last three centuries, when successful struggles against their foes produced new privileges, granted in order to recall the scattered

[1] Sanskrit, *Sāla*.

inhabitants. Thus one contains an abolition of the monopoly of tobacco;[1] another, the remission of tax on printed cloths, with permission to the country manufacturers to sell their goods free of duty at the neighbouring towns. To a third, a mercantile city, the abolition of war contributions,[2] and the establishment of its internal judicial authority. Nay, even where good manners alone are concerned, the lawgiver appears, and with an amusing simplicity:[3] "From the public feast none shall attempt to carry anything away." "None shall eat after sunset," shows that a Jain obtained the edict. To yoke the bullock or other animal for any work on the sacred Amavas,[4] is also declared punishable. Others contain revocations of vexatious fees to officers of the crown; "of beds and quilts[5]"; "the seizure of the carts, implements, or cattle of the husbandmen,"[6]—the sole boon in our own Magna Charta demanded for the husbandman. These and several others, of which copies are annexed, need not be repeated. If even from such memoranda a sufficient number could be collected of each prince's reign up to the olden time, what more could we desire to enable us to judge of the genius of their princes, the wants and habits of the people, their acts and occupations? The most ancient written customary law of France is A.D. 1088,[7] at which time Mewar was in high [135] prosperity; opposing, at the head of a league far more powerful than France could form for ages after, the progress of revolution and foreign conquest. Ignorance, sloth, and all the vices which wait on and result from continual oppression in a perpetual struggle for existence of ages' duration, gradually diminished the reverence of the inhabitants themselves for these relics of the wisdom of their forefathers. In latter years, they so far forgot the ennobling feeling and respect for 'the stone which told' their once exalted condition, as to convert the materials of the temple in which many of these stood into places of abode. Thus many a valuable relic is built up in the castles of their barons, or buried in the rubbish of the fallen pile.

[1] See Appendix, No. XII.
[2] See Appendix, No. XIII.
[3] See Appendix, No. XIV.
[4] 'Full moon' (See Appendix, No. XIII.).
[5] It is customary, when officers of the Government are detached on service, to exact from the towns where they are sent both bed and board.
[6] Seized for public service, and frequently to exact a composition in money.
[7] Hallam, vol. i. p. 197.

Books of Grants.—We have, however, the books of grants to the chiefs and vassals, and also the grand rent-roll of the country. These are of themselves valuable documents. Could we but obtain those of remoter periods, they would serve as a commentary on the history of the country, as each contains the detail of every estate, and the stipulated service, in horse and foot, to be performed for it. In later times, when turbulence and disaffection went unpunished, it was useless to specify a stipulation of service that was nugatory; and too often the grants contained but the names of towns and villages, and their value; or if they had the more general terms of service, none of its details.[1] From all these, however, a sufficiency of customary rules could easily be found to form the written law of fiefs in Rajasthan. In France, in the sixteenth century, the variety of these customs amounted to two hundred and eighty-five, of which only sixty[2] were of great importance. The number of consequence in Mewar which have come to my observation is considerable, and the most important will be given in the Appendix. Were the same plan pursued there as in that ordinance which produced the laws of Pays Coutumiers[3] of France, viz. ascertaining those of each district, the materials are ready.

Such a collection would be amusing, particularly if the traditionary were added to the engraved laws. They would often appear jejune, and might involve contradictions; but we should see the wants of the people; and if ever our connexion (which God forbid!) should be drawn closer, we could then legislate without offending national customs or religious prejudices. Could this, by any instinctive [136] impulse or external stimulus, be effected by themselves, it would be the era of their emersion from long oppression, and might lead to better notions of government, and consequent happiness to them all.

Noble Origin of the Rājput Race.—If we compare the antiquity and illustrious descent of the dynasties which have ruled, and some which continue to rule, the small sovereignties of Rajasthan, with many of celebrity in Europe, superiority will often attach to the Rajput. From the most remote periods we can trace nothing ignoble, nor any vestige of vassal origin. Reduced in

[1] Some of these, of old date, I have seen three feet in length.

[2] Hallam, vol. i. p. 199.

[3] Hallam notices these laws by this technical phrase.

power, circumscribed in territory, compelled to yield much of their splendour and many of the dignities of birth, they have not abandoned an iota of the pride and high bearing arising from a knowledge of their illustrious and regal descent. On this principle the various revolutions in the Rana's family never encroached; and the mighty Jahangir himself, the Emperor of the Moguls, became, like Caesar, the commentator on the history of the tribe of Sesodia.[1] The potentate of the twenty-two Satrapies of Hind dwells with proud complacency on this Rajput king having made terms with him. He praises heaven, that what his immortal ancestor Babur, the founder of the Mogul dynasty, failed to do, the project in which Humayun had also failed, and in which the illustrious Akbar, his father, had but partial success, was reserved for him. It is pleasing to peruse in the commentaries of these conquerors, Babur and Jahangir, their sentiments with regard to these princes. We have the evidence of Sir Thomas Roe, the ambassador of Elizabeth to Jahangir, as to the splendour of this race: it appears throughout their annals and those of their neighbours.

The Rāthors of Mārwār.—The Rathors can boast a splendid pedigree; and if we cannot trace its source with equal certainty to such a period of antiquity as the Rana's, we can, at all events, show the Rathor monarch wielding the sceptre at Kanauj, at the time the leader of an unknown tribe of the Franks was paving the way towards the foundation of the future kingdom of France. Unwieldy greatness caused the sudden fall of Kanauj in the twelfth century, of which the existing line of Marwar is a renovated scion.[2]

The Kachhwāhas of Amber.—Amber is a branch of the once illustrious and ancient [137] Nishadha, now Narwar, which produced the ill-fated prince whose story[3] is so interesting. Revolution and conquest compelled them to quit their ancestral abodes. Hindustan was then divided into no more than four great kingdoms. By Arabian[4] travellers we have a confused picture of

[1] Sesodia is the last change of name which the Rana's race has undergone. It was first Suryavansa, then Grahilot or Guhilot, Aharya, and Sesodia. These changes arise from revolutions and local circumstances.

[2] [The Rāthor dynasty of Kanauj is a myth (Smith, *EHI*, 385).]

[3] Nala and Damayanti.

[4] *Relations anciennes des Voyageurs*, par Renaudot.

these States. But all the minor States, now existing in the west, arose about the period when the feudal system was approaching maturity in France and England.

The others are less illustrious, being the descendants of the great vassals of their ancient kings.

The Sesodias of Mewār.—Mewar exhibits a marked difference from all the other States in her policy and institutions. She was an old-established dynasty when these renovated scions were in embryo. We can trace the losses of Mewar, but with difficulty her acquisitions; while it is easy to note the gradual aggrandisement of Marwar and Amber, and all the minor States. Marwar was composed of many petty States, whose ancient possessions formed an allodial vassalage under the new dynasty. A superior independence of the control of the prince arises from the peculiarity of the mode of acquisition; that is, with rights similar to the allodial vassals of the European feudal system.

Pride of Ancestry.—The poorest Rajput of this day retains all the pride of ancestry, often his sole inheritance; he scorns to hold the plough, or to use his lance but on horseback. In these aristocratic ideas he is supported by his reception amongst his superiors, and the respect paid to him by his inferiors. The honours and privileges, and the gradations of rank, amongst the vassals of the Rana's house, exhibit a highly artificial and refined state of society. Each of the superior rank is entitled to a banner, kettle-drums preceded by heralds and silver maces, with peculiar gifts and personal honours, in commemoration of some exploit of their ancestors.

Armorial Bearings.—The martial Rajputs are not strangers to armorial bearings,[1] now so indiscriminately used in Europe.

[1] It is generally admitted that armorial bearings were little known till the period of the Crusades, and that they belong to the east. The twelve tribes of Israel were distinguished by the animals on their banners, and the sacred writings frequently allude to the 'Lion of Judah.' The peacock was a favourite armorial emblem of the Rajput warrior; it is the bird sacred to their Mars (Kumara), as it was to Juno, his mother, in the west. The feather of the peacock decorates the turban of the Rajput and the warrior of the Crusade, adopted from the Hindu through the Saracens. "Le paon a toujours été l'emblême de la noblesse. Plusieurs chevaliers ornaient leurs casques des plumes de cet oiseau; un grand nombre de familles nobles le portaient dans leur blazon ou sur leur cimier; quelques-uns n'en portaient que la queue" (Art. "Armoirie," *Dict. de l'ancien Régime*).

The great banner of Mewar exhibits a golden sun [138] on a crimson field; those of the chiefs bear a dagger. Amber displays the *panchranga*, or five-coloured flag. The lion rampant on an argent field is extinct with the State of Chanderi.[1]

In Europe these customs were not introduced till the period of the Crusades, and were copied from the Saracens; while the use of them amongst the Rajput tribes can be traced to a period anterior to the war of Troy. In the Mahabharat, or great war, twelve hundred years before Christ, we find the hero Bhishma exulting over his trophy, the banner of Arjuna, its field adorned with the figure of the Indian Hanuman.[2] These emblems had a religious reference amongst the Hindus, and were taken from their mythology, the origin of all devices.

The Tribal Palladium.—Every royal house has its palladium, which is frequently borne to battle at the saddle-bow of the prince. Rao Bhima Hara, of Kotah, lost his life and protecting deity together. The late celebrated Khichi [3] leader, Jai Singh, never took the field without the god before him. 'Victory to Bajrang' was his signal for the charge so dreaded by the Mahratta, and often has the deity been sprinkled with his blood and that of the foe. Their ancestors, who opposed Alexander, did the same, and carried the image of Hercules (*Baldeva*) at the head of their array.[4]

Banners.—The custom (says Arrian) of presenting banners as an emblem of sovereignty over vassals, also obtained amongst the tribes of the Indus when invaded by Alexander. When he conquered the Saka and tribes east of the Caspian, he divided the provinces amongst the princes of the ancient families, for which they paid homage, engaged to serve with a certain quota of troops, and received from his own hand a banner; in all of which he followed the customs of the country. But in these we see only the outline of the system; we must descend to more

[1] I was the first European who traversed this wild country, in 1807, not without some hazard. It was then independent: about three years after it fell a prey to Sindhia. [Several ancient dynasties used a crest (*lânchhana*), and a banner (*dhvaja*): see the list in *BG*, i. Part ii. 299.]

[2] The monkey-deity. [Known as Bajrang, Skt. vajranga, 'of powerful frame.']

[3] The Khichis are a branch of the Chauhans, and Khichiwara lies east of Haravati.

[4] [Quintus Curtius, viii. 14, 46; Arrian, *Indika*, viii.]

modern days to observe it more minutely. A grand picture is drawn of the power of Mewar, when the first grand irruption of the Muhammadans occurred in the first century of their era; when "a hundred[1] kings, its allies and dependents, had their thrones raised in Chitor," for its defence and their own individually [139], when a new religion, propagated by the sword of conquest, came to enslave these realms. This invasion was by Sind and Makran; for it was half a century later ere 'the light' shone from the heights of Pamir[2] on the plains of the Jumna and Ganges.

From the commencement of this religious war in the mountains westward of the Indus, many ages elapsed ere the 'King of the Faith' obtained a seat on the throne of Yudhishthira. Chand, the bard, has left us various valuable memorials of this period, applicable to the subject historically as well as to the immediate topic. Visaladeva, the monarch whose name appears on the pillar of victory at Delhi, led an army against the invader, in which, according to the bard, "the banners of eighty-four princes were assembled." The bard describes with great animation the summons sent for this magnificent feudal levy from the heart of Antarbedi,[3] to the shores of the western sea, and it coincides with the record of his victory, which most probably this very army obtained for him. But no finer picture of feudal manners exists than the history of Prithwiraja, contained in Chand's poems. It is surprising that this epic should have been allowed so long to sleep neglected: a thorough knowledge of it, and of others of the same character, would open many sources of new knowledge, and enable us to trace many curious and interesting coincidences.[4]

[1] See Annals of Mewar, and note from D'Anville.

[2] The Pamir range is a grand branch of the Indian Caucasus. Chand, the bard, designates them as the "Parbat Pat Pamir," or Pamir Lord of Mountains. From Pahār and Pamir the Greeks may have compounded Paropanisos, in which was situated the most remote of the Alexandrias. [?]

[3] The space between the grand rivers Ganges and Jumna, well known as the Duab.

[4] Domestic habits and national manners are painted to the life, and no man can well understand the Rajput of yore who does not read these. Those were the days of chivalry and romance, when the assembled princes contended for the hand of the fair, who chose her own lord, and threw to the object of her choice, in full court, the *barmala*, or garland of marriage. Those were the days which the Rajput yet loves to talk of, when the glance

In perusing these tales of the days that are past, we should be induced to conclude that the Kuriltai of the Tatars, the Chaugan of the Rajput, and the Champ de Mars of the Frank, had one common origin.

Influence of Caste.—Caste has for ever prevented the inferior classes of society from being incorporated with this haughty *noblesse*. Only those of pure blood in both lines can hold fiefs of the crown. The highest may marry the daughter of a Rajput, whose sole [140] possession is a 'skin of land':[1] the sovereign himself is not degraded by such alliance. There is no moral blot, and the operation of a law like the Salic would prevent any political evil resulting therefrom. Titles are granted, and even fiefs of office, to ministers and civil servants not Rajputs; they are, however, but official, and never confer hereditary right. These official fiefs may have originally arisen, here and in Europe, from the same cause; the want of a circulating medium to pay the offices. The Mantris[2] of Mewar prefer estates to pecuniary stipend, which gives more consequence in every point of view. All the higher offices—as cup-bearer, butler, stewards of the household, wardrobe, kitchen, master of the horse—all these are enumerated as ministerialists[3] at the court of Charlemagne in the dark ages of Europe, and of whom we have the duplicates. These are what the author of the Middle Ages designates as "improper feuds."[4] In Mewar the prince's architect, painter, physician, bard, genealogist, heralds, and all the generation of the foster-brothers, hold lands. Offices are hereditary in this patriarchal government; their services personal. The title even appends to the family, and if the chance of events deprive them of the substance, they are seldom left destitute. It is not uncommon to see three or four with the title of pardhan or premier.[5]

---

of an eye weighed with a sceptre: when three things alone occupied him: his horse, his lance, and his mistress; for she is but the third in his estimation, after all: to the two first he owed her.

[1] Charsa, a 'hide or skin' [see p. 156 above].

[2] 'Ministers,' from *Mantra*, 'mystification' ['a sacred text, spell'].

[3] It is probably of Teutonic origin, and akin to *Mantri*, which embraces all the ministers and councillors of loyalty (Hallam, p. 195). [?]

[4] Hallam, p. 193.

[5] One I know, in whose family the office has remained since the period of Prithwiraja, who transferred his ancestor to the service of the Rana's

But before I proceed further in these desultory and general remarks, I shall commence the chief details of the system as described in times past, and, in part, still obtaining in the principality of the Rana of Mewar As its geography and distribution are fully related in their proper place, I must refer the reader to that for a preliminary understanding of its localities.

Estates of Chief and Fiscal Land.—The local disposition of the estates was admirably contrived. Bounded on three sides, the south, east, and west, by marauding barbarous tribes of Bhils, Mers, and Minas, the circumference of this circle was subdivided into estates for the chiefs, while the *khalisa*, or fiscal land, the best and richest, was in the heart of the country, and consequently well protected [141]. It appears doubtful whether the khalisa lands amounted to one-fourth of those distributed in grant to the chiefs. The value of the crown demesne as the nerve and sinew of sovereignty, was well known by the former heads of this house. To obtain any portion thereof was the reward of important services; to have a grant of a few acres near the capital for a garden was deemed a high favour; and a village in the amphitheatre or valley, in which the present capital is situated, was the *ne plus ultra* of recompense. But the lavish folly of the present prince, out of this tract, twenty-five miles in circumference, has not preserved a single village in his khalisa. By this distribution, and by the inroads of the wild tribes in the vicinity, or of Moguls and Mahrattas, the valour of the chiefs were kept in constant play.

The country was partitioned into districts, each containing from fifty to one hundred towns and villages, though sometimes exceeding that proportion. The great number of Chaurasis [1] leads to the conclusion that portions to the amount of eighty-four had been the general subdivision. Many of these yet remain:

---

house seven hundred years ago. He is not merely a nominal hereditary minister, for his uncle actually held the office; but in consequence of having favoured the views of a pretender to the crown, its active duties are not entrusted to any of the family.

[1] The numeral eighty-four. [In the ancient Hindu kingdoms the full estate was a group of 84 villages, smaller units being called Byālisa, 42, or Ch ubīsa, 24 (Baden-Powell, *The Village Community*, 198, and see a valuable article in Elliot, *Supplemental Glossary*, 178 ff.]

as the 'Chaurasi' of Jahazpur and of Kumbhalmer: tantamount to the old 'hundreds' of our Saxon ancestry. A circle of posts was distributed, within which the quotas of the chiefs attended, under 'the Faujdar of the Sima' (*vulgo* Sim), or commander of the border. It was found expedient to appoint from court this lord of the frontier, always accompanied by a portion of the royal insignia, standard, kettle-drums, and heralds, and being generally a civil officer, he united to his military office the administration of justice.[1] The higher vassals never attended personally at these posts, but deputed a confidential branch of their family, with the quota required. For the government of the districts there were conjoined a civil and a military officer: the latter generally a vassal of the second rank. Their residence was the chief place of the district, commonly a stronghold.

The division of the chiefs into distinct grades, shows a highly artificial state of society.

First class.—We have the Sixteen, whose estates were from fifty thousand to one hundred thousand rupees and upwards, of yearly rent. These appear in the [142] presence only on special invitation, upon festivals and solemn ceremonies, and are the hereditary councillors of the crown.[2]

Second class, from five to fifty thousand rupees. Their duty is to be always in attendance. From these, chiefly, faujdars and military officers are selected.[2]

Third class is that of Gol [2] holding lands chiefly under five thousand rupees, though by favour they may exceed this limit. They are generally the holders of separate villages and portions of land, and in former times they were the most useful class to the prince. They always attended on his person, and indeed formed his strength against any combination or opposition of the higher vassals.

Fourth class.—The offsets of the younger branches of the Rana's own family, within a certain period, are called the *babas*, literally 'infants,' and have appanages bestowed on them. Of

[1] Now each chief claims the right of administering justice in his own domain, that is, in civil matters; but in criminal cases they ought not without the special sanction of the crown. Justice, however, has long been left to work its own way, and the self-constituted tribunals, the panchayats, sit in judgment in all cases where property is involved.

[2] See Appendix, No. XX.

this class are Shahpura and Banera; too powerful for subjects.[1] They hold on none of the terms of the great clans, but consider themselves at the disposal of the prince. These are more within the influence of the crown. Allowing adoption into these houses, except in the case of near kindred, is assuredly an innovation; they ought to revert to the crown, failing immediate issue, as did the great estate of Bhainsrorgarh, two generations back. From these to the holder of a *charsa*, or hide of land, the peculiarity of tenure and duties of each will form a subject for discussion.

Revenues and Rights of the Crown.—I need not here expatiate upon the variety of items which constitute the revenues of the prince, the details of which will appear in their proper place. The land-tax in the khalisa demesne is, of course, the chief source of supply; the transit duties on commerce and trade, and those of the larger towns and commercial marts, rank next. In former times more attention was paid to this important branch of income, and the produce was greater because less shackled. The liberality on the side of the crown was only equalled by the integrity of the merchant, and the extent to which it was carried would imply an almost Utopian degree of perfection in their mutual qualities of liberality and honesty; the one, perhaps, generating the other. The remark of a merchant recently, on the vexatious train of duties and espionage attending their collection, is not merely figurative: "our ancestors tied their invoice to the horns of the oxen[2] at the first frontier post of customs, and no intermediate questions [143] were put till we passed to the opposite or sold our goods, when it was opened and payment made accordingly; but now every town has its rights." It will be long ere this degree of confidence is restored on either side; extensive demand on the one is met by fraud and evasion on the other, though at least one-half of these evils have already been subdued.

Mines and Minerals.—The mines were very productive in former times, and yielded several lacs to the princes of Mewar.[3]

[1] [They are heads of the Rānāwat sub-tribe. The latter enjoys the right, on succession, of having a sword sent to him with full honours, on receipt of which he goes to Udaipur to be installed (Erskine ii. A. 92).]

[2] Oxen and carts are chiefly used in the *Tandas*, or caravans, for transportation of goods in these countries; camels further to the north.

[3] [On the mines of Mewār, see *IA*, i. 63 f.]

The rich tin mines of Jawara produced at one time a considerable proportion of silver. Those of copper are abundant, as is also iron on the now alienated domain on the Chambal; but lead least of all.[1]

The marble quarries also added to the revenue; and where there is such a multiplicity of sources, none are considered too minute to be applied in these necessitous times.

Barār.—*Barar* is an indefinite term for taxation, and is connected with the thing taxed: as *ghanim-barar*,[2] 'war-tax'; *ghar ginti-barar*,[3] 'house-tax'; *hal-barar*, 'plough-tax'; *neota-barar*, 'marriage-tax'; and others, both of old and new standing. The war-tax was a kind of substitute for the regular mode of levying the rents on the produce of the soil; which was rendered very difficult during the disturbed period, and did not accord with the wants of the prince. It is also a substitute in those mountainous regions, for the *jarib*,[4] where the produce bears no proportion to the cultivated surface; sometimes from poverty of soil, but often from the reverse, as in Kumbhalmer, where the choicest crops are produced on the cultivated terraces, and on the sides of its mountains, which abound with springs, yielding the richest canes and cottons, and where experiment has proved that four crops can be raised in the same patch of soil within the year.

The offering on confirmation of estates (or fine on renewal) is now, though a very small, yet still one source of supply; as is the annual and triennial payment of the quit-rents of the Bhumia chiefs. Fines in composition of offences may also be mentioned; and they might be larger, if more activity were introduced in the detection of offenders [144].

These governments are mild in the execution of the laws;

[1] The privilege of coining is a reservation of royalty. No subject is allowed to coin gold or silver, though the Salumbar chief has on sufferance a copper currency. The mint was a considerable source of income, and may be again when confidence is restored and a new currency introduced. The Chitor rupee is now thirty-one per cent inferior to the old Bhilara standard, and there was one struck at the capital even worse, and very nearly as bad as the *moneta nigra* of Philip the Fair of France, who allowed his vassals the privilege of coining it. [For an account of the past and present coinage of Mewār, see W. W. Webb, *Currencies of the Hindu States of Rajputana*, 3 ff.]

[2] Enemy.

[3] Numbering of houses.

[4] A measure of land [usually 55 English yards].

and a heavy fine has more effect (especially on the hill tribes) than the execution of the offender, who fears death less than the loss of property.

Khar-Lakar.—The composition for 'wood and forage' afforded a considerable supply. When the princes of Mewar were oftener in the tented field than in the palace, combating for their preservation, it was the duty of every individual to store up wood and forage for the supply of the prince's army. What originated in necessity was converted into an abuse and annual demand. The towns also supplied a certain portion of provisions; where the prince halted for the day these were levied on the community; a goat or sheep from the shepherd, milk and flour from the farmer. The maintenance of these customs is observable in taxes, for the origin of which it is impossible to assign a reason without going into the history of the period; they scarcely recollect the source of some of these themselves. They are akin to those known under the feudal tenures of France, arising from exactly the same causes, and commuted for money payments; such as the *droit de giste et de chevauche.*[1] Many also originated in the perambulations of these princes to visit their domains;[2] a black year in the calendar to the chief and the subject. When he honoured the chief by a visit, he had to present horses and arms, and to entertain his prince, in all which honours the cultivators and merchants had to share. The duties on the sale of spirits, opium, tobacco, and even to a share of the garden-stuff, affords also modes of supply [145].[3]

CHAPTER 2

Legislative Authority.—During the period still called 'the good times of Mewar,' the prince, with the aid of his civil council, the four ministers of the crown and their deputies, promulgated all the legislative enactments in which the general rights and wants of the community were involved. In these the martial vassals

[1] Hallam, vol. i. p. 232.

[2] Hume describes the necessity for our earlier kings making these tours to consume the produce, being in kind. So it is in Mewar; but I fancy the supply was always too easily convertible into circulating medium to be the cause there.

[3] See Appendix, No. X.

or chiefs had no concern : a wise exclusion, comprehending also their immediate dependents, military, commercial, and agricultural. Even now, the little that is done in these matters is effected by the civil administration, though the Rajput Pardhans have been too apt to interfere in matters from which they ought always to be kept aloof, being ever more tenacious of their own rights than solicitous for the welfare of the community.

Panchāyats.—The neglect in the legislation of late years was supplied by the self-constituted tribunals, the useful panchayats, of which enough has been said to render further illustration unnecessary. Besides the resident ruler of the district, who was also a judicial functionary, there was, as already stated, a special officer of the government in each frontier thana, or garrison post. He united the triple occupation of embodying the quotas, levying the transit duties, and administering justice, in which he was aided at the chabutra [1] or court, by assembling the Chauthias or assessors of justice. Each town and village has its chauthia, the members of which are elected by their fellow-citizens, and remain as long as they conduct themselves impartially in disentangling the intricacies of complaints preferred to them.

They are the aids to the Nagarseth, or chief magistrate, an hereditary office in every large city in Rajasthan. Of this chauthia the Patel and Patwari [2] are generally members. The former of these, like the Dasaundhi of the Mahrattas, resembles in his duties the decanus of France and the tithing-man in England. The chauthia and panchayat of these districts are analogous to the assessors of [146] justice called *scabini* [3] in France, who held the office by election or the concurrence of the people. But these are the special and fixed council of each town; the general panchayats are formed from the respectable population at large, and were formerly from all classes of society.

The chabutras, or terraces of justice, were always established in the khalisa, or crown demesne. It was deemed a humiliating intrusion if they sat within the bounds of a chief. To 'erect the flag' within his limits, whether for the formation of defensive posts or the collection of duties, is deemed a gross breach of his

[1] Literally 'terrace,' or 'altar.'

[2] [Headman and accountant.]

[3] They were considered a sort of jury, bearing a close analogy to the *judices selecti*, who sat with the praetor in the tribunal of Rome (Hallam).

privileged independence, as to establish them within the walls of his residence would be deemed equal to sequestration. It often becomes necessary to see justice enforced on a chief or his dependent, but it begets eternal disputes and disobedience, till at length they are worried to compliance by rozina.

Rozīna.—When delay in these matters, or to the general commands of the prince, is evinced, an officer or herald is deputed with a party of four, ten, or twenty horse or foot, to the fief of the chief, at whose residence they take up their abode; and carrying, under the seal, a warrant to furnish them with specified daily (*rozina*) rations, they live at free quarters till he is quickened into compliance with the commands of the prince. This is the only accelerator of the slow movements of a Rajput chieftain in these days, whether for his appearance at court or the performance of an act of justice. It is often carried to a harassing excess, and causes much complaint.

In cases regarding the distribution of justice or the internal economy of the chief's estates, the government officers seldom interfere. But of their panchayats I will only remark, that their import amongst the vassals is very comprehensive; and when they talk of the '*panch*,' it means the 'collective wisdom.' In the reply to the remonstrance of the Deogarh vassals,[1] the chief promises never to undertake any measure without their deliberation and sanction.

On all grand occasions where the general peace or tranquillity of the government is threatened, the chiefs form the council of the sovereign. Such subjects are always first discussed in the domestic councils of each chief; so that when the [147] *witenagemot* of Mewar was assembled, each had prepared himself by previous discussion, and was fortified by abundance of advice.

To be excluded the council of the prince is to be in utter disgrace. These grand divans produce infinite speculation, and the ramifications which form the opinions are extensive. The council of each chief is, in fact, a miniature representation of the sovereign's. The greater sub-vassals, his civil pardhan, the mayor of the household, the purohit,[2] the bard, and two or three of the most intelligent citizens, form the minor councils, and all are separately deliberating while the superior court is in discussion. Thus is collected the wisdom of the magnates of Rajwara.

[1] See Appendix, No. III. [2] Family priest.

Military Service.—In Mewar, during the days of her glory and prosperity, fifteen thousand horse, bound by the ties of fidelity and service, followed their prince into the field, all supported by lands held by grant; from the chief who headed five hundred of his own vassals, to the single horseman.

Knight's Fee or Single Horsemen.—A knight's fee in these States varies. For each thousand rupees of annual rent, never less than two, and generally three horsemen were furnished; and sometimes three horse and three foot soldiers, according to the exigencies of the times when the grant was conferred. The different grants [1] appended will show this variety, and furnish additional proof that this, and all similar systems of policy, must be much indebted to chance for the shape they ultimately take. The knight's fee, when William the Conqueror partitioned England into sixty thousand such portions, from each of which a soldier's service was due, was fixed at £20. Each portion furnished its soldier or paid escuage. The knight's fee of Mewar may be said to be two hundred and fifty rupees, or about £30.

Limitations of Service.—In Europe, service was so restricted that the monarch had but a precarious authority. He could only calculate upon forty days' annual service from the tenant of a knight's fee. In Rajasthan it is very different: "at home and abroad, service shall be performed when demanded"; such is the condition of the tenure.

For state and show, a portion of the greater vassals [2] reside at the capital for [148] some months, when they have permission to retire to their estates, and are relieved by another portion. On the grand military festival the whole attend for a given time; and when the prince took the field, the whole assembled at their own charge; but if hostilities carried them beyond the frontier they were allowed certain rations.

Escuage or Scutage.—Escuage or scutage, the phrase in Europe to denote the amercement [3] for non-attendance, is also known and exemplified in deeds. Failure from disaffection, turbulence, or pride, brought a heavy fine; the sequestration of the whole or part of the estate.[4] The princes of these States

[1] See Appendix, Nos. IV. V. and VI.

[2] See Appendix, No. XX. art. 6; the treaty between the chiefs and his vassals defining service.

[3] Appendix, No. XVI.

[4] Both of which I have witnessed.

would willingly desire to see escuage more general. All have made this first attempt towards an approximation to a standing army; but, though the chiefs would make compensation to get rid of some particular service, they are very reluctant to renounce lands, by which alone a fixed force could be maintained. The rapacity of the court would gladly fly to scutages, but in the present impoverished state of the fiefs, such if injudiciously levied would be almost equivalent to resumption; but this measure is so full of difficulty as to be almost impracticable.

Inefficiency of this Form of Government.—Throughout Rajasthan the character and welfare of the States depend on that of the sovereign: he is the mainspring of the system—the active power to set and keep in motion all these discordant materials; if he relax, each part separates, and moves in a narrow sphere of its own. Yet will the impulse of one great mind put the machine in regular movement, which shall endure during two or three imbecile successors, if no fresh exterior force be applied to check it. It is a system full of defects; yet we see them so often balanced by virtues, that we are alternately biassed by these counteracting qualities; loyalty and patriotism, which combine a love of the institutions, religion, and manners of the country, are the counterpoise to systematic evil. In no country has the system ever proved efficient. It has been one of eternal excitement and irregular action; inimical to order, and the repose deemed necessary after conflict for recruiting the national strength. The absence of an external foe was but the signal for disorders within, which increased to a terrific height in the feuds of the two great rival factions of Mewar, the clans of [149] Chondawat [1] and Saktawat,[2] as the weakness of the prince augmented by the abstraction of his personal domain, and the diminution of the services of the third class of vassals (the Gol), the personal retainers of the crown; but when these feuds broke out, even with the enemy at their gates, it required a prince of great nerve and talent to regulate them. Yet is there a redeeming quality in the

[1] A clan called after Chonda, eldest son of an ancient Rana, who resigned his birthright.

[2] Sakta was the son of Rana Udai Singh, founder of Udayapura, or Udaipur. The feuds of these two clans, like those of the Armagnacs and Bourguignons, "qui couvrirent la France d'un crêpe sanglant," have been the destruction of Mewar. It requires but a change of names and places, while reading the one, to understand perfectly the history of the other.

system, which, imperfect as it is, could render such perilous circumstances but the impulse to a rivalry of heroism.

Rivalry of the Chondāwat and Saktāwat Sub-clans.—When Jahangir had obtained possession of the palladium of Mewar, the ancient fortress of Chitor, and driven the prince into the wilds and mountains of the west, an opportunity offered to recover some frontier lands in the plains, and the Rana with all his chiefs was assembled for the purpose. But the Saktawats asserted an equal privilege with their rivals to form the vanguard;[1] a right which their indisputable valour (perhaps superior to that of the other party) rendered not invalid. The Chondawats claimed it as an hereditary privilege, and the sword would have decided the matter but for the tact of the prince. "The harawal to the clan which first enters Untala," was a decision which the Saktawat leader quickly heard; while the other could no longer plead his right, when such a gauntlet was thrown down for its maintenance.

Untala is the frontier fortress in the plains, about eighteen miles east of the capital, and covering the road which leads from it to the more ancient one of Chitor. It is situated on a rising ground, with a stream flowing beneath its walls, which are of solid masonry, lofty, and with round towers at intervals.[2] In the centre was the governor's house, also fortified. One gate only gave admission to this castle.

The clans, always rivals in power, now competitors in glory, moved off at the same time, some hours before daybreak—Untala the goal, the harawal the reward! Animated with hope—a barbarous and cruel foe the object of their prowess—their wives and families spectators, on their return, of the meed of enterprise; the bard [150], who sang the praise of each race at their outset, demanding of each materials for a new wreath, supplied every stimulus that a Rajput could have to exertion.

The Saktawats made directly for the gateway, which they reached as the day broke, and took the foe unprepared; but the walls were soon manned, and the action commenced. The Chondawats, less skilled in topography, had traversed a swamp, which retarded them—but through which they dashed, fortunately meeting a guide in a shepherd of Untala. With more foresight than their opponents, they had brought ladders. The

[1] Harāwal.

[2] It is now in ruins, but the towers and part of the walls are still standing.

chief led the escalade, but a ball rolled him back amidst his vassals; it was not his destiny to lead the harawal! Each party was checked. The Saktawat depended on the elephant he rode, to gain admission by forcing the gate; but its projecting spikes deterred the animal from applying its strength. His men were falling thick around him, when a shout from the other party made him dread their success. He descended from his seat, placed his body on the spikes, and commanded the driver, on pain of instant death, to propel the elephant against him. The gates gave way, and over the dead body of their chief his clan rushed to the combat! But even this heroic surrender of his life failed to purchase the honour for his clan. The lifeless corpse of his rival was already in Untala, and this was the event announced by the shout which urged his sacrifice to honour and ambition. When the Chondawat chief fell, the next in rank and kin took the command. He was one of those arrogant, reckless Rajputs, who signalized themselves wherever there was danger, not only against men but tigers, and his common appellation was the Benda Thakur ('mad chief') of Deogarh. When his leader fell, he rolled the body in his scarf; then tying it on his back, scaled the wall, and with his lance having cleared the way before him he threw the dead body over the parapet of Untala, shouting, "The vanguard to the Chondawat! we are first in!" The shout was echoed by the clan, and the rampart was in their possession nearly at the moment of the entry of the Saktawats. The Moguls fell under their swords: the standard of Mewar was erected in the castle of Untala, but the leading of the vanguard remained with the Chondawats[1] [151].

This is not the sole instance of such jealousies being converted

[1] An anecdote appended by my friend Amra (the bard of the Sangawats, a powerful division of the Chondawats, whose head is Deogarh, often alluded to, and who alone used to lead two thousand vassals into the field) was well attested. Two Mogul chiefs of note were deeply engaged in a game of chess when the tumult was reported to them. Feeling confident of success, they continued their game; nor would they desist till the inner castle of this 'donjon keep' was taken, and they were surrounded by the Rajputs, when they coolly begged they might be allowed to terminate their game. This the enemy granted; but the loss of their chiefs had steeled their breasts against mercy, and they were afterwards put to death. [Compare the similar case of Ganga, Rāja of Mysore, who was surprised, by the treachery of his ministers, while occupied in a game of chess (L. Rice, *Mysore Gazetteer* (1897), i. 319.]

into a generous and patriotic rivalry; many others could be adduced throughout the greater principalities, but especially amongst the brave Rathors of Marwar.

It was a nice point to keep these clans poised against each other; their feuds were not without utility, and the tact of the prince frequently turned them to account. One party was certain to be enlisted on the side of the sovereign, and this alone counterbalanced the evil tendencies before described. To this day it has been a perpetual struggle for supremacy; and the epithets of 'loyalist' and 'traitor' have been alternating between them for centuries, according to the portion they enjoyed of the prince's favour, and the talents and disposition of the heads of the clans to maintain their predominance at court. The Saktawats are weaker in numbers, but have the reputation of greater bravery and more genius than their rivals. I am inclined, on the whole, to assent to this opinion; and the very consciousness of this reputation must be a powerful incentive to its preservation.

When all these governments were founded and maintained on the same principle, a system of feuds, doubtless, answered very well; but it cannot exist with a well-constituted monarchy. Where individual will controls the energies of a nation, it must eventually lose its liberties. To preserve their power, the princes of Rajasthan surrendered a portion of theirs to the emperors of Delhi. They made a nominal surrender to him of their kingdoms receiving them back with a sanad, or grant, renewed on each lapse: thereby acknowledging him as lord paramount. They received, on these occasions, the khilat of honour and investiture, consisting of elephants, horses, arms, and jewels; and to their hereditary title of 'prince' was added by the emperor, one of dignity, *mansab*.[1] Besides this acknowledgment of supremacy, they offered *nazarana*[2] and homage, especially on the festival of Nauroz (the new year), engaging to attend the royal presence when required, at the head of a stipulated number of their vassals. The emperor presented them with a royal standard, kettle-drums, and other insignia, which headed the array of each prince. Here we have all the chief incidents of a great feudal sovereignty. Whether the Tatar sovereigns borrowed these customs from their

[1] ['Office, prerogative.' For a full account of the Mansab system, see Irvine, *Army of the Indian Moghuls*, 3 ff.]

[2] Fine of relief.

princely vassals, or brought them from the highlands of Asia, from the Oxus [152] and Jaxartes, whence, there is little doubt, many of these Sachha Rajputs originated, shall be elsewhere considered.

Akbar's Policy towards the Rājputs.—The splendour of such an array, whether in the field or at the palace, can scarcely be conceived. Though Humayun had gained the services of some of the Rajput princes, their aid was uncertain. It was reserved for his son, the wise and magnanimous Akbar, to induce them to become at once the ornament and support of his throne. The power which he consolidated, and knew so well to wield, was irresistible; while the beneficence of his disposition, and the wisdom of his policy, maintained what his might conquered. He felt that a constant exhibition of authority would not only be ineffectual but dangerous, and that the surest hold on their fealty and esteem would be the giving them a personal interest in the support of the monarchy.

Alliances between Moguls and Rājputs.—Akbar determined to unite the pure Rajput blood to the scarcely less noble stream which flowed from Aghuz Khan, through Jenghiz, Timur, and Babur, to himself, calculating that they would more readily yield obedience to a prince who claimed kindred with them, than to one purely Tatar; and that, at all events, it would gain the support of their immediate kin, and might in the end become general. In this supposition he did not err. We are less acquainted with the obstacles which opposed his first success than those he subsequently encountered; one of which neither he nor his descendants ever overcame in the family of Mewar, who could never be brought to submit to such alliance.

Amber, the nearest to Delhi and the most exposed, though more open to temptation than to conquest, in its then contracted sphere, was the first to set the example.[1] Its Raja Bhagwandas gave his daughter to Humayun;[2] and subsequently this practice became so common, that some of the most celebrated emperors were the offspring of Rajput princesses. Of these, Salim, called after his accession, Jahangir; his ill-fated son, Khusru; Shah

[1] [There were earlier instances of alliances between Muhammadan princes and Hindus. The mother of Fīroz Shāh, born A.D. 1309, was a Bhatti lady: Khizr Khān married Deval Devi, a Vāghela lady of Gujarāt (Elliot-Dowson, iii. 271 f., 545; Elphinstone, 395).]

[2] [There is no evidence for this statement (Smith, *Akbar*, 58, 225).]

Jahan ;[1] Kambakhsh,[2] the favourite of his father ; Aurangzeb, and his rebellious son Akbar, whom his Rajput kin would have placed on the throne had his genius equalled their power, are the most prominent instances. Farrukhsiyar, when the empire began to totter, furnished the last instance of a Mogul sovereign [153] marrying a Hindu princess,[3] the daughter of Raja Ajit Singh, sovereign of Marwar.

These Rajput princes became the guardians of the minority of their imperial nephews, and had a direct stake in the empire, and in the augmentation of their estates.

Rājputs in the Imperial Service.—Of the four hundred and sixteen Mansabdars, or military commanders of Akbar's empire, from leaders of two hundred to ten thousand men, forty-seven were Rajputs, and the aggregate of their quotas amounted to fifty-three thousand horse :[4] exactly one-tenth of the united Mansabdars of the empire, or five hundred and thirty thousand horse.[5] Of the forty-seven Rajput leaders, there were seventeen whose mansabs were from one thousand to five thousand horse, and thirty from two hundred to one thousand.

The princes of Amber, Marwar, Bikaner, Bundi, Jaisalmer, Bundelkhand, and even Shaikhawati, held mansabs of above one thousand ; but Amber only, being allied to the throne, had the dignity of five thousand.

The Raja Udai Singh of Marwar, surnamed the Fat, chief of

[1] The son of the Princess Jodh Bai, whose magnificent tomb still excites admiration at Sikandra, near Agra.

[2] 'Gift of Love.' [Kāmbakhsh had a Hindu wife, Kalyān Kumāri, daughter of Amar Chand and sister of Sagat Singh, Zamīndār of Manoharpur. Professor Jadunath Sarkar has been unable to trace a Hindu wife of Akbar, son of Aurangzeb.]

[3] To this very marriage we owe the origin of our power. When the nuptials were preparing, the emperor fell ill. A mission was at that time at Delhi from Surat, where we traded, of which Mr. Hamilton was the surgeon. He cured the king, and the marriage was completed. In the oriental style, he desired the doctor to name his reward ; but instead of asking anything for himself, he demanded a grant of land for a factory on the Hoogly for his employers. It was accorded, and this was the origin of the greatness of the British empire in the East. Such an act deserved at least a column ; but neither "storied urn nor animated bust" marks the spot where his remains are laid [C. R. Wilson, *Early Annals of the English in Bengal*, ii. 235, see p. 468 below].

[4] Abu-l Fazl [*Āīn*, i. 308 ff.].

[5] The infantry, regulars, and militia, exceeded 4,000,000.

the Rathors, held but the mansab of one thousand, while a scion of his house, Rae Singh of Bikaner, had four thousand. This is to be accounted for by the dignity being thrust upon the head of that house. The independent princes of Chanderi, Karauli, Datia, with the tributary feudatories of the larger principalities, and members of the Shaikhawat federation, were enrolled on the other grades, from four to seven hundred. Amongst these we find the founder of the Saktawat clan, who, quarrelling with his brother, Rana Partap of Mewar, gave his services to Akbar. In short it became general, and what originated in force or persuasion, was soon coveted from interested motives; and as nearly all the States submitted in [154] time to give queens to the empire, few were left to stigmatize this dereliction from Hindu principle.

Akbar thus gained a double victory, securing the good opinions as well as the swords of these princes in his aid. A judicious perseverance would have rendered the throne of Timur immovable, had not the tolerant principles and beneficence of Akbar, Jahangir, and Shah Jahan been lost sight of by the bigoted and bloodthirsty Aurangzeb; who, although while he lived his commanding genius wielded the destinies of this immense empire at pleasure, alienated the affections, by insulting the prejudices, of those who had aided in raising the empire to the height on which it stood. This affection withdrawn, and the weakness of Farrukhsiyar substituted for the strength of Aurangzeb, it fell and went rapidly to pieces. Predatory warfare and spoliation rose on its ruins. The Rajput princes, with a short-sighted policy, at first connived at, and even secretly invited the tumult; not calculating on its affecting their interests. Each looked to the return of ancient independence, and several reckoned on great accession of power. Old jealousies were not lessened by the part which each had played in the hour of ephemeral greatness; and the prince of Mewar, who preserved his blood uncontaminated, though with loss of land, was at once an object of respect and envy to those who had forfeited the first pretensions [1] of a Rajput. It was the only ovation the Sesodia [2] had to boast for centuries of oppression and spoliation, whilst their neighbours

[1] See, in the Annals of Mewar, the letter of Raē Singh of Bikaner (who had been compelled to submit to this practice), on hearing that Rana Partap's reverses were likely to cause a similar result. It is a noble production, and gives the character of both.

[2] The tribe to which the princes of Mewar belonged.

were basking in court favour. The great increase of territory of these princes nearly equalled the power of Mewar, and the dignities thus acquired from the sons of Timur, they naturally wished should appear as distinguished as his ancient title. Hence, while one inscribed on his seal "The exalted in dignity, a prince amongst princes, and king of kings,"[1] the prince of Mewar preserved his royal simplicity in "Maharana Bhima Singh, son of Arsi." But this is digression.

Results of Feudalism.—It would be difficult to say what would be the happiest form of government for these States without reference to their neighbours. Their own feudal customs would seem to have worked well. The experiment of centuries has secured [155] to them political existence, while successive dynasties of Afghans and Moguls, during eight hundred years, have left but the wreck of splendid names. Were they to become more monarchical, they would have everything to dread from unchecked despotism, over which even the turbulence of their chiefs is a salutary control.

Were they somewhat more advanced towards prosperity, the crown demesne redeemed from dissipation and sterility, and the chiefs enabled to bring their quotas into play for protection and police, recourse should never be had to bodies of mercenary troops, which practice, if persevered in, will inevitably change their present form of government. This has invariably been the result, in Europe as well as Rajasthan, else why the dread of standing armies ?

Employment of Mercenaries.—Escuage is an approximating step. When Charles VII. of France[2] raised his companies of ordnance, the basis of the first national standing army ever embodied in Europe, a tax called 'taille' was imposed to pay them, and Guienne rebelled. Kotah is a melancholy instance of subversion of the ancient order of society. Mewar made the experiment from necessity sixty years ago, when rebellion and invasion conjoined ; and a body of Sindis were employed, which completed their disgust, and they fought with each other till almost mutually exterminated, and till all faith in their prince was lost. Jaipur had adopted this custom to a greater extent ; but it was an ill-paid band, neither respected at home nor feared

[1] *Raj Rajeswara*, the title of the prince of Marwar : the prince of Amber, *Raj Rajindra*.

[2] Hallam, vol. i. p. 117.

abroad. In Marwar the feudal compact was too strong to tolerate it, till Pathan predatory bands, prowling amidst the ruins of Mogul despotism, were called in to partake in each family broil; the consequence was the weakening of all, and opening the door to a power stronger than any, to be the arbiter of their fate.

General Duties of the Pattāwat, or Vassal Chief of Rājasthān.—"The essential principle of a fief was a mutual contract of support and fidelity. Whatever obligations it laid upon the vassal of service to his lord, corresponding duties of protection were imposed by it on the lord towards his vassal. If these were transgressed on either side, the one forfeited his land, the other his signiory or rights over it."[1] In this is comprehended the very foundation of feudal policy, because in its simplicity we recognize first principles involving mutual preservation. The best [156] commentary on this definition of simple truth will be the sentiments of the Rajputs themselves in two papers: one containing the opinions of the chiefs of Marwar on the reciprocal duties of sovereign and vassal;[2] the other, those of the sub-vassals of Deogarh, one of the largest fiefs in Rajasthan, of their rights, the infringement of them, and the remedy.[3]

If, at any former period in the history of Marwar, its prince had thus dared to act, his signiory and rights over it would not have been of great value; his crown and life would both have been endangered by these turbulent and determined vassals. How much is comprehended in that manly, yet respectful sentence: "If he accepts our services, then he is our prince and leader; if not, but our equal, and we again his brothers, claimants of and laying claim to the soil." In the remonstrance of the sub-vassals of Deogarh, we have the same sentiments on a reduced scale. In both we have the ties of blood and kindred, connected with and strengthening national policy. If a doubt could exist as to the principle of fiefs being similar in Rajasthan and in Europe, it might be set at rest by the important question long agitated by the feodal lawyers in Europe, "whether the vassal is bound to follow the standard of his lord against his own kindred or against his sovereign": which in these States is illustrated by a simple and universal proof. If the question were put to a Rajput to whom his service is due, whether to his chief or his sovereign, the

[1] Hallam, vol. i. p. 173. [2] See Appendix, No. I.
[3] See Appendix, Nos. II. and III.

reply would be, *Raj ka malik wuh, pat*[1] *ka malik yih*: 'He is the Sovereign of the State, but this is my *head*': an ambiguous phrase, but well understood to imply that his own immediate chief is the only authority he regards.

This will appear to militate against the right of remonstrance (as in the case of the vassals of Deogarh), for they look to the crown for protection against injustice; they annihilate other rights by admitting appeal higher than this. Every class looks out for some resource against oppression. The sovereign is the last applied to on such occasions, with whom the sub-vassal has no bond of connexion. He can receive no favour, nor perform any service, but through his own immediate superior; and presumes not to question (in cases not personal to himself) the propriety of his chief's actions, adopting implicitly his feelings [157] and resentments. The daily familiar intercourse of life is far too engrossing to allow him to speculate, and with his lord he lives a patriot or dies a traitor. In proof of this, numerous instances could be given of whole clans devoting themselves to the chief against their sovereign;[2] not from the ties of kindred, for many were aliens to blood; but from the ties of duty, gratitude, and all that constitutes clannish attachment, superadded to feudal obligation. The sovereign, as before observed, has nothing to do with those vassals not holding directly from the crown; and those who wish to stand well with their chiefs would be very slow in receiving any honours or favours from the general fountain-head. The Deogarh chief sent one of his sub-vassals to court on a mission; his address and deportment gained him favour, and his consequence was increased by a seat in the presence of his sovereign. When he returned, he found this had lost him the favour of his chief, who was offended, and conceived a jealousy both of his prince and his servant. The distinction paid to the latter was, he said, subversive of his proper authority, and the vassal incurred by his vanity the loss of estimation where alone it was of value.

Obligations of a Vassal.—The attempt to define all the obligations of a vassal would be endless: they involve all the duties of kindred in addition to those of obedience. To attend the court

[1] *Pat* means 'head,' 'chief.'

[2] The death of the chief of Nimaj, in the Annals of Marwar, and Sheogarh Feud, in the Personal Narrative, Vol. II.

of his chief; never to absent himself without leave; to ride with him a-hunting; to attend him at the court of his sovereign or to war, and even give himself as a hostage for his release; these are some of the duties of a vassal.

CHAPTER 3

Feudal Incidents.—I shall now proceed to compare the more general obligations of vassals, known under the term of 'Feudal Incidents' in Europe, and show their existence in Rajasthan. These were six in number: 1. Reliefs; 2. Fines of alienation; 3. Escheats; 4. Aids; 5. Wardship; 6. Marriage [158].

Relief.—The first and most essential mark of a feudal relation exists in all its force and purity here: it is a perpetually recurring mark of the source of the grant, and the solemn renewal of the pledge which originally obtained it. In Mewar it is a virtual and *bona fide* surrender of the fief and renewal thereof. It is thus defined in European polity: "A relief[1] is a sum of money due from every one of full age taking a fief by descent." It was arbitrary, and the consequent exactions formed a ground of discontent; nor was the tax fixed till a comparatively recent period.

By Magna Charta reliefs were settled at rates proportionate to the dignity of the holder.[2] In France the relief was fixed by the customary laws at one year's revenue.[3] This last has long been the settled amount of *nazarana*, or fine of relief, in Mewar.

[1] "Plusieurs possesseurs de fiefs, ayant voulu en laisser perpétuellement la propriété à leurs descendans, prirent des arrangemens avec leur Seigneur; et, outre ce qu'ils donnèrent pour faire le marché, ils s'engagèrent, eux et leur postérité, à abandonner pendant une année, au Seigneur, la jouissance entière du fief, chaque fois que le dit fief changerait de main. C'est ce qui forma le droit de *relief*. Quand un gentilhomme avait dérogé, il pouvait effacer cette tache moyennant finances, et ce qu'il payait s'appelait *relief*, il recevait pour quittance des lettres de *relief* ou de réhabilitation." (Art. 'Relief, *Dict. de l'anc. Régime*).

[2] Namely, "the heir or heirs of an earl, for an entire earldom, one hundred pounds; the heir or heirs of a baron, for an entire barony, one hundred marks; the heir or heirs of a knight, for a whole knight's fee, one hundred shillings at most" (Art. III. Magna Charta).

[3] "Le droit de rachat devoit se payer à chaque mutation d'héritier, et se paya même d'abord en ligne directe.—La coutume la plus générale l'avait fixé à une année du revenue" (*L'Esprit des Loix*, livre xxxi. chap. xxxiii.)

Fine paid on Succession.—On the demise of a chief, the prince immediately sends a party, termed the *zabti* (sequestrator), consisting of a civil officer and a few soldiers, who take possession of the State in the prince's name. The heir sends his prayer to court to be installed in the property, offering the proper relief. This paid, the chief is invited to repair to the presence, when he performs homage, and makes protestations of service and fealty; he receives a fresh grant, and the inauguration terminates by the prince girding him with a sword, in the old forms of chivalry. It is an imposing ceremony, performed in a full assembly of the court, and one of the few which has never been relinquished. The fine paid, and the brand buckled to his side, a steed, turban, plume, and dress of honour given to the chief, the investiture [1] is [159] complete; the sequestrator returns to court, and the chief to his estate, to receive the vows and congratulations of his vassals.[2]

In this we plainly perceive the original power (whether exercised or not) of resumption. On this subject more will appear in treating of the duration of grants. The *kharg bandhai*, or 'binding of the sword,' is also performed when a Rajput is fit to bear arms; as amongst the ancient German tribes, when they put into the hands of the aspirant for fame a lance. Such are the substitutes for the *toga virilis* of the young Roman. The Rana himself is thus ordained a knight by the first of his vassals in dignity, the chief of Salumbar.

Renunciation of Reliefs.—In the demoralization of all those States, some of the chiefs obtained renunciation of the fine of

[1] That symbolic species of investiture denominated 'improper investiture,' the delivery of a turf, stone, and wand, has its analogies amongst the mountaineers of the Aravalli. The old baron of Badnor, when the Mer villages were reduced, was clamorous about his feudal rights over those wild people. It was but the point of honour. From one he had a hare, from another a bullock, and so low as a pair of sticks which they use on the festivals of the Holi. These marks of vassalage come under the head of 'petite serjanteri' (petit serjeantry) in the feudal system of Europe (see Art. XLI. of Magna Charta).

[2] [" All Rājput Jāgīrdārs, or holders of assigned lands, pay *nazarāna* on the accession of a new Mahārāna, and on certain other occasions, while most of them pay a fine called *Kaid* ['imprisonment'] on succeeding to these estates. On the death of a Rājput Jāgīrdār, his estates immediately revert to the Darbār, and so remain until his son or successor is recognized by the Mahārāna, when the grant is renewed, and a fresh lease taken " (Erskine ii. A. 71).]

relief, which was tantamount to making a grant in perpetuity, and annulling the most overt sign of paramount sovereignty. But these and many other important encroachments were made when little remained of the reality, or when it was obscured by a series of oppressions unexampled in any European State.

It is in Mewar alone, I believe, of all Rajasthan, that these marks of fealty are observable to such an extent. But what is remarked elsewhere upon the fiefs being movable, will support the doctrine of resumption though it might not be practised: a prerogative may exist without its being exercised.

Fine of Alienation.—Rajasthan never attained this refinement indicative of the dismemberment of the system; so vicious and self-destructive a notion never had existence in these States. Alienation does not belong to a system of fiefs: the lord would never consent to it, but on very peculiar occasions.

In Cutch, amongst the Jareja [1] tribes, sub-vassals may alienate their estates; but this privilege is dependent on the mode of acquisition. Perhaps the only knowledge we have in Rajasthan of alienation requiring the sanction of the lord paramount, is in donations for pious uses: but this is partial. We see in the remonstrance of the Deogarh vassals the opinion they entertained of their lord's alienation of their sub-fees to strangers, and without the Rana's consent; which, with a similar train of conduct, produced sequestration of his fief till they were reinducted [160].

Tenants of the Crown may Alienate.—The agricultural tenants, proprietors of land held of the crown, may alienate their rights upon a small fine, levied merely to mark the transaction. But the tenures of these non-combatants and the holders of fees are entirely distinct, and cannot here be entered on, further than to say that the agriculturist is, or was, the proprietor of the soil; the chief, solely of the tax levied thereon. But in Europe the alienation of the *feudum paternum* was not good without the consent of the kindred in the line of succession.[2] This would involve sub-infeudation and frerage, which I shall touch on distinctly, many of the troubles of these countries arising therefrom.

[1] Jareja is the title of the Rajput race in Cutch; they are descendants of the Yadus, and claim from Krishna. In early ages they inhabited the tracts on the Indus and in Seistan [p. 102 above].

[2] Wright on Tenures, *apud* Hallam, vol. i. p. 185.

Escheats and Forfeitures.—The fiefs which were only to descend in lineal succession reverted to the crown on failure of heirs, as they could not be bequeathed by will. This answers equally well for England as for Mewar. I have witnessed escheats of this kind, and foresee more, if the pernicious practice of unlimited adoption do not prevent the Rana from regaining lands, alienated by himself at periods of contention. Forfeitures for crimes must, of course, occur, and these are partial or entire, according to the delinquency.

In Marwar, at this moment, nearly all the representatives of the great fiefs of that country are exiles from their homes: a distant branch of the same family, the prince of Idar, would have adopted a similar line of conduct but for a timely check from the hand of benevolence.[1]

There is, or rather was, a class of lands in Mewar appended to the crown, of which it bestowed life-rents on men of merit. These were termed Chhorutar, and were given and taken back, as the name implies; in contradistinction to grants which, though originating in good behaviour, not only continued for life but descended in perpetuity. Such places are still so marked in the rent-roll, but they are seldom applied to the proper purpose.

Aids.—Aids, implying 'free gifts,' or 'benevolences,' as they were termed in a European code, are well known. The *barar* (war-tax) is well understood in Mewar, and is levied on many occasions for the necessities of the prince or the head of a clan. It is a curious fact, that the *dasaundh*, or 'tenth,' in Mewar, as in Europe, was the [161] stated sum to be levied in periods of emergency or danger. On the marriage of the daughters of the prince, a benevolence or contribution was always levied: this varied. A few years ago, when two daughters and a granddaughter were married to the princes of Jaisalmer, Bikaner, and Kishangarh, a schedule of one-sixth, to portion the three, was made out; but it did not realize above an eighth. In this aid the civil officers of government contribute equally with the others. It is a point of honour with all to see their sovereign's daughters married, and for once the contribution merited the name of benevolence.

[1] The Hon. Mr. Elphinstone, Governor of Bombay. As we prevented the spoliation of Idar by the predatory powers, we are but right in seeing that the head does not become the spoliator himself, and make these brave men "wish any change but that which we have given them."

But it is not levied solely from the coffers of the rich; by the chiefs it is exacted of their tenantry of all classes, who, of course, wish such subjects of rejoicing to be of as rare occurrence as possible.

"These feudal aids are deserving of our notice as the commencement of taxation, of which they long answered the purpose, till the craving necessities and covetous policy of kings established for them more durable and onerous burthens." [1]

The great chiefs, it may be assumed, were not backward, on like occasions, to follow such examples, but these gifts were more voluntary. Of the details of aids in France we find enumerated, "paying the relief to the suzerain on taking possession of his lands"; [2] and by Magna Charta our barons could levy them on the following counts: to make the baron's eldest son a knight, to marry his eldest daughter, or to redeem his person from captivity. The latter is also one occasion for the demand in all these countries. The chief is frequently made prisoner in their predatory invasions, and carried off as a hostage for the payment of a war contribution. Everything disposable is often got rid of on an occasion of this kind. Cœur de Lion would not have remained so long in the dungeons of Austria had his subjects been Rajputs. In Amber the most extensive benevolence, or *barar*,[3] is on the marriage of the Rajkumar, or heir apparent.

Wardship.—This does exist, to foster the infant vassal during minority; but often terminating, as in the system of Europe, in the nefarious act of defrauding a helpless infant, to the pecuniary benefit of some court favourite. It is accordingly [162] here undertaken occasionally by the head of the clan; but two strong recent instances brought the dark ages, and the purchase of wardships for the purpose of spoliation, to mind. The first was in the Deogarh chief obtaining by bribe the entire management of the lands of Sangramgarh, on pretence of improving them for the infant, Nahar Singh, whose father was incapacitated by derangement. Nahar was a junior branch of the clan Sangawat, a subdivision of the Chondawat clan, both Sesodias of the Rana's blood. The object, at the time, was to unite them to Deogarh, though he pleaded duty as head of the clan. His nomination of young Nahar as his own heir gives a colouring of truth to his

[1] Hallam. [2] Ducange, *apud* Hallam.

[3] *Barar* is the generic name for taxation.

intentions; and he succeeded, though there were nearer of kin, who were set aside (at the wish of the vassals of Deogarh and with the concurrence of the sovereign) as unfit to head them or serve him.

Another instance of the danger of permitting wardships, particularly where the guardian is the superior in clanship and kindred, is exemplified in the Kalyanpur estate in Mewar. That property had been derived from the crown only two generations back, and was of the annual value of ten thousand rupees. The mother having little interest at court, the Salumbar chief, by bribery and intrigue, upon paying a fine of about one year's rent, obtained possession—ostensibly to guard the infant's rights; but the falsehood of this motive was soon apparent. There were duties to perform on holding it which were not thought of. It was a frontier post, and a place of rendezvous for the quotas to defend that border from the incursions of the wild tribes of the south-west. The Salumbar chief, being always deficient in the quota for his own estate, was not likely to be very zealous in his muster-roll for his ward's, and complaints were made which threatened a change. The chief of Chawand was talked of as one who would provide for the widow and minor, who could not perform the duties of defence.

The sovereign himself often assumes the guardianship of minors; but the mother is generally considered the most proper guardian for her infant son. All others may have interests of their own; she can be actuated by his welfare alone. Custom, therefore, constitutes her the guardian; and with the assistance of the elders of the family, she rears and educates the young chief till he is fit to be girded with the sword [163].[1]

The Faujdar, or military manager, who frequently regulates the household as well as the subdivisions of the estate, is seldom of the kin or clan of the chief: a wise regulation, the omission of which has been known to produce, in these *maires du palais* on a small scale, the same results as will be described in the larger. This officer, and the civil functionary who transacts all the pecuniary concerns of the estate, with the mother and her family, are always considered to be the proper guardians of the minor. 'Blood which could not inherit,' was the requisite for a guardian

[1] The charter of Henry I. promises the custody of heirs to the mother or next of kin (Hallam, vol. ii. p. 429).

in Europe,[1] as here; and when neglected, the results are in both cases the same.

Marriage.—Refinement was too strong on the side of the Rajput to admit this incident, which, with that of wardship (both partial in Europe), illustrated the rapacity of the feudal aristocracy. Every chief, before he marries, makes it known to his sovereign. It is a compliment which is expected, and is besides attended with some advantage, as the prince invariably confers presents of honour, according to the station of the individual.

No Rajput can marry in his own clan; and the incident was originated in the Norman institutes, to prevent the vassal marrying out of his class, or amongst the enemies of his sovereign.[2]

Thus, setting aside marriage (which even in Europe was only partial and local) and alienation, four of the six chief incidents marking the feudal system are in force in Rajasthan, viz. relief, escheats, aids, and wardships.

Duration of Grants.—I shall now endeavour to combine all the knowledge I possess with regard to the objects attained in granting lands, the nature and durability of these grants, whether for life and renewable, or in perpetuity. I speak of the rules as understood in Mewar. We ought not to expect much system in what was devoid of regularity, even according to the old principles of European feudal law, which, though now reduced to some fixed principles, originated in, and was governed by, fortuitous circumstances; and after often changing its character, ended in despotism, oligarchy, or democracy.

Classes of Landholders.—There are two classes of Rajput landholders in Mewar, though the one greatly exceeds the other in number. One is the Girasia Thakur, or lord; the other the Bhumia. The Girasia chieftain is he who holds (*giras*) by grant (*patta*) of the [164] prince, for which he performs service with specified quotas at home and abroad, renewable at every lapse, when all the ceremonies of resumption,[3] the fine of relief,[4] and the investiture take place.

The Bhumia does not renew his grant, but holds on prescriptive

[1] Hallam, vol. i. p. 190.

[2] [The rule of tribal exogamy, whatever may be its origin, is much more primitive than the author supposed (Sir J. G. Frazer, *Totemism and Exogamy*, i. 54 ff.).]

[3] *Zabti*, 'sequestration.'

[4] *Nazarana*.

possession. He succeeds without any fine, but pays a small annual quit-rent, and can be called upon for local service in the district which he inhabits for a certain period of time. He is the counterpart of the allodial proprietor of the European system, and the real zamindar of these principalities. Both have the same signification ; from *bhum* and *zamin*, 'land' : the latter is an exotic of Persian origin.

Girāsia.—Girasia is from *giras*, 'a subsistence' ; literally and familiarly 'a mouthful.' Whether it may have a like origin with the Celtic word *gwas*,[1] said to mean 'a servant,'[2] and whence the word vassal is derived, I shall leave to etymologists to decide, who may trace the resemblance to the *girasia*, the vassal chieftain of the Rajputs. All the chartularies or pattas[3] commence, "To . . . *giras* has been ordained."

Whether Resumable.—It has always been a subject of doubt whether grants were resumable at pleasure, or without some delinquency imputable to the vassal. Their duration in Europe was, at least, the life of the possessor, when they reverted[4] to the fisc. The whole of the ceremonies in cases of such lapse are decisive on this point in Mewar. The right to resume, therefore, may be presumed to exist ; while the non-practice of it, the formalities of renewal being gone through, may be said to render the right a dead letter. But to prove its existence I need only mention, that so late as the reign of Rana Sangram,[5] the fiefs of Mewar were actually movable ; and little more than a century and a half has passed since this practice ceased. Thus a Rathor would shift, with family, chattels, and retainers, from the north into the wilds of Chappan ;[6] while the Saktawat relieved would

[1] It might not be unworthy of research to trace many words common to the Hindu and the Celt ; or to inquire whether the Kimbri, the Juts or Getae, the Sakasena, the Chatti of the Elbe and Cimbric Chersonese, and the ancient Britons, did not bring their terms with their bards and *vates* (the Bhats and Bardais) from the highland of Scythia east of the Caspian, which originated the nations common to both, improved beyond the Wolga and the Indus [?].

[2] Hallam, vol. i. 155. [Welsh, Cornish *gwas*, 'a servant.']

[3] *Patta*, a 'patent' or 'grant' ; *Pattāwat*, 'holder of the fief or grant.'

[4] Montesquieu, chaps. xxv., liv., xxxi.

[5] Ten generations ago. [At present an estate is not liable to confiscation save for some gross political offence (Erskine ii. A. 71).]

[6] The mountainous and woody region to the south-west, dividing Mewar from Gujarat.

occupy the plains at the foot of the Aravalli;[1] or a Chondawat would exchange his [165] abode on the banks of the Chambal with a Pramara or Chauhan from the table-mountain, the eastern boundary of Mewar.[2]

Since these exchanges were occurring, it is evident the fiefs (*pattas*) were not grants in perpetuity. This is just the state of the benefices in France at an early period, as described by Gibbon, following Montesquieu: "Les bénéfices étoient amovibles; bientôt ils les rendirent perpétuels, et enfin héréditaires."[3] This is the precise gradation of fiefs in Mewar; movable, perpetual, and then hereditary. The sons were occasionally permitted to succeed their fathers;[4] an indulgence which easily grew into a right, though the crown had the indubitable reversion. It is not, however, impossible that these changes[5] were not of ancient authority, but arose from the policy of the times to prevent infidelity.

We ought to have a high opinion of princes who could produce an effect so powerful on the minds of a proud and turbulent nobility. The son was heir to the title and power over the vassals' personals and movables, and to the allegiance of his father, but to nothing which could endanger that allegiance.

A proper apportioning and mixture of the different clans was another good result to prevent their combinations in powerful families, which gave effect to rebellion, and has tended more than external causes to the ruin which the State of Mewar exhibits.

[1] The grand chain dividing the western from the central States of Rajasthan.

[2] Such changes were triennial; and, as I have heard the prince himself say, so interwoven with their customs was this rule that it caused no dissatisfaction; but of this we may be allowed at least to doubt. It was a perfect check to the imbibing of local attachment; and the prohibition against erecting forts for refuge or defiance, prevented its growth if acquired. It produced the object intended, obedience to the prince, and unity against the restless Mogul. Perhaps to these institutions it is owing that Mewar alone never was conquered by the kings during the protracted struggle of seven centuries; though at length worried and worn out, her power expired with theirs, and predatory spoliation completed her ruin.

[3] Gibbon, *Misc. Works*, vol. iii. p. 189; *Sur le système féodal surtout en France.*

[4] Hallam, quoting Gregory of Tours; the picture drawn in A.D. 595.

[5] "Fiefs had partially become hereditary towards the end of the first race: in those days they had not the idea of an 'unalienable fief.'" Montesquieu, vol. ii. p. 431. The historian of the Middle Ages doubts if ever they were resumable at pleasure, unless from delinquency.

Nobility: Introduction of Foreign Stocks.—Throughout the various gradations of its nobility, it was the original policy to introduce some who were foreign in country and blood. Chiefs of the Rathor, Chauhan, Pramara, Solanki, and Bhatti tribes were intermingled. Of these several were lineal descendants of the most ancient races of the kings of Delhi and Anhilwara Patan;[1] and from these, in order to preserve the purity of blood, the princes of Mewar took their wives, when the other princes of Hind assented to [166] the degradation of giving daughters in marriage to the emperors of Delhi. The princes of Mewar never yielded in this point, but preserved their ancient manners amidst all vicissitudes. In like manner did the nobles of the Rana's blood take daughters from the same tribes; the interest of this foreign race was therefore strongly identified with the general welfare, and on all occasions of internal turmoil and rebellion they invariably supported their prince. But when these wise institutions were overlooked, when the great clans increased and congregated together, and the crown demesne was impoverished by prodigality, rebellions were fostered by Mahratta rapacity, which were little known during the lengthened paramount sway of the kings of Delhi. This foreign admixture will lead us to the discussion of the different kinds of grants: a difference, perhaps, more nominal than real, but exhibiting a distinction so wide as to imply grants resumable and irresumable.

Kāla Pattas.—It is elsewhere related that two great clans, descendants of the Ranas Rae Mall and Udai Singh, and their numerous scions, forming subdivisions with separate titles or patronymics, compose the chief vassalage of this country.

Exogamy.—Chondawat and Saktawat are the stock; the former is subdivided into ten, the latter into about six clans. Rajputs never intermarry with their own kin: the prohibition has no limit; it extends to the remotest degree. All these clans are resolvable into the generic term of 'the race' or Kula Sesodia. A Sesodia man and woman cannot unite in wedlock—all these are therefore of the blood royal; and the essayists on population would have had a fine field in these quarters a century ago, ere constant misery had thinned the country, to trace the numerous

[1] The Nahlwara of D'Anville and the Arabian travellers of the eighth century, the capital of the Balhara kings.

progeny of Chonda and Sakta in the Genesis[1] of Mewar. The Bhat's genealogies would still, to a certain extent, afford the same means.

Descent gives a strength to the tenure of these tribes which the foreign nobles do not possess; for although, from all that has been said, it will be evident that a right of reversion and resumption existed (though seldom exercised, and never but in cases of crime), yet the foreigner had not this strength in the soil, even though of twenty generations' duration. The epithet of *kala patta*, or 'black grant,' attaches to the foreign grant, and is admitted by the holder, from which the kinsman thinks himself exempt. It is virtually a grant resumable; nor can the possessors feel that security which the other widely affiliated aristocracies afford [167]. When, on a recent occasion, a revision of all the grants took place, the old ones being called in to be renewed under the sign-manual of the reigning prince, the minister himself visited the chief of Salumbar, the head of the Chondawats, at his residence at the capital, for this purpose. Having become possessed of several villages in the confusion of the times, a perusal of the grant would have been the means of detection; and on being urged to send to his estate for it, he replied, pointing to the palace, "My grant is in the foundation of that edifice": an answer worthy of a descendant of Chonda, then only just of age. The expression marks the spirit which animates this people, and recalls to mind the well-known reply of our own Earl Warenne, on the very same occasion, to the *quo warranto* of Edward: "By their swords my ancestors obtained this land, and by mine will I maintain it."

Hence it may be pronounced that a grant of an estate is for the life of the holder, with inheritance for his offspring in lineal descent or adoption, with the sanction of the prince, and resumable for crime or incapacity:[2] this reversion and power of resumption being marked by the usual ceremonies on each lapse

[1] *Janam*, 'birth'; *es*, 'lord' or 'man.' [See p. 24 above.]

[2] "La loi des Lombards oppose les bénéfices à la propriété. Les historiens, les formules, les codes des différens peuples barbares, tous les monumens qui nous restent, sont unanimes. Enfin, ceux qui ont écrit le livre des fiefs, nous apprennent, que d'abord les Seigneurs purent les ôter à leur volonté, qu'ensuite ils les assurèrent pour un an, et après les donnèrent pour la vie" (*L'Esprit des Loix*, chap. xvi. livre 30).

of the grantee, of sequestration (*zabti*), of relief (*nazarana*), of homage and investiture of the heir. Those estates held by foreign nobles differ not in tenure ; though, for the reasons specified, they have not the same grounds of security as the others, in whose welfare the whole body is interested, feeling the case to be their own : and their interests, certainly, have not been so consulted since the rebellions of S. 1822,[1] and subsequent years. Witness the Chauhans of Bedla and Kotharia (in the Udaipur valley), and the Pramar of the plateau of Mewar, all chiefs of the first rank.

The difficulty and danger of resuming an old-established grant in these countries are too great to be lightly risked. Though in all these estates there is a mixture of foreign Rajputs, yet the blood of the chief predominates ; and these must have a leader of their own, or be incorporated in the estates of the nearest of kin. This increase might not be desirable for the crown, but the sub-vassals cannot be turned [168] adrift ; a resumption therefore in these countries is widely felt, as it involves many. If crime or incapacity render it necessary, the prince inducts a new head of that blood ; and it is their pride, as well as the prince's interest, that a proper choice should be made. If, as has often occurred, the title be abolished, the sub-vassals retain their sub-infeudations, and become attached to the crown.

Many estates were obtained, during periods of external commotion, by threats, combination, or the avarice of the prince—his short-sighted policy, or that of his ministers—which have been remedied in the late reorganization of Mewar ; where, by retrograding half a century, and bringing matters as near as possible to the period preceding civil dissension, they have advanced at least a century towards order.

Bhūmia, the Allodial Proprietor.—It is stated in the historical annals of this country that the ancient clans, prior to Sanga Rana,[2] had ceased, on the rising greatness of the subsequent new division of clans, to hold the higher grades of rank ; and had, in fact, merged into the general military landed proprietors of this country under the term *bhumia*, a most expressive and comprehensive name, importing absolute identity with the soil : *bhum* meaning 'land,' and being far more expressive than the new-

[1] A.D. 1766.

[2] Contemporary and opponent of Sultan Babur.

fangled word, unknown to Hindu India, of *zamindar*, the 'land-holder' of Muhammadan growth. These Bhumias, the scions of the earliest princes, are to be met with in various parts of Mewar; though only in those of high antiquity, where they were defended from oppression by the rocks and wilds in which they obtained a footing; as in Kumbhalmer, the wilds of Chappan, or plains of Mandalgarh, long under the kings, and where their agricultural pursuits maintained them.

Their clannish appellations, Kumbhawat, Lunawat, and Ranawat, distinctly show from what stem and when they branched off; and as they ceased to be of sufficient importance to visit the court on the new and continually extending ramifications, they took to the plough. But while they disdained not to derive a subsistence from labouring as husbandmen, they never abandoned their arms; and the Bhumia, amid the crags of the alpine Aravalli where he pastures his cattle or cultivates his fields, preserves the erect mien and proud spirit of his ancestors, with more tractability, and less arrogance and folly, than his more [169] courtly but now widely separated brethren, who often make a jest of his industrious but less refined qualifications.[1] Some of these yet possess entire villages, which are subject to the payment of a small quit-rent: they also constitute a local militia, to be called in by the governor of the district, but for which service they are entitled to rations or *peti*.[2] These, the allodial [3] tenantry of our

[1] Many of them taking wives from the degraded but aboriginal races in their neighbouring retreats, have begot a mixed progeny, who, in describing themselves, unite the tribes of father and mother.

[2] Literally, 'a belly-full.'

[3] Allodial property is defined (Hallam, vol. i. p. 144) as "land which had descended by inheritance, subject to no burthen but public defence. It passed to all the children equally; in failure of children, to the nearest kindred." Thus it is strictly the *Miras* or *Bhum* of the Rajputs: inheritance, patrimony. In Mewar it is divisible to a certain extent; but in Cutch, to infinity: and is liable only to local defence. The holder of bhum calls it his *Adyapi*, *i.e.* of old, by prescriptive right; not by written deed. Montesquieu, describing the conversion of allodial estates into fiefs, says, "These lands were held by Romans or Franks (*i.e.* freemen) not the king's vassals," viz. lands exterior and anterior to the monarchy. We have Rathor, Solanki, and other tribes, now holding bhum in various districts, whose ancestors were conquered by the Sesodias, but left in possession of small portions insufficient to cause jealousy. Some of these may be said to have converted their lands into fiefs, as the Chauhan lord of ——, who served the Salumbar chief.

feudal system, form a considerable body in many districts, armed with matchlock, sword, and shield. In Mandalgarh, when their own interests and the prince's unite (though the rapacity of governors, pupils of the Mahratta and other predatory schools, have disgusted these independents), four thousand Bhumias could be collected. They held and maintained without support the important fortress of that district, during half a century of turmoil, for their prince. Mandalgarh is the largest district of Mewar, and in its three hundred and sixty towns and villages many specimens of ancient usage may be found. The Solanki held largely here in ancient days, and the descendant of the princes of Patan still retains his Bhum and title of Rao.[1]

Feudal Militia.—All this feudal militia pay a quit-rent to the crown, and perform local but limited service on the frontier garrison ; and upon invasion,[2] when the *Kher* is called out, the whole are at the disposal of the prince on furnishing rations only. They assert that they ought not to pay this quit-rent and perform service also ; but this may be doubted, since the sum is so small. To elude it, they often performed service under some powerful chief, where faction or court interest [170] caused it to be winked at. To serve without a *patta* is the great object of ambition. *Ma ka bhum*, 'my land,' in their Doric tongue, is a favourite phrase.[3]

[1] Amidst ruins overgrown with forest, I discovered on two tables of stone the genealogical history of this branch, which was of considerable use in elucidating that of Anhilwara, and which corresponded so well with the genealogies of a decayed bard of the family, who travelled the country for a subsistence, that I feel assured they formerly made good use of these marble records.

[2] See Appendix, Nos. XVI. and XVII.

[3] I was intimately acquainted with, and much esteemed, many of these Bhumia chiefs—from my friend Paharji (the rock), Ranawat of Amargarh, to the Kumbhawat of Sesoda on the highest point, lord of the pass of the Aravalli ; and even the mountain lion, Dungar Singh who bore amongst us, from his old raids, the familiar title of Roderic Dhu. In each situation I have had my tents filled with them ; and it was one of the greatest pleasures I ever experienced, after I had taken my leave of them, perhaps for ever, crossed the frontiers of Mewar, and encamped in the dreary pass between it and Marwar, to find that a body of them had been my guards during the night. This is one of the many pleasing recollections of the past. Fortunately for our happiness, the mind admits their preponderance over opposite feelings. I had much to do in aiding the restoration of their past condition ; leaving, I believe, as few traces of error in the mode as could be expected, where so many conflicting interests were to be reconciled.

Circumstances have concurred to produce a resemblance even to the refined fiction of giving up their allodial property to have it conferred as a fief. But in candour it should be stated, that the only instances were caused by the desire of being revenged on the immediate superiors of the vassals. The Rathor chief of Dabla held of his superior, the Raja of Banera, three considerable places included in the grant of Banera. He paid homage, an annual quit-rent, was bound to attend him personally to court, and to furnish thirty-five horse in case of an invasion. During the troubles, though perfectly equal to their performance, he was remiss in all these duties. His chief, with returning peace, desired to enforce the return to ancient customs, and his rights so long withheld; but the Rathor had felt the sweets of entire independence, and refused to attend his summons. To the warrant he replied, "his head and Dabla were together"; and he would neither pay the quit-rent nor attend his court. This refractory spirit was reported to the Rana; and it ended in Dabla being added to the fisc, and the chief's holding the rest as a vassal of the Rana, but only to perform local service. There are many other petty free proprietors on the Banera estate, holding from small portions of land to small villages; but the service is limited and local in order to swell the chief's miniature court. If they accompany him, he must find rations for them and their steeds.

So cherished is this tenure of Bhum, that the greatest chiefs are always solicitous to obtain it, even in the villages wholly dependent on their authority: a decided proof of its durability above common grants. The various modes in which it is acquired, and the precise technicalities which distinguished its tenure, as well as the privileges attached to it, are fully developed in translations of different deeds on the subject [171].[1]

Rajas of Banera and Shāhpura.—We have also, amongst the nobility of Mewar, two who hold the independent title of prince or raja, one of whom is by far too powerful for a subject. These are the Rajas of Banera and Shahpura, both of the blood royal. The ancestor of the first was the twin-brother of Rana Jai Singh; the other, a Ranawat, branched off from Rana Udai Singh.

They have their grants renewed, and receive the khilat of investiture; but they pay no relief, and are exempt from all but personal attendance at their prince's court, and the local

[1] See Appendix.

service of the district in which their estates are situated. They have hitherto paid but little attention to their duties, but this defect arose out of the times. These lands lying most exposed to the imperial headquarters at Ajmer, they were compelled to bend to circumstances, and the kings were glad to confer rank and honour on such near relations of the Rana's house. He bestowed on them the titles of Raja, and added to the Shahpura chief's patrimony a large estate in Ajmer, which he now holds direct of the British Government, on payment of an annual tribute.

Form and Substance of Grant.—To give a proper idea of the variety of items forming these chartularies, I append several [1] which exhibit the rights, privileges, and honours, as well as the sources of income, while they also record the terms on which they are granted. Many royalties have been alienated in modern times by the thoughtless prodigality of the princes; even the grand mark of vassalage, the fine of relief, has been forgiven to one or two individuals; portions of transit duties, tolls on ferries, and other seignorial rights; coining copper currency; exactions of every kind, from the levy of toll for night protection of merchandise and for the repairs of fortifications, to the share of the depredations of the common robber, will sufficiently show the demoralization of the country.

Division of Pattas, or Sub-infeudation.—Many years ago, when the similarity of the systems first struck my attention, I took one of the grants or *pattas* of a great vassal of Jaipur, and dissected it in all its minutiae, with the aid of a very competent authority who had resided as one of the managers of the chief. This document, in which the subdivision of the whole clan is detailed, materially aided me in developing the system [172].

The court and the household economy of a great chieftain is a miniature representation of the sovereign's: the same officers, from the pardhan, or minister, to the cup-bearer (*paniyari*), as well as the same domestic arrangements. He must have his *shish-mahall*,[2] his *bari-mahall*,[3] and his *mandir*,[4] like his prince.

[1] See Appendix, Nos. IV., V., VI.

[2] Mirror apartments. [To meet the demand for the glass mosaics seen in the palaces of Rājputāna, the Panjab, and Burma, the industry of blowing glass globes, silvered inside, came into existence. The globes are broken into fragments, and set in cement (in Burma in laquer), and used to decorate the walls (Watt, *Comm. Prod.* 563, 717 f.). There is a Shīsh Mahall in the Agra Fort.]

[3] Gardens on the terrace within the palace.

[4] Private temple of worship.

He enters the *dari-sala*, or carpet hall, the minstrel [1] preceding him rehearsing the praises of his family; and he takes his seat on his throne, while the assembled retainers, marshalled in lines on the right and left, simultaneously exclaim, "Health to our chief!" which salutation he returns by bowing to all as he passes them. When he is seated, at a given signal they all follow the example, and shield rattles against shield as they wedge into their places.

We have neither the kiss nor individual oaths of fidelity administered. It is sufficient, when a chief succeeds to his patrimony, that his '*an*' [2] is proclaimed within his *sim* or boundary. Allegiance is as hereditary as the land: "I am your child; my head and sword are yours, my service is at your command." It is a rare thing for a Rajput to betray his Thakur, while the instances of self-devotion for him are innumerable: many will be seen interspersed in these papers. Base desertion, to their honour be it said, is little known, and known only to be execrated. Fidelity to the chief, Swamidharma, is the climax of all the virtues. The Rajput is taught from his infancy, in the song of the bard, to regard it as the source of honour here, and of happiness hereafter. The poet Chand abounds with episodes on the duty and beauty of fidelity; nor does it require a very fervid imagination to picture the affections which such a life is calculated to promote, when the chief is possessed of the qualities to call them forth. At the chase his vassals attend him: in the covert of the forest, the ground their social board, they eat their repast together, from the venison or wild boar furnished by the sport of the day; nor is the cup neglected. They are familiarly admitted at all times to his presence, and accompany him to the court of their mutual sovereign. In short, they are inseparable.[3]

Their having retained so much of their ancient manners and customs, during [173] centuries of misery and oppression, is the best evidence that those customs were riveted to their very souls. The Rajput of character is a being of the most acute sensibility;

[1] Dholi.

[2] *An* is the oath of allegiance. Three things in Mewar are royalties a subject cannot meddle with: 1, *An*, or oath of allegiance; 2, *Dan*, or transit dues on commerce; 3, *Khan*, or mines of the precious metals.

[3] I rather describe what they were, than what they are. Contentions and poverty have weakened their sympathies and affections; but the mind of philanthropy must hope that they will again become what they have been.

where honour is concerned, the most trivial omission is often ignorantly construed into an affront.

Provision for Chief's Relations.—In all the large estates the chief must provide for his sons or brothers, according to his means and the number of immediate descendants. In an estate of sixty to eighty thousand rupees of annual rent, the second brother might have a village of three to five thousand of rent. This is his patrimony (*bapota*): he besides pushes his fortune at the court of his sovereign or abroad. Juniors share in proportion. These again subdivide, and have their little circle of dependents. Each new family is known by the name of the founder conjoined to that of his father and tribe: *Man Meghsinghgot Saktawat*; that is, 'Man, family of Megh, tribe Saktawat.' The subdivisions descend to the lowest denomination.

Charsa.—*Charsa*, a 'hide of land,' or about sufficient to furnish an equipped cavalier. It is a singular coincidence that the term for the lowest subdivision of land for military service should be the same amongst the Rajputs as in the English system. Besides being similar in name, it nearly corresponds in actual quantity. From the beginning of the Anglo-Saxon government the land was divided into hides, each comprehending what could be cultivated by a single plough.[1] Four hides constituted one knight's fee,[2] which is stated to be about forty acres. The Charsa may have from twenty-five to thirty bighas; which are equal to about ten acres—the Saxon hide.

For what these minor vassals held to be their rights on the great pattawats, the reader is again referred to the letter of protest of the inferior pattawats of the Deogarh estate—it may aid his judgement; and it is curious to observe how nearly the subject of their prayer to the sovereign corresponded with the edict of Conrad of Italy,[3] in the year 1037, which originated in

[1] Millar's *Historical View of the English Government*, p. 85. [See p. 156 above.]

[2] Hume, *History of England*, Appendix II. vol. ii. p. 291.

[3] "1. That no man should be deprived of his fief, whether held of the emperor or mesne lord, but by the laws of the empire and *judgement of his peers*. 2. That from such judgement the vassal might appeal to his sovereign. 3. That fiefs should be inherited by sons and their children, or in their failure by brothers, provided they were *feuda paterna*, such as had descended from the father. 4. That the lord should not alienate the fief of his vassal without his consent.'

disagreements between the great lords and their vassals on the subject of sub-infeudations [174].

The extent to which the subdivision before mentioned is carried in some of the Rajput States, is ruinous to the protection and general welfare of the country. It is pursued in some parts till there is actually nothing left sufficiently large to share, or to furnish subsistence for one individual: consequently a great deprivation of services to the State ensues. But this does not prevail so much in the larger principalities as in the isolated tributary Thakurats or lordships scattered over the country; as amongst the Jarejas of Cutch, the tribes in Kathiawar, and the small independencies of Gujarat bordering on the greater western Rajput States. This error in policy requires to be checked by supreme authority, as it was in England by Magna Charta,[1] when the barons of those days took such precautions to secure their own seignorial rights.

Brotherhood.—The system in these countries of minute subdivision of fiefs is termed *bhayyad*,[2] or brotherhood, synonymous to the tenure by frerage of France, but styled only an approximation to sub-infeudation.[3] "Give me my *bat* (share)," says the Rajput, when he attains to man's estate, 'the bat of the bhayyad,' the portion of the frerage; and thus they go on clipping and paring till all are impoverished. The 'customs' of France[4] preserved the dignities of families and the indivisibility of a feudal homage, without exposing the younger sons of a gentleman to beggary and dependence. It would be a great national benefit if some means could be found to limit this subdivision, but it is an evil difficult of remedy. The divisibility of the Cutch and Kathiawar frerage, carried to the most destructive extent, is productive of litigation, crime, and misery. Where it has proper limits it is useful; but though the idea of each rood supporting its man is very poetical, it does not and cannot answer in practice. Its limit in Mewar we would not undertake to assert, but the vassals are careful not to let it become too small; they send the extra numbers to seek their fortunes abroad. In this custom, and the difficulty of finding *daejas*, or dowers, for their daughters,

[1] By the revised statute, *Quia emptores*, of Edw. I., which forbids it in excess, under penalty of forfeiture (Hallam, vol. i. p. 184).

[2] *Bhayyad*, 'frerage.'

[3] Hallam, vol. i. p. 186.

[4] *Ibid.*

we have the two chief causes of infanticide amongst the Rajputs, which horrible practice was not always confined to the female.

The author of the Middle Ages exemplifies ingeniously the advantages of sub-[175]infeudation, by the instance of two persons holding one knight's fee; and as the lord was entitled to the service of one for forty days, he could commute it for the joint service of the two for twenty days each. He even erects as a maxim on it, that "whatever opposition was made to the rights of sub-infeudation or frerage, would indicate decay in the military character, the living principle of feudal tenure";[1] which remark may be just where proper limitation exists, before it reaches that extent when the impoverished vassal would descend to mend his shoes instead of his shield. Primogeniture is the corner-stone of feudality, but this unrestricted sub-infeudation would soon destroy it.[2] It is strong in these States; its rights were first introduced by the Normans from Scandinavia. But more will appear on this subject and its technicalities, in the personal narrative of the author.

CHAPTER 4

Rakhwāli.—I now proceed to another point of striking resemblance between the systems of the east and west, arising from the same causes—the unsettled state of society, and the deficiency of paramount protection. It is here called *rakhwali*,[3] or 'preservation'; the *salvamenta* of Europe.[4] To a certain degree it always existed in these States; but the interminable predatory

[1] Hallam, vol. i. p. 186.

[2] "Le *droit d'aînesse* a causé, pendant l'existence du régime féodal, une multitude de guerres et de procès. Notre histoire nous présente, à chaque page, des cadets réduits à la mendicité, se livrant à toutes sortes de brigandages pour réparer les torts de la fortune; des aînés, refusant la légitime à leurs frères; des cadets, assassinant leur aîné pour lui succéder, etc." (see article, 'Droit d'aînesse,' *Dict. de l'Ancien Régime*).

[3] See Appendix, Nos. VII., VIII., and IX.

[4] This is the '*sauvement* ou *vingtain*' of the French system: there it ceased with the cause. "Les guerres (feudal) cessèrent avec le régime féodal, et les paysans n'eurent plus besoin de la protection du Seigneur; on ne les força pas moins de réparer son château, et de lui payer le droit qui se nommait de *sauvement* ou *vingtain*" (Art. 'Château,' *Dict. de l'Ancien Régime*).

warfare of the last half century increased it to so frightful an extent that superior authority was required to redeem the abuses it had occasioned. It originated in the necessity of protection; and the modes of obtaining it, as well as the compensation [176] when obtained, were various. It often consisted of money or kind on the reaping of each harvest: sometimes in a multiplicity of petty privileges and advantages, but the chief object was to obtain *bhum*: and here we have one solution of the constituted *bhumia*,[1] assimilating, as observed, to the allodial proprietor. Bhum thus obtained is irrevocable; and in the eager anxiety for its acquisition we have another decided proof of every other kind of tenure being deemed resumable by the crown.

It was not unfrequent that application for protection was made to the nearest chief by the tenants of the fisc; a course eventually sanctioned by the Government, which could not refuse assent where it could not protect. Here, then, we revert to first principles; and 'seignorial rights' may be forfeited, when they cease to yield that which ought to have originated them, viz. benefit to the community. Personal service at stated periods, to aid in the agricultural[2] economy of the protector, was sometimes stipulated, when the husbandmen were to find implements and cattle,[3] and to attend whenever ordered. The protected calls the chief 'patron'; and the condition may not unaptly be compared to that of personal commendation,[4] like *salvamenta*, founded on the disturbed state of society. But what originated thus was often continued and multiplied by avarice, and the spirit of rapine, which disgraced the Rajput of the last half century, though he had abundance of apologies for 'scouring the country.' But all *salvamenta* and other marks of vassalage, obtained during these times of desolation, were annulled in the settlement which took place between the Rana and his chiefs, in A.D. 1818[5] [177].

[1] The chief might lose his *patta* lands, and he would then dwindle down into the *bhumia* proprietor, which title only lawless force could take from him. See Appendix, No. IX.

[2] See Appendix, No. X., Art. II.

[3] This species would come under the distinct term of Hydages due by soccage vassals, who in return for protection supply carriages and work (Hume, vol. ii. p. 308).

[4] Hallam, vol. i. p. 169.

[5] In indulging my curiosity on this subject, I collected some hundred

But the crown itself, by some singular proceeding, possesses, or did possess, according to the *Patta Bahi*, or Book of Grants, considerable *salvamenta* right, especially in the districts between the new and ancient capitals, in sums of from twenty to one hundred rupees in separate villages.

To such an extent has this *rakhwali* [1] been carried when protection was desired, that whole communities have ventured their liberty, and become, if not slaves, yet nearly approaching the condition of slaves, to the protector. But no common visitation ever leads to an evil of this magnitude. I mention the fact merely to show that it does exist ; and we may infer that the chief, who has become the arbiter of the lives and fortunes of his followers, must have obtained this power by devoting all to their protection. The term thus originated, and probably now (with many others) written for the first time in English letters in this sense, is *Basai*.

---

engagements, and many of a most singular nature. We see the chieftain stipulating for fees on marriages ; for a dish of the good fare at the wedding feast, which he transfers to a relation of his district if unable to attend himself ; portions of fuel and provender ; and even wherewithal to fill the wassail cup in his days of merriment. The Rajput's religious notions are not of so strict a character as to prevent his even exacting his *rakhwali* dues from the church lands, and the threat of slaughtering the sacred flock of our Indian Apollo has been resorted to, to compel payment when withheld. Nay, by the chiefs it was imposed on things locomotive : on caravans, or Tandas of merchandise, wherever they halted for the day, *rakhwali* was demanded. Each petty chief through whose district or patch of territory they travelled, made a demand, till commerce was dreadfully shackled ; but it was the only way in which it could be secured. It was astonishing how commerce was carried on at all ; yet did the cloths of Dacca and the shawls of Kashmir pass through all such restraints, and were never more in request. Where there is demand no danger will deter enterprise ; and commerce flourished more when these predatory armies were rolling like waves over the land, than during the succeeding halcyon days of pacification.

[1] The method by which the country is brought under this tax is as follows : " When the people are almost ruined by continual robberies and plunders, the leader of the band of thieves, or some friend of his, proposes that, for a sum of money annually paid, he will keep a number of men in arms to protect such a tract of ground, or as many parishes as submit to the contribution. When the terms are agreed upon he ceases to steal, and thereby the contributors are safe : if any one refuse to pay, he is immediately plundered. To colour all this villainy, those concerned in the robberies pay the tax with the rest ; and all the neighbourhood must comply or be undone. This is the case (among others), with the whole low country of the shire of Ross " (Extract from Lord Lovat's Memorial to George I. on the State of the Highlands of Scotland, in A.D. 1724).

Basāi, Slavery.—Slavery is to be found in successive stages of society of Europe, but we have no parallel in Rajwara (at least in name) to the agricultural serfs and *villains* of Europe; nor is there any intermediate term denoting a species of slavery between the *Gola* [1] of the Hindu chief's household and the free Rajput but the singular one of *basai*, which must be explained, since it cannot be translated. This class approximates closely to the *tributarii* and *coloni*, perhaps to the *servi*, of the Salic Franks, "who were cultivators of the earth, and subject to residence upon their master's estate, though not destitute of property or civil rights." [2] Precisely the condition of the cultivator in Haraoti who now tills for a taskmaster the fields he formerly owned, degraded to the name of *hali*,[3] a ploughman.

"When small proprietors," says Hallam, "lost their lands by mere rapine, we may believe their liberty was hardly less endangered." The *hali* of Haraoti knows the bitter truth of this inference, which applies to the subject immediately before us, [178] the *basai*. The portion of liberty the latter has parted with, was not originally lost through compulsion on the part of the protector, but from external violence, which made this desperate remedy necessary. Very different from the *hali* of Kotah, who is servile though without the title—a serf in condition but without the patrimony; compelled to labour for subsistence on the land he once owned; chained to it by the double tie of debt and strict police; and if flight were practicable, the impossibility of bettering his condition from the anarchy around would render it unavailing. This is not the practice under the patriarchal native government, which, with all its faults, retains the old links of society, with its redeeming sympathies; but springs from a *maire du palais*, who pursued an unfeeling and mistaken policy towards this class of society till of late years. Mistaken ambition was the origin of the evil; he saw his error, and remedied it in time to prevent further mischief to the State. This octogenarian ruler, Zalim Singh of Kotah, is too much of a philosopher and politician to let passion over-

[1] In Persian *ghulām*, literally 'slave'; evidently a word of the same origin with the Hindu *gola*. [The words have no connexion.]

[2] Hallam, vol. i. p. 217.

[3] From *hal*, 'a plough.' *Syl* is 'a plough' in Saxon (Turner's *Anglo-Saxons*). The *h* and *s* are permutable throughout Rajwara. [The words have no connexion.] In Marwar, *Salim Singh* is pronounced *Halim Hingh.*

come his interests and reputation; and we owe to the greatest despot a State ever had the only regular charter which at present exists in Rajasthan, investing a corporate body with the election of their own magistrates and the making of their own laws, subject only to confirmation; with all the privileges which marked in the outset the foundation of the free cities of Europe, and that of boroughs in England.

It is true that, in detached documents, we see the spirit of these institutions existing in Mewar, and it is as much a matter of speculation, whether this wise ruler promulgated this novelty as a trap for good opinions, or from policy and foresight alone: aware, when all around him was improving, from the shackles of restraint being cast aside, that his retention of them must be hurtful to himself. Liberality in this exigence answered the previous purpose of extortion. His system, even then, was good by comparison; all around was rapine, save in the little oasis kept verdant by his skill, where he permitted no other oppression than his own.

This charter is appended [1] as a curiosity in legislation, being given thirty years ago. Another, for the agriculturists' protection, was set up in A.D. 1821. No human being prompted either; though the latter is modelled from the proceedings in Mewar, and may have been intended, as before observed, to entrap applause.

In every district of Haraoti the stone was raised to record this ordinance [179].

Gola—Das (*Slaves*).—Famine in these regions is the great cause of loss of liberty: thousands were sold in the last great famine. The predatory system of the Pindaris and mountain tribes aided to keep it up. Here, as amongst the Franks, freedom is derived through the mother. The offspring of a *goli* [2] or *dasi* must be a slave. Hence the great number of golas in Rajput families, whose illegitimate offspring are still adorned in Mewar, as our Saxon slaves were of old, with a silver ring round the left ankle, instead of the neck. They are well-treated, and are often amongst the best of the military retainers; [3] but are generally esteemed in proportion to the quality of the mother, whether Rajputni, Muslim, or of the degraded tribes: they hold confidential places

[1] See Appendix, No. XI. [2] Female slave.
[3] See Appendix, No. XIX.

about the chiefs of whose blood they are. The great-grandfather of the late chief of Deogarh used to appear at court with three hundred *golas* [1] on horseback in his train, the sons of Rajputs, each with a gold ring round his ankle: men whose lives were his own. This chief could then head two thousand retainers, his own vassals.[2]

Slavery due to Gambling.—Tacitus [3] describes the baneful effects of gambling amongst the German tribes, as involving personal liberty; their becoming slaves, and being subsequently sold by the winner. The Rajput's passion for gaming, as remarked in the history of the tribes, is strong; and we can revert to periods long anterior to Tacitus, and perhaps before the woods of Germany were peopled with the worshippers of Tuisto, for the antiquity of this vice amongst the Rajput warriors, presenting a highly interesting picture of its pernicious effects. Yudhishthira having staked and lost the throne of India to Duryodhana, to recover it hazarded the beautiful and virtuous Draupadi. By the loaded dice of his foes she became the *goli* of the Kaurava, who, triumphing in his pride, would have unveiled her in public; but the deity presiding over female modesty preserved her from the rude gaze of the assembled host; the miraculous scarf lengthened as he withdrew it, till tired, he desisted at the instance of superior interposition. Yudhishthira, not satisfied with this, staked twelve years of his personal liberty, and became an exile from the haunts of Kalindi, a wanderer in the wilds skirting the distant ocean [180].

The illegitimate sons of the Rana are called *das*, literally 'slave': they have no rank, though they are liberally provided

[1] The reader of Dow's translation of Ferishta [i. 134] may recollect that when Kutbu-d-din was left the viceroy of the conqueror he is made to say: "He gave the country to Gola the son of Pittu Rai." ["He delivered over the country to the Gola, or natural son, of Pithow Ray" (Briggs' trans. i. 128).] Dow mistakes this appellation of the natural brother of the last Hindu sovereign for a proper name. He is mentioned by the bard Chand in his exploits of Prithwiraja.

[2] I have often received the most confidential messages, from chiefs of the highest rank, through these channels. [There are, at the present day, several bastard castes originally composed of the illegitimate children of men of rank, Rājputs, Brāhmans, Mahājans, and others. These are now recruited from the descendants of such persons, and from recently born illegitimate children (*Census Report, Rajputana*, 1911, i. 249 f.).]

[3] *Germania*, xxiv.

for. *Basai* signifies 'acquired slavery'; in contradistinction to *gola*, 'an hereditary slave.' The gola can only marry a goli: the lowest Rajput would refuse his daughter to a son of the Rana of this kind. The basai can redeem [1] his liberty: the gola has no wish to do so, because he could not improve his condition nor overcome his natural defects. To the basai nothing dishonourable attaches: the class retain their employments and caste, and are confined to no occupation, but it must be exercised with the chief's sanction. Individuals reclaimed from captivity, in gratitude have given up their liberty: communities, when this or greater evils threatened, have done the same for protection of their lives, religion, and honour. Instances exist of the population of towns being in this situation. The greater part of the inhabitants of the estate of Bijolli are the basai of its chief, who is of the Pramara tribe: they are his subjects; the Rana, the paramount lord, has no sort of authority over them. Twelve generations have elapsed since his ancestor conducted this little colony into Mewar, and received the highest honours and a large estate on the plateau of its border, in a most interesting country.[2]

The only badge denoting the basai is a small tuft of hair on the crown of the head. The term interpreted has nothing harsh in it, meaning 'occupant, dweller, or settler.' The numerous towns in India called *Basai* have this origin: chiefs abandoning their ancient haunts, and settling [3] with all their retainers and chattels in new abodes. From this, the town of Basai near Tonk (Rampura), derived its name, when the Solanki prince was compelled to abandon his patrimonial lands in Gujarat; his subjects of all

[1] The *das* or 'slave' may hold a fief in Rajasthan, but he never can rise above the condition in which this defect of birth has placed him. "L'affranchissement consistait à sortir de la classe des serfs, par l'acquisition d'un fief, ou seulement d'un fonds. La nécessité où s'étaient trouvés les seigneurs féodaux de vendre une partie de leurs terres, pour faire leurs équipages des croisades, avait rendu ces acquisitions communes; mais le fief n'anoblissait qu'à la troisième génération." Serfs who had twice or thrice been champions, or saved the lives of their masters, were also liberated. "Un évêque d'Auxerre déclara qu'il n'affranchirait gratuitement, qui que ce soit, s'il n'avait reçu quinze blessures à son service" (see Article 'Affranchissement,' *Dict. de l'ancien Régime*).

[2] I could but indistinctly learn whether this migration, and the species of paternity here existing, arose from rescuing them from Tatar invaders, or from the calamity of famine.

[3] *Basna*, 'to settle.'

classes accompanying him voluntarily, in preference to submitting to foreign rule. Probably the foundation of Bijolli was similar; though only the name of Basai now attaches to the inhabitants. It is not uncommon [181], in the overflowing of gratitude, to be told, "You may sell me, I am your basai." [1]

Private Feuds—Composition.—In a state of society such as these sketches delineate, where all depends on the personal character of the sovereign, the field for the indulgence of the passions, and especially of that most incident to the uncontrollable habits of such races—revenge—must necessarily be great. Private feuds have tended, with the general distraction of the times, to desolate this country. Some account of their mode of prosecution, and the incidents thence arising, cannot fail to throw additional light on the manners of society, which during the last half-century were fast receding to a worse than semi-barbarous condition, and, aided by other powerful causes, might have ended in entire annihilation. The period was rapidly advancing, when this fair region of Mewar, the garden of Rajasthan, would have reverted to its primitive sterility. The tiger and the wild boar had already become inmates of the capital, and the bats flitted undisturbed in the palaces of her princes. The antecourts, where the chieftains and their followers assembled to grace their prince's cavalcade, were overgrown with dank shrubs and grass, through which a mere footpath conducted the 'descendant of a hundred kings' to the ruins of his capital.

In these principalities the influence of revenge is universal. Not to prosecute a feud is tantamount to an acknowledgement of self-degradation; and, as in all countries where the laws are insufficient to control individual actions or redress injuries, they have few scruples as to the mode of its gratification. Hence

[1] I had the happiness to be the means of releasing from captivity some young chiefs, who had been languishing in Mahratta fetters as hostages for the payment of a war contribution. One of them, a younger brother of the Purawat division, had a mother dying to see him; but though he might have taken her house in the way, a strong feeling of honour and gratitude made him forgo this anxious visit: "I am your Rajput, your gola, your basai." He was soon sent off to his mother. Such little acts, mingling with public duty, are a compensation for the many drawbacks of solitude, gloom, and vexation, attending such situations. They are no sinecures or beds of roses—ease, comfort, and health, being all subordinate considerations.

feuds are entailed with the estates from generation to generation. To sheathe the sword till 'a feud is balanced' (their own idiomatic expression), would be a blot never to be effaced from the escutcheon.

In the Hindu word which designates a feud we have another of those striking coincidences in terms to which allusion has already been made: *vair* is 'a feud,' *vairi*, 'a foe.' The Saxon term for the composition of a feud, *wergild*, is familiar to every man. In some of these States the initial vowel is hard, and [182] pronounced *bair*. In Rajasthan, *bair* is more common than *vair*, but throughout the south-west *vair* only is used. In these we have the original Saxon word *war*,[1] the French *guer*. The Rajput *wergild* is land or a daughter to wife. In points of honour the Rajput is centuries in advance of our Saxon forefathers, who had a legislative remedy for every bodily injury, when each finger and toe had its price.[2] This might do very well when the injury was committed on a hind, but the Rajput must have blood for blood. The monarch must be powerful who can compel acceptance of the compensation, or *mund-kati*.[3]

The prosecution of a feud is only to be stopped by a process which is next to impracticable; namely, by the party injured volunteering forgiveness, or the aggressor throwing himself as a suppliant unawares on the clemency of his foe within his own domains: a most trying situation for each to be placed in, yet

[1] Gilbert on *Tenures*, art. "Warranty," p. 169. [Wergild, *wer*, 'man,' *gield*, *gieldan*; *vair* is Skt. *vira*, 'hero'; O.E. *wer*, O.H.G. *werran*, 'to embroil,' Fr. *guerre*.]

[2] "The great toe took rank as it should be, and held to double the sum of the others, for which ten scyllinga was the value without the nail, which was thirty scealta to boot" (Turner's *Anglo-Saxons*, vol. ii. p. 133).

[3] Appendix, No. XVIII. The laws of composition were carried to a much greater extent amongst the Hindu nations than even amongst those of the Anglo-Saxons, who might have found in Manu all that was ever written on the subject, from the killing of a Brahman by design to the accidental murder of a dog. The Brahman is four times the value of the soldier, eight of the merchant, and sixteen times of the Sudra. "If a Brahman kill one of the soldier caste (without malice), a bull and one thousand cows is the fine of expiation. If he slays a merchant, a bull and one hundred cows is the fine. If a Sudra or lowest class, ten white cows and a bull to the priest is the expiation" [*Laws*, xi. 127 ff.]. Manu legislated also for the protection of the brute creation, and if the priest by chance kills a cat, a frog, a dog, a lizard, an owl, or a crow, he must drink nothing but milk for three days and nights, or walk four miles in the night.

not unexampled, and revenge in such a case would entail infamy. It was reserved for these degenerate days to produce such an instance.

Amargarh-Shāhpura Feud.—The Raja of Shahpura, one of the most powerful of the chiefs of Mewar, and of the Rana's blood, had a feud with the Ranawat chief, the Bhumia proprietor of Amargarh. Ummeda,[1] the chief of Shahpura, held two estates: one was the grant of the kings of Delhi, the other of his own sovereign, and each amounting to £10,000 [2] of annual rent, besides the duties on commerce. His estate in Mewar was in the district of Mandalgarh, where also lay his antagonist's; their bounds were in common and some of the lands were intermixed: this led to disputes, threats, and blows, even in the towns of their fathers, between their husbandmen. The Bhumia Dilel was much less powerful; he was lord of only ten villages, not yielding above £1200 a year; but they were compact and well managed, and he was [183] popular amongst his brethren, whose swords he could always command. His castle was perched on a rock, and on the towers facing the west (the direction of Shahpura) were mounted some swivels: moreover a belt of forest surrounded it, through which only two or three roads were cut, so that surprise was impossible. Dilel had therefore little to fear, though his antagonist could bring two thousand of his own followers against him. The feud burned and cooled alternately; but the Raja's exposed villages enabled Dilel to revenge himself with much inferior means. He carried off the cattle, and sometimes the opulent subjects, of his foe, to his donjon-keep in Amargarh for ransom. Meanwhile the husbandmen of both suffered, and agriculture was neglected, till half the villages held by Ummeda in Mandalgarh became deserted. The Raja had merited this by his arrogance and attempts to humble Dilel, who had deserved more of the sympathies of his neighbours than his rival, whose tenants were tired of the payments of *barchi-dohai*.[3]

[1] *Ummeda*, 'hope.'

[2] Together £20,000, equal to £100,000 of England, if the respective value of the necessaries of life be considered.

[3] *Barchi* is 'a lance.' In these marauding days, when there was a riever in every village, they sallied out to 'run the country,' either to stop the passenger on the highway or the inhabitant of the city. The lance at his breast, he would call out *dohai*, an invocation of aid. During harvest time *barchi-dohai* used to be exacted.

Ummeda was eccentric, if the term be not too weak to characterize acts which, in more civilized regions, would have subjected him to coercion. He has taken his son and suspended him by the cincture to the pinnacle of his little chapel at Shahpura, and then called on the mother to come and witness the sight. He would make excursions alone on horseback or on a swift camel, and be missing for days. In one of these moods he and his foe Dilel encountered face to face within the bounds of Amargarh. Dilel only saw a chief high in rank at his mercy. With courtesy he saluted him, invited him to his castle, entertained him, and pledged his health and forgiveness in the *munawwar piyala*:[1] they made merry, and in the cup agreed to extinguish the remembrance of the feud.

Both had been summoned to the court of the sovereign. The Raja proposed that they should go together, and invited him to go by Shahpura. Dilel accordingly saddled his twenty steeds, moved out his equipage, and providing himself with fitting raiment, and funds to maintain him at the capital, accompanied the Raja to receive the return of his hospitality. They ate from the same platter,[2] drank of the same cup and enjoyed the song and dance. They even went together to [184] their devotions, to swear before their deity what they had pledged in the cup—oblivion of the past. But scarcely had they crossed the threshold of the chapel, when the head of the chief of Amargarh was rolling on the pavement, and the deity and the altar were sprinkled with his blood! To this atrocious and unheard-of breach of the laws of hospitality, the Raja added the baseness of the pilferer, seizing on the effects of his now lifeless foe. He is said, also, with all the barbarity and malignity of long-treasured revenge, to have kicked the head with his foot, apostrophising it in the pitiful language of resentment. The son of Dilel, armed for revenge, collected all his adherents, and confusion was again commencing its reign. To prevent this, the Rana compelled restitution of the horses and effects; and five villages from the estate of the Raja were the *mund-kati* (wergild) or compensation to the son of Dilel. The rest of the estate of the murderer was eventually sequestrated by the crown.

[1] 'Cup of invitation.' [*Munawwar*, Pers. 'bright, splendid.']

[2] This is a favourite expression, and a mode of indicating great friendship: 'to eat of the same platter (*thali*), and drink of the same cup (*piyala*).'

The feuds of Arja and Sheogarh are elsewhere detailed, and such statements could be multiplied. Avowal of error and demand of forgiveness, with the offer of a daughter in marriage, often stop the progress of a feud, and might answer better than appearing as a suppliant, which requires great delicacy of contrivance.[1] Border disputes[2] are most prolific in the production of feuds, and the Rajput lord-marchers have them entailed on them as regularly as their estates. The border chiefs of Jaisalmer and Bikaner carry this to such extent that it often involved both states in hostilities. The *vair* and its composition in Mandalgarh will, however, suffice for the present to exemplify these things.

Rajput Pardhans or Premiers.—It would not be difficult, amongst the *Majores Domus Regiae* of these principalities, to find parallels to the *Maires du Palais* of France. Imbecility in the chief, whether in the east or west, must have the same consequences; and more than one State in India will present us with the joint appearance of the phantom and the substance of royalty. The details of [185] personal attendance at court will be found elsewhere. When not absent on frontier duties, or by permission at their estates, the chiefs resided with their families at the capital; but a succession of attendants was always secured, to keep up its splendour and perform personal service at the palace. In Mewar, the privileges and exemptions of the higher class are such as to exhibit few of the marks of vassalage observable at other courts. Here it is only on occasion of particular festivals and solemnities that they ever join the prince's cavalcade, or attend at court. If full attendance is required, on the reception of ambassadors, or in discussing matters of general policy, when

[1] The Bundi feud with the Rana is still unappeased, since the predecessor of the former slew the Rana's father. It was an indefensible act, and the Bundi prince was most desirous to terminate it. He had no daughter to offer, and hinted a desire to accompany me *incog.* and thus gain admission to the presence of the Rana. The benevolence and generosity of this prince would have insured him success; but it was a delicate matter, and I feared some exposure from any arrogant hot-headed Rajput ere the scene could have been got up. The Raja Bishan Singh of Bundi is since dead [in 1828]; a brave and frank Rajput; he has left few worthier behind. His son [Rām Singh, 1821–89], yet a minor, promises well. The protective alliance, which is to turn their swords into ploughshares, will prevent their becoming foes; but they will remain sulky border-neighbours, to the fostering of disputes and the disquiet of the merchant and cultivator.

[2] Sim—Kankar.

they have a right to hear and advise as the hereditary council (*panchayat*) of the State, they are summoned by an officer, with the prince's *juhar*,[1] and his request. On grand festivals the great *nakkaras*, or kettle-drums, beat at three stated times; the third is the signal for the chief to quit his abode and mount his steed. Amidst all these privileges, when it were almost difficult to distinguish between the prince and his great chiefs, there are occasions well understood by both, which render the superiority of the former apparent: one occurs in the formalities observed on a lapse; another, when at court in personal service, the chief once a week mounts guard at the palace with his clan. On these occasions the vast distance between them is seen. When the chief arrives in the grand court of the palace with his retainers, he halts under the balcony till intimation is given to the prince, who from thence receives his obeisance and duty. This over, he retires to the great *darikhana*, or hall of audience, appropriated for these ceremonies, where carpets are spread for him and his retainers. At meals the prince sends his compliments, requesting the chief's attendance at the *rasora*[2] or 'feasting hall,' where with other favoured chiefs he partakes of dinner with the prince. He sleeps in the hall of audience, and next morning with the same formalities takes his leave. Again, in the summons to the presence from their estates, instant obedience is requisite. But in this, attention to their rank is studiously shown by *ruqa*, written by the private secretary, with the sign-manual of the prince attached, and sealed with the private finger-ring. For the inferior grades, the usual seal of state entrusted to the minister is used.

But these are general duties. In all these States some great court favourite [186], from his talents, character, or intrigue, holds the office of premier. His duties are proportioned to his wishes, or the extent of his talents and ambition; but he does not interfere with the civil administration, which has its proper minister. They, however, act together. The Rajput premier is the military minister, with the political government of the

[1] A salutation, only sent by a superior to an inferior.

[2] The kitchen is large enough for a fortress, and contains large eating halls. Food for seven hundred of the prince's court is daily dressed. This is not for any of the personal servants of the prince, or female establishments; all these are separate.

fiefs; the civil minister is never of this caste. Local customs have given various appellations to this officer. At Udaipur he is called *bhanjgarh*; at Jodhpur, *pardhan*; at Jaipur (where they have engrafted the term used at the court of Delhi) *musahib*; at Kotah, *kiladar*, and *diwan* or regent. He becomes a most important personage, as dispenser of the favours of the sovereign. Through him chiefly all requests are preferred, this being the surest channel to success. His influence, necessarily, gives him unbounded authority over the military classes, with unlimited power over the inferior officers of the State. With a powerful body of retainers always at his command, it is surprising we have not more frequently our 'mayors of Burgundy and Dagoberts,'[1] our 'Martels and Pepins,' in Rajasthan.

We have our hereditary Rajput premiers in several of these States: but in all the laws of succession are so regulated that they could not usurp the throne of their prince, though they might his functions.

When the treaty was formed between Mewar and the British Government, the ambassadors wished to introduce an article of guarantee of the office of pardhan to the family of the chief noble of the country, the Rawat of Salumbar. The fact was, as stated, that the dignity was hereditary in this family; but though the acquisition was the result of an act of virtue, it had tended much towards the ruin of the country, and to the same cause are to be traced all its rebellions.

The ambassador was one of the elders of the same clan, being the grand uncle of the hereditary pardhan. He had taken a most active share in the political events of the last thirty years, and had often controlled the councils of his prince during this period,

[1] Dagobert commended his wife and son Clovis to the trust of Ega, with whom she jointly held the care of the palace. On his death, with the aid of more powerful lords, she chose another mayor. He confirmed their grants for life. They made his situation hereditary; but which could only have held good from the crowd of imbeciles who succeeded Clovis, until the descendant of this mayor thrust out his children and seized the crown. This change is a natural consequence of unfitness; and if we go back to the genealogies (called sacred) of the Hindus, we see there a succession of dynasties forced from their thrones by their ministers. Seven examples are given in the various dynasties of the race of Chandra. (See Genealogical Tables, No. II.) [The above is in some ways inaccurate, but it is unnecessary to correct it, as it is not connected with the question of premiers in Rājputāna: see *EB*, xvii. 938.]

SALÚMBAR.

To face page 216.

and actually held the post of premier himself when stipulating [187] for his minor relative. With the ascendancy he exercised over the prince, it may be inferred that he had no intention of renouncing it during his lifetime; and as he was educating his adopted heir to all his notions of authority, and initiating him in the intrigues of office, the guaranteed dignity in the head of his family would have become a nonentity,[1] and the Ranas would have been governed by the deputies of their mayors. From both those evils the times have relieved the prince. The crimes of Ajit had made his dismissal from office a point of justice, but imbecility and folly will never be without 'mayors.'

When a Rana of Udaipur leaves the capital, the Salumbar chief is invested with the government of the city and charge of the palace during his absence. By his hands the sovereign is girt with the sword, and from him he receives the mark of inauguration on his accession to the throne. He leads, by right, the van in battle; and in case of the siege of the capital, his post is the *surajpol*,[2] and the fortress which crowns it, in which this family had a handsome palace, which is now going fast to decay.

It was the predecessor of the present chief of Salumbar who set up a pretender and the standard of rebellion; but when foreign aid was brought in, he returned to his allegiance and the defence of the capital. Similar sentiments have often been awakened in patriotic breasts, when roused by the interference of foreigners in their internal disputes. The evil entailed on the State by these hereditary offices will appear in its annals.

[1] So many sudden deaths had occurred in this family, that the branch in question (Ajit Singh's) were strongly suspected of 'heaping these mortal murders on their crown,' to push their elders from their seats. The father of Padma, the present chief, is said to have been taken off by poison; and Pahar Singh, one generation anterior, returning grievously wounded from the battle of Ujjain, in which the southrons first swept Mewar, was not permitted to recover. The mother of the present young chief of the Jhala tribe of the house of Gogunda, in the west, was afraid to trust him from her sight. She is a woman of great strength of mind and excellent character, but too indulgent to an only son. He is a fine bold youth, and, though impatient of control, may be managed. On horseback with his lance, in chase of the wild boar, a more resolute cavalier could not be seen. His mother, when he left the estate alone for court, which he seldom did without her accompanying him, never failed to send me a long letter, beseeching me to guard the welfare of her son. My house was his great resort: he delighted to pull over my books, or go fishing or riding with me.

[2] *Surya*, 'sun'; and *pol*, 'gate.' *Poliya*, 'a porter.'

In Marwar the dignity is hereditary in the house of Awa; but the last brave chief who held it became the victim of a revengeful and capricious sovereign,[1] [188] who was jealous of his exploits; and dying, he bequeathed a curse to his posterity who should again accept the office. It was accordingly transferred to the next in dignity, the house of Asop. The present chief, wisely distrusting the prince whose reign has been a series of turmoils, has kept aloof from court. When the office was jointly held by the chiefs of Nimaj and Pokaran, the tragic end of the former afforded a fine specimen of the prowess and heroism of the Rathor Rajput. In truth, these pardhans of Marwar have always been mill-stones round the necks of their princes; an evil interwoven in their system when the partition of estates took place amidst the sons of Jodha in the infancy of this State. It was, no doubt, then deemed politic to unite to the interests of the crown so powerful a branch, which when combined could always control the rest; but this gave too much equality.

The Chief of Pokaran.—Deo Singh, the great-grandfather of the Pokaran chief alluded to, used to sleep in the great hall of the palace with five hundred of his clan around him. "The throne of Marwar is in the sheath of my dagger," was the repeated boast of this arrogant chieftain. It may be anticipated that either he or his sovereign would die a violent death. The lord of Pokaran was entrapped, and instant death commanded; yet with the sword suspended over his head, his undaunted spirit was the same as when seated in the hall, and surrounded by his vassals. "Where, traitor, is now the sheath that holds the fortunes of Marwar?" said the prince. The taunt recoiled with bitterness when he loftily replied, "With my son at Pokaran I have left it." No time was given for further insult; his head rolled at the steps of the palace; but the dagger of Pokaran still haunts the imaginations of these princes, and many attempts have been made to get possessed of their stronghold on the edge of the desert.[2] The narrow escape of the present chief will be related hereafter, with the sacrifice of his friend and coadjutor, the chief of Nimaj.

[1] "The *cur* can bite," the reply of this chief, either personally, or to the person who reported that his sovereign so designated him, was never forgiven.

[2] His son, Sabal Singh, followed in his footsteps, till an accidental cannon-shot relieved the terrors of the prince.

Premiers in Kotah and Jaisalmer.—In Kotah and Jaisalmer the power of the ministers is supreme. We might describe their situation in the words of Montesquieu. "The Pepins kept their princes in a state of imprisonment in the palace, showing them once a year to the people. On this occasion they made such ordinances as were directed [189] by the mayor; they also answered ambassadors, but the mayor framed the answer."[1]

Like those of the Merovingian race, these puppets of royalty in the east are brought forth to the Champ de Mars once a year, at the grand military festival, the Dasahra. On this day, presents provided by the minister are distributed by the prince. Allowances for every branch of expenditure are fixed, nor has the prince the power to exceed them. But at Kotah there is nothing parsimonious, though nothing superfluous. On the festival of the birth of Krishna, and other similar feasts, the prince likewise appears abroad, attended by all the insignia of royalty. Elephants with standards precede; lines of infantry and guns are drawn up; while a numerous cavalcade surrounds his person. The son of the minister sometimes condescends to accompany his prince on horseback; nor is there anything wanting to magnificence, but the power to control or alter any part of it. This failing, how humiliating to a proud mind, acquainted with the history of his ancestors and imbued with a portion of their spirit, to be thus muzzled, enchained, and rendered a mere pageant of state! This chain would have been snapped, but that each link has become adamantine from the ties this ruler has formed with the British Government. He has well merited our protection; though we never contemplated to what extent the maintenance of these ties would involve our own character. But this subject is connected with the history of an individual who yields to none of the many extraordinary men whom India has produced, and who required but a larger theatre to have drawn the attention of the world. His character will be further elucidated in the Annals of Haravati [190].

[1] *L'Esprit des Loix*, chap. vi. livre 31.

CHAPTER 5

Adoption.—The hereditary principle, which perpetuates in these States their virtues and their vices, is also the grand preservative of their political existence and national manners : it is an imperishable principle, which resists time and innovation : it is this which made the laws of the Medes and Persians, as well as those of the Rajputs, unalterable. A chief of Mewar, like his sovereign, never dies : he disappears to be regenerated. '*Le roi est mort, vive le roi !*' is a phrase, the precise virtue of which is there well understood. Neither the crown nor the greater fiefs are ever without heirs. Adoption is the preservative of honours and titles ; the great fiefs of Rajasthan can never become extinct.[1] But, however valuable this privilege, which the law of custom has made a right, it is often carried to the most hurtful and foolish extent. They have allowed the limit which defined it to be effaced, and each family, of course, maintains a custom, so soothing to vanity, as the prospect of having their names revived in their descendants. This has resulted from the weakness of the prince and the misery of the times. Lands were bestowed liberally which yielded nothing to their master, who, in securing a nominal obedience and servitude, had as much as the times made them worth when given ; but with returning prosperity and old customs, these great errors have become too visible. Adoptions are often made during the life of the incumbent when without prospect of issue. The chief and his wife first agitate the subject in private ; it is then confided to the little council of the fief, and when propinquity and merit unite, they at once petition the prince to confirm their wishes, which are generally acceded to. So many interests are to be consulted on this occasion, that the blind partiality of the chief to any particular object is always counterpoised by the elders of the clan, who must have a pride in seeing a proper Thakur[2] at their head, and who prefer the nearest of kin, to prevent the disputes which would be attendant on neglect in this point [191].

[1] [The abandonment of the policy of escheat or lapse, and the recognition of the right of adoption were announced by Lord Canning in 1859.]

[2] As in Deogarh.

On sudden lapses, the wife is allowed the privilege, in conjunction with those interested in the fief, of nomination, though the case is seldom left unprovided for: there is always a presumptive heir to the smallest sub-infeudation of these estates. The wife of the deceased is the guardian of the minority of the adopted.

The Case of Deogarh.—The chief of Deogarh, one of the sixteen Omras[1] of Mewar, died without issue. On his death-bed he recommended to his wife and chiefs Nahar Singh for their adoption. This was the son of the independent chieftain of Sangramgarh, already mentioned. There were nearer kin, some of the seventh and eighth degrees, and young Nahar was the eleventh. It was never contemplated that the three last gigantic[2] chieftains of Deogarh would die without issue, or the branches, now claimants from propinquity, would have been educated to suit the dignity; but being brought up remote from court, they had been compelled to seek employment where obtainable, or to live on the few acres to which their distant claim of birth restricted them. Two of these, who had but the latter resource to fly to, had become mere boors; and of two who had sought service abroad by arms, one was a cavalier in the retinue of the prince, and the other a hanger-on about court: both dissipated and unfitted, as the frerage asserted, 'to be the chieftains of two thousand Rajputs, the sons of one father.'[3] Much interest and intrigue were carried on for one of these, and he was supported by the young prince and a faction. Some of the senior Pattawats of Deogarh are men of the highest character, and often lamented the sombre qualities of their chief, which prevented the clan having that interest in the State to which its extent and rank entitled it. While these intrigues were in their infancy, they adopted a decided measure; they brought home young Nahar from his father's residence, and 'bound round his head the turban of the deceased.' In his name the death of the late chief was announced. It was added, that he hoped to see his friends

[1] [Umara, plural of Amīr, 'a chief.']

[2] Gokuldas, the last chief, was one of the finest men I ever beheld in feature and person. He was about six feet six, perfectly erect, and a Hercules in bulk. His father at twenty was much larger, and must have been nearly seven feet high. It is surprising how few of the chiefs of this family died a natural death. It has produced some noble Rajputs.

[3] *Ek bap ka beta.*

after the stated days of *matam* or mourning; and he performed all the duties of the son of Deogarh, and lighted the funeral pyre.

When these proceedings were reported, the Rana was highly and justly incensed. The late chief had been one of the rebels of S. 1848;[1] and though pardon had been [192] granted, yet this revived all the recollection of the past, and he felt inclined to extinguish the name of Sangawat.[2]

In addition to the common sequestration, he sent an especial one with commands to collect the produce of the harvest then reaping, charging the sub-vassals with the design of overturning his lawful authority. They replied very submissively, and artfully asserted that they had only given a son to Gokuldas, not an heir to Deogarh; that the sovereign alone could do this, and that they trusted to his nominating one who would be an efficient leader of so many Rajputs in the service of the Rana. They urged the pretensions of young Nahar, at the same time leaving the decision to the sovereign. Their judicious reply was well supported by their ambassador at court, who was the bard of Deogarh, and had recently become, though *ex officio*, physician to the prince.[3] The point was finally adjusted, and Nahar was brought to court, and invested with the sword by the hand of the sovereign, and he is now lord of Deogarh Madri, one of the richest and most powerful fiefs[4] of Mewar Madri was the ancient name of the estate; and Sangramgarh, of which Nahar was the heir, was severed from it, but by some means had reverted to the crown, of which it now holds. The adoption of Nahar by Gokuldas leaves the paternal estate without an immediate heir; and his actual father being mad, if more distant claims are not admitted, it is probable that Sangramgarh will eventually revert to the fisc.

[1] A.D. 1792. [2] That of the clan of Deogarh.

[3] Apollo [Krishna] is the patron both of physicians and poets; and though my friend Amra does not disgrace him in either calling, it was his wit, rather than his medical degree, that maintained him at court. He said it was not fitting that the sovereign of the world should be served by clowns or opium-eaters; and that young Nahar, when educated at court under the Rana's example, would do credit to the country: and what had full as much weight as any of the bard's arguments was, that the fine of relief on the *Talwar bandhai* (or girding on of the sword) of a lac of rupees, should be immediately forthcoming.

[4] Patta. [About 30 miles south of Udaipur city.]

Reflections.—The system of feuds must have attained considerable maturity amongst the Rajputs, to have left such traces, notwithstanding the desolation that has swept the land: but without circumspection these few remaining customs will become a dead letter. Unless we abstain from all internal interference, we must destroy the links which connect the prince and his vassals; and, in lieu of a system decidedly imperfect, we should leave them none at all, or at least not a system of feuds, the only one they can comprehend. Our friendship has rescued them from exterior foes, and time will restore the rest. With the dignity and [193] establishments of their chiefs, ancient usages will revive; and *nazarana* (relief), *kharg bandhai* (investiture), *dasaundh* (aids or benevolence, literally 'the tenth'), and other incidents, will cease to be mere ceremonies. The desire of every liberal mind, as well as the professed wish of the British Government, is to aid in their renovation, and this will be best effected by not meddling with what we but imperfectly understand.[1]

We have nothing to apprehend from the Rajput States if raised to their ancient prosperity. The closest attention to their history proves beyond contradiction that they were never capable of uniting, even for their own preservation: a breath, a scurrilous stanza of a bard, has severed their closest confederacies. No national head exists amongst them as amongst the Mahrattas; and each chief being master of his own house and followers, they are individually too weak to cause us any alarm.

No feudal government can be dangerous as a neighbour; for defence it has in all countries been found defective; and for aggression, totally inefficient. Let there exist between us the most perfect understanding and identity of interests; the foundation-step to which is to lessen or remit the galling, and to us

[1] Such interference, when inconsistent with past usage and the genius of the people, will defeat the very best intentions. On the grounds of policy and justice, it is alike incumbent on the British Government to secure the maintenance of their present form of government, and not to repair, but to advise the repairs of the fabric, and to let their own artists alone be consulted. To employ ours would be like adding a Corinthian capital to a column of Ellora, or replacing the mutilated statue of Baldeva with a limb from the Hercules Farnese. To have a chain of prosperous independent States on our only exposed frontier, the north-west, attached to us from benefits, and the moral conviction that we do not seek their overthrow, must be a desirable policy.

contemptible tribute, now exacted, enfranchise them from our espionage and agency, and either unlock them altogether from our dangerous embrace, or let the ties between us be such only as would ensure grand results: such as general commercial freedom and protection, with treaties of friendly alliance. Then, if a Tatar or a Russian invasion threatened our eastern empire, fifty thousand Rajputs would be no despicable allies.[1]

Rajput Loyalty and Patriotism.—Let us call to mind what they did when they fought for Aurangzeb: they are still unchanged, if we give them the proper stimulus. Gratitude, honour, and fidelity, are terms which at one time were the foundation of all the virtues of a Rajput. Of the theory of these sentiments he is still enamoured; but, unfortunately, for his happiness, the times have left him but little scope for the practice [194] of them. Ask a Rajput which is the greatest of crimes? he will reply, '*gunchhor*,' 'forgetfulness of favours.'. This is his most powerful term for ingratitude. Gratitude with him embraces every obligation of life, and is inseparable from *swamidharma*, 'fidelity to his lord.' He who is wanting in these is not deemed fit to live, and is doomed to eternal pains in Pluto's[2] realm hereafter.[3]

"It was a powerful feeling," says an historian[4] who always identifies his own emotions with his subject, "which could make the bravest of men put up with slights and ill-treatment at the hand of their sovereign, or call forth all the energies of discontented exertion for one whom they never saw, and in whose character there was nothing to esteem. Loyalty has scarcely less tendency to refine and elevate the heart than patriotism itself." That these sentiments were combined, the past history of the Rajputs will show;[5] and to the strength of these ties do they

[1] [The author's prediction has been realized by recent events.]

[2] *Yamaloka.*

[3] The *gunchhor* (ungrateful) and *satchhor* (violator of his faith) are consigned, by the authority of the bard, to sixty-thousand years' residence in hell. Europeans, in all the pride of mastery, accuse the natives of want of gratitude, and say their language has no word for it. They can only know the *namak-haram* ['he that is false to his salt'] of the Ganges. *Gunchhor* is a compound of powerful import, as ingratitude and infidelity are the highest crimes. It means, literally, "abandoner (from *chhorna*, 'to quit') of virtue (*gun*)."

[4] Hallam, vol. i. p. 323.

[5] Of the effects of loyalty and patriotism combined, we have splendid examples in Hindu history and tradition. A more striking instance could

owe their political existence, which has outlived ages of strife. But for these, they would have been converts and vassals to the Tatars, who would still have been enthroned in Delhi. Neglect, oppression, and religious interference, sunk one of the greatest monarchies of the world ;[1] made Sivaji a hero, and converted the peaceful husbandmen of the Kistna and Godavari into a brave but rapacious soldier.

We have abundant examples, and I trust need not exclaim with the wise minister of Akbar, "who so happy as to profit by them ?"[2]

The Rajput, with all his turbulence, possesses in an eminent degree both loyalty and patriotism ; and though he occasionally exhibits his refractory spirit to his [195] father and sovereign,[3] we shall see of what he is capable when his country is threatened with dismemberment, from the history of Mewar, and the reign of Ajit Singh of Marwar. In this last we have one of the noblest examples history can afford of unbounded devotion. A prince, whom not a dozen of his subjects had ever seen, who had been concealed from the period of his birth throughout a tedious minority to avoid the snares of a tyrant,[4] by the mere magic of a name kept the discordant materials of a great feudal association

---

scarcely be given than in the recent civil distractions at Kotah, where a mercenary army raised and maintained by the Regent, either openly or covertly declared against him, as did the whole feudal body to a man, the moment their young prince asserted his subverted claims, and in the cause of their rightful lord abandoned all consideration of self, their families and lands, and with their followers offered their lives to redeem his rights or perish in the attempt. No empty boast, as the conclusion testified. God forbid that we should have more such examples of Rajput devotion to their sense of fidelity to their lords !

[1] See statement of its revenues during the last emperor, who had preserved the empire of Delhi united.

[2] Abu-l Fazl uses this expression when moralizing on the fall of Shihabu-d-din, king of Ghazni and first established monarch of India, slain by Prithwiraja, the Hindu sovereign of Delhi [*Āīn*, ii. 302]. [Muhammad Ghori, Shihābu-d-dīn, was murdered on the road to Ghazni by a fanatic of the Mulāhidah sect, in March, A.D. 1206 (*Tabakāt-ī-Nāsiri*, in Elliot-Dowson ii. 297, 235). According to the less probable account of Ferishta (Briggs, i. 185), he was murdered at Rohtak by a gang of Gakkhars or rather Khokhars (Rose, *Glossary*, ii. 275).]

[3] The Rajput, who possesses but an acre of land, has the proud feeling of common origin with his sovereign, and in styling him *bapji* (sire), he thinks of him as the common father or representative of the race. What a powerful incentive to action !

[4] Aurangzeb.

in subjection, till, able to bear arms, he issued from his concealment to head these devoted adherents, and reconquer what they had so long struggled to maintain. So glorious a contest, of twenty years' duration, requires but an historian to immortalize it. Unfortunately we have only the relation of isolated encounters, which, though exhibiting a prodigality of blood and acts of high devotion, are deficient in those minor details which give unity and interest to the whole.

Gallant Services to the Empire.—Let us take the Rajput character from the royal historians themselves, from Akbar, Jahangir, Aurangzeb. The most brilliant conquests of these monarchs were by their Rajput allies; though the little regard the latter had for opinion alienated the sympathies of a race, who when rightly managed, encountered at command the Afghan amidst the snows of Caucasus, or made the furthest Cheronese tributary to the empire. Assam, where the British arms were recently engaged, and for the issue of which such anxiety was manifested in the metropolis of Britain, was conquered by a Rajput prince,[1] whose descendant is now an ally of the British Government.

But Englishmen in the east, as elsewhere, undervalue everything not national. They have been accustomed to conquest, not reverses: though it is only by studying the character of those around them that the latter can be avoided and this superiority maintained. Superficial observers imagine that from lengthened predatory spoliation the energy of the Rajput has fled: an idea which is at once erroneous and dangerous. The vices now manifest from oppression will disappear [196] with the cause, and with reviving prosperity new feelings will be generated, and each national tie and custom be strengthened. The Rajput would glory in putting on his saffron robes[2] to fight for such a land, and for those who disinterestedly laboured to benefit it.

[1] Raja Man of Jaipur, who took Arakan, Orissa, and Assam. Raja Jaswant Singh of Marwar retook Kabul for Aurangzeb, and was rewarded by poison. Raja Ram Singh Hara, of Kotah, made several important conquests; and his grandson, Raja Isari Singh, and his five brothers, were left on one field of battle.

[2] When a Rajput is determined to hold out to the last in fighting, he always puts on a robe dyed in saffron. [This was the common practice, saffron being the colour of the bridal robe (Malcolm, *Memoir of Central India*, 2nd ed. i. 358; Grant Duff, *Hist. of the Mahrattas*, 317; Forbes, *Rāsmālā*, 408).]

Let us, then, apply history to its proper use. We need not turn to ancient Rome for illustration of the dangers inseparable from wide dominion and extensive alliances. The twenty-two Satrapies of India, the greater part of which are now the appanage of Britain, exhibited, even a century ago, one of the most splendid monarchies history has made known, too extensive for the genius of any single individual effectually to control. Yet was it held together, till encroachment on their rights, and disregard to their habits and religious opinions, alienated the Rajputs, and excited the inhabitants of the south to rise against their Mogul oppressors. 'Then was the throne of Aurangzeb at the mercy of a Brahman, and the grandson[1] of a cultivator in the province of Khandesh held the descendants of Timur pensioners on his bounty' [197].

[1] Sindhia

APPENDIX

PAPERS REFERRED TO IN THE SKETCH OF A FEUDAL SYSTEM IN RAJASTHAN

BEING

LITERAL TRANSLATIONS *from* INSCRIPTIONS *and* ORIGINAL DOCUMENTS, *most of which are in the* AUTHOR'S POSSESSION

No. I

Translation of a Letter from the expatriated Chiefs[1] *of Marwar to the Political Agent of the British Government, Western Rajput States.*

After compliments.

We have sent to you a confidential person, who will relate what regards us. The Sarkar Company are sovereigns of Hindustan, and you know well all that regards our condition. Although there is nothing which respects either ourselves or our country hid from you, yet is there matter immediately concerning us which it is necessary to make known.

Sri Maharaja and ourselves are of one stock, all Rathors. He is our head, we his servants: but now anger has seized him, and we are dispossessed of our country. Of the estates, our patrimony and our dwelling, some have been made khalisa,[2] and those who endeavour to keep aloof expect the same fate. Some under the most solemn pledge of security have been inveigled and suffered death, and others imprisoned. Mutasadis,[3] officers of

[1] The names omitted to prevent any of them falling a sacrifice to the blind fury of their prince. The brave chief of Nimaj has sold his life, but dearly. In vain do we look in the annals of Europe for such devotion and generous despair as marked his end, and that of his brave clan. He was a perfect gentleman in deportment, modest and mild, and head of a powerful clan.

[2] Fiscal, that is, sequestrated.

[3] Clerks, and inferior officers of government.

state, men of the soil and those foreign to it, have been seized, and the most unheard-of deeds and cruelties inflicted, which we cannot even write. Such a spirit has possessed his mind as never was known to any former prince of Jodhpur. His forefathers have reigned for generations; our forefathers were their ministers and advisers, and whatever was performed was by the collective wisdom of the council of our chiefs. Before the face of his ancestors, our own ancestors have slain and been slain; and in performing services to the kings,[1] they made the State of Jodhpur what it is. Wherever Marwar was concerned, there our fathers were to be found, and with their lives preserved the land. Sometimes our head was a minor; even then by the wisdom of our fathers and their services, the land was kept firm under our feet, and thus has it descended from generation to generation. Before his eyes (Raja Man's) we have performed good service: when at that perilous time the host of Jaipur[2] surrounded [198] Jodhpur on the field we attacked it; our lives and fortunes were at stake, and God granted us success; the witness is God Almighty. Now, men of no consideration are in our prince's presence; hence this reverse. *When our services are acceptable, then is he our lord; when not, we are again his brothers and kindred, claimants and laying claim to the land.*

He desires to dispossess us; but can we let ourselves be dispossessed? The English are masters of all India. The chief of —— sent his agent to Ajmer; he was told to go to Delhi. Accordingly Thakur —— went there, but no path was pointed out. If the English chiefs will not hear us, who will? The English allow no one's lands to be usurped, and our birthplace is Marwar—from Marwar we must have bread. A hundred thousand Rathors—where are they to go to? From respect to the English alone have we been so long patient, and without acquainting your government of our intentions, you might afterwards find fault; therefore we make it known, and we thereby acquit ourselves to you. What we brought with us from Marwar we have consumed, and even what we could get on credit; and now, when want must make us perish, we are ready and can do anything.[3]

The English are our rulers, our masters. Sri Man Singh has seized our lands; by your government interposing these troubles may be settled, but without its guarantee and intervention we can have no confidence whatever. Let us have a reply to our petition.

[1] Alluding to the sovereigns of Delhi. In the magnificent feudal assemblage at this gorgeous court, where seventy-six princes stood in the Divan (*Diwan-i-Khass*) each by a pillar covered with plates of silver, the Marwar prince had the right hand of all. I have an original letter from the great-grandfather of Raja Man to the Rana, elate with this honour.

[2] In 1806.

[3] The historian of the Middle Ages justly remarks, that "the most deadly hatred is that which men, exasperated by proscription and forfeitures, bear their country."

We will wait it in patience; but if we get none, the fault will not be ours, having given everywhere notice. Hunger will compel man to find a remedy. For such a length of time we have been silent from respect to your government alone: our own Sarkar is deaf to complaint. But to what extreme shall we wait? Let our hopes be attended to. Sambat 1878, Sawan sudi duj. (August 1821.)

True Translation:
(Signed) JAMES TOD.

No. II

Remonstrance of the Sub-Vassals of Deogarh against their chief, Rawat Gokul Das.

1. He respects not the privileges or customs established of old.

2. To each Rajput's house a charas [1] or hide of land was attached: this he has resumed.

3. Whoever bribes him is a true man: who does not, is a thief.

4. Ten or twelve villages established by his pattayats [2] he has resumed, and left their families to starve.

5. From time immemorial sanctuary (*saran*) has been esteemed sacred: this he has abolished.

6. On emergencies he would pledge his oath to his subjects (*ryots*), and afterwards plunder them.

7. In old times, it was customary when the presence of his chiefs and kindred was required, to invite them by letter: a fine is now the warrant of summons: thus lessening their dignity.

8. Such messengers, in former times, had a taka [3] for their ration (*bhatta*); now he imposes two rupees [199].

9. Formerly, when robberies occurred in the mountains within the limits of Deogarh, the loss was made good: now all complaint is useless, for his faujdar [4] receives a fourth of all such plunder. The Mers [5] range at liberty; but before they never committed murder: now they slay as well as rob our kin; nor is there any redress, and such plunder is even sold within the town of Deogarh.

10. Without crime, he resumes the lands of his vassals for the

[1] Hide or skin, from the vessel used in irrigation being made of leather.

[2] The vassals, or those holding fiefs (patta) of Deogarh.

[3] A copper coin, equal to twopence.

[4] Military commander; a kind of inferior *maire du palais*, on every Rajput chieftain's estate, and who has the military command of the vassals. He is seldom of the same family, but generally of another tribe.

[5] Mountaineers.

sake of imposition of fines; and after such are paid, he cuts down the green crops, with which he feeds his horses.

11. The cultivators[1] on the lands of the vassals he seizes by force, extorts fines, or sells their cattle to pay them. Thus cultivation is ruined and the inhabitants leave the country.

12. From oppression the town magistrates[2] of Deogarh have fled to Raepur. He lays in watch to seize and extort money from them.

13. When he summons his vassals for purposes of extortion and they escape his clutches, he seizes on their wives and families. Females, from a sense of honour, have on such occasions thrown themselves into wells.

14. He interferes to recover old debts, distraining the debtor of all he has in the world: half he receives.

15. If any one have a good horse, by fair means or foul he contrives to get it.

16. *When Deogarh was established, at the same time were our allotments: as is his patrimony, so is our patrimony.*[3] Thousands have been expended in establishing and improving them, yet our rank, privileges, and rights he equally disregards.

17. From these villages, founded by our forefathers, he, at will, takes four or five skins of land and bestows them on foreigners; and thus the ancient proprietors are reduced to poverty and ruin.

18. From of old, all his Rajput kin had daily rations, or portions of grain: for four years these rights have been abolished.

19. From ancient times the pattayats formed his council; now he consults only foreigners. What has been the consequence? the whole annual revenue derived from the mountains is lost.

20. From the ancient Bhum[4] of the Frerage[5] the mountaineers carry off the cattle, and instead of redeeming them, this faujdar sets the plunderers up to the trick of demanding rakhwali.[6]

21. Money is justice, and there is none other: whoever has money may be heard. The bankers and merchants have gone abroad for protection, but he asks not where they are.

22. When cattle are driven off to the hills, and we do ourselves justice and recover them, we are fined, and told that the mountaineers have his pledge. Thus our dignity is lessened. Or if

[1] Of the Jat and other labouring tribes.

[2] Chauthias. In every town there is an unpaid magistracy, of which the head is the Nagar Seth, or chief citizen, and the four Chauthias, tantamount to the Lord Mayor and Aldermen, who hold their courts and decide in all civil cases.

[3] Here are the precise sentiments embodied in the remonstrances of the great feudal chiefs of Marwar to their prince; see Appendix, No. I.

[4] The old allodial allotments.

[5] Bhayyad.

[6] The *salvamenta* of our feudal writers; the *blackmail* of the north.

we seize one of these marauders, a party is sent to liberate him, for which the faujdar [200] receives a bribe. Then a feud ensues at the instigation of the liberated Mer, and the unsupported Rajput is obliged to abandon his patrimony.[1] There is neither protection nor support. The chief is supine, and so regardless of honour, that he tells us to take money to the hills and redeem our property. Since this faujdar had power, 'poison has been our fate.' Foreigners are all in all, and the home-bred are set aside. Deccanis and plunderers enjoy the lands of his brethren. Without fault, the chiefs are deprived of their lands, to bring which into order time and money have been lavished. Justice there is none.

Our rights and privileges in his family are the same as his in the family of the Presence.[2] Since you[3] entered Mewar, lands long lost have been recovered. What crimes have we committed that at this day we should lose ours?

We are in great trouble.[4]

No. III

Maharaja Sri Gokuldas to the four ranks (*char misl*) of Pattayats of Deogarh, commanding. Peruse.

Without crime no vassal shall have his estate or charsas disseized. Should any individual commit an offence, it shall be judged by the *four ranks* (char misl), my brethren, and then punished. Without consulting them on all occasions I shall never inflict punishment.[5] To this I swear by Sri Nathji. No departure from this agreement shall ever occur. S. 1874; the 6th Pus.

[1] 'Watan.' [2] The Rana. [3] The Author.

[4] With the articles of complaint of the vassals of Deogarh and the short extorted charter, to avoid future cause for such, we may contrast the following: "Pour avoir une idée du brigandage que les nobles exerçaient à l'époque où les premières *chartes* furent accordées, il suffit d'en lire quelques-unes, et l'on verra que le seigneur y disait :—'Je promets de ne point *voler*, *extorquer* les biens et les meubles des habitans, de les délivrer des *toles* ou *rapines*, et autres *mauvaises coutumes*, et de ne plus commettre envers eux d'exactions.'—En effet, dans ces tems malheureux, vivres, meubles, chevaux, voitures, dit le savant Abbé de Mably, tout était enlevé par l'insatiable et aveugle avidité des seigneurs" (Art. 'Chartres,' *Dict. de l'Ancien Régime*).

[5] This reply to the remonstrance of his vassals is perfectly similar in point to the 43rd article of Magna Charta.

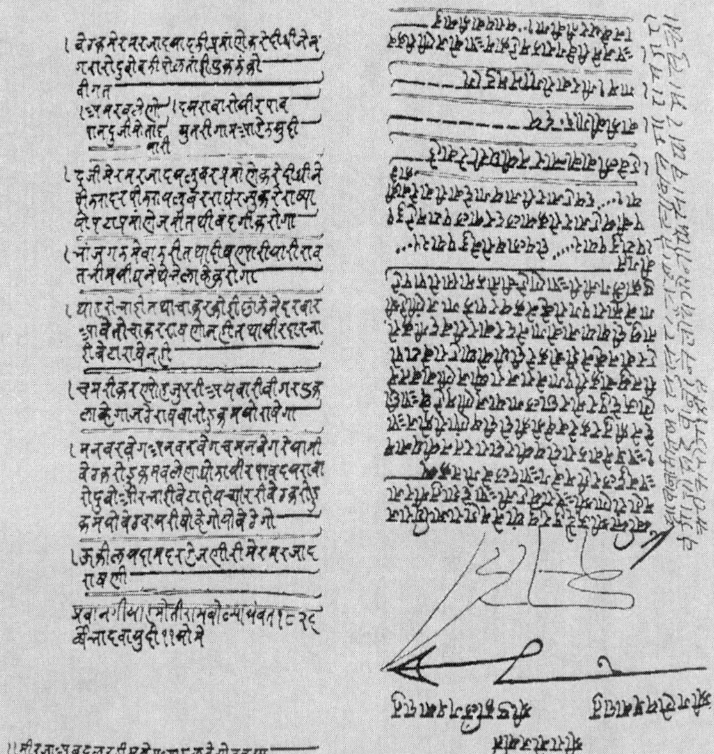

REPRODUCTION OF SANSKRIT GRANT.

To face page 232.

No. IV

Grant from Maharana Ari Singh, Prince of Mewar, to the Sindi Chief, Abdu-l Rahim Beg.

Ramji ![1]

Ganeshji ![1] Eklingji ![1]

Sri Maharaja Dhiraj Maharana Ari Singh to Mirza Abdu-l Rahim Beg Adilbegot, commanding.

Now some of our chiefs having rebelled and set up the impostor Ratna Singh, brought the [201] Deccani army and erected batteries against Udaipur, in which circumstances your services have been great and tended to the preservation of our sovereignty: therefore, in favour towards you, I have made this grant, which your children and children's children shall continue to enjoy. You will continue to serve faithfully; and whoever of my race shall dispossess you or yours, on him be Eklingji and the sin of the slaughter of Chitor.

Particulars.

1st. In estates, 200,000 rupees.

2nd. In cash annually, 25,000.

3rd. Lands outside the Debari gate, 10,000.

4th. As a residence, the dwelling-house called Bharat Singh's.

5th. A hundred bighas of land outside the city for a garden.

6th. The town of Mithun in the valley, to supply wood and forage.

7th. To keep up the tomb of Ajmeri Beg, who fell in action, one hundred bighas of land.

Privileges and Honours.

8th. A seat in Darbar and rank in all respects equal to the chieftain of Sadri.[2]

9th. Your kettle-drums (Nakkara) to beat to the exterior gate, but with one stick only.

10th. Amar Balaona,[3] and a dress of honour on the Dasahra[4] festival.

[1] Invocations to Ram, Ganesh (god of wisdom), and Eklinga, the patron-divinity of the Sesodia Guhilots.

[2] The first of the foreign vassals of the Rana's house. [Bari Sādri, about 50 miles E.S.E. of Udaipur city, held by the senior noble of Mewār, a Rājput of the Jhāla sub-sept, styled Rāja of Sādri (Erskine ii. A. 93).]

[3] A horse furnished by the prince, always replaced when he dies, therefore called Amar, or immortal.

[4] The grand military festival, when a muster is made of all the Rajput quotas.

11th. Drums to beat to Ahar. All other privileges and rank like the house of Salumbar.[1] Like that house, yours shall be from generation to generation; therefore according to the valuation of your grant you will serve.

12th. Your brothers or servants, whom you may dismiss, I shall not entertain or suffer my chief to entertain.

13th. The Chamars[2] and Kirania[3] you may use at all times when alone, but never in the Presence.

14th. Munawwar Beg, Anwar Beg, Chaman Beg, are permitted seats in front of the throne; Amar Balaona, and honorary dresses on Dasahra, and seats for two or three other relatives who may be found worthy the honour.

15th. Your agent (*Vakil*) shall remain at court with the privileges due to his rank.

By command:
SAH MOTI RAM BOLIA,
S. 1826 (A.D. 1770) Bhadon (August) sudi 11 Somwar (Monday).

No. V

Grant of the Patta of Bhainsror to Rawat Lal Singh, one of the sixteen great vassals of Mewar.

Maharaja Jagat Singh to Rawat Lal Singh Kesarisinghgot,[4] commanding.

Now to you the whole Pargana of Bhainsror[5] is granted as *Giras*, viz. [202]:

Town of Bhainsror . . .	3000	1500
Fifty-two others (names uninteresting), besides one in the valley of the capital. Total value . .	62,000	31,000[6]

With two hundred and forty-eight horse and two hundred and forty-eight foot, good horse and good Rajputs, you will perform service. Of this, forty-eight horse and forty-eight foot are excused for the protection of your fort; therefore with two hundred foot and two hundred horse you will serve when and wherever ordered. The first grant was given in Pus, S. 1798, when the income inserted was over-rated. Understanding this, the Presence (huzur) ordered sixty thousand of annual value to be attached to Bhainsror.

[1] The first of the home-chieftains.

[2] The tail of the wild ox, worn across the saddle-bow.

[3] An umbrella or shade against the sun; from *kiran*, 'a ray.'

[4] Clan (*got*) of Kesari Singh, one of the great branches of the Chondawats.

[5] On the left bank of the Chambal.

[6] To explain these double *rekhs*, or estimates, one is the full value, the other the deteriorated rate.

No. VI

Grant from Maharana Sangram Singh of Mewar to his Nephew, the Prince Madho Singh, heir-apparent to the principality of Jaipur.

Sri Ramjayati
(*Victory to Rama*).

Sri Ganesh Prasad (*By favour of Ganesh*). Sri Ekling Prasad (*By favour of Eklinga*).

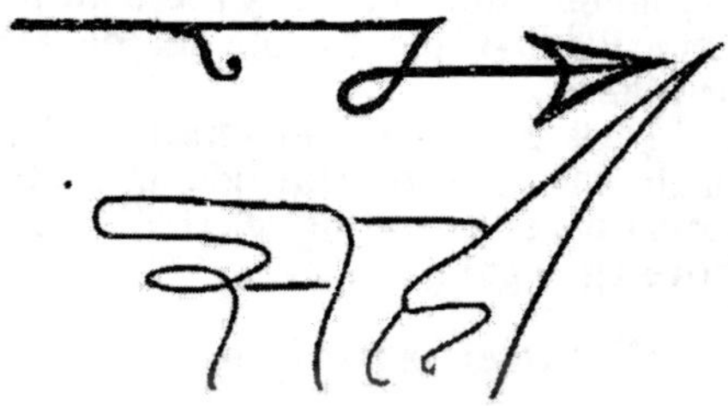

(*See notes 1 and 2 below.*)

Maharaja Dhiraj Maharana Sri Sangram Singh, Adisatu, commanding. To my nephew, Kunwar Madho Singhji, *giras* (a fief) has been granted, viz. :

The fief (*patta*) of Rampura ; therefore, with one thousand horse and two thousand foot, you will perform service during six months annually ; and when foreign service is required, three thousand foot and three thousand horse.

While the power of the Presence is maintained in these districts you will not be dispossessed.

By command :
Pancholi Raechand amd Mehta Mul Das.
S. 1785 (A.D. 1729) ; Chait sudi 7th ; Mangalwar (Tuesday).

Addressed in the Rana's own hand.

To my nephew Madho Singh[3] [203]. My child, I have given you Rampura : while mine, you shall not be deprived of it. Done.

[1] The bhala, or lance, is the sign-manual of the Salumbar chieftain, as hereditary premier of the state.

[2] Is a monogram forming the word *Sahai*, being the sign-manual of the prince.

[3] *Bhanaij* is sister's son ; as *Bhatija* is brother's son. It will be seen in the Annals, that to support this prince to the succession of the Jaipur Gaddi, both Mewar and Jaipur were ruined, and the power of the Deccanis established in both countries.

No. VII

Grant of Bhum Rakhwali (Salvamenta) from the village of Dongla to Maharaja Khushhal Singh.

S. 1806 (A.D. 1750), *the first of Sawan (July)*.

1st. A field of one hundred and fifty-one bighas, of which thirty-six are irrigated.

2nd. One hundred and two bighas of waste and unirrigated, viz. :

Six bighas cultivated by Govinda the oilman.
Three, under Hira and Tara the oilmen.
Seventeen cultivated by the mason Hansa, and Lal the oilman.
Four bighas of waste and forest land (*parti, aryana*) which belonged to Govinda and Hira, etc., etc.; and so on enumerating all the fields composing the above aggregate.

Dues and Privileges

Pieces of money . . 12.
Grain . . . . 24 maunds.
On the festivals of Rakhi, Diwali, and Holi, one copper coin from each house.
Serana . . . . at harvest.
Shukri from the Brahmans.
Transit duties for protection of merchandise, viz., a pice on every cart-load, and half a pice for each bullock.
Two platters on every marriage feast.

No. VIII

Grant of Bhum by the Inhabitants of Amli to Rawal Fateh Singh of Amet. S. 1814 (A.D. 1758)

The Ranawats Sawant Singh and Subhag Singh had Amli in grant; but they were oppressive to the inhabitants, slew the Patels Jodha and Bhagi, and so ill-treated the Brahmans, that Kusal and Nathu sacrificed themselves on the pyre. The inhabitants demanded the protection of the Rana, and the pattayats were changed; and now the inhabitants grant in rakhwali one hundred and twenty-five bighas as bhum to Fateh Singh [1] [204].

[1] This is a proof of the value attached to bhum, when granted by the inhabitants, as the first act of the new proprietor though holding the whole town from the crown, was to obtain these few bighas as bhum. After having been sixty years in that family, Amli has been resumed by the crown: the bhum has remained with the chief.

No. IX

Grant of Bhum by the Inhabitants of the Town of Dongla to Maharaja Zorawar Singh, of Bhindar.

To Sri Maharaja Zorawar Singh, the Patels, traders, merchants, Brahmans, and united inhabitants of Dongla, make agreement.

Formerly the 'runners' in Dongla were numerous: to preserve us from whom we granted bhum to the Maharaja. To wit:

One well, that of Hira the oilman.

One well, that of Dipa the oilman.

One well, that of Dewa the oilman.

In all, three wells, being forty-four bighas of irrigated (*piwal*), and one hundred and ninety-one bighas of unirrigated (*mal*) land. Also a field for juar.

Customs or Dignities (Maryad) attached to the Bhum.

1st. A dish (*kansa*) on every marriage.

2nd. Six hundred rupees ready cash annually.

3rd. All Bhumias, Girasias, the high roads, passes from raids and 'runners,' and all disturbances whatsoever, the Maharaja must settle.

When the Maharaja is pleased to let the inhabitants of Dongla reinhabit their dwellings, then only can they return to them.[1]

Written by the accountant Kacchia, on the full moon of Jeth, S. 1858, and signed by all the traders, Brahmans, and townspeople.

No. X

Grant of Bhum by the Prince of Mewar to an inferior Vassal.

Maharana Bhim Singh to Baba Ram Singh, commanding.

Now a field of two hundred and twenty-five bighas in the city of Jahazpur, with the black orchard (*sham bagh*) and a farm-house (*nohara*) for cattle, has been granted you in bhum.

Your forefathers recovered for me Jahazpur and served with fidelity; on which account this bhum is renewed. Rest assured no molestation shall be offered, nor shall any pattayat interfere with you.

Privileges.

One serana.[2]

Two halmas [205].[3]

[1] This shows how bhum was extorted in these periods of turbulence, and that this individual gift was as much to save them from the effects of the Maharaja's violence as to gain protection from that of others.

[2] A seer on each maund of produce.

[3] The labour of two ploughs (*hal*). *Halma* is the personal service of the

Offerings of coco-nuts on the Holi and Dasahra festivals.

From every hundred bullock-loads[1] of merchandise, twelve annas.

From every hundred and twenty-five ass-loads, six annas.

From each horse sold within Jahazpur, two annas.

From each camel sold, one anna.

From each oil-mill, one pula.

From each iron mine (*madri*), a quarter rupee.

From each distillation of spirits, a quarter rupee.

From each goat slain, one pice.

On births and marriages,[2] five platters (*kansa*).

The handful (*inch*) from every basket of greens.

With every other privilege attached to bhum.

Irrigated land (*piwal*) . . .	51 bighas.
Unirrigated land (*mal*) . . .	110 „
Mountain land (*magra*) . . .	40 „
Meadow land (*bira*)	25 „
	226 bighas.

Asarh (June) S. 1853 (A.D. 1797).

---

husbandman with his plough for such time as is specified. *Halma* is precisely the detested *corvée* of the French régime. "Les *corvées* sont tout ouvrage ou service, soit de corps ou de charrois et bêtes, pendant le jour, qui est dû à un seigneur. Il y avait deux sortes de *corvées* : les réelles et les personnelles, etc. Quelquefois le nombre des *corvées* était fixe : mais, le plus souvent, elles étaient à volonté du seigneur, et c'est ce qu'on appelait *corvées à merci*" (Art. 'Corvée,' *Dict. de l'anc. Régime*). Almost all the exactions for the last century in Mewar may come under this latter denomination.

[1] A great variety of oppressive imposts were levied by the chiefs during these times of trouble, to the destruction of commerce and all facility of travelling. Everything was subject to tax, and a long train of vexatious dues exacted for "repairs of forts, boats at ferries, night-guards, guards of passes," and other appellations, all having much in common with the 'Droit de *Péage*' in France. "Il n'y avait pas de ponts, de gués, de chaussées, d'écluses, de défilés, de portes, etc., où les féodaux ne fissent payer un droit à ceux que leurs affaires ou leur commerce forçaient de voyager" (*Dict. de l'anc. Régime*).

[2] The privileges of our Rajput chieftains on the marriages of their vassals and cultivating subjects are confined to the best dishes of the marriage feast or a pecuniary commutation. This is, however, though in a minor degree, one of the vexatious claims of feudality of the French system, known under the term *noçages*, where the seigneur or his deputy presided, and had the right to be placed in front of the bride, "et de chanter à la fin du répas, une chanson guillerette." But they even carried their insolence further, and "poussèrent leur mépris pour les villains (the agricultural classes of the Rajput system) jusqu'à exiger que leurs chiens eussent *leur couvert* auprès de la mariée, et qu'on les laissât manger sur la table" (Art. 'Noçages,' *Dict. de l'anc. Régime*).

No. XI

Charter of Privileges and Immunities granted to the town of Jhalrapatan, engraved on a Pillar in that City.

S. 1853 (A.D. 1797), corresponding with the Saka 1718, the sun being in the south, the season of cold, and the happy month of Kartika,[1] the enlightened half of the month, being Monday the full moon.

Maharaja Dhiraj Sri Ummed Singh Deo,[2] the Faujdar[3] Raj Zalim Singh [206] and Kunwar Madho Singh, commanding. To all the inhabitants of Jhalrapatan, Patels,[4] Patwaris,[5] Mahajans,[6] and to all the thirty-six castes, it is written.

At this period entertain entire confidenee, build and dwell.

Within this abode all forced contributions and confiseations are for ever abolished. The taxes called Bhalamanusi,[7] Anni,[8] and Rekha Barar,[9] and likewise all Bhetbegar,[10] shall cease.

To this intent is this stone erected, to hold good from year to year, now and evermore. There shall be no violence in this territory. This is sworn by the cow to the Hindu and the hog to the Musalman: in the presence of Captain Dilel Khan, Chaudhari Sarup Chand, Patel Lalo, the Mahesri Patwari Balkishan, the architect Kalu Ram, and the stone-mason Balkishan.

Parmo[11] is for ever abolished. Whoever dwells and traffics within the town of Patan, one half of the transit duties usually levied in Haravati are remitted; and all mapa (meter's) duties are for ever abolished.

No. XII

Abolitions, Immunities, Prohibitions, etc. etc. Inscription in the Temple of Lachhmi Narayan at Akola.

In former times tobacco was sold in one market only. Rana Raj Singh commanded the monopoly to be abolished. S. 1645.

Rana Jagat Singh prohibited the seizure of the cots and quilts by the officers of his government from the printers of Akola.

[1] December.
[2] The Raja of Kotah.
[3] Commander of the forces and regent of Kotah.
[4] Officers of the land revenue.
[5] Land accountants.
[6] The mercantile class.
[7] Literally 'good behaviour.'
[8] An agricultural tax.
[9] Tax for registering.
[10] This includes in one word the forced labour exacted from the working classes: the *corvée* of the French system.
[11] Grain thrown on the inhabitants at an arbitrary rate; often resorted to at Kotah, where the regent is farmer general.

No. XIII

Privileges and Immunities granted to the Printers of Calico and Inhabitants of the Town of Great Akola in Mewar.

Maharana Bhim Singh, commanding, to the inhabitants of Great Akola.

Whereas the village has been abandoned from the assignments levied by the garrison of Mandalgarh, and it being demanded of its population how it could again be rendered prosperous, they unanimously replied: "Not to exact beyond the dues and contributions (*dand dor*) established of yore; to erect the pillar promising never to exact above half the produce of the crops, or to molest the persons of those who thus paid their dues."

The Presence agreed, and this pillar has been erected. May Eklinga look to him who breaks this command. The hog to the Musalman and the cow to the Hindu.

Whatever contributions (*dand*) parmo,[1] puli,[2] heretofore levied shall be paid [207].

All crimes committed within the jurisdiction of Akola to be tried by its inhabitants, who will sit in justice on the offender and fine him according to his faults.

On Amavas [3] no work shall be done at the well [4] or at the oil-mill, nor printer put his dye-pot on the fire.[5]

Whoever breaks the foregoing, may the sin of the slaughter of Chitor be upon him.

This pillar was erected in the presence of Mehta Sardar Singh, Sanwal Das, the Chaudharis Bhopat Ram and Daulat Ram, and the assembled Panch of Akola.

Written by the Chaudhari Bhopji, and engraved by the stone-cutter Bhima.

S. 1856 (A.D. 1800)

No. XIV

Prohibition against Guests carrying away Provisions from the Public Feast.[6]

Sri Maharana Sangram Singh to the inhabitants of Marmi.

On all feasts of rejoicing, as well as those on the ceremonies

[1] Grain, the property of the government, thrown on the inhabitants for purchase at an arbitrary valuation.

[2] The handful from each sheaf at harvest.

[3] A day sacred to the Hindu, being that which divides the month.

[4] Meaning, they shall not irrigate the fields.

[5] This part of the edict is evidently the instigation of the Jains, to prevent the destruction of life, though only that of insects.

[6] The cause of this sumptuary edict was a benevolent motive, and to

for the dead, none shall carry away with them the remains of the feast. Whoever thus transgresses shall pay a fine to the crown of one hundred and one rupees. S. 1769 (A.D. 1713), Chait Sudi 7th.

No. XV

Maharana Sangram Singh to the merchants and bankers of Bakrol.

The custom of furnishing quilts (*sirak*) [1] of which you complain is of ancient date. Now when the collectors of duties, their officers, or those of the land revenue stop at Bakrol, the merchants will furnish them with beds and quilts. All other servants will be supplied by the other inhabitants.

Should the dam of the lake be in any way injured, whoever does not aid in its repair shall, as a punishment, feed one hundred and one Brahmans. Asarh 1715, or June A.D. 1659 [208].

No. XVI

Warrant of the Chief of Bijolli to his Vassal, Gopaldas Saktawat.

Maharaja Mandhata to Saktawat Gopaldas, be it known.

At this time a daily fine of four rupees is in force against you.

prevent the expenses on these occasions falling too heavily on the poorer classes. It was customary for the women to carry away under their petticoats (*ghaghra*) sufficient sweetmeats for several days' consumption. The great Jai Singh of Amber had an ordinance restricting the number of guests to fifty-one on these occasions, and prohibited to all but the four wealthy classes the use of sugar-candy: the others were confined to the use of molasses and brown sugar. To the lower vassals and the cultivators these feasts were limited to the coarser fare; to juar flour, greens and oil. A dyer who on the Holi feasted his friends with sweetmeats of fine sugar and scattered about balls made of brown sugar, was fined five thousand rupees for setting so pernicious an example. The *sadh*, or marriage present, from the bridegroom to the bride's father, was limited to fifty-one rupees. The great sums previously paid on this score were preventives of matrimony. Many other wholesome regulations of a much more important kind, especially those for the suppression of infanticide, were instituted by this prince.

[1] 'Defence against the cold weather' (*si*). This in the ancient French régime came under the denomination of "*Albergie* ou Hébergement, un droit royal. Par exemple, ce ne fut qu'après le règne de Saint Louis, et moyennant finances, que les habitans de Paris et de Corbeil s'affranchirent, les premiers de fournir au roi et à sa suite de bons oreillers et d'excellens lits de plumes, tant qu'il séjournait dans leur ville, et les seconds de le régaler quand it passait par leur bourg."

Eighty are now due; Ganga Ram having petitioned in your favour, forty of this will be remitted. Give a written declaration to this effect—that with a specified quota you will take the field; if not, you will stand the consequences.

Viz.: One good horse and one matchlock, with appurtenances complete, to serve at home and abroad (*des pardes*), and to run the country [1] with the Kher.

When the levy (*kher*) takes the field, Gopaldas must attend in person. Should he be from home, his retainers must attend, and they shall receive rations from the presence. Sawan sudi das (August 10) S. 1782.

No. XVII

Maharaja Udaikaran to the Saktawat Shambhu Singh. Be it known.

I had annexed Gura to the fisc, but now, from favour, restore it to you. Make it flourish, and serve me at home and abroad, with one horse, and one foot soldier.

When abroad you shall receive rations (*bhatta*) as follows:

Flour .	. 3 lb.
Pulse .	. 4 ounces.
Butter (*ghi*) .	2 pice weight.
Horses' feed .	4 seers at 22 takas each seer, of daily allowance.

[1] The 'Daurayat' or runners, the term applied to the bands who swept the country with their forays in those periods of general confusion, are analogous to the armed bands of the Middle Ages, who in a similar manner desolated Europe under the term *routiers*, tantamount to our *rabars* (on the road), the *labars* of the Pindaris in India. The Rajput Daurayat has as many epithets as the French *routier*, who were called *escorcheurs, tard veneurs* (of which class Gopaldas appears to have been), *mille-diables, Guilleries*, etc. From the Crusades to the sixteenth century, the nobles of Europe, of whom these bands were composed (like our Rajputs), abandoned themselves to this sort of life; who, to use the words of the historian, "préférèrent la vie vagabonde à laquelle ils s'étoient accoutumés dans le camp, à retourner cultiver leurs champs. C'est alors que se formèrent ces bandes qu'on vit parcourir le royaume et étendre sur toutes les provinces le fléau de leurs inclinations destructives, répandre partout l'effroi, la misère, le deuil et le désespoir; mettre les villes à contribution, piller et incendier les villages, égorger les laboureurs, et se livrer à des accès de cruauté qui font frémir" (*Dict. de l'ancien régime et des abus féodaux*, art. 'Routier,' p. 422).

We have this apology for the Rajput *routiers*, that the nobles of Europe had not; they were driven to it by perpetual aggressions of invaders. I invariably found that the reformed *routier* was one of the best subjects: it secured him from indolence, the parent of all Rajput vices.

If for defence of the fort you are required, you will attend with all your dependents, and bring your wife, family, and chattels; for which, you will be exempted from two years of subsequent service. Asarh 14, S. 1834 [209].

No. XVIII

Bhum in Mundkati, or Compensation for Blood, to Jeth Singh Chondawat.

The Patel's son went to bring home his wife with Jeth's Rajputs as a guard. The party was attacked, the guard killed, and there having been no redress for the murder, twenty-six bighas have been granted in mundkati [1] (compensation).

No. XIX

Rawat Megh Singh to his natural brother, Jamna Das, a patta (*fief*) has been granted, viz.:

The village of Rajpura, value . . .	Rupees 401
A garden of mogra flowers [2] . . .	11
Rupees . .	412

Serve at home and abroad with fidelity: contributions and aids pay according to custom, and as do the rest of the vassals. Jeth 14th, S. 1874

No. XX

Charter given by the Rana of Mewar, accepted and signed by all his Chiefs; defining the duties of the contracting Parties.
A.D. 1818.

Siddh Sri Maharana Dhiraj, Maharana Bhim Singh, to all the nobles my brothers and kin, Rajas, Patels, Jhalas, Chauhans, Chondawats, Panwars, Sarangdeots, Saktawats, Rathors, Ranawats, etc., etc.

Now, since S. 1822 (A.D. 1776), during the reign of Sri Ari Singhji,[3] when the troubles commenced, laying ancient usages aside, undue usurpations of the land have been made: therefore

[1] *Mund*, 'the head'; *kati*, 'cut.'

[2] [The double jasmine, *Jasminum sambac.*]

[3] The rebellion broke out during the reign of this prince.

on this day, Baisakh badi 14th, S. 1874 (A.D. 1818), the Maharana assembling all his chiefs, lays down the path of duty in new ordinances.

1st. All lands belonging to the crown obtained since the troubles, and all lands seized by one chief from another, shall be restored.

2nd. All Rakhwali,[1] Bhum, Lagat,[2] established since the troubles, shall be renounced.

3rd. Dhan,[3] Biswa,[4] the right of the crown alone, shall be renounced.

4th. No chiefs shall commit thefts or violence within the boundaries of their estates. They shall entertain no Thugs,[5] foreign thieves or thieves of the country, as Moghias,[5] Baoris,[5] Thoris:[5] but those who shall adopt peaceful habits may remain; but should any return to their old pursuits, their heads shall instantly be taken off. All property stolen shall be made good by the proprietor of the estate within the limits of which it is plundered [210].

5th. Home or foreign merchants, traders, Kafilas,[6] Banjaras,[7] who enter the country, shall be protected. In no wise shall they be molested or injured, and whoever breaks this ordinance, his estate shall be confiscated.

6th. According to command, at home or abroad service must be performed. Four divisions (*chaukis*) shall be formed of the chiefs, and each division shall remain three months in attendance at court, when they shall be dismissed to their estates. Once a year, on the festival of the Dasahra,[8] all the chiefs shall assemble with their quotas ten days previous thereto, and twenty days subsequent they shall be dismissed to their estates. On urgent occasions, and whenever their services are required, they shall repair to the Presence.

[1] Salvamenta.

[2] Dues.

[3] Transit duty.

[4] Ditto.

[5] Different descriptions of thieves. [The Moghias are settled principally in E. Mewār; if not identical with, they are closely allied to, the Bāori (Luard, *Ethnographic Survey, Central India*, App. V. 17 ff.). Gen. C. Hervey (*Some Records of Crime*, i. 386 ff.) makes frequent references to dacoities committed by them from their headquarters, Nīmach. The Bāori or Bāwariya are a notorious criminal tribe (Rose, *Glossary*, ii. 70 ff.; M. Kennedy, *Notes on Criminal Classes in Bombay Presidency*, 173 ff., 198 ff.). The Thori in Mārwār claim Rājput origin, and are connected with the Aheri, or nomad hunters (*Census Report, Mārwār*, 1891, ii. 194). According to Rose (*op. cit.* iii. 466) those in the Panjāb are rather vagrants than actual criminals.]

[6] Caravans of merchandise, whether on camels, bullocks, or in carts.

[7] Caravans of bullocks, chiefly for the transport of grain and salt.

[8] On this festival the muster of all the feudal retainers is taken by the Rana in person, and honorary dresses and dignities are bestowed.

7th. Every Pattawat holding a separate patta from the Presence shall perform separate service. They shall not unite or serve under the greater Pattawats : and the sub-vassals of all such chiefs shall remain with and serve their immediate Pattawat.[1]

8th. The Maharana shall maintain the dignities due to each chief according to his degree.

9th. The Ryots shall not be oppressed : there shall be no new exactions or arbitrary fines. This is ordained.

10th. What has been executed by Thakur Ajit Singh and sanctioned by the Rana, to this all shall agree.[2]

11th. Whosoever shall depart from the foregoing, the Maharana shall punish. In doing so the fault will not be the Rana's. Whoever fails, on him be the oath (*an*) of Eklinga and the Maharana.

[Here follow the signatures of all the chieftains of rank in Mewar, which it is needless to insert] [211].

[1] This article had become especially necessary, as the inferior chiefs, particularly those of the third class, had amalgamated themselves with the head of their clans, to whom they had become more accountable than to their prince.

[2] This alludes to the treaty which this chief had formed, as the ambassador of the Rana, with the British Government.

PALACE OF UDAIPUR.

To face page 247.

BOOK IV

ANNALS OF MEWĀR

CHAPTER 1

We now proceed to the history of the States of Rajputana, and shall commence with the Annals of Mewar, and its princes.

Titles of Mewār Chiefs: descent from the Sun.—These are styled Ranas, and are the elder branch of the Suryavansi, or 'children of the sun.' Another patronymic is Raghuvansi, derived from a predecessor of Rama, the focal point of each scion of the solar race. To him, the conqueror of Lanka,[1] the genealogists endeavour to trace the solar lines. The titles of many of these claimants are disputed; but the Hindu tribes yield unanimous suffrage to the prince of Mewar as the legitimate heir to the throne of Rama, and style him Hindua Suraj, or 'Sun of the Hindus.'[2] He is universally allowed to be the first of the 'thirty-six royal tribes'; nor has a doubt ever been raised respecting his purity of descent. Many of these tribes[3] have been swept away by time; and the genealogist, who abhors a vacuum in his mystic page, fills up their place with others, mere scions of some ancient but forgotten stem.

Stability of Mewār State.—With the exception of Jaisalmer, Mewar is the only dynasty of these races[3] which has outlived eight centuries of foreign domination, in the same lands where

[1] Said to be Ceylon; an idea scouted by the Hindus, who transfer Lanka to a very distant region. [The latter is certainly not the common belief.]

[2] This descendant of one hundred kings shows himself in cloudy weather from the *surya-gaukhra*, or 'balcony of the sun.'

[3] See *History of the Tribes*.

[212] conquest placed them. The Rana still possesses nearly the same extent of territory which his ancestors held when the conqueror from Ghazni first crossed the 'blue waters'[1] of the Indus to invade India; while the other families now ruling in the north-west of Rajasthan are the relics of ancient dynasties driven from their pristine seats of power, or their junior branches, who have erected their own fortunes. This circumstance adds to the dignity of the Ranas, and is the cause of the general homage which they receive, notwithstanding the diminution of their power. Though we cannot give the princes of Mewar an ancestor in the Persian Nushirwan, nor assert so confidently as Sir Thomas Roe his claims to descent from the celebrated Porus,[2] the opponent of Alexander, we can carry him into the regions of antiquity more remote than the Persian, and which would satisfy the most fastidious in respect to ancestry.

Origin of the Rājputs.—In every age and clime we observe the same eager desire after distinguished pedigree, proceeding from a feeling which, though often derided, is extremely natural. The Rajaputras are, however, scarcely satisfied with discriminating their ancestors from the herd of mankind. Some plume themselves on a celestial origin, whilst others are content to be demi-celestial; and those who cannot advance such lofty claims, rather than acknowledge the race to have originated in the ordinary course of nature, make their primeval parent of demoniac extraction; accordingly, several of the dynasties who cannot obtain a niche amongst the children of the sun or moon, or trace their descent from some royal saint, are satisfied to be considered the offspring of some Titan (*Daitya*). These puerilities are of modern fabrication, in cases where family documents have been lost, or emigration has severed branches from the parent stock; who, increasing in power, but ignorant of their birth, have had recourse to fable to supply the void. Various authors, borrowing from the same source, have assigned the seat of Porus to the Rana's

[1] *Nilab* from *nil*, 'blue,' and *ab*, 'water'; hence the name of the Nile in Egypt and in India [?]. *Sind*, or *Sindhu*, appears to be a Scythian word: *Sin* in the Tatar, *t sin* in Chinese, 'river.' [It is Sanskrit, meaning 'divider.'] Hence the inhabitants of its higher course termed it *aba sin*, 'parent stream'; and thus, very probably, *Abyssinia* was formed by the Arabians; 'the country on the Nile,' or *aba sin*. [Abyssinia is 'land of the Habashi, or negroes.']

[2] See p. 47 above.

family; and coincidence of name has been the cause of the family being alternately elevated and depressed. Thus the incidental circumstance of the word Rhamnae being found in Ptolemy's geography, in countries bordering on Mewar, furnishes our ablest geographers [1] with a reason [213] for planting the family there in the second century; while the commentators [2] on the geography of the Arabian travellers of the ninth and tenth centuries [3] discover sufficient evidence in "the kingdom of Rahmi, always at war with the Balhara sovereign," to consider him (notwithstanding Rahmi is expressly stated "not to be much considered for his birth or the antiquity of his kingdom") as the prince of Chitor, celebrated in both these points.

The translator of the *Periplus of the Erythrean Sea*, following D'Anville,[4] makes Ozene (Ujjain) the capital of a Porus,[5] who sent an embassy to Augustus to regulate their commercial intercourse, and whom he asserts to be the ancestor of the Rana. But to show how guarded we should be in admitting verbal resemblance to decide such points, the title of Rana is of modern adoption, even so late as the twelfth century; and was assumed in consequence of the victorious issue of a contest with the Parihara prince of Mandor, who bore the title of Rana, and who surrendered it with his life and capital to the prince of Mewar. The latter substituted it for the more ancient appellation of Rawal; [6] but it was not till the thirteenth century that the novel distinction was generally recognized by neighbouring powers. Although we

[1] D'Anville and Rennell. [The Rhamnae have been identified with the Brāhūi of Baluchistān (McCrindle, *Ptolemy*, 159). Lassen places them on the Nerbudda.]

[2] Maurice and others.

[3] *Relations anciennes des voyageurs*, par Renaudot.

[4] D'Anville (*Antiquités de l'Inde*) quotes Nicolas of Damascus as his authority, who says the letter written by Porus, prince of Ozene, was in the Greek character.

[5] This *Porus* is a corruption of *Puar*, once the most powerful and conspicuous tribe in India; classically written Pramara, the dynasty which ruled at Ujjain for ages. [This is not certain (Smith, *EHI*, 60, note).]

[6] *Rawal*, or *Raul*, is yet borne as a princely title by the Aharya prince of Dungarpur, and the Yadu prince of Jaisalmer, whose ancestors long ruled in the heart of Scythia. *Raoul* seems to have been titular to the Scandinavian chiefs of Scythic origin. The invader of Normandy was *Raoul*, corrupted to *Rollon* or *Rollo*. [The words, of course, have no connexion: Rāwal, Skt. *rājakula*, 'royal family.']

cannot for a moment admit the Rahmi, or even the Rhamnae of Ozene, to be connected with this family, yet Ptolemy appears to have given the real ancestor in his Baleokouroi, the Balhara monarchs of the Arabian travellers, the Valabhiraes of Saurashtra, who were the ancestors of the princes of Mewar.[1]

Before we proceed, it is necessary to specify the sources whence materials were obtained for the Annals of Mewar, and to give some idea of the character they merit as historical data [214].

Sources of the History.—For many years previous to sojourning at the court of Udaipur, sketches were obtained of the genealogy of the family from the rolls of the bards. To these was added a chronological sketch, drawn up under the eye of Raja Jai Singh of Amber, with comments of some value by him, and which served as a ground-work. Free access was also granted to the Rana's library, and permission obtained to make copies of such MSS. as related to his history. The most important of these was the Khuman Raesa,[2] which is evidently a modern work founded upon ancient materials, tracing the genealogy to Rama, and halting at conspicuous beacons in this long line of crowned heads, particularly about the period of the Muhammadan irruption in the tenth century, the sack of Chitor by Alau-d-din in the thirteenth century, and the wars of Rana Partap with Akbar, during whose reign the work appears to have been recast.

The next in importance were the Rajvilas, in the Vraj Bhakha, by Man Kabeswara;[3] and the Rajratnakar,[4] by Sudasheo Bhat: both written in the reign of Rana Raj Singh, the opponent of Aurangzeb: also the Jaivilas, written in the reign of Jai Singh, son of Raj Singh. They all commence with the genealogies of the

[1] The Balhara kings, and their capital Nahrwala, or Anhilwara Patan, have given rise to much conjecture amongst the learned. We shall, before this work is closed, endeavour to condense what has been said by ancient and modern authorities on the subject; and from manuscripts, ancient inscriptions, and the result of a personal visit to this ancient domain, to set the matter completely at rest. [See p. 122 above.] ["Hippokoura, the royal seat of Baleo Kouros" (*Periplus*, viii. 83). Baleo Kouros has been identified with Vilivāyakura, a name found on coins of the Andhra dynasty (*BG*, i. Part ii. 158; McCrindle, *Ptolemy*, 179).]

[2] *Khuman* is an ancient title of the earlier princes, and still used. It was borne by the son of *Bappa*, the founder, who retired to Transoxiana, and there ruled and died: the very country of the ancient Scythic *Khomani*.

[3] Lord of rhyme.

[4] Sea of gems.

family, introductory to the military exploits of the princes whose names they bear.

The Mamadevi Prasistha is a copy of the inscriptions[1] in the temple of 'the Mother of the Gods' at Kumbhalmer. Genealogical rolls of some antiquity were obtained from the widow of an ancient family bard, who had left neither children nor kindred to follow his profession. Another roll was procured from a priest of the Jains residing in Sandrai, in Marwar, whose ancestry had enjoyed from time immemorial the title of Guru, which they held at the period of the sack of Valabhipura in the fifth century, whence they emigrated simultaneously with the Rana's ancestors. Others were obtained from Jain priests at Jawad in Malwa. Historical documents possessed by several chiefs were readily furnished, and extracts were made from works, both Sanskrit and Persian, which incidentally mention the family. To these were added traditions or biographical anecdotes furnished in conversation by the Rana, or men of intellect amongst his chiefs [215], ministers, or bards, and inscriptions calculated to reconcile dates; in short, every corroborating circumstance was treasured up which could be obtained by incessant research during sixteen years. The Commentaries of Babur and Jahangir, the Institutes of Akbar, original grants, public and autograph letters of the emperors of Delhi and their ministers, were made to contribute more or less; yet, numerous as are the authorities cited, the result may afford but little gratification to the general reader, partly owing to the unpopularity of the subject, partly to the inartificial mode of treating it.

Kanaksen.—At least ten genealogical lists, derived from the most opposite sources, agree in making Kanaksen the founder of this dynasty; and assign his emigration from the most northern of the provinces of India to the peninsula of Saurashtra in S. 201, or A.D. 145. We shall, therefore, make this the point of outset; though it may be premised that Jai Singh, the royal historian and astronomer of Amber, connects the line with Sumitra (the fifty-sixth descendant from the deified Rama), who appears to have been the contemporary of Vikramaditya, A.C. 56.

The country of which Ayodhya (now Oudh) was the capital, and Rama monarch, is termed, in the geographical writings of the Hindus, Kosala; doubtless from the mother of Rama, whose

[1] These inscriptions will be described in the Personal Narrative.

name was Kausalya.[1] The first royal emigrant from the north is styled, in the Rana's archives, Kosala-putra, 'son of Kosala.'

Titles of the Chiefs.—Rama had two sons, Lava and Kusa: from the former the Rana's family claim descent. He is stated to have built Lahore, the ancient Lohkot;[2] and the branch from which the princes of Mewar are descended resided there until Kanaksen emigrated to Dwarka. The difficulty of tracing these races through a long period of years is greatly increased by the custom of changing the appellation of the tribe, from conquest, locality, or personal celebrity. Sen[3] seems to have been the martial termination for many generations: this was followed by Dit, or Aditya, a term for the 'sun.' The first change in the name of the tribe was on their expulsion from Saurashtra, when for the generic term of Suryavansi was substituted the particular appellation of Guhilot. This name was maintained till another event dispersed the family, and when they settled in [216] Ahar,[4] Aharya became the appellative of the branch. This continued till loss of territory and new acquisitions once more transferred the dynasty to Sesoda,[5] a temporary capital in the western mountains. The title of Ranawat, borne by all descendants of the blood royal since the eventful change which removed the seat of government from Chitor to Udaipur, might in time have superseded that of Sesodia, if continued warfare had not checked the increase of population; but the Guhilot branch of the Suryavansi still retain the name of Sesodia.

Having premised thus much, we must retrograde to the darker ages, through which we shall endeavour to conduct this celebrated dynasty, though the clue sometimes nearly escapes from our hands in these labyrinths of antiquity.[6] When it is recollected

[1] [It is the other way: Kausalya took her name from Kosala.]

[2] [See p. 116 above.]

[3] *Sen*, 'army'; *kanak*, 'gold.' [Kanaksen is entirely mythical. It has been suggested that the name is a reminiscence of the connexion of the great Kushān Emperor, Kanishka, with Gujarāt and Kāthiāwār (*BG*, i. Part i. 101).]

[4] Ahar, or Ar, is in the valley of the present capital, Udaipur.

[5] The origin of this name is from the trivial occurrence of the expelled prince of Chitor having erected a town to commemorate the spot, where after an extraordinarily hard chase he killed a hare (*sasu*).

[6] The wild fable which envelops or adorns the cradle of every illustrious family is not easily disentangled. The bards weave the web with skill, and it clings like ivy round each modern branch, obscuring the aged stem, in

to what violence this family has been subjected during the last eight centuries, often dispossessed of all but their native hills and compelled to live on their spontaneous produce, we could scarcely expect that historical records should be preserved. Chitor was thrice sacked and destroyed, and the existing records are formed from fragments, registers of births and marriages, or from the oral relations of the bards.

Legend of Kanaksen.—By what route Kanaksen, the first emigrant of the solar race, found his way into Saurashtra from Lohkot, is uncertain: he, however, wrested dominion from a prince of the Pramara race, and founded Birnagara in the second century (A.D. 144). Four generations afterwards, Vijayasen, whom the prince of Amber calls Nushirwan, founded Vijayapur, supposed to be where Dholka now stands, at the head of the Saurashtra peninsula.[1] Vidarba was also founded by him, the name of which was afterwards changed to Sihor. But the most celebrated was the capital, Valabhipura, which for years baffled all search, till it was revealed in its now humbled condition as Walai, ten miles west [217] of Bhaunagar. The existence of this city was confirmed by a celebrated Jain work, the Satrunjaya Mahatma.[2] The want of satisfactory proof of the Rana's emigration from thence was obviated by the most unexpected discovery of an inscription of the twelfth century, in a ruined temple on the tableland forming the eastern boundary of the Rana's present territory, which appeals to the 'walls of Valabhi' for the truth of the action it records. And a work written to commemorate the reign of Rana Raj Singh opens with these words: "In the west is Sorathdes,[3] a country well known: the barbarians invaded it, and conquered Bal-ka-nath;[4] all fell in the sack of Valabhipura, except the daughter of the Pramara." And the Sandrai

---

the time-worn branches of which monsters and demi-gods are perched, whose claims of affinity are held in high estimation by these 'children of the sun,' who would deem it criminal to doubt that the loin-robe (*dhoti*) of their great founder, Bapa Rawal, was less than five hundred cubits in circumference, that his two-edged sword (*khanda*), the gift of the Hindu Proserpine. weighed an ounce less than sixty-four pounds, or that he was an inch under twenty feet in height.

[1] [Vijayapur has been doubtfully identified with Bījapur in the Ahmadābād district (*BG*, i. Part i. 110).]

[2] Presented to the Royal Asiatic Society of London.

[3] Sorath or Saurashtra.

[4] The 'lord of Bal.'

roll thus commences: "When the city of Valabhi was sacked, the inhabitants fled and founded Bali, Sandrai, and Nadol in Mordar des."[1] These are towns yet of consequence, and in all the Jain religion is still maintained, which was the chief worship of Valabhipura when sacked by the 'barbarian.' The records preserved by the Jains give S.B. 205 (A.D. 524) as the date of this event.[2]

The tract about Valabhipura and northward is termed Bal, probably from the tribe of Bala, which might have been the designation of the Rana's tribe prior to that of Grahilot; and most probably Multan, and all these regions of the Kathi, Bala, etc., were dependent on Lohkot, whence emigrated Kanaksen; thus strengthening the surmise of the Scythic descent of the Ranas, though now installed in the seat of Rama. The sun was the deity of this northern tribe, as of the Rana's ancestry, and the remains of numerous temples to this grand object of Scythic homage are still to be found scattered over the peninsula; whence its name, Saurashtra, the country of the Sauras, or Sun-worshippers; the Surastrene or Syrastrene of ancient geographers; its inhabitants, the *Suros* (Σύρων) of Strabo.[3]

Besides these cities, the MSS. give Gayni[4] as the last refuge

[1] Mārwār.

[2] [The date of the fall of Valabhi is very uncertain (Smith, *EHI*, 315, note). It is said to have been destroyed in the reign of Silāditya VI., the last of the dynasty, about A.D. 776 (Duff, *Chronology of India*, 31, 67, 308).]

[3] [There is possibly a confusion with the Soras of Aelian (xv. 8) which has been identified by Caldwell (*Dravidian Grammar*, 17) with the Σῶραι of Ptolemy, and with the Chola kingdom of Southern India. Surāshtra or Saurāshtra, 'land of the Sus,' was afterwards Sanskritized into 'goodly country' (Monier Williams, *Skt. Dict.* s.v.; *BG*, i. Part i. 6).]

[4] Gaini, or Gajni, is one of the ancient names of Cambay (the port of Valabhipura), the ruins of which are about three miles from the modern city. Other sources indicate that these princes held possessions in the southern continent of India, as well as in the Saurashtra peninsula. Talatalpur Patan, on the Godavari, is mentioned, which tradition asserts to be the city of Deogir; but which, after many years' research, I discovered in Saurashtra, it being one of the ancient names of Kandala. In after times, when succeeding dynasties held the title of Balakarao, though the capital was removed inland to Anhilwara Patan, they still held possession of the western shore, and Cambay continued the chief port. [For the identification of Gajni with Cambay see *IA*, iv. 147; *BG*, vi. 213 note. The site of Devagiri has been identified with Daulatābād (*BG*, i. Part ii. 136; Beal, *Buddhist Records of the Western World*, ii. 255, note).]

of the family [218] when expelled Saurashtra. One of the poetic chronicles thus commences: "The barbarians had captured Gajni. The house of Siladitya was left desolate. In its defence his heroes fell; of his seed but the name remained."

Invaders of Saurāshtra.—These invaders were Scythic, and in all probability a colony from the Parthian kingdom, which was established in sovereignty on the Indus in the second century, having their capital at Saminagara, where the ancient Yadu ruled for ages: the Minnagara[1] of Arrian, and the Mankir of the Arabian geographers. It was by this route, through the eastern portion of the valley of the Indus, that the various hordes of Getae or Jats, Huns, Kamari, Kathi, Makwahana, Bala and Aswaria, had peopled this peninsula, leaving traces still visible. The period is also remarkable when these and other Scythic hordes were simultaneously abandoning higher Asia for the cold regions

[1] The position of Minnagara has occupied the attention of geographers from D'Anville to Pottinger. Sind being conquered by Omar, general of the caliph Al-Mansur (Abbasi), the name of Minagara was changed to Mansura, "une ville célèbre sur le rivage droit du Sind ou Mehran." "Ptolémée fait aussi mention de cette ville; mais en la déplaçant," etc. D'Anville places it about 26°, but not so high as Ulug Bég, whose tables make it 26° 40′. I have said elsewhere that I had little doubt that Minnagara, handed down to us by the author of the *Periplus* as the μετρόπολις τῆς Σκυθίας, was the Saminagara of the Yadu Jarejas, whose chronicles claim Seistān as their ancient possession, and in all probability was the stronghold (*nagara*) of Sambos, the opponent of Alexander. On every consideration, I am inclined to place it on the site of Sehwan. The learned Vincent, in his translation of the *Periplus*, enters fully and with great judgment upon this point, citing every authority, Arrian, Ptolemy, Al-Biruni, Edrisi, D'Anville, and De la Rochette. He has a note (26, p. 386, vol. i.) which is conclusive, could he have applied it: "Al-Birun [equi-distant] between Debeil and Mansura." D'Anville also says: "de Mansora à la ville nommée Birun, la distance est indiquée de quinze parasanges dans Abulféda," who fixes it, on the authority of Abu-Rehan (surnamed Al-Biruni from his birthplace), at 26° 40′. The ancient name of Haidarabad, the present capital of Sind, was Nerun (نيرون ;) or Nirun, and is almost equi-distant, as Abulfeda says, between Debal (Dewal or Tatta) and Mansura, Sehwan, or Minnagara, the latitude of which, according to my construction, is 26° 11′. Those who wish to pursue this may examine the *Éclaircissemens sur la Carte de l'Inde*, p. 37 *et seq.*, and Dr. Vincent's estimable translation, p. 386. [The site of Minnagara, like those of all the cities in the delta of the Indus, owing to changes in the course of the river, is very uncertain. Jhajhpur or Mungrapur has been suggested (McCrindle, *Ptolemy*, 72, *Periplus*, 1086 f.). Nirūn has been identified with Helāi, a little below Jarak, on the high road from Tatta to Haidarābād (Elliot-Dowson i. 400).]

of Europe and the warm plains of Hindustan. From the first to the sixth century of the Christian era, various records exist of these irruptions from the north. Gibbon, quoting De Guignes, mentions one in the second century, which fixed permanently in the Saurashtra peninsula; and the latter, from original authorities, describes another of the Getae or Jats, styled by the Chinese Yueh-chi, in the north of India.[1] But the authority directly in point is that of Cosmas, surnamed Indikopleustes, who was in India during the reign of Justinian, and that of the first monarch of the Chinese dynasty of Leam.[2] Cosmas [219] had visited Kalyan, included in the Balhara kingdom; and he mentions the Ephthalites, or White Huns, under their king Golas, as being established on the Indus at the very period of the invasion of Valabhipura.[3]

Arrian, who resided in the second century at Barugaza (Broach), describes a Parthian sovereignty as extending from the Indus to the Nerbudda.[4] Their capital has already been mentioned, Minnagara. Whether these, the Abtelites [5] of Cosmas, were the Parthian dynasty of Arrian, or whether the Parthians were supplanted by the Huns, we must remain in ignorance, but to one or the other we must attribute the sack of Valabhipura.

[1] See *History of the Tribes*, p. 107, and translation of Inscription No. I. *Vide* Appendix.

[2] Considerable intercourse was carried on between the princes of India and China from the earliest periods; but particularly during the dynasties of Sum, Leam and Tam, from the fourth to the seventh centuries, when the princes from Bengal and Malabar to the Panjab sent embassies to the Chinese monarchs. The dominions of these Hindu princes may yet be identified. [Cosmas flourished in the sixth century A.D., and never reached India proper (*EB*, vii. 214).]

[3] [Gollas was Mihiragula (Smith, *EHI*, 317).]

[4] [*Ibid.* 230 f.]

[5] D'Herbelot (vol. i. p. 179) calls them the Haiathelah or Indoscythae, and says that they were apparently from Thibet, between India and China. De Guignes (tome i. p. 325) is offended with this explanation, and says: "Cette conjecture ne peut avoir lieu, les Euthélites n'ayant jamais demeuré dans le Thibet." A branch of the Huns, however, did most assuredly dwell in that quarter, though we will not positively assert that they were the Abtelites. The Haihaya was a great branch of the Lunar race of Yayati, and appears early to have left India for the northern regions, and would afford a more plausible etymology for the Haiathelah than the Te-le, who dwelt on the waters (*ab*) of the Oxus. This branch of the Hunnish race has also been termed Nephthalite, and fancied one of the lost tribes of Israel [?].

The legend of this event affords scope for speculation, both as regards the conquerors and the conquered, and gives at least a colour of truth to the reputed Persian ancestry of the Rana : a subject which will be distinctly considered. The solar orb, and its type, fire, were the chief objects of adoration of Siladitya of Valabhipura. Whether to these was added that of the lingam, the symbol of Balnath (the sun), the primary object of worship with his descendants, may be doubted. It was certainly confined to these, and the adoption of 'strange gods' by the Suryavansi Guhilot is comparatively of modern invention.[1]

The Fountain of the Sun.—There was a fountain (*Surya-kunda*) 'sacred to the sun' at Valabhipura, from which arose, at the summons of Siladitya (according to the legend) the seven-headed horse Saptasva, which draws the car of Surya, to bear him to battle. With such an auxiliary no foe could prevail; but a wicked minister revealed to the enemy the secret of annulling this aid, by polluting the sacred fountain with blood. This accomplished, in vain did the prince call on Saptasva to save him from the strange and barbarous foe : the charm was broken, and with it sunk the dynasty of Valabhi. Who the 'barbarian' was that defiled with blood of kine [220] the fountain of the sun,[2] whether Getae, Parthian, or Hun, we are left to conjecture. The Persian, though he venerated the bull, yet sacrificed him on the

[1] Ferishta, in the early part of his history [i. Introd. lxviii f.], observes that, some centuries prior to Vikramaditya, the Hindus abandoned the simple religion of their ancestors, made idols, and worshipped the host of heaven, which faith they had from Kashmir, the foundry of magic superstition.

[2] Divested of allegory, it means simply that the supply of water was rendered impure, and consequently useless to the Hindus, which compelled them to abandon their defences and meet death in the open field. Alau-d-din practised the same *ruse* against the celebrated Achal, the Khichi prince of Gagraun, which caused the surrender of this impregnable fortress. "It matters not," observes an historian whose name I do not recollect, "whether such things are true, it is sufficient that they were believed. We may smile at the mention of the ghost, the evil genius of Brutus, appearing to him before the battle of Pharsalia ; yet it never would have been stated, had it not assimilated with the opinions and prejudices of the age." And we may deduce a simple moral from "the parent orb refusing the aid of his steed to his terrestrial offspring," viz. that he was deserted by the deity. Fountains sacred to the sun and other deities were common to the Persians, Scythians, and Hindus, and both the last offered steeds to him in sacrifice. Vide *History of the Tribes*, article 'Aswamedha,' p. 91.

altar of Mithras;[1] and though the ancient Guebre purifies with the urine[2] of the cow, he will not refuse to eat beef; and the iniquity of Cambyses, who thrust his lance into the flank of the Egyptian Apis, is a proof that the bull was abstractedly no object of worship. It would be indulging a legitimate curiosity, could we by any means discover how these 'strange' tribes obtained a footing amongst the Hindu races; for so late as seven centuries ago we find Getae, Huns, Kathi, Ariaspas, Dahae, definitively settled, and enumerated amongst the Chhattis rajkula. How much earlier the admission, no authority states; but mention is made of several of them aiding in the defence of Chitor, on the first appearance of the faith of Islam upwards of eleven hundred years ago.

CHAPTER 2

The Refugee Queen.—Of the prince's family, the queen Pushpavati alone escaped the sack of Valabhi, as well as the funeral pyre, upon which, on the death of Siladitya, his other wives were sacrificed. She was a daughter of the Pramara prince of Chandravati [221], and had visited the shrine of the universal mother, Amba-Bhavani, in her native land, to deposit upon the altar of the goddess a votive offering consequent to her expectation of offspring. She was on her return, when the intelligence arrived which blasted all her future hopes, by depriving her of her lord, and robbing him, whom the goddess had just granted to her prayers, of a crown. Excessive grief closed her pilgrimage. Taking refuge in a cave in the mountains of Malia, she was delivered of a son. Having confided the infant to a Brahmani of Birnagar named Kamlavati, enjoining her to educate the young prince as a Brahman, but to marry him to a Rajputni,[3] she

[1] The Baldan, or sacrifice of the bull to Balnath, is on record, though now discontinued amongst the Hindus. [*Baldān*=*balidāna*, 'a general offering to the gods.']

[2] Pinkerton, who is most happy to strengthen his aversion for the Celt, seizes on a passage in Strabo, who describes him as having recourse to the same mode of purification as the Guebre. Unconscious that it may have had a religious origin, he adduces it as a strong proof of the uncleanliness of their habits.

[3] [This corroborates Bhandarkar's theory that the Guhilots sprang from Nāgar Brāhmans.]

mounted the funeral pile to join her lord. Kamlavati, the daughter of the priest of the temple, was herself a mother, and she performed the tender offices of one to the orphan prince, whom she designated Goha, or 'cave-born.'[1] The child was a source of perpetual uneasiness to its protectors: he associated with Rajput children, killing birds, hunting wild animals, and at the age of eleven was totally unmanageable: to use the words of the legend, "How should they hide the ray of the sun?"

The Legend of Goha.—At this period Idar was governed by a chief of the savage race of Bhil; his name, Mandalika.[2] The young Goha frequented the forests in company with the Bhils, whose habits better assimilated with his daring nature than those of the Brahmans. He became a favourite with the Vanaputras, or 'children of the forest,' who resigned to him Idar with its woods and mountains. The fact is mentioned by Abu-l Fazl,[3] and is still repeated by the bards, with a characteristic version of the incident, of which doubtless there were many. The Bhils having determined in sport to elect a king, the choice fell on Goha; and one of the young savages, cutting his finger, applied the blood as the tīka of sovereignty to his forehead. What was done in sport was confirmed by the old forest chief. The sequel fixes on Goha the stain of ingratitude, for he slew his benefactor, and no motive is assigned in the legend for the deed. Goha's name became the patronymic of his descendants, who were styled Guhilot, classically Grahilot, in time softened to Gehlot.

We know very little concerning these early princes but that they dwelt in this mountainous region for eight generations; when the Bhils, tired of a foreign rule, assailed Nagaditya, the eighth prince, while hunting, and deprived him of life and Idar. The descendants of Kamlavati (the Birnagar Brahmani), who retained the office of priest in the family, were again the preservers of the line of Valabhi. The infant Bappa, son of Nagaditya [222], then only three years old, was conveyed to the fortress of Bhander,[4] where he was protected by a Bhil of Yadu descent.

[1] [This is a folk-etymology to explain the name Guhilot, probably derived from Guha or Guhasena (A.D. 559–67), the fourth and apparently the first great Valabhi monarch (*BG.* i. Part i. 85).]

[2] [Mandalika seems to mean 'ruler of a district' (*mandal*), (Bayley, *Dynasties of Gujarāt*, 183).]

[3] [*Āīn*, ii. 268.]

[4] Fifteen miles south-west of Jharol, in the wildest region in India. [In Gwalior State, *IGI*, viii. 72.]

Thence he was removed for greater security to the wilds of Parasar. Within its impervious recesses rose the three-peaked (*trikuta*) mountain, at whose base was the town of Nagindra,[1] the abode of Brahmans, who performed the rites of the 'great god.' In this retreat passed the early years of Bappa, wandering through these Alpine valleys, amidst the groves of Bal and the shrines of the brazen calf.

The most antique temples are to be seen in these spots—within the dark gorge of the mountain, or on its rugged summit—in the depths of the forest, and at the sources of streams, where sites of seclusion, beauty, and sublimity alternately exalt the mind's devotion. In these regions the creative power appears to have been the earliest, and at one time the sole, object of adoration, whose symbols, the serpent-wreathed phallus (lingam), and its companion, the bull, were held sacred even by the 'children of the forest.' In these silent retreats Mahadeva continued to rule triumphant, and the most brilliant festivities of Udaipur were those where his rites are celebrated in the nine days sacred to him, when the Jains and Vaishnavas mix with the most zealous of his votaries; but the strange gods from the plains of the Yamuna and Ganges have withdrawn a portion of the zeal of the Guhilots from their patron divinity Eklinga, whose diwan,[2] or vicegerent, is the Rana. The temple of Eklinga, situated in one of the narrow defiles leading to the capital, is an immense structure, though more sumptuous than elegant. It is built entirely of white marble, most elaborately carved and embellished; but lying in the route of a bigoted foe, it has undergone many dilapidations. The brazen bull, placed under his own dome, facing the sanctuary of the phallus, is nearly of the natural size, in a recumbent posture. It is cast (hollow) of good shape, highly polished and without flaw, except where the hammer of the Tatar had opened a passage in the hollow flank in search of treasure[3] [223].

The Marriage of Bappa.—Tradition has preserved numerous

[1] Or Nagda, still a place of religious resort, about ten miles north of Udaipur. Here I found several very old inscriptions relative to the family, which preserve the ancient denomination Gohil instead of Gehlot. One of these is about nine centuries old. [The ancient name was Nāgahrida (Erskine ii. A. 106).]

[2] Ekling-ka-Diwan is the common title of the Rana.

[3] Amongst the many temples where the brazen calf forms part of the establishment of Balkesar, there is one sacred to Nandi alone, at Nain in the valley. This lordly bull has his shrine attended as devoutly as was that

details of Bappa's[1] infancy, which resembles the adventures of every hero or founder of a race. The young prince attended the sacred kine, an occupation which was honourable even to the 'children of the sun,' and which they still pursue: possibly a remnant of their primitive Scythic habits. The pranks of the royal shepherd are the theme of many a tale. On the Jhal Jhulni, when swinging is the amusement of the youth of both sexes, the daughter of the Solanki chief of Nagda and the village maidens had gone to the groves to enjoy this festivity, but they were unprovided with ropes. Bappa happened to be at hand, and was called by the Rajput damsels to forward their sport. He promised to procure a rope if they would first have a game at marriage. One frolic was as good as another, and the scarf of the Solankini was united to the garment of Bappa, the whole of the village lasses joining hands with his as the connecting link; and thus they performed the mystical number of revolutions round an aged tree. This frolic caused his flight from Nagda, and originated his greatness, but at the same time burthened him with all these damsels; and hence a heterogeneous issue, whose descendants still ascribe their origin to the prank of Bappa round the old mango-tree of Nagda. A suitable offer being shortly after made for the young Solankini's hand, the family priests of the bridegroom, whose duty it was, by his knowledge of palmistry, to investigate the fortunes of the bride, discovered that she was already married: intelligence which threw the family into the greatest consternation.[2] Though Bappa's power over his brother shepherds was too strong to create any dread of disclosure as to his being the principal in this affair, yet was it too much to expect that a secret, in which no less than six hundred of the daughters of Eve were concerned, could long remain such? Bappa's mode of swearing his companions to secrecy is preserved. Digging a small pit, and taking a pebble in his hand, "Swear," cried he,

of Apis at Memphis; nor will Eklinga yield to his brother Serapis. The changes of position of the Apis at Nain are received as indications of the fruitfulness of the seasons, though it is not apparent how such are contrived.

[1] *Bappa* is not a proper name, it signifies merely a 'child.' [This is wrong: it is the old Prākrit form of *bāp*, 'father' (*IA*, xv. 275 f.; *BG*, i. Part i. 84).] He is frequently styled *Saila*, and in inscriptions *Sailadīsa*, 'the mountain lord.'

[2] [The legend implies that Bāpa, from association with Bhīls, was regarded to be of doubtful origin.]

"secrecy and obedience to me in good and in evil; that you will reveal to me all that you hear, and failing, desire that the good deeds of your forefathers may, like this pebble (dropping it into the pit) fall into the Washerman's well."[1] They took the oath. The Solanki chief, however, heard that [224] Bappa was the offender, who, receiving from his faithful scouts intimation of his danger, sought refuge in one of the retreats which abound in these mountains, and which in after-times proved the preservation of his race. The companions of his flight were two Bhils: one of Undri, in the valley of the present capital; the other of Solanki descent, from Oghna Panarwa, in the western wilds. Their names, Baleo and Dewa, have been handed down with Bappa's; and the former had the honour of drawing the tika of sovereignty with his own blood on the forehead of the prince, on the occasion of his taking the crown from the Mori.[2] It is pleasing to trace, through a series of ages, the knowledge of a custom still 'honoured in the observance.' The descendants of Baleo of Oghna and the Undri Bhil still claim the privilege of performing the tika on the inauguration of the descendants of Bappa.

Oghna Panarwa.—Oghna Panarwa is the sole spot in India which enjoys a state of natural freedom. Attached to no State, having no foreign communications, living under its own patriarchal head, its chief, with the title of Rana, whom one thousand hamlets scattered over the forest-crowned valleys obey, can, if requisite, appear at 'the head of five thousand bows.' He is a Bhumia Bhil of mixed blood, from the Solanki Rajput, on the old stock of pure (*ujla*) Bhils, the autochthones (if such there be of any country) of Mewar. Besides making the tika of blood from an incision in the thumb, the Oghna chief takes the prince by the arm and seats him on the throne, while the Undri Bhil holds the salver of spices and sacred grains of rice[3] used in making the tika.

[1] Deemed in the East the most impure of all receptacles. These wells are dug at the sides of streams, and give a supply of pure water filtering through the sand.

[2] [The right is said to have been enjoyed by the Bhīls till the time of Rāna Hamīr Singh, who died A.D. 1364, and it was recognised in Dungarpur till fairly recent times (Erskine ii. A. 228). The Jāts have the same right in Bīkaner (Rose, *Glossary*, ii. 301): Mers in Porbandar (Wilberforce-Bell, *Hist. of Kathiawad*, 53: Kandhs in Kalahandi (Russell, *Tribes and Castes Central Provinces*, iii. 465, and *cf.* ii. 280).]

[3] Hence, perhaps, the name *khushka* for tika. [*Khushka*, *khushk*, 'dry,'

But the solemnity of being seated on the throne of Mewar is so expensive, that many of these rites have fallen into disuse. Jagat Singh was the last prince whose coronation was conducted with the ancient magnificence of this princely house. It cost the sum of ninety lakhs of rupees (£1,125,000), nearly one entire year's revenue of the State in the days of its prosperity, and which, taking into consideration the comparative value of money, would amount to upwards of four millions sterling [1] [225].

To resume the narrative: though the flight of Bappa and its cause are perfectly natural, we have another episode; when the bard assuming a higher strain has recourse to celestial machinery for the *dénouement* of this simple incident: but "an illustrious race must always be crowned with its proper mythology." Bappa who was the founder of a line of a 'hundred kings,' feared as a monarch, adored as more than mortal, and, according to the legend, 'still living' (*charanjiva*), deserves to have the source of his pre-eminent fortune disclosed, which, in Mewar, it were sacrilege to doubt. While he pastured the sacred kine in the valleys of Nagindra, the princely shepherd was suspected of appropriating the milk of a favourite cow to his own use. He was distrusted and watched, and although indignant, the youth admitted that they had reason to suspect him, from the habitual dryness of the brown cow when she entered the pens at even.[2] He watched, and traced her to a narrow dell, when he beheld the udder spontaneously pouring its stores amidst the shrubs. Under a thicket

---

is plain boiled rice without seasoning.] Grains of ground rice in curds is the material of the primitive tika, which the author has had applied to him by a lady in Gujargarh, one of the most savage spots in India, amidst the *levée en masse*, assembled hostilely against him, but separated amicably.

[1] Such the pride of these small kingdoms in days of yore, and such their resources, till reduced by constant oppression! But their public works speak what they could do, and have done; witness the stupendous work of marble, and its adjacent causeway, which dams the lake of Rajsamand at Kankrauli, and which cost upwards of a million. When the spectator views this expanse of water, this 'royal sea' (*rajsamand*) on the borders of the plain; the pillar of victory towering over the plains of Malwa, erected on the summit of Chitor by Rana Mokal; their palaces and temples in this ancient abode; the regal residence erected by the princes when ejected, must fill the observer with astonishment at the resources of the State. They are such as to explain the metaphor of my ancient friend Zalim Singh, who knew better than we the value of this country: "Every pinch of the soil of Mewar contains gold."

[2] *Godhūli*, the dust raised at the time when the cows come home.

of cane a hermit was reposing in a state of abstraction, from which the impetuosity of the shepherd soon roused him. The mystery was revealed in the phallic symbol of the 'great God,' which daily received the lacteal shower, and raised such doubts of the veracity of Bappa.

No eye had hitherto penetrated into this natural sanctuary of the rites of the Hindu Creator, except the sages and hermits of ancient days (of whom this was the celebrated Harita),[1] whom this bounteous cow also fed.

Bappa related to the sage all he knew of himself, received his blessing, and retired ; but he went daily to visit him, to wash his feet, carry milk to him, and gather such wild flowers as were acceptable offerings to the deity. In return he received lessons of morality, and was initiated into the mysterious rites of Siva : and at length he was invested with the triple cordon of faith (*tin parwa zunnar*) [2] by the hands of the sage, who became his spiritual guide, and bestowed on his pupil the title of [226] 'Regent (Diwan) of Eklinga.' Bappa had proofs that his attentions to the saint and his devotions to Eklinga were acceptable, by a visit from his consort, 'the lion-born goddess.' From her hand he received the panoply of celestial fabrication, the work of Viswakarma (the Vulcan of Eastern mythology), which outvies all the arms ever forged for Greek or Trojan. The lance, bow, quiver, and arrows ; a shield and sword (more famed than Balisarda) [3] which the goddess girded on him with her own hand : the oath of fidelity and devotion was the 'relief' of this celestial investiture. Thus initiated into the mysteries of 'the first' (*adi*), admitted under the banners of Bhavani, Harita resolved to leave his pupil to his fortunes, and to quit the worship of the symbol for the presence of the deity in the mansions above. He informed Bappa of his design, and commanded him to be at the sacred spot early on the following morn ; but Bappa showed his materiality by oversleeping himself, and on reaching the spot the sage had already made some progress in his car, borne by the

[1] On this spot the celebrated temple of Eklinga was erected, and the present high priest traces sixty-six descents from Harita to himself. To him (through the Rana) I was indebted for the copy of the Sheo (*Siva*) Purana presented to the Royal Asiatic Society.

[2] [*Zunnār* is an Arabic word, the Hindi *janeo*.]

[3] [The sword stolen from Orlando by Brunello, given to Rogero (Ariosto, *Orlando Furioso*).]

Apsaras, or celestial messengers. He checked his aerial ascent to give a last token of affection to his pupil; and desiring him to reach up to receive his blessing, Bappa's stature was extended to twenty cubits; but as he did not reach the car, he was commanded to open his mouth, when the sage did what was recorded as performed, about the same period, by Muhammad, who spat into the mouth of his favourite nephew, Husain, the son of Ali. Bappa showed his disgust and aversion by blinking, and the projected blessing fell on his foot, by which squeamishness he obtained only invulnerability by weapons instead of immortality. The saint was soon lost in the cerulean space. Thus marked as the favourite of heaven, and having learned from his mother that he was nephew to the Mori prince of Chitor, he 'disdained a shepherd's slothful life,' and with some companions from these wilds quitted his retreat, and for the first time emerged into the plains. But, as if the brand of Bhavani was insufficient, he met with another hermit in the forest of the Tiger Mount,[1] the famed Gorakhnath, who presented to him the double-edged sword,[2] which, with the proper incantation, could 'sever rocks.' With this he opened the road to fortune leading to the throne of Chitor [227].

Chitor was at this period held by the Mori prince of the Pramar race, the ancient lords of Malwa, then paramount sovereigns of Hindustan: but whether this city was then the chief seat of power is not known. Various public works, reservoirs, and bastions, yet retain the name of this race.

Bappa's connexion with the Mori[3] obtained him a good recep-

[1] The *Nahra Magra*, seven miles from the eastern pass leading to the capital, where the prince has a hunting seat surrounded by several others belonging to the nobles, but all going to decay. The tiger and wild boar now prowl unmolested, as none of the 'unlicensed' dare shoot in these royal preserves.

[2] They surmise that this is the individual blade which is yet annually worshipped by the sovereign and chiefs on its appropriate day, one of the nine sacred to the god of war; a rite completely Scythic. I had this relation from the chief genealogists of the family, who gravely repeated the incantation: "By the preceptor, Gorakhnath and the great god, Eklinga; by Takshka the serpent, and the sage Harita; by Bhavani (Pallas) strike!"

[3] Bappa's mother was a Pramar, probably from Abu or Chandravati, near to Idar; and consequently Bappa was nephew to every Pramar in existence. [The Morya or Maurya sub-clan of the Pramārs still exists (*Census Report, Rajputana*, 1911, i. 255. For traces of the Mauryas in W. India see *BG*, i. Part ii. 284, note.]

tion; he was enrolled amongst the sawants or leaders, and a suitable estate conferred upon him. The inscription of the Mori prince's reign, so often alluded to, affords a good idea of his power, and of the feudal manners of his court. He was surrounded by a numerous nobility, holding estates on the tenure of military service, but whom he had disgusted by his neglect, and whose jealousy he had provoked by the superior regard shown to Bappa. A foreign foe appearing at this time, instead of obeying the summons to attend, they threw up their grants, and tauntingly desired him to call on his favourite.[1]

Bappa undertook the conduct of the war, and the chiefs, though dispossessed of their estates, accompanied him from a feeling of shame. The foe was defeated and driven out of the country; but instead of returning to Chitor, Bappa continued his course to the ancient seat of his family, Gajni, expelled the 'barbarian' called Salim, placed on the throne a chief of the Chaura tribe,[2] and returned with the discontented nobles. Bappa, on this occasion, is said to have married the daughter of his enemy. The nobles quitted Chitor, leaving their defiance with their prince. In vain were the spiritual preceptor (*Guru*) and foster-brother (*Dhabhai*) sent as ambassadors: their only reply was, that as they had 'eaten his salt,' they would forbear their vengeance for twelve months. The noble deportment of Bappa won their esteem, and they transferred to him their service and homage. With the temptation of a crown, the gratitude of the Grahilot was given to the winds. On return they assaulted and carried Chitor, and, in the words of the chronicle, "Bappa took Chitor from the Mori and became himself the mor (crown) of the land": he obtained by universal consent the title of 'sun of the Hindus (*Hindua suraj*), preceptor of princes (*Raj Guru*), and universal lord (*Chakravartin*)' [228].

He had a numerous progeny, some of whom returned to their ancient seats in Saurashtra, whose descendants were powerful chieftains in that tract so late as Akbar's reign.[3] Five sons went to Marwar, and the ancient Gohils 'of the land of Kher,' expelled

[1] We are furnished with a catalogue of the tribes which served the Mori prince, which is extremely valuable, from its acquainting us with the names of tribes no longer existing.

[2] [See p. 121, above.]

[3] See *Āīn*, ii. 247, which speaks of fifty thousand [8000] Guhilots in Sorath.

and driven to Gohilwal,[1] have lost sight of their ancestry, and by a singular fatality are in possession of the wreck of Valabhipura, ignorant of its history and their connexion with it, mixing with Arabs and following marine and mercantile pursuits; and the office of the bard having fallen into disrepute, they cannot trace their forefathers beyond Kherdhar.[2]

The close of Bappa's career is the strangest part of the legend, and which it might be expected they would be solicitous to suppress. Advanced in years, he abandoned his children and his country, carried his arms west to Khorasan, and there established himself, and married new wives from among the 'barbarians,' by whom he had a numerous offspring.[3]

Bappa had reached the patriarchal age of one hundred when he died. An old volume of historical anecdotes, belonging to the chief of Delwara, states that he became an ascetic at the foot of Meru, where he was buried alive after having overcome all the kings of the west, as in Ispahan, Kandahar, Kashmir, Irak, Iran, Turan, and Kafiristan; all of whose daughters he married, and by whom he had one hundred and thirty sons, called the Naus-shahra Pathans. Each of these founded a tribe, bearing the name of the mother. His Hindu children were ninety-eight in number, and were called Agni-upasi Suryavansi, or 'sunborn fire-worshippers.' The chronicles also record that (in like manner as did the subjects of the Bactrian king Menander, though from a different motive) the subjects of Bappa quarrelled for the disposal of his remains. The Hindu wished the fire to consume them; the 'barbarian' to commit them to earth; but on raising the pall while the dispute was raging, innumerable flowers of the lotus were found in the place of the remains of mortality: these were conveyed and planted in the lake. This is precisely what is related of the end of the Persian Nushirwan[4] [229].

[1] Pepara Guhilots.

[2] The 'land of Kher,' on the south-west frontier of Marwar, near the Luni river.

[3] The reigning prince told the author that there was no doubt of Bappa having ended his days among 'the Turks': a term now applied to all Muhammadans by the Hindu, but at that time confined to the inhabitants of Turkistan, the Turushka of the Puranas, and the Takshak of early inscriptions.

[4] [Recent inquiries identify Bappa, whose name is merely a title, with either Mahendrāji ii. or Kālbhoja, early chiefs of Mewār (Erskine ii. B. 8). It

The Question of Dates.—Having thus briefly sketched the history of the founder of the Guhilot dynasty in Mewar, we must now endeavour to establish the epoch of this important event in its annals. Although Bappa Rawal was nine generations after the sack of Valabhipura, the domestic annals give S. 191 (A.D. 135) for his birth; which the bards implicitly following, have vitiated the whole chronology. An important inscription [1] in a character little known, establishes the fact of the Mori dynasty being in possession of Chitor in S. 770 (A.D. 714). Now the annals of the Rana's house expressly state Bappa Rawal to be the nephew of the Mori prince of Chitor; that at the age of fifteen he was enrolled amongst the chieftains of his uncle, and that the vassals (before alluded to), in revenge for the resumption of their grants by the Mori, dethroned him and elevated as their sovereign the youthful Bappa. Notwithstanding this apparently irreconcilable anachronism, the family traditions accord with the inscription, except in date. Amidst such contradictions the development of the truth seemed impossible. Another valuable inscription of S. 1024 (A.D. 968), though giving the genealogy from Bappa to Sakti Kumar and corroborating that from Chitor, and which furnished convincing evidence, was not sanctioned by the prince or his chroniclers, who would admit nothing as valid that militated against their established era 191 for the birth of their founder. After six years' residence and unremitting search amid ruins, archives, inscriptions, traditions, and whatever could throw light upon this point, the author quitted Udaipur with all these doubts in his mind, for Saurashtra, to prosecute his inquiries in the pristine abodes of the race. Then it was that he was rewarded, beyond his most sanguine expectations, by the discovery of an inscription which reconciled these conflicting authorities and removed every difficulty. This marble, found in the celebrated temple of Somnath,[2] made mention of a distinct era, viz. the

has been suggested that his legend is mixed up with that of Bappa or Saila of Valabhi, the story of his retreat to Irān representing the latter being carried as a captive to Mansūra on the fall of Valabhi or Gandhār (*BG*, i. Part i. 94, note 2). In any case, the whole story is mere legend, a tale like that of the mysterious disappearance of Romulus and other kings (Sir J. Frazer, *Lectures on the Early History of the Kingship*, 269 ff.). A similar tale is told of Rāna Uda in later Mewār history.]

[1] *Vide* Appendix, Translation, No. II.

[2] See Translation, No. III.

Valabhi Samvat, as being used in Saurashtra; which era was three hundred and seventy-five years subsequent to Vikramaditya.[1]

On the sack of Valabhi thirty thousand families abandoned this 'city of a hundred temples,' and led by their priests found a retreat for themselves and their faith [230] in Mordardes (Marwar), where they erected the towns of Sandrai and Bali, in which latter we recognise the name of the eity whenee they were expelled. The religion of Valabhi, and consequently of the colonists, was the Jain; and it was by a priest descended from the survivors of this catastrophe, and still with their descendants inhabiting those towns, that these most important documents were furnished to the author. The Sandrai roll assigns the year 305 (Valabhi era) for the destruction of Valabhi: another, also from Jain authority, gives 205; and as there were but nine princes from Vijayasen, the founder, to its fall, we can readily believe the first a numerical error. Therefore 205+375=580 S. Vikrama (A.D. 524), for the invasion of Saurashtra by 'the barbarians from the north,' and saek of Valabhipura.

Now if from 770, the date of the Mori tablet, we deduet 580, there remains 190; justifying the pertinacity with which the chroniclers of Mewar adhered to the date given in their annals for the birth of Bappa, viz. 191: though they were ignorant that this period was dated from the flight from Valabhipura.

Bappa, when he sueceeded to the Mori prince, is said to have been fifteen years old; and his birth being one year anterior to the Mori inscription of 770+14=S.V. 784 (A.D. 728),[2] is the period for the foundation of the Guhilot dynasty in Mewar: sinee which, during a space of eleven hundred years, fifty-nine princes lineally descended from Bappa have sat on the throne of Chitor.

Though the bards and chroniclers will never forgive the temerity which thus curtails the antiquity of their founder, he is yet placed in the dawn of ehivalry, when the Carlovingian dynasty

[1] [The Valabhi era begins in A.D. 318–19.]

[2] This will make Bappa's attainment of Chitor fifteen years posterior to Muhammad bin Kasim's invasion. I have observed generally a discrepancy of ten years between the Samvat and Hegira; the Hegira reckoned from the sixteenth year of Muhammad's mission, and would if employed reconcile this difficulty. [The traditional dates are untrustworthy, being based on a confused reminiscence of Valabhi history (*IA*, xv. 275). A list of the chiefs of Mewār, with the dates as far as can be ascertained, is given by Erskine (ii. B. 8 ff.).]

was established in the west, and when Walid, whose bands planted 'the green standard' on the Ebro, was 'commander of the faithful.'

From the deserted and now forgotten 'city of the sun,' Aitpur, the abode of wild beasts and savage Bhils, another memorial [1] of the princes of Mewar was obtained. It relates to the prince Sakti Kumar. Its date is S. 1024 (A.D. 968), and it contains the names of fourteen of his ancestors in regular succession. Amongst these is Bappa, or Saila. When compared with the chronicles and [281] family archives, it was highly gratifying to find that, with the exception of one superfluous name and the transposition of others, they were in perfect accordance.

Hume says, "Poets, though they disfigure the most certain history by their fictions, and use strange liberties with truth, when they are the sole historians, as among the Britons, have commonly some foundation for their wildest exaggerations." The remark is applicable here; for the names which had been mouldering for nine centuries, far from the abode of man, are the same they had worked into their poetical legends. It was at this exact epoch that the arms of Islam, for the first time, crossed the Indus. In the ninety-fifth year of the Hegira,[2] Muhammad bin Kasim, the general of the Caliph Walid, conquered Sind, and penetrated (according to early Arabian authors) to the Ganges; and although Elmacin mentions only Sind, yet other Hindu States were at this period convulsed from the same cause: witness the overthrow of Manikrae of Ajmer, in the middle of the eighth century, by a foe 'coming in ships,' Anjar specified as the point where they landed. If any doubt existed that it was Kasim who advanced to Chitor [3] and was defeated by Bappa, it was set at rest by finding at this time in Chitor 'Dahir,[4] the prince of Debil.'

[1] See Translation of Inscription, No. IV.

[2] A.D. 713, or S. 769: the Inscription 770 of Man Mori, against whom came the 'barbarian.'

[3] I was informed by a friend, who had seen the papers of Captain Macmurdo, that he had a notice of Kasim's having penetrated to Dungarpur. Had this gentleman lived, he would have thrown much light on these Western antiquities. [Muhammad bin Kāsim does not seem to have attacked Ajmer: the place was not founded till A.D. 1000 (Watson, *Gazetteer*, i. A. 9).]

[4] By an orthographical error, the modern Hindu, ignorant of Debal, has written Delhi. But there was no lord of Delhi at this time: he is styled Dahir, Despat (lord) of Debal, from *des*, 'a country,' and *pat*, 'the head.'

Abu-l Fazl[1] records, from Arabian authorities, that Dahir was lord of Sind, and resided at his capital, Debal, the first place captured by Kasim in 95. His miserable end, and the destruction of his house, are mentioned by the historian, and account for the son being found with the Mori prince of Chitor.

Nine princes intervened between Bappa and Sakti Kumar, in two centuries (twenty-two years to each reign): just the time which should elapse from the founder, who 'abandoned his country for Iran,' in S. 820, or A.D. 764. Having thus established four epochs in the earlier history of the family, viz.—1 Kanaksen, A.D. 144; 2, Siladitya, and sack of Valabhi, A.D. 524; 3, Establishment in Chitor and Mewar, A.D. 720; 4, Sakti Kumar, A.D. 1068;[2] we may endeavour to relieve this narrative by the notices which regard their Persian descent [232].

CHAPTER 3

Connexion of the Rānas with Persia.—Historic truth has, in all countries, been sacrificed to national vanity: to its gratification every obstacle is made to give way; fictions become facts, and even religious prejudices vanish in this mirage of the imagination. What but this spurious zeal could for a moment induce any genuine Hindu to believe that, only twelve centuries ago, 'an eater of beef' occupied the chair of Rama, and enjoyed by universal acclaim the title of 'Sun of the Hindus'; or that the most ancient dynasty in the world could owe its existence to the last of the Sassanian kings:[3] that a slip from such a tree could be surreptitiously grafted on that majestic stem, which has flourished from the golden to the iron age, covering the land with its branches? That there existed a marked affinity in religious rites between the Rana's family and the Guebres, or ancient Persians, is evident. With both, the chief object of adoration was the sun; each bore the image of the orb on their banners. The chief day in the seven[4] was dedicated to the sun; to it is

[1] *Āīn*, ii. 344 f.

[2] [The dates are open to much question. It is known from inscriptions that Sakti Kumār was alive in A.D. 977.]

[3] Yezdegird died A.D. 651.

[4] *Surajwar*, or *Adityawar*, Sun-day; and the other days of the week, from the other planets, which Western nations have taken from the East.

sacred the chief gate of the city, the principal bastion of every fortress. But though the faith of Islam has driven away the fairy inhabitants from the fountains of Mithras, that of Surya has still its devotees on the summit of Chitor, as at Valabhi: and could we trace with accuracy their creeds to a distant age, we might discover them to be of one family, worshipping the sun at the fountains of the Oxus and Jaxartes.

The darkest period of Indian history is during the six centuries following Vikramaditya, which are scarcely enlightened by a ray of knowledge: but India was undergoing great changes, and foreign tribes were pouring in from the north. To this period, the sixth century, the genealogies of the Puranas are brought down, which expressly declare (adopting the prophetic spirit to conceal [233] the alterations and additions they then underwent) that at this time the genuine line of princes would be extinct, and that a mixed race would rule conjointly with foreign barbarians; as the Turushka, the Mauna,[1] the Yavan,[2] the Gorind, and

[1] See *History of the Tribes*, pp. 123, 135, articles 'Takshak,' and 'Jhala,' or *Makwahana*, in all probability the *Mauna* of the *Puranas* [?].

[2] The Yavan, or Greek princes, who apparently continued to rule within the Indus after the Christian era, were either the remains of the Bactrian dynasty or the independent kingdom of Demetrius or Apollodotus, who ruled in the Panjab, having as their capital Sagala, changed by Demetrius to Euthymedia. Bayer says, in his *Hist. Reg. Bact.*, p. 84: "I find from Claudius Ptolemy, that there was a city within the Hydaspes yet nearer the Indus, called Sagala, also Euthymedia; but I scarcely doubt that Demetrius called it Euthydemia, from his father, after his death and that of Menander. Demetrius was deprived of his patrimony A.U.C. 562." [The site of Sagala is uncertain—Chiniot, Shāhkot, Siālkot (*IGI*, ii. 80 f.; McCrindle, *Ptolemy*, 122 ff.).]

On this ancient city, Sagala, I have already said much; conjecturing it to be the Salbhanpura of the Yadus when driven from Zabulistan, and that of the Yueh-chi or Yuti, who were fixed there from Central Asia in the fifth century, and if so early as the second century, when Ptolemy wrote, may have originated the change of Yuti-media, the 'Central Yuti.' The numerous medals which I possess, chiefly found within the probable limits of the Greek kingdom of Sagala, either belong to these princes or the Parthian kings of Minnagara on the Indus. The legends are in Greek on one side, and in the Sassanian character on the reverse. Hitherto I have not deciphered the names of any but those of Apollodotus and Menander; but the titles of 'Great King,' 'Saviour,' and other epithets adopted by the Arsacidae, are perfectly legible. The devices, however, all incline me to pronounce them Parthian. It would be curious to ascertain how these Greeks and Parthians gradually merged into the Hindu population [see *IGI*, ii. 137].

Garddhabin.[1] There is much of truth in this; nor is it to be doubted that many of the Rajput tribes entered India from the north-west regions about this period. Gor and Gardhaba have the same signification; the first is Persian; the second its version in Hindi, meaning the 'wild ass,' an appellation of the Persian monarch Bahram, surnamed Gor from his partiality to hunting that animal. Various authorities state Bahramgor being in India in the fifth century, and his having there left progeny by a princess of Kanauj. A passage extracted by the author from an ancient Jain MS. indicates that "in S. 523 Raja Gardhabela, of Kakustha, or Suryavansa, ruled in Valabhipura." It has been surmised that Gardhabela was the son of Bahramgor, a son of whom is stated to have obtained dominion at Patan; which may be borne in mind when the authorities for the Persian extraction of the Rana's family are given.[2]

The Hindus, when conquered by the Muhammadans, naturally wished to gild the chains they could not break. To trace a common, though distant, origin with the conquerors was to remove some portion of the taint of dishonour which arose from giving their daughters in marriage to the Tatar emperors of Delhi; and a degree of satisfaction was derived from assuming that the blood thus corrupted once flowed from a common fountain[3] [234].

[1] [The list in the Vishnu Purāna (474 f.) gives 7 Abhīras, 10 Garddhabas, 16 Sakas, 14 Tushāras, 13 Mundas, 11 Maunas. On the impossibility of reducing the Purānic accounts to order see Smith, *EHI*, 274.]

[2] [Rawlinson (*Seventh Oriental Monarchy*, 298) regards the eastern adventure of Bahrāmgor, Varahran V., as mythical. Sykes (*Hist. of Persia*, i. 470) thinks they can hardly be authentic, "but I do not reject it as entirely devoid of historical basis."]

[3] The Hindu genealogist, in ignorance of the existence of Aghuz Khan, the Tatar patriarch, could not connect the chain of Chagatai with Chandra. The Brahman, better read, supplied the defect, and with his doctrine of the metempsychosis animated the material frame of the beneficent Akbar with the 'good genius' of a Hindu; and that of their mortal foe, Aurangzeb, with one of evil destiny, being that of Kalayavana, the foe of Krishna. They gravely assert that Akbar visited his ancient hermitage at the confluence of the Ganges and Jumna, and excavated the implements of penance used by him in his former shape, as one of the sages of ancient times; while such is their aversion to Aurangzeb, that they declare the final avatar, Time (*Kal*), on his white steed, will appear in his person. The Jaisalmer annals affirm that the whole Turkish (*Turushka*) race of Chagatai are of Yadu stock; while the Jam Jareja of Cutch traces his descent from the Persian Jamshid, contemporary with Solomon. These are curious claims, but the Rana's family would consider such vanity criminal.

Further to develop these claims of Persian descent, we shall commence with an extract from the Upadesa Prasād, a collection of historic fragments in the Magadhi dialect. "In Gujardes (Gujarat) there are eighty-four cities. In one of these, Kaira, resided the Brahman Devaditya, the expounder of the Vedas. He had an only child, Subhaga (*of good fortune*) by name, at once a maiden and a widow. Having learned from her preceptor the solar incantation, incautiously repeating it, the sun appeared and embraced her, and she thence became pregnant.[1] The affliction of her father was diminished when he discovered the parent; nevertheless [as others might be less charitable] he sent her with a female attendant to Valabhipura, where she was delivered of twins, male and female. When grown up the boy was sent to school; but being eternally plagued about his mysterious birth, whence he received the nickname of Ghaibi ('concealed'), in a fit of irritation he one day threatened to kill his mother if she refused to disclose the author of his existence. At this moment the sun revealed himself: he gave the youth a pebble, with which it was sufficient to touch his companions in order to overcome them. Being carried before the Balhara prince, who menaced Ghaibi, the latter slew him with the pebble, and became himself sovereign of Saurashtra, taking the name of Siladitya[2] (from *sila*, 'a stone or pebble,' and *aditya*, 'the sun'): his sister was married to the Raja of Broach." Such is the literal translation of a fragment totally unconnected with the history of the Rana's family, though evidently bearing upon it. The father of Siladitya, according to the Sandrai roll and other authorities of that period, is Suraj (the sun) Rao, though two others make a Somaditya intervene[3] [235].

[1] [For legends of women impregnated by the sun see Frazer, *Golden Bough*, Part vii. vol. i. 74 ff.]

[2] This is probably the Siladitya of the Satrunjaya Mahatma, who repaired the temple on Satrunjaya in S. 477 (A.D. 421). [A mere folk etymology—Sīlāditya, from *sil*, 'to worship,' *āditya*, 'the sun.']

[3] In perusing this fragment we are struck by the similarity of production of these Hindu Heliadae and that of the celebrated Tatar dynasty from which Jenghiz Khan was descended. The Niruns, or 'children of light,' were from an amour of the sun with Alung Goa, from which Jenghiz was the ninth in descent. Authorities quoted by Petis de la Croix, in his life of this conqueror, and likewise by Marigny, in his *History of the Saracens*, affirm Jenghiz Khan to be a descendant of Yazdegird, the last Sassanian prince. Jenghiz was an idolater, and hated the very name of Muhammadan [see

Let us see what Abu-l Fazl says of the descent of the Ranas from Nushirwan: "The chief of the State was formerly called Rāwal, but for a long time past has been known as Rāna. He is of the Ghelot clan, and pretends to descent from Noshirwān the Just. An ancestor of this family through the vicissitudes of fortune came to Berār and was distinguished as the chief of Narnālah. About eight hundred years previous to the present time[1] Narnālah was taken by the enemy and many were slain. One Bāpa, a child, was carried by his mother from this scene of desolation to Mewār, and found refuge with Rājah Mandalikh, a Bhīl."[2]

The work which has furnished all the knowledge which exists on the Persian ancestry of the Mewar princes is the *Maasiru-l-Umara*, or that (in the author's possession) founded on it, entitled *Bisatu-l-Ghanim*, or 'Display of the Foe,' written in A.H. 1204[3] [A.D. 1789]. The writer of this work styles himself Lachhmi Narayan Shafik Aurangabadi, or 'the rhymer of Aurangabad. He professes to give an account of Sivaji, the founder of the Mahratta empire; for which purpose he goes deep into the lineage of the Ranas of Mewar, from whom Sivaji was descended,[4] quoting

---

Howorth, *Hist. of the Mongols*, i. 37 ff.]. A courtier telling Aurangzeb of his celestial ancestry, gravely quoting the affair of the mother of the race of Timur with the sun, the bigoted monarch coarsely replied, "Mama qahba bud," which we will not translate.

[1] Akbar commenced his reign A.D. 1556, and had been forty years on the throne when the 'Institutes' were composed by the Abu-l Fazl. [The translation of Gladwin in the original text has been replaced by that of Jarrett, *Āīn*, ii. 268.]

[2] Orme [*Historical Fragments*, Notes, p. xxii] was acquainted with this passage, and shows his knowledge of the Hindu character by observing that it was a strange pedigree to assign a Hindu prince, for Khusru, of the religion of Zoroaster, though compelled to many abstinences, was not restrained from eating beef: and Anquetil du Perron says of the Parsis, their descendants, that they have refrained since their emigration from slaying the cow merely to please the Hindu.

[3] The cryptographic date is contained in the numerical value of the letters which compose the title:

B. S. A. T. a. l. G. N. A. E. M.	As the total is only 1183, either the date is wrong, or a deficient value given to the numerals.
2. 60. 1. 9. 1. 9. 1000. 50. 1. 10. 40.	

[4] Wilford, who by his indefatigable research and knowledge of Sanskrit had accumulated extensive materials, unhappily deteriorated by a too credulous imagination, yet containing much valuable matter available to those sufficiently familiar with the subject to select with safety, has touched on this, and almost on every other point in the circle of Hindu antiquities.

at length the Maasiru-l-Umara, from which the following is a literal translation: "It is well known that the Rajas of Udaipur are exalted over all the princes of Hind. Other Hindu princes, before they can succeed to the throne of their fathers, must receive the khushka, or tilak of regality and investiture, from them. This type of sovereignty is received with humility and veneration. The khushka of these princes is made with human blood: their title is Rana, and they deduce [236] their origin from Noshirwan-i-Adil (*i.e.* the Just), who conquered the countries of ——,[1] and many parts of Hindustan. During his lifetime his son Noshizad, whose mother was the daughter of Kaiser of Rum,[2] quitted the ancient worship and embraced the 'faith[3] of the Christians,' and with numerous followers entered Hindustan. Thence he marched a great army towards Iran, against his father Noshirwan; who despatched his general, Rambarzin,[4] with

Ali Ibrahim, a learned native of Benares, was Wilford's authority for asserting the Rana's Persian descent, who stated to him that he had seen the original history, which was entitled, Origin of the Peishwas from the Ranas of Mewar. (Ibrahim must have meant the Satara princes, whose ministers were the Peshwas.) From this authority three distinct emigrations of the Guebres, or ancient Persians, are recorded, from Persia into Gujarat. The first in the time of Abu Bakr, A.D. 631; the second on the defeat of Yazdegird, A.D. 651; and the third when the descendants of Abbas began to prevail, A.D. 749. Also that a son of Noshirwan landed near Surat with eighteen thousand of his subjects, from Laristan, and were well received by the prince of the country. Abu-l Fazl confirms this account by saying, "the followers of Zoroaster, when they fled from Persia, settled in *Surat*," the contracted term for the peninsular of Saurashtra, as well as the city of this name [*Āīn*, ii. 243].

[1] The names are obliterated in the original. Ferishta [i. Introd. lxxix] informs us that Ramdeo Rathor, sovereign of Kanauj, was made tributary by Firoz 'Sassan'; and that Partap Chand, who usurped the throne of Ramdeo, neglecting to pay this tribute, Noshirwan marched into India to recover it, and in his progress subdued Kabul and the Panjab. From the striking coincidence of these original and decisive authorities, we may rest assured that they had recourse to ancient records, both of the Guebres and the Hindus, for the basis of their histories, which research may yet discover.

[2] Maurice, emperor of Byzantium. [Sykes (*Hist. of Persia*, ii. 495) calls the son of Nushirwān Nushishad, and mentions his rebellion against his father. There seems to be no evidence that Nushishad reached India: he was slain after he revolted (Malcolm, *Hist. Persia*, 2nd ed. i. 112 ff.).]

[3] *Din-i-Tarsar*. See Ebn Haukal, art. 'Serir,' or Russia; whose king, a son of Bahram Chassin, whom he styles a *Tersar* or Christian, first possessed it about the end of the sixth century.

[4] The *Verames* of Western historians [Malcolm, *op. cit.* i. 113].

numerous forces to oppose him. An action ensued, in which Noshizad was slain; *but his issue remained in Hindustan, from whom are descended the Ranas of Udaipur.* Nushirwan had a wife from the Khakhan [1] of China, by whom he had a son called Hormuz, declared heir to the throne shortly before his death. As according to the faith of the fire-worshippers [2] it is not customary either to bury or to burn the dead, but to leave the corpse exposed to the rays of the sun, so it is said the body of Nushirwan has to this day suffered no decay, but is still fresh."

I now come to the account of Yazd, "the son of Shahriyar, the son of Khusru Parves, the son of Hormuz, the son of Nushirwan.

"Yazd was the last king of Ajám. It is well known he fought many battles with the Muhammadans. In the fifteenth year of the caliphat, Rustam, son of Ferokh, a great chief, was slain in battle by Saad-bin-wakas, who commanded for Omar, which was the death-blow to the fortunes of the house of Sassan: so that a remnant of it did not remain in A.H. 31, when Iran was seized by the Muhammadans. This battle had lasted four days when Rustam Ferokzad was slain by the hand of Hilkal, the son of Al Kumna, at Saad's command [237]; though Firdausi asserts by Saad himself. Thirty thousand Muslims were slain, and the same number of the men of Ajam. To count the spoils was a torment. During this year (the thirty-first), the sixteenth of the prophet,[3] the era of the Hegira was introduced. In A.H. 17 Abu Musa of Ashur seized Hormuz, the son of the uncle of Yazdegird, whom he sent with Yazdegird's daughter to Imam Husain, and another daughter to Abubakr.

"Thus far have I [4] extracted from the history of the fire-worshippers. He who has a mind to examine these, let him do so. The people of the religion of Zardusht have a full knowledge

[1] *Khakhan* was the title of the kings of Chinese Tartary. It was held by the leader of the Huns, who at this period held power on the Caspian: it was also held by the Urus, Khuzr, Bulgar, Serir, all terms for Russia, before its *Kaisar* was cut down into *Tzar*, for the original of which, the kings of Rome, as of Russia, were indebted to the Sanskrit *Kesar*, a " lion ' [Lat. Caesar] (*vide* Ibn Haukal, art. 'Khozr').

[2] Din-i-Majusi; literally, 'faith of the Magi.'

[3] Muhammad, born A.D. 578; the Hegira, or flight, A.D. 622.

[4] It must be borne in mind that it is the author of the *Mausiru-l-Umara*, not the rhymer of Aurungabad, who is speaking.

of all these events, with their dates; for the pleasure of their lives is the obtaining accounts of antiquity and astronomical knowledge, and their books contain information of two and three thousand years. It is also told, that when the fortunes of Yazdegird were on the wane, his family dispersed to different regions. The second daughter, Shahr Banu, was married to Imam Husain,[1] who, when he fell a martyr (shahid), an angel carried her to heaven. The third daughter, Banu, was seized by a plundering Arab and carried into the wilds of Chichik, thirty coss from Yazd. Praying to God for deliverance, she instantly disappeared; and the spot is still held sacred by the Parsis, and named 'the secret abode of perfect purity.' Hither, on the twenty-sixth of the month Bahman, the Parsis yet repair to pass a month in pilgrimage, living in huts under indigenous vines skirting the rock, out of whose fissures water falls into a fountain below: but if the unclean approach the spring, it ceases to flow.

"Of the eldest daughter of Yazdegird, Maha Banu, the Parsis have no accounts; but the books of Hind give evidence to her arrival in that country, and that from her issue is the tribe Sesodia. But, at all events, this race is either of the seed of Nushishad, the son of Nushirwan, or of that of the daughter of Yazdegird."[2]

Thus have we adduced, perhaps, all the points of evidence for the supposed Persian origin of the Rana's family. The period of the invasion of Saurashtra by Nushishad, who mounted the throne A.D. 531, corresponds well with the sack of Valabhi, A.D. 524 [238]. The army he collected in Laristan to depose his father might have been from the Parthians, Getae, Huns, and other Scythic races then on the Indus, though it is unlikely, with such an object in view as the throne of Persia, that he would waste his strength in Saurashtra. Khusru Parvez, grandson of Nushirwan

[1] [This is the Persian tradition (Sykes, *op. cit.* ii. 44).]

[2] For the extract from "The Annals of Princes (*Maasiru-l-Umara*)" let us laud the memory of the rhymer of Aurungabad. An original copy, which I in vain attempted to procure in India, is stated by Sir William Ouseley to be in the British Museum. We owe that country a large debt, for we have robbed her of all her literary treasures, leaving them to sleep on the shelves of our public institutions. [There is no real evidence of the Persian descent of the Rānas, and it has been suggested that the story is based on the fire symbols on the coinage found in Kāthiawār and Mewār, these, though in the main Indo-Scythic, betraying from about sixth century a more direct Sassanian influence (*BG*, i. Part i. 102). At the same time recent discoveries indicate Persian influence in N. India.]

the great, and who assumed this title according to Firdausi, married Marian, the daughter of Maurice, the Greek emperor of Byzantium. She bore him Shirauah (the Siroes of the early Christian writers), who slew his father. It is difficult to separate the actions of the two Nushirwans, and still more to say which of them merited the epithet of *adil*, or 'just.'

According to the 'Tables' in Moreri,[1] Nushishad, son of Khusru the Great, reigned from A.D. 531 to 591. This is opposed to the *Maasiru-l-Umara*, which asserts that he was slain during his rebellion. Siroes, son of Khusru (the second Nushirwan) by his wife Marian, alternately called the friend and foe of the Christians, did raise the standard of revolt, and met the fate attributed to Nushishad; on which Yazdegird, his nephew, was proclaimed. The crown was intended for Shirauah's younger brother, which caused the revolt, during which the elder sought refuge in India.

These revolutions in the Sassanian house were certainly simultaneous with those which occurred in the Rana's, and no barrier existed to the political intercourse at least between the princely worshippers of Surya and Mithras. It is, therefore, curious to speculate even on the possibility of such a pedigree to a family whose ancestry is lost in the mists of time; and it becomes interesting when, from so many authentic sources, we can raise testimonies which would furnish, to one even untinctured with the love of hypothesis, grounds for giving ancestors to the Ranas in Maurice of Byzantium and Cyrus (Khusru) of Persia [239]. We have a singular support to these historic relics in a geographical fact, that places on the site of the ancient Valabhi a city called Byzantium, which almost affords conclusive proof that it must have been the son of Nushirwan who captured Valabhi and Gajni, and destroyed the family of Siladitya; for it would be a legitimate occasion to name such conquest after the city where his Christian mother had had birth.[2] Whichever of the propositions we adopt at the command of the author of The Annals of Princes, namely, "that the Sesodia race is of the seed of Nushishad, son of Nushirwan, or of that of Mahabanu, daughter of Yazdegird," we arrive at a singular and startling conclusion, viz. that the 'Hindua

[1] Vide *Grand Dictionnaire Historique.*

[2] [Byzantium cannot have been a Greek colony, the name apparently representing Vijayanta, now Vijayadurga, the southern entrance of the Vāghotan River in Ratnagiri (McCrindle, *Ptolemy*, 47; *BG*, i. Part ii. 174 f.).]

Suraj, descendant of a hundred kings,' the undisputed possessor of the honours of Rama, the patriarch of the Solar race, is the issue of a Christian princess: that the chief prince amongst the nations of Hind can claim affinity with the emperors of 'the mistress of the world,' though at a time when her glory had waned, and her crown had been transferred from the Tiber to the Bosphorus.

But though I deem it morally impossible that the Ranas should have their lineage from any *male* branch of the Persian house, I would not equally assert that Mahabanu, the fugitive daughter of Yazdegird, may not have found a husband, as well as sanctuary, with the prince of Saurashtra; and she may be the Subhagna (mother of Siladitya), whose mysterious amour with the 'sun'[1] compelled her to abandon her native city of Kaira. The son of Marian had been in Saurashtra, and it is therefore not unlikely that her grandchild should there seek protection in the reverses of her family.

The Salic law is here in full force, and honours, though never acquired by the female, may be stained by her; yet a daughter of the noble house of Sassan might be permitted to perpetuate the line of Rama without the reproach of taint.[2]

We shall now abandon this point to the reader, and take leave

[1] It will be recollected that the various authorities given state Raja Suraj (*sun*), of Kakustha race, to be the father of Siladitya. *Kakustha* is a term used synonymously with *Suryavansa*, according to the Solar genealogists. Those who may be inclined to the Persian descent may trace it from *Kaikaus*, a well-known epithet in the Persian dynasties. I am unacquainted with the etymology of Kakustha; but it may possibly be from *ka*, 'of or belonging to,' *Kusa* (Cush), the second son of Rama [?]. I have already hinted that the Assyrian Medes might be descendants of Hyaspa, a branch of the Indu-Mede of the family of Yayati which bore the name of *Kausika*. [The reference in the text may be to Kakutstha, grandson of Ikshwāku, who is said to have taken his name because he stood on the hump (*Kukuda*) of Indra when he was turned into a bull (Wilson, *Vishnu Purāna*, 361).]

[2] "The moral consequence of a pedigree," says Hume, "is differently marked by the influence of law and custom. The male sex is deemed more noble than the female. The association of our ideas pursues the regular descent of honour and estates from father to son, and their wives, however essential, are considered only in the light of foreign auxiliaries" (*Essays*, vol. ii. p. 192). Not unlike the Rajput axiom, though more coarsely expressed; "It is, who planted the tree, not where did it grow," that marks his idea of the comparative value of the side whence honours originate; though purity of blood in both lines is essential.

of Yazdegird,[1] the last of the house of Sassan, in the words of the historian of Rome: "Avec lui, on voit périr pour jamais la gloire et l'empire des Perses. Les rochers du Mazendaran et les sables du Kerman, furent les seuls [2] asiles que les vainqueurs laissèrent aux sectateurs de Zoroastre" [3] [240].

CHAPTER 4

Samarsi, Samar Singh.—Having established Bappa on the throne of Chitor S. 784 (A.D. 728), we will proceed to glean from the annals, from the period of his departure for Iran, S. 820 (A.D. 764) to another halting point—the reign of Samarsi, S. 1249 (A.D. 1193); [4] an important epoch, not only in the history of Mewar, but to the whole Hindu race; when the diadem of sovereignty was torn from the brow of the Hindu to adorn that of the Tatar. We shall not, however, overleap the four intervening centuries, though we may not be able to fill up the reigns of the eighteen princes [5] whose "banner at this time was a golden sun on a crimson field," [6] and several of whose names yet live recorded "with an iron pen on the rock" of their native abodes.

An intermediate period, from Bappa to Samarsi, that of Sakti Kumar, is fixed by the Aitpur inscription in S. 1024 (A.D. 968);

[1] A new era had commenced, not of Yazdegird's accession, as is supposed, which would have been vain indeed, when the throne was tottering under him, but consequent to the completion of the grand cycle of 1440 years. He was slain at Merv in A.D. 651, the 31st of the Hegira; on the eleventh year of which, or A.D. 632 (according to Moreri), he commenced his reign.

[2] Gibbon was wrong. India afforded them an asylum, and their issue constitutes the most wealthy, the most respected, and the most enlightened part of the native community of Bombay and the chief towns of that presidency.

[3] Gibbon, *Miscellaneous Works*, 'Sur la Monarchie des Mèdes,' vol. iii.

[4] ["We now know that Samar Singh was alive up to 1299, only four years before Alāu-d-dīn's siege of Chitor, and that in several inscriptions his dates are given as 1273, 1274, 1285, etc. . . . Instead of being the father of Karan Singh I., as stated by Tod, Samar Singh came eight generations after him, and was the father of Ratan Singh I., who, according to Muhammadan historians, was the ruler of Chitor during the reign of Alāu-d-dīn, and the husband of Padmini" (Erskine ii. A. 14 f.)]

[5] See Genealogical Table.

[6] This, according to the roll, was the standard of Bappa.

and from the more perishable yet excellent authority of an ancient Jain MS. the era of Allat, the ancestor of Sakti Kumar, was S. 922 (A.D. 866), four generations anterior. From Bappa's departure for Iran, in A.D. 764, to the subversion of Hindu dominion in the reign of Samarsi, in A.D. 1193, we find recorded an intermediate Islamite invasion. This was during the reign of Khuman, between A.D. 812 and 836, which event forms the chief subject of the Khuman-Raesa, the most ancient of the poetic chronicles of Mewar [241].

As the history of India at this period is totally dark, we gladly take advantage of the lights thus afforded. By combining these facts with what is received as authentic, though scarcely less obscure or more exact than these native legends, we may furnish materials for the future historian. With this view, let us take a rapid sketch of the irruptions of the Arabians into India, from the rise of Islamism to the foundation of the Ghaznivid empire, which sealed the fate of the Hindus. The materials are but scanty. El-Makin, in his history of the Caliphs, passes over such intercourse almost without notice. Abu-l-Fazl, though not diffuse, is minute in what he does say, and we can confide in his veracity. Ferishta has a chapter devoted to this subject, which merits a better translation than yet exists.[1] We shall, however, in the first place, touch on Bappa's descendants, till we arrive at the point proper for the introduction of the intended sketch.

Of the twenty-four tribes of Guhilot, several issued from the founder, Bappa. Shortly after the conquest of Chitor, Bappa proceeded to Saurashtra and married the daughter of Yusufgol, prince of the island of Bandardiva.[2] With his bride he conveyed

[1] Amongst the passages which Dow [i. 37] has slurred over in his translation is the interesting account of the origin of the Afghans; who, when they first came in contact with those of the new faith, in A.H. 62, dwelt around the Koh-i-Sulaiman. Ferishta, quoting authority, says: "The Afghans were Copts, ruled by Pharaun, many of whom were converted to the laws and religion of Moses; but others, who were stubborn in their worship to their gods, fled towards Hindustan, and took possession of the country adjoining the Koh-i-Sulaiman. They were visited by Kasim from Sind, and in the 143rd year of the Hegira had possessed themselves of the provinces of Kirman, Peshawar, and all within their bounds (*sinoran*)," which Dow has converted into a province. The whole geographical description of the Kohistan, the etymology of the term *Rohilla*, and other important matter, is omitted by him [see Briggs, trans. i. 6 f.].

[2] [The island Diu.] Yūsufgol is stated to have held Chaul on the main-

to Chitor the statue of Vyanmata, the tutelary goddess of her race, who still divides with Eklinga the devotion of the Guhilot princes. The temple in which he enshrined this islandic goddess yet stands on the summit of Chitor, with many other monuments assigned by tradition to Bappa. This princess bore him Aparajit, who from being born in Chitor was nominated successor to the throne, to the exclusion of his less fortunate elder brother, Asil (born of the daughter of the Kaba (Pramara) prince of Kalibao near Dwaraka), who, however, obtained possessions in Saurashtra, and founded a race called the Asila Guhilots,[1] whose descendants were so numerous, even in Akbar's reign, as to [242] be supposed able to bring into the field fifty thousand men at arms. We have nothing important to record of the actions of Aparajit, who had two sons, Kalbhoj[2] and Nandkumar. Kalbhoj succeeded Aparajit, and his warlike qualities are extolled in an inscription discovered by the author in the valley of Nagda. Nandkumar slew Bhimsen Dor (*Doda*), and possessed himself of Deogarh in the Deccan.

Khumān I.—Khuman succeeded Kalbhoj. His name is remarkable in the history of Mewar. He came to the throne at the

---

land. He was most probably the father of Vanaraja Chawara, the founder of Patan Anhilwara, whose ancestors, on the authority of the Kumarpal Charitra, were princes of Bandardiva, held by the Portuguese since the time of Albuquerque, who changed its name to Deo. [But Yūsufgol, if he existed, must have been a Musalmān. Vanarāja Chāwara was son of Jayasekhara, said to have been slain in battle, A.D. 696, leaving his wife pregnant (*BG*, i. Part i. 150 f.). Yūsufgol does not appear in the local history.]

[1] The ancient roll from which this is taken mentions Asil giving his name to a fortress, called Asilgarh. His son, Bijai Pal, was slain in attempting to wrest Khambayat (Cambay) from Sangram Dabhi. One of his wives, from a violent death, was prematurely delivered of a boy, called Setu; and as, in such cases, the Hindu supposes the deceased to become a discontented spirit (*churail*), Churaila became the name of the tribe. Bija, the twelfth from Asil, obtained Sonal from his maternal uncle, Khengar Dabhi, prince of Girnar, but was slain by Jai Singh Deo, prince of Surat. From these names compounded, Dabi and Churaila, we may have the Dabiśalima of Mahmud. [The Asil Guhilots are now included in the Mers of the Kāthiawār coast; their numbers are exaggerated in the text (*Āīn*, ii. 247; *BG*, ix. Part i. 126).] [See p. 266 above.]

[2] Also called Karna. He it was who excavated the Boraila lake, and erected the grand temple of Eklinga on the site of the hermitage of Harita, whose descendant, the present officiating priest, reckons sixty-six descents, while the princes of Mewar amount to seventy-two in the same period.

beginning of the ninth century, when Chitor was assailed by another formidable invasion of Muhammadans. The chief object of the Khuman Raesa is to celebrate the defence made on this occasion, and the value of this Raesa consists in the catalogue of the princes who aided in defending this bulwark of the Hindu faith. The bard, in an animated strain, makes his sovereign on this occasion successfully defend the 'crimson standard' of Mewar, treat with contempt the demand for tribute, and after a violent assault, in which the 'barbarian' is driven back, follow and discomfit him in the plan, carrying back the hostile leader, Mahmud, captive. With this event, which introduces the name of Mahmud two centuries before the conqueror of Ghazni, we will pause, and resume the promised sketch of the intercourse of Arabia and Hindustan at this period.

The Muhammadan Invasion, A.D. **644-55.**—The first intimation of the Moslems attempting the invasion of India is during the caliphat of Omar, who built the port of Bassorah at the mouth of the Tigris, chiefly to secure the trade of Gujarat and Sind; into which latter country a powerful army penetrated under Abul Aas,[1] who was killed in battle at Aror. The Caliph Osman, who succeeded Omar, sent to explore the state of India, while he prepared an army to invade it in person: a design which he never fulfilled. The generals of the Caliph Ali made conquests in Sind, which they abandoned at Ali's death. While Yazid was governor of Khorasan several attempts were made on India, as also during the caliphat of Abdu-l Malik, but without any lasting [243] results. It was not till the reign of Walid[2] that any successful invasion took place. He not only finally conquered Sind and the adjoining continent of India, but rendered tributary all that part of India on this side the Ganges.[3] What an exalted idea must we not form of the energy and rapidity of such conquests, when we find the arms of Islam at once on the Ganges and the Ebro, and two regal dynasties simultaneously cut off, that of Roderic, the last of the Goths of Andaloos, and Dahir Despati in the valley of the Indus. It was in A.H. 99 (A.D. 712, S. 774) that Muhammad bin Kasim vanquished and slew Dahir,

[1] [Ferishta (i. 2) calls him Sayyid bin Abiu-l-Aas.]

[2] See Table next page.

[3] Marigny (quoting El-Makin), *Hist. of the Arabians*, vol. ii. p. 283; *Mod. Univ. Hist.* vol. ii. p. 47.

GUHILOT AND CONTEMPORARY PRINCES[1]

Guhilot Princes.	Eras.		Caliphs of Baghdad and Kings of Ghazni.	Eras.		Remarks.
	Samvat.	Christian.		A.H.	A.D.	
			Caliphs of Baghdad.			
Bappa, born.	769	713	Walid (7th Ummaiya Caliph)	86 to 96	705 to 715	Conquered India to the Ganges.
—— obtained Chitor.	784	728	Omar II. (9th do.)	99 to 102	718 to 721	Sindi conquered. The Mori prince of Chitor attacked by Muhammad (son of Kasim), the General of Omar.
—— governs Mewar	..	..	Hasham (10th do.)	104 to 125	723 to 742	Battle of Tours, A.D. 732, and defeat of the Caliph's army, under Abdulrahman, by Charles Martel.
—— abandons Chitor.	820	764	Al-Mansur Abbasi (2nd do.)	136 to 158	754 to 775	Final conquest of Sind, and the name of its capital, Aror, changed to Mansura. Bappa, founder of the Guhilot race in Mewar, retires to Iran.
Aparajit. Kalbhoj	..	..	Harunu-r-rashid (5th do.)	170 to 193	786 to 809	Partition of the caliphat amongst Harun's sons. The second, Al-Mamun, obtains Zabulistan, Sind, and India, and ruled them till A.D. 813, when he became Caliph.
Khuman	868 to 892	812 to 836	Al-Mamun (7th do.)	198 to 218	813 to 833	Invasion and attack on Chitor from Zabulistan.
Bhartaribhat. Singhji. Allat. Narabahan. Salivahan.			*Kings of Ghazni.*			
Sakti Kumar	1024	968	Alptigin	350	957	Inscription of Sakti-kumar from ruins of Aitpur.
Amba Pasao. Naravarman	..	..	Sabuktigin	367	977	Invasion of India.
Jasuvarman [or Kirtivarman]	..	..	Mahmud	387 to 418	997 to 1027	Invasions of India, destruction of Aitpur.

[1] [The Mewār dates are quite untrustworthy (see Erskine iii. B. 8 f.).]

prince of Sind, after numerous conflicts. Amongst the spoils of victory sent to the caliph on this occasion were the daughters of the subjugated monarch, who were the cause of Kasim's destruction,[1] when he was on the eve of carrying the war against Raja [244] Harchand of Kanauj. Some authorities state that he actually prosecuted it; and as Sind remained a dependency of the caliphat during several successive reigns, the successor of Kasim may have executed his plans. Little is said of India from this period to the reign of Al-Mansur, except in regard to the rebellion of Yazid in Khorasan, and the flight of his son to Sind. The eight sovereigns, who rapidly followed, were too much engaged with the Christians of the west and the Huns on the Caspian to think of India. Their armies were then in the heart of France, which was only saved from the Koran by their overthrow at Tours by Charles Martel.

Al-Mansur, when only the lieutenant of the Caliph Abbas, held the government of Sind and of India, and made the island of Bakhar on the Indus, and the adjacent Aror,[2] the ancient capital, his residence, naming it Mansura; and it was during his government that Bappa Rawal abandoned Chitor for Iran.

The celebrated Harunu-r-rashid, contemporary of Charlemagne, in apportioning his immense empire amongst his sons, gave to the second, Al-Mamun, Khorasan, Zabulistan, Kabulistan, Sind, and Hindustan.[3] Al-Mamun, on the death of Harun, deposed his brother, and became caliph in A.H. 198 or A.D. 813, and ruled to 833, the exact period of the reign of Khuman, prince of Chitor. The domestic history brings the enemy assailant of Chitor from Zabulistan; and as the leader's name is given *Mahmud Khorasan Pat*, there can be little doubt that it is an error arising from ignorance of the copyist, and should be *Mamun*.

[1] "The two young princesses, in order to revenge the death of their father, represented falsely to the Khalif that Muhammad bin Kasim had been connected with them. The Khalif, in a rage, gave order for Muhammad bin Kasim to be sewed up in a raw hide, and sent in that condition to court. When the mandate arrived at Tatta, Kasim was prepared to carry an expedition against Harchand, monarch of Kanauj. When he arrived at court, the Khalif showed him to the daughters of Dahir, who expressed their joy upon beholding their father's murderer in such a condition" [*Āīn*, ii. 345; Elliot-Dowson i. 209 f.].

[2] Aror is seven miles east of Bakhar.

[3] Marigny, vol. iii. p. 83; *Univ. Hist.* vol. ii. p. 162.

Mahmūd's Invasion.—Within twenty years after this event, the sword of conquest and conversion was withdrawn from India, and Sind was the only province left to Mutawakkil (A.D. 850 [847-861]), the grandson of Harun, for a century after whom the throne of Baghdad, like that of ancient Rome, was sold by her praetorians to the highest bidder. From this time we find no mention whatever of Hindustan, or even of Sind, until Sabuktigin,[1] governor of Khorasan, hoisted the standard of independent sovereignty at Ghazni. In A.H. 365 (A.D. 974) he carried his arms [245] across the Indus, forcing the inhabitants to abandon the religion of their ancestors, and to read the Koran from the altars of Bal and Krishna. Towards the close of this century he made his last invasion, accompanied by his son, the celebrated Mahmud, destined to be the scourge of the Hindu race, who early imbibed the paternal lesson inculcating the extirpation of infidels. Twelve several visitations did Mahmud make with his Tatar hordes, sweeping India of her riches, destroying her temples and architectural remains, and leaving the country plunged in poverty and ignorance. From the effect of these incursions she never recovered; for though she had a respite of a century between Mahmud and the final conquest, it was too short to repair what it had cost ages to rear: the temples of Somnath, of Chitor, and Girnar are but types of the magnificence of past times. The memorial of Sakti Kumar proves him to have been the contemporary of Sabuktigin, and to one of his son's visitations is attributed the destruction of the 'city of the sun' (Aitpur),[2] his capital.

Attack on Chitor.—Having thus condensed the little information afforded by Muhammadan historians of the connexion between the caliphs of Baghdad and princes of Hind, from the first to the end of the fourth century of the Hegira, we shall revert to the first recorded attack on the Mori prince of Chitor, which brought Bappa into notice. This was either by Yazid or Muhammad bin Kasim from Sind.[3] Though in the histories of the caliphs we can only expect to find recorded those expeditions

[1] His father's name was Aliptigin, termed a slave by Ferishta and his authorities; though El-Makin gives him an ancestor in Yazdegird. [He was a slave (Elliot-Dowson iv. 159).]

[2] *Ait*, contracted from *Aditya*: hence *Itwar*, 'Sunday.'

[3] [This is not corroborated by Musulmān authorities.]

which were successful, or had some lasting results, there are inroads of their revolted lieutenants or their frontier deputies, which frequently, though indistinctly, alluded to in Hindu annals, have no place in Muhammadan records. Throughout the period mentioned there was a stir amongst the Hindu nations, in which we find confusion and dethronement from an unknown invader, who is described as coming sometimes by Sind, sometimes by sea, and not unfrequently as a demon and magician; but invariably as *mlechchha*, or 'barbarian.'[1] From S. 750 to S. 780 (A.D. 694 to [246] 724), the annals of the Yadus, the Chauhans, the Chawaras, and the Guhilots, bear evidence to simultaneous convulsions in their respective houses at this period. In S. 750 (A.H. 75) the Yadu Bhatti was driven from his capital Salpura in the Panjab, across the Sutlej into the Indian desert; the invader named Farid. At the same period Manika Rae, the Chauhan prince of Ajmer, was assailed and slain.[2]

[1] Even from the puerilities of Hindu legends something may be extracted. A mendicant dervesh, called Roshan Ali (*i.e.* the '*light* of Ali'), had found his way to Garh Bitli (the ancient name of the Ajmer fortress), and having thrust his hand into a vessel of curds destined for the Raja, had his finger cut off. The disjointed member flew to Mecca, and was recognized as belonging to the saint. An army was equipped in the disguise of horse-merchants, which invaded Ajmer, whose prince was slain. May we not gather from this incident that an insult to the first Islamite missionary, in the person of Roshan Ali, brought upon the prince the arms of the Caliph? The same Chauhan legends state that Ajaipal was prince of Ajmer at this time; that in this invasion by sea he hastened to Anjar (on the coast of Cutch), where he held the 'guard of the ocean' (*Samudra ki Chauki*), where he fell in opposing the landing. An altar was erected on the spot, on which was sculptured the figure of the prince on horseback, with his lance at rest, and which still annually attracts multitudes at the 'fair (Mela) of Ajaipal.' The subsequent invasion alluded to in the text, of S. 750 (A.D. 694), is marked by a curious anecdote. When the 'Asurs' had blockaded Ajmer, Lot, the infant son of Manika Rae, was playing on the battlements, when an arrow from the foe killed the heir of Ajmer, who has ever since been worshipped amongst the lares and penates of the Chauhans; and as he had on a silver chain anklet at the time, this ornament is forbid to the children of the race. In all these Rajput families there is a putra (*adolescens*) amongst the penates, always one who has come to an untimely end, and chiefly worshipped by females; having a strong resemblance to the rites in honour of Adonis. We have traced several Roman and Grecian terms to Sanskrit origin; may we add that of *lares*, from *larla*, 'dear' or 'beloved'? [?].

[2] [The story is "puerile and fictitious: independent of which the Arabs had quite enough to do nearer home" (Elliot-Dowson i. 426).]

The Muster of the Clans.—The first of the Khichi princes who occupied the Duab of Sindsagar in the Panjab, as well as the ancestor of the Haras established in Golkonda, was expelled at the same time. The invader is treated in the genuine Hindu style as a Danava, or demon, and is named Ghairaram [1] (*i.e.* restless), from Kujliban,[2] a term geographically given to a portion of the Himalaya mountains about the glaciers of the Ganges. The ancestor of the founder of Patan was expelled from his petty islandic dominion on the coast of Saurashtra at the same time. This is the period when Yazid was the caliph's lieutenant in Khorasan, and when the arms of Walid conquered to the Ganges; nor is there a doubt that Yazid or Kasim was the author of all these revolutions in the Hindu dynasties. We are supported in this by the names of the princes contained in the catalogue who aided to defend Chitor and the Mori prince on this occasion. It is evident that Chitor was, alternately with Ujjain, the seat of sovereignty of the Pramara at this period, and, as it became the rallying point of the Hindus, that this race was the first in consequence.[3] We find the prince of Ajmer, and the quotas of

[1] [Persian : not a likely name.]

[2] Signifying 'Elephant forests,' and described in a Hindu map (stamped on cloth and painted) of India from Kujliban to Lanka, and the provinces west of the Indus to Calcutta; presented by me to the Royal Asiatic Society.

[3] The list of the vassal princes at the court of the Mori confirms the statement of the bard Chand, of the supremacy of Ram Pramara, and the partition of his dominion, as described (see p. 63, note) amongst the princes who founded separate dynastics at this period; hitherto in vassalage or subordinate to the Pramara. We can scarcely suppose the family to have suffered any decay since their ancestor, Chandragupta, connected by marriage with as well as the ally of the Grecian Seleucus, and who held Greeks in his pay. From such connexion, the arts of sculpture and architecture may have derived a character hitherto unnoticed. Amidst the ruins of Barolli are seen sculptured the Grecian helmet; and the elegant ornament, the Kumbha, or 'vessel of desire,' on the temple of Annapurna (*i.e.* 'giver of food'), the Hindu Ceres, has much affinity to the Grecian device. From the inscription (see No. 2) it is evident that Chitor was an appanage of Ujjain, the seat of Pramar empire. Its monarch, Chandragupta (Mori [Maurya]), degraded into the barber (Maurya) tribe, was the descendant of Srenika, prince of Rajagriha, who, according to the Jain work, Kalpadruma Kalka, flourished in the year 477 before Vikramaditya, and from whom Chandragupta was the thirteenth in descent. The names as follows: Kanika, Udsen, and nine in succession of the name of Nanda, thence called the Nau-nanda. These, at twenty-two years to a reign (see p. 64), would give 286 years, which—477 = 191 S.V. + 56 = 247 A.C. Now it was in A.C. 260,

Saurashtra and Gujarat [247]; Angatsi, lord of the Huns; Busa, the lord of the North; Sheo, the prince of the Jarejas; the Johya, lord of Jangaldes; the Aswaria, the Sepat, the Kulhar, the Malan, the Ohir, the Hul, and many others, having nothing of the Hindu in name, now extinct. But the most conspicuous is 'Dahir Despati from Debal.' This is erroneously written Delhi, the seat of the Tuars; whereas we recognize the name of the prince of Sind, slain by Kasim, whose expatriated son doubtless found refuge in Chitor.[1]

The Defeat of the Enemy.—This attack on the Mori prince was defeated chiefly through the bravery of the youthful Guhilot. The foe from Kujliban, though stated to have advanced by Mathura, retreated by Saurashtra and Sind, pursued by Bappa. He found the ancient seat of his ancestors, Gajni,[2] still in the possession of the 'Asur': a term as well as *mlechchha*, or 'barbarian,' always given to the Islamite at this period. Salim, who held Gajni, was attacked and forced to surrender, and Bappa in-

---

according to Bayer, that the treaty was formed between Seleucus and Chandragupta; so that this scrap of Jain history may be regarded as authentic and valuable. Asoka (a name of weight in Jain annals) succeeded Chandragupta. He by Kunala, whose son was Samprati, with whose name ends the line of Srenika, according to the authority from which I made the extract. The name of Samprati is well known from Ajmer to Saurashtra, and his era is given in a valuable chronogrammatic catalogue in an ancient Jain manuscript from the temple of Nadol, at 202 of the Virat Samvat. He is mentioned both traditionally and by books as the great supporter of the Jain faith, and the remains of temples dedicated to Mahavira, erected by this prince, yet exist at Ajmer, on Abu, Kumbhalmer, and Girnar. [Much of this needs correction, which cannot be done in the limits of a note. For the Nanda dynasty see Smith, *EHI*, 40, and for Chandragupta Maurya and Asoka, 115 ff.]

[1] [This and the second catalogue are fictions. They conflict with the conditions then existing in Gujarāt, and such motley arrays are a favourite bardic theme (Forbes, *Rāsmāla*, 31, note; *ASR*, ii. 379).]

[2] It has already been stated that the ancient name of Cambay was Gaini or Gajni, whose ruins are three miles from the present city [see p. 254 above]. There is also a Gajni on the estuary of the Mahi, and Abu-l Fazl incidentally mentions a Gajnagar as one of the most important fortresses of Gujarat, belonging to Ahmad Shah; in attempting to obtain which by stratagem, his antagonist, Hoshang, king of Malwa, was made prisoner. I am unaware of the site of this place, though there are remains of an extensive fortress near the capital, founded by Ahmad, and which preserves no name. It may be the ancient Gajnagar. [The Author confuses the place in Gujarāt with Jājnagar or Jājpur in Orissa, captured through a stratagem by Hoshang (*Āīn*, ii. 219; Ferishta iv. 178; *BG*, i. Part i. 359).]

ducted into this stronghold of his ancestors a nephew of his own. It is no less singular than honourable to their veracity that the annals should record the fact, so contrary to their religion, of Bappa having married the daughter of the conquered Salim ; and we have a right to infer that it was from the influence acquired by this union that he ultimately abandoned the sovereignty of Mewar and the title of 'Hindua Suraj' to become the founder of the 'one hundred and thirty tribes of Naushahra [248] Pathans' of the west. It is fair to conclude from all these notices regarding the founder of the Guhilot race in Chitor that he must have abjured his faith for that of Islam ; and it is probable (though the surmise must ever remain unproved) that, under some new title applicable to such change, we may have, in one of the early distinguished leaders of 'the Faith,' the ancestor of the Guhilots.

Khumān II.—Let us now proceed to the next irruption of the Islamite invaders in the reign of Khuman, from A.D. 812 to 836. Though the leader of this attack is styled 'Mahmud Khorasan Pat,' it is evident from the catalogue of Hindu princes who came to defend Chitor that this 'lord of Khorasan' was at least two centuries before the son of Sabuktigin; and as the period is in perfect accordance with the partition of the caliphat by Harun amongst his sons, we can have no hesitation in assigning such invasion to Mamun, to whose share was allotted Khorasan, Sind, and the Indian dependencies. The records of this period are too scanty to admit of our passing over in silence even a barren catalogue of names, which, as texts, with the aid of collateral information, may prove of some benefit to the future antiquarian and historian.

"From Gajni came the Guhilot ; the Tak from Asir ; from Narlai the Chauhan ; the Chalukya from Rahargarh ; from Setubandha the Jarkhera ; from Mandor the Khairavi ; from Mangrol the Makwahana ; from Jethgarh the Joria ; from Taragarh the Rewar ; the Kachhwaha from Narwar ; from Sanchor the Kalam ; from Junagarh the Dasanoh ; from Ajmer the Gaur ; from Lohadargarh the Chandano ; from Dasaundi the Dor ; from Delhi the Tuar ; from Patan the Chawara, preserver of royalty (*Rajdhar*) ; from Jalor the Sonigira ; from Sirohi the Deora ; from Gagraun the Khichi ; the Jadon from Junagarh ; the Jhala from Patri ; from Kanauj the Rathor ; from Chotiala the Bala ; from Piramgarh the Gohil ; from Jaisalgarh the Bhatti ; the

Busa from Lahore ; the Sankhla from Roneja ; the Sehat from Kherligarh ; from Mandalgarh the Nikumbha ; the Bargujar from Rajor ; from Karangarh the Chandel ; from Sikar the Sikarwal ; from Umargarh the Jethwa ; from Pali the Bargota ; from Khantargarh the Jareja ; from Jirga the Kherwar ; from Kashmir the Parihara."

Of the Guhilot from Gajni we have said enough ; nor shall we comment on the Tak, or his capital, Asir, which now belongs to the British Government. The Chauhan, who came from Narlai, was a celebrated branch of the Ajmer [249] house, and claims the honour of being the parent of the Sonigiras of Jalor and the Deoras of Sirohi. Nadol is mentioned by Ferishta as falling a prey to one of Mahmud's invasions, who destroyed its ancient temples ; but from erroneous punctuation it is lost in the translation as Bazule.[1] Of Rahargarh and the Jarkhera from Setubandha (on the Malabar coast) nothing is known.[2] Of the Khairavi from Mandor we can only say that it appears to be a branch of the Pramaras (who reckoned Mandor one of the nine strongholds, '*Nau-kot*,' under its dominion), established anterior to the Pariharas, who at this period had sovereignty in Kashmir. Both the Dor and his capital, Dasaundi, are described in ancient books as situated on the Ganges below Kanauj.

It is a subject of regret that the annals do not mention the name of the Tuar prince of Delhi, which city could not have been refounded above a century when this call was made upon its aid. Abu-l Fazl, Ferishta, their translators, and those who have followed them have been corrected by the *Edinburgh Review*, whose critical judgment on this portion of ancient history is eminently good. I possess the original Hindu record used by Abu-l Fazl, which gives S. 829 for the first Anangpal instead of S. 429 ; and

[1] I presented to the Royal Asiatic Society two inscriptions from Nadol, one dated S. 1024, the other 1039. They are of Prince Lakha, and state as instances of his power that he collected the transit duties at the further barrier of Patan, and levied tribute from the prince of Chitor. He was the contemporary of Mahmud, who devastated Nadol. I also discovered inscriptions of the twelfth century relative to this celebrated Chauhan family, in passing from Udaipur to Jodhpur. [Dow (i. 170) writes "Tilli and Buzule"; Briggs (i. 196) has "Baly and Nadole"; Elliot-Dowson (ii. 229) writes "Pāli and Nandūl," the differences being due to misreading of the Arabic script.]

[2] [Setubandha is the causeway made by Rāma to Lanka or Ceylon (*IGI*, v. 81).]

as there were but nineteen princes who intervened until his dynasty was set aside by the Chauhan, it requires no argument to support the *four* instead of *eight* centuries. The former will give the just average of twenty-one years to a reign. The name of Anangpal was titular in the family, and the epithet was applied to the last as to the first of the race.

The name of the Chawara prince of Patan (Anhilwara) being recorded amongst the auxiliaries of Khuman, is another satisfactory proof of the antiquity of this invasion; for this dynasty was extinct, and succeeded by the Solankis, in S. 998 (A.D. 942), fifty years prior to Mahmud of Ghazni, who captured Patan during the reign of Chawand, the second Solanki prince.[1]

The Sonigira, who came from Jalor, is a celebrated branch of the Chauhan race, but we are ignorant of the extent of time that it held this fortress: and as nothing can invalidate the testimonies afforded by the names of the Chawara of [250] Patan, the Kachhwaha of Narwar, the Tuar of Delhi, and the Rathor from Kanauj, there can be no hesitation at pointing out the anachronisms of the chronicle, which states the Deora from Sirohi, the Khichi from Gagraun, or the Bhatti from Jaisalgarh, amongst the levies on this occasion; and which we must affirm to be decided interpolations, the two first being at that period in possession of the Pramara, and the latter not erected for three centuries later. That the Deoras, the Khichis, and the Bhattis came to the aid of Khuman, we cannot doubt; but the copyist, ignorant even of the names of the ancient capitals of these tribes, Chhotan, Sindsagar, and Tanot, substituted those which they subsequently founded.

The Jadon (Yadu) from Junagarh (Girnar) was of the race of Krishna, and appeared long to have held possession of this territory; and the names of the Khengars, of this tribe, will remain as long as the stupendous monuments they reared on this sacred hill. Besides the Jadon, we find Saurashtra sending forth the Jhalas, the Balas, and the Gohils to the aid of the descendant of the lord of Valabhipura, whose paramount authority they once all acknowledged, and who appeared to have long maintained influence in that distant region.

Of the tribe of Busa, who left their capital, Lahore, to succour

[1] [Chāmunda reigned A.D. 997–1010; Anhilwāra was captured under Bhima I. (1022–64).]

Chitor, we have no mention, further than the name being enumerated amongst the unassigned tribes of Rajputs.[1] Ferishta frequently notices the princes of Lahore in the early progress of Islamism, though he does not tell us the name of the tribe. In the reign of the caliph Al-Mansur, A.H. 143 (A.D. 761), the Afghans of Kirman and Peshawar, who, according to this authority, were a Coptic colony expelled from Egypt,[2] had increased in such numbers as to abandon their residence about the 'hill of Sulaiman,' and crossing the Indus, wrested possessions from the Hindu princes of Lahore. This frontier warfare with a tribe which, though it had certainly not then embraced the faith of Islam, brought to their succour the forces of the caliph in Zabulistan, so that in five months seventy battles were fought with varied success; but the last, in which the Lahore prince carried his arms to Peshawar,[3] produced a peace. Hence arose a union of interests between them and the hill tribe of Gakkhar, and all the Kohistan west of the Indus was ceded to them [251] on the condition of guarding this barrier into Hindustan against invasion. For this purpose the fortress of Khaibar was erected in the chief pass of the Koh-i-Daman. For two centuries after this event Ferishta is silent on this frontier warfare, stating that henceforth Hindustan was only accessible through Sind. When Aliptigin first crossed the Indus, the prince of Lahore and the Afghans still maintained this alliance and united to oppose him. Jaipal was then prince of Lahore; and it is on this event that Ferishta, for the first time, mentions the tribe of Bhatti,[4] "at the advice of whose prince he conferred the command of the united forces on an Afghan chief," to whom he assigned the provinces of Multan and Lamghan. From this junction of interests the princes of Lahore enjoyed comparative security, until Sabuktigin and Mahmud compelled the Afghans to serve them: then Lahore was captured. The territory dependent upon Lahore, at this period, extended from Sirhind to Lamghan, and from Kashmir to Multan. Bhatinda divided with Lahore the residence of its princes. Their first encounter was at Lingham, on which occasion young Mahmud first distinguished himself, and as the historian says, "the eyes

[1] See p. 144. [2] [Ferishta i. 6.]

[3] The scene of action was between Peshawar and Kirman, the latter lying ninety miles south-west of the former.

[4] Dow omits this in his translation [see Briggs i. Introd. 9, i. 16].

of the heavens were obscured at seeing his deeds."[1] A tributary engagement was the result, which Jaipal soon broke; and being aided by levies from all the princes of Hindustan, marched an army of one hundred thousand men against Sabuktigin, and was again defeated on the banks of the Indus. He was at length invested and taken in Bhatinda by Mahmud, when he put himself to death.[2] The successors of Jaipal are mentioned merely as fugitives, and always distinct from the princes of Delhi. It is most probable that they were of the tribe termed Busa in the annals of Mewar, possibly a subdivision of another; though Ferishta calls the prince of Lahore a Brahman.

The Sankhla from Roneja. Both tribe and abode are well known: it is a subdivision of the Pramara. Harbuji Sankhla was the Paladin of Marwar, in which Roneja was situated.

The Sehat from Kherligarh was a northern tribe, dwelling about the Indus, and though entirely unknown to the modern genealogists of India, is frequently mentioned in the early history of the Bhattis, when their possessions extended on both sides of the Hyphasis. As intermarriages between the Bhattis and Sehats are [252] often spoken of, it must have been Rajput. It most probably occupied the province of Swat, the Suvat of D'Anville, a division of the province of Ashthanagar, where dwelt the Assakenoi of Alexander; concerning which this celebrated geographer says, "Il est mention de Suvat comme d'un canton du pays d'Ash-nagar dans la même géographie turque" (*Ecl.* p. 25). The whole of this ground was sacred to the Jadon tribe from the most remote antiquity, from Multan, the hills of Jud, to Aswinikot (the Tshehin-kote of D'Anville), which, built on the point of confluence of the Choaspes of the Greeks with the Indus, marks the spot where dwelt the Assakenoi, corroborated by the Puranas, which mention the partition of all these territories amongst the sons of Bajaswa, the lord of Kampilnagara, the grand subdivision of the Yadu race. In all likelihood the Sehat, who came to the aid of Khuman of Chitor, was a branch of these Assakenoi, the opponents of Alexander.[3] The modern town of Dinkot

[1] The sense of this passage has been quite perverted by Dow [see Briggs i. 16].

[2] [See Smith, *EHI*, 382.]

[3] [The capital of the Assakenoi was Massaga, near the Malakand Pass (Smith, *EHI*, 54; McCrindle, *Alexander*, 334 f.).]

appears to occupy the site of Aswinikot, though D'Anville feels inclined to carry it into the heart of Bajaur and place it on the rock (*silla*) Aornos.[1] Such the Sehat; not improbably the Soha, one of the eight subdivisions of the Yadu.[2] When, in S. 785, the Bhatti chief Rao Tanu was driven across the Sutlej, the Sehats are mentioned with other tribes as forming the army of Husain Shah, with the Barahas, the Judis, and Johyas (the Juds and Jinjohyas of Babur), the Butas, and the 'men of Dud.'

The Chandel, from Karangarh, occupied the tracts now termed Bundelkhand.

We shall pass over the other auxiliary tribes and conclude with the Parihar, who came from Kashmir on this occasion; a circumstance entirely overlooked in the dissertation on this tribe;[3] nor does this isolated fact afford room for further discussion on a race which expelled the Pramaras from Mandor.

Such aids, who preserved Khuman when assailed by the 'Khorasan Pat,' fully demonstrate the antiquity of the annals, which is further attested by inscriptions. Khuman fought twenty-four great battles, and his name, like that of Caesar, became a family distinction. At Udaipur, if you make a false step, or even sneeze, you hear the ejaculation of 'Khuman aid you!' Khuman, by the advice of the Brahmans, resigned the gaddi to his younger son, Jograj; but again resumed [253] it, slaying his advisers and execrating the name of Brahman, which he almost exterminated in his own dominions. Khuman was at length slain by his own son, Mangal; but the chiefs expelled the parricide, who seized upon Lodorwa in the northern desert, and there established the Mangalia Guhilots.

Bhartribhat III.—Bhartribhat (familiarly Bhato) succeeded. In his reign, and in that of his successor, the territory dependent on Chitor was greatly increased. All the forest tribes, from the banks of the Mahi to Abu, were subjugated, and strongholds erected, of which Dharangarh and Ujargarh still remain to maintain them. He established no less than thirteen[4] of his sons in

[1] [For the site see Smith, *EHI*, 56, note 2.]

[2] See p. 104. [3] See p. 119 f.

[4] By name, Kulanagar, Champaner, Choreta, Bhojpur, Lunara, Nimthor, Sodara, Jodhgarh, Sandpur, Aitpur, and Gangabheva. The remaining two are not mentioned.

independent possessions in Malwa and Gujarat, and these were distinguished as the Bhatera Guhilots.

We shall now leap over fifteen generations; which, though affording a few interesting facts to the antiquary, would not amuse the general reader. We will rest satisfied with stating that the Chauhans of Ajmer and the Guhilots of Chitor were alternately friends and foes; that Durlabh Chauhan was slain by Bersi Rawal in a grand battle fought at Kawaria, of which the Chauhan annals state 'that their princes were now so powerful as to oppose the chief of Chitor.' Again, in the next reign, we find the renowned Bisaldeo, son of Durlabh, combining with Rawal Tejsi of Chitor to oppose the progress of Islamite invasion: facts recorded by inscriptions as well as by the annals. We may close these remarks on the fifteen princes, from Khuman to Samarsi, with the words of Gibbon on the dark period of Guelphic annals: "It may be presumed that they were illiterate and valiant; that they plundered in their youth, and reared churches in their old age; that they were fond of arms, horses, and hunting"; and, we may add, continued bickering with their vassals within when left unemployed by the enemy from without [254].

CHAPTER 5

ALTHOUGH the whole of this chain of ancestry, from Kanaksen in the second, Vijaya the founder of Valabhi in the fourth, to Samarsi in the thirteenth century, cannot be discriminated with perfect accuracy, we may affirm, to borrow a metaphor, that "the two extremities of it are riveted in truth": and some links have at intervals been recognized as equally valid. We will now extend the chain to the nineteenth century.

Samar Singh, Samarsi: The Tuars of Delhi.—Samarsi was born in S. 1206.[1] Though the domestic annals are not silent on his acts, we shall recur chiefly to the bard of Delhi [2] for his char-

[1] [For the error in his date see p. 281 above.]

[2] The work of Chand is a universal history of the period in which he wrote. In the sixty-nine books, comprising one hundred thousand stanzas, relating to the exploits of Prithiraj, every noble family of Rajasthan will find some record of their ancestors. It is accordingly treasured amongst the archives of each race having any pretensions to the name of Rajput.

acter and actions, and the history of the period. Before we proceed, however, a sketch of the political condition of Hindustan during the last of the Tuar sovereigns of Delhi, derived from this authority and in the bard's own words, may not be unacceptable. "In Patan is Bhola Bhim the Chalukya, of iron frame.[1] On the mountain Abu, Jeth Pramara, in battle immovable as the star of the north. In Mewar is Sâmar Singh, who takes tribute from the mighty, a wave of iron in the path of Delhi's foe. In the midst of all, strong in his own strength, Mandor's prince, the arrogant Nahar Rao, the might of Maru, fearing none. In Delhi the chief of all [255] Ananga, at whose summons attended the princes of Mandor, Nagor, Sind, Jalwat,[2] and others on its confines, Peshawar, Lahore, Kangra, and its mountain chiefs, with Kasi,[3] Prayag,[4] and Garh Deogir. The lords of Simar [5] were in constant danger of his power." The Bhatti, since their expulsion from Zabulistan, had successively occupied as capitals, Salivahanapur in the Panjab, Tanot, Derawar, which last they founded, and the ancient Lodorwa, which they conquered in the desert; and at the period in question were constructing their present residence, Jaisalmer. In this nook they had been fighting for centuries

---

From this he can trace his martial forefathers who 'drank of the wave of battle' in the passes of Kirman when the 'cloud of war rolled from Himachal to the plains of Hindustan. The wars of Prithiraj, his alliances, his numerous and powerful tributaries, their abodes and pedigrees, make the works of Chand invaluable as historic and geographical memoranda, besides being treasures in mythology, manners, and the annals of the mind. To read this poet well is a sure road to honour, and my own Guru was allowed, even by the professional bards, to excel therein. As he read I rapidly translated about thirty thousand stanzas. Familiar with the dialects in which it is written, I have fancied that I seized occasionally the poet's spirit; but it were presumption to suppose that I embodied all his brilliancy, or fully comprehended the depth of his allusions. But I knew for whom he wrote. The most familiar of his images and sentiments I heard daily from the mouths of those around me, the descendants of the men whose deeds he rehearses. I was enabled thus to seize his meaning, where one more skilled in poetic lore might have failed, and to make my prosaic version of some value. [For Chand Bardāi see Grierson, *Modern Literary History of Hindustan*, 3 f.]

[1] [Bhīma II., Chaulukya, known as Bhola, 'the simpleton,' A.D. 1179–1242.]

[2] Unknown, unless the country on the 'waters' (*jal*) of Sind.

[3] Benares.

[4] Allahabad.

[5] The cold regions (*si*, 'cold').

with the lieutenants of the Caliph at Aror, occasionally redeeming their ancient possessions as far as the city of the Tak on the Indus. Their situation gave them little political interest in the affairs of Hindustan until the period of Prithiraj, one of whose principal leaders, Achales, was the brother of the Bhatti prince. Anangpal, from this description, was justly entitled to be termed the paramount sovereign of Hindustan; but he was the last of a dynasty of nineteen princes, who had occupied Delhi nearly four hundred years, from the time of the founder Bilan Deo, who, according to a manuscript in the author's possession, was only an opulent Thakur when he assumed the ensigns of royalty in the then deserted Indraprastha, taking the name of Anangpal,[1] ever after titular in the family. The Chauhans of Ajmer owed at least homage to Delhi at this time, although Bisaldeo had rendered it almost nominal; and to Someswar, the fourth in deseent, Anangpal was indebted for the preservation of this supremacy against the attempts of Kanauj, for which service he obtained the Tuar's daughter in marriage, the issue of which was Prithiraj, who when only eight years of age was proclaimed successor to the Delhi throne.

Prithiraj.—Jaichand of Kanauj and Prithiraj bore the same relative situation to Anangpal; Bijaipal, the father of the former, as well as Someswar, having had a daughter of the Tuar to wife. This originated the rivalry between the Chauhans and Rathors, which ended in the destruction of both. When Prithiraj mounted the throne of Delhi, Jaichand not only refused to acknowledge his supremacy, but set forth his own claims to this distinction. In these he was supported by the prince of Patan [256] Anhilwara (the eternal foe of the Chauhans), and likewise by the Parihars of Mandor. But the affront given by the latter, in refusing to fulfil the contract of bestowing his daughter on the young Chauhan, brought on a warfare, in which this first essay was but the presage of his future fame. Kanauj and Patan had recourse to the dangerous expedient of entertaining bands of Tatars, through whom the sovereign of Ghazni was enabled to take advantage of their internal broils.

[1] *Ananga* is a poetical epithet of the Hindu Cupid, literally 'incorporeal'; but, according to good authority, applicable to the founder of the desolate abode, *palna* being 'to support,' and *anga*, with the primitive *an*, 'without body.'

Samarsi, prince of Chitor, had married the sister of Prithiraj, and their personal characters, as well as this tie, bound them to each other throughout all these commotions, until the last fatal battle on the Ghaggar. From these feuds Hindustan never was free. But unrelenting enmity was not a part of their character: having displayed the valour of the tribe, the bard or Nestor of the day would step in, and a marriage would conciliate and maintain in friendship such foes for two generations. From time immemorial such has been the political state of India, as represented by their own epics, or in Arabian or Persian histories: thus always the prey of foreigners, and destined to remain so. Samarsi had to contend both with the princes of Patan and Kanauj; and although the bard says "he washed his blade in the Jumna," the domestic annals slur over the circumstance of Siddharaja-Jayasingha having actually made a conquest of Chitor; for it is not only included in the eighteen capitals enumerated as appertaining to this prince, but the author discovered a tablet [1] in Chitor, placed there by his successor, Kumarpal, bearing the date S. 1206, the period of Samarsi's birth. The first occasion of Samarsi's aid being called in by the Chauhan emperor was on the discovery of treasure at Nagor, amounting to seven millions of gold, the deposit of ancient days. The princes of Kanauj and Patan, dreading the influence which such sinews of war would afford their antagonist, invited Shihabu-d-din to aid their designs of humiliating the Chauhan, who in this emergency sent an embassy to Samarsi. The envoy was Chand Pundir, the vassal chief of Lahore, and guardian of that frontier. He is conspicuous from this time to the hour "when he planted his lance at the ford of the Ravi," and fell in opposing the passage of Shihabu-d-din. The presents he carries, the speech with which he greets the Chitor prince, his reception, reply, and dismissal are all preserved by [257] Chand. The style of address and the apparel of Samarsi betoken that he had not laid aside the office and ensigns of a 'Regent of Mahadeva.' A simple necklace of the seeds of the lotus adorned his neck; his hair was braided, and he is addressed as Jogindra, or chief of ascetics. Samarsi proceeded to Delhi; and it was arranged, as he was connected by marriage with the prince of Patan, that Prithiraj should march against this prince, while he should oppose the army from Ghazni. He

[1] See Inscription No. 5.

(Samarsi) accordingly fought several indecisive battles, which gave time to the Chauhan to terminate the war in Gujarat and rejoin him. United, they completely discomfited the invaders, making their leader prisoner. Samarsi declined any share of the discovered treasure, but permitted his chiefs to accept the gifts offered by Chauhan. Many years elapsed in such subordinate warfare, when the prince of Chitor was again constrained to use his buckler in defence of Delhi and its prince, whose arrogance and successful ambition, followed by disgraceful inactivity, invited invasion with every presage of success. Jealousy and revenge rendered the princes of Patan, Kanauj, Dhar, and the minor courts indifferent spectators of a contest destined to overthrow them all.

The Death of Samar Singh.—The bard gives a good description of the preparations for his departure from Chitor, which he was destined never to see again. The charge of the city was entrusted to a favourite and younger son, Karna: which disgusted the elder brother, who went to the Deccan to Bidar, where he was well received by an Abyssinian chief,[1] who had there established himself in sovereignty. Another son, either on this occasion or on the subsequent fall of Chitor, fled to the mountains of Nepal, and there spread the Guhilot line.[2] It is in this, the last of the books of Chand, termed *The Great Fight*, that we have the character of Samarsi fully delineated. His arrival at Delhi is hailed with songs of joy as a day of deliverance. Prithiraj and his court advance seven miles to meet him, and the description of the greeting of the king of Delhi and his sister, and the chiefs on either side who recognize ancient friendships, is most animated. Samarsi reads his brother-in-law an indignant lecture on his unprincely inactivity, and throughout the book divides attention with him.

In the planning of the campaign, and march towards the Ghaggar to meet the foe [258], Samarsi is consulted, and his opinions are recorded. The bard represents him as the Ulysses of the host: brave, cool, and skilful in the fight; prudent, wise, and eloquent in council; pious and decorous on all occasions; beloved by his own chiefs, and reverenced by the vassals of the Chauhan. In the line of march no augur or bard could better

[1] Styled Habshi Padshah.

[2] [The Gorkhas or Gurkhas are said to have reached Nepal through Kumaun after the fall of Chitor (*IGI*, xix. 32).]

explain the omens, none in the field better dress the squadrons for battle, none guide his steed or use his lance with more address. His tent is the principal resort of the leaders after the march or in the intervals of battle, who were delighted by his eloquence or instructed by his knowledge. The bard confesses that his precepts of government are chiefly from the lips of Khuman;[1] and of his best episodes and allegories, whether on morals, rules for the guidance of ambassadors, choice of ministers, religious or social duties (but especially those of the Rajput to the sovereign), the wise prince of Chitor is the general organ.

On the last of three days' desperate fighting Samarsi was slain, together with his son Kalyan, and thirteen thousand of his household troops and most renowned chieftains.[2] His beloved Pirtha, on hearing the fatal issue, her husband slain, her brother captive, the heroes of Delhi and Chitor "asleep on the banks of the Ghaggar, in the wave of the steel," joined her lord through the flame, nor waited the advance of the Tatar king, when Delhi was carried by storm, and the last stay of the Chauhans, Prince Rainsi, met death in the assault. The capture of Delhi and its monarch, the death of his ally of Chitor, with the bravest and best of their troops, speedily ensured the further and final success of the Tatar arms; and when Kanauj fell, and the traitor to his nation met his fate in the waves of the Ganges, none were left to contend with Shihabu-d-din the possession of the regal seat of the Chauhan. Scenes of devastation, plunder, and massacre commenced, which lasted through ages; during which nearly all that was sacred in religion or celebrated in art was destroyed by these ruthless and barbarous invaders. The noble Rajput, with a spirit of constancy and enduring courage, seized every opportunity to turn upon his oppressor. By his perseverance and valour he wore out entire dynasties of foes, alternately yielding 'to his fate,' or restricting the circle of conquest. Every road in Rajasthan was moistened with torrents of blood of the [259] spoiled and the spoiler. But all was of no avail; fresh supplies were ever pouring in, and dynasty succeeded dynasty, heir to the same remorseless feeling which sanctified murder, legalized spoliation, and deified destruc-

[1] I have already mentioned that Khuman became a patronymic and title amongst the princes of Chitor.

[2] [The battle was fought at Tarāīn or Talāwari in the Ambāla District, Panjāb, in 1192.]

tion. In these desperate conflicts entire tribes were swept away whose names are the only memento of their former existence and celebrity.

Gallant Resistance of the Rājputs.—What nation on earth would have maintained the semblance of civilization, the spirit or the customs of their forefathers, during so many centuries of overwhelming depression but one of such singular character as the Rajput? Though ardent and reckless, he can, when required, subside into forbearance and apparent apathy, and reserve himself for the opportunity of revenge. Rajasthan exhibits the sole example in the history of mankind of a people withstanding every outrage barbarity can inflict, or human nature sustain, from a foe whose religion commands annihilation, and bent to the earth, yet rising buoyant from the pressure, and making calamity a whetstone to courage. How did the Britons at once sink under the Romans, and in vain strive to save their groves, their druids, or the altars of Bal from destruction! To the Saxons they alike succumbed; they, again, to the Danes; and this heterogeneous breed to the Normans. Empire was lost and gained by a single battle, and the laws and religion of the conquered merged in those of the conquerors. Contrast with these the Rajputs; not an iota of their religion or customs have they lost, though many a foot of land. Some of their States have been expunged from the map of dominion; and, as a punishment of national infidelity, the pride of the Rathor, and the glory of the Chalukya, the overgrown Kanauj and gorgeous Anhilwara, are forgotten names! Mewar alone, the sacred bulwark of religion, never compromised her honour for her safety, and still survives her ancient limits; and since the brave Samarsi gave up his life, the blood of her princes has flowed in copious streams for the maintenance of this honour, religion, and independence.

Karan Singh I.: Ratan Singh.—Samarsi had several sons;[1] but Karna was his heir, and during his minority his mother, Kuramdevi, a princess of Patan, nobly maintained what his father left. She headed her Rajputs and gave battle[2] in person to Kutbu-d-din,

[1] Kalyanrae, slain with his father; Kumbhkaran, who went to Bidar; a third, the founder of the Gorkhas. [This assertion, based on the authority of Chand, is incorrect, Samar Singh being misplaced, and succeeded by Ratan Singh (Erskine ii. A. 146).]

[2] This must be the battle mentioned by Ferishta (see Dow, p. 169, vol. ii.).

near [260] Amber, when the viceroy was defeated and wounded. Nine Rajas, and eleven chiefs of inferior dignity with the title of Rawat, followed the mother of their prince.

Karna (the radiant) succeeded in S. 1249 (A.D. 1193); but he was not destined to be the founder of a line in Mewar.[1] The annals are at variance with each other on an event which gave the sovereignty of Chitor to a younger branch, and sent the elder into the inhospitable wilds of the west, to found a city[2] and perpetuate a line.[3] It is stated generally that Karna had two sons, Mahup and Rahup; but this is an error: Samarsi and Surajmall were brothers: Karna was the son of the former and Mahup was his son, whose mother was a Chauhan of Bagar. Surajmall had a son named Bharat, who was driven from Chitor by a conspiracy. He proceeded to Sind, obtained Aror from its prince, a Musalman, and married the daughter of the Bhatti chief of Pugal, by whom he had a son named Rahup. Karna died of grief for the loss of Bharat and the unworthiness of Mahup, who abandoned him to live entirely with his maternal relations, the Chauhans.

The Sonigira chief of Jalor had married the daughter of Karna,

[1] He had a son, Sarwan, who took to commerce. Hence the mercantile Sesodia caste, Sarwania.

[2] Dungarpur, so named from *dungar*, 'a mountain.'

[3] [The facts are that after "Karan Singh the Mewār family divided into two branches—one with the title of Rāwal, the other Rāna. In the first, or Rāwal, branch were Khem or Kshem Singh, the eldest son of Karan Singh, Sāmant Singh, Kumār Singh, Mathan Singh, Padam Singh, Jeth Singh, Tej Singh, Samar Singh, and Ratan Singh, all of whom reigned at Chitor; while in the Rāna branch were Rāhup, a younger son of Karan Singh, Narpat, Dinkaran, Jaskaran, Nāgpāl. Puranpāl, Prithi Pāl, Bhuvān Singh, Bhīm Singh, Jai Singh, and Lakshman Singh, who ruled at Sesoda, and called themselves Sesodias. Thus, instead of having to fit in something like ten generations between Samar Singh, who, as we know, was alive in 1299, and the siege of Chitor, which certainly took place in 1303, we find that those ten princes were not descendants of Samar Singh at all, but the contemporaries of his seven immediate predecessors on the *gaddi* of Chitor and of himself, and that both Ratan Singh, the son of Samar Singh, and Lakshman Singh, the contemporary of Ratan Singh, were descended from a common ancestor, Karan Singh I., nine and eleven generations back respectively. It is also possible to reconcile the statement of the Musalmān historians that Ratan Singh (called Rāī Ratan) was ruler of Chitor during the siege—a statement corroborated by an inscription at Rājnagar—with the generally accepted story that it was Rāna Lakshman Singh who fell in defence of the fort" (Erskine ii. A. 15).]

by whom he had a child named Randhol,[1] whom by treachery he placed on the throne of Chitor, slaying the chief Guhilots. Mahup being unable to recover his rights, and unwilling to make any exertion, the chair of Bappa Rawal would have passed to the Chauhans but for an ancient bard of the house. He pursued his way to Aror, held by old Bharaṭ as a fief of Kabul. With the levies of Sind he marched to claim the right abandoned by Mahup and at Pali encountered and defeated the Sonigiras. The retainers of Mewar flocked to his standard, and by their aid he enthroned himself in Chitor. He sent for his father and mother, Ranangdevi, whose dwelling on the Indus was made over to a younger brother, who bartered his faith for Aror, and held it as a vassal of Kabul.

Rāhup.—Rahup obtained Chitor in S. 1257 (A.D. 1201), and shortly after sustained the attack of Shamsu-d-din, whom he met and overcame in a battle at Nagor. Two [261] great changes were introduced by this prince; the first in the title of the tribe, to Sesodia; the other in that of its prince, from Rawal to Rana. The puerile reason for the former has already been noticed;[2] the cause of the latter is deserving of more attention. Amongst the foes of Rahup was the Parihar prince of Mandor: his name Mokal, with the title of Rana. Rahup seized him in his capital and brought him to Sesoda, making him renounce the rich district of Godwar and his title of Rana, which he assumed himself, to denote the completion of his feud. He ruled thirty-eight years in a period of great distraction, and appears to have been well calculated, not only to uphold the fallen fortunes of the State, but to rescue them from utter ruin. His reign is the more remarkable by contrast with his successors, nine of whom are 'pushed from their stools' in the same or even a shorter period than that during which he upheld the dignity.

From Rahup to Lakhamsi [Lakshman Singh], in the short space of half a century, nine princes of Chitor were crowned, and at nearly equal intervals of time followed each other to 'the mansions of the sun.' Of these nine, six fell in battle. Nor did they meet their fate at home, but in a chivalrous enterprise to redeem the sacred Gaya from the pollution of the barbarian.

[1] So pronounced, but properly written Randhaval, 'the standard of the field.'

[2] See note, p. 252.

For this object these princes successively fell, but such devotion inspired fear, if not pity or conviction, and the bigot renounced the impiety which Prithimall purchased with his blood, and until Alau-d-din's reign, this outrage to their prejudices was renounced. But in this interval they had lost their capital, for it is stated as the only occurrence in Bhonsi's[1] reign that he [262] "recovered Chitor" and made the name of Rana be acknowledged by all. Two memorials are preserved of the nine princes from Rahup to Lakhamsi, and of the same character: confusion and strife within and without. We will, therefore, pass over these to another grand event in the vicissitudes of this house, which possesses more of romance than of history, though the facts are undoubted.

[1] His second son, Chandra, obtained an appanage on the Chambal, and his issue, well known as Chandarawats, constituted one of the most powerful vassal clans of Mewar. Rampura (Bhanpura) was their residence, yielding a revenue of nine lakhs (£110,000), held on the tenure of service which, from an original grant in my possession from Rana Jagat Singh to his nephew Madho Singh, afterwards prince of Amber, was three thousand horse and foot (see p. 235), and the fine of investiture was seventy-five thousand rupees. Madho Singh, when prince of Amber, did what was invalid as well as ungrateful; he made over this domain, granted during his misfortunes, to Holkar, the first limb lopped off Mewar. The Chandarawat proprietor continued, however, to possess a portion of the original estate with the fortress of Amad, which it maintained throughout all the troubles of Rajwara till A.D. 1821. It shows the attachment to custom that the young Rao applied and received 'the sword' of investiture from his old lord paramount, the Rana, though dependent on Holkar's forbearance. But a minority is proverbially dangerous in India. Disorder from party plots made Amad troublesome to Holkar's government, which as his ally and preserver of tranquillity we suppressed by blowing up the walls of the fortress. This is one of many instances of the harsh, uncompromising nature of our power, and the anomalous description of our alliances with the Rajputs. However necessary to repress the disorder arising from the claims of ancient proprietors and the recent rights of Holkar, or the new proprietor, Ghafur Khan, yet surrounding princes, and the general population, who know the history of past times, lament to see a name of five hundred years' duration thus summarily extinguished, which chiefly benefits an upstart Pathan. Such the vortex of the ambiguous, irregular, and unsystematic policy, which marks many of our alliances, which protect too often but to injure, and gives to our office of general arbitrator and high constable of Rajasthan a harsh and unfeeling character. Much of this arises from ignorance of the past history; much from disregard of the peculiar usages of the people; or from that expediency which too often comes in contact with moral fitness, which will go on until the day predicted by the Nestor of India, when "*one sikka* (seal) alone will be used in Hindustan."

CHAPTER 6

Lakhamsi : Lachhman Singh.—Lakhamsi[1] succeeded his father in S. 1331 (A.D. 1275), a memorable era in the annals, when Chitor, the repository of all that was precious yet untouched of the arts of India, was stormed, sacked, and treated with remorseless barbarity by the Pathan [Khilji] emperor, Alau-d-din. Twice it was attacked by this subjugator of India. In the first siege it escaped spoliation, though at the price of its best defenders : that which followed is the first successful assault and capture of which we have any detailed account.

Bhim Singh : Padmini.—Bhimsi was the uncle of the young prince, and protector during his minority. He had espoused the daughter of Hamir Sank (Chauhan) of Ceylon, the cause of woes unnumbered to the Sesodias. Her name was Padmini,[2] a title bestowed only on the superlatively fair, and transmitted with renown to posterity by tradition and the song of the bard. Her beauty, accomplishments, exaltation, and destruction, with other incidental circumstances, constitute the subject of one of the most popular traditions of Rajwara. The Hindu bard recognizes the fair, in preference to fame and love of conquest, as the motive for the attack of Alau-d-din, who [263] limited his demand to the possession of Padmini ; though this was after a long and fruitless siege. At length he restricted his desire to a mere sight of this extraordinary beauty, and acceded to the proposal of beholding her through the medium of mirrors. Relying on the faith of the Rajput, he entered Chitor slightly guarded, and having gratified his wish, returned. The Rajput, unwilling to be outdone in confidence, accompanied the king to the foot of the fortress, amidst many complimentary excuses from his guest at the trouble he thus occasioned. It was for this that Ala risked his own safety, relying on the superior faith of the Hindu. Here he had an

[1] [Rāna Lachhman Singh was not, strictly speaking, ruler of Chitor. He belonged to the Rāna branch, and succeeded Jai Singh. When Chitor was invested he came to help his relation, Rāwal Ratan Singh, husband of Padmini, and ruler of Chitor, and was killed, with seven of his sons (Erskine ii. B. 10).]

[2] ['The Lotus.' Ferishta in his account of the siege says nothing of Padmini (i. 353 f.). Her story is told in *Āīn*, ii. 269 f.]]

ambush ; Bhimsi was made prisoner, hurried away to the Tatar camp, and his liberty made dependent on the surrender of Padmini.

The Siege of Chitor.—Despair reigned in Chitor when this fatal event was known, and it was debated whether Padmini should be resigned as a ransom for their defender. Of this she was informed, and expressed her acquiescence. Having provided wherewithal to secure her from dishonour, she communed with two chiefs of her own kin and clan of Ceylon, her uncle Gora, and his nephew Badal, who devised a scheme for the liberation of their prince without hazarding her life or fame. Intimation was dispatched to Ala that on the day he withdrew from his trenches the fair Padmini would be sent, but in a manner befitting her own and his high station, surrounded by her females and handmaids ; not only those who would accompany her to Delhi, but many others who desired to pay her this last mark of reverence. Strict commands were to be issued to prevent curiosity from violating the sanctity of female decorum and privacy. No less than seven hundred covered litters proceeded to the royal camp. In each was placed one of the bravest of the defenders of Chitor, borne by six armed soldiers disguised as litter-porters. They reached the camp. The royal tents were enclosed with *kanats* (walls of cloth) ; the litters were deposited, and half an hour was granted for a parting interview between the Hindu prince and his bride. They then placed their prince in a litter and returned with him, while the greater number (the supposed damsels) remained to accompany the fair to Delhi.[1] But Ala had no intention to permit Bhimsi's return, and was becoming jealous of the long interview he enjoyed, when, instead of the prince and Padmini, the devoted band issued from their litters : but Ala was too well guarded. Pursuit was ordered, while these covered the retreat till they perished to a man. A fleet horse was in reserve for [264] Bhimsi, on which he was placed, and in safety ascended the fort, at whose outer gate the host of Ala was encountered. The choicest of the heroes of Chitor met the assault. With Gora and Badal at their head, animated by the noblest sentiments, the deliverance of their chief and the honour of their queen, they devoted them-

[1] [A folk-tale of the 'Horse of Troy' type, common in India; see Rhys Davids, *Buddhist India*, 4 f. ; Ferishta ii. 115 ; Grant Duff, *Hist. Mahrattas*, 64, note ; cf. Herodotus v. 20.]

selves to destruction, and few were the survivors of this slaughter of the flower of Mewar. For a time Ala was defeated in his object, and the havoc they had made in his ranks, joined to the dread of their determined resistance, obliged him to desist from the enterprise.

Mention has already been made of the adjuration, "by the sin of the sack of Chitor." Of these sacks they enumerate *three and a half*. This is the 'half'; for though the city was not stormed, the best and bravest were cut off (*sakha*). It is described with great animation in the Khuman Raesa. Badal was but a stripling of twelve, but the Rajput expects wonders from this early age. He escaped, though wounded, and a dialogue ensues between him and his uncle's wife, who desires him to relate how her lord conducted himself ere she joins him. The stripling replies: "He was the reaper of the harvest of battle; I followed his steps as the humble gleaner of his sword. On the gory bed of honour he spread a carpet of the slain; a barbarian prince his pillow, he laid him down, and sleeps surrounded by the foe." Again she said: "Tell me, Badal, how did my love (*piyar*) behave?" "Oh! mother, how further describe his deeds when he left no foe to dread or admire him?" She smiled farewell to the boy, and adding, "My lord will chide my delay," sprung into the flame.

Alau-d-din, having recruited his strength, returned to his object, Chitor. The annals state this to have been in S. 1346 (A.D. 1290), but Ferishta gives a date thirteen years later.[1] They had not yet recovered the loss of so many valiant men who had sacrificed themselves for their prince's safety, and Ala carried on his attacks more closely, and at length obtained the hill at the southern point, where he entrenched himself. They still pretend to point out his trenches; but so many have been formed by subsequent attacks that we cannot credit the assertion. The poet has found in the disastrous issue of this siege admirable materials for his song. He represents the Rana, after an arduous day, stretched on his pallet, and during a night of watchful anxiety, pondering on the means by which he might preserve from the general destruction one at least of his twelve sons; when a voice [265] broke on his solitude, exclaiming, "*Main bhukhi*

[1] [Chitor was captured in August 1303 (Ferishta i. 353; Elliot-Dowson iii. 77).]

ho "; [1] and raising his eyes, he saw, by the dim glare of the chiragh,[2] advancing between the granite columns, the majestic form of the guardian goddess of Chitor. "Not satiated," exclaimed the Rana, "though eight thousand of my kin were late an offering to thee?" "I must have regal victims; and if twelve who wear the diadem bleed not for Chitor, the land will pass from the line." This said, she vanished.

On the morn he convened a council of his chiefs, to whom he revealed the vision of the night, which they treated as the dream of a disordered fancy. He commanded their attendance at midnight; when again the form appeared, and repeated the terms on which alone she would remain amongst them. "Though thousands of barbarians strew the earth, what are they to me? On each day enthrone a prince. Let the kirania,[3] the chhatra and the chamara,[3] proclaim his sovereignty, and for three days let his decrees be supreme: on the fourth let him meet the foe and his fate. Then only may I remain."

Whether we have merely the fiction of the poet, or whether the scene was got up to animate the spirit of resistance, matters but little, it is consistent with the belief of the tribe; and that the goddess should openly manifest her wish to retain as her tiara the battlements of Chitor on conditions so congenial to the warlike and superstitious Rajput was a gage readily taken up and fully answering the end. A generous contention arose amongst the brave brothers who should be the first victim to avert the denunciation. Arsi urged his priority of birth: he was proclaimed, the umbrella waved over his head, and on the fourth day he surrendered his short-lived honours and his life. Ajaisi, the next in birth, demanded to follow; but he was the favourite son of his father, and at his request he consented to let his brothers precede him. Eleven had fallen in turn, and but one victim remained to the salvation of the city, when the Rana, calling his chiefs around him, said, "Now I devote myself for Chitor."

The Johar.—But another awful sacrifice was to precede this act of self-devotion in that horrible rite, the *Johar*,[4] where the

[1] 'I am hungry.' [2] Lamp.

[3] These are the insignia of royalty. The *kirania* is a parasol, from *kiran*, 'a ray': the *chhatra* is the umbrella, always red; the *chamara*, the flowing tail of the wild ox, set in a gold handle, and used to drive away the flies.

[4] [Sir G. Grierson informs me that *Johar* or *Jauhar* is derived from *Jatu-*

females are immolated to preserve them from pollution or captivity. The funeral pyre was lighted within the 'great subterranean retreat,' in chambers impervious to the light [266] of day, and the defenders of Chitor beheld in procession the queens, their own wives and daughters, to the number of several thousands. The fair Padmini closed the throng, which was augmented by whatever of female beauty or youth could be tainted by Tatar lust. They were conveyed to the cavern, and the opening closed upon them, leaving them to find security from dishonour in the devouring element.

A contest now arose between the Rana and his surviving son; but the father prevailed, and Ajaisi, in obedience to his commands, with a small band passed through the enemy's lines, and reached Kelwara in safety. The Rana, satisfied that his line was not extinct, now prepared to follow his brave sons; and calling around him his devoted clans, for whom life had no longer any charms, they threw open the portals and descended to the plains, and with a reckless despair carried death, or met it, in the crowded ranks of Ala. The Tatar conqueror took possession of an inanimate capital, strewed with brave defenders, the smoke yet issuing from the recesses where lay consumed the once fair object of his desire; and since this devoted day the cavern has been sacred: no eye has penetrated its gloom, and superstition has placed as its guardian a huge serpent, whose 'venomous breath' extinguishes the light which might guide intruders to 'the place of sacrifice.'

The Conquests of Alāu-d-dīn.—Thus fell, in A.D. 1303, this celebrated capital, in the round of conquest of Alau-d-din, one of the most vigorous and warlike sovereigns who have occupied

griha, 'a house built of lac or other combustibles,' in allusion to the story in the *Mahābhārata* (i. chap. 141-151) of the attempted destruction of the Pāndavas by setting such a building on fire. For other examples of the rite see Ferishta i. 59 f.; Elliot-Dowson i. 313, 536 f., iii. 426, 433, iv. 277, 402, v. 101; Forbes, *Rās Māla*, 286; Malcolm, *Memoir Central India*, 2nd ed. i. 483. For recent cases Irvine, *Army of the Indian Moghuls*, 242; *Punjab Notes and Queries*, iv. 102 ff.]

[1] The Author has been at the entrance of this retreat, which, according to the Khuman Raesa, conducts to a subterranean palace, but the mephitic vapours and venomous reptiles did not invite to adventure, even had official situation permitted such slight to these prejudices. The Author is the only Englishman admitted to Chitor since the days of Herbert, who appears to have described what he saw.

the throne of India. In success, and in one of the means of attainment, a bigoted hypocrisy, he bore a striking resemblance to Aurangzeb; and the title of 'Sikandaru-s-Sani,' or the second Alexander, which he assumed and impressed on his coins, was no idle vaunt. The proud Anhilwara, the ancient Dhar and Avanti, Mandor and Deogir, the seats of the Solankis, the Pramaras, the Pariharas and Taks, the entire Agnikula race, were overturned for ever by Ala. Jaisalmer, Gagraun, Bundi, the abodes of the Bhatti, the Khichi, and the Hara, with many of minor importance, suffered all the horrors of assault from this foe of the race, though destined again to raise their heads. The Rathors of Marwar and the [267] Kachhwahas of Amber were yet in a state of insignificance: the former were slowly creeping into notice as the vassals of the Pariharas, while the latter could scarcely withstand the attacks of the original Mina population. Ala remained in Chitor some days, admiring the grandeur of his conquest; and having committed every act of barbarity and wanton dilapidation which a bigoted zeal could suggest, overthrowing the temples and other monuments of art, he delivered the city in charge to Maldeo, the chief of Jalor, whom he had conquered and enrolled amongst his vassals. The palace of Bhim and the fair Padmini alone appears to have escaped the wrath of Ala; it would be pleasing could we suppose any kinder sentiment suggested the exception, which enables the author of these annals to exhibit the abode of the fair of Ceylon.

The Flight of Rāna Ajai Singh.—The survivor of Chitor, Rana Ajaisi, was now in security at Kelwara, a town situated in the heart of the Aravalli mountains, the western boundary of Mewar, to which its princes had been indebted for twelve centuries of dominion. Kelwara is at the highest part of one of its most extensive valleys, termed the Shero Nala, the richest district of this Alpine region. Guarded by faithful adherents, Ajaisi cherished for future occasion the wrecks of Mewar. It was the last behest of his father that when he attained 'one hundred years' (a figurative expression for dying) the son of Arsi, the elder brother, should succeed him. This injunction, from the deficiency of the qualities requisite at such a juncture in his own sons, met a ready compliance. Hamir was this son, destined to redeem the promise of the genius of Chitor and the lost honours of his race, and whose birth and early history fill many a page of their annals. His

PALACE OF RĀNA BHĪM AND PADMINI.

To face page 312.

father, Arsi, being out on a hunting excursion in the forest of Ondua, with some young chiefs of the court, in pursuit of the boar entered a field of maize, when a female offered to drive out the game. Pulling one of the stalks of maize, which grows to the height of ten or twelve feet, she pointed it, and mounting the platform made to watch the corn, impaled the hog, dragged him before the hunters, and departed. Though accustomed to feats of strength and heroism from the nervous arms of their country-women, the act surprised them. They descended to the stream at hand, and prepared the repast, as is usual, on the spot. The feast was held, and comments were passing on the fair arm which had transfixed the boar, when a ball of clay from a sling fractured a limb of the prince's steed. Looking in the direction whence it [268] came, they observed the same damsel, from her elevated stand,[1] preserving her fields from aerial depredators; but seeing the mischief she had occasioned she descended to express her regret and then returned to her pursuit. As they were proceeding homewards after the sports of the day, they again encountered the damsel, with a vessel of milk on her head, and leading in either hand a young buffalo. It was proposed, in frolic, to overturn her milk, and one of the companions of the prince dashed rudely by her; but without being disconcerted, she entangled one of her charges with the horse's limbs and brought the rider to the ground. On inquiry the prince discovered that she was the daughter of a poor Rajput of the Chandano tribe.[2] He returned the next day to the same quarter and sent for her father, who came and took his seat with perfect independence close to the prince, to the merriment of his companions, which was checked by Arsi asking his daughter to wife. They were yet more surprised by the demand being refused. The Rajput, on going home, told the more prudent mother, who scolded him heartily, made him recall the refusal, and seek the prince. They were married, and Hamir was the son of the Chandano Rajputni.[3]

[1] A stand is fixed upon four poles in the middle of a field, on which a guard is placed armed with a sling and clay balls, to drive away the ravens, peacocks, and other birds that destroy the corn.

[2] One of the branches of the Chauhan.

[3] [The same tale is told of Dhadīj, grandson of Prithirāj, the ancestor of the Dahiya Jāts (Rose, *Glossary*, ii. 220; Risley, *People of India*, 2nd ed., 179 f.).]

He remained little noticed at the maternal abode till the catastrophe of Chitor. At this period he was twelve years of age, and had led a rustic life, from which the necessity of the times recalled him.

Mewār occupied by the Musalmāns: The Exploit of Hamir.— Mewar was now occupied by the garrisons of Delhi, and Ajaisi had besides to contend with the mountain chiefs, amongst whom Munja Balaicha was the most formidable, who had, on a recent occasion, invaded the Shero Nala, and personally encountered the Rana, whom he wounded on the head with a lance. The Rana's sons, Sajansi and Ajamsi, though fourteen and fifteen, an age at which a Rajput ought to indicate his future character, proved of little aid in the emergency. Hamir was summoned, and accepted the feud against Munja, promising to return successful or not at all. In a few days he was seen entering the pass of Kelwara with Munja's head at his saddle-bow. Modestly placing the trophy at his uncle's feet, he exclaimed: "Recognize the head of your foe!" Ajaisi 'kissed his beard,'[1] and observing that fate had stamped empire on his forehead, impressed [269] it with a tika of blood from the head of the Balaicha. This decided the fate of the sons of Ajaisi; one of whom died at Kelwara, and the other, Sajansi, who might have excited a civil war, was sent from the country.[2] He departed for the Deccan, where his issue was destined to avenge some of the wrongs the parent country had sustained, and eventually to overturn the monarchy of Hindustan; for Sajansi was the ancestor of Sivaji, the founder of the Satara throne, whose lineage[3] is given in the chronicles of Mewar.

[1] This is an idiomatic phrase; Hamir could have had no beard.

[2] *Des desa.*

[3] Ajaisi, Sajansi, Dalipji, Sheoji, Bhoraji, Deoraj, Ugarsen, Mahulji, Kheluji, Jankoji, Satuji, Sambhaji, Sivaji (the founder of the Mahratta nation), Sambhaji, Ramraja, usurpation of the Peshwas. The Satara throne, but for the jealousies of Udaipur, might on the imbecility of Ramraja have been replenished from Mewar. It was offered to Nathji, the grandfather of the present chief Sheodan Singh, presumptive heir to Chitor. Two noble lines were reared from princes of Chitor expelled on similar occasions; those of Sivaji and the Gorkhas of Nepal. [This pedigree is largely the work of the bards. But the Mahrattas, who seem to be chiefly sprung from the Kunbi peasantry, claim Rājput origin, and several of their clans bear Rājput names. It is said that in 1836 the Rāna of Mewār was satisfied that the Bhonslas and certain other families had the right to be regarded as Rājputs (*Census Report, Bombay*, 1901, i. 184 f.; Russell, *Tribes and Castes Central Provinces*, iv. 199 ff.).]

Rāna Hamīr Singh, A.D. **1301–64.**—Hamir succeeded in S. 1357 (A.D. 1301), and had sixty-four years granted to him to redeem his country from the ruins of the past century, which period had elapsed since India ceased to own the paramount sway of her native princes. The day on which he assumed the ensigns of rule he gave, in the *tika daur*, an earnest of his future energy, which he signalized by a rapid inroad into the heart of the country of the predatory Balaicha, and captured their stronghold Pusalia. We may here explain the nature of this custom of a barbaric chivalry.

The Inaugural Foray.—The tika daur signifies the foray of inauguration, which obtained from time immemorial on such events, and is yet maintained where any semblance of hostility will allow its execution. On the morning of installation, having previously received the tika of sovereignty, the prince at the head of his retainers makes a foray into the territory of any one with whom he may have a feud, or with whom he may be indifferent as to exciting one ; he captures a stronghold or plunders a town, and returns with the trophies. If amity should prevail with all around, which the prince cares not to disturb, they have still a mock representation of the custom. For many reigns after the Jaipur princes united their fortunes to the throne of Delhi their frontier town, Malpura, was the object of the tika daur of the princes of Mewar.

Chitor under a Musalmān Garrison.—" When Ajmall [1] went another road," as the bard figuratively describes the demise of Rana Ajaisi, " the son of Arsi unsheathed the sword, thence never stranger to his hand." ' Maldeo remained with the royal garrison at Chitor,[2] but Hamir [270] desolated their plains, and left to his enemies only the fortified towns which could safely be inhabited. He commanded all who owned his sovereignty either to quit their abodes, and retire with their families to the shelter of the hills on the eastern and western frontiers, or share the fate of the public enemy. The roads were rendered impassable from his parties, who issued from their retreats in the Aravalli, the security

[1] This is a poetical version of the name of Ajaisi ; a liberty frequently taken by the bards for the sake of rhyme.

[2] [From an inscription at Chitor it appears that the fort remained in the charge of Muhammadans up to the time of Muhammad Tughlak (1324–51), who appointed Māldeo of Jālor governor (Erskine ii. A. 16).]

of which baffled pursuit. This destructive policy of laying waste the resources of their own country, and from this asylum attacking their foes as opportunity offered, has obtained from the time of Mahmud of Ghazni in the tenth, to Muhammad, the last who merited the name of Emperor of Delhi, in the eighteenth century.

Resistance of Hamīr Singh.—Hamir made Kelwara [1] his residence, which soon became the chief retreat of the emigrants from the plains. The situation was admirably chosen, being covered by several ranges, guarded by intricate defiles, and situated at the foot of a pass leading over the mountain into a still more inaccessible retreat (where Kumbhalmer now stands),[2] well watered and wooded, with abundance of pastures and excellent indigenous fruits and roots. This tract, above fifty miles in breadth, is twelve hundred feet above the level of the plains and three thousand above the sea, with a considerable quantity of arable land, and free communication to obtain supplies by the passes of the western declivity from Marwar, Gujarat, or the friendly Bhils, of the west, to whom this house owes a large debt of gratitude. On various occasions the communities of Oghna and Panarwa furnished the princes of Mewar with five thousand bowmen, supplied them with provisions, or guarded the safety of their families when they had to oppose the foe in the field. The elevated plateau of the eastern frontier presented in its forests and dells many places of security ; but Ala [3] traversed these in person, destroying as he went : neither did they possess the advantages of climate and natural productions arising from the elevation of the other. Such was the state of Mewar : its places of strength occupied by the foe, cultivation and peaceful objects neglected from the persevering hostility of Hamir, when a proposal of marriage came from the Hindu governor of Chitor, which was immediately accepted, contrary to the [271] wishes of the prince's advisers.

The Recovery of Chitor.—Whether this was intended as a snare

[1] The lake he excavated here, the Hamir-talao, and the temple of the protecting goddess on its bank, still bear witness of his acts while confined to this retreat.

[2] See Plate, view of Kumbhalmer.

[3] I have an inscription, and in Sanskrit, set up by an apostate chief or bard in his train, which I found in this tract.

to entrap him, or merely as an insult, every danger was scouted by Hamir which gave a chance to the recovery of Chitor. He desired that '*the coco-nut*[1] *might be retained*,' coolly remarking on the dangers pointed out, "My feet shall at least tread in the rocky steps in which my ancestors have moved. A Rajput should always be prepared for reverses; one day to abandon his abode covered with wounds, and the next to reascend with the *maur* (crown) on his head." It was stipulated that only five hundred horse should form his suite. As he approached Chitor, the five sons of the Chauhan advanced to meet him, but on the portal of the city no toran,[2] or nuptial emblem, was suspended. He, however, accepted the unsatisfactory reply to his remark on this indication of treachery, and ascended for the first time the ramp of Chitor. He was received in the ancient halls of his ancestors by Rao Maldeo, his son Banbir, and other chiefs, *with folded hands*. The bride was brought forth, and presented by her father without any of the solemnities practised on such occasions; 'the knot of their garments tied and their hands united,' and thus they were left. The family priest recommended patience, and Hamir

[1] This is the symbol of an offer of marriage.

[2] The toran is the symbol of marriage. It consists of three wooden bars, forming an equilateral triangle; mystic in shape and number, and having the apex crowned with the effigies of a peacock, it is placed over the portal of the bride's abode. At Udaipur, when the princes of Jaisalmer, Bikaner, and Kishangarh simultaneously married the two daughters and granddaughter of the Rana, the torans were suspended from the battlements of the tripolia, or three-arched portal, leading to the palace. The bridegroom, on horseback, lance in hand, proceeds to break the toran (*toran torna*), which is defended by the damsels of the bride, who from the parapet assail him with missiles of various kinds, especially with a crimson powder made from the flowers of the *palasa*, at the same time singing songs fitted to the occasion, replete with double-entendres. At length the toran is broken amidst the shouts of the retainers; when the fair defenders retire. The similitude of these ceremonies in the north of Europe and in Asia increases the list of common affinities, and indicates the violence of rude times to obtain the object of affection; and the lance, with which the Rajput chieftain breaks the toran, has the same emblematic import as the spear, which, at the marriage of the nobles in Sweden, was a necessary implement in the furniture of the marriage chamber (vide Mallett, *Northern Antiquities*). [The custom perhaps represents a symbol of marriage by capture, but it has also been suggested that it symbolizes the luck of the bride's family which the bridegroom acquires by touching the arch with his sword (see Luard, *Ethnographic Survey Central India*, 22; Enthoven, *Folk-lore Notes Gujarāt*, 69; Russell, *Tribes and Castes Central Provinces*, ii. 410).]

retired with his bride to the apartments allotted for them. Her kindness and vows of fidelity overcame his sadness upon learning that he had married a widow. She had been wedded to a chief of the Bhatti tribe, shortly afterwards slain, and when she was so young as not to recollect even his appearance. He ceased to lament the insult when she herself taught him how it might be avenged, and that it might even lead to the recovery of Chitor. It is a privilege possessed by the bridegroom to have one specific favour complied with as a part of the dower (*daeja*), and Hamir was instructed by his bride to ask for Jal, one of the civil [272] officers of Chitor, and of the Mehta tribe. With his wife so obtained, and the scribe whose talents remained for trial, he returned in a fortnight to Kelwara. Khetsi was the fruit of this marriage, on which occasion Maldeo made over all the hill tracts to Hamir. Khetsi was a year old when one of the penates (Khetrpal) [1] was found at fault, on which she wrote to her parents to invite her to Chitor, that the infant might be placed before the shrine of the deity. Escorted by a party from Chitor, with her child she entered its walls; and instructed by the Mehta, she gained over the troops who were left, for the Rao had gone with his chief adherents against the Mers of Madri. Hamir was at hand. Notice that all was ready reached him at Bagor. Still he met opposition that had nearly defeated the scheme; but having forced admission, his sword overcame every obstacle, and the oath of allegiance (*an*) was proclaimed from the palace of his fathers.

The Sonigira on his return was met with 'a salute of arabas,' [2] and Maldeo himself carried the account of his loss to the Khilji king Mahmud, who had succeeded Ala. The 'standard of the sun' once more shone refulgent from the walls of Chitor, and was the signal for return to their ancient abodes from their hills and hiding-places to the adherents of Hamir. The valleys of Kumbhalmer and the western highlands poured forth their 'streams of men,' while every chief of true Hindu blood rejoiced at the prospect of once more throwing off the barbarian yoke. So powerful was this feeling, and with such activity and skill did Hamir follow up this favour of fortune, that he marched to meet Mahmud,

1 [Khetrpāl, Kshetrapāla, is guardian of the field (*Kshetra*).]

2 A kind of arquebuss [properly the gun-carriage. Irvine, *Army of the Indian Moghuls*, 140 ff.]

who was advancing to recover his lost possessions. The king unwisely directed his march by the eastern plateau, where numbers were rendered useless by the intricacies of the country. Of the three steppes which mark the physiognomy of this tract, from the first ascent from the plain of Mewar to the descent at Chambal, the king had encamped on the central, at Singoli, where he was attacked, defeated, and made prisoner by Hamir, who slew Hari Singh, brother of Banbir, in single combat. The king suffered a confinement of three months in Chitor, nor was liberated till he had surrendered Ajmer, Ranthambor, Nagor, and Sui Sopur, besides paying fifty lakhs of rupees and one hundred elephants. Hamir would exact no promise of cessation from further inroads, but contented himself with assuring him that from such he should be prepared to defend Chitor, not within, but without the walls [273].[1]

Banbir, the son of Maldeo, offered to serve Hamir, who assigned the districts of Nimach, Jiran, Ratanpur, and the Kerar to maintain the family of his wife in becoming dignity; and as he gave the grant he remarked: "Eat, serve, and be faithful. You were once the servant of a Turk, but now of a Hindu of your own faith; for I have but taken back my own, the rock moistened by the blood of my ancestors, the gift of the deity I adore, and who will maintain me in it; nor shall I endanger it by the worship of a fair face, as did my predecessor." Banbir shortly after carried Bhainsror by assault, and this ancient possession guarding the Chambal was again added to Mewar. The chieftains of Rajasthan rejoiced once more to see a Hindu take the lead, paid willing homage, and aided him with service when required.

The Power of Rāna Hamīr Singh.—Hamir was the sole Hindu prince of power now left in India: all the ancient dynasties were

[1] Ferishta does not mention this conquest over the Khilji emperor; but as Mewar recovered her wonted splendour in this reign, we cannot doubt the truth of the native annals. [There is a mistake here. The successor of Alāu-d-dīn was Kutbu-d-dīn Mubārak, who came to the throne in 1316. Ferishta says that Rāī Ratan Singh of Chitor, who had been taken prisoner in the siege, was released by the cleverness of his daughter, and that Alāu-d-dīn ordered his son, Khizr Khān, to evacuate the place, on which the Rāī became tributary to Alāu-d-dīn. Also in 1312 the Rājputs threw the Muhammadan officers over the ramparts and asserted their independence (Ferishta, trans. Briggs, i. 363, 381). Erskine says that the attack was made by Muhammad Tughlak (1324–51).]

crushed, and the ancestors of the present princes of Marwar and Jaipur brought their levies, paid homage, and obeyed the summons of the prince of Chitor, as did the chiefs of Bundi, Gwalior, Chanderi, Raesin, Sikri, Kalpi, Abu, etc.

Extensive as was the power of Mewar before the Tatar occupation of India, it could scarcely have surpassed the solidity of sway which she enjoyed during the two centuries following Hamir's recovery of the capital. From this event to the next invasion from the same Cimmerian abode, led by Babur, we have a succession of splendid names recorded in her annals, and though destined soon to be surrounded by new Muhammadan dynasties, in Malwa and Gujarat as well as Delhi, yet successfully opposing them all. The distracted state of affairs when the races of Khilji, Lodi, and Sur alternately struggled for and obtained the seat of dominion, Delhi, was favourable to Mewar, whose power was now so consolidated that she not only repelled armies from her territory, but carried war abroad, leaving tokens of victory at Nagor, in Saurashtra, and to the walls of Delhi.

Public Works.—The subjects of Mewar must have enjoyed not only a long repose, but high prosperity during this period, judging from their magnificent public works, when a triumphal [274] column must have cost the income of a kingdom to erect, and which ten years' produce of the crown-lands of Mewar could not at this time defray. Only one of the structures prior to the sack of Chitor was left entire by Ala, and is yet existing, and this was raised by private and sectarian hands. It would be curious if the unitarian profession of the Jain creed was the means of preserving this ancient relic from Ala's wrath.[1] The princes of this house were great patrons of the arts, and especially of architecture; and it is a matter of surprise how their revenues, derived chiefly from the soil, could have enabled them to expend so much on these objects and at the same time maintain such armies as are enumerated. Such could be effected only by long prosperity and a mild, paternal system of government; for the subject had his monuments as well as the prince, the ruins of which may yet be discovered in the more inaccessible or deserted portions of Rajasthan. Hamir died full of years, leaving a name still

[1] [The Jain tower, known as Kirtti Stamb, 'pillar of fame,' erected in the twelfth or thirteenth century by Jīja, a Bagherwāl Mahājan, and dedicated to Ādināth, the first Jain Tīrthankara or saint.]

honoured in Mewar, as one of the wisest and most gallant of her princes, and bequeathing a well-established and extensive power to his son.

Kshetra or Khet Singh, A.D. 1364–82.—Khetsi succeeded in S. 1421 (A.D. 1365) to the power and to the character of his father. He captured Ajmer and Jahazpur from Lila Pathan, and reannexed Mandalgarh, Dasor, and the whole of Chappan (for the first time) to Mewar. He obtained a victory over the Delhi monarch Humayun [1] at Bakrol; but unhappily his life terminated in a family broil with his vassal, the Hara chief of Bumbaoda, whose daughter he was about to espouse.

Laksh Singh, A.D. 1382–97.—Lakha Rana, by this assassination, mounted the throne in Chitor in S. 1439 (A.D. 1373). His first act was the entire subjugation of the mountainous region of Merwara, and the destruction of its chief stronghold, Bairatgarh, where he erected Badnor. But an event of much greater importance than settling his frontier, and which most powerfully tended to the prosperity of the country, was the discovery of the tin and silver mines of Jawara, in the tract wrested by Khetsi from the Bhils of Chappan.[2] Lakha Rana has the merit of having first worked them, though their existence is superstitiously alluded to so early as the period of the founder. It is said the 'seven metals' (*haft-dhat*)[3] were formerly [275] abundant; but this appears figurative. We have no evidence for the gold, though silver, tin, copper, lead, and antimony were yielded in abundance (the first two from the same matrix), but the tin that has been extracted for many years past yields but a small portion of silver.[4] Lakha Rana defeated the Sankhla Rajputs of Nagarchal,[5] at Amber. He encountered the emperor Muhammad Shah Lodi, and on one

[1] [The contemporary of Khet Singh at Delhi was Fīroz Shāh Tughlak.]

[2] [The mines at Jāwar, sixteen miles south of Udaipur city, produce lead, zinc, and some silver. The mention of tin in the text seems wrong (Watt, *Dict. Econ. Prod.* vi. Part iv. 356; *Comm. Prod.* 1077).]

[3] *Haft-dhat*, corresponding to the planets, each of which ruled a metal: hence Mihr, 'the sun,' for gold; Chandra, 'the moon,' for silver.

[4] They have long been abandoned, the miners are extinct, and the protecting deities of mines are unable to get even a flower placed on their shrines, though some have been reconsecrated by the Bhils, who have converted Lakshmi into Sitalamata (Juno Lucina), whom the Bhil females invoke to pass them through danger.

[5] Jhunjhunu, Singhana, and Narbana formed the ancient Nagarchal territory.

occasion defeated a royal army at Badnor; but he carried the war to Gaya, and in driving the barbarian from this sacred place was slain.[1] Lakha is a name of celebrity, as a patron of the arts and benefactor of his country. He excavated many reservoirs and lakes, raised immense ramparts to dam their waters, besides erecting strongholds. The riches of the mines of Jawara were expended to rebuild the temples and palaces levelled by Ala. A portion of his own palace yet exists, in the same style of architecture as that, more ancient, of Ratna and the fair Padmini; and a minster (*mandir*) dedicated to the creator (Brahma), an enormous and costly fabric, is yet entire. Being to 'the One,' and consequently containing no idol, it may thus have escaped the ruthless fury of the invaders.

Lakha had a numerous progeny, who have left their clans called after them, as the Lunawats and Dulawats, now the sturdy allodial proprietors of the Alpine regions bordering on Oghna, Panarwa, and other tracts in the Aravalli.[2] But a circumstance which set aside the rights of primogeniture, and transferred the crown of Chitor from his eldest son, Chonda, to the younger, Mokal, had nearly carried it to another line. The consequences of making the elder branch a powerful vassal clan with claims to the throne, and which have been the chief cause of its subsequent prostration, we will reserve for another chapter [276].

CHAPTER 7

If devotion to the fair sex be admitted as a criterion of civilization, the Rajput must rank high. His susceptibility is extreme, and fires at the slightest offence to female delicacy, which he never forgives. A satirical impromptu, involving the sacrifice

[1] [There was no Sultān Muhammad Shāh Lodi, and that dynasty did not begin till 1451. Fīroz Shāh (1351–88) was contemporary of Laksh Singh at Delhi. It is not likely that a Rājput in the fourteenth century conducted a campaign at Gayā in Bengal; but, according to Har Bilas Sarda, author of a recent monograph on Rāna Kūmbha, the fact is corroborated by inscriptions, Peterson, *Bhaunagar Inscriptions*, 96, 117, 119.]

[2] The Sarangdeot chief of Kanor (on the borders of Chappan), one of the sixteen lords of Mewar, is also a descendant of Lakha, as are some of the tribes of Sondwara, about Pharphara and the ravines of the Kali Sind.

of Rajput prejudices, dissolved the coalition of the Rathors and Kachhwahas, and laid each prostrate before the Mahrattas, whom when united they had crushed: and a jest, apparently trivial, compromised the right of primogeniture to the throne of Chitor, and proved more disastrous in its consequences than the arms either of Moguls or Mahrattas.

Chonda renounces his Birthright.—Lakha Rana was advanced in years, his sons and grandsons established in suitable domains, when 'the coco-nut came' from Ranmall, prince of Marwar, to affiance his daughter with Chonda, the heir of Mewar. When the embassy was announced, Chonda was absent, and the old chief was seated in his chair of state surrounded by his court. The messenger of Hymen was courteously received by Lakha, who observed that Chonda would soon return and take the gage; "for," added he, drawing his fingers over his moustaches, "I don't suppose you send such playthings to an old greybeard like me." This little sally was of course applauded and repeated; but Chonda, offended at delicacy being sacrificed to wit, declined accepting the symbol which his father had even in jest supposed might be intended for him: and as it could not be returned without gross insult to Ranmall, the old Rana, incensed at his son's obstinacy, agreed to accept it himself, provided Chonda would swear to renounce his birthright in the event of his having a son, and be to the child but the 'first of his Rajputs.' He swore by Eklinga to fulfil his father's wishes.

Rāna Mokal, A.D. **1397–1433.**—Mokalji was the issue of this union, and had attained the age of five when the Rana resolved to signalize his finale by a raid against the enemies of their faith [277], and to expel the 'barbarian' from the holy land of Gaya. In ancient times this was by no means uncommon, and we have several instances in the annals of these States of princes resigning 'the purple' on the approach of old age, and by a life of austerity and devotion, pilgrimage and charity, seeking to make their peace with heaven "for the sins inevitably committed by all who wield a sceptre." But when war was made against their religion by the Tatar proselytes to Islam, the Sutlej and the Ghaggar were as the banks of the Jordan—Gaya, their Jerusalem, their holy land; and if there destiny filled his cup, the Hindu chieftain was secure of beatitude,[1] exempted from the troubles of 'second

[1] *Mukti.*

birth';[1] and borne from the scene of probation in celestial cars by the Apsaras,[2] was introduced at once into the 'realm of the sun.'[3] Ere, however, the Rana of Chitor journeyed to this bourne, he was desirous to leave his throne unexposed to civil strife. The subject of succession had never been renewed; but discussing with Chonda his warlike pilgrimage to Gaya, from which he might not return, he sounded him by asking what estates should be settled on Mokal. "The throne of Chitor," was the honest reply; and to set suspicion at rest, he desired that the ceremony of installation should be performed previous to Lakha's departure. Chonda was the first to pay homage and swear obedience and fidelity to his future sovereign: reserving, as the recompense of his renunciation, the first place in the councils, and stipulating that in all grants to the vassals of the crown, his symbol (the lance) should be superadded to the autograph of the prince. In all grants the lance of Salumbar[4] still precedes the monogram of the Rana.[5]

The sacrifice of Chonda to offended delicacy and filial respect was great, for he had all the qualities requisite for command. Brave, frank, and skilful, he conducted all public affairs after his father's departure and death, to the benefit of the minor and the State. The queen-mother, however, who is admitted as the natural guardian of her infant's rights on all such occasions, felt umbrage and discontent at her loss of power; forgetting that, but for Chonda, she would never [278] have been mother to the Rana of Mewar. She watched with a jealous eye all his proceedings; but it was only through the medium of suspicion she could accuse the integrity of Chonda, and she artfully asserted that, under colour of directing state affairs, he was exercising absolute sovereignty, and that if he did not assume the title of Rana, he would reduce it to an empty name. Chonda, knowing the purity of his own motives, made liberal allowance for maternal solicitude; but upbraiding the queen with the injustice of her suspicions,

[1] This is a literal phrase, denoting further transmigration of the soul, which is always deemed a punishment. The soldier who falls in battle in the faithful performance of his duty is alone exempted, according to their martial mythology, from the pains of 'second birth.'

[2] The fair messengers of heaven.

[3] *Suraj Mandal.*

[4] The abode of the chief of the various clans of Chondawat.

[5] *Vide* p. 235.

and advising a vigilant care to the rights of Sesodias, he retired to the court of Mandu, then rising into notice, where he was received with the highest distinctions, and the district of Halar [1] was assigned to him by the king.

Rāthor Influence in Mewār.—His departure was the signal for an influx of the kindred of the queen from Mandor. Her brother Jodha (who afterwards gave his name to Jodhpur) was the first, and was soon followed by his father, Rao Ranmall, and numerous adherents, who deemed the arid region of Maru-des, and its rabri, or maize porridge, well exchanged for the fertile plains and wheaten bread of Mewar.

Raghudeva, the Mewār Hero.—With his grandson on his knee, the old Rao "would sit on the throne of Bappa Rawal, on whose quitting him for play, the regal ensigns of Mewar waved over the head of Mandor." This was more than the Sesodia nurse [2] (an important personage in all Hindu governments) could bear, and bursting with indignation, she demanded of the queen if her kin was to defraud her own child of his inheritance. The honesty of the nurse was greater than her prudence. The creed of the Rajput is to 'obtain sovereignty,' regarding the means as secondary and this avowal of her suspicions only hastened their designs. The queen soon found herself without remedy, and a remonstrance to her father produced a hint which threatened the existence of her offspring. Her fears were soon after augmented by the assassination of Raghudeva, the second brother of Chonda, whose estates were Kelwara and Kawaria. To the former place, where he resided aloof from the court, Rao Ranmall sent a dress of honour, which etiquette requiring him to put on when presented, the prince was assassinated in the act. Raghudeva was so much beloved for his virtues, courage, and manly beauty, that his [279] murder became martyrdom, and obtained for him divine honours, and a place amongst the *Di Patres* (*Pitrideva*) of Mewar. His image is on every hearth, and is daily worshipped with the Penates. Twice in the year his altars receive public homage from every Sesodia, from the Rana to the serf.[3]

[1] [Hālār in W. Kāthiāwār (*BG*, viii. 4).]

[2] The *Dhāi*. The *Dhābhāis*, or 'foster-brothers,' often hold lands in perpetuity, and are employed in the most confidential places; on embassies, marriages, etc.

[3] On the 8th day of the Dasahra, or 'military festival,' when the levies

The Expulsion of the Rāthor Party.—In this extremity the queen-mother turned her thoughts to Chonda, and it was not difficult to apprise him of the danger which menaced the race, every place of trust being held by her kinsmen, and the principal post of Chitor by a Bhatti Rajput of Jaisalmer Chonda, though at a distance, was not inattentive to the proverbially dangerous situation of a minor amongst the Rajputs. At his departure he was accompanied by two hundred Aherias or huntsmen, whose ancestors had served the princes of Chitor from ancient times. These had left their families behind, a visit to whom was the pretext for their introduction to the fort. They were instructed to get into the service of the keepers of the gates, and, being considered more attached to the place than to the family, their object was effected. The queen-mother was counselled to cause the young prince to descend daily with a numerous retinue to give feasts to the surrounding villages, and gradually to increase the distance, but not to fail on the 'festival of lamps'[1] to hold the feast (*got*) at Gosunda.[2]

These injunctions were carefully attended to. The day arrived, the feast was held at Gosunda; but the night was closing in, and no Chonda appeared. With heavy hearts the nurse, the Purohit,[3] and those in the secret moved homeward, and had reached the eminence called Chitori, when forty horsemen passed them at the gallop, and at their head Chonda in disguise, who by a secret sign paid homage as he passed to his younger

---

are mustered at the Chaugan, or 'Champ de Mars,' and on the 10th of Chait his altars are purified, and his image is washed and placed thereon. Women pray for the safety of their children; husbands, that their wives may be fruitful. Previously to this, a son of Bappa Rawal was worshipped; but after the enshrinement of Raghudeva, the adoration of Kulisputra was gradually abolished. Nor is this custom confined to Mewar: there is a deified *Putra* in every Rajput family—one who has met a violent death. Besides Eklinga, the descendants of Bappa have adopted numerous household divinities: the destinies of life and death, Baenmata the goddess of the Chawaras, Nagnachian the serpent divinity of the Rathors, and Khetrapal, or 'fosterer of the field,' have with many others obtained a place on the Sesodia altars. This festival may not unaptly be compared to that of Adonis amongst the Greeks, for the *Putra* is worshipped chiefly by women.

[1] The *Diwali*, from *diwa*, 'a lamp.' This festival is in honour of Lakshmi, goddess of wealth.

[2] Seven miles south of Chitor, on the road to Malwa.

[3] The family priest and instructor of youth.

brother and sovereign. Chonda and [280] his band had reached the Rampol,[1] or upper gate, unchecked. Here, when challenged, they said they were neighbouring chieftains, who, hearing of the feast at Gosunda, had the honour to escort the prince home. The story obtained credit; but the main body, of which this was but the advance, presently coming up, the treachery was apparent. Chonda unsheathed his sword, and at his well-known shout the hunters were speedily in action. The Bhatti chief, taken by surprise, and unable to reach Chonda, launched his dagger at and wounded him, but was himself slain; the guards at the gates were cut to pieces, and the Rathors hunted out and killed without mercy.

Death of Rāo Ranmall.—The end of Rāo Ranmall was more ludicrous than tragical. Smitten with the charms of a Sesodia handmaid of the queen, who was compelled to his embrace, the old chief was in her arms, intoxicated with love, wine, and opium, and heard nothing of the tumult without. A woman's wit and revenge combined to make his end afford some compensation for her loss of honour. Gently rising, she bound him to his bed with his own Marwari turban:[2] nor did this disturb him, and the messengers of fate had entered ere the opiate allowed his eyes to open to a sense of his danger. Enraged, he in vain endeavoured to extricate himself; and by some tortuosity of movement he got upon his legs, his pallet at his back like a shell or shield of defence. With no arms but a brass vessel of ablution, he levelled to the earth several of his assailants, when a ball from a matchlock extended him on the floor of the palace. His son Jodha was in the lower town, and was indebted to the fleetness of his steed for escaping the fate of his father and kindred, whose bodies strewed the *terre-pleine* of Chitor, the merited reward of their usurpation and treachery.

The Revenge of Chonda.—But Chonda's revenge was not yet satisfied. He pursued Rao Jodha, who, unable to oppose him, took refuge with Harbuji Sankhla, leaving Mandor to its fate. This city Chonda entered by surprise, and holding it till his sons Kantatji and Manjaji arrived with reinforcements, the Rathor treachery was repaid by their keeping possession of the capital during twelve years. We might here leave the future founder

1 *Rampol*, 'the gate of Ram.'

2 Often sixty cubits in length.

of Jodhpur, had not this feud led to the junction of the rich [281] province of Godwar to Mewar, held for three centuries and again lost by treachery. It may yet involve a struggle between the Sesodias and Rathors.[1]

"Sweet are the uses of adversity." To Jodha it was the first step in the ladder of his eventual elevation. A century and a half had scarcely elapsed since a colony, the wreck of Kanauj, found an asylum, and at length a kingdom, taking possession of one capital and founding another, abandoning Mandor and erecting Jodhpur. But even Jodha could never have hoped that his issue would have extended their sway from the valley of the Indus to within one hundred miles of the Jumna, and from the desert bordering on the Sutlej to the Aravalli mountains: that one hundred thousand swords should at once be in the hands of Rathors, 'the sons of one father' (*ek Bap ke Betan*).

If we slightly encroach upon the annals of Marwar, it is owing to its history and that of Mewar being here so interwoven, and the incidents these events gave birth so illustrative of the national character of each, that it is, perhaps, more expedient to advert to the period when Jodha was shut out from Mandor, and the means by which he regained that city, previous to relating the events of the reign of Mokal.

Harbuji Sānkhla.—Harbuji Sankhla, at once a soldier and a devotee, was one of those Rajput cavaliers '*sans peur et sans reproche*,' whose life of celibacy and perilous adventure was mingled with the austere devotion of an ascetic; by turns aiding with his lance the cause which he deemed worthy, or exercising an unbounded hospitality towards the stranger. This generosity had much reduced his resources when Jodha sought his protection. It was the eve of the *Sada-bart*, one of those hospitable rites which, in former times, characterized Rajwara. This 'perpetual charity' supplies food to the stranger and traveller, and is distributed not only by individual chiefs and by the government, but by subscriptions of communities. Even in Mewar, in her present impoverished condition, the offerings to the gods in support of their shrines and the establishment of the *Sada-bart* were simultaneous. Hospitality is a virtue pronounced to belong more peculiarly to a semi-barbarous condition. Alas! for refinement

[1] [Godwār, including the Bāli and Desuri districts in S.E. Mārwār, is now known as the Desuri Hukūmat: see Erskine iii. A. 180 f.]

and ultra-civilization, strangers to the happiness enjoyed by Harbuji Sankhla. Jodha, with one hundred and twenty followers, came to solicit the 'stranger's fare': but unfortunately it was too late, the *Sada-bart* had been distributed. In this exigence, Harbuji recollected that there was a wood [282] called *mujd*,[1] used in dyeing, which among other things in the desert regions is resorted to in scarcity. A portion of this was bruised, and boiled with some flour, sugar, and spices, making altogether a palatable pottage; and with a promise of better fare on the morrow, it was set before the young Rao and his followers, who, after making a good repast, soon forgot Chitor in sleep. On waking, each stared at his fellow, for their mustachios were dyed with their evening's meal; but the old chief, who was not disposed to reveal his expedient, made it minister to their hopes by giving it a miraculous character, and saying "that as the grey of age was thus metamorphosed into the tint of morn[2] and hope, so would their fortunes become young, and Mandor again be theirs."

Elevated by this prospect, they enlisted Harbuji on their side. He accompanied them to the chieftain of Mewa, "whose stables contained one hundred chosen steeds." Pabuji, a third independent of the same stamp, with his 'coal-black steed,' was gained to the cause, and Jodha soon found himself strong enough to attempt the recovery of his capital. The sons of Chonda were taken by surprise: but despising the numbers of the foe, and ignorant who were their auxiliaries, they descended sword in hand to meet the assailants. The elder[3] son of Chonda with

[1] The wood of Solomon's temple is called *almug*; the prefix *al* is merely the article [?]. This is the wood also mentioned in the annals of Gujarat, of which the temple to Adinath was constructed. It is said to be indestructible even by fire. It has been surmised that the fleets of Tyre frequented the Indian coast: could they thence have carried the *Almujd* for the temple of Solomon? [Almug, according to the *Encyclopædia Biblica* (i. 1196) is either Brazil-wood or red sandalwood (*Pterocarpus santalinus*). Sir G. Watt, who has kindly examined the question, thinks it very improbable that the *mujd* of the text is almug wood, because neither the true sandalwood (*Santalum album*) nor the red sandalwood (*Pterocarpus santalinus*) is found in Rājputāna. He identifies the *mujd* of the text with *Moringa concanensis*, a small tree found wild in Sind and the Konkan, which yields a gum of considerable value, and its congener *Moringa pterygosperma* (*Comm. Prod.* 784), the horse-radish tree of India, is used as a dye in Jamaica, and probably could be so used in India.]

[2] This wood has a brownish-red tint.

[3] This is related with some variation in other annals of the period.

many adherents was slain; and the younger, deserted by the subjects of Mandor, trusted to the swiftness of his horse for escape; but being pursued, was overtaken and killed on the boundary of Godwar. Thus Jodha, in his turn, was revenged, but the 'feud was not balanced.' Two sons of Chitor had fallen for one chief of Mandor. But wisely reflecting on the original aggression, and the superior power of Mewar, as well as his being indebted for his present success to foreign aid, Jodha sued for peace, and offered as the *mundkati*, or 'price of blood,' and 'to quench the feud,' that the spot where Manja fell should be the future barrier of the two States. The entire province of Godwar was comprehended in the cession, which for three centuries withstood every contention, till the internal dissensions of the last half century, which grew out of the cause by which [283] it was obtained, and the change of succession in Mewar severed this most valuable acquisition.[1]

Who would imagine, after such deadly feuds between these rival States, that in the very next succession these hostile frays were not only buried in oblivion, but that the prince of Marwar abjured 'his turban and his bed' till he had revenged the assassination of the prince of Chitor, and restored his infant heir to his rights? The annals of these States afford numerous instances of the same hasty, overbearing temperament governing all; easily moved to strife, impatient of revenge, and steadfast in its gratification. But this satisfied, resentment subsides. A daughter of the offender given to wife banishes its remembrance, and when the bard joins the lately rival names in the couplet, each will complacently curl his mustachio over his lip as he hears his 'renown expand like the lotus,' and thus 'the feud is extinguished.' Thus have they gone on from time immemorial, and will continue, till what we may fear to contemplate. They have now neither friend nor foe but the British. The Tatar invader sleeps in his tomb, and the Mahratta depredator is muzzled and enchained. To return.

[1] There is little hope, while British power acts as high constable and keeper of the peace in Rajwara, of this being recovered: nor, were it otherwise, would it be desirable to see it become an object of contention between these States. Marwar has attained much grandeur since the time of Jodha, and her resources are more unbroken than those of Mewar, who, if she could redeem, could not, from its exposed position, maintain the province against the brave Rathor.

Mokal, A.D. 1397–1433.—Mokal, who obtained the throne by Chonda's surrender of his birthright, was not destined long to enjoy the distinction, though he evinced qualities worthy of heading the Sesodias. He ascended the throne in S. 1454 (A.D. 1398), at an important era in the history of India; when Timur, who had already established the race of Chagatai in the kingdoms of Central Asia, and laid prostrate the throne of Byzantium, turned his arms towards India. But it was not a field for his ambition; and the event is not even noticed in the annals of Mewar: a proof that it did not affect their repose. But they record an attempted invasion by the king of Delhi, which is erroneously stated to have been by Firoz Shah. A grandson of this prince had indeed been set up, and compelled to flee from the arms of Timur, and as the direction of his flight was Gujarat, it is not unlikely that the recorded attempt to penetrate by the passes of Mewar may have been his [284]. Be this as it may, the Rana Mokal anticipated and met him beyond the passes of the Aravalli, in the field of Raepur, and compelled him to abandon his enterprise. Pursuing his success, he took possession of Sambhar and its salt lakes, and otherwise extended and strengthened his territory, which the distracted state of the empire consequent to Timur's invasion rendered a matter of little difficulty. Mokal finished the palace commenced by Lakha, now a mass of ruins; and erected the shrine of Chaturbhuja, 'the four-armed deity,' [1] in the western hills.

Lāl Bāi.—Besides three sons, Rana Mokal had a daughter, celebrated for her beauty, called Lal Bai, or 'the ruby.' She was betrothed to the Khichi chieftain of Gagraun, who at the Hathleva [2] demanded the pledge of succour on foreign invasion. Dhiraj, the son of the Khichi, had come to solicit the stipulated aid against Hoshang of Malwa, who had invested their capital. The Rana's headquarters were then at Madri, and he was employed in quelling a revolt of the mountaineers, when Dhiraj arrived and obtained the necessary aid. Madri was destined to be the scene of the termination of Mokal's career: he was assassinated by his uncles, the natural brothers of his father, from an unintentional offence, which tradition has handed down in all its details.

[1] [The four-armed Vishnu, the favourite deity of the Mertia Rāthors (*Census Report, Rajputana*, 1891, ii. 26).]

[2] The ceremony of joining hands.

Assassination of Rāna Mokal.—Chacha and Mera were the natural sons of Khetsi Rana (the predecessor of Lakha); their mother a fair bandmaid of low descent, generally allowed to be a carpenter's daughter. 'The fifth sons of Mewar' (as the natural children are figuratively termed) possess no rank, and though treated with kindness, and entrusted with confidential employments, the sons of the chiefs of the second class take precedence of them, and 'sit higher on the carpet.' These brothers had the charge of seven hundred horse in the train of Rana Mokal at Madri. Some chiefs at enmity with them, conceiving that they had overstepped their privileges, wished to see them humiliated. Chance procured them the opportunity: which, however, cost their prince his life. Seated in a grove with his chiefs around him, he inquired the name of a particular tree. The Chauhan chief, feigning ignorance, whispered him to ask either of the brothers; and not perceiving their scope, he artlessly did so. "Uncle, what tree is this?" The sarcasm thus prompted they considered as reflecting on their birth (being sons [285] of the carpenter's daughter), and the same day, while Mokal was at his devotions, and in the act of counting his rosary, one blow severed his arm from his body, while another stretched him lifeless. The brothers, quickly mounting their steeds, had the audacity to hope to surprise Chitor, but the gates were closed upon them.

Rāna Kūmbha, A.D. **1433–68.**—Though the murder of Mokal is related to have no other cause than the sarcasm alluded to, the precautions taken by the young prince Kumbha,[1] his successor, would induce a belief that this was but the opening of a deep-laid conspiracy. The traitors returned to the stronghold near Madri, and Kumbha trusted to the friendship and good feeling of the prince of Marwar in this emergency. His confidence was well repaid. The prince put his son at the head of a force, and the retreat of the assassins being near his own frontier, they were encountered and dislodged. From Madri they fled to Pai, where they strengthened a fortress in the mountains named Ratakot; a lofty peak of the compound chain which encircles Udaipur, visible from the surrounding country, as are the remains of this stronghold of the assassins. It would appear that their

[1] [His mother was a Pramār, Subhāgya Devi, daughter of Rāja Jaitmall, Sānkhla.]

lives were dissolute, for they had carried off the virgin daughter of a Chauhan, which led to their eventual detection and punishment. Her father, Suja, had traced the route of the ravishers, and, mixing with the workmen, found that the approaches to the place of their concealment were capable of being scaled. He was about to lay his complaint before his prince, when he met the cavalcade of Kumbha and the Rathor. The distressed father, 'covering his face,' disclosed the story of his own and daughter's dishonour. They encamped till night at Delwara, when, led by the Chandana, they issued forth to surprise the authors of so many evils.

Suja and the Tiger.—Arrived at the base of the rock, where the parapet was yet low, they commenced the escalade, aided by the thick foliage. The path was steep and rugged, and in the darkness of the night each had grasped his neighbour's skirt for security. Animated by a just revenge, the Chauhan (Suja) led the way, when on reaching a ledge of the rock the glaring eyeballs of a tigress flashed upon him. Undismayed, he squeezed the hand of the Rathor prince who followed him, and who on perceiving the object of terror instantly buried his poignard in her heart This omen was superb. They soon reached the summit. Some had ascended the parapet; others were scrambling over, when the minstrel [286] slipping, fell, and his drum, which was to have accompanied his voice in singing the conquest, awoke by its crash the daughter of Chacha. Her father quieted her fears by saying it was only "the thunder and the rains of Bhadon": to fear God only and go to sleep, for their enemies were safe at Kelwa. At this moment the Rao and his party rushed in. Chacha and Mera had no time to avoid their fate. Chacha was cleft in two by the Chandana, while the Rathor prince laid Mera at his feet, and the spoils of Ratakot were divided among the assailants.

CHAPTER 8

Rāna Kūmbha, A.D. **1433-68.**—Kumbha succeeded his father in S. 1475 (A.D. 1419); [1] nor did any symptom of dissatisfaction

[1] [The dates given in the margin are based on recently found inscriptions (Har Bilas Sarda, *Maharana Kumbha: Sovereign, Soldier, Scholar*, Ajmer, 1917, p. 2.]

appear to usher in his reign, which was one of great success amidst no common difficulties. The bardic historians[1] do as much honour to the Marwar prince, who had made common cause with their sovereign in revenging the death of his father, as if it had involved the security of his crown; but this was a precautionary measure of the prince, who was induced thus to act from several motives, and, above all, in accordance with usage, which stigmatizes the refusal of aid when demanded: besides 'Kumbha was the nephew of Marwar.'

It has rarely occurred in any country to have possessed successively so many energetic princes as ruled Mewar through several centuries. She was now in the middle path of her glory, and enjoying the legitimate triumph of seeing the foes of her religion captives on the rock of her power. A century had elapsed since the bigot Ala had wreaked his vengeance on the different monuments of art. Chitor had recovered the sack, and new defenders had sprung up in the place [287] of those who had fallen in their 'saffron robes,' a sacrifice for her preservation. All that was wanting to augment her resources against the storms which were collecting on the brows of Caucasus and the shores of the Oxus, and were destined to burst on the head of his grandson Sanga, was effected by Kumbha; who with Hamir's energy, Lakha's taste for the arts, and a genius comprehensive as either and more fortunate, succeeded in all his undertakings, and once more raised the 'crimson banner' of Mewar upon the banks of the Ghaggar, the scene of Samarsi's defeat. Let us contrast the patriarchal Hindu governments of this period with the despotism of the Tatar invader.

From the age of Shihabu-d-din, the conqueror of India, and his contemporary Samarsi, to the time we have now reached, two entire dynasties, numbering twenty-four emperors and one empress, through assassination, rebellion, and dethronement, had followed in rapid succession, yielding a result of only nine years to a reign. Of Mewar, though several fell in defending their altars at home or their religion abroad, eleven princes suffice to fill the same period.

It was towards the close of the Khilji dynasty that the satraps

[1] The *Raj Ratana*, by Ranchhor Bhat, says: "The Mandor Rao was pardhan, or premier to Mokal, and conquered Nawa and Didwana for Mewar."

of Delhi shook off its authority and established subordinate kingdoms: Bijapur and Golkonda in the Deccan; Malwa, Gujarat, Jaunpur in the east; and even Kalpi had its king. Malwa and Gujarat had attained considerable power when Kumbha ascended the throne. In the midst of his prosperity these two States formed a league against him, and in S. 1496 (A.D. 1440) both kings, at the head of powerful armies, invaded Mewar. Kumbha met them on the plains of Malwa bordering on his own State, and at the head of one hundred thousand horse and foot and fourteen hundred elephants, gave them an entire defeat, carrying captive to Chitor Mahmud the Khilji sovereign of Malwa.

Abu-l Fazl relates this victory, and dilates on Kumbha's greatness of soul in setting his enemy at liberty, not only without ransom but with gifts.[1] Such is the character of the Hindu: a mixture of arrogance, political blindness, pride, and generosity. To spare a prostrate foe is the creed of the Hindu cavalier, and he carries all such maxims to excess. The annals, however, state that Mahmud was confined six months in Chitor; and that the trophies of conquest were retained we have evidence from Babur, who mentions receiving from the son of his opponent, Sanga, the crown of the Malwa king.

The Tower of Victory.—But there is a more durable [288] monument than this written record of victory: the triumphal pillar in Chitor, whose inscriptions detail the event, "when, shaking the earth, the lords of Gujarkhand and Malwa, with armies overwhelming as the ocean, invaded Medpat." Eleven years after this event Kumbha laid the foundations of this column, which was completed in ten more: a period apparently too short to place "this ringlet on the brow of Chitor, which makes her look down upon Meru with derision." We will leave it, with the aspiration that it may long continue a monument of the fortune of its founders.[2]

It would appear that the Malwa king afterwards united his

[1] [It is the generosity of Rāna Sanga to Muzaffar Shāh of which Abu-l Fazl speaks (*Āīn*, ii. 221).]

[2] [The Musalmān historians give a different account. Ferishta says that Mahmūd stormed the lower part of Chitor, and that the Rāna fled (iv. 209). At any rate, Mahmūd erected a tower of victory at Māndu (*IGI*, xvii. 173). The result was probably indecisive. For Kūmbha's pillar see Fergusson, *Hist. Indian Architecture*, ii. 59; Smith, *HFA*. 202 f.]

arms with Kumbha, as, in a victory gained over the imperial forces at Jhunjhunu, when 'he planted his standard in Hissar,' the Malwa troops were combined with those of Mewar. The imperial power had at this period greatly declined: the Khutba was read in the mosques in the name of Timur, and the Malwa king had defeated, single-handed, the last Ghorian sultan of Delhi.

The Fortresses of Mewār.—Of eighty-four fortresses for the defence of Mewar, thirty-two were erected by Kumbha. Inferior only to Chitor is that stupendous work called after him Kumbhalmer,[1] 'the hill of Kumbha,' from its natural position, and the works he raised, impregnable to a native army. These works were on the site of a more ancient fortress, of which the mountaineers long held possession. Tradition ascribes it to Samprati Raja, a Jain prince in the second century, and a descendant of Chandragupta;[2] and the ancient Jain temples appear to confirm the tradition. When Kumbha captured Nagor he brought away the gates, with the statue of the god Hanuman, who gives his name to the gate which he still guards. He also erected a citadel on a peak of Abu, within the fortress of the ancient Pramara, where he often resided. Its magazine and alarm-tower still bear Kumbha's name; and in a rude temple the bronze effigies of Kumbha and his father still receive divine honours.[3] Centuries have passed since the princes of Mewar had influence here, but the incident marks the vivid remembrance of their condition. He fortified the passes between the western frontier and Abu, and erected the fort Vasanti near the present Sirohi, and that of Machin, to defend the Shéro Nala and Deogarh against the Mers of Aravalli. He re-established Ahor and other smaller [289] forts to overawe the Bhumia[4] Bhil of Jharol and Panarwa, and defined the boundaries of Marwar and Mewar.

Temples.—Besides these monuments of his genius, two consecrated to religion have survived: that of Kumbha Sham, on Abu, which, though worthy to attract notice elsewhere, is here eclipsed by a crowd of more interesting objects; the other, one

[1] Pronounced *Kumalmer*.

[2] [Grandson of Asoka (Smith, *EHI*, 192 f.).]

[3] [For the Ābu temples see Tod, *Western India*, 75 ff.: Erskine iii. A. 295.]

[4] A powerful phrase, indicating 'possessor of the soil.'

of the largest edifices existing, cost upwards of a million sterling, towards which Kumbha contributed eighty thousand pounds. It is erected in the Sadri pass leading from the western descent of the highlands of Mewar, and is dedicated to Rishabhadeva.[1] Its secluded position has preserved it from bigoted fury, and its only visitants now are the wild beasts who take shelter in its sanctuary. Kumbha Rana was also a poet: but in a far more elevated strain than the troubadour princes, his neighbours, who contented themselves with rehearsing their own prowess or celebrating their lady's beauty. He composed a *tika*, or appendix to the 'Divine Melodies,'[2] in praise of Krishna. We can pass no judgment on these inspirations of the royal bard, as we are ignorant whether any are preserved in the records of the house: a point his descendant, who is deeply skilled in such lore, might probably answer.

Mira Bāi.—Kumbha married a daughter of the Rathor of Merta, the first of the clans of Marwar. Mira Bai[3] was the most celebrated princess of her time for beauty and romantic piety. Her compositions were numerous, though better known to the worshippers of the Hindu Apollo than to the ribald bards. Some of her odes and hymns to the deity are preserved and admired. Whether she imbibed her poetic piety from her husband, or

[1] The Rana's minister, of the Jain faith, and of the tribe Porwar (one of the twelve and a half divisions), laid the foundation of this temple in A.D. 1438. It was completed by subscription. It consists of three stories, and is supported by numerous columns of granite, upwards of forty feet in height. The interior is inlaid with mosaics of cornelian and agate. The statues of the Jain saints are in its subterranean vaults. We could not expect much elegance at a period when the arts had long been declining, but it would doubtless afford a fair specimen of them, and enable us to trace their gradual descent in the scale of refinement. This temple is an additional proof of the early existence of the art of inlaying. That I did not see it is now to me one of the many vain regrets which I might have avoided.

[2] *Gita Govinda.*

[3] [She was daughter of Ratiya Rāna, and was married to Kūmbha in 1413. Her great work is the Rāg Gobind (Grierson, *Modern Literature of Hindustan*, 12; Macauliffe, *The Sikh Religion*, vi. 342 ff.; *IA*, xxv. 19, xxxii. 329 ff.; *ASR*, xxiii. 106). As an illustration of the uncertainty of early Mewār history, according to Har Bilas Sarda, author of the monograph on Rāna Kūmbha, Mīra Bāi was not wife of Kūmbhā, but of Bhojrāj, son of Rāna Sanga. She was daughter of Ratan Singh of Merta, fourth son of Rāo Duda (A.D. 1461–62). She was married to Bhojrāj A.D. 1516, and died in 1546.]

whether from her he caught the sympathy which produced the 'sequel to the songs of Govinda,' we cannot determine. Her history is a romance, and her excess of devotion at every shrine of the favourite deity with the fair of Hind, from the Yamuna to 'the world's end,' [1] gave rise to many [290] tales of scandal. Kumbha mixed gallantry with his warlike pursuits. He carried off the daughter of the chief of Jhalawar, who had been betrothed to the prince of Mandor: this renewed the old feud, and the Rathor made many attempts to redeem his affianced bride. His humiliation was insupportable, when through the purified atmosphere of the periodical rains "the towers of Kumbhalmer became visible from the castle of Mandor, and the light radiated from the chamber of the fair through the gloom of a night in Bhadon,[2] to the hall where he brooded o'er his sorrows." It was surmised that this night-lamp was an understood signal of the Jhalani, who pined at the decree which ambition had dictated to her father, in consigning her to the more powerful rival of her affianced lord. The Rathor exhausted every resource to gain access to the fair, and had once nearly succeeded in a surprise by escalade, having cut his way in the night through the forest in the western and least guarded acclivity: but, as the bard equivocally remarks, "though he cut his way through the *jhal* (brushwood), he could not reach the *Jhalani*."

The Assassination of Rāna Kūmbha, A.D. **1468.**—Kumbha had occupied the throne half a century; he had triumphed over the enemies of his race, fortified his country with strongholds, embellished it with temples, and with the superstructure of her fame had laid the foundation of his own—when, the year which should have been a jubilee was disgraced by the foulest blot in the annals; and his life, which nature was about to close, terminated by the poignard of an assassin—that assassin, his son!

Rāna Uda, A.D. **1468-73.**—This happened in S. 1525 (A.D. 1469). Uda was the name of the parricide, whose unnatural ambition, and impatience to enjoy a short lustre of sovereignty, bereft of life the author of his existence. But such is the detestation which marks this unusual crime that, like that of the Venetian traitor, his name is left a blank in the annals, nor is Uda known but by the epithet *Hatyara*, 'the murderer.' Shunned by his kin, and compelled to look abroad for succour to maintain him

[1] *Jagat Khunt*, or Dwarka. [2] The darkest of the rainy months.

on the throne polluted by his crime, Mewar in five years of illegitimate rule lost half the consequence which had cost so many to acquire. He made the Deora prince independent in Abu, and bestowed Sambhar, Ajmer, and adjacent districts on the prince of Jodhpur[1] as the price of his friendship. But, a prey to remorse, he felt that he [291] could neither claim regard from, nor place any dependence upon, these princes, though he bribed them with provinces. He humbled himself before the king of Delhi, offering him a daughter in marriage to obtain his sanction to his authority; "but heaven manifested its vengeance to prevent this additional iniquity, and preserve the house of Bappa Rawal from dishonour." He had scarcely quitted the divan (*diwan-khana*), on taking leave of the king, when a flash of lightning struck the *Haiyara* to the earth, whence he never arose.[2] The bards pass over this period cursorily, as one of their race was the instrument of Uda's crime.

Banishment of the Chārans.—There has always been a jealousy between the Mangtas, as they term all classes 'who extend the palm,' whether Brahmans, Yatis, Charans, or Bhats; but since Hamir, the Charan influence had far eclipsed the rest. A Brahman astrologer predicted Kumbha's death through a Charan, and as the class had given other cause of offence, Kumbha banished the fraternity his dominions, resuming all their lands: a strong measure in those days, and which few would have had nerve to attempt or firmness to execute. The heir-apparent, Raemall, who was exiled to Idar for what his father deemed an impertinent curiosity,[3] had attached one of these bards to his suite, whose ingenuity got the edict set aside, and his race restored to their lands and the prince's favour. Had they taken off the Brahman's head, they might have falsified the prediction which unhappily was too soon fulfilled.[4]

[1] Jodha laid the foundation of his new capital in S. 1515 [A.D. 1459], ten years anterior to the event we are recording.

[2] [See p. 268 above.]

[3] He had observed that his father, ever since the victory over the king at Jhunjhunu, before he took a seat, thrice waved his sword in circles over his head, pronouncing at the same time some incantation. Inquiry into the meaning of this was the cause of his banishment.

[4] During the rains of 1820, when the author was residing at Udaipur, the Rana fell ill; his complaint was an intermittent (which for several years returned with the monsoon), at the same time that he was jaundiced with

Rāna Rāemall, A.D. 1473-1508.—Raemall succeeded in S. 1530 (A.D. 1474) by his own valour to the seat of Kumbha. He had fought and defeated the usurper, who on this occasion fled to the king of Delhi and offered him a daughter of Mewar. After his death in the manner described, the Delhi monarch, with Sahasmall [292] and Surajmall, sons of the parricide, invaded Mewar, encamping at Siarh, now Nathdwara. The chiefs were faithful to their legitimate prince, Raemall, and aided by his allies of Abu and Girnar, at the head of fifty-eight thousand horse and eleven thousand foot, he gave battle to the pretender and his imperial ally at Ghasa. The conflict was ferocious. 'The streams ran blood,' for the sons of the usurper were brave as lions; but the king was so completely routed that he never again entered Mewar.

Raemall bestowed one daughter on Surji (Yadu), the chief of Girnar; and another on the Deora, Jaimall of Sirohi, confirming his title to Abu as her dower. He sustained the warlike reputation of his predecessors, and carried on interminable strife with Ghiyasu-d-din of Malwa, whom he defeated in several pitched battles, to the success of which the valour of his nephews, whom he had pardoned, mainly contributed. In the last of these encounters the Khilji king sued for peace, renouncing the pretensions he had formerly urged.[1] The dynasty of Lodi next enjoyed the imperial bauble, and with it Mewar had to contest her northern boundary.

The Sons of Rāna Rāemall.—Raemall had three sons, celebrated

bile. An intriguing Brahman, who managed the estates of the Rana's eldest sister, held also the twofold office of physician and astrologer to the Rana. He had predicted that year as one of evil in his horoscope, and was about to verify the prophecy, since, instead of the active medicines requisite, he was administering the *Haft dhat*, or 'seven metals,' compounded. Having a most sincere regard for the Rana's welfare, the author seized the opportunity of a full court being assembled on the distribution of swords and coco-nuts preparatory to the military festival, to ask a personal favour. The Rana, smiling, said that it was granted, when he was entreated to leave off the poison he was taking. He did so; the amendment was soon visible, and, aided by the medicines of Dr. Duncan, which he readily took, his complaint was speedily cured. The 'man of fate and physic' lost half his estates, which he had obtained through intrigue. He was succeeded by Amra the bard, who is not likely to ransack the pharmacopoeia for such poisonous ingredients; his ordinary prescription being the 'amrit.'

[1] [Ferishta does not mention these campaigns (iv. 236 ff.), and Ghiyāsu-d-din (A.D. 1469–99) is said to have spent his life in luxury and never to have left his palace (*BG*, i. Part i. 362 ff.).]

in the annals of Rajasthan: Sanga, the competitor of Babur, Prithiraj, the Rolando of his age, and Jaimall. Unhappily for the country and their father's repose, fraternal affection was discarded for deadly hate, and their feuds and dissensions were a source of constant alarm. Had discord not disunited them, the reign of Raemall would have equalled any of his predecessors. As it was, it presented a striking contrast to them: his two elder sons banished; the first, Sanga, self-exiled from perpetual fear of his life, and Prithiraj, the second, from his turbulence; while the youngest, Jaimall, was slain through his intemperance. A sketch of these feuds will present a good picture of the Rajput character, and their mode of life when their arms were not required against their country's foes.

Sanga[1] and Prithiraj were the offspring of the Jhali queen; Jaimall was by another mother. What moral influence the name he bore had on Prithiraj we can surmise only from his actions, which would stand comparison with those of his prototype [293] the Chauhan of Delhi, and are yet the delight of the Sesodia. When they assemble at the feast after a day's sport, or in a sultry evening spread the carpet on the terrace to inhale the leaf or take a cup of kusumbha,[2] a tale of Prithiraj recited by the bard is the highest treat they can enjoy. Sanga, the heir-apparent, was a contrast to his brother. Equally brave, his courage was tempered by reflection; while Prithiraj burned with a perpetual thirst for action, and often observed "that fate must have intended him to rule Mewar." The three brothers, with their uncle, Surajmall, were one day discussing these topics, when Sanga observed that, though heir to 'the ten thousand towns' of Mewar, he would waive his claims, and trust them, as did the Roman brothers, to the omen which should be given by the priestess of Charani Devi at Nahra Magra,[3] the 'Tiger's Mount.' They repaired to her abode. Prithiraj and Jaimall entered first, and seated themselves on a pallet: Sanga followed and took possession of the panther hide of the prophetess; his uncle, Surajmall, with one knee resting thereon. Scarcely had Prithiraj disclosed their errand, when the sibyl pointed to the panther-hide[4] as the decisive omen

[1] His name classically is Sangram Singh, 'the lion of war.'

[2] [Infusion of opium.]

[3] About ten miles east of Udaipur.

[4] *Singhasan* is the ancient term for the Hindu throne, signifying 'the

of sovereignty to Sanga, with a portion to his uncle. They received the decree as did the twins of Rome. Prithiraj drew his sword and would have falsified the omen, had not Surajmall stepped in and received the blow destined for Sanga, while the prophetess fled from their fury. Surajmall and Prithiraj were exhausted with wounds, and Sanga fled with five sword-cuts and an arrow in his eye, which destroyed the sight for ever. He made for the sanctuary of Chaturbhuja, and passing Sivanti, took refuge with Bida (Udawat), who was accoutred for a journey, his steed standing by him. Scarcely had he assisted the wounded heir of Mewar to alight when Jaimall galloped up in pursuit. The Rathor guarded the sanctuary, and gave up his life in defence of his guest, who meanwhile escaped.

Retirement of Sanga.—Prithiraj recovered from his wounds; and Sanga, aware of his implacable enmity, had recourse to many expedients to avoid discovery. He, who at a future period leagued a hundred thousand men against the descendant of Timur, was compelled to associate with goat-herds, expelled the peasant's abode as too stupid [294] to tend his cattle, and, precisely like our Alfred the Great, having in charge some cakes of flour, was reproached with being more desirous of eating than tending them. A few faithful Rajputs found him in this state, and, providing him with arms and a horse, they took service with Rao Karamchand, Pramar, chief of Srinagar,[1] and with him 'ran the country.' After one of these raids, Sanga one day alighted under a banian tree, and placing his dagger under his head, reposed, while two of his faithful Rajputs, whose names are preserved,[2] prepared his repast, their steeds grazing by them. A ray of the sun penetrating the foliage, fell on Sanga's face, and discovered a snake, which, feeling the warmth, had uncoiled itself and was rearing its crest over the head of the exile:[3] a bird of omen[4] had perched itself

lion-seat.' Charans, bards, who are all *Maharajas*, 'great princes,' by courtesy, have their seats of the hide of the lion, tiger, panther, or black antelope.

[1] Nearly ten miles south-east of Ajmer.

[2] Jai Singh Baleo and Jaimu Sindhal.

[3] [A common folk-tale, told of Malhar Rāo Holkar and many other princes (Crooke, *Popular Religion Northern India*, ii. 142; Malcolm, *Memoir of Central India*, 2nd ed. i. 143 f.; E. S. Hartland, *Ritual and Belief*, 323 f.).]

[4] Called the *devi*, about the size of the wagtail, and like it, black and white.

on the crested serpent, and was chattering aloud. A goat-herd named Maru, 'versed in the language of birds,' passed at the moment Sanga awoke. The prince repelled the proffered homage of the goat-herd, who, however, had intimated to the Pramara chief that he was served by 'royalty.'[1] The Pramara kept the secret, and gave Sanga a daughter to wife, and protection till the tragical end of his brother called him to the throne.

The Adventures of Prithirāj.—When the Rana heard of the quarrel which had nearly deprived him of his heir, he banished Prithiraj, telling him that he might live on his bravery and maintain himself with strife. With but five horse[2] Prithiraj quitted the paternal abode, and made for Bali in Godwar. These dissensions following the disastrous conclusion of the last reign, paralysed the country, and the wild tribes of the west and the mountaineers of the Aravalli so little respected the garrison of Nadol (the chief town of Godwar), that they carried their depredations to the plains. Prithiraj halted at Nadol, and having to procure some necessaries pledged a ring to the merchant who had sold it to him; the merchant recognized the prince, and learning the cause of his disguise, proffered his services in the scheme which the prince had in view for the restoration of order in Godwar, being determined to evince to his father that he had resources independent of birth. The Minas were the aboriginal proprietors of all these regions; the Rajputs were interlopers and conquerors. A Rawat of this tribe had regained their ancient haunts, and held his petty court at the [295] town of Narlai in the plains, and was even served by Rajputs. By the advice of Ojha, the merchant, Prithiraj enlisted himself and his band among the adherents of the Mina. On the Aheria, or 'hunter's festival,' the vassals have leave to rejoin their families. Prithiraj, who had also obtained leave, rapidly retraced his steps, and despatching his Rajputs to dislodge the Mina, awaited the result in ambush at the gate of the town. In a short time the Mina appeared on horseback, and in full flight to the mountains for security. Prithiraj pursued, overtook, and transfixed him with his lance to a kesula tree, and setting fire to the village, he slew the Minas as they sought to escape the flames. Other towns shared the same fate, and all the

[1] Chhatrdhāri.

[2] The names of his followers were, Jasa Sindhal, Sangam (Dabhi), Abha, Jana, and a Badel Rathor.

province of Godwar, with the exception of Desuri, a stronghold of the Madrecha Chauhans, fell into his power. At this time Sada Solanki, whose ancestor had escaped the destruction of Patan and found refuge in these mountainous tracts, held Sodhgarh. He had espoused a daughter of the Madrecha, but the grant of Desuri and its lands [1] in perpetuity easily gained him to the cause of Prithiraj.

Prithiraj having thus restored order in Godwar, and appointed Ojha and the Solanki to the government thereof, regained the confidence of his father; and his brother Jaimall being slain at this time, accelerated his forgiveness and recall. Ere he rejoins Raemall we will relate the manner of this event. Jaimall was desirous to obtain the hand of Tara Bai, daughter of Rao Surthan,[2] who had been expelled Toda by the Pathans. The price of her hand was the recovery of this domain: but Jaimall, willing to anticipate the reward, and rudely attempting access to the fair, was slain by the indignant father. The quibbling remark of the bard upon this event is that "Tara was not the star (*tara*) of his destiny." At the period of this occurrence Sanga was in concealment, Prithiraj banished, and Jaimall consequently looked to as the heir of Mewar. The Rana, when incited to revenge, replied with a magnanimity which deserves to be recorded, "that he who had thus dared to insult the honour of a [296] father, and that father in distress, richly merited his fate"; and in proof of his disavowal of such a son he conferred on the Solanki the district of Badnor.

Prithirāj recalled.—This event led to the recall of Prithiraj, who eagerly took up the gage disgraced by his brother. The adventure was akin to his taste. The exploit which won the hand of the fair Amazon, who, equipped with bow and quiver, subsequently accompanied him in many perilous enterprises, will be elsewhere related.

[1] The grant in the preamble denounces a curse on any of Prithiraj's descendants who should resume it. I have often conversed with this descendant, who held Sodhgarh and its lands, which were never resumed by the princes of Chitor, though they reverted to Marwar. The chief still honours the Rana, and many lives have been sacrificed to maintain his claims, and with any prospect of success he would not hesitate to offer his own.

[2] This is a genuine Hindu name, 'the Hero's refuge,' from *sur*, 'a warrior,' and *than*, 'an abode.'

Surajmall (the uncle), who had fomented these quarrels, resolved not to belie the prophetess if a crown lay in his path. The claims acquired from his parricidal parent were revived when Mewar had no sons to look to. Prithiraj on his return renewed the feud with Surajmall, whose 'vaulting ambition' persuaded him that the crown was his destiny, and he plunged deep into treason to obtain it. He joined as partner in his schemes Sarangdeo, another descendant of Lakha Rana, and both repaired to Muzaffar, the sultan of Malwa.[1] With his aid they assailed the southern frontier, and rapidly possessed themselves of Sadri, Bataro, and a wide tract extending from Nai to Nimach, attempting even Chitor. With the few troops at hand Raemall descended to punish the rebels, who met the attack on the river Gambhir.[2] The Rana, fighting like a common soldier, had received two-and-twenty wounds, and was nearly falling through faintness, when Prithiraj joined him with one thousand fresh horse, and reanimated the battle. He selected his uncle Surajmall, whom he soon covered with wounds. Many had fallen on both sides, but neither party would yield; when worn out they mutually retired from the field, and bivouacked in sight of each other.

Interview between Prithirāj and Sūrajmall.—It will show the manners and feelings so peculiar to the Rajput, to describe the meeting between the rival uncle and nephew,—unique in the details of strife, perhaps, since the origin of man. It is taken from a MS. of the Jhala chief who succeeded Surajmall in Sadri. Prithiraj visited his uncle, whom he found in a small tent reclining on a pallet, having just had 'the barber' (*nai*) to sew up his wounds. He rose, and met his nephew with the customary respect, as if nothing unusual had occurred; but the exertion caused some of the wounds to open afresh, when the following dialogue ensued:

Prithiraj.—" Well, uncle, how are your wounds ? "

Surajmall.—" Quite healed, my child, since I have the pleasure of seeing you " [297].

Prithiraj.—" But, uncle (*kaka*), I have not yet seen the Diwanji.[3] I first ran to see you, and I am very hungry; have you anything to eat ? "

[1] [There is an error here: there was no contemporary Sultan of Mālwa of this name.]

[2] Near Chitor.

[3] 'Regent'; the title the Rana is most familiarly known by.

Dinner was soon served, and the extraordinary pair sat down and 'ate off the same platter';[1] nor did Prithiraj hesitate to eat the *pan*,[2] presented on his taking leave.

Prithiraj.—" You and I will end our battle in the morning, uncle."

Surajmall.—" Very well, child; come early!"

They met; but Sarangdeo bore the brunt of the conflict, receiving thirty-five wounds. During "four gharis[3] swords and lances were plied, and every tribe of Rajput lost numbers that day"; but the rebels were defeated and fled to Sadri, and Prithiraj returned in triumph, though with seven wounds, to Chitor. The rebels, however, did not relinquish their designs, and many personal encounters took place between the uncle and nephew: the latter saying he would not let him retain "as much land of Mewar as would cover a needle's point"; and Suja[4] retorting, that he would allow his nephew to redeem only as much "as would suffice to lie upon." But Prithiraj gave them no rest, pursuing them from place to place. In the wilds of Batara they formed a stockaded retreat of the dhao tree,[5] which abounds in these forests. Within this shelter, horses and men were intermingled: Suja and his coadjutor communing by the night-fire in their desperate plight, when their cogitations were checked by the rush and neigh of horses. Scarcely had the pretender exclaimed "This must be my nephew!" when Prithiraj dashed his steed through the barricade and entered with his troops. All was confusion, and the sword showered its blows indiscriminately. The young prince reached his uncle, and dealt him a blow which would have levelled him, but for the support of Sarangdeo, who upbraided him, adding that "a buffet now was more than a score of wounds in former days": to which Suja rejoined, "only when dealt by my nephew's hand." Suja demanded a parley; and calling on the prince to stop the combat, he continued: "If I am killed, it matters not—my children are Rajputs, they will run the [298] country to find support; but if you are slain, what

[1] *Thali*, 'a brass platter.' This is the highest mark of confidence and friendship.

[2] This compound of the betel or areca-nut, cloves, mace, *Terra japonica*, and prepared lime, is always taken after meals, and has not unfrequently been a medium for administering poison.

[3] Hours of twenty-two minutes each.

[4] Familiar contraction of Surajmall.

[5] [*Anogeissus latifolia*.]

will become of Chitor? My face will be blackened, and my name everlastingly reprobated."

The sword was sheathed, and as the uncle and nephew embraced, the latter asked the former, "What were you about, uncle, when I came?"—"Only talking nonsense, child, after dinner." "But with me over your head, uncle, as a foe how could you be so negligent?"—"What could I do? you had left me no resource, and I must have some place to rest my head!" There was a small temple near the stockade, to which in the morning Prithiraj requested his uncle to accompany him to sacrifice to Kali,[1] but the blow of the preceding night prevented him. Sarangdeo was his proxy. One buffalo had fallen, and a goat was about to follow, when the prince turned his sword on Sarangdeo. The combat was desperate; but Prithiraj was the victor, and the head of the traitor was placed as an offering on the altar of Time. The Gaunda[2] was plundered, the town of Batara recovered, and Surajmall fled to Sadri, where he only stopped to fulfil his threat, "that if he could not retain its lands he would make them over to those stronger than the king";[3] and having distributed them amongst Brahmans and bards, he finally abandoned Mewar. Passing through the wilds of Kanthal,[4] he had an omen which recalled the Charani's prediction: "a wolf endeavouring in vain to carry off a kid defended by maternal affection." This was interpreted as 'strong ground for a dwelling.' He halted, subdued the aboriginal tribes, and on this spot erected the town and stronghold of Deolia, becoming lord of a thousand villages, which have descended to his offspring, who now enjoy them under British protection. Such was the origin of Partabgarh Deolia.[5]

[1] The Hindu Proserpine, or Calligenia. Is this Grecian handmaid of Hecate also Hindu, 'born of time' (*Kali-janama*)? [Καλλιγένεια, 'bearer of fair offspring,' has, of course, no connexion with Kāli.]

[2] Gaunda, or Gaunra, is the name of such temporary places of refuge; the origin of towns bearing this name.

[3] Such grants are irresumable, under the penalty of sixty thousand years in hell. This fine district is eaten up by these mendicant Brahmans. One town alone, containing 52,000 bighas (about 15,000 acres) of rich land, is thus lost; and by such follies Mewar has gradually sunk to her present extreme poverty.

[4] [Kānthal, in Partābgarh State, is the boundary (*Kāntha*) between Mewār on the north, Bāgar on the west, and Mālwa on the east and south.]

[5] [The statement in the text that Sūrajmall, son of Uda, retired to

Prithirāj poisoned: Death of Rāna Rāemall.—Prithiraj was poisoned by his brother-in-law, of Abu, whom he had punished for maltreating his sister, and afterwards confided in. His death was soon followed by that of Rana Raemall, who, though not equal to his predecessors, was greatly respected, and maintained the dignity of his station amidst no ordinary calamities [290].[1]

CHAPTER 9

Rāna Sanga or Sangrām Singh; A.D. 1508-27.—Sangram, better known in the annals of Mewar as Sanga (called Sanka by the Mogul historians),[2] succeeded in S. 1565 (A.D. 1509). With this prince Mewar reached the summit of her prosperity. To use their own metaphor, "he was the kalas[3] on the pinnacle of her glory." From him we shall witness this glory on the wane; and though many rays of splendour illuminated her declining career, they served but to gild the ruin.

The imperial chair, since occupied by the Tuar descendant of the Pandus, and the first and last of the Chauhans, and which had been filled successively by the dynasties of Ghazni and Ghor, the Khilji and Lodi, was now shivered to pieces, and numerous petty thrones were constructed of its fragments. Mewar little dreaded these imperial puppets, "when Amurath to Amurath succeeded," and when four kings reigned simultaneously between Delhi and Benares.[4] The kings of Malwa, though leagued with those of Gujarat, conjoined to the rebels, could make no impression on Mewar when Sanga led her heroes. Eighty thousand horse, seven Rajas of the highest rank, nine Raos, and one hundred and four chieftains bearing the titles of Rawal and Rawat, with five hundred war elephants, followed him into the field. The princes of Marwar and Amber[5] did him homage, and the Raos of Gwalior

---

Deolia is incorrect. Sūrajmall was first-cousin, not son of Uda, and it was his great-grandson, Bīka, who conquered the Kānthal and founded the town of Deolia at least fifty years later (Erskine ii. A. 197).]

[1] The walls of his palace are still pointed out.

[2] [*Āīn*, ii. 270.]

[3] The ball or urn which crowns the pinnacle (*sikhar*).

[4] Delhi, Bayana, Kalpi, and Jaunpur.

[5] Prithiraj was yet but Rao of Amber, a name now lost in Jaipur. The

Ajmer, Sikri, Raesen,[1] Kalpi, Chanderi [300], Bundi, Gagraun, Rampura, and Abu, served him as tributaries or held of him in chief.

Sanga did not forget those who sheltered him in his reverses. Karamchand of Srinagar had a grant of Ajmer and the title of Rao for his son Jagmall, the reward of his services in the reduction of Chanderi.

The Administration and Wars of Rāna Sanga.—In a short space of time, Sanga entirely allayed the disorders occasioned by the intestine feuds of his family; and were it permitted to speculate on the cause which prompted a temporary cession of his rights and his dignities to his more impetuous brother, it might be discerned in a spirit of forecast, and of fraternal and patriotic forbearance, a deviation from which would have endangered the country as well as the safety of his family. We may assume this, in order to account for an otherwise pusillanimous surrender of his birthright, and being in contrast to all the subsequent heroism of his life, which, when he resigned, was contained within the wreck of a form. Sanga organized his forces, with which he always kept the field, and ere called to contend with the descendant of Timur, he had gained eighteen pitched battles against the kings of Delhi and Malwa. In two of these he was opposed by Ibrahim Lodi in person, at Bakrol and Ghatoli, in which last battle the imperial forces were defeated with great slaughter, leaving a prisoner of the blood royal to grace the triumph of Chitor. The Pilakhal (yellow rivulet) near Bayana became the northern boundary of Mewar, with the Sind River to the east,—touching Malwa to the south, while his native hills were an impenetrable barrier to the west. Thus swaying, directly or by control, the greater part of Rajasthan, and adored by the Rajputs for the possession of those qualities they hold in estimation, Sanga was ascending to the pinnacle of distinction; and had not fresh hordes of Usbeks and Tatars from the prolific shores of the Oxus and Jaxartes again poured down on the devoted plains

twelve sons of this prince formed the existing subdivisions or clans of the Kachhwahas, whose political consequence dates from Humayun, the son and successor of Babur.

[1] [Sīkri, afterwards Fatehpur Sīkri, the site of Akbar's palace; Rāēsen in Bhopāl State (*IGI*, xxi. 62 f.).]

of Hindustan, the crown of the Chakravartin [1] might again have encircled the brow of a Hindu, and the banner of supremacy been transferred from Indraprastha to the battlements of Chitor. But Babur arrived at a critical time to rally the dejected followers of the Koran, and to collect them around his own victorious standard.

Invasions from Central Asia.—From the earliest recorded periods of her history, India has been the prey of [301] the more hardy population from the central regions of Asia. From this fact we may infer another, namely, that its internal form of government was the same as at the present day, partitioned into numerous petty kingdoms, of tribes and clans, of a feudal federation, a prey to all the jealousies inseparable from such a condition. The historians of Alexander bear ample testimony to such form of government, when the Panjab alone possessed many sovereigns, besides the democracies of cities. The Persians overran it, and Darius the Mede accounted India the richest of his satrapies. The Greeks, the Parthians have left in their medals the best proofs of their power ; the Getae or Yuti followed ; and from the Ghori Shihabu-d-din to the Chagatai Babur, in less than three centuries, five invasions are recorded, each originating a dynasty. Sanga's opponent was the last, and will continue so until the rays of knowledge renovate the ancient nursery of the human race,—then may end the anomaly in the history of power, of a handful of Britons holding the succession to the Mede, the Parthian, and the Tatar. But, however surprise may be excited at witnessing such rapidity of change, from the physical superiority of man over man, it is immeasurably heightened at the little moral consequence which in every other region of the world has always attended such concussions. Creeds have changed, races have mingled, and names have been effaced from the page of history ; but in this corner of civilization we have no such result, and the Rajput remains the same singular being, concentrated in his prejudices, political and moral, as in the days of Alexander, desiring no change himself, and still less to cause any in others. Whatever be the conservative principle, it merits a philosophic analysis ; but more, a proper application and direction, by those to whom the destinies of this portion of the globe are confided ;

[1] Universal potentate: ["he whose chariot wheels run everywhere without obstruction"]; the Hindus reckon only six of these in their history.

for in this remote spot there is a nucleus of energy, on which may accumulate a mass for our support or our destruction.

To return : a descendant of the Turushka of the Jaxartes, the ancient foe of the children of Surya and Chandra, was destined to fulfil the prophetic Purana which foretold dominion "to the Turushka, the Yavan," and other foreign races in Hind ; and the conquered made a right application of the term Turk, both as regards its ancient and modern signification, when applied to the conquerors from Turkistan. Babur, the opponent of Sanga, was king of Ferghana, and of Turki race. His dominions were on both sides the Jaxartes, a portion of ancient [302] Sakatai, or Sakadwipa (Scythia), where dwelt Tomyris the Getic queen immortalized by Herodotus, and where her opponent erected Cyropolis, as did in after-times the Macedonian his most remote Alexandria. From this region did the same Getae, Jat, or Yuti, issue, to the destruction of Bactria, two centuries before the Christian era, and also five subsequent thereto to found a kingdom in Northern India. Again, one thousand years later, Babur issued with his bands to the final subjugation of India. As affecting India alone, this portion of the globe merits deep attention ; but as the *officina gentium*, whence issued those hordes of Asii, Jats, or Yeuts (of whom the Angles were a branch), who peopled the shores of the Baltic, and the precursors of those Goths who, under Attila and Alaric, altered the condition of Europe, its importance is vastly enhanced.[1] But on this occasion it was not redundant population which made the descendant of Timur and Jenghiz abandon the Jaxartes for the Ganges, but unsuccessful ambition : for Babur quitted the delights of Samarkand as a fugitive, and commenced his enterprise, which gave him the throne of the Pandus, with less than two thousand adherents.

Character of Bābur.—The Rajput prince had a worthy antagonist in the king of Ferghana. Like Sanga, he was trained in the school of adversity, and like him, though his acts of personal heroism were even romantic, he tempered it with that discretion which looks to its results. In A.D. 1494, at the tender age of twelve, he succeeded to a kingdom ; ere he was sixteen he defeated several confederacies and conquered Samarkand, and in two short years again lost and regained it. His life was a tissue

[1] [As usual, the Indian Jāts are identified with the Getae, Iutae or Iuti, Jutes of Bede.]

of successes and reverses; at one moment hailed lord of the chief kingdoms of Transoxiana; at another flying, unattended, or putting all to hazard in desperate single combats, in one of which he slew five champions of his enemies. Driven at length from Ferghana, in despair he crossed the Hindu-Kush, and in 1519 the Indus. Between the Panjab and Kabul he lingered seven years, ere he advanced to measure his sword with Ibrahim of Delhi. Fortune returned to his standard; Ibrahim was slain, his army routed and dispersed, and Delhi and Agra opened their gates to the fugitive king of Ferghana. His reflections on success evince it was his due: "Not to me, O God! but to thee, be the victory!" says the chivalrous Babur. A year had elapsed in possession of Delhi, ere he ventured against the most powerful of his antagonists, Rana Sanga of Chitor.

With all Babur's qualities as a soldier, supported by the hardy clans of the 'cloud mountains' (*Belut Tagh*) [303] of Karateghin,[1]

[1] [The author borrows from Elphinstone, *Caubul*, i. 118.] The literary world is much indebted to Mr. Erskine for his *Memoirs of Baber*, a work of a most original stamp and rare value for its extensive historical and geographical details of a very interesting portion of the globe. The king of Ferghana, like Caesar, was the historian of his own conquests, and unites all the qualities of the romantic troubadour to those of the warrior and statesman. It is not saying too much when it is asserted, that Mr. Erskine is the only person existing who could have made such a translation, or preserved the great charm of the original—its elevated simplicity; and though his modesty makes him share the merit with Dr. Leyden, it is to him the public thanks are due. Mr. Erskine's introduction is such as might have been expected from his well-known erudition and research, and with the notes interspersed adds immensely to the value of the original. [A new translation by Mrs. Beveridge is in course of publication.] With his geographical materials, those of Mr. Elphinstone, and the journal of the *Voyage d'Orenbourg à Bokhara*, full of merit and modesty, we now possess sufficient materials for the geography of the nursery of mankind. I would presume to amend one valuable geographical notice (Introd. p. 27), and which only requires the permutation of a vowel, Kas-*mer* for Kas-*mir*; when we have, not 'the country of the Kas,' but the *Kasia Montes* (mer) of Ptolemy: the Kho (*mer*) Kas, or *Caucasus*. *Mir* has no signification, *Mer* is 'mountain' in Sanskrit, as is *Kho* in Persian. [The origin of the name Kashmīr is very doubtful: but the view in the text cannot be accepted (see Stein, *Rājatarangini*, ii. 353, 386; Smith, *EHI*, 38, note; *IA*, xliii. 143 ff.).] *Kas* was the race inhabiting these: and *Kasgar*, the Kasia Regio of Ptolemy [Chap. 15]. *Gar* [or *garh*] is a Sanskrit word still in use for a 'region,' as *Kachhwahagar*, *Gujargar*. [See Elliot, *Supplementary Glossary*, 237.] A new edition of Erskine's translation, edited by Professor White King, is in course of publication.

RUINS OF THE FORTRESS OF BAYĀNA.

To face page 352.

the chances were many that he and they terminated their career on the 'yellow rivulet' of Bayana. Neither bravery nor skill saved him from this fate, which he appears to have expected. What better proof can be desired than Babur's own testimony to the fact, that a horde of invaders from the Jaxartes, without support or retreat, were obliged to entrench themselves to the teeth in the face of their Rajput foe, alike brave and overpowering in numbers? To ancient jealousies he was indebted for not losing his life instead of gaining a crown, and for being extricated from a condition so desperate that even the frenzy of religion, which made death martyrdom in "this holy war," scarcely availed to expel the despair which so infected his followers, that in the bitterness of his heart he says "there was not a single person who uttered a manly word, nor an individual who delivered a courageous opinion."

The Battle of Khānua, March 16, 1527.—Babur advanced from Agra and Sikri to oppose Rana Sanga, in full march to attack him at the head of almost all the princes of Rajasthan. Although the annals state some points which the imperial historian has not recorded, yet both accounts of the conflict correspond in all the essential details. On the 5th of Kartik, S. 1584 [1] (A.D. 1528), according to the annals, the Rana raised the siege of Bayana, and at Khanua encountered the advanced guard of the Tatars, amounting to fifteen hundred men, which was entirely destroyed; the fugitives carrying to the main body the accounts of the disaster, which paralysed their energies, and made them entrench for security, instead of advancing with the confidence of victory. Reinforcements met the same fate, and were pursued to the camp. Accustomed to reverses, Babur met the check without dismay, and adopted every precaution [304] that a mind fertile in expedients could suggest to reassure the drooping spirits of his troops. He threw up entrenchments, in which he placed his artillery, connecting his guns by chains, and in the more exposed parts *chevaux de frise*, united by leather ropes: a precaution

[1] According to the *Memoirs of Baber*, February 11, 1527. [The battle was fought at Khānua or Kanwāha, now in the Bharatpur State, about twenty miles from Agra (Abu-l Fazl, *Akbarnāma*, i. 259 f.; Ferishta ii. 55), on March 16, 1527. Ferishta says that the provocation came from Rāna Sanga, who attacked Nāzim Khān, Governor of Bayāna, on which the latter appealed to Bābur (ii. 51). Bābur says that Sanga broke his engagement (Elliot-Dowson iv. 264; Badaoni, *Muntakhabu-t-tawārīkh*, i. 444, 470).]

continued in every subsequent change of position. Everything seemed to aid the Hindu cause: even the Tatar astrologer asserted that as Mars was in the west, whoever should engage coming from the opposite quarter should be defeated. In this state of total inactivity, blockaded in his encampment, Babur remained near a fortnight, when he determined to renounce his besetting sin, and merit superior aid to extricate himself from his peril: the *naïveté* of his vow must be given in his own words.[1]

[1] "On Monday, the 23rd of the first Jemadi, I had mounted to survey my posts, and in the course of my ride was seriously struck with the reflection, that I had always resolved, one time or another, to make an effectual repentance, and that some traces of a hankering after the renunciation of forbidden works had ever remained in my heart: I said to myself, 'O, my soul.'

(*Persian Verse.*)

"'How long wilt thou continue to take pleasure in sin?
Repentance is not unpalatable—taste it.

(*Turki Verse.*)

"'How great has been thy defilement from sin!
How much pleasure thou didst take in despair!
How long hast thou been the slave of thy passions!
How much of thy life hast thou thrown away!
Since thou hast set out on a holy war,
Thou hast seen death before thine eyes for thy salvation.
He who resolves to sacrifice his life to save himself
Shall attain that exalted state which thou knowest.
Keep thyself far away from all forbidden enjoyments;
Cleanse thyself from all thy sins.'

"Having withdrawn myself from such temptation, I vowed never more to drink wine. Having sent for the gold and silver goblets and cups, with all the other utensils used for drinking parties, I directed them to be broken, and renounced the use of wine, purifying my mind. The fragments of the goblets and other utensils of gold and silver I directed to be divided among derwishes and the poor. The first person who followed me in my repentance was Asas, who also accompanied me in my resolution of ceasing to cut the beard, and of allowing it to grow. That night and the following, numbers of Amirs and courtiers, soldiers, and persons not in the service, to the number of nearly three hundred men, made vows of reformation. The wine which we had with us we poured on the ground. I ordered that the wine brought by Baba Dost should have salt thrown into it, that it might be made into vinegar. On the spot where the wine had been poured out I directed a wāīn to be sunk and built of stone, and close by the wāīn an almshouse to be erected. In the month of Moharrem in the year 935, when I went to visit Gualiar, in my way from Dholpur to Sikri, I found this wāīn completed. I had previously made a vow, that if I gained the victory over Rana Sanka the Pagan, I would remit the Temgha (or stamp-tax) levied from Musulmans.

But the destruction of the wine flasks would appear only to have added to the existing consternation, and made him, as a last resort, appeal to their faith. Having addressed them in a speech of [305] manly courage, though bordering on despair, he seized the happy moment that his exhortation elicited, to swear them on the Koran to conquer or perish.[1] Profiting by this excitement, he broke up his camp, to which he had been confined nearly a month, and marched in order of battle to a position two miles in advance, the Rajputs skirmishing up to his guns. With-

At the time when I made my vow of penitence, Derwish Muhammed Sarban and Sheikh Zin put me in mind of my promise. I said, 'You did right to remind me of this: I renounce the tomgha in all my dominions, so far as concerns Musulmans'; and I sent for my secretaries, and desired them to write and send to all my dominions firmans conveying intelligence of the two important incidents that had occurred" (*Memoirs of Baber*, p. 354). [Elliot-Dowson iv. 269.]

[1] "At this time, as I have already observed, in consequence of preceding events, a general consternation and alarm prevailed among great and small. There was not a single person who uttered a manly word, nor an individual who delivered a courageous opinion. The Vazirs, whose duty it was to give good counsel, and the Amirs, who enjoyed the wealth of kingdoms, neither spoke bravely, nor was their counsel or deportment such as became men of firmness. During the whole course of this expedition, Khalifeh conducted himself admirably, and was unremitting and indefatigable in his endeavours to put everything in the best order. At length, observing the universal discouragement of my troops, and their total want of spirit, I formed my plan. I called an assembly of all the Amirs and officers, and addressed them: 'Noblemen and soldiers! Every man that comes into the world is subject to dissolution. When we are passed away and gone, God only survives, unchangeable. Whoever comes to the feast of life must, before it is over, drink from the cup of death. He who arrives at the inn of mortality must one day inevitably take his departure from that house of sorrow, the world. How much better it is to die with honour than to live with infamy!

"'With fame, even if I die, I am contented;
Let fame be mine, since my body is death's.

"'The most high God has been propitious to us, and has now placed us in such a crisis, that if we fall in the field we die the death of martyrs; if we survive, we rise victorious, the avengers of the cause of God. Let us, then, with one accord, swear on God's holy word, that none of us will even think of turning his face from this warfare, nor desert from the battle and slaughter that ensues, till his soul is separated from his body.'

"Master and servant, small and great, all with emulation, seizing the blessed Koran in their hands, swore in the form that I had given. My plan succeeded to admiration, and its effects were instantly visible far and near, on friend and foe" (*Memoirs of Baber*, p. 357).

out a regular circumvallation, his movable pallisadoes and guns chained, he felt no security. The inactivity of Sanga can scarcely escape censure, however we may incline to palliate it by supposing that he deemed his enemy in the toils, and that every day's delay brought with it increased danger to him. Such reasoning would be valid, if the heterogeneous mass by which the prince of Mewar was surrounded had owned the same patriotic sentiments as himself: but he ought to have known his countrymen, nor overlooked the regulating maxim of their ambition, *get land.* Delay was fatal to this last coalition against the foes of his race. Babur is silent on the point to which the annals ascribe their discomfiture, a negotiation pending his blockade at Khanua; but these have preserved it, with the name of the traitor who sold the cause of his country. The negotiation[1] had reached this point, that on condition of Babur being left Delhi and its dependencies, the Pilakhal at Bayana should be the boundary of their respective dominions, and even an annual tribute was offered to the Rana [306]. We can believe that in the position Babur then was, he would not scruple to promise anything. The chief of Raesen, by name Salehdi, of the Tuar tribe, was the medium of communication, and though the arrangement was negatived, treason had effected the salvation of Babur.

On March 16 the attack commenced by a furious onset on the centre and right wing of the Tatars, and for several hours the conflict was tremendous. Devotion was never more manifest on the side of the Rajput, attested by the long list of noble names amongst the slain as well as the bulletin of their foe, whose artillery made dreadful havoc in the close ranks of the Rajput cavalry, which could not force the entrenchments, nor reach the infantry which defended them. While the battle was still doubtful, the Tuar traitor who led the van (*harawal*) went over to Babur, and Sanga was obliged to retreat from the field, which in the onset promised a glorious victory, himself severely wounded and the choicest of his chieftains slain: Rawal Udai[2] Singh of

[1] Babur says, "Although Rana Sanka (Sanga) the Pagan, when I was at Cabul, sent me ambassadors, and had arranged with me that if I would march upon Delhi he would on Agra; but when I took Delhi and Agra, the Pagan did not move" (*Memoirs of Baber*, p. 339).

[2] In the translation of Babur's *Memoirs*, Udai Singh is styled 'Wali of the country,' confounding him with Udai Singh, successor of Sanga.

Dungarpur, with two hundred of his clan; Ratna of Salumbar, with three hundred of his Chondawat kin; Raemall Rathor, son of the prince of Marwar, with the brave Mertia leaders Khetsi and Ratna; Ramdas the Sonigira Rao; Uja the Jhala; Gokuldas Pramara; Manikchand and Chandrbhan, Chauhan chiefs of the first rank in Mewar; besides a host of inferior names.[1] Hasan Khan of Mewat, and a son of the last Lodi king of Delhi, who coalesced with Sanga, were amongst the killed.[2] Triumphal pyramids were raised of the heads of the slain, and on a hillock which overlooked the field of battle a tower of skulls was erected; and the conqueror assumed the title of *Ghazi*, which has ever since been retained by his descendants.

The Death of Rāna Sanga.—Sanga retreated towards the hills of Mewat, having announced his fixed determination never to re-enter Chitor but with victory. Had his life been spared to his country, he might have redeemed the pledge; but the year of his defeat was the last of his existence, and he died at Baswa,[3] on the frontier of Mewat, not without suspicion of poison. It is painful to record the surmise that his ministers prompted the deed, and the cause is one which would fix a deep stain on the country; namely, the purchase by regicide of inglorious ease and stipulated safety, in [307] preference to privations and dangers, and to emulating the manly constancy of their prince, who resolved to make the heavens his canopy till his foe was crushed—a determination which was pursued with the most resolute perseverance by some of his gallant successors.

Evils resulting from Polygamy.—Polygamy is the fertile source of evil, moral as well as physical, in the East. It is a relic of barbarism and primeval necessity, affording a proof that

He was Wali (sovereign) of Dungarpur, not 'Oodipoor,' which was not then in existence. [Erskine, in his later work (*Hist. India*, i. 473, note), admits his error.]

[1] [A list of the slain, nearly identical, is given by Abu-l Fazl, *Akbarnāma*, i. 265.]

[2] [The author confuses Hasan Khān, Mewāti, an important officer (Ferishta ii. 55; Bayley, *Muhammad Dynasties of Gujarāt*, 278), whom Badaoni (*Muntakhabu-t-tawārikh*, i. 447) calls a Jogi in form and appearance, with Hasan Khān, Lodi (*Āīn*, i. 503).]

[3] [About eighty-five miles north-north-west of Jaipur city. Bābur says that he intended to pursue Sanga to Chitor, but was prevented by the defeat of his forces advancing on Lucknow (Elliot-Dowson iv. 277).]

ancient Asia is still young in knowledge. The desire of each wife,[1] that her offspring should wear a crown, is natural; but they do not always wait the course of nature for the attainment of their wishes, and the love of power too often furnishes instruments for any deed, however base. When we see, shortly after the death of Sanga, the mother of his second son intriguing with Babur, and bribing him with the surrender of Ranthambhor and the trophy of victory, the crown of the Malwa king, to supplant the lawful heir, we can easily suppose she would not have scrupled to remove any other bar. On this occasion, however, the suspicion rests on the ministers alone. That Babur respected and dreaded his foe we have the best proof in his not risking another battle with him; and the blame which he bestows on himself for the slackness of his pursuit after victory is honourable to Sanga, who is always mentioned with respect in the commentaries of the conqueror: and although he generally styles him the Pagan, and dignifies the contest with the title of "the holy war," yet he freely acknowledges his merit when he says, "Rana Sanga attained his present high eminence by his own valour and his sword."

Appearance of Rāna Sanga.—Sanga Rana was of the middle stature, but of great muscular strength; fair in complexion, with unusually large eyes, which appear to be peculiar to his descendants.[2] He exhibited at his death but the fragments of a warrior: one eye was lost in the broil with his brother; an arm in an action with the Lodi king of Delhi, and he was a cripple owing to a limb being broken by a cannon-ball in another [308]; while he counted eighty wounds from the sword or the lance on various parts of his body. He was celebrated for energetic

[1] The number of queens is determined only by state necessity and the fancy of the prince. To have them equal in number to the days of the week is not unusual, while the number of *handmaids* is unlimited. It will be conceded that the prince who can govern such a household, and maintain equal rights when claims to pre-eminence must be perpetually asserted, possesses no little tact. The government of the kingdom is but an amusement compared with such a task, for it is within the *Rawala* that intrigue is enthroned.

[2] I possess his portrait, given to me by the present Rana, who has a collection of full-lengths of all his royal ancestors, from Samarsi to himself, of their exact heights and with every bodily peculiarity, whether of complexion or form. They are valuable for the costume. He has often shown them to me while illustrating their actions.

enterprise, of which his capture of Muzaffar, king of Malwa, in his own capital, is a celebrated instance; and his successful storm of the almost impregnable Ranthambhor, though ably defended by the imperial general Ali, gained him great renown. He erected a small palace at Khanua, on the line which he determined should be the northern limit of Mewar; and had he been succeeded by a prince possessed of his foresight and judgment, Babur's descendants might not have retained the sovereignty of India. A cenotaph long marked the spot where the fire consumed the remains of this celebrated prince. Sanga had seven sons, of whom the two elder died in non-age. He was succeeded by the third son,

Rāna Ratan Singh II., A.D. 1527-31.—Ratna (S. 1586, A.D. 1530) possessed all the arrogance and martial virtue of his race. Like his father, he determined to make the field his capital, and commanded that the gates of Chitor never should be closed, boasting that "its portals were Delhi and Mandu." Had he been spared to temper by experience the exuberance of youthful impetuosity, he would have well seconded the resolution of his father, and the league against the enemies of his country and faith. But he was not destined to pass the age always dangerous to the turbulent and impatient Rajput, ever courting strife if it would not find him. He had married by stealth the daughter of Prithiraj of Amber, probably before the death of his elder brothers made him heir to Chitor. His double-edged sword, the proxy of the Rajput cavalier, represented Ratna on this occasion.[1] Unfortunately it was kept but too secret; for the Hara prince of Bundi,[2] in ignorance of the fact, demanded and obtained her to wife, and carried her to his capital. The consequences are attributable to the Rana alone, for he ought, on coming to the throne, to have espoused her; but his vanity was flattered at the mysterious transaction, which he deemed would prevent all application for the hand of his 'affianced' (*manga*). The bards of Bundi are rather pleased to record the power of their

[1] [The practice of sending his sword to represent the bridegroom probably originated in the desire for secrecy, and has since been observed, as among the Rāj Gonds of the Central Provinces, for the sake of convenience, and in order to avoid expense (Forbes, *Rāsmāla*, 624; *BG*, ix. Part i. 143, 145 f.; Russell, *Tribes and Castes, Central Provinces*, iii. 77).]

[2] Surajmall.

princes, who dared to solicit and obtain the hand of the 'bride' of Chitor. The princes of Bundi had long been attached to the Sesodia house: and from the period when their common ancestors fought together on the banks of the Ghaggar against [309] Shihabu-d-din, they had silently grown to power under the wing of Mewar, and often proved a strong plume in her pinion. The Hara inhabited the hilly tract on her eastern frontier, and though not actually incorporated with Mewar, they yet paid homage to her princes, bore her ensigns and titles, and in return often poured forth their blood. But at the tribunal of Ananga,[1] the Rajput scattered all other homage and allegiance to the winds. The maiden of Amber saw no necessity for disclosing her secret or refusing the brave Hara, of whom fame spoke loudly, when Ratna delayed to redeem his proxy.

Death of Rāna Ratan Singh.—The unintentional offence sank deep into the heart of the Rana, and though he was closely connected with the Hara, having married his sister, he brooded on the means of revenge, in the attainment of which he sacrificed his own life as well as that of his rival. The festival of the Aheria[2] (the spring hunt), which has thrice been fatal to the princes of Mewar, gave the occasion, when they fell by each other's weapons. Though Ratna enjoyed the dignity only five years, he had the satisfaction to see the ex-king of Ferghana, now founder of the Mogul dynasty of India, leave the scene before him, and without the diminution of an acre of land to Mewar since the fatal day of Bayana. Rana Ratna was succeeded by his brother,

Rāna Bikramajīt, A.D. **1531–35.**—Bikramajit,[3] in S. 1591 (A.D. 1535). This prince had all the turbulence, without the redeeming qualities of character, which endeared his brother to his subjects; he was insolent, passionate, and vindictive, and utterly regardless of that respect which his proud nobles rigidly exacted. Instead of appearing at their head, he passed his time amongst wrestlers and prize-fighters, on whom and a multitude

[1] The Hindu Cupid, implying 'incorporeal,' from *anga*, 'body,' with the privative prefix '*an*.'

[2] I have given the relation of this duel in the narrative of my journeys on my visit to the cenotaph of Ratna, erected where he fell. It was the pleasure of my life to listen to the traditional anecdotes illustrative of Rajput history on the scenes of their transactions.

[3] The Bhakha orthography for Vikramaditya.

of 'paiks,' or foot soldiers, he lavished those gifts and that approbation, to which the aristocratic Rajput, the equestrian order of Rajasthan, arrogated exclusive right. In this innovation he probably imitated his foes, who had learned the superiority of infantry, despised by the Rajput, who, except in sieges, or when 'they spread the carpet and hamstrung their steeds,' held the foot-soldier very cheap. The use of artillery was now becoming general, and the [310] Muslims soon perceived the necessity of foot for their protection: but prejudice operated longer upon the Rajput, who still curses 'those vile guns,' which render of comparatively little value the lance of many a gallant soldier; and he still prefers falling with dignity from his steed to descending to an equality with his mercenary antagonist.

An open rupture was the consequence of such innovation, and (to use the figurative expression for misrule) 'Papa Bai ka Raj'[1] was triumphant; the police were despised; the cattle carried off by the mountaineers from under the walls of Chitor; and when his cavaliers were ordered in pursuit, the Rana was tauntingly told to send his paiks.

The Attack by Bahādur, Sultān of Gujarāt.—Bahadur, sultan of Gujarat, determined to take advantage of the Rajput divisions, to revenge the disgrace of the defeat and captivity of his predecessor Muzaffar.[2] Reinforced by the troops of Mandu, he marched against the Rana, then encamped at Loicha, in the Bundi territory. Though the force was overwhelming, yet with the high courage which belonged to his house, Bikramajit did not hesitate to give battle; but he found weak defenders in his mercenary paiks, while his vassals and kin not only kept aloof, but marched off in a body to defend Chitor, and the posthumous son of Sanga Rana, still an infant.

[1] The government of Papa Bai, a princess of ancient time, whose mismanaged sovereignty has given a proverb to the Rajput. [Major Luard informs me that Pāpa Bāi is said to have been the daughter of a Rājput of Siddal. She and Shiral Seth, a corn-merchant who, in return for his penances, asked to be made a king for three *ghatikas* (twenty-four minutes each), and gave indiscriminately alms to rich and poor, are bywords for foolish extravagance. She is worshipped at a shrine in Ujjain by all who desire good crops, especially sugar. Another name for such a period of misrule is Harbong kā rāj (Elliot, *Supplemental Glossary*, 466 ff.).]

[2] Taken by Prithiraj and carried to Rana Raemall, who took a large sum of money and seven hundred horses as his ransom.

There is a sanctity in the very name of Chitor, which from the earliest times secured her defenders; and now, when threatened again by 'the barbarian,' such the inexplicable character of the Rajput, we find the heir of Surajmall abandoning his new capital of Deolia, to pour out the few drops which yet circulated in his veins in defence of the abode of his fathers.

'The son of Bundi,' with a brave band of five hundred Haras, also came; as did the Sonigira and Deora Raos of Jalor and Abu, with many auxiliaries from all parts of Rajwara. This was the most powerful effort hitherto made by the sultans of Central India, and European artillerists[1] are recorded in these [311] annals as brought to the subjugation of Chitor. The engineer is styled 'Labri Khan of Fringan,' and to his skill Bahadur was indebted for the successful storm which ensued. He sprung a mine at the 'Bika rock,' which blew up forty-five cubits of the rampart, with the bastion where the brave Haras were posted. The Bundi bards dwell on this incident, which destroyed their prince and five hundred of his kin. Rao Durga, with the Chondawat chieftains Sata and Dudu and their vassals, bravely defended the breach and repelled many assaults; and, to set an example of courageous devotion, the queen-mother Jawahir Bai, of Rathor race, clad in armour, headed a sally in which she was slain. Still the besiegers gained ground, and the

[1] We have, in the poems of Chand, frequent indistinct notices of firearms, especially the nal-gola or *tube*-ball; but whether discharged by percussion or the expansive force of gunpowder is dubious. The poet also repeatedly speaks of "the volcano of the field," giving to understand great guns; but these may be interpolations, though I would not check a full investigation of so curious a subject by raising a doubt. Babur was the first who introduced field guns in the Muhammadan wars, and Bahadur's invasion is the first notice of their application in sieges, for in Alau-d-din's time, in the thirteenth century, he used the catapult or battering-ram, called manjanik. To these guns Babur was indebted for victory over the united cavalry of Rajasthan. They were served by Rumi Khan, probably a Roumeliot, or Syrian Christian. The Franks (Faringis), with Bahadur, must have been some of Vasco di Gama's crew. [For the use of artillery in Mogul times see the full account by Irvine (*Army of the Indian Moghuls*, 113 ff.). Manjanīk is the Greek μάγγανον. Rūmi Khān was an Ottoman Turk, called Khudāwand Khān, who learned the science in Turkish service (Erskine, *Hist. of India*, ii. 49; *Āīn*, i. 441). Akbar is said to have used Chinese artillery, and to have employed English gunners from Surat (Manucci i. 139; Irvine, *op. cit.* 152).]

last council convened was to concert means to save the infant son of Sanga from this imminent peril.

Crowning of a New Rāna.—But Chitor can only be defended by royalty, and again they had recourse to the expedient of crowning a king, as a sacrifice to the dignity of the protecting deity of Chitor. Baghji, prince of Deolia, courted the insignia of destruction; the banner of Mewar floated over him, and the golden sun from its sable field never shone more refulgent than when the *changi*[1] was raised amidst the shouts of her defenders over the head of the son of Surajmall.

The Johar.—The infant, Udai Singh, was placed in safety with Surthan, prince of Bundi,[2] the garrison put on their saffron robes, while materials for the *johar* were preparing. There was little time for the pyre. The bravest had fallen in defending the breach, now completely exposed. Combustibles were quickly heaped up in reservoirs and magazines excavated in the rock, under which gunpowder was strewed. Karnavati, mother of the prince, and sister to the gallant Arjun Hara, led the procession of willing victims to their doom, and thirteen thousand females were thus swept at once from the record of life. The gates were thrown open, and the Deolia chief, at the head of the survivors, with a blind and impotent despair, rushed on his fate [312].

Bahadur must have been appalled at the horrid sight on viewing his conquest;[3] the mangled bodies of the slain, with hundreds in the last agonies from the poniard or poison, awaiting death as less dreadful than dishonour and captivity.[4] To use the emphatic

[1] The *Changi*, the chief insignia of regality in Mewar, is a sun of gold in the centre of a disc of black ostrich feathers or felt, about three feet in diameter, elevated on a pole, and carried close to the prince. It has something of a Scythic cast about it. What *changi* imports I never understood. [Probably Pers. *chang*, 'anything bent.']

[2] The name of the faithful Rajput who preserved Udai Singh, Chakasen Dhundera, deserves to be recorded.

[3] The date, "Jeth sudi 12th, S. 1589," A.D. 1533, and according to Ferishta A.H. 949, A.D. 1532–33. [Chitor was taken in 1534. The *Mirāt-i-Sikandari* states that on March 24, 1533, Bahādur received the promised tribute, and moved his camp from Chitor (Bayley, *Muhammadan Dynasties of Gujarāt*, 372).]

[4] From ancient times, leading the females captive appears to have been the sign of complete victory. Rajput inscriptions often allude to "a conqueror beloved by the wives of his conquered foe," and in the early parts

words of the annalist, "the last day of Chitor had arrived." Every clan lost its chief, and the choicest of their retainers; during the siege and in the storm thirty-two thousand Rajputs were slain. This is the second *sakha* of Chitor.

Bahadur had remained but a fortnight, when the tardy advance of Humayun with his succours warned him to retire.[1] According to the annals, he left Bengal at the solicitation of the queen Karnavati; but instead of following up the spoil-encumbered foe, he commenced a pedantic war of words with Bahadur, punning on the word 'Chitor.' Had Humayun not been so distant, this catastrophe would have been averted, for he was bound by the laws of chivalry, the claims of which he had acknowledged, to defend the queen's cause, whose knight he had become. The relation of the peculiarity of a custom analogous to the taste of the chivalrous age of Europe may amuse. When her Amazonian sister the Rathor queen was slain, the mother of the infant prince took a surer method to shield him in demanding the fulfilment of the pledge given by Humayun when she sent the Rakhi to that monarch.

The Rākhi.—'The festival of the bracelet' (*Rakhi*) is in spring, and whatever its origin, it is one of the few when an intercourse of gallantry of the most delicate nature is established between the fair sex and the cavaliers of Rajasthan. Though the bracelet may be sent by maidens, it is only on occasions of urgent necessity or danger. The Rajput dame bestows with the Rakhi the title of adopted brother; and while its acceptance secures to her all the protection of a *cavalière servente*, scandal itself never suggests any other tie to his devotion. He may hazard his life in her cause, and yet never receive a smile in reward, for he cannot even see the fair object who, as brother of her adoption, has constituted him her defender. But there is a charm in the mystery of such connexion, never endangered by close observation, and the loyal to the fair may well attach a value [313] to the public recognition of being the Rakhi-band Bhai, the 'bracelet-bound brother' of a princess. The intrinsic value of such pledge is

of Scripture the same notion is referred to. The mother of Sisera asks' "Have they not divided the prey; to every man a damsel or two?" (Judges v. 30.)

[1] [Ferishta ii. 75 f. Badaoni says that Humāyūn hesitated to interfere because Bahādur was attacking an infidel (*Muntakhabu-t-tawārīkh*, i. 453 f.).]

never looked to, nor is it requisite it should be costly, though it varies with the means and rank of the donor, and may be of flock silk and spangles, or gold chains and gems. The acceptance of the pledge and its return is by the *kachhli,* or corset, of simple silk or satin, of gold brocade and pearls. In shape or application there is nothing similar in Europe, and as defending the most delicate part of the structure of the fair, it is peculiarly appropriate as an emblem of devotion. A whole province has often accompanied the Kachhli, and the monarch of India was so pleased with this courteous delicacy in the customs of Rajasthan, on receiving the bracelet of the princess Karnavati, which invested him with the title of her brother, and uncle and protector to her infant Udai Singh, that he pledged himself to her service, "even if the demand were the castle of Ranthambhor." Humayun proved himself a true knight, and even abandoned his conquests in Bengal when called on to redeem his pledge and succour Chitor, and the widows and minor sons of Sanga Rana.[1] Humayun had the highest proofs of the worth of those courting his protection; he was with his father Babur in all his wars in India, and at the battle of Bayana his prowess was conspicuous, and is recorded by Babur's own pen. He amply fulfilled his pledge, expelled the foe from Chitor, took Mandu by assault, and, as some revenge for her king's aiding the king of Gujarat, he sent for the Rana Bikramajit, whom, following their own notions of

[1] Many romantic tales are founded on 'the gift of the Rakhi.' The author, who was placed in the enviable situation of being able to do good, and on the most extensive scale, was the means of restoring many of these ancient families from degradation to affluence. The greatest reward he could, and the only one he would, receive, was the courteous civility displayed in many of these interesting customs. He was the Rakhi-band Bhai of, and received 'the bracelet' from, three queens of Udaipur, Bundi, and Kotah, besides Chand Bai, the maiden sister of the Rana; as well as many ladies of the chieftains of rank, with whom he interchanged letters. The sole articles of 'barbaric pearl and gold,' which he conveyed from a country where he was six years supreme, are these testimonies of friendly regard. Intrinsically of no great value, they were presented and accepted in the ancient spirit, and he retains them with a sentiment the more powerful, because he can no longer render them any service. [The Rākhi (Skt. *raksha,* 'protection') is primarily a protective amulet assumed at the full moon of Sāwan (July-August) (Forbes, *Rāsmāla,* 609). It was worn on this date to avert the unhealthiness of the rainy season. Jahāngir and Akbar followed the custom, introduced by their Hindu ladies (Jahangir, *Memoirs,* 246; Badaoni, *op. cit.* ii. 269).]

investiture, he girt with a sword in the captured citadel of his foe.[1]

The Muhammadan historians, strangers to their customs, or the secret motives which caused the emperor to abandon Bengal, ascribe it to the Rana's solicitation ; but we may credit the annals, which are in unison with the chivalrous notions of the Rajputs, into which succeeding monarchs, the great Akbar, his son [314] Jahangir, and Shah Jahan, entered with delight ; and even Aurangzeb, two of whose original letters to the queen-mother of Udaipur are now in the author's possession, and are remarkable for their elegance and purity of diction, and couched in terms perfectly accordant with Rajput delicacy.[2]

Restoration of Bikramajit.—Bikramajit, thus restored to his capital, had gained nothing by adversity ; or, to employ the words of the annalist, "experience had yielded no wisdom." He renewed all his former insolence to his chiefs, and so entirely threw aside his own dignity, and, what is of still greater consequence, the reverence universally shown to old age, as to strike in open court Karamchand of Ajmer, the protector of his father Sanga in his misfortunes. The assembly rose with one accord at this indignity to their order ; and as they retired, the Chondawat leader Kanji, the first of the nobles, exclaimed, "Hitherto, brother chiefs, we have had but a smell of the blossom, but now we shall be obliged to eat the fruit" ; to which the insulted Pramara added, as he hastily retired, "To-morrow its flavour will be known."

Though the Rajput looks up to his sovereign as to a divinity, and is enjoined implicit obedience by his religion, which rewards him accordingly hereafter, yet this doctrine has its limits, and precedents are abundant for deposal, when the acts of the prince may endanger the realm. But there is a bond of love as well as of awe which restrains them, and softens its severity in the paternity of sway ; for these princes are at once the father and king of their people : not in fiction, but reality—for he is the

[1] [Probably policy, rather than romance, caused Humāyūn to interfere.]

[2] He addresses her as "dear and virtuous sister," and evinces much interest in her welfare. We are in total ignorance of the refined sentiment which regulates such a people—our home-bred prejudices deem them beneath inquiry ; and thus indolence and self-conceit combine to deprive the benevolent of a high gratification.

representative of the common ancestor of the aristocracy—the sole lawgiver of Rajasthan.

Death of Rāna Bikramajīt.—Sick of these minors (and they had now a third in prospect), which in a few years had laid prostrate the throne of Mewar, her nobles on leaving their unworthy prince repaired to Banbir, the natural son of the heroic Prithiraj, and offered "to seat him on the throne of Chitor." He had the virtue to resist the solicitation; and it was only on painting the dangers which threatened the country, if its chief at such a period had not their confidence, that he gave his consent. The step between the deposal and death of a king is necessarily short [315], and the cries of the females, which announced the end of Bikramajit, were drowned in the acclamations raised on the elevation of the *changi* over the head of the bastard Banbir.

CHAPTER 10

Rāna Banbīr Singh, A.D. 1535–37.—A few hours of sovereignty sufficed to check those 'compunctious visitings' which assailed Banbir ere he assumed its trappings, with which he found himself so little encumbered that he was content to wear them for life. Whether this was the intention of the nobles who set aside the unworthy son of Sanga, there is abundant reason to doubt; and as he is subsequently branded with the epithet of 'usurper' it was probably limited, though unexpressed, to investing him with the executive authority during the minority of Udai Singh. Banbir, however, only awaited the approach of night to remove with his own hands the obstacle to his ambition.

The Escape of Udai Singh, the Heir.—Udai Singh was about six years of age. "He had gone to sleep after his rice and milk," when his nurse was alarmed by screams from the rawala,[1] and the Bari [2] coming in to take away the remains of the dinner, informed her of the cause, the assassination of the Rana. Aware that one murder was the precursor of another, the faithful nurse put her

[1] The seraglio, or female palace.

[2] Bari, Nai, are names for the barbers, who are the *cuisiniers* of the Rajputs. [The special duty of the Bāri is making leaf-platters from which Hindus eat: he is also a domestic servant, but does not, like the Nāi, work as a barber.]

charge into a fruit basket and, covering it with leaves, she delivered it to the Bari, enjoining him to escape with it from the fort. Scarcely had she time to substitute her own infant in the room of the prince, when Banbir, entering, inquired for him. Her lips refused their office; she pointed to the cradle, and beheld the murderous steel buried in the heart of her babe [316]. The little victim to fidelity was burnt amidst the tears of the rawala, the inconsolable household of their late sovereign, who supposed that their grief was given to the last pledge of the illustrious Sanga. The nurse (*Dhai*) was a Rajputni of the Khichi tribe, her name Panna, or 'the Diamond.' Having consecrated with her tears the ashes of her child, she hastened after that she had preserved. But well had it been for Mewar had the poniard fulfilled its intention, and had the annals never recorded the name of Udai Singh in the catalogue of her princes.

The faithful barber was awaiting the nurse in the bed of the Berach River, some miles west of Chitor, and fortunately the infant had not awoke until he descended the city. They departed for Deolia, and sought refuge with Singh Rao, the successor to Baghji, who fell for Chitor; who dreading the consequence of detection, they proceeded to Dungarpur. Rawal Askaran then ruled this principality, which, as well as Deolia, was not only a branch, but the elder branch, of Chitor. With every wish to afford a shelter, he pleaded the danger which threatened himself and the child in such a feeble sanctuary. Pursuing a circuitous route through Idar, and the intricate valleys of the Aravalli, by the help and with the protection of its wild inmates, the Bhils, she gained Kumbhalmer. The resolution she had formed was bold as it was judicious. She demanded an interview with the governor, Asa Sah his name, of the mercantile tribe of Depra,[1] and a follower of the theistical tenets of the Jains. The interview being granted, she placed the infant in his lap, and bid him "guard the life of his sovereign." He felt perplexed and alarmed: but his mother, who was present, upbraided him for his scruples. "Fidelity," said she, "never looks at dangers or difficulties. He is your master, the son of Sanga, and by God's blessing the result will be glorious." Having thus fulfilled her trust, the faithful Panna

[1] [Dr. Tessitori states that the true form of the name is Dahīpra or Dahīpura, and they seem to be the same as the Depla of Gujarāt, where they are said to have been originally Lohānas (*BG*, ix. Part i. 122).]

withdrew from Kumbhalmer to avoid the suspicion which a Rajputni about a Srawak's [1] child would have occasioned, as the heir of Chitor was declared to be the nephew of the Depra.

The Boyhood of Udai Singh.—Suspicions were often excited regarding Asa's nephew; once, especially, on the anniversary (*samvatsara*) of the governor's father, when "the Rajput guests being in one rank, and the men of wealth in another, young Udai seized a vessel of curds, which no intreaty could prevail on him to relinquish, deriding their threats" [317]. Seven years elapsed before the secret transpired; at length self-revealed, from the same independent bearing. On occasion of a visit from the Sonigira chief, Udai was sent to receive him, and the dignified manner in which he performed the duty convinced the chief 'he was no nephew to the Sah.' Rumour spread the tale, and brought not only the nobles of Mewar, but adjacent chiefs, to hail the son of Sanga Rana. Sahidas of Salumbar, the representative of Chonda, Jaga of Kelwa, Sanga of Bagor, all chiefs of the clans of Chondawat; the Chauhans of Kotharia and Bedla, the Pramar of Bijolia Akhiraj (Sonigira), Prithiraj of Sanchor, and Lunkaran Jethawat, repaired to Kumbhalmer, when all doubt was removed by the testimony of the nurse, and of her coadjutor in the preservation of the child.

Installation of Rāna Udai Singh, A.D. **1537-72.**—A court was formed, when the faithful Asa Sah resigned his trust and placed the prince of Chitor 'in the lap of the Kotharia Chauhan,' as the 'great ancient' [2] among the nobles of Mewar, who was throughout acquainted with the secret, and who, to dissipate the remaining scruples which attached to the infant's preservation, 'ate off the same platter with him.' The Sonigira Rao did not hesitate to affiance to him his daughter, and it was accepted by his advisers, notwithstanding the interdict of Hamir to any intermarriage with the Sonigira, since the insult of giving the widow to his bed. Udai received the tika of Chitor in the castle of Kumbha, and the homage of nearly all the chiefs of Mewar.

The tidings soon reached the usurper, who had not borne his

[1] The laity of the Jain persuasion are so called [*srāvak*, meaning 'a disciple'].

[2] *Bara* 'great,' *būrha* 'aged'; the 'wise elder' of Rajasthan, where old age and dignity are synonymous.

faculties meekly since his advancement; but having seized on the dignity, he wished to ape all the customs of the legitimate monarchs of Chitor, and even had the effrontery to punish as an insult the refusal of one of the proud sons of Chonda to take the *dauna* from his bastard hand.

The Dauna, a Recognition of Legitimacy.—The *dauna*, or *daua*, is a portion of the dish of which the prince partakes, sent by his own hand to whomsoever he honours at the banquet. At the rasora, or refectory, the chiefs who are admitted to dine in the presence of their sovereign are seated according to their rank. The repast is one of those occasions when an easy familiarity is permitted, which, though unrestrained, never exceeds the bounds [318] of etiquette, and the habitual reverence due to their father and prince. When he sends, by the steward of the kitchen, a portion of the dish before him, or a little from his own *kansa*, or plate, all eyes are guided to the favoured mortal, whose good fortune is the subject of subsequent conversation. Though, with the diminished lustre of this house, the *dauna* may have lost its former estimation, it is yet received with reverence; but the extent of this feeling, even so late as the reign of Arsi Rana, the father of the reigning prince, the following anecdote will testify. In the rebellion during this prince's reign, amongst the ancient customs which became relaxed, that of bestowing the *dauna* was included; and the Rana conferring it on the Rathor prince of Kishangarh, the Bijolia chief, one of the sixteen superior nobles of Mewar, rose and left the presence, observing, "Neither the Kachhwaha nor the Rathor has a right to this honour, nor can we, who regard as sanctified even the leavings of your repast, witness this degradation; for the Thakur of Kishangarh is far beneath me." To such extent is this privilege even yet carried, and such importance is attached from habit to the personal character of the princes of Mewar, that the test of regal legitimacy in Rajasthan is admission to eat from the same plate (*kansa*) with the Rana: and to the refusal of this honour to the great Man Singh of Amber may be indirectly ascribed the ruin of Mewar.[1]

It may therefore be conceived with what contempt the haughty nobility of Chitor received the mockery of honour from the hand of this 'fifth son of Mewar'; and the Chondawat chief had the boldness to add to his refusal, "that an honour from the

[1] [On the privilege of eating with the Rāna see p. 213 above.]

hand of a true son of Bappa Rawal became a disgrace when proffered by the offspring of the handmaid Sitalseni." The defection soon became general, and all repaired to the valley of Kumbhalmer to hail the legitimate son of Mewar. A caravan of five hundred horses and ten thousand oxen, laden with merchandise from Cutch, the dower of Banbir's daughter, guarded by one thousand Gaharwar Rajputs, was plundered in the passes : a signal intimation of the decay of his authority, and a timely supply to the celebration of the nuptials of Udai Rana with the daughter of the Rao of Jalor. Though the interdict of Hamir was not forgotten, it was deemed that the insult given by Banbir Sonigira was amply effaced by his successor's redemption of the usurpation of Banbir Sesodia. The marriage was solemnized at Bali, within the limits of Jalor, and the [319] customary offerings were sent or given by all the princes of Rajasthan. Two chiefs only, of any consequence, abstained from attending on their lawful prince on this occasion, the Solanki of Maholi and Maloji of Tana. In attacking them, the bastard was brought into conflict; but Maloji was slain and the Solanki surrendered.

Deposition of Rāna Banbīr Singh.—Deserted by all, Banbir held out in the capital; but his minister admitted, under the garb of a reinforcement with supplies, a thousand resolute adherents of the prince : the keepers of the gates were surprised and slain, and the *an* of Udai Singh was proclaimed. Banbir was even permitted to retire with his family and his wealth. He sought refuge in the Deccan, and the Bhonslas of Nagpur are said to derive their origin from this spurious branch of Chitor.[1]

Rāna Udai Singh, A.D. **1537-72.**—Rana Udai Singh ascended the throne in S. 1597 (A.D. 1541–2). Great were the rejoicings on the restoration of this prince. 'The song of joy,'[2] which was composed on the occasion, is yet a favourite at Udaipur, and on the festival of Isani (the Ceres of Rajasthan), the females still chant in chorus the 'farewell to Kumbhalmer.'[3] But the evil days of Mewar which set in with Sanga's death, and were accelerated by the fiery valour of Ratna and the capricious conduct of Bikramajit, were completed by an anomaly in her annals : a coward succeeding a bastard to guide the destinies of the Sesodias. The

[1] [There seems no basis for this tradition. The Bhonslas sprang from a Marātha headman of Deora in Sātāra (*IGI*, xviii. 306).]

[2] Suhaila.

[3] Kumbhalmer bidaona.

vices of Ratna and his brother were virtues compared to this physical defect, the consequences of which destroyed a great national feeling, the opinion of its invincibility.

His Character.—" Woe to the land where a minor rules or a woman bears sway ! " exclaims the last of the great bards [1] of Rajasthan ; but where both were united, as in Mewar, the measure of her griefs was full. Udai Singh had not one quality of a sovereign ; and wanting martial virtue, the common heritage of his race, he was destitute of all. Yet he might have slumbered life away in inglorious repose during the reign of Humayun, or the contentions of the Pathan usurpation ; but, unhappily for Rajasthan, a prince was then rearing who forged fetters for the Hindu race which enthralled them for ages ; and though the corroding hand of time left but their fragments, yet even now, though emancipated, they bear the indelible marks of the manacle ; not like the galley slave's, physical and exterior, but deep mental scars, never to be effaced. Can a nation which has run its long career of glory be [320] regenerated ? Can the soul of the Greek or the Rajput be reanimated with the spark divine which defended the kunguras [2] of Chitor or the pass of Thermopylae ? Let history answer the question.

Birth of Akbar.—In the same year that the song of joy was raised in the cloud-capped [3] palace of Kumbhalmer for the deliverance of Udai Singh, the note of woe was pealed through the walls of Umarkot, and given to the winds of the desert, to proclaim the birth [4] of an infant destined to be the greatest monarch who ever swayed the sceptre of Hindustan. In an oasis of the Indian desert, amidst the descendants of the ancient Sogdoi [5] of Alexander, Akbar first saw the light ; his father a fugitive, the diadem torn from his brows, its recovery more improbable than was its acquisition by Babur. The ten years which had elapsed since Humayun's accession were passed in perpetual strife with his brothers, placed according to custom in subordinate governments. Their selfish ambition met its reward ; for with the fall of Humayun their own was ensured, when Sher Shah displaced the dynasty of Chagatai for his own, the Pathan (or Sur).

[1] Chand, the heroic bard of the last Hindu emperor. [Cf. *Ecclesiastes*, x. 16.]

[2] Battlements. [3] *Badal Mahall.* [4] November 23, A.D. 1542.

[5] The Sodhas, a branch of the Pramaras, see p. 111.

Defeat and Flight of Humāyūn, A.D. **1540.**—From the field of battle at Kanauj, where Humayun left his crown, his energetic opponent gave him no respite, driving him before him from Agra to Lahore. Thence, with his family and a small band of adherents, alternately protected and repelled by Hindu chieftains, he reached the valley of Sind, where he struggled to maintain himself amidst the greatest privations, attempting in succession each stronghold on the Indus, from Multan to the ocean. Foiled in every object, his associates made rebels by distress, he abandoned them for the more dubious shelter of the foes of his race. Vain were his solicitations to Jaisalmer and Jodhpur; and though it cannot be matter of wonder that he found no commiseration from either Bhatti or Rathor, we must reprobate the unnational conduct of Maldeo, who, the Mogul historian says, attempted to make him captive. From such inhospitable treatment the royal exile escaped by again plunging into the desert, where he encountered, along with the tender objects of his solicitude, hardships of the most appalling description, until sheltered by the Sodha prince of Umarkot. The high courage and the virtues of this monarch increase that interest in his sufferings which royalty in distress never fails to awaken by its irresistible influence [321] upon our sympathies; and they form an affecting episode in the history of Ferishta.[1] Humayun, though more deeply skilled in the

[1] "Humaioon mounted his horse at midnight and fled towards Amercot, which is about one hundred coss from Tatta. His horse, on the way, falling down dead with fatigue, he desired Tirdi Beg, who was well mounted, to let him have his; but so ungenerous was this man, and so low was royalty fallen, that he refused to comply with his request. The troops of the raja being close to his heels, he was necessitated to mount a camel, till one Nidim Koka, dismounting his own mother, gave the king her horse, and, placing her on the camel, ran himself on foot by her side.

"The country through which they fled being an entire sandy desert, the troop began to be in the utmost distress for water. Some ran mad, others fell down dead; nothing was heard but dreadful screams and lamentations. To add, if possible, to this calamity, news arrived of the enemy's near approach. Humaioon ordered all those who could fight to halt, and let the women and baggage move forward. The enemy not making their appearance, the king rode on in front to see how it fared with his family.

"Night, in the meantime, coming on, the rear lost their way, and in the morning were attacked by a party of the enemy. Shech Ali, with about twenty brave men, resolved to sell his life dear. Having repeated the creed of martyrdom, he rushed upon the enemy, and the first arrow having reached the heart of the chief of the party, the rest were by the valour of his handful

mysteries of astrology than any professed seer of his empire, appears never to have enjoyed that prescience which, according to the initiated in the science, is to be obtained from accurate observation :

And coming events cast their shadows before ;

for, could he, by any prophetic power, have foreseen that the cloud which then shaded his fortunes, was but the precursor of glory to his race, he would have continued his retreat from the sheltering sand-hills of Umarkot with very different sentiments from those which accompanied his flight into Persia [322].

Early Years of Akbar.—Humayun educated the young Akbar

---

put to flight. The other Moguls joined in the pursuit, and took many of the camels and horses. They then continued their march, found the king sitting by a well which he had fortunately found, and gave him an account of their adventure.

"Marching forward the next day from this well, they were more distressed than before, there being no water for two days' journey. On the fourth day of their retreat they fell in with another well, which was so deep, that the only bucket they had took a great deal of time in being wound up, and therefore a drum was beat to give notice to the caffilas when the bucket appeared, that they might repair by turns to drink. The people were so impatient for the water, that as soon as the first bucket appeared, ten or twelve of them threw themselves upon it before it quite reached the brim of the well, by which means the rope broke, and the bucket was lost, and several fell headlong after it. When this fatal accident happened, the screams and lamentations of all became loud and dreadful. Some lolling out their tongues, rolled themselves in agony on the hot sand ; while others, precipitating themselves into the well, met with an immediate, and consequently an easier death. What did not the unhappy king feel, when he saw this terrible situation of his few faithful friends !

"The next day, though they reached water, was not less fatal than the former. The camels, who had not tasted water for several days, now drank so much that the greatest part of them died. The people, also, after drinking, complained of an oppression of the heart, and in about half an hour a great part of them expired.

"A few, with the king, after this unheard-of distress, reached Amercote. The raja, being a humane man, took compassion on their misfortunes : he spared nothing that could alleviate their miseries, or express his fidelity to the king.

"At Amercote, upon Sunday the fifth of Rigib, in the year nine hundred and forty-nine, the prince Akber was brought forth by Hamida Banu Begum. The king, after returning thanks to God, left his family under the protection of Raja Rana, and, by the aid of that prince, marched against Bicker." Dow's *Ferishta* [2nd ed. ii. 136 ff. Compare that of Briggs ii. 93 ff.].

in the same school of adversity in which he had studied under Babur. Between the Persian court and his ancient patrimony in Transoxiana, Kandahar, and Kashmir, twelve years were passed in every trial of fortune. During this short period, India, always the prize of valour, had witnessed in succession six [1] kings descended from the Pathan 'Lion' (*sher*), of whom the last, Sikandar, was involved in the same civil broils which brought the crown to his family. Humayun, then near Kashmir, no sooner observed the tide of events set counter to his foe, than he crossed the Indus and advanced upon Sirhind, where the Pathan soon appeared with a tumultuous array. The impetuosity of young Akbar brought on a general engagement, which the veterans deemed madness. Not so Humayun, who gave the command to his boy, whose heroism so excited all ranks, that they despised the numbers of the enemy, and gained a glorious victory. This was the presage of his future fame; for Akbar was then but twelve years of age,[2] the same period of life at which his grandfather, Babur, maintained himself on the throne of Farghana. Humayun, worthy of such a son and such a sire, entered Delhi in triumph; but he did not long enjoy his recovered crown. His death will appear extraordinary, according to the erroneous estimate formed of Eastern princes: its cause was a fall from the terrace of his library;[3] for, like every individual of his race, he was not merely a patron of literature, but himself a scholar. Were we to contrast the literary acquirements of the Chagatai princes with those of their contemporaries of Europe, the balance of lore would be found on the side of the Asiatics, even though Elizabeth and Henry IV. of France were in the scale. Amongst the princes from the Jaxartes are historians, poets, astronomers, founders of systems of government and religion, warriors, and great captains, who claim our respect and admiration.

Akbar's Struggle for the Empire.—Scarcely had Akbar been seated on the throne, when Delhi and Agra were wrested from him, and a nook of the Panjab constituted all his empire: but by the energetic valour of the great Bairam Khan, his lost sovereignty was regained with equal rapidity, and established by the wisdom

[1] [Four are usually reckoned: Islām Shāh, Muhammad Shāh Ādil, Ibrāhim Shāh, and Sikandar Shāh.]

[2] A.D. 1554.

[3] [At the Sher Mandal in Purāna Kila, Delhi, on January 24, 1556.]

of this Sully [1] of Hindustan on a rock. Kalpi, Chanderi, Kalanjar, all Bundelkhand and Malwa, were soon attached to the empire, and at the early age of eighteen Akbar assumed the uncontrolled [323] direction of the State. He soon turned his attention towards the Rajputs; and whether it was to revenge the inhospitality of Maldeo towards his father, he advanced against the Rathors, and stormed and took Merta, the second city in Marwar. Raja Biharimall [or Bahar Mall] of Amber anticipated the king, enrolled himself and son Bhagwandas amongst his vassals, gave the Chagatai a daughter to wife, and held his country as a fief of the empire. But the rebellions of the Usbek nobles, and the attempts of former princes to regain their lost power, checked for a time his designs upon Rajasthan. These matters adjusted, and the petty sovereigns in the East (to whom the present monarch of Oudh is as Alexander) subjected to authority, he readily seized upon the provocation which the sanctuary given to Baz Bahadur of Malwa and the ex-prince of Narwar afforded, to turn his arms against Chitor.[2]

Comparison of Akbar with Rāna Udai Singh.—Happy the country where the sovereignty is in the laws, and where the monarch is but the chief magistrate of the State, unsubjected to those vicissitudes which make the sceptre in Asia unstable as a pendulum, kept in perpetual oscillation by the individual passions of her princes; where the virtues of one will exalt her to the summit of prosperity, as the vices of a successor will plunge her into the abyss of degradation. Akbar and Udai Singh furnish the corollary to this self-evident truth.

The Rana was old enough to philosophize on 'the uses of adversity'; and though the best of the 'great ancients' had fallen in defence of Chitor, there were not wanting individuals capable of instilling just and noble sentiments into his mind: but it was of that common character which is formed to be

[1] There are excellent grounds for a parallel between Akbar and Henry IV. and between Bairam and Sully, who were, moreover, almost contemporaries. The haughty and upright Bairam was at length goaded from rebellion to exile, and died by assassination only four years after Akbar's accession. [January 31, 1561.] The story is one of the most useful lessons of history. [The life of Akbar has been fully told, with much new evidence, by V. A. Smith, *Akbar the Great Mogul*, 1917.]

[2] A.H. 975, or A.D. 1567.

controlled by others; and an artful and daring concubine stepped in, to govern Udai Singh and Mewar.

Akbar was not older when he came to the throne [1] of Delhi than Udai Singh when he ascended that of Mewar. Nor were his hopes much brighter; but the star which beamed upon his cradle in the desert, conducted to his aid such counsellors as the magnanimous Bairam, and the wise and virtuous Abu-l Fazl. Yet it may be deemed hardly fair to contrast the Rajput with the Mogul: the one disciplined into an accurate knowledge of human nature, by experience of the [324] mutability of fortune; the other cooped up from infancy in a valley of his native hills, his birth concealed, and his education restricted.[2]

Akbar was the real founder of the empire of the Moguls, the first successful conqueror of Rajput independence: to this end his virtues were powerful auxiliaries, as by his skill in the analysis of the mind and its readiest stimulant to action, he was enabled to gild the chains with which he bound them. To these they became familiarized by habit, especially when the throne exerted its power in acts gratifying to national vanity, or even in ministering to the more ignoble passions. But generations of the martial races were cut off by his sword, and lustres rolled away ere his conquests were sufficiently confirmed to permit him to exercise the beneficence of his nature, and obtain by the universal acclaim of the conquered, the proud epithet of Jagad Guru, or 'guardian of mankind.' He was long ranked with Shihabu-d-din, Ala, and other instruments of destruction, and with every just claim; and, like these, he constructed a Mimbar [3] for the Koran from the altars of Eklinga. Yet he finally succeeded in healing the wounds his ambition had inflicted, and received from millions that meed of praise which no other of his race ever obtained.

The absence of the kingly virtues in the sovereign of Mewar filled to the brim the bitter cup of her destiny. The guardian goddess of the Sesodias had promised never to abandon the rock of her pride while a descendant of Bappa Rawal devoted himself to her service. In the first assault by Ala, twelve crowned heads

[1] A.D. 1556; both were under thirteen years of age.

[2] If we argue this according to a Rajput's notions, he will reject the compromise, and say that the son of Sanga should have evinced himself worthy of his descent, under whatever circumstances fortune might have placed him.

[3] The pulpit or platform of the Islamite preachers.

defended the 'crimson banner' to the death. In the second, when conquest led by Bajazet [1] came from the south, the chieftain of Deolia, a noble scion of Mewar, "though severed from her stem," claimed the crown of glory and of martyrdom. But on this, the third and grandest struggle, no regal victim appeared to appease the Cybele of Chitor, and win her to retain its 'kunguras' [2] as her coronet. She fell! the charm was broken; the mysterious tie was severed for ever which connected [325] Chitor with perpetuity of sway to the race of Guhilot. With Udai Singh fled the "fair face" which in the dead of night unsealed the eyes of Samarsi, and told him "the glory of the Hindu was departing": [3] with him, that opinion, which for ages esteemed her walls the sanctuary of the race, which encircled her with a halo of glory, as the palladium of the religion and the liberties of the Rajputs.

To traditions such as these, history is indebted for the noblest deeds recorded in her page; and in Mewar they were the covert impulse to national glory and independence. For this the philosopher will value the relation; and the philanthropist as being the germs or nucleus of resistance against tyrannical domination. Enveloped in a wild fable, we see the springs of their prejudices and their action: batter down these adamantine walls of national opinion, and all others are but glass. The once invincible Chitor is now pronounced indefensible. "The abode of regality, which for a thousand years reared her head above all the cities of Hindustan," is become the refuge of wild beasts, which seek cover in her temples; and this erst sanctified capital is now desecrated as the dwelling of evil fortune, into which the entrance of her princes is solemnly interdicted.

Akbar besieges Chitor, September, A.D. 1567.—Ferishta mentions but one enterprise against Chitor, that of its capture; but the annals record another, when Akbar was compelled to relinquish the undertaking.[4] The successful defence is attributed to the

[1] Malik Bāyazīd was the name of the Malwa sovereign ere he came to the throne, corrupted by Europeans to Bajazet. He is always styled 'Baz Bahadur' in the annals of Mewar.

[2] Battlements.

[3] The last book of Chand opens with this vision.

[4] [Ferishta ii. 299 ff. "It does not appear when that attempt was made, and it is difficult to find a place for it in Abu-l Fazl's chronology, but there is also difficulty in believing the alleged fact to be an invention" (Smith, *Akbar, the Great Mogul*, 81).]

masculine courage of the Rana's concubine queen, who headed the sallies into the heart of the Mogul camp, and on one occasion to the emperor's headquarters. The imbecile Rana proclaimed that he owed his deliverance to her; when the chiefs, indignant at this imputation on their courage, conspired and put her to death. Internal discord invited Akbar to reinvest Chitor; he had just attained his twenty-fifth year, and was desirous of the renown of capturing it. The site of the royal Urdu,[1] or camp, is still pointed out. It extended from the village of Pandauli[2] along the high road to Basai, a distance of ten miles. The headquarters of Akbar are yet marked by a pyramidal column of marble, to which tradition has assigned the [326] title of Akbar ka diwa, or 'Akbar's lamp.'[3] Scarcely had Akbar sat down before Chitor, when the Rana was compelled (say the annals) to quit it; but the necessity and his wishes were in unison. It lacked not, however, brave defenders. Sahidas, at the head of a numerous band of the descendants of Chonda, was at his post,

[1] Of which *horde* is a corruption.

[2] There are two villages of this name. This is on the lake called Mansarowar on whose bank I obtained that invaluable inscription (see No. 2) in the nail-headed character, which settled the establishment of the Guhilot in Chitor, at a little more than (as Orme has remarked) one thousand years. To the eternal regret of my Yati Guru and myself, a barbarian Brahman servant, instead of having it copied, broke the venerable column to bring the inscription to Udaipur.

[3] It is as perfect as when constructed, being of immense blocks of compact white limestone, closely fitted to each other; its height thirty feet, the base a square of twelve, and summit four feet, to which a staircase conducts. A huge concave vessel was then filled with fire, which served as a night-beacon to this ambulatory city, where all nations and tongues were assembled, or to guide the foragers. Akbar, who was ambitious of being the founder of a new faith as well as kingdom, had tried every creed, Jewish, Hindu, and even made some progress in the doctrines of Christianity, and may have in turn affected those of Zardusht, and assuredly this pyramid possesses more of the appearance of a pyreum than a 'diwa'; though either would have fulfilled the purport of a beacon. [Mr. V. A. Smith, quoting Kavi Rāj Shyāmal Dās, 'Antiquities at Nagari' (*JASB*, Part i. vol. lvi. (1887), p. 75), corrects the statements in this note. There was no interior staircase, and more accurate measurements are: height, 36 ft. 7 in.; 14 ft. 1 in. square at base; 3 ft. 3 in. square at apex. The tower is solid for 4 ft., then hollow for 20 ft., and solid again up to the top. The building may be very ancient, though used by Akbar as alleged by popular tradition; probably a wooden ladder gave access to the chamber and to the summit. The original purpose of the building, which stands near Nagari, some six miles N.E. of Chitor, is uncertain (*Akbar the Great Mogul*, 86, note).]

'the gate of the sun'; there he fell resisting the entrance of the foe, and there his altar stands, on the brow of the rock which was moistened with his blood. Rawat Duda of Madri led 'the sons of Sanga.'[1] The feudatory chiefs of Bedla and Kotharia, descended from Prithiraj of Delhi—the Pramar of Bijolia—the Jhala of Sadri—inspired their contingents with their brave example: these were all home chieftains. Another son of Deolia again combated for Chitor, with the Sonigira Rao of Jalor—Isaridas Rathor, Karamchand Kachhwaha,[2] with Duda Sadani,[3] and the Tuar prince of Gwalior, were distinguished amongst the foreign auxiliaries on this occasion.

Jaimall and Patta.—But the names which shine brightest in this gloomy page of the annals of Mewar, which are still held sacred by the bard and the true Rajput, and immortalized by Akbar's own pen, are Jaimall of Badnor and Patta of Kelwa, both of the sixteen superior vassals of Mewar. The first was a Rathor of the Mertia house, the bravest of the brave clans of Marwar; the other was head of the Jagawats, another grand shoot from Chonda. The names of Jaimall and Patta are 'as household words,' inseparable in Mewar, and will be honoured while the Rajput retains a shred of his inheritance or a spark of his ancient recollections. Though deprived of the stimulus which would have been given had their prince been a witness of their deeds, heroic achievements such as those already recorded were conspicuous on this occasion; and many a fair form threw the buckler over the scarf, and led the most desperate sorties [327].

When Salumbar[4] fell at the gate of the sun, the command devolved on Patta of Kelwa. He was only sixteen:[5] his father had fallen in the last shock, and his mother had survived but to rear this the sole heir of their house. Like the Spartan mother of old, she commanded him to put on the 'saffron robe,' and to die for Chitor: but surpassing the Grecian dame, she illustrated

[1] The Sangawats, not the sons of Rana Sanga, but of a chieftain of Chonda's kin, whose name is the patronymic of one of its principal subdivisions, of whom the chief of Deogarh is now head (see p. 188).

[2] Of the Panchaenot branch.

[3] One of the Shaikhavat subdivisions.

[4] The abode of the Chondawat leader. It is common to call them by the name of their estates.

[5] [He must have been older, as he left two sons, and had already served in defence of Merta (Smith, *op. cit.* 88).]

her precept by example; and lest any soft 'compunctious visitings' for one dearer than herself might dim the lustre of Kelwa, she armed the young bride with a lance, with her descended the rock, and the defenders of Chitor saw her fall, fighting by the side of her Amazonian mother. When their wives and daughters performed such deeds, the Rajputs became reckless of life. They had maintained a protracted defence, but had no thoughts of surrender, when a ball struck Jaimall, who took the lead on the fall of the kin of Mewar. His soul revolted at the idea of ingloriously perishing by a distant blow. He saw there was no ultimate hope of salvation, the northern defences being entirely destroyed, and he resolved to signalize the end of his career. The fatal Johar was commanded, while eight thousand Rajputs ate the last 'bira'[1] together, and put on their saffron robes; the gates were thrown open, the work of destruction commenced, and few survived 'to stain the yellow mantle' by inglorious surrender. Akbar entered Chitor, when thirty thousand of its inhabitants became victims to the ambitious thirst of conquest of this 'guardian of mankind.' All the heads of clans, both home and foreign, fell, and seventeen hundred of the immediate kin of the prince sealed their duty to their country with their lives. The Tuar chief of Gwalior appears to have been the only one of note who was reserved for another day of glory.[2] Nine queens, five princesses (their daughters), with two infant sons, and the families of all the chieftains not at their estates, perished in the flames or in the assault of this ever memorable day. Their divinity had indeed deserted them; for it was on Adityawar, the day of the sun,[3] he shed for the last time a ray of glory on Chitor. The rock of their strength was despoiled; the temples, the palaces dilapidated: and, to complete her humiliation and his triumph, Akbar bereft her of all the symbols of [328] regality: the nakkaras,[4] whose reverberations proclaimed, for miles

[1] The bira, or pan, the aromatic leaf so called, enveloping spices, *terra japonica*, calcined shell-line, and pieces of the areca nut, is always presented on taking leave.

[2] [His name appears to have been Sālivāhan, and as he had married a Sesodia princess, he was bound to fight for the Rāna (*ASR*, ii. 394).]

[3] "Chait sudi igārahwān, S. 1624," 11th Chait, or May, A.D. 1568. [The Musalmān writers give February 23, 1568 (*Akbarnāma*, ii. 471; Elliot-Dowson v. 327; *cf.* Badaoni ii. 111).]

[4] Grand kettle-drums, about eight or ten feet in diameter.

around, the entrance and exit of her princes; the candelabras from the shrine of the 'great mother,' who girt Bappa Rawal with the sword with which he conquered Chitor; and, in mockery of her misery, her portals, to adorn his projected capital, Akbarabad.[1]

Akbar claimed the honour of the death of Jaimall by his own hand: the fact is recorded by Abu-l Fazl, and by the emperor Jahangir, who conferred on the matchlock which aided him to this distinction the title of Sangram.[2] But the conqueror of Chitor evinced a more exalted sense, not only of the value of his conquest, but of the merits of his foes, in erecting statues to the names of Jaimall and Patta at the most conspicuous entrance of his palace at Delhi; and they retained that distinction even when Bernier was in India.[3]

The Sin of the Capture of Chitor.—When the Carthaginian gained the battle of Cannae, he measured his success by the bushels of rings taken from the fingers of the equestrian Romans

[1] The *tija sakha Chitor ra*, or 'third sack of Chitor,' was marked by the most illiterate atrocity, for every monument spared by Ala or Bayazid was defaced, which has left an indelible stain on Akbar's name as a lover of the arts, as well as of humanity. Ala's assault was comparatively harmless, as the care of the fortress was assigned to a Hindu prince; and Bayazid had little time to fulfil this part of the Mosaic law, maintained with rigid severity by the followers of Islamism. Besides, at those periods, they possessed both the skill and the means to reconstruct: not so after Akbar, as the subsequent portion of the annals will show but a struggle for existence. The arts do not flourish amidst penury: the principle to construct cannot long survive, when the means to execute are fled; and in the monumental works of Chitor we can trace the gradations of genius, its splendour and decay. [There is no good evidence that Akbar destroyed the buildings (Smith, *op. cit.* 90).]

[2] "He (Akber) named the matchlock with which he shot Jeimul *Singram*, being one of great superiority and choice, and with which he had slain three or four thousand birds and beasts" (*Jahangir-namah*). [Ed. Rogers-Beveridge 45; *Āīn*, i. 116, 617; Badaoni ii. 107.]

[3] "I find nothing remarkable at the entry but two great elephants of stone, which are in the two sides of one of the gates. Upon one of them is the statue of Jamel (Jeimul), that famous raja of Cheetore, and upon the other Potter (Putta) his brother. These are two gallant men that, together with their mother, who was yet braver than they, cut out so much work for Ekbar; and who, in the sieges of towns which they maintained against him, gave such extraordinary proofs of their generosity, that at length they would rather be killed in the outfalls (sallies) with their mother, than submit; and for this gallantry it is, that even their enemies thought them worthy to have these statues erected to them. These two great elephants, together with the two resolute men sitting on them, do at the first entry into this

CHITOR.

To face page 382.

who fell in that memorable field. Akbar estimated his, by the quantity of cordons (*zunnar*) of [329] distinction taken from the necks of the Rajputs, and seventy-four mans and a half[1] are the recorded amount. To eternize the memory of this disaster, the numerals '74½' are *talak*, or accursed.[2] Marked on the banker's letter in Rajasthan it is the strongest of seals, for 'the sin of the slaughter of Chitor'[3] is thereby invoked on all who violate a letter under the safeguard of this mysterious number. He would be a fastidious critic who stopped to calculate the weight of these cordons of the Rajput cavaliers, probably as much over-rated as the trophies of the Roman rings, which are stated at three and a half bushels. It is for the moral impression that history deigns to note such anecdotes, in themselves of trivial import. So long as '74½' shall remain recorded, some good will result from the calamity, and may survive when the event which caused it is buried in oblivion.

Escape of Rāna Udai Singh: Foundation of Udaipur.—When Udai Singh abandoned Chitor, he found refuge with the Gohil in the forests of Rajpipli. Thence he passed to the valley of the

---

fortress make an impression of I know not what greatness and awful terror" (*Letter written at Delhi, 1st July 1663, from edition printed in London in 1684*, in the author's possession). [Ed. V. A. Smith, 256.] Such the impression made on a Parisian a century after the event: but far more powerful the charm to the author of these annals, as he pondered on the spot where Jaimall received the fatal shot from Sangram, or placed flowers on the conotaph that marks the fall of the son of Chonda and the mansion of Patta, whence issued the Sesodia matron and her daughter. Every foot of ground is hallowed by ancient recollections. [For the question of these statues see V. A. Smith, *HFA*, 426; *ASR*, i. 225 ff.; Manucci, ii. 11.]

In these the reader may in some degree participate, as the plate gives in the distance the ruins of the dwellings both of Jaimall and Patta on the projection of the rock, as well as 'the ringlet on the forehead of Chitor,' the column of victory raised by Lakha Rana.

[1] The *man* is of four seers: the maund is forty, or seventy-five pounds. Dow, calculating all the captured wealth of India by the latter, has rendered many facts improbable. [The *man* in the *Āīn* was 55½ lbs.]

[2] [Sir H. M. Elliot proved that the use of 74½ is merely a modification of the figures 74+⅙, meaning apparently 84, a sacred number (*Supplemental Glossary*, 197). In the Central Provinces it is said that it originated in Jahāngīr's slaughter of the Nāgar Brāhmans, when 7450 of them threw away their sacred cords and became Sūdras to save their lives (Russell, *Tribes and Castes*, ii. 395).]

[3] '*Chitor marya ra pap*': *ra* is the sign of the genitive, in the Doric tongue of Mewar, the *ka* of the refined.

Giro in the Aravalli, in the vicinity of the retreat of his great ancestor Bappa, ere he conquered Chitor. At the entrance of this valley, several years previous to this catastrophe, he had formed the lake, still called after him Udai Sagar, and he now raised a dyke between the mountains which dammed up another mountain stream. On the cluster of hills adjoining he raised the small palace called Nauchauki, around which edifices soon arose, and formed a city to which he gave his own name, Udaipur,[1] henceforth the capital of Mewar.

Death of Rāna Udai Singh.—Four years had Udai Singh survived the loss of Chitor, when he expired at Gogunda, at the early age of forty-two ; yet far too long for his country's honour and welfare. He left a numerous issue of twenty-five legitimate sons, whose descendants, all styled Ranawat, pushed aside the more ancient stock, and form that extensive clan distinctively termed the Babas, or 'infants,' of Mewar, whether Ranawats, Purawats, or Kanawats. His last act was to entail with a barren sceptre contention upon his children ; for, setting aside the established laws of primogeniture, he proclaimed his favourite son Jagmall his successor.

Jagmall proclaimed Rāna.—In Mewar there is no interregnum : even the ceremony of *matam* (mourning) is held at the [330] house of the family priest while the palace is decked out for rejoicing. On the full moon of the spring month of Phalgun, while his brothers and the nobles attended the funeral pyre, Jagmall took possession of the throne in the infant capital, Udaipur : but even while the trumpets sounded, and the heralds called aloud "May the king live for ever!" a cabal was formed round the bier of his father.

Jagmall deposed in favour of Rāna Partāp Singh.—It will be borne in mind that Udai Singh espoused the Sonigira princess ; and the Jalor Rao, desirous to see his sister's son have his right, demanded of Kistna, the 'great ancient' of Mewar and the leader of the Chondawats, how such injustice was sanctioned by him. "When a sick man has reached the last extreme and asks for milk to drink, why refuse it ?" was the reply ; with the addition : "The Sonigira's nephew is my choice, and my stand by Partap." Jagmall had just entered the Rasora, and Partap was saddling

[1] Classically *Udayapura*, the city of the East ; from *udaya* (*oriens*), the point of sunrise, as *asta* (west) is of sunset.

for his departure, when Rawat Kistna entered, accompanied by the ex-prince of Gwalior. Each chief took an arm of Jagmall, and with gentle violence removed him to a seat in front of the 'cushion' he had occupied; the hereditary premier remarking, "You had made a mistake, Maharaj; that place belongs to your brother": and girding Partap with the sword (the privilege of this house), thrice touching the ground, hailed him king of Mewar. All followed the example of Salumbar. Scarcely was the ceremony over, when the young prince remarked, it was the festival of the Aheria, nor must ancient customs be forgotten: "Therefore to horse, and slay a boar to Gauri,[1] and take the omen for the ensuing year." They slew abundance of game, and in the mimic field of war, the nobles who surrounded the gallant Partap anticipated happier days for Mewar [331].

CHAPTER 11

Rāna Partāp Singh, A.D. **1572–97.**—Partap[2] succeeded to the titles and renown of an illustrious house, but without a capital, without resources, his kindred and clans dispirited by reverses: yet possessed of the noble spirit of his race, he meditated the recovery of Chitor, the vindication of the honour of his house, and the restoration of its power. Elevated with this design, he hurried into conflict with his powerful antagonist, nor stooped to calculate the means which were opposed to him. Accustomed to read in his country's annals the splendid deeds of his forefathers, and that Chitor had more than once been the prison of their foes, he trusted that the revolutions of fortune might co-operate with his own efforts to overturn the unstable throne of Delhi. The reasoning was as just as it was noble; but whilst he gave loose to those lofty aspirations which meditated liberty to Mewar, his crafty opponent was counteracting his views by a scheme of policy which, when disclosed, filled his heart with

[1] Ceres—The Aheria, or *Mahurat ka Shikar*, will be explained in the Personal Narrative, as it would here break the connexion of events.

[2] [Partāp Singh is usually called by the Muhammadans Rāna Kīka, *Kīka* (in Mārwār *gīga*, in Mālwa *Kūka*), meaning 'a small boy' (*Āīn*, i. 339; Elliot-Dowson v. 397, 410).]

anguish. The wily Mogul arrayed against Partap his kindred in faith as well as blood. The princes of Marwar, Amber, Bikaner, and even Bundi, late his firm ally, took part with Akbar and upheld despotism. Nay, even his own brother, Sagarji,[1] deserted him, and received, as the price of his treachery, the ancient capital of his race, and the title which that possession conferred [332].

Rāna Partâp Singh resists the Moguls.—But the magnitude of the peril confirmed the fortitude of Partap, who vowed, in the words of the bard, "to make his mother's milk resplendent"; and he amply redeemed his pledge. Single-handed, for a quarter of a century did he withstand the combined efforts of the empire; at one time carrying destruction into the plains, at another flying from rock to rock, feeding his family from the fruits of his native hills, and rearing the nursling hero Amra, amidst savage beasts and scarce less savage men, a fit heir to his prowess and revenge. The bare idea that "the son of Bappa Rawal should bow the head to mortal man," was insupportable; and he spurned every overture which had submission for its basis, or the degradation of uniting his family by marriage with the Tatar, though lord of countless multitudes.

The brilliant acts he achieved during that period live in every valley; they are enshrined in the heart of every true Rajput, and many are recorded in the annals of the conquerors. To recount them all, or relate the hardships he sustained, would be to pen what they would pronounce a romance who had not traversed the country where tradition is yet eloquent with his exploits, or conversed with the descendants of his chiefs, who

[1] Sagarji held the fortress and lands of Kandhar. His descendants formed an extensive clan called Sagarawats, who continued to hold Kandhar till the time of Sawai Jai Singh of Amber, whose situation as one of the great tatraps of the Mogul court enabled him to wrest it from Sagarji's issue, upon sheir refusal to intermarry with the house of Amber. The great Mahabat Khan, the most intrepid of Jahangir's generals, was an apostate Sagarawat. They established many chieftainships in Central India, as Umri Bhadaura, Ganeshganj, Digdoli; places better known to Sindhia's officers than to the British. [It is remarkable that the author believed that Mahābat Khān was a Rājput. This man, the De Montfort of Jahāngīr, had such close Hindu affinities and associations that he was thought to be a Hindu. He was a Musulmān, Zamāna Beg of Kābul, best known for his arrest of Jahāngīr in 1628. He died in 1644. (Jahāngīr, *Memoirs*, Rogers-Beveridge i. 24; *Āīn*, i. 337 f., 347, 371, 414; Elphinstone, *Hist. of India*, 567.)]

cherish a recollection of the deeds of their forefathers, and melt, as they recite them, into manly tears.[1]

Partap was nobly supported; and though wealth and fortune tempted the fidelity of his chiefs, not one was found base enough to abandon him. The sons of Jaimall shed their blood in his cause, along with the successors of Patta—the house of Salumbar redoubled the claims of Chonda to fidelity; and these five lustres of adversity are the brightest in the chequered page of the history of Mewar. Nay, some chiefs, attracted by the very desperation of his fortunes, pressed to his standard, to combat and die with Partap. Amongst these was the Delwara chief, whose devotion gained him the prince's 'right hand.'

The Vow of Rāna Partāp Singh.—To commemorate the desolation of Chitor, which the bardic historian represents as a 'widow' despoiled of the ornaments to her loveliness, Partap interdicted to himself and his successors every article of luxury or pomp, until the insignia of her glory should be redeemed. The gold and silver dishes were laid aside [333] for *pattras*[2] of leaves; their beds henceforth of straw, and their beards left untouched. But in order more distinctly to mark their fallen fortune and stimulate to its recovery, he commanded that the martial *nakkaras*, which always sounded in the van of battle or processions, should follow in the rear. This last sign of the depression of Mewar still survives; the beard is yet untouched by the shears; and even in the subterfuge by which the patriot king's behest is set aside, we have a tribute to his memory: for though his descendant eats off gold and silver, and sleeps upon a bed, he places the leaves beneath the one and straw under the other.[3]

Often was Partap heard to exclaim, "Had Udai Singh never been, or none intervened between him and Sanga Rana, no

[1] I have climbed the rocks, crossed the streams, and traversed the plains which were the theatre of Partap's glory, and conversed with the lineal descendants of Jaimall and Patta on the deeds of their forefathers, and many a time has the tear started in their eye at the tale they recited.

[2] The first invented drinking cup or eating vessel being made from the leaf (*pat*) of particular trees, especially the palasa (*Butea frondosa*) and bar (*Ficus religiosa*). The cups of a beautiful brown earthenware, made at Kotharia, are chiefly *pateras*, of a perfectly classical shape. Query, the Roman *patera*, or the Greek *ποτήρ*, or Saxon *pot*? [*patera*, *pateo*, 'to lie open'; *pot*. O.E. *pott*, Lat. *potus*, 'drinking.']

[3] [For some further details see *Rāsmāla*, 307.]

Turk should ever have given laws to Rajasthan." Hindu society had assumed a new form within the century preceding: the wrecks of dominion from the Jumna and Ganges had been silently growing into importance; and Amber and Marwar had attained such power, that the latter single-handed coped with the imperial Sher Shah; while numerous minor chieftainships were attaining shape and strength on both sides the Chambal. A prince of commanding genius alone was wanting, to snatch the sceptre of dominion from the Islamite. Such a leader they found in Sanga, who possessed every quality which extorts spontaneous obedience, and the superiority of whose birth, as well as dignity, were admitted without cavil, from the Himalaya to Rameswaram.[1] These States had powerful motives to obey such a leader, in the absence of whom their ancient patrimony was lost; and such they would have found renewed in Sanga's grandson, Partap, had Udai Singh not existed, or had a less gifted sovereign than Akbar been his contemporary.

With the aid of some chiefs of judgment and experience, Partap remodelled his government, adapting it to the exigencies of the times and to his slender resources. New grants were issued, with regulations defining the service required. Kumbhalmer, now the seat of government, was strengthened, as well as Gogunda and other mountain fortresses; and, being unable to keep the field in the plains [334] of Mewar, he followed the system of his ancestors, and commanded his subjects, on pain of death, to retire into the mountains. During the protracted contest, the fertile tracts watered by the Banas and the Berach, from the Aravalli chain west to the eastern tableland, were *be chiragh*, 'without a lamp.'

Many tales are related of the unrelenting severity with which Partap enforced obedience to this stern policy. Frequently, with a few horse, he issued forth to see that his commands were obeyed. The silence of the desert prevailed in the plains; grass had usurped the place of the waving corn; the highways were choked with the thorny babul,[2] and beasts of prey made their abode in the habitations of his subjects. In the midst of this desolation, a single goatherd, trusting to elude observation, disobeyed his prince's injunction, and pastured his flock in the

[1] The bridge of Rama, the southern point of the peninsula [*IGI*, xxi. 173 ff.]

[2] *Mimosa* [*Acacia*] *Arabica*.

luxuriant meadows of Untala, on the banks of the Banas. After a few questions, he was killed and hung up *in terrorem*. By such patriotic severity Partap rendered 'the garden of Rajasthan' of no value to the conqueror, and the commerce already established between the Mogul court and Europe, conveyed through Mewar from Surat and other ports, was intercepted and plundered.

Akbar attacks Rāna Partāp Singh, A.D. **1576.**—Akbar took the field against the Rajput prince, establishing his headquarters at Ajmer. This celebrated fortress, destined ultimately to be one of the twenty-two subahs of his empire and an imperial residence, had admitted for some time a royal garrison. Maldeo of Marwar, who had so ably opposed the usurper Sher Shah, was compelled to follow the example of his brother prince, Bhagwandas of Amber, and to place himself at the footstool of Akbar: only two years subsequent to Partap's accession, after a brave but fruitless resistance in Merta and Jodhpur, he sent his son, Udai Singh, to pay homage to the king.[1] Akbar received him at Nagor, on his route to Ajmer, on which occasion the Raos of Mandor were made Rajas; and as the heir of Marwar was of uncommon bulk, the title by which he was afterwards known in Rajasthan was Mota Raja,[2] and henceforth the descendants of the kings of Kanauj had the 'right hand' of the emperor of the Moguls. But the Rathor was greater in his native pride than with all the accession of dignity or power which accrued on his sacrifice of Rajput principles [335]. Udai 'le gros' was the first of his race who gave a daughter in marriage to a Tatar. The bribe for which he bartered his honour was splendid; for four provinces,[3] yielding £200,000 of annual revenue, were given in exchange for Jodh Bai,[4] at once doubling the fisc of Marwar. With such examples

[1] A.H. 977, A.D. 1569. [*Āīn*, i. 429 f.]

[2] There is less euphony in the English than in the French designation, Udai '*le Gros*.' [Erskine (iii. A. 58) with less probability says it may mean 'great, potent, good.']

[3] Godwar, Rs. 900,000; Ujjain, 249,914; Debalpur, 182,500; Badnawar, 250,000.

[4] The magnificent tomb of Jodh Bai, the mother of Shah Jahan, is at Sikandra, near Agra, and not far from that in which Akbar's remains are deposited. [Jodh Bāi is a title, meaning 'Jodhpur lady.' There were some doubts about her identity, but she was certainly daughter of Udai Singh and wife of Jahāngīr (*Āīn*, i. 619). For her tomb see Sleeman, *Rambles*, 348.]

as Amber and Marwar, and with less power to resist the temptation, the minor chiefs of Rajasthan, with a brave and numerous vassalage, were transformed into satraps of Delhi, and the importance of most of them was increased by the change. Truly did the Mogul historian designate them "at once the props and the ornaments of the throne."

Rāna Partāp Singh deserted by Rājput Princes.—But these were fearful odds against Partap: the arms of his countrymen thus turned upon him, derived additional weight from their self-degradation, which kindled into jealousy and hatred against the magnanimous resolution they wanted the virtue to imitate. When Hindu prejudice was thus violated by every prince in Rajasthan (that of Bundi alone excepted [1]), the Rana renounced all alliance with those who were thus degraded; and in order to carry on the line, he sought out and incorporated with the first class of nobles of his own kin the descendants of the ancient princes of Delhi, of Patan, of Marwar, and of Dhar. To the eternal honour of Partap and his issue be it told, that to the very close of the monarchy of the Moguls, they not only refused such alliance with the throne, but even with their brother princes of Marwar and Amber. It is a proud triumph of virtue to record, from the autograph letters of the most powerful of their princes, Bakhta Singh and Jai Singh, that whilst they had risen to greatness from the surrender of principle, as Mewar had decayed from her adherence to it, they should, even while basking in court favour, solicit, and that humbly, to be readmitted to the honour of matrimonial intercourse—'to be purified,' 'to be regenerated,' 'to be made Rajputs': and that this was granted only on condition of their abjuring the contaminating practice which had disunited them for more than a century; with the additional stipulation, that the issue of marriage with the house [336] of Mewar should be the heirs to those they entered: conditions which the decline of the empire prevented from being broken.

Rāja Mān Singh and Rāna Partāp Singh.—An anecdote illustrative of the settled repugnance of this noble family to sully the purity of its blood may here be related, as its result had a

[1] The causes of exemption are curious, and are preserved in a regular treaty with the emperor, a copy of which the author possesses, which will be given in *The Annals of Bundi.*

material influence on its subsequent condition. Raja Man, who had succeeded to the throne of Amber, was the most celebrated of his race, and from him may be dated the rise of his country. This prince exemplified the wisdom of that policy which Babur adopted to strengthen his conquest; that of connecting his family by ties of marriage with the Hindus. It has been already related, that Humayun espoused a daughter of Bhagwandas, consequently Raja Man was brother-in-law to Akbar.[1] His courage and talents well seconded this natural advantage, and he became the most conspicuous of all the generals of the empire. To him Akbar was indebted for half his triumphs. The Kachhwaha bards find a delightful theme in recounting his exploits, from the snow-clad Caucasus to the shores of the 'golden Chersonese.'[2] Let the eye embrace these extremes of his conquests, Kabul and the Paropanisos of Alexander, and Arakan (a name now well known) on the Indian Ocean; the former reunited, the latter subjugated, to the empire by a Rajput prince and a Rajput army. But Akbar knew the master-key to Hindu feeling, and by his skill overcame prejudices deemed insurmountable, and many are the tales yet told of their blind devotion to their favourite emperor.

Raja Man was returning from the conquest of Sholapur to Hindustan when he invited himself to an interview with Partap, then at Kumbhalmer, who advanced to the Udaisagar to receive him. On the mound which embanks this lake a feast was pre-

[1] [Akbar married a daughter of Rāja Bihāri Mall and sister of Bhagwāndās (*Āīn*, i. 310, 339). There is no evidence of the marriage of Humāyūn into this family.]

[2] When Raja Man was commanded to reduce the revolted province of Kabul, he hesitated to cross the Indus, the Rubicon of the Hindu, and which they term *Atak*, or 'the barrier,' as being the limit between their faith and the barbarian. On the Hindu prince assigning this as his reason for not leading his Rajputs to the snowy Caucasus, the accomplished Akbar sent him a couplet in the dialect of Rajasthan:—

"Sabhi bhūmi Gopāl kī	"The whole earth is of God,
Jā men Atak kaba,	In which he has placed the Atak.
Jā ke man men atak he,	The mind that admits *impediments*
Soī Atak raha."	Will always find an Atak."

[Dr. Tessitori, whose version is given, remarks that the popular form of the third line is: Bhītar tāti pāp ki.] This delicate irony succeeded when stronger language would have failed.

pared for the prince of Amber. The board was spread, the Raja summoned, and Prince Amra appointed to wait upon him; but no Rana appeared, for whose absence apologies alleging headache were urged by his son, with the request [337] that Raja Man would waive all ceremony, receive his welcome, and commence. The prince, in a tone at once dignified and respectful, replied: "Tell the Rana I can divine the cause of his headache; but the error is irremediable, and if he refuses to put a plate (*kansa*) before me, who will?" Further subterfuge was useless. The Rana expressed his regret; but added, that "he could not eat with a Rajput who gave his sister to a Turk, and who probably ate with him." Raja Man was unwise to have risked this disgrace: and if the invitation went from Partap, the insult was ungenerous as well as impolitie; but of this he is acquitted. Raja Man left the feast untouched, *save the few grains of rice he offered to Anndeva,*[1] *which he placed in his turban*, observing as he withdrew: "It was for the preservation of your honour that we sacrificed our own, and gave our sisters and our daughters to the Turk; but abide in peril, if such be your resolve, for this country shall not hold you"; and mounting his horse he turned to the Rana, who appeared at this abrupt termination of his visit, "If I do not humble your pride, my name is not Man": to which Partap replied, "he should always be happy to meet him"; while some one, in less dignified terms, desired he would not forget to bring his '*Phupha*' [father's sister's husband], Akbar. The ground was deemed impure where the feast was spread: it was broken up and lustrated with the water of the Ganges, and the chiefs who witnessed the humiliation of one they deemed apostate, bathed and changed their vestments, as if polluted by his presence. Every act was reported to the emperor, who was exasperated at the insult thus offered to himself, and who justly dreaded the revival of those prejudices he had hoped were vanquished; and it hastened the first of those sanguinary battles which have immortalised the name of Partap: nor will Haldighat be forgotten while a Sesodia occupies Mewar, or a bard survives to relate the tale.

Salim's Campaign, A.D. 1576.—Prince Salim, the heir of

[1] The Hindus, as did the Greeks and other nations of antiquity, always made offering of the first portion of each meal to the gods. Anndeva, 'the god of food.'

Delhi,[1] led the war, guided by the counsels of Raja Man and the distinguished apostate son of Sagarji, Mahabat Khan. Partap trusted to his native hills and the valour of twenty-two thousand Rajputs to withstand the son of Akbar. The divisions of the royal army encountered little opposition at the exterior defiles by which they penetrated the western side of the [338] Aravalli, concentrating as they approached the chief pass which conducted to the vulnerable part of this intricate country.

Battle of Haldīghāt or Gogūnda, June 18, 1576.—The range to which Partap was restricted was the mountainous region around, though chiefly to the west of the new capital. From north to south, Kumbhalmer to Rakhabhnath,[2] about eighty miles in length; and in breadth, from Mirpur west to Satola east, about the same. The whole of this space is mountain and forest, valley and stream. The approaches to the capital from every point to the north, west, and south are so narrow as to merit the term of defile; on each side lofty perpendicular rocks, with scarcely breadth for two carriages abreast, across which are those ramparts of nature termed *Col* in the mountain scenery of Europe, which occasionally open into spaces sufficiently capacious to encamp a large force. Such was the plain of Haldighat, at the base of a neck of mountain which shut up the valley and rendered it almost inaccessible.[3] Above and below the Rajputs were posted, and on the cliffs and pinnacles overlooking the field of battle, the faithful aborigines, the Bhil, with his natural weapon the bow and arrow, and huge stones ready to roll upon the combatant enemy.

At this pass Partap was posted with the flower of Mewar, and glorious was the struggle for its maintenance. Clan after clan followed with desperate intrepidity, emulating the daring of their prince, who led the crimson banner into the hottest part of the field. In vain he strained every nerve to encounter Raja Man; but though denied the luxury of revenge on his Rajput foe, he

[1] [This is impossible, because Salīm, afterwards the Emperor Jahāngīr, was only in his seventh year. The generals in command were Mān Singh and Āsaf Khān.]

[2] [Rakhabhdev, with a famous Jain temple, forty miles south of Udaipur city (Erskine ii. A. 118).]

[3] Whoever has travelled through the Oberhasli of Meyringen, in the Oberland Bernois, requires no description of the alpine Aravalli. The Col de Balme, in the vale of Chamouni, is, on a larger scale, the Haldighat of Mewar.

made good a passage to where Salim commanded. His guards fell before Partap, and but for the steel plates which defended his howda, the lance of the Rajput would have deprived Akbar of his heir. His steed, the gallant Chetak, nobly seconded his lord, and is represented in all the historical drawings of this battle with one foot raised upon the elephant of the Mogul, while his rider has his lance propelled against his foe. The conductor, destitute of the means of defence, was slain, when the infuriated animal, now without control, carried off Salim. On this spot the carnage was immense: the Moguls eager to defend Salim; the heroes of Mewar to second their prince, who had already received seven wounds [339].[1] Marked by the 'royal umbrella,' which he would not lay aside, and which collected the might of the enemy against him, Partap was thrice rescued from amidst the foe, and was at length nearly overwhelmed, when the Jhala chief gave a signal instance of fidelity, and extricated him with the loss of his own life. Mana seized upon the insignia of Mewar, and rearing the 'gold sun' over his own head, made good his way to an intricate position, drawing after him the brunt of the battle, while his prince was forced from the field. With all his brave vassals the noble Jhala fell; and in remembrance of the deed his descendants have, since the day of Haldighat, borne the regal ensigns of Mewar, and enjoyed 'the right hand of her princes.'[2] But this desperate valour was unavailing against such a force, with a numerous field artillery and a dromedary corps mounting swivels; and of twenty-two thousand Rajputs assembled on that day for the defence of Haldighat, only eight thousand quitted the field alive.[3]

The Escape of Rāna Partāp Singh.—Partap, unattended, fled on the gallant Chetak, who had borne him through the day, and who saved him now by leaping a mountain stream when closely pursued by two Mogul chiefs, whom this impediment momentarily

[1] Three from the spear, one shot, and three by the sword.

[2] The descendants of Mana yet hold Sadri and all the privileges obtained on this occasion. Their kettle-drums beat to the gate of the palace, a privilege allowed to none besides, and they are addressed by the title of *Raj*, or royal.

[3] [The battle fought on June 18, 1576, is known to Musalmān historians as the battle of Khamnaur or Khamnor, twenty-six miles north of Udaipur city (Badaoni ii. 237; *Akbarnāma*, iii. 244 ff.; Elliot-Dowson v. 398; *Āīn*, i. 339; Smith, *Akbar the Great Mogul*, 151 ff.).]

checked. But Chetak, like his master, was wounded; his pursuers gained upon Partap, and the flash from the flinty rock announced them at his heels, when, in the broad accents of his native tongue, the salutation *Ho! nila ghora ra aswar*, 'Ho! rider of the blue horse,' made him look back, and he beheld but a single horseman: that horseman his brother.

Sakta, whose personal enmity to Partap had made him a traitor to Mewar, beheld from the ranks of Akbar the 'blue horse' flying unattended. Resentment was extinguished, and a feeling of affection, mingling with sad and humiliating recollections, took possession of his bosom. He joined in the pursuit, but only to slay the pursuers, who fell beneath his lance; and now, for the first time in their lives, the brothers embraced in friendship. Here Chetak fell, and as the Rana unbuckled his caparison to place it upon Ankara, presented to him by his brother, the noble steed expired. An altar was raised, and yet marks the spot, where Chetak[1] died; and the entire scene may be seen painted on the walls of half the houses of the capital [340].

The greeting between the brothers was necessarily short; but the merry Sakta, who was attached to Salim's personal force, could not let it pass without a joke; and inquiring "how a man felt when flying for his life?" he quitted Partap with the assurance of reunion the first safe opportunity. On rejoining Salim, the truth of Sakta was greatly doubted when he related that Partap had not only slain his pursuers, but his own steed, which obliged him to return on that of the Khorasani. Prince Salim pledged his word to pardon him if he related the truth; when Sakta replied, "The burthen of a kingdom is on my brother's shoulders, nor could I witness his danger without defending him from it." Salim kept his word, but dismissed the future head of the Saktawats. Determined to make a suitable nazar on his introduction, he redeemed Bhainsror by a *coup de main*, and joined Partap at Udaipur, who made him a grant of the conquest, which long remained the chief abode of the Saktawats;[2] and

[1] 'Chetak ka Chabutra' is near to Jharol.

[2] The mother of Sakta was the *Baijiraj*, 'Royal Mother' (Queen Dowager) of Mewar. She loved this son, and left Udaipur to superintend his household at Bhainsror: since which renunciation of rank to affection, the mothers of the senior branch of Saktawat are addressed Baijiraj. [Bhainsror is now held by a Chondāwat Rāwat.]

since the day when this, their founder, preserved the life of his brother and prince against his Mogul pursuers, the birad of the bard to all of his race is *Khorasani Multani ka Agal*, 'the barrier to Khorasan and Multan,' from which countries were the chiefs he slew.

On the 7th of Sawan, S. 1632 (July, A.D. 1576), a day ever memorable in her annals, the best blood of Mewar irrigated the pass of Haldighat. Of the nearest kin of the prince five hundred were slain: the exiled prince of Gwalior, Ramsah, his son Khanderao, with three hundred and fifty of his brave Tuar clan, paid the debt of gratitude with their lives. Since their expulsion by Babur they had found sanctuary in Mewar, whose princes diminished their feeble revenues to maintain inviolable the rites of hospitality.[1] Mana, the devoted Jhala, lost one hundred and fifty of his vassals, and every house of Mewar mourned its chief support.

Siege of Kumbhalmer.—Elate with victory, Salim left the hills. The rainy season had set in, which impeded operations, and obtained for Partap a few months of repose; but with the spring the foe returned, when he was again defeated,[2] and took post in Kumbhalmer, which was invested by the Koka, Shahbaz Khan. He here made a gallant and [341] protracted resistance, and did not retire till insects rendered the water of the Naugun well, their sole resource, impure.[3] To the treachery of the Deora chief of Abu, who was now with Akbar, this deed is imputed. Partap thence withdrew to Chawand,[4] while Bhan, the Sonigira chief, defended the place to the last, and was slain in the assault. On this occasion also fell the chief bard of Mewar, who inspired by his deeds, as well as by his song, the spirit of resistance to the 'ruthless king,' and whose laudatory couplets on the deeds of his lord are still in every mouth. But the spirit of poesy died not with him, for princes and nobles, Hindu and

[1] Eight hundred rupees, or £100 daily, is the sum recorded for the support of this prince.

[2] The date of this battle is Magh Sudi 7, S. 1633, A.D. 1577.

[3] [For the career of Shāhbaz Khān, known as Koka or 'foster-brother,' who died in 1600, see *Āīn*, i. 399 ff. Kūmbhalmer was captured in 1578–9 (Elliot-Dowson v. 410, vi. 58). "About 1578" (Erskine ii. A. 116).]

[4] A town in the heart of the mountainous tract on the south-west of Mewar, called Chappan, containing about three hundred and fifty towns and villages, peopled chiefly by the aboriginal Bhils.

Turk, vied with each other in exalting the patriot Partap, in strains replete with those sentiments which elevate the mind of the martial Rajput, who is inflamed into action by this national excitement.

Further Imperialist Advance.—On the fall of Kumbhalmer, the castles of Dharmeti and Gogunda were invested by Raja Man. Mahabat Khan took possession of Udaipur; and while a prince of the blood [1] cut off the resources furnished by the inhabitants of Oghna Panarwra, Khan Farid invaded Chappan, and approached Chawand from the south. Thus beset on every side, dislodged from the most secret retreats, and hunted from glen to glen, there appeared no hope for Partap: yet, even while his pursuers deemed him panting in some obscure lurking-place, he would by mountain signals reassemble his bands, and assail them unawares and often unguarded. By a skilful manœuvre, Farid, who dreamed of nothing less than making the Rajput prince his prisoner, was blocked up in a defile and his force cut off to a man. Unaccustomed to such warfare, the mercenary Moguls became disgusted in combating a foe seldom tangible; while the monsoon swelled the mountain streams, filling the reservoirs with mineral poisons and the air with pestilential exhalations. The periodical rains accordingly always brought some respite to Partap.

Years thus rolled away, each ending with a diminution of his means and an increase to his misfortunes. His family was his chief source of anxiety: he dreaded their captivity, an apprehension often on the point of being realised. On one occasion they were saved by the faithful Bhils of Kava, who carried them in wicker baskets and concealed them in the tin mines of Jawara, where they guarded [342] and fed them. Bolts and rings are still preserved in the trees about Jawara and Chawand, to which baskets were suspended, the only cradles of the royal children of Mewar, in order to preserve them from the tiger and the wolf. Yet amidst such complicated evils the fortitude of Partap remained unshaken, and a spy sent by Akbar represented the Rajput and his chiefs seated at a scanty meal, maintaining all the etiquette observed in prosperity, the Rana bestowing the *dauna* to the most deserving, and which, though only of the wild fruit of the country, was received with all the reverence of better

[1] Called Ami Sah in the Annals.

days. Such inflexible magnanimity touched the soul of Akbar,[1] and extorted the homage of every chief in Rajasthan; nor could those who swelled the gorgeous train of the emperor withhold their admiration. Nay, these annals have preserved some stanzas addressed by the Khankhanan,[2] the first of the satraps of Delhi, to the noble Rajput, in his native tongue, applauding his valour and stimulating his perseverance: "All is unstable in this world: land and wealth will disappear, but the virtue of a great name lives for ever. Patta[3] abandoned wealth and land, but never bowed the head: alone, of all the princes of Hind, he preserved the honour of his race."

But there were moments when the wants of those dearer than his own life almost excited him to frenzy. The wife of his bosom was insecure, even in the rock or the cave; and his infants, heirs to every luxury, were weeping around him for food: for with such pertinacity did the Mogul myrmidons pursue them, that "five meals have been prepared and abandoned for want of opportunity to eat them." On one occasion his queen and his son's wife were preparing a few cakes from the flour of the meadow grass,[4] of which one was given to each; half for the present, the rest for a future meal. Partap was stretched beside them pondering on his misfortunes, when a piercing cry from his daughter roused him from reflection: a wild cat had darted on the reserved portion of food, and the agony of hunger made her shrieks insupportable. Until that moment his fortitude had been unsubdued. He had beheld his sons and his kindred fall around him on the field without emotion—"For this the Rajput was born"; but the lamentation of his children for food "unmanned him." He cursed the name of royalty, if only to be enjoyed on such conditions, and he demanded of Akbar a mitigation of his hardships [343].

Submission of Rāna Partāp Singh.—Overjoyed at this indication of submission, the emperor commanded public rejoicings, and exultingly showed the letter to Prithiraj, a Rajput compelled to follow the victorious car of Akbar. Prithiraj was the younger

[1] [Akbar was anxious to destroy Partāp, but he could not carry on a guerilla campaign in Rājputana, and he had work to do elsewhere (Smith, *Akbar the Great Mogul*, 153).]

[2] [Mirza Abdu-r-rahīm, son of Bairām Khān (*Āīn*, i. 334).]

[3] A colloquail contraction for Partap.

[4] Called *Mol*.

brother of the prince of Bikaner,[1] a State recently grown out of the Rathors of Marwar, and which, being exposed in the flats of the desert, had no power to resist the example of its elder, Maldeo. Prithiraj was one of the most gallant chieftains of the age, and like the Troubadour princes of the west, could grace a cause with the soul-inspiring effusions of the muse, as well as aid it with his sword: nay, in an assembly of the bards of Rajasthan, the palm of merit was unanimously awarded to the Rathor cavalier. He adored the very name of Partap, and the intelligence filled him with grief. With all the warmth and frankness of his nature, he told the king it was a forgery of some foe to the fame of the Rajput prince. "I know him well," said he; "for your crown he would not submit to your terms." He requested and obtained permission from the king to transmit by his courier a letter to Partap, ostensibly to ascertain the fact of his submission, but really with the view to prevent it. On this occasion he composed those couplets, still admired, and which for the effect they produced will stand comparison with any of the *sirventes* of the Troubadours of the west.[2]

"The hopes of the Hindu rest on the Hindu; yet the Rana forsakes them. But for Partap, all would be placed on the same level by Akbar; for our chiefs have lost their valour and our females their honour. Akbar is the broker in the market of our race: all has he purchased but the son of Uda; he is beyond his price. What true Rajput would part with honour for nine days (*nauroza*); yet how many have bartered it away? Will Chitor come to this market, when all have disposed of the chief article of the Khatri? Though Patta has squandered away wealth, yet this treasure has he preserved. Despair has driven man to this mart, to witness their dishonour: from such infamy the descendant of Hamir alone has been preserved. The world asks, whence the concealed aid of Partap? None but the soul of manliness and his sword: with it, well has he maintained the Khatri's pride. This broker in the market [344] of men will one day be overreached; he cannot live for ever: then will our race come to Partap, for the seed of the Rajput to sow in our desolate

[1] [Rāō Singh (1571–1611).]

[2] It is no affectation to say that the spirit evaporates in the lameness of the translation. The author could feel the force, though he failed to imitate the strength, of the original.

lands. To him all look for its preservation, that its purity may again become resplendent."

Rally of Rāna Partāp Singh.—This effusion of the Rathor was equal to ten thousand men; it nerved the drooping mind of Partap, and roused him into action: for it was a noble incentive to find every eye of his race fixed upon him.

The Nauroza.—The allusion of the princely poet in the phrase, "bartering their honour on the Nauroza," requires some explanation. The Nauroza, or 'New Year's Day,' when the sun enters Aries, is one of great festivity among the Muhammadan princes of the East; but of that alluded to by Prithiraj we can form an adequate idea from the historian Abu-l Fazl.[1]

It is not New Year's Day, but a festival especially instituted by Akbar, and to which he gave the epithet Khushroz, 'day of pleasure,' held on the ninth day (*nauroza*), following the chief festival of each month. The court assembled, and was attended by all ranks. The queen also had her court, when the wives of the nobles and of the Rajput vassal princes were congregated. But the Khushroz was chiefly marked by a fair held within the precincts of the court, attended only by females. The merchants' wives exposed the manufactures of every clime, and the ladies of the court were the purchasers.[2] "His majesty is also there in disguise, by which means he learns the value of merchandise, and hears what is said of the state of the empire and the character of the officers of government." The ingenuous Abu-l Fazl thus

[1] [*Āīn*, i. 276 f.; *Memoirs of Jahāngīr*, trans. Rogers-Beveridge, 48 f.]

[2] At these royal fairs were also sold the productions of princely artisans, male and female, and which, out of compliment to majesty, made a bounteous return for their industry. It is a fact but little known, that most Asiatic princes profess a trade: the great Aurangzeb was a cap-maker, and sold them to such advantage on these 'ninth day' fairs, that his funeral expenses were by his own express command defrayed from the privy purse, the accumulation of his personal labour. A delightful anecdote is recorded of the Khilji king Mahmud, whose profession was literary, and who obtained good prices from his Omrahs for his specimens of calligraphy. While engaged in transcribing one of the Persian poets, a professed scholar, who with others attended the conversazione, suggested an emendation, which was instantly attended to, and the supposed error remedied. When the Mullah was gone, the monarch erased the emendation and re-inserted the passage. An Omrah had observed and questioned the action, to which the king replied: "It was better to make a blot in the manuscript than wound the vanity of a humble scholar." [Ferishta tells the story of Nāsiru-d-dīn Mahmūd, i. 246.]

softens down the unhallowed purpose of this day; but posterity cannot admit that the great Akbar was to obtain these results amidst the Pushto jargon of the dames of Islam, or the mixed Bhakha of the fair of [345] Rajasthan. These 'ninth day fairs' are the markets in which Rajput honour was bartered, and to which the brave Prithiraj makes allusion.[1]

Akbar and Rajput Ladies.—It is scarcely to be credited that a statesman like Akbar should have hazarded his popularity or his power, by the introduction of a custom alike appertaining to the Celtic races of Europe as to these the Goths of Asia;[2] and that he should seek to degrade those whom the chances of war had made his vassals, by conduct so nefarious and repugnant to the keenly cherished feelings of the Rajput. Yet there is not a shadow of doubt that many of the noblest of the race were dishonoured on the Nauroza; and the chivalrous Prithiraj was only preserved from being of the number by the high courage and virtue of his wife, a princess of Mewar, and daughter of the founder of the Saktawats. On one of these celebrations of the

[1] [Compare the later accounts of these fairs by Bernier 272 f.; and Manucci i. 195. Aurangzeb transferred the Nauroz rejoicings to the coronation festival in Ramazān (Jadunath Sarkar, *Life of Aurangzib*, iii. 93). The ladies of the Mughal court usually spoke, not Pushto, but Turki.]

[2] This laxity, as regards female delicacy, must have been a remnant of Scythic barbarism, brought from the banks of the Jaxartes, the land of the Getae, where now, as in the days of Tomyris, a shoe at the door is a sufficient barrier to the entrance of many Tatar husbands. It is a well-known fact, also, that the younger son in these regions inherited a greater share than the elder, which is attributed to their pastoral habits, which invited early emigration in the elder sons. This habit prevailed with the Rajput tribes of very early times, and the annals of the Yadus, a race allied to the Yuti-Getae, or Jāt, afford many instances of it. Modified it yet exists amongst the Jarejas (of the same stock), with whom the sons divide equally; which custom was transmitted to Europe by these Getic hordes, and brought into England by the *Jut* brothers, who founded the kingdom of Kent (*kanthi*, 'a coast' in Gothic and Sanskrit), where it is yet known as *Gavelkind*. In English law it is termed *borough-English*. In Scotland it existed in barbarous times, analogous to those when the Nauroza was sanctioned; and the lord of the manor had privileges which rendered it more than doubtful whether the first-born was natural heir: hence, the youngest was the heir. So in France, in ancient times; and though the '*droit de Jambage*' no longer exists, the term sufficiently denotes the extent of privilege, in comparison with which the other rights of '*Noçages*,' the seigneur's feeding his greyhounds with the best dishes and insulting the bride's blushes with ribald songs, were innocent. [The ethnological views in this note do not deserve notice.]

Khushroz, the monarch of the Moguls was struck with the beauty of the daughter of Mewar, and he singled her out from amidst the united fair of Hind as the object of his passion. It is not improbable that an ungenerous feeling united with that already impure, to despoil the Sesodias of their honour, through a princess of their house under the protection of the sovereign. On retiring from the fair, she found herself entangled amidst the labyrinth of apartments by which egress was purposely ordained, when Akbar stood before her: but instead of acquiescence, she drew a poniard from her corset, and held it to his breast, dictating, and making him repeat, the oath of renunciation of the infamy to all her race. The anecdote is accompanied in the original with many dramatic circumstances. The guardian goddess of Mewar, the terrific Mata, appears on her tiger in the subterranean passage of this palace of pollution, to strengthen her mind by a solemn denunciation [346], and her hand with a weapon to protect her honour. Rae Singh, the elder brother of the princely bard, had not been so fortunate; his wife wanted either courage or virtue to withstand the regal tempter, and she returned to their dwelling in the desert despoiled of her chastity, but loaded with jewels; or, as Prithiraj expresses it: "She returned to her abode, tramping to the tinkling sound of the ornaments of gold and gems on her person; but where, my brother, is the moustache[1] on thy lip?"

Adventures of Rāna Partāp Singh.—It is time to return to the Aravalli, and to the patriot prince Partap. Unable to stem the torrent, he had formed a resolution worthy of his character; he determined to abandon Mewar and the blood-stained Chitor (no longer the stay of his race), and to lead his Sesodias to the Indus, plant the 'crimson banner' on the insular capital of the Sogdoi, and leave a desert between him and his inexorable foe. With his family, and all that was yet noble in Mewar, his chiefs and vassals, a firm and intrepid band, who preferred exile to degradation, he descended the Aravalli, and had reached the confines of the desert, when an incident occurred which made him change his measures, and still remain a dweller in the land of his forefathers. If the historic annals of Mewar record acts of unexampled severity,

[1] The loss of this is the sign of mourning. [There is naturally no confirmation of these anecdotes in the Musalmān historians, but they possibly may be true.]

they are not without instances of unparalleled devotion. The minister of Partap, whose ancestors had for ages held the office, placed at his prince's disposal their accumulated wealth, which, with other resources, is stated to have been equivalent to the maintenance of twenty-five thousand men for twelve years. The name of Bhama Sah is preserved as the saviour of Mewar. With this splendid proof of gratitude, and the *sirvente* of Prithiraj as incitements, he again "screwed his courage to the sticking-place," collected his bands, and while his foes imagined that he was endeavouring to effect a retreat through the desert, surprised Shahbaz in his camp at Dawer, whose troops were cut in pieces. The fugitives were pursued to Amet, the garrison of which shared the same fate. Ere they could recover from their consternation, Kumbhalmer was assaulted and taken; Abdulla and his garrison were put to the sword, and thirty-two fortified posts in like manner carried by surprise, the troops being put to death without mercy. To use the words of the annals: "Partap made a desert of Mewar; he made an [347] offering to the sword of whatever dwelt in its plains": an appalling but indispensable sacrifice. In one short campaign (S. 1586, A.D. 1530), he had recovered all Mewar, except Chitor, Ajmer, and Mandalgarh; and determining to have a slight ovation in return for the triumph Raja Man had enjoyed (who had fulfilled to the letter his threat, that Partap should "live in peril"), he invaded Amber, and sacked its chief mart of commerce, Malpura.

Udaipur was also regained; though this acquisition was so unimportant as scarcely to merit remark. In all likelihood it was abandoned from the difficulty of defending it, when all around had submitted to Partap; though the annals ascribe it to a generous sentiment of Akbar, prompted by the great Khankhanan, whose mind appears to have been captivated by the actions of the Rajput prince.[1] An anecdote is appended to account for Akbar's relaxation of severity, but it is of too romantic a nature even for this part of their annals.

Mewār left in Peace by the Imperialists.—Partap was indebted to a combination of causes for the repose he enjoyed during the latter years of his life; and though this may be ascribed principally to the new fields of ambition which occupied the Mogul arms, we are authorized also to admit the full weight of the influence that

[1] [See p. 398, above.]

the conduct of the Hindu prince exerted upon Akbar, together with the general sympathy of his fellow-princes, who swelled the train of the conqueror, and who were too powerful to be regarded with indifference.

Repose was, however, no boon to the noblest of his race. A mind like Partap's could enjoy no tranquillity while, from the summit of the pass which guarded Udaipur, his eye embraced the Kunguras of Chitor, to which he must ever be a stranger. To a soul like his, burning for the redemption of the glory of his race, the mercy thus shown him, in placing a limit to his hopes, was more difficult of endurance than the pangs of fabled Tantalus. Imagine the warrior, yet in manhood's prime, broken with fatigues and covered with scars, from amidst the fragments of basaltic ruin [1] (fit emblem of his own condition !), casting a wistful eye to [348] the rock stained with the blood of his fathers ; whilst in the 'dark chamber' of his mind the scenes of glory enacted there appeared with unearthly lustre. First, the youthful Bappa, on whose head was the 'mor he had won from the Mori' : [2] the warlike Samarsi, arming for the last day of Rajput independence, to die with Prithiraj on the banks of the Ghaggar : again, descending the steep of Chitor, the twelve sons of Arsi, the crimson banner floating around each, while from the embattled rock the guardian goddess looked down on the carnage which secured a perpetuity of sway. Again, in all the pomp of sacrifice, the Deolia chiefs, Jaimall and Patta ; and like the Pallas of Rajasthan, the Chondawat dame, leading her daughter into the ranks of destruction : examples for their sons' and husbands' imitation. At length clouds of darkness dimmed the walls of Chitor : from her battle-

[1] These mountains are of granite and close-grained quartz ; but on the summit of the pass there is a mass of columnar rocks, which, though the author never examined them very closely, he has little hesitation in calling basaltic. Were it permitted to intrude his own feelings on his reader, he would say, he never passed the portals of Debari, which close the pass leading from Chitor to Udaipur, without throwing his eye on this fantastic pinnacle and imagining the picture he has drawn. Whoever, in rambling through the 'eternal city,' has had his sympathy awakened in beholding at the Porta Salaria the stone seat where the conqueror of the Persians and the Goths, the blind Belisarius, begged his daily dole,—or pondered at the unsculptured tomb of Napoleon upon the vicissitudes of greatness, will appreciate the feeling of one who, in sentiment, had identified himself with the Rajputs, of whom Partap was justly the model.

[2] [A pun on *maur*, 'a crown,' and the Maurya tribe.]

ments 'Kungura Rani'[1] had fled; the tints of dishonour began to blend with the visions of glory; and lo! Udai Singh appeared flying from the rock to which the honour of his house was united. Aghast at the picture his fancy had portrayed, imagine him turning to the contemplation of his own desolate condition, indebted for a cessation of persecution to the most revolting sentiment that can assail an heroic mind—compassion; compared with which scorn is endurable, contempt even enviable: these he could retaliate; but for the high-minded, the generous Rajput, to be the object of that sickly sentiment, pity, was more oppressive than the arms of his foe.

The Last Days of Rāna Partāp.—A premature decay assailed the pride of Rajasthan; a mind diseased preyed on an exhausted frame, and prostrated him in the very summer of his days. The last moments of Partap were an appropriate commentary on his life, which he terminated, like the Carthaginian, swearing his successor to eternal conflict against the foes of his country's independence. But the Rajput prince had not the same joyful assurance that inspired the Numidian Hamilcar; for his end was clouded with the presentiment that his son Amra would abandon his fame for inglorious repose. A powerful sympathy is excited by the picture which is drawn of this final scene. The dying hero is represented in a lowly dwelling; his chiefs, the faithful companions of many a glorious day, awaiting round his pallet the dissolution of their prince, when a groan of mental anguish made Salumbar inquire [349], "What afflicted his soul that it would not depart in peace?" He rallied: "It lingered," he said, "for some consolatory pledge that his country should not be abandoned to the Turk"; and with the death-pang upon him, he related an incident which had guided his estimate of his son's disposition, and now tortured him with the reflection that for personal ease he would forgo the remembrance of his own and his country's wrongs.

On the banks of the Pichola, Partap and his chiefs had constructed a few huts[2] (the site of the future palace of Udaipur),

[1] 'The queen of battlements,' the turreted Cybele of Rajasthan.

[2] This magnificent lake is now adorned with marble palaces. Such was the wealth of Mewar even in her decline. [The lake is said to have been constructed by a Banjāra at the end of the fourteenth century, and the embankment was built by Rāna Udai Singh in 1560. The lake is 2½ miles

to protect them during the inclemency of the rains in the day of their distress. Prince Amra, forgetting the lowliness of the dwelling, a projecting bamboo of the roof caught the folds of his turban and dragged it off as he retired. A hasty emotion, which disclosed a varied feeling, was observed with pain by Partap, who thence adopted the opinion that his son would never withstand the hardships necessary to be endured in such a cause. "These sheds," said the dying prince, "will give way to sumptuous dwellings, thus generating the love of ease; and luxury with its concomitants will ensue, to which the independence of Mewar, which we have bled to maintain, will be sacrificed: and you, my chiefs, will follow the pernicious example." They pledged themselves, and became guarantees for the prince, "by the throne of Bappa Rawal," that they would not permit mansions to be raised till Mewar had recovered her independence. The soul of Partap was satisfied, and with joy he expired.

Thus closed the life of a Rajput whose memory is even now idolized by every Sesodia, and will continue to be so, till renewed oppression shall extinguish the remaining sparks of patriotic feeling. May that day never arrive! yet if such be her destiny, may it, at least, not be hastened by the arms of Britain!

It is worthy the attention of those who influence the destinies of States in more favoured climes, to estimate the intensity of feeling which could arm this prince to oppose the resources of a small principality against the then most powerful empire of the world, whose armies were more numerous and far more efficient than any ever led by the Persian against the liberties of Greece. Had Mewar possessed her Thucydides or her Xenophon, neither the wars of the Peloponnesus nor the retreat of the 'ten thousand' would have yielded more diversified incidents for [350] the historic muse, than the deeds of this brilliant reign amid the many vicissitudes of Mewar. Undaunted heroism, inflexible fortitude, that which 'keeps honour bright,' perseverance,—with fidelity such as no nation can boast, were the materials opposed to a soaring ambition, commanding talents, unlimited means, and the fervour of religious zeal; all, however, insufficient to contend with one unconquerable mind. There is not a pass in the alpine Aravalli

---

long, and 1¼ broad, with an area of over one square mile. In the middle stand the island palaces, the Jagmandir and the Jagniwās (Erskine ii. A. 109).]

that is not sanctified by some deed of Partap,—some brilliant victory or, oftener, more glorious defeat. Haldighat is the Thermopylae of Mewar; the field of Dawer her Marathon.

CHAPTER 12

Rāna Amar Singh I., A.D. **1597-1620.**—Of the seventeen sons of Partap, Amra, who succeeded him, was the eldest. From the early age of eight to the hour of his parent's death, he had been his constant companion and the partner of his toils and dangers. Initiated by his noble sire in every act of mountain strife, familiar with its perils, he entered on his career [1] in the very flower of manhood, already attended by sons able to maintain whatever his sword might recover of his patrimony.

Akbar, the greatest foe of Mewar, survived Partap nearly eight years.[2] The vast field in which he had to exert the resources of his mind, necessarily withdrew him from a scene where even success ill repaid the sacrifices made to attain it. Amra was left in perfect repose during the remainder of this monarch's life, which it was not wisdom to disturb by the renewal of a contest against the colossal power of the Mogul. An extended reign of more than half a century permitted Akbar to consolidate the vast empire he had erected, and to model the form of his [351] government, which displays, as handed down by Abu-l Fazl, an incontestable proof of his genius as well as of his natural beneficence. Nor would the Mogul lose, on being contrasted with the contemporary princes of Europe: with Henry IV. of France, who, like himself, ascended a throne weakened by dissension; with Charles V., alike aspiring to universal sway; or the glorious queen of our own isle, who made advances to Akbar and sent him an embassy.[3] Akbar was fortunate as either Henry

[1] S. 1653, A.D. 1597.

[2] [It has now been established by Mr. V. A. Smith that Akbar died on October 17, O.S., October 27, N.S., 1605 (*IA*, xliv. November 1915).]

[3] The embassy under Sir Thomas Roe was prepared by Elizabeth, but did not proceed till the accession of James. He arrived just as Mewar had bent her head to the Mogul yoke, and speaks of the Rajput prince Karan, whom he saw at court as a hostage for the treaty, with admiration. [The embassy was in India from 1615 to 1619. Roe's Journal has been edited by W. Foster, Hakluyt Society, 1899.]

or Elizabeth in the choice of his ministers. The lofty integrity, military genius, and habits of civil industry, for which Sully was distinguished, found their parallel in Bairam; and if Burleigh equalled in wisdom, he was not superior in virtue to Abu-l Fazl, nor possessed of his excessive benevolence. Unhappily for Mewar, all this genius and power combined to overwhelm her. It is, however, a proud tribute to the memory of the Mogul that his name is united with that of his rival Partap in numerous traditionary couplets honourable to both; and if the Rajput bard naturally emblazons first on his page that of his own hero, he admits that none other but Akbar can stand a comparison with him; thereby confirming the eulogy of the historian of his race, who, in summing up his character, observes that, "if he sometimes did things beneath the dignity of a great king, he never did anything unworthy of a good man." But if the annalist of the Bundi State can be relied upon, the very act which caused Akbar's death will make us pause ere we subscribe to these testimonies to the worth of departed greatness, and, disregarding the adage of only speaking good of the dead, compel us to institute, in imitation of the ancient Egyptians, a posthumous inquest on the character of the monarch of the Moguls. The Bundi records are well worthy of belief, as diaries of events were kept by her princes, who were of the first importance in this and the succeeding reigns: and they may be more likely to throw a light upon points of character of a tendency to disgrace the Mogul king, than the historians of his court, who had every reason to withhold such. A desire to be rid of the great Raja Man of Amber, to whom he was so much indebted, made the emperor descend [352] to act the part of the assassin. He prepared a *ma'ajun*, or confection, a part of which contained poison; but, caught in his own snare, he presented the innoxious portion to the Rajput and ate that drugged with death himself.[1] We have a sufficient clue to the motives which influenced Akbar to a deed so unworthy of him, and which were more fully developed in the reign of his successor; namely, a design on the part of Raja Man to alter the succession, and that Khusru, his nephew, should succeed instead of Salim. With such a motive, the aged emperor might have admitted with less scruple the advice which prompted an act he dared not openly undertake, without exposing

[1] [The question has been discussed in the *Būndi Annals*, below.]

the throne in his latter days to the dangers of civil contention, as Raja Man was too powerful to be openly assaulted.

The Administration of Rāna Amar Singh.—Let us return to Mewar. Amra remodelled the institutions of his country, made a new assessment of the lands and distribution of the fiefs, apportioning the service to the times. He also established the gradation of ranks such as yet exists, and regulated the sumptuary laws even to the tie of a turban,[1] and many of these are to be seen engraved on pillars of stone in various parts of the country.

The repose thus enjoyed realized the prophetic fears of Partap, whose admonitions were forgotten. Amra constructed a small palace on the banks of the lake, named after himself 'the abode of immortality,'[2] still remarkable for its Gothic contrast to the splendid marble edifice erected by his successors, now the abode of the princes of Mewar.

Jahāngīr attacks Mewār.—Jahangir had been four years on the throne, and having overcome all internal dissension, resolved to signalize his reign by the subjugation of the only prince who had disdained to acknowledge the paramount power of the Moguls; and assembling the royal forces, he put them in motion for Mewar.

Amra, between the love of ease and reputation, wavered as to the conduct he should adopt; nor were sycophants wanting who

> Counselled ignoble ease and peaceful sloth,
> Not peace:

and dared to prompt his following the universal contagion, by accepting the imperial farman. In such a state of mind the chiefs found their prince, when [353] they repaired to the new abode to warn him, and prepare him for the emergency. But the gallant Chondawat, recalling to their remembrance the dying behest of their late glorious head, demanded its fulfilment. All resolved to imitate the noble Partap,

> . . . preferring
> Hard liberty before the easy yoke
> Of servile pomp.

Chief of Salūmbar intervenes.—A magnificent mirror of

[1] The *Amrasahi pagri*, or turban, is still used by the Rana and some nobles on court days, but the foreign nobility have the privilege, in this respect, of conforming to their own tribes. [2] *Amara mahall.*

European fabrication adorned the embryo palace. Animated with a noble resentment at the inefficacy of his appeal to the better feelings of his prince, the chieftain of Salumbar hurled 'the slave of the carpet'[1] against the splendid bauble, and starting up, seized his sovereign by the arm and moved him from the throne. "To horse, chiefs!" he exclaimed, "and preserve from infamy the son of Partap." A burst of passion followed the seeming indignity, and the patriot chief was branded with the harsh name of traitor; but with his sacred duty in view, and supported by every vassal of note, he calmly disregarded the insult. Compelled to mount his steed, and surrounded by the veterans and all the chivalry of Mewar, Amra's passion vented itself in tears of indignation. In such a mood the cavalcade descended the ridge, since studded with palaces, and had reached the spot where the temple of Jagannath now stands, when he recovered from this fit of passion; the tear ceased to flow, and passing his hand over his moustache,[2] he made a courteous salutation to all, entreating their forgiveness for this omission of respect; but more especially expressing his gratitude to Salumbar, he said, "Lead on, nor shall you ever have to regret your late sovereign." Elevated with every sentiment of generosity and valour, they passed on to Dawer, where they encountered the royal army led by the brother of the Khankhanan, as it entered the pass, and which, after a long and sanguinary combat, they entirely defeated.[3]

Defeat of the Imperialists.—The honours of the day are chiefly attributed to the brave Kana, uncle to the Rana, and ancestor of that numerous clan called after him Kanawats. A truce followed this battle, but it was of short duration; for another and yet more murderous conflict took place in the spring of 1666, in the pass of the sacred Ranpur [354], where the imperial army, under its leader Abdulla, was almost exterminated;[4] though with the loss of the best and bravest of the chiefs of Mewar,

[1] A small brass ornament placed at the corners of the carpet to keep it steady.

[2] This is a signal both of defianee and self-gratulation.

[3] S. 1664, A.D. 1608.

[4] Phalgun 7th, S. 1666, the spring of A.D. 1610. Ferishta [Dow iii. 37] misplaces this battle, making it immediately precede the invasion under Khurram. The defeats of the Mogul forces are generally styled 'recalls of the commander.'

whose names, however harsh, deserve preservation.[1] A feverish exultation was the fruit of this victory, which shed a hectic flush of glory over the declining days of Mewar, when the crimson banner once more floated throughout the province of Godwar.

Jahāngīr establishes Sagra as Rāna.—Alarmed at these successive defeats, Jahangir, preparatory to equipping a fresh army against Mewar, determined to establish a new Rana, and to instal him in the ancient seat of power, Chitor, thus hoping to withdraw from the standard of Amra many of his adherents. The experiment evinced at least a knowledge of their prejudices; but, to the honour of Rajput fidelity, it failed. Sagra, who abandoned Partap and went over to Akbar, was selected;[2] the sword of investiture was girded on him by the emperor's own hands, and under the escort of a Mogul force he went to reign amidst the ruins of Chitor. Her grandeur, even in desolation, is beautifully depicted at this very period by the chaplain to the embassy from Elizabeth to Jahangir, the members composing which visited the capital of the Sesodias in their route to Ajmer.[3]

For seven years Sagra had a spurious homage paid to him amidst this desolation, the ruined pride of his ancestors. But

[1] Dudo, Sangawat of Deogarh, Narayandas, Surajmall, Askarn, all Sesodias of the first rank; Puran Mall, son of Bhan, the chief of the Saktawats; Haridas Rathor, Bhopat the Jhala of Sadri, Kahirdas Kachhwaha, Keshodas Chauhan of Bedla, Mukunddas Rathor, Jaimallot, of the blood of Jaimall.

[2] [When Partāp was attacked by Akbar, Sakra, as he is called, paid his respects at court, and was appointed Commander of 200 (*Aīn*, i. 519).]

[3] "Chitor, an antient great kingdom, the chief city so called, which standeth upon a mighty hill flat on the top, walled about at the least ten English miles. *There appear to this day above a hundred ruined churches, and divers fair palaces, which are lodged in like manner among the ruins, besides many exquisite pillars of carved stone, and the ruins likewise of a hundred thousand stone houses, as many English by their observation have guessed.* There is but one ascent unto it, cut out of a firm rock, to which a man must pass through four (sometime very magnificent) gates. *Its chief inhabitants at this day are Ziim and Ohim, birds and wild beasts; but the stately ruins thereof give a shadow of its beauty while it flourished in its pride.* It was won from Ramas, an ancient Indian prince, who was forced to live himself ever after on high mountainous places adjoining to that province, and his posterity to live there ever since. Taken from him it was by Achabar Padsha (the father of that king who lived and reigned when I was in these parts) after a very long siege, which famished the besieged, without which it could never have been gotten." [E. Terry, *A Voyage to East-India*, 1777, p. 77 f.]

it is gratifying to record, that not even by this recreant son of Chitor could the impressions formed in contemplating such scenes be resisted; and Sagra, though flinty as the rock to a brother and nephew, could not support the silent admonition of the altars of the heroes who had fallen in her defence. The triumphal column raised for victory over a combination of [355] kings, was a perpetual memento of his infamy; nor could he pass over one finger's breadth of her ample surface, without treading on some fragment which reminded him of their great deeds and his own unworthiness. We would be desirous of recording, that a nobler remembrancer than 'coward conscience,' animated the brother of Partap to an act of redeeming virtue; but when the annals tell us, that "the terrific Bhairon (the god of battle) openly manifested his displeasure," it is decisive that it was not less the wish for greatness, than the desire to be "without the illness should attend it"; and sending for his nephew, he restored to him Chitor, retiring to the isolated Kandhar.[1] Some time after, upon going to court, and being upbraided by Jahangir, he drew his dagger and slew himself in the emperor's presence: an end worthy of such a traitor.[2]

Conquests of Rāna Amar Singh I.—Amra took possession of the seat of his ancestors; but wanting the means to put it in defence, the acquisition only served to increase the temporary exultation. The evil resulting from attaching so much consequence to a capital had been often signally manifested; as to harass the enemy from their mountains, and thereby render his conquests unavailing, was the only policy which could afford the chance of independence. With Chitor the Rana acquired, by surrender or assault, possession of no less than eighty of the chief towns and fortresses of Mewar: amongst them Untala, at whose capture occurred the patriotic struggle between the clans of Chondawat and Saktawat for the leading of the vanguard, elsewhere related.[3] On this memorable storm, besides the leaders

[1] An isolated rock in the plain between the confluence of the Parbati and Chambal, and the famous Ranthambhor. The author has twice passed it in his travels in these regions.

[2] It was one of his sons who apostatized from his faith, who is well known in the imperial history as Mahabat Khan, beyond doubt the most daring chief in Jahangir's reign [see p. 386, above]. This is the secret of his bond of union with prince Khurram (Shah Jahan), himself half a Rajput. It was with his Rajputs Mahabat did that daring deed, making Jahangir prisoner in his own camp, in the zenith of his power.

[3] Page 175, above.

of the rival bands, five of the infant clan Saktawat, consisting but of sixteen brave brothers, with three of the house of Salumbar, perished, struggling for the immortality promised by the bard. We may here relate the rise of the Saktawats, with which is materially connected the future history of Mewar.

Sakta and the Saktāwats.—Sakta was the second of the twenty-four sons of Udai Singh. When only five years of age, he discovered that fearless temperament which marked his manhood [356]. The armourer having brought a new dagger to try its edge by the usual proof on thinly spread cotton, the child asked the Rana "if it was not intended to cut bones and flesh," and seizing it, tried it on his own little hand. The blood gushed on the carpet, but he betrayed no symptom of pain or surprise. Whether his father admitted the tacit reproof of his own want of nerve, or that it recalled the prediction of the astrologers, who, in casting Sakta's horoscope, had announced that he was to be "the bane of Mewar," he was incontinently commanded to be put to death, and was carried off for this purpose, when saved by the Salumbar chief, who arrested the fiat, sped to the Rana, and begged his life as a boon, promising, having no heirs, to educate him as the future head of the Chondawats. The Salumbar chief had children in his old age, and while wavering between his own issue and the son of his adoption, the young Sakta was sent for to court by his brother Partap. The brothers for a considerable time lived on the most amicable footing, unhappily interrupted by a dispute while hunting, which in time engendered mutual dislike. While riding in the ring, Partap suddenly proposed to decide their quarrel by single combat, "to see who was the best lancer." Not backward, Sakta replied, "Do you begin"; and some little time was lost in a courteous struggle for the first spear, when, as they took their ground and agreed to charge together, the Purohit[1] rushed between the combatants and implored them not to ruin the house. His appeal, however, being vain, there was but one way left to prevent the unnatural strife: the priest drew his dagger, and plunging it in his breast, fell a lifeless corpse between the combatants. Appalled at the horrid deed, 'the blood of the priest on their head,' they desisted from their infatuated aim. Partap, waving his hand, commanded Sakta to quit his dominions, who bowing retired,

[1] Family priest.

and carried his resentments to Akbar. Partap performed with the obsequies of this faithful servant many expiatory rites, and made an irrevocable grant of Salera to his son, still enjoyed by his descendants, while a small column yet identifies the spot of sacrifice to fidelity. From that hour to the memorable day when the founder of the Saktawats gained the birad of the race '*Khurasan Multan ka Aggal*,' on the occasion of his saving his sovereign flying from the field, the brothers had never beheld each other's face [357].

Sakta had seventeen sons, all of whom, excepting the heir of Bhainsror,[1] attended his obsequies. On return from this rite they found the gates barred against them by Bhanji, now chief of the Saktawats, who told them " there were too many mouths," and that they must push their fortunes elsewhere while he attended his sovereign with the quota of Bhainsror. They demanded their horses and their arms, if such were his pleasure; and electing Achal as their head (whose wife was then pregnant), they took the route to Idar, which had recently been acquired by a junior branch of the Rathors of Marwar.[2] They had reached Palod when the pangs of childbirth seized the wife of Achal; and being rudely repulsed by the Sonigira vassal of Palod, who refused her shelter at such a moment, they sought refuge amidst the ruins of a temple.[3] It was the shrine of Mata Janavi, 'the mother of births,' the Juno Lucina of the Rajputs. In a corner of the sanctuary they placed the mother of a future race; but the rain, which fell in torrents, visibly affected the ruin. A beam of stone gave way, which but for Bala would have crushed her: he supported the sinking roof on his head till the brothers cut down a babul tree, with which they propped it and relieved him. In this retreat Asa (*Hope*) was born, who became the parent of an extensive branch known as the Achalis Saktawats.

The 'Great Mother' was propitious. The parent of '*Hope*' was soon enabled to resume her journey for Idar, whose chief received them with open arms, and assigned lands for their

[1] I have visited the cenotaphs of Sakta and his successors at the almost insulated Bhainsror on the Chambal. The castle is on a rock at the confluence of the black Bamani and the Chambal.

[2] [Idar was not occupied by the Rāthors till 1728 (*IGI*, xiii. 325).]

[3] Probably the identical temple to the Mother, in which I found a valuable inscription of Kumarpal of Anhilwara Patan, dated S. 1207. Palod is in the district of Nimbahera, now alienated from Mewar, and under that upstart Pathan, Amir Khan.

support. Here they had been some time when the Rana's prime minister passed through Idar from a pilgrimage to Satrunjaya.[1] A violent storm would have thrown down the tent in which was his wife, but for the exertion of some of the brothers; and the minister, on learning that it was to the near kin of his sovereign he was indebted for this kindness, invited them to Udaipur, taking upon him to provide for them with their own proper head, which they declined without a special invitation. This was not long wanting; for Amra [358] was then collecting the strength of his hills against the king, and the services of the band of brothers, his kinsmen, were peculiarly acceptable. The first act of duty, though humble, is properly recorded, as ennobled by the sentiment which inspired it, and the pictured scene is yet preserved of Bala and Jodha collecting logs of wood for a night fire in the mountain bivouac for their kinsman and sovereign. In the more brilliant exploit which followed Bala took the lead, and though the lord of Bhainsror was in camp, it was Bala who obtained the leading of the vanguard: the commencement of that rivalry of clanship from whence have resulted some of the most daring, and many of the most merciless deeds in the history of Mewar. The right to lead in battle belonged to the Chondawats, and the first intimation the chieftain had of his prince's inconsiderate insult was from the bard incessantly repeating the 'birad' of the clan, until 'the portal of the ten thousand' of Mewar deemed him mad. "Not so," replied he; "but it is, perhaps, the last time your ears may be gratified with the watchword of Chonda, which may to-morrow be given as well as the Harawal to the Saktawats." An explanation followed, and the assault of Untala ensued, which preserved the rights of the Chondawats, though nobly contested by their rivals. The vassal of Bakrol carried the tidings of the successful assault to the Rana, who arrived in time to receive the last obeisance of Bala, whose parting words to his prince were seized on by the bard and added to the birad of the clan: and although, in sloth and opium, they now "lose and neglect the creeping hours of time," yet whenever a Saktawat chief enters the court of his sovereign, or takes his seat amongst his brother chiefs, the bards still salute him with the dying words of Bala:

---

[1] One of the five sacred mounts of the Jains, of whose faith was the minister. Of these I shall speak at length in the Personal Narrative. [*IGI*, xix. 316 ff.]

"*Dūna dātār.*
Chauguna junjhār,
Khurāsān Multān ka āggāl."[1]

Then passing the hand over his moustache, for a moment the escalade of Untala flits before his vision, where Bala, Achalis, Jodha, Dilla, and Chaturbhan, five of the seventeen sons of Sakta, fell for the maintenance of the post of honour [359]. Bhanji soon after performed a service which obtained him the entire favour of his prince, who, returning from Ratlam, was insulted by the Rathors of Bhindar, which was punished by the Saktawat, who took the town by assault, expelling the aggressors. Amra added it to his fief of Bhainsror, and since the latter was bestowed on the rival clan, Bhindar has continued the chief residence of the leader of the Saktawats. Ten chiefs[2] have followed in regular

[1] 'Double gifts, fourfold sacrifice.' Meaning, with increase of their prince's favour the sacrifice of their lives would progress; and which, for the sake of euphony probably, preceded the birad won by the founder, '*the barrier to Khurasan and Multan.*'

The *Birad* of the Chondawats is: *Das sahas Mewār ka bar Kewār,* 'the portal of the ten thousand [towns] of Mewār.' It is related that Sakta, jealous of so sweeping a birad, complained that nothing was left for him: when the master bard replied, he was *Kewār ka aggal,* the bar which secures the door (*Kewār*).

[2] Sakta.—17 sons.
|
Bhanji.
|
Dayāl. | Ber. | Man. | Gokuldās. | Pūran Mall.
|
Sabal Singh.
|
Mokham Singh.
|
Amar Singh.
|
Prithi Singh.
|
Jeth Singh.
|
Ummed Singh.
|
Kushāl Singh.
|
Zorāwar,

[to whom succeeded in order Hamīr Singh, Madan Singh, Kesari Singh, and Mādho Singh, the present Mahārāja, who succeeded in 1900 (Erskine ii. A. 99).]

succession, whose issue spread over Mewar, so that in a few generations after Sakta, their prince could muster the swords of ten thousand Saktawats; but internal feuds and interminable spoliation have checked the progress of population, and it might be difficult now to assemble half that number of the 'children of Sakta' fit to bear arms.

Renewed Attack by Jahāngīr. Battle of Khāmnor.—To return. These defeats alarmed Jahangir, who determined to equip an overwhelming force to crush the Rana. To this end he raised the imperial standard at Ajmer, and assembled the expedition under his immediate inspection, of which he appointed his son Parvez commander, with instructions on departure "that if the Rana or his elder son Karan should repair to him, to receive them with becoming attention, and to offer no molestation to the country."[1] But the Sesodia prince little thought of submission: on the contrary, flushed with success, he gave the royal army the meeting at a spot oft moistened with blood, the pass of Khamnor,[2] leading into the heart of the hills. The imperial army was disgracefully beaten, and fled, pursued with great havoc, towards Ajmer. The Mogul historian admits it to have been a glorious day for Mewar. He describes Parvez entangled in the passes, dissensions in his camp, his supplies cut off, and under all [360] these disadvantages attacked; his precipitate flight and pursuit, in which the royal army lost vast numbers of men.[3] But Jahangir in his diary slurs it over, and

[1] A.D. 1611.

[2] Translated 'Brampoor' in Dow's *Ferishta*, and transferred to the Deccan; and the pass (*bāla-ghāt*) rendered the Bālaghāt mountains of the south. There are numerous similar errors. [The Author seems to be mistaken. Dow (iii. 39) speaks of "Brampour, the capital of the Rana's dominions." Khāmnor is in W. Mewār, a little distance south of Nāthdwāra.]

[3] The details of battles, unless accompanied by exploits of individuals, are very uninteresting. Under this impression, I have suppressed whatever could impair the current of action by amplification, otherwise not only the Rajput bard, but the contemporary Mogul historian, would have afforded abundant matter; but I have deemed both worthy of neglect in such cases. Ferishta's history is throughout most faulty in its geographical details, rendered still more obscure from the erroneous orthography, often arising from mistaken punctuation of the only translation of this valuable work yet before the public. There is one gentleman (Lieut.-Col. Briggs) well qualified to remedy these defects, and who, with a laudable industry, has made

simply remarks: "Fearing that Khusrau's affair might be prolonged, I ordered my son Parwīz to leave some of the Sardārs to look after the Rānā, and to come to Agra with Āsaf Khān and a body of those nearly connected with him in the service."[1]

This son, tutored by the great Mahabat Khan, fared no better than Parvez; he was routed and slain. But the Hydra was indestructible; for every victory, while it cost the best blood of Mewar, only multiplied the number of her foes. Seventeen pitched battles had the illustrious Rajput fought since the death of his father: but the loss of his experienced veterans withered the laurels of victory, nor had he sufficient repose either to husband his resources or to rear his young heroes to replace them. Another and yet more mighty army was assembled under Prince Khurram, the ablest of the sons of Jahangir, and better known in history as Shah Jahan, when emperor of the Moguls.

Again did the Rana with his son Karan collect the might of their hills; but a handful of warriors was all their muster to meet the host of Delhi, and the 'crimson banner,' which for more than eight hundred years had waved in proud independence over the heads of the Guhilots, was now to be abased to the son of Jahangir. The Emperor's own pen shall narrate the termination of this strife.

"My chief object, after my visit to the Khwāja [the tomb of Mu'īnu-d-dīn Chishti, the saint of Ajmer] was to put a stop to the affair of the rebel Rānā. On this account I determined to remain myself at Ajmīr and send on Bābā Khurram, my fortunate son. This idea was a very good one, and on this account, on the 6th of Day [tenth month of the solar year] at the hour fixed on, I dispatched him in happiness and triumph. I presented him with a *qabā* (outer coat) of gold brocade with jewelled flowers and pearls round the flowers, a brocaded turban with strings of pearls, a gold woven sash with chains of pearls, one of my private elephants called Fath Gaj, with trappings, a splendid horse, a

---

an entire translation of the works of Ferishta, besides collating the best MSS. of the original text. It is to be hoped he will present his performance to the public. [This appeared in four volumes, 1829; reprinted, Calcutta, 1908.]

[1] [*Memoirs of Jahāngīr*, trans. Rogers-Beveridge, p. 70. The incorrect versions of this and other passages in the text have been replaced from the recent translation and that in Elliot-Dowson.]

jewelled sword, with a *phūl katāra* (dagger). In addition to the men first appointed to this duty under the leadership of Khān A'zam, I sent 12,000 more horse with my son, and honoured their *khil'at* (wearing robes of honour) leaders." [1]

On 14th Isfandārmuz [twelfth month of the solar year] "a representation came from my son Bābā Khurram that the elephant 'Ālam Gumān [' arrogant of the earth '], of which the Rānā was very fond, together with seventeen 'Ālamgumān other elephants, had fallen into the hands of the victorious army." [2] Jahāngīr rode this elephant on the second day of the New Year, which began on 21st March 1614.[3]

" In the month of Bahman [eleventh solar month] there came pieces of good news, one after the other. The first was that the Rānā Amar Singh had elected for obedience and service to the Court. The circumstances of this affair are these. Sultān Khurram, by dint of placing a great many posts, especially in some places where most people said it was impossible to place them on account of the badness of the air and water and the wild nature of the localities, and by dint of moving the royal forces one after another in pursuit, without regard to the heat or excessive rain, and making prisoners of the inhabitants of that region, brought matters with the Rānā to such a pass that it became clear to him that if this should happen to him again he must either fly the country or be made prisoner. Being without remedy, he chose obedience and loyalty, and sent to my fortunate son his maternal uncle Subhkaran, with Haridās Jhālā, who was one of the two men in his confidence, and petitioned that if that fortunate son would ask forgiveness for his offences and tranquillize his mind, and obtain for him the auspicious sign-manual (*panja*,[4] the mark of the Emperor's five fingers), he would himself

[1] [*Memoirs*, 256.] [2] [*Ibid.* 259.] [3] [*Ibid.* 260.]

[4] The giving the hand amongst all nations has been considered as a pledge for the performance or ratification of some act of importance, and the custom amongst the Scythic or Tatar nations, of transmitting its impress as a substitute, is here practically described. I have seen the identical Farman in the Rana's archives. The hand being immersed in a compost of sandalwood, is applied to the paper, and the palm and five fingers (*panja*) are yet distinct. In a masterly delineation of Oriental manners (*Carne's Letters from the East*) is given an anecdote of Muhammad, who, unable to sign his name to a convention, dipped his hand in ink, and made an impression therewith. It is evident the Prophet of Islam only followed an ancient solemnity, of the same import as that practised by Jahangir.

wait on my son, and would send his son and successor, Karan Singh, or he, after the manner of other Rājas, would be enrolled among the servants of the Court and do service. He also begged that he himself might be excused from coming to Court on account of his old age. Accordingly, my son sent them in company with his own Dīwān, Mullā Shukru-llah, whom after the conclusion of this business I dignified with the title of Afzal Khān, and Sundar Dās, his major-domo, who, after the matter was settled, was honoured with the title of Rāy Rayān, to the exalted Court, and represented the circumstances. My lofty mind was always desirous, as far as possible, not to destroy the old families. The real point was that as Rānā Amar Singh and his fathers, proud in the strength of the hilly country and their abodes, had never seen or obeyed any of the kings of Hindustan, this should be brought about in my reign. At the request of my son, I forgave the Rānā's offences, and gave a gracious farmān that should satisfy him, and impressed on it the mark of my auspicious palm. I also wrote a farmān of kindness to my son that if he could arrange to settle the matter I should be much pleased. My son also sent them [perhaps the uncle and Haridās, or the farmāns] with Mullā Shukru-llah and Sundar Dās to the Rānā to console him and make him hopeful of the royal favour. They gave him the gracious farmān with the sign-manual of the auspicious hand, and it was settled that on Sunday, the 26th of the month Bahman, he and his sons should come and pay their respects to my son."[1]

"In the end of this month, when I was employed in hunting in the environs of Ajmīr, Muhammad Beg, an attendant on my fortunate son Sultān Khurram, came and brought a report from that son, and stated that the Rānā had come with his sons and paid his respects to the prince: the details would be made known by the report. I immediately turned the face of supplication to the Divine Court, and prostrated myself in thanksgiving. I presented a horse, an elephant, and a jewelled dagger to the aforesaid Muhammad Khān, and honoured him with the title of Zu-l-faqār Khān ['Lord of the sword']."[2]

"From the report it appeared that on Sunday the 26th Bahman, the Rānā paid his respects to my fortunate son with the politeness and ritual that servants pay their respects, and pro-

[1] [*Memoirs*, 272 ff.] [2] [*Ibid.* 275.]

duced as offerings a famous large ruby that was in his house, with some decorated articles and seven elephants, some of them fit for the private stud, and which had not fallen into our hands, and were the only ones left him, and nine horses. My son also behaved to him with perfect kindness. When the Rānā clasped his feet and asked forgiveness for his faults, he took his hand and placed it on his breast, and consoled him in such a manner as to comfort him. He presented him with a superb dress of honour, a jewelled sword, a horse with a jewelled saddle, and a private elephant with silver housings, and as there were not more than 100 men with him who were worthy of complete robes of honour, he gave 100 *sarupā* [dresses] and 50 horses and 12 jewelled *khapwā* [daggers]. As it is the custom of the Zamīndārs [1] that the son who is the heir-apparent should not go with his father to pay his respects to a king or prince,[2] the Rānā observed this custom, and did not bring with him Karan, the son who had received the *tīkā* [forehead mark of inauguration]. As the hour (fixed by astrology) of his departure of that son of lofty fortune from that place was the end of that same day, he gave him leave, so that, having himself gone, he might send Karan to pay his respects. To him also he gave a superb dress of honour, a jewelled sword and dagger, a horse with a gold saddle, and a special elephant, and on the same day, taking Karan in attendance, he proceeded towards the illustrious Court." [3]

"In my interview with Sultan Khurram on his arrival at Ajmer,[4] he represented that if it was my pleasure he would present the prince Karan, whom I accordingly desired him to bring. He arrived, paid his respects, *and his rank was commanded to be, at the request of my son, immediately on my right hand*, and I rewarded him with suitable khilats. As Karan, owing to the rude life he had led in his native hills, was extremely shy, and unused to the pageantry and experience of a court, in order to reconcile and give him confidence I daily gave him some testimonies of my

[1] [The Rāna is purposely treated as a mere landowner under the State.]

[2] This was to avoid treachery. I have often had the honour to receive the descendant princes, father and son, 'of these illustrious ones' together (note by the Author).

[3] [*Memoirs*, 275 f.]

[4] [The remaining part of the narrative is fairly correct, and has been allowed to stand, with necessary corrections in transliteration of proper names.]

regard and protection, and in the second day of his service I gave him a jewelled dagger, and on the third a choice steed of Irak with rich caparisons; and on the same day, I took him with me to the queen's court, when the queen, Nur Jahan, made him splendid khilats, elephant and horse caparisoned, sword, etc. The same day I gave him a rich necklace of pearls, another day an elephant, and it was my wish to give him rarities and choice things of every kind. I gave him three royal hawks and three gentle falcons trained to the hand,[1] a coat of mail, chain and plate armour, and two rings of value; and, on the last day of the month, carpets, state cushions, perfumes, vessels of gold, and a pair of the bullocks of Gujarat.[2]

"10th year.[3] At this time I gave prince Karan leave to return to his jagir;[4] when I bestowed on him an elephant, horse, and a pearl necklace valued at 50,000 rupees (£5000); and from the day of his repairing to my court to that of his departure, the value of the various gifts I presented him exceeded ten lakhs of rupees (£125,000), exclusive of one hundred and ten horses, five elephants, or what my son Khurram gave him. I sent Mubarik Khan along with [364] him, by whom I sent an elephant, horse, etc., and various confidential messages to the Rana.

"On the 8th Safar[5] of the 10th year of the H. 1024 Karan was elevated to the dignity of a Mansabdar[6] of five thousand, when I presented him with a bracelet of pearls, in which was a ruby of great price.

"24th Muharram,[7] 10th year (A.D. 1615), Jagat Sing, son of Karan, aged twelve years, arrived at court and paid his respects, and presented the arzis of his father and grandfather, Rana Amra Singh. *His countenance carried the impression of his*

[1] Baz and Tura.

[2] [On the famous oxen of Gujarat see Forbes, *Rāsmāla*, 540; Watt, *Comm. Prod.* 733 ff.]

[3] Of his reign.

[4] Such was now the degraded title of the ancient, independent sovereign Mewar. Happy Partap, whose ashes being mingled with his parent earth, was spared his country's humiliation!

[5] [The second month of the Musalmān calendar.]

[6] With this the annals state the restoration of many districts: the Kherar, Phulia, Badnor, Mandalgarh, Jiran, Nimach, and Bhainsror, with supremacy over Deolia, and Dungarpur.

[7] [The first month of the Muhammadan year.]

illustrious extraction,[1] *and I delighted his heart with presents and kindness.*

[1] It must have been this grandson of Amra of whom Sir Thomas Roe thus writes: "The right issue of Porus is here a king in the midst of the Mogul's dominions, never subdued till last year; and, to say the truth, he is rather bought than conquered: won to own a superior by gifts and not by arms. The pillar erected by Alexander is yet standing at Delhi, the ancient seat of Rama, the successor of Porus" (*Extract of a letter to the Archbishop of Canterbury, dated at Ajmere, January* 29, 1615).

Copy of a letter written by the great Mogul unto King James, in the Persian tongue, here faithfully translated, which was as follows:

"Unto a king rightly descended from his ancestors, bred in military affairs, clothed with honour and justice, a commander worthy of all command, strong and constant in the religion which the great prophet Christ did teach, King James, whose love hath bred such an impression in my thoughts as shall never be forgotten; but as the smell of amber, or as a garden of fragrant flowers, whose beauty and odour is still increasing, so, be assured, my love shall still grow and increase with yours.

"The letters which you sent me in the behalf of your merchants I have received, whereby I rest satisfied of your tender love towards me, desiring you not to take it ill, that I have not wrote to you heretofore: this present letter I send to you to renew our loves, and herewith do certifie you, that I have sent forth my firmaunes throughout all my countries to this effect, that if any English ships or merchants shall arrive in any of my ports, my people shall permit and suffer them to do what they please, freely in their merchandising causes, aiding and assisting them in all occasion of injuries that shall be offered them, that the least cause of discourtesie be not done unto them; that they may be as free, or freer than my own people.

"And as now, and formerly, I have received from you divers tokens of your love; so I shall still desire your mindfulness of me by some novelties from your countries, as an argument of friendship betwixt us, for such is the custom of princes here.

"And for your merchants, I have given express order through all my dominions, to suffer them to buy, sell, transport, and carry away at their pleasure, without the lett or hinderance of any person whatsoever, all such goods and merchandises as they shall desire to buy; and let this my letter as fully satisfie you in desired peace and love, as if my own son had been messenger to ratifie the same.

"And if any in my countries, not fearing God, nor obeying their king, or any other void of religion, should endeavour to be an instrument to break this league of friendship, I would send my son Sultan Caroom, a souldier approved in the wars, to cut him off, that no obstacle may hinder the continuance and increase of our affections.

"When your majesty shall open this letter, let your royal heart be as fresh as a small garden, let all people make reverence at your gate. Let your throne be advanced higher. Amongst the greatness of the kings of the prophet Jesus, let your majesty be the greatest; and all monarchs derive their wisdom and counsel from your breast, as from a fountain, that

"On the 10th Shaban,[1] Jagat Singh had permission to return to his house. At his departure I presented him with 20,000 rupees, a horse, elephant, and khilats [365]; and to Haridas Jhala, preceptor of Prince Karan, 5000 rupees, a horse, and khilat; and I sent by him six golden images[2] to the Rana.

"28th Rabiu-l-Ākhir,[3] 11th year. *The statues of the Rana and Karan, sculptured in white marble, I desired should have inscribed the date in which they were prepared and presented, and commanded they should be placed in the gardens at Agra.*[4]

"In the 11th year of my reign an arzi from Itimad Khan acquainted me that Sultan Khurram had entered the Rana's country, and that prince and his son had both exchanged visits with my son; and that from the tribute, consisting of seven elephants, twenty-seven saddle horses, trays of jewels, and ornaments of gold, my son took three horses and returned all the rest, and engaged that Prince Karan and fifteen hundred Rajput horse should remain with him in the wars.

"In the 13th year Prince Karan repaired to my court, then at Sindla, to congratulate me on my victories and conquest of the Deccan, and presented 100 mohars,[5] 1000 rupees, nazarana, and effects in gold and jewels to the amount of 21,000 rupees, hardy

---

the law of the majesty of Jesus may receive, and flourish under your protection.

"The letters of love and friendship which you sent me, the present tokens of your good affection towards me, I have received by the hands of your ambassadour, Sir Thomas Row, who well deserveth to be your trusty servant, delivered to me in an acceptable and happy hour; upon which mine eyes were so fixed, that I could not easily remove them unto any other objects, and have accepted them with great joy and delight, etc."

The last letter had this beginning: "How gracious is your majesty, whose greatness God preserve. As upon a rose in a garden, so are mine eyes fixed upon you. God maintain your estate, that your monarchy may prosper and be augmented; and that you may obtain all your desires worthy the greatness of your renown; and as the heart is noble and upright, so let God give you a glorious reign, because you strongly defend the law of the majesty of Jesus, which God made yet more flourishing, for that it was confirmed by miracles, etc." (*Della Valle*, p. 473).

[1] [Sha'bān, the eighth month.]

[2] There are frequent mention of such images (*putlis*), but I know not which they are. [The word in the original is *Shoshpari*, 'golden maces.']

[3] [The fourth month.]

[4] [On these statues see Smith, *HFA*, 426 ff.]

[5] Golden suns, value £1 : 12s.

elephants and horses; the last I returned, but kept the rest, and next day presented him a dress of honour; and from Fatehpur gave him his leave, with elephant, horse, sword, and dagger, and a horse for his father.

"14th year of my reign. On the 17th Rabiu-l-awwal,[1] 1029 H., I received intelligence of the death of Rana Amra Singh.[2] To Jagat Singh, his grandson, and Bhim Singh, his son, in attendance, I gave khilats, and dispatched Raja Kishordas[3] with the farman conferring benefits and with the dignity of Rana, the khilat of investiture, choice horses, and a letter of condolence suitable to the occasion to Prince Karan. 7th Shawwal.[4] Biharidas Brahman I dispatched with a [366] farman to Rana Karan, desiring that his son with his contingent should attend me."

Treatment of the Rāna by Jahāngīr.—To have generalized this detail of the royal historian would have been to lessen the interest of this important period in the annals of Mewar. Jahangir merits to have his exultation, his noble and unostentatious conduct, described by his own pen, the extreme minuteness of which description but increases the interest. With his self-gratulation, he bears full testimony to the gallant and long-protracted resistance of the Rajputs; and while he impartially, though rather erroneously, estimates their motives and means of opposition, he does Amra ample justice in the declaration, that he did not yield until he had but the alternative of captivity or exile; and with a magnanimity above all praise, he records the Rajput prince's salvo for his dignity, "that he would hold himself excused from attending in person." The simple and naïve declaration of his joy, "his going abroad on 'Alam Guman," the favourite elephant of the Rana which had been captured, on learning his submission, is far stronger than the most pompous testimony of public rejoicing. But there is a heart-stirring philanthropy in the conduct of the Mogul which does him immortal honour; and in commanding his son "to treat the illustrious one according to his heart's wishes," though he so long and so signally had foiled the royal armies, he proved himself worthy of the good fortune he acknowledges, and well shows his

[1] [The third month.] [2] [He died in 1620.]

[3] Increasing the respect to the Ranas by making a prince the bearer of the farman.

[4] [The tenth month.]

sense of the superiority of the chief of all the Rajputs, by placing the heir of Mewar, even above all the princes of his own house, 'immediately on his right hand.' Whether he attempts to relieve the shyness of Karan, or sets forth the princely appearance of Jagat Singh, we see the same amiable feeling operating to lighten the chains of the conquered. But the shyness of Karan deserved a worthier term: he felt the degradation which neither the statues raised to them, the right hand of the monarch, the dignity of a 'commander of five thousand,' or even the restoration of the long-alienated territory could neutralize, when the kingdom to which he was heir was called a fief (*jagir*), and himself, 'the descendant of a hundred kings,' a vassal (*jagirdar*) of the empire, under whose banner, which his ancestors had so signally opposed, he was now to follow with a contingent of fifteen hundred Rajput horse.

Seldom has subjugated royalty met with such consideration; yet, to a lofty mind like Amra's, this courteous condescension but increased the severity of endurance [367]. In the bitterness of his heart he cursed the magnanimity of Khurram, himself of Rajput blood [1] and an admirer of Rajput valour, which circumstance more than the force of his arms had induced him to surrender; for Khurram demanded but the friendship of the Rajput as the price of peace, and to withdraw every Muhammadan from Mewar if the Rāna would but receive the emperor's farman outside of his capital. This his proud soul rejected; and though he visited Prince Khurram as a friend, he spurned the proposition of acknowledging a superior, or receiving the rank and titles awaiting such an admission. The noble Amra, who—

Rather than be less,
Cared not to be at all—

took the resolution to abdicate [2] the throne he could no longer hold but at the will of another. Assembling his chiefs, and

[1] Khurram was son of a Rajput princess of Amber [whose name, according to Beale, was Balmati] of the Kachhwaha tribe, and hence his name was probably *Kurm*, synonymous to *kachhwa*, a tortoise. The bards are always punning upon it. [The Persian word *khurram*, 'glad, joyful,' has, of course, no connexion with Hindi *kurm*, 'a tortoise.']

[2] Surrendered S. 1672, A.D. 1616 (according to Dow, S. 1669, A.D. 1613); died 1621 [1620. There seems to be no corroboration of his abdication.]

disclosing his determination, he made the *tika* on his son's forehead; and observing that the honour of Mewar was now in his hands, forthwith left the capital and secluded himself in the Nauchauki:[1] nor did he from that hour cross its threshold, but to have his ashes deposited with those of his fathers.

Character of Rāna Amar Singh.—All comment is superfluous on such a character as Rana Amra. He was worthy of Partap and his race. He possessed all the physical as well as mental qualities of a hero, and was the tallest and strongest of all the princes of Mewar. He was not so fair as they usually are, and he had a reserve bordering upon gloominess, doubtless occasioned by his reverses, for it was not natural to him; he was beloved by his chiefs for the qualities they most esteem, generosity and valour, and by his subjects for his justice and kindness, of which we can judge from his edicts, many of which yet live on the column or the rock [368].

CHAPTER 13

Rāna Karan Singh II., A.D. **1620–28.**—Karan, or Karna (*the radiant*), succeeded to the last independent king of Mewar, S. 1677, A.D. 1621. Henceforth we shall have to exhibit these princely 'children of the sun' with diminished lustre, moving as satellites round the primary planet; but, unaccustomed to the laws of its attraction, they soon deviated from the orbit prescribed, and in the eccentricity of their movements occasionally displayed their unborrowed effulgence. For fifteen hundred years we have traced each alternation of the fortune of this family, from their establishment in the second, to their expulsion in the fifth century from Saurashtra by the Parthians; the acquisition and loss of Idar; the conquest and surrender of Chitor; the rise of Udaipur

[1] It must have been here that Sultan Khurram visited the Rana. The remains of this palace, about half a mile without the city wall (north), on a cluster of hills, are yet in existence. It was built by Udai Singh on the banks of a lake, under which are gardens and groves, where the author had the Rana's permission to pitch his tents in the hottest months. [When Khurram was in revolt against his father, he stayed at first in the Rāna's palace; but as his followers little respected Rājput prejudices, he removed to the Jagmandir, and the island became his home till shortly before his father's death (Erskine ii. A, 109).]

and abasement of the red flag to Jahangir; and we shall conclude with not the least striking portion of their history, their unity of interests with Britain.

Karan was deficient neither in courage nor conduct; of both he had given a decided proof, when, to relieve the pecuniary difficulties of his father, with a rapidity unparalleled, he passed through the midst of his foes, surprised and plundered Surat, and carried off a booty which was the means of protracting the evil days of his country. But for the exercise of the chief virtue of the Rajput, he [369] had little scope throughout his reign, and fortunately for his country the powerful esteem and friendship which Jahangir and Prince Khurram evinced for his house, enabled him to put forth the talents he possessed to repair past disasters. He fortified the heights round the capital, which he strengthened with a wall and ditch, partly enlarged the noble dam which retains the waters of the Pichola, and built that entire portion of the palace called the Rawala, still set apart for the ladies of the court.

Terms between Rāna Karan Singh and Jahāngīr.—When Rana Amra made terms with Jahangir, he stipulated, as a salvo for his dignity and that of his successors, exemption from all personal attendance; and confined the extent of homage to his successors receiving, on each lapse of the crown, the farman or imperial decree in token of subordination, which, more strongly to mark their dependent condition, the Rana was to accept without the walls of his capital; accordingly, though the heirs-apparent of Mewar [1] attended the court, they never did as Rana. Partly to lessen the weight of this sacrifice to independence, and partly to exalt the higher grade of nobles, the princes of the blood-royal of Mewar were made to rank below the Sixteen, a fictitious diminution of dignity which, with similar acts peculiar to this house, enhanced the self-estimation of the nobles, and made them brave every danger to obtain such sacrifices to the ruling passion of the Rajput, a love of distinction.[2] It is mentioned by the emperor

[1] The contingent of Mewar was one thousand horse.

[2] During the progress of my mediation between the Rana and his nobles, in 1818, the conduct of the lineal representative of Jaimall, the defender of Chitor against Akbar, was striking. Instead of surrendering the lands which he was accused of usurping, he placed himself at the door of the threshold of the palace, whence he was immovable. His claims were left to my adjudication: but he complained with great heat of the omission of cere-

RĀJMAHALL.

To face page 428.

that he placed the heir-apparent of Mewar immediately on his right hand, over all the princes of Hindustan; consequently the superior nobles of Mewar, who were all men of royal descent, deemed themselves, and had their [370] claims admitted, to rank above their peers at other courts, and to be seated almost on an equality with their princes.[1]

Sesodias in the Imperial Service.—The Sesodia chieftains were soon distinguished amongst the Rajput vassals of the Mogul, and had a full share of power. Of these Bhim, the younger brother of Karan, who headed the quota of Mewar, was conspicuous, and became the chief adviser and friend of Sultan Khurram, who well knew his intrepidity. At his son's solicitation, the emperor conferred upon him the title of Raja, and assigned a small principality on the Banas for his residence, of which Toda was the capital. Ambitious of perpetuating a name, he erected a new city and palace on the banks of the river, which he called Rajmahall, and which his descendants held till about forty years ago. The ruins of Rajmahall[2] bear testimony to the architectural taste

monials, and especially of the prostration of honours by the prince. I incautiously remarked that these were trivial compared with the other objects in view, and begged him to disregard it. "Disregard it! why, it was for these things my ancestors sacrificed their lives; when such a band * as this on my turban was deemed ample reward for the most distinguished service, and made them laugh at wounds and hardships!" Abashed at the inconsiderate remark which provoked this lofty reproof, I used my influence to have the omission rectified: the lands were restored, and the enthusiastic reverence with which I spoke of Jaimall would have obtained even greater proof of the Badnor chief's regard for the fame of his ancestors than the surrender of them implied. Who would not honour this attachment to such emblems in the days of adversity?

[1] This was conceded, as the following anecdote will attest. When the first Peshwa [Bālaji Visvanāth (1707–20)] appeared at the Jaipur court he was accompanied by the Salumbar chieftain. The Jaipur prince divided his gaddi (*cushion*) with the Peshwa, and the latter made room for the Salumbar chief upon it, observing that their privileges and rank were similar. The same Peshwa had the address to avoid all discussion of rank at Udaipur, by alleging the prerogative of his order to '*spread his cloth in front of the throne*,' a distinction to which every priest is entitled.

[2] The plate represents Rajmahall, on the Banas, now in the fief of Rao Chand Singh, one of the Jaipur nobles, whose castle of Duni is in the

* *Balaband*, a fillet or band, sometimes embroidered; often, as in the present case, of silk or gold thread knotted, and tassels tied round the turban. *Balaband* is synonymous with diadem.

of this son of Mewar, as do the fallen fortunes of his descendant to the instability of power : the lineal heir of Raja Bhim serves the chief of Shahpura on half a crown a day!

Revolt and Death of Bhīm Singh.—Jahangir, notwithstanding his favours, soon had a specimen of the insubordinate spirit of Bhim. Being desirous to separate him from Sultan Khurram, who aspired to the crown in prejudice to his elder brother Parvez, he appointed Bhim to the government of Gujarat, which was distinctly refused. Detesting Parvez, who, it will be recollected, invaded Mewar, and was foiled for his cruelty on this occasion, Bhim advised his friend at once to throw off the mask, if he aspired to reign. Parvez was slain,[1] and Khurram manifested his guilt by flying to arms [371]. He was secretly supported by a strong party of the Rajput interest, at the head of which was Gaj Singh of Marwar, his maternal grandfather, who cautiously desired to remain neutral. Jahangir advanced to crush the incipient revolt; but dubious of the Rathor (Gaj Singh), he gave the van to Jaipur, upon which the prince furled his banners and determined to be a spectator. The armies approached and were joining action, when the impetuous Bhim sent a message to the Rathor either to aid or oppose them. The insult provoked him to the latter course, and Bhim's party was destroyed, himself slain,[2] and Khurram and Mahabat Khan compelled to seek refuge

---

distance. There are many picturesque scenes of this nature on the Banas. Duni made a celebrated defence against Sindhia's army in 1808, and held out several months, though the Mahratta prince had an army of forty thousand men and a park of eighty pieces of cannon to oppose two hundred Rajputs. They made sorties, captured his foragers, cut his batteries to pieces, and carried off his guns (of which they had none), and, placing them on their walls, with his own shot made the whole army change position, beyond matchlock range. At last their inexpertness rendered them useless, and they obtained honourable terms. On one occasion the foragers of our escort were returning, and met Sindhia's coming away without their guns and cattle, which had just been taken from them. Our lads, from fellowship, volunteered to recover them, and returned on the captors, who gave them up (if my memory deceive me not) without a struggle, and from respect to the red coat!

[1] [Parvez died at Burhānpur, Nimār District, Central Provinces, in his thirty-eighth year, on October 28, 1626.]

[2] Man Singh, chief of the Saktawats, and his brother Gokuldas, were Bhim's advisers, and formed with Mahabat Khan the junta who ruled the Mogul heir-apparent. Man held Sanwar in the Khairar, and was celebrated

in Udaipur. In this asylum he remained undisturbed: apartments in the palace were assigned to him; but his followers little respecting Rajput prejudices, the island became his residence, on which a sumptuous edifice was raised, adorned with a lofty dome crowned with the crescent. The interior was decorated with mosaic, in onyx, cornelian, jaspers, and agates, rich Turkey carpets, etc.; and that nothing of state might be wanting to the royal refugee, a throne was sculptured from a single block of serpentine, supported by quadriform female Caryatidae. In the court a little chapel was erected to the Muhammadan saint Madar,[1] and here the prince with his court resided, every wish anticipated, till a short time before his father's death, when he retired into Persia.[2]

Such was Rajput gratitude to a prince who, when the chances of war made him victor over them, had sought unceasingly to mitigate the misery attendant on the loss of independence! It is pleasing to record to the honour of this calumniated race, that these feelings on the part of Karan were not transient; and that so far from expiring with the object,

> The debt immense of endless gratitude

was transmitted as an heirloom to his issue; and though two centuries have fled, during which Mewar had suffered every

---

in Amra's wars as the great champion of the Sesodias. He counted above eighty wounds, and had at various times "sent a *ser* (two pounds) of exfoliated bone to the Ganges." Such was the affection between Man and Bhim, that they concealed the death of the latter, sending him food in Bhim's name; but he no sooner learned the truth than he tore away the bandages and expired. Of Gokuldas the bard says, in allusion to the peaceful reign of Karan, "The wreath of Karan's renown was fading, but Gokul revived it with his blood." It was with the Sesodia Rajputs and the Saktawats that Mahabat performed the most daring exploit in Mogul history, making Jahangir prisoner in his own camp: but it is too long for insertion in a note. [This occurred in 1626; see Elphinstone, *Hist. of India*, 568.]

[1] [The saint Madār is said to have been a Jew from Aleppo who lived from A.D. 1050 to 1433, and was buried at Makanpur in the Cawnpur District, where pilgrims visit his tomb (*IGI*, xvii. 43; *Dabistan*, trans. Shea-Troyer iii. 244 ff.).]

[2] Contemporary historians say to Golkonda. [Khurram was prevented by bad health from going to Persia, and proceeded to the Deccan, whence he returned after his father's death (Elphinstone, *op. cit.* 573; Elliot-Dowson vi. 433, 437, 445).]

variety of woe, pillaged by Mogul [372], Pathan, and Mahratta, yet the turban of Prince Khurram, the symbol of fraternity,[1] has been preserved, and remains in the same folds as when transferred from the head of the Mogul to that of the Rajput prince. The shield is yet held as the most sacred of relics, nor will the lamp which illumines the chapel of Madar want oil while the princes of Udaipur have wherewithal to supply it.[2]

Death of Rāna Karan Singh.—Rana Karan had enjoyed eight years of perfect tranquillity when he was gathered to his fathers. The sanctuary he gave Prince Khurram had no apparent effect on Jahangir, who doubtless believed that the Rana did not sanction the conduct of his brother Bhim. He was succeeded by his son Jagat Singh, 'the lion of the world,' in S. 1684 (A.D. 1628).

Rāna Jagat Singh I., A.D. 1628-52.—The Emperor Jahangir died shortly after his accession [October 28, 1627], and while Khurram was in exile. This event, which gave the throne to the friend of his house, was announced to him by the Rana, who sent his brother and a band of Rajputs to Surat to form the cortege of the emperor, who repaired directly to Udaipur; and it was in the Badal Mahall ('the cloud saloon') of his palace that he was first saluted by the title of 'Shah Jahan,' by the satraps and tributary princes of the empire.[3] On taking leave, the new monarch restored five alienated districts, and presented the Rana

[1] An exchange of turbans is the symbol of fraternal adoption.

[2] It is an affecting proof of the perpetuity of true gratitude,

"Which owing, owes not,"

as well as of religious toleration, to find the shrine of the Muhammadan saint maintained in this retreat of the Sesodias, and the priest and establishment kept up, though the son of their benefactor persecuted them with unrelenting barbarity. Are these people worth conciliating? or does the mist of ignorance and egotism so blind us that we are to despise the minds hidden under the cloak of poverty and long oppression? The orange-coloured turban, and the shield of Shah Jahan, have been brought from their sacred niche for my view: that I looked on them with sentiments of reverence, as relics consecrated by the noblest feeling of the mind, will be credited. I bowed to the turban with an irresistible impulse, and a fervour as deep as ever did pilgrim before the most hallowed shrine.

[3] Ferishta [Dow iii. 99], whose geography is often quite unintelligible, omits this in his history, and passes the king direct to Ajmer: but the annals are fuller, and describe the royal insignia conveyed by Mahabat, Abdulla, Khan Jahan, and his secretary Sadullah.

JAGMANDIR PALACE, UDAIPUR.

To face page 432.

with a ruby of inestimable value, giving him also permission to reconstruct the fortifications of Chitor.[1]

The twenty-six years during which Jagat Singh occupied the throne passed in uninterrupted tranquillity: a state unfruitful to the bard, who flourishes only amidst agitation and strife. This period was devoted to the cultivation of the peaceful arts, especially architecture; and to Jagat Singh Udaipur is indebted for those magnificent works which bear his name, and excite our astonishment, after all the disasters we have related, at the resources he found to accomplish them [373].

Erection of Buildings at Udaipur.—The palace on the lake (covering about four acres), called the Jagniwas, is entirely his work, as well as many additions to its sister isle, on which is the Jagmandir.[2] Nothing but marble enters into their composition; columns, baths, reservoirs, fountains, all are of this material, often inlaid with mosaics, and the uniformity pleasingly diversified by the light passing through glass of every hue. The apartments are decorated with historical paintings in water-colours, almost meriting the term fresco from their deep absorption in the wall, though the darker tints have blended with and in part obscured the more delicate shades, from atmospheric causes. The walls, both here and in the grand palace, contain many medallions, in considerable relief, in gypsum, portraying the principal historical events of the family, from early periods even to the marriage pomp of the present Rana. Parterres of flowers, orange and lemon groves, intervene to dispel the monotony of the buildings, shaded by the wide-spreading tamarind and magnificent evergreen khirni;[3] while the graceful palmyra and coco wave their plume-like branches over the dark cypress or cooling plantain. Detached colonnaded refectories are placed on the water's edge for the chiefs, and extensive baths for their use. Here they listened to the tale of the bard, and slept off their noonday opiate amidst

[1] [According to Manucci (i. 214 f.) Shāhjahān ordered his Wazīr S'adullah Khān to prepare a campaign against the Rāna, but the plan was disclosed by a woman, and the Rāna made terms, ceded territory, and paid a sum of money. Shāhjahān is said to have destroyed the fortifications of Chitor, on the ground that they had been repaired without his father's permission.]

[2] 'The minster of the world.' [According to Erskine (ii. A. 109) the Jagmandir was built by Jagat Singh I. (1628–52); the Jagniwās by Jagat Singh II. (1734–51).]

[3] [*Wrightia tinctoria* (Watt, *Comm. Prod.* 1131 f.).]

the cool breezes of the lake, wafting delicious odours from myriads of the lotus-flower which covered the surface of the waters; and as the fumes of the potion evaporated, they opened their eyes on a landscape to which not even its inspirations could frame an equal: the broad waters of the Pichola, with its indented and well-wooded margin receding to the terminating point of sight, at which the temple of Brahmpuri opened on the pass of the gigantic Aravalli, the field of the exploits of their forefathers. Amid such scenes did the Sesodia princes and chieftains recreate during two generations, exchanging the din of arms for voluptuous inactivity.

Jagat Singh was a highly respected prince, and did much to efface the remembrance of the rude visitations of the Moguls. The dignity of his character, his benevolence of address and personal demeanour, secured the homage of all who had access to him, and are alike attested by the pen of the emperor, the ambassador of England, and the chronicles of Mewar. He had the proud satisfaction [374] of redeeming the ancient capital from ruin; rebuilding the "chaplet bastion,[1] restoring the portals, and replacing the pinnacles on the temples of Chitrakot." By a princess of Marwar he left two sons, the eldest of whom succeeded.

Rāna Rāj Singh, A.D. 1652–80.—Raj Singh (the royal lion) mounted the throne in S. 1710 (A.D. 1654). Various causes over which he had no control combined, together with his personal character, to break the long repose his country had enjoyed. The emperor of the Moguls had reached extreme old age, and the ambition of his sons to usurp his authority involved every Rajput in support of their individual pretensions. The Rana inclined to Dara,[2] the legitimate heir to the throne, as did nearly the whole Rajput race; but the battle of Fatehabad[3] silenced every pretension, and gave the lead to Aurangzeb, which he maintained by the sacrifice of whatever opposed his ambition. His father, brothers, nay, his own offspring, were in turn victims to that thirst for power which eventually destroyed the monarchy of the Moguls.

[1] The *Mala Burj*, a 'chaplet bastion' blown up by Akbar, is a small fortress of itself.

[2] I have copies of the original letters written by Dara, Suja, Murad, and Aurangzeb on this occasion, each soliciting the Rana's aid.

[3] [Samūgarh, afterwards called Fatehābād, May 20, 1658 (Jadunāth Sarkar, *Life of Aurangzib*, ii. 32 ff.; Manucci i. 270 ff.; Bernier 49 ff.).]

The policy introduced by their founder, from which Akbar, Jahangir, and Shah Jahan had reaped so many benefits, was unwisely abandoned by the latter, who of all had the most powerful reasons for maintaining those ties which connected the Rajput princes with his house. Historians have neglected to notice the great moral strength derived from this unity of the indigenous races with their conquerors ; for during no similar period was the empire so secure, nor the Hindu race so cherished, as during the reigns of Jahangir and Shah Jahan : the former born from a Rajput princess of Amber, and the latter from the house of Marwar. Aurangzeb's unmixed Tatar blood brought no Rajput sympathies to his aid ; on the contrary, every noble family shed their best blood in withstanding his accession, and in the defence of Shah Jahan's rights, while there was a hope of success. The politic Aurangzeb was not blind to this defect, and he tried to remedy it in his successor ; for both his declared heir, Shah Alam, and Azam, as well as his favourite grandson,[1] were the offspring of Rajputnis ; but, uninfluenced himself by such predilections, his bigotry outweighed his policy, and he visited the Rajputs with an unrelenting and unwise persecution [375].

We shall pass the twice-told tale of the struggle for power which ended in the destruction of the brothers, competitors with Aurangzeb : this belongs to general history, not to the annals of Mewar ; and that history is in every hand,[2] in which the magnanimity of Dara,[3] the impetuosity of Murad, and the activity of Suja met the same tragical end.

Princes contemporary with Aurangzeb.—It has seldom occurred that so many distinguished princes were contemporary as during the reign of Aurangzeb. Every Rajput principality had a head above mediocrity in conduct as in courage. Jai Singh of Amber,

[1] Kambakhsh (son of Jodhpuri, not Udaipuri), 'the gift of Cupid.' Of this the Greeks made Cambyses. [Kāmbakhsh was son of Udaipuri, the youngest and best-loved concubine of Aurangzeb (Judunath Sarkar i. 64). Cambyses is Old Persian Kābuzīya or Kambuzīya (Maspero, *Passing of the Empires*, 655, note).]

[2] Bernier, who was an eye-witness of these transactions, describes them far better than the Mogul historians, and his accounts tally admirably with the Rajput annals. [But he is not always to be trusted (Jadunath Sarkar ii. 10, note).]

[3] [The proper form is Dāra Shukoh or Shikoh, 'equal in splendour to Darius.']

surnamed 'the Mirza Raja'; Jaswant Singh of Marwar, with the Haras of Bundi and Kotah; the Rathors of Bikaner, and Bundelas of Orchha and Datia, were men whose prejudices, properly consulted, would have rendered the Mogul power indissoluble: but he had but one measure of contumely for all, which inspired Sivaji with designs of freedom to Maharashtra, and withdrew every sentiment of support from the princes of Rajasthan. In subtlety and the most specious hypocrisy, in that concentration of resolve which confides its deep purpose to none, in every qualification of the warrior or scholar,[1] Aurangzeb had

[1] We possess a most erroneous idea of the understanding of Asiatic princes, and the extent of its cultivation. Aurangzeb's rebuke to his tutor Mulla Sale [Mulla Sālih, Bernier 154; Manucci ii. 30], who beset him with a sycophantic intrusion on his coming to the throne, may correct this, and, with the letter of Rana Raj Singh, give the European world juster notions of the powers of mind both of Hindu and Muhammadan. It is preserved by Bernier, who had ample opportunity to acquire a knowledge of them. (*From an edition in the author's possession, printed* A.D. 1684, *only three years after these events.*)

"'What is it you would have of me, Doctor? Can you reasonably desire I should make you one of the chief Omrahs of my court? Let me tell you, if you had instructed me as you should have done, nothing would be more just; for I am of this persuasion, that a child well educated and instructed is as much, at least, obliged to his master as to his father. But where are those good documents you have given me? In the first place, you have taught me that all that Frangistan (so it seems they call Europe) was nothing but I know not what little island, of which the greatest king was he of Portugal, and next to him he of Holland, and after him he of England: and as to the other kings, as those of France and Andalusia, you have represented them to me as our petty Rajas; telling me that the kings of Indostan were far above them all together, and that they were the true and only Houmayous, the Ekbars, the Jehan-Guyres, the Chah-Jehans, the fortunate ones, the great ones, the conquerors and kings of the world; and that Persia and Usbec, Kachguer, Tartar and Catay, Pegu, China and Matchina did tremble at the name of the kings of Indostan. Admirable geography! You should rather have taught me exactly to distinguish all those different states of the world, and well to understand their strength, their way of fighting, their customs, religions, governments, and interests; and, by the perusal of solid history, to observe their rise, progress, decay, and whence, how, and by what accidents and errors those great changes and revolutions of empires and kingdoms have happened. I have scarce learnt of you the name of my grandsires, the famous founders of this empire: so far were you from having taught me the history of their life, and what course they took to make such great conquests. You had a mind to teach me the Arabian tongue, to read and to write. I am much obliged to you, forsooth, for having made me lose so much time upon a language that

no superior amongst the many distinguished [376] of his race; but that sin by which 'angels fell' had steeped him in an ocean of guilt, and not only neutralized his natural capacities, but converted the means for unlimited power into an engine of self-

requires ten or twelve years to attain to its perfection; as if the son of a king should think it to be an honour to him to be a grammarian or some doctor of the law, and to learn other languages than those of his neighbours, when he cannot well be without them; he, to whom time is so precious for so many weighty things, which he ought by times to learn. As if there were any spirit that did not with some reluctancy, and even with a kind of debasement, employ itself in so sad and dry an exercise, so longsom and tedious, as is that of learning words.'

"Thus did Arung-Zebe resent the pedantic instructions of his tutor; to which 'tis affirmed in that court, that after some entertainment which he had with others, he further added the following reproof:

"'Know you not, that childhood well govern'd, being a state which is ordinarily accompanied with an happy memory, is capable of thousands of good precepts and instructions, which remain deeply impressed the whole remainder of a man's life, and keep the mind always raised for great actions? The law, prayers, and science, may they not as well be learned in our mother-tongue as in Arabick? You told my father, Chah Jehan, that you would teach me philosophy. 'Tis true, I remember very well, that you have entertain'd me for many years with airy questions of things that afford no satisfaction at all to the mind, and are of no use in humane society, empty notions and mere phancies, that have only this in them, that they are very hard to understand and very easie to forget, which are only capable to tire and spoil a good understanding, and to breed an opinion that is insupportable. I still remember, that after you had thus amused me, I know not how long, with your fine philosophy, all I retained of it was a multitude of barbarous and dark words, proper to bewilder, perplex, and tire out the best wits, and only invented the better to cover the vanity and ignorance of men like yourself, that would make us believe that they know all, and that under those obscure and ambiguous words are hid great mysteries which they alone are capable to understand. If you had season'd me with that philosophy which formeth the mind to ratiocination, and insensibly accustoms it to be satisfied with nothing but solid reasons, if you had given me those excellent precepts and doctrines which raise the soul above the assaults of fortune, and reduce her to an unshakeable and always equal temper, and permit her not to be lifted up by prosperity nor debased by adversity; if you had taken care to give me the knowledge of what we are and what are the first principles of things, and had assisted me in forming in my mind a fit idea of the greatness of the universe, and of the admirable order and motion of the parts thereof; if, I say, you had instilled into me this kind of philosophy, I should think myself incomparably more obliged to you than Alexander was to his Aristotle, and believe it my duty to recompense you otherwise than he did him. Should not you, instead of your flattery, have taught me somewhat of that point so important to a

destruction. "This hypocrisy," says the eloquent Orme,[1] "encreased with his power, and in order to palliate to his Mahomedan subjects the crimes by which he had become their sovereign, he determined to enforce the conversion of the Hindoos by the severest penalties, and even threatned the sword; as if the blood of his subjects were to wash away the stains, with which he was imbrued by the blood of his family. . . . Labour left the field and industry the loom, until the decrease of the revenues drew representations from the governors of the provinces; which induced Aurungzebe to substitute a capitation tax[2] as the ballance of the account between the two religions." The same historian justly characterizes this enactment as one so contrary to all notions of sound policy, as well as of the feelings of humanity, that "reflection seeks the motive with amazement." In this amazement we might remain, nor seek to develop the motive, did not the ample page of history in all [377] nations disclose that in the name of religion more blood has been shed, and more atrocity committed, than by the united action of the whole catalogue of the passions. Muhammad's creed was based on conversion, which, by whatever means effected, was a plenary atonement for every crime. In obedience thereto Aurangzeb acted; but though myriads of victims who clung to their faith were sacrificed by him at the fiat of this gladiatorial prophet, yet nor these, nor the scrupulous fulfilment of fanatic observances, could soothe at the dread hour the perturbations of the 'still small voice' which whispered the names of father, brother, son, bereft by him of life. Eloquently does he portray these terrors in his letters to his grandson on his death-bed, wherein he says, "Whichever way I look, I see only the divinity"—and that an offended divinity [378].[3]

---

king, which is, what the reciprocal duties are of a sovereign to his subjects and those of subjects to their sovereign; and ought not you to have considered, that one day I should be obliged with the sword to dispute my life and the crown with my brothers? Is not that the destiny almost of all the sons of Indostan? Have you ever taken any care to make me learn, what 'tis to besiege a town or to set an army in array? For these things I am obliged to others, not at all to you. Go, and retire to the village whence you are come, and let nobody know who you are or what is become of you.'" [For another version of this speech see Bernier 154 ff., Manucci ii. 30 ff.]

[1] [*Historical Fragments of the Mogul Empire*, ed. 1782, p. 101. The quotation in the text has been corrected.]

[2] The Jizya.

[3] I deem it right, in order further to illustrate the cultivated understand-

Rāna Rāj Singh defies Aurangzeb.—Raj Singh had signalized his accession by the revival of the warlike Tika-daur, and plundered

---

ing of Aurangzeb, to annex the letters written to his sons a few days before his death. With such talents, with so just a conception as these and the rebuke to his tutor evince of his knowledge of the right, what might he not have been had not fell ambition misguided him!

"To Shaw Azim Shaw. [Shāh Āzam Shāh.]

"Health to thee! my heart is near thee. Old age is arrived: weakness subdues me, and strength has forsaken all my members. I came a stranger into this world, and a stranger I depart. I know nothing of myself, what I am, and for what I am destined. The instant which passed in power, hath left only sorrow behind it. I have not been the guardian and protector of the empire. My valuable time has been passed vainly. I had a patron in my own dwelling (conscience), but his glorious light was unseen by my dim sight. Life is not lasting, there is no vestige of departed breath, and all hopes from futurity are lost. The fever has left me, but nothing of me remains but skin and bone. My son (Kaum Buksh), though gone towards Beejapore, is still near; and thou, my son, are yet nearer. The worthy of esteem, Shaw Aulum, is far distant; and my grandson (Azeem Ooshaun), by the orders of God, is arrived near Hindostan. The camp and followers, helpless and alarmed, are like myself, full of affliction, restless as the quicksilver. Separated from their lord, they know not if they have a master or not.

"I brought nothing into this world, and, except the infirmities of man, carry nothing out. I have a dread for my salvation, and with what torments I may be punished. Though I have strong reliance on the mercies and bounty of God, yet, regarding my actions, fear will not quit me; but when I am gone, reflection will not remain. Come then what may, I have launched my vessel to the waves. Though Providence will protect the camp, yet, regarding appearances, the endeavours of my sons are indispensably incumbent. Give my last prayers to my grandson (Bedar Bukht), whom I cannot see, but the desire affects me. The Begum (his daughter) appears afflicted; but God is the only judge of hearts. The foolish thoughts of women produce nothing but disappointment. Farewell! farewell! farewell!" [This letter is printed by H. Bilimoria, *Letters of Aurangzeb*, 71 f.]

"To the Prince Kaum Buksh. [Kāmbakhsh.]

"My son, nearest to my heart. Though in the height of my power, and by God's permission, I gave you advice, and took with you the greatest pains, yet, as it was not the divine will, you did not attend with the ears of compliance. Now I depart a stranger, and lament my own insignificance, what does it profit me? I carry with me the fruits of my sins and imperfections. Surprising Providence! I came here alone, and alone I depart. The leader of this caravan hath deserted me. The fever which troubled me for twelve days has left me. Wherever I look, I see nothing but the divinity. My fears for the camp and followers are great: but, alas! I know not myself. My back is bent with weakness, and my feet have lost the powers of motion. The breath which rose is gone, and left not even

Malpura, which though on the Ajmer frontier, Shah Jahan, when advised to vengeance, replied "it was only a folly of his nephew."[1] An appeal to his gallantry made him throw down the gauntlet to Aurangzeb in the plenitude of his power, when the valour of the Sesodias again burst forth in all the splendour of the days of Partap; nor did the contest close till after a series of brilliant victories, and with the narrow escape from captivity of the Xerxes of Hindustan. The Mogul demanded the hand of the princess of Rupnagar, a junior branch of the Marwar house, and sent with the demand (a compliance with which was contemplated

---

hope behind it. I have committed numerous crimes, and know not with what punishments I may be seized. Though the protector of mankind will guard the camp, yet care is incumbent also on the faithful and my sons. When I was alive, no care was taken; and now I am gone, the consequence may be guessed. The guardianship of a people is the trust by God committed to my sons. Azim Shaw is near. Be cautious that none of the faithful are slain, or their miseries fall upon my head. I resign you, your mother and son, to God, as I myself am going. The agonies of death come upon me fast. Behadur Shaw is still where he was, and his son is arrived near Hindostan. Bedar Bukht is in Guzarat. Hyaut al Nissa, who has beheld no afflictions of time till now, is full of sorrows. Regard the Begum as without concern. *Odiporee,* your mother, was a partner in my illness, and wishes to accompany me in death; but every thing has its appointed time.*

"The domestics and courtiers, however deceitful, yet must not be ill-treated. It is necessary to gain your views by gentleness and art. Extend your feet no lower than your skirt. The complaints of the unpaid troops are as before. Dara Shekkoh, though of much judgment and good understanding, settled large pensions on his people, but paid them ill and they were ever discontented. I am going. Whatever good or evil I have done, it was for you. Take it not amiss, nor remember what offences I have done to yourself; that account may not be demanded of me hereafter. No one has seen the departure of his own soul; but I see that mine is departing" (*Memoirs of Eradut Khan*). See Scott's *Hist. of the Dekhan* [ii. Part iv.]. [This letter, with some variants, is printed by Bilimoria, 73 f.]

[1] The emperor was the adopted brother of Rana Karan.

---

* Orme [*Fragments*, 119] calls her a Cashmerian; certainly she was not a daughter of the Rana's family, though it is not impossible she may have been of one of the great families of Shahpura or Banera (then acting independently of the Rana), and her desire to burn shows her to have been Rajput. ["Such an inference is wrong, because a Hindu princess on marrying a Muslim king lost her caste and religion, and received Islamic burial. We read of no Rajputni of the harem of any of the Mughal emperors having burnt herself with her deceased husband, for the very good reason that a Muslim's corpse is buried and not burnt. Evidently Udipuri meant that she would kill herself in passionate grief on the death of Aurangzib" (Jadunath Sarkar i. 64, note).]

as certain) a cortège of two thousand horse to escort the fair to court. But the haughty Rajputni, either indignant at such precipitation or charmed with the gallantry of the Rana, who had evinced his devotion to the fair by measuring his sword with the head of her house, rejected with disdain the proffered alliance, and, justified by brilliant precedents in the romantic history of her nation, she entrusted her cause to the arm of the chief of the Rajput race, offering herself as the reward of protection. The family priest (her preceptor) deemed his office honoured by being the messenger of her wishes, and the billet he conveyed is incorporated in the memorial of this reign. "Is the swan to be the mate of the stork: a Rajputni, pure in blood, to be wife to the monkey-faced barbarian!" concluding with a threat of self-destruction if not saved from dishonour. This appeal, with other powerful motives, was seized on with avidity by the Rana as a pretext to throw away the scabbard, in order to illustrate the opening of a warfare, in which he determined to put all to the hazard in defence of his country and his faith. The issue was an omen of success to his warlike and [379] superstitious vassalage. With a chosen band he rapidly passed the foot of the Aravalli and appeared before Rupnagar, cut up the imperial guards, and bore off the prize to his capital. The daring act was applauded by all who bore the name of Rajput, and his chiefs with joy gathered their retainers around the 'red standard,' to protect the queen so gallantly achieved.

The Imposition of the Jizya or Capitation Tax.—The annalist of Rajputana is but an indifferent chronologist, and leaves us doubtful of the exact succession of events at this period. It was not, however, till the death of those two powerful princes, Jaswant Singh of Marwar and Jai Singh of Amber, both poisoned by command of the tyrant, the one at his distant government of Kabul, the other in the Deccan, that he deemed himself free to put forth the full extent of his long-concealed design, the imposition of the *jizya* or capitation tax on the whole Hindu race. But he miscalculated his measures, and the murder of these princes, far from advancing his aim, recoiled with vengeance on his head. Foiled in his plot to entrap the infant sons of the Rathor by the self-devotion of his vassals,[1] the compound treachery evinced that

[1] Two hundred and fifty Rajputs opposed five thousand of the Imperialists at a pass, till the family of Jaswant escaped.

their only hope lay in a deadly resistance. The mother of Ajit, the infant heir of Marwar, a woman of the most determined character, was a princess of Mewar, and she threw herself upon the Rana as the natural guardian of his rights, for sanctuary (*saran*) during the dangers of his minority. This was readily yielded, and Kelwa assigned as his residence, where under the immediate safeguard of the brave Durgadas Ajit resided,[1] while she nursed the spirit of resistance at home. A union of interests was cemented between these the chief States of Rajputana, for which they never before had such motive, and but for repeated instances of an ill-judged humanity, the throne of the Moguls might have been completely overturned [380].

Letter of Remonstrance to Aurangzeb.—On the promulgation of that barbarous edict, the *jizya*, the Rana remonstrated by letter, in the name of the nation of which he was the head, in a style of such uncompromising dignity, such lofty yet temperate resolve, so much of soul-stirring rebuke mingled with a boundless and tolerating benevolence, such elevated ideas of the Divinity with such pure philanthropy, that it may challenge competition with any epistolary production of any age, clime, or condition.[2]

[1] The Rana received the young Rathor with the most princely hospitality, and among other gifts a diamond worth ten thousand dinars is enumerated.

[2] This letter, first made known to Europe by Orme [*Fragments*, Notes, xciii. ff.], has by him been erroneously attributed to Jaswant Singh of Marwar, who was dead before the promulgation of the edict, as the mention of Ramsingh sufficiently indicates, whose father, Jai Singh, was contemporary with Jaswant, and ruled nearly a year after his death. My Munshi obtained a copy of the original letter at Udaipur, where it is properly assigned to the Rana. [Compare the version of this letter in Jadunath Sarkar (iii. 325 ff.), who remarks that "the internal evidence and biographical details of the writer apply to Shivaji and not to Raj Singh. In the penultimate paragraph of the letter *Rajah Ram Singh* is given for *Rana Raj Singh* by ASBMs and Orme; but no Jaipur chieftain could have been 'the head of the Hindus.'"] It were superfluous to give a translation after the elegant production of Sir W. B. Rouse.

"Letter from Rana Raj Singh to Aurangzeb.

"All due praise be rendered to the glory of the Almighty, and the munificence of your majesty, which is conspicuous as the sun and moon. Although I, your well-wisher, have separated from your sublime presence, I am nevertheless zealous in the performance of every bounden act of obedience and loyalty. My ardent wishes and strenuous services are employed to promote the prosperity of the Kings, Nobles, Mirzas, Rajahs, and Roys of the provinces of Hindostan, and the chiefs of Æraun, Turaun, Room, and Shawm,

In this are contained the true principles of Christianity, and to the illustrious Gentile, and such as acted as he did, was pointed

---

the inhabitants of the seven climates, and all persons travelling by land and by water. This my inclination is notorious, nor can your royal wisdom entertain a doubt thereof. Reflecting therefore on my former services, and your majesty's condescension, I presume to solicit the royal attention to some circumstances, in which the public as well as private welfare is greatly interested.

"I have been informed that enormous sums have been dissipated in the prosecution of the designs formed against me, your well-wisher; and that you have ordered a tribute to be levied to satisfy the exigencies of your exhausted treasury.

"May it please your majesty, your royal ancestor Mahomed Jelaul ul Deen Akbar, whose throne is now in heaven, conducted the affairs of this empire in equity and firm security for the space of fifty-two years, preserving every tribe of men in ease and happiness, whether they were followers of Jesus or of Moses, of David or Mahomed; were they Brahmins, were they of the sect of Dharians, which denies the eternity of matter, or of that which ascribes the existence of the world to chance, they all equally enjoyed his countenance and favour: insomuch that his people, in gratitude for the indiscriminate protection he afforded them, distinguished him by the appellation of *Juggut Gooroo* (Guardian of Mankind).

"His majesty Mahomed Noor ul Deen Jehangheer, likewise, whose dwelling is now in paradise, extended, for a period of twenty-two years, the shadow of his protection over the heads of his people; successful by a constant fidelity to his allies, and a vigorous exertion of his arm in business.

"Nor less did the illustrious Shah Jehan, by a propitious reign of thirty-two years, acquire to himself immortal reputation, the glorious reward of clemency and virtue.

"Such were the benevolent inclinations of your ancestors. Whilst they pursued these great and generous principles, wheresoever they directed their steps, conquest and prosperity went before them; and then they reduced many countries and fortresses to their obedience. During your majesty's reign, many have been alienated from the empire, and farther loss of territory must necessarily follow, since devastation and rapine now universally prevail without restraint. Your subjects are trampled under foot, and every province of your empire is impoverished; depopulation spreads, and difficulties accumulate. When indigence has reached the habitation of the sovereign and his princes, what can be the condition of the nobles? As to the soldiery, they are in murmurs; the merchants complaining, the Mahomedans discontented, the Hindoos destitute, and multitudes of people, wretched even to the want of their nightly meal, are beating their heads throughout the day in rage and desperation.

"How can the dignity of the sovereign be preserved who employs his power in exacting heavy tributes from a people thus miserably reduced? At this juncture it is told from east to west, that the emperor of Hindostan, jealous of the poor Hindoo devotee, will exact a tribute from Brahmins, Sanorahs, Joghies, Berawghies, Sanyasees; that, regardless of the illustrious

that golden sentence of toleration, "Those [381] who have not the law, yet do by nature the things contained in the law, shall be a law unto themselves."

Aurangzeb attacks Mewār.—This letter, the sanctuary afforded Ajit, and (what the historical parasite of the Mogul's life dared not indite [1]) the carrying off of his betrothed, made him pour out all the phials of his wrath against the devoted Mewar, and his preparations more resembled those for the conquest of a potent kingdom than the subjugation of a Rajput *zamindar*,[2] a vassal of that colossal empire on whose surface his domain was but a speck. In the very magnitude of these, the Suzerain of Hindustan paid the highest tribute of praise to the tributary Rajput, for he denuded the very extremities of his empire to assemble a host which he deemed must prove irresistible. Akbar was recalled from his province, Bengal; Azam from the distant Kabul; and even Muazzam (the Mogul's heir) from the war in the Deccan.

---

honour of his Timurean race, he condescends to exercise his power over the solitary inoffensive anchoret. If your majesty places any faith in those books, by distinction called divine, you will there be instructed that God is the God of all mankind, not the God of Mahomedans alone. The Pagan and the Mussulman are equally in His presence. Distinctions of colour are of His ordination. It is He who gives existence. In your temples, to His name the voice is raised in prayer; in a house of images, where the bell is shaken, still He is the object of adoration. To vilify the religion or customs of other men is to set at naught the pleasure of the Almighty. When we deface a picture, we naturally incur the resentment of the painter; and justly has the poet said, presume not to arraign or scrutinize the various works of power divine.

"In fine, the tribute you demand from the Hindoos is repugnant to justice: it is equally foreign from good policy, as it must impoverish the country: moreover, it is an innovation and an infringement of the laws of Hindostan. But if zeal for your own religion hath induced you to determine upon this measure, the demand ought, by the rules of equity, to have been made first upon Ramsing, who is esteemed the principal amongst the Hindoos. Then let your well-wisher be called upon, with whom you will have less difficulty to encounter; but to torment ants and flies is unworthy of an heroic or generous mind. It is wonderful that the ministers of your government should have neglected to instruct your majesty in the rules of rectitude and honour."

[1] It is well known that Aurangzeb forbade the continuation of the history of his life, subsequent to that portion comprehending the first ten years [the *Ālamgīrnāma*; see Jadunath Sarkar ii. 302].

[2] The epithet by which these Tatar sovereigns affected to call the indigenous (*bhumia*) princes.

With this formidable array [1] the emperor entered Mewar, and soon reduced the low countries, which experience had taught them were indefensible, the inhabitants previously retiring with their effects to the hills.[2] Chitor, Mandalgarh, Mandasor, Jiran, and many other strongholds were obtained after the usual form of opposition, and garrisoned by the Moguls. Meanwhile the Rana was animating the might of the Aravalli, where he meditated a resistance proportioned to the peril which threatened every cherished prejudice of his race: not the mere defence of dominion or dignity, but a struggle, *pro aris et focis*, around which rallied every Rajput with the most deadly determination. Even the primitive races of the western wilds, "the Palindas [3] and Palipats [3] (*lord of the passes*), with thousands of bows, and hearts devoted in the cause of Hindupat," [4] assembled round the red banner of Mewar. The Rana divided his forces into three bodies [382]. His eldest son, Jai Singh, was posted on the crest of the Aravalli, ready to act on the invaders from either side of the mountains. Prince Bhim was to the west, to keep up the communications with the outlets to Gujarat; while the Rana, with the main body, took post in the Nai defile, unassailable by the enemy, and hanging on his left flank, ready to turn it, and cut off all retreat the moment the Imperialists entered the mountains. Aurangzeb advanced to Debari, but instead of entering the valley of which it was the gorge, he halted, and by the advice of Tahawwar Khan [5] sent on Prince Akbar with fifty thousand men to the capital. This caution of the wily monarch saved him from the ably planned scheme of the Rajput prince, who evinced a thorough knowledge [6] of the topography of this intricate and

[1] There were no such field trains in Europe as those of the Moguls. Seventy pieces of heavy ordnance, sixty of horse artillery, and a dromedary corps three hundred strong, mounting swivels, accompanied the emperor on an excursion to Kashmir. Bernier, who gives this detail, describes what he saw [217 f.].

[2] [For this campaign see the account in Jadunath Sarkar, *Life of Aurangzib*, iii. 365 ff.]

[3] *Pāl* is the local term for these long defiles, the residence of the mountaineers: their *chiefs* are called *Indras*, *Pati*, in Bhakha, *Pat*.

[4] Chief of the Hindus.

[5] [In the text "Tyber" Khān. His original name was Jān Beg, also known as Bādshāh Kuli Khān, one of Aurangzeb's great nobles (Manucci ii. 239, note 3, 247, note). His tragical end is told later on.]

[6] The Saktawat leader, Gharibdas, has the merit of having prompted

romantic portion of his domain. The Girwa, emphatically 'the Circle,' from which the valley of the capital is named, has this form to the eye when viewing it from thence as a centre. It is, however, an irregular ellipse of about fourteen miles in length from south to north, and about eleven in breadth from east to west, the capital being situated towards the extremity of the transverse axis, having only the lake Pichola between it and the base of the Aravalli. The mountains of this circular (*girwa*) valley, ranging from eight to twelve hundred feet in height, are of primitive formation, and raise their fantastic pinnacles in every diversity of shape over each other. To the westward the grand chain rises two thousand feet above the plains, and might be termed the chord, of which the Girwa is an irregular segment of a circle, less in height, and far less compound in character. Towards the plains east, it has three practicable passes ; one, the more northern, by Delwara ; the other (central), by Debari ; a third, leading to the intricacies of Chappan, that of Nai. Of these three passes the emperor chose the most practicable, and encamped near the Udaisagar lake, on the left of its entrance.

The Advance of Prince Akbar.—Prince Akbar advanced. "Not a soul interrupted his progress to the city. Palaces, gardens, lakes, and isles met his eye, but no living thing : all was silence." Akbar encamped. Accustomed to this desertion from the desire of the people to avoid a licentious soldiery, and lulled into a hardy security, he was surprised [383] by the heir of Mewar. Some were praying, some feasting, some at chess : "they came to steal and yet fell asleep," says the annalist, and were dispersed with terrific and unrelenting slaughter. Cut off from the possibility of a junction with the emperor by a movement of a part of the Rana's personal force, Akbar attempted a retreat to the plains of Marwar by the route of Gogunda. It was a choice of evils, and he took the worst. The allodial vassals of the mountains, with the Bhil auxiliaries, outstripped his retreat, and blocked up farther egress in one of those long-extended valleys termed *Nal*, closed by a natural rampart or *Col*, on which they

---

this plan. His speech on the advance of Aurangzeb is given in the Annals ; and his advice, "Let the king have free entrance through the passes, shut him in, and make famine his foe," was literally followed, with the hard knocks, which being a matter-of-course accompaniment, the gallant Saktawat deemed it unnecessary to specify.

formed *abbatis* of trees, and manning the crests on each side, hurled destruction on the foe; while the prince, in like manner, blocked up the entrance and barred retrogression. Death menaced them in every form. For several days they had only the prospect of surrender to save them from famine and a justly incensed foe, when an ill-judged humanity on the part of Jai Singh saved them from annihilation. He admitted overtures, confided in protestations to renounce the origin of the war, and gave them guides to conduct them by the defile of Jhilwara, nor did they halt till protected by the walls of Chitor.[1]

[1] Orme, who has many valuable historical details of this period, makes Aurangzeb in person to have been in the predicament assigned by the annals to his son, and to have escaped from the operation of those high and gallant sentiments of the Rajput, which make him no match for a wily adversary.

"In the meantime Aurengzebe was carrying on the war against the Rana of Cheetore, and the Raja of Marwar, who on the approach of his army at the end of the preceding year, 1678, had abandoned the accessible country, and drew their herds and inhabitants into the vallies, within the mountains; the army advanced amongst the defiles with incredible labour, and with so little intelligence, that the division which moved with Aurengzebe himself was unexpectedly stopped by insuperable defences and precipices in front; whilst the Rajpoots in one night closed the streights in his rear, by felling the overhanging trees; and from their stations above prevented all endeavours of the troops, either within or without, from removing the obstacle. Udeperri, the favourite and Circassian wife of Aurengzebe, accompanied him in this arduous war, and with her retinue and escort was enclosed in another part of the mountains; her conductors, dreading to expose her person to danger or public view, surrendered. She was carried to the Rana, who received her with homage and every attention. Meanwhile the emperor himself might have perished by famine, of which the Rana let him see the risque, by a confinement of two days; when he ordered his Rajpoots to withdraw from their stations, and suffer the way to be cleared. As soon as Aurengzebe was out of danger, the Rana sent back his wife, accompanied by a chosen escort, who only requested in return that he would refrain from destroying the sacred animals of their religion which might still be left in the plains; but Aurengzebe, who believed in no virtue but self-interest, imputed the generosity and forbearance of the Rana to the fear of future vengeance, and continued the war. Soon after he was again well-nigh enclosed in the mountains. This second experience of difficulties beyond his age and constitution, and the arrival of his sons, Azim and Acbar, determined him not to expose himself any longer in the field, but to leave its operations to their conduct, superintended by his own instructions from Azmir; to which city he retired with the households of his family, the officers of his court, and his bodyguard of four thousand men, dividing the army between his two sons, who each had brought a considerable body of troops from their respective

Another body of the Imperialists, under the celebrated Dilir Khan,[1] who [384] entered by the Desuri Pass from Marwar (probably with a view of extricating Prince Akbar), were allowed to advance unopposed, and when in the long intricate gorge were assailed by Bikram Solanki[2] and Gopinath Rathor[3] (both nobles of Mewar), and after a desperate conflict entirely destroyed. On each occasion a vast booty fell into the hands of the Rajputs.

So ably concerted was this mountain warfare, that these defeats were the signal for a simultaneous attack by the Rana on Aurangzeb, who, with his son Azam, watched at Debari the result of the operations under Akbar and Dilir. The great home-clans had more than their wonted rivalry to sustain them, for the gallant Durgadas with the Rathor swords (*talwār Rāthorān*) whetted by an accumulation of wrongs, were to combat with them against their common oppressor ; and nobly did they contest the palm of glory. The tyrant could not withstand them : his guns, though manned by Franks, could not protect him against the just cause and avenging steel of the Rajput, and he was beaten and compelled to disgraceful flight, with an immense loss in men and equipment. The Rana had to lament many brave leaders, home and auxiliary ; and the imperial standard, elephants, and state equipage fell into his hands, the acquisition of Mohkam and the Saktawats. This glorious encounter occurred in the spring month of Phalgun, S. 1737, March A.D. 1681 [1680].

The discomfited forces formed a junction under the walls of Chitor, whence the emperor dictated the recall of his son, Prince Muazzam, from the Deccan, deeming it of greater moment to regain lost importance in the north than to prevent the independence of Sivaji. Meanwhile the activity of Sawaldas (descended from the illustrious Jaimall) cut off the communication between Chitor and Ajmer, and alarmed the tyrant for his personal safety. Leaving, therefore, this perilous warfare to his sons Azam and Akbar, with instructions how to act till reinforced,—foiled in his

governments. They continued the war each in a different part of the country, and neither at the end of the year had forced the ultimate passes of the mountains " [*Historical Fragments*, 110 f.].

[1] [Dilīr Khan, otherwise Jalāl Khān Dā'ūdzai, died at Aurangābād, 1682–83 (Manucci i. 243). Grant Duff speaks highly of his services in the Deccan (145 f.).]

[2] Chief of Rupnagar.

[3] Chief of Ghānerāo, in Godwar, now alienated from Mewar.

vengeance and personally disgraced, he abandoned Mewar, and at the head of his guards repaired to Ajmer. Thence he detached [1] Khan Rohilla, with twelve thousand men, against Sawaldas, with supplies and equipments for his sons. The Rathor, joined by the troops of Marwar, gave him the meeting at Pur Mandal, and defeated the Imperialists with great loss, driving them back on Ajmer [385].

Diversion made by the Rājputs.—While the Rana, his heir and auxiliaries, were thus triumphant in all their operations, Prince Bhim with the left division was not idle, but made a powerful diversion by the invasion of Gujarat, captured Idar, expelling Hasan and his garrison, and proceeding by Birnagar, suddenly appeared before Patan, the residence of the provincial satrap, which he plundered. Siddhpur, Modasa,[2] and other towns shared the same fate; and he was in full march to Surat, when the benevolence of the Rana, touched at the woes of the fugitives, who came to demand his forbearance, caused him to recall Bhim in the midst of his career.

Contrary to the Rajput character, whose maxim is *parcere subjectis*, they were compelled by the utter faithlessness of Aurangzeb (chiefly vulnerable through his resources) to retaliate his excesses; and Dayal Sah, the civil minister, a man of high courage and activity, headed another flying force, which ravaged Malwa to the Nerbudda and Betwa. Sarangpur, Dewas, Sironj, Mandu, Ujjain, and Chanderi were plundered, and numerous garrisons put to the sword; and, to use the words of the Chronicle, "husbands abandoned their wives and children, and whatever could not be carried off was given to the flames." For once they avenged themselves, in imitation of the tyrant, even on the religion of their enemies: "the Kazis were bound and shaved, and the Korans thrown into wells." The minister was unrelenting and made Malwa a desert, and from the fruits of his incursions repaired the resources of his master. Flushed with success, he formed a junction with the heir of Mewar, and gave battle to Azam near Chitor. On this occasion the flower of Mewar, with the Rathor and Khichi auxiliaries,[3] were engaged, and obtained

[1] [Some name is wanting here.]

[2] [Siddhpur, a famous place of pilgrimage in Baroda State (*IGI*, xxii. 358 f.); Modāsa, fifty-two miles north-east of Ahmadābād (*BG*, vi. 346).]

[3] Mokham and Ganga Saktawats, Ratan Chondawat of Salumbar,

a glorious victory, the Mogul prince being defeated and pursued with great slaughter to Ranthambhor, which he entered. This was a just revenge, for it was Azam who surprised Chitor the year preceding. In Mewar the contest terminated with the expulsion of the Imperialists from the country; when the Rana, in support of the rights of the minor prince of Marwar, united his arms to the forces of that state, and opened the campaign at Ghanerao, the chief town of [386] Godwar. The heroic mother of the infant Rathor prince, a daughter of Mewar, had, since the death of her husband, well supported his rights, having resisted every aggression and regained many lost advantages over their antagonist. Prince Bhim commanded the Sesodias, who formed a junction with the Rathors, and gave battle to the royal forces led by Akbar and Tahawwar Khan, whom they entirely defeated. The victory is chiefly attributed to a stratagem of a Rajput chief, who, having carried off five hundred camels from the Imperialists, conceived the idea of fixing torches to them and letting them loose in the royal camp; and, in the confusion produced by the charge of such a body, the Rajputs assaulted them.

Plan to dethrone Aurangzeb.—On their continued successes, the Rana and his allies meditated the project of dethroning the tyrant and setting up his son Akbar. The pernicious example of his father towards Shah Jahan was not lost upon Akbar, who favourably received the overture; but he wanted the circumspection which characterized Aurangzeb, whose penetration defeated the scheme when on the eve of execution.[1] Already had the Rajput armies united with Akbar, and the astrologer had fixed the day which was to exalt him; but the revealer of secrets baffled his own prediction by disclosing it to the emperor. Aurangzeb, attended only by his guards at Ajmer, had recourse to the same artifice which raised him to empire, in order to ward off this danger. Akbar was but one day's march distant; his elder sons, Muazzam and Azam, yet far off. Not a moment was to be lost: he penned a letter to his son, which by a spy was

Chandrasen Jhala of Sadri, Sabal Singh Chauhan of Bedla, Berisal Punwar of Bijolia. Four of the chiefs made speeches on the eve preceding the battle, which are recorded in the Chronicle.

[1] [For Akbar's rebellion see Jadunath Sarkar ii. 402 ff.; Elliot-Dowson vii. 298 ff.; Manucci ii. 243 ff.]

dropped in the tent of the Rajput leader Durgadas.[1] In this he applauded a pretended scheme by which Akbar was to fall upon them when they engaged the emperor. The same scheme had saved Sher Shah in this country from Maldeo, and has more recently been put in practice, and with like success, in the war with Sivaji. It succeeded. The Rajputs detached themselves from the prince who had apparently betrayed them. Tahawwar Khan, in despair, lost his life in an attempt to assassinate the emperor,[2] and before the artifice was discovered, the reinforcements under Muazzam and Azam arrived, and Aurangzeb was saved. The Rajputs still offered *saran* (refuge) to Akbar; but aware of his father's vigour of character, he deemed himself unsafe in his vicinage, and accepted the escort of five hundred Rajputs led by Durgadas [387], who cut their way through every opposition by the defiles of Mewar and Dungarpur, and across the Nerbudda, to the Mahratta leader Sambhaji, at Palargarh, whence he was shortly after conveyed in an English ship to Persia.[3]

Overtures for Peace.—" The escape of Acbar " (observes an historian,[4] who appreciated the importance of the transactions of this period) " to Sambagee, oppressed Aurengzebe with as much anxiety, as formerly the phantom of his brother Sujah amongst the Pitans; and the consequence of their alliance

[1] A portrait of this Rathor hero was given to the author of the present work by his descendants. He was chief of Dunara, on the Luni. He saved his young sovereign's life from the tyrant, and guarded him during a long minority, heading the Rathors in all the wars for the independence of his country. A bribe of forty thousand *gold suns* was sent to him by Azam *without stipulation*, when conveying Akbar out of danger. The object was obvious, yet the Mogul prince dared not even specify his wishes. It is needless to say that Durga spurned the offer. [For the flight of Akbar see Jadunath Sarkar ii. 415 ff.]

[2] [For the attempt of Tahawwar Khān to assassinate Aurangzeb see Manucci ii. 247 ff.; Jadunath Sarkar ii. 411 ff.]

[3] [Palargarh is perhaps Pālanpur (*IGI*, xix. 354). Akbar died in Persia, 1706.]

[4] " We are not without hopes that some of the many in India who have the means will supply the portions of information which are deficient in these fragments, and must otherwise always continue out of our reach. The knowledge is well worth the inquiry; for, besides the magnitude of the events and the energy of the characters which arise within this period, there are no states or powers on the continent of India, with whom our nation have either connection or concern, which do not owe the origin of their present condition to the reign of Aurengzebe, or to its influence on the reigns of his successors " (Orme's *Fragments* [Notes i. f.]).

became a nearer care than the continuance of the war against the Rajpoots, whose gallant activity prevented a speedy decision by the sword; but the dignity of the throne forbad any overtures of peace to a resistance which had attempted the deposal, if not the life, of the monarch. A Rajpoot officer, who had long served with distinction under Delire Khan, solved the difficulty: he quitted the army on the pretence of retiring to his own country and visited the Rana as from courtesy on his journey. The conversation turned on the war, which the Rajpoot perhaps really lamented, and he persuaded the Rana that although Aurengzebe would never condescend to make, he might accept overtures of peace: upon which he was empowered by the Rana to tender them."[1] The domestic annals confirm this account, and give the name of this mediator, Raja Shyam Singh of Bikaner; but the negotiation was infamously protracted to the rains, the period when operations necessarily cease, and by which time Aurangzeb had recruited his broken forces, and was again enabled to take the field; and it was concluded "without assertion or release of the capitation tax, but with the surrender of the districts taken from Chitor, and the State of Jodhpur was included in the treaty." How correctly this elegant historian had obtained a knowledge of those events, a translation of the treaty evinces.[2] But these

[1] [Orme, *Fragments*, 150 f.]

[2] "*Jawab-sowal* [treaty, 'question—answer'] *of Sur Singh (uncle of Rana Raj Singh) and Narhar Bhat with the Emperor.*

Panja, or impress of the Emperor's hand, with the word '*Manzuri*,' written by himself. *Manzuri* ('agreed').

"Your servants, according to your royal pleasure and summons, have been sent by the Rana to represent what is written underneath. We hope you will agree to these requests, besides others which will be made by Padam Singh.

"1. Let Chitor, with the districts adjacent appertaining thereto when it was inhabited, be restored.

"2. In such temples and places of Hindu religious resort as have been converted into mosques, the past cannot be recalled, but let this practice be abolished.

"3. The aid hitherto afforded to the empire by the Rana shall be continued, but let no additional commands be imposed.

"4. The sons and dependants of the deceased Raja Jaswant Singh so

occurrences belong to the succeeding reign, for the Rana died about this period,[1] from wounds and vexation.

Cruel Treatment of Rāja of Golkonda.—Once more we claim the reader's admiration on behalf of another patriot prince of Mewar, and ask him to contrast the indigenous Rajput with the emperor of the Moguls [388]; though to compare them would be manifestly unjust, since in every moral virtue they were antipodes to each other. Aurangzeb accumulated on his head more crimes than any prince who ever sat on an Asiatic throne. With all the disregard of life which marks his nation, he was never betrayed, even in the fever of success, into a single generous action; and, contrary to the prevailing principle of our nature, the moment of his foe's submission was that chosen for the malignant completion of his revenge: witness his scourging the prostrate King of Golkonda.[2] How opposite to the beneficence of the Rajput prince, who, when the most efficient means of self-defence lay in the destruction of the resources of his enemy, feeling for the miseries of the suffering population of his persecutor, recalled his son in the midst of victory! As a skilful general and gallant soldier, in the defence of his country, he is above all [389] praise. As a chivalrous Rajput, his braving all consequences when called upon to save the honour of a noble female of his race, he is without parallel. As an accomplished prince and benevolent man, his dignified letter of remonstrance to Aurangzeb on the promulgation of the capitation-edict, places him high in the scale of moral as well as intellectual excellence; and an additional evidence of both, and of his taste for the arts, is furnished by the formation of the inland lake, the Rajsamund, with a slight account of which, and the motives for its execution, we shall conclude the sketch of this glorious epoch in the annals of Mewar.

---

soon as enabled to perform their duties, we hope will have their country restored to them.*

"Respect prevents inferior demands. May the splendour of your fortune, like the sun illuminating the world, be for ever increasing and never set.

"The Arzi (requests) of your servants, Sur Singh and Narhar Bhat."

* S. 1737, A.D. 1681.

[1] It was to defend the rights of the heir of Marwar, as well as to oppose the odious *jizya*, that the Rana took to arms. Ajit was still under the Rana's safeguard.

[2] [Orme, *Fragments*, 217 f. A different story is told by Khāfi Khān (Elliot-Dowson vii. 334).]

The Rājsamund Lake.—This great national work is twenty-five miles north of the capital, and is situated on the declivity of the plain about two miles from the base of the Aravalli. A small perennial stream, called the Gomati or 'serpentine,'[1] flowing from these mountains, was arrested in its course, and confined by an immense embankment, made to form the lake called after himself, Rajsamund, or 'royal sea.' The *band* or dam forms an irregular segment of a circle, embracing an extent of nearly three miles, and encircling the waters on every side except the space between the north-west and north-east points. This barrier, which confines a sheet of water of great depth, and about twelve miles in circumference, is entirely of white marble, with a flight of steps of the same material, throughout this extent, from the summit to the water's edge; the whole buttressed by an enormous rampart of earth, which, had the projector lived, would have been planted with trees to form a promenade. On the south side are the town and fortress built by the Rana, and bearing his name, Rajnagar; and upon the embankment stands the temple of Kankroli, the shrine of one of the seven forms (*sarup*) of Krishna. The whole is ornamented with sculpture of tolerable execution for the age; and a genealogical sketch of the founder's family is inscribed in conspicuous characters. One million one hundred and fifty thousand pounds sterling,[2] contributed by the Rana, his chiefs and opulent subjects, was expended on this work, of which the material was from the adjacent quarries. But, magnificent, costly, and useful as it is, it derives its chief beauty from the benevolent motive to which it owes its birth: to alleviate the miseries of a starving population, and make their employment conducive to national benefit, during one of those awful visitations [390] of providence, famine, and pestilence with which these states are sometimes afflicted.

The Famine of A.D. 1662.—It was in S. 1717,[3] only seven years after the accession of Raj Singh, that these combined evils reached Mewar, less subject to them, owing to its natural advantages, than any other State in India;[4] and on Tuesday the 8th of Pus,

[1] [A common error; Gomati, meaning 'rich in cattle,' has no connexion with Hindi *ghūmna*, 'to twist.']

[2] Ninety-six lakhs of rupees [Erskine ii. A. 9].

[3] A.D. 1661.

[4] From all I could learn, it was the identical pestilence which has been ravaging India for the last ten years, erroneously called *cholera morbus*.

Hasti Nakshatra (constellation of the elephant), as fixed by the astrologer, the first stone was laid. "The chief of Mewar, deeply meditating on this extreme distress, determined to raise a monument, by which the wretched might be supported and his own name perpetuated. This was seven years in constructing, and at its commencement and termination all the rites of sacrifice and oblation were observed.

"The Rana went to implore favour at the temple of the 'four-armed'; for though Asarh[1] was over, not a drop of rain fell from the heavens; and, in like manner, the months of Sawan[1] and Bhadon[1] passed away. For want of water the world was in despair, and people went mad with hunger. Things unknown as food were eaten. The husband abandoned the wife, the wife the husband—parents sold their children—time increased the evil; it spread far and wide: even the insects died: they had nothing to feed on. Thousands of all ages became victims to hunger. Those who procured food to-day, ate twice what nature required. The wind was from the west, a pestilential vapour. The constellations were always visible at night, nor was there a cloud in the sky by day, and thunder and lightning were unknown. Such portents filled mankind with dread. Rivers, lakes, and fountains were dried up. Men of wealth meted out the portions of food. The ministers of religion forgot their duties. There was no longer distinction of caste, and the Sudra and Brahman were undistinguishable. Strength, wisdom, caste, tribe, all were abandoned, and food alone was the object. The Charbaran[2] threw away every symbol of separation; all was lost in hunger. Fruits, flowers, every vegetable thing, even trees were stripped of their bark, to appease the cravings [391] of hunger: nay, *man ate man*! Cities were depopulated. The seed of families was lost, the fishes were extinct, and the hope of all extinguished."[3]

About thirty-five years ago the same disease carried off multitudes in these countries. Orme [*Fragments*, 200] gives notice of something similar in A.D. 1684, in the imperial camp near Goa, when five hundred victims daily fell its prey. Mewar was not free from the last visitation of 1818, and the only son of the Rana was the first person attacked.

[1] The three months of rain, termed the *Barsat*. [Asārh is the month June to July, followed by Sāwan and Bhādon.]

[2] The four castes, sacerdotal, military, mercantile, and servile.

[3] From the *Raj Vilas*, the chronicle of the reign of Raj Singh.

Such is the simple yet terrific record of this pestilence, from which Mewar was hardly freed, when Aurangzeb commenced the religious warfare narrated, with all its atrocities, still further to devastate this fair region. But a just retribution resulted from this disregard to the character and prejudices of the Rajputs, which visited the emperor with shame, and his successors with the overthrow of their power.

CHAPTER 14

Rāna Jai Singh, A.D. 1680-98.—Rana Jai Singh took possession of the *Gaddi*[1] in S. 1737 (A.D. 1681). A circumstance occurred at his birth, which as descriptive of manners may deserve notice. A few hours only intervened between his entrance into the world and that of another son called Bhim. It is customary for the father to bind round the arm of the new-born infant a root of that species of grass called the *amardub*, the 'imperishable' *dub*, well known for its nutritive properties and luxuriant vegetation under the most intense heat.[2] The Rana first attached the ligature round the arm of the youngest, apparently an oversight, though in fact from superior affection for his mother. As the boys approached to manhood, the Rana, apprehensive that this preference might create dissension, one day drew his sword, and placing it in the hand of Bhim (the elder), said, it was better to use it at once on his brother, than hereafter to endanger the safety of the State. This [392] appeal to his generosity had an instantaneous effect, and he not only ratified, 'by his father's throne,'[3] the acknowledgment of the sovereign rights of his brother, but declared, to remove all fears, "he was not his son if he again drank water within the pass of Debari"; and, collecting his retainers, he abandoned Udaipur to court Fortune where she might be kinder. The day was sultry, and on reaching the barrier he halted under the shade of a sacred fig-tree to bestow a last look upon the place of his birth. His cup-bearer (*Paniyari*) brought his silver goblet filled from the cool fountain, but as he

[1] '*The Cushion*,' by which a Rajput throne is designated.

[2] [Dūb, *Cynodon dactylon*, the most common and useful Indian grass (Watt, *Comm. Prod.*, 463 f).]

[3] *Gaddi ki an.*

raised it to his lips, he recollected that his vow was incomplete while within the portal; he poured the libation on the earth in the name of the Supreme, and casting the cup as an offering to the deity of the fountain, the huge gates closed upon the valley. He proceeded to Bahadur Shah, who conferred upon him the dignity (*mansab*) of a leader of three thousand five hundred horse, with the Bawana, or fifty-two districts for their support: but quarrelling with the imperial general, he was detached with his contingent west of the Indus, where he died.[1]

Treaty between Rāna Jai Singh and Aurangzeb.—Let us return to Jai Singh (*the lion of victory*). He concluded a treaty with Aurangzeb, conducted by Prince Azam and Dilir Khan, who took every occasion to testify his gratitude for the clemency of Rana Raj Singh, when blockaded in the defiles of the Aravalli. At this conference, the Rana was attended by ten thousand horse and forty thousand foot, besides the multitude collected from the mountains to view the ceremony, above one hundred thousand souls, who set up a shout of joy at the prospect of revisiting the plains, which disconcerted Azam, while Dilir expatiated on the perils from which the Rana's generosity had liberated him. Azam, who said he was no stranger to the Rana's illustrious house, concluded a treaty on the spot, in which, as a salvo for the imperial dignity, a nominal fine and surrender of three districts were inserted for aiding Akbar's rebellion, and a hint that the regal colour (*crimson*) of his tents and umbrella [393] should be discontinued. That advantages were gained by the Rana, we may infer from Dilir's sons being left as hostages for Azam's good faith; a fact we learn from his farewell address to the Rana! "Your nobles are rude, and my children are the hostages of your safety; but if at the expense of their lives I can obtain the entire

[1] I give these anecdotes as related to me by his descendant and representative the Raja of Banora, while seated in a balcony of his castle overlooking the plains of Mewar. Often have I quenched my thirst at the fountain, and listened to their traditionary tales. It is a spot consecrated to recollections: every altar which rises around it is a text for the '*great ancients*' of the clans to expatiate on; and it is, moreover, a grand place of rendezvous, whether for the traveller or sportsman. Bhim dislocated his spine in a feat of strength. He was celebrated for activity, and could, while his steed was urged to his speed, disengage and suspend himself by the arms from the bough of a tree; and to one of these experiments he owed his death.

restoration of your country, keep your mind at ease, for there was friendship between your father and me."

The Jaisamund Lake.—But all other protection than what his sword afforded was futile; and though Dilir's intentions were noble, he had little control over events: in less than five years after his accession, the Rana was again forced to fly the plains for the inaccessible haunts of Kamori. Yet, in spite of these untoward circumstances and uninterrupted warfare, such were the resources of this little State that the Rana completed a work which perpetuates his name. He threw a dam across a break in the mountains, the channel of an ever-flowing stream, by which he formed the largest lake in India,[1] giving it his own name, the Jaisamund, or sea of victory. Nature had furnished the hint for this undertaking, for there had always existed a considerable volume of water; but the Rana had the merit of uniting these natural buttresses, and creating a little sea from the Dhebar pool, its ancient appellation. The circumference cannot be less than thirty miles, and the benefits to cultivation, especially in respect to the article of rice, which requires perpetual irrigation, were great. On this huge rampart he erected a palace for his favourite queen, Komaladevi, a princess of the Pramara race, familiarly known as the Ruthi Rani, or 'testy queen.'

Rana Jai Singh and his heir Amar Singh.—Domestic unhappiness appears to have generated in the Rana inaptitude to state affairs; and, unluckily, the favoured queen estranged him from his son. Amra, a name venerated in Mewar, was that of the heir of Jai Singh. His mother was of the Bundi house, a family which has performed great services to, and brought great calamities upon, the ancient sovereigns of Mewar. To the jealousies of the rival queens, one of them mother to the heir, the other the favourite of the sovereign, are attributed dissensions, which at such a juncture were a greater detriment than the loss of a battle, and which afford another illustration, if any were wanting, of the impolicy of polygamy. The annals of Mewar seldom exhibit those unnatural contentions for power, from which no other Hindu State was exempt; this was owing to the wholesome regulation of not investing the princes of the blood with any [394]

[1] [The Bhojpur lake, which covered an area of 250 square miles, was much larger, the Jaisamund covering only 21 square miles (Smith, *EHI*, 396; Erskine ii. A. 8 f.).]

political authority; and establishing as a counterpoise to natural advantages an artificial degradation of their rank, which placed them beneath the sixteen chief nobles of the State; which, while it exalted these in their own estimation, lessened the national humiliation, when the heirs-apparent were compelled to lead their quota in the *arrière-ban* of the empire.

Rebellion of Amar Singh.—Rana Jai Singh, who had evinced such gallantry and activity in the wars of Aurangzeb, now secluded himself with Komala in the retreat of Jaisamund, leaving Amra under the guidance of the Pancholi [1] minister, at the capital. But he having personally insulted this chief officer of the State, in consequence of receiving a rebuke for turning loose an infuriated elephant in the town, the Rana left his retreat, and visiting Chitor in his tour, arrived at Udaipur. Amra awaited not his father's arrival, but adding his mother's resentments to a feeling of patriotic indignation at the abasement his indolence produced, fled to Bundi, took up arms, and, joined by many of his own nobles and Hara auxiliaries, returned at the head of ten thousand men. Desirous of averting civil war, the Rana retired to Godwar beyond the Aravalli, whence he sent the Ghanerao chieftain, the first feudatory of that department, to expostulate with his son. But Amra, supported by three-fourths of the nobles, made direct for Kumbhalmer to secure the State treasure, saved by the Depra governor for his sovereign. A failure in this project, the knowledge that the Rathors fostered the quarrel with a view to obtain Godwar, and the determination of the few chiefs yet faithful [2] to the Rana, to defend the Jhilwara pass to the last, made the prince listen to terms, which were ratified at the shrine of Eklinga, whereby the Rana was to return to the capital, and the prince to abide in exile at the new palace during the life of his father, which closed twenty years after his accession. Had he maintained the reputation he established in his early years, the times were well calculated for the redemption of his country's independence; but documents which yet exist afford little reason to doubt that in his latter years a state of indolence,

[1] [Pancholi, Panchauli, of which the derivation is uncertain, perhaps *pancha-kula*, 'five houses,' is the local title of the Desi or Māthur Kāyasths, or writer caste (*Census Report Mārwār*, 1891, ii. 111).]

[2] Beri Sal of Bijolia, Kandal of Salumbar, Gopinath of Ghanerao, and the Solanki of Desuri.

having all the effects of imbecility, supervened, and but for the formation of 'the victorious sea,' would have left his name a blank in the traditional history of Mewar.

Rāna Amar Singh II., A.D. **1698–1710.**—Amra II., who succeeded in S. 1756 (A.D. 1700), had much of the gallantry [395] and active turn of mind of his illustrious namesake; but the degrading conflict with his father had much impaired the moral strength of the country, and counteracted the advantages which might have resulted from the decline of the Mogul power. The reigns of Raj Singh and Jai Singh illustrate the obvious truth, that on the personal character of the chief of a feudal government everything depends. The former, infusing by his talent and energy patriotic sentiments into all his subordinates, vanquished in a series of conflicts the vast military resources of the empire, led by the emperor, his sons, and chosen generals; while his successor, heir to this moral strength, and with every collateral aid, lowered her to a stage of contempt from which no talent could subsequently raise her.

Amra early availed himself of the contentions amongst the sons of Aurangzeb to anticipate events, and formed a private treaty [1] with the Mogul heir-apparent, Shah Alam, when com-

[1] "*Private Treaty between the Rana and Shah Alam Bahadur Shah, and bearing his sign-manual.*

"Six articles of engagement, just, and tending to the happiness of the people, have been submitted by you, and by me accepted, and with God's blessing shall be executed without deviation—

"1. The re-establishment of Chitor as in the time of Shah Jahan.

"2. Prohibition of kine-killing.*

---

* From the second of these articles, which alternate between stipulations of a temporal and spiritual nature, we may draw a lesson of great political importance. In all the treaties which have come under my observation, the insertion of an article against the slaughter of kine was prominent. This sacrifice to their national prejudices was the subject of discussion with every ambassador when the States of Rajasthan formed engagements with the British Government in 1817–18, "the prohibition of kine-killing within their respective limits." From the construction of our armies we could not guarantee this article, but assurances were given that every practical attention would be paid to their wishes; and kine are not absolutely slain within the jurisdiction of any of these Rajput princes. But even long habit, though it has familiarized, has not reconciled them to this revolting sacrifice; nor would the kine-killer in Mewar be looked upon with less detestation than was Cambyses by the Egyptians, when he thrust his lance into the flank of Apis. But in time this will be overlooked, and the verbal assurance

manded to the countries west of the Indus, on which occasion [396] the Mewar contingent[1] accompanied him, and fought several gallant actions under a Saktawat chieftain.

Breach between the Rājputs and the Mughal Empire.—It is important to study the events of this period, which involved the overthrow of the Mogul power, and originated that form of society which paved the way to the dominion of Britain in these distant regions. From such a review a political lesson of great value may be learned, which will show a beacon warning us against the danger of trusting to mere physical power, unaided

"3. The restoration of all the districts held in the reign of Shah Jahan.

"4. Freedom of faith and religious worship, as during the government of him whose *nest is Paradise* (Akbar).

"5. Whoever shall be dismissed by you shall receive no countenance from the king.

"6. The abrogation of the contingent for the service of the Deccan." *

[1] It consisted of twenty-two *Nakkaraband* chiefs, *i.e.* each entitled to a kettle-drum, and fifteen *Turais*, or chiefs, entitled to brass trumpets. ["As a mark of favour, kettle-drums (*naqqārah*) and the right to play them (*naubat*) might be granted to a subject, but he must be a man of the rank of 2000 sawār (troopers) or upwards. As an invariable condition, however, it was stipulated they should not be used when the Emperor was present, or within a certain distance from his residence" (Irvine, *Army of the Indian Moghuls*, 30, 208 f.).]

will become a dead letter; men of good intention will be lulled into the belief that, because not openly combated, the prejudice is extinct, and that homage to our power has obliterated this article of their creed. Thus Aurangzeb thought, but he avowedly and boldly opposed the religious opinions of his tributaries; we only hold them in contempt, and even protect them when productive of no sacrifice. Yet if we look back on the early page of history, we shall find both policy and benevolence combined to form this legislative protection to one of the most useful of domestic animals, and which would tempt the belief that Triptolemus, the lawgiver of Sparta, had borrowed from Manu [*Laws*, xi. 60, 69, 71], or rather from the still greater friends of dumb creatures, the Jains, in the law which exempted not only the lordly bull from the knife, but "every living thing."

* The Mewar contingent had been serving under Azam in the south, as the following letter from him to the Rana discloses:—"Be it known to Rana Amra Singh, your arzi [petition] arrived, and the accounts of your mother gave me great grief, but against the decrees of God there is no struggling. Pray for my welfare. Raja Rae Singh made a request for you; you are my own; rest in full confidence and continue in your obedience. The lands of your illustrious ancestors shall all be yours—but this is the time to evince your duty—the rest learn from your own servants—continue to think of me."

"Your Rajputs have behaved well."

by the latent, but more durable support of moral influence. When Aurangzeb neglected the indigenous Rajputs, he endangered the keystone of his power; and in despising opinion, though his energetic mind might for a time render him independent of it, yet long before his death the enormous fabric reared by Akbar was tottering to its foundation: demonstrating to conviction that the highest order of talent, either for government or war, though aided by unlimited resources, will not suffice for the maintenance of power, unsupported by the affections of the governed. The empire of Aurangzeb was more extensive than that of Britain at this day—the elements of stability were incomparably more tenacious: he was associated with the Rajputs by blood, which seemed to guarantee a respect for their opinions; he possessed the power of distributing the honours and emoluments of the state, when a service could be rewarded by a province,[1] drawing at will supplies of warriors from the mountains of the west, as a check on his indigenous subjects, while these left the plains of India to control the Afghan amidst the snows of Caucasus. But the most devoted attachment and most faithful service were repaid by insults to their habits, and the imposition of an obnoxious tax; and to the jizya, and the unwise pertinacity with which his successors adhered to it, must be directly ascribed the overthrow of the monarchy. No condition was exempted from this odious and impolitic assessment, which was deemed by the tyrant a mild substitute for the conversion he once meditated of the entire Hindu race to the creed of Islam.[2]

[1] In lieu of all, what reward does Britain hold out to the native population to be attached? Heavy duties exclude many products of their industry from the home market. The rates of pay to civil officers afford no security to integrity; and the faithful soldier cannot aspire to higher reward than £120 per annum, were his breast studded with medals. Even their prejudices are often too little considered, prejudices, the violation of which lost the throne of India, in spite of every local advantage, to the descendants of Aurangzeb.

[2] [Jizya, meaning 'tribute,' was a capitation tax imposed on subjects (*zimmi*) who did not follow the state religion, Islām. Its hardship lay in the fact that it was additional to, and about the same amount as the revenue demand, the latter being thus nearly doubled. Great merchants in the time of Aurangzeb paid Rs. 13.8; the middle class Rs. 6.12; the poor Rs. 3.8 per annum per head (Manucci ii. 234). On the *Jizya* see Hughes, *Dict. Islām*, 248; Smith, *Akbar the Great Mogul*, 65 f.; Keene, *Turks in India*, 153 ff.; Grant Duff, *Hist. of the Mahrattas*, 145; Jadunath Sarkar, *Life of Aurangzib*, iii. 305 ff.]

Rājput Apostates.—An abandonment of their faith was the Rajput's surest road to the tyrant's favour [397], and an instance of this dereliction in its consequences powerfully contributed to the annihilation of the empire. Rao Gopal, a branch of the Rana's family, held the fief of Rampura, on the Chambal,[1] and was serving with a select quota of his clan in the wars of the Deccan, when his son, who had been left at home, withheld the revenues, which he applied to his own use instead of remitting them to his father. Rao Gopal complained to the emperor; but the son discovered that he could by a sacrifice not only appease Aurangzeb, but attain the object of his wishes: he apostatized from his faith, and obtained the emperor's forgiveness, with the domain of Rampura. Disgusted and provoked at such infurious conduct, Rao Gopal fled the camp, made an unsuccessful attempt to redeem his estate, and took refuge with Rana Amra, his suzerain. This natural asylum granted to a chief of his own kin was construed by the tyrant into a signal of revolt, and Azam was ordered to Malwa to watch the Rana's motions: conduct thus characterized in the memoirs of a Rajput chieftain,[2] one of the most devoted to Aurangzeb, and who died fighting for his son. "The emperor showed but little favour to his faithful and most useful subjects the Rajputs, which greatly cooled their ardour in his service." The Rana took up arms, and Malwa joined the tumult; while the first irruption of the Mahrattas across the Nerbudda,[3] under Nima Sindhia, compelled the emperor to detach Raja Jai Singh to join Prince Azam. Amidst these accumulated troubles, the Mahrattas rising into importance, the Rajput feudatories disgusted and alienated, his sons and grandsons ready to commit each individual pretension to the decision of the sword, did Aurangzeb, after a reign of terror of half a century's duration, breathe his last on the 28th Zilqa'da, A.D. 1707 [February 21], at the city bearing his name—Aurangabad.

[1] Rampura Bhanpura (city of the sun) to distinguish it from Rampura *Tonk*. Rao Gopal was of the Chandarawat clan. See note, p. 306.

[2] Rao Dalpat Bundela of Datia, a portion of whose memoirs were presented to me by the reigning prince, his descendant.

[3] A.D. 1706–7. [The Mahrattas crossed the Nerbudda in 1705 (Grant Duff, *Hist. Mahrattas*, 177; Malcolm, *Memoir Central India*, i. 58 ff.). The latter remarks that they came to attack the government, not the people, and acted with the concurrence of the Hindu chiefs discontented with the policy of Aurangzeb.]

Shāh Alam Bahādur Shāh, Emperor, A.D. **1707-12.**—At his death his second son Azam assumed the imperial dignity, and aided by the Rajput princes of Datia and Kotah,[1] who had always served in his division, he marched to Agra to contest the legitimate claims of his eldest brother Muazzam, who was advancing from Kabul supported by the contingents of Mewar and Marwar, and all western Rajwara. The battle of Jajau [398][2] was fatal to Azam, who with his son Bedarbakht and the princes of Kotah and Datia was slain, when Muazzam ascended the throne under the title of Shah Alam Bahadur Shah. This prince had many qualities which endeared him to the Rajputs, to whom his sympathies were united by the ties of blood, his mother being a Rajput princess.[3] Had he immediately succeeded the beneficent Shah Jahan, the race of Timur, in all human probability, would have been still enthroned at Delhi, and might have presented a picture of one of the most powerful monarchies of Asia. But Aurangzeb had inflicted an incurable wound on the mind of the Hindu race, which for ever estranged them from his successors; nor were the virtues of Bahadur, during the short lustre of his sway, capable of healing it. The bitter fruit of a long experience had taught the Rajputs not to hope for amelioration from any graft of that stem, which, like the deadly Upas, had stifled the vital energies of Rajasthan, whose leaders accordingly formed a league for mutual preservation; which it would have been madness to dissolve merely because a fair portion of virtue was the inheritance of the tyrant's successor. They had proved that no act of duty or subserviency could guarantee them from the infatuated abuse of power, and they were at length steeled against every appeal to their loyalty, replying with a trite adage, which we may translate '*quem Deus vult perdere, prius dementat*,' —of common application with the Rajput in such a predicament.

The Rise of the Sikhs.—The emperor was soon made to perceive the little support he had in future to expect from the Rajputs. Scarcely had he quashed the pretensions of Kambakhsh, his youngest brother, who proclaimed himself emperor in the Deccan, than he was forced to the north, in consequence of an insurrection

[1] Rao Dalpat (Bundela), and Rao Ram Singh (Hara).

[2] [Twenty miles south of Agra, June 7, 1707.]

[3] [Nawāb Bāi, daughter of the Rāja of Rājauri, Kashmīr, who died in 1690 (Manucci ii. 57, note).]

of the Sikhs of Lahore. This singular race, the disciples (*sikhs*) of a teacher called Nanak, were the descendants of the Scythic Getae,[1] or Jat, of Transoxiana, who so early as the fifth century were established in the tract watered by the five arms (*Panjab*) of the Indus. Little more than a century has elapsed since their conversion from a spurious Hinduism to the doctrines of the sectarian Nanak, and their first attempt to separate themselves, in temporal as well as spiritual matters, from all control, and they are now the sole independent power within the limits [399] of the Mogul monarchy. On this occasion[2] the princes of Amber and Marwar visited the emperor, but left his camp without permission, and, as the historian[3] adds, manifested a design to struggle for independence. Such was the change in their mutual circumstances that the Mogul sent the heir-apparent to conciliate and conduct them to him; but they came at the head of all their native bands, when "they were gratified with whatever their insolence demanded":[4] a splenetic effusion of the historian, which well paints their altered position. From the royal *urdu*,[5] or camp, they repaired to Rana Amra at Udaipur, where a triple league was formed, which once more united them to the head of their nation. This treaty of unity of interests against the common foe was solemnized by nuptial engagements, from which those princes had been excluded since the reigns of Akbar and Partap. To be readmitted to this honour was the basis of this triple alliance, in which they ratified on oath the renunciation of all connexion, domestic or political, with the empire. It was, moreover, stipulated that the sons of such marriage should be heirs, or if the issue were females, that they should never be dishonoured by being married to a Mogul.

Sacrifice of the Right of Primogeniture.—But this remedy, as will be seen, originated a worse disease; it was a sacrifice of the rights of primogeniture (clung to by the Rajputs with extreme pertinacity), productive of the most injurious effects, which

[1] See *History of the Tribes*, article 'Jats,' p. 127.

[2] A.D. 1709–10.

[3] *Memoirs of Iradat Khan*, p. 58 [translated by Captain Jonathan Scott; extracts from the work of Irādat Khān will be found in Elliot-Dowson vii. 534 f.]; also autograph letters of all those princes, with files of the regular newspapers (*akhbars*) of the day, in my possession, dated from the emperor's camp.

[4] *Memoirs of Iradat Khan.*

[5] Hence the corruption of *horde*.

introdueed domestic strife, and called upon the stage an umpire not less baneful than the power from whose iron grasp they were on the point of freeing themselves : for although this treaty laid prostrate the throne of Babur, it ultimately introduced the Mahrattas as partisans in their family disputes, who made the bone of contention their own.

The injudicious support afforded by the emperor to the apostate chief of Rampura first brought the triple federation into action. The Rana, upholding the cause of Himmat Singh, made an attack on Rampura, which the apostate usurper Ratan Singh, now Raj Muslim Khan, defeated, and was rewarded for [400] it by the emperor.[1] But the same report conveyed to the king "that the Rana determined to lay waste his country, and retire to the hills,"[2] which was speedily confirmed by the unwelcome intelligence that Sawaldas, an officer of the Rana's, had attacked Firoz Khan, the governor of Pur Mandal, who was obliged to retreat with great loss to Ajmer ;[3] on which occasion this loyal descendant of the illustrious Jaimall lost his life.[4] The brave Durgadas, who conveyed the rebellious Akbar through all opposition to a place of refuge, again appeared upon the stage—his own prince being unable to protect him, he had found a safe asylum at Udaipur, and had the sum of five hundred rupees daily paid for his expenditure—a princely liberality. But the result of this combination was reserved for the following reigns, Shah Alam being carried off by poison,[5] ere he could correct the disorders which were rapidly breaking up the empire from the Hindu-Kush to the ocean. Had his life been spared, his talents for business, his experience, and courteous manners might have retarded the ruin of the monarchy, which the utter unworthiness of his successor sunk beyond the power of man to redeem. Every

[1] Newspapers, dated 3rd Rajab, San. 3—(3rd year of his reign).

[2] Newspapers, 10th Rajab, San. 3.

[3] Newspapers, 5th Shavval, San. 3.

[4] The following edict, which caused this action, I translated from the archives ; it is addressed to the son of Sawaldas :—"Maharana Amra Singh to Rathor Rae Singh Sawaldasot (race of Sawaldas)—Lay waste your villages and the country around you—your families shall have other habitations to dwell in—for particulars consult Daulat Singh Chondawat : obey these." Asoj, S. 1764 (Dec. A.D. 1708).

[5] [February 18] A.D. 1712. [The Musalmān authorities do not corroborate the assertion that he was poisoned.]

subsequent succession was through blood; and the sons of Shah Alam performed the part for which they had so many great examples. Two brothers,[1] Sayyids, from the town of Barha in the Duab, were long the Warwicks of Hindustan, setting up and plucking down its puppet kings at their pleasure; they had elevated Farrukhsiyar when the triumvirs of Rajasthan commenced their operations.

Farrukhsīyar, Emperor, A.D. 1712-19.—Giving loose to long-suppressed resentment, the Rajputs abandoned the spirit of toleration which it would have been criminal to preserve; and profiting by the lessons of their tyrants, they overthrew the mosques built on the sites of their altars, and treated the civil and religious officers of the government with indignity. Of these every town in Rajasthan had its *mulla* to proclaim the name of Muhammad, and its *kazi* for the administration of justice,—branches of government [401] entirely wrested from the hands of the native princes,[2] abusing the name of independence. But for a moment it was redeemed, especially by the brave Rathors, who had made a noble resistance, contesting every foot of land since the death of Jaswant Singh, and now his son Ajit entirely expelled the Moguls from Marwar. On this occasion the native forces of the triple alliance met at the salt lake of Sambhar, which was made the common boundary of their territory, and its revenues were equally divided amongst them.

The pageant of an emperor, guided by the Sayyids, or those who intrigued to supplant their ministry, made an effort to oppose the threatening measures of the Rajputs; and one of them, the Amiru-l-umara,[3] marched against Raja Ajit, who received private instructions from the emperor to resist his commander-in-chief, whose credit was strengthened by the means taken to weaken it, which engendered suspicions of treachery. Ajit leagued with the Sayyids, who held out to the Rathor an important share of power at court, and agreed to pay tribute and give a daughter in marriage to Farrukhsiyar.

[1] Husain Ali and Abdu-lla Khan.

[2] Next to kine-killing was the article inhibiting the introduction of the *Adalat*, or British courts of justice, into the Rajput States, in all their treaties with the British Government in A.D. 1817–18, the very name of which is abhorrent to a native.

[3] The title of Husain Ali,—as Kutbu-l-mulk (the axis of the State), was that of his brother Abdu-lla.

Marriage of Farrukhsiyar : Grant to the British.—This marriage yielded most important results, which were not confined to the Moguls or Rajputs, for to it may be ascribed the rise of the British power in India. A dangerous malady,[1] rendering necessary a surgical operation upon Farrukhsiyar, to which the faculty of the court were unequal, retarded the celebration of the nuptials between the emperor and the Rajput princess of Marwar, and even threatened a fatal termination. A mission from the British merchants at Surat was at that time at court, and, as a last resource, the surgeon attached to it was called in, who cured the malady, and made the emperor happy in his bride.[2] His gratitude was displayed with oriental magnificence. The emperor desired Mr. Hamilton to name [402] his reward, and to the disinterested patriotism of this individual did the British owe the first royal grant or farman, conferring territorial possession and great commercial privileges. These were the objects of the mission, which till this occurrence had proved unsuccessful.

This gorgeous court ought to have been, and probably was, impressed with a high opinion of the virtuous self-denial of the inhabitants of Britain; and if history has correctly preserved the transaction, some mark of public gratitude should have been forthcoming from those who so signally benefited thereby. But to borrow the phraseology of the Italian historian, "Obligations which do not admit of being fully discharged are often repaid with the coin of ingratitude": the remains of this man rest in the churchyard of Calcutta, without even a stone to mark the spot![3]

[1] A white swelling or tumour on the back.

[2] The ceremony is described, as it was celebrated, with true Asiatic pomp. "The Ameer-ool Omra conducted the festivities on the part of the bride, and the marriage was performed with a splendour and magnificence till then unseen among the princes of Hindust'han. Many pompous insignia were added to the royal cortège upon this occasion. The illuminations rivalled the planets, and seemed to upbraid the faint lustre of the stars. The nuptials were performed at the palace of the Ameer-ool Omra, whence the emperor conveyed his bride with the highest splendour of imperial pomp to the citadel, amidst the resoundings of musical instruments and the acclamations of the people" (Scott's *History of Aurangzeb's Successors*, vol. i. p. 132. [For the cure of Farrukhsīyar by Surgeon W. Hamilton see C. R. Wilson, *Early Annals of the English in Bengal*, ii. 235.]

[3] [There is a monument of Hamilton in St. John's Church, Calcutta (*IGI*, x. 280).]

The Jizya Reimposed.—This marriage, which promised a renewal of interests with the Rajputs, was soon followed by the revival of the obnoxious jizya. The character of this tax, though much altered from its original imposition by Aurangzeb, when it was at once financial and religious, was held in unmitigated abhorrence by the Hindus from the complex association; and although it was revived chiefly to relieve pecuniary wants, it kindled a universal feeling of hatred amongst all classes, and quenched the little zeal which the recent marriage had inspired in the Rajputs of the desert. The mode and channel of its introduction evinced to them that there was no hope that the intolerant spirit which originally suggested it would ever be subdued. The weak Farrukhsiyar, desirous of snapping the leading-strings of the Sayyids, recalled to his court Inayatu-lla Khan,[1] the minister of Aurangzeb, and restored to him his office of Diwan, who, to use the words of the historian of the period, "did not consult the temper of the times, so very different from the reign of Aurangzeb, and the revival of the *jizya* came with him." Though by no means severe in its operation, not amounting to three-quarters per cent on annual income,[2]—from which the lame, the blind, and very poor were exempt,—it nevertheless raised a general spirit of hostility, particularly from its retaining the insulting distinction of a 'tax on infidels.' Resistance to taxation appears to be a universal feeling, in which even the Asiatic forgets the divine right of sovereignty, and which throws us back on the pervading spirit of selfishness which [403] governs human nature. The *tamgha*,[3] or stamp tax, which preceded the *jizya*, would appear to have been as unsatisfactory as it was general, from the solemnity of its renunciation by Babur on the field of battle after the victory over infidels, which gave him the crown of India; and though we have no record of the jizya being its substitute, there are indications which authorize the inference.

[1] [Ināyatu-lla Khān, a Persian of Naishapur, was tutor of Zebu-n-nissa Begam, daughter of Aurangzeb, and held high office in his reign and in that of Farrukhsīyar. He died in 1726 (Beale, *s.v.*).]

[2] 13 rupees on every 2000 rupees.

[3] [Altamgha, 'the red seal,' technically 'a royal grant. On its remission by Bābur see Erskine, *Hist. of India*, i. 467. Elliot remarks that the *altamgha* as a tax was enforced as early as the time of Alāu-d-dīn and Fīroz Shāh (Elliot-Dowson iii. 365). For the use of the seal see *Memoirs of Jahāngīr*, trans. Rogers-Beveridge, 23.]

Rāna Amar Singh asserts Rājput Independence.—Rana Amra was not an idle spectator of these occurrences ; and although the spurious thirst for distinction so early broke up the alliance by detaching Ajit, he redoubled his efforts for personal independence, and with it that of the Rajput nation. An important document attests this solicitude, namely, a treaty [1] with the emperor, in which the second article stipulates emancipation from the galling *jizya*. It may be well to analyse this treaty, which attests the

[1] "*Memorandum of Requests.*

"1. The *Mansab* of 7000, the highest grade of rank.

"2. Farman of engagement under the *panja* private seal and sign that the jizya shall be abolished—that it shall no longer be imposed on the Hindu nation ; at all events, that none of the Chagatai race shall authorize it in Mewar. Let it be annulled.

"3. The contingent of one thousand horse for service in the Deccan to be excused.

"4. All places of Hindu faith to be rebuilt, with perfect freedom of religious worship.

"5. If my uncles, brothers, or chiefs, repair to the Presence, to meet no encouragement.

"6. The Bhumias of Doolia, Banswara, Dungarpur, and Sirohi, besides other zamindars over whom I am to have control, they shall not be admitted to the Presence.

"7. The forces I possess are my chiefs—what troops you may require for a given period, you must furnish with rations (*peti*), and when the service is over, their accounts will be settled.

"8. Of the Hakkdars, Zamindars, Mansabdars, who serve you with zeal and from the heart, let me have a list—and those who are not obedient I will punish ; but in effecting this no demand is to be made for *Paemali*." *

"List of the districts attached to the *Panjhazari*,† at present under sequestration, to be restored—Phulia, Mandalgarh, Badnor, Pur, Basar, Ghayaspur, Pardhar, Banswara, Dungarpur. Besides the 5000 of old, you had on ascending the throne granted an increase of 1000, and on account of the victory at Siusini 1000 more, of two and three horse." ‡

"Of three crores of *dams* ‖ in gift (*inam*), namely, two according to farman, and one for the payment of the contingent in the Deccan, and of which two are immediately required, you have given me in lieu thereof Sirohi.

"Districts now desired—Idar, Kekri, Mandal, Jahazpur, Malpur (and another illegible)."

* Destruction of property, alluding to the crops which always suffered in the movements of disorderly troops.

† Mansab of 5000.

‡ It was usual to allow two and three horses to each cavalier when favour was intended.

‖ 40 dams to the rupee.

altered condition of both parties. Its very title marks the subordination of the chief of the Rajputs; but while this is headed a 'Memorandum of Requests,' the eighth article discloses the effective means of the Rana, for there he assumes an air of protection towards the emperor. In the opening stipulation for the *mansab* of 7000, the [404] mind reverts to the great Amra, who preferred abdication to acknowledgment of a superior; but opinion had undergone a change as great as the mutual relations of the Rajputs. In temporal dignities other States had risen to an equality with Mewar, and all had learned to look on the Mogul as the fountain of honour. The abolition of the jizya, freedom from religious restraint, control over the ancient feudatories of his house, and the restoration of all sequestrations, distinguish the other articles, and amply attest the improving attitude of Mewar, and the rapid decay of the Mogul empire. The Mahrattas under Raja Sahu [1] were successfully prosecuting their peculiar system in the south, with the same feelings which characterized the early Gothic invaders of Italy; strangers to settled government, they imposed the taxes of *chauth* and *desmukhi*,[2] the *fourth* and *tenth* of all territorial income, in the countries they overran. The Jat tribes west of the Chambal likewise bearded their oppressors in this reign, by hoisting the standard of independence at the very threshold of their capital; and from the siege of Sinsini (mentioned in this treaty) to the last storm of Bharatpur, they maintained the consequence thus assumed.

Death of Rāna Amar Singh.—This treaty was the last act of Rana Amra's life; he died in A.D. 1716 [1710], leaving the reputation of an active and high-minded prince, who well upheld his station and the prosperity of his country, notwithstanding the anarchy of the period. His encouragement of agriculture and protection of manufactures are displayed in the edicts engraved on pillars, which will hand down his name to posterity. His memory is held in high veneration; nor do the Rajputs admit the absolute degradation of Mewar till the period of the second prince in succession to Amra [405].

[1] [Sāhu, 'the honest, respectable man,' a title given by Aurangzeb to Sivaji, son of Sambhaji (Grant Duff, 184).]

[2] [*Desmukhi* from *Sardesmukh*, an officer exercising police and revenue jurisdiction under the Marāthas. These taxes were confirmed in favour of Sivaji in 1665 (*Ibid.* 94).]

CHAPTER 15

Rāna Sangrām Singh II., A.D. 1710-34.—Sangram Singh (the lion of battle) succeeded; a name renowned in the annals of Mewar, being that of the opponent of the founder of the Moguls. He ascended the throne about the same time with Muhammad Shah,[1] the last of the race of Timur who deserved the name of emperor of India. During the reign of Sangram, from A.D. 1716 to 1734, this mighty empire was dismembered; when, in lieu of one paramount authority, numerous independent governments started up, which preserved their uncertain existence until the last revolution, which has given a new combination to these discordant materials—Muhammadan, Mahratta, and Rajput, in the course of one century under the dominion of a handful of Britons! Like the Satraps of the ancient Persian, or the Lieutenants of Alexander, each chief proclaimed himself master of the province, the government of which was confided to his loyalty and talents; and it cannot fail to diminish any regret at the successive prostration of Bengal, Oudh, Haidarabad, and other less conspicuous States, to remember that they were founded in rebellion, and erected on ingratitude; and that their rulers were destitute of those sympathies, which could alone give stability to their ephemeral greatness, by improving the condition of their subjects. With the Mahrattas the case is different: their emergence to power claims our admiration, when tyranny transformed the industrious husbandman, and the minister of religion, into a hardy and enterprising soldier, and a skilful functionary of government. Had their ambition been restrained within legitimate bounds, it would have been no less gratifying than politically and morally just that the family of Sivaji should have retained its [406] authority in countries which his active valour wrested from Aurangzeb. But the genius of conquest changed their natural habits; they devastated instead of consolidating; and in lieu of that severe and frugal simplicity, and that energy of enterprise, which were their peculiar characteristics, they became distinguished for mean parsimony, low cunning, and dastardly depredation. Had they, retaining their original character, been content with their proper sphere of action, the Deccan, they

[1] [September 29, 1719.]

might yet have held the sovereignty of that vast region, where their habits and language assimilated them with the people. But as they spread over the north they encountered national antipathies, and though professing the same creed, a wider difference in sentiment divided the Mahratta from the Rajput, than from the despots of Delhi, whose tyrannical intolerance was more endurable, because less degrading, than the rapacious meanness of the Southron. Rajasthan benefited by the demolition of the empire: to all but Mewar it yielded an extension of power. Had the national mind been allowed to repose, and its energies to recruit, after so many centuries of demoralization, all would have recovered their strength, which lay in the opinions and industry of the people, a devoted tenantry and brave vassalage, whom we have so often depicted as abandoning their habitations and pursuits to aid the patriotic views of their princes.

Deposition of Farrukhsīyar: Nizāmu-l-mulk.—The short reign of Farrukhsiyar was drawing to a close; its end was accelerated by the very means by which that monarch hoped to emancipate himself from the thraldom of the Sayyids, against whose authority the faction of Inayatu-lla was but a feeble counterpoise, and whose arbitrary habits, in the re-establishment of the jizya, lost him even the support of the father of his queen. It was on this occasion that the celebrated Nizamu-l-mulk,[1] the founder of the Haidarabad State, was brought upon the stage: he then held the unimportant charge of the district of Moradabad; but possessed of high talents, he was bought over, by the promise of the government of Malwa, to further the views of the Sayyids. Supported by a body of ten thousand Mahrattas, these makers of kings soon manifested their displeasure by the deposal of Farrukhsiyar, who was left without any support but that of the princes of Amber and Bundi. Yet they would never have abandoned him had he hearkened to their counsel to take the field, and trust his cause to them: but, cowardly and infatuated, he refused to quit the walls of his palace, and threw [407] himself upon the mercy of his enemies, who made him dismiss the faithful Rajputs and "admit a guard of honour of their troops into the citadel."[2]

[1] [Nizāmu-l-mulk, Asaf Jāh, titles of Chīn Qilich Khān, a Turkmān officer in the service of Aurangzeb, governor of the Deccan, died May 22, 1748.]

[2] Amongst the archives of the Rana to which I had access, I discovered

Murder of Farrukhsīyar, May 16, 1719.—Farrukhsiyar hoped for security in the inviolability of the harem—but he found no sanctuary even there: to use the words of the Mogul memoir, "night advanced, and day, like the fallen star of the emperor, sunk in darkness. The gates of the citadel were closed upon his friends: the Wazir and Ajit Singh remained within. This night was dreadful to the inhabitants of the city; no one knew what was passing in the palace, and the troops under the Amiru-l-umara, with ten thousand Mahrattas, remained under arms: morning came, and all hope was extinguished by the royal band (*Naubat*) announcing the deposal of Farrukhsiyar, in the proclamation of Rafiu-d-darajat, his successor." The interval between the deposal and the death of an Asiatic prince is short, and even while the heralds vociferated "long live the king!" to the new puppet, the bowstring was on the neck of the contemptible Farrukhsiyar.

---

an autograph letter of Raja Jai Singh, addressed at this important juncture to the Rana's prime minister, Biharidas.

"The Amiru-l-umara has arrived, and engagements through Balaji Pandit have been agreed to: he said that he always had friendship for me, but advised me to march, a measure alike recommended by Kishan Singh and Jiwa Lal. On this I presented an *arzi* to his Majesty, stated the advice, but desired to have his Majesty's commands; when the king sanctioning my leave, such being the general desire, on Thursday the 9th of Phālgun I moved, and pitched my tents at Sarbal Sarai. I told the Rao Raja (of Bundi) to accompany me, but it did not reach his mind, and he joined Kutbu-l-mulk, who gave him some horse, and made him encamp with Ajit Singh. Bhim Singh's (of Kotah) army arrived, and an engagement took place, in which Jeth Singh Hara was killed, and the Rao Raja fled to Allahwirdi Khan's sarai. I sent troops to his aid; the king has made over the baths and wardrobe to the Sayyids, who have everything their own way. You know the Sayyids; I am on my way back to my own country, and have much to say *vivâ voce* to the Huzur:* come and meet me. Phālgun, S. 19, 1775 (A.D. 1719)."

"Siddh Sri Maharaja dhiraj Sri Sangram Singhji; receive the *mujra* † of Raja Sawai Jai Singh. Here all is well; your welfare is desired; you are the chief, nor is there any separation of interests: my horses and Rajputs are at your service; command when I can be of use. It is long since I have seen the royal mother (Sri Baiji Raj); if you come this way, I trust she will accompany you. For news I refer you to Dip Chand Pancholi. Asoj 6, S. 1777."

---

* *Huzur* signifies the Presence. Such was the respectful style of the Amber prince to the Rana; to illustrate which I shall add another letter from the same prince, though merely complimentary, to the Rana.

† *Mujra* is a salutation of respect used to a superior.

Accession of Rafiu-d-darajāt.—The first act of the new reign (A.D. 1719) was one of conciliation towards Ajit Singh and the Rajputs, namely, the abrogation of the *jizya*; and the Sayyids further showed their disposition to attach them by conferring the important office of Diwan on one of their own faith: Raja Ratan Chand was accordingly inducted into the ministry in lieu of Inayatu-lla.

Accession of Roshan-Akhtar Muhammad Shah, A.D. **1719-48.**—Three phantoms of royalty flitted across the scene in a few months, till Roshan-Akhtar, the eldest son of Bahadur Shah, was [408] enthroned with the title of Muhammad Shah (A.D. 1720), during whose reign of nearly thirty years the empire was completely dismembered,[1] and Mahrattas from the south disputed its spoils with the Afghan mountaineers. The haughty demeanour of the Sayyids disgusted all who acted with them, especially their coadjutor the Nizam,[2] of whose talents, displayed in restoring Malwa to prosperity, they entertained a dread. It was impossible to cherish any abstract loyalty for the puppets they established, and treason lost its name, when the Nizam declared for independence, which the possession of the fortresses of Asir and Burhanpur enabled him to secure. The brothers had just cause for alarm. The Rajputs were called upon for their contingents,[3]

[1] [For a sketch of the history of this period see Keene, *Sketch of the History of Hindustan*, 304 ff.]

[2] Raja Jai Singh to Biharidas, the Rana's minister:—"You write that your Lord despatches money for the troops—I have no accounts thereof; put the treasure on camels and send it without delay. The Nawab Nizamu-l-mulk is marching rapidly from Ujjain, and Chhabile Ram is coming hither, and according to accounts from Agra he has crossed at Kalpi. Let the Diwan's army form a speedy junction. Make no delay; in supplies of cash everything is included." Bhadon, 4th S. 1776 (A.D. 1720).

[3] Letter from Raja Bakhta Singh of Nagor to Biharidas, the Rana's prime minister:—"Your letter was received, and its contents made me happy. Sri Diwan's *ruqa'* reached me and was understood. You tell me both the Nawabs (*Sayyids*) had taken the field, that both the Maharajas attended, and that your own army was about to be put in motion, for how could ancient friendships be severed? All was comprehended. But neither of the Nawabs will take the field, nor will either of the Maharajas proceed to the Deccan: they will sit and enjoy themselves quietly in talking at home. But should by some accident the Nawabs take the field, espouse their cause; if you cling to any other you are lost; of this you will be convinced ere long, so guard yourself—if you can wind up our own thread, don't give it to another to break—you are wise, and can anticipate intentions. Where there is such a servant as you, that house can be in no danger."

and the princes of Kotah and Narwar gallantly interposed their own retainers to cut off the Nizam from the Nerbudda, on which occasion the Kotah prince was slain. The independence of the Nizam led to that of Oudh. Saadat Khan was then but the commandant of Bayana, but he entered into the conspiracy to expel the Sayyids, and was one of those who drew lots to assassinate the Amiru-l-umara. The deed was put into execution on the march to reduce the Nizam, when Haidar Khan buried his poniard in the Amir's heart.[1] The emperor then in camp, being thus freed, returned against the Wazir, who instantly set up Ibrahim and marched against his opponents. The Rajputs wisely remained neutral, and both armies met. The decapitation of Ratan Chand was the signal for the battle, which was obstinate and bloody; the Wazir was made prisoner, and subjected to the bowstring. For the part Saadat Khan acted in the conspiracy he was honoured with the title of Bahadur Jang, and the government of Oudh. The Rajput princes paid their respects to the [409] conqueror, who confirmed the repeal of the *jizya*, and as the reward of their neutrality the Rajas of Amber and Jodhpur, Jai Singh and Ajit, were gratified, the former with the government of the province of Agra, the last with that of Gujarat and Ajmer, of which latter fortress he took possession. Girdhardas[2] was made governor of Malwa to oppose the Mahrattas, and the Nizam was invited from his government of Haidarabad to accept the office of wazir of the empire.

The Policy of Mewār.—The policy of Mewar was too isolated for the times; her rulers clung to forms and unsubstantial homage, while their neighbours, with more active virtue, plunged into the tortuous policy of the imperial court, and seized every opportunity to enlarge the boundaries of their States: and while Amber appropriated to herself the royal domains almost to the Jumna; while Marwar planted her banner on the battlements of Ajmer, dismembered Gujarat, and pushed her clans far into the desert, and even to 'the world's end';[3] Mewar confined her ambition to the control of her ancient feudatories of Abu,

[1] [Haidar Khān assassinated Husain Ali on September 18, 1720.]

[2] Girdhardas was a Nagar Brahman, son of Chhabile Ram, the chief secretary of Ratan Chand.

[3] Jagatkhunt, the Jagat point, of our maps, at Dwarka, where the Badhels, a branch of the Rathors, established themselves.

Idar, and the petty States which grew out of her, Dungarpur and Banswara. The motive for this policy was precisely the same which had cost such sacrifices in former times; she dreaded amalgamating with the imperial court, and preferred political inferiority to the sacrifice of principle. The internal feuds of her two great clans also operated against her aggrandizement; and while the brave Saktawat, Jeth Singh, expelled the Rathor from Idar, and subdued the wild mountaineers even to Koliwara, the conquest was left incomplete by the jealousy of his rival, and he was recalled in the midst of his success. From these and other causes an important change took place in the internal policy of Mewar, which tended greatly to impair her energies. To this period none of the vassals had the power to erect places of strength within their domains, which, as already stated, were not fixed, but subject to triennial change; their lands were given for subsistence, their native hills were their fortresses, and the frontier strongholds defended their families in time of invasion. As the Mogul power waned, the general defensive system was [410] abandoned, while the predatory warfare which succeeded compelled them to stud their country with castles, in order to shelter their effects from the Mahratta and Pathan, and in later times to protect rebels.

Rana Sangram ruled eighteen [twenty-four] years; under him Mewar was respected, and the greater portion of her lost territory was regained. His selection of Biharidas Pancholi evinced his penetration, for never had Mewar a more able or faithful minister, and numerous autograph letters of all the princes of his time attest his talent and his worth as the oracle of the period. He retained his office during three reigns: but his skill was unable to stem the tide of Mahratta invasion, which commenced on the death of Sangram.

Anecdotes of Rāna Sangrām Singh II.—Tradition has preserved many anecdotes of Sangram, which aid our estimate of Rajput character, whether in the capacity of legislators or the more retired sphere of domestic manners. They uniformly represent this Rana as a patriarchal ruler, wise, just, and inflexible,[1] steady in his application to business, regulating public and private

[1] In the dialect, *chhari mazbūt thi*, his rod was strong—a familiar phrase, which might be rendered 'sceptre'—a long rod with an iron spike on it, often placed before the *gaddi*, or throne.

expenditure, and even the sumptuary laws, which were rigidly adhered to, and on which the people still expatiate, giving homely illustrations of the contrast between them and the existing profusion. The Chauhan of Kotharia, one of the highest class of chieftains, had recommended an addition to the folds of the court robe, and as courtesy forbids all personal denial, his wish was assented to, and he retired to his estate pluming himself on his sovereign's acquiescence. But the Rana, sending for the minister, commanded the sequestration of two villages of Kotharia, which speedily reaching the ears of the chief, he repaired to court, and begged to know the fault which had drawn upon him this mark of displeasure. "None, Raoji; but on a minute calculation I find the revenue of these two villages will just cover the expense of the superfluity of garment which obedience to your wishes will occasion me, and as every iota of my own income is appropriated, I had no other mode of innovating on our ancient costume than by making you bear the charge attending a compliance with your suggestion." It will readily be believed, that the Chauhan prayed the [411] revocation of this edict, and that he was careful for the future of violating the sumptuary laws of his sovereign.

On another occasion, from lapse of memory or want of consideration, he broke the laws he had established, and alienated a village attached to the household. Each branch had its appropriate fund, whether for the kitchen, the wardrobe, the privy purse, the queens; these lands were called *thua*, and each had its officer, or *thuadar*, all of whom were made accountable for their trust to the prime minister; it was one of these he had alienated. Seated with his chiefs in the *rasora*, or banqueting-hall, there was no sugar forthcoming for the curds, which has a place in the dinner *carte* of all Rajputs, and he chid the superintendent for the omission. "Anndata" (giver of food), replied the officer, "the minister says you have given away the village set apart for sugar."—"Just," replied the Rana, and finished his repast without further remark, and without sugar to his curds.

Another anecdote will show his inflexibility of character, and his resistance to that species of interference in state affairs which is the bane of Asiatic governments. Sangram had recently emancipated himself from the trammels of a tedious minority, during which his mother, according to custom, acted a conspicuous part in the guardianship of her son and the State. The chieftain of Dariawad had his estate confiscated: but as the Rana never punished from passion or pardoned from weakness, none dared to plead his cause, and he remained proscribed from court during two years, when he ventured a petition to the queen-mother through the Bhandarins,[1] for the reversion of the decree, accompanied with a note for two lakhs of rupees,[2] and a liberal donation to the fair mediators. It was the daily habit of the Rana to pay his respects to his mother before dinner, and on one of these visits she introduced the Ranawat's request, and begged the restoration of the estate. It was customary, on the issue of every grant, that eight days should elapse from the mandate to the promulgation of the edict, to which eight official seals[3] were attached; but on the present occasion the Rana commanded the execution of the deed at once, and to have it ere he left the Rawala. On its being brought, he [412] placed it respectfully in his mother's hands, begging her to return the note to the Ranawat; having made this sacrifice to duty, he bowed and retired. The next day he commanded dinner an hour earlier, without the usual visit to the Rawala: all were surprised, but none so much as the queen-mother—the day passed—another came—still no visit, and to a confidential message, she received a ceremonious reply. Alarmed for the loss of her son's affections, she pondered on the cause, but could find none, except the grant—she entreated the minister's interference; he respectfully intimated that he was interdicted from the discussion of State affairs but with his sovereign—she had recourse to other expedients, which proving alike fruitless, she became sullen, punished her damsels without cause, and refused food: Sangram still remained obdurate. She talked of a pilgrimage to the Ganges, and befitting equipage and escort were commanded to attend her—the moment of departure was at hand, and yet he would not see her. She repaired by Amber on her route to Mathura, to worship the Apollo of Vraj,[4] when the great Raja Jai Singh (married to the Rana's sister)[5]

[1] The dames attendant on the queens,—the Lady Mashams of every female court in Rajasthan.

[2] £25,000.

[3] There were eight ministers; from this the Mahrattas had their *asht pardhans*, the number which formed the ministry of Rama.

[4] [Krishna.]

[5] I discovered the following letter from one of the princesses of Amber to Rana Sangram, written at this period; it is not evident in what relation

advanced, and conducted her to his new city of Jaipur, and to evince his respect "put his shoulder to the travelling litter or palki," and promised to return with her and be a suppliant to his brother-in-law for the restoration of his regard. She made a tour of the sacred places, and on return accepted the escort of the Prince of Amber. The laws of hospitality amongst the Rajputs are rigid: the Rana could not refuse to his guest the request for which he had left his capital: but averse to owing reconciliation to external intercession, and having done enough for the suppression of intrigue, he advanced to meet the cortège when within one march of Udaipur, as if to receive the Amber prince; but proceeding direct to his [413] mother's tents, he asked her blessing, and having escorted her to the palace, returned to greet and conduct his brother prince; all the allusion he made to the subject was in the simple but pithy expression, "family quarrels should be kept in the family."

Another anecdote shows him as the vigilant shepherd watching over the safety of his flock. As he sat down to dinner, tidings arrived of an invasion of the Malwa Pathans, who had rifled several villages at Mandasor, carrying the inhabitants into captivity. Pushing the platter from him, he ordered his armour, and the *nakkara* to beat the assemblage of his chieftains. With all speed a gallant band formed on the terrace below, but they prevailed on the Rana to leave the punishment of the desultory aggression to them, as unworthy of his personal interference. They de-

---

she stood to him, but I think she must have been his wife, and the sister of Jai Singh:

"To Siddh Sri Sangram Singh, happiness! the Kachhwaha Rani (*queen*) writes, read her *asis* * (blessing). Here all is well; the welfare of the Sri Diwanji is desired. You are very dear to me; you are great, the sun of Hindustan; if you do not thus act, who else can? the action is worthy of you; with your house is my entire friendship. From ancient times we are the Rajputs of your house, from which both Rajas † have had their consequence increased, and I belong to it of old, and expect always to be fostered by it, nor will the Sri Diwanji disappoint us. My intention was to proceed to the feet of the Sri Diwanji, but the wet weather has prevented me; but I shall soon make my appearance." S. 1778 (A.D. 1722).

---

* *Asis* is benediction, which only ladies and holy men employ in epistolary writing or in verbal compliment.

† Amber and Marwar; this expression denotes the letter to have been written on intermarriage with the Rana's house, and shows her sense of such honour.

parted: several hours after, the chief of Kanor arrived, having left a sick-bed, and with a tertian come in obedience to his sovereign's summons. Vain was his prince's dissuasion to keep him back, and he joined the band as they came up with the invaders. The foe was defeated and put to flight, but the sick chieftain fell in the charge, and his son was severely wounded by his side. On the young chief repairing to court he was honoured with a *bira* [1] from the Rana's own hand, a distinction which he held to be an ample reward for his wounds, and testimonial of the worth of his father. The existence of such sentiments are the strongest tests of character.

On another occasion, some parasite had insinuated suspicions against the chief of the nobles, the Rawat of Salumbar, who had just returned victorious in action with the royal forces at Malwa, and had asked permission to visit his family on his way to court. The Rana spurned the suspicion, and to show his reliance on the chief, he dispatched a messenger for Salumbar to wait his arrival and summon him to the presence. He had reached his domain, given leave to his vassals as they passed their respective abodes, dismounted, and reached the door of the Rawala, when the herald called aloud, "The Rana salutes you, Rawatji, and commands this letter." With his hand on the door where his wife and children awaited him, he demanded his horse, and simply leaving his 'duty for his mother,' he [414] mounted, with half a dozen attendants, nor loosed the rein until he reached the capital. It was midnight; his house empty; no servants; no dinner; but his sovereign had foreseen and provided, and when his arrival was announced, provender for his cattle, and vessels of provision prepared in the royal kitchen, were immediately sent to his abode. Next morning Salumbar attended the court. The Rana was unusually gracious, and not only presented him with the usual tokens of regard, a horse and jewels, but moreover a grant of land. With surprise he asked what service he had performed to merit such distinction, and from a sentiment becoming the descendant of Chonda solemnly refused to accept it; observing, that even if he had lost his head, the reward was

[1] The *bira* is the betel or pan-leaf folded up, containing aromatic spices, and presented on taking leave. The Kanor chieftain, being of the second grade of nobles, was not entitled to the distinction of having it from the sovereign's own hand.

excessive; but if his prince would admit of his preferring a request, it would be, that in remembrance of his sovereign's favour, when he, or his, in after times, should on the summons come from their estate to the capital, the same number of dishes from the royal kitchen should be sent to his abode: it was granted, and to this day his descendants enjoy the distinction. These anecdotes paint the character of Sangram far more forcibly than any laboured effort. His reign was as honourable to himself as it was beneficial to his country, in whose defence he had fought eighteen actions; but though his policy was too circumscribed, and his country would have benefited more by a surrender of some of those antique prejudices which kept her back in the general scramble for portions of the dilapidated monarchy of the Moguls, yet he was respected abroad, as he was beloved by his subjects, of whose welfare he was ever watchful, and to whose wants ever indulgent. Rana Sangram was the last prince who upheld the dignity of the *gaddi* of Bappa Rawal; with his death commenced Mahratta ascendancy, and with this we shall open the reign of his son and successor.

Rāna Jagat Singh II., A.D. 1734-51. Difficulties of Rājput Combination.—Jagat Singh II., the eldest of the four sons of Sangram, succeeded S. 1790 (A.D. 1734). The commencement of his reign was signalized by a revival of the triple alliance formed by Rana Amra, and broken by Raja Ajit's connexion with the Sayyids and the renewal of matrimonial ties with the empire, the abjuration whereof was the basis of the treaty. The present engagement, which included all the minor states, was formed at Hurra, a town in Mewar on the Ajmer frontier, where the confederate princes met at the head of their vassals. To insure unanimity, the Rana was invested with paramount control, and headed the forces which were [415] to take the field after the rains, already set in.[1] Unity of interests was the chief character

[1] Treaty.

Seal of Rana.

Sri Eklinga. (*a*)

Agreed.	Agreed.	
Sita Rama jayati. (*c*)	Vraj Adhis. (*b*)	Abhai Singh. (*d*)

(*a*) (*b*) (*c*). All these seals of Mewar, Marwar, and Amber bear respectively the names of the tutelary divinity of each prince and his tribe

of the engagement, had they adhered to which, not only the independence, but the aggrandisement, of Rajasthan, was in their power, and they might have alike defied the expiring efforts of Mogul tyranny, and the Parthian-like warfare of the Mahratta. They were indeed the most formidable power in India at this juncture; but difficult as it had ever proved to coalesce the Rajputs for mutual preservation, even when a paramount superiority of power, both temporal and spiritual, belonged to the Ranas, so now, since Amber and Marwar had attained an equality with Mewar, it was found still less practicable to prevent the operation of the principles of disunion. In fact, a moment's reflection must discover that the component parts of a great feudal federation, such as that described, must contain too many discordant particles—too many rivalries and national antipathies—ever cordially to amalgamate. Had it been otherwise, the opportunities were many and splendid for the recovery of Rajput freedom; but though individually enamoured of liberty, the universality of the sentiment prevented its realization: they never would submit to the control required to work it out, and this, the best opportunity which had ever occurred, was lost. A glance at the disordered fragments of the throne of Akbar will show the comparative strength of the Rajputs.

League of Nizamu-l-mulk with Rājputs and Marāthas.—

Swasti Sri! By the united chiefs the under-written has been agreed to, from which no deviation can take place. Sawan sudi 13, S. 1791 (A.D. 1735), Camp Hurra.

1. All are united, in good and in evil, and none will withdraw therefrom, on which oaths have been made, and faith pledged, which will be lost by whoever acts contrary thereto. The honour and shame of one is that of all, and in this everything is contained.
2. No one shall countenance the traitor of another.
3. After the rains the affair shall commence, and the chiefs of each party assemble at Rampura; and if from any cause the head cannot come, he will send his Kunwar (heir), or some personage of weight.
4. Should from inexperience such Kunwar commit error, the Rana alone shall interfere to correct it.
5. In every enterprise all shall unite to effect it.

(*a*) Ėklinga, or Mahadeva of the Sesodias of Mewar; (*b*) Vraj Adhis, the lord of Vraj, the country round Mathura; the epithet of Krishna; seal of the Hara prince; (*c*) Victory to Sita and Rama, the demi-god, ancestor of the princes of Amber; (*d*) Abhai Singh, prince of Marwar.

Nizamu-l-mulk had completely emancipated himself from his allegiance, and signalized his independence, by sending the head of the imperial general, who [416] ventured to oppose it, as that of a traitor, to the emperor. He leagued with the Rajputs, and instigated Bajirao to plant the Mahratta standard in Malwa and Gujarat. In defending the former, Dayya Bahadur fell;[1] and Jai Singh of Amber, being nominated to the trust, delegated it to the invader, and Malwa was lost. The extensive province of Gujarat soon shared the same fate; for in the vacillating policy of the court, the promise of that government to the Rathors had been broken, and Abhai Singh, son of Ajit, who had expelled Sarbuland Khan[2] after a severe contest, following the example of his brother prince of Amber, connived with the invaders, while he added its most northern districts to Marwar. In Bengal, Behar, and Orissa, Shujau-d-daula, and his deputy Allahwirdi Khan,[3] were supreme, and Safdar Jang[4] (son of Saadat Khan) was established in Oudh. The basest disloyalty marked the rise of this family, which owed everything to Muhammad Shah. It was Saadat Khan who invited Nadir Shah, whose invasion gave the final stab to the empire; and it was his son, Safdar Jang, who, when commandant of the artillery (*mir-i-atish*), turned it against his sovereign's palace, and then conveyed it to Oudh. Of the Diwans of Bengal we must speak only with reverence; but, whether they had any special dispensation, their loyalty to the descendant of Farrukhsiyar has been very little more distinguished than that of the satraps enumerated, though the original tenure of Bengal is still apparent, and the feudal obligation to the suzerain of Delhi manifested, in the homage of *petite serjanterie*, in transmitting with the annual fine of relief (one hundred mohars) the spices of the eastern archipelago. Yet of all those who gloried in the title of *fidwi padshah-i-ghazi*, the only 'slave of the victorious king,' who has been generous to him in the day of his distress, is the Diwan of Bengal, better known as the English

[1] [Sūbahdār of Mālwa, killed in battle at Tala near Dhār in 1732 (Grant Duff 227).]

[2] [Sarbuland Khān was superseded by Abhai Singh (*ibid.* 226).]

[3] [Mahābat Jang, in 1740 usurped the Government of Bengal, over which he reigned for sixteen years, died April 10, 1756 N.S., buried at Murshidābād (Beale, sv.).]

[4] [Nephew and son-in-law of Burhānu-l-mulk, Sa'ādat Khān, was appointed Wazīr in 1748, died October 17, 1754.]

East India Company. In the hour of triumph they rescued the blind and aged descendants of the illustrious Babur from a state of degradation and penury, and secured to him all the dignity and comfort which his circumstances could lead him to hope; and the present state of his family, contrasted with the thraldom and misery endured while fortune favoured the Mahratta, is splendid. Yet perhaps the most acute stroke of fortune to this fallen monarch was when the British governor of India lent his aid to the descendant of the rebellious Safdar Jang to mount the throne of Oudh, and to assume, in lieu of the title of wazir of the empire, that of king. We can [417] appreciate and commiserate the feeling; for the days of power were yet too recent [1] for Akbar Sani (the second) to receive such intelligence without a shock, or without comparing his condition with him whose name he bore. It is well to pause upon this page of eastern history, which is full of instruction; since by weighing the abuses of power, and its inevitable loss through placing a large executive trust in the hands of those who exercised it without sympathy towards the governed, we may at least retard the day of our decline.

Marātha Raids. The Campaign of Nādir Shāh.—The Mahratta establishments in Malwa and Gujarat constituted a nucleus for others to form upon, and like locusts, they crossed the Nerbudda in swarms; when the Holkars, the Sindhias, the Puars, and other less familiar names, emerged from obscurity; when the plough [2] was deserted for the sword, and the goat-herd [3] made a lance of his crook. They devastated, and at length settled upon, the lands of the indigenous Rajputs. For a time the necessity of unity made them act under one standard, and hence the vast masses under the first Bajirao, which bore down all opposition, and afterwards dispersed themselves over those long-oppressed regions. It was in A.D. 1735 that he first crossed the Chambal [4] and appeared before Delhi, which he blockaded, when his retreat was purchased by the surrender of the *chauth*, or fourth of the

[1] [Akbar Shāh II., King of Delhi, reigned from 1806 to 1827.] I have conversed with an aged Shaikh who recollected the splendour of Muhammad Shah's reign before Nadir's invasion. He was darogah (superintendent) to the Duab canal, and described to me the fête on its opening.

[2] Sindhia's family were husbandmen.

[3] Holkar was a goat-herd.

[4] The ford near Dholpur still is called Bhaoghat. [Bājirāo appeared at Delhi in 1736 (Grant Duff 226).]

gross revenues of the empire. The Nizam, dreading the influence such pusillanimous concession might exert upon his rising power, determined to drive the Mahrattas from Malwa, where, if once fixed, they would cut off his communications with the north. He accordingly invaded Malwa, defeated Bajirao in a pitched battle, and was only prevented from following it up by Nadir Shah's advance, facilitated by the Afghans, who, on becoming independent in Kabul, laid open the frontiers of Hindustan.[1] In this emergency, "great hopes were placed on the valour of the Rajputs"; but the spirit of devotion in this brave race, by whose aid the Mogul power was made and maintained, was irretrievably alienated, and not one of those high families, who had throughout been so lavish of their blood in its defence, would obey the summons to the royal standard, when the fate of India was decided on the plains of Karnal.[2] A sense [418] of individual danger brought together the great home feudatories, when the Nizam and Saadat Khan (now Wazir) united their forces under the imperial commander; but their demoralized levies were no match for the Persian and the northern mountaineer. The Amiru-l-umara was slain, the Wazir made prisoner, and Muhammad Shah and his kingdom were at Nadir's disposal. The disloyalty of the Wazir filled the capital with blood, and subjected his sovereign to the condition of a captive. Jealous of the Nizam, whose diplomatic success had obtained him the office of Amiru-l-umara, he stimulated the avarice of the conqueror by exaggerating the riches of Delhi, and declared that he alone could furnish the ransom negotiated by the Nizam. Nadir's love of gold overpowered his principle; the treaty was broken, the keys of Delhi were demanded, and its humiliated emperor was led in triumph through the camp of the conqueror, who, on March 8, A.D. 1739, took possession of the palace of Timur, and coined money bearing this legend:

King over the kings of the world
Is Nadir, king of kings, and lord of the period.

Plunder and Massacre at Delhi.—The accumulated wealth of India contained in the royal treasury, notwithstanding the lavish expenditure during the civil wars, and the profuse rewards

[1] A.D. 1740.

[2] [Near Pānipat, February 13, 1739 (Elphinstone 717).]

scattered by each competitor for dominion, was yet sufficient to gratify even avarice itself, amounting in gold, jewels, and plate to forty millions sterling, exclusive of equipages of every denomination. But this enormous spoil only kindled instead of satiating the appetite of Nadir, and a fine of two millions and a half was exacted, and levied with such unrelenting rigour and cruelty on the inhabitants, that men of rank and character could find no means of escape but by suicide. A rumour of this monster's death excited an insurrection, in which several Persians were killed. The provocation was not lost: the conqueror ascended a mosque,[1] and commanded a general massacre, in which thousands were slain. Pillage accompanied murder; whilst the streets streamed with blood, the city was fired, and the dead were consumed in the conflagration of their late habitations. If a single ray of satisfaction could be felt amidst such a scene of horror, it must have been when Nadir commanded the minister of the wretch who was the author of [419] this atrocity, the infamous Saadat Khan, to send, on pain of death, an inventory of his own and his master's wealth; demanding meanwhile the two millions and a half, the original composition settled by the Nizam, from the Wazir alone. Whether his 'coward conscience' was alarmed at the mischief he had occasioned, or mortification at discovering that his ambition had 'o'erleaped itself,' and recoiled with vengeance on his own head, tempted the act, it is impossible to discover, but the guilty Saadat became his own executioner. He swallowed poison;[2] an example followed by his diwan, Raja Majlis Rae, in order to escape the rage of the offended Nadir. By the new treaty, all the western provinces, Kabul, Tatta, Sind, and Multan, were surrendered and united to Persia, and on the vernal equinox, Nadir, gorged with spoil, commenced his march from the desolated Delhi.[3] The philo-

[1] It is yet pointed out to the visitor of this famed city. [The Golden Mosque of Roshanu-d-daula (Fanshawe, *Delhi Past and Present*, 50).]

[2] [This is not certain. Many officials committed suicide, and Sa'ādat Khān was believed to have been among these: it is certain that he died the night before the massacre (Keene, *Sketch Hist. Hindustan*, 324).]

[3] As the hour of departure approached, the cruelties of the ruthless invaders increased, to which the words of the narrator, an eye-witness, can alone do justice: "A type of the last day afflicted the inhabitants of this once happy city; hitherto it was a general massacre, but now came the murder of individuals. In every house was heard the cry of affliction.

sophic comment of the native historian on these events is so just, that we shall transcribe it verbatim. "The people of Hindustan at this period thought only of personal safety and gratification; misery was disregarded by those who escaped it, and man, centred wholly in self, felt not for his kind. This selfishness, destructive of public and private virtue, was universal in Hindustan at the invasion of Nadir Shah; nor have the people become more virtuous since, and consequently neither more happy nor more independent."

Results to the Rājputs.—At this eventful era in the political history of India, the Rajput nation had not only maintained their ground amidst the convulsions of six centuries under the paramount sway of the Islamite, but two of the three chief States, Marwar and [420] Amber, had by policy and valour created substantial States out of petty principalities, junior branches[1] from which had established their independence, and

---

Basant Rae, agent for pensions, killed his family and himself; Khalik Yar Khan stabbed himself; many took poison. The venerable chief magistrate was dishonoured by stripes; sleep and rest forsook the city. The officers of the court were beaten without mercy, and a fire broke out in the imperial *farash-khana*, and destroyed effects to the amount of a crore (a million sterling). There was a scarcity of grain, two seers of coarse rice sold for a rupee, and from a pestilential disorder crowds died daily in every street and lane. The inhabitants, like the affrighted animals of the desert, sought refuge in the most concealed corners. Yet four or five crores (millions) more were thus extracted." On the 5th April, Nadir's seals were taken off the imperial repositories, and his farmans sent to all the feudatories of the empire to notify the place and to inculcate obedience 'to his dear brother,' which, as a specimen of eastern diplomatic phraseology, is worth insertion. It was addressed to the Rana, the Rajas of Marwar and Amber, Nagor, Satara, the Peshwa Bajirao, etc. "Between us and our dear brother, Muhammad Shah, in consideration of the regard and alliances of the two sovereigns, the connexions of regard and friendship have been renewed, so that we may be esteemed as one soul in two bodies. Now our dear brother has been replaced on the throne of this extensive empire, and we are moving to the conquest of other regions, it is incumbent that ye, like your forefathers, walk in the path of submission and obedience to our dear brother, as they did to former sovereigns of the house of Timur. God forbid it; but if accounts of your rebelling should reach our ears, we will blot you out of the pages of the book of creation" ('Memoirs of Iradat Khan,' *Scott's History of Dekhan*, vol. ii. p. 213).

[1] Bikaner and Kishangarh arose out of Marwar, and Macheri from Amber; to which we might add Shaikhavati, which, though not separate, is tributary to Amber (now Jaipur).

still enjoy it under treaty with the British Government. Mewar at this juncture was defined by nearly the same boundaries as when Mahmud of Ghazni invaded her in the tenth century, though her influence over many of her tributaries, as Bundi, Abu, Idar, and Deolia, was destroyed. To the west, the fertile district of Godwar carried her beyond her natural barrier, the Aravalli, into the desert; while the Chambal was her limit to the east. The Khari separated her from Ajmer, and to the south she adjoined Malwa. These limits comprehended one hundred and thirty miles of latitude and one hundred and forty of longitude, containing 10,000 towns and villages, with upwards of a million sterling of revenue, raised from a fertile soil by an excellent agricultural population, a wealthy mercantile community, and defended by a devoted vassalage. Such was this little patriarchal State after the protracted strife which has been related; we shall have to exhibit her, in less than half a century, on the verge of annihilation from the predatory inroads of the Mahrattas.

The Coming of the Marāthas.—In order to mark with exactitude the introduction of the Mahrattas into Rajasthan, we must revert to the period [1] when the dastardly intrigues of the advisers of Muhammad Shah surrendered to them as tribute the *chauth*, or fourth of his revenues. Whether in the full tide of successful invasion, these spoilers deemed any other argument than force to be requisite in order to justify their extortions, they had in this surrender a concession of which the subtle Mahrattas were well capable of availing themselves; and as the Mogul claimed sovereignty over the whole of Rajasthan, they might plausibly urge their right of *chauth*, as applicable to all the territories subordinate to the empire.

The Rājput Coalition.—The rapidity with which these desultory bands flew from conquest to conquest appears to have alarmed the Rajputs, and again brought about a coalition, which, with the characteristic peculiarity of all such contracts, was commenced by matrimonial alliances. On this occasion, Bijai Singh, the heir of Marwar, was affianced to the Rana's daughter, who at the same time reconciled the princes [421] of Marwar and Amber, whose positions at the court of the Mogul often brought their national jealousies into conflict, as they alternately took the lead in his councils: for it was rare to find both in the same

[1] A.D. 1735.

line of politics. These matters were arranged at Udaipur.[1] But as we have often had occasion to observe, no public [422] or

[1] These documents are interesting, if merely showing the high respect paid by every Rajput prince to the Ranas of Mewar, and illustrating what is recorded in the reign of Partap, who abjured all intercourse with them.

No. 1.

"From Kunwar Bijai Singh of Marwar to the Maharana Sri-Sri-Sri.

"Jagat Singh's Presence—let my *mujra* (obedience) be known. You honoured me by sending Rawat Kesari Singh and Biharidas, and commanding a marriage connexion. Your orders are on your child's head. You have made me a servant. To everything I am agreed, and now I am your child; while I live I am yours. If a true Rajput, my head is at your disposal. You have made 20,000 Rathors your servants. If I fail in this, the Almighty is between us. Whoever is of my blood will obey your commands, and the fruit of this marriage shall be sovereign, and if a daughter, should I bestow her on the Turkana, I am no true Rajput. She shall be married to a proper connexion, and not without your advice; and even should Sri Bavaji (an epithet of respect to his father), or others of our elders, recommend such proceeding, I swear by God I shall not agree. I am the Diwan's, let others approve or disapprove. Asarh Sudi Punim, Full Moon, Thursday, S. 1791 (A.D. 1735-36)."

"*N.B.*—This deed was executed in the balcony of the Kishanbilas by Rawat Kesari Singh and Pancholi Biharidas, and written by Pancholi Lalji—namely, marriage-deed of Kunwar Bijai Singh, son of Bakht Singh."

No. 2.

"From Bijai Singh to Rana Jagat Singh.

"Here all is well. Preserve your friendship and favour for me, and give me tidings of your welfare. That day I shall behold you will be without price (*amolak*). You have made me a thorough Rajput—never shall I fail in whatever service I can perform. You are the father of all the tribes, and bestow gifts on each according to his worth—the support and preservation of all around you—to your enemy destruction; great in knowledge, and wise like Brahma. May the Lord of the world keep the Rana happy. Asarh 13."

No. 3.

"Raja Bakht Singh to the Rana.

"To Maharana Sri-Sri-Sri Jagat Singh, let Bakht Singh's respects (*mujra*) be made known. You have made me a thorough Rajput, and by such your favour is known to the world. What service I can perform, you will never find me backward. The day I shall see you I shall be happy, my heart yearns to be with you. Asarh 11."

No. 4.

"Sawai Jai Singh to the Rana.

"May the respects of Sawai Jai Singh be known to the Maharana. According to the Sri Diwan's commands (*hukm*), I have entered into terms of friendship with you (Abhai Singh of Marwar). For neither Hindu nor

general benefit ever resulted from these alliances, which were obstructed by the multitude of petty jealousies inseparable from clanship; even while this treaty was in discussion, the fruit of the triple league formed against the tyranny of Aurangzeb was about to show its baneful influence, as will presently appear.

Bājirāo visits Mewār. Negotiations with the Marāthas.—When Malwa was acquired by the Mahrattas, followed by the cession of the *chauth*, their leader, Bajirao, repaired to Mewar, where his visit created great alarm.[1] The Rana desired to avoid a personal

---

Musalman shall I swerve therefrom. To this engagement God is between us, and the Sri Diwanji is witness. Asarh Sudi 7."

No. 5.

"Raja Bakht Singh to the Rana.

"Your *Khas ruqa'* (note in the Rana's own hand) I received, read, and was happy. Jai Singh's engagement you will have received, and mine also will have reached you. At your commands I entered into friendship with him, and as to my preserving it have no doubts, for having given you as my guarantee, no deviation can occur; do you secure his. Whether you may be accounted my father, brother, or friend, I am yours; besides you I care for neither connexion nor kin. Asarh 6."

No. 6.

"From Raja Abhai Singh to the Rana.

"To the Presence of Maharana Jagat Singh, Maharaja Abhai Singh writes—read his respects (*mujra*). God is witness to our engagement, whoever breaks it may he fare ill. In good and in evil we are joined; with one mind let us remain united, and let no selfishness disunite us. Your chiefs are witnesses, and the true Rajput will not deviate from his engagement. Asoj 3, Thursday."

Abhai Singh and Bakht Singh were brothers, sons of Raja Ajit of Marwar, to whom the former succeeded, while Bakht Singh held Nagor independently. His son was Bijai Singh, with whom this marriage was contracted. He ultimately succeeded to the government of Marwar or Jodhpur. He will add another example of political expediency counteracting common gratitude, in seizing on domestic convulsions to deprive the Rana's grandson of the province of Godwar. Zalim Singh was the fruit of this marriage, who resided during his elder brother's (Fateh Singh) lifetime at Udaipur. He was brave, amiable, and a distinguished poet. The Yati (priest), who attended me during twelve years, my assistant in these researches, was brought up under the eye of this prince as his amanuensis, and from him he imbibed his love of history and poetry, in reading which he excelled all the bards of Rajwara.

[1] Letters from Rana Jagat Singh to Biharidas Pancholi.

No. 1.

"Swasti Sri, chief of ministers, Pancholiji, read my Juhar.* The remem-

---

* A compliment used from a superior to any inferior.

interview, and sent as his ambassadors [423], the chief of Salumbar and his prime minister, Biharidas. Long discussions followed as

brance of you never leaves me. The Deccani question you have settled well, but if a meeting is to take place,* let it be beyond Deolia—nearer is not advisable. Lessen the number of your troops, by God's blessing there will be no want of funds. Settle for Rampura according to the preceding year, and let Daulat Singh know the opportunity will not occur again. The royal mother is unwell. Gararao and Gaj Manik fought nobly, and Sundar Gaj played a thousand pranks.† I regretted your absence. How shall I send Sobharam? Asoj 6, S. 1791 (A.D. 1735)."

No. 2.—*To the Same.*

"I will not credit it, therefore send witnesses and a detail of their demands. Bajirao is come, and he will derive reputation from having compelled a contribution from me, besides his demand of land. He has commenced with my country, and will take twenty times more from me than other Rajas—if a proportionate demand, it might be complied with. Malhar came last year, but this was nothing—Bajirao this, and he is powerful. But if God hears me he will not get my land. From Devichand learn particulars.

"Thursday. S. 1792.

"At the Holi all was joy at the Jagmandir,‡ but what is food without salt? what Udaipur without Biharidas?"

No. 3.—*Same to the Same.*

"With such a man as you in my house I have no fears for its stability; but why this appearance of poverty? perhaps you will ask, what fault have you committed, that you sit and move as I direct? The matter is thus: money is all in all, and the troubles on foot can only be settled by you, and all other resolutions are useless. You may say, you have got nothing, and how can you settle them—but already two or three difficulties have occurred, in getting out of which, both your pinions and mine, as to veracity, have been broken, so that neither scheming nor wisdom is any longer available. Though you have been removed from me for some time, I have always considered you at hand; but now it will be well if you approach nearer to me, that we may raise supplies, for in the act of hiding you are celebrated, and the son ‖ (*beta*) hides none: therefore your hoarding is useless, and begets suspicions. Therefore, unless you have a mind to efface all regard for your master and your own importance at my court, you will get ready some jewels and bonds under good security and bring them to me. There

* To the Peshwa is the allusion.

† As the Rana never expected his confidential notes to be translated into English, perhaps it is illiberal to be severe on them; or we might say, his elephants are mentioned more *con amore* than his sick mother or state affairs. I obtained many hundreds of these autograph notes of this prince to his prime minister.

‡ The Hindu saturnalia held in the island, 'The Minster of the world.'

‖ The Rana always styled him 'father.'

to the mode of Bajirao's reception, which was settled to be on the same footing as the Raja of Banera,[1] and that he should be seated in front of the throne. A treaty followed, stipulating an annual

is no way but this to allay these troubles: but should you think you have got ever so much time, and that I will send for you at all events, then have I thrown away mine in writing you this letter. You are wise—look to the future, and be assured I shall write no second letter. S. 1792."

This letter will show that the office of prime minister is not a bed of roses. The immediate descendants of Biharidas are in poverty like their prince, though some distant branches of the family are in situations of trust; his ambassador to Delhi, and who subsequently remained with me as medium of communication with the Rana, was a worthy and able man—Kishandas Pancholi.

I shall subjoin another letter from the Satara prince to Rana Jagat Singh, though being without date it is doubtful whether it is not addressed to Jagat Singh the First; this is, however, unimportant, as it is merely one of compliment, but showing the high respect paid by the sovereign of the Peshwas to the house whence they originally sprung.

"Swasti Sri, worthy of all praise (*opma*), from whose actions credit results; the worshipper of the remover of troubles; the ambrosia of the ocean of the Rajput race * (*amrita ratnakara kshatriya kula*); resplendent as the sun; who has made a river of tears from the eyes of the wives of your warlike foes; in deeds munificent. Sriman Maharaja dhiraj Maharana Sri Jagat Singhji, of all the princes chief, Sriman Sahu Chatarpati Raja writes, read his Ram, Ram! Here all is well; honour me by good accounts, which I am always expecting, as the source of happiness.

"Your favour was received by the Pandit Pardhan) † with great respect; and from the period of the arrival of Raj Sri Rawat Udai Singh to this time my goodwill has been increasing towards him: let your favour between us be enlarged: what more can I write?"

[1] The descendant of Bhim, son of Rana Raj Singh. The seat assigned to Bajirao was made the precedent for the position of the representative of the British Government. [The Rāwat of Banera, on succession, has the right of receiving a sword, on the arrival of which he goes to Udaipur to be installed (Erskine ii. A. 92).]

* The ocean has the poetical appellation of *ratnakara*, or 'house of gems' ['mine of jewels']; the fable of the churning of the ocean is well known, when were yielded many bounties, of which the *amrita* or 'immortal food' of the gods was one, to which the Rana, as head of all the Rajput tribes, is likened.

† This expression induces the belief that the letter is written by the Peshwa in his sovereign's name, as they had at this time commenced their usurpation of his power. It was to the second Jagat Singh that an offer was made to fill the Satara throne by a branch of his family, then occupied by an imbecile. A younger brother of the Rana, the ancestor of the present heir presumptive, Sheodan Singh, was chosen, but intrigues prevented it, the Rana dreading a superior from his own family.

tribute, which remained in force during ten years,[1] when grasping at the whole they despised a part, and the treaty became a nullity.[2] The dissensions which arose soon after, in consequence of the Rajput engagements, afforded the opportunity sought for to mix in their internal concerns.

Right of Primogeniture.—It may be recollected that in the family engagements formed by Rana Amra there was an obligation to invest the issue of such marriage with the rights of primogeniture; and the death of Sawai Jai Singh[3] of Amber, two years after Nadir's invasion, brought that stipulation into effect. His eldest son, Isari Singh, was proclaimed Raja, but a strong party supported Madho Singh, the Rana's nephew, and the stipulated, against the natural order of succession. We are [424] left in doubt as to the real designs of Jai Singh in maintaining his guarantee, which was doubtless inconvenient; but that Madho Singh was not brought up to the expectation is evident, from his holding a fief of the Rana Sangram, who appropriated the domain of Rampura for his support, subject to the service of one thousand horse and two thousand foot, formally sanctioned by his father, who allowed the transfer of his services. On the other hand, the letter of permission entitles him *Kshema*, 'prosperous,' an epithet only applied to the heir-apparent of Jaipur. Five years, however, elapsed before any extraordinary exertions were made to annul the rights of Isari Singh, who led his vassals to the Sutlej in order to oppose the first invasion of the Duranis.[4] It would be tedious to give even an epitome of the intrigues for the development of this object, which properly belong to the annals of Amber, and whence resulted many of the troubles of Rajputana. The Rana took the field with his nephew, and was met by Isari Singh,[5] supported by the Mahrattas; but the Sesodias did not evince in the battle of Rajmahall that gallantry which must have its source in moral strength: they were defeated and fled. The Rana vented his indignation in a galling sarcasm;

[1] The amount was 160,000 rupees, divided into three shares of 53,333 0 4½ assigned to Holkar, Sindhia, and the Puar. The management was entrusted to Holkar; subsequently Sindhia acted as receiver-general. This was the only regular tributary engagement Mewar entered into.

[2] See letter No. 2, in note, p. 492.

[3] A.D. 1743.

[4] A.D. 1747.

[5] The great Jai Singh built a city which he called after himself, and henceforth Jaipur will supersede the ancient appellation, Amber.

he gave the sword of state to a common courtesan to carry in procession, observing "it was a woman's weapon in these degenerate times": a remark the degrading severity of which made a lasting impression in the decline of Mewar. Elated with this success, Isari Singh carried his resentments and his auxiliaries, under Sindhia, against the Haras of Kotah and Bundi, who supported the cause of his antagonist. Kotah stood a siege and was gallantly defended, and Sindhia (Apaji) lost an arm:[1] on this occasion both the States suffered a diminution of territory, and were subjected to tribute. The Rana, following the example of the Kachhwahas, called in as auxiliary Malhar Rao Holkar, and engaged to pay sixty-four lakhs of rupees (£800,000) on the deposal of Isari Singh. To avoid degradation this unfortunate prince resolved on suicide, and a dose of poison gave Madho Singh the *gaddi*, Holkar his bribe, and the Mahrattas a firm hold upon Rajasthan. Such was the cause of Rajput abasement; the moral force of the vassals was lost in a contest unjust in all its associations, and from this period we have only the degrading spectacle of civil strife and predatory spoliation till the existing treaty of A.D. 1817 [425].

Death of Rāna Jagat Singh II., A.D. **1751.**—In S. 1808 (A.D. 1752) Rana Jagat Singh died. Addicted to pleasure, his habits of levity and profusion totally unfitted him for the task of governing his country at such a juncture; he considered his elephant fights[2] of more importance than keeping down the Mahrattas. Like all his family, he patronized the arts, greatly enlarged the palace, and expended £250,000 in embellishing the islets of the Pichola. The villas scattered over the valley were all erected by him, and many of those festivals devoted to idleness and dissipation, and now firmly rooted at Udaipur, were instituted by Jagat Singh II.

[1] [Āpaji was one of Sindhia's best officers. Suffering from a painful disease, he committed suicide in 1797 by drowning himself in the Jumna (Compton, *European Military Adventurers*, 132).]

[2] See letters from Rana Jagat Singh to Biharidas, p 492.

CHAPTER 16

Rāna Partāp Singh II., A.D. 1751-54.—Partap II. succeeded in A.D. 1752. Of the history of this prince, who renewed the most illustrious name in the annals of Mewar, there is nothing to record beyond the fact, that the three years he occupied the throne were marked by so many Mahratta invasions [1] and war contributions. By a daughter of Raja Jai Singh of Amber he had a son, who succeeded him.

Rāna Rāj Singh II., A.D. 1754-61.—Rana Raj Singh II. was as little entitled to the name he bore as his predecessor. During the seven years he held the dignity at least seven shoals of the Southrons overran Mewar,[2] and so exhausted this country, that the Rana was compelled to ask pecuniary aid from the Brahman collector of the tribute, to enable him to marry the Rathor chieftain's daughter. On his death the order of succession retrograded, devolving on his uncle [426],

Rāna Ari Singh II., A.D. 1761-73.—Rana Arsi, in S. 1818, A.D. 1762. The levity of Jagat Singh, the inexperience of his successors Partap and Raj Singh, with the ungovernable temper of Rana Arsi, and the circumstances under which he succeeded to power, introduced a train of disorders which proved fatal to Mewar. Until this period not a foot of territory had been alienated. The wisdom of the Pancholi ministers, and the high respect paid by the organ of the Satara government, for a while preserved its integrity; but when the country was divided by factions, and the Mahrattas, ceasing to be a federate body, prowled in search of prey under leaders, each having an interest of his own, they formed political combinations to suit the ephemeral purposes of the former, but from which they alone reaped advantage. An attempt to depose Partap and set up his uncle Nathji introduced a series of rebellions, and constituted Malhar Rao Holkar, who had already become master of a considerable

[1] The leaders of these invasions were Satwaji, Jankoji, and Raghunath Rao.

[2] In S. 1812, Raja Bahadur; in 1813, Malhar Rao Holkar and Vitthal Rao; in 1814, Ranaji Burtia: in 1813 three war contributions were levied, namely, by Sudasheo Rao, Govind Rao, and Kanaji Jadon.

portion of the domain of Mewar, the umpire in their family disputes.

Malhār Rāo Holkar invades Mewār. Famine, A.D. 1764.—The ties of blood or of princely gratitude are feeble bonds if political expediency demands their dissolution ; and Madho Singh, when firmly established on the throne of Amber, repaid the immense sacrifices by which the Rana had effected it by assigning his fief of Rampura, which he had not a shadow of right to alienate, to Holkar : this was the first limb severed from Mewar.[1] Holkar had also become the assignee of the tribute imposed by Bajirao, but from which the Rana justly deemed himself exempt, when the terms of all further encroachment in Mewar were set at nought. On the plea of recovering these arrears, and the rent of some districts[2] on the Chambal, Malhar, after many threatening letters, invaded Mewar, and his threats of occupying the capital were only checked by draining their exhausted resources of six hundred thousand pounds.[3] In the same year[4] a famine afflicted them, when flour and tamarinds were equal in value, and were sold at the rate of a rupee for one pound and a half. Four years subsequent to this, civil war broke out and continued to influence all posterior proceedings, rendering [427] the inhabitants of this unhappy country a prey to every invader until 1817, when they tasted repose under British protection.

Civil War in Mewār. Revolt of Ratan Singh.—The real cause of this rebellion must ever remain a secret : for while some regard it as a patriotic effort on the part of the people to redeem themselves from foreign domination, others discover its motive in the selfishness of the hostile clans, who supported or opposed the succession of Rana Arsi. This prince is accused of having unfairly acquired the crown, by the removal of his nephew Raj Singh ; but though the traditional anecdotes of the period furnish

[1] This was in S. 1808 (A.D. 1752) ; portions, however, remained attached to the fisc of Mewar for several years, besides a considerable part of the feudal lands of the Chandarawat chief of Amad. Of the former, the Rana retained Hinglajgarh and the Tappas of Jarda Kinjera, and Budsu. These were surrendered by Raj Singh, who rented Budsu under its new appellation of Malhargarh.

[2] Budsu, etc.

[3] Holkar advanced as far as Untala, where Arjun Singh of Kurabar and the Rana's foster-brothers met him, and negotiated the payment of fifty-one lakhs of rupees.

[4] S. 1820, A.D. 1764.

strong grounds of suspicion, there is nothing which affords a direct confirmation of the crime. It is, however, a public misfortune when the line of succession retrogrades in Mewar: Arsi had no right to expect the inheritance he obtained, having long held a seat below the sixteen chief nobles; and as one of the 'infants' (*babas*) he was incorporated with the second class of nobles with an appanage of only £3000 per annum. His defects of character had been too closely contemplated by his compeers, and had kindled too many enmities, to justify expectation that the adventitious dignity he had attained would succeed in obliterating the memory of them; and past familiarity alone destroyed the respect which was exacted by sudden greatness. His insolent demeanour estranged the first of the home nobility, the Sadri chieftain,[1] whose ancestor at Haldighat acquired a claim to the perpetual gratitude of the Sesodias, while to an unfeeling pun on a personal defect of Jaswant Singh of Deogarh is attributed the hatred and revenge of this powerful branch of the Chondawats. These chiefs formed a party which eventually entrained many of lesser note to depose their sovereign, and immediately set up a youth called Ratna Singh, declared to be the posthumous son of the last Rana by the daughter of the chief of Gogunda, though to this hour disputes run high as to whether he was really the son of Raj Singh, or merely the puppet [428] of a faction. Be the fact as it may, he was made a rallying point for the disaffected, who soon comprehended the greater portion of the nobles, while out of the 'sixteen' greater chiefs five[2] only withstood the

[1] An autograph letter of this chief's to the minister of the day I obtained, with other public documents, from the descendant of the Pancholi:

"To Jaswant Rao Pancholi, Raj Rana Raghudeo writes. After compliments. I received your letter—from old times you have been my friend, and have ever maintained faith towards me, for I am of the loyal to the Rana's house. I conceal nothing from you, therefore I write that my heart is averse to longer service, and it is my purpose in Asarh to go to Gaya.* When I mentioned this to the Rana, he sarcastically told me I might go to Dwarka.† If I stay, the Rana will restore the villages in my fief, as during the time of Jethji. My ancestors have performed good service, and I have served since I was fourteen. If the Darbar intends me any favour, this is the time."

[2] Salumbar (Chondawat), Bijolia, Amet, Ghanerao, and Badnor.

---

* Gaya is esteemed the proper pilgrimage for the Rajputs.

† Dwarka, the resort for religious and unwarlike tribes.

defection: of these, Salumbar, the hereditary premier, at first espoused, but soon abandoned, the cause of the Pretender; not from the principle of loyalty which his descendants take credit for, but from finding the superiority of intellect of the heads of the rebellion [1] (which now counted the rival Saktawats) too powerful for the supremacy he desired. Basant Pal, of the Depra tribe, was invested with the office of Pardhan to the Pretender. The ancestor of this man accompanied Samarsi in the twelfth century from Delhi, where he held a high office in the household of Prithiraj, the last emperor of the Hindus, and it is a distinguished proof of the hereditary quality of official dignity to find his descendant, after the lapse of centuries, still holding office with the nominal title of Pardhan. The Futuri [2] (by which name the court still designates the Pretender) took post with his faction in Kumbhalmer; where he was formally installed, and whence he promulgated his decrees as Rana of Mewar. With that heedlessness of consequences and the political debasement which are invariable concomitants of civil dissension, they had the meanness to invite Sindhia to their aid, with a promise of a reward of more than one million sterling [3] on the dethronement of Arsi.

Zālim Singh of Kotah.—This contest first brought into notice one of the most celebrated Rajput chiefs of India, Zalim Singh of Kotah, who was destined to fill a distinguished part in the annals of Rajasthan, but more especially in Mewar, where his political sagacity first developed itself. Though this is not the proper place to delineate his history, which will occupy a subsequent portion of the work, it is impossible to trace the events with which he was so closely connected without adverting slightly to the part he acted in these scenes. The attack on Kotah, of which his father was military governor (during the struggle to place Madho Singh on the throne of Amber), by Isari Singh, in conjunction with Sindhia, was the first avenue to his distinguished career, leading to an acquaintance with the Mahratta chiefs, which linked him with their policy for more than half a century [429]. Zalim having lost his prince's favour, whose path in love

[1] Bhindir (Saktawat), Deogarh, Sadri, Gogunda, Delwara, Bedla, Kotharia, and Kanor.

[2] Agitator, or disturber.

[3] One crore and twenty-five lakhs.

he had dared to cross, repaired, on his banishment from Kotah, to the Rana, who, observing his talents, enrolled him amongst his chiefs, and conferred on him, with the title of Raj Rana, the lands of Chitarkhera for his support. By his advice the Mahratta leaders, Raghu Paigawala and Daula Miyan, with their bands, were called in by the Rana, who, setting aside the ancient Pancholi ministry, gave the seals of office to Agarji Mehta. At this period (S. 1824, A.D. 1768), Mahadaji Sindhia was at Ujjain, whither the conflicting parties hastened, each desirous of obtaining the chieftain's support. But the Pretender's proposals had been already entertained, and he was then encamped with Sindhia on the banks of the Sipra.[1]

Battle at the Sipra, and Siege of Udaipur, A.D. 1769.—The Rana's force, conducted by the chief of Salumbar, the Rajas of Shahpura and Banera, with Zalim Singh and the Mahratta auxiliaries, did not hesitate to attack the combined camp, and for a moment they were victorious, driving Mahadaji and the Pretender from the field, with great loss, to the gates of Ujjain. Here, however, they rallied, and being joined by a fresh body of troops, the battle was renewed with great disadvantage to the Rajputs, who, deeming the day theirs, had broken and dispersed to plunder. The chiefs of Salumbar, Shahpura, and Banera were slain, and the auxiliary Daula Miyan, Raja Man (ex-prince of Narwar), and Raj Kalyan, the heir of Sadri, severely wounded. Zalim Singh had his horse killed under him, and being left wounded on the field, was made prisoner, but hospitably treated by Trimbak Rao, father to the celebrated Ambaji. The discomfited troops retreated to Udaipur while the Pretender's party remained with Sindhia, inciting him to invest that capital and place Ratna on the throne. Some time, however, elapsed before he could carry this design into execution; when at the head of a large force the Mahratta chief gained the passes and besieged the city. The Rana's cause now appeared hopeless. Bhim Singh of Salumbar, uncle and successor to the chief slain at Ujjain, with the Rathor chief of Badnor (descendant of Jaimall), were the only nobles of high rank who defended their prince and capital in this emergency; but the energies of an individual saved both.

Amar Chand, Minister of Mewār.—Amra Chand Barwa, of the

[1] [The Sipra River in Mālwa, passes Ujjain, and finally joins the Chambal (*IGI*, xxiii. 14 f.).]

mercantile class, had held office in the preceding reigns, when his influence retarded the progress of evils which no human means could avert. He was now displaced, and little solicitous of recovering his [430] transient power, amidst hourly increasing difficulties, with a stubborn and unpopular prince, a divided aristocracy, and an impoverished country. He was aware also of his own imperious temper, which was as ungovernable as his sovereign's, and which experienced no check from the minor Partap, who regarded him as his father. During the ten years he had been out of office, mercenaries of Sind had been entertained and established on the forfeited lands of the clans, perpetuating discontent and stifling every latent spark of patriotism. Even those who did not join the Pretender remained sullenly at their castles, and thus all confidence was annihilated. A casual incident brought Amra forward at this critical juncture. Udaipur had neither ditch nor walls equal to its defence. Arsi was engaged in fortifying Eklinggarh, a lofty hill south of the city,[1] which it commanded, and attempting to place thereon an enormous piece of ordnance, but it baffled their mechanical skill to get it over the scraggy ascent. Amra happened to be present when the Rana arrived to inspect the proceedings. Excuses were made to avert his displeasure, when turning to the ex-minister, he inquired what time and expense ought to attend the completion of such an undertaking. The reply was, "A few rations of grain and some days": and he offered to accomplish the task, on condition that his orders should be supreme in the valley during its performance. He collected the whole working population, cut a road, and in a few days gave the Rana a salute from Eklinggarh. The foster-brother of the Rana had succeeded the Jhala chieftain, Raghu Deo, in the ministerial functions. The city was now closely invested on every side but the west, where communications were still kept open by the lake, across which the faithful mountaineers of the Aravalli, who in similar dangers never failed, supplied them with provisions. All defence rested on the fidelity of the mercenary Sindis, and they were at this very moment insolent in their clamours for arrears of pay. Nor were the indecisive measures daily passing before their eyes calculated to augment their respect, or stimulate their courage. Not satisfied with demands, they had the audacity to seize the

[1] [Eklinggarh, two miles south of Udaipur city; 2469 feet above sea-level.]

Rana by the skirt of his robe as he entered the palace, which was torn in the effort to detain him. The haughtiness of his temper gave way to this humiliating proof of the hopelessness of his condition; and while the Dhabhai (foster-brother) counselled escape by water to the mountains, whence he might gain Mandalgarh, the Salumbar chief confessed his inability to offer any advice [431] save that of recourse to Amra Chand. He was summoned, and the uncontrolled charge of their desperate affairs offered to his guidance. He replied that it was a task of which no man could be covetous, more especially himself, whose administration had formerly been marked by the banishment of corruption and disorder, for that he must now call in the aid of these vices, and assimilate the means to the times. "You know also," he added, "my defect of temper, which admits of no control. Wherever I am, I must be absolute—no secret advisers, no counteraction of measures. With finances ruined, troops mutinous, provisions expended, if you desire me to act, swear that no order, whatever its purport, shall be countermanded, and I may try what can be done: but recollect, Amra 'the just' will be the unjust, and reverse his former character." The Rana pledged himself by the patron deity to comply with all his demands, adding this forcible expression: "Should you even send to the queen's apartment and demand her necklace or *nathna*,[1] it shall be granted." The advice of the Dhabhai encountered the full flood of Amra's wrath. "The counsel is such as might be expected from your condition. What will preserve your prince at Mandalgarh if he flies from Udaipur, and what hidden resources have you there for your support? The project would suit you, who might resume your original occupation of tending buffaloes and selling milk, more adapted to your birth and understanding than state affairs; but these pursuits your prince has yet to learn." The Rana and his chiefs bent their heads at the bold bearing of Amra. Descending to the terrace, where the Sindi leaders and their bands were assembled, he commanded them to follow him, exclaiming, "Look to me for your arrears, and as for your services, it will be my fault if you fail." The mutineers, who had just insulted their sovereign, rose without reply, and in a body left the palace with Amra, who calculated their arrears

[1] The nose-jewel, which even to mention is considered a breach of delicacy.

and promised payment the next day. Meanwhile he commanded the bhandars (repositories) to be broken open, as the keeper of each fled when the keys of their trust were demanded. All the gold and silver, whether in bullion or in vessels, were converted into money—jewels were pledged—the troops paid and satisfied, ammunition and provisions laid in—a fresh stimulus supplied, the enemy held at defiance, and the siege prolonged during six months [432].

The Pretender's party had extended their influence over a great part of the crown domain, even to the valley of Udaipur; but unable to fulfil the stipulation to Sindhia, the baffled Mahratta, to whom time was treasure, negotiated with Amra to raise the siege, and abandon the Pretender on the payment of seventy lakhs. But scarcely was the treaty signed, when the reported disposition of the auxiliaries, and the plunder expected on a successful assault, excited his avarice and made him break his faith, and twenty lakhs additional were imposed. Amra tore up the treaty, and sent back the fragments to the faithless Mahratta with defiance. His spirit increased with his difficulties, and he infused his gallantry into the hearts of the most despairing. Assembling the Sindis and the home-clans who were yet true to their prince, he explained to them the transaction, and addressed them in that language which speaks to the souls of all mankind, and to give due weight to his exhortation, he distributed amongst the most deserving, many articles of cumbrous ornament lying useless in the treasury. The stores of grain in the city and neighbourhood, whether public or private, were collected and sent to the market, and it was proclaimed by beat of drum that every fighting man should have six months' provision on application. Hitherto grain had been selling at little more than a pound for the rupee, and these unexpected resources were matter of universal surprise, more especially to the besiegers.[1] The Sindis, having no longer cause for discontent, caught the spirit of the brave Amra, and went in a body to the palace to swear in public never to abandon the Rana, whom their leader, Adil Beg,[2] thus

[1] To Amra's credit it is related, that his own brother-in-law was the first and principal sufferer, and that to his remonstrance and hope that family ties would save his grain pits, he was told, that it was a source of great satisfaction that he was enabled through him to evince his disinterestedness.

[2] See grant to this chief's son, p. 233.

addressed : " We have long eaten your salt and received numerous favours from your house, and we now come to swear never to abandon you. Udaipur is our home, and we will fall with it. We demand no further pay, and when our grain is exhausted, we will feed on the beasts, and when these fail we will thin the ranks of the Southrons and die sword in hand." Such were the sentiments that Amra had inspired, the expression of which extorted tears from the Rana—a sight so unusual with this stern prince, as to raise frantic shouts from the Sindis and his Rajputs. The enthusiasm spread and was announced to Sindhia with all its circumstances by a general discharge of cannon on his advanced [433] posts. Apprehensive of some desperate display of Rajput valour, the wary Mahratta made overtures for a renewal of the negotiation. It was now Amra's turn to triumph, and he replied that he must deduct from the original terms the expense they had incurred in sustaining another six months' siege. Thus outwitted, Sindhia was compelled to accept sixty lakhs, and three-and-a-half for official expenses.[1]

Cessions made to Sindhia.—Thirty-three lakhs in jewels and specie, gold and silver plate, and assignments on the chiefs, were immediately made over to Sindhia, and lands mortgaged for the liquidation of the remainder. For this object the districts of Jawad, Jiran, Nimach, and Morwan were set aside to be superintended by joint officers of both governments, with an annual investigation of accounts. From S. 1825 to S. 1831 [A.D. 1768–74) no infringement took place of this arrangement ; but in the latter year Sindhia dismissed the Rana's officers from the management, and refused all further settlement ; and with the exception of a temporary occupation on Sindhia's reverse of fortune in S. 1851 [A.D. 1794], these rich districts have remained severed from Mewar. In S. 1831 [A.D. 1774] the great officers of the Mahratta federation began to shake off the trammels of the Peshwa's authority ; and Sindhia retained for the State of which he was the founder, all these lands except Morwan, which was made over to Holkar, who the year after the transaction demanded of the Rana the surrender of the district of Nimbahera, threatening, in the event of non-compliance, to repeat the part his predatory

[1] *Mutasadi kharch* [*mutasadi*, 'a clerk, accountant' ; *kharch*, 'expenses'] or douceur to the officers of government, was an authorized article of every Mahratta *mu'āmala*, or war contribution.

coadjutor Sindhia had just performed. The cession was unavoidable.

Thus terminated, in S. 1826 [A.D. 1769], the siege of Udaipur, with the dislocation of these fine districts from Mewar. But let it be remembered that they were only mortgaged :[1] and although the continued degradation of the country from the same causes has prevented their redemption, the claim to them has never been abandoned. Their recovery was stipulated by the ambassadors of the Rana in the treaty of A.D. 1817 with the British Government; but our total ignorance of the past transactions of these countries, added to our amicable relations with Sindhia [434], prevented any pledge of the reunion of these districts ; and it must ever be deeply lamented that, when the treacherous and hostile conduct of Sindhia gave a noble opportunity for their restoration, it was lost, from policy difficult to understand, and which must be subject to the animadversions of future historians of that important period in the history of India. It yet remains for the wisdom of the British Government to decide whether half a century's abeyance, and the inability to redeem them by the sword, render the claim a dead letter. At all events, the facts here recorded from a multiplicity of public documents, and corroborated by living actors[2] in the scene, may be useful at some future day, when expedience may admit of their being reannexed to Mewar.

Ratan Singh defeated.—Amra's defence of the capital, and the retreat of the Mahrattas, was a deathblow to the hopes of the Pretender, who had obtained not only many of the strongholds, but a footing in the valley of the capital. Rajnagar, Raepur, and Untala were rapidly recovered ; many of the nobles returned to the Rana and to their allegiance ; and Ratna was left in Kumbhalmer with the Depra minister, and but three of the sixteen principal nobles, namely Deogarh, Bhindir, and Amet. These contentions lasted till S. 1831 [A.D. 1774], when the chiefs above named also abandoned him, but not until their rebellion had cost the feather in the crown of Mewar. The rich province of Godwar, the most fruitful of all her possessions, and containing

[1] Little Maloni, now Gangapur, with its lands, was the only place decidedly alienated, being a voluntary gift to Sindhia, to endow the establishment of his wife, Ganga Bai, who died there.

[2] Zalim Singh of Kotah, and Lalaji Belal, both now dead.

the most loyal of her vassalage, the Ranawats, Rathors, and Solankis, was nearly all held on tenure of feudal service, and furnished three thousand horse besides foot, a greater number than the aggregate of the Chondawats. This district, which was won with the title of Rana from the Parihara prince of Mandor, before Jodhpur was built, and whose northern boundary was confirmed by the blood of the Chondawat chief in the reign of Jodha, was confided by the Rana to the care of Raja Bijai Singh of Jodhpur, to prevent its resources being available to the Pretender, whose residence, Kumbhalmer, commanded the approach to it: and the original treaty yet exists in which the prince of Marwar binds himself to provide and support a body of three thousand men for the Rana's service, from its revenues.

Assassination of Rāna Ari Singh, A.D. 1773.—This province might have been recovered; but the evil genius of Arsi Rana at this time led him to Bundi to [435] hunt at the spring festival (the Aheria), with the Hara prince, in spite of the prophetic warning of the suttee, who from the funeral pile denounced a practice which had already thrice proved fatal to the princes of Mewar.[1] Rana Arsi fell by the hand of the Bundi prince, and Godwar, withheld from his minor successor, has since remained severed. The Bundi heir, who perpetrated this atrocious assassination, was said to be prompted by the Mewar nobles, who detested their sovereign, and with whom, since the late events, it was impossible they could ever unite in confidence. Implacable in his disposition, he brooded over injuries, calmly awaiting the moment to avenge them. A single instance will suffice to evince this, as well as the infatuation of Rajput devotion. The Salumbar chief, whose predecessor had fallen in support of the Rana's cause at the battle of Ujjain, having incurred his suspicions, the Rana commanded him to eat the *pan* (betel leaf) presented on taking leave. Startled at so unusual an order, he remonstrated, but in vain; and with the conviction that it contained his death-warrant he obeyed, observing to the tyrant, "My compliance will cost you and your family dear": words fulfilled with fearful accuracy, for to this and similar acts is ascribed the murder of Arsi, and the completion

[1] [In 1382 Rāna Khet Singh was murdered by Lāl Singh of Banbaoda, brother of Bar Singh, Rāo of Būndi. Rāna Ratan Singh II. and Rāo Sūrajmall killed each other while shooting at Būndi in 1531. The feud between the two houses is not yet forgotten (Erskine ii. A. 25).]

of the ruin of the country. A colour of pretext was afforded to the Bundi chief in a boundary dispute regarding a patch of land yielding only a few good mangoes; but, even admitting this as a palliative, it could not justify the inhospitable act, which in the mode of execution added cowardice to barbarity: for while both were pursuing the boar, the Bundi heir drove his lance through the heart of the Rana. The assassin fell a victim to remorse, the deed being not only disclaimed, but severely reprobated by his father, and all the Hara tribe. A cenotaph still stands on the site of the murder, where the body of Arsi was consumed, and the feud between the houses remains unappeased.

Rāna Hamīr Singh II., A.D. 1773-78.—Rana Arsi left two sons, Hamir and Bhim Singh. The former, a name of celebrity in their annals, succeeded in S. 1828 (A.D. 1772) to the little enviable title of Rana. With an ambitious mother, determined to control affairs during his minority, a state pronounced by the bard peculiarly dangerous to a Rajput dynasty,—and the vengeful competition of the Salumbar chief (successor to the murdered noble), who was equally resolved to take the lead, combined with an unextinguishable enmity to the Saktawats, who supported the policy of the queen-mother [436], the demoralization of Mewar was complete: her fields were deluged with blood, and her soil was the prey of every paltry marauder.

Outbreak of the Sindis.—The mercenary Sindis, who, won by the enthusiasm of Amra, had for a moment assumed the garb of fidelity, threw it off at their prince's death, taking possession of the capital, which it will be remembered had been committed to the charge of the Salumbar chief, whom they confined and were about to subject to the torture of the hot iron[1] to extort their arrears of pay, when he was rescued from the indignity by the unlooked-for return of Amra from Bundi. This faithful minister determined to establish the rights of the infant prince against all other claimants for power. But he knew mankind, and had attained, what is still more difficult, the knowledge of himself. Aware that his resolution to maintain his post at all hazards, and against every competitor, would incur the imputation of self-interest, he, like our own Wolsey, though from far different motives, made an inventory of his wealth, in gold, jewels, and plate, even to his wardrobe, and sent the whole in trays to the

[1] A heated platter used for baking bread, on which they place the culprit.

queen-mother. Suspicion was shamed and resentment disarmed by this proceeding; and to repeated entreaties that he would receive it back he was inflexible, with the exception of articles of apparel that had already been in use. This imperious woman was a daughter of Gogunda. She possessed considerable talents, but was ruled by an artful *intrigante*, who, in her turn, was governed by a young *homme d'affaires*, then holding an inferior office, but who subsequently acted a conspicuous part; slew and was slain, like almost all who entered into the politics of this tempestuous period. The queen-mother, now supported by the Chondawats, opposed the minister, who maintained himself by aid of the Sindis, kept the Mahrattas from the capital, and protected the crown land; but the ungrateful return made to his long-tried fidelity rendered his temper ungovernable. Rampiyari [1] (such the name of the *intrigante*) repaired on one occasion to the office of the minister, and in the name of the regent queen reviled him for some supposed omission. Amra, losing all temper at this intrusion, applied to the fair abigail the coarsest epithets used to her sex, bidding her begone as a Kothi ki Rand (a phrase we shall not translate), which was reported with exaggeration to the queen, who threw herself into a litter and set off to the Salumbar chief. Amra, anticipating [437] an explosion, met the cavalcade in the street, and enjoined her instant return to the palace. Who dared disobey? Arrived at the door of the Rawala, he made his obeisance, and told her it was a disgrace to the memory of her lord that she should quit the palace under any pretext; that even the potter's wife did not go abroad for six months after her husband's death, while she, setting decorum at defiance, had scarcely permitted the period of mourning to elapse. He concluded by saying he had a duty to perform, and that he would perform it in spite of all obstacles, in which, as it involved her own and her children's welfare, she ought to cooperate, instead of thwarting him. But Baiji Raj (the royal mother) was young, artful, and ambitious, and persevered in her hostility till the demise of this uncompromising minister shortly after, surmised to be caused by poison. His death yielded a flattering comment on his life: he left not funds sufficient to cover the funeral expenses, and is, and will probably continue, the sole instance on record in Indian history of a minister

[1] 'The beloved of Rama.'

having his obsequies defrayed by subscription among his fellow-citizens.

The man who thus lived and thus died would have done honour to any, even the most civilized, country, where the highest incentives to public virtue exist. What, therefore, does not his memory merit, when amongst a people who, through long oppression, were likely to hold such feelings in little estimation, he pursued its dictates from principle alone, his sole reward that which the world could not bestow, the applause of the monitor within? But they greatly err who, in the application of their own overweening standard of merit, imagine there is no public opinion in these countries; for recollections of actions like this (of which but a small portion is related) they yet love to descant upon, and an act of vigour and integrity is still designated Amra-chanda;[1] evincing that if virtue has few imitators in this country, she is not without ardent admirers.

Revolt of the Chief of Begūn.—In S. 1831 (A.D. 1775) the rebellion of the Begun chief, head of a grand division of the Chondawats, the Meghawat, obliged the queen-mother to call upon Sindhia for his reduction, who recovered the crown lands he had usurped, and imposed on this refractory noble a fine of twelve lakhs of rupees, or £100,000 [438] sterling.[2] But instead of confining himself to punishing the guilty, and restoring the lands to the young Rana, he inducted his own son-in-law Berji Tap into the districts of Ratangarh Kheri and Singoli; and at the same time made over those of Irnia, Jath, Bichor, and Nadwai to Holkar, the aggregate revenue of which amounted to six lakhs annually. Besides these alienations of territory, the Mahrattas levied no less than four grand war contributions in S. 1830–31,[3] while in S. 1836[4] their rapacity exacted three more. Inability

[1] Amra Chand, it will be recollected, was the name of the minister.

[2] The treaty by which Sindhia holds these districts yet exists, which stipulates their surrender on the liquidation of the contribution. The Rana still holds this as a responsible engagement, and pleaded his rights in the treaty with the British Government in A.D. 1817–18. But half a century's possession is a strong bond, which we dare not break; though the claim now registered may hereafter prove of service to the family.

[3] 1830, Mahadaji Sindhia's contribution (*mu'āmala*) on account of Begun; 1831, Berji Tap's *mu'āmala* through Govind and Ganpat Rao; 1831, Ambaji Inglia, Bapu Holkar, and Daduji Pandit's joint *mu'āmala*.

[4] 1. Apaji and Makaji Getia, on Holkar's account; 2. Tukuji Holkar's, through Somji; 3. Ali Bahadur's, through Somji.

to liquidate these exorbitant demands was invariably a signal for further sequestration of land. Amidst such scenes of civil strife and external spoliation, one Mahratta following another in the same track of rapine, Hamir died before he had attained even Rajput majority,[1] in S. 1834 (A.D. 1778).

Recapitulation.—We may here briefly recapitulate the diminution of territory and wealth in Mewar from the period of the first Mahratta visitation in A.D. 1736, to the death of Hamir. It were a waste of time to enumerate the rapacious individuals who shared in the spoils of this devoted country. We may be content to say their name was 'legion.' These forty years were surcharged with evil. The Mogul princes observed at least the forms of government and justice, which occasionally tempered their aggressions; the Mahrattas were associations of vampires, who drained the very life-blood wherever the scent of spoil attracted them. In three payments we have seen the enormous sum of one crore and eighty-one lakhs,[2] upwards of two millions English money, exacted from Mewar, exclusive of individual contributions levied on chiefs, ministers, and the Pretender's party: and a schedule drawn up by the reigning prince of contributions levied up to his own time, amounts to £5,000,000 sterling. Yet the land would eventually have reimbursed [489] these sums, but the penalty inflicted for deficiencies of payment renders the evil irremediable; for the alienated territory which then produced an annual revenue of twenty-eight lakhs,[3] or £323,000 sterling, exceeds in amount the sum-total now left, whether fiscal or feudal, in the present impoverished state of the country.

[1] The age of eighteen.

[2] Namely,

		Lakhs
S. 1808,	by Rana Jagat Singh to Holkar	66
1820,	Partap and Arsi Rana to Holkar	51
1826,	Arsi Rana to Mahadaji Sindhia	64
	Total	181

[3]

		Lakhs
S. 1808,	Rampura, Bhanpura	9
1826,	Jawad, Jiran, Nimach, Nimbahera	$4\frac{1}{2}$
1831,	Ratangarh Kheri, Singoli, Irnia, Jath, Nadwai, etc. etc.	6
1831,	Godwar	9
	Total	$28\frac{1}{2}$

CHAPTER 17

Rāna Bhīm Singh, A.D. 1778-1828.—Rana Bhim Singh (the reigning prince), who succeeded his brother in S. 1834 (A.D. 1778), was the fourth minor in the space of forty years who inherited Mewar; and the half century during which he has occupied the throne has been as fruitful in disaster as any period of her history already recorded. He was but eight years of age on his accession, and remained under his mother's tutelage long after his minority had expired. This subjection fixed his character; naturally defective in energy, and impaired by long misfortune, he continued to be swayed by faction and intrigue. The cause of the Pretender, though weakened, was yet kept alive; but his insignificance eventually left him so unsupported, that his death is not even recorded [440].

Feud of Chondāwats and Saktāwats.—In S. 1840 (A.D. 1784) the Chondawats reaped the harvest of their allegiance and made the power thus acquired subservient to the indulgence of ancient animosities against the rival clan of Saktawat. Salumbar with his relatives Arjun Singh [1] of Kurabar and Partap Singh [2] of Amet, now ruled the councils, having the Sindi mercenaries under their leaders Chandan and Sadik at their command. Mustering therefore all the strength of their kin and clans, they resolved on the prosecution of the feud, and invested Bhindar, the castle of Mohkam the chief of the Saktawats, against which they placed their batteries.

Sangram Singh, a junior branch of the Saktawats, destined to play a conspicuous part in the future events of Mewar, was then rising into notice, and had just completed a feud with his rival the Purawat, whose abode, Lawa,[3] he had carried by escalade; and now, determined to make a diversion in favour of his chief, he invaded the estate of Kurabar, engaged against Bhindar, and

[1] Brother of Ajit, the negotiator of the treaty with the British.

[2] Chief of the Jagawat clan, also a branch of the Chondawats; he was killed in a battle with the Mahrattas.

[3] It is yet held by the successor of Sangram, whose faithful services merited the grant he obtained from his prince, and it was in consequence left unmolested in the arrangement of 1817, from the knowledge of his merits.

was driving off the cattle, when Salim Singh the heir of Kurabar intercepted his retreat, and an action ensued in which Salim[1] was slain by the lance of Sangram. The afflicted father, on hearing the fate of his son, 'threw the turban off his head,' swearing never to replace it till he had tasted revenge. Feigning a misunderstanding with his own party he withdrew from the siege, taking the road to his estate, but suddenly abandoned it for Sheogarh, the residence of Lalji the father of Sangram. The castle of Sheogarh, placed amidst the mountains and deep forests of Chappan, was from its difficulty of access deemed secure against surprise; and here Sangram had placed the females and children of his family. To this point Arjun directed his revenge, and found Sheogarh destitute of defenders save the aged chief; but though seventy summers had whitened his head, he bravely met the storm, and fell in opposing the foe; when the children of Sangram were dragged [441] out and inhumanly butchered, and the widow[2] of Lalji ascended the pyre. This barbarity aggravated the hostility which separated the clans, and together with the minority of their prince and the yearly aggressions of the Mahrattas, accelerated the ruin of the country. But Bhim Singh, the Chondawat leader, was governed by insufferable vanity, and not only failed in respect to his prince, but offended the queen regent. He parcelled out the crown domain from Chitor to Udaipur amongst the Sindi bands, and whilst his sovereign was obliged to borrow money to defray his marriage at Idar, this ungrateful noble had the audacity to disburse upwards of £100,000 on the marriage of his own daughter. Such conduct determined the royal mother to supplant the Chondawats, and calling in the Saktawats to her aid, she invested with power the chiefs of Bhindar and Lawa. Aware, however, that their isolated authority was insufficient to withstand their rivals, they looked abroad for support, and made an overture to Zalim Singh of Kotah, whose political and personal resentments to the Chonda-

[1] The father of Rawat Jawan Singh, whom I found at Udaipur as military minister, acting for his grand-uncle Ajit the organ of the Chondawats, whose head, Padam Singh, was just emerging from his minority. It was absolutely necessary to get to the very root of all these feuds, when as envoy and mediator I had to settle the disputes of half a century, and make each useful to detect their joint usurpations of the crown domain.

[2] She was the grandmother of Man Singh, a fine specimen of a Saktawat cavalier.

MAHĀRĀJA BHIM SINGH, PRINCE OF UDAIPUR.

To face page 512.

wats, as well as his connexion by marriage with their opponents, made him readily listen to it. With his friend the Mahratta, Lalaji Belal, he joined the Saktawats with a body of 10,000 men. It was determined to sacrifice the Salumbar chief, who took post in the ancient capital of Chitor, where the garrison was composed chiefly of Sindis, thus effacing his claim to his prince's gratitude, whom he defied, while the pretender still had a party in the other principal fortress, Kumbhalmer.

Battle of Lālsot, May 1787.—Such was the state of things, when the ascendancy of Mahadaji Sindhia received a signal check from the combined forces of Marwar and Jaipur ; and the battle of Lalsot, in which the Mahratta chief was completely defeated, was the signal for the Rajputs to resume their alienated territory.[1] Nor was the Rana backward on the occasion, when there appeared a momentary gleam of the active virtue of past days. Maldas Mehta was civil minister, with Mauji Ram as his deputy, both men of talent and energy. They first effected the reduction of Nimbahera and the smaller garrisons of Mahrattas in its vicinity, who from a sense of common danger assembled their detachments in Jawad, which was also invested. Sivaji Nana, the governor, capitulated, and was allowed to march out with his [442] effects. At the same time, the 'sons of the black cloud'[2] assembling, drove the Mahrattas from Begun, Singoli, etc., and the districts on the plateau ; while the Chondawats redeemed their ancient fief of Rampura, and thus for a while the whole territory was recovered. Elated by success, the united chiefs advanced to Chardu on the banks of the Rarkia, a streamlet dividing Mewar from Malwa, preparatory to further operations. Had these been confined to the maintenance of the places they had taken, and which had been withheld in violation of treaties, complete success might have crowned their efforts ; but in including Nimbahera in their capture they drew upon them the energetic Ahalya Bai, the regent-queen of the Holkar State, who unluckily for them was at hand and who coalesced with Sindhia's partisans to check

[1] [Lālsot, about 40 miles south of Jaipur city. For an account of the battle see Compton, *European Military Adventurers*, 346 f.]

[2] Megh Singh was the chief of Begun, and founder of that subdivision of the Chondawats called after him Meghawat, and his complexion being very dark (*kala*), he was called 'Kala Megh,' the 'black cloud.' His descendants were very numerous and very refractory.

this reaction of the Rajputs. Tulaji Sindhia and Sri Bhai, with five thousand horse, were ordered to support the discomfited Siva Nana, who had taken refuge in Mandasor, where he rallied all the garrisons whom the Rajputs had unwisely permitted to capitulate.

Defeat of the Rājputs. Murder of Somji.—On Tuesday, the 4th of Magh S. 1844,[1] the Rana's troops were surprised and defeated with great slaughter, the minister slain, the chiefs of Kanor and Sadri with many others severely wounded, and the latter made prisoner.[2] The newly made conquests were all rapidly lost, with the exception of Jawad, which was gallantly maintained for a month by Dip Chand, who, with his guns and rockets, effected a passage through the Mahrattas, and retired with his garrison to Mandalgarh. Thus terminated an enterprise which might have yielded far different results but for a misplaced security. All the chiefs and clans were united in this patriotic struggle except the Chondawats, against whom the queen-mother and the new minister, Somji, had much difficulty to contend for the establishment of the minor's authority. At length overtures were made to Salumbar, when the fair Rampiyari was employed to conciliate the obdurate chief, who condescended to make his appearance at Udaipur and to pay his respects to the prince. He pretended to enter into the views of the minister and to coalesce in his plans; but this was only a web to ensnare his victim, whose talent had diminished his authority, and was a bar to the prosecution of [443] his ambitious views. Somji was seated in his bureau when Arjun Singh of Kurabar and Sardar Singh[3] of Badesar entered, and the latter, as he demanded how he dared to resume his fief, plunged his dagger into the minister's breast. The Rana was passing the day at one of the villas in the valley called the Sahelia Bari, 'the garden of nymphs,' attended by Jeth Singh of Badnor, when the brothers[4] of the

[1] A.D. 1788.

[2] He did not recover his liberty for two years, nor till he had surrendered four of the best towns in his fief.

[3] Father of the present Hamir Singh, the only chief with whom I was compelled to use severity; but he was incorrigible. He was celebrated for his raids in the troubles, and from his red whiskers bore with us the name of the 'Red Riever' of Badesar—more of him by and by.

[4] Sheodas and Satidas, with their cousin Jaichand. They revenged their brother's death by that of his murderer, and were both in turn slain.

minister suddenly rushed into the presence to claim protection against the murderers. They were followed by Arjun of Kurabar, who had the audacity to present himself before his sovereign with his hands yet stained with the blood of Somji. The Rana, unable to punish the insolent chief, branding him as a traitor, bade him begone; when the whole of the actors in this nefarious scene, with their leader Salumbar, returned to Chitor. Sheodas and Satidas, brothers to the murdered minister, were appointed to succeed him, and with the Saktawats fought several actions against the rebels, and gained one decisive battle at Akola, in which Arjun of Kurabar commanded. This was soon balanced by the defeat of the Saktawats at Kheroda. Every triumph was attended with ruin to the country. The agriculturist, never certain of the fruits of his labour, abandoned his fields, and at length his country; mechanical industry found no recompense, and commerce was at the mercy of unlicensed spoliation. In a very few years Mewar lost half her population, her lands lay waste, her mines were unworked, and her looms, which formerly supplied all around, forsaken. The prince partook of the general penury; instead of protecting, he required protection; the bonds which united him with his subjects were snapped, and each individual or petty community provided for itself that defence which he could not give. Hence arose a train of evils: every cultivator, whether fiscal or feudal, sought out a patron, and [444] entered into engagements as the price of protection. Hence every Rajput who had a horse and lance, had his clients; and not a camel-load of merchandise could pass the abode of one of these cavaliers without paying fees. The effects of such disorder

---

Such were these times! The author more than once, when resuming the Chondawat lands, and amongst them Badesar, the fief of the son of Sardar, was told to recollect the fate of Somji; the advice, however, excited only a smile; he was deemed more of a Saktawat than a Chondawat, and there was some truth in it, for he found the good actions of the former far outweigh the other, who made a boast and monopoly of their patriotism. It was a curious period in his life; the stimulus to action was too high, too constant, to think of self; and having no personal views, being influenced solely by one feeling, the prosperity of all, he despised the very idea of danger, though it was said to exist in various shapes, even in the hospitable plate put before him! But he deemed none capable of such treachery, though once he was within a few minutes' march to the other world; but the cause, if the right one, came from his own *cuisinier*, or rather *boulanger*, whom he discharged.

were felt long after the cause ceased to exist, and claims difficult to adjust arose out of these licentious times, for the having prescriptive right was deemed sufficient to authorize their continuance.[1] Here were displayed the effects of a feudal association, where the powers of government were enfeebled. These feuds alone were sufficient to ruin the country; but when to such internal ills shoals of Mahratta plunderers were added, no art is required to describe the consequences.

Aid sought from Sindhia.—The Rana and his advisers at length determined to call in Sindhia to expel the rebellious Chondawats from the ancient capital; a step mainly prompted by Zalim Singh (now Regent of Kotah), who with the Rana's ministers was deputed to the Mahratta chieftain, then enjoying himself at the sacred lake of Pushkar.[2] Since the overthrow of Lalsot he had reorganized his brigades under the celebrated De Boigne,[3] through whose conduct he had redeemed his lost influence in Rajputana by the battles of Merta and Patan, in which the brave Rathors, after acts of the most devoted gallantry, were completely overthrown. Sindhia's plans coincided entirely with the object of the deputation, and he readily acquiesced in the Rana's desire. This event introduced on the political stage some of the most celebrated men of that day, whose actions offer a fair picture of manners, and may justify our entering a little into details.[4]

Negotiations by Zālim Singh.—Zalim Singh had for some years become regent of Kotah, and though to maintain himself in power, and the State he controlled in an attitude to compel the respect of surrounding foes, was no slight task, yet he found the field too contracted for his ambition, and his secret views had long been directed to permanent influence in Mewar. His skill in reading character convinced him that the Rana would be no

[1] See the Essay on a Feudal System.

[2] S. 1847 (A.D. 1791).

[3] [Count Benoit de Boigne, a Savoyard, born at Chambery, 1751: served under Mahādaji Sindhia, and won for him his battles of Pātan and Merta in 1790: defeated Holkar at Lakheri in 1793: resigned his command in 1795, and left India in the next year: died June 21, 1830 (Compton, *European Military Adventurers*, 15 ff.; Buckland, *Dict. of Indian Biography*, s.v.).]

[4] Acquired from the actors in those scenes: the prince, his ministers, Zalim Singh and the rival chiefs have all contributed.

bar to his wishes, the attainment of which, by giving him the combined resources of Haraoti and Mewar, would bestow the lead in Rajasthan. The Jaipur court he disregarded, whose effeminate army he had himself defeated single-handed [445] with the Kotah troops, and the influence he established amongst the leading chiefs of Marwar held out no fear of counteraction from that quarter. The stake was high, the game sure, and success would have opened a field to his genius which might have entirely altered the fate of Hindustan ; but one false move was irretrievable, and instead of becoming the arbitrator of India, he left only the reputation of being the Nestor of Rajputana.

The restriction of the Rana's power was the cloak under which he disguised all his operations, and it might have been well for the country had his plans succeeded to their full extent. To re-establish the Rana's authority, and to pay the charges of the reduction of Chitor, he determined that the rebels chiefly should furnish the means, and that from them and the fiscal lands, mostly in their hands, sixty-four lakhs should be levied, of which three-fifths should be appropriated to Sindhia, and the remainder to replenish the Rana's treasury. Preliminaries being thus arranged, Zalim was furnished with a strong corps under Ambaji Inglia ; while Sindhia followed, hanging on the Marwar frontier, to realize the contributions of that State. Zalim Singh and Ambaji moved towards Chitor, levying from the estates of those obnoxious to Zalim's views. Hamirgarh, whose chief, Dhiraj Singh, a man of talent and courage, was the principal adviser of Bhim Singh, the Salumbar chief, was besieged, and stood several assaults during six weeks' vigorous operations, when the destruction of the springs of the wells from the concussion of the guns compelled its surrender, and the estate was sequestrated. The force continued their progress, and after a trifling altercation at Basai, a Chondawat fief, also taken, they took up a position at Chitor, and were soon after joined by the main body under Sindhia.

Zālim Singh and Sindhia at Udaipur.—Zalim, to gratify Mahadaji's vanity, who was desirous of a visit from the Rana, which even the Peshwa considered an honour, proceeded to Udaipur to effect this object ; when the Rana, placing himself under his guidance, marched for this purpose, and was met at the Tiger Mount, within a few miles of his capital, by Sindhia, who received the Rana, and escorted him to the besieging army. But in this short interval, Ambaji, who remained with the army at Chitor, intrigued with the rebel Chondawat to supplant the predominant influence of his friend Zalim Singh, and seized the opportunity of his absence to counteract him, by [446] communicating his plans to Salumbar; aware that, unless he broke with Zalim, he could only hope to play a secondary part under him. Though the ulterior views of Zalim were kept to his own breast, they could not escape the penetration of the crafty Mahratta; his very anxiety to hide them furnished Ambaji with the means of detection. Had Zalim possessed an equal share of meanness with his political antagonist, he might have extricated himself from the snare; but once overreached, he preferred sinking to grasping at an unworthy support. Bhim Singh (Salumbar) privately negotiated with Ambaji the surrender of Chitor, engaging to humble himself before the Rana, and to pay a contribution of twenty lakhs, levied on the clans, provided Zalim Singh was ordered to retire. This suggestion, apparently founded on the rebellious chief's antipathy to Zalim, but in reality prompted by Ambaji, ensured the approbation, as it suited the views, of all parties, but especially Sindhia, who was desirous of repairing to Poona. Zalim, the sole obstacle to this arrangement, furnished to his enemies the means of escape from the dilemma, and lost the opportunity of realizing his long-cherished scheme of wielding the united resources of Mewar and Haraoti. Zalim had always preserved a strict amity with Ambaji wherever their interests did not clash, and his regard had the cement of gratitude to the Mahratta, whose father Trimbakji had saved Zalim's life and procured his liberty, when left wounded and a prisoner at the battle of Ujjain. On Zalim's return with the Rana, Ambaji touched on the terms of Bhim Singh's surrender, hinting that Zalim's presence was the sole obstacle to this desirable result; who, the more to mask his views, which any expressed reluctance to the measure might expose, went beyond probability in asseverations of readiness to be no bar to such arrangement, even so far as to affirm that, besides being tired of the business from the heavy expense it entailed on him, he had his prince's wish for his return to Kotah. There is one ingredient in Zalim's character, which has never been totally merged in the vices acquired from the tortuous policy of a long life, and which in the vigour of youth had full sway—namely, pride, one of the few virtues left to the Rajput, defrauded of many others by long oppression. But Zalim's pride was legitimate, being allied to honour, and it has retained him an evident superiority through all the mazes of ambition. Ambaji skilfully availed himself of this defect in his friend's political character. "A pretty [447] story, indeed!—you tell this to me! it might find credit with those who did not know you." The sarcasm only plunged him deeper into asseveration. "Is it then really your wish to retire?" "Assuredly." "Then," retorted the crafty Ambaji, "your wish shall be gratified in a few minutes." Giving him no time to retract, he called for his horse and galloped to Sindhia's tent. Zalim relied on Sindhia not acceding to the proposition; or if he did, that the Rana, over whom he imagined he had complete influence, would oppose it. His hopes of Sindhia rested on a promise privately made to leave troops under his authority for the restoration of order in Mewar; and a yet stronger claim, the knowledge that without Zalim he could not realize the stipulated sums for the expulsion of the Chondawat from Chitor. Ambaji had foreseen and prepared a remedy for these difficulties, and upon their being urged offered himself to advance the amount by bills on the Deccan. This argument was irresistible; money, and the consequent prosecution of his journey to Poona, being attained, Sindhia's engagements with Zalim and the Rana ceased to be a matter of importance. He nominated Ambaji his lieutenant, with the command of a large force, by whose aid he would reimburse himself for the sums thus advanced. Having carried his object with Sindhia, Ambaji proceeded direct from his tent to that of the Rana's ministers, Sheodas and Satidas, with whom, by the promise of co-operation in their views, and perfect subserviency to the Rana's interests, he was alike successful. Ambaji, with the rapidity necessary to ensure success, having in a few hours accomplished his purpose, hastened back to Zalim, to acquaint him that his wish to retire had met with general acquiescence; and so well did he manage, that the Rana's mace-bearer arrived at the same moment to announce that the khilat of leave awaited his acceptance. Zalim being thus outwitted, the Salumbar chief descended from Chitor, and touched the Rana's feet. Sindhia pursued his march to the Deccan, and Ambaji was left sole arbiter of Mewar. The Saktawats maintained the lead at court, and were not backward in consigning the estates of their rivals to the incubus now settled on the country: while the mortified Zalim, on his retreat, recorded his expenses, to be produced on some fitting occasion.

Sindhia's Instructions to Ambaji.—Ambaji remained eight years in Mewar, reaping its revenues and amassing those hoards of wealth which subsequently gave him the lead in Hindustan, and enabled him nearly to assert his independence. Yet, although he accumulated [448] £2,000,000 sterling from her soil,[1] exacting one-half of the produce of agricultural industry, the suppression of feuds and exterior aggressions gave to Mewar a degree of tranquillity and happiness to which she had long been a stranger. The instructions delivered to Ambaji were—

1. The entire restoration of the Rana's authority and resumption of the crown-lands from rebellious chiefs and mercenary Sindis.
2. The expulsion of the pretender from Kumbhalmer.
3. The recovery of Godwar from the Raja of Marwar.
4. To settle the Bundi feud for the murder of Rana Arsi.

A schedule (*pandhri*)[2] for the twenty lakhs stipulated was made and levied; twelve from the Chondawat estates and eight from the Saktawats; and the sum of sixty lakhs was awarded, besides the expense of Ambaji's army, when the other specified objects should be attained. Within two years the pretender was expelled Kumbhalmer, Jahazpur was recovered from a rebellious Ranawat, and the crown-lands[3] were redeemed from

[1] It was levied as follows:

Salumbar	Lakhs	3
Deogarh	„	3
Singingir Gosain, their adviser	„	2
Kosital	„	1
Amet	„	2
Kurabar	„	1
	Lakhs	12

[2] [Pāndhri, Pāndharapatti, a tax on shops, artisans, traders, and persons not engaged in agriculture, levied on their persons, implements, places of work, or traffic; the same as the Mahtarafa (Wilson, *Glossary*, s.v.).]

[3] Raepur Rajnagar from the Sindis; Gurla and Gadarmala from the Purawats; Hamirgarh from Sardar Singh, and Kurj Kawaria from Salumbar.

the nobles ; the personal domain of the Rana, agricultural and commercial, still realized nearly fifty lakhs of rupees. After these services, though Godwar was still unredeemed, the Bundi feud unappeased, and the lands mortgaged to the Mahrattas were not restored, Ambaji assumed the title of Subahdar of Mewar, and identified himself with the parties of the day. Yet so long as he personally upheld the interests of the Rana, his memory is done justice to, notwithstanding he never conformed to the strict letter of his engagements. The Rana's ministers, fearing lest their brother's fate should be theirs in the event of the Chondawats again attaining power, and deeming their own and their sovereign's security dependent on Ambaji's presence, made a subsidiary engagement with him, and lands to the amount of 75,000 rupees monthly, or eight lakhs annually, were appropriated for his force ; but so completely were the resources of the [449] country diverted from their honest use, that when, in S. 1851, a marriage was negotiated between the Rana's sister and the prince of Jaipur, the Rana was obliged to borrow £50,000 from the Mahratta commander to purchase the nuptial presents. The following year was marked by a triple event—the death of the queen-mother, the birth of a son and heir to the Rana, and the bursting of the embankment of the lake, which swept away a third of the city and a third of its inhabitants. Superstition attributed this catastrophe to the Rana's impiety, in establishing a new festival [1] to Gauri, the Isis of Rajasthan.

Anarchy in Mewār.—Ambaji, who was this year nominated by Sindhia his viceroy in Hindustan, left Ganesh Pant as his lieutenant in Mewar, with whom acted the Rana's officers, Sawai and Shirji Mehta ; [2] who applied themselves to make the most of their ephemeral power with so rapacious a spirit, that Ambaji was compelled to displace Ganesh Pant and appoint the celebrated Rae Chand. To him they would not yield, and each party formed a nucleus for disorder and misrule. It would be uninteresting

[1] In Bhadon, the third month of the rainy season. An account of this festival will hereafter be given.

[2] The first of these is now the manager of Prince Jawan Singh's estates, a man of no talent ; and the latter, his brother, was one of the ministers on my arrival at Udaipur. He was of invincible good humour, yet full of the spirit of intrigue, and one of the bars to returning prosperity. The cholera carried off this Falstaff of the court, not much to my sorrow.

and nauseating to the reader to carry him through all the scenes of villainy which gradually desolated this country; for whose spoil pilfering Mahrattas, savage Rohillas, and adventurous Franks were all let loose. The now humbled Chondawats, many of whose fiefs were confiscated, took to horse, and in conjunction with lawless Sindis scoured the country. Their estates were attacked, Kurabar was taken, and batteries were placed against Salumbar, whence the Sindis fled and found refuge in Deogarh. In this exigence, the Chondawats determined to send an envoy to Ambaji, who was then engaged in the siege of Datia; and Ajit Singh, since prominent in the intrigues of Mewar, was the organ of his clan on this occasion. For the sum of ten lakhs the avaricious Mahratta agreed to recall his deputy from Mewar,[1] to renounce Sheodas and the Saktawats, and lend his support to the Chondawats. The Salumbar chief again took the lead at court, and with Agarji Mehta[2] as minister, the Saktawats [450]

[1] S. 1853, A.D. 1797.

[2] This person was nominated the chief civil minister on the author's arrival at Udaipur, an office to which he was every way unequal. The affairs of Mewar had never prospered since the faithful Pancholis were deprived of power. Several productions of the descendants of Biharidas have fallen into my hands; their quaint mode of conveying advice may authorize their insertion here.

The Pancholis, who had performed so many services to the country, had been for some time deprived of the office of prime minister, which was disposed of as it suited the views of the factious nobles who held power for the time being; and who bestowed it on the Mehtas, Depras, or Dhabhais. Amongst the papers of the Pancholis, several addressed to the Rana and to Agarji Mehta, the minister of the day, are valuable for the patriotic sentiments they contain, as well as for the general light they throw upon the period. In S. 1853 (A.D. 1797) Amrit Rao devised a plan to remedy the evils that oppressed the country. He inculcated the necessity of dispensing with the interference of the Saktawats and Chondawats in the affairs of government, and strengthening the hands of the civil administration by admitting the foreign chieftains to the power he proposed to deprive the former of. He proceeds in the following quaint style:

"Disease fastened on the country from the following causes, envy and party spirit. With the Turks disease was introduced; but then the prince, his ministers, and chiefs, were of one mind, and medicine was ministered and a cure effected. During Rana Jai Singh's time the disorder returned, which his son Amra put down. He recovered the affairs of government from confusion, gave to every one his proper rank and dignity, and rendered all prosperous. But Maharana Sangram Singh put from under his wing the Chandarawat of Rampura, and thus a pinion of Mewar was broken. The calamity of Biharidas, whose son committed suicide, increased the diffi-

were attacked, the stipulated ten lakhs raised from their estates, and two fiefs of note, Hintha and Semari, confiscated [451].

culties. The arrival of the Deccanis under Bajirao, the Jaipur affair * and the defeat at Rajmahall, with the heavy expenditure thereby occasioned, augmented the disorder. Add to this in Jagat Singh's time the enmity of the Dhabhais towards the Pancholis, which lowered their dignities at home and abroad, and since which time every man has thought himself equal to the task of government. Jagat Singh was also afflicted by the rebellious conduct of his son Partap, when Shyama Solanki and several other chiefs were treacherously cut off. Since which time the minds of the nobles have never been loyal, but black and not to be trusted. Again, on the accession of Partap, Maharaja Nathji allowed his thoughts to aspire, from which all his kin suffered. Hence animosities, doubts, and deceits, arose on all sides. Add to this the haughty proceeding of Amra Chand now in office; and besides the strife of the Pancholis with each other, their enmity to the Depras. Hence parties were formed which completely destroyed the credit of all. Yet, notwithstanding, they abated none of their strife, which was the acme to the disease. The feud between Kuman Singh and the Saktawats for the possession of Hintha, aggravated the distresses. The treacherous murder of Maharaja Nathji, and the consequent disgust and retreat of Jaswant Singh of Deogarh; the setting up the impostor Ratna Singh and Jhala Raghudeo's struggle for office, with Amra Chand's entertaining the mercenaries of Sind, brought it to a crisis. The negligence arising out of luxury, and the intrigues of the Dhabhais of Rana Arsi, made it spread so as to defeat all attempt at cure. In S. 1829, on the treacherous murder of the Rana by the Bundi prince, and the accession of the minor Hamir, every one set up his own authority, so that there was not even the semblance of government. And now you (to the Rana), listening to the advice of Bhim Singh (Salumbar), and his brother, Arjun, have taken foreigners † into pay, and thus riveted all the former errors. You and Sri Baiji Raj (the royal mother), putting confidence in foreigners and Deccanis, have rendered the disease contagious; besides, your mind is gone. What can be done? Medicine may yet be had. Let us unite and struggle to restore the duties of the minister and we may conquer, or at least check its progress. If now neglected, it will hereafter be beyond human power. The Deccanis are the great sore. Let us settle their accounts, and at all events get rid of them, or we lose the land for ever. At this time there are treaties and engagements in every corner. I have touched on every subject. Forgive whatever is improper. Let us look the future in the face, and let chiefs, ministers, and all unite. With the welfare of the country all will be well. But this is a disease which, if not now conquered, will conquer us."

A second paper as follows:

"The disease of the country is to be considered and treated as a remittent.

* The struggle to place the Rana's nephew, Madho Singh, on the throne of Jaipur.

† The Pancholi must allude to the Mahratta subsidiary force under Ambaji.

Death of Mahādaji Sindhia, January 12, 1794.—The death of Mahadaji Sindhia,[1] and the accession of his nephew Daulatrao, his murder of the Shenvi Brahmans, and his quarrels with the Bais (' princesses,' wives of the deceased Sindhia), all occurred at this time, and materially influenced the events in Mewar. The power of Aṃbaji as Subahdar of Hindustan was strengthened by the minority of Sindhia, although contested by Lakwa and the Bais, supported by the Khichi prince, Durjan Sal, and the Datia Raja, who fought and died for the princesses. Lakwa wrote to the Rana to throw off Ambaji's yoke and expel his lieutenant; while Ambaji commanded his deputy to eject the Shenvi[2] Brah-

---

"Amra Singh cured it and laid a complete system of government and justice.

"In Sangram's time it once more gained ground.

"In Jagat Singh's time the seed was thrown into the ground thus obtained.

"In Partap's time it sprung up.

"In Raj Singh's time it bore fruit.

"In Rana Arsi's time it was ripe.

"In Hamir's time it was distributed, and all have had a share.

"And you, Bhim Singh (the present Rana), have eaten plentifully thereof. Its virtues and flavour you are acquainted with, and so likewise is the country; and if you take no medicine you will assuredly suffer much pain, and both at home and abroad you will be lightly thought of. Be not therefore negligent, or faith and land will depart from you."

A third paper to Agarji Mehta (then minister):

"If the milk is curdled it does not signify. Where there is sense butter may yet be extracted; and if the butter-milk (*chhachh*) is thrown away it matters not. But if the milk be curdled and black it will require wisdom to restore its purity. This wisdom is now wanted. The foreigners are the black in the curdled milk of Mewar. At all hazards remove them. Trust to them and the land is lost.

"In moonlight what occasion for a blue light? (*Chandra jot*).*

"Who looks to the false coin of the juggler?

"Do not credit him who tells you he will make a pigeon out of a feather.

"Abroad it is said there is no wisdom left in Mewar, which is a disgrace to her reputation."

[1] [Mahādaji Sindhia, commonly and erroneously called Mādhava Rāo, died near Poona, January 12, 1794. See his life by H. G. Keene, 'Rulers of India' series; Grant Duff, *Hist. of Mahrattas*, 343 ff.; W. Franklin, *Hist. of Shah-Aulum*, 119 ff.]

[2] There are three classes of Mahratta Brahmans: Shenvi, Prabhu, and Mahratta. Of the first was Lakwa, Balabha Tantia, Jiwa Dada, Sivaji Nana, Lalaji Pandit, and Jaswant Rao Bhao, men who held the mortgaged

---

* Literally, a 'moonlight.' The particular kind of firework which we call a 'blue light.'

mans, supporters of Lakwa, from all the lands in Mewar. To this end Ganesh Pant called on the Rana's ministers and chiefs, who, consulting thereon, determined to play a deep game; and while they apparently acquiesced in the schemes of Ganesh, they wrote the Shenvis to advance from Jawad and attack him, promising them support. They met at Sawa; Nana was defeated with the loss of his guns, and retired on Chitor. With a feint of support, the Chondawats made him again call in his garrison and try another battle, which he also lost and fled to Hamirgarh; then, uniting with his enemies, they invested the place with 15,000 men. Nana bravely maintained himself, making many sallies, in one of which both the sons of Dhiraj Singh, the chief of Hamirgarh, were slain. Shortly after, Nana was relieved by some battalions of the new raised regulars sent by Ambaji under Gulab Rao Kadam, upon which he commenced his retreat on Ajmer. At Musamusi he was forced to action, and success had nearly crowned the efforts of the clans, when a horseman, endeavouring to secure a mare, calling out [452], "*Bhagi! bhagi!*" "She flies! she flies!" the word spread, while those who caught her, exclaiming "*Milgayi! milgayi!*" "She is taken!" but equally significant with 'going over' to the enemy, caused a general panic, and the Chondawats, on the verge of victory, disgraced themselves, broke and fled. Several were slain, among whom was the Sindi leader Chandan. Shahpura opened its gates to the fugitives led by the Goliath of the host, the chief of Deogarh.[1] It was an occasion not to be lost by the bards of the rival clan, and many a ribald stanza records this day's disgrace. Ambaji's lieutenant, however, was so roughly handled that several chiefs redeemed their estates, and the Rana much of the fisc, from Mahratta control.

Contest of Ambaji and Lakwa.—Mewar now became the arena on which the rival satraps Ambaji and Lakwa contested the

---

lands of Mewar. [There are four groups of Marātha Brāhmans: Konkanasthas, Deshasthas, Karhādas, and Kanvas. The Prabhus are not Brāhmans, but the writer caste, like the Kāyasths of Hindustān (J. Wilson, *Indian Caste*, 1877, ii. 17 ff.). The word Shenvi is a corruption of *chhiyānavē*, 'ninety-six,' from the supposed number of their sections.]

[1] I knew him well. He stood six feet six inches, and was bulky in proportion. His limbs rivalled those of the Hercules Farnese. His father was nearly seven feet, and died at the early age of twenty-two, in a vain attempt to keep down, by regimen and medicine, his enormous bulk.

exalted office of Sindhia's lieutenancy in Hindustan. Lakwa was joined by all the chiefs of Mewar, his cause being their own; and Hamirgarh, still held by Nana's party, was reinvested. Two thousand shot had made a practicable breach, when Bala Rao Inglia, Bapu Sindhia, Jaswant Rao Sindhia, a brigade under the European 'Mutta field,' [1] with the auxiliary battalions of Zalim Singh of Kotah, the whole under the command of Ambaji's son, arrived to relieve the lieutenant. Lakwa raised the siege, and took post with his allies under the walls of Chitor; whilst the besieged left the untenable Ḥamirgarh, and joined the relief at Gosunda. The rival armies were separated only by the Berach river, on whose banks they raised batteries and cannonaded each other, when a dispute arose in the victor camp regarding the pay of the troops, between Bala Rao (brother of Ambaji) and Nana, and the latter withdrew and retreated to Sanganer. Thus disunited, it might have been expected that these congregated masses would have dissolved, or fallen upon each other, when the Rajputs might have given the *coup de grâce* to the survivors; but they were Mahrattas, and their politics were too complicated to end in simple strife: almost all the actors in these scenes lived to contest with, and be humiliated by, the British.

George Thomas.—The defection of Nana equalized the parties; but Bala Rao, never partial to fighting, opportunely recollected a debt of gratitude to Lakwa, to whose clemency he owed his life when taken by storm in Gugal Chapra. He also wanted money [453] to pay his force, which a private overture to Lakwa secured. They met, and Bala Rao retired boasting of his gratitude, to which, and the defection of Nana, soon followed by that of Bapu Sindhia, the salvation of Lakwa was attributed. Sutherland [2] with a brigade was detached by Ambaji to aid Nana: but a dispute depriving him of this reinforcement, he called in a partisan of more celebrity, the brave George Thomas.[3] Ambaji's

[1] [This is perhaps Captain Butterfield, who served in Sindhia's force under Colonel Sutherland. He behaved gallantly in action against Lakwa Dāda, for which he received a flattering letter from Perron: no further mention of him has been traced (Compton, *Military Adventurers*, 344).]

[2] [For Colonel Robert Sutherland, known to natives as 'Sutlej Sahib,' see Compton, 410 ff.]

[3] [For the remarkable career of George Thomas, who nearly succeeded in forming a kingdom of his own on the ruins of the Empire in N. India, see Compton, 109 f.; W. Franklin, *Military Memoirs of Mr. G. Thomas*, 1803.]

lieutenant and Lakwa were once more equal foes, and the Rana, his chiefs and subjects being distracted between these conflicting bands, whose leaders alternately paid their respects to him, were glad to obtain a little repose by espousing the cause of either combatant, whose armies during the monsoon encamped for six weeks within sight of each other.[1]

Pillage in Mewār.—Durjan Sal (Khichi), with the nobles of Mewar, hovered round Nana's camp with five thousand horse to cut off his supplies; but Thomas escorted the convoys from Shahpura with his regulars, and defied all their efforts. Thomas at length advanced his batteries against Lakwa, on whose position a general assault was about taking place, when a tremendous storm, with torrents of rain which filled the stream, cut off his batteries from the main body, burst the gates of Shahpura, his *point d'appui*, and laid the town in ruins.[2] Lakwa seized the moment, and with the Mewar chiefs stormed and carried the isolated batteries, capturing fifteen pieces of cannon; and the Shahpura Raja, threatened at once by his brother-nobles and the vengeance of heaven, refused further provision to Nana, who was compelled to abandon his position and retreat to Sanganer. The discomfited lieutenant vowed vengeance against the estates of the Mewar chieftains, and after the rains, being reinforced by Ambaji, again took the field. Then commenced a scene of carnage, pillage, and individual defence. The whole of the Chondawat estates under the Aravalli range were laid waste, their castles assaulted, some taken and destroyed, and heavy sums levied on all. Thomas besieged Deogarh and Amet, and both fought and paid. Kasital and Lasani were captured, and the latter razed for its gallant resistance. Thus they were proceeding in the work of destruction, when Ambaji [454] was dispossessed of the government of Hindustan, to which Lakwa was nominated,[3] and Nana was compelled to surrender all the fortresses and towns he held in Mewar.

[1] Both camps were on the right bank of the Banas: Lakwa's at Amli, about ten miles south of Shahpura, and Nana's at Kadera, between these towns.

[2] Lakwa at this time [S. 1856, A.D. 1799] put the Shahpura Raja in possession of the important fortress and district of Jahazpur, which, although the Rana consented to it, covertly receiving from the Raja two lakhs of rupees, disgusted the nobles with Lakwa.

[3] Balabha Tantia and Bakhshu Narayan Rao were Sindhia's ministers at this period, of the same tribe (the Shenvi) as Lakwa.

Daulat Rāo Sindhia reduces Mewār.—From this period must be dated the pretensions of Sindhia to consider Mewar as tributary to him. We have traced the rise of the Mahrattas, and the progress of their baneful influence in Mewar. The abstractions of territory from S. 1826 to 1831 [A.D. 1769–74], as pledges for contributions, satisfied their avarice till 1848 [A.D. 1791], when the Salumbar rebellion brought the great Sindhia to Chitor, leaving Ambaji as his lieutenant, with a subsidiary force, to recover the Rana's lost possessions. We have related how these conditions were fulfilled; how Ambaji, inflated with the wealth of Mewar, assumed almost regal dignity in Hindustan, assigning the devoted land to be governed by his deputies, whose contest with other aspirants made this unhappy region the stage for constant struggles for supremacy; and while the secret policy of Zalim Singh stimulated the Saktawats to cling to Ambaji, the Chondawats gave their influence and interest to his rival Lakwa. The unhappy Rana and the peasantry paid for this rivalry; while Sindhia, whose power was now in its zenith, fastened one of his desultory armies on Mewar, in contravention of former treaties, without any definite views, or even instructions to its commander. It was enough that a large body should supply itself without assailing him for prey, and whose services were available when required.

Lakwa Dāda Marātha Viceroy.—Lakwa, the new viceroy, marched to Mewar: Agarji Mehta was appointed minister to the Rana, and the Chondawats again came into power. For the sum of six lakhs Lakwa dispossessed the Shahpura of Jahazpur, for the liquidation of which thirty-six of its towns were mortgaged. Zalim Singh, who had long been manœuvring to obtain Jahazpur, administered to the necessities of the Mahratta, paid the note of hand, and took possession of the city and its villages. A contribution of twenty-four lakhs was imposed throughout the country, and levied by force of arms, after which first act of the new viceroy he quitted Mewar for Jaipur, leaving Jaswant Rao Bhao as his deputy. Mauji Ram, the deputy of Agarji (the Rana's minister), determined to adopt the European mode of discipline, now become general amongst all the native powers of India. But when the chiefs were [455] called upon to contribute to the support of mercenary regulars and a field-artillery, they evinced their patriotism by confining this zealous minister. Satidas was once more placed in power, and his brother Sheodas recalled from Kotah, whither he had fled from the Chondawats, who now appropriated to themselves the most valuable portions of the Rana's personal domain.

Holkar defeated at Indore. Plunder of Nāthdwāra: image removed.—The battle of Indore,[1] in A.D. 1802, where at least 150,000 men assembled to dispute the claim to predatory empire, wrested the ascendancy from Holkar, who lost his guns, equipage, and capital, from which he fled to Mewar, pursued by Sindhia's victorious army led by Sadasheo and Bala Rao. In his flight he plundered Ratlam, and passing Bhindar, the castle of the Saktawat chief, he demanded a contribution, from which and his meditated visit to Udaipur, the Rana and his vassal were saved by the activity of the pursuit. Failing in these objects, Holkar retreated on Nathdwara, the celebrated shrine of the Hindu Apollo.[2] It was here this active soldier first showed symptoms of mental derangement. He upbraided Krishna, while prostrate before his image, for the loss of his victory; and levied three lakhs of rupees on the priests and inhabitants, several of whom he carried to his camp as hostages for the payment. The portal (*dwara*) of the god (*Nath*) proving no bar either to Turk or equally impious Mahratta, Damodarji, the high priest, removed the god of Vraj from his pedestal and sent him with his establishment to Udaipur for protection. The Chauhan chief of Kotharia (one of the sixteen nobles), in whose estate was the sacred fane, undertook the duty, and with twenty horsemen, his vassals, escorted the shepherd god by intricate passes to the capital. On his return he was intercepted by a band of Holkar's troops, who insultingly desired the surrender of their horses. But the descendant of the illustrious Prithiraj preferred death to dishonour: dismounting, he hamstrung his steed, commanding his vassals to follow his example; and sword in hand courted his fate in the unequal conflict, in which he fell, with most of his gallant retainers. There are many such isolated exploits in the records of this eventful period, of which the Chauhans of Kotharia had their full share. Spoil, from whatever source, being welcome to these depredators, Nathdwara[3] remained long abandoned; and Apollo, after

[1] [October 14, 1801 (Grant Duff 555).] [2] [Krishna.]

[3] Five-and-twenty [about thirty] miles north of Udaipur. On this subject we shall have much to say hereafter.

six months' residence at Udaipur, finding [456] insufficient protection, took another flight to the mountains of Ghasyar, where the high priest threw up fortifications for his defence; and spiritual thunders being disregarded, the pontiff henceforth buckled on the armour of flesh, and at the head of four hundred cavaliers with lance and shield, visited the minor shrines in his extensive diocese.

The Inroad of Holkar.—To return to Holkar. He pursued his route by Banera and Shahpura, levying from both, to Ajmer, where he distributed a portion of the offerings of the followers of Krishna amongst the priests of Muhammad at the mosque of Khwaja Pir. Thence he proceeded towards Jaipur. Sindhia's leaders on reaching Mewar renounced the pursuit, and Udaipur was cursed with their presence, when three lakhs of rupees were extorted from the unfortunate Rana, raised by the sale of household effects and the jewels of the females of his family. Jaswant Rao Bhao, the Subahdar of Mewar, had prepared another schedule (*pandhri*), which he left with Tantia, his deputy, to realize. Then followed the usual scene of conflict—the attack of the chieftain's estates, distraining of the husbandman, seizure of his cattle, and his captivity for ransom, or his exile.

Mewār Quarrels.—The celebrated Lakwa, disgraced by his prince, died at this time [1] in sanctuary at Salumbar; and Bala Rao, brother to Ambaji, returned, and was joined by the Saktawats and the minister Satidas, who expelled the Chondawats for their control over the prince. Zalim Singh, in furtherance of his schemes and through hatred of the Chondawats, united himself to this faction, and Devi Chand, minister to the Rana, set up by the Chondawats, was made prisoner. Bala Rao levied and destroyed their estates with unexampled ferocity, which produced a bold attempt at deliverance. The Chondawat leaders assembled at the Chaugan (the *Champ de Mars*) to consult on their safety. The insolent Mahratta had preceded them to the palace, demanding the surrender of the minister's deputy, Mauji Ram. The Rana indignantly refused them—the Mahratta importuned, threatened, and at length commanded his troops to advance to the palace, when the intrepid minister pinioned the audacious plunderers, and secured his adherents (including their old enemy, Nana Ganesh), Jamalkar, and Uda Kunwar. The latter, a

[1] S. 1859 (A.D. 1803).

notorious villain, had an elephant's chain put round his neck, while Bala Rao was confined in a bath. The [457] leaders thus arrested, the Chondawats sallied forth and attacked their camp in the valley, which surrendered; though the regulars under Hearsey [1] retreated in a hollow square, and reached Gadarmala in safety. Zalim Singh determined to liberate his friend Bala Rao from peril; and aided by the Saktawats under the chiefs of Bhindar and Lawa, advanced to the Chaija Pass, one of the defiles leading to the capital. Had the Rana put these chiefs to instant death, he would have been justified, although he would have incurred the resentment of the whole Mahratta nation. Instead of this, he put himself at the head of a motley levy of six thousand Sindis, Arabs, and Gosains, with the brave Jai Singh and a band of his gallant Khichis, ever ready to poise the lance against a Mahratta. They defended the pass for five days against a powerful artillery. At length the Rana was compelled to liberate Bala Rao, and Zalim Singh obtained by this interference possession of the fortress and entire district of Jahazpur. A schedule of war contribution, the usual finale to these events, followed Bala's liberation, and no means were left untried to realize the exaction, before Holkar, then approaching, could contest the spoil.

Holkar plunders Udaipur.—This chief, having recruited his shattered forces, again left the south.[2] Bhindar felt his resentment for non-compliance with his demands on his retreat after the battle of Indore; the town was nearly destroyed, but spared for two lakhs of rupees, for the payment of which villages were assigned. Thence he repaired to Udaipur, being met by Ajit Singh, the Rana's ambassador, when the enormous sum of forty lakhs, or £500,000, was demanded from the country, of which one-third was commanded to be instantly forthcoming. The palace was denuded of everything which could be converted into gold; the females were deprived of every article of luxury and comfort: by which, with contributions levied on the city, twelve lakhs were

[1] [Hyder Young Hearsey (1782–3–1840), son of Captain Harry Thomas Hearsey by a Jāt lady, served Sindhia under Perron, and also George Thomas, joined Lord Lake at Dīg in 1804: taken prisoner in the Nepāl war of 1815: present at the siege of Bharatpur: died near Budāun (Buckland, *Dict. Indian Biography*, s.v.).]

[2] In S. 1860 (A.D. 1804).

obtained; while hostages from the household of the Rana and chief citizens were delivered as security for the remainder, and immured in the Mahratta camp. Holkar then visited the Rana. Lawa and Badnor were attacked, taken, and restored on large payments. Deogarh alone was mulcted four and a half lakhs. Having devastated Mewar during eight months, Holkar [458] marched to Hindustan,[1] Ajit Singh accompanying him as the Rana's representative; while Bala Ram Seth was left to levy the balance of the forty lakhs. Holkar had reached Shahpura when Sindhia entered Mewar, and their camps formed a junction to allow the leaders to organize their mutual plans of hostility to the British Government. These chieftains, in their efforts to cope with the British power, had been completely humiliated, and their resources broken. But Rajasthan was made to pay the penalty of British success, which riveted her chains, and it would be but honest, now we have the power, to diminish that penalty.

Sindhia and Holkar in Mewār.—The rainy season of A.D. 1805 found Sindhia and Holkar encamped in the plains of Badnor, desirous, but afraid, to seek revenge in the renewal of war. Deprived of all power in Hindustan, and of the choicest territory north and south of the Nerbudda, with numerous discontented armies now let loose on these devoted countries, their passions inflamed by defeat, and blind to every sentiment of humanity, they had no alternative to pacify the soldiery and replenish their own ruined resources but indiscriminate pillage. It would require a pen powerful as the pencil of Salvator Rosa to paint the horrors which filled up the succeeding ten years, to which the author was an eye-witness, destined to follow in the train of rapine, and to view in the traces of Mahratta camps[2] the desola-

[1] At this juncture an officer of Holkar's, Harnath Chela, on passing through Bansain, had some camels carried off by the Bhils of the Satola estate. Harnath summoned Gulab Singh Chondawat, who came with eight of his relatives, when he was told he should be detained till the cattle were restored; and in the morning, as the Mahratta mounted his elephant, he commanded the Raghaut chieftain to be seized. Gulab drew his sword and made at Harnath, but his sword broke in the howda, when he plunged his dagger into the elephant; but at length he and all his relations, who nobly plied their swords on the Mahrattas, were cut to pieces.

[2] [For a graphic account of these camps see T. D. Broughton, *Letters written in a Mahratta Camp during the year 1809*, ed. 1892.]

tion and political annihilation of all the central States of India,[1] several of which aided the British in their early struggle for dominion, but were now allowed to fall without a helping hand, the scapegoats of our successes. Peace between the Mahrattas and British was, however, doubtful, as Sindhia made the restoration of the rich provinces of Gohad and Gwalior a *sine qua non*: and unhappily for their legitimate ruler, who [459] had been inducted into the seat of his forefathers, a Governor-General (Lord Cornwallis) of ancient renown, but in the decline of life, with views totally unsuited to the times, abandoned our allies, and renounced all for peace, sending an ambassador[2] to Sindhia to reunite the bonds of 'perpetual friendship.'

Holkar saves Mewār from Sindhia.—The Mahratta leaders were anxious, if the war should be renewed, to shelter their families and valuables in the strongholds of Mewar, and their respective camps became the rendezvous of the rival factions. Sardar Singh, the organ of the Chondawats, represented the Rana at Sindhia's court, at the head of whose councils Ambaji had just been placed.[3] His rancour to the Rana was implacable, from the support given in self-defence to his political antagonist, Lakwa, and he agitated the partition of Mewar amongst the great Mahratta leaders. But whilst his baneful influence was preparing this result, the credit of Sangram Saktawat with Holkar counteracted it. It would be unfair and ungallant not to record that a fair suitor, the Baiza Bai,[4] Sindhia's wife, powerfully

[1] The Rana of Gohad and Gwalior, the Khichi chiefs of Raghugarh and Bahadurgarh, and the Nawab of Bhopal, made common cause with us in Warren Hastings' time. The first three possess not a shadow of independence; the last fortunately formed a link in our own policy, and Lord Hastings, in 1818, repaid with liberal interest the services rendered to the government of Warren Hastings in 1782. It was in his power, with equal facility, to have rescued all the other States, and to have claimed the same measure of gratitude which Bhopal is proud to avow. But there was a fatality in the desire to maintain terms with Sindhia, whose treachery to our power was overlooked.

[2] The author, then a subaltern, was attached to the suite of the ambassador, Mr. Græme Mercer. He left the subsidiary force at Gwalior in December 1805, and the embassy reached Sindhia's court in the spring of 1806, then encamped amidst the ruins of Mewar.

[3] The ministers of Sindhia were Ambaji, Bapu Chitnavis, Madhuba Huzuria, and Anaji Bhaskar.

[4] [Baiza Bāi, widow of Daulat Rāo Sindhia, who died in 1827, was an

contributed to the Rana's preservation on this occasion. This lady, the daughter of the notorious Sarji Rao, had unbounded power over Sindhia. Her sympathies were awakened on behalf of the supreme head of the Rajput nation, of which blood she had to boast, though she was now connected with the Mahrattas. Even the hostile clans stifled their animosities on this occasion, and Sardar Singh Chondawat left Sindhia's camp to join his rival Sangram with Holkar, and aided by the upright Kishandas Pancholi, united in their remonstrances, asking Holkar if he had given his consent to sell Mewar to Ambaji. Touched by the picture of the Rana's and their country's distresses, Holkar swore it should not be; advised unity amongst themselves, and caused the representatives of the rival clans 'to eat opium together.' Nor did he stop here, but with the envoys repaired to Sindhia's tents, descanted on the Rana's high descent, 'the master of their master's master,'[1] urging that it did not become them to overwhelm him, and that they should even renounce the mortgaged lands which their fathers had too long unjustly held, himself setting the example by the restitution of [460] Nimbahera. To strengthen his argument, he expatiated with Sindhia on the policy of conciliating the Rana, whose strongholds might be available in the event of a renewal of hostilities with the British. Sindhia appeared a convert to his views, and retained the envoys in his camp. The Mahratta camps were twenty miles apart, and incessant torrents of rain had for some days prevented all intercourse. In this interim, Holkar received intelligence that Bhairon Bakhsh, as envoy from the Rana, was in Lord Lake's camp negotiating for the aid of British troops, then at Tonk, to drive the Mahrattas from Mewar. The incensed Holkar sent for the Rana's ambassadors, and assailed them with a torrent of reproach; accusing them of treachery, he threw the newspaper containing the information at Kishandas, asking if that were the way in which the Mewaris kept faith with him? "I cared not to break with Sindhia in support of your master, and while combating the Farangis (Franks), when all the Hindus should be

unscrupulous, designing woman, whose intrigues at Gwalior forced her to take refuge in British territory. She returned after an interval and lived at Gwalior until her death in 1862 (*IGI*, xii. 424).]

[1] That is, chief of the race from which issued the Satārā sovereigns, whose minister, the Peshwa, accounted Sindhia and Holkar his feudatories.

as brothers, your sovereign the Rana, who boasts of not acknowledging the supremacy of Delhi, is the first to enter into arms with them. Was it for this I prevented Ambaji being fastened on you?" Kishandas here interrupted and attempted to pacify him, when Alikar Tantia, Holkar's minister, stopped him short, observing to his prince, "You see the faith of these Rangras;[1] they would disunite you and Sindhia, and ruin both. Shake them off: be reconciled to Sindhia, dismiss Sarji Rao, and let Ambaji be Subahdar of Mewar, or I will leave you and take Sindhia into Malwa." The other councillors, with the exception of Bhao Bhaskar, seconded this advice: Sarji Rao was dismissed; and Holkar proceeded northward, where he was encountered and pursued to the Panjab by the British under the intrepid and enterprising Lake, who dictated terms to the Mahratta at the altars of Alexander.[2]

Holkar protects Mewār Interests.—Holkar had the generosity to stipulate, before his departure from Mewar, for the security of the Rana and his country, telling Sindhia he should hold him personally amenable to him if Ambaji were permitted to violate his guarantee. But in his misfortunes this threat was disregarded, and a contribution of sixteen lakhs was levied immediately on Mewar; Sadasheo Rao, with Baptiste's[3] brigade, was detached from the camp in June 1806, for the double purpose of levying it, and driving from [461] Udaipur a detachment of the Jaipur prince's troops, bringing proposals and preliminary presents for this prince's marriage with the Rana's daughter.

The Tragedy of Krishna Kunwāri.—It would be imagined that the miseries of Rana Bhim were not susceptible of aggravation, and that fortune had done her worst to humble him; but his

[1] Rangra is an epithet applied to the Rajputs, implying turbulent, from *rana*, 'strife.' [Rāngar is the title of a body of turbulent, predatory Muhammadans, who claim Rājput descent, occupying parts of the E. Panjāb and W. districts of the Ganges-Jumna Duāb. The derivation suggested is very doubtful (Crooke, *Tribes and Castes, N.W.P. and Oudh*, v. 227 ff.).]

[2] [In October 1805 (Grant Duff 601).]

[3] [Jean Baptiste de la Fontaine Filoze (1775–1840) assisted in the campaign against Thomas in 1801. In the war with the English, part of his brigade under Dupont was defeated at Assaye. He was afterwards ill-treated by Sindhia, but was reinstated. Some of his descendants are still in Sindhia's service (Compton, *European Military Adventurers*, 352 ff.; Sleeman, *Rambles*, 115, note). He is frequently mentioned in Broughton, *Letters written in a Mahratta Camp*.]

pride as a sovereign and his feelings as a parent were destined to be yet more deeply wounded. The Jaipur cortège had encamped near the capital, to the number of three thousand men, while the Rana's acknowledgments of acceptance were dispatched, and had reached Shahpura. But Raja Man of Marwar also advanced pretensions, founded on the princess having been actually betrothed to his predecessor ; and urging that the throne of Marwar, and not the individual occupant, was the object, he vowed resentment and opposition if his claims were disregarded. These were suggested, it is said, by his nobles to cloak their own views ; and promoted by the Chondawats (then in favour with the Rana), whose organ, Ajit, was bribed to further them, contrary to the decided wishes of their prince.

Krishna Kunwari (the *Virgin* Krishna) was the name of the lovely object, the rivalry for whose hand assembled under the banners of her suitors (Jagat Singh of Jaipur and Raja Man of Marwar), not only their native chivalry, but all the predatory powers of India; and who, like Helen of old, involved in destruction her own and the rival houses. Sindhia having been denied a pecuniary demand by Jaipur, not only opposed the nuptials, but aided the claims of Raja Man, by demanding of the Rana the dismissal of the Jaipur embassy: which being refused, he advanced his brigades and batteries, and after a fruitless resistance, in which the Jaipur troops joined, forced the pass, threw a corps of eight thousand men into the valley, and following in person, encamped within cannon-range of the city. The Rana had now no alternative but to dismiss the nuptial cortège, and agree to whatever was demanded. Sindhia remained a month in the valley, during which an interview took place between him and the Rana at the shrine of Eklinga [462].[1]

[1] To increase his importance, Sindhia invited the British envoy and suite to be present on the occasion, when the princely demeanour of the Rana and his sons was advantageously contrasted with that of the Mahratta and his suite. It was in this visit that the regal abode of this ancient race, its isles and palaces, acted with irresistible force on the cupidity of this scion of the plough, who aspired to, yet dared not seat himself in, 'the halls of the Caesars.' It was even surmised that his hostility to Jaipur was not so much from the refused war-contribution, as from a mortifying negative to an audacious desire to obtain the hand of this princess himself. The impression made on the author upon this occasion by the miseries and noble appearance of 'this descendant of a hundred kings,' was never allowed to weaken,

Battle of Parbatsar. Defeat of the Mārwār Forces.—The heralds of Hymen being thus rudely repulsed and its symbols intercepted, the Jaipur prince prepared to avenge his insulted pride and disappointed hopes, and accordingly arrayed a force such as had not assembled since the empire was in its glory. Raja Man eagerly took up the gauntlet of his rival, and headed 'the swords of Maru.' But dissension prevailed in Marwar, where rival claimants for the throne had divided the loyalty of the clans, introducing there also the influence of the Mahrattas. Raja Man, who had acquired the sceptre by party aid, was obliged to maintain himself by it, and to pursue the demoralizing policy of the period by ranging his vassals against each other. These nuptials gave the malcontents an opportunity to display their long-curbed resentments, and following the example of Mewar, they set up a pretender, whose interests were eagerly espoused, and whose standard was erected in the array of Jaipur; the prince at the head of 120,000 men advancing against his rival, who with less than half the number met him at Parbatsar, on their mutual frontier. The action was short, for while a heavy cannonade opened on either side, the majority of the Marwar nobles went over to the pretender. Raja Man turned his poniard against himself: but some chiefs yet faithful to him wrested the weapon from his hand, and conveyed him from the field. He was pursued to his capital, which was invested, besieged, and gallantly defended during six months. The town was at length taken and plundered, but the castle of Jodha 'laughed a siege to scorn'; in time with the aid of finesse, the mighty host of Jaipur, which had consumed the forage of these arid plains for twenty miles around, began to crumble away; intrigue spread through every rank, and the siege ended in pusillanimity and flight. The Xerxes of Rajwara, the effeminate Kachhwaha, alarmed at length for his personal safety, sent on the spoils of

---

but kindled an enthusiastic desire for the restoration of his fallen condition, which stimulated his perseverance to obtain that knowledge by which alone he might be enabled to benefit him. Then a young *Sub.*, his hopes of success were more sanguine than wise; but he trusted to the rapid march of events, and the discordant elements by which he was surrounded, to effect the redemption of the prince from thraldom. It was a long dream—but after ten years of anxious hope, at length realized—and he had the gratification of being instrumental in snatching the family from destruction, and subsequently of raising the country to comparative prosperity.

Parbatsar and Jodhpur to his capital; but the brave nobles of Marwar, drawing the line between loyalty and patriotism, and determined that no trophy of Rathor degradation should be conveyed by the Kachhwahas from Marwar, attacked the cortège and redeemed the symbols of their disgrace. The colossal array of the invader was soon dismembered, and the 'lion of the world' (Jagat Singh), humbled and crestfallen [463], skulked from the desert retreat of his rival, indebted to a partisan corps for safety and convoy to his capital, around whose walls the wretched remnants of this ill-starred confederacy long lagged in expectation of their pay, while the bones of their horses and the ashes of their riders whitened the plain, and rendered it a Golgotha.[1]

Nawāb Amīr Khān.—By the aid of one of the most notorious villains India ever produced, the Nawab Amir Khan,[2] the pretender's party was treacherously annihilated. This man with his brigade of artillery and horse was amongst the most efficient of the foes of Raja Man; but the *auri sacra fames* not only made him desert the side on which he came for that of the Raja, but for a specific sum offer to rid him of the pretender and all his associates. Like Judas, he kissed whom he betrayed, took service with the pretender, and at the shrine of a saint of his own faith exchanged turbans with their leaders; and while the too credulous Rajput chieftains celebrated this acquisition to their party in the very sanctuary of hospitality, crowned by the dance and the song, the tents were cut down, and the victims thus enveloped, slaughtered in the midst of festivity by showers of grape.

Thus finished the under-plot; but another and more noble victim was demanded before discomfited ambition could repose, or the curtain drop on this eventful drama. Neither party

[1] I witnessed the commencement and the end of this drama, and have conversed with actors in all the intermediate scenes. In June 1806 the passes of Udaipur were forced; and in January 1808, when I passed through Jaipur in a solitary ramble, the fragments of this contest were scattered over its sandy plains.

[2] [Amīr Khān, ally of the Pindāris and ancestor of the present Nawābs of Tonk. A treaty between him and the British was signed on December 19, 1817, by which his State was recognized. He died in 1834. See his Life by Basāwan Lāl, translated by Thoby Prinsep; Malcolm, *Memoirs of Central India*, 2nd ed. ii. 325 ff.]

would relinquish his claim to the fair object of the war; and the torch of discord could be extinguished only in her blood. To the same ferocious Khan is attributed the unhallowed suggestion, as well as its compulsory execution. The scene was now changed from the desert castle of Jodha to the smiling valley of Udaipur, soon to be filled with funereal lamentation.

The Tragedy of Krishna Kunwāri.—Krishna Kunwari Bai, the 'Virgin Princess Krishna,' was in her sixteenth year: her mother was of the Chawara race, the ancient kings of Anhilwara. Sprung from the noblest blood of Hind, she added beauty of face and person to an engaging demeanour, and was justly proclaimed the 'flower of Rajasthan.' When the Roman father pierced the bosom of the dishonoured Virginia, appeased virtue applauded the deed. When Iphigenia was led to the sacrificial altar, the salvation of her country yielded a noble consolation. The votive victim of Jephthah's success had [464] the triumph of a father's fame to sustain her resignation, and in the meekness of her sufferings we have the best parallel to the sacrifice of the lovely Krishna: though years have passed since the barbarous immolation, it is never related but with a faltering tongue and moistened eyes, 'albeit unused to the melting mood.'

The rapacious and bloodthirsty Pathan, covered with infamy, repaired to Udaipur, where he was joined by the pliant and subtle Ajit. Meek in his demeanour, unostentatious in his habits; despising honours, yet covetous of power,—religion, which he followed with the zeal of an ascetic, if it did not serve as a cloak, was at least no hindrance to an immeasurable ambition, in the attainment of which he would have sacrificed all but himself. When the Pathan revealed his design, that either the princess should wed Raja Man, or by her death seal the peace of Rajwara, whatever arguments were used to point the alternative, the Rana was made to see no choice between consigning his beloved child to the Rathor prince, or witnessing the effects of a more extended dishonour from the vengeance of the Pathan, and the storm of his palace by his licentious adherents—the fiat passed that Krishna Kunwari should die.

But the deed was left for women to accomplish—the hand of man refused it. The Rawala[1] of an Eastern prince is a world within itself; it is the labyrinth containing the strings that move

[1] Harem.

the puppets which alarm mankind. Here intrigue sits enthroned, and hence its influenee radiates to the world, always at a loss to trace effects to their causes. Maharaja Daulat Singh,[1] descended four generations ago from one common ancestor with the Rana, was first sounded 'to save the honour of Udaipur'; but, horror-struck, he exclaimed, "Accursed the tongue that commands it! Dust on my allegiance, if thus to be preserved!" The Maharaja Jawandas, a natural brother, was then called upon; the dire necessity was explained, and it was urged that no common hand could be armed for the purpose. He accepted the poniard, but when in youthful loveliness Krishna appeared before him, the dagger fell from his hand, and he returned more wretched than the victim. The fatal purpose thus revealed, the shrieks of the frantic mother reverberated through the palace, as she implored mercy, or execrated the murderers of her child, who alone was resigned to her fate. But death was arrested, not averted [465]. To use the phrase of the narrator, "she was excused the steel—the cup was prepared,"—and prepared by female hands! As the messenger presented it in the name of her father, she bowed and drank it, sending up a prayer for his life and prosperity. The raving mother poured imprecations on his head, while the lovely victim, who shed not a tear, thus endeavoured to console her: "Why afflict yourself, my mother, at this shortening of the sorrows of life? I fear not to die! Am I not your daughter? Why should I fear death? We are marked out for sacrifice[2] from our birth; we scarcely enter the world but to be sent out again; let me thank my father that I have lived so long!"[3] Thus she conversed till the nauseating

[1] I knew him well—a plain honest man.

[2] Alluding to the custom of infanticide—here, very rare; indeed, almost unknown.

[3] With my mind engrossed with the scenes in which I had passed the better part of my life, I went two months after my return from Rajputana, in 1823, to York Cathedral, to attend the memorable festival of that year. The sublime recitations of Handel in 'Jephtha's Vow,' the sonorous woe of Sapio's 'Deeper and deeper still,' powerfully recalled the sad exit of the Rajputni; and the representation shortly after of Racine's tragedy of 'Iphigénie,' with Talma as Achille, Duchesnois as Clytemnestre, and a very interesting personation of the victim daughter of Agamemnon, again served to waken the remembrance of this sacrifice. The following passage, embodying not only the sentiments, but couched in the precise language in which the 'Virgin Krishna' addressed her father—proving that human

draught refused to assimilate with her blood. Again the bitter potion was prepared. She drained it off, and again it was rejected; but, as if to try the extreme of human fortitude, a third was administered; and, for the third time, Nature refused to aid the horrid purpose. It seemed as if the fabled charm, which guarded the life of the founder of her race,[1] was inherited by the Virgin Krishna. But the blood-hounds, the Pathan and Ajit, were impatient till their victim was at rest; and cruelty, as if gathering strength from defeat, made another and a fatal attempt. A powerful opiate was presented—*the kusumbha draught.*[2] She received it with a smile, wished the scene over, and drank it. The desires [466] of barbarity were accomplished. 'She slept!'[3] a sleep from which she never awoke.

The wretched mother did not long survive her child; nature was exhausted in the ravings of despair; she refused food; and her remains in a few days followed those of her daughter to the funeral pyre.

Even the ferocious Khan, when the instrument of his infamy, Ajit, reported the issue, received him with contempt, and spurned him from his presence, tauntingly asking "if this were the boasted Rajput valour?" But the wily traitor had to encounter language far more bitter from his political adversary, whom he detested. Sangram Saktawat reached the capital only four days after the catastrophe—a man in every respect the reverse of Ajit; audaciously brave, he neither feared the frown of his

---

nature was but one mode of expression for the same feelings—I am tempted to transcribe:

> . . . "Mon père,
> Cessez de vous troubler, vous n'êtes point trahi.
> Quand vous commanderez, vous serez obéi:
> Ma vie est votre bien. Vous voulez le reprendre,
> Vos ordres, sans détour, pouvaient se faire entendre;
> D'un œil aussi content, d'un cœur aussi soumis,
> Que j'acceptais l'époux que vous m'aviez promis,
> Je saurai, s'il le faut, victime obéissante
> Tendre au fer de Calchas une tête innocente;
> Et respectant le coup par vous-même ordonné,
> Vous rendre tout le sang que vous m'avez donné."

[1] Bappa Rawal.

[2] The kusumbha draught is made of flowers and herbs of a cooling quality; into this an opiate was introduced.

[3] The simple but powerful expression of the narrator.

sovereign nor the sword of his enemy. Without introduction he rushed into the presence, where he found seated the traitor Ajit. "Oh dastard! who hast thrown dust on the Sesodia race, whose blood which has flowed in purity through a hundred ages has now been defiled! this sin will check its course for ever; a blot so foul in our annals that no Sesodia[1] will ever again hold up his head! A sin to which no punishment were equal. But the end of our race is approaching! The line of Bappa Rawal is at an end! Heaven has ordained this, a signal of our destruction." The Rana hid his face with his hands, when turning to Ajit, he exclaimed, "Thou stain on the Sesodia race, thou impure of Rajput blood, dust be on thy head as thou hast covered us all with shame. May you die childless, and your name die with you![2] Why this indecent haste? Had the Pathan stormed the city? Had he attempted to violate the sanctity of the Rawala? And though he had, could you not die as Rajputs, like your ancestors? Was it thus they gained a name? Was it thus our race became renowned—thus they opposed the might of kings? Have you forgotten the Sakhas of Chitor? But whom do I address—not Rajputs? Had the honour of your females been endangered, had you sacrificed them all and rushed sword in hand on the enemy, your name would have lived, and the Almighty would have secured the seed of Bappa Rawal. But to owe preservation [467] to this unhallowed deed! You did not even await the threatened danger. Fear seems to have deprived you of every faculty, or you might have spared the blood of Sriji,[3] and if you did not scorn to owe your safety to deception, might have substituted some less noble victim! But the end of our race approaches!"

Fate of the Murderers.—The traitor to manhood, his sovereign, and humanity, durst not reply. The brave Sangram is now dead, but the prophetic anathema has been fulfilled. Of ninety-five children, sons and daughters, but one son (the brother of Krishna)[4] is left to the Rana; and though his two remaining daughters have been recently married to the princes of Jaisalmer and Bikaner, the Salic law, which is in full force in these States,

[1] The tribe of the Rana.

[2] That is, without adoption even to perpetuate it.

[3] A respectful epithet to the prince—*sire*.

[4] By the same mother.

precludes all honour through female descent. His hopes rest solely on the prince, Javana Singh,[1] and though in the flower of youth and health, the marriage bed (albeit boasting no less than four young princesses) has been blessed with no progeny.[2]

The elder brother of Javana[3] died two years ago. Had he lived he would have been Amra the Third. With regard to Ajit, the curse has been fully accomplished. Scarcely a month after, his wife and two sons were numbered with the dead; and the hoary traitor has since been wandering from shrine to shrine, performing penance and alms in expiation of his sins, yet unable to fling from him ambition; and with his beads in one hand, *Rama! Rama!* ever on his tongue, and subdued passion in his looks, his heart is deceitful as ever. Enough of him: let us exclaim with Sangram, "Dust on his head,"[4] which all the waters of the Ganges could not purify from the blood of the virgin Krishna, but

rather would the multitudinous sea incarnadine [468].

Amīr Khan rewarded by the British.—His coadjutor, Amir Khan, is now linked by treaties "in amity and unity of interests"

[1] He was nearly carried off by that awful scourge, the cholera, and, singular to remark, was the first person attacked at Udaipur. I remained by his bedside during the progress of this terrible visitation, and never shall I forget his grateful exclamation of surprise, when after a salutary sleep he opened his eyes to health. Shirji Mehta, his chief adviser and manager of his estates, merry as ever, though the heir of Mewar was given over, was seized with the complaint as his master recovered—was dead and his ashes blanching on the sands of the streamlet of Ar within twelve hours! Jovial and good-humoured as he was, "we could have better spared a better man." He was an adept in intrigue; of Ambaji's school; and till death shall extinguish the whole of this, and better morals are born, the country will but slowly improve. [Mahārāna Jawān Singh (1828–38) succeeded on the death of his father, Bhīm Singh, on March 31, 1828. He gave himself up to debauchery, and died without issue on August 30, 1838, being succeeded by his adopted son, Sardār Singh.]

[2] Since this work has gone to press, the author has been rejoiced to find that an heir has been born from the last marriage by a princess of Riwa of the Baghela tribe.

[3] See genealogical descendants of Rana Jagat Singh. Appendix, No. VIII.

[4] This was written at Udaipur in 1820. This old intriguer then attempted to renew the past, as the organ of the Chondawats, but his scheme ended in exile to the sacred city of Benares; and there he may now be seen with his rosary on the consecrated *ghat* of the Ganges.

with the sovereigns of India ; and though he has carried mourning into every house of Rajasthan, yet charity might hope forgiveness would be extended to him, could he cleanse himself from this deed of horror—'throwing this pearl away, richer than all his tribe!' His career of rapine has terminated with the caresses of the blind goddess, and placed him on a pinnacle to which his sword would never have traced the path. Enjoying the most distinguished post amongst the foreign chieftians of Holkar's State, having the regulars and park under his control, with large estates for their support, he added the epithet of traitor to his other titles, when the British Government, adopting the leading maxim of Asiatic policy, *divide et impera*, guaranteed to him the sovereignty of these districts on his abandoning the Mahrattas, disbanding his legions, and surrendering the park. But though he personally fulfilled not, nor could fulfil, one single stipulation, this man, whose services were not worth the pay of a single sepoy—who fled from his camp [1] unattended, and sought personal protection in that of the British commander—claimed and obtained the full price of our pledge, the sovereignty of about one-third of his master's dominions ; and the districts of Sironj, Tonk, Rampura, and Nimbahera, form the domain of the Nawab Amir Khan, etc., etc., etc.!! This was in the fitful fever of success, when our arms were everywhere triumphant. But were the viceroy of Hind to summon the forty tributaries [2] now covered by the aegis of British protection to a meeting, the murderer of Krishna would still occupy a place (though low) in this illustrious divan. Let us hope that his character being known, he would feel himself ill at ease ; and let us dismiss him likewise in the words of Sangram, "Dust on his head!"

The mind sickens at the contemplation of these unvarying scenes of atrocity ; but this unhappy State had yet to pass through two more lustres of aggravated sufferings (to which the author of these annals was an eye-witness) before their [469] termination, upon the alliance of Mewar with Britain. From the

[1] Brigadier-General Alexander Knox had the honour of dissolving these bands in the only way worthy of us. He marched his troops to take their guns and disperse their legions ; and, when in order of battle, the gallant General taking out his watch, gave them half an hour to reflect, their commander Jamshid, second only in villainy to his master, deeming 'discretion the better part of valour,' surrendered.

[2] There are full this number of princes holding under the British.

period of the forcing of the passes, the dismissal of the Jaipur embassy by Sindhia, and the murder of Krishna Kunwari, the embassy of Britain was in the train of the Mahratta leader, a witness of the evils described—a most painful predicament—when the hand was stretched out for succour in vain, and the British flag waved in the centre of desolation, unable to afford protection. But this day of humiliation is past, thanks to the predatory hordes who goaded us on to their destruction; although the work was incomplete, a nucleus being imprudently left in Sindhia for the scattered particles again to form.

Ruin of Mewār by the Marāthas.—In the spring of 1806, when the embassy entered the once-fertile Mewar, from whose native wealth the monuments the pencil will portray were erected, nothing but ruin met the eye—deserted towns, roofless houses, and uncultured plains. Wherever the Mahratta encamped, annihilation was ensured; it was a habit; and twenty-four hours sufficed to give to the most flourishing spot the aspect of a desert. The march of destruction was always to be traced for days afterwards by burning villages and destroyed cultivation. Some satisfaction may result from the fact, that there was scarcely an actor in these unhallowed scenes whose end was not fitted to his career. Ambaji was compelled to disgorge the spoils of Mewar, and his personal sufferings made some atonement for the ills he had inflicted upon her. This satrap, who had almost established his independence in the fortress and territory of Gwalior, suffered every indignity from Sindhia, whose authority he had almost thrown off. He was confined in a mean tent, manacled, suffered the torture of small lighted torches applied to his fingers, and even attempted suicide to avoid the surrender of his riches; but the instrument (an English penknife) was inefficient: the surgeon to the British embassy sewed up the wounds, and his coffers were eased of fifty-five lakhs of rupees! Mewar was, however, once more delivered over to him; he died shortly after. If report be correct, the residue of his treasures was possessed by his ancient ally, Zalim Singh. In this case, the old politician derived the chief advantage of the intrigues of S. 1848, without the crimes attendant on the acquisition.

Sindhia's father-in-law, when expelled that chief's camp, according to the treaty, enjoyed the ephemeral dignity of minister to the Rana, when he abstracted the most valuable records, especially those of the revenue [470].

Kumbhalmer was obtained by the minister Satidas from Jaswant Rao Bhao for seventy thousand rupees, for which assignments were given on this district, of which he retained possession. Amir Khan in A.D. 1809 led his myrmidons to the capital, threatening the demolition of the temple of Eklinga if refused a contribution of eleven lakhs of rupees. Nine were agreed to, but which by no effort could be raised, upon which the Rana's envoys were treated with indignity, and Kishandas [1] wounded. The passes were forced, Amir Khan entering by Debari, and his coadjutor and son-in-law, the notorious Jamshid, by the Chirwa, which made but a feeble resistance. The ruffian Pathans were billeted on the city, subjecting the Rana to personal humiliation, and Jamshid [2] left with his licentious Rohillas in the capital. The traces of their barbarity are to be seen in its ruins. No woman could safely venture abroad, and a decent garment or turban was sufficient to attract their cupidity.

Bāpu Sindhia Sūbahdār of Mewār.—In S. 1867 (A.D. 1811) Bapu Sindhia arrived with the title of Subahdar, and encamped in the valley, and from this to 1814 these vampires, representing Sindhia and Amir Khan, possessed themselves of the entire fiscal domain, with many of the fiefs, occasionally disputing for the spoils ; to prevent which they came to a conference at the Dhaula Magra (the white hill), attended by a deputation [3] from the Rana, when the line of demarcation was drawn between the spoilers. A schedule was formed of the towns and villages yet inhabited, the amount to be levied from each specified, and three and a half lakhs adjudged to Jamshid, with the same sum to Sindhia ; but this treaty was not better kept than the former ones. Mewar was rapidly approaching dissolution, and every

[1] This veteran attended me during all these troubles, as the medium of communication with the Rana. Though leagued with the Chondawats, he was a loyal subject and good servant. I saw him expire, and was of opinion, as well as the doctor who accompanied me, that his death was caused by poison. The general burst of sorrow from hundreds collected around his house, when the event was announced, is the best encomium on his public character.

[2] This monstrous villain (for he was a Goliath) died soon after Mewar was rescued, from a cancer in his back.

[3] Satidas, Kishandas, and Rup Ram.

sign of civilization fast disappearing; fields laid waste, cities in ruins, inhabitants exiled, chieftains demoralized, the prince and his family destitute of common comforts. Yet had Sindhia the audacity to demand compensation for the loss of his tribute stipulated to Bapu Sindhia [471],[1] who rendered Mewar a desert, carrying her chiefs, her merchants, her farmers, into captivity and fetters in the dungeons of Ajmer, where many died for want of ransom, and others languished till the treaty with the British, in A.D. 1817, set them free.

CHAPTER 18

Degraded Condition of the Rājputs.—The history of the Rana's family has now been traced through all the vicissitudes of its fortunes, from the second to the nineteenth century, whilst contending for existence, alternately with Parthians, Bhils, Tartars, and Mahrattas, till at length it has become tributary to Britain. The last chapter portrays the degraded condition of their princes, and the utter desolation of their country, in a picture which embodied the entire Rajput race. An era of repose at length dawned upon them. The destruction of that vast predatory system, under the weight of which the prosperity of these regions had so long been repressed, was effected by one short campaign in 1817; which if less brilliant than that of 1803, is inferior to none in political results. The tardy policy of the last-named period, at length accomplished, placed the power of Britain in the East on an expugnable position, and rescued the Rajputs from a progressing destruction.

Alliances with the British.—To prevent the recurrence of this predatory system it was deemed politic to unite all these settled States, alike interested with ourselves in its overthrow, in one grand confederation. Accordingly the Rajput States were

[1] Bapu Sindhia shortly outlived his expulsion from Ajmer, and as he had to pass through Mewar in his passage to his future residence, he was hooted by the population he had plundered. While I was attending the Rana's court, some one reporting Bapu Sindhia's arrival at his destination, mentioned that some pieces of ordnance formerly taken from Udaipur had, after saluting him, exuded a quantity of water, which was received with the utmost gravity by the court, until I remarked they were crying because they should never again be employed in plunder: an idea which caused a little mirth.

invited to shelter [472] under our protecting alliance; and with one exception (Jaipur), they eagerly embraced the invitation. The ambassadors of the various governments followed each other in quick succession to Delhi, where the treaties were to be negotiated, and in a few weeks all Rajputana was united to Britain by compacts of one uniform character;[1] insuring to them external protection with internal independence, as the price of acknowledged supremacy, and a portion of revenue to the protecting government. By this comprehensive arrangement, we placed a most powerful barrier between our territories and the strong natural frontier of India; and so long as we shall respect their established usages, and by contributing to the prosperity of the people preserve our motives from distrust, it will be a barrier impenetrable to invasion.

Treaty with Mewār.—Of all the princes who obtained succour at this momentous crisis in the political history of India, none stood more in need of it than the Rana of Udaipur. On January 16, 1818, the treaty was signed, and in February an envoy was nominated; who immediately proceeded to the Rana's court, to superintend and maintain the newly formed relations.[2] The right wing of the grand army[3] had already preceded him to compel the surrender of such territory as was unjustly held by the lawless partisans of Sindhia, and to reduce to obedience the refractory nobles, to whom anarchy was endeared from long familiarity. The strongholds in the plains as Raepur, Rajnagar, etc., soon surrendered; and the payment of the arrears of the garrison of Kumbhalmer put this important fortress in our possession.

In his passage from Jahazpur, which guards the range on the east to Kumbhalmer on the Aravalli west, a space of 140 miles, the limits of Mewar, only two thinly peopled towns were seen

[1] See Appendix, No. VIII., for treaty with the Rana.

[2] Commanded by Major-General Sir R. Donkin, K.C.B.

[3] The author had the honour to be selected by the Marquess of Hastings to represent him at the Rana's court, with the title of 'Political Agent to the Western Rajput States.' During the campaign of 1817–18 he was placed as the point of communication to the various divisions of the northern army; at the same time being intrusted with the negotiations with Holkar (previous to the rupture), and with those of Kotah and Bundi. He concluded the treaty with the latter State *en route* to Udaipur, where, as at the latter, there were only the benefits of moral and political existence to confer.

which acknowledged the Rana's authority. All was desolate; even the traces of the footsteps of man were effaced. The babul (*mimosa* [*acacia*] *Arabica*), and gigantic reed, which harboured the boar and the tiger, grew upon the highways; and every rising ground displayed a mass of ruin. Bhilwara, the commercial *entrepôt* of Rajputana, which ten years before contained six thousand [473] families, showed not a vestige of existence. All was silent in her streets—no living thing was seen except a solitary dog, that fled in dismay from his lurking-place in the temple, scared at the unaccustomed sight of man.[1]

Cession of Kumbhalmer.—An envoy was dispatched by the Rana to congratulate the Agent, who joined him in the British camp at Nathdwara; and while he returned to arrange the formalities of reception, the Agent obtained the cession of Kumbhalmer; which, with the acquisitions before mentioned, paved the way for a joyful reception. The prince, Javan Singh, with all the State insignia, and a numerous cortège, advanced to receive the mission, and conduct it to the capital. A spot was fixed on in a grove of palmyras, about two miles from the city, where carpets were spread, and where the prince received the Agent and suite in a manner at once courteous and dignified.[2] Of him it might have been said, in the language applied by Jahangir to the son of Rana Amra—"His countenance carried the impression of his illustrious extraction."

Arrival of the Author as Agent.—We entered the city [3] by the gate of the sun; and through a vista of ruin the mission was inducted into its future residence, once the abode of the fair Rampiyari.[4] Like all the mansions of Rajputana, it was a quadrangular pile, with an open paved area, the suites of apartments carried round the sides, with latticed or open corridors

[1] The author had passed through Bhilwara in May 1806, when it was comparatively flourishing. On this occasion (Feb. 1818) it was entirely deserted. It excited a smile, in the midst of regrets, to observe the practical wit of some of the soldiers, who had supplied the naked representative of Adinath with an apron—not of leaves, but scarlet cloth.

[2] The Agent had seen him when a boy, at a meeting already described; but he could scarcely have hoped to find in one, to the formation of whose character the times had been so unfavourable, such a specimen as this descendant of Partap.

[3] A description of the city and valley will be more appropriate elsewhere.

[4] See p. 508.

extending parallel to each suite. Another deputation with the *mehmani*, consisting of a hundred trays of sweetmeats, dried fruits, and a purse of one thousand rupees for distribution amongst the domestics, brought the Rana's welcome upon our arrival in his capital, and fixed the next day for our introduction at court.

At four in the afternoon, a deputation, consisting of the officiating prime minister, the representative of the Chondawats, with mace-bearers and a numerous escort, came to announce the Rana's readiness to receive the mission; which, with all the 'pomp and circumstance' peculiar to these countries, was marshalled in front of the residency, thronged by crowds of well-dressed [474] inhabitants, silently gazing at the unusual sight.[1] The grand Nakkaras having announced the Rana in court, the mission proceeded through streets which everywhere presented marks of rapine, hailed by the most enthusiastic greetings. "Jai! jai! Farangi ka Raj!" "Victory, victory to the English Government!" resounded from every tongue. The bards were not idle; and the unpoetic name of the Agent was hitched into rhyme. Groups of musicians were posted here and there, who gave a passing specimen of the *tappas*[2] of Mewar; and not a few of the fair, with brazen ewers of water on their heads, welcomed us with the *suhelia*, or songs of joy. Into each of these vessels the purse-bearer dropped a piece of silver; for neither the songs of the suhelia, the tappas of the minstrel, nor encomiastic stave of the bard, are to be received without some acknowledgement that you appreciate their merit and talents, however you may doubt the value they put upon your own. As we ascended the main street leading to the Tripolia, or triple portal, which guards the sacred enclosure, dense masses of people obstructed our progress, and even the walls of the temple of Jagannath were crowded. According to etiquette, we dismounted at the Porte, and proceeded on foot across the ample terrace; on which were drawn up a few elephants and horse, exercising for the Rana's amusement.

The Palace at Udaipur.—The palace is a most imposing pile,

[1] The escort consisted of two companies of foot, each of one hundred men, with half a troop of cavalry. The gentlemen attached to the mission were Captain Waugh (who was secretary and commandant of the escort), with Lieutenant Carey as his subaltern. Dr. Duncan was the medical officer.

[2] [Modes in music.]

of a regular form, built of granite and marble, rising at least a hundred feet from the ground, and flanked with octagonal towers, crowned with cupolas. Although built at various periods, uniformity of design has been very well preserved; nor is there in the East a more striking or majestic structure. It stands upon the very crest of a ridge running parallel to, but considerably elevated above, the margin of the lake. The terrace, which is at the east and chief front of the palace, extends throughout its length, and is supported by a triple row of arches from the declivity of the ridge. The height of this arcaded wall is fully fifty feet; and although all is hollow beneath, yet so admirably is it constructed, that an entire range of stables is built on the extreme verge of the terrace, on which the whole personal force of the Rana, elephants, horse, and foot, are often assembled. From this terrace the city and the valley lay before the spectator, whose vision is bounded only by the [475] hills shutting out the plains; while from the summit of the palace nothing obstructs its range over lake and mountain.

A band of Sindis guarded the first entrance to the palace; and being Saturday, the Saktawats were on duty in the great hall of assembly. Through lines of Rajputs we proceeded till we came to the marble staircase, the steps of which had taken the form of the segment of an ellipse, from the constant friction of the foot; an image of Ganesha guarded the ascent to the interior of the palace, and the apartment, or landing, is called Ganesha deori, from the Rajput Janus. After proceeding through a suite of saloons, each filled with spectators, the herald's voice announced to 'the lord of the world' that the English envoy was in his presence; on which he arose, and advanced a few paces in front of the throne, the chieftains standing to receive the mission. Everything being ruled by precedent, the seat allotted for the envoy was immediately in front and touching the royal cushion (*gaddi*): being that assigned to the Peshwa in the height of Mahratta prosperity, the arrangement, which was a subject of regular negotiation, could not be objected to. The apartment chosen for the initiatory visit was the Surya mahall, or 'hall of the sun,' so called from a medallion of the orb in basso-rilievo which decorates the wall. Close thereto is placed the Rana's throne, above which, supported by slender silver columns, rises a velvet canopy. The Gaddi, or throne, in the East is but a huge cushion, over which is thrown an embroidered velvet mantle. The chiefs of the higher grade, or 'the Sixteen,' were seated, according to their rank, on the right and left of the Rana; next and below these were the princes Amra and Javan Singh; and at right angles (by which the court formed three sides of a square), the chiefs of the second rank. The civil officers of the State were near the Rana in front, and the seneschal, butler, keeper of the wardrobe, and other confidential officers and inferior chieftains, formed a group standing on the extreme edge of the carpet.

The Rana's congratulations were hearty and sincere: in a few powerful expressions he depicted the miseries he had experienced, the fallen condition of his State, and the gratitude he felt to the British Government which had interposed between him and destruction; and which for the first moment of his existence allowed him to sleep in peace. There was an intense earnestness in every word he uttered, which, delivered with great fluency of speech and dignity of manner, inspired deep respect and sympathy. The Agent said that the Governor-General was no stranger to the [476] history of his illustrious family, or to his own immediate sufferings; and that it was his earnest desire to promote, by every means in his power, the Rana's personal dignity and the prosperity of his dominions. After conversing a few minutes, the interview was closed with presents to the Agent and suite: to the former a caparisoned elephant and horse, jewelled aigrette, and pearl necklace, with shawls and brocades; and with the customary presentation of essence of rose and the pan leaf the Rana and court rising, the envoy made his salaam and retired. In a short time the Rana, attended by his second son, ministers, and a select number of the chiefs, honoured the envoy with a visit. The latter advanced beyond his residence to meet the prince, who was received with presented arms by the guard, the officers saluting, and conducted to his throne, which had been previously arranged. Conversation was now unrestrained, and questions were demanded regarding everything which appeared unusual. After sitting half an hour, the Agent presented the Rana with an elephant and two horses, caparisoned with silver and gilt ornaments and velvet embroidered housings, with twenty-one shields [1] of shawls, brocades, muslins, and jewels; to prince Amra, unable from sickness to attend his father, a horse and

[1] The buckler is the tray in which gifts are presented by the Rajputs.

eleven shields; and to his brother, the second prince, Javan Singh, a horse and nine shields; to the ministers and chiefs according to rank: the whole entertainment costing about 20,000 rupees, or £2000. Amidst these ceremonials, receiving and returning visits of the Rana, his chiefs, his ministers, and men of influence and information commercial and agricultural, some weeks passed in silent observation, and in the acquisition of materials for action.[1]

Political Divisions of Mewār.—For the better comprehension of the internal relations, past and present, of Mewar [477], a sketch is presented, showing the political divisions of the tribes and the fiscal domain, from which a better idea may be formed of Rajput feudal economy than from a chapter of dissertation. The princes of Mewar skilfully availed themselves of their natural advantages in the partition of the country. The mountain-barriers east and west were allotted to the chiefs to keep the mountaineers and foresters in subjection, whose leading passes

[1] If we dare compare the moral economy of an entire people to the physical economy of the individual, we should liken this period in the history of Mewar to intermittent pulsation of the heart—a pause in moral as in physical existence; a consciousness thereof, inertly awaiting the propelling power to restore healthful action to a state of languid repose; or what the Rajput would better comprehend, his own condition when the opiate stimulant begins to dissipate, and mind and body are alike abandoned to helpless imbecility. Who has lived out of the circle of mere vegetation, and not experienced this temporary deprivation of moral vitality? for no other simile would suit the painful pause in the sympathies of the inhabitants of this once fertile region, where experience could point out but one page in their annals, one period in their history, when the clangour of the war trumpet was suspended, or the sword shut up in its scabbard. The portals of Janus at Rome were closed but twice in a period of seven hundred years; and in exactly the same time from the conquest by Shihabu-d-din to the great pacification, but twice can we record peace in Mewar—the reign of Numa has its type in Shah Jahan, while the more appropriate reign of Augustus belongs to Britain. Are we to wonder then that a chilling void now occupied (if the solecism is admissible) the place of interminable action? when the mind was released from the anxiety of daily, hourly, devising schemes of preservation, to one of perfect security—that enervating calm, in which, to use their own homely phrase, *Bher aur bakri ekhi thali se piye*, 'The wolf and the goat drank from the same vessel.' [Another, and more usual form is—*Āj kal, sher bakrī ek ghāt pāni pitē hain*, 'Nowadays the tiger and the goat drink from the same stream.'] But this unruffled torpidity had its limit: the Agrarian laws of Mewar were but mentioned, and the national pulse instantly rose.

were held by a lord-marcher, and the quotas of his quarter; and while strong forts guarded the exposed northern and southern entrances, the crown-land lay in the centre, the safest and the richest. The exterior, thus guarded by a cordon of feudal levies composed of the quotas of the greater fiefs; the minor and most numerous class of vassals, termed *gol,* literally 'the mass,' and consisting of ten thousand horse, each holding directly of the crown independent of the greater chiefs, formed its best security against both external aggression and internal commotions.

Desolation of Mewâr.—Such is a picture of the feudal economy of Mewar in the days of her renown; but so much had it been defaced through time and accident, that with difficulty could the lineaments be traced with a view to their restoration: her institutions a dead letter, the prince's authority despised, the nobles demoralized and rebellious, internal commerce abandoned, and the peasantry destroyed by the combined operation of war, pestilence, and exile. Expression might be racked for phrases which could adequately delineate the miseries all classes had endured. It is impossible to give more than a sketch of the state of the *das sahas Mewar*, 'the ten thousand townships' which once acknowledged her princes, and of which above three thousand still exist. All that remained to them was the valley of the capital; and though Chitor and Mandalgarh were maintained by the fidelity of the Rana's servants, their precarious revenues scarcely sufficed to maintain their garrisons. The Rana was mainly indebted to Zalim Singh of Kotah for the means of subsistence; for in the struggle for existence his chiefs thought only of themselves, of defending their own estates, or buying off their foes; while those who had succumbed took to horse, scoured the country, and plundered without distinction. Inferior clanships declared themselves independent of their superiors, who in their turn usurped the crown domain, or by bribing the necessities of their prince, obtained his patent for lands, to which, as they yielded him nothing, he became indifferent. The crown-tenants purchased of these chiefs the protection (*rakhwali*) which the [478] Rana could not grant, and made alienations of the crown taxes, besides private rights of the community, which were often extorted at the point of the lance. Feuds multiplied, and the name of each clan became the watchword of alarm or defiance to its neighbour: castles were assaulted, and their inmates, as at Sheogarh and Lawa, put to the sword; the Meras and Bhils descended from their hills, or emerged from their forests, and planted ambuscades for the traveller or merchant, whom they robbed or carried to their retreats, where they languished in durance till ransomed. Marriage processions were thus intercepted, and the honeymoon was passed on a cliff of the Aravalli, or in the forests on the Mahi. The Rajput, whose moral energies were blunted, scrupled not to associate and to divide the spoil with these lawless tribes, of whom it might be said, as of the children of Ishmael, "Their hands were against every man, and every man's hand against them." Yet notwithstanding such entire disorganization of society, external commerce was not stagnant; and in the midst of this rapine, the produce of Europe and Kashmir would pass each other in transit through Mewar, loaded it is true by a multiplicity of exactions, but guarded by those who scorned all law but the point of honour, which they were paid for preserving.

The Condition of Udaipur.—The capital will serve as a specimen of the country. Udaipur, which formerly reckoned fifty thousand houses within the walls, had not now three thousand occupied, the rest were in ruin, the rafters being taken for firewood. The realization of the spring harvest of 1818, from the entire fiscal land, was about £4000! Grain sold for seven sers the rupee, though thrice the quantity was procurable within the distance of eighty miles. Insurance from the capital to Nathdwara (twenty-five miles) was eight per cent. The Kotharia chief, whose ancestors are immortalized for fidelity, had not a horse to conduct him to his prince's presence, though his estates were of fifty thousand rupees annual value. All were in ruins; and the Rana, the descendant of those patriot Rajputs who opposed Babur, Akbar, and Aurangzeb, in the days of Mogul splendour, had not fifty horse to attend him, and was indebted for all the comforts he possessed to the liberality of Kotah.

Reorganization of the State.—Such was the chaos from which order was to be evoked. But the elements of prosperity, though scattered, were not extinct; and recollections of the past, deeply engraved in the national mind, became available to reanimate their moral and physical existence. To call these forth demanded only the exertion of moral [479] interference, and every other was rejected. The lawless freebooter, and even the savage Bhil, felt awed at the agency of a power never seen. To him moral opinion (compared with which the strength of armies is nought) was inexplicable, and he substituted in its stead another invisible power—that of magic: and the belief was current throughout the intricate region of the West, that a single individual could carry an army in his pocket, and that our power could animate slips of paper cut into the figures of armed men, from which no precaution could guard their retreats. Accordingly, at the mere name of the British power, rapine ceased, and the inhabitants of the wilds of the West, the 'forest lords,' who had hitherto laughed at subjection, to the number of seven hundred villages, put each the sign of the dagger to a treaty, promising abstinence from plunder and a return to industrious life—a single individual of no rank the negotiator. Moreover, the treaty was religiously kept for twelve months; when the peace was broken, not by them, but against them.

To the Rajput, the moral spectacle of a Peshwa marched into exile with all the quietude of a pilgrimage, effected more than twenty thousand bayonets, and no other auxiliary was required than the judicious use of the impressions from this and other passing events, to relay the foundations of order and prosperity—by never doubting the issue, success was insured. The British force, therefore, after the reduction of the plans enumerated, was marched to cantonments; the rest was left for time and reason to accomplish.

Form of Civil Government.—Before proceeding further, it may be convenient to sketch the form of civil government in Mewar, and the characters of its most conspicuous members: the former we shall describe as it was when the machine was in regular action; it will be found simple, and perfectly suited to its object.

There are four grand officers of the government:

1. The Pardhan, or prime minister.
2. Bakhshi, commander of the forces.
3. Suratnama, keeper of the records.
4. Sahai, keeper of the signet.[1]

The first, the Pardhan, or civil premier, must be of the non-

[1] Or rather, who makes the monogrammatic signet *Sahi* ('correct') to all deeds, grants, etc.

militant tribe. The whole of the territorial and financial arrangements are vested in him. He [480] nominates the civil governors of districts, and the collectors of the revenue and custom ; and has fourteen *thuas*, or departments, under him, which embrace all that relates to expenditure.

2. The Bakhshi must also be of a non-militant tribe, and one different from the Pardhan. His duties are mixed civil and military. He takes the musters, and pays mercenaries, or rations, to the feudal tenants when on extra service, and he appoints a deputy to accompany all expeditions, or to head frontier-posts, with the title of Faujdar, or commander. The royal insignia, the standard, and kettle-drums accompany him, and the highest nobles assemble under the general control of this civil officer, never under one of their own body. From the Bakhshi's bureau all patents are issued, as also all letters of sequestration of feudal land.

The Bakhshi has four secretaries :

1. Draws out deeds.
2. Accountant.
3. Recorder of all patents or grants.
4. Keeps duplicates.

3. The Suratnama [1] is the auditor and recorder of all the household expenditure and establishments, which are paid by his cheques. He has four assistants also, who make a daily report, and give a daily balance of accounts.

4. The Sahai. He is secretary both for home and foreign correspondence. He draws out the royal grants or patents of estates, and superintends the deeds of grant on copper-plate to religious establishments. Since the privilege appertaining to Salumbar, of confirming all royal grants with his signet the lance, has fallen into desuetude, the Sahai executes this military autograph.[2]

To all decrees, from the daily stipend to the *patta*, or patent of an estate, each minister must append his seal, so that there is a complete system of check. Besides these, the higher officers of government, there are thirty-six *karkhanas*, or inferior officers,

[1] [Properly Sūratnavīs, 'statement-writer.']

[2] The Salumbar chief had his deputy, who resided at court for this sole duty, for which he held a village. See p. 235.

appointed directly by the Rana, the most conspicuous of which are the justiciary,[1] the keepers of the register-office, of the mint, of the armoury, of the regalia, of the jewels, of the wardrobe, of the stables, of the kitchen, of the band, of the seneschalsy, and of the seraglio.

There was no want of aspirants to office, here hereditary; but it was vain to look [481] amongst the descendants of the virtuous Pancholi, or the severe Amrachand, and the prediction of the former, "Dust will cover the head of Mewar when virtue wanders in rags," was strictly fulfilled. There appeared no talent, no influence, no honesty; yet the deficiency was calculated to excite sorrow rather than surprise; to stimulate exertion on their behalf, rather than damp the hope of improvement; though all scope for action, save in the field of intrigue, was lost, and talent was dormant for want of exercise.

Incapacity of the Rāna.—The Rana's character was little calculated to supply his minister's deficiencies. Though perfectly versed in the past history of his country, its resources, and their management; though able, wise, and amiable, his talents were nullified by numerous weak points. Vain shows, frivolous amusements, and an ill-regulated liberality alone occupied him; and so long as he could gratify these propensities, he trusted complacently to the exertions of others for the restoration of order and his proper authority. He had little steadiness of purpose, and was particularly obnoxious to female influence. It is scarcely to be wondered that he coveted repose, and was little desirous to disturb the only moment his existence had presented of enjoying it, by inviting the turmoils of business. No man, however, was more capable of advising: his judgment was good, but he seldom followed its dictates; in short, he was an adept in theory, and a novice in practice. The only man about the court at once of integrity and efficiency was Kishandas, who had long acted as ambassador, and to whose assiduity the sovereign and the country owed much; but his services were soon cut off by death.

Such were the materials with which the work of reform commenced. The aim was to bring back matters to a correspondence with an era of their history, when the rights of the prince, the

[1] Niyao, Daftar, Taksala, Silah, Gaddi, Gahna, Kapra-bandar, Ghora, Rasora, Nakkar-khana, Jaleb, Rawala.

vassal, and the cultivator, were alike well defined—that of Amra Singh.

Relations of the Rāna with his Nobles.—The first point to effect was the recognition of the prince's authority by his nobles; the surest sign of which was their presence at the capital, where some had never been, and others only when it suited their convenience or their views. In a few weeks the Rana saw himself surrounded by a court such as had not been known for half a century. It created no small curiosity to learn by what secret power they were brought into each other's presence. Even the lawless Hamira, who but a short while before had plundered the marriage dower of the Hari queen [482] coming from Kotah, and the chief of the Sangawat clan, who had sworn "he might bend his head to woman, but never to his sovereign," left their castles of Badesar and Deogarh, and "placing the royal rescript on their heads," hastened to his presence; and in a few weeks the whole feudal association of Mewar was embodied in the capital.

Return of the Exiles.—To recall the exiled population was a measure simultaneous with the assembling of the nobles; but this was a work requiring time: they had formed ties, and incurred obligations to the societies which had sheltered them, which could not at once be disengaged or annulled. But wherever a subject of Mewar existed, proclamations penetrated, and satisfactory assurances were obtained, and realized to an extent which belied in the strongest manner the assertion that patriotism is unknown to the natives of Hindustan.' The most enthusiastic and cheering proofs were afforded that neither oppression from without, nor tyranny within, could expel the feeling for the *bapota*, the land of their fathers. Even now, though time has chastened the impressions, we should fear to pen but a tithe of the proofs of devotion of the husbandman of Mewar to the *solum natale*: it would be deemed romance by those who never contemplated humanity in its reflux from misery and despair to the 'sweet influences' of hope; he alone who had witnessed the day of trouble, and beheld the progress of desolation—the standing corn grazed by Mahratta horse—the rifled towns devoted to the flames—the cattle driven to the camp, and the chief men seized as hostages for money never to be realized—could appreciate their deliverance. To be permitted to see these evils banished, to behold the survivors of oppression congregated from the most distant provinces, many of them strangers to each other, and the aged and the helpless awaiting the lucky day to take possession of their ruined abodes, was a sight which memory will not part with. Thus on the 3rd of Sawan (July),[1] a favourite day with the husbandman, three hundred of all conditions, with their waggons and implements of labour, and preceded by banners and music, marched into Kapasan;[2] and Ganesha was once again invoked as they reconsecrated their dwellings, and placed his portrait as the Janus of the portals. On the same day, and within eight months subsequent to the signature of the treaty, above three hundred towns and villages were simultaneously reinhabited; and the land, which for many years had been a stranger to the plough-share, was broken up. Well might [483] the superstitious fancy that miracles were abroad; for even to those who beheld the work in progression it had a magical result, to see the waste covered with habitations, and the verdant corn growing in the fields where lately they had roused the boar from his retreat! It was a day of pride for Britain! By such exertions of her power in these distant lands her sway is hallowed. By Britain alone can this fair picture be defaced; the tranquillity and independence she has conferred, by her alone may be disturbed!

Attraction of Capital.—To these important preliminary measures, the assembly of the nobles and recall of the population, was added a third, without which the former would have been nugatory. There was no wealth, no capital, to aid their patriotism and industry. Foreign merchants and bankers had abandoned the devoted land; and those who belonged to it partook of her poverty and her shame. Money was scarce, and want of faith and credit had increased the usury on loans to a ruinous extent. The Rana borrowed at thirty-six per cent; besides twenty-five to forty per cent discount for his *barats*, or patents empowering collection on the land; a system pursued for some time even after his restoration to authority. His profusion exceeded even the rapidity of renovation; and the husbandman had scarcely broken up his long-waste fields, when a call was made by the harpies of the State for an advance on their produce, while he himself had been compelled to borrow at a like ruinous rate for

[1] [Sāwan sudi tij, third of the bright half of the month Sāwan (July to August), a festival celebrated throughout North India.]

[2] [About 45 miles north of Udaipur city.]

seed and the means of support, to be paid by expectations. To have hoped for the revival of prosperity amidst such destitution, moral and pecuniary, would have been visionary. It was as necessary to improve the one as to find the other; for poverty and virtue do not long associate, and certainly not in Mewar. Proclamations were therefore prepared by the Rana, inviting foreign merchants and bankers to establish connexions in the chief towns throughout the country; but as in the days of demoralization little faith was placed in the words of princes, similar ones were prepared by the Agent, guaranteeing the stipulations, and both were distributed to every commercial city in India. The result was as had been foreseen: branch banks were everywhere formed, and mercantile agents fixed in every town in the country, whose operations were only limited by the slow growth of moral improvement. The shackles which bound external commerce were at once removed, and the multifarious posts for the collections of transit duties abolished; in lieu of which chain of stations, all levies on goods in transit were confined to the frontiers. The scale of duties [484] was revised; and by the abolition of intermediate posts, they underwent a reduction of from thirty to fifty per cent. By this system, which could not for some time be comprehended, the transit and custom duties of Mewar made the most certain part of the revenue, and in a few years exceeded in amount what had ever been known.

Trade at Bhīlwāra.—The chief commercial mart, Bhilwara, which showed not a vestige of humanity, rapidly rose from ruin, and in a few months contained twelve hundred houses, half of which were occupied by foreign merchants. Bales of goods, the produce of the most distant lands, were piled up in the streets lately overgrown with grass, and a weekly fair was established for the home manufactures. A charter of privileges and immunities was issued, exempting them from all taxation for the first year, and graduating the scale for the future; calculated with the same regard to improvement, by giving the mind the full range of enjoying the reward of its exertions. The right of electing their own chief magistrates and the assessors of justice, was above all things indispensable, so as to render them as independent as possible of the needy servants of the court. A guard was provided by the government for their protection, and a competent authority nominated to see that the full extent of their privileges, and the utmost freedom of action, were religiously maintained. The entire success of this plan may at once be recorded to prevent repetition. In 1822, Bhilwara contained nearly three thousand dwellings, which were chiefly inhabited by merchants, bankers, or artisans. An entire new street had been constructed in the centre of the town, from the duties levied, and the shops and houses were rented at a moderate rate; while many were given up to the proprietors of their sites, returning from exile, on their paying the price of construction. But as there is no happiness without alloy, so even this pleasing picture had its dark shades to chasten the too sanguine expectation of imparting happiness to all. Instead of a generous emulation, a jealous competition checked the prosperity of Bhilwara: the base spirit of exclusive monopoly desired a distinction between the native and the stranger-merchant, for which they had a precedent in the latter paying an addition to the town-duty of metage (*mapa*). The unreasonableness of this was discussed, and it was shown to be more consonant to justice that he who came from Jaisalmer, Surat, Benares, or Delhi, should pay less than the merchant whose domicile was on the spot. When at length the parties acquiesced in this opinion, and were intreated and promised to know [485] none other distinction than that of 'inhabitant of Bhilwara,' sectarian differences, which there was less hope of reconciling, became the cause of disunion. All the Hindu merchants belong either to the Vaishnava or Jain sects; consequently each had a representative head, and 'the Five' for the adjudication of their internal arrangements; and these, the wise men of both parties, formed the general council for the affairs of Bhilwara. But they carried their religious differences to the judgement-seat, where each desired pre-eminence. Whether the point in dispute hinged on the interpretation of law, which with all these sects is of divine origin, or whether the mammon of unrighteousness was the lurking cause of their bickerings, they assuredly did much harm, for their appeals brought into play what of all things was least desired, the intrigues of the profligate dependents of the court. It will be seen hereafter,[1] in visits to Bhilwara, how these disputes were in some degree calmed. The leaders on both sides were distinctly given to understand they would be made to leave the place. Self-interest prevented this extremity; but from the

[1] In the Personal Narrative.

withdrawing of that active interference (which the state of the alliance did not indeed warrant, but which humanity interposed for their benefit) together with the effect of appeals to the court, it is to be apprehended that Bhilwara may fail to become what it was intended to be, the chief commercial mart of Central India.[1]

Reform of the Nobility.—Of the three measures simultaneously projected and pursued for the restoration of prosperity, the industrious portion has been described. The feudal interest remains, which was found the most difficult to arrange. The agricultural and commercial classes required only protection and stimulus, and we could repay the benefits their industry conferred by the lowest scale of taxation, which, though in fact equally beneficial to the government, was constructed as a boon. But with the feudal lords there was no such equivalent to offer in return for the sacrifices many had to make for the re-establishment of society. Those who were well inclined, like Kotharia, had everything to gain, and nothing left to surrender; while those who, like Deogarh, Salumbar, or Badnor, had preserved their power by foreign aid, intrigue, or prowess, dreaded the high price they might be called upon to pay [486] for the benefit of security which the new alliance conferred. All dreaded the word 'restitution,' and the audit of half a century's political accounts; yet the adjustment of these was the corner-stone of the edifice, which anarchy and oppression had dismantled. Feuds were to be appeased, a difficult and hazardous task; and usurpations, both on the crown and each other, to be redeemed. 'To bring the wolf and the goat to drink from the same vessel,' was a task of less difficulty than to make the Chondawat and Saktawat labour in concert for the welfare of the prince and the country. In fine, a better idea cannot be afforded of what was deemed the hopeless-

[1] Although Bhilwara has not attained that high prosperity my enthusiasm anticipated, yet the philanthropic Heber records that in 1825 (three years after I had left the country) it exhibited "a greater appearance of trade, industry, and moderate but widely diffused wealth and comfort, than he had witnessed since he left Dehli" [Diary, ed. 1861, ii. 56 f.]. The record of the sentiments of the inhabitants towards me, as conveyed by the bishop, was gratifying, though their expression could excite no surprise in any one acquainted with the characters and sensibilities of these people. [The author's anticipation of the prosperity of this town have not been completely realized; but it is still an important centre of trade, noted for the manufacture of cooking utensils, and possessing a ginning factory and a cotton-press (Erskine ii. A. 97 f.).]

ness of success than the opinion of Zorawar Singh, the chief of the latter clan, who had much to relinquish : " Were Parameswara (the Almighty) to descend, he could not reform Mewar." We judged better of them than they did of each other.

Negotiations with the Chiefs.—It were superfluous to detail all the preparatory measures for the accomplishment of this grand object ; the meetings and adjournments, which only served to keep alive discontent. On the 27th of April, the treaty with the British Government was read, and the consequent change in their relations explained. Meanwhile, a charter, defining the respective rights of the crown and of the chiefs, with their duties to the community, was prepared, and a day named for a general assembly of the chieftains to sanction and ratify this engagement. The 1st of May was fixed : the chiefs assembled ; the articles, ten in number, were read and warmly discussed ; when with unmeaning expressions of duty, and objections to the least prominent, they obtained through their speaker, Gokuldas of Deogarh, permission to reassemble at his house to consider them, and broke up with the promise to attend next day. The delay, as apprehended, only generated opposition, and the 2nd and 3rd passed in inter-communications of individual hope and fear. It was important to put an end to speculation. At noon, on the 4th of May, the grand hall was again filled, when the Rana, with his sons and ministers, took their seats. Once more the articles were read, objections raised and combated, and midnight had arrived without the object of the meeting being advanced, when an adjournment, proposed by Gokuldas, till the arrival of the Rana's plenipotentiary from Delhi, met with a firm denial ; and the Rana gave him liberty to retire, if he refused his testimony of loyalty. The Begun chief, who had much to gain, at length set the example, followed by the chiefs of Amet and Deogarh, and in succession by all the sixteen nobles, who also signed as the proxies of their [487] relatives, unable from sickness to attend. The most powerful of the second grade also signed for themselves and the absent of their clans, each, as he gave in his adhesion, retiring ; and it was three in the morning of the 5th of May ere the ceremony was over. The chief of the Saktawats, determined to be conspicuous, was the last of his own class to sign. During this lengthened and painful discussion of fifteen hours' continuance, the Rana conducted himself with such judgment and firmness, as to give

sanguine hopes of his taking the lead in the settlement of his affairs.

Enforcement of the Treaty.—This preliminary adjusted, it was important that the stipulations of the treaty [1] should be rigidly if not rapidly effected. It will not be a matter of surprise, that some months passed away before the complicated arrangements arising out of this settlement were completed; but it may afford just grounds for gratulation, that they were finally accomplished without a shot being fired, or the exhibition of a single British soldier in the country, nor, indeed, within one hundred miles of Udaipur. 'Opinion' was the sole and all-sufficient ally effecting this political reform. The Rajputs, in fact, did not require the demonstration of our physical strength; its influence had reached far beyond Mewar. When the few firelocks defeated hundreds of the foes of public tranquillity, they attributed it to 'the strength of the Company's salt,' [2] the moral agency of which was proclaimed the true basis of our power. 'Sachha Raj' was the proud epithet applied by our new allies to the British Government in the East; a title which distinguished the immortal Alfred, 'the upright.'

It will readily be imagined that a reform, which went to touch

[1] A literal translation of this curious piece of Hindu legislation will be found at the end of the Appendix. If not drawn up with all the dignity of the legal enactments of the great governments of the West, it has an important advantage in conciseness; the articles cannot be misinterpreted, and require no lawyer to expound them.

[2] "*Kampani Sahib ke namak ke zor se*" is a common phrase of our native soldiery; and "*Dohai! Kampani ki!*" is an invocation or appeal against injustice; but I never heard this watchword so powerfully applied as when a *Sub.* with the Resident's escort in 1812. One of our men, a noble young Rajput about nineteen years of age, and six feet high, had been sent with an elephant to forage in the wilds of Narwar. A band of at least fifty predatory horsemen assailed him, and demanded the surrender of the elephant, which he met by pointing his musket and giving them defiance. Beset on all sides, he fired, was cut down, and left for dead, in which state he was found, and brought to camp upon a litter. One sabre-cut had opened the back entirely across, exposing the action of the viscera, and his arms and wrists were barbarously hacked: yet he was firm, collected, and even cheerful; and to a kind reproach for his rashness, he said, "What would you have said, Captain Sahib, had I surrendered the Company's musket (*Kampani ki banduq*) without fighting?" From their temperate habits, the wound in the back did well; but the severed nerves of the wrists brought on a lockjaw of which he died. The Company have thousands who would alike die for their *banduq*. It were wise to cherish such feelings.

the entire feudal association, could not be accomplished without harassing and painful discussions [488], when the object was the renunciation of lands, to which in some cases the right of inheritance could be pleaded, in others, the cognisance of successful revenge, while to many prescriptive possession could be asserted. It was the more painful, because although the shades which marked the acquisition of such lands were varied, no distinction could be made in the mode of settlement, namely, unconditional surrender. In some cases, the Rana had to revoke his own grants, wrung either from his necessities or his weakness; but in neither predicament could arguments be adduced to soften renunciation, or to meet the powerful and pathetic and often angry appeals to justice or to prejudice. Counter-appeals to their loyalty, and the necessity for the re-establishment of their sovereign's just weight and influence in the social body, without which their own welfare could not be secured, were adduced; but individual views and passions were too absorbing to bend to the general interest. Weeks thus passed in interchange of visits, in soothing pride, and in flattering vanity by the revival of past recollections, which gradually familiarized the subject to the mind of the chiefs, and brought them to compliance. Time, conciliation, and impartial justice, confirmed the victory thus obtained; and when they were made to see that no interest was overlooked, that party views were unknown, and that the system included every class of society in its beneficial operation, cordiality followed concession. Some of these cessions were alienations from the crown of half a century's duration. Individual cases of hardship were unavoidable without incurring the imputation of favouritism, and the dreaded revival of ancient feuds, to abolish which was indispensable, but required much circumspection. Castles and lands in this predicament could therefore neither be retained by the possessor nor returned to the ancient proprietor without rekindling the torch of civil war. The sole alternative was for the crown to take the object of contention, and make compensation from its own domain. It would be alike tedious and uninteresting to enter into the details of these arrangements, where one chief had to relinquish the levy of transit duties in the most important outlet of the country, asserted to have been held during seven generations, as in the case of the chief of Deogarh. Of another (the Bhindar chief) who held forty-three towns and villages, in addition to his grant; of Amet, of

Badesar, of Dabla, of Lawa, and many others who held important fortresses of the crown independent of its will; and other claims, embracing every right [489] and privilege appertaining to feudal society; suffice it, that in six months the whole arrangements were effected.

The Case of Arja.—In the painful and protracted discussions attendant on these arrangements, powerful traits of national character were developed. The castle and domain of Arja half a century agò belonged to the crown, but had been usurped by the Purawats, from whom it was wrested by storm about fifteen years back by the Saktawats, and a patent sanctioning possession was obtained, on the payment of a fine of £1000 to the Rana. Its surrender was now required from Fateh Singh, the second brother of Bhindar, the head of this clan; but being regarded as the victorious completion of a feud, it was not easy to silence their prejudices and objections. The renunciation of the forty-three towns and villages by the chief of the clan caused not half the excitation, and every Saktawat seemed to forgo his individual losses in the common sentiment expressed by their head: "Arja is the price of blood, and with its cession our honour is surrendered." To preserve the point of honour, it was stipulated that it should not revert to the Purawats, but be incorporated with the fisc, which granted an equivalent; when letters of surrender were signed by both brothers, whose conduct throughout was manly and confiding.

Badnor and Amet.—The Badnor and Amet chiefs, both of the superior grade of nobles, were the most formidable obstacles to the operation of the treaty of the 4th of May. The first of these, by name Jeth Singh (*the victorious* [*chief*] *lion*), was of the Mertia clan, the bravest of the brave race of Rathor, whose ancestors had left their native abodes on the plains of Marwar, and accompanied the celebrated Mira Bai on her marriage with Rana Kumbha. His descendants, amongst whom was Jaimall, of immortal memory, enjoyed honour in Mewar equal to their birth and high deserts. It was the more difficult to treat with men like these, whose conduct had been a contrast to the general license of the times, and who had reason to feel offended, when no distinction was observed between them and those who had disgraced the name of Rajput. Instead of the submission expected from the Rathor, so overwhelmed was he from the magnitude of the claims, which amounted to a virtual extinction of his power, that he begged leave to resign his estates and quit the country. In prosecution of this design, he took post in the chief hall of the palace, from which no entreaties could make him move;[1] until the Rana, to [490] escape his importunities, and even restraint, obtained his promise to abide by the decision of the Agent. The forms of the Rana's court, from time immemorial, prohibit all personal communication between the sovereign and his chiefs in matters of individual interest, by which indecorous altercation is avoided. But the ministers, whose office it was to obtain every information, did not make a rigid scrutiny into the title-deeds of the various estates previous to advancing the claims of the crown. This brave man had enemies, and he was too proud to have recourse to the common arts either of adulation or bribery to aid his cause. It was a satisfaction to find that the two principal towns demanded of him were embodied in a grant of Sangram Singh's reign; and the absolute rights of the fisc, of which he had become possessed, were cut down to about fifteen thousand rupees of annual revenue. But there were other points on which he was even more tenacious than the surrender of these. Being the chief noble of the fine district of Badnor, which consisted of three hundred and sixty towns and villages, chiefly of feudal allotments (many of them of his own clan), he had taken advantage of the times to establish his influence over them, to assume the right of wardship of minors, and secure those services which were due to the prince, but which he wanted the power to enforce. The holders of these estates were of the third class of vassals or *gol* (the mass), whose services it was important to reclaim, and who constituted in past times the most efficient force of the Ranas, and were the preponderating balance of their authority when mercenaries were unknown in these patriarchal states. Abundant means towards a just investigation had been previously procured; and after some discussion, in which all admissible claims were recognized, and argument was silenced by incontrovertible facts, this chieftain relinquished all that was demanded, and sent in, as from himself, his written renunciation to his sovereign. However convincing the data by which his proper rights and those of his prince were defined, it was to feeling

[1] [An instance of the practice of 'sitting *dharna*' to enforce a claim (Yule-Burnell, *Hobson-Jobson*, 2nd ed. 315 f.).]

and prejudice that we were mainly indebted for so satisfactory an adjustment. An appeal to the name of Jaimall, who fell defending Chitor against Akbar,[1] and the contrast of his ancestor's loyalty and devotion with his own contumacy, acted as a talisman, and wrung tears from his eyes and the deed from his hand. It will afford some idea of the difficulties encountered, as well as the invidiousness of the task of arbitrating such matters, to give his own comment verbatim: "I remained faithful when his own kin deserted him, and was [491] one of four chiefs who alone of all Mewar fought for him in the rebellion; but the son of Jaimall is forgotten, while the 'plunderer' is his boon companion, and though of inferior rank, receives an estate which elevates him above me"; alluding to the chief of Badesar, who plundered the queen's dower. But while the brave descendant of Jaimall returned to Badnor with the marks of his sovereign's favour, and the applause of those he esteemed, the 'runner' went back to Badesar in disgrace, to which his prince's injudicious favour further contributed.

Hamira of Badesar.—Hamira of Badesar was of the second class of nobles, a Chondawat by birth. He succeeded to his father Sardar Singh, the assassin of the prime minister even in the palace of his sovereign;[2] into whose presence he had the audacity to pursue the surviving brother, destined to avenge him.[3] Hamira inherited all the turbulence and disaffection, with the estates, of his father; and this most conspicuous of the many lawless chieftains of the times was known throughout Rajasthan as Hamira 'the runner' (*daurayat*). Though not entitled to hold

[1] See p. 380. [2] See p. 514 and note.

[3] It will fill up the picture of the times to relate the revenge. When Jamshid, the infamous lieutenant of the infamous Amir Khan, established his headquarters at Udaipur, which he daily devastated, Sardar Singh, then in power, was seized and confined as a hostage for the payment of thirty thousand rupees demanded of the Rana. The surviving brothers of the murdered minister Somji 'purchased their foe' with the sum demanded, and anticipated his clansmen, who were on the point of effecting his liberation. The same sun shone on the head of Sardar, which was placed as a signal of revenge over the gateway of Rampiyari's palace. I had the anecdotes from the minister Siyahal, one of the actors in these tragedies, and a relative of the brothers, who were all swept away by the dagger. A similar fate often seemed to him, though a brave man, inevitable during these resumptions; which impression, added to the Rana's known inconstancy of favour, robbed him of half his energies.

lands beyond thirty thousand annually, he had become possessed to the amount of eighty thousand, chiefly of the fisc or *khalisa*, and nearly all obtained by violence, though since confirmed by the prince's patent. With the chieftain of Lawa (precisely in the same predicament), who held the fortress of Kheroda and other valuable lands, Hamira resided entirely at the palace, and obtaining the Rana's ear by professions of obedience, kept possession, while chiefs in every respect his superiors had been compelled to surrender; and when at length the Saktawat of Lawa was forbid the court until Kheroda and all his usurpations were yielded up, the son of Sardar displayed his usual turbulence, 'curled his moustache' at the minister, and hinted at the fate of his predecessor. Although none dared to imitate him, his stubbornness was not without admirers, especially among his own clan; and as it was too evident that fear or favour swayed the Rana, it was a case for the Agent's interference, the opportunity for which was soon afforded. When [492] forced to give letters of surrender, the Rana's functionaries, who went to take possession, were insulted, refused admittance, and compelled to return. Not a moment could be lost in punishing this contempt of authority; and as the Rana was holding a court when the report arrived, the Agent requested an audience. He found the Rana and his chiefs assembled in 'the balcony of the sun,' and amongst them the notorious Hamira. After the usual compliments, the Agent asked the minister if his master had been put in possession of Syana. It was evident from the general constraint, that all were acquainted with the result of the deputation; but to remove responsibility from the minister, the Agent, addressing the Rana as if he were in ignorance of the insult, related the transaction, and observed that his government would hold him culpable if he remained at Udaipur while his highness's commands were disregarded. Thus supported, the Rana resumed his dignity, and in forcible language signified to all present his anxious desire to do nothing which was harsh or ungracious; but that, thus compelled, he would not recede from what became him as their sovereign. Calling for a *bira*, he looked sternly at Hamira, and commanded him to quit his presence instantly, and the capital in an hour; and, but for the Agent's interposition, he would have been banished the country. Confiscation of his whole estate was commanded, until renunciation was completed. He departed that night; and, contrary to expectation, not only were all the usurpations surrendered, but, what was scarcely contemplated by the Agent, the Rana's flag of sequestration was quietly admitted into the fortress of Badesar.[1]

The Case of Āmli.—One more anecdote may suffice. The lands and fortress of Amli had been in the family of Amet since the year 27, only five years posterior to the date to which these arrangements extended ; their possession verged on half a century. The lords of Amet were of the Sixteen, and were chiefs of the clan Jagawat. The present representative enjoyed a fair character : he could, with the chief of Badnor, claim the succession of the loyal ; for Partap and Jaimall, their respective ancestors, were rivals and martyrs on that memorable day when the genius of Chitor abandoned the Sesodias. But the heir of Amet had not this alone [493] to support his claims ; for his predecessor Partap had lost his life in defending his country against the Mahrattas, and Amli had been his acquisition. Fateh Singh (such was his name) was put forward by the more artful of his immediate kin, the Chondawat interest ; but his disposition, blunt and impetuous, was little calculated to promote their views : he was an honest Rajput, who neither could nor cared to conceal his anger, and at a ceremonious visit paid him by the Agent, he had hardly sufficient control over himself to be courteous, and though he said nothing, his eyes, inflamed with opium and disdain, spoke his feelings. He maintained a dogged indifference, and was inaccessible to argument, till at length, following the example of Badnor, he was induced to abide by the Agent's mediation. He came attended by his vassals, who anxiously awaited the result, which an unpremeditated incident facilitated. After a long and fruitless expostulation, he had taken refuge in an obstinate silence ; and seated in a chair opposite to the envoy, with his shield in front, placed perpendicularly on his knees, and his arms and head

[1] Nearly twelve months after this, my public duty called me to Nimbahera *en route* to Kotah. The castle of Hamira was within an hour's ride, and at night he was reported as having arrived to visit me, when I appointed the next day to receive him. Early next morning, according to custom, I took my ride, with four of Skinner's Horse, and galloped past him, stretched with his followers on the ground not far from my camp, towards his fort. He came to me after breakfast, called me his greatest friend, "swore by his dagger he was my Rajput," and that he would be in future obedient and loyal ; but this, I fear, can never be.

reclined thereon, he continued vacantly looking on the ground. To interrupt this uncourteous silence in his own house, the envoy took a picture, which with several others was at hand, and placing it before him, remarked, "That chief did not gain his reputation for *swamidharma*[1] (loyalty) by conduct such as yours." His eyes suddenly recovered their animation and his countenance was lighted with a smile, as he rapidly uttered, "How did you come by this—why does this interest you?" A tear started in his eye as he added, "This is my father!"—"Yes," said the Agent, "it is the loyal Partap on the day he went forth to meet his death; but his name yet lives, and a stranger does homage to his fame."—"Take Amli, take Amli," he hurriedly repeated, with a suppressed tone of exultation and sorrow, "but forget not the extent of the sacrifice." To prolong the visit would have been painful to both, but as it might have been trusting too much to humanity to delay the resumption, the Agent availed himself of the moment to indite the *chhorchitthi*[2] of surrender for the lands.

With these instances, characteristic of individuals and the times, this sketch of the introductory measures for improving the condition of Mewar may be closed. To enter more largely in detail is foreign to the purpose of the work; nor is it requisite for the comprehension of the unity of the object, that a more minute dissection of the parts should be afforded. Before, however, we exhibit the [494] general results of these arrangements, we shall revert to the condition of the more humble, but a most important part of the community, the peasantry of Mewar; and embody, in a few remarks, the fruits of observation or inquiry, as to their past and present state, their rights, the establishment of them, their infringement, and restitution. On this subject much has been necessarily introduced in the sketch of the feudal system, where landed tenures were discussed; but it is one on which such a contrariety of opinion exists, that it may be desirable to show the exact state of landed tenures in a country, where Hindu manners should exist in greater purity than in any other part of the vast continent of India.

The Landed System.—The ryot (cultivator) is the proprietor of the soil in Mewar. He compares his right therein to the *akshay*

[1] Literally faith (*dharma*) to his lord (*swami*).
[2] Paper of relinquishment.

FACSIMILE OF NATIVE DRAWING OF PARTĀB SINGH AND RĀĒMALL.

To face page 572.

duba,[1] which no vicissitudes can destroy. He calls the land his *bapota*, the most emphatic, the most ancient, the most cherished, and the most significant phrase his language commands for patrimonial[2] inheritance. He has nature and Manu in support of his claim, and can quote the text, alike compulsory on prince and peasant, "cultivated land is the property of him who cut away the wood, or who cleared and tilled it,"[3] an ordinance binding on the whole Hindu race, and which no international wars, or conquest, could overturn. In accordance with this principle is the ancient adage, not of Mewar only but all Rajputana, *Bhog ra dhanni Raj ho : bhum ra dhanni ma cho :* 'the government is owner of the rent, but I am the master of the land.' With the toleration and benevolence of the race the conqueror is commanded "to respect the deities adored by the conquered, also their virtuous priests, and to establish the laws of the conquered nation as declared in their books."[4] If it were deemed desirable to recede to the system of pure Hindu agrarian law, there is no deficiency of materials. The customary laws contained in the various reports of able men, superadded to the general ordinances of Manu, would form a code at once simple and efficient: for though innovation from foreign conquest has placed many principles in abeyance, and modified others, yet he has observed to little purpose [495] who does not trace a uniformity of design, which at one time had ramified wherever the

[1] The *dūb* grass *Cynodon dactylon*] flourishes in all seasons, and most in the intense heats ; it is not only *amara* or 'immortal,' but *akshay*, 'not to be eradicated' ; and its tenacity to the soil deserves the distinction.

[2] From *bap*, 'father,' and the termination *of*, or *belonging to*, and by which clans are distinguished ; as Karansot, 'descended of Karan' ; Mansinghgot, 'descended of Mansingh.' It is curious enough that the mountain clans of Albania, and other Greeks, have the same distinguishing termination, and the Mainote of Greece and the Mairot of Rajputana alike signify *mountaineer*, or 'of the mountain,' *maina* in Albanian ; *mairu* or *meru* in Sanskrit. [The words have no connexion.]

[3] *Laws*, ix. 44.

[4] ["When he [the king] has gained victory, let him duly worship the gods and honour righteous Brāhmanas, let him grant exemptions, and let him cause promises of safety to be proclaimed. But having fully ascertained the wishes of all the (conquered), let him place then a relation of (the vanquished ruler on the throne), and let him impose his conditions. Let him make authoritative the lawful customs of the inhabitants, just as they are stated to be" (Manu, *Laws*, vii. 201 f., trans. Bühler, *Sacred Books of the East*, xxv. 248 f.).]

name of Hindu prevailed: language has been modified, and terms have been corrupted or changed, but the primary pervading principle is yet perceptible; and whether we examine the systems of Khandesh, the Carnatic, or Rajasthan, we shall discover the elements to be the same.

If we consider the system from the period described by Arrian, Curtius, and Diodorus, we shall see in the government of townships each commune an '*imperium in imperio*'; a little republic, maintaining its municipal legislation independent of the monarchy, on which it relies for general support, and to which it pays the *bhog*, or tax in kind, as the price of this protection; for though the prescribed duties of kings are as well defined by Manu[1] as by any jurisconsult in Europe, nothing can be more lax than the mutual relations of the governed and governing in Hindu monarchies, which are resolved into unbounded liberty of action. To the artificial regulation of society, which leaves all who depend on manual exertion to an immutable degradation, must be ascribed these multitudinous governments, unknown to the rest of mankind, which, in spite of such dislocation, maintain the bonds of mutual sympathies. Strictly speaking, every State presents the picture of so many hundred or thousand minute republics, without any connexion with each other, giving allegiance (*an*) and rent (*bhog*) to a prince, who neither legislates for them, nor even forms a police for their internal protection. It is consequent on this want of paramount interference that, in matters of police, of justice, and of law, the communes act for themselves; and from this want of paternal interference only have arisen those courts of equity, or arbitration, the *panchayats*.

But to return to the freehold ryot of Mewar, whose *bapota* is the *watan* and the *miras* of the peninsula—words of foreign growth, introduced by the Muhammadan conquerors; the first (Persian) is of more general use in Khandesh; the other (Arabic)

[1] ["Let him [the king] cause his annual revenue in his kingdom to be collected by trusty (officials), let him obey the sacred law (in his transactions with) the people, and behave as a father to all men" (Manu, *Laws*, vii. 80). "Not to turn back in battle, to protect the people, to honour the Brāhmanas, is the best means for a king to secure happiness" (*ib.* vii. 88). "From the people let him (the king) learn (the theory) of the (various) trades and professions" (*ib.* vii. 43). "But (he who is given) to these vices (loses) even his life" (*ib.* vii. 46), trans. Bühler, *Sacred Books of the East*, xxv.]

in the Carnatic. Thus the great Persian moralist Saadi exemplifies its application: "If you desire to succeed to your father's inheritance (*miras*), first obtain his wisdom" [496].

While the term *bapota* thus implies the inheritance or patrimony, its holder, if a military vassal, is called Bhumia, a term equally powerful, meaning one actually identified with the soil (*bhum*), and for which the Muhammadan has no equivalent but in the possessive compound *watandar*, or *mirasdar*. The Caniatchi[1] of Malabar is the Bhumia of Rajasthan.

The emperors of Delhi, in the zenith of their power, bestowed the epithet zamindar upon the Hindu tributary sovereigns: not out of disrespect, but in the true application of their own term Bhumia Raj, expressive of their tenacity to the soil; and this fact affords additional evidence of the proprietary right being in the cultivator (*ryot*), namely, that he alone can confer the freehold land, which gives the title of Bhumia, and of which both past history and present usage will furnish us with examples. When the tenure of land obtained from the cultivator is held more valid than the grant of the sovereign, it will be deemed a conclusive argument of the proprietary right being vested in the ryot. What should induce a chieftain, when inducted into a perpetual fief, to establish through the ryot a right to a few acres in bhum, but the knowledge that although the vicissitudes of fortune or of favour may deprive him of his aggregate signiorial rights, his claims, derived from the spontaneous favour of the commune, can never be set aside; and when he ceases to be the lord, he becomes a member of the commonwealth, merging his title of Thakur, or Signior, into the more humble one of Bhumia, the allodial tenant of the Rajput feudal system, elsewhere discussed.[2] Thus we have touched on the method by which he acquires this distinction, for protecting the community from violence; and if left destitute by the negligence or inability of the government, he is vested with the rights of the crown, in its share of the *bhog* or rent. But when their own land is in the predicament called *galita*, or reversions from lapses to the commune, he is 'seised' in

[1] *Cani*, 'land,' and *atchi*, 'heritage': *Report*, p. 289.—I should be inclined to imagine the *atchi*, like the *ot* and *awat*, Rajput terminations, implying clanship. [Tamil *kāniyātchi*, 'that which is held in free and hereditary property'; *kāni*, 'land,' *ātchi*, 'inheritance' (Wilson, *Glossary*, *s.v.*; *Madras Manual of Administration*, iii. 58).]

[2] See p. 195.

all the rights of the former proprietor; or, by internal arrangements, they can convey such right by cession of the commune.

The Bhūmia.—The privilege attached to the *bhum*,[1] and acquired from the community by the protection afforded to it, is the most powerful argument for the recognition of its original rights. The Bhumia, thus vested, may at pleasure drive his own plough [497], the right to the soil. His *bhum* is exempt from the *jarib* (measuring rod); it is never assessed, and his only sign of allegiance is a quit-rent, in most cases triennial, and the tax of *kharlakar*,[2] a war imposition, now commuted for money. The State, however, indirectly receives the services of these allodial tenants, the yeomen of Rajasthan, who constitute, as in the districts of Kumbhalmer and Mandalgarh, the landwehr, or local militia. In fact, since the days of universal repose set in, and the townships required no protection, an arrangement was made with the Bhumias of Mewar, in which the crown, foregoing its claim of quit-rent, has obtained their services in the garrisons and frontier stations of police at a very slight pecuniary sacrifice.

Such are the rights and privileges derived from the ryot cultivator alone. The Rana may dispossess the chiefs of Badnor, or Salumbar, of their estates, the grant of the crown—he could not touch the rights emanating from the community; and thus the descendants of a chieftain, who a few years before might have followed his sovereign at the head of one hundred cavaliers, would descend into the humble foot militia of a district. Thousands are in this predicament: the Kanawats, Lunawats, Kumbhawats, and other clans, who, like the Celt, forget not their claims of birth in the distinctions of fortune, but assert their propinquity as "brothers in the nineteenth or thirtieth degree to the prince" on the throne. So sacred was the tenure derived from the ryot, that even monarchs held lands in *bhum* from their subjects, for an instance of which we are indebted to the great poetic historian of the last Hindu king. Chand relates, that when his sovereign, the Chauhan, had subjugated the kingdom of Anhilwara[3] from the Solanki, he returned to the nephew of the

[1] See p. 195.

[2] See Sketch of Feudal System, p. 170.

[3] Nahrwala of D'Anville; the Balhara sovereignty of the Arabian travellers of the eighth and ninth centuries. I visited the remains of this city on my last journey, and from original authorities shall give an account of this ancient emporium of commerce and literature.

conquered prince several districts and seaports, and all the bhum held by the family. In short, the Rajput vaunts his aristocratic distinction derived from the land; and opposes the title of 'Bhumia Raj,' or government of the soil, to the 'Bania Raj,' or commercial government, which he affixes as an epithet of contempt to Jaipur: where "wealth accumulates and men decay."

In the great 'register of patents' (*patta bahi*) of Mewar we find a species of [498] *bhum* held by the greater vassals on particular crown lands; whether this originated from inability of ceding entire townships to complete the estate to the rank of the incumbent, or whether it was merely in confirmation of the grant of the commune, could not be ascertained. The benefit from this *bhum* is only pecuniary, and the title is '*bhum rakhwali*'[1] or land [in return for] 'preservation.' Strange to say, the crown itself holds '*bhum rakhwali*' on its own fiscal demesnes consisting of small portions in each village, to the amount of ten thousand rupees in a district of thirty or forty townships. This species, however, is so incongruous that we can only state it does exist: we should vainly seek the cause for such apparent absurdity, for since society has been unhinged, the oracles are mute to much of antiquated custom.

Occupiers' Rights in the Land.—We shall close these remarks with some illustrative traditions and yet existing customs, to substantiate the ryot's right in the soil of Mewar. After one of those convulsions described in the annals, the prince had gone to espouse the daughter of the Raja of Mandor, the (then) capital of Marwar. It is customary at the moment of *hathleva*, or the junction of hands, that any request preferred by the bridegroom to the father of the bride should meet compliance, a usage which has yielded many fatal results; and the Rana had been prompted on this occasion to demand a body of ten thousand Jat cultivators to repeople the deserted fisc of Mewar. An assent was given to the unprecedented demand, but when the inhabitants were thus despotically called on to migrate, they denied the power and refused. "Shall we," said they, "abandon the lands of our inheritance (*bapota*), the property of our children, to accompany a stranger into a foreign land, there to labour for him? Kill us you may, but never shall we relinquish our inalienable rights." The Mandor prince, who had trusted to this reply, deemed himself

[1] Salvamenta of the European system.

exonerated from his promise, and secured from the loss of so many subjects: but he was deceived. The Rana held out to them the enjoyment of the proprietary rights escheated to the crown in his country, with the lands left without occupants by the sword, and to all, increase of property. When equal and absolute power was thus conferred, they no longer hesitated to exchange the arid soil of Marwar for the garden of Rajwara; and the descendants of these Jats still occupy the flats watered by the Berach and Banas [499].

In those districts which afforded protection from innovation, the proprietary right of the ryot will be found in full force; of this the populous and extensive district of Jahazpur, consisting of one hundred and six townships, affords a good specimen. There are but two pieces of land throughout the whole of this tract the property of the crown, and these were obtained by force during the occupancy of Zalim Singh of Kotah. The right thus unjustly acquired was, from the conscientiousness of the Rana's civil governor, on the point of being annulled by sale and reversion, when the court interfered to maintain its proprietary right to the tanks of Loharia and Itaunda, and the lands which they irrigate, now the *bhum* of the Rana.[1] This will serve as an illustration how *bhum* may be acquired, and the annals of Kotah will exhibit, unhappily for the ryots of that country, the almost total annihilation of their rights, by the same summary process which originally attached Loharia to the fisc.

The power of alienation being thus proved, it would be superfluous to insist further on the proprietary right of the cultivator of the soil.

Proprietary Rights in Land.—Besides the ability to alienate as demonstrated, all the overt symbols which mark the proprietary right in other countries are to be found in Mewar; that of entire conveyance by sale, or temporary by mortgage; and numerous instances could be adduced, especially of the latter. The fertile lands of Horla, along the banks of the Khari, are almost all mortgaged, and the registers of these transactions form two

[1] The author has to acknowledge with regret that he was the cause of the Mina proprietors not re-obtaining their *bapota*: this arose, partly from ignorance at the time, partly from the individual claimants being dead. and more than all, from the representation that the intended sale originated in a bribe to Sadaram the governor, which, however, was not the case.

considerable volumes, in which great variety of deeds may be discovered: one extended for one hundred and one years;[1] when redemption was to follow, without regard to interest on the one hand, or the benefits from the land on the other, but merely by repayment of the sum borrowed. To maintain the interest during abeyance, it is generally stipulated that a certain portion of the harvest shall be reserved for the mortgagee—a fourth, a fifth, or *gugri*—a share so small as to be valued only as a mark of proprietary recognition.[2] The mortgagees were chiefly of the commercial classes of the large frontier towns; in [500] many cases the proprietor continues to cultivate for another the lands his ancestor mortgaged four or five generations ago, nor does he deem his right at all impaired. A plan had been sketched to raise money to redeem these mortgages, from whose complex operation the revenue was sure to suffer. No length of time or absence can affect the claim to the *bapota*, and so sacred is the right of absentees, that land will lay sterile and unproductive from the penalty which Manu denounces on all who interfere with their neighbour's rights: "for unless there be an especial agreement between the owner of the land and the seed, the fruits belong clearly to the land-owner"; even "if seed conveyed by water or by wind should germinate, the plant belongs to the land-owner, the mere sower takes not the fruit."[3] Even crime and the extreme sentence of the law will not alter succession to property, either to the military or cultivating vassal; and the old Kentish adage, probably introduced by the Jats from Scandinavia, who under Hengist established that kingdom of the heptarchy, namely:

> The father to the bough,
> And the son to the plough

---

[1] Claims to the *bapota* appear to be maintainable if not alienated longer than one hundred and one years; and undisturbed possession (no matter how obtained) for the same period appears to confer this right. The *miras* of Khandesh appears to have been on the same footing. See Mr. Elphinstone's *Report*, October 25, 1819, ed. 1872, p. 17 f., quoted in *BG*, xii. 266. [The word *mīrās* means 'inherited estate,' the right of disposal of which rests with the holder. The Jāts certainly did not bring the custom to Kent.]

[2] The *sawmy begum* of the peninsula in *Fifth Report*, pp. 356-57; correctly *swami bhoga*, 'lord's rent,' in Sanskrit.

[3] Manu, *Laws*, ix. 52-54, on the *Servile Classes*. [Bühler's version differs, but the meaning is practically the same as that of the text.]

is practically understood by the Jats and Bhumias[1] of Mewar, whose treason is not deemed hereditary, nor a chain of noble acts destroyed because a false link was thrown out. We speak of the military vassals—the cultivator cannot aspire to so dignified a crime as treason.

Village Officials : the Patel.—The officers of the townships are the same as have been so often described, and are already too familiar to those interested in the subject to require illustration. From the Patel, the Cromwell of each township, to the village gossip, the ascetic Sannyasi, each deems his office, and the land he holds in virtue thereof in perpetuity, free of rent to the State, except a small triennial quit-rent,[2] and the liability, like every other branch of the State, to two war taxes.[3]

Opinions are various as to the origin and attributes of the Patel, the most important personage in village sway, whose office is by many deemed foreign to the pure Hindu system, and to which language even his title is deemed alien. But there is no doubt that both office and title are of ancient growth, and even etymological rule proves the Patel to be head (*pati*) of the community.[4] The office of Patel [501] of Mewar was originally elective ; he was '*primus inter pares*,' the constituted attorney or representative of the commune, and as the medium between the cultivator and the government, enjoyed benefits from both. Besides his *bapota*, and the *serano*, or one-fortieth of all produce from the ryot, he had a remission of a third or fourth of the rent from such extra lands as he might cultivate in addition to his patrimony. Such was the Patel, the link connecting the peasant with the government, ere predatory war subverted all order :

1 Patel. 2 Patel *barar*.

3 The Gharginti *barar*, and Kharlakar, or *wood and forage*, explained in the Feudal System.

4 In copper-plate grants dug from the ruins of the ancient Ujjain (presented to the Royal Asiatic Society), the prince's patents (*patta*) conferring gifts are addressed to the *Patta-silas* and Ryots. I never heard an etymology of this word, but imagine it to be from *patta*, 'grant,' or 'patent,' and *sila*, which means a nail, or sharp instrument ; [? *sila*, the stone on which the grant is engraved] ; metaphorically, that which binds or unites these patents ; all, however, having *pati*, or chief, as the basis (see *Transactions of the Royal Asiatic Society*, vol. i. p. 237). [*Pati*, 'chief,' has no connexion with *patta*, 'a grant,' the latter being the origin of *patel*. For the position of the Patel see Baden-Powell, *The Indian Village Community*, 10 ff. ; Malcolm, *Memoir of Central India*, 2nd ed. ii. 14 ff.]

but as rapine increased, so did his authority. He became the plenipotentiary of the community, the security for the contribution imposed, and often the hostage for its payment, remaining in the camp of the predatory hordes till they were paid off. He gladly undertook the liquidation of such contributions as these perpetual invaders imposed. To indemnify himself, a schedule was formed of the share of each ryot, and mortgage of land, and sequestration of personal effects followed till his avarice was satisfied. Who dared complain against a Patel, the intimate of Pathan and Mahratta commanders, his adopted patrons? He thus became the master of his fellow-citizens; and, as power corrupts all men, their tyrant instead of their mediator. It was a system necessarily involving its own decay; for a while glutted with plenty, but failing with the supply, and ending in desolation, exile, and death. Nothing was left to prey on but the despoiled carcase; yet when peace returned, and in its train the exile ryot to reclaim the *bapota*, the vampire Patel was resuscitated, and evinced the same ardour for supremacy, and the same cupidity which had so materially aided to convert the fertile Mewar to a desert. The Patel accordingly proved one of the chief obstacles to returning prosperity; and the attempt to reduce this corrupted middle-man to his original station in society was both difficult and hazardous, from the support they met in the corrupt officers at court, and other influences 'behind the curtain.' A system of renting the crown lands deemed the most expedient to advance prosperity, it was incumbent to find a remedy for this evil. The mere name of some of these petty tyrants inspired such terror as to check all desire of return to the country; but the origin of the institution of the office and its abuses being ascertained, it was imperative, though difficult, to restore the one and banish the other. The original elective right in many townships was therefore returned to the ryot, who nominated new Patels [502], his choice being confirmed by the Rana, in whose presence investiture was performed by binding a turban on the elected, for which he presented his *nazar*. Traces of the sale of these offices in past times were observable; and it was deemed of primary importance to avoid all such channels for corruption, in order that the ryot's election should meet with no obstacle. That the plan was beneficial there could be no doubt; that the benefit would be permanent, depended, unfortunately, on circumstances which those most anxious had not the means to control: for it must be recollected, that although "personal aid and advice might be given when asked," all internal interference was by treaty strictly, and most justly, prohibited.

After a few remarks on the mode of levying the crown-rents, we shall conclude the subject of village economy in Mewar, and proceed to close this too extended chapter with the results of four years of peace and the consequent improved prosperity.

Modes of Collecting Rents.—There are two methods of levying the revenues of the crown on every description of corn—*kankut* and *batai*, for on sugar-cane, poppy, oil, hemp, tobacco, cotton, indigo, and garden stuffs, a money payment is fixed, varying from two to six rupees per bigha. The *kankut*[1] is a conjectural assessment of the standing crop, by the united judgement of the officers of government, the Patel, the Patwari, or registrar, and the owner of the field. The accuracy with which an accustomed eye will determine the quantity of grain on a given surface is surprising: but should the owner deem the estimate overrated, he can insist on *batai*, or division of the corn after it is threshed; the most ancient and only infallible mode by which the dues either of the government or the husbandman can be ascertained. In the *batai* system the share of the government varies from one-third to two-fifths of the spring harvest, as wheat and barley; and sometimes even half, which is the invariable proportion of the autumnal crops. In either case, *kankut* or *batai*, when the shares are appropriated, those of the crown may be commuted to a money payment at the average rate of the market. The *kut* is the most liable to corruption. The ryot bribes the collector, who will underrate the crop; and when he betrays his duty, the *shahnah*, or watchman, is not likely to be honest: and as the *makai*, or Indian corn, the grand autumnal crop of Mewar, is eaten green, the crown may be defrauded of half its dues. The system is one of uncertainty, from which eventually the ryot derives no advantage, though it [503] fosters the cupidity of patels and collectors; but there was a *barar*, or tax, introduced to make up for this deficiency, which was in proportion to the quantity cultivated, and its amount at the mercy of the officers. Thus the ryot went to work with a mill-stone round his neck; instead of the exhilarating reflection that every hour's additional

[1] [*Kan*, 'grain,' *kūt*, 'valuation,' *batāi* from *batānā*, 'to divide.']

labour was his own, he saw merely the advantage of these harpies, and contented himself with raising a scanty subsistence in a slovenly and indolent manner, by which he forfeited the ancient reputation of the Jat cultivator of Mewar.

Improvement in the Condition of the People.—Notwithstanding these and various other drawbacks to the prosperity of the country, in an impoverished court, avaricious and corrupt officers, discontented Patels, and bad seasons, yet the final report in May 1822 could not but be gratifying when contrasted with that of February 1818. In order to ascertain the progressive improvement, a census had been made at the end of 1821, of the three central fiscal districts [1] watered by the Berach and Banas. As a specimen of the whole, we may take the *tappa* or subdivision of Sahara. Of its twenty-seven villages, six were inhabited in 1818, the number of families being three hundred and sixty-nine, three-fourths of whom belonged to the resumed town of Amli. In 1821 nine hundred and twenty-six families were reported, and every village of the twenty-seven was occupied, so that population had almost trebled. The number of ploughs was more than trebled, and cultivation quadrupled; and though this, from the causes described, was not above one-third of what real industry might have effected, the contrast was abundantly cheering. The same ratio of prosperity applied to the entire crown demesne of Mewar. By the recovery of Kumbhalmer, Raepur, Rajnagar, and Sadri-Kanera from the Mahrattas; of Jahazpur from Kotah; of the usurpations of the nobles; together with the resumption of all the estates of the females of his family, a task at once difficult and delicate; [2] and by the subjugation of the mountain districts of Merwara, a thousand towns and villages were united to form the fiscal demesne of the Rana, composing twenty-four districts of various magnitudes, divided, as in ancient times, and with the primitive [504] appellations, into portions tantamount to the

[1] Mui, Barak, and Kapasan.

[2] To effect this, indispensable alike for unity of government and the establishment of a police, the individual statements of their holders were taken for the revenues they had derived from them, and money payments three times the amount were adjudged to them. They were gainers by this arrangement, and were soon loaded with jewels and ornaments, but the numerous train of harpies who cheated them and abused the poor ryot were eternally at work to defeat all such beneficial schemes; and the counteraction of the intrigues was painful and disgusting.

tithings and hundreds of England, the division from time immemorial amongst the Hindus.[1] From these and the commercial duties [2] a revenue was derived sufficient for the comforts, and even the dignities of the prince and his court, and promising an annual increase in the ratio of good government : but profusion scattered all that industry and ingenuity could collect ; the artificial wants of the prince perpetuated the real necessities of the peasant, and this, it is to be feared, will continue till the present generation shall sleep with their forefathers.

Abstract of the Fiscal Revenues of Mewar in the years 1818–19–20–21–22.

Spring harvest of 1818	Rs. 40,000	
,, 1819	451,281	
,, 1820	659,100	
,, 1821	1,018,478	
,, 1822	936,640	The active superintendence of the British Agent being almost entirely withdrawn.

Abstract of Commercial Duties included in the above.

In 1818	*Nominal*	
1819	Rs. 96,683	
1820	165,108	
1821	220,000	Farmed for three years, from 1822, for 750,000 rupees, which was assigned by the Rana for the liquidation of tribute fallen in arrear.
1822	217,000	

Mines and Minerals.—There are sources of wealth in Mewar yet untouched, and to which her princes owe much of their power. The tin mines of Jawara and Dariba alone, little more than half a century ago, yielded above three lakhs annually ;[3]

[1] Manu [*Laws*, vii. 119] ordains the division into tens, hundreds, and thousands.

[2] Farmed for the ensuing three years, from 1822, for seven lakhs of rupees.

[3] In S. 1816, Jawara yielded Rs. 222,000 and Dariba Rs. 80,000. The tin of these mines contains a portion of silver. [What the Author calls the tin mines are probably the lead and zinc mines at Jāwar, 16 miles south of Udaipur city. They seem now to be exhausted, and search might be made for other untouched pockets of ore. Those at Dariba, which formerly yielded a considerable revenue, have long been closed (Erskine ii. A. 53).]

besides rich copper mines in various parts. From such, beyond a doubt, much of the wealth of Mewar was extracted, but the miners are now dead, and the mines filled with water. An attempt was made to work them, but it was so unprofitable that the design was soon abandoned.

Nothing will better exemplify the progress of prosperity than the comparative population of some of the chief towns before, and after, four years of peace :

	No. of houses in 1818.	No. of houses in 1822.
Udaipur	3,500	10,000
Bhilwara	*not one*	2,700
Pur	200	1,200
Mandal	80	400
Gosunda	60	350 [505]

The Feudal Lands.—The feudal lands, which were then double the fiscal, did not exhibit the like improvement, the merchant and cultivator residing thereon not having the same certainty of reaping the fruits of their industry ; still great amelioration took place, and few were so blind as not to see their account in it.[1] The earnestness with which many requested the Agent to back their expressed intentions with his guarantee to their communities of the same measure of justice and protection as the fiscal tenants enjoyed was proof that they well understood the benefits of reciprocal confidence ; but this could not be tendered without danger. Before the Agent left the country he greatly withdrew from active interference, it being his constant, as it was his last impressive lesson, that they should rely upon themselves if they desired to retain a shadow of independence. To give an idea of the improved police, insurance which has been described as amounting to eight per cent in a space of twenty-five miles became almost nominal, or one-fourth of a rupee per cent from one frontier to the other. It would, however, have been quite Utopian to have expected that the lawless tribes would remain in that stupid subordination which the unexampled state

[1] There are between two and three thousand towns, villages, and hamlets, besides the fiscal land of Mewar ; but the tribute of the British Government is derived only from the fiscal ; it would have been impossible to collect from the feudal lands, which are burthened with service, and form the army of the State.

of society imposed for a time (as described in the opening of these transactions), when they found that real restraints did not follow imaginary terrors. Had the wild tribes been under the sole influence of British power, nothing would have been so simple as effectually, not only to control, but to conciliate and improve them; for it is a mortifying truth, that the more remote from civilization, the more tractable and easy was the object to manage, more especially the Bhil.[1] But these children of nature were incorporated in the demesnes of the feudal chiefs, who when they found our system did not extend to perpetual control, returned to their old habits of oppression: this provoked retaliation, which to subdue requires more power than the Rana yet possesses, and, in the anomalous state of our alliances, will always be an embarrassing task to whosoever may exercise political control.

In conclusion, it is to be hoped that the years of oppression that have swept the land will be held in remembrance by the protecting power, and that neither petulance nor indolence will lessen the benevolence which restored life to Mewar, or mar the picture of comparative happiness it created.

[1] Sir John Malcolm's wise and philanthropic measures for the reclamation of this race in Malwa will support my assertions [*Memoir of Central India*, 2nd ed. i. 516 ff., ii. 179 ff.].

The Sixteen chief Nobles of Mewar, their Titles, Names, Clans, Tribes, Estates, number of Villages in each, and their Value.

Title.	Names.	Clan.	Tribe.	Estate.	Number of Villages.	Value, A.D. 1760.	REMARKS.
Raj	Chandan Singh	Jhala	Jhala	Sadri	127	100,000	These estates are all diminished one-half in nominal amount; and their revenues still more.
Rao	Partap Singh	Chauhan	Chauhan	Bedla	80	100,000	
Rao	Mohkam Singh	Chauhan	Chauhan	Kotharia	65	80,000	
Rawat	Padma Singh	Chondawat	Sesodia	Salumbar	85	84,000	Would realize this if cultivated.
Thakur	Zorawar Singh	Mertia	Rathor	Ghanerao	100	100,000	This chief ceases to be one of the 16 since the Rana lost the province of Godwar.
Rao	Keshodas	—	Pramar	Bijolia	40	45,000	Would realize this if cultivated.
Rawat	Gokuldas	Sangawat	Sesodia	Deogarh	125	80,000	Would realize more if cultivated.
Rawat	Maha Singh	Meghawat	Sesodia	Begun	150	200,000	This includes usurpations — now seized by Sindhia. The estate would realize 70,000 if cultivated.
Raj	Kalyan Singh	Jhala	Jhala	Delwara	125	100,000	Would realize two-thirds if cultivated.
Rawat	Salim Singh	Jagawat	Sesodia	Amet	60	60,000	Do., do.
Raj	Chhattar Sal	Jhala	Jhala	Gogunda	50	50,000	Would realize this if cultivated.
Rawat	Fateh Singh	Sarangdevot	Sesodia	Kanor	50	95,000	Would realize half if cultivated.
Maharaja	Zorawar Singh	Saktawat	Sesodia	Bhindar	64	64,000	Would realize this if cultivated.
Thakur	Jeth Singh	Mertia	Rathor	Badnor	80	80,000	Do., do.
Rawat	Salim Singh	Saktawat	Sesodia	Bansi	40	40,000	These chiefs have lost all their influence and half their estates.
Rao	Surajmall	Chauhan	Chauhan	Parsoli	40	40,000	
Rawat	Kesari Singh	Kishanawat	Sesodia	Bhainsror	60	60,000	These chiefs have taken rank on the depression of the above—they never appear at court on the same day.
Rawat	Jawan Singh	Kishanawat	Sesodia	Kurabar	35	35,000	
Total number and estimated value of their estates sixty years ago, omitting Bhainsror and Kurabar, then enrolled in the second grade of chieftains.					1,181	1,310,000	

Note.—The inferior grades possessed estates to a still larger amount, conjointly yielding a revenue of thirty lakhs of rupees; and as each thousand rupees of estate furnished on emergency three horses completely equipped, the feudal interest could supply nine thousand horse besides foot, of which they make little account. [Accounts of the present condition of these nobles will be found in Erskine ii. A. under the headings of their estates.]

ANNALS AND ANTIQUITIES
OF
RAJASTHAN

COLONEL JAMES TOD.

(By permission of Lt.-Col. C. D. Blunt-Mackenzie, R.A.)

Frontispiece.

ANNALS AND ANTIQUITIES OF RAJASTHAN

OR THE CENTRAL AND WESTERN RAJPUT STATES OF INDIA

BY

LIEUT.-COL. JAMES TOD
LATE POLITICAL AGENT TO THE WESTERN RAJPUT STATES

EDITED WITH AN INTRODUCTION AND NOTES BY
WILLIAM CROOKE, C.I.E.
HON, D.SC. OXON., B.A., F.R.A.I.,
LATE OF THE INDIAN CIVIL SERVICE

IN THREE VOLUMES
VOL. II

GYAN

Published by

Gyan Publishing House
5, Ansari Road
Daryaganj, New Delhi-110002
Phone: 011-47034999, 9811692060
E-mail: books@gyanbooks.com

Distribution Network
gyanbooks.com
India, USA, Canada, UK, Australia, France

ISBN : 978-81-212-3130-5 (Set)
ISBN : 978-81-212-4824-2 (HB)
First Published, London, 1920

2nd Impression 2020

Printed at: Gyan Press, Delhi.

Annals and Antiquities of Rajasthan Vol. II
Author: James Tod

ANNALS AND ANTIQUITIES

OF

RAJASTHAN

OR THE CENTRAL AND WESTERN RAJPUT STATES OF INDIA

BY

LIEUT.-COL. JAMES TOD

LATE POLITICAL AGENT TO THE WESTERN RAJPUT STATES

EDITED WITH AN INTRODUCTION AND NOTES BY

WILLIAM CROOKE, C.I.E.

HON. D.SC. OXON., B.A., F.R.A.I.

LATE OF THE INDIAN CIVIL SERVICE

IN THREE VOLUMES

VOL. II

HUMPHREY MILFORD

OXFORD UNIVERSITY PRESS

LONDON EDINBURGH GLASGOW NEW YORK

TORONTO MELBOURNE BOMBAY

1920

CONTENTS

BOOK IV—*continued*

ANNALS OF MEWAR

CHAPTER 19

CHAPTER 20

CHAPTER 21

CHAPTER 22

CHAPTER 23

CHAPTER 24

PERSONAL NARRATIVE

CHAPTER 25

CHAPTER 26

CHAPTER 29

CHAPTER 30

BOOK V

ANNALS OF MARWAR

CHAPTER 1

CHAPTER 2

CHAPTER 3

CHAPTER 4

CHAPTER 5

CHAPTER 6

CHAPTER 7

CHAPTER 8

CHAPTER 9

CHAPTER 10

CHAPTER 11

CHAPTER 12

PAGE

CHAPTER 13

CHAPTER 14

CHAPTER 15

CHAPTER 16

PAGE

BOOK VI

ANNALS OF BIKANER

CHAPTER 1

CHAPTER 2

CHAPTER 3

BOOK VII

ANNALS OF JAISALMER

CHAPTER 1

PAGE

CHAPTER 2

CHAPTER 3

CHAPTER 4

CHAPTER 5

CHAPTER 6

CHAPTER 7

ILLUSTRATIONS

ANNALS AND ANTIQUITIES OF RAJASTHAN

BOOK IV—*Continued*

RELIGIOUS ESTABLISHMENTS, FESTIVALS, AND CUSTOMS OF MEWĀR

CHAPTER 19

Influence of the Priesthood.—In all ages the ascendancy of the hierarchy is observable; it is a tribute paid to religion through her organs. Could the lavish endowments and extensive immunities of the various religious establishments in Rajasthan be assumed as criteria of the morality of the inhabitants, we should be authorized to assign them a high station in the scale of excellence. But they more frequently prove the reverse of their position; especially the territorial endowments, often the fruits of a death-bed repentance,[1] which, prompted by superstition or fear, compounds for past crimes by posthumous profusion, although vanity not rarely lends her powerful aid. There is scarcely a State in Rajputana in which one-fifth of the soil is not assigned for the support of the temples, their ministers, the secular Brahmans, bards, and [508] genealogists. But the evil was not always so extensive; the abuse is of modern growth.

Weighing of Princes against Gold.—An anecdote related of the Rajas of Marwar and Amber, always rivals in war, love, and folly,

[1] Manu commands, "Should the king be near his end through some incurable disease, he must bestow on the priests all his riches accumulated from legal fines: and having duly committed his kingdom to his son, let him seek death in battle, or, if there be no war, by abstaining from food" (*Laws*, ix. 323). The annals of all the Rajput States afford instances of obedience to this text of their divine legislator. [The injunction to seek death by starvation is an addition by the commentator, and is not included in the original text.]

will illustrate the motives of these dismemberments. During the annual pilgrimage to the sacred lake of Pushkar, it is the custom for these lords of the earth to weigh their persons against all that is rare, in gold, gems, and precious cloths ; which are afterwards distributed to the priests.[1] The Amber chief had the advantage of a full treasury and a fertile soil, to which his rival could oppose a more extended sway over a braver race ; but his country was proverbially poor, and at Pushkar, the weight of the purse ranks above the deeds of the sword. As these princes were suspended in the scale, the Amber Raja, who was balanced against the more costly material, indirectly taunted his brother-in-law on the poverty of his offerings, who would gladly, like the Roman, have made up the deficiency with his sword. But the Marwar prince had a minister of tact, at whose suggestion he challenged his rival (of Amber) to equal him in the magnitude of his gift to the Brahmans. On the gage being accepted, the Rathor exclaimed, "Perpetual charity (*sasan*)[2] of all the lands held by the Brahmans in Marwar!" His unreflecting rival had commenced the redemption of his pledge, when his minister stopped the half-uttered vow, which would have impoverished the family for ever ; for there were ten Brahmans in Amber who followed secular employments, cultivating or holding lands in usufruct, to one in Marwar. Had these lords of the earth been left to their misguided vanity, the fisc of each state would have been seriously curtailed.

Grants to Brāhmans and Devotees.—The Brahmans, Sannyasis, and Gosains are not behind those professional flatterers, the Bards ; and many a princely name would have been forgotten but for the record of the gift of land. In Mewar, the lands in *sasan*, or religious grants, amount in value to one-fifth of the

[1] [The practice of a devotee weighing himself against gold was common in ancient Hindu times, was known as *tulāpurushadāna*, and is still performed by the Mahārāja of Travancore (Thurston, *Tribes and Castes of S. India*, vii. 202 ff. ; *BG*, i. Part ii. 415 ; Forbes, *Rāsmāla*, 84). Akbar used to have himself weighed against precious substances twice a year, on his solar and lunar birthdays, the articles being given to Brāhmans, and Jahāngīr followed the same custom (*Āīn*, i. 266 ff. ; Elliot-Dowson v. 307, 453 ; *Memoirs of Jahāngīr*, trans. Rogers-Beveridge, 78, 81, 111, 183).]

[2] [Sāsan, a grant by charter of rent-free lands, made in favour of Brāhmans and devotees. For the formula used in such grants see Barnett, *Antiquities of India*, 129.]

revenue of the State, and the greater proportion of these has arisen out of the prodigal mismanagement of the last century. The dilapidated state of the country, on the general pacification in A.D. 1818, afforded a noble opportunity to redeem in part these alienations, without the penalty of denunciation attached to the resumer of sacred charities. But death, famine, and exile, which had left but few of the grantees in a capacity to return and reoccupy the lands, in vain coalesced to restore the fisc of Mewar. The Rana dreaded a "sixty thousand [509] years' residence in hell," and some of the finest land of his country is doomed to remain unproductive. In this predicament is the township of Menal,[1] with 50,000 bighas (16,000 acres), which with the exception of a nook where some few have established themselves, claiming to be descendants of the original holders, are condemned to sterility, owing to the agricultural proprietors and the rent-receiving Brahmans being dead; and apathy united to superstition admits their claims without inquiry.

The antiquary, who has dipped into the records of the dark period in European church history, can have ocular illustration in Rajasthan of traditions which may in Europe appear questionable. The vision of the Bishop of Orleans,[2] who saw Charles Martel in the depths of hell, undergoing the tortures of the damned, for having stripped the churches of their possessions, "thereby rendering himself guilty of the sins of all those who had endowed them," would receive implicit credence from every Hindu, whose ecclesiastical economy might both yield and derive illustration from a comparison, not only with that of Europe, but with the more ancient Egyptian and Jewish systems, whose endowments, as explained by Moses and Ezekiel, bear a strong analogy to his

[1] [Menāl, Mahānāl, 'the great chasm,' in the Begun Estate, E. Mewār.]

[2] "Saint Eucher, évêque d'Orléans, eut une vision qui étonna les princes. Il faut que je rapporte à ce sujet la lettre que les évêques, assemblés à Reims, écrivent à Louis-le-Germanique, qui étoit entré dans les terres de Charles le Chauve, parce qu'elle est très-propre à nous faire voir quel étoit, dans ces temps-là, l'état des choses, et la situation des esprits. Ils disent que 'Saint Eucher ayant été ravi dans le ciel, il vit Charles Martel tourmenté dans l'enfer inférieur par l'ordre des saints qui doivent assister avec Jésus-Christ au jugement dernier; qu'il avoit été condamné à cette peine avant le temps pour avoir dépouillé les églises de leurs biens, et s'être par là rendu coupable des péchés de tous ceux qui les avoient dotées'" (Montesquieu, *L'Esprit des Lois*, livre xxxi. chap. xi. p. 460).

own. The disposition of landed property in Egypt, as amongst the ancient Hindus, was immemorially vested in the cultivator; and it was only through Joseph's ministry in the famine that "the land became Pharaoh's, as the Egyptians sold every man his field." [1] And the coincidence is manifest even in the tax imposed on them as occupants of their inheritance, being one-fifth of the crops to the king, while the maximum rate among the Hindus is a sixth.[2] The Hindus also, in visitations such as that which occasioned the dispossession of the ryots of Egypt, can mortgage or sell their patrimony (*bapota*). Joseph did not attempt to infringe the privileges of the sacred order when the whole of Egypt became crown-land, "except the lands of the priests, which became not Pharaoh's"; and these priests, according to Diodorus, held for themselves and the sacrifices no less than one-third of the lands of Egypt. But we learn from [510] Herodotus, that Sesostris, who ruled after Joseph's ministry, restored the lands to the people, reserving the customary tax or tribute.[3]

The prelates of the middle ages of Europe were often completely feudal nobles, swearing fealty and paying homage as did the lay lords.[4] In Rajasthan, the sacerdotal caste not bound to the altar may hold lands and perform the duties of vassalage: [5] but of late years, when land has been assigned to religious establishments, no reservation has been made of fiscal rights, territorial or commercial. This is, however, an innovation; since, formerly, princes never granted, along with territorial assignments, the prerogative of dispensing justice, of levying transit duties, or exemption from personal service of the feudal tenant who held on the land thus assigned. Well may Rajput heirs exclaim with the grandson of Clovis, "our exchequer is impoverished, and our riches are transferred to the clergy." [6] But Chilperic had the courage to recall the grants of his predecessors, which, however, the pious Gontram re-established. Many Gontrams could be found, though but few Chilperics, in Rajasthan: we have, indeed,

[1] Genesis xlvii. 20-26.

[2] Manu, *Laws*, vii. 130.

[3] *Origin of Laws and Government*, vol. i. p. 54, and vol. ii. p. 13. [Herodotus ii. 109.]

[4] Hallam, *Middle Ages*, vol. ii. p. 212.

[5] "A Brahman unable to subsist by his duties just mentioned (sacerdotal), may live by the duty of a soldier" (Manu x. 81).

[6] Montesquieu.

one in Jograj,[1] the Rana's ancestor, almost a contemporary of the Merovingian king, who not only resumed all the lands of the Brahmans, but put many of them to death, and expelled the rest his dominions.[2]

It may be doubted whether vanity and shame are not sufficient in themselves to prevent a resumption of the lands of the Mangtas or mendicants, as they style all those 'who extend the palm,' without the dreaded penalty, which operates very slightly on the sub-vassal or cultivator, who, having no superfluity, defies their anathemas when they attempt to wrest from him, by virtue of the crown-grant, any of his long-established rights. By these, the threat of impure transmigration is despised; and the Brahman may spill his blood on the threshold of his dwelling or in the field in dispute, which will be relinquished by the owner but with his life. The Pat Rani, or chief queen, on the death of Prince Amra, the heir-apparent, in 1818, bestowed a grant of fifteen bighas of land, in one of the central districts, on a Brahman who had assisted in the funeral rites of her son. With grant in hand [511], he hastened to the Jat proprietor, and desired him to make over to him the patch of land. The latter coolly replied that he would give him all the prince had a right to, namely the tax. The Brahman threatened to spill his own blood if he did not obey the command, and gave himself a gash in a limb; but the Jat was inflexible, and declared that he would not surrender his patrimony (*bapota*) even if he slew himself.[3] In short, the

[1] [One of the legendary Rānas, twenty-fifth on the list, to whom no date can be assigned.]

[2] "Le clergé recevoit tant, qu'il faut que, dans les trois races, on lui ait donné plusieurs fois tous les biens du royaume. Mais si les rois, la noblesse, et le peuple, trouvèrent le moyen de leur donner tous leurs biens, ils ne trouvèrent pas moins celui de les leur ôter" (Montesquieu, *L'Esprit des Lois*, livre xxxi. chap. x.).

[3] These worshippers of God and Mammon, when threats fail, have recourse to maiming, and even destroying, themselves, to gain their object. In 1820, one of the confidential servants of the Rana demanded payment of the petty tax called *gugri*, of one rupee on each house, from some Brahmans who dwelt in the village, and which had always been received from them. They refused payment, and on being pressed, four of them stabbed themselves mortally. Their bodies were placed upon biers, and funeral rites withheld till punishment should be inflicted on the priest-killer. But for once superstition was disregarded, and the rights of the Brahmans in this community were resumed. See Appendix to this Part, No. I [p. 644].

ryot of Mewar would reply, even to his sovereign, if he demanded his field, in the very words of Naboth to Ahab, king of Israel, when he demanded the vineyard contiguous to the palace: "The Lord forbid it me that I should give the inheritance of my fathers unto thee."

Tithes, Temples.—But the tithes, and other small and legally established rights of the hierarchy, are still religiously maintained. The village temple and the village priest are always objects of veneration to the industrious husbandman, on whom superstition acts more powerfully than on the bold marauding Rajput, who does not hesitate to demand salvamenta (*rakhwali*) from the lands of Kanhaiya or Eklinga. But the poor ryot of the nineteenth century of Vikrama has the same fears as the peasants of Charlemagne, who were made to believe that the ears of corn found empty had been devoured by infernal spirits, reported to have said they owed their feast to the non-payment of tithes.[1]

Political Influence of Brāhmans.—The political influence of the Brahmans is frequently exemplified in cases alike prejudicial to the interests of society and the personal welfare of the sovereign. The latter is often surrounded by lay-Brahmans as confidential servants, in the capacities of butler, keeper of the wardrobe, or seneschal,[2] besides the Guru or domestic chaplain, who to the duty of ghostly comforter sometimes joins that of [512] astrologer

[1] "Mais le bas peuple n'est guère capable d'abandonner ses intérêts par des exemples. Le synode de Francfort lui présenta un motif plus pressant pour payer les dîmes. On y fit un capitulaire dans lequel il est dit que, dans la dernière famine, on avoit trouvé les épis de blé vides, qu'ils avoient été dévorés par les démons, et qu'on avoit entendu leurs voix qui reprochoient de n'avoir pas payé la dîme: et, en conséquence, il fut ordonné à tous ceux qui tenoient les biens ecclésiastiques de payer la dîme, et, en conséquence encore, on l'ordonna à tous" (*L'Esprit des Lois*, livre xxxi. chap. xii.).

[2] These lay Brahmans are not wanting in energy or courage; the sword is as familiar to them as the *mala* (chaplet). The grandfather of Ramnath, the present worthy seneschal of the Rana, was governor of the turbulent district of Jahazpur, which has never been so well ruled since. He left a curious piece of advice to his successors, inculcating vigorous measures. "With two thousand men you may eat *khichri*; with one thousand *dalbhat*; with five hundred *juti* (the *shoe*)." *Khichri* is a savoury mess of pulse, rice, butter, and spices; *dalbhat* is simple rice and pulse; *the shoe* is indelible disgrace.

and physician, in which case God help the prince![1] These Gurus and Purohits, having the education of the children, acquire immense influence, and are not backward in improving "the greatness thrust upon them." They are all continually importuning their prince for grants of land for themselves and the shrines they are attached to; and every chief, as well as every influential domestic, takes advantage of ephemeral favour to increase the endowments of his tutelary divinity. The Peshwas of Satara are the most striking out of numerous examples.

In the dark ages of Europe the monks are said to have prostituted their knowledge of writing to the forging of charters in their own favour: a practice not easily detected in the days of ignorance.[2] The Brahmans, in like manner, do not scruple to employ this method of augmenting the wealth of their shrines; and superstition and indolence combine to support the deception

[1] Manu, in his rules on government, commands the king to impart his momentous counsel and entrust all transactions to a learned and distinguished Brahman (*Laws*, vii. 58). There is no being more aristocratic in his ideas than the secular Brahman or priest, who deems the bare name a passport to respect. The Kulin Brahman of Bengal piques himself upon this title of nobility granted by the last Hindu king of Kanauj (whence they migrated to Bengal), and in virtue of which his alliance in matrimony is courted. But although Manu has imposed obligations towards the Brahman little short of adoration, these are limited to the "learned in the Vedas": he classes the unlearned Brahman with "an elephant made of wood, or an antelope of leather"; nullities, save in name. And he adds further, that "as liberality to a fool is useless, so is a Brahman useless if he read not the holy texts": comparing the person who gives to such an one, to a husbandman "who, sowing seed in a barren soil, reaps no gain"; so the Brahman "obtains no reward in heaven." These sentiments are repeated in numerous texts, holding out the most powerful inducements to the sacerdotal class to cultivate their minds, since their power consists solely in their wisdom. For such, there are no privileges too extensive, no homage too great. "A king, even though dying with want, must not receive any tax from a Brahman learned in the Vedas." His person is sacred. "Never shall the king slay a Brahman, though convicted of all possible crimes," is a premium at least to unbounded insolence, and unfits them for members of society, more especially for soldiors; banishment, with person and property untouched, is the declared punishment for even the most heinous crimes. "A Brahman may seize without hesitation, if he be distressed for a subsistence, the goods of his Sudra slave." But the following text is the climax: "What prince could gain wealth by oppressing those [Brahmans], who, if angry, could frame other worlds, and regents of worlds, and could give birth to new gods and mortals?" (Manu, *Laws*, ii. iii. vii. viii. ix.).

[2] Hallam's *Middle Ages*, vol. i. p. 204.

There is not a doubt that the grand charter of Nathdwara was a forgery, in which the prince's butler was bribed to aid; and report alleges that the Rana secretly favoured an artifice which regard to opinion prevented him from overtly promulgating. Although the copper-plate had been buried under ground, and came out disguised with a coating of verdigris, there were marks which proved the date of its execution to be false. I have seen charters which, it has been gravely asserted, were granted by Rama upwards of three thousand years ago! Such is the origin assigned to one found in a well at the ancient Brahmpuri, in the valley of the capital. If there be sceptics as to its validity, they are silent ones; and this copper-plate of the brazen age [513] is worth gold to the proprietor.[1] A census[2] of the three central districts of Mewar discovered that more than twenty thousand acres of these fertile lands, irrigated by the Berach and Banas rivers, were distributed in isolated portions, of which the mendicant castes had the chief share, and which proved fertile sources of dispute to the husbandman and the officers of the revenue. From the mass of title-deeds of every description by which these lands were held, one deserves to be selected, on account of its being pretended to have been written and bestowed on the incumbent's ancestor by the deity upwards of three centuries ago, and which has been maintained as a *bona-fide* grant of Krishna[3] ever since. By such credulity and apathy are the Rajput States influenced: yet let the reader check any rising feeling of contempt for Hindu legislation, and cast a retrospective glance at the page of European church history, where he will observe in the time of the most potent of our monarchs that the clergy possessed one-half of the soil:[4] and the chronicles of France will show him Charlemagne on his death-bed, bequeathing two-thirds of his domains to the church, deeming the remaining third sufficient for the ambition of four sons. The same dread of futurity, and the hope to expiate the sins of a life, at its

[1] These forgeries of charters cannot be considered as invalidating the arguments drawn from them, as we may rest assured nothing is introduced foreign to custom, in the items of the deeds.

[2] Suggested by the Author, and executed under his superintendence, who waded through all these documents, and translated upwards of a hundred of the most curious.

[3] See the Appendix to this Part, No. II [p. 644].

[4] Hallam.

close, by gifts to the organs of religion, is the motive for these unwise alienations, whether in Europe or in Asia. Some of these establishments, and particularly that at Nathdwara, made a proper use of their revenues in keeping up the Sada-Brat, or perpetual charity, though it is chiefly distributed to religious pilgrims: but among the many complaints made of the misapplication of the funds, the diminution of this hospitable right is one; while, at other shrines, the avarice of the priests is observable in the coarseness of the food dressed for sacrifice and offering.

Tithes levied by Brāhmans.—Besides the crown-grants to the greater establishments, the Brahmans received petty tithes from the agriculturist, and a small duty from the trader, as *mapa* or metage, throughout every township, corresponding with the scale of the village-chapel. An inscription found by the author at the town of Palod,[1] and dated nearly seven centuries back, affords a good specimen of the claims of the village [514] priesthood. The following are among the items. The *serana,* or a *ser,* in every *maund,* being the fortieth part of the grain of the *unalu,* or summer-harvest; the *karpa,* or a bundle from every sheaf of the autumnal crops, whether *makai* (Indian corn), *bajra* or *juar* (maize) [millet], or the other grains peculiar to that season.[2]

They also derive a tithe from the oil-mill and sugar-mill, and receive a *kansa* or platter of food on all rejoicings, as births, marriages, etc., with *charai,* or the right of pasturage on the village common; and where they have become possessed of landed property they have *halma,* or unpaid labour in man and beasts, and implements, for its culture: an exaction well known in Europe as one of the detested *corvées* of the feudal system of France,[3] the abolition of which was the sole boon the English husbandman obtained by the charter of Runymede. Both the chieftain and the priest exact *halma* in Rajasthan; but in that country it is mitigated, and abuse is prevented, by a sentiment unknown to the feudal despot of the middle ages of Europe, and

[1] See Appendix to this Part, No. III [p. 645].

[2] Each bundle consists of a specified number of ears, which are roasted and eaten in the unripe state with a little salt. [A *ser* or *seer* = 2·057 lbs. avoirdupois.]

[3] *Dict. de l'Ancien Régime,* p. 131, art. "Corvée."

which, though difficult to define, acts imperceptibly, having its source in accordance of belief, patriarchal manners, and clannish attachments.

Privileges of Saivas and Jains.—I shall now briefly consider the privileges of the Saivas and Jains—the orthodox and heterodox sects of Mewar; and then proceed to those of Vishnu, whose worship is the most prevalent in these countries, and which I am inclined to regard as of more recent origin.

Worship of Siva.—Mahadeva, or Iswara, is the tutelary divinity of the Rajputs in Mewar; and from the early annals of the dynasty appears to have been, with his consort Isani, the sole object of Guhilot adoration. Iswara is adored under the epithet of Eklinga,[1] and is either worshipped in his monolithic symbol, or as Iswara Chaumukhi, the quadriform divinity, represented by a bust with four faces. The sacred bull, Nandi, has his altar attached to all the shrines of Iswara, as was that of Mneves or Apis to those of the Egyptian Osiris. Nandi has occasionally his separate shrines, and there is one in the valley of Udaipur which has the reputation of being oracular as regards the seasons. The bull was the steed of Iswara, and [515] carried him in battle; he is often represented upon it, with his consort Isani, at full speed. I will not stop to inquire whether the Grecian fable of the rape of Europa[2] by the tauriform Jupiter may not be derived, with much more of their mythology, from the Hindu pantheon; whether that pantheon was originally erected on the Indus, or

[1] That is, with *one (ek) lingam* or phallus—the symbol of worship being a single cylindrical or conical stone. There are others, termed *Sahaslinga* and *Kotiswara*, with a thousand or a million of phallic representatives, all minutely carved on the monolithic emblem, having then much resemblance to the symbol of Bacchus, whose orgies, both in Egypt and Greece, are the counterpart of those of the Hindu Baghis, thus called from being clad in a tiger's or leopard's hide: Bacchus had the panther's for his covering. There is a very ancient temple to Kotiswara at the *embouchure* of the eastern arm of the Indus; and here are many to Sahaslinga in the peninsula of Saurashtra. [Bacchus has no connexion with a Hindu tiger-god.]

[2] It might have appeared fanciful, some time ago, to have given a Sanskrit derivation to a Greek proper name: but Europa might be derived from *Surupa*, 'of the beautiful face'—the initial syllable *su* and *eu* having the same signification in both languages, namely, *good*—*Rupa* is 'countenance.' [Europa is probably Assyrian *ereb*, *irib*, 'land of the rising sun' (*EB*, ix. 907). Another explanation is that it is a cult title, meaning 'goddess of the flourishing willow-withies' (A. B. Cook, *Zeus*, 531).]

the Ganges, or the more central scene of early civilization, the banks of the Oxus. The bull was offered to Mithras by the Persian, and opposed as it now appears to Hindu faith, he formerly bled on the altars of the Sun-god, on which not only the Baldan,[1] 'offering of the bull,' was made, but human sacrifices.[2] We do not learn that the Egyptian priesthood presented the kindred of Apis to Osiris, but as they were not prohibited from eating beef, they may have done so.

The Temple of Eklinga.—The shrine of Eklinga is situated in a defile about six [twelve] miles north of Udaipur. The hills towering around it on all sides are of the primitive formation, and their scarped summits are clustered with honeycombs.[3] There are abundant small springs of water, which keep verdant numerous shrubs, the flowers of which are acceptable to the deity; especially the *kaner* or oleander, which grows in great

[1] In this sacrifice four altars are erected, for offering the flesh to the four gods, Lakshmi-Narayana, Umamaheswar, Brahma, and Ananta. The nine planets, and Prithu, or the earth, with her ten guardian-deities, are worshipped. Five *Vilwa*, five *Khadira*, five *Palasha*, and five *Udumbara* posts are to be erected, and a bull tied to each post. Clarified butter is burnt on the altar, and pieces of the flesh of the slaughtered animals placed thereon. This sacrifice was very common (Ward, *On the Religion of the Hindus*, vol. ii. p. 263). [Balidāna, 'an offering to the gods.']

[2] First a covered altar is to be prepared; sixteen posts are then to be erected of various woods; a golden image of a man, and an iron one of a goat, with golden images of Vishnu and Lakshmi, a silver one of Siva, with a golden bull, and a silver one of Garuda 'the eagle,' are placed upon the altar. Animals, as goats, sheep, etc., are tied to the posts, and to one of them, of the wood of the *mimosa*, is to be tied the human victim. Fire is to be kindled by means of a burning glass. The sacrificing priest, *hota*, strews the grass called *dub* or immortal, round the sacred fire. Then follows the burnt sacrifice to the ten guardian deities of the earth—to the nine planets, and to the Hindu Triad, to each of whom clarified butter is poured on the sacred fire one thousand times. Another burnt-sacrifice, to the sixty-four inferior gods, follows, which is succeeded by the sacrifice and offering of all the other animals tied to the posts. The human sacrifice concludes, the sacrificing priest offering pieces of the flesh of the victim to each god as he circumambulates the altar (*ibid*, 260).

[3] This is to be taken in its literal sense; the economy of the bee being displayed in the formation of extensive colonies which inhabit large masses of black comb adhering to the summits of the rocks. According to the legends of these tracts, they were called in as auxiliaries on Muhammadan invasions, and are said to have thrown the enemy more than once into confusion. [Stories of idols protected from desecration by swarms of hornets are common (*BG*, viii. 401; Sleeman, *Rambles*, 54).]

luxuriance on the Aravalli. Groves of bamboo and mango were formerly common, according to tradition; but although it is deemed sacrilege to thin the groves of Bal,[1] the bamboo has been nearly destroyed: there are, however, still many trees sacred to the deity scattered around. It would be difficult to convey a just [516] idea of a temple so complicated in its details. It is of the form commonly styled pagoda, and, like all the ancient temples of Siva, its *sikhara,* or pinnacle, is pyramidal. The various orders of Hindu sacred architecture are distinguished by the form of the *sikhara,* which is the portion springing from and surmounting the perpendicular walls of the body of the temple. The *sikhara* of those of Siva is invariably pyramidal, and its sides vary with the base, whether square or oblong. The apex is crowned with an ornamental figure, as a sphinx, an urn, a ball, or a lion, which is called the *kalas.* When the *sikhara* is but the frustum of a pyramid, it is often surmounted by a row of lions, as at Bijolia. The fane of Eklinga is of white marble and of ample dimensions. Under an open-vaulted temple supported by columns, and fronting the four-faced divinity, is the brazen bull Nandi, of the natural size; it is cast, and of excellent proportions. The figure is perfect, except where the shot or hammer of an infidel invader has penetrated its hollow flank in search of treasure. Within the quadrangle are miniature shrines, containing some of the minor divinities.[2] The high-priest of Eklinga, like all his order, is doomed to celibacy, and

[1] See Appendix to this Part, No. IV [p. 645].

[2] In June 1806 I was present at a meeting between the Rana and Sindhia at the shrine of Eklinga. The rapacious Mahratta had just forced the passes to the Rana's capital, which was the commencement of a series of aggressions involving one of the most tragical events in the history of Mewar—the immolation of the Princess Krishna and the subsequent ruin of the country. I was then an *attaché* of the British embassy to the Mahratta prince, who carried the ambassador to the meeting to increase his consequence. In March 1818 I again visited the shrine, on my way to Udaipur, but under very different circumstances—to announce the deliverance of the family from oppression, and to labour for its prosperity. While standing without the sanctuary, looking at the quadriform divinity, and musing on the changes of the intervening twelve years, my meditations were broken by an old Rajput chieftain, who, saluting me, invited me to enter and adore Baba Adam, 'Father Adam,' as he termed the phallic emblem. I excused myself on account of my boots, which I said I could not remove, and that with them I would not cross the threshold: a reply which pleased them, and preceded me to the Rana's court.

the office is continued by adopted disciples. Of such spiritual descents they calculate sixty-four since the Sage Harita, whose benediction obtained for the Guhilot Rajput the sovereignty of Chitor, when driven from Saurashtra by the Parthians.

The priests of Eklinga are termed Gosain or Goswami, which signifies 'control over the senses'! The distinguishing mark of the faith of Siva is the crescent on the forehead:[1] the hair is braided and forms a tiara round the head, and with its folds a chaplet of the lotus-seed is often entwined. They smear the body with ashes, and use garments dyed of an orange hue. They bury their dead in a sitting [517] posture, and erect tumuli over them, which are generally conical in form.[2] It is not uncommon for priestesses to officiate in the temple of Siva. There is a numerous class of Gosains who have adopted celibacy, and who yet follow secular employments both in commerce and arms. The mercantile Gosains[3] are amongst the richest individuals in India, and there are several at Udaipur who enjoy high favour, and who were found very useful when the Mahrattas demanded a war-contribution, as their privileged character did not prevent their being offered and taken as hostages for its payment. The Gosains who profess arms, partake of the character of the knights of St. John of Jerusalem. They live in monasteries scattered over the country, possess lands, and beg, or serve for pay when called upon. As defensive soldiers, they are good. Siva, their patron, is the god of war, and like him they make great use of intoxicating herbs, and even of spirituous liquors. In Mewar they can always muster many hundreds of the Kanphara[4] Jogi, or 'split-ear ascetics,' so called from the habit of piercing the ear and placing therein a ring of the conch-shell, which is their battle-

[1] Siva is represented with three eyes: hence his title of Trinetra and Trilochan, the Triophthalmic Jupiter of the Greeks. From the fire of the central eye of Siva is to proceed Pralaya, or the final destruction of the universe: this eye placed vertically, resembling the flame of a taper, is a distinguishing mark on the foreheads of his votaries.

[2] I have seen a cemetery of these, each of very small dimensions, which may be described as so many concentric rings of earth, diminishing to the apex, crowned with a cylindrical stone pillar. One of the disciples of Siva was performing rites to the manes, strewing leaves of an evergreen [probably bel, *Aegle marmelos*] and sprinkling water over the graves.

[3] For a description of these, vide *Transactions of the Royal Asiatic Society*, vol. i. p. 217.

[4] [The more usual form is Kanphata, with the same meaning.]

trumpet. Both Brahmans and Rajputs, and even Gujars, can belong to this order, a particular account of whose internal discipline and economy could not fail to be interesting. The poet Chand gives an animated description of the body-guard of the King of Kanauj, which was composed of these monastic warriors.

Priestly Functions of the Mewār Rānas.—The Ranas of Mewar, as the diwans, or vicegerents of Siva, when they visit the temple supersede the high priest in his duties, and perform the ceremonies, which the reigning prince does with peculiar correctness and grace.[1]

Privileges of Jains.—The shrine of Eklinga is endowed with twenty-four large villages from the fisc, besides parcels of land from the chieftains; but the privileges of the tutelary divinity have been waning since Kanhaiya fixed his residence amongst them; and as the priests of Apollo complained that the god was driven from the sacred mount [518] Govardhana, in Vraj, by the influence of those of Jupiter[2] with Shah Jahan, the latter may now lament that the day of retribution has arrived, when propitiation to the Preserver is deemed more important than to the Destroyer. This may arise from the personal character of the high priests, who, from their vicinity to the court, can scarcely avoid mingling in its intrigues, and thence lose in character: even the Ranis do not hesitate to take mortgages on the estates of Bholanath.[3] We shall not further enlarge on the immunities to Eklinga, or the forms in which they are conveyed, as these will be fully discussed in the account of the shrine of Krishna; but proceed to notice the privileges of the heterodox Jains—the Vidyavan[4] or Magi of Rajasthan. The numbers and power of

[1] The copy of the *Siva Purana* which I presented to the Royal Asiatic Society was obtained for me by the Rana from the temple of Eklinga.

[2] Jiva-pitri, the 'Father of Life,' would be a very proper epithet for Mahadeva, the creative 'power,' whose Olympus is Kailas. [Jīva-pitri means 'a child whose father is alive.' Jupiter = Skt. Dyaus-pitā.]

[3] Bholanath, or the 'Simple God,' is one of the epithets of Siva, whose want of reflection is so great that he would give away his own divinity if asked.

[4] Vidyavan, the 'Man of Secrets or Knowledge,' is the term used by way of reproach to the Jains, having the import of *magician*. Their opponents believe them to be possessed of supernatural skill; and it is recorded of the celebrated Amara, author of the *Kosa* or dictionary called after him, that he m raculously "made the full moon appear on Amavas"—the ides of the month, when the planet is invisible.

these sectarians are little known to Europeans, who take it for granted that they are few and dispersed. To prove the extent of their religious and political power, it will suffice to remark that the pontiff of the Khadatara-gachchha,[1] one of the many branches of this faith, has 11,000 clerical disciples scattered over India; that a single community, the Osi or Oswal,[2] numbers 100,000 families; and that more than half [519] of the mercantile wealth of India passes through the hands of the Jain laity. Rajasthan and Saurashtra are the cradles of the Buddhist or Jain faith, and three out of their five sacred mounts, namely, Abu, Palitana,[3] and Girnar, are in these countries. The officers

[1] Khadatara signifies 'true' [?], an epithet of distinction which was bestowed by that great supporter of the Buddhists or Jains, Siddharaj, king of Anhilwara Patan, on one of the branches (*gachchha*), in a grand religious disputation (*badha*) at that capital in the eleventh century. The celebrated Hemacharya was head of the *Khadatara-gachchha*; and his spiritual descendant honoured Udaipur with his presence in his visit to his dioceses in the desert in 1821. My own Yati tutor was a disciple of Hemacharya, and his *pattravali*, or pedigree, registered his descent by spiritual successions from him. [For the Jain gachchhas see Bühler, *The Indian Sect of the Jainas*, 77 ff. As usual, the author confounds Jains with Buddhists.] This pontiff was a man of extensive learning and of estimable character. He was versed in all the ancient inscriptions, to which no key now exists, and deciphered one for me which had been long unintelligible. His travelling library was of considerable extent, though chiefly composed of works relating to the ceremonies of his religion: it was in the charge of two of his disciples remarkable for talent, and who, like himself, were perfectly acquainted with all these ancient characters. The pontiff kindly permitted my Yati to bring for my inspection some of the letters of invitation written by his flocks in the desert. These were rolls, some of them several feet in length, containing pictured delineations of their wishes. One from Bikaner represented that city, in one division of which was the school or college of the Jains, where the Yatis were all portrayed at their various studies. In another part, a procession of them was quitting the southern gate of the city, the head of which was in the act of delivering a scroll to a messenger, while the pontiff was seen with his cortège advancing in the distance. To show the respect in which these high priests of the Jains are held, the princes of Rajputana invariably advance outside the walls of their capital to receive and conduct them to it—a mark of respect paid only to princes. On the occasion of the high priest of the *Khadataras* passing through Udaipur, as above alluded to, the Rana received him with every distinction.

[2] So called from the town of Osi or Osian, in Marwar [about 30 miles N. of Jodhpur city].

[3] Palitana, or 'the abode of the Pali' [?], is the name of the town at the foot of the sacred mount Satrunjaya (signifying 'victorious over the foe'), on which the Jain temples are sacred to Buddhiswara, or the 'Lord of the

of the State and revenue are chiefly of the Jain laity, as are the majority of the bankers, from Lahore to the ocean. The chief magistrate and assessors of justice, in Udaipur and most of the towns of Rajasthan, are of this sect; and as their voluntary duties are confined to civil cases, they are as competent in these as they are the reverse in criminal cases, from their tenets forbidding the shedding of blood. To this leading feature in their religion they owe their political debasement: for Kumarpal, the last king of Anhilwara of the Jain faith, would not march his armies in the rains, from the unavoidable sacrifice of animal life that must have ensued. The strict Jain does not even maintain a lamp during that season, lest it should attract moths to their destruction.

Absence of Intolerance.—The period of sectarian intolerance is now past; and as far as my observation goes, the ministers of Vishnu, Siva, and Buddha view each other without malignity; which feeling never appears to have influenced the laity of either sect, who are indiscriminately respectful to the ministers of all religions, whatever be their tenets. It is sufficient that their office is one of sanctity, and that they are ministers of the Divinity, who, they say, excludes the homage of none, in whatever tongue or whatever manner he is sought; and with this spirit of entire toleration, the devout missionary, or Mulla, would in no country meet more security or hospitable courtesy than among the Rajputs. They must, however, adopt the toleration they would find practised towards themselves, and not exclude, as some of them do, the races of Surya and Chandra from divine mercy, who, with less arrogance, and more reliance on the compassionate nature of the Creator, say, he has established a variety of paths by which the good may attain beatitude.

Mewar has, from the most remote period, afforded a refuge to

Buddhists' [?]. I have little doubt that the name of Palitana is derived from the pastoral (*pali*) Scythic invaders bringing the Buddhist faith in their train —a faith which appears to me not indigenous to India [?]. Palestine, which, with the whole of Syria and Egypt, was ruled by the Hyksos or Shepherd kings, who for a season expelled the old Coptic race, may have had a similar import to the *Palitana* founded by the Indo-Scythic Pali. The Author visited all these sacred mounts. [The Author describes Pālitāna in *WI*, 274 ff.; see also *BG*, viii. 603 f. All this confusion between Buddhists and Jains and the suggested derivation, in which the Author unfortunately relied on Wilford (*Asiatic Researches*, iii. 72 ff., viii. 321), are out of date.]

the followers of the Jain faith, which was the religion of Valabhi, the first capital of the Rana's ancestors, and many monuments attest the support this family has granted to its [520] professors in all the vicissitudes of their fortunes. One of the best preserved monumental remains in India is a column most elaborately sculptured, full seventy feet in height, dedicated to Parsvanath, in Chitor.[1] The noblest remains of sacred architecture, not in Mewar only, but throughout Western India, are Buddhist or Jain;[2] and the many ancient cities where this religion was fostered, have inscriptions which evince their prosperity in these countries, with whose history their own is interwoven. In fine, the necrological records of the Jains bear witness to their having occupied a distinguished place in Rajput society; and the privileges they still enjoy, prove that they are not overlooked. It is not my intention to say more on the past or present history of these sectarians, than may be necessary to show the footing on which their establishments are placed; to which end little is required beyond copies of a few simple warrants and ordinances in their favour.[3] Hereafter I may endeavour to add something to the knowledge already possessed of these deists of Rajasthan, whose singular communities contain mines of knowledge hitherto inaccessible to Europeans. The libraries of Jaisalmer in the desert, of Anhilwara, the cradle of their faith, of Cambay, and other places of minor importance, consist of thousands of volumes. These are under the control, not of the priests alone, but of communities of the most wealthy and respectable amongst the laity, and are preserved in the crypts of their temples, which precaution ensured their preservation, as well as that of the statues of their deified teachers, when the temples themselves were destroyed by the Muhammadan invaders, who paid more deference to the images of Buddha than those of Siva or Vishnu. The preservation of the former may be owing to the natural formation of their statues; for while many of Adinath, of Nemi, and of Parsva have escaped the hammer, there is scarcely an

[1] [The Kīrtti-Stambha, erected by a merchant named Jīja in the twelfth century A.D., and dedicated to Ādināth, the first Jain Tīrthakara (Fergusson, *Hist. Indian Architecture*, ii. 57 ff.; Erskine ii. A. 104).]

[2] [Buddhism and Jainism are again confused. For Buddhist remains in Rājputāna see *IGI*, xxi. 103.]

[3] See Appendix to this Part [p. 645].

Apollo or a Venus, of any antiquity, entire, from Lahore to Rameswaram. The two arms of these theists sufficed for their protection; while the statues of the polytheists have met with no mercy.

Grant of Rāna Rāj Singh.—No. V.[1] is the translation of a grant by the celebrated Rana Raj Singh, the gallant and successful opponent of Aurangzeb in many a battle. It is at once of a general and special nature, containing a confirmation of the old privileges of the sect, and a mark of favour to a priest of some distinction, called Mana. It is well known [521] that the first law of the Jains, like that of the ancient Athenian lawgiver Triptolemus, is, "Thou shalt not kill," a precept applicable to every sentient thing. The first clause of this edict, in conformity thereto, prohibits all innovation upon this cherished principle; while the second declares that even the life which is forfeited to the laws is immortal (*amara*) if the victim but passes near their abodes. The third article defines the extent of *saran*, or sanctuary, the dearest privilege of the races of these regions. The fourth article sanctions the tithes, both on agricultural and commercial produce; and makes no distinction between the Jain priests and those of Siva and Vishnu in this source of income, which will be more fully detailed in the account of Nathdwara. The fifth article is the particular gift to the priest; and the whole closes with the usual anathema against such as may infringe the ordinance.

The Jain Retreat.—The edicts Nos. VI. and VII.,[2] engraved on pillars of stone in the towns of Rasmi and Bakrol, further illustrate the scrupulous observances of the Rana's house towards the Jains; where, in compliance with their peculiar doctrine, the oil-mill and the potter's wheel suspend their revolutions for the four months in the year when insects most abound.[3] Many others of a similar character could be furnished, but these remarks may be concluded with an instance of the influence of the Jains on Rajput society, which passed immediately under the Author's

[1] See Appendix to this part [p. 645].

[2] See Appendix to this article [p. 646].

[3] [This is the Pachusan, the four months of Jain retreat, the Vassa or Vassavâsa of the Buddhists. It was held in the rainy season, during which travelling was forbidden, in order to avoid injury to the insect life which abounds at this time (*BG*, ix. Part i. 113 f.; Kern, *Manual of Indian Buddhism*, 80 f.).]

eye. In the midst of a sacrifice to the god of war, when the victims were rapidly falling by the scimitar, a request preferred by one of them for the life of a goat or a buffalo on the point of immolation, met instant compliance, and the animal, become *amara* or immortal, with a garland thrown round his neck, was led off in triumph from the blood-stained spot.

Nāthdwāra.—This is the most celebrated of the fanes of the Hindu Apollo. Its etymology is 'the portal (*dwara*) of the god' (*nath*), of the same import as his more ancient shrine of Dwarka[1] at the 'world's end.' Nathdwara is twenty-two [thirty] miles N.N.E. of Udaipur, on the right bank of the Banas. Although the principal resort of the followers of Vishnu, it has nothing very remarkable in its structure or situation. It owes its celebrity entirely to the image of Krishna, said to [522] be the same that has been worshipped at Mathura ever since his deification, between eleven and twelve hundred years before Christ.[2] As containing the representative of the mildest of the gods of Hind, Nathdwara is one of the most frequented places of pilgrimage, though it must want that attraction to the classical Hindu which the caves of Gaya, the shores of the distant Dwarka, or the pastoral Vraj,[3] the place of the nativity of Krishna, present to his imagination; for though the groves of Vindra,[4] in which

[1] Dwarka is at the point called Jagat Khunt, of the Saurashtra peninsula. *Ka* is the mark of the genitive case [?]: *Dwarkanath* would be the 'gate of the god' ['Lord of Dvārakā'].

[2] Fifty-seven descents are given, both in their sacred and profane genealogies, from Krishna to the princes supposed to have been contemporary with Vikramaditya. The Yadu Bhatti or Shama Bhatti (the Ahsham Bhatti of Abu-l Fazl) [*Āīn*, ii. 339], draw their pedigree from Krishna or Yadunath, as do the Jarejas of Cutch.

[3] With Mathura as a centre and a radius of eighty miles, describe a circle: all within it is Vraj, which was the seat of whatever was refined in Hinduism, and whose language, the Vraj-bhasha, was the purest dialect of India. Vraj is tantamount to the land of the Suraseni, derived from Sursen, the ancestor of Krishna, whose capital, Surpuri, is about fifty miles south of Mathura on the Yamuna (Jumna). The remains of this city (Surpuri) the Author had the pleasure of discovering. The province of the Surseni, or Suraseni, is defined by Manu [*Laws*, ii. 19, vii. 193, who calls them Surasenakas], and particularly mentioned by the historians of Alexander.

[4] Vindravana, or the 'forests of Vindra,' in which were placed many temples sacred to Kanhaiya, is on the Yamuna, a few miles above Mathura. A pilgrimage to this temple is indispensable to the true votary of Krishna.

Kanhaiya disported with the Gopis, no longer resound to the echoes of his flute ; though the waters of the Yamuna [1] are daily polluted with the blood of the sacred kine, still it is the holy land of the pilgrim, the sacred Jordan of his fancy, on whose banks he may sit and weep, as did the banished Israelite of old, the glories of Mathura, his Jerusalem !

It was in the reign of Aurangzeb that the pastoral divinity was exiled from Vraj, that classic soil which, during a period of two thousand eight hundred years, had been the sanctuary of his worshippers. He had been compelled to occasional flights during the visitations of Mahmud and the first dynasties of Afghan invaders ; though the more tolerant of the Mogul kings not only reinstated him, but were suspected of dividing their faith between Kanhaiya and the prophet. Akbar was an enthusiast in the mystic poetry of Jayadeva, which paints in glowing colours the loves of Kanhaiya and Radha, in which lovely personification the refined Hindu abjures all sensual interpretation, asserting its character of pure spiritual love.[2]

The Mughals and Krishna Worship.—Jahangir, by birth half a Rajput, was equally indulgent to the worship of Kanhaiya : but Shah Jahan, also the son of a Rajput princess, inclined to the [523] doctrines of Siva, in which he was initiated by Siddhrup the Sannyasi. Sectarian animosity is more virulent than faiths totally dissimilar. Here we see Hindu depressing Hindu : the followers of Siva oppressing those of Kanhaiya ; the priests of Jupiter driving the pastoral Apollo from the Parnassus of Vraj. At the intercession, however, of a princess of Udaipur, he was replaced on his altar, where he remained till Aurangzeb became emperor of the Moguls. In such detestation did the Hindus hold

[1] This river is called the Kal Yamuna, or black Yamuna, and Kalidah or the 'black pool,' from Kanhaiya having destroyed the hydra Kaliya which infested it. Jayadeva calls the Yamuna 'the blue daughter of the sun.'

[2] [The popular worship of Krishna and Rādha is decidedly erotic.] It affords an example of the Hindu doctrine of the Metempsychosis, as well as of the regard which Akbar's toleration had obtained him, to mention, that they held his body to be animated by the soul of a celebrated Hindu gymnosophist : in support of which they say he (Akbar) went to his accustomed spot of penance (*tapasya*) at the confluence of the Yamuna and Ganges, and excavated the implements, namely, the tongs, gourd, and deer-skin, of his anchorite existence. [For the tale of Akbar and the Brāhman Mukunda see *Asiatic Researches*, ix. 158.]

this intolerant king, that in like manner as they supposed the beneficent Akbar to be the devout Mukund in a former birth, so they make the tyrant's body enclose the soul of Kalyavana the foe of Krishna, ere his apotheosis, from whom he fled to Dwarka, and thence acquired the name of Ranchhor.[1]

The Image of Krishna removed to Mewār. Founding of Nāthdwāra. — When Aurangzeb proscribed Kanhaiya, and rendered his shrines impure throughout Vraj, Rana Raj Singh "offered the heads of one hundred thousand Rajputs for his service," and the god was conducted by the route of Kotah and Rampura to Mewar. An omen decided the spot of his future residence. As he journeyed to gain the capital of the Sesodias the chariot-wheel sunk deep into the earth and defied extrication; upon which the Saguni (augur) interpreted the pleasure of the god, that he desired to dwell there. This circumstance occurred at an inconsiderable village called Siarh, in the fief of Delwara, one of the sixteen nobles of Mewar. Rejoiced at this decided manifestation of favour, the chief hastened to make a perpetual gift of the village and its lands, which was speedily confirmed by the patent of the Rana.[2] Nathji (*the* god) was removed from his car, and in due time a temple was erected for his reception, when the hamlet of Siarh became the town of Nathdwara, which now contains many thousand inhabitants of all denominations, who, reposing under the especial protection of the god, are exempt from every mortal tribunal. The site is not uninteresting, nor devoid of the means of defence. To the east it is shut in by a cluster of hills, and to the westward flows the Banas, which nearly bathes the extreme points of the hills. Within these bounds is the sanctuary (*saran*) of Kanhaiya, where the criminal is free from pursuit; nor dare the rod of justice appear on the mount, or the foot of the pursuer pass the stream; neither within it can blood be spilt, for the pastoral Kanhaiya delights not in offerings of

[1] *Ran*, the 'field of battle,' *chhor*, from *chhorna*, 'to abandon.' Hence Ranchhor, one of the titles under which Krishna is worshipped at Dwarka, is most unpropitious to the martial Rajput. Kalyavana, the foe from whom he fled, and who is figured as a serpent, is doubtless the Tak, the ancient foe of the Yadus, who slew Janamejaya, emperor of the Pandus. [Kālyavana has been identified with Gonanda I. of Kashmīr, but was more probably one of the Bactrian chiefs of the Panjāb (Growse, *Mathura*, 3rd ed. 56).]

[2] See Appendix to this Part, No. VIII [p. 647].

this kind [524].[1] The territory contains within its precincts abundant space for the town, the temple, and the establishments of the priests, as well as for the numerous resident worshippers, and the constant influx of votaries from the most distant regions,

> From Samarcand, by Oxus, Temir's throne,
> Down to the golden Chersonese,

who find abundant shelter from the noontide blaze in the groves of tamarind, pipal, and semal,[2] where they listen to the mystic hymns of Jayadeva. Here those whom ambition has cloyed, superstition unsettled, satiety disgusted, commerce ruined, or crime disquieted, may be found as ascetic attendants on the mildest of the gods of India. Determined upon renouncing the world, they first renounce the ties that bind them to it, whether family, friends, or fortune, and placing their wealth at the disposal of the deity, stipulate only for a portion of the food dressed for him, and to be permitted to prostrate themselves before him till their allotted time is expired. Here no blood-stained sacrifice scares the timid devotee; no austerities terrify, or tedious ceremonies fatigue him; he is taught to cherish the hope that he has only to ask for mercy in order to obtain it; and to believe that the compassionate deity who guarded the lapwing's nest[3] in the

[1] [The right of sanctuary was maintained until quite recent times (Erskine ii. A. 120).]

[2] The cotton tree, *Bombax malabaracum*, which grows to an immense height.

[3] Whoever has unhooded the falcon at a lapwing, or even scared one from her nest, need not be told of its peculiarly distressing scream, as if appealing to sympathy. The allusion here is to the lapwing scared from her nest, as the rival armies of the Kurus and Pandus joined in battle, when the compassionate Krishna, taking from an elephant's neck a war-bell (*viraghanta*), covered the nest, in order to protect it. When the majority of the feudal nobles of Marwar became self-exiled, to avoid the almost demoniac fury of their sovereign, since his alliance with the British Government, Anar Singh, the chief of Ahor, a fine specimen of the Rathor Rajput, brave, intelligent, and amiable, was one day lamenting, that while all India was enjoying tranquillity under the shield of Britain, they alone were suffering from the caprice of a tyrant; concluding a powerful appeal to my personal interposition with the foregoing allegory, and observing on the beauty of the office of mediator: "You are all-powerful," added he, "and we may be of little account in the grand scale of affairs; but Krishna condescended to protect even the lapwing's egg in the midst of battle." This brave man knew my anxiety to make their peace with their sovereign,

midst of myriads of combatants, who gave beatitude to the courtesan [1] who as the wall crushed her pronounced the name of 'Rama,' will not withhold it from him who has quitted the world and its allurements that he may live only in his presence, be fed by the food prepared for himself, and yield up his last sigh invoking the name of Hari. There [525] have been two hundred individuals at a time, many of whom, stipulating merely for food, raiment, and funeral rites, have abandoned all to pass their days in devotion at the shrine: men of every condition, Rajput merchant, and mechanic; and where sincerity of devotion is the sole expiation, and gifts outweigh penance, they must feel the road smooth to the haven of hope.

Benefactions to Nāthdwāra.—The dead stock of Krishna's shrine is augmented chiefly by those who hold life "unstable as the dew-drop on the lotus"; and who are happy to barter "the wealth of Ormuz and of Ind" for the intercessional prayers of the high priest, and his passport to Haripur, the heaven of Hari. From the banks of the Indus to the mouths of the Ganges, from the coasts of the Peninsula to the shores of the Red Sea, the gifts of gratitude or of fear are lavishly poured in; and though the unsettled aspect of the last half-century curtailed the transmission of the more bulky but least valuable benefactions, it less affected the bills of exchange from the successful sons of commerce, or the legacies of the dead. The safe arrival of a galleon from Sofala or Arabia produced as much to the shrine as to the insurance office, for Kanhaiya is the Saint Nicholas of the Hindu navigator, as was Apollo to the Grecian and Celtic sailors, who purchased the charmed arrows of the god to calm the troubled

---

and being acquainted with the allegory, I replied with some fervour, in the same strain, "Would to God, Thakur Sahib, I had the *viraghanta* to protect you." The effect was instantaneous, and the eye of this manly chieftain, who had often fearlessly encountered the foe in battle, filled with tears as, holding out his hand, he said, "At least you listen to our griefs, and speak the language of friendship. Say but the word, and you may command the services of twenty thousand Rathors." There is, indeed, no human being more susceptible of excitement, and, under it, of being led to any desperate purpose, whether for good or for evil, than the Rajput.

[1] Chand, the bard, gives this instance of the compassionate nature of Krishna, taken, as well as the former, from the *Mahabharata*. [On Krishna worship see J. Kennedy, *JRAS*, October 1907, p. 960 ff.]

sea.[1] A storm accordingly yields in proportion to its violence, or to the nerve of the owner of the vessel. The appearance of a long-denied heir might deprive him of half his patrimony, and force him to lament his parent's distrust in natural causes; while the accidental mistake of touching forbidden food on particular fasts requires expiation, not by flagellation or seclusion, but by the penance of the purse.

There is no donation too great or too trifling for the acceptance of Krishna, from the baronial estate to a patch of meadow-land; from the gemmed coronet to adorn his image, to the widow's mite; nor, as before observed, is there a principality [526] in India which does not diminish its fisc to add to his revenues. What effect the milder rites of the shepherd-god have produced on the adorers of Siva we know not, but assuredly Eklinga, the tutelary divinity of Mewar, has to complain of being defrauded of half his dues since Kanhaiya transferred his abode from the Yamuna to the Banas; for the revenues assigned to Kanhaiya, who under the epithet of 'Yellow mantle'[2] has a distinguished niche in the domestic chapel of the Rana, far exceed those of the Avenger. The grants or patents of Hindupati,[3] defining the

[1] Near the town of Avranches, on the coast of Normandy, is a rock called Mont St. Michel, in ancient times sacred to the Galli or Celtic Apollo, or Belenus; a name which the author from whom we quote observes, "certainly came from the East, and proves that the littoral provinces of Gaul were visited by the Phoenicians."—"A college of Druidical priestesses was established there, who sold to seafaring men certain arrows endowed with the peculiar virtue of allaying storms, if shot into the waves by a young mariner. Upon the vessel arriving safe, the young archer was sent by the crew to offer thanks and rewards to the priestesses. His presents were accepted in the most graceful manner; and at his departure the fair priestesses, who had received his embraces, presented to him a number of shells, which afterwards he never failed to use in adorning his person" (*Tour through France*).

When the early Christian warrior consecrated this mount to his protector St. Michel, its name was changed from *Mons Jovis* (being dedicated to Jupiter) to *Tumba*, supposed from *tumulus*, a mound; but as the Saxons and Celts placed pillars on all these mounts, dedicated to the Sun-god Belenus, Bal, or Apollo, it is not unlikely that *Tumba* is from the Sanskrit *thambha*, or *sthambha*, 'a pillar' [?].

[2] [Pītāmbara.]

[3] *Hindupati*, vulgo *Hindupat*, 'chief of the Hindu race,' is a title justly appertaining to the Ranas of Mewar. It has, however, been assumed by chieftains scarcely superior to some of his vassals, though with some degree of pretension by Sivaji, who, had he been spared, might have worked the redemption of his nation, and of the Rana's house, from which he sprung.

privileges and immunities of the shrine, are curious documents.[1]

Rights of Sanctuary.—The extension of the sanctuary beyond the vicinage of the shrine became a subject of much animadversion; and in delegating judicial authority over the whole of the villages in the grant to the priests, the Rana committed the temporal welfare of his subjects to a class of men not apt to be lenient in the collection of their dues, which not unfrequently led to bloodshed. In alienating the other royalties, especially the transit duties, he was censured even by the zealots. Yet, however important such concessions, they were of subordinate value to the rights of sanctuary, which were extended to the whole of the towns in the grant, thereby multiplying the places of refuge for crime, already too numerous.

Violation of Sanctuary.—In all ages and countries the rights of sanctuary have been admitted, and however they may be abused, their institution sprung from humane motives. To check the impulse of revenge and to shelter the weak from oppression are noble objects, and the surest test of a nation's independence is the extent to which they are carried. From the remotest times *saran* has been the most valued privilege of the Rajputs, the lowest of whom deems his house a refuge against the most powerful. But we merely propose to discuss the sanctuary of holy places, and more immediately that of the shrine of Kanhaiya. When Moses, after the Exodus, made a division of the lands of Canaan amongst the Israelites, and appointed "six cities to be the refuge of him who had slain unwittingly, from the avenger of blood,"[2] the intention was not to afford facilities for eluding justice, but to check the hasty impulse of revenge; for the slayer was only to be protected "until he stood before the congregation for judgment, or until the death of the high-priest" [527], which event appears to have been considered as the termination of revenge.[3] The infraction of political sanctuary (*saran torna*)

[1] See Appendix to this paper, Nos. IX. and X [p. 647].

[2] Numbers, chap. xxxv. 11, 12.

[3] Numbers, chap. xxxv. 25, and Joshua, chap. xx. 6. There was an ancient law of Athens analogous to the Mosaic, by which he who committed '*chance-medley*' should fly the country for a year, during which his relatives made satisfaction to the relatives of the deceased. The Greeks had *asyla* for every description of criminals, which could not be violated without infamy. Gibbon [ed. W. Smith, iv. 377 f.] gives a memorable instance of

often gives rise to the most inveterate feuds; and its abuse by the priests is highly prejudicial to society. Moses appointed but six cities of refuge to the whole Levite tribe; but the Rana has assigned more to one shrine than the entire possessions of that branch of the Israelites who had but forty-two cities, while Kanhaiya has forty-six.[1] The motive of sanctuary in Rajasthan may have been originally the same as that of the divine legislator; but the privilege has been abused, and the most notorious criminals deem the temple their best safeguard. Yet some princes have been found hardy enough to violate, though indirectly, the sacred *saran*. Zalim Singh of Kotah, a zealot in all the observances of religion, had the boldness to draw the line when selfish priestcraft interfered with his police; and though he would not demand the culprit, or sacrilegiously drag him from the altar, he has forced him thence by prohibiting the admission of food, and threatening to build up the door of the temple. It was thus the Greeks evaded the laws, and compelled the criminal's surrender by kindling fires around the sanctuary.[2] The towns of Kanhaiya did not often abuse their privilege; but the Author once had to interpose, where a priest of Eklinga gave asylum to a felon who had committed murder within the bounds of his domain of Pahona. As this town, of eight thousand rupees annual revenue belonging to the fisc, had been gained by a forged charter, the Author was glad to seize on the occasion to recommend its resumption, though he thereby incurred the penalty for seizing church land, namely "sixty thousand years in hell." The unusual occurrence created a sensation, but it was so indisputably just that not a voice was raised in opposition.

Endowments of Nāthdwāra.—Let us revert to the endowments of Nathdwara. Herodotus[3] furnishes a powerful instance of

---

disregard to the sanctuary of St. Julian in Auvergne, by the soldiers of the Frank king Theodoric, who divided the spoils of the altar, and made the priests captives: an impiety not only unsanctioned by the son of Clovis, but punished by the death of the offenders, the restoration of the plunder, and the extension of the right of sanctuary five miles around the sepulchre of the holy martyr.

[1] [The chief sanctuaries in Rājputāna are: Nāgor; Barli, a few miles distant; Chaupāsni; Udaimandir and Mahmandir, close to Jodhpur. The system is a serious obstacle to the detection of crime (General Hervey, *Some Records of Crime*, i. 122 f., ii. 327 ff.).]

[2] [Smith, *Dictionary of Greek and Roman Antiquities*, 3rd ed. i. 235.]

[3] [iv. 33; L. R. Farnell, *Cults of the Greek States*, iv. 101 ff.]

the estimation in which sacred offerings were held by the nations of antiquity. He observes that these were transmitted from the remotest nations of Scythia to Delos in Greece ; a range far less extensive than the offerings to the [528] Dewal of Apollo in Mewar. The spices of the isles of the Indian archipelago ; the balmy spoils of Araby the blest ; the nard or frankincense of Tartary ; the raisins and pistachios of Persia ; every variety of saccharine preparation, from the shakkarkhand (sugar-candy) of the celestial empire, with which the god sweetens his evening repast, to the more common sort which enters into the *peras* of Mathura, the food of his infancy ;[1] the shawls of Kashmir, the silks of Bengal, the scarfs of Benares, the brocades of Gujarat,

> . . . the flower and choice
> Of many provinces from bound to bound,

all contribute to enrich the shrine of Nathdwara. But it is with the votaries of the maritime provinces of India that he has most reason to be satisfied ; in the commercial cities of Surat, Cambay, Muskat-mandavi, etc., etc., where the Mukhyas, or comptrollers deputed by the high priest, reside, to collect the benefactions, and transmit them as occasion requires. A deputy resides on the part of the high priest at Multan, who invests the distant worshippers with the initiative cordon and necklace. Even from Samarkand the pilgrims repair with their offerings ; and a sum, seldom less than ten thousand rupees, is annually transmitted by the votaries from the Arabian ports of Muscat, Mocha, and Jiddah ; which contribution is probably augmented not only by the votaries who dwell at the mouths of the Volga[2] [529],

[1] [*Perā*, a sweetmeat made of cream, sugar and spices, for which Mathura is famous.]

[2] Pallas gives an admirable and evidently faithful account of the worship of Krishna and other Hindu divinities in the city of Astrakhan, where a Hindu mercantile colony is established. They are termed Multani, from the place whence they migrated—Multan, near the Indus. This class of merchants of the Hindu faith is disseminated over all the countries, from the Indus to the Caspian : and it would have been interesting had the professor given us any account of their period of settlement on the western shore of the Caspian Sea. In costume and feature, as represented in the plate given by that author, they have nothing to denote their origin ; though their divinities might be seated on any altar on the Ganges. The Multanis of Indeskoi Dvor, or 'Indian court,' at Astrakhan, have erected a pantheon, in which Krishna, the god of all Vaishnava merchants, is seated in front of

but by the Samoyede[1] of Siberia. There is not a petty retailer professing the Vishnu creed who does not carry a tithe of his

Jagannath, Rama, and his brothers, who stand in the background; while Siva and his consort Ashtabhuja 'the eight-armed,' form an intermediate line, in which is also placed a statue which Pallas denominates Murali; but Pallas mistook the flute (*murali*) of the divine Krishna for a rod. The principal figure we shall describe in his own words. "In the middle was placed a small idol with a very high bonnet, called Gupaledshi. At its right there was a large black stone, and on the left two smaller ones of the same colour, brought from the Ganges, and regarded by the Hindus as sacred. These fossils were of the species called Sankara, and appeared to be an impression of a bivalve muscle." Minute as is the description, our judgment is further aided by the plate. Gupaledshi is evidently Gopalji, the pastoral deity of Vraj (from *gao*, a cow, and *pala*, a herdsman). The head-dress worn by him and all the others is precisely that still worn by Krishna, in the sacred dance at Mathura: and so minute is the delineation that even the *pera* or sugar-ball is represented, although the professor appears to have been ignorant of its use, as he does not name it. He has likewise omitted to notice the representation of the sacred mount of Govardhana, which separates him from the Hindu Jove and the turreted Cybele (Durga), his consort. The black stones are the Salagramas, worshipped by all Vaishnavas. In the names of 'Khandigana and Gori,' though the first is called a lion saddled, and the other a male divinity, we easily recognise Nandi, the bull-attendant (*Gana*) of Siva and his consort Gauri. Were all travellers to describe what they see with the same accuracy as Pallas, they would confer important obligations on society, and might defy criticism. It is with heartfelt satisfaction I have to record, from the authority of a gentleman who has dwelt amongst the Hindkis of Astrakhan, that distance from their ancient abodes has not deteriorated their character for uprightness. Mr. Mitchell, from whose knowledge of Oriental languages the Royal Asiatic Society will some day derive benefit, says that the reputation of these Hindu colonists, of whom there are about five hundred families, stands very high, and that they bear a preference over all the merchants of other nations settled in this great commercial city.

[1] Other travellers besides Pallas have described Hinduism as existing in the remote parts of the Russian empire, and if nominal resemblances may be admitted, we would instance the strong analogy between the *Samoyedes* and *Tchoudes* of Siberia and Finland and the Syama Yadus and Joudes of India [?]. The languages of the two former races are said to have a strong affinity, and are classed as Hindu-Germanic by M. Klaproth, on whose learned work, *Asia Polyglotta*, M. Rémusat has given the world an interesting *critique*, in his *Mélanges Asiatiques* (tome i. p. 267), in which he traces these tribes to Central Asia; thus approaching the land of the Getae or Yuti. Now the Yutis and Yadus have much in their early history to warrant the assertion of more than nominal analogy. The annals of the Yadus of Jaisalmer state that long anterior to Vikrama they held dominion from Ghazni to Samarkand: that they established themselves in those regions after the Mahabharata, or great war; and were again

trade to the stores: and thus caravans of thirty and forty cars, double-yoked, pass twice or thrice annually by the upper road to Nathdwara. These pious bounties are not allowed to moulder in the *bhandars*: the apparel is distributed with a liberal hand as the gift of the deity to those who evince their devotion; and the edibles enter daily into the various food prepared at the shrine.

Food offered to Deities.—It has been remarked by the celebrated Goguet[1] that the custom of offering food to the object of divine homage had its origin in a principle of gratitude, the repast being deemed hallowed by presenting the first portion to him who gave it, since the devotee was unable to conceive aught more acceptable than that whereby life is sustained. From the earliest period such offerings have been tendered; and in the burnt-offering (*hom*) of Abel, of the firstling of the flock, and the first portion of the repast presented by the Rajput to Annadeva[2] 'the nourisher,' the motive is the same. But the *parsad* (such is the denomination of the food sacred to Kanhaiya) is deemed unlucky, if not unholy; a prejudice arising from the heterogeneous sources whence it is supplied—often from bequests of the dead. The Mukhyas [530] of the temple accordingly carry the sacred food to wheresoever the votaries dwell, which proves an irresistible stimulus to backward zeal, and produces an ample return. At

impelled, on the rise of Islamism, within the Indus. As Yadus of the race of Sham or Syam (a title of Krishna), they would be Sama-Yadus; in like manner as the *Bhatti* tribe are called *Shama-bhatti*, the Ahsham Bhatti of Abu-l Fazl. The race of *Joude* was existing near the Indus in the Emperor Babur's time, who describes them as occupying the mountainous range in the first Duab, the very spot mentioned in the annals of the Yadus as their place of halt, on quitting India twelve centuries before Christ, and thence called Jadu or Yadu-ka-dang, the 'hills of Jadu or Yadu.' The peopling of all these regions, from the Indus to remote Tartary, is attributed to the race of Ayu or Indu, both signifying the moon, of which are the Haihayas, Aswas (*Asi*), Yadus, etc., who spread a common language over all Western Asia. Amongst the few words of Hindu-Germanic origin which M. Rémusat gives to prove affinity between the Finnish and Samoyede languages is "*Miel*, *Mod*, dans le dialecte Caucasien, et *Méd*, en Slave," and which, as well as *mead*, the drink of the Scandinavian warrior, is from the Sanskrit *Madhu*, a bee [honey]. Hence intoxicating beverage is termed *Madhva*, which supplies another epithet for Krishna, *Madhu* or *Madhava*. [These speculations possess no value.]

1 *Origin of Laws and Government.*

2 Literally 'the giver of food.'

the same time are transmitted, as from the god, dresses of honour corresponding in material and value with the rank of the receiver: a diadem, or fillet of satin and gold, embroidered; a *dagla*, or quilted coat of gold or silver brocade for the cold weather; a scarf of blue and gold; or if to one who prizes the gift less for its intrinsic worth than as a mark of special favour, a fragment of the garland worn on some festival by the god; or a simple necklace, by which he is inaugurated amongst the elect.[1]

Lands dedicated to the Shrine.—It has been mentioned that the lands of Mewar appropriated to the shrine are equal in value to a baronial appanage, and, as before observed, there is not a principality in India which does not assign a portion of its domain or revenue to this object. The Hara princes of Kotah and Bundi are almost exclusive worshippers of Kanhaiya, and the regent Zalim Singh is devoted to the maintenance of the dignity of the establishment. Everything at Kotah appertains to Kanhaiya. The prince has but the usufruct of the palace, for which £12,000 are annually transmitted to the shrine. The grand lake east of the town, with all its finny tenants, is under his especial protection;[2] and the extensive suburb adjoining, with its rents, lands, and transit duties, all belong to the god. Zalim Singh moreover transmits to the high priest the most valuable shawls, broadcloths, and horses; and throughout the long period of predatory warfare he maintained two Nishans,[3] of a hundred firelocks each, for the protection of the temple His favourite son also, a child of love, is called Gordhandas, the 'slave of Gordhan,' one of the many titles of Kanhaiya. The prince of Marwar went mad from the murder of the high priest of Jalandhara, the epithet

[1] *Kanhaiya ka kantha bāndhna,* 'to bind on [the neck] the chaplet of Kanhaiya,' is the initiatory step.

[2] I had one day thrown my net into this lake, which abounded with a variety of fish, when my pastime was interrupted by a message from the regent, Zalim Singh: "Tell Captain Tod that Kotah and all around it are at his disposal; but these fish belong to Kanhaiya." I, of course, immediately desisted, and the fish were returned to the safeguard of the deity. [The killing of fish at certain lakes and streams is forbidden on account of their harmlessness (*ahimsā*), and thus naturally associated with the cult of a gentle deity like Krishna, and because they are believed to contain the spirits of the dead (Stein, *Rājatarangini*, i. 185; Crooke, *Things Indian*, 221 ff.).]

[3] A Nishan, or standard, is synonymous with a company.

given to Kanhaiya in that State; and the Raja of Sheopur,[1] the last of the Gaurs, lost his sovereignty by abandoning the worship of Har for that of Hari. The 'slave' of Radha[2] (such was the name of this prince) almost lived in the temple, and used to dance before the statue. Had he upheld the rights of him who wields [531] the trident, the tutelary deity of his capital, Sivapur, instead of the unwarlike divinity whose unpropitious title of Ranchhor should never be borne by the martial Rajput, his fall would have been more dignified, though it could not have been retarded when the overwhelming torrent of the Mahrattas under Sindhia swept Rajwara.[3]

Grants to the High Priest.—A distinction is made between the grants to the temple and those for the personal use of the pontiff, who at least affects never to apply any portion of the former to his own use, and he can scarcely have occasion to do so; but when from the stores of Apollo could be purchased the spices of the isles, the fruits of Persia, and the brocades of Gujarat, we may indulge our scepticism in questioning this forbearance: but the abuse has been rectified, and traffic banished from the temple. The personal grant (Appendix, No. XI.) to the high priest ought alone to have sufficed for his household expenditure, being twenty thousand rupees per annum, equal to £10,000 in Europe. But the ten thousand towns of Mewar, from each of which he levied a crown, now exist only in the old rent-roll, and the heralds of Apollo would in vain attempt to collect their tribute from two thousand villages.

The Appendix, No. XII., being a grant of privileges to a minor shrine of Kanhaiya, in his character of Muralidhar or 'flute-player,' contains much information on the minutiae of benefactions, and will afford a good idea of the nature of these revenues.

Effects of Krishna-worship on the Rājputs.—The predominance

[1] Sheopur or Sivapur, the city of Sheo or Siva, the god of war, whose battle-shout is *Har*; and hence one of Vishnu's epithets, as Hari is that of Krishna or Kanhaiya.

[2] Radha was the name of the chief of the Gopis or nymphs of Vraj, and the beloved of Kanhaiya.

[3] In October 1807 I rambled through all these countries, then scarcely known by name to us. At that time Sheopur was independent, and its prince treated me with the greatest hospitality. In 1809 I witnessed its fall, when following with the embassy in the train of the Mahratta leader. [It is now included in the Gwalior State (*IGI*, xxii. 271 f.).]

of the mild doctrines of Kanhaiya over the dark rites of Siva, is doubtless beneficial to Rajput society. Were the prevention of female immolation the sole good resulting from their prevalence, that alone would conciliate our partiality; a real worshipper of Vishnu should forbid his wife following him to the pyre, as did recently the Bundi prince. In fact, their tenderness to animal life is carried to nearly as great an excess as with the Jains, who shed no blood. Celibacy is not imposed upon the priests of Kanhaiya, as upon those of Siva: on the contrary, they are enjoined to marry, and the priestly office is hereditary by descent. Their wives do not burn, but are committed, like themselves, to the earth. They inculcate tenderness towards all beings; though whether this feeling influences the mass, must depend on the soil which receives the seed, for the outward ceremonies of religion cost far less effort than the practice or essentials. I have often [532] smiled at the incessant aspirations of the Macchiavelli of Rajasthan, Zalim Singh, who, while he ejaculated the name of the god as he told his beads, was inwardly absorbed by mundane affairs; and when one word would have prevented a civil war, and saved his reputation from the stain of disloyalty to his prince, he was, to use his own words, "at four-score years and upwards, laying the foundation for another century of life." And thus it is with the prince of Marwar, who esteems the life of a man or a goat of equal value when prompted by revenge to take it. Hope may silence the reproaches of conscience, and gifts and ceremonies may be deemed atonement for a deviation from the first principle of their religion—a benevolence which should comprehend every animated thing. But fortunately the princely worshippers of Kanhaiya are few in number: it is to the sons of commerce we must look for the effects of these doctrines; and it is my pride and duty to declare that I have known men of both sects, Vaishnava and Jain, whose integrity was spotless, and whose philanthropy was unbounded.

CHAPTER 20

Krishna.—Hari, Krishna, familiarly Kanhaiya,[1] was of the celebrated tribe of Yadu, the founder of the fifty-six tribes[2] who obtained the universal sovereignty of India, and descended from Yayati, the third son[3] of Swayambhuva Manu,[4] or 'The Man, Lord of the earth,' whose daughter Ila[5] (*Terra*) was espoused by Budha (Mercury), son of Chandra[6] (the Moon), whence the Yadus are styled Chandravansi, or 'children of the moon.' Budha was therefore worshipped as the great [533] ancestor (*Pitrideva*) of the lunar race; and previous to the apotheosis of Krishna, was adored by all the Yadu race. The principal shrine of Budha was at Dwarka, where he still receives adoration as Budha Trivikrama.[7] Kanhaiya lived towards the conclusion of the brazen age, calculated to have been about 1100 to 1200 years before Christ.[8] He was born to the inheritance of Vraj,

[1] [Derived, through the Prākrit, from Krishna.]

[2] *Chhappan kula Yadava.*

[3] *Qu.* Japhet ? [?].

[4] Also called *Vaivaswata Manu*—'the man, son of the sun.'

[5] Ila, the earth—the Saxon *Ertha*. The Germans chiefly worshipped Tuisco or Teutates and Ertha, who are the Budha or Ila of the Rajputs [?].

[6] A male divinity with the Rajputs, the Tatars, and ancient Germans.

[7] 'Triple Energy' ['he who strides over the three worlds'], the Hermes Triplex of the Egyptians. [There is no cult of Budha at Dwārka.]

[8] I shall here subjoin an extract of the rise and progress of Vaishnavism as written at my desire by the Mukhya of the temple:

"Twenty-five years of the Dwapar (the brazen age) were yet unexpired, when the incarnation (*avatar*) of Sri Krishna took place. Of these, eleven were passed at Gokul,* and fourteen at Mathura. There he used to manifest himself personally, especially at Govardhan. But when the Kaliyug (the iron age) commenced, he retired to Dwarka, an island separated by the ocean from Bharatkand,† where he passed a hundred years before he went to heaven. In Samvat 937 (A.D. 881) God decreed that the Hindu faith should be overturned, and that the Turushka‡ should rule. Then the

* A small town in the Jumna, below Mathura. Hence one of Krishna's titles is Gokulnath, 'Lord of Gokul.'

† The channel which separates the island of Dwarka from the mainland is filled up, except in spring tides. I passed it when it was dry.

‡ We possess no record of the invasion of India in A.D. 881, by the Turki tribes, half a century after Mamun's expedition from Zabulistan against Chitor, in the reign of Rawal Khuman [?].

the country of the Suraseni, comprehending the territory round Mathura for a space of eighty miles, of which he was unjustly deprived in his infancy by his relative Kansa. From its vicinity to Delhi we may infer either that there was no lord paramount amongst the Yadus of this period, or that Krishna's family held as vassals of Hastinapur, then, with Indraprastha or Delhi, the chief seat of Yadu power. There were two princes named Surasen amongst the immediate predecessors of Krishna : one, his grandfather, the other eight generations anterior. Which of these was the founder of Suryapur on the Yamuna, the capital of the Yadus,[1] we know not, but we may assume that the first gave his name to the region around Mathura, described by Arrian as the country of the Suraseni. Alexander was in India probably about eight centuries after the deification of Krishna, and it is satisfactory to find that the inquiries he instituted into the genealogy of the dynasty then ruling on the [534] Yamuna correspond very closely with those of the Yadus of this distant period ; and combined with what Arrian says of the origin of the Pandus, it appears indisputable that the descendants of this powerful branch of the Yadus ruled on the Yamuna when the Macedonian erected the

---

jizya, or capitation tax, was inflicted on the head of the Hindu. Their faith also suffered much from the Jains and the various infidel (*asura*) sects which abounded. The Jains were so hostile, that Brahma manifested himself in the shape of Sankaracharya who destroyed them and their religion at Benares. In Gujarat, by their magic, they made the moon appear at Amavas.* Sankara foretold to its prince, Siddhraj,† the flood then approaching, who escaped in a boat and fled to Toda, on which occasion all the Vidyas ‡ (magicians) in that country perished." [For a more correct version of Krishna's legend see Growse, *Mathura*, 3rd ed. ; for Vaishnavism, R. G. Bhandarkar, "Vaisnavism, Saivism and Minor Religious Systems," in *Grundriss Indo-Arischen Philologie und Altertumskunde*, 1913.]

[1] For an account of the discovery of the remains of this ancient city, see *Transactions of the Royal Asiatic Society*, vol. i. p. 314.

---

* The ides of the month, when the moon is obscured.

† He ruled Samvat 1151 (A.D. 1095) to S. 1201 (A.D. 1145).

‡ Still used as a term of reproach to the Jains and Buddhists, in which, and other points, as *Ari* (the foe, qu. *Aria* ?), they bear a strong resemblance to the followers of the Arian Zardusht, or Zoroaster. Amongst other peculiarities, the ancient Persian fire-worshipper, like the present Jain, placed a bandage over the mouth while worshipping.

altars of Greece on the Indus. That the personage whose epithets of Krishna-Syam designate his colour as 'the Black Prince,' was in fact a distinguished chief of the Yadus, there is not a shadow of doubt; nor that, after his death, they placed him among the gods as an incarnation of Vishnu or the Sun; and from this period we may induce the Hindu notion of their Trinity. Arrian [1] enumerates the names of Boudyas (Βουδύας) and Kradeuas (Κραδεύας) amongst the early ancestors of the tribe then in power, which would alone convince us that Alexander had access to the genealogies of the Puranas; for we can have little hesitation in affirming these to be Budha and Kroshti, ancestors of Krishna; and that "Mathora and Cleisobora, the chief cities of the Suraseni," are the Mathura and Suryapur occupied by the descendants of Sursen.[2] Had Arrian afforded as many hints for discussing the analogy between the Hindu and Grecian Apollos as he has for the Hercules of Thebes and India, we might have come to a conclusion that the three chief divinities [3] of Egypt, Greece, and India had their altars first erected on the Indus, Ganges, and Jumna.

Sun and Moon Worship.—The earliest objects of adoration in these regions were the sun and moon, whose names designated the two grand races, Surya and Chandra of Indu. Budha, son of Indu, married Ila, a grandchild of Surya, from which union sprung the Indu race. They deified their ancestor Budha, who continued to be the chief object of adoration until Krishna: hence the worship of Balnath [4] and Budha [5] were coeval. That the Nomadic tribes of Arabia, as well as those of Tartary and India, adored the same objects, we learn from the earliest writers; and Job, the probable contemporary of Hasti, the founder of the first capital of the Yadus on the Ganges, boasts in the midst of his griefs that he had always remained uncorrupted by the Sabaeism which surrounded him. "If I beheld the sun when it shined, or the moon walking in brightness, and my mouth had kissed my hand, this also were an iniquity to be punished by the

[1] [Arrian, *Indika*, viii.]

[2] [Growse (*Mathura*, 279) suggests that Cleisobora is Krishnapura, 'Krishna's city.']

[3] Hercules, Mercury, and Apollo; *Balaram*, *Budha*, and *Kanhaiya*.

[4] The 'God Bal,' the Vivifier, the Sun [?].

[5] Budha signifies 'wisdom.'

judge, for I should have denied the [535] God that is above."[1] That there were many Hindus who, professing a pure monotheism like Job, never kissed the hand either to Surya or his herald Budha, we may easily credit from the sublimity of the notions of the 'One God,' expressed both by the ancients and moderns, by poets and by princes, of both races ;[2] but more especially by the sons of Budha, who for ages bowed not before graven images, and deemed it impious to raise a temple to

The Spirit in whose honour shrines are weak.

Hence the Jains, the chief sect of the Buddhists,[3] so called from adoring the spirit (Jina), were untinctured with idolatry until the apotheosis of Krishna,[4] whose mysteries superseded the simpler worship of Budha. Neminath (the deified Nemi) was the pontiff of Budha, and not only the contemporary of Krishna, but a Yadu, and his near relation ; and both had epithets denoting their complexion ; for Arishta, the surname of Nemi, has the same import as Syam and Krishna, 'the black,' though the latter is of a less Ethiopic hue than Nemi.[5] It was anterior to this schism amongst the sons of Budha that the creative power was degraded under sensual forms, when the pillar rose to Bal or Surya in Syria and on the Ganges : and the serpent, "subtlest beast of all the field," worshipped as the emblem of wisdom (Budha), was conjoined with the symbol of the creative power, as at the shrine of Eklinga, where the brazen serpent is wreathed round the lingam.[6] Budha's descendants, the Indus, preserved

[1] Job chap. xxxi. 26, 27, 28.

[2] Chand, the bard, after having separately invoked the three persons of the Hindu triad, says that he who believes them distinct, "hell will be his portion."

[3] [The Jains were not a Buddhist sect.]

[4] A very curious cause was assigned by an eminent Jain priest for the innovation of enshrining and worshipping the forms of the twenty-four pontiffs: namely, that the worship of Kanhaiya, before and after the apotheosis, became quite a rage amongst the women, who crowded his shrines, drawing after them all the youth of the Jains ; and that, in consequence, they made a statue of Neminath to counteract a fervour that threatened the existence of their faith. It is seldom we are furnished with such rational reasons for religious changes.

[5] [Neminātha was the twenty-second Jain Tīrthakara or deified saint. Arishta means 'unhurt, perfect.']

[6] It was the serpent (Budha) who ravished Ila, daughter of Ikshwaku, the son of Manu, whence the distinctive epithet of his descendants in the

the Ophite sign of their race, when Krishna's followers adopted the eagle as his symbol. These, with the adorers of Surya, form the three idolatrous classes of India, not confined to its modern [536] restricted definition, but that of antiquity, when Industhan or Indu-Scythia extended from the Ganges to the Caspian. In support of the position that the existing polytheism was unknown on the rise of Vaishnavism, we may state, that in none of the ancient genealogies do the names of such deities appear as proper names in society, a practice now common ; and it is even recorded that the rites of magic, the worship of the host of heaven, and of idols, were introduced from Kashmir, between the periods of Krishna and Vikrama. The powers of nature were personified, and each quality, mental and physical, had its emblem, which the Brahmans taught the ignorant to adopt as realities, till the pantheon become so crowded that life would be too short to acquire even the nomenclature of their 'thirty-three millions of gods.'[1] No object was too high or too base, from the glorious Orb to the Rampi, or paring-knife of the shoemaker. In illustration of the increase of polytheism, I shall describe the seven forms under which Krishna is worshipped, whose statues are established in the various capitals of Rajasthan, and are occasionally brought together at the festival of Annakuta at Nathdwara.

The international wars of the Suryas and the Yadu races, as described in the Ramayana and Mahabharata, are lost between allegory and literal interpretation. The Suryas, or Saivas, were depressed; and the Indus, who counted 'fifty-six' grand tribes, under the appellations of Takshak, 'serpent,' Aswa, 'horse,' Sasa, 'hare,' etc., etc., had paramount sway. Krishna's schism produced a new type, that of the eagle, and the wars of

East, *Manus*, or men, the very tradition on an ancient sculptured column in the south of India, which evidently points to the primeval mystery. In Portici there is an exact *lingam* entwined with a brazen serpent, brought from the temple of Isis at Pompeii: and many of the same kind, in mosaic, decorate the floors of the dwelling-houses. But the most singular coincidence is in the wreaths of *lingams* and the *yoni* over the door of the minor temple of Isis at Pompeii; while on another front is painted the rape of Venus by Mercury (Budha and Ila). The Lunar race, according to the Puranas, are the issue of the rape of Ila by Budha. *Aphah* is a serpent in Hebrew. *Ahi* and *Sarpa* are two of its many appellations in Sanskrit. [These speculations are now obsolete.]

[1] *Taintīs kror devata.*

the schismatics were depicted under their respective emblems, the eagle and serpent, of which latter were the Kauravas and Takshaks,[1] the political adversaries of the Pandus, the relatives of Krishna. The [537] allegory of Krishna's eagle pursuing the serpent Budha, and recovering the books of science and religion with which he fled, is an historical fact disguised: namely, that of Krishna incorporating the doctrines of Budha with his own after the expulsion of the sect from India. Dare we further attempt to lift the veil from this mystery, and trace from the seat of redemption of lost science its original source?[2] The Gulf of Cutch, the point where the serpent attempted to escape, has been from time immemorial to the present day the entrepôt for the commerce of Sofala, the Red Sea, Egypt, and Arabia. There

[1] The Mahabharata records constant wars from ancient times amongst the children of Surya (the sun), and the Tak or Takshak (serpent races). The horse of the sun, liberated preparatory to sacrifice, by the father of Rama, was seized by the Takshak Ananta; and Janamejaya, king of Delhi, grandson of Pandu, was killed by one of the same race. In both instances the Takshak is literally rendered the *snake*. The successor of Janamejaya carried war into the seats of this Tak or serpent race, and is said to have sacrificed 20,000 of them in revenge; but although it is specifically stated that he subsequently compelled them to sign tributary engagements (*paenama*), the Brahmans have nevertheless distorted a plain historical fact by a literal and puerile interpretation. The Paraitakai (*Mountain-Tak*) of Alexander were doubtless of this race, as was his ally Taxiles, which appellation was titular, as he was called Omphis till his father's death. It is even probable that this name is the Greek Ὄφις, in which they recognized the tribe of the Tak or Snake. Taxiles may be compounded of *is*, 'lord or chief,' *sila*, 'rock or mountain,' and Tak, 'lord of the mountain Tak,' whose capital was in the range west of the Indus. We are indebted to the Emperor Babur for the exact position of the capital of this celebrated race, which he passed in his route of conquest. We have, however, an intermediate notice of it between Alexander and Babur, in the early history of the Yadu Bhatti, who came in conflict with the Taks on their expulsion from Zabulistan and settlement in the Panjab. [The Paraitakai or Paraitakenai have no connexion with Tāk or Takshak, the first part of the name perhaps representing Skt. *parvata*, 'a mountain,' or *pahār* in the modern dialect. They lived in the hill country between the rivers Oxus and Jaxartes (McCrindle, *Alexander*, 57). Omphis represents the Āmbhi, king of Taxila, a name supposed to mean 'rock of the Tāk tribe' (*ibid.* 413; Smith, *EHI*, 60), or, more probably, 'city of cut stone.']

[2] The Buddhists appeared in this peninsula and the adjacent continent was the cradle of Buddhism, and here are three of the 'five' sacred mounts of their faith, *i.e.* Girnar, Satrunjaya and Abu. The Author purposes giving, hereafter, an account of his journey through these classic regions. [He refers to Jains; Buddhism arose in Bihār.]

Budha Trivikrama, or Mercury, has been and is yet invoked by the Indian mariners, especially the pirates of Dwarka. Did Budha or Mercury come from, or escape to the Nile? Is he the Hermes of Egypt to whom the 'four books of science,' like the four Vedas [1] of the Hindus, were sacred? The statues of Nemi,[2] the representative of Budha, exactly resemble in feature the bust of young Memnon.[3]

I have already observed that Krishna, before his own deification, worshipped his great ancestor Budha; and his temple at Dwarka rose over the ancient shrine of the latter, which yet stands. In an inscription from the cave of Gaya their characters are conjoined: "Hari who is Budha." According to Western mythology, Apollo and Mercury exchanged symbols, the caduceus for the lyre; so likewise in India their characters intermingle: and even the Saiva propitiates Hari as the mediator and disposer of the 'divine spark' (*jyoti*) to its reunion with the 'parent-flame':—thus, like Mercury, he may be said to be the conveyer of the souls of the dead. Accordingly in funeral lamentation his name only is invoked, and *Hari-bol! Hari-bol!* is emphatically pronounced by those conveying the corpse to its final abode. The *vahan* (*qu.* the Saxon *van*?) or celestial car of Krishna, in which the souls (*ansa*) of the just are conveyed to Suryamandal, the 'mansion of the sun,' is painted like himself, blue (indicative of space, or as Ouranos), with the eagle's head; and here he partakes of the Mercury of the [538] Greeks, and of Oulios, the preserver or saviour, one of the titles of Apollo at Delos.[4]

1 The Buddhists and Jains are stigmatized as *Vidyavan*, which, signifying 'possessed of science,' is interpreted 'magician.'

2 He is called Arishta-Nemi, 'the black Nemi,' from his complexion.

3 [The connexion of Hindu with Egyptian beliefs is no longer admitted.]

4 The Sun-god (Kan, according to Diodorus) is the Minos of the Egyptians. The hieroglyphics at Turin represent him with the head of an ibis, or eagle, with an altar before him, on which a shado places his offerings, namely, a goose, cakes of bread, and flowers of the lotus, and awaits in humble attitude his doom. In Sanskrit the same word means *soul*, *goose*, and *swan* [?], and the Hindu poet is always punning upon it; though it might be deemed a levity to represent the immaterial portion under so unclassical an emblem. The lotus flowers are alike sacred to the Kan of the Egyptians as to Kanhaiya the mediator of the Hindus, and both are painted blue and bird-headed. The claims of Kanhaiya (contracted Kan) as the sun divinity of the Hindus will be abundantly illustrated in the account of the festivals. [The above theories are obsolete.]

The Forms of Krishna.—The Tatar nations, who are all of Indu race, like the Rajputs and German tribes, adored the moon as a male divinity, and to his son, Budha, they assign the same character of mediator. The serpent is alike the symbol of the Budha of the Hindus, the Hermes of the Egyptians, and the Mercury of Greece: and the allegory of the dragon's teeth, the origin of letters, brought by Cadmus from Egypt, is a version of the Hindu fable of Kanhaiya (Apollo) wresting the Vedas (secrets) from Budha or wisdom (Hermes), under his sign, the serpent or dragon. We might still further elucidate the resemblance, and by an analysis of the titles and attributes of the Hindu Apollo, prove that from the Yamuna may have been supplied the various incarnations of this divinity, which peopled the pantheons of Egypt, Greece, and Rome. As Nomios, who attended the herds of Admetus, we have Nonita,[1] the infantine appellation of Kanhaiya, when he pastured the kine of Kesava in the woods of Vindra, whence the ceremony of the sons of princes assuming the crook, and on particular days tending the flocks.[2] As Muralidhara, or the 'flute-holder,' Kanhaiya is the god of music; and in giving him the shepherd's reed instead of the *vina* or lyre, we may conjecture that the simple bamboo (*bans*) which formed the first flute (*bansli*) was in use before the *chahtara*,[3] the Grecian cithara,[4] the first invented lyre of Apollo. Thus from the six-

[1] I do not mean to derive any aid from the resemblance of names, which is here merely accidental. [Nonīta probably=*navanīta*, 'fresh butter,' a dairy god (Macdonell-Keith, *Vedic Index*, i. 437).]

[2] When I heard the octogenarian ruler of Kotah ask his grandson, "Bapalal, have you been tending the cows to-day?" my surprise was converted into pleasure on the origin of the custom being thus classically explained.

[3] From *chha*, 'six,' and *tar*, 'a string or wire.'

[4] Strabo says the Greeks consider music as originating from Thrace and Asia, of which countries were Orpheus, Musaeus, etc.; and that others "who regard all Asia, as far as India, as a country sacred to Dionysus (Bacchus), attribute to that country the invention of nearly all the science of music. We perceive them sometimes describing the cithara of the Asiatic, and sometimes applying to flutes the epithet of Phrygian. The names of certain instruments, such as the *nabla*, and others likewise, are taken from barbarous tongues." This *nabla* of Strabo is possibly the *tabla*, the small tabor of India. If Strabo took his orthography from the Persian or Arabic, a single point would constitute the difference between the *N* (ن) and the *T* (ت). [The Arabic *tabl, tabla*, has no connexion with Greek νάβλα, Hebrew *nevel*.]

wired instrument of the Hindus we have the Greek cithara, the English cithern, and the Spanish guitar of modern [539] days. The Greeks, following the Egyptians, had but six notes, with their lettered symbols; and it was reserved for the Italians to add a seventh. Guido Aretine, a monk in the thirteenth century, has the credit of this. I, however, believe the Hindus numbered theirs from the heavenly bodies—the Sun, Moon, Mercury, Venus, Mars, Jupiter, Saturn,—hence they had the regular octave, with its semi-tones: and as, in the pruriency of their fancy, they converted the ascending and descending notes into *grahas*, or planetary bodies, so they may have added them to the harmonious numbers, and produced the *nauragini*, their *nine* modes of music.[1] Could we affirm that the hymns composed and set to music by Jayadeva, nearly three thousand years ago,[2] and still chanted in honour of the Apollo of Vraj, had been handed down with the sentiments of these mystic compositions (and Sir W. Jones sanctions the idea), we should say, from their simplicity, that the musicians of that age had only the diatonic scale; but we have every reason to believe, from the very elaborate character of their written music, which is painful and discordant to the ear from its minuteness of subdivision, that they had also the chromatic scale, said to have been invented by Timotheus in the time of Alexander, who might have carried it from the banks of the Indus.

The Rāsmandal Dance.—In the mystic dance, the *Rasmandal*, yet imitated on the annual festival sacred to the sun-god Hari, he is represented with a radiant crown in a dancing attitude, playing on the flute to the nymphs encircling him, each holding a musical instrument.

[1] An account of the state of musical science amongst the Hindus of early ages, and a comparison between it and that of Europe, is yet a desideratum in Oriental literature. From what we already know of the science, it appears to have attained a theoretical precision yet unknown to Europe, and that at a period when even Greece was little removed from barbarism. The inspirations of the bards of the first ages were all set to music; and the children of the most powerful potentates sang the episodes of the great epics of Valmiki and Vyasa. There is a distinguished member of the Royal Asiatic Society, and perhaps the only one, who could fill up this hiatus; and we may hope that the leisure and inclination of the Right Honourable Sir Gore Ousely will tempt him to enlighten us on this most interesting point.

[2] [The lyrical drama of Jayadeva, *Gītagovinda*, dates from the twelfth century A.D. (Macdonell, *Hist. Sanskrit Literature*, 344 f.).]

In song and dance about the sacred hill;
Mystical dance, which yonder starry sphere
Of planets and of fixed in all her wheels
Resembles nearest; mazes intricate,
Eccentric, intervolved, yet regular
Then most, when most irregular they seem;
And in their motions harmony divine
So smooths her charming tones that God's own ear
Listens delighted.

MILTON, *Paradise Lost*, Book v. 619–27.

These nymphs are also called the *nauragini*, from *raga*, a mode of song over which each presides, and *naurasa*, or 'nine passions,' excited by the powers [540] of harmony. May we not in this trace the origin of Apollo and the sacred nine? In the manner described above, the *rasmandal* is typical of the zodiacal phenomena; and in each sign a musical nymph is sculptured in alto-relievo, in the vaulted temples dedicated to the god,[1] or in secular edifices by way of ornament, as in the triumphal column of Chitor. On the festival of the Janam,[2] or 'birth-day,' there is a scenic representation of Kanhaiya and the Gopis: when are rehearsed in the mellifluous accents of the Ionic land of Vraj, the songs of Jayadeva, as addressed by Kanhaiya to Radha and her companions. A specimen of these, as translated by that elegant scholar, Sir W. Jones, may not be considered inappropriate here.

The Songs of Jayadeva.—I have had occasion to remark elsewhere,[3] that the Rajput bards, like the heroic Scalds of the north, lose no opportunity of lauding themselves; of which Jayadeva, the bard of the Yadus, has set an eminent example in the opening of 'the songs of Govinda.'

"If thy soul be delighted with the remembrance of Hari, or sensible to the raptures of love, listen to the voice of Jayadeva, whose notes are both sweet and brilliant."

[1] I have often been struck with a characteristic analogy in the sculptures of the most ancient Saxon cathedrals in England and on the Continent, to Kanhaiya and the Gopis. Both may be intended to represent divine harmony. Did the Asi and Jits of Scandinavia, the ancestors of the Saxons, bring them from Asia?

[2] [The Janamashtami, Krishna's birthday, is celebrated on the 8th dark half of Sāwan (July–August).]

[3] *Trans. Royal Asiatic Society*, vol. i. p. 146.

KANHAIYA AND RĀDHA.

To face page 630.

The poet opens the first interview of Krishna and Radha with an animated description of a night in the rainy season, in which Hari is represented as a wanderer, and Radha, daughter of the shepherd Nanda, is sent to offer him shelter in their cot.[1] Nanda thus speaks to Radha : " The firmament is obscured by clouds ; the woodlands are black with Tamala trees ; that youth who roves in the forest will be fearful in the gloom of night ; go, my daughter, bring the wanderer to my rustic mansion. Such was the command of Nanda the herdsman, and hence arose the love of Radha and Madhava." [2]

The poet proceeds to apostrophize Hari, which the Hindu bard terms *rupaka*, or ' personal description ' :

" Oh thou who reclinest on the bosom of Kamala, whose ears flame with gems, and whose locks are embellished with sylvan flowers ; thou, from whom the [541] day-star derived his effulgence, who slewest the venom-breathing Kaliya, who beamedst like a sun on the tribe of Yadu, that flourished like a lotus ; thou, who sittest on the plumage of Garuda, who sippest nectar from the radiant lips of Padma, as the fluttering chakora drinks the moonbeams ; be victorious, O Hari."

Jayadeva then introduces Hari in the society of the pastoral nymphs of Vraj, whom he groups with admirable skill, expressing the passion by which each is animated towards the youthful prince with great warmth and elegance of diction. But Radha, indignant that he should divide with them the affection she deemed exclusively her own, flies his presence. Hari, repentant and alarmed, now searches the forest for his beloved, giving vent at each step to impassioned grief. " Woe is me ! she feels a sense of injured honour, and has departed in wrath. How will she conduct herself ? How will she express her pain in so long a separation ? What is wealth to me ? What are numerous attendants ? What the pleasures of the world ? How can I invite thee to return ? Grant me but a sight of thee, oh ! lovely Radha, for my passion torments me. O God of love ! mistake me not for Siva. Wound me not again. I love already but too passionately ; yet have I lost my beloved. Brace not thy bow, thou conqueror of the world ! My heart is already pierced by arrows from Radha's eyes, black and keen as those of the antelope."

[1] [Rādha was daughter of Vrishabhānu.]

[2] *Madho* in the dialect of Vraj.

Radha relents and sends a damsel in quest of Hari, whom she finds in a solitary arbour on the banks of the Yamuna. She describes her mistress as animated by the same despair which controls him:

"Her face is like a water-lily veiled in the dew of tears, and her eyes are as moons eclipsed. She draws thy picture and worships it, and at the close of every sentence exclaims, 'O Madhava, at thy feet am I fallen!' Then she figures thee standing before her: she sighs, she smiles, she mourns, she weeps. Her abode, the forest—herself through thy absence is become a timid roe, and love is the tiger who springs on her, like Yama, the genius of death. So emaciated is her beautiful body, that even the light garland which waves o'er her bosom is a load. The palm of her hand supports her aching temple, motionless as the crescent rising at eve. Thus, O divine healer, by the nectar of thy love [542] must Radha be restored to health; and if thou refusest, thy heart must be harder than the thunder-stone."[1]

The damsel returns to Radha and reports the condition of Hari, mourning her absence: "Even the hum of the bee distracts him. Misery sits fixed in his heart, and every returning night adds anguish to anguish." She then recommends Radha to seek him. "Delay not, O loveliest of women; follow the lord of thy heart. Having bound his locks with forest flowers, he hastens to yon arbour, where a soft gale breathes over the banks of Yamuna, and there pronouncing thy name, he modulates his divine reed. Leave behind thee, O friend, the ring which tinkles on thy delicate ankle when thou sportest in the dance. Cast over thee thy azure mantle and run to the shady bower."

But Radha, too weak to move, is thus reported to Hari by the same fair mediator: "She looks eagerly on all sides in hope of thy approach: she advances a few steps and falls languid to the ground. She weaves bracelets of fresh leaves, and looking at herself in sport, exclaims, behold the vanquisher of Madhu! Then she repeats the name of Hari, and catching at a dark blue cloud,[2] strives to embrace it, saying, 'It is my beloved who approaches.'"

[1] We meet with various little philosophical phenomena used as similes in this rhapsody of Jayadeva. These aërolites, mentioned by a poet the contemporary of David and Solomon, are but recently known to the European philosopher. [But one was worshipped at Rome in B.C. 204.]

[2] This is, in allusion to the colour of Krishna, a dark blue.

Midnight arrives, but neither Hari nor the damsel returns, when she gives herself up to the frenzy of despair, exclaiming: "The perfidy of my friend rends my heart. Bring disease and death, O gale of Malaya! receive me in thy azure wave, O sister of Yama,[1] that the ardour of my heart may be allayed."

The repentant Hari at length returns, and in speech well calculated to win forgiveness, thus pleads his pardon:

"Oh! grant me a draught of honey from the lotus of thy mouth: or if thou art inexorable, grant me death from the arrows of thine eyes; make thy arms my chains: thou art my ornament; thou art the pearl in the ocean of my mortal birth! Thine eyes, which nature formed like blue water-lilies, are become through thy resentment like petals of the crimson lotus! Thy silence affects me; oh! speak with the voice of music, and let thy sweet accents allay my ardour" [543].

"Radha with timid joy, darting her eyes on Govinda while she musically sounded the rings of her ankles and the bells of her zone,[2] entered the mystic bower of her beloved. His heart was agitated by her sight, as the waves of the deep are affected by the lunar orb.[3] From his graceful waist flowed a pale yellow robe,[4] which resembled the golden dust of the water-lily scattered over its blue petals.[5] His locks interwoven with blossoms, were like a cloud variegated by the moonbeam. Tears of transport gushed in a stream from the full eyes of Radha, and their watery glances beamed on her best beloved. Even shame, which had before taken its abode in their dark pupils, was itself ashamed,[6] and departed when the fawn-eyed Radha gazed on the bright face of Krishna."

[1] The Indian Pluto; she is addressing the Yamuna.

[2] Thus the ancient statues do not present merely the sculptor's fancy in the zone of bells with which they are ornamented.

[3] This is a favourite metaphor with the bards of India, to describe the alternations of the exciting causes of love; and it is yet more important as showing that Jayadeva was the philosopher as well as the poet of nature, in making the action of the moon upon the tides the basis of this beautiful simile.

[4] This yellow robe or mantle furnishes another title of the Sun-god, namely, *Pitambara*, typical of the resplendence which precedes his rising and setting.

[5] It will be again necessary to call to mind the colour of Krishna, to appreciate this elegant metaphor.

[6] This idea is quite new.

The poet proceeds to describe Apollo's bower on the sable Yamuna, as 'Love's recess'; and sanctifies it as

> . . . The ground
> Where early Love his Psyche's zone unbound.[1]

In the morning the blue god aids in Radha's simple toilet. He stains her eye with antimony "which would make the blackest bee envious," places "a circle of musk on her forehead," and intertwines "a chaplet of flowers and peacock's feathers in her dark tresses," replacing "the zone of golden bells." The bard concludes as he commenced, with an eulogium on the inspirations of his muse, which it is evident were set to music. "Whatever is delightful in the modes of music, whatever is graceful in the fine strains of poetry, whatever is exquisite in the sweet art of love, let the happy and wise learn from the songs of Jayadeva."

The Rāsmandal Dance.—This mystic dance, the *rasmandal*, appears analogous to the Pyrrhic dance, or the fire-dance of the Egyptians. The movements of those who personate the deity and his fair companions are full [544] of grace, and the dialogue is replete with harmony.[2] The Chaubes [3] of Mathura and Vindravana have considerable reputation as vocalists; and the effect of the modulated and deep tones of the adult blending with the clear treble of the juvenile performers, while the time is marked by the cymbal or the soothing monotony of the tabor, accompanied occasionally by the *murali* or flute, is very pleasing.

[1] *Childe Harold*, Canto iii.

[2] The anniversary of the birth of Kanhaiya is celebrated with splendour at Sindhia's court, where the author frequently witnessed it, during a ten years' residence.

[3] The priests of Kanhaiya, probably so called from the *chob* or club with which, on the annual festival, they assault the castle of Kansa, the tyrant usurper of Krishna's birthright, who, like Herod, ordered the slaughter of all the youth of Vraj, that Krishna might not escape. These *Chaubēs* are most likely the *Sobii* of Alexander, who occupied the chief towns of the Panjab, and who, according to Arrian, worshipped Hercules (Hari-kul-es, chief of the race of Hari), and were armed with clubs. The mimic assault of Kansa's castle by some hundreds of these robust church militants, with their long clubs covered with iron rings, is well worth seeing. [The Chaubē Brāhmans of Mathura do not take their name from *Chob*, 'a club,' but from Skt. *Chaturvedin*, 'learned in the four Vedas.' By the Sobii the Author means the Sibi or Sivaya, inhabiting a district between the Hydaspes and the Indus (McCrindle, *Alexander*, 366). They have no possible connexion with the Mathura Chaubēs.]

Govardhana.—We have a Parnassus in Govardhana, from which sacred hill the god derives one of his principal epithets, Gordhan or Gordhannath, 'God of the mount of wealth.' [1] Here he first gave proofs of miraculous power, and a cave in this hill was the first shrine, on his apotheosis, whence his miracles and oracles were made known to the Yadus. From this cave (*gupha*) is derived another of his titles—Guphnath, 'Lord of the cave,' distinct from his epithet Gopinath, 'Lord of the Gopis,' [2] or pastoral nymphs. On the annual festival held at Govardhana, the sacred mount is purified with copious oblations of milk, for which all the cows of the district are in requisition.

Cave Worship of Krishna.—The worship of Krishna in ancient days, like that of Apollo amongst the Greeks, was chiefly celebrated in caves, of which there were many scattered over India. The most remarkable were those of Govardhana in Vraj; Gaya in Bihar; Gopnath on the shores of Saurashtra; and Jalandhara [3] on the Indus. In these dark and mysterious retreats superstition had her full influence over the votaries who sought the commands and deprecated the wrath of the deity: but, as the Mukhya told the author, "the age of oracles and miracles is past"; and the new wheel, which was miraculously furnished each revolving year to supply the place of that which first indicated his desire to abide at Nathdwara, is no longer forthcoming. The old one, which was the signal of his wish, is, however, preserved as a relic, and greatly reverenced. The statue now worshipped at Nathdwara, as the representative of 'the god of the mount' [545], is said to be the identical image raised in the cave of Govardhana, and brought thence by the high priest Balba.[4]

[1] [Govardhana means 'nourisher of cattle.']

[2] [The title Guphanātha is not recorded.]

[3] Jalandhara on the Indus is described by the Emperor Babur as a very singular spot, having numerous caves. The deity of the caves of Jalandhara is the tutelary deity of the Prince of Marwar. [When the body of Daksha was cut up, the breast fell at Jālandhar; the Daitya king, Jālandhara, was crushed by Siva under the Jawālamukhi hill (*Āīn*, ii. 314 f.).]

[4] [Cave worship does not seem to be specially connected with the cult of Krishna. The mention of the cave at Govardhan seems to refer to the legend of Krishna protecting the people of Braj from a storm sent by Indra, by holding the hill over them (Growse, *op. cit.* 60). The Gaya caves are Buddhistic, and have no connexion with Krishna (*IGI*, xii. 198 f.). Guphanāth does not seem to be a Krishna title, and the cave of Gopnāth in Kāthiāwar is said to derive its name from Gopsinghji, a Gohil prince, who reigned in the sixteenth century (*BG*, viii. 445).]

Krishna a Dragon-Slayer.—As the destroyer of Kaliyanag, 'the black serpent,' which infested the waters of the Yamuna, Kanhaiya has the character of the Pythic Apollo. He is represented dragging the monster from the 'black stream,' and bruising him with his foot. He had, however, many battles with his hydra-foe ere he vanquished him, and he was once driven by Kalayavana from Vraj to Dwarka, whence his title of Ranchhor. Here we have the old allegory of the schismatic wars of the Buddhists and Vaishnavas.

Parallels to Krishna in other Mythologies.—Diodorus informs us that *Kan* was one of the titles of the Egyptian Apollo as the sun; and this is the common contraction for Kanhaiya, whose colour is a dark cerulean blue (*nila*): and hence his name Nilanath, who, like the Apollo of the Nile, is depicted with the human form and eagle-head, with a lotus in his hand. S and H are permutable letters in the Bhakha, and Syam or Sham, the god of the Yamuna, may be the *Ham* or Hammon of Egypt. Hari accompanied Rama to Lanka, as did the Egyptian Apollo, Rameses-Sesostris, on his expedition to India: both were attended in their expedition by an army of Satyrs, or tribes bearing the names of different animals: and as we have the Aswas, the Takshaks, and the Sasas of the Yadu tribes, typified under the horse, the serpent, and the hare, so the races of Surya, of which Rama was the head, may have been designated Riksh and Hanuman, or bears and monkeys. The distance of the Nile from the Indian shore forms no objection; the sail spread for Ceylon could waft the vessel to the Red Sea, which the fleets of Tyre, of Solomon, and Hiram covered about this very time. That the Hindus navigated the ocean from the earliest ages, the traces of their religion in the isles of the Indian archipelago sufficiently attest; but on this subject we have already said enough.

The coincidence between the most common epithets of the Apollos of Greece and India, as applied to the sun, are peculiarly striking. Hari, as Bhannath, 'the lord of beams,' is Phoebus, and his heaven is Haripur (Heliopolis), or 'city of Hari.'[1] Helios (Ἥλιος) was a title of Apollo, whence the Greeks had their

[1] "In Hebrew *heres* signifies the sun, but in Arabic the meaning of the radical word is to guard, preserve; and of *haris*, guardian, preserver" (Volney's *Ruins of Empires*, p. 316). [Needless to say, Elysium (Ἠλύσιον πεδίον) has no connexion with Ἥλιος, the sun.]

Elysium, the Haripur or Bhanthan (the abode of the sun), the highest of the [546] heavens or abodes of bliss of the martial Rajput. Hence the eagle (the emblem of Hari as the sun) [1] was adopted by the western warrior as the symbol of victory.

The Di Majores of the Rajput are the same in number and title as amongst the Greeks and Romans, being the deities who figuratively preside over the planetary system. Their grades of bliss are therefore in unison with the eccentricity of orbit of the planet named. On this account Chandra or Indu, the moon, being a mere satellite of Ila, the earth, though probably originating the name of the Indu race, is inferior in the scale of blissful abodes to that of his son Budha or Mercury, whose heliacal appearance gave him importance even with the sons of Vaivasvata, the sun. From the poetic seers of the martial races we learn that there are two distinct places of reward ; the one essentially spiritual, the other of a material nature. The bard inculcates that the warrior who falls in battle in the fulfilment of his duty, "who abandons life through the wave of steel," will know no "second birth," but that the unconfined spark (*jyotis*) will reunite to the parent orb. The doctrine of transmigration through a variety of hideous forms may be considered as a series of purgatories.

The Greeks and Celts worshipped Apollo under the title of Carneios,[2] which "selon le scholiaste de Théocrite" is derived from Carnos, "qui ne prophétisoit que des malheurs aux Héraclides lors de leur incursion dans le Péloponnèse. Un d'eux appelé *Hippotés, le tua d'un coup de flèche.*" Now one of the titles of the Hindu Apollo is Karna, 'the radiant' ; from *karna*, 'a ray' ; and when he led the remains of the Harikulas in company

[1] The heaven of Vishnu, Vaikuntha, is entirely of gold, and 80,000 miles in circumference. Its edifices, pillars, and ornaments are composed of precious stones. The crystal waters of the Ganges form a river in Vaikuntha, where are lakes filled with blue, red, and white water-lilies, each of a hundred and even a thousand petals. On a throne glorious as the meridian sun resting on water-lilies, is Vishnu, with Lakshmi or Sri, the goddess of abundance (the Ceres of the Egyptians and Greeks), on his right hand, surrounded by spirits who constantly celebrate the praise of Vishnu and Lakshmi, who are served by his votaries, and to whom the eagle (*garuda*) is door-keeper (Extract from the Mahabharata—See Ward on the *History and Religion of the Hindus*, vol. ii. p. 14).

[2] [Apollo Κάρνειος was probably 'the horned god,' connected with κέρας, 'a horn,' as a deity of herdsmen (Farnell, *Cults of the Greek States*, iv. 131).]

with Baldeva (the god of strength), and Yudhishthira, after the great international war, into the Peloponnesus of Saurashtra, they were attacked by the aboriginal Bhils, one of whom slew the divine Karna with an arrow. The Bhils claim to be of Hayavansa, or the race of Haya, whose chief seat was at Maheswar on the Nerbudda: the assassin of Karna would consequently be Hayaputra, or descendant of Haya[1] [547].

The most celebrated of the monuments commonly termed Druidic, scattered throughout Europe, is at Carnac in Brittany, on which coast the Celtic Apollo had his shrines, and was propitiated under the title of Karneios, and this monument may be considered at once sacred to the manes of the warriors and the sun-god Karneios. Thus the Roman Saturnalia, the *carnivale*, has a better etymology in the festival to Karneios, as the sun, than in the 'adieu to flesh' during the fast. The character of this festival is entirely oriental, and accompanied with the licentiousness which belonged to the celebration of the powers of nature. Even now, although Christianity has banished the grosser forms, it partakes more of a Pagan than a Christian ceremony.

The Annakūta Festival.—Of the festivals of Krishna the Annakuta is the most remarkable;[2] when the seven statues were brought from the different capitals of Rajasthan, and mountains (*kuta*) of food (*anna*) piled up for their repast, at a given signal are levelled by the myriads of votaries assembled from all parts. About eighty years ago, on a memorable assemblage at the Annakuta, before warfare had devastated Rajasthan, and circumscribed the means of the faithful disciples of Hari, amongst the multitude of Vaishnavas of every region were almost all the Rajput princes; Rana Arsi of Mewar, Raja Bijai Singh of Marwar, Raja Gaj Singh of Bikaner, and Bahadur Singh of Kishangarh. Rana Arsi presented to the god a *tora*, or massive golden anklet-chain set with emeralds: Bijai Singh a diamond necklace worth

[1] Supposing these coincidences in the fabulous history of the ancient nations of Greece and Asia to be merely fortuitous, they must excite interest; but conjoined with various others in the history of the Herikulas of India and the Heraclidae of Greece, I cannot resist the idea that they were connected [?].

[2] [The Annakūta festival, held on the first day of the light half of Kārttik (Oct.–Nov.). This was the old name of the hill which Krishna held aloft to protect his people (Growse, *op. cit.* 300).]

twenty-five thousand rupees: the other princes according to their means. They were followed by an old woman of Surat, with infirm step and shaking head, who deposited four coppers in the hand of the high-priest, which were received with a gracious smile, not vouchsafed to the lords of the earth. "The Rand is in luck," whispered the chief of Kishangarh to the Rana. Soon afterwards the statue of Hari was brought forth, when the same old woman placed at its feet a bill of exchange for seventy thousand rupees. The mighty were humbled, and the smile of the Gosain was explained. Such gifts, and to a yet greater amount, are, or were, by no means uncommon from the sons of commerce, who are only known to belong to the flock from the distinguishing necklace of the sect.[1]

Interruption of Worship.—The predatory system which reduced these countries to a state of the most degraded anarchy, greatly diminished the number of pilgrimages to Nathdwara [548]; and the gods of Vraj had sufficient prescience to know that they could guard neither their priests nor followers from the Pathan and Mahratta, to whom the crown of the god, or the *nathna* (nose-jewel) of Radha, would be alike acceptable: nor would they have scrupled to retain both the deities and priests as hostages for such imposition as they might deem within their means. Accordingly, of late years, there had been no congress of the gods of Vraj, who remained fixtures on their altars till the halcyon days of A.D. 1818 permitted their liberation.[2]

Seven Forms of Krishna.—The seven statues of Kanhaiya were brought together by the high-priest Balba, who established

[1] Gibbon records a similar offering of 200,000 sesterces to the Roman church, by a stranger, in the reign of Decius [ed. W. Smith, ii. 190].

[2] I enjoyed no small degree of favour with the supreme pontiff of the shrine of Apollo and all his votaries, for effecting a meeting of the seven statues of Vishnu in 1820. In contriving this I had not only to reconcile ancient animosities between the priests of the different shrines, in order to obtain a free passport for the gods, but to pledge myself to the princes in whose capitals they were established, for their safe return: for they dreaded lest bribery might entice the priests to fix them elsewhere, which would have involved their loss of sanctity, dignity, and prosperity. It cost me no little trouble, and still more anxiety, to keep the assembled multitudes at peace with each other, for they are as outrageous as any sectarians in contesting the supreme power and worth of their respective forms (*rupa*). Yet they all separated, not only without violence, but without even any attempt at robbery, so common on such occasions.

the festival of the Annakuta. They remained in the same sanctuary until the time of Girdhari, the grandson of Balba, who having seven sons, gave to each a rupa or statue, and whose descendants continue in the office of priest. The names and present abodes of the gods are as follows:

Nathji, the god, or Gordhannath, god of the mount Nathdwara.

1. Nonita	Nathdwara.
2. Mathuranath	Kotah.
3. Dwarkanath	Kankroli.[1]
4. Gokulnath, or Gokulchandrama .	Jaipur.
5. Yadunath	Surat.
6. Vitthalnath[2]	Kotah.
7. Madan Mohana	Jaipur.

Nathji is not enumerated amongst the forms; he stands supreme.

Nonita, or Nonanda, the juvenile Kanhaiya, has his altar separate, though close to Nathji. He is also styled Balamukund, 'the blessed child,'[3] and is depicted as an infant with *pera*[4] or comfit-ball in his hand. This image, which was one of the penates of a former age, and which, since the destruction of the shrines of [549] Krishna by the Islamites, had lain in the Yamuna, attached itself to the sacerdotal zone (Janeo) of the high-priest Balba, while he was performing his ablutions, who, carrying it home, placed it in a niche of the temple and worshipped it: and Nonanda yet receives the peculiar homage of the high-priest and his family as their household divinity. Of the second image, Mathuranath, there is no particular mention: it was at one time at Khamnor in Mewar, but is now at Kotah.

Balkrishna, the third son, had Dwarkanath, which statue, now at Kankroli in Mewar, is asserted to be the identical image that

[1] [Kānkroli, 36 miles N.E. of Udaipur city: the image is said to have been brought from Mathura A.D. 1669 (Erskine ii. A. 113).]

[2] [The form of Vishnu worshipped at Pāndharpur in Sholapur District. The name is probably a local corruption of Vishnupati, 'Lord Vishnu,' through the forms Bistu or Bittu (*IA*, iv. 361).]

[3] [Said to mean 'the child, giver of liberation.']

[4] The *pera* of Mathura can only be made from the waters of the Yamuna, from whence it is still conveyed to Nonanda at Nathdwara, and with curds forms his evening repast.

received the adoration of Raja Amaraka, a prince of the solar race who lived in the Satya Yuga, or silver age. The 'god of the mount' revealed himself in a dream to his high-priest, and told him of the domicile of this his representative at Kanauj. Thither Balba repaired, and having obtained it from the Brahman, appointed Damodardas Khatri to officiate at his altar.

The fourth statue, that of Gokulnath, or Gokul Chandrama (*i.e.* the *moon* of Gokul), had an equally mysterious origin, having been discovered in a deep ravine on the banks of the river; Balba assigned it to his brother-in-law. Gokul is an island on the Jumna,[1] a few miles below Mathura, and celebrated in the early history of the pastoral divinity. The residence of this image at Jaipur does not deprive the little island of its honours as a place of pilgrimage; for the 'god of Gokul' has an altar on the original site, and his rites are performed by an aged priestess, who disowns the jurisdiction of the high-priest of Nathdwara, both in the spiritual and temporal concerns of her shrine; and who, to the no small scandal of all who are interested in Apollo, appealed from the fiat of the high-priest to the British court of justice. The royal grants of the Mogul emperors were produced, which proved the right to lie in the high-priest, though a long period of almost undisturbed authority had created a feeling of independent control in the family of the priestess, which they desired might continue. A compromise ensued, when the Author was instrumental in restoring harmony to the shrines of Apollo.

The fifth, Yadunath, is the deified ancestor of the whole Yadu race. This image, now at Surat, formerly adorned the shrine of Mahaban near Mathura which was destroyed by Mahmud [550].

The sixth, Vitthalnath, or Pandurang,[2] was found in the Ganges at Benares, Samvat 1572 (A.D. 1516), from which we may judge of their habit of multiplying divinities.

The seventh, Madan Mohana, 'he who intoxicates with desire,' the seductive lover of Radha and the Gopis, has his rites performed by a female. The present priestess of Mohana is the mother of Damodara, the supreme head of all who adore the Apollo of Vraj.

[1] [Gokul is not an island, but a suburb of Mahāban in Mathura District.

[2] [Pāndurang is said to mean 'white-coloured'; but others believe it to be the Sanskritized form of Pandaraga, that is, 'belonging to Pandargē,' the old name of Pāndharpur (*BG*, xx. 423).]

The Pontiff of Nāthdwāra.—I am not aware of the precise period of Balba Acharya, who thus collected the seven images of Krishna now in Rajasthan; but he must have lived about the time of the last of the Lodi kings, at the period of the conquest of India by the Moguls (A.D. 1526). The present pontiff, Damodara, as before said, is his lineal descendant; and whether in addressing him verbally or by letter he is styled Maharaja or 'great prince.' [1]

As the supreme head of the Vishnu sect his person is held to be Ansa, or 'a portion of the divinity'; and it is maintained that so late as the father of the present incumbent, the god manifested himself and conversed with the high-priest. The present pontiff is now about thirty years of age. He is of a benign aspect, with much dignity of demeanour: courteous, yet exacting the homage due to his high calling: meek, as becomes the priest of Govinda, but with the finished manners of one accustomed to the first society. His features are finely moulded, and his complexion good. He is about the middle size, though as he rises to no mortal, I could not exactly judge of his height. When I saw him he had one only daughter, to whom he is much attached. He has but one wife, nor does Krishna allow polygamy to his priest. In times of danger, like some of his prototypes in the dark ages of Europe, he poised the lance, and found it more effective than spiritual anathemas, against those who would first adore the god, and then plunder him. Such were the Mahratta chiefs, Jaswant Rao Holkar and Bapu Sindhia. Damodara accordingly made the [551] tour of his extensive diocese at the head of four hundred horse, two standards of foot, and two field-pieces. He rode the finest mares in the country; laid aside his

[1] Gosain is a title more applicable to the *célibataire* worshippers of Hara than of Hari—of Jupiter than of Apollo. It is alleged that the Emperor Akbar first bestowed this epithet on the high-priest of Krishna, whose rites attracted his regard. They were previously called Dikshit, 'one who performs sacrifice,' a name given to a very numerous class of Brahmans. The *Gotrācharya*, or genealogical creed of the high-priest, is as follows: "*Tailang Brahman, Bharadwaja gotra,** *Gurukula,*† *Taittari sakha*; *i.e.* Brahman of Telingana, of the tribe of Bharadwaja, of the race of Guru, of the branch Taittari."

* Bhāradwaja was a celebrated founder of a sect in the early ages.

† Guru is an epithet applied to Vrishapati, 'Lord of the bull,' the Indian Jupiter, who is called the Guru, preceptor or guardian of the gods. [Brihaspati, 'Lord of prayer,' the regent of the planet Jupiter, is confused with Vrishapati, 'Lord of the bull,' an epithet of Siva.]

pontificals for the quilted *dagla*, and was summoned to matins by the kettle-drum instead of the bell and cymbal. In this he only imitated Kanhaiya, who often mixed in the ranks of battle, and "dyed his saffron robe in the red-stained field." Had Damodara been captured on one of these occasions by any marauding Pathan, and incarcerated, as he assuredly would have been, for ransom, the marauder might have replied to the Rana, as did the Plantagenet king to the Pope, when the surrender of the captive church-militant bishop was demanded, "Is this thy son Joseph's coat?" But, notwithstanding this display of martial principle, which covered with a helmet the shaven crown, his conduct and character are amiable and unexceptionable, and he furnishes a striking contrast to the late head of the Vishnu establishments in Marwar, who commenced with the care of his master's conscience, and ended with that of the State; meek and unassuming till he added temporal[1] to spiritual power, which developed unlimited pride, with all the qualities that too often wait on "a little brief authority," and to the display of which he fell a victim. Damodara,[2] similarly circumstanced, might have evinced the same failings, and have met the same end; but though endeavours were made to give him political influence at the Rana's court, yet, partly from his own good sense, and partly through the dissuasion of the Nestor of Kotah (Zalim Singh), he was not entrained in the vortex of its intrigues, which must have involved the sacrifice of wealth and the proper dignity of his station [552].

[1] The high-priest of Jalandharnath used to appear at the head of a cavalcade far more numerous than any feudal lord of Marwar. A sketch of this personage will appear elsewhere. These Brahmans were not a jot behind the ecclesiastical lords of the Middle Ages, who are thus characterized: "Les seigneurs ecclésiatiques, malgré l'humilité chrétienne, ne se sont pas montrés moins orgueilleux que les nobles laïcs. Le doyen du chapitre de Notre Dame du Port, à Clermont, pour montrer sa grande noblesse, officiait avec toute la pompe féodale. Étant à l'autel, il avait l'oiseau sur la perche gauche, et on portait devant lui la hallebarde; on la lui portait aussi de la même manière pendant qu'on chantait l'évangile, et aux processions il avait lui-même l'oiseau sur le poing, et il marchait à la tête de ses serviteurs, menant ses chiens de chasse" (*Dict. de l'Anc. Régime*, p. 380).

[2] The first letter I received on reaching England after my long residence in India was from this priest, filled with anxious expressions for my health. and speedy return to protect the lands and sacred kine of Apollo.

APPENDIX

No. I

Grant of the Rathor Rani, the Queen-Mother of Udaipur, on the death of her Son, the Heir-Apparent, Prince Amra.

Siddh Sri Bari [1] Rathorji to the Patels and inhabitants of Girwa.[2] The four bighas of land, belonging to the Jat Roga, have been assigned to the Brahman Kishna on the Anta Samya (final epoch) of Lalji.[3] Let him possess the rents thereof.[4] The dues for wood and forage (*khar lakar*) contributions (*barar*) are renounced by the State in favour of the Brahmans.

Samvat 1875, Amavas 15th of Asoj, A.D. 1819.

No. II

Grant held by a Brahman of Birkhera.

"A Brahman's orphan was compelled by hunger to seek sustenance in driving an oil-mill; instead of oil the receptacle was filled with blood. The frightened oilman demanded of the child who he was; 'A Brahman's orphan,' was the reply. Alarmed at the enormity of his guilt in thus employing the son of a priest, he covered the palm of his hand with earth, in which he sowed the tulasi seed,[5] and went on a pilgrimage to Dwarka.

[1] The great Rathor queen. There were two of this tribe; she was the queen-mother.

[2] [The tract in the centre of the State, including Udaipur city.]

[3] An endearing epithet, applied to children, from *larla*, beloved.

[4] It is customary to call these grants to religious orders 'grants of land,' although they entitle only the rents thereof; for there is no seizin of the land itself, as numerous inscriptions testify, and which, as well as the present, prove the proprietary right to be in the cultivator only. The *tamba-pattra*,* or copper-plate patent (by which such grants are probably designated) of Yasodharman,† the Pramara prince of Ujjain, seven hundred years ago, is good evidence that the rents only are granted; he commands the crown tenants of the two villages assigned to the temple "to pay all dues as they arise—money-rent—first share of produce," not a word of seizing of the soil. See *Transactions of the Royal Asiatic Society*, vol. i. p. 223.

[5] [The sacred basil plant, *Ocymum sanctum*.]

---

* To distinguish them from grants of land to feudal tenants, which patents (*patta*) are manuscript.

† [He defeated Mihiragula, leader of the White Huns, about A.D. 528 (Smith, *EHI*, 318).]

He demanded the presence (*darsana*) of the god; the priests pointed to the ocean, when he plunged in, and had an interview with Dwarkanath, who presented him with a written order on the Rana for forty-five bighas of land. He returned and threw the writing before the Rana, on the steps of the temple of Jagannath. The Rana read the writing of the god, placed it on his head, and immediately made out the grant. This is three hundred and fifty years ago, as recorded by an inscription on stone, and his descendant, Kosala, yet enjoys it."

(A true Translation.) J. Tod.

No. III

The Palod inscription is unfortunately mislaid; but in searching for it, another was discovered from Aner, four miles southwest of the ancient Morwan, where there is a temple to the four-armed divinity (Chaturbhuja), endowed in Samvat 1570, by Rana Jagat Singh [553]. On one of the pillars of the temple is inscribed a voluntary gift made in Samvat 1845, and signed by the village Panch, of the first-fruits of the harvest, namely, two sers and a half (five pounds weight) from each *khal* [1] of the spring, and the same of the autumnal harvests.

No. IV

Sri Amra Sing (II.) etc., etc.

Whereas the shrine of Sri Pratap-Iswara (the God of Fortune) has been erected in the meadows of Rasmi, all the groves and trees are sacred to him; whoever cuts down any of them is an offender to the State, and shall pay a fine of three hundred rupees, and the *ass* [2] shall be the portion of the officers of government who suffer it.

Pus. 14, Samvat 1712 (A.D. 1656).

No. V

Maharana Sri Raj Singh, commanding.

To the Nobles, Ministers, Patels,[3] Patwaris,[3] of the ten thousand [villages] of Mewar (*das sahas Mewar-ra*), according to your stations—read!

1. From remote times, the temples and dwellings of the Jains

[1] A *khal* is one of the heaps after the corn is thrashed out, about *five maunds* [400 lbs.].

[2] The *gadha-ghal* is a punishment unknown in any but the Hindu code; the hieroglyphic import appears on the pillar, and must be seen to be understood.

[3] Revenue officers.

have been authorized; let none therefore within their boundaries carry animals to slaughter—this is their ancient privilege.

2. Whatever life, whether man or animal, passes their abode for the purpose of being killed, is saved (*amara*).[1]

3. Traitors to the State, robbers, felons escaped confinement, who may fly for sanctuary (*saran*) to the dwellings (*upasra*)[2] of the Yatis,[3] shall not there be seized by the servants of the court.

4. The *kunchi*[4] (handful) at harvest, the *mutthi* (handful) of *kirana*, the charity lands (*dholi*), grounds, and houses, established by them in the various towns, shall be maintained.

5. This ordinance is issued in consequence of the representation of the Rikh[5] Mana, to whom is granted fifteen bighas of *adhan*[6] land, and twenty-five of *maleti*.[6] The same quantity of each kind in each of the districts of Nimach and Nimbahera.—Total in three districts, forty-five bighas of *adhan*, and seventy-five of *mal*[7] (554).

On seeing this ordinance, let the land be measured and assigned, and let none molest the Yatis, but foster their privileges. Cursed be he who infringes them—the cow to the Hindu—the hog and corpse to the Musalman.

(By command.)

Samvat 1749, Magh sudi 5th, A.D. 1693. SAH DYAL (Minister).

No. VI

Maharaja Chhattar Singh (one of the Rana's sons), commanding.

In the town of Rasmi, whoever slays sheep, buffaloes, goats, or other living thing, is a criminal to the State; his house, cattle, and effects shall be forfeited, and himself expelled the village.

(By command).

Pus Sudi 14, Samvat 1705, A.D. 1649.

The Pancholi DAMAKA DAS.

[1] Literally 'immortal,' from *mara*, 'death,' and the privative prefix.

[2] Schools or colleges of the Yatis.

[3] Priests of the Jains.

[4] *Kunchi* and *mutthi* are both a 'handful'; the first is applied to grain in the stalk at harvest time; the other to such edibles in merchandise as sugar, raisins, etc., collectively termed *kirana*.

[5] *Rikh*[*rishi*] is an ancient title applied to the highest class of priests; *Rikh-Rikhsha-Rikhiswara*, applied to royalty in old times.

[6] *Adhan* is the richest land, lying under the protection of the town walls; *mal* or *maleti* land is land not irrigated from wells.

[7] In all a hundred and twenty bighas, or about forty acres.

No. VII

Maharana Jai Singh to the inhabitants of Bakrol; printers, potters, oilmen, etc., etc., commanding.

From the 11th Asarh (June) to the full moon of Asoj (September), none shall drain the waters of the lake; no oil-mill shall work, or earthen vessel be made, during these the four rainy months.[1]

No. VIII

Maharana Sri Jagat Singh II., commanding.

The village of Siarh in the hills, of one thousand rupees yearly rent, having been chosen by Nathji (*the* god) for his residence, and given up by Rana Raghude,[2] I have confirmed it. The Gosain [3] and his heirs shall enjoy it for ever.

Samvat 1793, A.D. 1737.

No. IX

Siddh Sri Maharaja Dhiraj, Maharana Sri Bhim Singhji, commanding.

The undermentioned towns and villages were presented to Sriji [4] by copper-plate. The revenues (*hasil*) [5] contributions (*barar*), taxes, dues (*lagat-be-lagat*), trees, shrubs, foundations and boundaries (*nim-sim*), shall all belong to Sriji. If of my seed, none will ever dispute this [555].

The ancient copper-plate being lost, I have thus renewed it.

[1] [For the annual Jain retreat see p. 606, above.]

[2] The chief of Delwara.

[3] There are other grants later than this, which prove that all grants were renewed in every new reign. This grant also proves that no chief has the power to alienate without his sovereign's sanction.

[4] Epithet indicative of the greatness of the deity.

[5] Here is another proof that the sovereign can only alienate the revenues (*hasil*); and though everything upon and about the grant, yet *not the soil*, The *nim-sim* is almost as powerful an expression as the old grant to the Rawdons—

"From earth to heaven,
From heaven to hell,
For thee and thine
Therein to dwell."

Here follows a list of thirty-four entire towns and villages, many from the fisc, or confirmations of the grants of the chiefs, besides various parcels of arable land, from twenty to one hundred and fifty bighas, in forty-six more villages, from chiefs of every class, and patches of meadowland (*bira*) in twenty more.

No. X

Sri Maharana Bhima Singhji, commanding.

To the towns of Sriji, or to the [personal] lands of the Gosainji,[1] no molestation shall be offered. No warrants or exactions shall be issued or levied upon them. All complaints, suits, or matters, in which justice is required, originating in Nathdwara, shall be settled there; none shall interfere therein, and the decisions of the Gosainji I shall invariably confirm. The town and transit duties [2] (of Nathdwara and villages pertaining thereto), the assay (*parkhai*) [2] fees from the public markets, duties on precious metals (*kasoti*),[2] all brokerage (*dalali*), and dues collected at the four gates; all contributions and taxes of whatever kind, are presented as an offering to Sriji; let the income thereof be placed in Sriji's coffers.

All the products of foreign countries imported by the Vaishnavas,[3] whether domestic or foreign, and intended for consumption at Nathdwara,[4] shall be exempt from duties. The right of sanctuary (*saran*) of Sriji, both in the town and in all his other villages,[5] will be maintained: the Almighty will take cognisance of any innovation. Wherefore, let all chiefs, farmers of duties, beware of molesting the goods of Nathji (*the* god), and wherever such may halt, let guards be provided for their security, and let each chief convey them through his bounds in safety. If of my blood, or if my servants, this warrant will be obeyed for ever and for ever. Whoever resumes this grant will be a caterpillar in hell during 60,000 years.

[1] The high-priest.

[2] All these are royalties, and the Rana was much blamed, even by his Vaishnava ministers, for sacrificing them even to Kanhaiya.

[3] Followers of Vishnu, Krishna, or Kanhaiya, chiefly mercantile.

[4] Many merchants, by the connivance of the conductors of the caravans of Nathji's goods, contrived to smuggle their goods to Nathdwara, and to the disgrace of the high-priest or his underlings, this traffic was sold for their personal advantage. It was a delicate thing to search these caravans, or to prevent the loss to the State from the evasion of the duties. The Rana durst not interfere lest he might incur the penalty of his own anathemas. The Author's influence with the high-priest put a stop to this.

[5] This extent of sanctuary is an innovation of the present Rana's, with many others equally unwise.

By command—through the chief butler (*Paneri*) Eklingdas: written by Surat Singh, son of Nathji Pancholi, Magh sudi 1st, Samvat 1865; A.D. 1809.

No. XI

Personal grant to the high-priest, Damodarji Maharaj.

Swasti Sri, from the abode at Udaipur, Maharana Sri Bhim Singhji, commanding [556].

To all the chieftains, landholders, managers of the crown and *deorhi*[1] lands, to all Patels, etc., etc., etc. As an offering to the Sri Gosainji two rupees have been granted in every village throughout Mewar, one in each harvest—let no opposition be made thereto. If of my kin or issue, none will revoke this—the *an* (oath of allegiance) be upon his head. By command, through Parihara Mayaram, Samvat 1860, Jeth sudi 5th Mangalwar; A.D. 1804.

At one side of the patent, in the Rana's own hand, "An offering to Sri Girdhariji[2] Maharaj—If of my issue none will disobey—who dares, may the Almighty punish!"

No. XII

Maharana Bhim Singh, commanding.

To the Mandir (*minster*) of Sri Murali Manohar (*flute delighting*), situated on the dam of the lake at Mandalgarh, the following grant has been made, with all the dues, income, and privileges, viz.:

1. The hamlet called Kotwalkhera, with all thereto appertaining.
2. Three rupees' worth of saffron monthly from the transit duty *chabutra*.[3]
3. From the police-office of Mandalgarh:

   Three tunics (*baga*) for the idol on each festival, viz. Ashtami, Jaljatra, and Vasant Panchami.[4]

   Five rupees' worth of oil[5] on the Jaljatra, and two and a half in the full moon of Karttik [Oct.–Nov.].

[1] Lands for the queens or others of the immediate household.

[2] Father of the present high-priest, Damodarji.

[3] [Office, properly 'a platform.']

[4] [Festivals of Krishna's birthday, the water festival, the spring festival.]

[5] Amongst the items of the Chartulary of Dunfermline is the tithe of the oil of the Greenland whale fisheries.

4. Both gardens under the dam of the lake, with all the fruits and flowers thereof.

5. The *Inch*[1] on all the vegetables appertaining to the prince.

6. *Kunchi* and *dalali*, or the handful at harvest, and all brokerage.

7. The income arising from the sale of the estates is to be applied to the repairs of the temple and dam.

Margsir [Nov.–Dec.] Sudi 1, Samvat 1866; A.D. 1810 [557].

CHAPTER 21

The Importance of Mythology.—It has been observed by that philosophical traveller, Dr. Clarke, that, "by a proper attention to the vestiges of ancient superstition, we are sometimes enabled to refer a whole people to their original ancestors, with as much, if not more certainty, than by observations made upon their language; because the superstition is engrafted upon the stock, but the language is liable to change."[2] Impressed with the justness, as well as the originality of the remark, I shall adopt it as my guide in the observations I propose to make on the religious festivals and superstitions of Mewar. However important may be the study of military, civil, and political history, the science is incomplete without mythological history; and he is little imbued with the spirit of philosophy who can perceive in the fables of antiquity nothing but the extravagance of a fervid imagination. Did no other consequence result from the study of mythology than the fact that, in all ages and countries, man has desecrated his reason, and voluntarily reduced himself below the level of the brutes that perish, it must provoke inquiry into the cause of this degradation. Such an investigation would develop, not only the source of history, the handmaid of the arts and sciences, but the origin and application of the latter, in a theogony typical of the seasons, their changes, and products. Thus mythology may be considered the parent of all history.

The Aboriginal Tribes.—With regard, however, to the rude tribes who still inhabit the mountains and fastnesses of India,

[1] A handful of every basket of vegetables sold in the public markets.

[2] *Travels in Scandinavia*, vol. i. p. 33.

and who may be regarded as the aborigines of that country, the converse of this doctrine is more probable. Not their language only, but [558] their superstitions, differ from those of the Rajputs: though, from a desire to rise above their natural condition, they have engrafted upon their own the most popular mythologies of their civilized conquerors, who from the north gradually spread themselves over the continent and peninsula, even to the remote isles of the Indian Ocean. Of the primitive inhabitants we may enumerate the Minas, the Meras, the Gonds, the Bhils, the Sahariyas, the Savaras, the Abhiras, the Gujars, and those who inhabit the forests of the Nerbudda, the Son, the Mahanadi, the mountains of Sarguja, and the lesser Nagpur; many of whom are still but little removed from savage life, and whose dialects are as various as their manners. These are content to be called the 'sons of the earth,' [1] or 'children of the forest,' [2] while their conquerors, the Rajputs, arrogate celestial descent.[3] How soon after the flood the Suryas, or sun-worshippers, entered India Proper, must ever remain uncertain.[4] It is sufficient that they were anterior in date to the Indus, or races tracing their descent from the moon (*Ind*); as the migration of the latter from the central lands of Indo-Scythia was antecedent to that of the Agnikulas, or fire-worshippers, of the Snake race, claiming Takshak as their original progenitor. The Suryas,[5] who migrated both to the East and West, as population became redundant in these fertile regions, may be considered the Celtic, as the Indu-Getae may be accounted the Gothic, races of India.[6] To attempt to discriminate these different races, and mark the shades which once separated them, after a system of priestcraft has amalgamated the mass, and identified their superstitions, would be

[1] *Bhumiputra.* [2] *Vanaputra.*

[3] Suryas and Induputras.

[4] [For the Vedic cult of Sūrya see Macdonell, "Vedic Mythology," *Grundriss der Indo-Arischen Philologie und Altertumskunde*, 1897, p. 30 ff.]

[5] The Sauromatae or Sarmatians of early Europe, as well as the Syrians, were most probably colonies of the same Suryavansi who simultaneously peopled the shores of the Caspian and Mediterranean, and the banks of the Indus and Ganges. Many of the tribes described by Strabo as dwelling around the Caspian are enumerated amongst the thirty-six royal races of India. One of these, the Sakasenae, supposed to be the ancestors of our own Saxon race, settled themselves on the Araxes in Armenia, adjoining Albania. [There are no grounds for these comparisons.]

[6] [There are no grounds for this classification.]

fruitless; but the observer of ancient customs may, with the imperfect guidance of peculiar rites, discover things, and even names, totally incongruous with the Brahmanical system, and which could never have originated within the Indus or Atak,—the Rubicon of Gangetic antiquaries, who fear to look beyond that stream for the origin of tribes. A residence amongst the Rajputs would lead to a disregard of such boundaries, either to the moral or physical man, as the annals of Mewar abundantly testify.

Comparative Study of Festivals.—Sir Wm. Jones remarks, "If the festivals of the old Greeks, Persians, Romans [559], Egyptians, and Goths could be arranged with exactness in the same form with the Indian, there would be found a striking resemblance among them; and an attentive comparison of them all might throw great light on the religion, and perhaps on the history, of the primitive world."

Analogies to Rājput Customs in Northern Europe.—In treating of the festivals and superstitions of the Rajputs, wherever there may appear to be a fair ground for supposing an analogy with those of other nations of antiquity, I shall not hesitate to pursue it. The proper names of many of the martial Rajputs would alone point out the necessity of seeking for a solution of them out of the explored paths; and where Sanskrit derivation cannot be assigned, as it happens in many instances, we are not, therefore, warranted in the hasty conclusion that the names must have been adopted since the conquests of Mahmud or Shihabu-d-din, events of comparatively modern date. Let us at once admit the hypothesis of Pinkerton,—the establishment of an original Indu-Getic or Indo-Scythic empire, "extending from the Caspian to the Ganges"; or if this conjecture be too extensive or too vague, let us fix the centre of this Madhya-Bhumi in the fertile region of Sogdiana;[1] and from the lights which modern history affords on the many migrations from this nursery of mankind,

[1] Long after the overthrow of the Greek kingdom of Bactria by the Yuti or Getes [Sakas] this region was popular and flourishing. In the year 120 before Christ, De Guignes says: "Dans ce pays on trouvait d'excellens grains, du vin de vigne, plus de cent villes, tant grandes que petites. Il est aussi fait mention du Tahia situé au midi du Gihon, et où il y a de grandes villes murées. Le général chinois y vit des toiles de l'Inde et autres marchandises, etc., etc." (*Hist. Gén. des Huns*, vol. i. p. 51).

even since the time of Muhammad, let us form an opinion of those which have not been recorded, or have been conveyed by the Hindus only in imperfect allegory; and with the aid of ancient customs, obsolete words, and proper names, trace them to Indo-Scythic colonies grafted on the parent stock. The Puranas themselves bear testimony to the incorporation of Scythic tribes with the Hindus, and to the continual irruptions of the Saka, the Pahlavas, the Yavanas,[1] the Turushkas, names conspicuous amongst the races of Central Asia, and recorded in the pages of the earliest Western historians. Even so early as the period of Rama, when furious international wars were carried on between the military and sacerdotal classes for supremacy, we have the names of these tribes recorded as auxiliaries [560] to the priesthood; who, while admitting them to fight under the banners of Siva, would not scruple to stamp them with the seal of Hinduism. In this manner, beyond a doubt, at a much later period than the events in the Ramayana, these tribes from the North either forced themselves among, or were incorporated with, 'the races of the sun.' When, therefore, we meet with rites in Rajputana and in ancient Scandinavia, such as were practised amongst the Getic nations on the Oxus, why should we hesitate to assign the origin of both to this region of earliest civilization? When we see the ancient Asii, and the Iutae, or Jutes, taking omens from the white steed of Thor, shut up in the temple at Upsala; and in like manner, the Rajput of past days offering the same animal in sacrifice to the sun, and his modern descendant taking the omen from his neigh, why are we to refuse our assent to the common origin of the superstition practised by the Getae of the Oxus? Again, when we find the 'homage to the sword' performed by all the Getic races of antiquity in Dacia, on the Baltic, as well as by the modern Rajput, shall we draw no conclusion from this testimony of the father of history, who declares that such rites

[1] Yavan or Javan is a celebrated link of the Indu (*lunar*) genealogical chain; nor need we go to Ionia for it, though the Ionians may be a colony descended from Javan, the ninth from Yayati, who was the third son of Ayu, the ancestor of the Hindu as well as of the Tatar Induvansi. [Yavana is the general term for a foreigner, especially the non-Hindu tribes of the N.W. Frontier, and those beyond them.] The Asuras, who are so often described as invaders of India, and which word has ordinarily a mere irreligious acceptation, I firmly believe to mean the Assyrians. [This theory was adopted by J. Fergusson, *Cave Temples of India*, 34.]

were practised on the Jaxartes in the very dawn of knowledge ? [1] Moreover, why hesitate to give Eastern etymologies for Eastern rites, though found on the Baltic ? The antiquary of the North (Mallet) may thus be assisted to the etymon of 'Tir-sing,' the enchanted sword of Angantýr, in *tir*, 'water,' and *singh*, 'a lion'; *i.e.* in water or spirit like a lion; for even *pani*, the common epithet for water, is applied metaphorically to 'spirit.' [2]

It would be less difficult to find Sanskrit derivations for many of the proper names in the Edda, than to give a Sanskrit analysis of many common amongst the Rajputs, which we must trace to an Indo-Scythic root: [3] such as Eyvorsél, Udila, Attitai, Pujun, Hamira,[4] and numerous other proper names of warriors. Of tribes: the Kathi, Rajpali, Mohila, Sariaspah, Aswaria (*qu.* Assyrian ?), Banaphar, Kamari. Silara, Dahima, etc. Of mountains: Drinodhar, Arbuda, Aravalli, Aravindha (the root *ara*, or mountain, being Scythic, and the expletive adjunct Sanskrit), 'the hill of Budha,' 'of strength,' 'of limit.' To all such as cannot be [561] resolved into the cognate language of India, what origin can we assign but Scythic ? [5]

Festivals in Mewār. Naurātri Festival.—In a memoir prepared for me by a well-informed public officer in the Rana's court, on the chief festivals celebrated in Mewar, he commenced with those following the autumnal equinox, in the month Asoj or Aswini,

[1] [Such analogies of custom do not prove ethnical identity.]

[2] [The theory breaks down, because the name of the sword of Argantýr was Tyrfing, or better Tyrfingr, the derivation of which word, as Mr. H. M. Chadwick kindly informs me, according to Vigfússon's *Icelandic Dictionary*, is from *tyrfi*, a resinous fir-tree used for kindling a fire, because the sword flamed like resinous wood.]

[3] See Turner's *History of Anglo-Saxons* for Indo-Scythic words.

[4] There were no less than four distinguished leaders of this name amongst the vassals of the last Rajput emperor of Delhi; and one of them, who turned traitor to his sovereign and joined Shihabu-d-din, was actually a Scythian, and of the Gakkhar race, which maintained their ancient habits of polyandry even in Babur's time. The Haoli Rao Hamira was lord of Kangra and the Gakkhars of Pamir.

[5] Turner, when discussing the history of the Sakai, or Sakaseni, of the Caspian, whom he justly supposes to be the Saxons of the Baltic, takes occasion to introduce some words of Scythic origin (preserved by ancient writers), to almost every one of which, without straining etymology, we may give a Sanskrit origin. [There is no ground for ascribing a Scythic origin to the proper names in the text.]

opening with the Nauratri, sacred to the god of war. Their fasts are in general regulated by the moon; although the most remarkable are solar, especially those of the equinoxes and solstices, and the Sankrantis, or days on which the sun enters a new sign. The Hindu solar year anciently commenced on the winter solstice, in the month Pausha, and was emphatically called 'the morning of the gods'; also Sivaratri, or night of Siva, analogous, as has been before remarked, to the 'mother night,' which ushered in the new year of the Scandinavian Asi, and other nations of Asiatic origin dwelling in the north.

The Repose of Vishnu.—They term the summer solstice in the month of Asarh, 'the night of the gods,' because Vishnu (as the sun) reposes during the four rainy months on his serpent couch. The lunar year of 360 days was more ancient than the solar, and

---

	Scythic.	Sanskrit or Bhakha.
Exampaios	sacred ways	*Agham* is the sacred book; *pai* and *pada*, a foot; *pantha*, a path.
Arimu	one	*Ad is the first*; whence *Adima*, or man.
Spou	an eye.	
Oior	a man.	
Pata	to kill	*Badh*, to kill.
Tahiti	the chief deity is Vesta	Tap is heat or flame; the type of Vesta.
Papaios	,, ,, Jupiter	Baba, or Bapa, the universal father. The Hindu Jivapitri, or *Father* of Life [?].
Oitosuros	,, ,, Apollo	Aitiswara, or Sun-God, applicable to Vishnu, who has every attribute of Apollo; from *ait*, contraction of *aditya*, the sun.
Artimpasa, or Aripasa	,, ,, Venus	Apsaras because born from the froth or essence, '*sara*,' of the waters, '*ap*' ['going in the water'].
Thamimasadus	,, ,, Neptune	Thoenatha; or *God of the Waters*.
Apia	wife of Papaios, or Earth	Amba, Ama, Uma, is the *universal mother*; wife of 'Baba Adam,' as they term the universal father.

See Turner's *History of the Anglo-Saxons*, vol. i. p. 35. [Many of the identifications are obsolete.]

commenced with the month of Asoj or Aswini: "the moon being at the full when that name was imposed on the first lunar station of the Hindu ecliptic."[1]

According to another authority, the festivals commenced on Amavas, or the Ides of Chait, near which the vernal equinox falls, the opening of the modern solar year; when, in like manner as at the commencement of the lunar year in Asoj, they [562] dedicate the first nine days of Chait (also called Nauratri) to Iswara and his consort Isani.

Having thus specified both modes of reckoning for the opening of the solar and lunar years, I shall not commence the abstract of the festivals of Mewar with either, but follow the more ancient division of time, when the year closed with the winter solstice in the month of Pus, consequently opening the new year with Magh. By this arrangement, we shall commence with the spring festivals, and let the days dedicated to mirth and gaiety follow each other; preferring the natural to the astrological year, which will enable us to preserve the analogy with the northern nations of Europe, who also reckoned from the winter solstice. The Hindu divides the year into six seasons, each of two months; namely, Vasanta, Grishma, Varsha, Sarad, Sisira, Sita; or spring, summer, rainy, sultry, dewy, and cold.

It is not, however, my intention to detail all the fasts and festivals which the Rajput of Mewar holds in common with the Hindu nation, but chiefly those restricted to that State, or such as are celebrated with local peculiarity, or striking analogies to those of Egypt, Greece, or Scandinavia. The goddess who presides over mirth and idleness preferred holding her court amidst the ruins of Udaipur to searching elsewhere for a dwelling. This determination to be happy amidst calamity, individual and national, has made the court proverbial in Rajwara, in the adage, '*sat bara, aur nau teohara*,' *i.e.* nine holidays out of seven days. Although many of these festivals are common to India, and their maintenance is enjoined by religion, yet not only the prolongation and repetition of some, but the entire institution of others, as well as the peculiar splendour of their solemnization, originate with the prince; proving how much individual example may nfluence the manners of a nation.

[1] Sir W. Jones, "On the Lunar Year of the Hindus," *Asiatic Researches*, vol. iii. p. 257.

Spring Festival, Vasant Panchami.—By the arrangement we have adopted, the lovely Vasanti, goddess of the spring, will usher in the festivals of Mewar. In 1819 her rites were celebrated in the kalends of January, and even then, on the verge of the tropic, her birth was premature.

The opening of the spring being on the 5th of the month Magha, is thence called the Vasant panchami, which in 1819 fell on the 30th of January; consequently the first of Pus (the antecedent month), the beginning of the old Hindu [563] year, or 'the morning of the gods,' fell on the 25th of December. The Vasant continues forty days after the panchami, or initiative fifth, during which the utmost license prevails in action and in speech; the lower classes regale even to intoxication on every kind of stimulating confection and spirituous beverage, and the most respectable individuals, who would at other times be shocked to utter an indelicate allusion, roam about with the groups of bacchanals, reciting stanzas of the warmest description in praise of the powers of nature, as did the conscript fathers of Rome during the Saturnalia. In this season, when the barriers of rank are thrown down, and the spirit of democracy is let loose, though never abused, even the wild Bhil, or savage Mer, will leave his forest or mountain shade to mingle in the revelries of the capital; and decorating his ebon hair or tattered turban with a garland of jessamine, will join the clamorous parties which perambulate the streets of the capital. These orgies are, however, reserved for the conclusion of the forty days sacred to the goddess of nature.

Bhān Saptami Festival.—Two days following the initiative fifth is the Bhan saptami or 'seventh [day] of the sun,' also called 'the birth of the sun,' with various other metaphorical denominations.[1] On this day there is a grand procession of the Rana, his chiefs and vassals, to the Chaugan, where the sun is worshipped. At the Jaipur court, whose princes claim descent from Kusa, the second son of Rama, the Bhan saptami is peculiarly sacred. The chariot of the sun, drawn by eight horses, is taken from the temple dedicated to that orb, and moved in procession: a ceremony otherwise never observed but on the inauguration of a new prince.

[1] Bhaskara saptami, in honour of the sun, as a form of Vishnu (Varaha Purana) Makari, from the sun entering the constellation *Makara* (Pisces), the first of the solar Magha (see *Asiatic Researches*, vol. iii. p. 273).

Sun Worship.—In the mythology of the Rajputs, of which we have a better idea from their heroic poetry than from the legends of the Brahmans, the sun-god is the deity they are most anxious to propitiate; and in his honour they fearlessly expend their blood in battle, from the hope of being received into his mansion. Their highest heaven is accordingly the Bhanuthan or Bhanuloka, the 'region of the sun': and like the Indu-Scythic Getae, the Rajput warrior of the early ages sacrificed the horse in his honour,[1] and dedicated to him the first day of the week, namely, Adityawar, contracted to Itwar, also called Thawara[2] [564].

The more we attend to the warlike mythology of the north, the more apparent is its analogy with that of the Rajputs, and the stronger ground is there for assuming that both races inherited their creed from the common land of the Yuti of the Jaxartes. What is a more proper etymon for Scandinavian, the abode of the warriors who destroyed the Roman power, than Skanda, the Mars or Kumara of the Rajputs? perhaps the origin of the Cimbri, derived by Mallet from koempfer, 'to fight.'

Thor, in the eleventh fable of the Edda, is denominated Asa-Thor,[3] the 'lord Thor,' called the Celtic Mars by the Romans. The chariot of Thor is ignobly yoked compared with the car of Surya; but in the substitution of the he-goats for the seven-headed horse Saptasva we have but the change of an adjunct depending on clime, when the Yuti migrated from the plains of Scythia, of which the horse is a native, to Yutland, of whose mountains the goat was an inhabitant prior to any of the race of Asi. The northern warrior makes the palace of the sun-god Thor the most splendid of the celestial abodes, "in which are

[1] See Vol. I. p. 91.

[2] This word appears to have the same import as Thor, the sun-god and war divinity of the Scandinavians. [? *Thāwar*, Saturday; Skt. *sthāvara*, 'stationary.']

[3] Odin is also called *As* or 'lord'; the Gauls also called him Oes or Es, and with a Latin termination Hesus, whom Lucan calls Esus; Edda, vol. ii. pp. 45-6. The celebrated translator of these invaluable remnants of ancient superstitions, by which alone light can be thrown on the origin of nations, observes that Es or Oes is the name for God with all the Celtic races. So it was with the Tuscans, doubtless from the Sanskrit, or rather from a more provincial tongue, the common contraction of Iswara, the Egyptian Osiris, the Persian Syr, the sun-god. [These words have, of course, no connexion. Syria perhaps derives its name from the Suri, a north-Euphratian tribe (*Encyclopaedia Biblica*, iv. 4815).]

five hundred and forty halls": vying with the Suryamandala, the supreme heaven of the Rajput. Whence such notions of the Aswa races of the Ganges, and the Asi of Scandinavia, but from the Scythic Saka, who adored the solar divinity under the name of 'Gaeto-Syrus,'[1] the Surya of the Sachha Rajput; and as, according to the commentator on the Edda, "the ancient people of the north pronounced the *th* as the English now do *ss*," the sun-god *Thor* becomes *Sor*, and is identified still more with Surya whose worship no doubt gave the name to that extensive portion of Asia called Συρία, as it did to the small peninsula of the Sauras, still peopled by tribes of Scythic origin. The Sol of the Romans has probably the same Celto-Etrurian origin; with those tribes the sun was the great object of adoration, and their grand festival, the winter solstice, was called Yule, Hiul, Houl, "which even at this day signifies the Sun, in the language of Bas-Bretagne and Cornwall."[2] On the conversion of the descendants of these Scythic Yeuts, who, according to [565] Herodotus, sacrificed the horse (*Hi*) to the sun (*El*), the name of the Pagan jubilee of the solstice was transferred to the day of Christ's nativity, which is thus still held in remembrance by their descendants of the north.[3]

Sun Worship at Udaipur.—At Udaipur the sun has universal precedence; his portal (*Suryapol*) is the chief entrance to the city; his name gives dignity to the chief apartment or hall (*Suryamahall*) of the palace; and from the balcony of the sun (*Suryagokhra*) the descendant of Rama shows himself in the dark monsoon as the sun's representative. A huge painted sun of gypsum in high relief, with gilded rays, adorns the hall of audience, and in front of it is the throne. As already mentioned, the sacred standard bears his image,[4] as does that Scythic part of the regalia called the *changi*, a disc of black felt or ostrich feathers, with a

[1] Which Mallet, from Hesychius, interprets 'good star.' [The name Goetosyrus or Octosyrus (Herodotus iv. 59) is so uncertain in form that it is useless to propose etymologies for it (E. H. Minns, *Scythians and Greeks*, 86). Rawlinson (*Herodotus*, 3rd ed. ii. 93) compares Greek *αἶθος*, Skt. *sūrya*, in the sense 'bright, burning Sun.']

[2] Mallet's *Northern Antiquities*, vol. ii. p. 42.

[3] [Much of this is from Sir W. Jones, Wilford and Paterson (*Asiatic Researches*, i. 253, iii. 141, viii. 48). Herodotus (i. 216) ascribes the custom of Sun sacrifice to the Massagetae.]

[4] [The Mughal emperors followed the same practice (Manucci i. 98).]

plate of gold to represent the sun in its centre, borne upon a pole. The royal parasol is termed *kirania*, in allusion to its shape, like a ray (*kiran*) of the orb. The last day but one of the month of Magha is called Sivaratri (night of Siva), and is held peculiarly sacred by the Rana, who is styled the Regent of Siva. It is a rigid fast, and the night is passed in vigils, and rites to the phallic representative of Siva.

The Spring Hunt.—The merry month of Phalgun is ushered in with the Aheria, or spring-hunt.[1] The preceding day the Rana distributes to all his chiefs and servants either a dress of green, or some portion thereof, in which all appear habited on the morrow, whenever the astrologer has fixed the hour for sallying forth to slay the boar to Gauri, the Ceres of the Rajputs: the Aheria is therefore called the Mahurat ka shikar, or the chase fixed astrologically. As their success on this occasion is ominous of future good, no means are neglected to secure it, either by scouts previously discovering the lair, or the desperate efforts of the hunters to slay the boar when roused. With the sovereign and his sons all the chiefs sally forth, each on his best steed, and all animated by the desire to surpass each other in acts of prowess and dexterity. It is very rare that in some one of the passes or recesses of the valley the hog is not found; the spot is then surrounded by the [566] hunters, whose vociferations soon start the *dukkara*,[2] and frequently a drove of hogs. Then each cavalier impels his steed, and with lance or sword, regardless of rock, ravine, or tree, presses on the bristly foe, whose knowledge of the country is of no avail when thus circumvented, and the ground soon reeks with gore, in which not unfrequently is mixed that of horse or rider. On the last occasion there occurred fewer casualties than usual; though the Chondawat Hamira, whom we nicknamed the 'Red Riever,' had his leg broken, and the second

[1] In his delight for this diversion, the Rajput evinces his Scythic propensity. The grand hunts of the last Chauhan emperor often led him into warfare, for Prithiraj was a poacher of the first magnitude, and one of his battles with the Tatars was while engaged in field sports on the Ravi. The heir of Jenghiz Khan was chief huntsman, the highest office of the State amongst the Scythic Tatars; as Ajanbahu, alike celebrated in either field of war and sport, was chief huntsman to the Chauhan emperor of Delhi, whose bard enters minutely into the subject, describing all the variety of dogs of chase.

[2] A hog in Hindi; in Persian *khuk*, nearly our *hog* [?].

son of Sheodan Singh, a near relation of the Rana, had his neighbour's lance driven through his arm. The young chief of Salumbar was amongst the distinguished of this day's sport. It would appal even an English fox-hunter to see the Rajputs driving their steeds at full speed, bounding like the antelope over every barrier —the thick jungle covert, or rocky steep bare of soil or vegetation,—with their lances balanced in the air, or leaning on the saddle-bow slashing at the boar.

The royal kitchen moves out on this occasion, and in some chosen spot the repast is prepared, of which all partake, for the hog is the favourite food of the Rajput, as it was of the heroes of Scandinavia. Nor is the *munawwar piyala*, or invitation cup, forgotten; and having feasted, and thrice slain their bristly antagonist, they return to the capital, where fame had already spread their exploits—the deeds done by the *barchhi* (lance) of Padma,[1] or the *khanda* (sword) blow of Hamira,[2] which lopped the head of the foe of Gauri. Even this martial amusement, the Aheria, has a religious origin. The boar is the enemy of Gauri of the Rajputs; it was so held of Isis by the Egyptians, of Ceres by the Greeks, of Freya by the north-man, whose favourite food was the hog: and of such importance was it deemed by the Franks, that the second chapter of the Salic law is entirely penal with regard to the stealers of swine. The heroes of the Edda, even in Valhalla, feed on the fat of the wild boar Saehrimner, while "the illustrious father of armies fattens his wolves Geri and Freki, and takes no other nourishment himself than the interrupted quaffing of wine": quite the picture of Har, the Rajput god of war, and his sons the Bhairavas, Krodha, and Kala, metaphorically called the 'sons of slaughter.' We need hardly repeat that the cup of the Scandinavian god of war, like that of the Rajputs, is the human skull (*khopra*) [567].[3]

The Phāg or Holi Festival.—As Phalgun advances, the bacchanalian mirth increases; groups are continually patrolling the streets, throwing a crimson powder at each other, or ejecting a solution of it from syringes, so that the garments and visages of all are one mass of crimson. On the 8th, emphatically called

1 Chief of Salumbar.

2 Chief of Hamirgarh.

3 [On the slaughter of the boar representing a corn-spirit see Sir J. Frazer, *The Golden Bough*, 3rd ed. Part v. vol. i. 298 ff.; Robertson Smith, *Religion of the Semites*, 2nd ed. 290 f.]

the Phag, the Rana joins the queens and their attendants in the palace, when all restraint is removed and mirth is unlimited. But the most brilliant sight is the playing of the Holi on horseback, on the terrace in front of the palace. Each chief who chooses to join has a plentiful supply of missiles, formed of thin plates of mica or talc, enclosing this crimson powder, called *abira*, which with the most graceful and dextrous horsemanship they dart at each other, pursuing, caprioling, and jesting. This part of it much resembles the Saturnalia of Rome of this day, when similar missiles are scattered at the Carnivâle. The last day or Punon ends the Holi, when the Nakkaras from the Tripolia summon all the chiefs with their retinues to attend their prince, and accompany him in procession to the Chaugan, their Champ de Mars. In the centre of this is a long *sala* or hall, the ascent to which is by a flight of steps: the roof is supported by square columns without any walls, so that the court is entirely open. Here, surrounded by his chiefs, the Rana passes an hour, listening to the songs in praise of Holika, while a scurrilous *kavya* or couplet from some wag in the crowd reminds him, that exalted rank is no protection against the license of the spring Saturnalia; though 'the Diwan of Eklinga' has not to reproach himself with a failure of obedience to the rites of the goddess, having fulfilled the command 'to multiply,' more than any individual in his kingdom.[1] While the Rana and his chiefs are thus amused above, the buffoons and itinerant groups mix with the cavalcade, throw powder in their eyes, or deluge their garments with the crimson solution. To resent it would only expose the sensitive party to be laughed at, and draw upon him a host of these bacchanals: so that no alternative exists between keeping entirely aloof or mixing in the fray [568].[2]

[1] He has been the father of more than one hundred children, legitimate and illegitimate, though very few are living.

[2] That this can be done without any loss of dignity by the *Sahib log* (a name European gentlemen have assumed) is well known to those who may have partaken of the hospitalities of that honourable man, and brave and zealous officer, Colonel James Skinner, C.B., at Hansi. That his example is worthy of imitation in the mode of commanding, is best evinced by the implicit and cheerful obedience his men pay to his instructions when removed from his personal control. He has passed through the ordeal of nearly thirty years of unremitted service, and from the glorious days of Delhi and Laswari under Lake, to the last siege of Bharatpur, James Skinner

On the last day, the Rana feasts his chiefs, and the camp breaks up with the distribution of *khanda nariyal*, or swords and coco-nuts, to the chiefs and all "whom the king delighteth to honour." These *khandas* are but 'of lath,' in shape like the Andrea Ferrara, or long cut-and-thrust, the favourite weapon of the Rajput. They are painted in various ways, like Harlequin's sword, and meant as a burlesque, in unison with the character of the day, when war is banished, and the multiplication,[1] not the destruction, of man is the behest of the goddess who rules the spring. At nightfall, the forty days conclude with 'the burning of the Holi,' when they light large fires, into which various substances, as well as the crimson *abira*, are thrown, and around which groups of children are dancing and screaming in the streets like so many infernals. Until three hours after sunrise of the new month of Chait, these orgies are continued with increased vigour, when the natives bathe, change their garments, worship, and return to the rank of sober citizens; and princes and chiefs receive gifts from their domestics.[2]

Chait.—The first of this month is the Samvatsara (vulg. Chamchari), or anniversary of the death of the Rana's father, to whose memory solemn rites are performed both in the palace and at Ara, the royal cemetery, metaphorically termed Mahasati, or place of 'great faith.' Thither the Rana repairs, and offers oblations to the *manes* of his father; and after purifying in the Gangabheva, a rivulet which flows through the middle of 'the abode of silence,' he returns to the palace.

On the 3rd, the whole of the royal insignia proceeds to Bedla, the residence of the Chauhan chief (one of the Sixteen), within the valley of the capital, in order to convey the Rao to court. The Rana advances to the Ganesa Deori[3] to receive him; when,

---

has been second to none. In obtaining for this gallant and modest officer the order of the Bath, Lord Combermere must have been applauded by every person who knows the worth of him who bears it, which includes the whole army of Bengal. [James Skinner, 1778–1841. See Compton, *Military Adventurers*, 389 ff.; Buckland, *Dict. Indian Biography*, s.v.

[1] Evinced in the presentation of the *sriphala*, the fruit of *Sri*, which is the coco-nut, emblematic of fruitfulness.

[2] Another point of resemblance to the Roman Saturnalia.

[3] A hall so called in honour of Ganesa, or Janus, whose effigies adorn the entrance. [Janus probably = Dianus: Ganesa, 'lord of the troops of inferior deities' (*gana*).]

after salutation, the sovereign and his chief return to the great hall of assembly, hand in hand, but that of the Chauhan above or upon his sovereign's. In this ceremony we have another singular memorial of the glorious days of Mewar, when almost every chieftain established by deeds of devotion a right to the eternal gratitude of their princes; the decay of whose [569] power but serves to hallow such reminiscences. It is in these little acts of courteous condescension, deviations from the formal routine of reception, that we recognize the traces of Rajput history; for inquiry into these customs will reveal the incident which gave birth to each, and curiosity will be amply repaid, in a lesson at once of political and moral import. For my own part, I never heard the kettledrum of my friend Raj Kalyan strike at the sacred barrier, the Tripolia, without recalling the glorious of memory his ancestor at the Thermopylae of Mewar;[1] nor looked on the autograph lance, the symbol of the Chondawats, without recognizing the fidelity of the founder of the clan;[2] nor observed the honours paid to the Chauhans of Bedla and Kotharia, without the silent tribute of applause to the manes of their sires.

Sitala's Festival.—Chait badi sat, or '7th of [the dark fortnight] Chait,' is in honour of the goddess Sitala, the protectress of children: all the matrons of the city proceed with their offerings to the shrine of the goddess, placed upon the very pinnacle of an isolated hill in the valley. In every point of view, this divinity is the twin-sister of the Mater Montana,[3] the guardian of infants amongst the Romans, the Grecian or Phrygian Cybele.

Birthday of the Rana.—This is also the Rana's birthday,[4] on which occasion all classes flock with gifts and good wishes that "the king may live for ever"; but it is in the penetralia of the Rawala, where the profane eye enters not, that the greatest festivities of this day are kept.

New Year's Day. The Festival of Flowers.—Chait Sudi 1st (15th of the month) is the opening of the luni-solar year of Vikramaditya. Ceremonies, which more especially appertain to the Nauratri of Asoj, are performed on this day; and the sword is worshipped

[1] See p. 394. [2] See p. 324.
[3] [See Hastings, *Encyclopaedia of Religion and Ethics*, viii. 868 f.]
[4] It fell on the 18th March 1819.

in the palace. But such rites are subordinate to those of the fair divinity, who still rules over this the smiling portion of the year. Vasanti has ripened into the fragrant Flora, and all the fair of the capital, as well as the other sex, repair to the gardens and groves, where parties assemble, regale, and swing, adorned with chaplets of roses, jessamine, or oleander, when the Naulakha gardens may vie with the Tivoli of Paris. They return in the evening to the city.

The Festival of Flowers.—The Rajput Floralia ushers in the rites of the beneficent Gauri, which continue nine days, the number sacred to the creative [570] power. These vie with the Cerealia of Rome, or the more ancient rites of the goddess of the Nile: I shall therefore devote some space to a particular account of them.[1]

Ganggor Festival.—Among the many remarkable festivals of Rajasthan, kept with peculiar brilliancy at Udaipur, is that in honour of Gauri, or Isani, the goddess of abundance, the Isis of Egypt, the Ceres of Greece. Like the Rajput Saturnalia, which it follows, it belongs to the vernal equinox, when nature in these regions proximate to the tropic is in the full expanse of her charms, and the matronly Gauri casts her golden mantle over the beauties of the verdant Vasanti.[2] Then the fruits exhibit their promise to the eye; the koil fills the ear with melody; the air is impregnated with aroma, and the crimson poppy contrasts with the spikes of golden grain, to form a wreath for the beneficent Gauri.

Gauri is one of the names of Isa or Parvati, wife of the greatest of the gods, Mahadeva or Iswara, who is conjoined with her in these rites, which almost exclusively appertain to the women. The meaning of Gauri is 'yellow,' emblematic of the ripened harvest, when the votaries of the goddess adore her effigies, which are those of a matron painted the colour of ripe corn; and though her image is represented with only two hands, in one of which she holds the lotos, which the Egyptians regarded as emblematic of reproduction, yet not unfrequently they equip her with the warlike conch, the discus, and the club, to denote that the goddess, whose gifts sustain life, is likewise accessary to the loss of it: uniting, as Gauri and Kali, the characters of life and death, like

[1] [For festivals in honour of Gauri see *IA*, xxxv. (1906) 61.]

[2] Personification of spring.

the Isis and Cybele of the Egyptians. But here she is only seen as Annapurna, the benefactress of mankind. The rites commence when the sun enters Aries (the opening of the Hindu year), by a deputation to a spot beyond the city, "to bring earth for the image of Gauri." [1] When this is formed, a smaller one of Iswara is made, and they are placed together; a small trench is then excavated, in which barley is sown; the ground is irrigated and artificial heat supplied till the grain germinates, when the females join hands and dance round it, invoking the blessings of Gauri on their husbands.[2] The young corn is then taken up, distributed, and presented by the females to the men, who wear it in their turbans. Every wealthy family has its image, or at least every purwa or subdivision of the city. These and other [571] rites known only to the initiated having been performed for several days within doors, they decorate the images, and prepare to carry them in procession to the lake. During these days of preparation, nothing is talked of but Gauri's departure from the palace; whether she will be as sumptuously apparelled as in the year gone by; whether an additional boat will be launched on the occasion; though not a few forget the goddess altogether in the recollection of the gazelle eyes (*mrig-nayani*) and serpentine locks (*nagini-zulf*) [3] of the beauteous handmaids who are selected to attend her. At length the hour arrives, the martial nakkaras give the signal "to the cannonier without," and speculation is at rest when the guns on the summit of the castle of Eklinggarh announce that Gauri has commenced her excursion to the lake.

The Bathing of the Goddess.—The cavalcade assembles on the magnificent terrace, and the Rana, surrounded by his nobles, leads the way to the boats, of a form as primitive as that which conveyed the Argonauts to Colchis. The scenery is admirably adapted for these fêtes, the ascent being gradual from the margin of the lake, which here forms a fine bay, and gently rising to the crest of the ridge on which the palace and dwellings of the chiefs are built. Every turret and balcony is crowded with spectators,

[1] Here we have Gauri as the type of the earth.

[2] [The Gardens of Adonis, for which see Sir J. Frazer, *Adonis, Attis, Osiris*, 3rd ed. i. 236 ff.]

[3] Here the Hindu mixes Persian with his Sanskrit, and produces the mongrel dialect Hindi.

from the palace to the water's edge; and the ample flight of marble steps which intervene from the Tripolia, or triple portal, to the boats, is a dense mass of females in variegated robes, whose scarfs but half conceal their ebon tresses adorned with the rose and the jessamine. A more imposing or more exhilarating sight cannot be imagined than the entire population of a city thus assembled for the purpose of rejoicing; the countenance of every individual, from the prince to the peasant, dressed in smiles. Carry the eye to heaven, and it rests on 'a sky without a cloud': below is a magnificent lake, the even surface of the deep blue waters broken only by palaces of marble, whose arched piazzas are seen through the foliage of orange groves, plantain, and tamarind; while the vision is bounded by noble mountains, their peaks towering over each other, and composing an immense amphitheatre. Here the deformity of vice intrudes not; no object is degraded by inebriation: no tumultuous disorder or deafening clamour, but all await patiently, with eyes directed to the Tripolia, the appearance of Gauri. At length the procession is seen winding down the steep, and in the midst [572], borne on a *pat*,[1] or throne, gorgeously arrayed in yellow robes, and blazing with 'barbaric pearl and gold,' the goddess appears; on either side the two beauties wave the silver *chamara* over her head, while the more favoured damsels act as harbingers, preceding her with wands of silver: the whole chanting hymns. On her approach, the Rana, his chiefs and ministers rise and remain standing till the goddess is seated on her throne close to the water's edge, when all bow, and the prince and court take their seats in the boats. The females then form a circle around the goddess, unite hands, and with a measured step and various graceful inclinations of the body, keeping time by beating the palms at particular cadences, move round the image singing hymns, some in honour of the goddess of abundance, others on love and chivalry; and embodying little episodes of national achievements, occasionally sprinkled with *double entendre*, which excites a smile and significant nod from the chiefs, and an inclination of the head of the fair choristers. The festival being entirely female, not a single male mixed in the immense groups, and even Iswara himself, the husband of Gauri, attracts no attention, as appears from his ascetic or mendicant form begging his dole

[1] Takht, Pat, Persian and Sanskrit, alike meaning *board*.

from the bounteous and universal mother. It is taken for granted that the goddess is occupied in bathing all the time she remains, and ancient tradition says death was the penalty of any male intruding on these solemnities; but the present prince deems them so fitted for amusement, that he has even instituted a second Ganggor. Some hours are thus consumed, while easy and good-humoured conversation is carried on. At length, the ablutions over, the goddess is taken up, and conveyed to the palace with the same forms and state. The Rana and his chiefs then unmoor their boats, and are rowed round the margin of the lake, to visit in succession the other images of the goddess, around which female groups are chanting and worshipping, as already described, with which ceremonies the evening closes, when the whole terminates with a grand display of fireworks, the finale of each of the three days dedicated to Gauri.

Considerable resemblance is to be discerned between this festival of Gauri and that in honour of the Egyptian Diana [1] at Bubastis, and Isis at Busiris, within the [573] Delta of the Nile, of which Herodotus says: "They who celebrate those of Diana embark in vessels; the women strike their tabors, the men their flutes; the rest of both sexes clap their hands, and join in chorus. Whatever city they approach, the vessels are brought on shore; the women use ungracious language, dance, and indelicately throw about their garments." [2] Wherever the rites of Isis prevailed, we find the boat introduced as an essential emblem in her worship, whether in the heart of Rajasthan, on the banks of the Nile, or in the woods of Germany. Bryant [3]

[1] The Ephesian Diana is the twin sister of Gauri, and can have a Sanskrit derivation in Devianna, 'the goddess of food,' contracted Deanna, though commonly Anna-de or Anna-devi, and Annapurna, 'filling with food,' or the nourisher, the name applied by 'the mother of mankind,' when she places the repast before the messenger of heaven:

"Heavenly Stranger, please to taste
These bounties, which our Nourisher, from whom
All perfect good, unmeasured out, descends,
To us for food and for delight, hath caused
The earth to yield."

Paradise Lost, Bk. v. 397-401.

[Diana is the feminine form of Dianus, Janus.]

[2] ii. 59-64.

[3] *Analysis of Ancient Mythology*, p. 312.

furnishes an interesting account from Diodorus and Curtius, illustrated by drawings from Pocock, from the temple of Luxor, near Carnac, in the Thebaid, of 'the ship of Isis,' carrying an ark; and from a male figure therein, this learned person thinks it bears a mysterious allusion to the deluge. I am inclined to deem the personage in the ark Osiris, husband of Isis, the type of the sun arrived in the sign of Aries (of which the ram's heads ornamenting both the prow and stem of the vessel are typical), the harbinger of the annual fertilizing inundation of the Nile: evincing identity of origin as an equinoctial festival with that of Gauri (Isis) of the Indu-Scythic races of Rajasthan.

The German Suevi adored Isis, and also introduced a ship in her worship, for which Tacitus [1] is at a loss to account, and with his usual candour says he has no materials whence to investigate the origin of a worship denoting the foreign origin of the tribe. This Isis of the Suevi was evidently a form of Ertha, the chief divinity of all the Saxon races, who, with her consort Teutates or Hesus [2] (Mercury), were the chief deities of both the Celtic and early Gothic races: the [574] Budha and Ila of the Rajputs; in short, the earth,[3] the prolific mother, the Isis of Egypt, the Ceres of Greece, the Annapurna (giver of food) of the Rajputs. On some ancient temples dedicated to this Hindu Ceres we have sculptured on the frieze and pedestal of the columns the emblem of abundance, termed the *kamakumbha*, or vessel of desire, a vase of elegant form, from which branches of the palm are gracefully pendent. Herodotus says that similar water-vessels, filled

[1] [*Germania*, ix.]

[2] Hesus is probably derived from Iswara, or Isa, *the* god. Toth was the Egyptian, and Teutates the Scandinavian, Mercury. I have elsewhere attempted to trace the origin of the Suevi, Su, or Yeuts of Yeutland (Jutland), to Yute, Getae, or Jat, of Central Asia, who carried thence the religion of Buddha into India as well as to the Baltic. There is little doubt that the races called Jotner, Jaeter, Jotuns, Jaets, and Yeuts, who followed the Asi into Scandinavia, migrated from the Jaxartes, the land of the great Getae (Massagetae); the leader was supposed to be endued with supernatural powers, like the Buddhist, called Vidiavan, or magician, whose haunts adjoined Aria, the cradle of the Magi. They are designated Aripunta [?], under the sign of a serpent, the type of Budha; or Ahriman, 'the foe of man.' [Much of this crude speculation is taken from Wilford (*Asiatic Researches*, iii. 133).]

[3] The German Ertha, to show her kindred to the Ila of the Rajputs, had her car drawn by a cow, under which form the Hindus typify the earth (*prithivi*).

with wheat and barley, were carried in the festival of Isis; and all who have attended to Egyptian antiquities are aware that the god Canopus is depicted under the form of a water-jar, or Nilometer, whose covering bears the head of Osiris.

The Agastya Festival.—To render the analogy perfect between the vessels emblematic of the Isis of the Nile and the Ganges, there is a festival sacred to the sage Agastya, who presides over the star Canopus, when the sun enters Virgo (*Kanya*). The *kamakumbha* is then personified under the epithet *kumbhayoni*, and the votary is instructed to pour water into a sea-shell, in which having placed white flowers and unground rice, turning his face to the south, he offers it with this incantation: "Hail, Kumbhayoni, born in the sight of Mitra and Varuna (the sun and water divinities), bright as the blossom of the *kusa* (grass), who sprung from Agni (fire) and the Maruts." By the prefix of Ganga (the river) to Gauri, we see that the Ganggor festival is essentially sacred to a river-goddess, affording additional proof of the common origin of the rites of the Isis of Egypt and India.

The Egyptians, according to Plutarch, considered the Nile as flowing from Osiris, in like manner as the Hindu poet describes the fair Ganga flowing from the head of Iswara, which Sir W. Jones thus classically paints in his hymn to Ganga:

Above the reach of mortal ken,
On blest Coilasa's top, where every stem
Glowed with a vegetable gem,
Mahesa stood, the dread and joy of men;
While Parvati, to gain a boon,
Fixed on his locks a beamy moon,
And hid his frontal eye in jocund play,
With reluctant sweet delay;
All nature straight was locked in dim eclipse,
Till Brahmins pure, with hallowed lips
And warbled prayers, restored the day,
When Ganga from his brow, with heavenly fingers prest,
Sprang radiant, and descending, graced the caverns of the west [575].

The Goddess Ganga.—Ganga, the river-goddess, like the Nile, is the type of fertility, and like that celebrated stream, has her source amidst the eternal glaciers of Chandragiri or Somagiri (the mountains of the moon); the higher peaks of the gigantic

COLUMNS OF TEMPLES AT CHANDRĀVATI.

To face page 670.

Himalaya, where Parvati is represented as ornamenting the tiara of Iswara "with a beamy moon." In this metaphor, and in his title of Somanatha (lord of the moon), we again have evidence of Iswara, or Siva, after representing the sun, having the satellite moon as his ornament.[1] His Olympus, Kailasa, is studded with that majestic pine, the cedar; thence he is called Kedarnath, 'lord of the cedar-trees.'[2] The mysteries of Osiris and those of Eleusis[3] were of the same character, commemorative of the first germ of civilization, the culture of the earth, under a variety of names, Ertha, Isis, Diana, Ceres, Ila. It is a curious fact that in the terra-cotta images of Isis, frequently excavated about her temple at Paestum,[4] she holds in her right hand an exact representation of the Hindu lingam and yoni combined; and on the Indian expedition to Egypt, our Hindu soldiers deemed themselves amongst the altars of their own god Iswara (Osiris), from the abundance of his emblematic representatives.

The Aghori Ascetics.—In the festival of Ganggor, as before mentioned, Iswara yields to his consort Gauri, and occupies an unimportant position near her at the water's edge, meanly clad, smoking intoxicating herbs, and, whether by accident or design, holding the stalk of an onion in full blossom as a mace or club—a plant regarded by some of the Egyptians with veneration, and held by the Hindus generally in detestation: and why they should on such an occasion thus degrade Iswara, I know not. Onion-juice is reluctantly taken when prescribed medicinally, as a powerful stimulant, by those who would reject spirituous liquors; and there are classes, as the Aghori, that worship Iswara in his most degraded form, who will not only devour raw flesh, but that of man; and to whom it is a matter of perfect

[1] Let it be borne in mind that Indu, Chandra, Soma, are all epithets for 'the moon,' or as *he* is classically styled (in an inscription of the famous Kumarpal, which I discovered in Chitor), Nisanath, the ruler of darkness (Nisa).

[2] [Kedārnāth has, of course, no connexion with the *cedar* tree. The origin of the name 'Lord of Kedār' is unknown; probably Kedār was an old cult title of Siva.]

[3] I have before remarked that a Sanskrit etymology might be given to this word in Ila and Isa, *i.e.* 'the goddess of the earth' [?] [p. 636, note].

[4] I was informed at Naples that four thousand of these were dug out of one spot, and I obtained while at Paestum many fragments and heads of this goddess.

indifference whether the victim was slaughtered or died a natural death For the honour of humanity, such monsters are few in number; but that they practise [576] these deeds I can testify, from a personal visit to their haunts, where I saw the cave of one of these Troglodyte monsters, in which by his own command he was inhumed; and which will remain closed, until curiosity and incredulity greater than mine may disturb the bones of the Aghori of Abu.

The ὠμοφαγία, or eating raw flesh with the blood, was a part of the secret mysteries of Osiris, in commemoration of the happy change in the condition of mankind from savage to civilized life, and intended to deter by disgust the return thereto.[1]

The Buddhists pursued this idea to excess; and in honour of Adiswara, the First, who from his abode of Meru taught them the arts of agriculture, they altogether abandoned that type of savage life, the eating of the flesh of animals,[2] and confined themselves to the fruits of the earth. With these sectarian anti-idolaters, who are almost all of Rajput descent, the beneficent Lakshmi, Sri, or Gauri, is an object of sincere devotion.

Affinities of Hindu to other Mythologies.—But we must close this digression; for such is the affinity between the mythology of India, Greece, and Egypt, that a bare recapitulation of the numerous surnames of the Hindu goddess of abundance would lead us beyond reasonable limits; all are forms of Parvati or Durga Mata, the Mater Montana of Greece and Rome, an epithet of Cybele or Vesta (according to Diodorus), as the guardian goddess of children, one of the characters of the Rajput 'Mother of the Mount,' whose shrine crowns many a pinnacle in Mewar; and who, with the prolific Gauri, is amongst the amiable forms of the universal mother, whose functions are more varied and extensive than her sisters of Egypt and of Greece. Like the Ephesian Diana, Durga wears the crescent on her head. She is also 'the turreted Cybele,' the guardian goddess of all places of strength (*durga*),[3] and like her she is drawn or carried by the lion. As Mata Janavi, 'the Mother of Births,' she is Juno

[1] Prichard's *Researches into the Physical History of Man*, p. 369. [For a full discussion of ὠμοφαγία see Miss J. E. Harrison, *Prolegomena to the Study of Greek Religion*, 483 ff.]

[2] The Buddhists of Tartary make no scruple of eating flesh.

[3] *Durga*, 'a fort'; as Suvarnadurg, 'the golden castle,' etc., etc.

Lucina: as Padma, 'whose throne is the lotos,' she is the fair Isis of the Nile: as Tripura,[1] 'governing the three worlds,' and Atmadevi, 'the Goddess of Souls,' she is the Hecate Triformis of the Greeks. In short, her power is manifested under every form from the birth, and all the [577] intermediate stages until death; whether Janavi, Gauri, or the terrific Kali, the Proserpine or Kalligeneia of the West.

Whoever desires to witness one of the most imposing and pleasing of Hindu festivals, let him repair to Udaipur, and behold the rites of the lotus-queen Padma, the Gauri of Rajasthan.

Chait (Sudi) 8th, which, being after the Ides, is the 23rd of the month, is sacred to Devi, the goddess of every tribe; she is called Asokashtami, and being the ninth night (*nauratri*) from the opening of their Floralia, they perform the *homa*, or sacrifice of fire. On this day a grand procession takes place to the Chaugan, and every Rajput worships his tutelary divinity.

The Birth of Rāma.—Chait (Sudi) 9th is the anniversary of Rama, the grand beacon of the solar race, kept with great rejoicings at Udaipur. Horses and elephants are worshipped, and all the implements of war. A procession takes place to the Chaugan, and the succeeding day, called the Dasahra or tenth, is celebrated in Asoj.

The Festival of Kamadeva.—The last days of spring are dedicated to Kamadeva, the god of love. The scorching winds of the hot season are already beginning to blow, when Flora droops her head, and "the god of love turns anchorite"; yet the rose continues to blossom, and affords the most fragrant chaplets for the Rajputnis, amidst all the heats of summer. Of this the queen of flowers, the jessamine (*chameli*), white and yellow, the mogra,[2] the champaka, that flourish in extreme heat, the ladies form garlands, which they twine in their dark hair, weave into bracelets, or wear as pendent collars. There is no city in the East where the adorations of the sex to Kamadeva are more fervent than in 'the city of the rising sun' (Udayapura). On the 13th and 14th of Chait they sing hymns handed down by the sacred bards:

"Hail, god of the flowery bow:[3] hail, warrior with a fish on

[1] Literally *Tripoli*, 'the three cities,' *pura*, *polis*.

[2] [The double jasmin (*Michelia champaka*).]

[3] Cupid's bow is formed of a garland of flowers.

thy banner! hail, powerful divinity, who causeth the firmness of the sage to forsake him!"

"Glory to Madana, to Kama,[1] the god of gods; to Him by whom Brahma [578], Vishnu, Siva, and Indra are filled with emotions of rapture!"—*Bhavishya Purana.*[2]

Festivals in the month Baisākh: April-May.—There is but one festival in this month of any note, when the grand procession denominated the 'Nakkara ki aswari' (from the equestrians being summoned, as already described, by the grand kettledrums from the Tripolia), takes place; and this is against the canons of the Hindu church, being instituted by the present Rana in S. 1847, a memorable year in the calendar. It was in this year, on the 2nd of Baisakh, that he commanded a repetition of the rites of Gauri, by the name of the Little Ganggor; but this act of impiety was marked by a sudden rise of the waters of the Pichola, the bursting of the huge embankment, and the inundation of the lake's banks, to the destruction of one-third of the capital: life, property, mansions, trees, all were swept away in the tremendous rush of water, whose ravages are still marked by the site of streets and bazaars now converted into gardens or places of recreation, containing thousands of acres within the walls, subdivided by hedges of the cactus, the natural fence of Mewar, which alike thrives in the valley or covers the most barren spots of her highest hills. But although the superstitious look grave, and add that a son was also taken from him on this very day, yet the Rana persists in maintaining the fête he established; the barge is manned, he and his chiefs circumnavigate the Pichola, regale on ma'ajun, and terrify Varuna (the water-god) with the pyrotechnic exhibitions.

Although the court calendar of Udaipur notices only those festivals on which State processions occur, yet there are many minor fêtes, which are neither unimportant nor uninteresting. We shall enumerate a few, alike in Baisakh, Jeth, and Asarh, which are blank as to the Nakkara Aswari.

Savitrivrata Festival.—On the 29th Baisakh there is a fast common to India peculiar to the women, who perform certain rites under the sacred fig-tree (the *vata* or *pipal*), to preserve

[1] Madana, he who intoxicates with desire (*kama*), both epithets of the god of love. The festivals on the 13th and 14th are called Madana trayodasi (the tenth) and Chaturdasi (fourteenth).

[2] *Asiatic Researches,* vol. iii. p. 278.

them from widowhood; and hence the name of the fast Savitri-vrata.[1]

Festivals in the month Jeth: May-June.—On the 2nd of Jeth, when the sun is in the zenith, the Rajput ladies commemorate the birth of the sea-born goddess Rambha, the queen of the naiads or Apsaras,[2] whose birth, like that of Venus, was from the froth of the waters; and [579] hence the Rajput bards designate all the fair messengers of heaven by the name of Apsaras, who summon the 'chosen' from the field of battle, and convey him to the 'mansion of the sun.'[3]

The Aranya-Shashthi Festival.—On the 6th of Jeth the ladies have another festival called the Aranya Shashthi, because on this day those desirous of offspring walk in the woods (*aranya*) to gather and eat certain herbs. Sir W. Jones has remarked the analogy between this and the Druidic ceremony of gathering the mistletoe (also on the Shashthi, or 6th day of the moon), as a preservative against sterility.

Festivals in the month Āsārh: June-July.—Asarh, the initiative month of the periodical rains, has no particular festivity at Udaipur, though in other parts of India the Rathayatra, or procession of the car of Vishnu or Jagannatha (lord of the universe) is well known: this is on the 2nd and the 11th, 'the night of the gods,' when Vishnu (the sun) reposes four months.

Festivals in the month Sāwan: July-August.—Sawan, classically Sravana. There are two important festivals, with processions, in this month.

The Tij.—The third, emphatically called 'the Tij' (third), is sacred to the mountain goddess Parvati, being the day on which, after long austerities, she was reunited to Siva: she accordingly declared it holy, and proclaimed that whoever invoked her on that day should possess whatever was desired. The Tij is

[1] [Savitri-vrata means 'the vow to Savitri,' and has no connexion with the *vata* or banyan-tree. But the tree is worshipped in connexion with it on 15th light or dark fortnight of the month Jeth (*Census Report, Baroda*, 1901, i. 127).]

[2] *Ap*, 'water,' and *sara*, 'froth or essence.' [The word means 'going in the waters, or between the waters of the clouds.']

[3] The Romans held the calends of June (generally Jeth) sacred to the goddess Carna, significant of the sun. Carneus was the sun-god of the Celts, and a name of Apollo at Sparta, and other Grecian cities. The Karneia was a festival in honour of Apollo.

accordingly reverenced by the women, and the husbandman of Rajasthan, who deems it a most favourable day to take possession of land, or to reinhabit a deserted dwelling. When on the expulsion of the predatory powers from the devoted lands of Mewar, proclamations were disseminated far and wide, recalling the expatriated inhabitants, they showed their love of country by obedience to the summons. Collecting their goods and chattels, they congregated from all parts, but assembled at a common rendezvous to make their entry to the *bapota*, 'land of their sires,' on the Tij of Sawan. On this fortunate occasion, a band of three hundred men, women, and children, with colours flying, drums beating, the females taking precedence with brass vessels of water on their heads, and chanting the *suhaila* (song of joy), entered the town of Kapasan, to revisit their desolate dwellings [580], and return thanks on their long-abandoned altars to Parvati [1] for a happiness they had never contemplated.

Red garments are worn by all classes on this day, and at Jaipur clothes of this colour are presented by the Raja to all the chiefs. At that court the Tij is kept with more honour than at Udaipur. An image of Parvati on the Tij, richly attired, is borne on a throne by women chanting hymns, attended by the prince and his nobles. On this day, fathers present red garments and stuffs to their daughters.

The Nāgpanchami Festival: Serpent Worship.—The 5th is the Nagpanchami, or day set apart for the propitiation of the chief of the reptile race, the Naga or serpent. Few subjects have more occupied the notice of the learned world than the mysteries of Ophite worship, which are to be traced wherever there existed a remnant of civilization, or indeed of humanity; among the savages of the savannahs [2] of America, and the magi of Fars, with whom it was the type of evil,—their Ahrimanes.[3] The Nagas, or serpent-genii of the Rajputs, have a semi-human structure, precisely as Diodorus describes the snake-mother of

[1] The story of the vigils of Parvati, preparatory to her being reunited to her lord, consequent to her sacrifice as *Sati*, is the counterpart of the Grecian fable of Cybele, her passion for, and marriage with, the youth Atys or *Papas*, the *Baba*, or universal father, of the Hindus.

[2] How did a word of Persian growth come to signify 'the boundless brake' of the new world?

[3] *Ari*, 'a foe'; *manus*, 'man.' [Angro Mainyush, 'destructive spirit.']

the Scythae, in whose country originated this serpent-worship, engrafted on the tenets of Zardusht, of the Puranas of the priesthood of Egypt, and on the fables of early Greece.[1] Dupuis, Volney, and other expounders of the mystery, have given an astronomical solution to what they deem a varied ramification of an ancient fable, of which that of Greece, 'the dragon guarding the fruits of Hesperides,' may be considered the most elegant version. Had these learned men seen those ancient sculptures in India, which represent 'the fall,' they might have changed their opinion. The traditions of the Jains or Buddhists (originating in the land of the Takshaks,[2] or Turkistan) assert the creation of the human species in pairs, called *jugal*, who fed off the ever-fructifying *kalpa-vriksha*, which possesses all the characters of the Tree of Life, like it bearing

> Ambrosial fruit of vegetable gold;

which was termed *amrita*, and rendered them immortal. A drawing, brought by [581] Colonel Coombs, from a sculptured column in a cave temple in the south of India, represents the first pair at the foot of this ambrosial tree, and a serpent entwined among the heavily laden boughs, presenting to them some of the fruit from his mouth. The tempter appears to be at that part of his discourse, when

> . . . his words, replete with guile,
> Into her heart too easy entrance won:
> Fixed on the fruit she gazed.

This is a curious subject to be engraved on an ancient pagan temple; if Jain or Buddhist, the interest would be considerably enhanced. On this festival, at Udaipur, as well as throughout India, they strew particular plants about the threshold, to prevent the entrance of reptiles.

The Rākhi Festival.—This festival, which is held on the last day of Sawan, was instituted in honour of the good genii, when Durvasas the sage instructed Salono (the genius or nymph presiding over the month of Sawan) to bind on *rakhis*, or bracelets, as charms to avert evil. The ministers of religion and females alone are privileged to bestow these charmed wrist-bands. The ladies of

[1] [There is no reason to believe that snake-worship was not independently practised in India.]

[2] This is the snake-race of India, the foes of the Pandus.

Rajasthan, either by their handmaids or the family priests, send a bracelet as the token of their esteem to such as they adopt as brothers, who return gifts in acknowledgement of the honour. The claims thus acquired by the fair are far stronger than those of consanguinity: for illustration of which I may refer to an incident already related in the annals of this house.[1] Sisters also present their brothers with clothes on this day, who make an offering of gold in return.[2]

This day is hailed by the Brahmans as indemnifying them for their expenditure of silk and spangles, with which they decorate the wrists of all who are likely to make a proper return.

Festivals in the month Bhādon: August-September.—On the 3rd there is a grand procession to the Chaugan; and the 8th, or Ashtami, is the birth of Krishna, which will be described at large in an account of Nathdwara. There are several holidays in this month, when the periodical [582] rains are in full descent; but that on the last but one (Sudi 14, or 29th) is the most remarkable.

Ancestor Worship.—On this day[3] commences the worship of the ancestorial manes (the Pitrideva, or *father-gods*) of the Rajputs, which continues for fifteen days. The Rana goes to the cemetery at Ara, and performs at the cenotaph of each of his forefathers the rites enjoined, consisting of ablutions, prayers, and the hanging of garlands of flowers, and leaves sacred to the dead, on their monuments. Every chieftain does the same amongst the altars of the 'great ancients' (*bara burha*); or, if absent from their estates, they accompany their sovereign to Ara.

[1] See p. 364.

[2] I returned from three to five pieces of gold for the *rakhis* sent by my adopted sisters; from one of whom, the sister of the Rana, I annually received this pledge by one of her handmaids; three of them I have yet in my possession, though I never saw the donor, who is now no more. I had, likewise, some presented through the family priest, from the Bundi queen-mother, with whom I have conversed for hours, though she was invisible to me; and from the ladies of rank of the chieftains' families, but one of whom I ever beheld, though they often called upon me for the performance of brotherly offices in consequence of such tie. There is a delicacy in this custom, with which the bond uniting the cavaliers of Europe to the service of the fair, in the days of chivalry, will not compare.

[3] Sacred to Vishnu, with the title of *Ananta*, or infinite—*Bhavishyottara*. (See *Asiatic Researches*, vol. iii. p. 291.) Here Vishnu appears as 'lord of the manes.'

CHAPTER 22

Khadga Sthapana, Sword Worship.—The festival in which this imposing rite occurs is the Nauratri,[1] sacred to the god of war, commencing on the first of the month Asoj. It is essentially martial, and confined to the Rajput, who on the departure of the monsoon finds himself at liberty to indulge his passion whether for rapine or revenge, both which in these tropical regions are necessarily suspended during the rains. Arguing from the order of the passions, we may presume that the first objects of emblematic worship were connected with war [583], and we accordingly find the highest reverence paid to arms by every nation of antiquity. The Scythic warrior of Central Asia, the intrepid Gete, admitted no meaner representative of the god of battle than his own scimitar.[2] He worshipped it, he swore by it; it was buried with him, in order that he might appear before the martial divinity in the other world as became his worshipper on earth: for the Gete of Transoxiana, from the earliest ages, not only believed in the soul's immortality, and in the doctrine of rewards and punishments hereafter, but, according to the father of history, he was a monotheist; of which fact he has left a memorable proof in the punishment of the celebrated Anacharsis, who, on his return from a visit to Thales and his brother philosophers of Greece, attempted to introduce into the land of the Saka (Sakatai) the corrupted polytheism of Athens.

If we look westward from this the central land of earliest

[1] Nauratri may be interpreted the nine days' festival, or the 'new night' [?].

[2] "It was natural enough," says Gibbon, "that the Scythians should adore with peculiar devotion the god of war; but as they were incapable of forming either an abstract idea, or a corporeal representation, they worshipped their tutelar deity under the symbol of an iron cimeter. If the rites of Scythia were practised on this solemn occasion,* a lofty altar, or rather pile of faggots, three hundred yards in length and in breadth, was raised in a spacious plain; and the sword of Mars was placed erect on the summit of this rustic altar, which was annually consecrated by the blood of sheep, horses, and of the hundredth captive" (Gibbon's *Roman Empire*, ed. W. Smith, iv. 194 f.).

* Attila dictating the terms of peace with the envoys of Constantinople, at the city of Margus, in Upper Moesia.

civilization, to Dacia, Thrace, Pannonia, the seats of the Thyssagetae or western Getae, we find the same form of adoration addressed to the emblem of Mars, as mentioned by Xenophon in his memorable retreat, and practised by Alaric and his Goths, centuries afterwards, in the Acropolis of Athens. If we transport ourselves to the shores of Scandinavia, amongst the Cimbri and Getae of Jutland, to the Ultima Thule, wherever the name of Gete prevails, we shall find the same adoration paid by the Getic warrior to his sword.

The Frisian Frank also of Gothic race, adhered to this worship, and transmitted it with the other rites of the Getic warrior of the Jaxartes; such as the adoration of the steed, sacred to the sun, the great god of the Massagetae, as well as of the Rajput, who sacrificed it at the annual feast, or with his arms and wife burnt it on his funeral pile. Even the kings of the 'second race' kept up the religion of their Scythic sires from the Jaxartes, and the bones of the war-horse of Chilperic were exhumed with those of the monarch. These rites, as well as those long-cherished chivalrous notions, for which the Salian Franks have ever been conspicuous [584], had their birth in Central Asia; for though contact with the more polished Arab softened the harsh character of the western warrior, his thirst for glory, the romantic charm which fed his passion, and his desire to please the fair, he inherited from his ancestors on the shores of the Baltic, which were colonized from the Oxus. Whether Charlemagne addressed his sword as Joyeuse,[1] or the Scandinavian hero Angantýr as the enchanted blade Tyrfing (Hialmar's bane), each came from one common origin, the people which invented the custom of Khadga Sthapana, or 'adoration of the sword.' But neither the falchion 'made by the dwarfs for Suafurlama,' nor the redoubled sword of Bayard with which he dubbed the first Francis,—not even the enchanted brand of Ariosto's hero, can for a moment compare with the double-edged khanda (scimitar) annually worshipped by the chivalry of Mewar. Before I descant on this monstrous blade, I shall give an abstract of the ceremonies on each of the nine days sacred to the god of war.

The Dasahra Festival.—On the 1st of Asoj, after fasting, ablution, and prayer on the part of the prince and his household, the double-edged khanda is removed from the hall of arms

[1] St. Palaye, *Memoirs of Ancient Chivalry*, p. 305.

(*ayudhsala*), and having received the homage (*puja*) of the court, it is carried in procession to the Kishanpol (gate of Kishan), where it is delivered to the Raj Jogi,[1] the Mahants, and band of Jogis assembled in front of the temple of Devi '*the* goddess,' adjoining the portal of Kishan.[2] By these, the monastic militant adorers of Hara, the god of battle, the brand emblematic of the divinity is placed[3] on the altar before the image of his divine consort. At three in the afternoon the nakkaras, or grand kettle-drums, proclaim from the Tripolia[4] the signal for the assemblage of the chiefs with their retainers; and the Rana and his cavalcade proceed direct to the stables, when a buffalo is sacrificed in honour of the war-horse. Thence the procession moves to the temple of Devi, where the Raja Krishan (*Godi*) has proceeded. Upon this, the Rana seats himself close to the Raj Jogi, presents two pieces of [585] silver and a coco-nut, performs homage to the sword (*khadga*), and returns to the palace.

Asoj 2nd. In similar state he proceeds to the Chaugan, their Champ de Mars, where a buffalo is sacrificed; and on the same day another buffalo victim is felled by the nervous arm of a Rajput, near the Toranpol, or triumphal gate. In the evening the Rana goes to the temple of Amba Mata, the universal mother, when several goats and buffaloes bleed to the goddess.

The 3rd. Procession to the Chaugan, when another buffalo is offered; and in the afternoon five buffaloes and two rams are sacrificed to Harsiddh Mata.[5]

On the 4th, as on every one of the nine days, the first visit is to the Champ de Mars: the day opens with the slaughter of a buffalo. The Rana proceeds to the temple of Devi, when he worships the sword, and the standard of the Raj Jogi, to whom, as the high-priest of Siva, the god of war, he pays homage, and

[1] Raj Jogi is the chief of the ascetic warriors; the Mahants are commanders [the term being usually applied to the abbot of a monastery]. More will be said of this singular society when we discuss the religious institutions of Mewar.

[2] The god Krishna is called Kishan in the dialects.

[3] This is the *sthapana* of the sword, literally its inauguration or induction, for the purposes of adoration.

[4] Tripolia, or triple portal.

[5] [The chief centres of worship of Harsiddh Māta are Gāndhari and Ujjain. It is said that her image stood on the sea-shore, and that she used to swallow all the vessels that passed by (R. E. Enthoven, *Folklore Notes Gujarāt*, 5; *BG*, ix. Part i. 226).]

makes offering of sugar, and a garland of roses. A buffalo having been previously fixed to a stake near the temple, the Rana sacrifices him with his own hand, by piercing him from his travelling throne (raised on men's shoulders and surrounded by his vassals) with an arrow. In the days of his strength, he seldom failed almost to bury the feather in the flank of the victim ; but on the last occasion his enfeebled arm made him exclaim with Prithiraj, when, captive and blind, he was brought forth to amuse the Tartar despot, "I draw not the bow as in the days of yore."

On the 5th, after the usual sacrifice at the Chaugan, and an elephant fight, the procession marches to the temple of Asapurna (Hope) ; a buffalo and a ram are offered to the goddess adored by all the Rajputs, and the tutelary divinity of the Chauhans. On this day the lives of some victims are spared at the intercession of the Nagar-Seth, or chief-magistrate,[1] and those of his faith, the Jains.

On the 6th, the Rana visits the Chaugan, but makes no sacrifice. In the afternoon, prayers and victims to Devi ; and in the evening the Rana visits Bhikharinath, the chief of the Kanphara Jogis, or split-ear ascetics

The 7th. After the daily routine at the Chaugan, and sacrifices to Devi (the goddess of destruction), the chief equerry is commanded to adorn the steeds with their new caparisons, and lead them to be bathed in the lake. At night, the sacred fire (*hom*) is kindled, and a buffalo and a ram are sacrificed to Devi ; the Jogis [586] are called up and feasted on boiled rice and sweetmeats. On the conclusion of this day, the Rana and his chieftains visit the hermitage of Sukharia Baba, an anchorite of the Jogi sect.

8th. There is the *homa*, or fire-sacrifice in the palace. In the afternoon, the prince, with a select cavalcade, proceeds to the village of Samina, beyond the city walls, and visits a celebrated Gosain.[2]

9th. There is no morning procession. The horses from the royal stables, as well as those of the chieftains, are taken to the

[1] [Formerly an important personage, but his authority has now much decreased (*BG*, ix. Part i. 96).]

[2] On this day sons visit and pay adoration to their fathers. The diet is chiefly of vegetables and fruits. Brahmans with their unmarried daughters are feasted, and receive garments called *chunri* from their chiefs. [This is a kind of cloth dyed by partly tying it in knots, which escape the action of the dye.]

lake, and bathed by their grooms, and on returning from purification they are caparisoned in their new housings, led forth, and receive the homage of their riders, and the Rana bestows a largess on the master of the horse, the equerries, and grooms. At three in the afternoon, the nakkaras having thrice sounded, the whole State insignia, under a select band, proceed to Mount Matachal, and bring home the sword. When its arrival in the court of the palace is announced, the Rana advances and receives it with due homage from the hands of the Raj Jogi, who is presented with a khilat; while the Mahant, who has performed all the austerities during the nine days, has his *patra* [1] filled with gold and silver coin. The whole of the Jogis are regaled, and presents are made to their chiefs. The elephants and horses again receive homage, and the sword, the shield, and spear are worshipped within the palace. At three in the morning the prince takes repose.

The 10th, or Dasahra,[2] is a festival universally known in India, and respected by all classes, although entirely military, being commemorative of the day on which the deified Rama commenced his expedition to Lanka for the redemption of Sita; [3] the 'tenth of Asoj' is consequently deemed by the Rajput a fortunate day for warlike enterprise. The day commences with a visit from the [587] prince or chieftain to his spiritual guide. Tents and carpets are prepared at the Chaugan or Matachal mount, where the artillery is sent; and in the afternoon the Rana, his chiefs, and their retainers repair to the field of Mars, worship the *khejra* tree,[4] liberate the *nilkanth* or jay (sacred to Rama), and return amidst a discharge of guns.

[1] The Jogi's *patra* is not so revolting as that of their divinity Hara (the god of war), which is the human *cranium*; this is a hollow gourd.

[2] From *das*, the numeral *ten*; *the* tenth. [It means 'the feast that removes ten sins.']

[3] In this ancient story we are made acquainted with the distant maritime wars which the princes of India carried on. Even supposing Ravana's abode to be the insular Ceylon, he must have been a very powerful prince to equip an armament sufficiently numerous to carry off from the remote kingdom of Kosala the wife of the great king of the Suryas. It is most improbable that a petty king of Ceylon could wage equal war with a potentate who held the chief dominion of India; whose father, Dasaratha, drove his victorious car (*ratha*) over every region (*desa*), and whose intercourse with the countries beyond the Brahmaputra is distinctly to be traced in the Ramayana. [Dasaratha has no connexion with *desa*: the name means 'he who possesses ten (*dasa*) chariots (*ratha*).']

[4] [*Prosopis spicigera.*]

11th. In the morning, the Rana, with all the State insignia, the kettledrums sounding in the rear, proceeds towards the Matachal mount, and takes the muster of his troops, amidst discharges of cannon, tilting, and display of horsemanship. The spectacle is imposing even in the decline of this house. The hilarity of the party, the diversified costume, the various forms, colours, and decorations of the turbans, in which some have the heron plume, or sprigs from some shrub sacred to the god of war; the clusters of lances, shining matchlocks, and black bucklers, the scarlet housings of the steeds, and waving pennons, recall forcibly the glorious days of the devoted Sanga, or the immortal Partap, who on such occasions collected round the black *changi* and crimson banner of Mewar a band of sixteen thousand of his own kin and clan, whose lives were their lord's and their country's. The shops and bazaars are ornamented with festoons of flowers and branches of trees, while the costliest cloths and brocades are extended on screens, to do honour to their prince; the *toran* (or triumphal arch) is placed before the tent, on a column of which he places one hand as he alights, and before entering makes several circumambulations. All present offer their *nazars* to the prince, the artillery fires, and the bards raise 'the song of praise,' celebrating the glories of the past; the fame of Samra, who fell with thirteen thousand of his kin on the Ghaggar; of Arsi and his twelve brave sons, who gave themselves as victims for the salvation of Chitor; of Kumbha, Lakha, Sanga, Partap, Amra, Raj, all descended of the blood of Rama, whose exploits, three thousand five hundred years before, they are met to celebrate. The situation of Matachal is well calculated for such a spectacle, as indeed is the whole ground from the palace through the Delhi portal to the mount, on which is erected one of the several castles commanding the approaches to the city. The fort is dedicated to Mata, though it would not long remain stable (*achal*) before a battery of thirty-six pounders. The guns are drawn up about the termination of the slope of the natural glacis; the Rana and his court remain on horseback [588] half up the ascent; and while every chief or vassal is at liberty to leave his ranks, and "witch the world with noble horsemanship," there is nothing tumultuous, nothing offensive in their mirth.

The steeds purchased since the last festival are named, and as the cavalcade returns, their grooms repeat the appellations of each as the word is passed by the master of the horse; as Baj Raj, 'the royal steed'; Hayamor, 'the chief of horses'; Manika, 'the gem'; Bajra, 'the thunderbolt,' etc., etc. On returning to the palace, gifts are presented by the Rana to his chiefs. The Chauhan chief of Kotharia claims the apparel which his prince wears on this day, in token of the fidelity of his ancestor to the minor, Udai Singh, in Akbar's wars. To others, a fillet or *balaband* for the turban is presented; but all such compliments are regulated by precedent or immediate merit.

The Toran Arch.—Thus terminates the Nauratri festival sacred to the god of war, which in every point of view is analogous to the autumnal festival of the Scythic warlike nations, when these princes took the muster of their armies, and performed the same rites to the great celestial luminary.[1] I have presented to the antiquarian reader these details, because it is in minute particulars that analogous customs are detected. Thus the temporary *toran*, or triumphal arch, erected in front of the tent at Mount Matachala would scarcely claim the least notice, but that we discover even in this emblem the origin of the triumphal arches of antiquity, with many other rites which may be traced to the Indo-Scythic races of Asia. The *toran* in its original form consisted of two columns and an architrave, constituting the number three, sacred to Hara, the god of war. In the progress of the arts the architrave gave way to the Hindu arch, which consisted of two or more ribs without the keystone, the apex being the perpendicular junction of the archivaults; nor is the arc of the *toran* semicircular, or any segment of a circle, but with that graceful curvature which stamps with originality one of the arches of the Normans, who may have brought it from their ancient seats on the Oxus, whence it may also have been [589] carried within the Indus. The cromlech, or trilithic altar in the centre

[1] "A la première lune de chaque année, tous ces officiers, grands et petits, tenoient une assemblée générale à la cour du Tanjou, et y faisoient un sacrifice solennel: à la cinquième lune, ils s'assembloient à Lumtching, où ils sacrifioient au ciel, à la terre, aux esprits, et aux ancêtres. Il se tenoit encore une grande assemblée à Tai-lin dans l'automne, parce qu'alors les chevaux étoient plus gras, et on y faisoit en même-tems le dénombrement des hommes et des troupeaux; mais tous les jours le Tanjou sortoit de son camp, le matin pour adorer le soleil, et le soir la lune. Sa tente étoit placée à gauche, comme le côté le plus honorable chez ces peuples, et regardoit le couchant" (*Avant J.-C.* 209; *L'Histoire Générale des Huns*, vol. i. p. 24).

of all those monuments called Druidic, is most probably a *toran*, sacred to the Sun-god Belenus, like Har, or Balsiva, the god of battle, to whom as soon as a temple is raised the *toran* is erected, and many of these are exquisitely beautiful.

Gates.—An interesting essay might be written on portes and *torans*, their names and attributes, and the genii presiding as their guardians. Amongst all the nations of antiquity, the portal has had its peculiar veneration: to pass it was a privilege regarded as a mark of honour. The Jew Haman, in the true Oriental style, took post at the king's gate as an inexpugnable position. The most pompous court in Europe takes its title from its *porte*, where, as at Udaipur, all alight. The Tripolia, or triple portal, the entry to the magnificent terrace in front of the Rana's palace, consists, like the Roman arcs of triumph, of three arches, still preserving the numeral sacred to the god of battle, one of whose titles is Tripura, which may be rendered Tripoli, or lord of the three places of abode, or cities, but applied in its extensive sense to the three worlds, heaven, earth, and hell. From the Sanskrit *Pola* we have the Greek πύλη, *a gate*, or pass; and in the guardian or *Polia*, the πυλωρός or porter; while to this *langue mère* our own language is indebted, not only for its portes and porters, but its doors (*dwara*).[1] Pylos signified also a pass; so in Sanskrit these natural barriers are called *Palas*, and hence the poetical epithet applied to the aboriginal mountain tribes of Rajasthan, namely, Palipati and Palindra, 'lords of the pass.'[2]

Ganesa.—One of the most important of the Roman divinities was Janus, whence Januae, or portals, of which he was the guardian.[3] A resemblance between the Ganesa of the Hindu pantheon and the Roman Janus has been pointed out by Sir W. Jones, but his analogy extended little beyond nominal similarity. The fable of the birth of Ganesa furnishes us with the origin of the worship of Janus, and as it has never been given, I shall transcribe it from the bard Chand. Ganesa is the chief of the genii[4] attendant on the god of war, and was expressly formed by

[1] [There is no Skt. word *pola*, 'gate'; the Hindi *pol*, *paul* is Skt. *pura dvāra*, 'city entrance.']

[2] [The words *pol* and *pāl* are not connected.]

[3] Hence may be found a good etymology of *janizary*, the guardian of the *serai*, a title left by the lords of Eastern Rome for the Porte. [Turkish *yeni-tsheri*, 'new soldiery.']

[4] In Sanskrit *gana* (pronounced as *gun*), the *jinn* of the Persians, trans-

Uma, the Hindu Juno, to guard the entrance of her caverned retreat in the [590] Caucasus, where she took refuge from the tyranny of the lord of Kailasa (Olympus), whose throne is fixed amidst eternal snows on the summit of this peak of the gigantic Caucasus (*Koh-khasa*).[1]

"Strife arose between Mahadeo and the faithful Parvati: she fled to the mountains and took refuge in a cave. A crystal fountain tempted her to bathe, but shame was awakened; she dreaded being seen. Rubbing her frame, she made an image of man; with her nail she sprinkled it with the water of life, and placed it as guardian at the entrance of the cave." Engrossed with the recollection of Parvati,[2] Siva went to Karttikeya[3] for tidings of his mother, and together they searched each valley and recess, and at length reached the spot where a figure was placed at the entrance of a cavern. As the chief of the gods prepared to explore this retreat, he was stopped by the Polia. In a rage he struck off his head with his discus (*chakra*), and in the gloom discovered the object of his search. Surprised and dismayed, she demanded how he obtained ingress: "Was there no guardian at the entrance?" The furious Siva replied that he had cut off his head. On hearing this, the mountain-goddess was enraged, and weeping, exclaimed, "You have destroyed my child." The god, determined to recall him to life, decollated a young elephant, replaced the head he had cut off, and naming him Ganesa, decreed that in every resolve his name should be the first invoked.

---

muted to *genii*; here is another instance in point of the alternation of the initial, and softened by being transplanted from Indo-Scythia to Persia, as *Ganes* was *Janus* at Rome. [*Gana* and *Jinn*, *Ganesa* and *Janus*, have no connexion.]

[1] The *Casius Mons* of Ptolemy. [The derivation of the word Caucasus is unknown.]

[2] Parvati, 'the mountain goddess,' was called Sati, or 'the faithful,' in her former birth. She became the mother of Jahnavi, the river (*Ganga*) goddess.

[3] Karttikeya, the son of Siva and Parvati, the Jupiter and Juno of the Hindu theogony, has the leading of the armies of the gods, delegated by his father; and his mother has presented to him her peacock, which is the steed of this warlike divinity. He is called Karttikeya from being nursed by six females called Krittika, who inhabit six of the seven stars composing the constellation of the Wain, or Ursa Major. Thus the Hindu Mars, born of Jupiter and Juno, and nursed by Ursa Major, is, like all other theogonies, an astronomical allegory. There is another legend of the birth of Mars, which I shall give in the text.

Invocation of the Bard to Ganesa.

"Oh, Ganesa! thou art a mighty lord; thy single tusk [1] is beautiful, and demands the tribute of praise from the Indra of song.[2] Thou art the chief of the human race; the destroyer of unclean spirits; the remover of fevers, whether daily or tertian. Thy bard sounds thy praise; let my work be accomplished!"

Thus Ganesa is the chief of the Di minores of the Hindu pantheon, as the etymology of the word indicates,[3] and like Janus, was entrusted with the gates of heaven [591]; while of his right to preside over peace and war, the fable related affords abundant testimony. Ganesa is the first invoked and propitiated [4] on every undertaking, whether warlike or pacific. The warrior implores his counsel; the banker indites his name at the commencement of every letter; the architect places his image in the foundation of every edifice; and the figure of Ganesa is either sculptured or painted at the door of every house as a protection against evil. Our Hindu Janus is represented as four-armed, and holding the disk (*chakra*), the war-shell, the club, and the lotos. Ganesa is not, however, *bifrons*, like the Roman guardian of portals. In every transaction he is *adi*, or the first, though the Hindu does not, like the Roman, open the year with his name. I shall conclude with remarking that one of the portes of every Hindu city is named the Ganesa Pol, as well as some conspicuous entrance to the palace: thus Udaipur has its Ganesa dwara, who also gives a name to the hall, the Ganesa deori; and his shrine will be found on the ascent of every sacred mount, as at Abu, where it is placed close to a fountain on the abrupt face about twelve hundred feet from the base. There is likewise a hill sacred to him in Mewar called Ganesa Gir, tantamount to the Mons Janiculum of the eternal city. The companion of this divinity is a rat, who indirectly receives a portion of homage, and with full as much right as the bird emblematic of Minerva.[5]

[1] This elephant-headed divinity has but one tusk.

[2] The bard thus modestly designates himself.

[3] Chief (*isa*) of the gana (*genii*) or attendants on Siva.

[4] So he was at Rome, and his statue held the keys of heaven in his right hand, and, like Ganesa, a rod (the *ankus*) in his left.

[5] [The rat is the emblem of Ganesa probably because, like Apollo Smintheus, he protects the crops from vermin (Frazer, *The Golden Bough*, 3rd ed. Part v. vol. ii. 282 f.).]

We have abandoned the temple of the warlike divinity (Devi), the sword of Mars, and the triumphal *toran*, to invoke Ganesa. It will have been remarked that the Rana aids himself to dismount by placing his hand on one of the columns of the *toran*, an act which is pregnant with a martial allusion, as are indeed the entire ceremonials of the " worship of the sword."

Analogies to Western Customs. Oaths by the Sword.—It might be deemed folly to trace the rites and superstitions of so remote an age and nation to Central Asia ; but when we find the superstitions of the Indo-Scythic Getae prevailing within the Indus, in Dacia, and on the shores of the Baltic, we may assume their common origin ; for although the worship of arms has prevailed among all warlike tribes, there is a peculiar respect paid to the sword amongst the Getic races. The Greeks and Romans paid devotion to their arms, and swore by them. The Greeks brought their habits from ancient Thrace, where the custom existed of presenting as the greatest gift that peculiar kind of sword called *acinaces*,[1] which we dare not derive from the Indo-Scythic or Sanskrit *asi*, a [592] sword. When Xenophon,[2] on his retreat, reached the court of Seuthes, he agreed to attach his corps to the service of the Thracian. His officers on introduction, in the true Oriental style, presented their *nazars*, or gifts of homage, excepting Xenophon, who, deeming himself too exalted to make the common offering, presented his sword, probably only to be touched in recognition of his services being accepted. The most powerful oath of the Rajput, next to his sovereign's throne (*gaddi ka an*), is by his arms, *ya silah ka an*, ' by this weapon ! ' as, suiting the action to the word, he puts his hand on his dagger, never absent from his girdle. *Dhal, tarwar, ka an*, ' by my sword and shield ! ' The shield is deemed the only fit vessel or salver on which to present gifts ; and accordingly at a Rajput court, shawls, brocades, scarfs, and jewels are always spread before the guest on bucklers.[3]

In the Runic " incantation of Hervor," daughter of Angantýr, at the tomb of her father, she invokes the dead to deliver the enchanted brand Tyrfing, or " Hjalmr's bane," which, according

[1] [Persian *āhanak*, ' a sword of steel.']   [2] [*Anabasis*, vii. 2.]

[3] The Gothic invaders of Italy inaugurated their monarch by placing him upon a shield, and elevating him on their shoulders in the midst of his army.

to Getic custom, was buried in his tomb; she adjures him and his brothers "by all their arms, their shields, etc." It is depicted with great force, and, translated, would deeply interest a Rajput, who might deem it the spell by which the *Khanda* of Hamira, which he annually worships, was obtained.

Incantation

Hervor—"Awake, Angantýr! Hervor, the only daughter of thee and Suafu, doth awaken thee. Give me out of the tomb the tempered sword which the dwarfs made for Suafurlama.

"Can none of Eyvors' [1] sons speak with me out of the habitations of the dead? Hervardur,[1] Hurvardur?" [1]

The tomb at length opens, the inside of which appears on fire, and a reply is sung within:

Angantýr—"Daughter Hervor, full of spells to raise the dead, why dost thou call so? I was not buried either by father or friends; two who lived after me got Tyrfing, one of whom is now in possession thereof [593]."

Hervor—"The dead shall never enjoy rest unless Angantýr deliver me Tyrfing, that cleaveth shields, and killed Hjalmr." [2]

Angantýr—"Young maid, thou art of manlike courage, who dost rove by night to tombs, with spear engraven with magic spells,[3] with helm and coat of mail, before the door of our hall."

Hervor—"It is not good for thee to hide it."

Angantýr—"The death of Hjalmr [4] lies under my shoulders; it is all wrapt up in fire: I know no maid that dares to take this sword in hand."

Hervor—"I shall take in hand the sharp sword, if I may

[1] All these proper names might have Oriental etymologies assigned to them; Eyvor-sail is the name of a celebrated Rajput hero of the Bhatti tribe, who were driven at an early period from the very heart of Scythia, and are of Yadu race.

[2] This word can have a Sanskrit derivation from *haya*, 'a horse'; *marna*, 'to strike or kill'; *Hjalmr*, 'the horse-slayer.' [These theories are of no value.]

[3] The custom of engraving incantations on weapons is also from the East, and thence adopted by the Muhammadan, as well as the use of phylacteries. The name of the goddess guarding the tribe is often inscribed, and I have had an entire copy of the Bhagavadgita taken from the turban of a Rajput killed in action: in like manner the Muhammadans place therein the Koran.

[4] The metaphorical name of the sword Tyrfing.

obtain it. I do not think that fire will burn which plays about the site of deceased men." [1]

Angantýr—"Take and keep Hjalmr's bane: touch but the edges of it, there is poison in them both; [2] it is a most cruel devourer of men." [3]

The Magic Sword of Mewār.—Tradition has hallowed the two-edged sword (*khanda*) of Mewar, by investing it with an origin as mysterious as "the bane of Hjalmr." It is supposed to be the enchanted weapon fabricated by Viswakarma,[4] with which the Hindu Proserpine girded the founder of the race, and led him forth to the conquest of Chitor.[5] It remained the great heirloom of her princes till the sack of Chitor by the Tatar Ala, when Rana Arsi and eleven of his brave sons devoted themselves at the command of the guardian goddess of their race, and their capital falling into the hands of the invader, the last scion of Bappa became a fugitive amidst the mountains of the west. It was then the Tatar inducted the Sonigira Maldeo [594], as his lieutenant, into the capital of the Guhilots. The most celebrated of the poetic chronicles of Mewar gives an elaborate description of the subterranean palace in Chitor, in one of whose entrances the dreadful sacrifice was perpetuated to save the honour of Padmini and the fair of Chitor from the brutalized Tatars.[6] The curiosity of Maldeo was more powerful than his superstition, and he determined to explore these hidden abodes, though reputed to be guarded by the serpent genii attendant on Nagnaicha, the

[1] I have already mentioned these fires (see p. 89), which the northern nations believed to issue from the tombs of their heroes, and which seemed to guard their ashes; them they called Hauga Elldr, or 'the sepulchral fires,' and they were supposed more especially to surround tombs which contained hidden treasures. These supernatural fires are termed Shihaba by the Rajputs. When the intrepid Scandinavian maiden observes that she is not afraid of the flame burning her, she is bolder than one of the boldest Rajputs, for Sri-kishan, who was shocked at the bare idea of going near these sepulchral lights, was one of the three non-commissioned officers who afterwards led thirty-two firelocks to the attack and defeat of 1500 Pindaris.

[2] Like the Rajput Khanda, Tyrfing was double-edged; the poison of these edges is a truly Oriental idea.

[3] This poem is from the Hervarer Saga, an ancient Icelandic history. See Edda, vol. ii. p. 192.

[4] The Vulcan of the Hindus.

[5] For an account of the initiation to arms of Bappa, the founder of the Guhilots, see p. 264 [Vol. I.].

[6] See p. 311 [Vol. I.].

ancient divinity of its Takshak founders.[1] Whether it was through the identical caverned passage, and over the ashes of those martyred Kaminis,[2] that he made good his way into those rock-bound abodes, the legend says not; but though

> In darkness, and with dangers compassed round,
> And solitude,

the intrepid Maldeo paused not until he had penetrated to the very bounds of the abyss, where in a recess he beheld the snaky sorceress and her sister crew seated round a cauldron, in which the materials of their incantation were solving before a fire that served to illume this abode of horror. As he paused, the reverberation of his footsteps caused the infernal crew to look athwart the palpable obscure of their abode, and beholding the audacious mortal, they demanded his intent. The valiant Sonigira replied that he did not come as a spy,

> With purpose to explore or to disturb
> The secrets of their realm,

but in search of the enchanted brand of the founder of the Guhilots. Soon they made proof of Maldeo's hardihood. Uncovering the cauldron, he beheld a sight most appalling: amidst divers fragments of animals was the arm of an infant. A dish of this horrid repast was placed before him, and a silent signal made for him to eat. He obeyed, and returned the empty platter: it was proof sufficient of his worth to wear the enchanted blade, which, drawn forth from its secret abode, was put into the hand of Maldeo, who bowing, retired with the trophy [595].

Rana Hamira recovered this heirloom of his house, and with it the throne of Chitor, by his marriage with the daughter of the

[1] The Mori prince, from whom Bappa took Chitor, was of the Tak or Takshak race [?], of whom Nagnaicha or Nagini Mata was the mother, represented as half woman and half serpent; the sister of the mother of the Scythic race, according to their legends; so that the deeper we dive into these traditions, the stronger reason we shall find to assign a Scythic origin to all these tribes. As Bappa, the founder of the Guhilots, retired into Scythia and left his heirs to rule in India, I shall find fault with no antiquary who will throw overboard all the connexion between Kanaksen, the founder of the Valabhi empire, and Sumitra, the last of Rama's line. Many rites of the Rama's house are decidedly Scythic.

[2] [Lovely maidens.]

Sonigira, as related in the annals.[1] Another version says it was Hamira himself who obtained the enchanted sword, by his incantations to Charani Devi, or the goddess of the bards, whom he worshipped.

The Birth of Kumāra.—We shall conclude this account of the military festival of Mewar with the birth of Kumara, the god of war, taken from the most celebrated of their mythological poems, the Ramayana, probably the most ancient book in the world.[2] "Mena, daughter of Meru, became the spouse of Himavat, from whose union sprung the beauteous Ganga, and her sister Uma. Ganga was sought in marriage by all the celestials; while Uma, after a long life of austerity, was espoused by Rudra."[3] But neither sister was fortunate enough to have offspring, until Ganga became pregnant by Hutasana (regent of fire), and "Kumara, resplendent as the sun, illustrious as the moon, was produced from the side of Ganga." The gods, with Indra at their head, carried him to the Krittikas[4] to be nursed, and he became their joint care. "As he resembled the fire in brightness, he received the name of Skanda, when the immortals, with Agni (fire) at their head, anointed him as general of the armies of the gods."[5]—"Thus (the bard Valmiki speaks), oh! Rama, have I related the story of the production of Kumar."

[1] See p. 317 [Vol. I.].

[2] ["The kernel of the Rāmāyana was composed before 500 B.C., while the more recent portions was probably not added till the second century B.C., and later" (Macdonell, *Hist. Sanskrit Literature*, 309).]

[3] One of the names of the divinity of war, whose images are covered with vermilion in imitation of blood. (*Qy.* the German *roodur*, 'red') [596]. [Rudra, 'the roarer,' originally "god of storms."]

[4] The Pleiades.

[5] The festival of the birth of this son of Ganga, or Jahnavi, is on the 10th of Jeth. Sir W. Jones gives the following couplet from the Sancha: "On the 10th of Jyaishtha, on the bright half of the month, on the day of Mangala,* son of the earth, when the moon was in Hasta, this daughter of Jahnu brought from the rocks, and ploughed over the land inhabited by mortals."

* Mangala is one of the names (and perhaps one of the oldest) of the Hindu Mars (Kumara), to whom the Wodens-dag of the Northmen, the Mardi of the French, the Dies Martis of the Romans, are alike sacred. Mangala also means 'happy,' the reverse of the origin of Mongol, said to mean 'sad' ['brave']. The juxtaposition of the Rajput and Scandinavian days of the week will show that they have the same origin:

This is a very curious relic of ancient mythology, in which we may trace the most material circumstances of the birth of the Roman divinity of war. Kumara (Mars) was the son of Jahnavi (Juno), and born, like the Romans, without sexual intercourse, but by the agency of Vulcan (regent of fire). Kumara has the peacock (sacred to Juno likewise) as his companion; and as the Grecian goddess is feigned to have her car drawn by peacocks, so Kumara (the evil-striker) [1] has a peacock for his steed [596].

Ganga, 'the river goddess,' has some of the attributes of Pallas, being like the Athenian maid (Ganga never married) born from the head of Jove. The bard of the silver age makes her fall from a glacier of Kailasa (Olympus) on the head of the father of the gods, and remain many years within the folds of his tiara (*jata*), until at length being liberated, she was precipitated into the plains of Aryavarta. It was in this escape that she burst her rocky barrier (the Himalaya), and on the birth of Kumara exposed those veins of gold called *jambunadi*, in colour like the jambu fruit, probably alluding to the veins of gold discovered in the rocks of the Ganges in those distant ages.

The Winter Season.—The last day of the month Asoj ushers in the Hindu winter (*sarad rit*). On this day, nothing but white vestments and silver (*chandi*) ornaments are worn, in honour of the moon (Chandra), who gives his [2] name to the

Pale and common drudge
'Tween man and man.

[1] [Kumāra probably means 'easily dying.']

[2] It will be recollected that the moon with the Rajputs as with the Scandinavians is a male divinity. The Tatars, who also consider him a male divinity, pay him especial adoration in this autumnal month.

Rajput.	Scandinavian and Saxon.	Rajput.	Scandinavian and Saxon.
Suryavar	Sun-day.	Brihaspativar (*a*)	Thors-day.
Som, or Induvar	Moon-day.	Sukravar (*b*)	Frey-day.
Budhvar	Tuis-day.	Sani, or Sanichara -var	Satur-day (*c*)
Mangalvar	Wodens-day.		

(*a*) Brihaspati, 'he who rides on the bull'; the steed of the Rajput god of war [probably 'lord of prayer,' or 'of increase,' confounded in the original note with Vrishapati, 'Lord of the bull,' a title of Siva.]

(*b*) Sukra is a Cyclop, regent of the planet Venus.

(*c*) [See Max Müller, *Selected Essays*, 1881, ii. 460 ff.]

This year there was an entire intercalary month : such are called *Laund.* There is a procession of all the chiefs to the Chaugan ; and on their return, a full court is held in the great hall, which breaks up with 'obeisance to the lamp' (*jot ka mujra*), whose light each reverences ; when the candles are lit at home, every Rajput, from the prince to the owner of a "skin (*charsa*) of land," seated on a white linen cloth, should worship his tutelary divinity, and feed the priests with sugar and milk.

Karttika.—This month is peculiarly sacred to Lakshmi, the goddess of wealth, the Juno Moneta of the Romans. The 13th is called the Dhanteras, or thirteenth [day] of wealth, when gold and silver coin are worshipped, as the representatives of the goddess, by her votaries of all classes, but especially by the mercantile [597]. On the 14th, all anoint with oil, and make libations thereof to Yama, the judge of departed spirits. Worship (*puja*) is performed to the lamp, which represents the god of hell, and is thence called Yamadiwa, 'the lamp of Pluto'; and on this day partial illumination takes place throughout the city.

The Diwāli, or Festival of Lamps.—On the Amavas, or Ides of Karttik, is one of the most brilliant fêtes of Rajasthan, called the Diwali, when every city, village, and encampment exhibits a blaze of splendour. The potters' wheels revolve for weeks before solely in the manufacture of lamps (*diwa*), and from the palace to the peasant's hut every one supplies himself with them, in proportion to his means, and arranges them according to his fancy. Stuffs, pieces of gold, and sweetmeats are carried in trays and consecrated at the temple of Lakshmi, the goddess of wealth, to whom the day is consecrated. The Rana on this occasion honours his prime minister with his presence to dinner ; and this chief officer of the State, who is always of the mercantile caste, pours oil into a terra-cotta lamp, which his sovereign holds; the same libation of oil is permitted by each of the near relations of the minister. On this day, it is incumbent upon every votary of Lakshmi to try the chance of the dice, and from their success in the Diwali, the prince, the chief, the merchant, and the artisan foretell the state of their coffers for the ensuing year.

Lakshmi, though on this festival depicted under the type of riches, is evidently the beneficent Annapurna in another garb, for the agricultural community place a corn-measure filled with grain and adorned with flowers as her representative ; or, if they adorn her effigies, they are those of Padma, the water-nymph, with a lotos in one hand, and the *pasa* (or fillet for the head) in the other. As Lakshmi was produced at "the Churning of the Ocean," and hence called one of the "fourteen gems," she is confounded with Rambha, chief of the Apsaras, the Venus of the Hindus. Though both were created from the froth (*sara*) of the waters (*ap*),[1] they are as distinct as the representations of riches and beauty can be. Lakshmi became the wife of Vishnu, or Kanhaiya, and is placed at the feet of his marine couch when he is floating on the chaotic waters. As his consort, she merges into the character of Sarasvati, the goddess of eloquence, and here we have the combination of Minerva and Apollo. As of Minerva, the owl [598] is the attendant of Lakshmi ;[2] and when we reflect that the Egyptians, who furnished the Grecian pantheon, held these solemn festivals, also called "the feast of lamps," in honour of Minerva at Sais, we may deduce the origin of this grand Oriental festival from that common mother-country in Central Asia, whence the Diwali radiated to remote China, the Nile, the Ganges, and the shores of the Tigris ; for the Shab-i-barat of Islam is but "the feast of lamps" of the Rajputs. In all these there is a mixture of the attributes of Ceres and Proserpine, of Plutus and Pluto. Lakshmi partakes of the attributes of both the first, while Kuvera,[3] who is conjoined with her, is Plutus : as Yama is Pluto, the infernal judge. The consecrated lamps and the libations of oil are all dedicated to him ; and "torches and flaming brands are likewise kindled and consecrated, to burn the bodies of kinsmen who may be dead in battle in a foreign land, and light them through the shades of death to the mansion of Yama."[4]

Festival of Yama.—To the infernal god Yama, who is "the son of the sun," the second day following the Amavas, or Ides of Karttika, is also sacred ; it is called the Bhratri dvitiya, or 'the brothers' second,' because the river-goddess Yamuna on this day

[1] [Apsaras means 'going in the waters, or in the waters of the clouds.']

[2] [The owl is a bird of ill omen, and does not seem to be associated with Lakshmi except in Bengal.]

[3] The Hindu god of riches.

[4] Yamala is the great god of the Finlanders (Clarke).

entertained her brother (*bhratri*) Yama, and is therefore consecrated to fraternal affection. At the hour of curfew (*godhuli*),[1] when the cattle return from the fields, the cow is worshipped, the herd having been previously tended. From this ceremony no rank is exempted on the preceding day, dedicated to Krishna: prince and peasant all become pastoral attendants on the cow, as the form of Prithivi,[2] or the earth.

The Annakūta Festival.—The 1st (Sudi), or 16th of Karttika, is the grand festival of Annakuta, sacred to the Hindu Ceres, which will be described with its solemnities at Nathdwara. There is a State procession, horse-races, and elephant-fights at the Chaugan; the evening closes with a display of fireworks.

The Jaljātra Festival.—The 14th (Sudi), or 29th, is another solemn festival in honour of Vishnu. It is called the Jaljatra, from being performed on the water (*jal*). The Rana, chiefs, ministers, and citizens go in procession to the lake, and adore the "spirit of the waters," on which floating lights are placed, and the whole surface is illuminated by a grand display of pyrotechny. On this day "Vishnu rises from his slumber of four [599] months";[3] a figurative expression to denote the sun's emerging from the cloudy months of the periodical flood.

The Makara Sankrānti Festival.—The next day (the Punim, or last day of Karttika), being the Makara sankranti, or autumnal equinox, when the sun enters the zodiacal sign Makara,[4] or Pisces, the Rana and chiefs proceed in state to the Chaugan, and play at ball on horseback. The entire last half of the month Karttika, from Amavas (the Ides) to the Punim, is sacred to Vishnu; who is declared by the Puranas to represent the sun, and whose worship, that of water, and the floating-lights placed thereon—all objects emblematic of fecundity—carry us back to the point whence we started—the adoration of the powers of nature: clearly proving all mythology to be universally founded on an astronomical basis.

[1] From *go*, 'a cow' [*dhūli*, 'the dust raised by them as they return to the stall'].

[2] See anecdote in Chap. 21, which elucidates this practice of princes becoming herdsmen.

[3] Matsya Purana. [Vishnu is generally said to wake on the Deothān, 11th light half of Kārttik.]

[4] [Makara, a kind of shark or sea-monster, marks the 10th sign of the Zodiac, Capricorn.]

Mitra Saptami, Bhāskara Saptami Festivals.—In the remaining months of Aghan, or Margsir, and Pus, there are no festivals in which a state procession takes place, though in each there are marked days, kept not only by the Rajputs, but generally by the Hindu nation; especially that on the 7th of Aghan, which is called Mitra Saptami, or 7th of Mithras, and like the Bhaskara Saptami or the 7th of Magha, is sacred to the sun as a form of Vishnu. On this seventh day occurred the descent of the river-goddess (Ganga) from the foot of Vishnu; or the genius of fertilization, typified under the form of the river-goddess, proceeding from the sun, the vivifying principle, and impended over the head of Iswara, the divinity presiding over generation, in imitation of which his votary pours libations of water (if possible from the sacred river Ganga) over his emblem, the lingam or phallus: a comparison which is made by the bard Chand in an invocation to this god, for the sake of contrasting his own inferiority "to the mighty bards of old."

"The head of Is [1] is in the skies; on his crown falls the ever-flowing stream (Ganga); but on his statue below, does not his votary pour the fluid from his *patra*?"

Phallicism.—No satisfactory etymology has ever been assigned for the phallic emblem of generation, adored by Egyptian, Greek, Roman, and even by the Christian, which may be from the same primeval language that formed the Sanskrit.

Phalisa is the 'fructifier,' from *phala*, 'fruit,' and *Isa*, 'the god.' [2] Thus the type of Osiris can have a definite interpretation, still wanting to the lingam of Iswara [600]. Both deities presided over the streams which fertilized the countries in which they received divine honours: Osiris over the Nile, from 'the mountains of the moon,' in Ethiopia,[3] Iswara over the Indus [4] (also called the Nil), and the Ganges from Chandragiri, 'the mountains of the moon,' on a peak of whose glaciers he has his throne.

[1] Iswara, Isa, or as pronounced, Is.

[2] [Monier-Williams in his *Sanskrit Dict.* records no such form as *phalīsa*. φαλλός = Lat. *palus*, English *pole*, *pale*. The Author follows Wilford (*Asiatic Researches*, iii. 135 f.).]

[3] 'The land of the sun' (*aditya*). [This is impossible. The true derivation is unknown; to the Greeks the word meant 'swarthy-faced.']

[4] Ferishta calls the Indus the Nilab, or 'blue waters'; it is also called Abusin, the 'father of streams.'

Siva and the Sun.—Siva occasionally assumes the attributes of the sun-god; they especially appertain to Vishnu, who alone is styled "immortal, the one, creator, and uncreated"; and in whom centre all the qualities (*gunan*), which have peopled the Hindu pantheon with their ideal representatives. The bard Chand, who has embodied the theological tenets of the Rajputs in his prefatory invocation to every divinity who can aid his intent, apostrophizes Ganesa, and summons the goddess of eloquence (Sarasvati) "to make his tongue her abode"; deprecates the destroying power, "him whom wrath inhabits," lest he should be cut off ere his book was finished; and lauding distinctly each member of the triad (*trimurti*), he finishes by declaring them one, and that "whoever believes them separate, hell will be his portion." Of this One the sun is the great visible type, adored under a variety of names, as Surya, Mitra, Bhaskar, Vivasvat, Vishnu, Kaṛna, or Kana, likewise an Egyptian epithet for the sun.[1]

The emblem of Vishnu is Garuda, or the eagle,[2] and the Sun-god both of the Egyptians and Hindus is typified with the bird's head. Aruna (the dawn), brother of Garuda, is classically styled the charioteer of Vishnu, whose two sons, Sampati and Jatayu, attempting in imitation of their father to reach the sun, the wings of the former were burnt and he fell to the earth: of this the Greeks may have made their fable of Icarus.[3]

Festivals in Honour of Vishnu.—In the chief zodiacal phenomena, observation will discover that Vishnu is still the object of worship. The Phuladola,[4] or Floralia, in the vernal equinox, is so called from the image of Vishnu being carried in a *dola*, or ark, covered with garlands of flowers (*phula*). Again, in the month of Asarh, the commencement of [601] the periodical rains, which

[1] According to Diodorus Siculus. [Rudra-Siva has a benign side to his character, and may be associated with the Sun (R. G. Bhandarkar, *Vaisnavism, Saivism and Minor Religious Systems*, 105). But the Author, in his constant references to "Bāl"-Siva, has pressed this conception to an excessive length.]

[2] The vulture and crane, which soar high in the heavens, are also called *garuda*, and vulgarly *gidh*. The ibis is of the crane or heron kind.

[3] Phaeton was the son of Cephalus and Aurora. The former answers to the Hindu bird-headed messenger of the sun. Aruna is the Aurora of the Greeks, who with more taste have given the dawn a female character.

[4] Also called Dolayatra.

date from the summer solstice, the image of Vishnu is carried on a car, and brought forth on the first appearance of the moon, the 11th of which being the solstice, is called "the night of the gods." Then Vishnu reposes on his serpent-couch until the cessation of the flood on the 11th of Bhadon, when "he turns on his side." [1]

The 4th is also dedicated to Vishnu under his infantine appellation Hari (Ἥλιος), because when a child "he hid himself in the moon." We must not derogate from Sir W. Jones the merit of drawing attention to the analogy between these Hindu festivals on the equinoxes, and the Egyptian, called the entrance of Osiris into the moon, and his confinement in an ark. But that distinguished writer merely gives the hint, which the learned Bryant aids us to pursue, by bringing modern travellers to corroborate the ancient authorities: the drawings of Pocock from the sun temple of Luxor to illustrate Plutarch, Curtius, and Diodorus. Bryant comes to the same conclusion with regard to Osiris enclosed in the ark, which we adopt regarding Vishnu's repose during the four months of inundation, the period of fertilization. I have already, in the rites of Annapurna, the Isis of the Egyptians, noticed the crescent form of the ark of Osiris, as well as the ram's-head ornaments indicative of the vernal equinox, which the Egyptians called Phamenoth, being the birthday of Osiris, or the sun; the Phag, or Phalgun month of the Hindus; the Phagesia of the Greeks, sacred to Dionysus.[2]

The Argonauts.—The expedition of Argonauts in search of the golden fleece is a version of the arkite worship of Osiris, the Dolayatra of the Hindus: and Sanskrit etymology, applied to the vessel of the Argonauts, will give the sun (*argha*) god's (*natha*) entrance into the sign of the Ram. The Tauric and Hydra foes, with which Jason had to contend before he obtained the fleece of Aries, are the symbols of the sun-god, both of the Ganges and the Nile; and this fable, which has occupied almost every pen of antiquity, is clearly astronomical, as the names alone of the

[1] Bhagavat and Matsya Puranas. See Sir W. Jones on the lunar year of the Hindus, *Asiatic Researches*, vol. iii. p. 286.

[2] [Mr. F. Ll. Griffith tells me that this comes from a French translation of Plutarch, *De Iside et Osiride*, cap. xii. (birth of Osiris on the first of the epagomenal days). This entry of Osiris into the moon seems to mean his conception rather than his birth. Φαμενώθ is the name of the seventh month, about 25th February.]

Arghanath, sons of Apollo, Mars, Mercury, Sol, Arcus or Argus,[1] Jupiter, Bacchus, etc., sufficiently testify, whose voyage is entirely celestial.

Egyptian Influence on Hindu Mythology.—If it be destined that any portion of the veil which covers these ancient mysteries [602], connecting those of the Ganges with the Nile, shall be removed, it will be from the interpretation of the expedition of Rama, hitherto deemed almost as allegorical as that of the Arghanaths. I shall at once assume an opinion I have long entertained, that the western coast of the Red Sea was the Lanka of the memorable exploit in the history of the Hindus. If Alexander from the mouths of the Indus ventured to navigate those seas with his frail fleet of barks constructed in the Panjab, what might we not expect from the resources of the King of Kosala, the descendant of Sagara, emphatically called the sea-king, whose " 60,000 sons " were so many mariners, and who has left his name as a memorial of his marine power at the island (*Sagar*) at the embouchure of the main arm of the Ganges, and to the ocean itself, also called Sagara? If the embarkation of Ramesa and his heroes for the redemption of Sita had been from the Gulph of Cutch, the grand emporium from the earliest ages, the voyage of Rama would have been but the prototype of that of the Macedonians; but local tradition has sanctified Rameswaram, the southern part of the peninsula, as the rendezvous of his armament. The currents in the Straits of Manar, curiosity, or a wish to obtain auxiliaries from this insular kingdom, may have prompted the visit to Ceylon; and hence the vestiges there found of this event. But even from this " utmost isle, Taprobane," the voyage across the Erythrean Sea is only twenty-five degrees of longitude, which with a flowing sail they would run down in ten or twelve days. The only difficulty which occurs is in the synchronical existence of Rama and the Pharaoh[2] of Moses, which would tend to the opposite of my hypothesis, and show that India received her Phallic rites, her architecture, and symbolic mythology from the Nile, instead of planting them there.

" Est-ce l'Inde, la Phénicie, l'Éthiopie, la Chaldée, ou l'Égypte,

[1] *Arka*, 'the sun,' in Sanskrit. [This is due to Wilford (*Asiatic Researches*, iii. 134) and is, of course, impossible.]

[2] Pha-ra is but a title, 'the king.' [Egyptian Pr'o, 'the great house.']

qui a vu naître ce culte ? ou bien le type en a-t-il été fourni aux habitans de ces contrées, par une nation plus ancienne encore ? " asks an ingenious but anonymous French author, on the origin of the Phallic worship.[1] Ramesa, chief of the Suryas, or sun-born race, was king of the city designated from his mother, Kausalya, of which Ayodhya was the capital. His sons were Lava and Kusa, who originated the races we may term the Lavites and Kushites, or Kushwas of India.[2] Was then Kausalya [603] the mother of Ramesa, a native of Aethiopia,[3] or Kusadwipa, 'the land of Cush'? Rama and Krishna are both painted blue (*nila*), holding the lotus, emblematic of the Nile. Their names are often identified. Ram-Krishna, the bird-headed divinity, is painted as the messenger of each, and the historians of both were contemporaries. That both were real princes there is no doubt, though Krishna assumed to be an incarnation of Vishnu, as Rama was of the sun. Of Rama's family was Trisankha,[4] mother of the great apostle of Buddha, whose symbol was the serpent; and the followers of Buddha assert that Krishna and this apostle, whose statues are facsimiles of those of Memnon, were cousins. Were the Hermetic creed and Phallic rites therefore received from the Ethiopic Cush? Could emblematic relics be discovered in the caves of the Troglodytes, who inhabited the range of mountains on the Cushite shore of the Arabian straits, akin to those of Ellora and Elephanta,[5] whose style discloses physical, mythological, as well as architectural affinity to the Egyptian, the question would at once be set at rest.

I have derived the Phallus from Phalisa, the chief fruit. The Greeks, who either borrowed it from the Egyptians or had it from the same source, typified the Fructifier by a pineapple, the

[1] *Des divinités génératives: ou du culte du Phallus chez les anciens et les modernes* (Paris).

[2] Of the former race the Ranas of Mewar, of the latter the princes of Narwar and Amber, are the representatives.

[3] Aethiopia, 'the country of the sun'; from *Ait*, contraction of Aditya. Aegypt may have the same etymology, *Aitia* [see p. 699 above].

[4] [The Author may refer to Pārsvanātha, 23rd Jain Tīrthakara, whose symbol was his serpent; but his mother was Vāmadevi. Trisala was mother of the 24th Tīrthakara, Mahāvira or Vardhamāna, but his cognizance was a lion.]

[5] It is absurd to talk of these being modern; decipher the characters thereon, and then pronounce their antiquity. [Ellora, 5th to 9th or 10th centuries A.D.; Elephanta, 8th to 10th (*IGI*, xii. 22, 4).]

form of which resembles the Sitaphala,[1] or fruit of Sita, whose rape by Ravana carried Rama from the Ganges over many countries ere he recovered her.[2] In like manner Gauri, the Rajput Ceres, is typified under the coco-nut, or sriphala,[3] the chief of fruit, or fruit sacred to Sri, or Isa (Isis), whose other elegant emblem of abundance, the kamakumbha, is drawn with branches of the palmyra,[4] or coco-tree, gracefully pendent from the vase (*kumbha*).

The Sriphala [5] is accordingly presented to all the votaries of Iswara and Isa on the conclusion of the spring-festival of Phalguna, the Phagesia of the Greeks, the [604] Phamenoth of the Egyptian, and the Saturnalia of antiquity; a rejoicing at the renovation of the powers of nature; the empire of heat over cold—of light over darkness.[6]

[1] Vulg. *Sharifa.*

[2] Rama subjected her to the fiery ordeal, to discover whether her virtue had suffered while thus forcibly separated.

[3] Vulg. *Nariyal.*

[4] Palmyra is Sanskrit corrupted, and affords the etymology of Solomon's city of the desert, Tadmor. The ث p, by the retrenchment of a single diacritical point, becomes ت t; and the ل (*l*) and د (*d*) being permutable, Pal becomes Tad, or Tal—the Palmyra, which is the Mor, or chief of trees; hence Tadmor, from its date-trees [?].

[5] The Jayaphala, 'the fruit of victory,' is the nutmeg; or, as a native of Java, Javuphala, 'fruit of Java,' is most probably derived from Jayadiva, 'the victorious isle.' [The nutmeg is Jātiphala: Java is *yavadwīpa*, 'island of barley.']

[6] The Kamari of the Saura tribes, or sun-worshippers of Saurashtra, claims descent from the bird-god of Vishnu (who aided Rama * to the discovery of Sita), and the Makara † or crocodile, and date the monstrous conception from that event, and their original abode from Sankodra Bet, or island of Sankodra. Whether to the Dioscorides at the entrance of the Arabian Gulf this name was given, evidently corrupted from Sankhadwara to Socotra, we shall not stop to inquire. Like the isle in the entrance of the Gulf of Cutch, it is the *dwara* or portal to the Sinus Arabicus, and the pearl-shell (*sankha*) there abounds. This tribe deduce their origin from Rama's expedition, and allege that their Icthyiopic mother landed them where they still reside. Wild as is this fable, it adds support to this hypothesis. [The Sanskrit name of Bet Island ("Bate" in the text) is Sankhuddhāra, from the conch fishery. Socotra is Dwīpa Sukhadāra, 'island of pleasure' (not Sakhādāra, as in *EB*, xxv. 355) (Yule, *Marco Polo*, 1st ed. ii. 342).]

---

* Rama and Vishnu interchange characters.

† It is curious that the designation of the tribe Kamar is a transposition of Makar, for the final letter of each is mute.

The analogy between the goddess of the spring Saturnalia, Phalguni, and the Phagesia of the Greeks, will excite surprise; the word is not derived from (φαγεῖν) eating, with the Rajput votaries of Holika, as with those of the Dionysia of the Greeks; but from *phalguni*, compounded of *guna*, 'quality, virtue, or characteristic,' and *phala*, 'fruit'; in short, the fructifier. From φαλλός,[1] to which there is no definite meaning, the Egyptian had the festival Phallica, the Holika of the Hindus. *Phula* and *phala*, flower and fruit, are the roots of all, Floralia and Phalaria, the Phallus of Osiris, the Thyrsus of Bacchus, or Lingam of Iswara, symbolized by the *Sriphala*, or *Ananas*, the 'food of the gods,'[2] or the Sitaphala of the Helen of Ayodhya.

From the existence of this worship in Congo at this day, the author already quoted asks if it may not have originated in Ethiopia, "qui, comme le témoignent plusieurs écrivains de l'antiquité, a fourni ses dieux à l'Égypte." On the first of the five complementary days called "ἐπαγόμεναι ἡμέραι" preceding New Year's Day, the Egyptians celebrated the birth of the sun-god Osiris, in a similar manner as the Hindus do their solstitial festival, "the morning of the gods," the Hiul of Scandinavia; on which occasion, "on promenait en procession une figure d'Osiris, dont le Phallus était triple"; a number, he adds, expressing "la pluralité indéfinie." The number three is sacred to Iswara, chief of the Trimurti or Triad, whose statue adorns the junction (*sangam*) of all triple streams; hence called Triveni, who is [605] Trinetra, or 'three-eyed,' and Tridanta, or 'god of the trident'; Triloka, 'god of the triple abode, heaven, earth, and hell'; Tripura, of the triple city, to whom the Tripoli or triple gates are sacred, and of which he has made Ganesa the Janitor, or guardian. The grotesque figure placed by the Hindus during the Saturnalia in the highways, and called Nathurama

[1] See Lempriere, arts. *Phagesia* and *Phallica*. "L'Abbé Mignot pense que le *Phallus* est originaire de l'Assyrie et de la Chaldée, et que c'est de ce pays que l'usage de consacrer ce symbole de la génération a passé en Égypte. Il croit, d'après le savant Le Clerc, que le nom de ce symbole est phénicien: qu'il dérive de *Phalou* qui, dans cette langue, signifie une *chose secrète* et *cachée*, et du verbe *phala*, qui veut dire *être tenu secret*." *

[2] *Anna*, 'food,' and *asa* or *isa*, 'the god.' [Ananas comes from Brazilian *Nana* or *Nanas* (Yule, *Hobson-Jobson*, 2nd ed. 25).]

* *Des divinités génératives.*

(the god Rama), is the counterpart of the figure described by Plutarch as representing Osiris, "ce soleil printanier," in the Egyptian Saturnalia or Phamenoth. Even Ramisa and Ravana may, like Osiris and Typhon, be merely the ideal representatives of light and darkness; and the chaste Sita, spouse of the Surya prince, the astronomical Virgo, only a zodiacal sign.[1]

Wide Extension of Hindu Mythology.—That a system of Hinduism pervaded the whole Babylonian and Assyrian empires, Scripture furnishes abundant proofs, in the mention of the various types of the sun-god Balnath, whose pillar adorned "every mount" and "every grove"; and to whose other representative, the brazen calf (*nandi*), the 15th of each month (*amavas*)[2] was especially sacred. It was not confined to these celebrated regions of the East, but was disseminated throughout the earth; because from the Aral to the Baltic, colonies were planted from that central region,[3] the cradle of the Suryas and the Indus, whose branches (*sakha*),[4] the Yavan, the Aswa, and the Meda, were the progenitors of the Ionians, the Assyrians, and the Medes;[5] while in later times, from the same teeming region, the Galati and Getae,[6] the Kelts and Goths, carried modifications of the system to the shores of Armorica and the Baltic, the cliffs of Caledonia, and the remote isles of the German Ocean. The monumental circles sacred to the sun-god Belenus at once existing in that central region,[7] in India,[8] and throughout Europe, is

[1] [It is unnecessary to discuss these theories, which are based on incorrect assumptions and obsolete etymologies.]

[2] The Hindus divide the month into two portions called *pakh* or fortnights. The first is termed *badi*, reckoning from the 1st to the 15th, which day of partition is called *amavas*, answering to the Ides of the Romans, and held by the Hindus as it was by the Jews in great sanctity. The last division is termed *sudi*, and they recommence with the initial numeral, thence to the 30th or completion, called *punim*; thus instead of the 16th, 17th, etc., of the month, they say *Sudi ekam* (1st), *Sudi duj* (3rd).

[3] Sogdiana and Transoxiana.

[4] Hence the word Saka [?].

[5] See Genealogical Table No. 2 for these names. The sons of the three Midas, pronounced Mede, founded kingdoms at the precise point of time, according to calculation from the number of kings, that Assyria was founded.

[6] The former were more pastoral, and hence the origin of their name, corrupted to Keltoi. The Getae or Jats pursued the hunter's occupation, living more by the chase, though these occupations are generally conjoined in the early stages of civilization.

[7] Rubruquis and other travellers.

[8] Colonel Mackenzie's invaluable and gigantic collection.

conclusive. The apotheosis of the patriarch Noah, whom the Hindu styles Manu-Vaivaswata, '*the* man, son of the sun,' may have originated the Dolayatra of the Hindus, the ark of Osiris [606], the ship of Isis amongst the Suevi, in memory of "the forty days" noticed in the traditions of every nation of the earth.

The time may be approaching when this worship in the East, like the Egyptian, shall be only matter of tradition; although this is not likely to be effected by such summary means as were adopted by Cambyses, who slew the sacred Apis and whipped his priests, while their Greek and Roman conquerors adopted and embellished the Pantheon of the Nile.[1] But when Christianity reared her severe yet simple form, the divinities of the Nile, the Pantheon of Rome, and the Acropolis of Athens, could not abide her awful majesty. The temples of the Alexandrian Serapis were levelled by Theophilus,[2] while that of Osiris at Memphis became a church of Christ. "Muni de ses pouvoirs, et escorté d'une foule de moines, il mit en fuite les prêtres, brisa les idoles, démolit les temples, ou y établit des monastères."[3] The period for thus subverting idolatry is passed: the religion of Christ is not of the sword, but one enjoining peace and goodwill on earth. But as from him "to whom much is given," much will be required, the good and benevolent of the Hindu nations may have ulterior advantages over those Pharisees who would make a monopoly even of the virtues; who "see the mote in their neighbour's eye, but cannot discern the beam in their own." While, therefore, we strive to impart a purer taste and better faith, let us not imagine that the minds of those we would reform are the seats of impurity, because, in accordance with an idolatry coeval with the flood, they continue to worship mysteries opposed to our own modes of thinking [607].

[1] Isis and Osiris, Serapis and Canopus, Apis and Ibis, adopted by the Romans, whose temples and images, yet preserved, will allow full scope to the Hindu antiquary for analysis of both systems. The temple of Serapis at Pozzuoli is quite Hindu in its ground plan.

[2] In the reign of Theodosius.

[3] *Du Culte*, etc., etc., p. 47.

CHAPTER 23

The Character of the Rājput. Influence of Custom.—The manners of a nation constitute the most interesting portion of its history, but a thorough knowledge of them must be the fruit of long and attentive observation: an axiom which applies to a people even less inaccessible than the Rajputs. The importance and necessity of such an illustration of the Rajput character, in a work like the present, call for and sanction the attempt, however inadequate the means. Of what value to mankind would be the interminable narrative of battles, were their moral causes and results passed by unheeded? Although both the Persian and Hindu annalists not unfrequently unite the characters of moralist and historian, it is in a manner unsuitable to the subject, according to the more refined taste of Europe. In the poetic annals of the Rajput, we see him check his war-chariot, and when he should be levelling his javelin, commence a discourse upon ethics; or when the battle is over, the Nestor or Ulysses of the host converts his tent into a lyceum, and delivers lectures on morals or manners. But the reflections which should follow, and form the corollary to each action, are never given; and even if they were, though we might comprehend the moral movements of a nation, we should still be unable to catch the minute shades of character that complete the picture of domestic life, and which are to be collected from those familiar sentiments uttered in social intercourse, when the mind unbends and nature throws aside the trammels of education and of ceremony. Such a picture would represent the manners, which are continually undergoing modifications, in contradistinction to the morals of society; the latter, having a fixed creed for their basis, are definite and unchangeable. The *chal* of the Rajput, like the *mores* of the Romans, or *costumi* of modern Italy, is significant alike of mental and external habit. In the moral point of view it is the path chalked out for him by the sages of antiquity [608]; in the personal, it is that which custom has rendered immutable. *Kaisi buri chal men chalta*, 'in what a bad path does he march!' says the moralist: *Bap, Dada ki chal chhori*, 'he abandons the usages of his ancestors,' says the stickler for custom, in Rajasthan.[1]

Rājput Morals.—The grand features of morality are few, and nearly the same in every nation not positively barbarous. The principles contained in the Decalogue form the basis of every code—of Manu and of Muhammad, as well as of Moses. These are grand landmarks of the truth of divine history; and are confirmed by the less important traits of personal customs and religious rites, which nations the most remote from each other continue to hold in common. The Koran we know to have been founded on the Mosaic law; the Sastra of Manu, unconsciously, approaches still more to the Jewish Scriptures in spirit and intention; and from its pages might be formed a manual of moral instruction, which, if followed by the disciples of the framer, might put more favoured societies to the blush.

Variety of Customs due to Environment.—As it has been observed in a former part of this work, the same religion governing all must tend to produce a certain degree of mental uniformity. The shades of moral distinction which separate these races are almost imperceptible: while you cannot pass any grand natural barrier without having the dissimilarity of customs and manners forced upon your observation. Whoever passes from upland Mewar, the country of the Sesodias, into the sandy flats of Marwar, the abode of the Rathors, would feel the force of this remark. Innovations proceeding from external causes, such as conquest by irreligious foes, and the birth of new sects and schisms, operate important changes in manners and customs. We can only pretend, however, to describe facts which are obvious, and those which history discloses, whence some notions may be formed of the prevailing traits of character in the Rajput; his ideas of virtue and vice, the social intercourse and familiar courtesies of Rajasthan, and their recreations, public and private.

"The manners of a people," says the celebrated Goguet, "always bear a proportion to the progress they have made in the arts and sciences." If by this test we trace the analogy between past and existing manners amongst the Rajputs, we must conclude at once that they have undergone a decided

[1] ["The custom handed down in regular succession since time immemorial among the four chief castes and the mixed races of that country, is called the conduct of virtuous men" (Manu, *Laws*, ii. 18).]

PORTRAITS OF A RĀJPUTNI, A RĀJPUT, A MEWĀTI AND GUSĀIN.

To face page 708.

deterioration. Where can we look for sages like those whose systems of philosophy were the [609] prototypes of those of Greece: to whose works Plato, Thales, and Pythagoras were disciples? Where shall we find the astronomers, whose knowledge of the planetary system yet excites wonder in Europe, as well as the architects and sculptors, whose works claim our admiration, and the musicians, "who could make the mind oscillate from joy to sorrow, from tears to smiles, with the change of modes and varied intonation." [1] The manners of those days must have corresponded with this advanced stage of refinement, as they must have suffered from its decline: yet the homage paid by Asiatics to precedent has preserved many relics of ancient customs, which have survived the causes that produced them.

Treatment of Women by the Rājputs.—It is universally admitted that there is no better criterion of the refinement of a nation than the condition of the fair sex therein. As it is elegantly expressed by Comte Ségur, "Leur sort est un boussole sûr pour le premier regard d'un étranger qui arrive dans un pays inconnu." [2] Unfortunately, the habitual seclusion of the higher classes of females in the East contracts the sphere of observation in regard to their influence on society; but, to borrow again from our ingenious author, "les hommes font les lois, les femmes font les mœurs"; and their incarceration in Rajasthan by no means lessens the application of the adage to that country. Like the magnetic power, however latent, their attraction is not the less certain. "C'est aux hommes à faire des grandes choses, c'est aux femmes à les inspirer," is a maxim to which every Rajput cavalier would subscribe, with whom the age of chivalry is not fled, though ages of oppression have passed over him. He knows there is no retreat into which the report of a gallant action will not penetrate, and set fair hearts in motion to be the object of his search. The bards, those chroniclers of fame, like the Jongleurs of old, have everywhere access, to the palace as to the hamlet; and a brilliant exploit travels with all the rapidity of a comet, and clothed with the splendid decorations of poetry, from the

[1] So says Valmiki, the author of the oldest epic in existence, the Ramayana [see p. 693 above].

[2] *Les Femmes, leur condition et leur influence dans l'ordre social,* vol. i. p. 10.

Indian desert to the valley of the Jumna. If we cannot paint the Rajput dame as invested with all the privileges which Ségur assigns to the first woman, " compagne de l'homme et son égale, vivant par lui, pour lui, associée à son bonheur, à ses plaisirs, à la puissance qu'il exerçait sur ce vaste univers," she is far removed from the condition which demands commiseration [610].

The Seclusion of Women.—Like the ancient German or Scandinavian, the Rajput consults her in every transaction; from her ordinary actions he draws the omen of success, and he appends to her name the epithet of *devi*, or 'godlike.' The superficial observer, who applies his own standard to the customs of all nations, laments with an affected philanthropy the degraded condition of the Hindu female, in which sentiment he would find her little disposed to join. He particularly laments her want of liberty, and calls her seclusion imprisonment. Although I cordially unite with Ségur, who is at issue with his compatriot Montesquieu on this part of discipline, yet from the knowledge I do possess of the freedom, the respect, the happiness, which Rajput women enjoy, I am by no means inclined to deplore their state as one of captivity. The author of the *Spirit of Laws*, with the views of a closet philosopher, deems seclusion necessary from the irresistible influence of climate on the passions; while the chivalrous Ségur, with more knowledge of human nature, draws the very opposite conclusion, asserting all restraints to be injurious to morals. Of one thing we are certain, seclusion of females could only originate in a moderately advanced stage of civilization. Amongst hunters, pastors, and cultivators, the women were required to aid in all external pursuits, as well as internal economy. The Jews secluded not their women, and the well, where they assembled to draw water, was the place where marriages were contracted, as with the lower classes in Rajputana. The inundations of the Nile, each house of whose fertile valleys was isolated, is said to have created habits of secluding women with the Egyptians; and this argument might apply to the vast valleys of the Indus and Ganges first inhabited, and which might have diffused example with the spread of population. Assuredly, if India was colonized from the cradle of nations, Central Asia, they did not thence bring these notions within the Indus; for the Scythian women went to the opposite extreme, and were polyandrists.[1] The desire of eradicating those impure habits, described by Herodotus, that the slipper at the tent-door should no longer be a sign, may have originated the opposite extreme in a life of entire seclusion. Both polygamy and polyandry originated in a mistaken view of the animal economy, and of the first great command to people the earth: the one was general amongst all the nations [611] of antiquity; the other rare, though to be found in Scythia, India, and even amongst the Natchez, in the new world; but never with the Rajput, with whom monogamy existed during the patriarchal ages of India, as amongst the Egyptians.[2] Of all the nations of the world who have habituated the female to a restricted intercourse with society, whether Grecian, Roman, Egyptian, or Chinese, the Rajput has given least cause to provoke the sentiment of pity; for if deference and respect be proofs of civilization, Rajputana must be considered as redundant in evidence of it. The uxoriousness of the Rajput might be appealed to as indicative of the decay of national morals; "chez les barbares (says Ségur) les femmes ne sont rien: les mœurs de ces peuples s'adoucissent-t'-elles, on compte les femmes pour quelque chose: enfin, se corrompent-elles, les femmes sont tout"; and whether from this decay, or the more probable and amiable cause of seeking, in their society, consolation for the loss of power and independence, the women are nearly everything with the Rajput.

It is scarcely fair to quote Manu as an authority for the proper treatment of the fair sex, since many of his dicta by no means tend to elevate their condition. In his lengthened catalogue of things pure and impure he says, however, "The mouth of a woman is constantly pure,"[3] and he ranks it with the running waters and the sunbeam; he suggests that their names should be "agreeable, soft, clear, captivating the fancy, auspicious, ending in long vowels, resembling words of benediction."[4]

[1] So are some of the Hindu races in the mountainous districts about the Himalaya, and in other parts of India. This curious trait in ancient manners is deserving of investigation: it might throw some light on the early history of the world. [" Each man has but one wife, yet all the women are held in common: for this is a custom of the Massagetae, and not of the Scythians, as the Greeks wrongly say" (Herodotus i. 216). For polyandry in India see Risley, *The People of India*, 2nd ed. 206 ff.]

[2] [Polygamy does to some extent prevail (*Census Report, Rājputāna*, 1911, i. 157 f.)]

[3] *Laws*, v. 130.

[4] *Ibid.* ii. 33.

"Where females are honoured" (says Manu), "there the deities are pleased; but where dishonoured, there all religious rites become useless": and he declares, "that in whatever house a woman not duly honoured pronounces an imprecation, that house, with all that belongs to it, shall utterly perish." [1] "Strike not, even with a blossom, a wife guilty of a hundred faults," [2] says another sage: a sentiment so delicate, that Reginald de Born, the prince of troubadours, never uttered any more refined.

However exalted the respect of the Rajput for the fair, he nevertheless holds that

> Nothing lovelier can be found
> In woman, than to study household good [612].

The Chief of Sādri and his Wife.—In the most tempestuous period of the history of Mewar, when the Ranas broke asunder the bonds which united them to the other chiefs of Rajasthan, and bestowed their daughters on the foreign nobles incorporated with the higher class of their own kin, the chief of Sadri, so often mentioned, had obtained a princess to wife. There was a hazard to domestic happiness in such unequal alliance, which the lord

[1] *Digest of Hindu Law*, Colebrooke, vol. ii. p. 209 [Manu iii. 55-8].

[2] Of all the religions which have diversified mankind, whatever man might select, woman should choose the Christian. This alone gives her just rank in the scale of creation, whether arising from the demotic principle which pervades our faith, or the dignity conferred on the sex in being chosen to be the mother of the Saviour of man. In turning over the pages of Manu we find many mortifying texts, which I am inclined to regard as interpolations; as the following, so opposed to the beautiful sentiment above quoted: "A wife, a son, a servant, a pupil, and a younger brother, may be corrected when they commit faults with a rope, or the small thong of a cane" [viii. 299]. Such texts might lead us to adopt Ségur's conclusions, that ever since the days of the patriarchs women were only brilliant slaves—victims, who exhibited, in the wreaths and floral coronets which bedecked them, the sacrifices to which they were destined. In the patriarchal ages their occupations were to season the viands, and bake the bread, and weave cloth for the tents: their recreations limited to respire the fresh evening air under the shade of a fig tree, and sing canticles to the Almighty. Such a fate, indeed, must appear to a Parisian dame, who passes her time between the Feydeau and Tivoli, and whose daily promenade is through the Champs Élysées, worse than death: yet there is no positive hardships in these employments, and it was but the fair division of labour in the primitive ages, and that which characterizes the Rajputni of the present day.

of Sadri soon experienced. To the courteous request, "Ranawatji, fill me a cup of water," he received a contemptuous refusal, with the remark, that "The daughter of a hundred kings would not become cup-bearer to the chieftain of Sadri."—"Very well," replied the plain soldier, "you may return to your father's house, if you can be of no use in mine." A messenger was instantly sent to the court, and the message, with every aggravation, was made known; and she followed on the heels of her messenger. A summons soon arrived for the Sadri chief to attend his sovereign at the capital. He obeyed; and arrived in time to give his explanation just as the Rana was proceeding to hold a full court. As usual, the Sadri chief was placed on his sovereign's right hand, and when the court broke up, the heir-apparent of Mewar, at a preconcerted sign, stood at the edge of the carpet, performing the menial office of holding the slippers of the chief. Shocked at such a mark of extreme respect, he stammered forth some words of homage, his unworthiness, etc.; to which the Rana replied, "As my son-in-law, no distinction too great can be conferred: take home your wife, she will never again refuse you a cup of water" [613].[1]

Could authority deemed divine ensure obedience to what is considered a virtue in all ages and countries, the conjugal duties of the Rajputs are comprehended in the following simple text: "Let mutual fidelity continue to death; this, in few words, may be considered as the supreme law between husband and wife."[2]

Devotion of Rājput Women.—That this law governed the

[1] Manu lays down some plain and wholesome rules for the domestic conduct of the wife; above all, he recommends her to "preserve a cheerful temper," and "frugality in domestic expenses" [*Laws*, v. 150]. Some of his texts savour, however, more of the anchorite than of a person conversant with mankind; and when he commands the husband to be reverenced as a god by the virtuous wife, even though enamoured of another woman, it may be justly doubted if ever he found obedience thereto; or the scarcely less difficult ordinance, "for a whole year let a husband bear with his wife who treats him with aversion," after which probation he is permitted to separate [ix. 77]. It is very likely the Rajputs are more in the habit of quoting the first of these texts than of hearing the last: for although they have a choice at home, they are not ashamed to be the avowed admirers of the Aspasias and Phrynes of the capital; from the same cause which attracted Socrates and made Pericles a slave and which will continue until the united charms of the dance and the song are sanctioned to be practised by the *légitimes* within.

[2] Manu ix. 101.

Rajputs in past ages, as well as the present, in as great a degree as in other stages of society and other countries, we cannot doubt. Nor will the annals of any nation afford more numerous or more sublime instances of female devotion, than those of the Rajputs; and such would never have been recorded, were not the incentive likely to be revered and followed. How easy would it be to cite examples for every passion which can actuate the human mind! Do we desire to see a model of unbounded devotion, resignation, and love, let us take the picture of Sita, as painted by the Milton of their silver age, than which nothing more beautiful or sentimental may be culled even from Paradise Lost. Rama was about to abandon his faithful wife for the purpose of becoming a Vana-prastha or hermit, when she thus pours out her ardent desire to partake of his solitude.

> A woman's bliss is found, not in the smile
> Of father, mother, friend, nor in herself:
> Her husband is her only portion here,
> Her heaven hereafter. If thou indeed
> Depart this day into the forest drear,
> I will precede, and smooth the thorny way.
>
> A gay recluse
> On thee attending, happy shall I feel
> Within the honey-scented grove to roam,
> For thou e'en here canst nourish and protect;
> And therefore other friend I cannot need.
> To-day most surely with thee will I go,
> And thus resolved, I must not be deny'd.
> Roots and wild fruit shall be my constant food;
> Nor will I near thee add unto thy cares,
> Nor lag behind, nor forest-food refuse,
> But fearless traverse every hill and dale.
>
> Thus could I sweetly pass a thousand years;
> But without thee e'en heaven would lose its charms [614].
>
> Pleased to embrace thy feet, I will reside
> In the rough forest as my father's house.
> Void of all other wish, supremely thine,
> Permit me this request—I will not grieve,
> I will not burden thee—refuse me not.
> But shouldst thou, Raghuvu, this prayer deny
> Know, I resolve on death.

Vide Ward, *On the History, Literature, and Mythology of the Hindus*, ed. 1815, ii. p. 308 ff. [Cp. Manu, vi. 2 ff.]

The publication of Mr. Wilson's specimens of the Hindu drama has put the English public in possession of very striking features of ancient Hindu manners, amongst which conjugal fidelity and affection stand eminently conspicuous. The Uttara Rama Charitra, the Vikrama and Urvasi, and the Mudra Rakshasa, contain many instances in point. In the latter piece occurs an example, in comparatively humble life, of the strong affection of a Hindu wife. Chandana Das, like Antonio in the *Merchant of Venice*, is doomed to die, to save his friend. His wife follows him to the scene of execution, with their only child, and the succeeding dialogue ensues :

Chand. Withdraw, my love, and lead our boy along.
Wife. Forgive me, husband,—to another world
Thy steps are bound, and not to foreign realms,
Whence in due time thou homeward wilt return ;
No common farewell our leave-taking now
Admits, nor must the partner of thy fate
Leave thee to trace thy solitary way.
Chand. What dost thou mean ?
Wife. To follow thee in death.
Chand. Think not of this—our boy's yet tender years
Demand affectionate and guardian care.
Wife. I leave him to our household gods, nor fear
They will desert his youth :—come, my dear boy,
And bid thy sire a long and last farewell.

The Tale of Dewaldai.—The annals of no nation on earth record a more ennobling or more magnanimous instance of female loyalty than that exemplified by Dewaldai, mother of the Bannaphar brothers, which will at once illustrate the manners of the Rajput fair, and their estimation and influence in society.

The last Hindu emperor of Delhi, the chivalrous Prithiraj of the Chauhan race, had abducted the daughter of the prince of Sameta. Some of the wounded who had covered his retreat were assailed and put to death by Parmal, the Chandel prince of Mahoba.[1] In order to avenge this insult, the emperor had no sooner conveyed his bride to Delhi than he invaded the territory of the Chandel, whose troops were cut to pieces at Sirswa,[2] the

[1] [Parmāl or Paramardi Chandel (A.D. 1165–1203). He was defeated by Prithirāj Chauhān in 1182.]

[2] On the Pahuj, and now belonging to the Bundela prince of Datia. The author has been over this field of battle.

advanced post of his kingdom. While [615] pursuing his success, the Chandel called a council, and by the advice of his queen Malandevi demanded a truce of his adversary, on the plea of the absence of his chieftains Alha and Udala. The brother of the bard of Mahoba was the envoy, who found the Chauhan ready to cross the Pahuj. He presented his gifts, and adjured him, "as a true Rajput, not to take them at such disadvantage." The gifts were accepted, and the Chauhan pledged himself, "albeit his warriors were eager for the fight," to grant the truce demanded; and having dismissed the herald, he inquired of his own bard, the prophetic Chand, the cause of the disaffection which led to the banishment of the Bannaphar; to which he thus replies: "Jasraj was the leader of the armies of Mahoba when his sovereign was defeated and put to flight by the wild race of Gonds; Jasraj repulsed the foe, captured Garha their capital, and laid his head at his sovereign's feet. Parmal returning with victory to Mahoba, in gratitude for his service, embraced the sons of Jasraj, and placed them in his honours and lands, while Malandevi the queen made no distinction between them and her son." The fief of the young Bannaphar [1] chieftains was at the celebrated fortress Kalanjar, where their sovereign happening to see a fine mare belonging to Alha, desired to possess her, and being refused, so far forgot past services as to compel them to abandon the country. On retiring they fired the estates of the Parihara chief who had instigated their disgrace. With their mother and families they repaired to Kanauj, whose monarch received them with open arms, assigning lands for their maintenance. Having thus premised the cause of banishment, Chand conducts us to Kanauj, at the moment when Jagnakh the bard was addressing the exiles on the dangers of Mahoba.

War with Prithirāj.—"The Chauhan is encamped on the plains of Mahoba; Narsingh and Birsingh have fallen, Sirswa is given to the flames, and the kingdom of Parmal laid waste by the Chauhan. For one month a truce has been obtained: while to you I am sent for aid in his griefs. Listen, O sons of Bannaphar; sad have been the days of Malandevi since you left Mahoba! Oft she looks towards Kanauj; and while she recalls you to

[1] [On the Bannāphar sept, from which sprang the heroes Alha and Udal, see Crooke, *Tribes and Castes North-West Provinces*, i. 137 ff.; their bravery forms the subject of numerous ballads (*ASR*, ii. 455 ff.).]

mind, tears gush from her eyes and she exclaims, 'The fame of the Chandel is departing'; but when gone, O sons of Jasraj, great will be your self-accusing sorrow: yet, think of Mahoba."

"Destruction to Mahoba! Annihilation to the Chandel who, without fault [616], expelled us our home: in whose service fell our father, by whom his kingdom was extended. Send the slanderous Parihara—let him lead your armies against the heroes of Delhi. Our heads were the pillars of Mahoba; by us were the Gonds expelled, and their strongholds Deogarh and Chandbari added to his sway. We maintained the field against the Jadon, sacked Hindaun,[1] and planted his standard on the plains of Katehr.[2] It was I (continued Alha) who stopped the sword of the conquering Kachhwaha[3]—The amirs of the Sultan fled before us.—At Gaya we were victorious, and added Rewa[4] to his kingdom. Antarved[5] I gave to the flames, and levelled to the ground the towns of Mewat.[6] From ten princes did Jasraj bring spoil to Mahoba. This have we done; and the reward is exile from our home! Seven times have I received wounds in his service, and since my father's death gained forty battles; and from seven has Udala conveyed the record of victory[7] to Parmal. Thrice my death seemed inevitable. The honour of his house I have upheld—yet exile is my reward!"

The bard replies—"The father of Parmal left him when a child to the care of Jasraj. Your father was in lieu of his own; the son should not abandon him when misfortune makes him call on you. The Rajput who abandons his sovereign in distress will be plunged into hell. Then place on your head the loyalty of your father. Can you desire to remain at Kanauj while he is in

[1] Hindaun was a town dependent on Bayana, the capital of the Jadons, whose descendants still occupy Karauli and Sri Mathura.

[2] [The modern Rohilkhand Division.]

[3] Rao Pajun of Amber, one of the great vassals of the Chauhan, and ancestor of the present Raja of Jaipur.

[4] In the original, "the land of the Baghel to that of the Chandel." Rewa is capital of [or leading State in] Baghelkhand, founded by the Baghela Rajputs, a branch of the Solanki kings of Anhilwara.

[5] Antarved, the Duab, or Mesopotamia of the Jumna and Ganges.

[6] A district S.W. of Delhi, notorious for the lawless habits of its inhabitants: a very ancient Hindu race, but the greater part forced proselytes to the faith of Islam. In the time of Prithiraj the chief of Mewat was one of his vassals.

[7] *Jayapattra*, or 'bulletin of victory.'

trouble, who expended thousands in rejoicings for your birth? Malandevi (the queen), who loves you as her own, presses your return. She bids me demand of Dewaldai fulfilment of the oft-repeated vow, that your life and Mahoba, when endangered, were inseparable. The breaker of vows, despised on earth, will be plunged into hell, there to remain while sun and moon endure."

Dewaldai heard the message of the queen. "Let us fly to Mahoba," she [617] exclaimed. Alha was silent, while Udala said aloud, "May evil spirits seize upon Mahoba!—Can we forget the day when, in distress, he drove us forth?—Return to Mahoba—let it stand or fall, it is the same to me; Kanauj is henceforth my home."

"Would that the gods had made me barren," said Dewaldai, "that I had never borne sons who thus abandon the paths of the Rajput, and refuse to succour their prince in danger!" Her heart bursting with grief, and her eyes raised to heaven, she continued: "Was it for this, O universal lord, thou mad'st me feel a mother's pangs for these destroyers of Bannaphar's fame? Unworthy offspring! the heart of the true Rajput dances with joy at the mere name of strife—but ye, degenerate, cannot be the sons of Jasraj—some carl must have stolen to my embrace, and from such ye must be sprung." The young chiefs arose, their faces withered in sadness. "When we perish in defence of Mahoba, and covered with wounds, perform deeds that will leave a deathless name; when our heads roll in the field—when we embrace the valiant in fight, and treading in the footsteps of the brave, make resplendent the blood of both lines, even in the presence of the heroes of the Chauhan, then will our mother rejoice."

The envoy having, by this loyal appeal of Dewaldai, attained the object of his mission, the brothers repair to the monarch of Kanauj,[1] in order to ask permission to return to Mahoba; this is granted, and they are dismissed with magnificent gifts, in which the bardic herald participated;[2] and the parting valediction was

[1] Jaichand was then king of this city, only second to Delhi. He was attacked in 1193 (A.D.) by Shihabu-d-din, after his conquest of the Chauhan, driven from his kingdom, and found a watery grave in the Ganges. [The battle was fought at Chandāwar in the Etāwa District, A.D. 1194 (Smith, *EHI*, 385).]

[2] Jagnakh had two villages conferred upon him, besides an elephant and a dress.

"preserve the faith of the Rajputs." The omens during the march were of the worst kind: as Jagnakh expounded them, Alha with a smile replied, "O bard, though thou canst dive into the dark recesses of futurity, to the brave all omens are happy,[1] even though our heroes shall fall, and the fame of the Chandel must depart; thus in secret does my soul assure me." The saras[2] was alone on the right—the eagle as he flew dropped his prey—the chakwa[3] separated from his mate—drops fell from the eyes of the warlike steed—the siyal[4] sent forth sounds of lamentation; spots were seen on the disc of the sun" [618]. The countenance of Lakhan fell;[5] these portents filled his soul with dismay: but Alha said, "though these omens bode death, yet death to the valiant, to the pure in faith, is an object of desire not of sorrow. The path of the Rajput is beset with difficulties, rugged, and filled with thorns; but he regards it not, so it but conducts to battle."—"To carry joy to Parmala alone occupied their thoughts: the steeds bounded over the plain like the swift-footed deer." The brothers, ere they reached Mahoba, halted to put on the saffron robe, the sign of "no quarter" with the Rajput warrior. The intelligence of their approach filled the Chandela prince with joy, who advanced to embrace his defenders, and conduct them to Mahoba; while the queen Malandevi came to greet Dewaldai, who with the herald bard paid homage, and returned with the queen to the city. Rich gifts were presented, gems resplendent with light. The queen sent for Alha, and extending her hands over his head, bestowed the *asis*[6] (blessing as kneeling he swore his head was with Mahoba, and then waved a vessel filled with pearls over his head, which were distributed to his followers.[7]

1 [Compare *Iliad*, xii. 237 ff.]

2 The phenicopteros. [The great crane, *Grus antigone*.]

3 A large red duck, the emblem of fidelity with the Rajputs. [The Brahmani duck, *Anas casarca*.]

4 The jackal.

5 Commander of the succours of Kanauj.

6 *Asis* is a form of benediction only bestowed by females and priests: it is performed by clasping both hands over the person's head, and waving a piece of silver or other valuable over him, which is bestowed in charity [the object being to disperse evil influence].

7 This is a very ancient ceremony, and is called *Nicharavali* [or *ārti*]. The Author has frequently had a large salver filled with silver coin waved

The bardic herald was rewarded with four villages. We are then introduced to the Chauhan camp and council, where Chand the bard is expatiating on the return of the Bannaphars with the succours of Kanauj. He recommends his sovereign to send a herald to the Chandel to announce the expiration of the truce, and requiring him to meet him in the field, or abandon Mahoba. According to the bard's advice, a dispatch was transmitted to Parmal, in which the cause of war was recapitulated—the murder of the wounded; and stating that, according to Rajput faith, he had granted seven days beyond the time demanded, "and although so many days had passed since succour had arrived from Kanauj, the lion-horn had not yet sounded (*singhnad*)": adding, "if he abandon all desire of combat, let him proclaim his vassalage to Delhi, and abandon Mahoba."

Parmal received the hostile message in despair; but calling his warriors around him, he replied to the herald of the Chauhan, that "on the day of the sun, the first of the month, he would join him in strife" [619].

"On the day sacred to Sukra (Friday), Prithiraj sounded the shell, while the drums thrice struck proclaimed the truce concluded.[1] The standard was brought forth, around which the warriors gathered; the cup circulated, the prospect of battle filled their souls with joy. They anointed their bodies with fragrant oils, while the celestial Apsaras with ambrosial oils and heavenly perfumes anointed their silver forms, tinged their eyelids, and prepared for the reception of heroes.[2] The sound of the war-shell reached Kailas; the abstraction of Iswara was at an end—joy seized his soul at the prospect of completing his chaplet of skulls (*mundamala*). The Yoginis danced with joy, their faces sparkled with delight, as they seized their vessels to drink the blood of the slain. The devourers of flesh, the Palankashas, sung

---

over his head, which was handed for distribution amongst his attendants. It is most appropriate from the fair, from whom also he has had this performed by their proxies, the family priest or female attendants.

[1] The sankh, or war-shell, is thrice sounded, and the nakkaras strike thrice, when the army is to march; but should it after such proclamation remain on its ground, a scape-goat is slain in front of the imperial tent.

[2] This picture recalls the remembrance of Hacon and the heroes of the north; with the Valkyries or choosers of the slain; the celestial maids of war of Scandinavia.

songs of triumph at the game of battle between the Chauhan and Chandel."

In another measure, the bard proceeds to contrast the occupations of his heroes and the celestials preparatory to the combat, which descriptions are termed *rupaka.* "The heroes gird on their armour, while the heavenly fair deck their persons. They place on their heads the helm crowned with the war-bell (*viragantha*), these adjust the corset; they draw the girths of the war-steed, the fair of the world of bliss bind the anklet of bells; nets of steel defend the turban's fold, they braid their hair with golden flowers and gems; the warrior polishes his falchion—the fair tints the eyelid with *anjan*;[1] the hero points his dagger, the fair paints a heart on her forehead; he braces on his ample buckler—she places the resplendent orb in her ear; he binds his arms with a gauntlet of brass—she stains her hands with the henna. The hero decorates his hand with the tiger-claw[2]—the Apsaras ornaments with rings and golden bracelets; the warrior shakes the ponderous lance—the heavenly fair the garland of love[3] to decorate those who fall in the fight; she binds on a necklace of pearls, he a *mala* of the tulasi.[4] The warrior strings his bow—the fair assume their killing [620] glances. Once more the heroes look to their girths, while the celestial fair prepare their cars."

After the bard has finished his *rupaka*, he exclaims, "Thus says Chand, the lord of verse; with my own eyes have I seen what I describe." It is important to remark, that the national faith of the Rajput never questions the prophetic power of their chief bard, whom they call Trikala, or cognoscent of the past, the present, and the future—a character which the bard has enjoyed in all ages and climes; but Chand was the last whom they admitted to possess supernatural vision.

[1] [Collyrium.]

[2] Baghnakh or Naharnakh. [This weapon is best known by its use by Sivaji when he slew Afzu-l Khān in 1659 at Pratāpgarh (Grant Duff, *Hist. Mahrattas*, 78). Four specimens in the Indian Museum are described, with an illustration, by Hon. W. Egerton (*Illustrated Handbook of Indian Arms*, 115).]

[3] Barmala.

[4] *Mala*, a necklace. The *tulasi* [the plant *Olymum sanctum*] or *rudraksha* [the nuts of *Elaeocarpus ganitrus*, the former worn by Vaishnavas, the latter by Saivas] had the same estimation amongst the Hindus that the mistletoe had amongst the ancient Britons, and was always worn in battle as a charm.

We must now return to Mahoba, where a grand council had assembled at a final deliberation; at which, shaded by screens, the mother of the Bannaphars, and the queen Malandevi, were present. The latter thus opens the debate: "O mother of Alha, how may we succeed against the lord of the world?[1] If defeated, lost is Mahoba; if we pay tribute, we are loaded with shame." Dewaldai recommends hearing *seriatim* the opinions of the chieftains, when Alha thus speaks: "Listen, O mother, to your son; he alone is of pure lineage who, placing loyalty on his head, abandons all thoughts of self, and lays down his life for his prince; my thoughts are only for Parmal. If she lives she will show herself a woman, or emanation of Parvati.[2] The warriors of Sambhar shall be cut in pieces. I will so illustrate the blood of my fathers, that my fame shall last for ever. My son Indal, O prince! I bequeath to you, and the fame of Dewaldai is in your keeping."

The queen thus replies: "The warriors of the Chauhan are fierce as they are numerous; pay tribute, and save Mahoba." The soul of Udala inflamed, and turning to the queen, "Why thought you not thus when you slew the defenceless? but then I was unheard. Whence now your wisdom? thrice I beseeched you to pardon. Nevertheless, Mahoba is safe while life remains in me, and in your cause, O Parmal! we shall espouse celestial brides."

"Well have you spoken, my son," said Dewaldai, "nothing now remains but to make thy parent's milk resplendent by thy deeds. The call of the peasant driven [621] from his home meets the ear, and while we deliberate, our villages are given to the flames." But Parmal replied: "Saturn[3] rules the day, tomorrow we shall meet the foe." With indignation Alha turned to the king: "He who can look tamely on while the smoke ascends from his ruined towns, his fields laid waste, can be no Rajput—he who succumbs to fear when his country is invaded, his body will be plunged into the hell of hells, his soul a wanderer in the world of spirits for sixty thousand years; but the warrior

[1] Prithiraj.

[2] A Rajput never names his wife. Here it is evidently optional to the widow to live or die, though Alha shows his wish for her society above. See chapter on Satis, which will follow.

[3] Sanichar.

who performs his duty will be received into the mansion of the sun, and his deeds will last for ever."

But cowardice and cruelty always accompany each other, nor could all the speeches of the brothers "screw his courage to the sticking place." Parmal went to his queen, and gave fresh vent to his lamentation. She upbraided his unmanly spirit, and bid him head his troops and go forth to the fight. The heroes embraced their wives for the last time, and with the dawn performed their pious rites. The Bannaphar offered oblations to the nine planets, and having adored the image of his tutelary god, he again put the chain round his neck;[1] then calling his son Indal, and Udala his brother, he once more poured forth his vows to the universal mother "that he would illustrate the name of Jasraj, and evince the pure blood derived from Dewaldai, whene'er he met the foe."—"Nobly have you resolved," said Udala, "and shall not my *kirwan*[2] also dazzle the eyes of Sambhar's lord? shall he not retire from before me?"—"Farewell, my children," said Dewaldai, "be true to your salt, and should you lose your heads for your prince, doubt not you will obtain the celestial crown." Having ceased, the wives of both exclaimed, "What virtuous wife survives her lord? for thus says Gauriji,[3] 'the woman, who survives her husband who falls in the field of battle, will never obtain bliss, but wander a discontented ghost in the region of unhallowed spirits.'"

This is sufficient to exhibit the supreme influence of women, not only on, but also in society.

The extract is taken from the Bardic historian, when Hindu customs were pure, and the Chauhan was paramount sovereign of India. It is worth while to compare it with another written six centuries after the conquest by the Muhammadans; although six dynastics—namely, Ghazni, Ghor, Khilji [622], Sayyid, Lodi, and Mogul, numbering more than thirty kings, had intervened, yet the same uncontrollable spirit was in full force, unchangeable even in misfortune. Both Hindu and Persian historians expatiate with delight on the anecdote; but we prefer the narrative of the ingenuous Bernier, under whose eye the incident occurred.

[1] It was a *jantar* or phylactery of Hanuman the monkey deity; probably a magical stanza, with his image.

[2] A crooked scimitar.

[3] One of the names of Mena or Parvati. This passage will illustrate the subject of Satis in a future chapter.

Jaswant Singh and his Wife.—In the civil war for empire amongst the sons of Shah Jahan, when Aurangzeb opened his career by the deposal of his father and the murder of his brothers, the Rajputs, faithful to the emperor, determined to oppose him. Under the intrepid Rathor Jaswant Singh, thirty thousand Rajputs, chiefly of that clan, advanced to the Nerbudda, and with a magnanimity amounting to imprudence, they permitted the junction of Murad with Aurangzeb, who, under cover of artillery served by Frenchmen, crossed the river almost unopposed. Next morning the action commenced, which continued throughout the day. The Rajputs behaved with their usual bravery; but were surrounded on all sides, and by sunset left ten thousand dead on the field.[1] The Maharaja retreated to his own country, but his wife, a daughter of the Rana of Udaipur, " disdained (says Ferishta) to receive her lord, and shut the gates of the castle."

Bernier, who was present, says, " I cannot forbear to relate the fierce reception which the daughter of the Rana gave to her husband Jeswunt Singh [Jessom Seingue], after his defeat and flight. When she heard he was nigh, and had understood what had passed in the battle; that he had fought with all possible courage; that he had but four or five hundred men left; and at last, no longer able to resist the enemy, had been forced to retreat; instead of sending some one to condole him in his misfortunes, she commanded in a dry mood to shut the gates of the castle, and not to let this infamous man enter; that he was not her husband; that the son-in-law of the great Rana could not have so mean a soul; that he was to remember, that being grafted into so illustrious a house, he was to imitate its virtue; in a word, he was to vanquish, or to die. A moment after, she was of another humour; she commands a pile of wood to be laid, that she might

[1] " 'Tis a pleasure (says Bernier) to see them with the fume of opium in their heads, embrace each other when the battle is to begin, and give their mutual farewells, as men resolved to die." [Ed. 1914, p. 40. The battle of Dharmāt was fought on the banks of the river Sipra (*IGI*, xxi. 14 f.) on 15th April, 1658. Manucci was not present, but gives an account derived from Aurangzeb's artillery officers of the battle at Dharmātpur, about 14 miles from Ujjain (i. 259 f., and see Jadunath Sarkar, *Life of Aurangzeb*, ii. 1 ff.). The latter (ii. 20 f.) speaks highly of the valour of Jaswant Singh, but Khāfi Khan (Elliot-Dowson vii. 219) says that he acted in a cowardly way. The account quoted by the author is not in the original work of Ferishta, but in Dow's continuation (ed. 1812, iii. 206 f).].

burn herself; that they abused her; that her husband must needs be dead; that it could not be otherwise. And a little while after, she was seen to change countenance, to [623] fall into a passion, and break into a thousand reproaches against him. In short, she remained thus transported eight or nine days, without being able to resolve to see her husband, till at last her mother coming, brought her in time to herself, composed by assuring her that as soon as the Raja had but refreshed himself he would raise another army to fight Aurangzeb, and repair his honour. By which story one may see," says Bernier, "a pattern of the courage of the women in that country"; and he adds this philosophieal corollary on this and the custom of satis, which he had witnessed: "There is nothing which opinion, prepossession, custom, hope, and the point of honour, may not make men do or suffer." [1]

The Tale of Sanjogta.—The romantic history of the Chauhan emperor of Delhi abounds in sketches of female character; and in the story of his carrying off Sanjogta, the princess of Kanauj, we have not only the individual portrait of the Helen of her country, but in it a faithful picture of the sex. We see her, from the moment when, rejecting the assembled princes, she threw the "garland of marriage" round the neck of her hero, the Chauhan, abandon herself to all the influences of passion—mix in a combat of five days' continuance against her father's array, witness his overthrow, and the carnage of both armies, and subsequently, by her seductive charms, lulling her lover into a neglect of every princely duty. Yet when the foes of his glory and power invade India, we see the enchantress at once start from her trance of pleasure, and exchanging the softer for the sterner passions, in accents not less strong because mingled with deep affection, she conjures him, while arming him for the battle, to die for his fame, declaring that she will join him in "the mansions of the sun." Though it is difficult to extract, in passages sufficiently condensed, what may convey a just idea of this heroine, we shall attempt it in the bard's own language, rendered into prose. He announces the tidings of invasion by the medium of a dream, which the Chauhan thus relates:

[1] Bernier's *History of the Late Revolution o the Empire of the Mogul*, fol. p. 13, ed. 1684 [ed. 1914, p. 40 f., where a somewhat different version is given].

"'This night, while in the arms of sleep, a fair, beautiful as Rambha, rudely seized my arm; then she assailed you, and while you were struggling, a mighty elephant,[1] infuriated, and hideous as a demon, bore down upon me. Sleep fled—nor Rambha nor demon remained—but my heart was panting, and [624] my quivering lips muttering *Har! Har!*[2] What is decreed the gods only know.'

"Sanjogta replied, 'Victory and fame to my lord! O, sun of the Chauhans, in glory, or in pleasure, who has tasted so deeply as you? To die is the destiny not only of man but of the gods: all desire to throw off the old garment; but to die well is to live for ever. Think not of self, but of immortality; let your sword divide your foe, and I will be your *ardhanga*[3] hereafter.'

The king sought the bard, who expounded the dream, and the Guru wrote an incantation, which he placed in his turban. A thousand brass vessels of fresh milk were poured in libations to the sun and moon. Ten buffaloes were sacrificed to the supporters of the globe, and gifts were made to all. But will offerings of blood or libations of milk arrest what is decreed? If by these man could undo what is ordained, would Nala or the Pandus have suffered as they did?"

While the warriors assemble in council to consult on the best mode of opposing the Sultan of Ghazni, the king leaves them to deliberate, in order to advise with Sanjogta. Her reply is curious:

"Who asks woman for advice? The world deems their understanding shallow; even when truths issue from their lips, none listen thereto. Yet what is the world without woman? We have the forms of Sakti[4] with the fire of Siva; we are at once thieves and sanctuaries; we are vessels of virtue and of vice—of knowledge and of ignorance. The man of wisdom, the astrologer, can from the books calculate the motion and course of the planets; but in the book of woman he is ignorant: and this is not a saying of to-day, it ever has been so: our book has not been mastered, therefore, to hide their ignorance, they say,

[1] It is deemed unlucky to see this emblem of Ganesa in sleep.

[2] The battle-shout of the Rajput. [Hara, a title of Siva.]

[3] 'Half-body,' which we may render, in common phraseology, 'other half.'

[4] [The impersonation of the female energy.]

in woman there is no wisdom! Yet woman shares your joys and your sorrows. Even when you depart from the mansion of the sun, we part not. Hunger and thirst we cheerfully partake with you; we are as the lakes, of which you are the swans; what are you when absent from our bosoms?"

The army having assembled, and all being prepared to march against the Islamite, in the last great battle which subjugated India, the fair Sanjogta armed her lord for the encounter. "In vain she sought the rings of his corslet; her eyes were [625] fixed on the face of the Chauhan, as those of the famished wretch who finds a piece of gold. The sound of the drum reached the ear of the Chauhan; it was as a death-knell on that of Sanjogta: and as he left her to head Delhi's heroes, she vowed that henceforward water only should sustain her. "I shall see him again in the region of Surya, but never more in Yoginipur." [1] Her prediction was fulfilled: her lord was routed, made captive and slain; and, faithful to her vow, she mounted the funeral pyre.

The Queen of Ganor.—Were we called upon to give a pendant for Lucretia, it would be found in the queen of Ganor.[2] After having defended five fortresses against the foe, she retreated to her last stronghold on the Nerbudda, and had scarcely left the bark, when the assailants arrived in pursuit. The disheartened defenders were few in number, and the fortress was soon in possession of the foe, the founder of the family now ruling in Bhopal. The beauty of the queen of Ganor was an allurement only secondary to his desire for her country, and he invited her to reign over it and him. Denial would have been useless, and would have subjected her to instant coercion, for the Khan awaited her reply in the hall below; she therefore sent a message of assent, with a complimentary reflection on his gallant conduct and determination of pursuit; adding, that he merited her hand for his bravery, and might prepare for the nuptials, which should be celebrated on the terrace of the palace. She demanded two hours for unmolested preparation, that she might appear in appropriate attire, and with the distinction her own and his rank demanded.

[1] Delhi ["the city of the witch or sorceress"].

[2] [The "Ganore" of the text possibly represents the town of Ganora in the Bānswāra State. There is another place of the same name in Gwalior.]

Ceremonials, on a scale of magnificence equal to the shortness of the time, were going on. The song of joy had already stifled the discordant voice of war, and at length the Khan was summoned to the terrace. Robed in the marriage garb presented to him by the queen, with a necklace and aigrette of superb jewels from the coffers of Ganor, he hastened to obey the mandate, and found that fame had not done justice to her charms. He was desired to be seated, and in conversation full of rapture on his side, hours were as minutes while he gazed on the beauty of the queen. But presently his countenance fell—he complained of heat; punkas and water were brought, but they availed him not, and he began to tear the bridal garments from his frame, when the queen thus addressed him [626]: "Know, Khan, that your last hour is come; our wedding and our death shall be sealed together. The vestments which cover you are poisoned; you had left me no other expedient to escape pollution." While all were horror-struck by this declaration, she sprung from the battlements into the flood beneath. The Khan died in extreme torture, and was buried on the road to Bhopal; and, strange to say, a visit to his grave has the reputation of curing the tertian of that country.[1]

Rāja Jai Singh and his Wife.—We may give another anecdote illustrative of this extreme delicacy of sentiment, but without so tragical a conclusion. The celebrated Raja Jai Singh of Amber

[1] [Several of our best authorities—Sir Lauder Brunton, Sir G. Birdwood, Professors A. Keith and A. Doran of the Royal College of Surgeons—have kindly investigated the question of death by poisoned robes, of which various instances are reported in this work. The general result is that it is doubtful if any known poison could be used in this way. Sir Lauder Brunton remarks that a paste of the seeds of *Abrus precatorius* is used for killing animals. Dr. N. Chevers (*Manual of Medical Jurisprudence in India*, p. 299) writes: "Any one who has noticed how freely a robust person in India perspires through a thin garment can understand that, if a cloth were thoroughly impregnated with the cantharidine of that very powerful vesicant, the *Telini*, the result would be as dangerous as an extensive burn." For *telini* (*Mylabris punctum*), used as a substitute for *Cantharis vesicatoria*, see Sir G. Watt (*Dict. Economic Products of India*, v. 309). Manucci (i. 149) says that Akbar placed such poisons in charge of a special officer. The stock classical case is that of Herakles killed by an ointment made from the blood of Nessus. An old writer, W. Ramesey (*Of Poisons* (1660), p. 14 f.) speaks of poisoning done in this way: but he regards some of "these and the like storeyes to be merely Fabulous . . . and rather to be attributed to the Subtilty, Craft, and Malice of the Devill" (12 series, *Notes and Queries*, i. (1916) p. 417).]

had espoused a princess of Haraoti, whose manners and garb, accordant with the simplicity of that provincial capital, subjected her to the badinage of the more refined court of Amber, whose ladies had added the imperial costume to their own native dress. One day being alone with the prince, he began playfully to contrast the sweeping jupe of Kotah with the more scanty robe of the belles of his own capital; and taking up a pair of scissors, said he would reduce it to an equality with the latter. Offended at such levity, she seized his sword, and assuming a threatening attitude, said, "that in the house to which she had the honour to belong, they were not habituated to jests of this nature; that mutual respect was the guardian, not only of happiness but of virtue"; and she assured him, that if he ever again so insulted her, he would find that the daughter of Kotah could use a sword more effectively than the prince of Amber the scissors; adding, that she would prevent any future scion of her house from being subjected to similar disrespect, by declaring such intermarriages *talak*, or forbidden, which interdict I believe yet exists.[1]

A Courageous Rājput Woman.—I will append an anecdote related by the celebrated Zalim Singh, characteristic of the presence of mind, prowess, and physical strength of the Rajput women. To attend and aid in the minutiae of husbandry is by no means uncommon with them, as to dress and carry the meals of their husbands to the fields is a general practice. In the jungle which skirts the knolls of Pachpahar, a huge bear assaulted a Rajputni as she was carrying her husband's dinner. As he approached with an air of gallantry upon his hind-legs, doubting whether the food or herself [627] were the intended prey, she retreated behind a large tree, round the trunk of which Bruin, still in his erect attitude, tried all his powers of circumvention to seize her. At length, half exhausted, she boldly grasped his paws, and with so vigorous a hold that he roared with pain, while in vain, with his short neck, did he endeavour to reach the powerful hand which fixed him. While she was in this dilemma, a Pardesi (a foreign soldier of the State) happened to be passing

[1] The physician (unless he unite with his office that of ghostly comforter) has to feel the pulse of his patient with a curtain between them, through a rent, in which the arm is extended. [See the amusing account by Fryer (*New Account of E. India and Persia*, Hakluyt Society, ed. i. 326 f.).]

to the garrison of Gagraun, and she called out to him in a voice of such unconcern to come and release her for a time, that he complied without hesitation. She had not retired, however, above a dozen yards ere he called loudly for her return, being scarcely able to hold his new friend; but laughingly recommending perseverance, she hastened on, and soon returned with her husband, who laid the monster prostrate with his matchlock, and rescued the Pardesi from his unpleasing predicament.[1]

Such anecdotes might be multiplied *ad infinitum*; but I will conclude with one displaying the romantic chivalry of the Rajput, and the influence of the fair in the formation of character; it is taken from the annals of Jaisalmer, the most remote of the States of Rajasthan, and situated in the heart of the desert, of which it is an oasis.

The Wedding of Sādhu.—Raningdeo was lord of Pugal, a fief of Jaisalmer; his heir, named Sadhu, was the terror of the desert, carrying his raids even to the valley of the Indus, and on the east to Nagor. Returning from a foray, with a train of captured camels and horses, he passed by Aurint, where dwelt Manik Rao, the chief of the Mohils, whose rule extended over 1440 villages. Being invited to partake of the hospitality of the Mohil, the heir of Pugal attracted the favourable regards of the old chieftain's daughter:

> She loved him for the dangers he had passed;

for he had the fame of being the first riever of the desert. Although betrothed to the heir of the Rathor of Mandor, she signified her wish to renounce the throne to be the bride of the chieftain of Pugal; and in spite of the dangers he provoked, and contrary to the Mohil chief's advice, Sadhu, as a gallant Rajput, dared not reject the overture, and he promised "to accept the coco,"[2] if sent in form to Pugal [628]. In due time it came, and the nuptials were solemnized at Aurint. The dower was splendid; gems of high price, vessels of gold and silver, a golden bull, and a train of thirteen *dewadharis*,[3] or damsels of wisdom and penetration.

[1] [This is a stock story (Risley, *The People of India*, 2nd ed. 179 f.; Rose, *Glossary*, ii. 220; cf. Herodotus v. 12).]

[2] Sriphala.

[3] Literally 'lamp-holders'; such is the term applied to these handmaids; who invariably form a part of the *daeja* or 'dower.' [The custom

Arankanwal, the slighted heir of Mandor, determined on revenge, and with four thousand Rathors planted himself in the path of Sadhu's return, aided by the Sankhla Mehraj, whose son Sadhu had slain. Though entreated to add four thousand Mohils to his escort, Sadhu deemed his own gallant band of seven hundred Bhattis sufficient to convey his bride to his desert abode, and with difficulty accepted fifty, led by Meghraj, the brother of the bride.

The rivals encountered at Chondan, where Sadhu had halted to repose; but the brave Rathor scorned the advantage of numbers, and a series of single combats ensued, with all the forms of chivalry. The first who entered the lists was Jaitanga, of the Pahu clan, and of the kin of Sadhu. The enemy came upon him by surprise while reposing on the ground, his saddle-cloth for his couch, and the bridle of his steed twisted round his arm; he was soon recognized by the Sankhla, who had often encountered his prowess, on which he expatiated to Arankanwal, who sent an attendant to awake him; but the gallant Panch Kalyan (for such was the name of his steed) had already performed this service, and they found him upbraiding white-legs [1] for treading upon him. Like a true Rajput, "*toujours prêt*," he received the hostile message, and sent the envoy back with his compliments, and a request for some *amal* or opium, as he had lost his own supply. With all courtesy this was sent, and prepared by the domestics of his antagonist; after taking which he lay down to enjoy the customary siesta. As soon as he awoke, he prepared for the combat, girt on his armour, and having reminded Panch Kalyan of the fields he had won, and telling him to bear him well that day, he mounted and advanced. The son of Chonda admiring his sang-froid, and the address with which he guided his steed, commanded Jodha Chauhan, the leader of his party, to encounter the Pahu. "Their two-edged swords soon clashed in combat"; but the gigantic Chauhan fell beneath the Bhatti, who, warmed

---

of sending handmaids with the bride, the girls often becoming concubines of the bridegroom, is common (Russell, *Tribes and Castes Central Provinces*, i. 63, ii. 77). In Gujarāt they are known as Goli or Vadhāran, and are sometimes married to the Khawās, or male slaves of the harem (*BG*, ix. Part i. 147, 235).]

[1] Panch Kalyan is generally, if not always, a chestnut, having four white legs, with a white nose and list or star.

with the fight, plunged amidst his foes, encountering all he deemed worthy of his assault.

The fray thus begun, single combats and actions of equal parties followed, the [629] rivals looking on. At length Sadhu mounted: twice he charged the Rathor ranks, carrying death on his lance; each time he returned for the applause of his bride, who beheld the battle from her car. Six hundred of his foes had fallen, and nearly half his own warriors. He bade her a last adieu, while she exhorted him to the fight, saying, "she would witness his deeds, and if he fell, would follow him even in death." Now he singled out his rival Arankanwal,[1] who was alike eager to end the strife, and blot out his disgrace in his blood. They met: some seconds were lost in a courteous contention, each yielding to his rival the first blow, at length dealt out by Sadhu on the neck of the disappointed Rathor. It was returned with the rapidity of lightning, and the daughter of the Mohil saw the steel descend on the head of her lover. Both fell prostrate to the earth: but Sadhu's soul had sped; the Rathor had only swooned. With the fall of the leaders the battle ceased; and the fair cause of strife, Karamdevi, at once a virgin, a wife, and a widow, prepared to follow her affianced. Calling for a sword, with one arm she dissevered the other, desiring it might be conveyed to the father of her lord—"tell him such was his daughter." The other she commanded to be struck off, and given, with her marriage jewels thereon, to the bard of the Mohils. The pile was prepared on the field of battle; and taking her lord in her embrace, she gave herself up to the devouring flames. The dissevered limbs were disposed of as commanded; the old Rao of Pugal caused the one to be burnt, and a tank was excavated on the spot, which is still called after the heroine, "the lake of Karamdevi."

This encounter took place in S. 1462, A.D. 1406. The brunt of the battle fell on the Sankhlas, and only twenty-five out of three hundred and fifty left the field with their leader, Mehraj, himself severely wounded. The rejected lover had four brothers dangerously hurt; and in six months the wounds of Arankanwal opened afresh: he died, and the rites to the manes of these rivals

[1] *Arankanwal*, 'the lotos of the desert,' from *aranya* (Sanskrit), 'a waste,' and *kamala* (pronounced *kanwal*), 'a lotos': classically it should be written *aranykamala*; I write it as pronounced.

in love, the *chhamasa*[1] of Sadhu, and the *duadasa*[2] of Arankanwal, were celebrated on the same day.

Without pausing to trace the moral springs of that devotion which influenced the Mohila maiden, we shall relate the sequel to the story (though out of place)[3] in illustration of the prosecution of feuds throughout Rajasthan. The fathers [630] now took up the quarrel of their sons; and as it was by the prowess of the Sankhla vassal of Mandor that the band of Sadhu was discomfited, the old Rao, Raningdeo, drew together the lances of Pugal, and carried destruction into the fief of Mehraj. The Sankhlas yield in valour to none of the brave races who inhabit the "region of death"; and Mehraj was the father of Harbuji Sankhla, the Palladin of Marudes, whose exploits are yet the theme of the erratic bards of Rajasthan. Whether he was unprepared for the assault, or overcome by numbers, three hundred of his kin and clan moistened the sand-hills of the Luni with their blood. Raningdeo, flushed with revenge and laden with spoil, had reached his own frontier, when he was overtaken by Chonda of Mandor, alike eager to avenge the loss of his son Arankanwal, and this destructive inroad on his vassal. A desperate conflict ensued, in which the Rao of Pugal was slain; and the Rathor returned in triumph to Mandor.

Unequal to cope with the princes of Mandor, the two remaining sons of Raningdeo, Tana and Mera, resolved to abandon their faith, in order to preserve the point of honour, and "to take up their father's feud."[4] At this period the king, Khizr Khan,[5] was at Multan; to him they went, and by offers of service and an open apostacy, obtained a force to march against Chonda, who had recently added Nagor to his growing dominions. While the brothers were thus negotiating, they were joined by Kilan, the third son of their common sovereign, the Rawal of Jaisalmer, who advised the use of *chal*, which with the Rajput means indifferently stratagem or treachery, so that it facilitates revenge. With the ostensible motive of ending their feuds, and restoring tranquillity to their borderers, whose sole occupation was watch-

[1] The rites to the manes on the completion of the 'sixth month.'

[2] The rites to the manes on the 'twelfth day.'

[3] The greater portion of these anecdotes, the foundation of national character, will appear in the respective annals.

[4] *Bap ra wair lena.*

[5] [Khizr Khān, of the Sayyid dynasty of Delhi, was left in charge by Timūr, and died A.D. 1421.]

ing, burning, and devastating, Kilan offered a daughter in marriage to Chonda, and went so far as to say, that if he suspected aught unfair, he would, though contrary to custom and his own dignity, send the Bhatti princess to Nagor. This course being deemed the wisest, Chonda acquiesced in his desire "to extinguish the feud (*wair bujhana*)."

Nāgor taken by Stratagem.—Fifty covered chariots were prepared as the nuptial cortège, but which, instead of the bride and her handmaids, contained the bravest men of Pugal.[1] These were preceded by a train of horses led by Rajputs, of whom seven hundred also attended the camels laden with baggage, provisions, and gifts, while a small armed [631] retinue brought up the rear. The king's troops, amounting to one thousand horse, remained at a cautious distance behind. Chonda left Nagor to meet the cavalcade and his bride, and had reached the chariots ere his suspicions were excited. Observing, however, some matters which little savoured of festivity, the Rathor commenced his retreat. Upon this the chiefs rushed from their chariots and camels, and the royal auxiliaries advancing, Chonda was assailed and fell at the gate of Nagor; and friend and foe entering the city together, a scene of general plunder commenced.

Once more the feud was balanced; a son and a father had fallen on each side, and the petty Rao of Pugal had bravely maintained the *wair* against the princes of Mandor. The point of honour had been carried to the utmost bound by both parties, and an opportunity of reconciliation was at hand, which prevented the shadow of disgrace either to him who made or him who accepted the overture. The Rathors dreaded the loss of the recent acquisition, Nagor, and proposed to the Bhattis to seal their pacification with the blood of their common foe. United, they fell on the spoil-encumbered Tatars, whom they slew to a man.[2] Their father's feud thus revenged, the sons of Raningdeo (who, as apostates from their faith, could no longer hold Pugal in fief, which was retained by Kilan, who had aided their revenge) retired amongst the Abobaria Bhattis, and their descendants are now styled Momin Musalman Bhatti.

[1] [For this legend see Vol. I. p. 308 above.]

[2] Khizr Khan succeeded to the throne of Delhi in A.D. 1414 [or rather, was left in charge of Delhi by Timūr, and died A.D. 1421], and according to the Jaisalmer annals the commencement of these feuds was in A.D. 1406.

From such anecdotes it will be obvious wherein consists the point of honour with the Rajputs ; and it is not improbable that the very cause which has induced an opinion that females can have no influence on the lords of the creation, namely, their seclusion, operates powerfully in the contrary way.

Influence of Women on Rājput Society.—In spite of this seclusion, the knowledge of their accomplishments and of their personal perfections, radiates wherever the itinerant bard can travel. Though invisible themselves, they can see ; and accident often favours public report, and brings the object of renown within the sphere of personal observation : as in the case of Sadhu and the Mohila maiden. Placed behind screens, they see the youths of all countries, and there are occasions when permanent impressions are made, during tournaments and other martial exercises. Here we have just seen that the passion of the [632] daughter of the Mohil was fostered at the risk of the destruction not only of her father's house, but also that of her lover ; and as the fourteen hundred and forty towns, which owned the sway of the former, were not long after absorbed into the accumulating territory of Mandor, this insult may have been the cause of the extirpation of the Mohils, as it was of the Bhattis of Pugal.

The influence of women on Rajput society is marked in every page of Hindu history, from the most remote periods. What led to the wars of Rama ? the rape of Sita. What rendered deadly the feuds of the Yadus ? the insult to Draupadi. What made prince Nala an exile from Narwar ? his love for Damayanti. What made Raja Bhartari abandon the throne of Avanti ? the loss of Pingali. What subjected the Hindu to the dominion of the Islamite ? the rape of the princess of Kanauj. In fine, the cause which overturned kingdoms, commuted the sceptre to the pilgrim's staff, and formed the groundwork of all their grand epics, is woman. In ancient, and even in modern times, she had more than a negative in the choice of a husband, and this choice fell on the gallant and the gay. The fair Draupadi was the prize of the best archer, and the Pandu Bhima established his fame, and bore her from all the suitors of Kampila. The princess of Kanauj, when led through ranks of the princes of Hind, each hoping to be the object of her choice, threw the marriage-garland (*barmala*) over the neck of the effigy of the Chauhan, which her father in derision had placed as porter at the gate. Here was incense to fame and incentive to gallantry ! [1]

In the same manner, as related in another part of this work, did the princess of Kishangarh invite Rana Raj Singh to bear her from the impending union with the emperor of the Moguls ; and abundant other instances could be adduced of the free agency of these invisibles.

It were superfluous to reason on the effects of traditional histories, such as these, on the minds and manners of the females of Rajasthan. They form the amusement of their lives, and the grand topic in all their conversaziones ; they read them with the Purohit, and they have them sung by the itinerant bard or Dholi minstrel [633], who disseminates them wherever the Rajput name extends. The Rajput mother claims her full share in the glory of her son, who imbibes at the maternal fount his first rudiments of chivalry ; and the importance of this parental instruction cannot be better illustrated than in the ever-recurring simile, " make thy mother's milk resplendent " ; the full force of which we have in the powerful, though overstrained expression of the Bundi queen's joy on the announcement of the heroic death of her son : " the long-dried fountain at which he fed, jetted forth as she listened to the tale of his death, and the marble pavement, on which it fell, rent asunder." Equally futile would it be to reason on the intensity of sentiment thus implanted in the infant Rajput, of whom we may say without metaphor, the shield is his cradle, and daggers his playthings ; and with whom the first commandment is, " avenge thy father's feud " ; on which they can heap text upon text, from the days of the great Pandu moralist Vyasa to the not less influential bard of their nation, the Trikala Chand.

[1] The Samnite custom, so lauded by Montesquieu as the reward of youthful virtue, was akin in sentiment to the Rajput, except that the fair Rajputni made herself the sole judge of merit in her choice. It was more calculated for republican than aristocratic society : " On assembloit tous les jeunes gens, et on les jugeoit ; celui qui était déclaré le meilleur de tout prenoit pour sa femme la fille qu'il vouloit : l'amour, la beauté, la chastité, la vertu, la naissance, les richesses même, tout cela était, pour ainsi dire, la dot de la vertu." It would be difficult, adds Montesquieu, to imagine a more noble recompense, or one less expensive to a petty State, or more influential on the conduct of both sexes (*L'Esprit des Lois*, chap. xvi. livre vii.).

CHAPTER 24

The Immolation of Women.—We now proceed to consider another trait of Rajput character, exemplified in the practice of female immolation, and to inquire whether religion, custom, or affection has most share in such sacrifiee. To arrive at the origin of this rite, we must trace it to the recesses of mythology, where we shall discover the precedent in the example of Sati, who to avenge an insult to Iswara, in her own father's omission to ask her lord to an entertainment, consumed herself in the presence of the assembled gods. With this act of fealty (*sati*) the name of Daksha's daughter has been identified; and her regeneration and reunion to her husband, as the mountain-nymph Mena, or Parvati, furnish the incentive to similar [634] acts. In the history of these celestial beings, the Rajputni has a memorable lesson before her, that no domestic differences can afford exemption from this proof of faith: for Jupiter and Juno were not more eminent examples of connubial discord than Mena and Siva, who was not only alike unfaithful, but more cruel, driving Mena from his Olympus (Kailas), and forcing her to seek refuge in the murky caverns of Caucasus. Female immolation, therefore, originated with the sun-worshipping Saivas, and was common to all those nations who adored this the most splendid object of the visible creation. Witness the Scythic Gete or Jat warrior of the Jaxartes, who devoted his wife, horse, arms, and slaves, to the flames; the "giant Gete" of Scandinavia, who forgot not on the shores of the Baltic his Transoxianian habits; and the Frisian Frank and Saxon descended from him, who ages after omitted only the female. Could we assign the primary cause of a custom so opposed to the first law of nature with the same certainty that we can prove its high antiquity, we might be enabled to devise some means for its abolition. The chief characteristic of Satiism is its expiating quality: for by this act of faith, the Sati not only makes atonement for the sins of her husband, and secures the remission of her own, but has the joyful assurance of reunion to the object whose beatitude she procures. Having once imbibed this doctrine, its fulfilment is powerfully aided by that heroism of character inherent to the Rajputni; though we see that the stimulant of religion requires no aid even in the timid female of Bengal, who, relying on the promise of regeneration, lays her head on the pyre with the most philosophical composure.

Nothing short of the abrogation of the doctrines which pronounce such sacrifices exculpatory can be effectual in preventing them; but this would be to overturn the fundamental article of their creed, the notion of metempsychosis. Further research may disclose means more attainable, and the sacred Shastras are at once the surest and the safest. Whoever has examined these is aware of the conflict of authorities for and against cremation; but a proper application of them (and they are the highest who give it not their sanction) has, I believe, never been resorted to. Vyasa, the chronicler of the Yadus, a race whose manners were decidedly Scythic, is the great advocate for female sacrifice: he (in the Mahabharata) pronounces the expiation perfect. But Manu inculcates no such doctrine [635]; and although the state of widowhood he recommends might be deemed onerous by the fair sex of the west, it would be considered little hardship in the east. "Let her emaciate her body, by living voluntarily on pure flowers, roots, and fruit; but let her not, when her lord is deceased, even pronounce the name of another man." Again he says, "A virtuous wife ascends to heaven, if, after the decease of her lord, she devote herself to pious austerity; but a widow, who slights her deceased husband by marrying again, brings disgrace on herself here below, and shall be excluded from the seat of her lord." [1]

These and many other texts, enjoining purity of life and manners to the widow, are to be found in this first authority, but none demanding such a cruel pledge of affection. Abstinence from the common pursuits of life, and entire self-denial, are rewarded by "high renown in this world, and in the next the abode of her husband"; and procure for her the title of "*sadhwi*, or the virtuous." These are deemed sufficient pledges of affection by the first of sages.[2] So much has been written on this subject that we shall not pursue it further in this place; but proceed to consider a still more inhuman practice, infanticide.

[1] Manu, *Laws*, v. 157, 160, 161.

[2] Were all Manu's maxims on this head collected, and with other good authorities, printed, circulated, and supported by Hindu missionaries, who might be brought to advocate the abolition of Satiism, some good might be effected. Let every text tending to the respectability of widowhood be made prominent, and degrade the opponents by enumerating the weak

Although custom sanctions, and religion rewards, a Sati, the victim to marital selfishness, yet, to the honour of humanity, neither traditionary adage nor religious text can be quoted in support of a practice so revolting as infanticide. Man alone, of the whole animal creation, is equal to the task of destroying his offspring [636]: for instinct preserves what reason destroys. The wife is the sacrifice to his egotism, and the progeny of her own sex to his pride; and if the unconscious infant should escape the influence of the latter, she is only reserved to become the victim of the former at the period when life is most desirous of extension. If the female reasoned on her destiny, its hardships are sufficient to stifle all sense of joy, and produce indifference to life. When a female is born, no anxious inquiries await the mother—no greetings welcome the newcomer, who appears an

---

points they abound in. Instance the polyandry which prevailed among the Pandus, whose high priest Vyasa was an illegitimate branch; though above all would be the efficacy of the abolition of polygamy, which in the lower classes leaves women destitute, and in the higher condemns them to mortification and neglect. Whatever result such a course might produce, there can be no danger in the experiment. Such sacrifices must operate powerfully on manners; and, barbarous as is the custom, yet while it springs from the same principle, it ought to improve the condition of women, from the fear that harsh treatment of them might defeat the atonement hereafter. Let the advocate for the abolition of this practice by the hand of power read attentively Mr. Colebrooke's essay, "On the Duties of a Faithful Hindu Widow," in the fourth volume of the *Asiatic Researches* [*Essays on the Religion and Philosophy of the Hindus*, ed. 1858, p. 70 ff.], to correct the notion that there is no adequate religious ordinance for the horrid sacrifice. Mr. C. observes (p. 220): "Though an alternative be allowed, the Hindu legislators have shown themselves disposed to encourage widows to burn themselves with their husband's corpse." In this paper he will find too many authorities deemed sacred for its support; but it is only by knowing the full extent of the prejudices and carefully collecting the conflicting authorities, that we can provide the means to overcome it. Jahangir legislated for the abolition of this practice by successive ordinances. At first he commanded that no woman, being mother of a family, should under any circumstances be permitted, however willing, to immolate herself; and subsequently the prohibition was made entire when the slightest compulsion was required, "whatever the assurances of the people might be." The royal commentator records no reaction. We might imitate Jahangir, and adopting the partially prohibitive ordinance, forbid the sacrifice where there was a family to rear. [The early texts on the subject of Sati have been collected by H. H. Wilson, *Essays and Lectures chiefly on the Religion of the Hindus*, 1881, ii. 270 ff. Also see Max Müller, *Selected Essays on Language, Mythology, and Religion*, 1881, i. 332 ff.]

intruder on the scene, which often closes in the hour of its birth. But the very silence with which a female birth is accompanied forcibly expresses sorrow; and we dare not say that many compunctious visitings do not obtrude themselves on those who, in accordance with custom and imagined necessity, are thus compelled to violate the sentiments of nature. Families may exult in the Satis which their cenotaphs portray,[1] but none ever heard a Rajput boast of the destruction of his infant progeny.

The Origin of Infanticide.—What are the causes, we may ask, sufficiently powerful to induce the suppression of a feeling which every sentient being has in common for its offspring? To suppose the Rajput devoid of this sentiment would argue his deficiency in the ordinary attributes of humanity: often is he heard to exclaim, "Accursed the day when a woman child was born to me!" The same motive which studded Europe with convents, in which youth and beauty were immured until liberated by death, first prompted the Rajput to infanticide: and, however revolting the policy, it is perhaps kindness compared to incarceration. There can be no doubt that monastic seclusion, practised by the Frisians in France, the Langobardi in Italy, and the Visigoths in Spain, was brought from Central Asia, the cradle of the Goths.[2] It is, in fact, a modification of the same feeling which characterizes the Rajput and the ancient German warrior —the dread of dishonour to the fair: the former raises the poniard

[1] [On Sati shrines and records of their deaths at Bikaner see General G. Hervey, *Some Records of Crime*, i. 209 f., 238 ff.]

[2] The Ghakkars, a Scythic race inhabiting the banks of the Indus, at an early period of history were given to infanticide. "It was a custom among them," says Ferishta, "as soon as a female child was born, to carry her to the market-place and there proclaim aloud, holding the child in one hand and a knife in the other, that any person who wanted a wife might now take her; otherwise she was immediately put to death. By this means they had more men than women, which occasioned the custom of several husbands to one wife. When this wife was visited by one of her husbands, she set up a mark at the door, which being observed by any of the others who might be coming on the same errand, he immediately withdrew till the signal was taken away."

[This quotation from Ferishta is taken from Dow (2nd ed. i. 138 f.). Compare Briggs' trans., i. 183 f. This account is denied by the present members of the tribe (Rose, *Glossary*, ii. 275). Much that is said about them refers to the Khokhar tribe (Elliot-Dowson v. 166, note).]

to the breast of his wife rather than witness her captivity, and he gives the opiate to the infant, whom, if he cannot portion and marry to her equal, he dare not see degraded [637].

Infanticide.—Although religion nowhere authorizes this barbarity, the laws which regulate marriage amongst the Rajputs powerfully promote infanticide. Not only is intermarriage prohibited between families of the same clan (*khanp*), but between those of the same tribe (*got*); and though centuries may have intervened since their separation, and branches thus transplanted may have lost their original patronymic, they can never be regrafted on the original stem: for instance, though eight centuries have separated the two grand subdivisions of the Guhilots, and the younger, the Sesodia, has superseded the elder, the Aharya, each ruling distinct States, a marriage between any of the branches would be deemed incestuous: the Sesodia is yet brother to the Aharya, and regards every female of the race as his sister. Every tribe has therefore to look abroad, to a race distinct from its own, for suitors for the females. Foreign war, international feuds, or other calamities affect tribes the most remote from each other; nor can war or famine thin the clans of Marwar, without diminishing the female population of Amber: thus both suffer in a twofold degree. Many virtuous and humane princes have endeavoured to check or mitigate an evil, in the eradication of which every parental feeling would co-operate. Sumptuary edicts alone can control it; and the Rajputs were never sufficiently enamoured of despotism to permit it to rule within their private dwellings. The plan proposed, and in some degree followed by the great Jai Singh of Amber, might with caution be pursued, and with great probability of success. He submitted to the prince of every Rajput State a decree, which was laid before a convocation of their respective vassals, in which he regulated the *daeja* or dower, and other marriage expenditure, with reference to the property of the vassal, limiting it to one year's income of the estate. This plan was, however, frustrated by the vanity of the Chondawat of Salumbar, who expended on the marriage of his daughter a sum even greater than his sovereign could have afforded; and to have his name blazoned by the bards and genealogists, he sacrificed the beneficent views of one of the wisest of the Rajput race. Until vanity suffers itself to be controlled, and the aristocratic Rajput submit to republican simplicity,[1] the evils arising from nuptial profusion will not cease. Unfortunately, those who could check it find their interest in stimulating it, namely, the whole class of Mangtas [638] (mendicants), bards, minstrels, jugglers, Brahmans who assemble on these occasions, and pour forth their epithalamiums in praise of the virtue of liberality. The Bardais are the grand recorders of fame, and the volume of precedent is always recurred to, in citing the liberality of former chiefs ; while the dread of their satire (*visarva*, literally ' poison ')[2] shuts the eyes of the chiefs to consequences, and they are only anxious to maintain the reputation of their ancestors, though fraught with future ruin. " The Dahima emptied his coffers " (says Chand, the pole-star of the Rajputs) " on the marriage of his daughter with Prithiraj ; but he filled them with the praises of mankind." The same bard retails every article of these *daejas* or ' dowers,' which thus become precedents for future ages; and the " *lakh pasarna*,"[3] then established for the chief bardai, has become a model to posterity. Even now the Rana of Udaipur, in his season of poverty, at the recent marriage of his daughters bestowed " the gift of a lakh " on the chief bard ; though the articles of gold, horses, clothes, etc., were included in the estimate, and at an undue valuation, which rendered the gift not quite so precious as in the days of the Chauhan. Were bonds taken from all the feudal chiefs, and a penal clause inserted, of forfeiture of their fief by all who exceeded a fixed nuptial expenditure, the axe would be laid to the root, the evil would be checked, and the heart of many a mother (and we may add father) be gladdened, by preserving at once the point of honour and their child. When ignorance declaims against the gratuitous love of murder amongst these brave men, our contempt is excited equally by its short-sighted conclusions, and the affected philanthropy which overlooks all remedy but the " *sic volo*." Sir John Shore,[4] when acting on the suggestions of

[1] Could they be induced to adopt the custom of the ancient Marsellois, infanticide might cease : " Marseille fut la plus sage des républiques de son temps : les dots ne pourraient passer cents écus en argent, et cinq en habits, dit Strabon " (*De l'Esprit des Lois*, chap. xv. liv. v. 21).

[2] [Dr. L. P. Tesitori writes that the true form of this word is *risar*, ' satire,' which has no connexion with *vis*, ' poison.']

[3] [This term and the custom of extravagant gifts at marriages still prevail. *Pasārna* means ' to scatter, display ' (Russell, *Tribes and Castes Central Provinces*, ii. 256).]

[4] [*Asiatic Researches*, iv. 353 f. ; *Calcutta Review*, i. 377.]

the benevolent Duncan for the suppression of this practice amongst the Rajkumars, judged more wisely as a politician, and more charitably in his estimate of human motives. "A prohibition," says he, "enforced by the denunciation of the severest temporal penalties, would have had little efficacy in abolishing a custom which existed in opposition to the feelings of humanity and natural affection"; but "the sanction of that religion which the Rajkumars professed was appealed to in aid of the ordinances of civil authority; and an engagement binding themselves to desist from the barbarous practice was prepared, and circulated for signature amongst the Rajkumars." It may well be doubted how far this influence could extend, when the root of the evil [639] remained untouched, though not unseen, as the philanthropic Duncan pointed out in the confession of the Rajkumars: "all unequivocally admitted it, but all did not fully acknowledge its atrocity; and the only reason they assigned for the inhuman practice was the great expense of procuring suitable matches for their daughters, if they allowed them to grow up." The Rajkumar is one of the Chauhan sakha, chief of the Agnikulas, and in proportion to its high and well-deserved pretensions on the score of honour, it has more infanticides than any other of the "thirty-six royal races." Amongst those of this race out of the pale of feudalism, and subjected to powers not Rajput, the practice is fourfold greater, from the increased pressure of the cause which gave it birth, and the difficulty of establishing their daughters in wedlock. Raja Jai Singh's enactment went far to remedy this. Conjoin his plan with Mr. Duncan's, provide dowers, and infanticide will cease. It is only by removing the cause that the consequences can be averted.[1]

As to the almost universality of this practice amongst the Jarejas, the leading cause, which will also operate to its continuance, has been entirely overlooked. The Jarejas were Rajputs, a subdivision of the Yadus; but by intermarriage with the Muhammadans, to whose faith they became proselytes, they lost their caste. Political causes have disunited them from the Muhammadans, and they desire again to be considered as pure Rajputs; but having been contaminated, no Rajput will intermarry with them. The owner of a hyde of land, whether Sesodia,

[1] [For recent measures proposed for reduction of marriage expenses, see Risley, *The People of India*, 2nd ed. 195 ff.]

Rathor, or Chauhan, would scorn the hand of a Jareja princess. Can the "*sic volo*" be applied to men who think in this fashion?

Johar.—Having thus pointed out the causes of the sacrifice of widows and of infants, I shall touch on the yet more awful rite of Johar, when a whole tribe may become extinct, of which several instances have been recorded in the annals of Mewar. To the fair of other lands the fate of the Rajputni must appear one of appalling hardship. In each stage of life death is ready to claim her; by the poppy at its dawn, by the flames in riper years; while the safety of the interval depending on the uncertainty of war, at no period is her existence worth a twelvemonth's purchase. The loss of a battle, or the capture of a city, is a signal to avoid captivity and its horrors, which to the Rajputni are worse than death. To the doctrines of Christianity Europe owes the boon of protection to the helpless and the fair, who are [640] comparatively safe amidst the vicissitudes of war; to which security the chivalry of the Middle Ages doubtless contributed. But it is singular that a nation so refined, so scrupulous in its ideas with regard to females, as the Rajput, should not have entered into some national compact to abandon such proof of success as the bondage[1] of the sex. We can enter into the feeling, and applaud the deed, which ensured the preservation of their honour by the fatal johar, when the foe was the brutalized Tatar. But the practice was common in the international wars of the Rajputs; and I possess numerous inscriptions (on stone and on brass) which record as the first token of victory the captive wives of the foeman. When "the mother of Sisera looked out of the window, and cried through the lattice, Why tarry the wheels of his chariot—have they not sped? have they not divided the prey; to every man a damsel or two?"[2] we have a perfect picture of the Rajput mother expecting her son from the foray.

The Jewish law with regard to female captives was perfectly analogous to that of Manu; both declare them "lawful prize," and both Moses and Manu establish rules sanctioning the marriage of such captives with the captors. "When a girl is made captive by her lover, after a victory over her kinsman," marriage "is permitted by law."[3] That forcible marriage in the Hindu law

[1] *Banda* is 'a bondsman' in Persian; *Bandi*, 'a female slave' in Hindi. [These words have no connexion with "bondage."]

[2] Judges v. 28-30.

[3] Manu, *Laws*, iii. 26.

termed Rakshasa, namely, "the seizure of a maiden by force from her house while she weeps and calls for assistance, after her kinsman and friends have been slain in battle,"[1] is the counterpart of the ordinance regarding the usage of a captive in the Pentateuch,[2] excepting the "shaving of the head," which is the sign of complete slavery with the Hindu.[3] When Hector, anticipating his fall, predicts the fate which awaits Andromache, he draws a forcible picture of the misery of the Rajput; but the latter, instead of a lachrymose and enervating harangue as he prepared for the battle with the same chance of defeat, would have spared her the pain of plying the "Argive loom" by her death. To prevent such degradation, the brave [641] Rajput has recourse to the johar, or immolation of every female of the family: nor can we doubt that, educated as are the females of that country, they gladly embrace such a refuge from pollution. Who would not be a Rajput in such a case? The very term widow (*rand*) is used in common parlance as one of reproach.[4]

Manu commands that whoever accosts a woman shall do so

[1] Manu, *Laws*, iii. 33.

[2] "When thou goest forth to war against thine enemies, and the Lord thy God hath delivered them into thine hands, and thou hast taken them captive, and seest among the captives a beautiful woman, and hast a desire unto her, that thou wouldest have her to thy wife; then thou shalt bring her home to thine house, and she shall shave her head, and pare her nails; and she shall put the raiment of her captivity from off her, and shall remain in thine house, and bewail her father and her mother a full month: and after that thou shalt go in unto her, and be her husband, and she shall be thy wife" (Deut. xxi. 10, 11, 12, 13).

[3] [On head-shaving as a mark of slavery see *Jātaka*, Cambridge trans., v. 125; Anantha Krishna Iyer, *Tribes and Castes of Cochin*, ii. 337; *BG*, ix. Part i. 232.]

[4] I remember in my subaltern days, and wanderings through countries then little known, one of my Rajput soldiers at the well, impatient for water, asked a woman for the rope and bucket by the uncivil term of *rand*: "*Main Rajputni che,*" 'I am a Rajputni,' she replied in the Hara dialect, to which tribe she belonged, "*aur Rajput ki ma cho,*" 'and the mother of Rajputs.' At the indignant reply the hands of the brave Kalyan were folded, and he asked her forgiveness by the endearing and respectful epithet of "mother." It was soon granted, and filling his brass vessel, she dismissed him with the epithet of "son," and a gentle reproof. Kalyan was himself a Rajput, and a bolder lives not, if he still exists; this was in 1807, and in 1817 he gained his sergeant's knot, as one of the thirty-two firelocks of my guard, who led the attack, and defeated a camp of fifteen hundred Pindaris.

by the title of "sister,"[1] and that "way must be made for her, even as for the aged, for a priest, a prince, or a bridegroom"; and in the admirable text on the laws of hospitality, he ordains that "pregnant women, brides, and damsels shall have food before all the other guests"[2]; which, with various other texts, appears to indicate a time when women were less than now objects of restraint; a custom attributable to the paramount dominion of the Muhammadans, from whose rigid system the Hindus have borrowed. But so many conflicting texts are to be found in the pages of Manu, that we may pronounce the compilation never to have been the work of the same legislator: from whose dicta we may select with equal facility texts tending to degrade as to exalt the sex. For the following he would meet with many plaudits: "Let women be constantly supplied with ornaments at festivals and jubilees, for if the wife be not elegantly attired, she will not exhilarate her husband. A wife gaily adorned, the whole house is embellished."[3] In the following text he pays an unequivocal compliment to her power: "A female is able to draw from the right path in this life, not a fool only, but even a sage, and can lead him in subjection to desire or to wrath." With this acknowledgment from the very fountain of authority, we have some ground for asserting that *les femmes font les mœurs*, even in Rajputāna; and that though immured and invisible, their influence on society is not less certain than if they moved in the glare of open day.

Position of Rājput Women.—Most erroneous ideas have been formed of the Hindu female from the pictures drawn by those who never left the banks of the Ganges. They are represented [642] as degraded beings, and that not one in many thousands can even read. I would ask such travellers whether they know the name of Rajput, for there are few of the lowest chieftains whose daughters are not instructed both to read and write; though the customs of the country requiring much form in epistolary writing, only the signature is made to letters. But of their intellect, and knowledge of mankind, whoever has had to converse with a Rajputni guardian of her son's rights, must draw a very different conclusion.[4] Though excluded by the

[1] *Laws*, ii. 129. [2] *Ibid.* iii. 114.

[3] *Ibid.* iii. 57, 60, 61, 62, 63.

[4] I have conversed for hours with the Bundi queen-mother on the affairs

Salic law of India from governing, they are declared to be fit regents during minority; and the history of India is filled with anecdotes of able and valiant females in this capacity.[1]

Rājput Character.—The more prominent traits of character will be found disseminated throughout the annals; we shall therefore omit the customary summaries of nationalities, those fanciful debtor and creditor accounts, with their balanced amount, favourable or unfavourable according to the disposition of the observer; and from the anecdotes through these pages leave the reader to form his own judgement of the Rajput. High courage, patriotism, loyalty, honour, hospitality, and simplicity are qualities which must at once be conceded to them; and if we cannot vindicate them from charges to which human nature in every clime is obnoxious; if we are compelled to admit the deterioration of moral dignity, from the continual inroads of, and their consequent collision with, rapacious conquerors; we must yet admire the quantum of virtue which even oppression and bad example have failed to banish. The meaner vices of deceit and falsehood, which the delineators of national character attach to the Asiatic without distinction, I deny to be universal with the Rajputs, though some tribes may have been obliged from position to use these shields of the weak against continuous oppression. Every court in Rajasthan has [643] its characteristic epithet; and there is none held more contemptible than the affix

of her government and welfare of her infant son, to whom I was left guardian by his dying father. She had adopted me as her brother; but the conversation was always in the presence of a third person in her confidence, and a curtain separated us. Her sentiments showed invariably a correct and extensive knowledge, which was equally apparent in her letters, of which I had many. I could give many similar instances.

[1] Ferishta in his history [ii. 217 ff.] gives an animated picture of Durgavati, queen of Garha, defending the rights of her infant son against Akbar's ambition. Like another Boadicea, she headed her army, and fought a desperate battle with Asaf Khan, in which she was wounded and defeated; but scorning flight, or to survive the loss of independence, she, like the antique Roman in such a predicament, slew herself on the field of battle. [For Durgāvati see Badaoni, trans. W. H. Lowe, ii. 65; Elliot-Dowson v. 169, 288, vi. 118 ff.; Sleeman, *Rambles*, 190 f.]

Whoever desires to judge of the comparative fidelity of the translations of this writer, by Dow [ii. 224 ff.] and Briggs, cannot do better than refer to this very passage. The former has clothed it in all the trappings of Ossianic decoration: the latter gives "a plain unvarnished tale," which ought to be the aim of every translator.

of *jhutha darbar*, 'the lying court,' applied to Jaipur; while the most comprehensive measure of praise is the simple epithet of *sachha*,[1] 'the truth-teller.' Again, there are many shades between deceit and dissimulation: the one springs from natural depravity; the other may be assumed, as with the Rajput, in self-defence. But their laws, the mode of administering them, and the operation of external causes, must be attentively considered before we can form a just conclusion of the springs which regulate the character of a people. We must examine the opinions of the competent of past days, when political independence yet remained to the Rajputs, and not found our judgment of a nation upon a superficial knowledge of individuals. To this end I shall avail myself of the succinct but philosophical remarks of Abu-l-fazl, the wise minister of the wise Akbar, which are equally applicable to mankind at large, as to the particular people we are treating of. "If," he says, speaking of the Hindus, "a diligent investigator were to examine the temper and disposition of the people of each tribe, he would find every individual differing in some respect or other. Some among them are virtuous in the highest degree, and others carry vice to the greatest excess. They are renowned for wisdom, disinterested friendship, obedience to their superiors, and many other virtues: but, at the same time, there are among them men whose hearts are obdurate and void of shame, turbulent spirits, who for the merest trifle will commit the greatest outrages."[2]

Again: "The Hindus are religious, affable, courteous to strangers, cheerful, enamoured of knowledge, lovers of justice, able in business, grateful, admirers of truth, and of unbounded fidelity in all their dealings. Their character shines brightest in adversity. Their soldiers (the Rajputs) know not what it is to fly from the field of battle: but when the success of the combat becomes doubtful, they dismount from their horses, and throw away their lives in payment of the debt of valour."[3]

I shall conclude this chapter with a sketch of their familiar habits, and a few of their indoor and outdoor recreations.

Introduction of Melons, Grapes, Tobacco, Opium: the Use of Opium.—To Babur, the founder of the Mogul dynasty, India is

[1] *Sachha* is very comprehensive; in common parlance it is the opposite of 'untrue'; but it means 'loyal, upright, just.'

[2] [*Āīn*, iii. 114.]

[3] [*Ibid.* iii. 8.]

indebted for the introduction [644] of its melons and grapes; and to his grandson Jahangir for tobacco.[1] For the introduction of opium we have no date, and it is not even mentioned in the poems of Chand.[2] This pernicious plant has robbed the Rājput of half his virtues; and while it obscures these, it heightens his vices, giving to his natural bravery a character of insane ferocity, and to the countenance, which would otherwise beam with intelligence, an air of imbecility. Like all stimulants, its effects are magical for a time; but the reaction is not less certain: and the faded form or amorphous bulk too often attest the debilitating influence of a drug which alike debases mind and body. In the more ancient epics we find no mention of the poppy-juice as now used, though the Rajput has at all times been accustomed to his *madhava ra piyala*, or 'intoxicating cup.' The essence,[3] whether of grain, of roots, or of flowers, still welcomes the guest, but is secondary to the opiate. *Amal lar khana*, 'to eat opium together.' is the most inviolable pledge; and an agreement ratified by this ceremony is stronger than any adjuration. If a Rajput pays a visit, the first question is, *amal khaya*? 'have you had your opiate?'—*amal khao*, 'take your opiate.' On a birthday, when all the chiefs convene to congratulate their brother on another 'knot to his years,' the large cup is brought forth, a lump of opiate put therein, upon which water is poured, and by the aid of a stick a solution is made, to which each helps his neighbour, not with a glass, but with the hollow of his hand held to his mouth. To judge by the wry faces on this occasion, none can like it, and to get rid of the nauseous taste, comfit-balls are handed round. It is curious to observe the animation it inspires; a Rajput is

[1] The autobiography of both these noble Tatar princes are singular compositions, and may be given as standards of Eastern intellectual acquirement. They minutely note the progress of refinement and luxury. [The sweet melon was probably introduced from Persia, but some varieties of the plant seem to be indigenous. India, however, has a strong claim to ancient cultivation of the vine. Doubtless to the Portuguese may be assigned the credit of having conveyed both the tobacco plant and the knowledge of its properties to India and China (Watt, *Econ. Dict.* ii. 626, 628, vi. Part iv. 263, v. 361; *Id. Comm. Prod.* 437 f., 796, 1112; Yule, *Hobson-Jobson*, 2nd ed. 924 ff.)].

[2] [If the Greeks discovered opium, the Arabs were chiefly concerned in disseminating in the East the knowledge of the plant and its uses (Watt, *Econ. Dict.* vi. Part i. 24 ff.; *Comm. Prod.* 846).]

[3] *'Araq*, 'essence'; whence *arrack* and *rack*.

fit for nothing without his *amal*, and I have often dismissed their men of business to refresh their intellects by a dose, for when its effects are dissipating they become mere logs [645].[1] Opium to the Rajput is more necessary than food, and a suggestion to the Rana to tax it highly was most unpopular. From the rising generation the author exacted promises that they would resist initiation in this vice, and many grew up in happy ignorance of the taste of opium. He will be the greatest friend to Rajasthan who perseveres in eradicating the evil. The valley of Udaipur is a poppy garden, of every hue and variety, whence the Hindu Sri may obtain a coronet more variegated than ever adorned the Isis of the Nile.

Pledge by eating Opium.—A pledge once given by the Rajput, whether ratified by the "eating opium together," "an exchange of turbans," or the more simple act of "giving the right hand," is maintained inviolable under all circumstances.

Hunting and other Sports.—Their grand hunts have been described. The Rajput is fond of his dog and his gun. The former aids him in pulling down the boar or hare, and with the stalking-horse he will toil for hours after the deer. The greater

[1] Even in the midst of conversation, the eye closes and the head nods as the exciting cause is dissipating, and the countenance assumes a perfect vacuity of expression. Many a chief has taken his siesta in his chair while on a visit to me: an especial failing of my good friend Raj Kalyan of Sadri, the descendant of the brave Shama, who won "the right hand" of the prince at Haldighat. The lofty turban worn by the Raj, which distinguishes this tribe (the Jhala), was often on the point of tumbling into my lap, as he unconsciously nodded. When it is inconvenient to dissolve the opium, the chief carries it in his pocket, and presents it, as we would a pinch of snuff in Europe. In my subaltern days the chieftain of Senthal, in Jaipur, on paying me a visit, presented me with a piece of opium, which I took and laid on the table. Observing that I did not eat it, he said he should like to try the *Farangi ka amal*, 'the opiate of the Franks.' I sent him a bottle of powerful Schiedam, and to his inquiry as to the quantity of the dose, I told him he might take from an eighth to the half, as he desired exhilaration or oblivion. We were to have hunted the next morning; but having no sign of my friend, I was obliged to march without ascertaining the effect of the barter of *aphim* for the waters of Friesland; though I have no doubt that he found them quite Lethean. [The Rājputs ascribed a divine power to opium owing to the mental exhilaration caused by the drug: hence the taking of it with a chief was a form of solemn communion, and a renewal of the pledge of loyalty (Russell, *Tribes and Castes, Central Provinces*, i. 170, iii. 164, iv. 425). For opium drinking among Rājputs see Malcolm, *Memoir, Central India*, 2nd ed. ii. 146 f.; Forbes, *Rāsmāla*, 557).]

chieftains have their *ramnas* or preserves, where poaching would be summarily punished, and where the slaughter of all kinds of beasts, elk, hog, hyena, tiger, boar, deer, wild-dog, wolf, or hare, is indiscriminate. Riding in the ring with the lance in tournaments, without the spike, the point being guarded; defence of the sword against the lance, with every variety of "noble horsemanship," such as would render the most expert in Europe an easy prey to the active Rajput, are some of the chief exercises. Firing at a mark with a matchlock, in which they attain remarkable accuracy of aim; and in some parts of the country throwing a dart or javelin from horseback, are favourite amusements. The practice of the bow is likewise a main source of pastime, and in the manner there adopted it requires both dexterity and strength [1] [646]. The Rajput is not satisfied if he cannot bury his arrow either in the earthern target, or in the buffalo, to the feather. The use of the bow is hallowed; Arjuna's bow in the "great war," and that of the Chauhan king, Prithiraj, with which the former gained Draupadi and the latter the fair Sanjogta, are immortalized like that of Ulysses. In these martial exercises the youthful Rajput is early initiated, and that the sight of blood may be familiar, he is instructed, before he has strength to wield a sword, to practise with his boy's scimitar on the heads of lambs and kids. His first successful essay on the animals '*ferae naturae*' is a source of congratulation to his whole family.[2] In this manner the spirit of chivalry is continually fed, for everything around him speaks of arms and strife. His very amusements are warlike; and the dance and the song, the burthen of which is the record of his successful gallantry, so far from enervating, serve as fresh incitements to his courage.

Wrestling.—The exhibition of the Jethis, or wrestlers,[3] is another mode of killing time. It is a state concern for every prince or chief to entertain a certain number of these champions

[1] [The use of the bow has now disappeared except among forest tribes. For its use in Mogul times see Irvine, *Army of the Indian Moghuls*, 91 ff.]

[2] The author has now before him a letter written by the queen-mother of Bundi desiring his rejoicings on Lalji, 'the beloved's,' *coup d'essai* on a deer, which he had followed most pertinaciously to the death. On this occasion a court was held, and all the chiefs presented offerings and congratulations.

[3] [For the Jethi wrestlers in S. India see Thurston, *Tribes and Castes*, ii. 456 ff.]

of the glove. Challenges are sent by the most celebrated from one court to another; and the event of the *akhara*, as the arena is termed, is looked to with great anxiety.

Armouries.—No prince or chief is without his *silah-khana*, or armoury, where he passes hours in viewing and arranging his arms. Every favourite weapon, whether sword, matchlock, spear, dagger, or bow, has a distinctive epithet. The keeper of the armoury is one of the most confidential officers about the person of the prince. These arms are beautiful and costly. The *sirohi*,[1] or slightly curved blade, is formed like that of Damascus, and is the greatest favourite of all the variety of sabres throughout Rajputana. The long cut-and-thrust, like the Andrea Ferrara, is not uncommon; nor the *khanda*, or double-edged sword. The matchlocks both of Lahore and the country are often highly finished and inlaid with mother-of-pearl and gold: those of Bundi are the best. The shield of the rhinoceros-hide offers the best resistance, and is often ornamented with animals, beautifully painted, and enamelled in gold and silver. The bow is of buffalo-horn, and the arrows of reed, and barbed in a variety of fashions, as the crescent, the trident, the snake's tongue, and other fanciful forms.

Sheodān Singh. Music.—The Maharaja Sheodan Singh (whose family are heirs presumptive to the throne) was one of my constant visitors; and the title of 'adopted brother,' which he conferred upon me, allowed him to make his visits unreasonably long. The Maharaja had many excellent qualities. He was the best shot in Mewar; he was well read in the classic literature of his nation; deeply versed in the secrets of the chronicles, not only of Mewar but of all Rajwara; conversant with all the mysteries of the bard, and could improvise on every occasion. He was a proficient in musical science [647], and could discourse most fluently on the whole theory of Sangita, which comprehends vocal and instrumental harmony. He could explain each of the *ragas*, or musical modes, which issued from the five mouths of Siva and his consort Mena, together with the almost endless variations of the *ragas*, to each of which are allotted six

[1] [It takes its name from the town where they were made. The blade is slightly curved, one specimen being rather narrower and lighter than the ordinary sword (*talwār*), (Egerton, *Handbook of Indian Arms*, 1880, p. 105; Irvine, *Army of the Indian Moghuls*, 76 f.).]

consorts or *raginis*. He had attached to his suite the first vocalists of Mewar, and occasionally favoured me by letting them sing at my house. The chief cantatrice had a superb voice, a contralto of great extent, and bore the familiar appellation of 'Catalani.' Her execution of all the *basant* or 'spring-songs,' and the *megh* or 'cloud-songs' of the monsoon, which are full of melody, was perfect. But she had a rival in a singer from Ujjain, and we made a point of having them together, that emulation might excite to excellence. The chieftain of Salumbar, the chief of the Saktawats, and others, frequently joined these parties, as well as the Maharaja: for all are partial to the dance and the song, during which conversation flows unrestrained. Saadatu-lla, whose execution on the guitar would have secured applause even at the Philharmonic, commanded mute attention when he played a *tan* or symphony, or when, taking any of the simple *tappas* of Ujjain as a theme, he wandered through a succession of voluntaries. In summer these little parties were held on the terrace or the house-top, where carpets were spread under an awning, while the cool breezes of the lake gave life after the exhaustion of a day passed under 96° of Fahrenheit. The subjects of their songs are various, love, glory, satire, etc. I was invited to similar assemblies by many of the chiefs; though none were so intellectual as those of the Maharaja. On birthdays or other festivals the chief Bardai often appears, or the bard of any other tribe who may happen to be present. Then all is mute attention, broken only by the emphatic "*wah, wah!*" the measured nod of the head, or fierce curl of the moustache, in token of approbation or the reverse.[1]

The Maharaja's talents for amplification were undoubted, and by more than one of his friends this failing was attributed to his long residence at the court of Jaipur, whose cognomen will not have been forgotten. He had one day been amusing us with feats of his youth, his swimming from island to island, and [648] bestriding the alligators for an excursion.[2] Like Tell, he had

[1] Poetic impromptus pass on these occasions unrestricted by the fear of the critic, though the long yawn now and then should have given the hint to my friend the Maharaja that his verses wanted Attic. But he had certainly talent, and he did not conceal his light, which shone the stronger from the darkness that surrounded him: for poverty is not the school of genius, and the trade of the schoolmaster has ever been the least lucrative in a capital where rapine has ruled.

[2] There are two of these alligators quite familiar to the inhabitants of

placed a mark on his son's head and hit it successfully. He could kill an eagle on the wing, and divide a ball on the edge of a knife, the knife itself unseen. While running on in this manner, my features betraying some incredulity, he insisted on redeeming his word. A day was accordingly appointed, and though labouring under an ague, he came with his favourite matchlocks. The more dangerous experiment was desisted from, and he commenced by dividing the ball on the knife. This he placed perpendicularly in the centre of an earthen vessel filled with water; and taking his station at about twenty paces, perforated the centre of the vessel, and allowed you to take up the fragments of the ball; having previously permitted you to load the piece, and examine the vessel, which he did not once approach himself. Another exhibition was striking an orange from a pole without perforating it. Again, he gave the option of loading to a bystander, and retreating a dozen paces, he knocked an orange off untouched by the ball, which, according to a preliminary proviso, could not be found: the orange was not even discoloured by the powder. He was an adept also at chess [1] and chaupar, and could carry on a conversation by stringing flowers in a peculiar manner. If he plumed himself upon his pretensions, his vanity was always veiled under a demeanour full of courtesy and grace; and Maharaja Sheodan Singh would be esteemed a well-bred and well-informed man at the most polished court of Europe.

Every chief has his band, vocal and instrumental; but Sindhia, some years since, carried away the most celebrated vocalists of Udaipur. The Rajputs are all partial to music. The tappa is the favourite measure. Its chief character is plaintive simplicity; and it is analogous to the Scotch, or perhaps still more to the Norman.[2]

Udaipur, who come when called "from the vasty deep" for food; and I have often exasperated them by throwing an inflated bladder, which the monsters greedily received, only to dive away in angry disappointment. It was on these that my friend affirmed he had ventured.

[1] *Chaturanga*, so called from imitating the formation of an army. The 'four' (*chatur*) 'bodied' (*anga*) array; or elephants, chariots, horse, and foot. His chief antagonist at chess was a blind man of the city. [*Chaupar* is played with oblong dice on a board with two transverse bars in the form of a cross, like *chausar* and *pachīsī.*]

[2] The *tappa* belongs to the very extremity of India, being indigenous as far as the Indus and the countries watered by its arms; and though the

The Rana, who is a great patron of the art, has a small band of musicians, whose only instrument is the *shahna*, or hautboy. They played their national [649] tappas with great taste and feeling; and these strains, wafted from the lofty terrace of the palace in the silence of the night, produced a sensation of delight not unmixed with pain, which its peculiarly melancholy character excites. The Rana has also a few flute or flageolet players, who discourse most eloquent music. Indeed, we may enumerate this among the principal amusements of the Rajputs; and although it would be deemed indecorous to be a performer, the science forms a part of education.[1]

Who that has marched in the stillness of night through the mountainous regions of Central India, and heard the warder sound the *turai* from his turreted abode, perched like an eyrie on the mountain-top, can ever forget its graduated intensity of sound, or the emphatic *ham! ham!* 'all's well," which follows the lengthened blast of the cornet reverberating in every recess.[2]

Bagpipes.—A species of bagpipe, so common to all the Celtic races of Europe, is not unknown to the Rajputs. It is called the *mashak*,[3] but is only the rudiment of that instrument whose

---

peculiar measure is common in Rajasthan, the prefix of *panjabi* shows its origin. I have listened at Caen to the viola or hurdy-gurdy, till I could have fancied myself in Mewar.

[1] Chand remarks of his hero, the Chauhan, that he was "master of the art," both vocal and instrumental. Whether profane music was ever common may be doubted; but sacred music was a part of early education with the sons of kings. Rama and his brothers were celebrated for the harmonious execution of episodes from the grand epic, the Ramayana. The sacred canticles of Jayadeva were set to music, and apparently by himself, and are yet sung by the Chaubes. The inhabitants of the various monastic establishments chant their addresses to the deity; and I have listened with delight to the modulated cadences of the hermits, singing the praises of Pataliswara from their pinnacled abode of Abu. It would be injustice to touch incidentally on the merits of the minstrel Dholi, who sings the warlike compositions of the sacred Bardai of Rajasthan.

[2] The *turai* is the sole instrument of the many of the trumpet kind which is not dissonant. The Kotah prince has the largest band, perhaps, in those countries; instruments of all kinds—stringed, wind, and percussion. But as it is formed by rule, in which the sacred and shrill conch-shell takes precedence, it must be allowed that it is anything but harmonious.

[3] [*Mashak* is the name of the leather water-bag. One of the late Rājas of Jind in the Panjāb had a bagpipe band, the musicians wearing kilts and

peculiar influence on the physical, through the moral agency of man, is described by our own master-bard. They have likewise the double flageolet; but in the same ratio of perfection to that of Europe as the *mashak* to the heart-stirring pipe of the north. As to their lutes, guitars, and all the varieties of tintinnabulants (as Dr. Johnson would call them), it would fatigue without interesting the reader to enumerate them.

Literature among the Rajputs. Observatories.—We now come to the literary attainments of the lords of Rajasthan, of whom there is none without sufficient clerkship to read his grant or agreement for *rakhwali* or blackmail; and none either so ignorant, or so proud, as the boasted ancestral wisdom of England, whose barons could not even sign their names to the great charter of their liberties. The Rana of Udaipur has unlimited command of [650] his pen, and his letters are admirable; but we may say of him nearly what was remarked of Charles the Second—"he never wrote a foolish thing, and seldom did a wise one." The familiar epistolary correspondence of the princes and nobles of Rajasthan would exhibit abundant testimony of their powers of mind: they are sprinkled with classical allusions, and evince that knowledge of mankind which constant collision in society must produce. A collection of these letters, which exist in the archives of every principality, would prove that the princes of this country are upon a par with the rest of mankind, not only in natural understanding, but, taking their opportunities into account, even in its cultivation. The prince who in Europe could quote Hesiod and Homer with the freedom that the Rana does on all occasions Vyasa and Valmiki, would be accounted a prodigy; and there is not a divine who could make application of the ordinances of Moses with more facility than the Rana of those of their great lawgiver Manu. When they talk of the wisdom of their ancestors, it is not a mere figure of speech. The instruction of their princes is laid down in rules held sacred, and must have been far more onerous than any system of European university education, for scarcely a branch of human knowledge is omitted. But the cultivation of the mind, and the arts of polished life, must always flourish in the ratio of a nation's

---

pink leggings to make them look like their Highland originals. The Yanādis, a forest tribe in Madras, play the bagpipe (Thurston, *Tribes and Castes*, vii. 431).]

prosperity, and from the decline of the one, we may date the deterioration of the other with the Rajput. The astronomer has now no patron to look to for reward ; there is no Jai Singh to erect such stupendous observatories as he built at Delhi, Benares, Ujjain, and at his own capital ;[1] to construct globes and armillary spheres, of which, according to their own and our system, the Kotah prince has two, each three feet in diameter. The same prince (Jai Singh) collated De la Hire's tables with those of Ulugh Beg, and presented the result to the last emperor of Delhi, worthy the name of the Great Mogul. To these tables he gave the name of *Zij Muhammad Shahi.* It was Jai Singh who, as already mentioned, sought to establish sumptuary laws throughout the nation, to regulate marriages, and thereby prevent infanticide ; and who left his name to the capital he founded, the first in Rajasthan.

But we cannot march over fifty miles of country without observing traces of the genius, talent, and wealth of past days : though—whether the more abstruse sciences, or the lighter arts which embellish life—all are now fast disappearing [651]. Whether in the tranquillity secured to them by the destruction of their predatory foes, these arts and sciences may revive, and the nation regain its elevated tone, is a problem which time alone can solve.

Household Furniture.—In their household economy, their furniture and decorations, they remain unchanged during the lapse of a thousand years. No chairs, no couches adorn their sitting apartments, though the painted and gilded ceiling may be supported by columns of serpentine, and the walls one mass of mirrors, marble, or china ;—nothing but a soft carpet, hidden by a white cloth, on which the guests seat themselves according to rank. In fine, the quaint description of the chaplain to the first embassy which England sent to India, more than two hundred years ago, applies now, as it probably will two hundred years hence. " And now for the furniture the greatest men have in them [their houses], it is *curta supellex,* very little, they (the rooms) being not beautified with hangings, nor with anything besides to line their walls ; for they have no chairs, stools, couches,

[1] [For these observatories see A. ff. Garrett, Pandit Chandradhar Guleri, *The Jaipur Observatory and its Builder*, Allahabad, 1902 ; Fanshawe, *Delhi Past and Present*, 247 f. ; M. A. Sherring, *The Sacred City of the Hindus*, 131 ff. ; *Asiatic Researches*, v. 177 ff.]

tables, beds enclosed with canopies, or curtains, in any of their rooms. And the truth is, that if they had them, the extreme heat would forbid the use of many of them ; all their bravery is upon their floors, on which they spread most excellent carpets." [1]

Dress.—It were useless to expatiate on dress, either male or female, the fashion varying in each province and tribe, though the texture and materials are everywhere the same : cotton in summer, and quilted chintz or broadcloth in winter. The ladies have only three articles of *parure*; the *ghaghra*, or 'petticoat'; the *kanchuli*, 'or corset' ; and the *dopatta*, or 'scarf,' which is occasionally thrown over [652] the head as a veil. Ornaments are without number. For the men, trousers of every shape and calibre, a tunic girded with a ceinture, and a scarf, form the wardrobe of every Rajput. The turban is the most important part of the dress, and is the unerring mark of the tribe ; the form and

[1] [E. Terry, *A Voyage to East India*, ed. 1777, p. 185.] Those who wish for an opinion "of the most excellent moralities which are to be observed amongst the people of these nations" cannot do better than read the 14th section of the observant, intelligent, and tolerant chaplain, who is more just, at least on one point, than the modern missionary, who denies to the Hindu filial affection. "And here I shall insert another most needful particular to my present purpose which deserves a most high commendation to be given unto that people in general, how poor and mean soever they be; and that is, the great exemplary care they manifest in their piety to their parents, that notwithstanding they serve for very little, but five shillings a moon for their whole livelihood and subsistence, yet if their parents be in want, they will impart, at the least, half of that little towards their necessities, choosing rather to want themselves than that their parents should suffer need." It is in fact one of the first precepts of their religion. The Chaplain thus concludes his chapter "On the Moralities of the Hindu" [232 f.]: "O! what a sad thing is it for Christians to come short of Indians, even in moralities; come short of those, who themselves believe to come short of heaven!" The Chaplain closes his interesting and instructive work with the subject of Conversion, which is as remote from accomplishment at this day as it was at that distant period. "Well known it is that the Jesuits there, who, like the Pharisees that would 'compass sea and land to make one proselyte' (Matt. xxiii. 15), have sent into Christendom many large reports of their great conversions of infidels in East India. But all these boastings are but reports; the truth is, that they have there spilt the precious water of Baptism upon some few faces, working upon the necessity of some poor men, who for want of means, which they give them, are contented to wear crucifixes; but for want of knowledge in the doctrine of Christianity are only in name Christians." *

* *A Voyage to East India*, 427.

fashion are various, and its decorations differ according to time and circumstances. The *balaband*, or 'silken fillet,' was once valued as the mark of the sovereign's favour, and was tantamount to the courtly "orders" of Europe. The colour of the turban and tunic varies with the season; and the changes are rung upon crimson, saffron, and purple, though white is by far the most common. Their shoes are mere slippers, and sandals are worn by the common classes. Boots are yet used in hunting or war, made of chamois leather, of which material the warrior often has a doublet, being more commodious, and less oppressive, than armour. The dagger or poniard is inseparable from the girdle.

Cookery, Medicine.—The culinary art will be discussed elsewhere, together with the medical, which is very low, and usurped by empyrics, who waste alike the purse and health of the ignorant by the sale of aphrodisiacs, which are sought after with great avidity. Gums, metals, minerals, all are compounded, and for one preparation, while the author was at Udaipur, 7000 rupees (nearly £1000) were expended by the court-physician.

Superstitions.—Their superstitions, incantations, charms, and phylacteries against danger, mental or bodily, will appear more appropriately where the subject is incidently introduced [653].

PERSONAL NARRATIVE OF THE AUTHOR

CHAPTER 25

Leaving Udaipur.—*October* 11, 1819.—Two years had nearly sped since we entered the valley of Udaipur, the most diversified and most romantic spot on the continent of India. In all this time none of us had penetrated beyond the rocky barrier which formed the limit of our horizon, affording the vision a sweep of six miles radius. Each hill and dale, tower and tree, had become familiar to us; every altar, cenotaph, and shrine had furnished its legend, till tradition was exhausted. The ruins were explored, their inscriptions deciphered, each fantastic pinnacle had a name, and the most remarkable chieftains and servants of the court had epithets assigned to them, expressive of some quality or characteristic. We had our 'Red Reaver,' our 'Roderic Dhu,' and a 'Falstaff,' at the court; our 'Catalani,' our 'Vestris,' in the song or the ballet. We had our palace in the city, our cutter on the lake, our villa in the woods, our fairy-islands in the waters; streams to angle in, deer to [654] shoot, much, in short, to please the eye and gratify the taste:—yet did ennui intrude, and all panted to escape from the "happy valley," to see what was in the world beyond the mountains. In all these twenty moons, the gigantic portals of Debari, which guard the entrance of the Girwa,[1] had not once creaked on their hinges for our egress; and though from incessant occupation I had wherewithal to lessen the *taedium vitae*, my companions not having such resources,

[1] The amphitheatre, or circle. [The valley of Udaipur.]

VALLEY OF UDAIPUR.

To face page 760.

it was in vain that, like the sage Imlac, I urged them not to feel dull in this "blissful captivity": the scenery had become hideous, and I verily believe had there been any pinion-maker in the capital of the Sesodias, they would have essayed a flight, though it might have terminated in the lake. Never did Rasselas sigh more for escape. At length the day arrived, and although the change was to be from all that constitutes the enchantments of vision, from wood and water, dale and mountain, verdure and foliage, to the sterile plains of the sandy desert of Marwar, it was sufficient that it was change. Our party was composed of Captain Waugh, Lieutenant Carey, and Dr. Duncan, with the whole of the escort, consisting of two companies of foot and sixty of Skinner's Horse, all alike delighted to quit the valley where each had suffered more or less from the prevalent fevers of the monsoon, during which the valley is peculiarly unhealthy, especially to foreigners, when the wells and reservoirs overflow from the springs which break in, impregnated with putrid vegetation and mineral poisons, covering the surface with a bluish oily fluid. The art of filtrating water to free it from impurities is unknown to the Rajputs, and with some shame I record that we did not make them wiser, though they are not strangers to the more simple process, adopted throughout the desert, of using potash and alum; the former to neutralize the salt and render the water more fit for culinary purposes; the latter to throw down the impurities held suspended. They also use an alkaline nut in washing, which by simply steeping emits a froth which is a good substitute for soap.[1]

On the 12th October, at five A.M., our trumpet sounded to horse, and we were not slow in obeying the summons; the "yellow boys" with their old native commandant looking even more cheerful than usual as we joined them. Skinner's Horse[2] wear a jamah or tunic of yellow broadcloth, with scarlet turbans and cincture. Who [655] does not know that James Skinner's men are the most orderly in the Company's service, and that in every

[1] *Sabun*, in the lingua franca of India, signifies 'soap.' [The soap-nut tree (*sapindus mukorossi*), the fruit of which is used for washing clothes and the hair (Watt, *Comm. Prod.* 979).]

[2] [Raised by James Skinner (1778-1841), known as "The Yellow Boys," in 1823; 1st Irregular Cavalry (Skinner's Horse), 1840; 1st Bengal Cavalry, 1861 (F. G. Cardew, *Sketch of the Services of the Bengal Native Army to the Year 1895*).]

other qualification constituting the efficient soldier, they are second to none? On another signal which reverberated from the palace, where the drums announced that the descendant of Surya was no sluggard, we moved on through the yet silent capital towards the gate of the sun, where we found drawn up the quotas of Bhindar, Delwara, Amet, and Bansi, sent as an honorary guard by the Rana, to escort us to the frontiers. As they would have been an incumbrance to me and an inconvenience to the country, from their laxity of discipline, after chatting with their leader, during a sociable ride, I dismissed them at the pass, with my respects to the Rana and their several chieftains. We reached the camp before eight o'clock, the distance being only thirteen miles. The spot chosen (and where I afterwards built a residence) was a rising ground between the villages of Merta and Tus, sprinkled with trees, and for a space of four miles clear of the belt of forest which fringes the granite barriers of the valley. It commanded an entire view of the plains in the direction of Chitor, still covered, excepting a patch of cultivation here and there, with jungle. The tiger-mount, its preserves of game, and the mouldering hunting-seats of the Rana and his chieftains, were three miles to the north; to the south, a mile distant, we had the Berach River, abounding in trout; and the noble lake whence it issues, called after its founder the Udai Sagar, was not more than three to the west. For several reasons it was deemed advisable to choose a spot out of the valley; the health of the party, though not an unimportant, was not a principal motive for choosing such a distance from the court. The wretchedness in which we found it rendered a certain degree of interference requisite, and it was necessary that they should shake this off, in order to preserve their independence. It was dreaded lest the aid requested by the Rana, from the peculiar circumstances on our first going amongst them, might be construed as a precedent for the intrusion of advice on after occasions. The distance between the court and the agent of the British Government was calculated to diminish this impression, and obliged them also to trust to their own resources, after the machine was once set in motion. On the heights of Tus our tents were pitched, the escort paraded, and St. George's flag displayed. Here camels, almost wild, were fitted for the first time with the pack-saddle, lamenting in discordant gutturals the [656] hardship of their fate, though luckily ignorant of the difference between grazing whither they listed in the happy valley, and carrying a load in "the region of death," where they would only find the thorny mimosa or prickly *phog*[1] to satisfy their hunger.

Pallāna.—*October* 13.—There being no greater trial of patience than the preparations for a march after a long halt, we left the camp at daybreak amidst the most discordant yells from the throats of a hundred camels, which drowned every attempt to be heard, while the elephants squeaked their delight in that peculiar treble which they emit when happy. There was one little fellow enjoying himself free from all restraints of curbs or pack-saddles, and inserting his proboscis into the sepoy's baggage, whence he would extract a bag of flour, and move off, pursued by the owner; which was sure to produce shouts of mirth to add to the discord. This little representative of Ganesa was only eight years old, and not more than twelve hands high. He was a most agreeable pet, though the proofs he gave of his wisdom in trusting himself amidst the men when cooking their dinners, were sometimes disagreeable to them, but infinitely amusing to those who watched his actions. The rains having broken up unusually late, we found the boggy ground, on which we had to march, totally unable to bear the pressure of loaded cattle; even the ridges, which just showed their crests of quartz above the surface, were not safe. Our route was over a fine plain well wooded and watered, soil excellent, and studded with numerous large villages; yet all presenting uniformly the effects of warfare and rapine. The landscape, rendered the more interesting by our long incarceration in the valley, was abstractedly pleasing. On our left lay the mountains enclosing the capital, on one of whose elevated peaks are the ruins of Ratakot, overlooking all around; while to the east the eye might in vain seek for a boundary. We passed Deopur, once a township of some consequence, and forming part of the domain of the Bhanej,[2] Zalim Singh, the

[1] [*Calligonum polygonoides*, a shrub on which camels live for the greater part of the year.]

[2] *Bhanej*, or 'nephew,' a title of courtesy enjoyed by every chieftain who marries a daughter or immediate kinswoman of the Rana's house. [When Bhīm Singh succeeded in 1793, his first act was to drive his uncle, Zālim Singh, the son of a Mewār princess, from Jodhpur. He took refuge in

heir of Marwar, whose history, if it could be given here, would redeem the nobles of Rajputana from the charge of being of uncultivated intellect. In listening to [657] his biography, both time and place were unheeded; the narrator, my own venerable Guru,[1] had imbibed much of his varied knowledge from this accomplished chieftain, to whom arms and letters were alike familiar. He was the son of Raja Bijai Singh and a princess of Mewar: but domestic quarrels made it necessary to abandon the paternal for the maternal mansion, and a domain was assigned by the Rana, which put him on a footing with his own children. Without neglecting any of the martial amusements and exercises of the Rajput, he gave up all those hours, generally devoted to idleness, to the cultivation of letters. He was versed in philosophical theology, astronomy, and the history of his country; and in every branch of poesy, from the sacred canticles of Jayadeva to the couplets of the modern bard, he was an adept. He composed and improvised with facility, and his residence was the rendezvous for every bard of fame. That my respected tutor did not overrate his acquirements, I had the best proof in his own, for all which (and he rated them at an immeasurable distance compared with the subject of his eulogy) he held himself indebted to the heir of Marwar, who was at length slain in asserting his right to the throne in the desert.

Rām Singh and the Rāja of Narsinghgarh. The Oswāl Mahājans.—After a four hours' march, picking our way amidst swamps and treacherous bogs, we reached the advanced tents at Pallana. Like Deopur, it presented the spectacle of a ruin, a corner of which held all its inhabitants; the remains of temples and private edifices showed what it had once been. Both towns formerly belonged to the fisc of the Rana, who, with his usual improvidence, on the death of his nephew included them in the grant to the temple of Kanhaiya. I found at my tents the minister's right hand, Ram Singh Mehta; Manikchand, the Diwan or factotum of the chieftain of Bhindar; and the ex-Raja

---

Udaipur, and passed the rest of his days in literary pursuits. He was a man of charm and ability, a gallant soldier, no mean poet. He died in the prime of life in British Merwāra in 1799 (Erskine iii. A. 70).]

[1] My guide or instructor, Yati Gyanchandra, a priest of the Jain sect, who had been with me ten years. To him I owe much, for he entered into all my antiquarian pursuits with zeal.

of Narsinghgarh, now an exile at Udaipur.[1] The first was a fine specimen of the non-militant class of these countries, and although he had seldom passed the boundaries of Mewar, no country could produce a better specimen of a courteous gentleman: his figure tall, deportment easy, features regular and handsome, complexion fair, with a fine slightly-curled beard and mustachios jet black. Ram Singh, without being conceited, is aware that nature has been indulgent to him, and without any foppery he pays great attention to externals. He is always elegantly attired, and varies with good taste the colours of his turban and ceinture, though his loose tunics are always white; the aroma of the *itr* is the only mark of the dandy about him: and this forms no criterion [658], as our red coats attest, which receive a sprinkling at every visit. With his dagger and pendent tassel, and the *balaband* or purple cordon (the Rana's gift) round his turban, behold the servant "whom the king delighteth to honour." As he has to support himself by paying court to the Rana's sister, the queens, and other fair influentials behind the curtain, his personal *attraits* are no slight auxiliaries. He is of the Jain faith, and of the tribe of Osi, which now reckons one hundred thousand families, all of Rajput origin, and descendants of the Agnikula stock. They proselytized in remote antiquity, and settling at the town of Osi in Marwar, retain this designation, or the still more common one of Oswal. It was from the Pramara and Solanki branches of the Agnikula race that these assumed the doctrines of Buddha or Jaina: not however from the ranks of the Brahmans, but, as I firmly believe, from that faith, whatever it was, which these Scythic or Takshak tribes brought from beyond the Indus. In like manner we found the Chauhan (also an Agnikula) regenerated by the Brahmans on Mount Abu; while the fourth tribe, the Parihara (ancient sovereigns of Kashmir), have left traces in the monuments of their capital, Mandor, that they espoused the then prevailing faith of Rajasthan, namely, that of Buddha.[2]

Mānikchand.—Manikchand, also of the Jain faith, but of a different tribe (the Sambhari), was in all the reverse of Ram Singh.

[1] [A chiefship in Central India under the Bhopāl Agency. In 1819 Subhāg Singh becoming imbecile was replaced by his son Chain Singh, after whose death in 1824 he was restored (*IGI*, xviii. 353).]

[2] [As usual, Jainism and Buddhism are confounded.]

He was tall, thin, rather bent, and of swarthy complexion, and his tongue and his beads were in perpetual motion. He had mixed in all the intrigues of the last quarter of a century, and, setting Zalim Singh of Kotah aside, had more influenced events than any individual now alive. He was the organ of the Saktawats, and the steward and counsellor of the head of this clan, the Bhindar chief; and being accordingly the irreconcilable foe of the Chondawats, had employed all the resources of his talents and his credit to effect their humiliation. To this end, he has leagued with Sindis, Pathans, and Mahrattas, and would not have scrupled to coalesce with his Satanic Majesty, could he thereby have advanced their revenge: in pursuance of which he has been detained in confinement as a hostage, put to torture from inability to furnish the funds he would unhesitatingly promise for aid, and all the while sure of death if he fell into the hands of his political antagonists. His talent and general information made him always a welcome guest: which was wormwood to the Chondawats, who laid claim to a monopoly of patriotism, and stigmatized the Saktawats as the destroyers [659] of Mewar, though in truth both were equally blind to her interests in their contests for supremacy. He was now beyond fifty, and appeared much older; but was cheerful, good-humoured, and conversant in all the varied occurrences of the times. He at length completely established himself in the Rana's good graces, who gave his elder son a confidential employment. Had he lived, he would have been conspicuous, for he had all the talent of his father, with the personal adjuncts possessed by Ram Singh; but being sensitive and proud, he swallowed poison, in consequence it was said of the severity of an undeserved rebuke from his father, and died generally regretted. I may here relate the end of poor Manika. It was on the ground we had just quitted that he visited me for the last time, on my return from the journey just commenced. He had obtained the contract for the whole transit duties of the State, at the rate of 250,000 rupees per annum. Whether from the corruption of his numerous deputy collectors, his own cupidity, or negligence, he professed his inability to fulfil the contract by nearly a sixth of the amount, though from his talents and promises, a perfect establishment of this important department, which had been taken from others on his account, was expected. It was difficult to judge charitably of his assertions, without giving occasion to his enemies to put a wrong construction on the motives. He pitched his tent near me, and requested an interview. He looked very disconsolate, and remarked, that he had seven several times left his tent, and as often turned back, the bird of omen having each time passed him on the adverse side; but that at length he had determined to disregard it, as having forfeited confidence, he was indifferent to the future. He admitted the profligacy of his inferiors, whom he had not sufficiently superintended, and took his leave, promising by assiduity to redeem his engagements, though his past character for intrigue made his asseverations doubtful. Again failing to make good his promises, or, as was surmised, having applied the funds to his own estate, he took *saran* with the Raja of Shahpura; where, mortified in all probability by the reflection of the exultation of his rivals over his disgrace, and having lost the confidence of his own chief when he obtained that of the Rana, he had recourse to the usual expedient of these countries when "perplexed in the extreme,"—took poison and died.

The Rāja of Narsinghgarh.—The last of the trio of visitors on this occasion, the Raja of Narsinghgarh, is now, as before stated, in exile. He is of the tribe of Umat, one of thirty-six divisions [660] of the Pramaras,[1] settled during fifteen generations in Central India, and giving the name of Umatwara to the petty sovereignty of which Narsinghgarh is the capital. Placed in the very heart of the predatory hordes, the Pindaris and Mahrattas occupied almost every village that owned their sway, and compelled him to the degradation of living under Holkar's orange standard, which waved over the battlements of his abode. To one or other of the great Mahratta leaders, Sindhia and Holkar, all the petty princes were made tributary dependents, and Umatwara had early acknowledged Holkar, paying the annual sum of eighty thousand rupees: but this vassalage did not secure the Raja from the ravages of the other spoliators, nor from the rapacity of the myrmidons of his immediate lord paramount. In 1817, when

[1] One of the four Agnikulas. [The Umats were not a distinguished tribe until Achal Singh, Dīwān of Narsinghgarh, married his son to a near relation of the Mahārāna of Udaipur, and since this alliance many of the principal Mālwa families eat with the Rājas of Umatwāra (Malcolm, *Memoir of Central India*, 2nd ed. ii. 130 f.). For a full and slightly different account see *IGI*, xviii. 382 ff.]

these countries, for the first time in many centuries, tasted the blessings of peace, Umatwara was, like Mewar, a mass of ruins, its fertile lands being overgrown with the thorny *mimosa* or the useful *kesula*. The Raja partook of the demoralization around him; he sought refuge in opium and arak from his miseries, and was totally unfitted to aid in the work of redemption when happier days shone upon them. His son Chain Singh contrived to escape these snares, and was found in every respect competent to co-operate in the work of renovation, and through the intervention of the British agent (Major Henley), an arrangement was effected by which the Raja retired on a stipend and the son carried on the duties of government in his name.[1]

It was unfortunate for these ancient races, that on the fortunate occasion presented in 1817–18, when both Sindhia and Holkar aimed at the overthrow of our power (the one treacherously cloaking his views, the other disclosing them in the field), our policy did not readily grasp it, to rescue all these States from ruin and dependence. Unfortunately, their peculiar history was little known, or it would have been easily perceived that they presented the exact materials we required between us and the entire occupation of the country. But there was then a strong notion afloat of a species of balance of power, and it was imagined that these demoralized and often humiliated Mahrattas were the fittest materials to throw into the scale—against I know not what, except ourselves: for assuredly the day of our reverses will be a jubilee to them, and will level every spear that they can bring against our existence. They would merit contempt if they acted [661] otherwise. Can they cease to remember that the orange flag which waved in triumph from the Sutlej to the Kistna has been replaced by the cross of St. George? But the snake which flutters in tortuous folds thereon, fitting crest for the wily Mahratta, is only scathed, and may yet call forth the lance of the red cross knight to give the coup de grace.[2] Let it then be remembered that, both as regards good policy and justice, we owe to these States—independence.

To what does our interference with Umatwara tend, but to realize the tribute of Holkar; to fix a millstone round their necks,

[1] [Chain Singh quarrelled with the Political Agent, attacked the British forces at Sehore, and was killed in the battle in 1824 (*IGI*, xviii. 383).]

[2] Sindhia's flag is a snake *argent* on an *orange* field.

which, notwithstanding the comparative happiness they enjoy, will keep them always repining, and to secure which will make our interference eternal. Had a due advantage been taken of the hostilities in 1817, it might have obviated these evils by sending the predatory sovereign of half a century's duration to a more restricted sphere. It may be said that it is easy to devise plans years after the events which immediately called for them: these not only were mine at the time, but were suggested to the proper authorities; and I am still disposed to think my views correct.

After chatting some time with the two chiefs described, and presenting them with *itr* and *pan*,[1] they took leave.

Nāthdwāra.—*October* 14.—Marched at daybreak, and found the route almost impracticable for camels, from the swampy nature of the soil. The country is much broken with irregular low ridges of micaceous schist, in the shape of a chine or hog's back, the crest of which has throughout all its length a vein of quartz piercing the slate, and resembling a back-bone; the direction of these veins is uniformly N.N.E., and the inclination about 75° to the east. Crossed the Nathdwara ridge, about four hundred feet in height, and, like the hills encircling the valley, composed of a brown granite intersected with protruding veins of quartz, incumbent on blue compact slate. The ascent was a mile and a half east of the town, and on the summit, which is table-land, there are two small lakes, whence water-courses conduct streams on each side of the road to supply the temple and the town. There are noble trees planted on either side of these rivulets, forming a delightful shade. As we passed through the town to our encampment on the [662] opposite side of the Banas River, the inhabitants crowded the streets, shouting their grateful acknowledgments to the power which had redeemed the sacred precincts of Kanhaiya from the scenes of turpitude amidst which they had grown up. They were all looking forward with much pleasure to the approaching festival of Annakuta.

[1] *Pān*, 'the leaf'; *parna* and *pattra*, the Sanskrit for 'a leaf'; and hence *panna*, 'a leaf or sheet of paper'; and *patra*, 'a plate of metal or sacrificial cup,' because these vessels were first made of leaves. I was amused with the coincidence between the Sanskrit and Tuscan *panna*. That lovely subject by Raphael, the "Madonna impannata," in the Pitti Palace at Florence, is so called from the subdued light admitted through the window, the panes of which are of paper. [The words have no connexion.]

October 15.—Halted to allow the baggage to join, which, partly from the swamps and partly from the intractable temper of the cattle, we have not seen since we parted company at Merta. Received a visit from the Mukhya of the temple, accompanied by a pilgrim in the person of a rich banker of Surat. A splendid quilted cloak of gold brocade, a blue scarf with a deep border of gold, and an embroidered band for the head, were brought to me as the gift of the god through his high-priest, in testimony of my zeal. I was also honoured with a tray of the sacred food, which consisted of all the dried fruits, spices, and aromatics of the East. In the evening I had a portion of the afternoon repast, consisting of a preparation of milk ; but the days of simplicity are gone, and the Apollo of Vraj has his curds adulterated with rose-water and amber. Perhaps, with the exception of Lodi, where is fabricated the far-famed Parmesan, whose pastures maintain forty thousand kine, there is no other place known which possesses more than the city of the Hindu Apollo, though but a tenth of that of Lodi. But from the four thousand cows, the expenditure of milk and butter for the votaries of Kanhaiya may be judged. I was entertained with the opinions of the old banker on the miraculous and oracular power of the god of Nathdwara. He had just been permitted to prostrate himself before the car which conveyed the deity from the Yamuna, and held forth on the impiety of the age, in withholding the transmission of the miraculous wheels from heaven, which in former days came once in six months. The most devout alone are permitted to worship the chariot of Kanhaiya. The garments which decorate his representative are changed several times a day, to imitate the different stages of his existence, from the youthful Bala to the conqueror of Kansa ; or, as the Surat devotee said in broken English, " Oh, sir, he be much great god ; he first of all ; and he change from de balak, or child, to de fierce chief, with de bow and arrow a hees hands " ; while the old Mukhya, whose office it is to perambulate the whole continent of India as one of the couriers of Kanhaiya, lifted up his eyes as he ejaculated, " Sri Krishna ! Sri Krishna ! " I gave him a paper [663] addressed to all officers of the British Government who might pass through the lands of the church, recommending the protection of the peacocks and pipal trees, and to forbear polluting the precincts of the god with the blood of animals. To avoid offending against their prejudices in this particular, I crossed the river, and killed our fowls within our own sanctuary, and afterwards concealed the murder by burying the feathers.

Sagacity of Elephants. Usarwās.—*October* 16.—There is nothing so painful as sitting down inactive when the mind is bent upon an object. Our escort was yet labouring in the swamps, and as we could not be worse off than we were, we deemed it better to advance, and accordingly decamped in the afternoon, sending on a tent to Usarwas; but though the distance was only eight miles we were benighted, and had the comfort to find old Fateh, "the victorious," floundering with his load in a bog, out of which he was picking his way in a desperate rage. It is generally the driver's fault when such an accident occurs: for if there be but a foot's breadth of sound footing, so sensible is the animal, that he is sure to avoid danger if left to his own discretion and the free use of his proboscis, with which he thumps the ground as he cautiously proceeds step by step, giving signals to his keeper of the safety or the reverse of advancing, as clearly as if he spoke. Fateh's signals had been disregarded, and he was accordingly in a great passion at finding himself abused, and kept from his cakes and butter, of which he had always thirty pounds' weight at sunset. The sagacity of the elephant is well known, and was in no instance better displayed than in the predicament above described. I have seen the huge monster in a position which to him must have been appalling; but, with an instinctive reliance on others, he awaited in tolerable patience the arrival of materials for his extrication, in the shape of fascines and logs of wood, which being thrown to him, he placed deliberately in front, and making a stout resistance with head, teeth, and foot, pressing the wood, he brought up one leg after the other in a most methodical and pioneer-like manner, till he delivered himself from his miry prison. Fateh did not require such aid; but, aware that the fault was not his, he soon indignantly shook the load off his back, and left them to get it out in any manner they chose.

Wolves.—Waited to aid in reloading, and it being already dusk, pushed on with my dog Belle, who, observing a couple of animals, darted off into the jungles, and led me after her as fast as the devious paths in such a savage scene would permit. But I [664] soon saw her scampering down the height, the game, in the shape of two huge wolves, close at her heels, and delighted to find rescue at hand. I have no doubt their retreat from my favourite greyhound was a mere *ruse de guerre* to lead her beyond supporting distance, and they had nearly effected their object: they went off in a very sulky and leisurely manner. In my subaltern days, when with the subsidiary force in Gohad, I remember scouring the tremendous ravines near the Antri Pass to get a spear at a wolf, my companion (Lieut. now Lieut.-Col. T. D. Smith) and myself were soon surrounded by many scores of these hungry animals, who prowled about our camp all night, having carried off a child the night before. As we charged in one direction, they gave way; but kept upon our quarters without the least fear, and seemingly enjoyed the fun. I do not recollect whether it excited any other feeling than mirth. They showed no symptom of ferocity, or desire to make a meal of us; or a retreat from these ravines, with their superior topographical knowledge, would doubtless have been difficult.

The Banās River. The Fairy Gift Legend.—We passed the Banas River, just escaping from the rock-bound barriers, our path almost in contact with the water to the left. The stream was clear as crystal, and of great depth; the banks low and verdant, and fringed with wood. It was a lovely, lonely spot, and well deserved to be consecrated by legendary tale. In ancient times, ere these valleys were trod by the infidel Tatar, coco-nuts were here presented to the genius of the river, whose arm appeared above the waters to receive them; but ever since some unhallowed hand threw a stone in lieu of a coco-nut, the arm has been withdrawn.[1] Few in fact lived, either to supply or keep alive the traditions which lend a charm to a journey through these wild scenes, though full of bogs and wolves. We reached our journey's end very late, and though no tents were up, we had the consolation to spy the cook in a snug corner with a leg of mutton before some blazing logs, round which he had placed the wall of a tent to check the force of the mountain air. We all congregated round the cook's fire, and were infinitely happier in the prospect before us, and with the heavens for our canopy, than with all our accustomed conveniences and fare. Every one this day had taken his own road, and each had his adventure to relate. Our repast was delicious; nor did any favourable

[1] [A variant of the well-known Fairy Gift legend (Crooke, *Popular Religion and Folklore of N. India*, 2nd ed. i. 287 ff.).]

account reach us of tents or other luxuries to mar our enjoyments, till midnight, when the fly of the doctor's tent arrived, of which we availed ourselves as a protection against the heavy dews of [665] the night; and though our bivouac was in a ploughed field, and we were surrounded by wild beasts in a silent waste, they proved no drawbacks to the enjoyment of repose.

Halted the 17th, to collect the dislocated baggage; for although such scenes, seasoned with romance, might do very well for *us*, our followers were ignorant of the name of Ann Radcliffe or other conjurers; and though admirers of tradition, like myself, preferred it after dinner. Usarwas is a valuable village, but now thinly inhabited. It was recently given by the Rana, with his accustomed want of reflection, to a Charan bard, literally for an old song. But even this folly was surpassed on his bestowing the township of Sesoda,[1] in the valley in advance, the place from which his tribe takes its appellation, on another of the fraternity, named Kishna, his master bard, who has the art to make his royal patron believe that opportunity alone is wanting to render his name as famed as that of the illustrious Sanga, or the immortal Partap. I received and returned the visit of an ascetic Sannyasi, whose hermitage was perched upon a cliff not far from our tents. Like most of his brethren, he was intelligent, and had a considerable store of local and foreign legends at command. He was dressed in a loose orange-coloured anga or tunic, with a turban of the same material, in which was twisted a necklace of the lotus-kernel;[2] he had another in his hand, with which he repeated the name of the deity at intervals. He expressed his own surprise and the sentiments of the inhabitants at the tranquillity they enjoyed, without any tumultuary cause being discoverable; and said that we must be something more than human. This superstitious feeling for a while was felt as well by the prince and the turbulent chief, as by the anchorite of Usarwas.

Samecha.—*October* 18.—Marched at daybreak to Samecha, distance twelve miles. Again found our advanced elephant and

[1] [The home of the Rāna branch of Guhilots, who take the name of Sesodia from it, while Chitor was the capital of the Rāwal branch of the ruling house (Erskine ii. A. 15).]

[2] [Lotus nuts are used for necklaces, but Sannyāsis usually wear those of the *rudrāksha* (*Elaeocarpus ganitrus*) (Watt, *Econ. Dict.* v. 345; *Comm. Prod.* 511).]

breakfast-tent in a swamp: halted to extricate him from his difficulties. The road from Nathdwara is but a footpath, over or skirting a succession of low broken ridges, covered with prickly shrubs, as the Khair, the Karil, and Babul.[1] At the village of Gaon Gura, midway in the morning's journey, we entered the alpine valley called the Shera Nala. The village of Gura is placed in the opening or break in the range through which the river flows, whose serpentine meanderings indicate the only road up this majestic valley. On the banks, or in its bed, which we frequently crossed, lay [666] the remainder of this day's march. The valley varies in breadth, but is seldom less than half a mile, the hills rising boldly from their base; some with a fine and even surface covered with mango trees, others lifting their splintered pinnacles into the clouds. Nature has been lavish of her beauties to this romantic region. The *gular* or wild fig, the *sitaphal* or custard-apple, the peach or *aru badam* (almond-peach),[2] are indigenous and abundant; the banks of the stream are shaded by the withy, while the large trees, the useful mango and picturesque tamarind, the sacred pipal and bar, are abundantly scattered with many others, throughout. Nor has nature in vain appealed to human industry and ingenuity to second her intents.

Terrace Cultivation.—From the margin of the stream on each side to the mountain's base they have constructed a series of terraces rising over each other, whence by simple and ingenious methods they raise the waters to irrigate the rich crops of sugar-cane, cotton, and rice, which they cultivate upon them. Here we have a proof that ingenuity is the same, when prompted by necessity, in the Jura or the Aravalli. Wherever soil could be found, or time decomposed these primitive rocks, a barrier was raised. When discovered, should it be in a hollow below, or on the summit of a crag, it is alike greedily seized on: even there water is found, and if you leave the path below and ascend a hundred feet above the terraces, you will discover pools or reservoirs dammed in with massive trees, which serve to irrigate such insulated spots, or serve as nurseries to the young rice-plants. Not unfrequently, their labour is entirely destroyed, and the dykes swept away by the periodical inundations; for we observed the high-water mark in the trees considerably up the

[1] [*Acacia catechu, Capparis aphylla, Acacia arabica.*]

[2] [*Ficus glomerata, Annona squamosa, Prunus persica.*]

acclivity. The rice crop was abundant, and the *juar* [millet] or maize was thriving, but scanty; the standard autumnal crop which preceded it, the *makai*, or 'Indian corn,' had been entirely devoured by the locust. The sugar-cane, by far the most valuable product of this curious region, was very fine but sparingly cultivated, from the dread of this insect, which for the last three years had ravaged the valley. There are two species of locusts, which come in clouds, darkening the air, from the desert: the *pharka* and the *tiri* are their names;[1] the first is the great enemy of our incipient prosperity. I observed a colony some time ago proceeding eastward with a rustling, rushing sound, like a distant torrent, or the wind in a forest at the fall of the leaf. We have thus to struggle against natural and artificial obstacles to the rising energies of the country; and dread of the *pharkas* deters speculators [667] from renting this fertile tract, which almost entirely belongs to the fisc. Its natural fertility cannot be better demonstrated than in recording the success of an experiment, which produced five crops, from the same piece of ground, within thirteen months. It must, however, be understood that two of these are species of millet, which are cut in six weeks from the time of sowing. A patch of ground, for which the cultivator pays six rupees rent, will produce sugar-cane six hundred rupees in value: but the labour and expense of cultivation are heavy, and cupidity too often deprives the husbandman of the greater share of the fruits, ninety rupees having been taken in arbitrary taxes, besides his original rent.

The air of this elevated region gave vigour to the limbs, and appetite to the disordered stomach. There was an exhilarating *fraîcheur*, which made us quite frantic; the transition being from 96° of Fahrenheit to English summer heat. We breakfasted in a verdant spot under the shade of a noble fig-tree fanned by the cool breezes from the mountains.

Samecha Town. Rājpūt Bhūmias.—Samecha consists of three separate hamlets, each of about one hundred houses. It is situated at the base of a mountain distinctively termed Rana Pag, from a well-known path, by which the Ranas secured their retreat to the upland wilds when hard pushed by the Moguls.

[1] [Our knowledge of Indian locusts is still imperfect, the best-known varieties being the Bombay and the North-West (Watt, *Econ. Dict.* vi. Part i. 154 f.; *Comm. Prod.* 686).]

It also leads direct to the capital of the district, avoiding the circuitous route we were pursuing. Samecha is occupied by the Kumbhawats, descendants of Rana Kumbha, who came in a body with their elders at their head to visit me, bringing the famed *kakri* [1] of the valley (often three feet in length), curds, and a kid as gifts. I rose to receive these Rajaputras, the Bhumias or yeomen of the valley; and though undistinguishable in dress from the commonest cultivator, I did homage to their descent. Indeed, they did not require the auxiliaries of dress, their appearance being so striking as to draw forth the spontaneous exclamation from my friends, "what noble-looking fellows!" Their tall and robust figures, sharp aquiline features, and flowing beards, with a native dignity of demeanour (though excepting their chiefs, who wore turbans and scarfs, they were in their usual labouring dresses, immense loose breeches and turbans), compelled respect and admiration. Formerly they gave one hundred matchlocks for garrison duty at Kumbhalmer; but the Mahrattas have pillaged and impoverished them. These are the real allodial tenants of the land, performing personal local service, and paying an annual quit-rent. I conciliated their good opinion by [668] talking of the deeds of old days, the recollection of which a Rajput never outlives. The assembly under the fig-tree was truly picturesque, and would have furnished a good subject for Gerard Dow. Our baggage joined us at Samecha; but many of our camels were already worn out by labouring through swamps, for which they are by nature incapacitated.

October 19.—Marched to Kelwara, the capital of this mountainous region, and the abode of the Ranas when driven from Chitor and the plains of the Banas; on which occasion these valleys received and maintained a great portion of the population of Mewar. There is not a rock or a stream that has not some legend attached to it, connected with these times. The valley presents the same features as already described. Passed a cleft in the mountain on the left, through which a stream rushes, called the "elephant's pool"; a short cut may be made by the foot passenger to Kelwara, but it is too intricate for any unaccustomed to these wilds to venture. We could not ascertain the origin of the "elephant's pool," but it is most likely connected with ancient warfare. Passed the village of Murcha, held by a

[1] [A kind of cucumber, *Cucumis utilissimus* (Watt, *Comm. Prod.* 439).]

CITADEL OF THE HILL FORTRESS OF KŪMBHALMER.

To face page 776.

Rathor chieftain. On the margin of a small lake adjoining the village, a small and very neat sacrificial altar attracted my regard; and not satisfied with the reply that it was *sati ka makan*, 'the place of faith,' I sent to request the attendance of the village seer. It proved to be that of the ancestor of the occupant: a proof of devotion to her husband, who had fallen in the wars waged by Aurangzeb against this country; when, with a relic of her lord, she mounted the pyre. He is sculptured on horseback, with lance at rest, to denote that it is no churl to whom the record is devoted.

Near the "elephant's pool," and at the village of Kherli, two roads diverge: one, by the Bargula *nal* or pass, conducts direct to Nathdwara; the other, leading to Rincher, and the celebrated shrine of the four-armed god,[1] famed as a place of pilgrimage. The range on our left terminating abruptly, we turned by Uladar to Kelwara, and encamped in a mango-grove, on a tableland half a mile north of the town. Here the valley enlarges, presenting a wild, picturesque, and rugged appearance. The barometer indicated about a thousand feet of elevation above the level of Udaipur, which is about two thousand above the sea: yet we were scarcely above the base of the alpine cliffs which towered around us on all sides. It was the point of divergence for the waters, which, from the numerous fountains in [669] these uplands, descended each declivity, to refresh the arid plains of Marwar to the west, and to swell the lakes of Mewar to the east. Previous to the damming of the stream which forms that little ocean, the Kankroli lake, it is asserted that the supply to the west was very scanty, nearly all flowing eastward, or through the valley; but since the formation of the lake, and consequent saturation of the intermediate region, the streams are ever flowing to the west. The spot where I encamped was at least five hundred feet lower than Aret pol, the first of the fortified barriers leading to Kumbhalmer, whose citadel rose more than seven hundred feet above the *terre-pleine* of its outworks beneath.

Kūmbhalmer Fort. Mahārāja Daulat Singh.—The Maharaja Daulat Singh, a near relative of the Rana, and governor of Kumbhalmer, attended by a numerous suite, the crimson standard, trumpets, kettledrums, seneschal, and bard, advanced several miles to meet and conduct me to the castle. According to

[1] [Chaturbhuja Vishnu.]

etiquette, we both dismounted and embraced, and afterwards rode together conversing on the affairs of the province, and the generally altered condition of the country. Daulat Singh, being of the immediate kin of his sovereign, is one of the Babas or infants of Mewar, enumerated in the tribe called Ranawat, with the title of Maharaja. Setting aside the family of Sheodan Singh, he is the next in succession to the reigning family. He is one of the few over whom the general demoralization has had no power, and remains a simple-minded straightforward honest man; blunt, unassuming, and courteous. His rank and character particularly qualify him for the post he holds on this western frontier, which is the key to Marwar. It was in February 1818 that I obtained possession of this place (Kumbhalmer), by negotiating the arrears of the garrison. Gold is the cheapest, surest, and most expeditious of all generals in the East, amongst such mercenaries as we had to deal with, who change masters with the same facility as they would their turban. In twenty-four hours we were put in possession of the fort, and as we had not above one-third of the stipulated sum in ready cash, they without hesitation took a bill of exchange, written on the drum-head, on the mercantile town of Pali in Marwar: in such estimation is British faith held, even by the most lawless tribes of India! Next morning we saw them winding down the western declivity, while we quietly took our breakfast in an old ruined temple. During this agreeable employment, we were joined by Major Macleod, of the artillery, sent by General Donkin to report on the facilities of reducing the place by siege, and [670] his opinion being, that a gun could not be placed in position in less than six weeks, the grilling spared the European force in such a region was well worth the £4000 of arrears. My own escort and party remained in possession for a week, until the Rana sent his garrison. During these eight days our time was amply occupied in sketching and deciphering the monumental records of this singularly diversified spot. It would be vain to attempt describing the intricacies of approach to this far-famed abode, whose exterior is delineated by the pencil. A massive wall, with numerous towers and pierced battlements, having a strong resemblance to the Etruscan, encloses a space of some miles extent below, while the pinnacle or *sikhara* rises, like the crown of the Hindu Cybele, tier above tier of battlements, to the summit, which is crowned with the

Badal Mahall, or 'cloud-palace' of the Ranas. Thence the eye ranges over the sandy deserts and the chaotic mass of mountains, which are on all sides covered with the cactus, which luxuriates amidst the rocks of the Aravalli. Besides the Aret [1] pol, or barrier thrown across the first narrow ascent, about one mile from Kelwara, there is a second called the Halla [2] pol, intermediate to the Hanuman [3] pol, the exterior gate of the fortress, between which and the summit there are three more, viz. the gate of victory, the sanguinary gate, and that of Rama, besides the last, or Chaugan [4] pol. The barometer stood, at half-past seven A.M., 26° 65′; thermometer 58° Fahr. at the Aret pol: and on the summit at nine, while the thermometer rose to 75°, the barometer had only descended 15′, and stood at 26° 50′,[5] though we had ascended full six hundred feet.

A Jain Temple.—Admitting the last range as our guide, the peak of Kumbhalmer will be 3353 [6] feet above the level of the ocean. Hence I laid down the positions of many towns far in the desert. Here were subjects to occupy the pencil at least for a month; but we had only time for one of the most interesting views, the Jain temple before the reader, and a sketch of the fortress itself, both finished on the spot. The design of this temple is truly classic. It consists only of the sanctuary, which has a vaulted dome and colonnaded portico all round. The architecture is undoubtedly Jain, which is as distinct in character from the Brahmanical as their religion. There is a chasteness and simplicity in this specimen of monotheistic worship, affording a wide contrast to the elaborately sculptured shrines of the Saivas, and [671] other polytheists of India. The extreme want of decoration best attests its antiquity, entitling us to attribute it to that period when Samprati Raja, of the family of Chandragupta, was paramount sovereign over all these regions (two hundred years before Christ); [7] to whom tradition ascribes the most ancient monu-

[1] ['The Barrier.'] [2] ['The Onset.']

[3] ['That of the monkey god,' a common guardian of forts.]

[4] [Chaugān, 'the Parade Ground.']

[5] At four o'clock P.M., same position, thermometer 81°; barometer, 26° 85′. [6] [3658 feet.]

[7] [Samprati was grandson of Asoka, and he is credited with the erection of many Jain buildings (Smith, *EHI*, 192 f.; *BG*. i. Part i. 15). From the picture of the temple given by the author, and from an inscription of the reign of Rāna Sangrām Singh (A.D. 1508–27), it could not have been more

ments of this faith, yet existing in Rajasthan and Saurashtra. The proportions and forms of the columns are especially distinct from the other temples, being slight and tapering instead of massive, the general characteristic of Hindu architecture; while the projecting cornices, which would absolutely deform shafts less slight, are peculiarly indicative of the Takshak architect.[1] Samprati was the fourth prince in descent from Chandragupta, of the Jain faith, and the ally of Seleucus, the Grecian sovereign of Bactriana. The fragments of Megasthenes, ambassador from Seleucus, record that this alliance was most intimate; that the daughter of the Rajput king was married to Seleucus, who, in return for elephants and other gifts, sent a body of Greek soldiers to serve Chandragupta. It is curious to contemplate the possibility, nay the probability, that the Jain temple now before the reader may have been designed by Grecian artists, or that the taste of the artists among the Rajputs may have been modelled after the Grecian. This was our temple of Theseus in Mewar. A massive monolithic emblem of black marble of the Hindu Pitrideva had been improperly introduced into the shrine of the worshippers of the "spirit alone." Being erected on the rock, and chiselled from the syenite on which it stands, it may bid defiance to time. There was another sacred structure in its vicinity, likewise Jain, but of a distinct character; indeed, offering a perfect contrast to that described. It was three stories in height; each tier was decorated with numerous massive low columns, resting on a sculptured panelled parapet, and sustaining the roof of each story, which, being very low, admitted but a broken light to break the pervading gloom. I should imagine that the sacred architects of the East had studied effect equally with the preservers of learning and the arts in the dark period of Europe, when those monuments, which must ever be her pride, arose on the ruins of paganism. How far the Saxon or Scandinavian pagan contributed to the general design of such structures may be doubted; but that their decorations, especially the

than three centuries old when he saw it (*IA*, ii. 205). There are two temples, one consisting of a square sanctuary with a vaulted dome, and surrounded by a colonnade of elegant pillars: the second is of peculiar design, having three stories, each tier being decorated with massive low columns (Erskine ii. A. 116).]

[1] See note, p. 37, above.

JAIN TEMPLE
In the Fortress of Kûmbhalmer.

To face page 780.

grotesque, have a powerful resemblance to the most ancient Hindu-Scythic, there is no question, as I shall hereafter more particularly point out [672].

Who, that has a spark of imagination, but has felt the indescribable emotion which the gloom and silence of a Gothic cathedral excites? The very extent provokes a comparison humiliating to the pigmy spectator, and this is immeasurably increased when the site is the mountain pinnacle, where man and his works fade into nothing in contemplating the magnificent expanse of nature. The Hindu priest did not raise the temple for heterogeneous multitudes: he calculated that the mind would be more highly excited when left to its solitary devotions, amidst the silence of these cloistered columns, undisturbed save by the monotony of the passing bell, while the surrounding gloom is broken only by the flare of the censer as the incense mounts above the altar.

Temple of Māma Devi.—It would present no distinct picture to the eye were I to describe each individual edifice within the scope of vision, either upwards towards the citadel, or below. Looking down from the Jain temple towards the pass, till the contracting gorge is lost in distance, the gradually diminishing space is filled with masses of ruin. I will only notice two of the most interesting. The first is dedicated to Mama Devi, 'the mother of the gods,' whose shrine is on the brow of the mountain overlooking the pass. The goddess is placed in the midst of her numerous family, including the greater and lesser divinities. They are all of the purest marble, each about three feet in height, and tolerably executed, though evidently since the decline of the art, of which very few good specimens exist executed within the last seven centuries. The temple is very simple and primitive, consisting but of a long hall, around which the gods are ranged, without either niche or altar.

The most interesting portion of this temple is its court, formed by a substantial wall enclosing a tolerable area. The interior of this wall had been entirely covered with immense tables of black marble, on which was inscribed the history of their gods, and, what was of infinitely greater importance, that of the mortal princes who had erected the tablets in their honour. But what a sight for the antiquary! Not one of the many tables was entire; the fragments were strewed about, or placed in position to receive the flesh-pots of the sons of Ishmael, the mercenary Rohilla Afghan [673].[1]

Memorial of Prithirāj and Tāra Bāi.—On quitting the temple of Mama Devi, my attention was attracted by a simple monumental shrine on the opposite side of the valley, and almost in the gorge of the pass. It was most happily situated, being quite isolated, overlooking the road leading to Marwar, and consisted of a simple dome of very moderate dimensions, supported by columns, without any intervening object to obstruct the view of the little monumental altar arising out of the centre of the platform. It was the Sybilline temple of Tivoli in miniature. To it, over rock and ruin, I descended. Here repose the ashes of the Troubadour of Mewar, the gallant Prithiraj and his heroine wife, Tara Bai, whose lives and exploits fill many a page of the legendary romances of Mewar.

This fair 'star' (*tara*) was the daughter of Rao Surthan, the chieftain of Badnor. He was of the Solanki tribe, the lineal descendant of the famed Balhara kings of Anhilwara. Thence expelled by the arms of Ala in the thirteenth century, they migrated to Central India, and obtained possession of Tonk-Toda and its lands on the Banas, which from remote times had been occupied (perhaps founded) by the Taks, and hence bore the name of Taksilanagar, familiarly Takatpur and Toda.[2] Surthan had been deprived of Toda by Lila the Afghan, and now

[1] These people assert their Coptic origin: being driven from Egypt by one of the Pharaohs, they wandered eastwards till they arrived under that peak of the mountains west of the Indus called Sulaiman-i-koh, or 'Hill of Solomon,' where they halted. Others draw their descent from the lost tribes. They are a very marked race, and as unsettled as their forefathers, serving everywhere. They are fine gallant men, and, when managed by such officers as Skinner, make excellent and orderly soldiers; but they evince great contempt for the eaters of swine, who are their abomination. [The Rohillas, 'Highlanders,' are a Pathān tribe which occupied Rohilkhand after the death of Aurangzeb, A.D. 1707 (Crooke, *Tribes and Castes N.W.P. and Oudh*, iv. 165 f.).]

[2] From the ruins of its temples, remnants of Takshak architecture, the amateur might speedily fill a portfolio. This tract abounds with romantic scenery: Rajmahall on the Banas, Gokaran, and many others. Herbert calls Chitor the abode of Taxiles, the ally of Alexander. The Taks were all of the race of Puru, so that Porus is a generic, not a proper name. This Taksilanagar has been a large city. We owe thanks to the Emperor Babur, who has given us the position of the city of Taxiles, where Alexander left it, west of the Indus. [The Tāk tribe had no connexion with Chitor.]

RUINS IN KŪMBHALMER.

To face page 782.

occupied Badnor at the foot of the Aravalli, within the bounds of Mewar. Stimulated by the reverses of her family, and by the incentives of its ancient glory, Tara Bai, scorning the habiliments and occupations of her sex, learned to guide the war-horse, and throw with unerring aim the arrow from his back, even while at speed. Armed with the bow and quiver, and mounted on a fiery Kathiawar, she joined the cavalcade in their unsuccessful attempts to wrest Toda from the Afghan. Jaimall, the third son of Rana Raemall, in person made proposals for her hand. "Redeem Toda," said the star of Badnor, "and my hand is thine." He assented to the terms: but evincing a rude determination to be possessed of the prize ere he had earned it, he was slain by the indignant father. Prithiraj, the brother of the deceased, was then in exile in Marwar; he had just signalized his valour, and ensured his father's forgiveness, the redemption of Godwar,[1] and the [674] catastrophe at Badnor determined him to accept the gage thrown down to Jaimall. Fame and the bard had carried the renown of Prithiraj far beyond the bounds of Mewar; the name alone was attractive to the fair, and when thereto he who bore it added all the chivalrous ardour of his prototype, the Chauhan, Tara Bai, with the sanction of her father, consented to be his, on the simple asseveration that "he would restore to them Toda, or he was no true Rajput." The anniversary of the martyrdom of the sons of Ali was the season chosen for the exploit.[2] Prithiraj formed a select band of five hundred cavaliers, and accompanied by his bride, the fair Tara, who insisted on partaking his glory and his danger, he reached Toda at the moment the *ta'aziya* or bier containing the martyr-brothers was placed in the centre of the *chauk* or 'square.' The prince, Tara Bai, and the faithful Sengar chief, the inseparable companion of Prithiraj, left their cavalcade and joined the procession as it passed under the balcony of the palace in which the Afghan was putting on his dress preparatory to descending. Just as he had asked who were the strange horsemen that had joined the throng, the lance of Prithiraj and an arrow from the bow of his Amazonian bride stretched him on the floor. Before the crowd recovered from the panic, the three had reached the gate of the town, where their exit was obstructed by an elephant. Tara Bai with her

[1] See p. 344 [Vol. I.].

[2] [The Muharram festival.]

scimitar divided his trunk, and the animal flying, they joined their cavalcade, which was close at hand.

The Afghans were encountered, and could not stand the attack. Those who did not fly were cut to pieces; and the gallant Prithiraj inducted the father of his bride into his inheritance. A brother of the Afghans, in his attempt to recover it, lost his life. The Nawab Mallu Khan then holding Ajmer determined to oppose the Sesodia prince in person; who, resolved upon being the assailant, advanced to Ajmer, encountered his foe in the camp at daybreak, and after great slaughter entered Garh Bitli, the citadel, with the fugitives. "By these acts," says the chronicle, "his fame increased in Rajwara: one thousand Rajputs, animated by the same love of glory and devotion, gathered round the *nakkaras* of Prithiraj. Their swords shone in the heavens, and were dreaded on the earth; but they aided the defenceless."

Another story is recorded and confirmed by Muhammadan writers as to the result, though they are ignorant of the impulse which prompted the act. Prithiraj on some [675] occasion found the Rana conversing familiarly with an ahadi [1] of the Malwa king, and feeling offended at the condescension, expressed himself with warmth. The Rana ironically replied: "You are a mighty seizer of kings; but for me, I desire to retain my land." Prithiraj abruptly retired, collected his band, made for Nimach, where he soon gathered five thousand horse, and reaching Dipalpur, plundered it, and slew the governor. The king on hearing of the irruption left Mandu at the head of what troops he could collect; but the Rajput prince, in lieu of retreating, rapidly advanced and attacked the camp while refreshing after the march. Singling out the royal tent, occupied by eunuchs and females, the king was made captive, and placed on an express camel beside the prince, who warned the pursuers to follow peaceably, or he would put his majesty to death; adding that he intended him no harm, but that after having made him "touch his father's feet," he should restore him to liberty. Having carried him direct to Chitor and to his father's presence, he turned to him saying, "Send for your friend the ahadi, and ask

[1] [Ahadi, 'single, alone,' like our warrant-officer, a gentleman trooper in the Mughal service, so called because they offered their services singly, and did not attach themselves to any chief (*Āīn*, i. 20, note; Irvine, *Army of the Indian Moghuls*, 43).]

him who this is?" The Malwa king was detained a month within the walls of Chitor, and having paid his ransom in horses, was set at liberty with every demonstration of honour.[1] Prithiraj returned to Kumbhalmer, his residence, and passed his life in exploits like these from the age of fourteen to twenty-three, the admiration of the country and the theme of the bard.

It could not be expected that long life would be the lot of one who thus courted distinction, though it was closed neither by shot nor sabre, but by poison, when on the eve of prosecuting his unnatural feud against his brother Sanga, the place of whose retreat was made known by his marriage with the daughter of the chieftain of Srinagar, who had dared to give him protection in defiance of his threats.

At the same time he received a letter from his sister, written in great grief, complaining of the barbarous treatment of her lord, the Sirohi prince, from whose tyranny she begged to be delivered and to be restored to the paternal roof; since whenever he had indulged too freely in the 'essence of the flower,' or in opium, he used to place her under the bedstead, and leave her to sleep on the floor. Prithiraj instantly departed, reached Sirohi at midnight, scaled the palace, and interrupted the repose of Pabhu Rao by placing his poniard at his throat. His wife, notwithstanding his cruelty, complied with his humiliating appeal for mercy, and begged his life, which was granted on condition of his standing as a suppliant with his wife's [676] shoes on his head, and touching her feet, the lowest mark of degradation. He obeyed, was forgiven, and embraced by Prithiraj, who became his guest during five days. Pabhu Rao was celebrated for a confection, of which he presented some to his brother at parting. He partook of it as he came in sight of Kumbhalmer; but on reaching the shrine of Mama Devi was unable to proceed. Here he sent a message to the fair Tara to come and bid him farewell; but so subtle was the poison, that death had overtaken him ere she descended from the citadel. Her resolution was soon formed; the pyre was erected, and with the mortal remains of the chivalrous Prithiraj in her embrace, she sought "the regions of the sun."

[1] [This is the Rājput story which lacks confirmation from Muhammadan sources. The captive may have been Ghiyāsū-d-dīn of Mālwa, or Muzaffar Shāh of Gujarāt; but it is probably fiction invented by the Mewār bards (Erskine ii. A. 18).]

Such the end of the Sesodia prince, and the star of Badnor. From such instances we must form our opinion of the manners of these people. But for the poisoned confection of the chief of Sirohi, Prithiraj would have had the glory of opposing himself to Babur, instead of his heroic brother and successor, Sanga.[1] Whether, from his superior ardour of temperament, and the love of military glory which attracted similarly constituted minds to his fortunes, he would have been more successful than his brother, it is futile to conjecture.

The Frontier of Mārwār.—*October* 20.—Halted till noon, that the men might dress their dinners, and prepare for the descent into "the region of death," or Marwar. The pass by which we had to gain it was represented as terrific; but as both horse and elephant, with the aid of the hatchet, will pick their way wherever man can go, we determined to persevere. Struck the camp at noon, when the baggage filed off, halting ourselves till three; the escort and advanced tents, and part of the cuisine being ordered to clear the pass, while we designed to spend the night midway, in a spot forming the natural boundary of Mewar and Marwar, reported to be sufficiently capacious. Rumour had not magnified the difficulties of the descent, which we found strewed with our baggage, arresting all progress for a full hour. For nearly a mile there was but just breadth sufficient to admit the passage of a loaded elephant, the descent being at an angle of 55° with the horizon, and streams on either side rushing with a deafening roar over their rugged beds. As we gained a firmer footing at the base of this first descent, we found that the gallant Manika, the gift of my friend the Bundi prince, had missed his footing and rolled down the steep, breaking the cantle of the saddle; a little farther appeared the cook, hanging in dismay over the scattered implements of his art, his camel remonstrating against the [677] replacing of his *kajavas* or panniers. For another mile it became more gentle, when we passed under a tower of Kumbhalmer, erected on a scarped projection of the rock, full five hundred feet above us. The scenery was magnificent; the mountains rising on each side in every variety of form, and their summits, as they caught a ray of the departing sun, reflecting on our sombre path a momentary gleam from the masses of rose-coloured quartz which crested them. Noble

[1] See Annals, p. 353.

forest trees covered every face of the hills and the bottom of the glen, through which, along the margin of the serpentine torrent which we repeatedly crossed, lay our path. Notwithstanding all our mishaps, partly from the novelty and grandeur of the scene, and partly from the invigorating coolness of the air, our mirth became wild and clamorous : a week before I was oppressed with a thousand ills ; and now I trudged the rugged path, leaping the masses of granite which had rolled into the torrent.

There was one spot where the waters formed a pool or *dah*. Little Carey determined to trust to his pony to carry him across, but deviating to the left, just as I was leaping from a projecting ledge, to my horror, horse and rider disappeared. The shock was momentary, and a good ducking the only result, which in the end was the luckiest thing that could have befallen him. On reaching the Hathidarra, or 'barrier of the elephant' (a very appropriate designation for a mass of rock serving as a rampart to shut up the pass), where we had intended to remain the night, we found no spot capacious enough even for a single tent. Orders accordingly passed to the rear for the baggage to collect there, and wait the return of day to continue the march. The shades of night were fast descending, and we proceeded almost in utter darkness towards the banks of the stream, the roar of whose waters was our guide, and not a little perplexed by the tumultuous rush which issued from every glen, to join that we were seeking. Towards the termination of the descent the path became wider, and the voice of the waters of a deeper and hoarser tone, as they glided to gain the plains of Marwar. The vault of heaven, in which there was not a cloud, appeared as an arch to the perpendicular cliffs surrounding us on all sides, and the stars beamed with peculiar brilliancy from the confined space through which we viewed them. As we advanced in perfect silence, fancy busily at work on what might befall our straggling retinue from the ferocious tiger or plundering mountaineer, a gleam of light suddenly flashed upon us on emerging from the brushwood, and disclosed a party of dismounted cavaliers seated round their night-fires under some magnificent fig-trees [678].[1]

Meeting with the Mers.—Halted, and called a council of war to determine our course : we had gained the spot our guides had assigned as the only fitting one for bivouac before we reached the

[1] The bar or banyan tree, *Ficus Indica*.

plains beyond the mountains; it afforded shade from the dews, and plenty of water. The *munitions de bouche* having gone on was a good argument that we should follow; but darkness and five miles more of intricate forest, through a path from which the slightest deviation, right or left, might lead us into the jaws of a tiger, or the toils of the equally savage Mer, decided us to halt. We now took another look at the group above-mentioned. Though the excitement of the morning was pretty well chilled by cold and hunger (poor sharpeners of the imagination), it was impossible to contemplate the scene before us without a feeling of the highest interest. From twenty-five to thirty tall figures, armed at all points, were sitting or reposing in groups round their watch-fires, conversing and passing the pipe from hand to hand, while their long black locks, and motley-fashioned turbans, told that they belonged to Marudesa. A rude altar, raised in honour of some "gentle blood" shed by the murky mountaineer, served as a place of rest for the chief of the party, distinguished by the gold band in his turban, and his deer-skin doublet. I gave the usual salutation of "Rama, Rama," to the chief and his party, and inquired after the health of their chieftain of Ghanerao, to whose courtesy I found I owed this mark of attention. This was the boundary between the two States of Marwar and Mewar, since the district of Godwar was lost by the latter about fifty years ago. The spot has been the scene of many a conflict, and a closer approach disclosed several other altars raised in honour of the slain; each represented a cavalier mounted on his war-steed, with his lance poised, denoting that in such attitude he fell in defending the pass, or redeeming the cattle from the plundering mountain Mer. A square tablet placed on each contained the date on which he gained "the mansions of the sun." Midnight being past, and bringing no hope of our appetites growing by what they might feed upon, Dr. Duncan and Captain Waugh took the *jhul*, or broadcloth-housing, from the elephant, and rolling themselves in it, followed the example of the chieftain and reposed upon the ashes of the brave, on an altar adjoining the one he occupied. I soon left them in happy forgetfulness of tigers, Meras, hunger, and all the fatigues of the day, and joined the group to listen to the tale with which they enlivened the midnight hour. This I can repeat, but it would have required the pencil of a master to paint the scene. It was a subject for

KOLI AND BHIL.
(The Foresters of Rājputana.)

CHĀRAN OR BARD.

To face page 788.

Salvator Rosa; though I should [679] have been perfectly satisfied with one of Captain Waugh's delineations, had he been disposed at that moment to exert the pictorial art. Several of my friends had encountered the mountaineer on this very spot; and these humble cenotaphs, covering the ashes of their kin, recalled events not likely to be repeated in these halcyon days, when the names of Bhil and Mer cease to be the synonyms of plunderer. As there may be no place more appropriate for a sketch of the mountaineers, the reader may transport himself to the glen of Kumbhalmer, and listen to the history of one of the aboriginal tribes of Rajasthan [680].

CHAPTER 26

The Mer Tribe.—The Mer or Mera is the mountaineer of Rajputana, and the country he inhabits is styled Merwara, or 'the region of hills.' The epithet is therefore merely local, for the Mer is but a branch of the Mina or Maina, one of the aborigines of India. He is also called Merot and Merawat; but these terminations only more correctly define his character of mountaineer.[1] Merwara is that portion of the Aravalli chain between Kumbhalmer and Ajmer, a space of about ninety miles in length, and varying in breadth from six to twenty. The general character of this magnificent rampart, in the natural and physical geography of Rajputana, is now sufficiently familiar. It rises from three to four thousand feet above the level of the sea, and abounds with a variety of natural productions. In short, I know no portion of the globe which would yield to the scientific traveller more abundant materials for observation than the alpine Aravalli. The architectural antiquary might fill his portfolio, and natural history would receive additions to her page in every department,

[1] *Meru* is 'a [fabulous] mountain' in Sanskrit; Merawat and Merot, 'of or belonging to the mountain.' I have before remarked that the name of the Albanian mountaineer, Mainote, has the same signification. I know not the etymology of *Mina*, of which the Mer is a branch. [Needless to say, whatever the meaning of the title Mer may be, it has no connexion with Mt. Meru. The traditions of the Mers point to Mīna ancestry. For the Mīna tribe see Rose, *Glossary*, iii. 102 ff.; Watson, *Rajputāna Gazetteer*, i. A. 20 ff.]

and especially in botany and zoology.[1] I [681] should know no higher gratification than to be of a scientific party to anatomize completely this important portion of India. I would commence on the Gujarat, and finish on the Shaikhawat frontier. The party should consist of a skilful surveyor, to lay down on a large scale a topographical chart of the mountains; several gentlemen thoroughly versed in natural history; able architectural and landscape draughtsmen, and the antiquary to transcribe ancient inscriptions, as well as to depict the various races. The "Aravalli delineated," by the hand of science, would form a most instructive and delightful work.

A minute account of the Mer, his habits and his history, would be no unimportant feature: but as this must be deferred, I will, in the meanwhile, furnish some details to supply the void.

The Mers are a branch of the Chitas, an important division of the Minas.[2] I shall elsewhere enter at large into the history of this race, which consists of as many branches as their conquerors, the Rajputs. All these wild races have the vanity to mingle their pedigree with that of their conquerors, though in doing so they stigmatize themselves. The Chita-Minas accordingly claim descent from a grandson of the last Chauhan emperor of Delhi. Anhul and Anup were the sons of Lakha, the nephew of the Chauhan king. The coco-nut was sent from Jaisalmer, offering princesses of that house in marriage: but an investigation into their maternal ancestry disclosed that they were the issue of a

[1] I had hoped to have embodied those subjects with, and thereby greatly to have increased the interest, of my work; but just as Lord Hastings had granted my request, that an individual eminently qualified for those pursuits should join me, a Higher Power deemed it fit to deny what had been long near my heart.

The individual, John Tod, was a cousin of my own, and possessed an intellect of the highest order. He was only twenty-two years of age when he died, and had only been six months in India. He was an excellent classical scholar, well versed in modern languages and every branch of natural history. His manners, deportment, and appearance were all in unison with these talents. Had it pleased the Almighty to have spared him, this work would have been more worthy of the public notice. [An officer named Tod was murdered at Nāhar Magra, near Udaipur, in May 1804 (Malcolm, *Memoir Central India*, 2nd ed. i. 237).]

[2] [The Mers are supposed to be a foreign tribe, like the Gurjaras and Mālavas, which passed into Kāthiāwār through the Panjāb, Sind, and N. Gujarāt (*BG*, i. Part i. 136 ff.; Elliot-Dowson i. 519 ff.).]

Mina concubine: and their birth being thus revealed, they became exiles from Ajmer, and associates with their maternal relatives.

Anhul espoused the daughter of a Mina chieftain, by whom he had Chita, whose descendants enjoy almost a monopoly of power in Merwara. The sons of Chita, who occupied the northern frontier near Ajmer, became Muhammadans about fifteen generations ago, when Duda, the sixteenth from the founder of the race, was created Dawad Khan by the Hakim of Ajmer; and as Hathun was his residence, the "Khan of Hathun" signified the chief of the Merots. Chang, Jhak, and Rajosi are the principal towns adjoining Hathun. Anup also took a Mina wife, by whom he had Barar, whose descendants have continued true [682] to their original tenets. Their chief places are Barar, Berawara, Mandila, etc. Though the progeny of these Minas may have been improved by the infusion of Rajput blood, they were always notorious for their lawless habits, and for the importance attached to them so far back as the period of Bisaldeo, the celebrated prince of Ajmer, whom the bard Chand states to have reduced them to submission, making them "carry water in the streets of Ajmer." Like all mountaineers, they of course broke out whenever the hands of power were feeble. In the battle between the Chauhans of Ajmer and the Parihars of Mandor, a body of four thousand Mer bowmen served Nahar Rao, and defended the pass of the Aravalli against Prithiraj in this his first essay in arms. Chand thus describes them: [1] "Where hill joins hill, the Mer and Mina thronged. The Mandor chief commanded that the pass should be defended—four thousand heard and obeyed, each in form as the angel of death—men who never move without the omen, whose arrow never flies in vain—with frames like Indra's bolt—faithful to their word, preservers of the land and the honour [2] of Mandor; whose fortresses have to this day remained unconquered—who bring the spoils of the plains to their dwellings. Of these in the dark recesses of the mountains four thousand lay concealed, their crescent-formed arrows beside them. Like the envenomed serpent, they wait in silence the advance of the foe.

[1] I cannot discover by what part of the range the invasion of Mandor was attempted; it might have been the pass we are now in, for it is evident it was not from the frontier of Ajmer.

[2] *Laj* is properly 'shame,' which word is always used in lieu of honour: *laj rakho*, 'preserve my shame,' *i.e.* my honour from shame.

Prithirāj attacks the Mers.—"Tidings reached the Chauhan that the manly Mina, with bow in hand, stood in the mountain's gorge. Who would be bold enough to force it? his rage was like the hungry lion's when he views his prey. He called the brave Kana, and bade him observe those wretches as he commanded him to clear the pass. Bowing he departed, firm as the rock on which he trod. He advanced, but the mountaineer (Mer) was immovable as Sumeru. Their arrows, carrying death, fly like Indra's bolts—they obscure the sun. Warriors fall from their steeds, resounding in their armour as a tree torn up by the blast. Kana quits the steed; hand to hand he encounters the foe; the feathery shafts, as they strike fire, appear like birds escaping from the flames. The lance flies through the breast, appearing at the back [683], like a fish escaping through the meshes of a net. The evil spirits dance in the mire of blood. The hero of the mountain [1] encountered Kana, and his blow made him reel; but like lightning it was returned, and the mountaineer fell: the crash was as the shaking of Sumeru. At this moment Nahar arrived, roaring like a tiger for his prey: he called aloud to revenge their chief, his brother,[2] and fresh vigour was infused into their souls. On the fall of the mountain-chief, the Chauhan commanded the 'hymn of triumph'[3] to be sounded; it startled the mountaineer, but only to nerve his soul afresh. In person the Chauhan sought his foe. The son of Somesa is a bridegroom. His streaming standards flutter like the first falls of rain in Asarh, and as he steps on the bounds which separate Mandor from Ajmer, 'Victory! victory!' is proclaimed. Still the battle rages. Elephants roar, horses neigh, terror stalks everywhere. The aids of Girnar[4] and of Sind now appeared for Mandor, bearing banners of every colour, varied as the flowers of the spring. Both arrays were clad in mail; their eyes and their finger-nails alone were exposed; each invoked his tutelary protector as he wielded the *dodhara*.[5] Prithiraj was refulgent as Indra; the Parihar's brightness was as the morning star; each was clad in armour of proof, immovable as gods in mortal form. The sword of the Chauhan descended on the steed of the Parihar;

[1] Parbat Vira.

[2] The Parihar prince bestowed this epithet merely in compliment.

[3] *Sindhu Raga.*

[4] [The sacred Jain mountain in Kāthiāwār.]

[5] With two (*do*) edges (*dhara*).

but as he fell, Nahar sprung erect, and they again darted on each other, their warriors forming a fortress around the persons of their lords. Then advanced the standards of the Pramar, like a black rolling cloud, while the lightnings flashed from his sword. Mohana, the brother of Mandor, received him; they first examined each other—then joining in the strife, the helm of the Pramar was cleft in twain. Now advanced Chawand, the Dahima; he grasped his iron lance,[1]—it pierced the Parihar, and the head appeared like a serpent looking through the door in his back. The flame (*jyot*) united with the fire from which it sprung, while the body fell on its parent earth. By his devotion the sins of his life were forgiven. Nobly did the tiger (Nahar) of Mandor meet the lion of the world. He called aloud, 'Hold your ground as did Bal Raja of old.' Again the battle rages—Durga gluts herself with blood [684]—the air resounds with the clash of arms and the rattling of banners—the Aswar[2] rains on the foe—Khetrpal[3] sports in the field of blood—Mahadeva fills his necklace—the eagle gluts itself on the slain—the mien of the warriors expands as does the lotos at the sunbeam—the war-song resounds—with a branch of the tulasi on the helm, adorned in the saffron robe, the warriors on either side salute each other." The bard here exclaims, "But why should I enlarge on this encounter?"—but as this digression is merely for breathing time, we shall not follow him, the object being to introduce the mountain Mer, whom we now see *hors de combat*.

Character of the Mers.—Admitting the exaggeration of the poet, the Mer appears to have been in the twelfth century what he is in the nineteenth, a bold, licentious marauder. He maintained himself throughout the whole of the Mogul domination, alternately succumbing and depredating; and since the Mahrattas crippled these countries, the Mer had regained all his consequence, and was rapidly encroaching upon his Rajput suzerain. But when in 1821 their excesses made it imperative to reduce their holds and fastnesses, they made no stand against the three battalions of sepoys sent against them, and the whole tract was

[1] *Sang* is the iron lance, either wholly of iron, or having plates for about ten feet; these weapons are much used in combats from camels in the Desert.

[2] 'Sword'—*Aswar* in the dialect.

[3] [The field guardian deity.]

compelled to obedience ; not, however, till many of the descendants of Chita and Barar had suffered both in person and property.[1] The facility with which we reduced to entire subjection this extensive association of plunderers, for centuries the terror of these countries, occasioned no little astonishment to our allies. The resistance was indeed contemptible, and afforded a good argument against the prowess of those who had tolerated the existence of a gang at once so mischievous and weak. But this was leaping to a conclusion without looking beneath the surface, or to the moral and political revolution which enervated the arms of Mer and Mahratta, Pindari and Pathan. All rose to power from the common occupation of plunderers, aided by the national jealousies of the Rajputs. If the chieftains of Mewar leagued to assault the mountaineers, they found refuge and support in Marwar ; and as their fortresses at all times presented a sanctuary, their Rawats or leaders obtained consequence amongst all parties by granting it. Every Mer community, accordingly, had a perfect understanding with the chieftain whose lands were contiguous to their own, and who enjoyed rights granted by the Rana over these nominal subjects. These rights were all of a feudal nature, as *rakhwali* or 'blackmail' [685], and those petty proofs of subordination, entitled in the feudal law of Europe "petit serjanterie." The token might be a colt, a hawk, or a bullock, and a *nazarana*, or pecuniary acknowledgement, perhaps only of half-a-crown on the chieftain's birthday, or on the Rajput Saturnalia, the Holi. But all these petty causes for assimilation between the Rajput and the lawless Mer were overlooked, as well as the more powerful one which rendered his arms of no avail. Every door was hermetically sealed against him ; wherever he looked he saw a foe—the magical change bewildered him ; and when their Khan and his adherents were assailed while in fancied security, and cut off in a midnight attack, his self-confidence was annihilated—he saw a red-coat in every glen, and called aloud for mercy.

The Merwāra Battalion.—A corps of these mountaineers, commanded by English officers, has since been formed, and I have no doubt may become useful.[2] Notwithstanding their lawless

[1] [For an account of the Mer rebellion in 1820 and its suppression see Watson, *Rājputāna Gazetteer*, i. A. 14.]

[2] [The 44th Merwāra Infantry, formerly known as the Merwāra Battalion,

habits, they did not neglect agriculture and embanking, as described in the valley of Shera Nala, and a district has been formed in Merwara which in time may yield a lakh of rupees annually to the state.

Marriage Customs.—Some of their customs are so curious, and so different from those of their lowland neighbours, that we may mention a few. Leaving their superstitions as regards omens and auguries, the most singular part of their habits, till we give a detailed sketch of the Minas hereafter, I will notice the peculiarity of their notions towards females. The Mer, following the customary law handed down from his rude ancestry, and existing long before the written law of Manu, has no objection to a widow as a wife. This contract is termed *nata*, and his civilized master levies a fine or fee of a rupee and a quarter for the licence, termed *kagli*. On such marriage the bridegroom must omit in the *maur*, or nuptial coronet, the graceful palmyra leaf, and substitute a small branch of the sacred pipal wreathed in his turban. Many of the forms are according to the common Hindu ritual. The *sat-phera*, or seven perambulations round the jars filled with grain, piled over each other—the *ganth-jora*, or uniting the garments—and the *hathleva*, or junction of hands of bride and bridegroom, are followed by the Mers. Even the northern clans, who are converts to Islam, return to their ancient habits on this occasion, and have a Brahman priest to officiate. I discovered, on inquiring into the habits of the Mers, that they are not the only race which did not refuse to wed a widow, and that both Brahmans and Rajputs have from ancient times been accustomed not to consider it derogatory [686].[1] Of the former, the sacerdotal class, the Nagda[2] Brahmans, established at this town long before the Guhilots obtained power in Mewar. Of the Rajputs, they are all of the most ancient tribes, now the allodial vassals or Bhumias of Rajputana, as the Chinana, Kharwar, Uten, Daya, names better known in the mystic page of the

---

formed in 1822, did good service in the Mutiny of 1857, and in the Afghān campaign of 1878 (Watson, *Gazetteer*, i. A. 119 ff.; Cardew, *Sketch of the Services of the Bengal Native Army*, 338 ff.)].

[1] [No class of Brāhmans or Rājputs, claiming respectability, now permits widow marriage.]

[2] [Nāgda, near the shrine of Eklingji, one of the most ancient places in Mewār.]

chronicle than now, though occasionally met with in the valleys of the Aravalli. But this practice, so little known, gives rise to an opinion, that many of the scrupulous habits regarding women are the inventions of the priests of more modern days. The facilities for separation are equally simple. If tempers do not assimilate, or other causes prompt them to part, the husband tears a shred from his turban, which he gives to his wife, and with this simple bill of divorce, placing two jars filled with water on her head, she takes whatever path she pleases, and the first man who chooses to ease her of her load becomes her future lord. This mode of divorce is practised not only amongst all the Minas, but by Jats, Gujars, Ahirs, Malis, and other Sudra tribes. *Jehar le aur nikali*, 'took the jar and went forth,' is a common saying amongst the mountaineers of Merwara.

Oaths, Food, Omens.—Their invocations and imprecations are peculiar. The Chita or northern Mer, since he became acquainted with the name of the prophet, swears by 'Allah,' or by his first proselyte ancestor, 'Duda Dawad Khan,' or the still more ancient head of the races, '*Chita, Barar ka an*.' The southern Mers also use the latter oath: "By my allegiance to Chita and Barar"; and they likewise swear by the sun, '*Suraj ka Sagun*,' and '*Nath ka Sagun*'; or their ascetic priest, called the Nath. The Muhammadan Mer will not now eat hog; the southron refuses nothing, though he respects the cow from the prejudices of those around him, and to please the Nath or Jogi, his spiritual guide. The partridge and the *maloli*,[1] or wag-tail, are the chief birds of omen with him, and the former 'clamouring' on the left, when he commences a foray, is a certain presage of success. To conclude; colonies of the Mers or Meras will be found as far north as the Chambal, and even in the peninsula of Saurashtra. Merwara is now in subjection to the Rana of Mewar, who has erected small forts amidst the most influential communities to overawe them. The whole tract has been assessed; the chiefs of the districts being brought to the Rana's presence presented *nazarana*, swore fidelity, and received according to their rank gold bracelets or turbans. It was an era in the annals of Mewar to see the accumulated arms of Merwara piled upon the [687] terrace of the palace at the capital; but these measures were subsequent to our sojourn

[1] [Elsewhere known as Khanjarit or Khanjan, a well-known bird of omen.]

in the glen of Kumbhalmer, from which we have yet to issue to gain Marwar.

The Chief of Gokulgarh.—*October* 21.—All hailed the return of daylight with reverence. Captain Waugh and the Doctor uncoiled from the elephant's *jhul*, and I issued from my palki, which had proved a welcome retreat against the chills of the night air. By thirst and hunger our appetite for the picturesque was considerably abated, and the contemplation of the spot where we had bivouaced in that philosophical spirit of silence, which all have experienced who have made a long march before breakfast, lost much of its romantic interest. Nevertheless, could I have consulted merely my own wishes, I would have allowed my friends and escort to follow the canteen, and have pursued an intricate path which branched off to the right, to have had the chance of an interview with the outlaw of Gokulgarh.

This petty chieftain, who enjoyed the distinctive epithet of outlaw (*barwatia*), was of the Sonigira clan (a branch of the Chauhans), who for centuries were the lords of Jalor. He was a vassal of Marwar, now sovereign of Jalor, and being expelled for his turbulence by his prince, he had taken post in the old ruined castle of Gokulgarh, on a cliff of the Aravalli, and had become the terror of the country. By his knowledge of the intricacies of the mountains, he eluded pursuit; and his misdeeds being not only connived at, but his spoils participated by the chief of Deogarh, in whose fief was his haunt, he was under no apprehension of surprise. Inability either to seize the Barwatia, or drive him from his retreat, formed a legitimate excuse for the resumption of Gokulgarh, and the dues of 'blackmail' he derived from its twelve dependent villages. The last act of the Sonigira was most flagrant; he intercepted in the plains of Godwar a marriage procession, and made captives the bridegroom and bride, whom he conveyed to Gokulgarh, where they long languished for want of ransom. A party was formed to lie in wait for him; but he escaped the snare, and his retreat was found empty. Such was the state of society in these districts. The form of outlawry is singular in this country, where the penal laws are satisfied with banishment, even in cases of treason, instead of the sanguinary law of civilization. The criminal against whom the sentence of exile is pronounced being called into his prince's presence, is clad in black vestments, and placed upon a black steed, his arms and shield all of the same sombre hue of mourning and [688] disgrace ; he is then left to gain the frontier by himself. This custom is very ancient : the Pandu brothers were 'Barwatias'[1] from the Jumna three thousand years ago. The Jaisalmer annals relate the solemnity as practised towards one of their own princes ; and the author, in the domestic dissensions of Kotah, received a letter from the prince, wherein he demands either that his rights should be conceded, or that the government would bestow the "black garment," and leave him to his fate.

The Chief of Ghānērāo.—Conversing on these and similar subjects with my Marwari friends, we threaded our way for five miles through the jungles of the pass, which we had nearly cleared, when we encountered the chieftain of Ghanerao at the head of his retinue, who of his own accord, and from a feeling of respect to his ancient sovereign the Rana, advanced thus far to do me honour. I felt the compliment infinitely the more, as it displayed that spirit of loyalty peculiar to the Rajput, though the step was dangerous with his jealous sovereign, and ultimately was prejudicial to him. After dismounting and embracing, we continued to ride to the tents, conversing on the past history of the province, of his prince, and the Rana, after whom he affectionately inquired. Ajit Singh is a noble-looking man, about thirty years of age, tall, fair, and sat his horse like a brave Rathor cavalier. Ghanerao is the chief town of Godwar, with the exception of the commercial Pali, and the garrison-post Desuri. From this important district the Rana could command four thousand Rathors holding lands on the tenure of service, of whom the Ghanerao chief, then one of the sixteen nobles of Mewar, was the head. Notwithstanding the course of events had transferred the province, and consequently his services, from the Rana of Udaipur to the Raja of Jodhpur, so difficult is it to eradicate old feelings of loyalty and attachment, that the present Thakur preferred having the sword of investiture bound on him by his ancient and yet nominal suzerain, rather than by his actual sovereign. For this undisguised mark of feeling, Ghanerao was denuded of its walls, which were levelled to the ground ; a perpetual memento of disgrace and an incentive to vengeance : and whenever the day arrives that the Rana's herald may salute him with the old motto,

[1] This term is a compound of *bāhar* and *watan*, literally 'ex patria.'

"Remember Kumbhalmer," he will not be deaf to the call. To defend this post was the peculiar duty of his house, and often have his ancestors bled in maintaining it against the Mogul. Even now [689], such is the inveteracy with which the Rajput clings to his honours, that whenever the Ghanerao chief, or any of his near kin, attend the Rana's court, he is saluted at the porte, or at the champ de Mars, by a silver mace-bearer from the Rana, with the ancient war-cry, "Remember Kumbhalmer," and he still receives on all occasions of rejoicing a khilat from that prince. He has to boast of being of the Rana's blood, and is by courtesy called "the nephew of Mewar." The Thakur politely invited me to visit him; but I was aware that compliance would have involved him in difficulties with his jealous prince, and made excuses of fatigue, and the necessity of marching next morning, the motives of which he could not misunderstand.

Our march this morning was but short, and the last two miles were in the plains of Marwar, with merely an occasional rock. Carey joined us, congratulating himself on the ducking which had secured him better fare than we had enjoyed in the pass of Kumbhalmer, and which fastened both on Waugh and myself violent colds. The atmospheric change was most trying: emerging from the cold breezes of the mountains to 96° of Fahrenheit, the effect was most injurious: it was 58° in the morning of our descent into the glen. Alas! for my surviving barometer! Mahesh, my amanuenis, who had been entrusted with it, joined us next day, and told me the quicksilver had contrived to escape; so I lost the opportunity of comparing the level of the desert with the plains of Marwar.

The Chief of Rūpnagar.—*October* 27.—Halted to collect the scattered baggage, and to give the men rest; the day was nearly over before the whole came up, each party bringing lamentable reports of the disastrous descent. I received a visit from the chief of Rupnagar, who, like the Thakur of Ghanerao, owes a divided allegiance to the courts on each side the mountains. His castle, which gives him rank as one of the most conspicuous of the second grade of the Rana's nobles, was visible from the camp, being placed on the western face of the mountains, and commanding a difficult passage across them. From thence he looks down upon Desuri and his ancient patrimony, now transferred with Godwar to the Rathor prince; and often has he measured his lance with the present occupants to retain his ancient *bhum*, the right derived from the cultivating proprietor of the soil. The chief of Rupnagar is of the Solanki race, a lineal descendant of the sovereigns of Nahrwala, and the inheritor [690] of the war-shell of the celebrated monarch Siddhraj,[1] one of the most powerful who ever sat on an eastern throne, and who occupied that of Anhilwara from A.D. 1094, during half a century, celebrated as a patron of literature and the arts. When in the thirteenth century this State was destroyed, the branches found refuge, as already described, in Mewar; for the ancestor of Rupnagar was brother to the father of "the star of Badnor," and was invested with the estate and lands of Desuri by the same gallant prince who obtained her hand by the recovery of her father's estates. The anecdote is worthy of relation, as showing that the Rajput will stop at nothing "to obtain land." The intestine feuds amongst Rana Raemall's sons, and his constant warfare with the kings of Delhi and Malwa, made his authority very uncertain in Godwar. The Mina and Mer possessed themselves of lands in the plains, and were supported by the Madrecha descendant of the once independent Chauhan sovereigns of Nadol, the ancient capital of this region. Sand, the Madrecha, had obtained possession of Desuri, the garrison town. To expel him, the prince had recourse to Sada, the Solanki, whose son was married to the daughter of the Madrecha. The bribe for the reward of this treachery was to be the grant in perpetuity of Desuri and its lands. Sada's son readily entered into the scheme; and to afford facilities for its execution he went with his wife to reside at Desuri. It was long before an opportunity offered; but at length the marriage of the young Madrecha to the daughter of Sagra the Balecha was communicated to the Solanki by his son; who told his father "to watch the smoke ascending from the tower of Desuri," as the signal for the attempt to get possession. Anxiously did Sand watch from his castle of Sodhgarh the preconcerted sign, and when the volume of black smoke ascended, he rushed down from the Aravalli at the head of his retainers. The mother-in-law of the young Solanki sent to know why he should make a smoke as if he were burning a corpse, when her son must be returning with his bride. Soon she heard the clash of arms; the Solankis had entered and fired the town,

[1] He ruled from A.D. 1094 to 1143.

and the bridal party appeared before success was attained. Spears and swords were plied. "'Ware the bull!" (*sand*), said the Madrecha, as he encountered his foe. "My name is the lion (*singh*) who will [691] devour the bull," replied the Solanki. The contest was fierce, but the Madrechas were slain, and in the morn Prithiraj was put in possession of Desuri. He drew out a grant upon the spot, inserting in it a curse against any of Sesodia blood who might break the bond which had restored the Rathor authority in Godwar. Although seventeen generations have passed since this event, the feud has continued between the descendants of the lion of Sodhgarh and the bull of Desuri, though the object of dissension is alienated from both.

The Chief of Ghānērāo. The Rājputs of Mewār and Mārwār compared.—I could well have dispensed with visits this day, the thermometer being 96°; I was besides devoured with inflammatory cold; but there was no declining another polite visit of the chieftain of Ghanerao. His retinue afforded a good opportunity of contrasting the Sesodia Rajput of fertile Mewar with the Rathors of Marwar, and which on the whole would have been favourable to the latter, if we confined our view to those of the valley of Udaipur, or the mountainous region of its southern limit, where climate and situation are decidedly unfavourable. There the Rajput may be said not only to deteriorate in muscular form and strength, but in that fairness of complexion which distinguishes him from the lower orders of Hindus. But the danger of generalizing on such matters will be apparent when it is known that there is a cause continually operating to check and diminish the deteriorating principle arising from the climate and situation (or, as the Rajput would say, from the *hawa pani*, 'air and water') of these unhealthy tracts; namely, the continual influx of the purest blood from every region in Rajputana: and the stream which would become corrupt if only flowing from the commingling of the Chondawats of Salumbar and the Jhalas of Gogunda (both mountainous districts), is refreshed by that of the Rathors of Godwar, the Chauhans of Haraoti, or the Bhatti of the desert. I speak from conviction, the chieftains above mentioned affording proofs of the evil resulting from such repeated intermarriages; for, to use their own adage, "a raven will produce a raven." But though the personal appearanee of the chieftain of Gogunda might exclude him from the table of the sixteen barons of Mewar, his son by a Rathor mother may be exhibited as a redeeming specimen of the Jhalas, and one in every way favourable of the Rajput of Mewar. On such occasion, also, as a formal visit, both chieftain and retainers appear under every advantage of dress and decoration; for even the form of the turban may improve the contour of the face, though [692] the Mertias of Ghanerao have nothing so decidedly peculiar in this way as those of other clans.

After some discourse on the history of past days, with which, like every respectable Rajput, I found him perfectly conversant, the Ghanerao chief took his leave with some courteous and friendly expressions. It is after such a conversation that the mind disposed to reflection will do justice to the intelligence of these people: I do not say this with reference to the baron of Ghanerao, but taking them generally. If by history we mean the relation of events in succession, with an account of the leading incidents connecting them, then are all the Rajputs versed in this science; for nothing is more common than to hear them detail their immediate ancestry or that of their prince for many generations, with the events which have marked their societies. It is immaterial whether he derives this knowledge from the chronicle, the chronicler, or both: it not only rescues him from the charge of ignorance, but suggests a comparison between him and those who constitute themselves judges of nationalities by no means unfavourable to the Rajput.

Godwār.—*October* 28.—Marched at daybreak. The Thakur sent a confidential vassal to accompany me through his domain. We could now look around us, as we receded from the Alpine Aravalli, with nothing to obstruct the vision, over the fertile plains of Godwar. We passed near Ghanerao, whose isolated portals, without tower or curtain to connect them, have a most humiliating appearance. It is to Raja Bhim, some twenty years ago, that their chieftains owe this degradation, in order to lessen their ability to recover the province for its ancient master the Rana. It was indeed one of the gems of his crown, as it is the only dazzling one in that of Marwar. While we marched over its rich and beautiful plains, well watered, well wooded, and abounding in fine towns, I entered into conversation with the Rana's envoy, who joined me on the march. Kishandas has already been mentioned as one of the few men of integrity and wisdom who had been spared to be useful to his country. He was a mine of ancient lore, and his years, his situation, and his character gave force to his sentiments of determined independence. He was as quick as touchwood, which propensity occasionally created a wordy war between me and my friend, who knew my respect for him. "Restore us Godwar," was his abrupt salutation as he joined me on the march: to which, being a little vexed, as the point could not be agitated by our government, I said in reply, "Why did you [693] let them take it?—where has the Sesodia sword slept this half century?" Adding, "God Almighty never intended that the region on this side the mountains should belong to Mewar;—nature's own hand has placed the limit between you." The old envoy's blood was roused as he exclaimed, "Even on this principle Godwar is ours, for nature has marked our limit by stronger features than mountains. Observe, as you advance, and you will find to the further limit of the province every shrub and flower common to Mewar; pass that limit but a few yards, and they are lost:

"Ānwal, ānwal Mewār:
Bāwal, bāwal Mārwār.

"Wherever the anwal puts forth its yellow blossoms, the land is of right ours; we want nothing more. Let them enjoy their stunted babuls, their karil, and the ak; but give us back our sacred pipal, and the anwal of the border." [1] In truth, the transition is beyond credence marked: cross but a shallow brook, and you leave all that is magnificent in vegetation; the pipal, bar, and that species of the mimosa resembling the cypress, peculiar to Godwar, are exchanged for the prickly shrubs, as the wild caper, jawas, and many others, more useful than ornamental, on which the camel browses.[2] The argument was, however, more ingenious than just, and the old envoy was here substituting the effect for the cause; but he shall explain in his own words why Flora should be permitted to mark the line of demarcation instead of the rock-enthroned (*Durga*) Cybele. The legend now repeated is historical, and the leading incidents of it have already been touched upon;[3] I shall therefore condense the Pancholi's descrip-

[1] [*Ānwal, āonla, Phyllanthus emblica; bāwal, babūl, Acacia arabica; karīl, Capparis aphylla; āk, Calotropis gigantea; pīpal, Ficus religiosa.*]

[2] [*Bar, Ficus bengalensis; jawās, Hedysarum alhagi.*]

[3] See p. 325.

tion into a summary analysis of the cause why the couplet of the bard should be deemed "confirmation strong" of the bounds of kingdoms. These traditionary couplets, handed down from generation to generation, are the most powerful evidence of the past, and they are accordingly employed to illustrate the Khyats or annals, of Rajputana. When, towards the conclusion of the fourteenth century, the founder of the Chondawats repaid the meditated treachery of Ranmall of Mandor by his death, he took possession of that capital and the entire country of the Rathors (then but of small extent), which he held for several years. The heir of Mandor became a fugitive, concealing himself in the fastnesses of the Aravalli, with little hope that [694] his name (Jodha) would become a patronymic, and that he would be honoured as the second founder of his country: that Mandor itself should be lost in Jodhpur. The recollection of the feud was almost extinct; the young Rana of Chitor had passed the years of Rajput minority, and Jodha continued a fugitive in the wilds of Bhandak-parao, with but a few horse in his train, indebted to the resources of some independents of the desert for the means of subsistence. He was discovered in this retreat by a Charan or bard, who, without aspiring to prophetic powers, revealed to him that the intercession of the queen-mother of Chitor had determined the Rana to restore him to Mandor. Whether the sister of Jodha, to give éclat to the restoration, wished it to have the appearance of a conquest, or whether Jodha, impatient for possession, took advantage of circumstances to make his entrance one of triumph, and thereby redeem the disgrace of a long and humiliating exile, it is difficult to decide; for while the annals of Mewar make the restoration an act of grace, those of Marwar give it all the colours of a triumph. Were the point worthy of discussion, we should say both accounts were correct. The Rana had transmitted the recall of Chonda from Mandor, but concealed from him the motive, and while Jodha even held in his possession the Rana's letter of restoration, a concatenation of circumstances, in which "the omen" was predominant, occurred to make him anticipate his induction by a measure more consonant to the Rajput, a brilliant *coup de main*. Jodha had left his retreat in the Run[1] to make known to Harbuji Sankhla, Pabuji, and other rievers

[1] An alp, or spot in these mountainous regions, where springs, pasture, and other natural conveniences exist.

of the desert, the changes which the bard had communicated. While he was there, intelligence was brought that Chonda, in obedience to his sovereign's command, had proceeded to Chitor. That same night "the bird of omen perched on Jodha's lance, and the star which irradiated his birth shone bright upon it." The bard of Mandor revealed the secret of heaven to Jodha, and the heroes in his train: "Ere that star descends in the west, your pennon will wave on the battlements of Mandor." Unless, however, this "vision of glory" was merely mental, Jodha's star must have been visible in daylight; for they could never have marched from the banks of the Luni, where the Sankhla resided, to Mandor, between its rising and setting. The elder son of Chonda had accompanied his father, and they had proceeded two coss in their [695] journey, when a sudden blaze appeared in Mandor: Chonda pursued his route, while his son Manja returned to Mandor. Jodha was already in possession; his *an* had been proclaimed, and the two other sons of Chonda had fallen in its defence. Manja, who fled, was overtaken and slain on the border. These tidings reached Chonda at the pass of the Aravalli; he instantly returned to Mandor, where he was met by Jodha, who showed him the letters of surrender for Mandor, and a command that he should fix with him the future boundary of each State. Chonda thought that there was no surer line of demarcation than that chalked out by the hand of nature; and he accordingly fixed that wherever the "yellow blossom" was found, the land should belong to his sovereign, and the bard was not slow in perpetuating the decree. Such is the origin of

Ānwal, ānwal Mewār :
Bāwal, bāwal Mārwār.

The brave and loyal founder of the Chondawats, who thus sacrificed his revenge to his sovereign's commands, had his feelings in some degree propitiated by this arrangement, which secured the entire province of Godwar to his prince: his son Manja fell, as he touched the region of the anwalas, and this cession may have been in '*mundkati*,' the compromise of the price of blood. By such traditional legends, not less true than strange, and to which the rock sculptures taken from Mandor bear evidence, even to the heroes who aided Jodha in his enterprise, the anwal of the Rajputs has been immortalized, like the humble broom of the French, whose planta-genesta has distinguished the loftiest name in chivalry, the proudest race emblazoned on the page of heraldry.

Notwithstanding the crops had been gathered, this tract contrasted favourably with Mewar, although amidst a comparative prosperity we could observe the traces of rapine; and numerous stories were rehearsed of the miseries inflicted on the people by the rapacious followers of Amir Khan. We crossed numerous small streams flowing from the Aravalli, all proceeding to join the "Salt River," or Luni. The villages were large and more populous; yet was there a dulness, a want of that hilarity which pervaded the peasantry of Mewar, in spite of their misfortunes. The Rajputs partook of the feeling, the cause of which a little better acquaintance with their headquarters soon revealed. Mewar had passed through the period [696] of reaction, which in Marwar was about to display itself, and was left unfortunately to its own control, or with only the impulse of a long suppressed feeling of revenge in the bosom of its prince, and the wiles of a miscreant minister, who wished to keep him in durance, and the country in degradation.

Nādol.—It creates a refreshing sensation to find the camp pitched in a cool and shaded spot; and at Nadol[1] we had this satisfaction. Here again there was no time for recreation, for there was abundant, nay, overwhelming matter both for the pen and the pencil; but my readers must be satisfied with the imperfect delineations of the first. Nadol is still a place of some consequence, though, but for its temples, we should not have supposed it to have been the capital of a province. With its neighbour, Narlai, five miles to the westward, it was the abode of a branch of the Chauhans of Ajmer, established at a very early period. From Nadol sprung the Deoras of Sirohi, and the Sonigiras of Jalor. The former still maintain their ground, in spite of all attempts of the Rathors; but the Sonigira, who was immortalized by his struggle against the second Ala, is blotted from the list of independent States; and this valuable domain, consisting of three hundred and sixty towns, is now incorporated with Jodhpur.

There is no spot in Rajputana that does not contain some record of the illustrious Chauhan; and though every race has

[1] [About seventy miles south-south-west of Jodhpur city.]

had its career of glory, the sublimity of which, the annals of the Sesodias before the reader sufficiently attest, yet with all my partiality for those with whom I long resided, and with whose history I am best acquainted, my sense of justice compels me to assign the palm of martial intrepidity to the Chauhan over all the "royal races" of India. Even the bards, to whatever family they belong, appear to articulate the very name as if imbued with some peculiar energy, and dwell on its terminating nasal with peculiar complacency. Although they had always ranked high in the list of chivalry, yet the seal of the order was stamped on all who have the name of Chauhan, since the days of Prithiraj, the model of every Rajput, and who had a long line of fame to maintain. Of the many names familiar to the bard is Guga of Bhatinda, who with forty-seven sons "drank of the stream of the sword" on the banks of the Sutlej, in opposing Mahmud.[1] This conqueror proceeded through the desert to the attack of Ajmer, the chief abode of this race, where his arms were disgraced, the invader wounded, and forced to relinquish his enterprise [697]. In his route to Nahrwala and Somnath he passed Nadol,[2] whose prince hesitated not to measure his sword even with Mahmud. I was fortunate enough to obtain an inscription regarding this prince, the celebrated Lakha, said to be the founder of this branch from Ajmer, of which it was a fief—its date S. 1039 (A.D. 983).[3] The fortress attributed to Lakha is on the declivity

[1] [Bhatinda, now Govindgarh, in the Patiāla State (*IGI*, xii. 343). The author's accounts of Gūga or Gugga are contradictory (see Index, *s.v.*). For this famous saga see Temple, *Legends of the Panjāb*, i. 121 ff., iii. 261 ff. The cult of the hero has passed as far south as Gujarāt, his festival being held on 9th dark half of Bhādon (Aug.-Sept.), known as Gūga navami (*BG*, ix. Part i. 524 f.).]

[2] Ferishta, or his copyist, by a false arrangement of the points, has lost Nadole in Buzule, using the ب for the ن and the ذ for the د. [It was Kutbu-d-dīn who, on his way to Gujarāt, passed the forts of "Tilli and Buzule" (Dow, ed. 1812, i. 147). Briggs (Ferishta i. 196) writes "Baly and Nadole." In the *Tāju-l-Ma-āsir* of Hasan Nizāmi the names are given as "Pāli and Nandūl" (Elliot-Dowson ii. 229). This illustrates the difficulty of tracing place names in the Muhammadan historians.]

[3] [Towards the end of the tenth century, Lākhan or Lakshman Singh, a younger brother of Wākpatirāj, the Chauhān Rāja of Sāmbhar, settled at Nādol, and his descendants ruled the territory till their defeat by Kutbu-d-dīn Ībak in 1206-10 (Erskine iii. A. 181 f.).]

of a low ridge to the westward of the town, with square towers of ancient form, and built of a very curious conglomerate of granite and gneiss, of which the rock on which it stands is composed. There was a second inscription, dated S. 1024 (A.D. 968), which made him the contemporary of the Rana's ancestor, Sakti Kumar of Aitpur, a city also destroyed, more probably by the father of Mahmud. The Chauhan bards speak in very lofty terms of Rao Lakha, who "collected transit dues from the further gate of Anhilwara, and levied tribute from the prince of Chitor."

Remains at Nādol.—It is impossible to do full justice to the architectural remains, which are well worthy of the pencil. Here everything shows that the Jain faith was once predominant, and that their arts, like their religion, were of a character quite distinct from those of Siva. The temple of Mahavira, the last of their twenty-four apostles, is a very fine piece of architecture. Its vaulted roof is a perfect model of the most ancient style of dome in the East; probably invented anterior to the Roman. The principle is no doubt the same as the first substitute of the arch, and is that which marked the genius of Caesar in his bridge over the Rhone, and which appears over every mountain torrent of the ancient Helvetii, from whom he may have borrowed it.[1] The principle is that of a horizontal instead of a radiating pressure. At Nadol the stones are placed by a gradual projection one over the other, the apex being closed by a circular key-stone. The angles of all these projections being rounded off, the spectator looking up can only describe the vault as a series of gradually diminishing amulets or rings converging to the apex. The effect is very pleasing, though it furnishes a strong argument that the Hindus first became acquainted with the perfect arch through their conquerors. The *toran*, in front of the altar of Mahavira, is exquisitely sculptured, as well as several statues of marble, discovered about one hundred and fifty years ago in the bed of the river, when it changed its course. It is not unlikely that they were buried during Mahmud's invasion. But [698] the

[1] [The temple of Mahāvīra contains three inscriptions, dated A.D. 1609, recording its construction from charitable funds. Garrett disputes the author's reference to Caesar, as the buildings are not superior to many others in Rājputāna (*ASR*, xxiii. (1887) 93).]

most singular structure of Nadol is a reservoir, called the *chana ki baoli*, from the cost of it being paid by the return of a single grain of pulse (*chana*). The excavation is immense; the descent is by a flight of grey granite steps, and the sides are built up from the same materials by piling blocks upon blocks of enormous magnitude, without the least cement.

Inscriptions and Coins.—My acquisitions here were considerable. Besides copies of inscriptions made by my Sanskrit scribes, I obtained two originals on brass. Of one of these, dated S. 1218, the memorial of Alandeva, I append a translation,[1] which may be considered curious as a formula of endowment of the Jains. I likewise procured several isolated MS. leaves of very great value, relative to the thirty-six royal races, to the ancient geography of India, and to the founding of ancient cities; also a catalogue of longevity of plants and animals, and an extract from a work concerning the descendants of Srenika and Samprati, the potent princes of the Jain faith between Mahavira and Vikrama. However meagre these fragments may be, I have incorporated their contents into my mosaic. I also made valuable additions to my collection of medals, for I obtained coins of Mahmud, Balban, and Ala, surnamed Khuni, or 'the sanguinary'; and another of a conqueror equally meriting that title, Nadir Shah. But these were of little consequence compared with what one of my envoys brought from Narlai—a small bag full of curious hieroglyphical (if I may so use the term) medals of the Chauhan princes.[2] One side represents a warrior on horseback, compounded out of a character to which I have applied the above term; on some there was a bull; while others, retaining the original reverse, have on the obverse the titles of the first Islamite conquerors, in the same manner as the currency of France bears the effigies of Louis XVI. and the emblems of the Republic. Whoever will pay a visit to Nadol will find his labour amply rewarded; I had only leisure to glean a few of these relics, which yet formed a rich harvest. Narlai, Bali, Desuri, Sadri, all ancient seats of the Jains, will yield medals, MSS., and rare specimens of the architectural art. From Abu to Mandor, the

[1] See Appendix, No. VII.

[2] These will appear more appropriately in a disquisition on Hindu medals found by me in India, in the *Transactions of the Royal Asiatic Society*. [The well-known "Bull and Horseman" type (*IGI*, ii. 142 f.).]

antiquary might fill many portfolios, and collect matter for volumes of the ancient history of this people, for this is the cradle of their faith. That I was enabled to obtain so much during a rapid march through the country arose partly from previous [699] knowledge, partly from the extent of my means, for I had flying detachments to the right and left of my route, consisting of intelligent natives of each city, accompanied by pandits for deciphering, and others for collecting whatever was the object of research; who, at the close of each day, brought me the fruits of their inquiries. When any remarkable discovery was made, I followed it up in person, or by sending those in whom I could confide. This is not mentioned from a spirit of egotism, but to incite others to the pursuit by showing the rewards which await such research.

Indara.—*October* 29.—Camp at Indara, eleven miles. This small town, placed on the north bank of one of the nameless feeders of the 'salt river,' is the boundary of Godwar; here the reign of the yellow anwal terminates, and here commences Marusthali, or 'the region of death.' The transition is great. We can look back upon fertility, and forward on aridity, which does not, however, imply sterility: for that cunning artist, nature, compensates the want of verdure and foliage to the inhabitants of the desert by many spontaneous bounties. An entire race of cucurbitaceous plants is the eleemosynary equivalent for the mango and exotics of the central lands of Rajputana; while indigenous poverty sends forth her commercial sons from Osi, Pali, and Pokaran, to bring wealth from the Ganges and the Kistna, to the Luni, or to the still more remote oasis, Jaisalmer. From Indara everything assumed a new character: the sand, of which we had before scarcely a sprinkling, became occasionally heavy; the shallow beds of the numerous streams were white with saline incrustations; and the vegetable creation had been gradually diminishing, from the giant race of the sacred fig-tree with leaf "broad as Amazonian targe," to the dwarfish shrubs of the desert. At once the satiric stanza of the bard of a more favoured region was brought to my mind, and as I repeated it to my old friend the Rana's envoy, he enjoyed the confession, and afresh urged his wish that nature should decide the question of their boundaries:

Āk ra jhonpra,
Phog ra vār,
Bājra ri roti,
Motham hari dāl,
Dekho ho Raja, teri Marwar.

'Huts of the āk,
Barriers of thorns,
Bread of maize,
Lentils of the vetch,
Behold Raja, your Marwar!' [700].

Construction of Villages.—The villages are of a construction totally distinct from anything we have seen, and more approaching the wigwam of the western world. Every commune is surrounded with a circumvallation of thorns, *kanta ka kot,* and the stacks of *bhus*, or 'chaff,' which are placed at intervals, give it the appearance of a respectable fortification. These *bhus* stacks are erected to provide provender for the cattle in scanty rainy seasons, when the parched earth denies grass, or full crops of maize. They are erected to the height of twenty or thirty feet, coated with a cement of earth and cow-dung, and with a sprinkling of thorns, to prevent the fowls of the air from reposing in them. In this manner, with a little fresh coating, they will exist ten years, being only resorted to on emergencies, when the kine may be said to devour the village walls. Their appearance is a great relief to the monotony of the march through the desert; which, however, cannot strictly be said to commence till you cross the Luni.

Pāli.—*October* 30.—A long march of twenty-one miles, in which there was little to record, brought us to Pali, the great commercial mart of western Rajwara. Like everything else in these regions it bore the marks of rapine; and as in the civil wars of this State its possession was of great importance to either party, the fortifications were razed at the desire of the inhabitants, who did not admire the noise of war within their gates. From the same feeling, when it was proposed to gird the sister mart, Bhilwara, with walls, the opposition to it was universal. The remnants of the walls lend it an air of desolation.[1] The town is overrated at ten thousand houses. As an emporium its reputation is of ancient

[1] [All traces of these walls have disappeared, but in Jūna or 'Old' Pāli there are some fine temples (*ASR*, xxiii. (1887) 86 ff.).]

date: and, politically, it is connected with the establishment of the reigning family in these regions. A community of Brahmans then held Pali in grant from the princes of Mandor: whence comes a numerous class, termed Paliwal, who follow mercantile pursuits. It was in S. 1212 (A.D. 1156) that Siahji, the founder of the Rathor dynasty and son to the emperor of Kanauj, passed Pali on his return from a pilgrimage from Dwarka to the Ganges. The Brahmans sent a deputation to relieve them from two great enemies to their repose, namely, the Minas of the Aravalli, and the lions, which had become very numerous. Siahji relieved them from both; but the opportunity "to acquire land" was too good to be lost, and on the festival of the Holi he put the leading Brahmans to death, and took possession of Pali.

The Commerce of Pāli.—Commerce, in these regions, is the basis of liberty: even despotism is [701] compelled to leave it unrestrained. Pali, like Bhilwara, Jhalrapatan, Rani, and other marts, enjoys the right of electing its own magistrates, both for its municipal regulations, and the arbitration of all matters connected with commercial pursuits. It was commerce which freed Europe from the bondage of feudality; and the towns above cited only require the same happy geographical position, to play the part of the Hanse towns of Europe. Like Bhilwara, Pali has its own currency, which, amidst universal deterioration, it has retained undebased. From remote times, Pali has been the connecting link between the sea-coast and northern India. Commercial houses established at Muskat-Mandavi, Surat, and Navanagar transmit the products of Persia, Arabia, Africa, and Europe, receiving those of India and Thibet. To enumerate all the articles, it would be necessary to name the various products of each: from the coast, elephants' teeth, rhinoceros' hides, copper, tin, pewter, dates dried and moist,[1] of which there is an immense consumption in these regions: gum-arabic, borax, coco-nuts, broad-cloths, striped silks, called *patang*; various dyes, particularly the *kermes* or crimson; drugs, especially the oxides of arsenic and quicksilver; spices, sandal-wood, camphor, tea, *momiai* or mummy,[2] which is much sought after in medicine, and

[1] The *kharak* and *pind khajūr*. [*Kharak* is the stage when the date becomes red or yellow, according to variety; *pind*, when it is quite ripe (Watt, *Econ. Dict.* vi. Part i. 205).]

[2] *Mom* in the language of Egypt signifies 'wax,' says some ancient

JĀT PEASANT OF MĀRWĀR.

RĀJPUT FOOT-SOLDIER OF MĀRWĀR.

To face page 812.

green glass (*kanch*). From Bahawalpur, soda (*sajji*),[1] the dyes called *al*[2] and *majith*,[3] matchlocks, dried fruits, asafoetida, Multan chintzes, and wood for household furniture. From Kotah and Malwa, opium and chintzes. From Jaipur, various cloths and sugars. From Bhuj, swords and horses.

The exports of home production are the two staple articles of salt and woollens; to which we may add coarse cotton cloths, and paper made in the town of Pali. The *lois*, or blankets, are disseminated throughout India, and may be had at from four to sixty rupees per pair; scarfs and turbans are made of the same material, but not for exportation. But salt is the chief article of export, and the duties arising therefrom equal half the land revenue of the country. Of the *agars*, or 'salt lakes,' Pachbhadra, Phalodi, and Didwana are the principal, the first being several miles in circuit [702].

The commercial duties of Pali yielded 75,000 rupees annually, a large sum in a poor country like Marwar.

Chāran and Bhāt Carriers.—The Charans and Bhats, or bards and genealogists, are the chief carriers of these regions: their sacred character overawes the lawless Rajput chief; and even the savage Koli and Bhil, and the plundering Sahariya of the desert, dread the anathema of these singular races, who conduct the caravans through the wildest and most desolate regions. The traveller avails himself of such convoy who desires to proceed to the coast by Jalor, Bhinmal, Sanchor, and Radhanpur, whence he may pursue his route to Surat, or Muskat-Mandavi.

Pungiri Temple.—To the east of Pali about ten miles, there is an isolated hill, called Pungiri, 'the hill of virtue,' which is crowned with a small temple, said to have been conveyed by a Buddhist magician from Palitana in Saurashtra. Wherever this ancient and numerous sect exists, magical skill is always asserted.

---

authority: so it is the usual name of that article in Persian. *Mummy* is probably thence derived. I remember playing a trick on old Silu, our *khabardar* [spy] at Sindhia's camp, who had been solicited to obtain a piece of *momiai* for a chieftain's wife. As we are supposed to possess everything valuable in the healing art, he would take no refusal; so I substituted a piece of indiarubber. [For the virtues of *momiāi* see Crooke, *Popular Religion and Folklore of N. India*, ii. 176 ff.]

[1] [Barilla, Watt, *Econ. Prod.* 112 f.]

[2] [*Morinda citrifolia, ibid.* 783 f.]

[3] [Madder, *Rubia cordifolia, ibid.* 926 f.]

Here we found our old friend, Gough, who had been rambling to the south-west amongst Sahariya, Khosas,[1] and all the wild beings of these uncivilized tracts, in search of new breeds of horses. Halted to enjoy his society.

Kairla, 30th.

Rohat, 31st.

Khānkāni.—*November* 1.—Khankani, on the north bank of the Luni. There was nothing to arrest attention between Pali and the Luni: all is flat and lonely in the thirty miles which intervene. Our halts were at Kairla, which has two small salt lakes, whence its name; in fact, this superabundant product, *khar*, or salt, gives its name to streams and towns. Both Kairla and Rohat, the intermediate places of halt, are feudal estates, and both chiefs had been involved in the recent civil dissensions: Rohat was under the ban.

Bhāt Customs. Coercion by Threat of Human Sacrifice.—Here I had an exemplification of the vulgar adage, "two of a trade," etc. Pema Naik, the leader of one of the largest *tandas*, or caravans, which frequent the desert for salt, had left his convoy, and with his brethren came to exhibit his wounds and fractures received in a fray with the leaders of another caravan. Both were Bhats; Pema was the head of the Bamania Bhats, so called from the place of their abode, and he counted forty thousand beasts of burthen under his control. Shama had no distinctive epithet: he had no home separate from [703] his *tanda*. His little State when not in motion was on the highways; hence those who dwell entirely with their cattle are styled *upapanti*, 'on the road.' Shama had taken advantage of the greater portion of Pema's caravan being detached to revenge an ancient feud; and had shown himself quite an adept in club-law, as the broken heads of his opponents disclosed. To reconcile them was impossible; and as the case was to be decided, not by the scales of abstract justice but by calculating which contributed most in duties, Pema by this summary process, more than from sympathy to his wounded honour, gained a victory by the exclusion of his rival. As before observed, these classes take advantage of their sacred character amongst the Rajputs to become the general

[1] [The Khosa is a Baloch tribe, many of them found in Sind, where, it is said, they were given lands by the Emperor Humāyūn (*Census Report, Baluchistan*, 1901, i. 95 f.).]

carriers of the country: but the advantage which might result to the State from the respect paid to them is neutralized by their avarice and constant evasion of the payment of all established duties. A memorable example of this kind occurred during the reign of Amra the First with the ancestor of this same Pema. The Rana would not submit to the insolent demands of the Bhats, when they had recourse to one of the most sanguinary sacrifices ever recorded—the threat alone of which is generally sufficient to extort acquiescence and concession. But the firmness of Amra has been recorded: and he braved them. Collecting the elder portion of their community, men, women, and youths of both sexes, they made a sacrifice to the number of eighty souls with their daggers in the court of the palace. The blood of the victims was on the Rana's head.[1] It was a species of excommunication, which would have unsettled a weaker reason; for the Rajput might repose after the murder of a Brahman, but that of the prophetic Vates would rise against him here and hereafter. For once they encountered a mind too strong to be shaken; Amra banished the whole fraternity of Bamania Bhats from his dominions, and the town of Bamani reverted to the fisc. The edict remained uncancelled until these days, when amongst the industrious of all classes whom the proclamations[2] brought once more to Mewar, came Pema and his brethren. Although tradition had preserved the causes of their exile, it had made no alteration in their sentiments and opinions, and the dagger was always at hand, to be sheathed in their own flesh whenever provocation called it from the girdle. Pema beset the Rana in all his rides, demanding a reduction [704] or rather abolition of duties for his *tanda*; and at length he took up a position on the terrace fronting the 'balcony of the sun,' threatening a *chandni*,[3] for such is the

[1] [Numerous instances of this custom among Bhāts will be found in *BG*, ix. Part i. 209 ff.] [2] See Vol. I. p. 561.

[3] [Platts (*Hindustāni Dict.*, *s.v.*) gives *chāndni*, 'moonlight'; *chāndni mār-jāna*, 'to be moonstruck, paralysed by a stroke of the moon'; *chāndni karan*, 'the practice of Brāhmans and others wounding themselves in order to extort the payment of a debt.' Here the threat is fear of the ghost of the man who took his life. Sir G. Grierson notes that in Gujarāti and Marāthi *chāndi karun* means 'to reduce to white ashes,' hence 'to ruin or destroy completely.' Here *chāndi*, usually meaning 'silver,' means 'anything white,' and hence 'white ashes.' This, he suggests, seems to be a more probable explanation than 'moonstruck.']

term applied to this suicidal revenge. The Rana, who had not the nerve of his ancestor, sent to me to beseech my interference: with his messenger, one from me returned to invite the Bhats to a settlement. They came, as fine, robust, intrepid a set as I ever saw. We soon came to issue: I urged that duties must be paid by all who chose to frequent the passes of Mewar, and that they would get nothing by their present silly mode of endeavouring to obtain remission; that if they would give a written agreement to abide by the scale of duties laid down, they should receive exemption for five hundred out of the forty thousand bullocks of their *tanda*, and be reinducted into Bamani; if not, there were daggers (showing them some on the table), and they might begin as soon as they pleased. I added that, in addition to Rana Amra's penalty of banishment, I would recommend confiscation of their entire caravan. Pema was no fool: he accepted Bamani, and the *muafi* for five hundred, and that day received his gold bracelets and clothes of investiture for Bamani from the Rana.

Jhālamand.—*November* 2.—Jhalamand, ten miles. Although within one march of Jodhpur, we were obliged to make an intermediate halt, in order to arrange the ceremonials of reception; a grave matter with all the magnates of the East, who regulate all such affairs by slavish precedent and ancestral wisdom. On such a novel occasion as the reception of an English envoy at this desert court, they were a good deal puzzled how to act. They could very well comprehend how an ambassador direct from majesty should be received, and were not unfamiliar with the formula to be observed towards a viceregal legation. But the present case was an anomaly: the Governor of all India, of course, could appear only as the first servant of a commercial body, which, with whatever privileges invested, never could be made to rank with royalty or its immediate emanation. Accordingly, this always proved a clog to our diplomatic missions, until the diffusion of our power from the Indus to the ocean set speculation at rest on the formalities of reception of the Company's ambassadors. On the other hand, the eternal rotation of military adventurers enjoying ephemeral power, such as the commanders of the myrmidons of Sindhia and Holkar, compelled all the Rajput princes to forgo much of their dignity; and men like Amir Khan, Jean Baptiste, or Bapu Sindhia, who but a [705] short time ago would have deemed themselves honoured with a seat in the ante-chamber, claimed equality of reception with princes. Each made it a subject for boasting, how far he had honoured himself by the humiliation of the descendant of the emperor of Kanauj, or the scion of Rama. At the same time, as the world is always deceived by externals, it was difficult to concede a reception less distinguished than that granted to the leader of a Mahratta horde; and here their darling precedent was available. To what distance did the Raja send the *istikbal* to meet Amir Khan? what was the rank of the chieftains so deputed? and to what point did the "offspring of the sun" condescend to advance in person to receive this "lord of the period"? All these, and many similar questions, were propounded through the Wakil, who had long been with me, to his sovereign, to whose presence he proceeded in order that they might be adjusted, while I halted at Jhalamand, only five miles from the capital. However individually we may despise these matters, we have no option, as public servants, but to demand the full measure of honour for those we represent. As the present would also regulate future receptions, I was compelled to urge that the Raja would best consult his own dignity by attending to that of the government I represented, and distinctly signified that it could never be tolerated that he should descend to the very foot of his castle to honour Amir Khan, and await the English envoy almost on the threshold of his palace. It ended, as such matters generally do in those countries, by a compromise: it was stipulated that the Raja should receive the mission in his *palki* or litter, at the central barrier of descent.[1] These preliminaries being arranged, we left Jhalamand in the afternoon, that we might not derange the habits of slumber of those who were to conduct us to the capital. About half-way we were met by the great feudatory chieftains of Pokaran and Nimaj, then lords of the ascendant, and the joint advisers of their sovereign. We dismounted, embraced, complimented each other in the customary phraseology; then remounted, and rode together until we reached the tents, where, after I had requested them to be the bearers of my homage to their sovereign, we mutually saluted and parted.

[1] Mr. Wilder, the superintendent of Ajmer, was deputed by General Sir D. Ochterlony, in December 1818, to the court of Jodhpur, and was very courteously received by the Raja.

The Chief of Pokaran.—Salim Singh [1] was the name of the lord of Pokaran, the most wealthy and the [706] most powerful of all the baronies of Marwar. His castle and estate (wrested from Jaisalmer) are in the very heart of the desert; the former is strong both by position and art. It is a family which has often shaken the foundation of the throne of Marwar. During four generations have its bold and turbulent chiefs made the most resolute of these monarchs tremble. Deo Singh, the great grandfather of the present chief, used to sleep in the hall of the royal palace, with five hundred of his Champawats, of which clan he is the chief. "The throne of Marwar is within the sheath of my dagger," was the boast, as elsewhere mentioned, of this haughty noble to his sovereign. His son, Sabal Singh, followed his father's steps, and even dethroned the great Bijai Singh: a cannon-shot relieved the prince from this terror of his reign. Sawai Singh, his son and successor, acted the same part towards Raja Bhim, and was involved in the civil wars which commenced in 1806, when he set up the pretender, Dhonkal Singh. The catastrophe of Nagor, in which Amir Khan acted the assassin of the Champawat and all his associates, relieved Raja Man from the evil genius of his house; and the honours this prince heaped on the son of the Champawat, in giving him the first office in the State, were but a trap to ensnare him. From this he escaped, or his life and the honours of Pokaran would have been lost together. Such is a rapid sketch of the family of the chief who was deputed to meet me. He was about thirty-five years of age; his appearance, though not prepossessing, was dignified and commanding. In person he was tall, but more powerful than athletic; his features were good, but his complexion was darker than in general amongst the chieftains of Marwar.

The Chief of Nimāj.—His companion, and associate in the councils of his prince, was in every point of personal appearance the reverse of this portrait. Surthan Singh was chief of the Udawats, a clan which can muster four thousand swords, all residing on the land skirting the Aravalli; and of which his

[1] The sibilant is the *Shibboleth* of the Rajput of Western India, and will always detect him. The 'lion' (*singh*) of Pokaran is degraded into 'asafoetida' (*hing*); as *Halim Hing*. [Pokaran, 85 miles N.W. of Jodhpur city, held by the premier noble of the Champāwat clan of Rāthors.]

residence Nimaj,[1] Raepur, and Chandawal are the principal fiefs. Surthan was a fine specimen of the Rajput; his figure tall and graceful; his complexion fair; his deportment manly and mild; in short, he was a thorough gentleman in appearance, understanding, and manners.

It would be impossible to relate here all the causes which involved him in the catastrophe from which his coadjutor escaped. It was the misfortune of Surthan to have been associated with Salim Singh; but his past services to his prince amply counterbalanced this party bias. It was he who prevented his sovereign from [707] sheathing a dagger in his heart on the disgraceful day at Parbatsar; and he was one of the four chieftains of all Marwar who adhered to his fortunes when beset by the united force of Rajputana. He was also one of the same four who redeemed the spoils of their country from the hands of the multitudinous array which assaulted Jodhpur in 1806, and whose fate carried mourning into every house of Rajasthan.[2] The death of Surthan Singh was a prodigal sacrifice, and caused a sensation of universal sorrow, in which I unfeignedly participated. His gallant bearing was the theme of universal admiration; nor can I give a better or a juster idea of the chivalrous Rajput than by inserting a literal translation of the letter conveying the account of his death, about eight months after my visit to Jodhpur.

"Jodhpur, 2d Asarh, or 28th June 1820.

"On the last day of Jeth (the 26th June), an hour before daybreak, the Raja sent the Aligols,[3] and all the quotas of the chiefs, to the number of eight thousand men, to attack Surthan Singh. They blockaded his dwelling in the city, upon which for three watches they kept up a constant fire of great guns and small arms. Surthan, with his brother Sur Singh, and his kindred and clan, after a gallant defence, at length sallied forth, attacked the foreigners sword in hand, and drove them back. But who can oppose their prince with success? The odds were too great,

[1] [Nīmāj, about 60 miles E.S.E. of Jodhpur city, fief of a noble of the Udāwat Rāthors.]

[2] See Vol. I. p. 539 for the murder of the princess of Udaipur, one of its results.

[3] The mercenary Rohilla battalions, who are like the Walloons and independent companies which formed the first regular armies of Europe. ['Aligol, 'noble troop' (Yule, *Hobson-Jobson*, 2nd ed. 15.]

and both brothers fell nobly. Nagoji and forty of the bravest of the clan fell with the Thakur brothers, and forty were severely wounded. Eighty, who remained, made good their retreat with their arms to Nimaj.[1] Of the Raja's troops, forty were killed on the spot, and one hundred were wounded. Twenty of the townsfolk suffered in the fray.

"The Pokaran chief, hearing of this, saddled; but the Maharaja sent Sheonath Singh of Kuchaman, the chief of Bhadrajan, and others, to give him confidence, and induce him to stay; but he is most anxious to get away. My nephew and fifteen of my followers were slain on this occasion. The Nimaj chief fell as became a Rathor. The world exclaims 'applause,' and both Hindu and Turk say he met [708] his death nobly. Sheonath Singh, Bakhtawar Singh, Rup Singh, and Anar Singh,[2] performed the funeral rites."

Such is the Rajput, when the point of honour is at stake! Not a man of his clan would have surrendered while their chief lived to claim their lives; and those who retreated only preserved them for the support of the young lord of the Udawats [709]!

CHAPTER 27

City and Fort of Jodhpur.—The sand, since we crossed the Luni, had become gradually heavier, and was quite fatiguing as we approached the capital of "the region of death"; but the Marwaris and the camels appeared to move through it as briskly as our men would on the plains of the Ganges. The view before the reader will give a more correct idea of the 'city of Jodha' than the most laboured description. The fort is erected on a mole projecting from a low range of hills, so as to be almost isolated, while, being higher than the surrounding objects, it is not commanded. This table-ridge (mountain we can scarcely term it, since its most elevated portion is not more than three hundred feet in height) is a curious feature in these regions of

[1] Which they afterwards nobly defended during many months.

[2] The last, a brave and excellent man, was the writer of this letter. He, who had sacrificed all to save his prince, and, as he told me himself, supported him, when proscribed by his predecessor, by the sale of all his property, even to his wife's jewels, yet became an exile, to save his life from an overwhelming proscription. To the anomalous state of our alliances with these States is to be ascribed many of these mischiefs.

TOWN AND FORT OF JODHPUR.
(From the south-east.)

To face page 820.

uninterrupted aridity. It is about twenty-five miles in length, and, as far as I could determine from a bird's-eye view and from report, between two and three in breadth, the capital being placed on the highest part at the southern extremity, and may be said to be detached from it. The northern point, which is the highest, and on which the palace is built, is less than three hundred feet. Everywhere it is scarped, but especially at this point, against which the batteries of the League [1] were directed in 1806, at least a hundred and twenty feet of perpendicular height. Strong walls and numerous round and square towers encircle the crest of the hill, encompassing a space of great extent, as may be judged from the dimensions of the base, said to be four miles in circuit. Seven barriers are thrown across the circuitous ascent, each having immense portals and their separate guards. There are two small lakes under the walls: the Rani Talab, or 'Queen's Lake,' to the east; and the Gulab Sagar, or 'Rose-water Sea,' to the south, from [710] which the garrison draws up water in buckets. There is also inside a *kund*, or reservoir, about ninety feet in depth, excavated from the rock, which can be filled from these tanks; and there are likewise wells within, but the water is brackish. Within are many splendid edifices, and the Raja's residence is a succession of palaces, each prince since the founder having left memorials of his architectural taste. The city to the eastward of the citadel is encompassed by a strong wall, three coss, or nearly six miles, in extent, on which a hundred and one bastions or towers are distributed; on the rampart are mounted several *rahkalas* [2] or swivels. There are seven gates to the capital, each bearing the name of the city to which it leads. The streets are very regular, and adorned with many handsome edifices of free-stone, of which the ridge is composed. The number of families some years ago was stated to be 20,000, probably 80,000 souls, an estimate far too great for the present day.[3] The Gulab Sagar is the favourite lounge of the inhabitants, who recreate amongst its gardens; and, strange to say, the most incomparable pomegranates (*anar*) are produced in it, far superior even to those of Kabul, which they resemble in the peculiarity of being *be-dana*,

[1] [Of Jagat Singh of Jaipur and Amīr Khān.]

[2] [*Rahkala* is properly the carriage on which a field-piece is mounted: then, a swivel-gun (Irvine, *Army of the Indian Moghuls*, 140).]

[3] [The population of the city in 1911 was 79,756.]

'without grain': rather a misnomer for a fruit, the characteristic of which is its granulations; but this is in contradistinction to those of India, which are all grain and little pulp. The *anars* of the Kagli-ka-bagh, or 'Ravens' Garden,' are sent to the most remote parts as presents. Their beautiful ruby tint affords an abundant resource for metaphor to the Rajput bard, who describes it as "sparkling in the ambrosial cup."[1]

Reception by the Rāja.—On the 4th the Raja received us with due form, advancing beyond the second gate of descent; when, after salutations and greetings, he returned according to etiquette. Giving him time to make his arrangements, we advanced slowly through lines of his clansmen to the upper area, where a display of grandeur met our view for which we were totally unprepared, and far eclipsing the simple and unostentatious state of the Rana. Here everything was imitative of the imperial court of Delhi, where the Rathor, long pre-eminent, had "the right hand of the king of the world." Lines of gold and silver mace-bearers deafened us with the titles of "Raj-Raj-Iswara!" 'the king, the lord of kings!' into whose presence, through mazes of intricate courts filled with his chivalry, all hushed into that mysterious silence which is invariably observed on such occasions, we were at length ushered [711].

Rāja Mān Singh.—The King of Maru arose from his throne, and advanced a few paces, when he again courteously received the envoy and suite, who were here introduced. The hall of reception was of great extent: from its numerous square columns it is styled Sahas stambha, 'the thousand-columned hall.' They were more massive than elegant; and being placed in parallel rows, at not more than twelve feet from each other, they gave an air of cumbrous, if not clumsy grandeur to an immense apartment, the ceiling of which was very low. About the centre, in a niche or recess, the royal *gaddi* or 'cushion' was placed, over which was raised a richly embroidered canopy, supported by silver-gilt columns. On the Rana's right hand were placed those whom the king honoured, the chieftains of Pokaran and Nimaj, who would have been less at their ease had they known that all the distinctions they then enjoyed were meshes to ensnare them. Several other chieftains and civil officers, whose names would but little interest the reader, were placed around. The wakil, Bishan

[1] *Amrit ra piyala.*

Ram, was seated near me, almost in front of the Raja. The conversation was desultory and entirely complimentary; affording, however, abundant opportunity to the Raja to display his proficiency in that mixed language, the Hindustani, which he spoke with great fluency and much greater purity than those who resided about the court at Delhi. In person the Raja is above the common height, possessing considerable dignity of manner, though accompanied by the stiffness of habitual restraint. His demeanour was commanding and altogether princely; but there was an entire absence of that natural majesty and grace which distinguished the prince of Udaipur, who won without exertion our spontaneous homage. The features of Raja Man are good: his eye is full of intelligence; and though the ensemble of his countenance almost denotes benevolence, yet there is ever and anon a doubtful expression, which, with a peculiarly formed forehead, gave a momentary cast of malignity to it. This might have been owing to that deep dissimulation, which had carried him through a trial of several years' captivity, during which he acted the maniac and the religious enthusiast, until the assumed became in some measure his natural character.

The biography of Man Singh would afford a remarkable picture of human patience, fortitude, and constancy, never surpassed in any age or country. But in this school of adversity he also took lessons of cruelty: he learned therein to master or rather disguise his passions; and though he showed not the ferocity of the tiger, he acquired [712] the still more dangerous attribute of that animal—its cunning. At that very time, not long after he had emerged from his seclusion, while his features were modelled into an expression of complaisant self-content, indicative of a disdain of human greatness, he was weaving his web of destruction for numberless victims who were basking in the sunshine of his favour. The fate of one of them has been already related.[1]

Descent of the Rāthors.—The Rathor, like many other dynasties not confined to the East, claims celestial descent. Of their Bhat, we may say what Gibbon does of the Belgic genealogist who traced the illustrious house of Este from Romulus, that "he riots in all the lust of fiction, and spins from his own bowels a lineage of some thousand years." We are certain that there were sovereigns of Kanauj in the fifth century, and it is very probable

[1] See p. 820.

that they ruled there prior to the era of Christianity. But this is accounted nothing by these lovers of antiquity, who never stop short of Swayambhuva,[1] and the ark, in which the antediluvian records of the Rathors may have been preserved with those of the De Courcys. But we will not revert to those "happy times, when a genealogical tree would strike its root into any soil, and the luxuriant plant could flourish and fructify without a seed of truth." Then the ambition of the Rathor for a solar pedigree could be gratified without difficulty.

But it requires neither Bhat nor bard to illustrate its nobility: a series of splendid deeds which time cannot obliterate has emblazoned the Rathor name on the historical tablet. Where all these races have gained a place in the temple of fame, it is almost invidious to select; but truth compels me to place the Rathor with the Chauhan, on the very pinnacle. The names of Chonda and Jodha are sufficient to connect Siahji, the founder, a scion of Kanauj, with his descendant, Raja Man:[2] the rest

> Were long to tell; how many battles fought;
> How many kings destroyed, and kingdoms won.

Let us, therefore, put forth our palm to receive the itr from his august hand, and the pan, acknowledged by a profound salaam, and bringing the right hand to my cocked hat, which etiquette requires we should "apply to the proper use:—'tis for the head," even in the presence. At all the native courts the head is covered, and the *en bas* left bare. It would be sadly indecorous to walk in soiled boots over their [713] delicate carpets, covered with white linen, the general seat. The slippers are left at the door, and it is neither inconvenient nor degrading to sit in your socks. The Raja presented me with an elephant and horse caparisoned, an aigrette, necklace, brocades, and shawls, with a portion according to rank to the gentlemen who accompanied me.

On the 6th I paid the Raja another visit, to discuss the affairs of his government. From a protracted conversation of several hours, at which only a single confidential personal attendant of the prince was present, I received the most convincing proofs of his intelligence, and minute knowledge of the past history, not of his own country alone, but of India in general. He was remark-

[1] ['The self-existent.']

[2] [The Rāthor dynasty of Kanauj is a myth (Smith, *EHI*, 385, note 1).]

ably well read; and at this and other visits he afforded me much instruction. He had copies made for me of the chief histories of his family, which are now deposited in the library of the Royal Asiatic Society. He entered deeply into the events of his personal history, and recounted many of the expedients he was obliged to have recourse to in order to save his life, when, in consequence of the murder of his Guru (not only his spiritual but his temporal guide, counsellor, and friend), he relinquished the reins of power, and acquiesced in their assumption by his son. The whole transaction is still involved in mystery, which the Raja alone can unravel. We must enter so far into the State secrets of the court as to disclose the motive for such an act as the destruction of the brave Surthan, and introduce to the reader another high priest of the Rajputs as a pendant for the oracle of the Apollo of Nathdwara.

The parricidal murder of Raja Ajit has been the destruction of Marwar, and even "unto the third and fourth generation" Providence would seem to have visited the act with its vengeance. The crown, which in a few years more would have been transmitted by nature's law, was torn from the brow of this brave prince, who has redeemed his lost inheritance from Aurangzeb, by the unhallowed arm of his eldest son Abhai Singh; instigated thereto by an imperial bribe of the viceroyalty of Gujarat. His brother, Bakhta Singh, was made almost independent in Nagor by the concession of Abhai and the sanad and titles of his sovereign; and the contests between their issue have moistened the sands of Marwar with the richest blood of her children. Such is the bane of feudal dominion—the parent of the noblest deeds and the deepest crimes.

Deonāthji, the High Priest.—Raja Man, accordingly, came to the throne with all the advantages and [714] disadvantages of such a state of things; and he was actually defending his existence in Jalor against his cousin and sovereign, when an unexpected event released him from his perils, and placed him on the throne. Bhim Singh had destroyed almost every branch of the blood-royal, which might have served as a nucleus for those intestine wars which desolated the country, and young Man, the sole intervening obstacle to the full accomplishment of his wishes, was reduced to the last extremity, and on the eve of surrendering himself and Jalor to this merciless tyrant, when he was relieved from his perilous situation. He attributed his escape to the intercession of the high priest of Marwar, the spiritual leader of the Rathors. This hierarch bore the title of divinity, or Nathji: his praenomen of Deo or Deva was almost a repetition of his title; and both together, Deonath, cannot be better rendered than by 'Lord God.' Whether the intercession of this exalted personage was purely of a moral nature, as asserted, or whether Raja Bhim was removed from this vain world to the heaven of Indra by means less miraculous than prayer is a question on which various opinions are entertained; but all agree that nothing could have been better timed for young Man, the sole victim required to fill up the measure of Bhim's sanguinary policy. When suicide was the sole alternative to avoid surrender to the fangs of this Herod of the Desert, the high priest, assuming the mantle of prophecy, pronounced that no capitulation was inscribed in the book of fate—whose page revealed brighter days for young Man. Such prophets are dangerous about the persons of princes, who seldom fail to find the means to prevent their oracles from being demented. A dose of poison, it is said, was deemed a necessary adjunct to render efficacious the prayers of the pontiff; and they conjointly extricated the young prince from a fate which was deemed inevitable, and placed him on the regal cushion of Marwar. The gratitude of Raja Man had no limits—no honours, no grants were sufficient to mark his sense of obligation. The royal mantle was hallowed by the tread of this sainted being; and the throne itself was exalted when Deonath condescended to share it with his master, who, while this proud priest muttered forth his mysterious benedictions, with folded hands stood before him to receive the consecrated garland. Lands in every district were conferred upon the Nath, until his estates, or rather those of the church of which he was the head, far exceeded in extent those of the proudest nobles of the land, his income [715] amounting to a tenth of the revenues of the State. During the few years he held the keys of his master's conscience, which were conveniently employed to unlock the treasury, he erected no less than eighty-four mandirs, or places of worship, with monasteries adjoining them, for his well-fed lazy chelas or disciples, who lived at free quarters on the labour of the industrious. Deonath was a striking example of the identity of human nature, under whatever garb and in whatever clime; whether under the cowl or the coronet, in the cold clime of Europe, or in the deserts of India. This Wolsey of Marudes exercised his hourly-increasing power to the disgust and alienation of all but his infatuated prince. He leagued with the nominal minister, Induraj, and together they governed the prince and country. Such characters, when exceeding the sphere of their duties, expose religion to contempt. The degradation which the haughty grandees of Marwar experienced made murder in their eyes a venial offence, provoked as they were by the humiliations they underwent through the influence of this arrogant priest, whose character may be given in the language of Gibbon, merely substituting Deonath of Marwar for Paul of Samosata: "His ecclesiastical jurisdiction was venal and rapacious; he extorted frequent contributions from the most opulent of the faithful, and converted to his own use a considerable part of the public revenue. His council chamber and his throne, the splendour with which he appeared in public, the suppliant crowd who solicited his attention, and the perpetual hurry of business in which he was involved, were circumstances much better suited to the state of a civil magistrate than to the humility of a primitive bishop."[1] But his "full-blown pride" at length burst under him. Sequestrations from the estates of the chief barons of Maru became frequent in order to swell his rent-roll for the support of his establishments; his retinue on ordinary occasions surpassed that of any chieftain, and not unfrequently he was attended by the whole insignia of the State—the prince attending on such ceremonies. On these occasions the proud Rajput felt that he folded his hands, not to his sovereign, but to his sovereign's sovereign; to a vindictive and vainglorious priest, who, amidst the mummeries and artifices of religious rites, gratified an inordinate vanity, while he mortified their pride and diminished their revenues. The hatred of such men is soon followed by their vengeance; and though they would not dye their own daggers in his blood, they soon found agents in a race who know not mercy, the myrmidons of [716] that villain Amir Khan, under whose steel, and within the precincts of the palace, Deonath fell a victim. It has been surmised that Raja Man was privy to the murder; that if he did not command or even sanction it, he used no means to prevent it. There are but two in this life who can reveal this mystery—the

[1] [*Decline and Fall*, ed. W. Smith, ii. 262.]

Raja, and the *bourreau en chéf* of Rajasthan, the aforesaid Amir Khan.

The murder of the high priest was but a prolongation of the drama, in which we have already represented the treacherous destruction of the chieftain of Pokaran and his kindred; and the immolation of Krishna Kunwari, the Helen of Rajasthan. The attack on the gallant Surthan, who conducted us from Jhalamand to the capital, sprung from the seed which was planted so many years back; nor was he the last sacrifice: victim after victim followed in quick succession until the Caligula of the Desert, who could "smile and stab," had either slain or exiled all the first chieftains of his State. It would be a tedious tale to unravel all these intrigues; yet some of them must be told, in order to account for the ferocity of this man, now a subordinate ally of the British Government in the East.

Accession of Rāja Mān Singh.—It was in A.D. 1804 [1] that Raja Man exchanged the defence of Jalor for the throne of Jodhpur. His predecessor, Raja Bhim, left a widow pregnant; she concealed the circumstance, and when delivered, contrived to convey the child in a basket to Sawai Singh of Pokaran. During two years he kept the secret: he at length convened the Marwar chieftains, with whose concurrence he communicated it to Raja Man, demanding the cession of Nagor and its dependencies as a domain for this infant, named Dhonkal Singh, the heir-apparent of Marwar. The Raja promised compliance if the mother confirmed the truth of the statement. Whether her personal fears overcame her maternal affection, or the whole was an imposture of Pokaran, she disclaimed the child. The chiefs, though not satisfied, were compelled to appear contented with the result of this appeal; and for some years the matter seemed at rest. But this calm was only the presage of a storm, which shook to its base the political edifice of Marwar, and let loose upon her cities a torrent of predatory foes; it dethroned her prince, and, what the planner could not have contemplated, involved his own destruction. The effects of this treachery have for ever destroyed all confidence between the chief and the entire feudal interest. The Pokaran chief, after failing to establish the [717] claims of Dhonkal Singh as pretender to the throne, sent him for safety

[1] The date of his accession is the 5th of the month Margsir, S. 1860 [A.D. 1803].

to the Shaikhawat chief of Khetri,[1] one of the independent nobles of the Jaipur family. Here he left him till an opportunity again arrived to bring him upon the scene, which was afforded by the contest between the princes of Marwar and Jaipur for the hand of the Rana's daughter. This rivalry, the effects of which are already related, and which brought into conflict all the northern powers of India, was, in fact, only the under-plot of the deep-laid policy of Sawai. When once the gauntlet was thrown down for the hand of this fair lady, the Pokaran chief stepped in with the pretended son of Raja Bhim, whose cause, from the unpopularity of Raja Man, soon brought to his standard almost all the feudality of Marwar. The measures which followed, and the catastrophe, the death of Krishna Kunwari, have already been related.[2] The assassination of the chief of Pokaran was simultaneous with these events; and it was shortly after that the murder of the pontiff Deonath took place.

Insanity of Rāja Mān Singh.—After being relieved from all external foes by his own strength of mind, and the aid of a few friends whom no reverse could estrange from him, Raja Man either fell, or affected to fall, into a state of mental despondency bordering on insanity. Suspicious of every one, he would only eat from the hands of his wife, who prepared his food herself; he became sullen and morose; he neglected public business; and finally withdrew entirely from the world. The attempt to rouse him from this real or pretended stupor was fruitless; he did nothing but lament the death of Deonath, and pour forth prayers to the deity. In this state, he was easily induced to associate his son in the government, and he bestowed upon him with his own hand the *tika* of command. Chhattar Singh was the name of the prince, who was still in his minority; thoughtless, and of dissolute habits, he soon gave himself up to the guidance of a junta of the chiefs, who proclaimed Akhai Chand, of the mercantile caste, the chief civil minister of the State.

British Control of Mārwār. Restoration and Policy of Rāja Mān Singh.—Such was the condition of Marwar from A.D. 1809 to 1817. At this period the progress of events made the English arbiters of the destinies of Rajasthan. The regent of Marwar sent an ambassador to treat; but before the treaties were ratified and exchanged the young regent was dead. Various causes were

[1] [About 80 miles N. of Jaipur city.]

[2] Vol. I. page 535.

assigned [718] for his death: by some his dissolute habits, occasioning premature decay; by others, with more probability, the dagger of an indignant Rajput, the honour of whose daughter he had clandestinely attempted. Upon this event, and the change of political circumstances, the chiefs had no alternative but to turn to the secluded prince. If but one half is true that I have heard, and from authority of high credit, the occupations of the years which the Raja passed between the murder of the priest and the death of his son might be deemed an atonement for the deepest crimes. When messengers announced the fate of his son, and that State necessity recalled him to the helm of affairs, he appeared unable to comprehend them. He had so long acted the maniac that he had nearly become one: his beard was never touched, and his hair, clotted and foul, gave him an expression of idiocy; yet throughout these long years he was resolutely tenacious of life. The party who governed the son and the State had their own menials to wait upon him, and many were the attempts to poison him by their means; in avoiding which his simulated madness was so perfect that they deemed he had "a charmed life." But he had one faithful servant, who throughout this dreadful trial never forsook him, and who carried him food in his turban to replace that which was suspected. When by degrees he was led to understand the emergency, and the necessity of leaving his prison, he persevered in his apparent indifference to everything earthly, until he gathered information and the means for a terrible reaction. The treaty with the English put the ball at his foot: he very soon perceived that he might command a force to put down disorder—such was even volunteered; but with admirable penetration he trusted to the impression of this knowledge amongst his chiefs, as a sufficient auxiliary. By disseminating it, he paralysed that spirit which maintained rights in the soil of Marwar nearly concurrent with those of the sovereign. No higher compliment could be paid to British ascendancy than the sentiments of Raja Man and his nobles; and no better illustration is on record of the opinion of our power than that its name alone served the Raja's purpose in subjugating men, who, scarcely knowing fear, yet reposing partly on our justice, though mainly on the utter hopelessness of resisting us, were deprived of all moral courage.

In refusing the aid of a mere physical force, the Raja availed himself of another weapon; for by this artifice he threw the chiefs off their guard, who confided in his [719] assumed desire to forget the past. Intrigues for power and patronage seemed to strengthen this confidence; and Salim Singh of Pokaran, the military Maire du palais or Bhanjgarh, and Akhai Chand, retained as civil prime minister, were opposed by Jodhraj Singwi, who headed the aspirants to supplant them. The Raja complained of their interested squabbles, but neither party dreamed that they were fostered by him to cloak his deep-laid schemes. Akhai Chand had been minister throughout the son's administration; the political and pecuniary transactions of the State were known chiefly to him; to cut him off would have been poor revenge, and Raja Man was determined not only to extract from him all the knowledge of State matters transacted during his seclusion, but to make himself master of his coffers, and neither would have been attained by simple murder. Akhai Chand was not blind to the dangers of his position; he dreaded the *appui* his sovereign derived from the English, and laboured to inspire the Raja with distrust of their motives. It suited his master's views to flatter this opinion; and the minister and his adherents were lulled into a fatal security.

Maladministration of Rāja Mān Singh.—Such were the schemes concocting when I visited this court, which were revealed by succeeding events. At this time the Raja appeared in a state of mental depression, involved in difficulties, cautious, fearful of a false step, and surrounded by the satellites of the miscreant Akhai Chand, who, if he could no longer incarcerate his person, endeavoured to seal up the mind of his prince from all communication with those who might stimulate him to exertion. But all his arts only served to entangle him in the web then weaving for his life. The Raja first made him the means of destroying the most powerful of his chieftains, Surthan being the primary sacrifice to his sanguinary proscription; many others followed, until the best of the feudal chieftains sought refuge from his fury in exile, and found the saran (sanctuary) they sought in the surrounding States, the majority in Mewar. The day of vengeance at length arrived, and the minister and his partisans were transferred from their position at the helm of the State to a dungeon. Deceived with hopes of life, and compelled by the application of some summary methods of torture, Akhai Chand gave in a schedule of forty lakhs of property, of which the Raja realized a large portion, and then dismissed him to the other world. Nagoji, the kiladar,[1] and Mulji Dandal, both favourites and advisers of the Raja's [720] late son, returned on the strength of a general amnesty, and forgot they had been traitors. The wealth which prodigality had heaped upon them, consisting of many of the crown jewels, being recovered, their worldly accounts were settled by a cup of poison, and their bodies thrown over the battlements. Success, and the taste of blood, whetted rather than appeased the appetite of Raja Man. He was well seconded by the new minister, Fateh Raj, the deadly opponent of Akhai Chand, and all the clan of Champawats, whom he deemed the authors of the murder of his brother Induraj, slain at the same time with Deonath. Each day announced a numerous list of victims, either devoted to death, or imprisoned and stripped of their wealth. The enormous sum of a crore of rupees has been stated as the amount of the confiscations.

All these atrocities occurred within six months after my visit to this court, and about eighteen from the time it was received into protective alliance with the British Government. The anomalous condition of all our connexions with the Rajput States has already been described : and if illustration of those remarks be required, it is here in awful characters. We had tied up our own hands : "internal interference" had been renounced, and the sequestration of every merchant's property, who was connected with the Mehta faction, and the exile of the nobles, had no limit but the will of a bloodthirsty and vindictive tyrant. The objects of his persecution made known everywhere the unparalleled hardships of their case, and asserted that nothing but respect for the British Government prevented their doing themselves justice. In no part of the past history of this State could such proscription of the majority of the kin and clan of the prince have taken place. The dread of our intervention, as an umpire favourable to their chief, deprived them of hope ; they knew that if we were exasperated there was no saran to protect them. They had been more than twelve months in this afflicting condition when I left the country ; nor have I heard that anything has been done to relieve them, or to adjust these intestine broils. It is abandoning them to that spirit of revenge which is a powerful

[1] Commandant of the fortress [*qil'adār*].

ingredient in their nature, and held to be justifiable by any means when no other hope is left them. In all human probability, Raja Man will end his days by the same expedient which secured him from the fury of his predecessor.[1]

Interview with Rāja Mān Singh.—Having lifted the mantle which veiled the future, my reader must forget all that [721] has been said to the disadvantage of Raja Man, and see only the dignified, the courteous, and the well-instructed gentleman and prince. I cannot think that the Raja had coolly formed to himself the plan of the sanguinary measures he subsequently pursued, and which it would require a much more extended narrative to describe. We discoursed freely on past history, in which he was well read, as also in Persian, and his own native dialects. He presented me with no less than six metrical chronicles of his house; of two, each containing seven thousand stanzas, I made a rough translation. In return, I had transcribed and sent to him Ferishta's great *History of the Mahomedan Power in India*, and *Khulasatu-t-tawarikh*,[2] a valuable epitome of the history of Hindustan. I little imagined that I should then have to exhibit him otherwise than his demeanour and instructive discourse made him appear to me. In our graver conversation I was amused with a discourse on the rules of government, and instructions for the guidance of ambassadors, which my better acquaintance with Chand discovered to be derived from that writer. He carried me, accompanied by a single domestic, to various apartments in the palace, whence he directed my view across the vast plains of the desert, whose monarch I envied not. The low hills in the vicinity alone broke the continuity of this arid region, in which a few isolated nim trees were thinly scattered, to remind one of the absence of all that is grand in vegetation. After a visit of several hours, I descended to my tent, and found my friends, Captain Waugh and Major Gough, just returned from a successful chase of an antelope, which, with the aid of some Rohilla greyhounds, they had run down. I attributed their success to the heavy

[1] [In 1839, in consequence of the misgovernment of Mān Singh, a force was sent by the British Government and Jodhpur was occupied. He entered into a treaty securing a cessation of his tyrannical acts. He died on September 5, 1843.]

[2] [An abstract of the *Khulāsatu-t-tawārīkh* of Subhān Rāe is given in Elliot-Dowson viii. 5 ff.]

sands, on which I have witnessed many pulled down by dogs of little speed; but the secret was revealed on this animal being sent to the *cuisinier*. On depriving him of his hide, between it and the flesh the whole carcase was covered with a large, inert, amorphous white maggot. The flesh was buried in the sands, and no venison appeared again on my table while in India.[1]

Mandor. Rāthor Cenotaphs.—*November* 8.—I set out early this morning to ramble amidst the ruins of the ancient capital, Mandor, an important link in the chain of archaeological research, before the *panchranga*, or 'five-coloured banner' of Maru was prostrated to the crescent. Attended by an escort provided by the Raja, I left the perambulator behind; but as the journey occupied an hour and a quarter, and at a very slow pace, the distance must be under five miles. I proceeded through the Sojat gate, to [722] gain the road leading to Nagor; shortly after which I passed the Maha Mandir, or 'Grand Minster,' the funds for the erection of which were provided by Raja Man on his escape from ruin at Jalor. I skirted the range, gradually decreasing in height for three miles, in a N.N.E. direction. We then altered our course to N.N.W., and entered the gorge of the mountains which envelop all that is hallowed of the relics of the princes of this house. The pass is narrow; the cliffs are almost perpendicular, in which are numerous caves, the abodes of ascetics. The remains of fortifications thrown across, to bar the entrance of the foe to the ancient capital of the Pariharas, are still visible: a small stream of pure and sweet water issues from this opening, and had a watercourse under an archway. After proceeding a little farther, the interval widened, and passing through the village, which does not exceed two hundred houses, our attention was attracted by a line of lofty temples, rising in graduated succession. These proud monuments proved to be the cenotaphs of the Rathors, erected on the spots where the funeral pyre consumed the crowned heads of Maru, who seldom burnt alone, but were accompanied by all that made life agreeable or poisoned its enjoyment. The small brook already mentioned flows past the southern extremity of

[1] [Professor E. B. Poulton kindly sends a note from Colonel J. W. Yerbury, who writes: "Although no record exists of the occurrence of Hypoderma in Hindustan, I think there is no doubt that the maggots are the larvae of either *H. diaua* or *H. acteon*. They have been found in antelopes—*Antelope saiga*—and *dorcas* brought to Italy from the East."]

the chief line of monuments, which extend from south to north. At the former point stands that of Rao Maldeo, the gallant opponent of Sher Shah, the brave usurper of the throne of the Moguls. The farther point terminates with that of Maharaja Ajit Singh; while the princes in regular succession, namely, Sur Singh, Udai Singh, Gaj Singh, and Jaswant Singh, fill up the interval.

These dumb recorders of a nation's history attest the epochs of Marwar's glory, which commenced with Maldeo, and ended with the sons of Ajit. The temple-monument of Maldeo, which yet throws into shade the still more simple shrines of Chonda, and Jodha, contrasted with the magnificent mausoleum of Raja Ajit, reads us a lesson on the advancement of luxurious pomp in this desert State. The progression is uniform, both in magnitude and elegance, from Maldeo's who opposed on equal terms the Afghan king (whose memorable words, "I had nearly lost the throne of India for a handful of barley,"[1] mark at once the gallantry and the poverty of those whom he encountered), to the last great prince Ajit. Even that of Raja Gaj is plain, compared to his successor's. These monuments are all erected of a very close-grained freestone, of a dark brown or red [723] tint, with sufficient hardness to allow the sculptor to indulge his fancy. The style of architecture, or rather the composition, is mixed, partaking both of the Saivite and the Buddhist; but the details are decidedly Jain, more especially the columns, which are of the same model as those in Kumbhalmer. I speak more especially of those of Rajas Jaswant and Ajit, drawings of which, on a large scale, executed by the Raja's chief architect, I brought to Europe; but which it would be too expensive to have engraved. They are raised on immense terraces, faced with large blocks of well-polished freestone. That of Jaswant is somewhat ponderous and massive; but Ajit's rises with great elegance and perfect symmetry of proportion.

On ascending the terrace you enter through a lofty vaulted porch supported by handsome columns to the sanctum, which is a pyramidal temple, four stories in height, in the Saivite style,

[1] [Sher Shāh, after his victory over Rāja Māldeo in A.D. 1544, said that "for a handful of millet (*juār*) he had almost lost the empire of India" (Ferishta ii. 123; Manucci i. 117). The author quotes this saying twice later on.]

crowned by the *sikhar* and *kalas*, elsewhere described. The sculptural ornaments are worthy of admiration, both for their design and effect; and the numerous columns on the basement, and different stages of ascent, give an air of so much majesty that one might deem these monuments more fitting sepulture for the Egyptian Cheops than a shrine—over what? not even the ashes of the desert king, which were consigned in an urn to the bosom of the Ganges. If the foundations of these necrological monuments have been equally attended to with the superstructure, they bid fair to convey to remote posterity the recollection of as conspicuous a knot of princely characters as ever followed each other in the annals of any age or country. Let us place them in juxtaposition with the worthies of Mewar and the illustrious scions of Timur, and challenge the thrones of Europe to exhibit such a contemporaneous display of warriors, statesmen, or scholars.

Mewar.	Marwar.	Delhi.
Rana Sanga	Rao Maldeo	Babur and Sher Shah.
	Rao Sur Singh	Humayun.
Rana Partap	Raja Udai Singh	Akbar.
Rana Amra I. Rana Karan	Raja Gaj Singh	Jahangir and Shah Jahan.
Rana Raj	Raja Jaswant Singh	Aurangzeb.
Rana Jai Singh Rana Amra II.	Raja Ajit Singh	All the competitors for the throne after Farrukhsiyar [724].

From Maldeo to Udai *le gros* the first *Raja* (hitherto *Raos*) of Marwar, and the friend of Akbar, to Jaswant, the implacable foe of Aurangzeb, and Ajit, who redeemed his country from oppression, all were valiant men and patriotic princes.

"Where were the lions' cubs," I asked of my conductor, "the brave sons of Ajit, who erected this monument to his manes, and who added provinces to his dominions?" He pointed to two sheds, where the *kriya karma*[1] was performed; there was

> No funeral urn
> To mark their obsequies:

[1] [Funeral rite.]

but these lowly sheds told, in more forcible, more emphatic language, the cause of this abrupt transition from grandeur to humility than pen ever wrote; and furnished the moral epilogue to the eventful drama of the lives of these kings of the desert. Abhai Singh's parricidal hand bereft his father of life; yet though his career was one splendid tissue of success and honour, leaving his dominions more than doubled, the contentions of his issue with that of his brother Bakhta Singh, alike accessory, it is said, to the crime, have entailed endless misery upon Marwar, and left them not the power, if they had the inclination, to house his ashes. In the same line with the parricide and his brave brother is the humble monument of the great Bijai Singh, whose life till towards its close was a continued tide of action. I could not avoid an exclamation of surprise: "Shame to the country," I said, "that has neglected to enshrine the ashes of a name equal to the proudest!" His three sons, amongst them Zalim Singh, with the sketch of whom this narrative opened, have their shrines close to his; and but a few yards removed are those of Raja Bhim, and his elder brother Guman (who died in his minority), the father of the reigning prince, Raja Man. The last, which closed the line, pertained to Chhattar Singh, who, in all probability, was saved by death from the murder of his parent. I passed it in disgust, asking who had been so foolish as to entomb his ashes better than those of some of the worthies of his race? I found that it was the act of maternal fondness.

Ancestor Worship. Sati.—The Amavas (the Ides) and the Sankrantis (when the sun enters a new sign of the Zodiac) of every month are sacred to the Pitrideva, on which days it is incumbent on the reigning prince to "give water" to his ancestors. But the ignorance of my conductor deprived me of much information which I anticipated [725]; and had I not been pretty well read in the chronicles of the Rathors, I should have little enjoyed this visit to a "nation's dust." They related one fact, which was sufficient to inspire horror. No less than sixty-four females accompanied the shade of Ajit to the mansion of the sun. But this is twenty short of the number who became Satis when Raja Budh Singh of Bundi was drowned! The monuments of this noble family of the Haras are far more explicit than those of the Rathors, for every such Sati is sculptured on a small altar in the centre of the cenotaph: which speaks in distinct language the all-powerful motive, vanity, the principal incentive to these tremendous sacrifices. Budh Singh was a contemporary of Ajit, and one of the most intrepid generals of Aurangzeb; the period elapsed is about one hundred and twenty years. Mark the difference! When his descendant, my valued friend, the Rao Raja Bishan Singh, died in 1821, his last commands were that none should give such a proof of their affection. He made me guardian of his infant heir;—in a few days I was at Bundi, and his commands were religiously obeyed.

In this account are enumerated the monumental relics below the fort. Upon the mountain, and beyond the walls of the fortress of Mandor, are the *dewals* of Rao Ranmall, Rao Ganga, and Chonda, who conquered Mandor from the Parihars. Within a hundred yards of this trio of worthies of this house is a spot set apart for the queens who die natural deaths. But this is anticipating; let me in form conduct my readers step by step from the cemetery of the Rathors to the Cyclopean city of the Parihars.

Whoever has seen Cortona, Volterra, or others of the ancient Tuscan cities can form a correct idea of the walls of Mandor, which are precisely of the same ponderous character. It is singular that the ancient races of India, as well as of Europe (and whose name of Pali is the synonym of Galati or Keltoi) should, in equal ignorance of the mechanical arts, have piled up these stupendous monuments, which might well induce their posterity to imagine "there were giants in those days." This western region, in which I include nearly all Rajputana and Saurashtra, has been the peculiar abode of these "pastor kings," who have left their names, their monuments, their religion and sacred character as the best records of their supremacy. The Rajpali, or 'Royal Pastors,' are enumerated as one of the thirty-six royal races of ancient days: the city of Palitana, 'the abode of the Pali,' in Saurashtra (built [726] at the foot of Mount Satrunjaya, sacred to Buddha), and Pali in Godwar, are at once evidences of their political consequence and the religion they brought with them; while the different nail-headed characters are claimed by their descendants, the sectarian Jains of the present day.[1] There is scarcely an ancient city in Rajputana whence I have not

[1] [There is no evidence that the name Pālitāna is connected with a Pāli tribe.]

obtained copies of inscriptions from columns and rocks, or medals, gold, silver, and copper, bearing this antique character. All are memorials of these races, likewise termed Takshak, the Scythic conquerors of India, ancestors of many of the Rajputs, whose history the antiquary will one day become better acquainted with. The Parihara, it will be recollected, is one of the four Agnikulas: races who obtained a footing in India posterior to the Suryas and Indus. I omitted, however, to mention, in the sketch of the Pariharas, that they claim Kashmir as the country whence they migrated into India: the period is not assigned, but it was when the schismatic wars between the Saivites and Buddhists were carrying on; and it would appear that the former found proselytes and supporters in many of these Agnikulas. But of the numerical extent of the followers of this faith we have this powerful evidence, namely, that three-fourths of the mercantile classes of these regions are the descendants of the martial conquerors of India, and that seven out of the ten and a half niyats or tribes, with their innumerable branches, still profess the Jain faith, which, beyond controversy, was for ages paramount in this country.

The Walls of Mandor.—Let us now ascend the paved causeway to this gigantic ruin, and leave the description of the serpentine Nagda, which I threaded to its source in the glen of Panchkunda, till our return. Half-way up the ascent is a noble *baoli*, or 'reservoir,' excavated from the solid rock, with a facing of cut stone and a noble flight of steps: on which, however, two enormous *gulars* [1] or wild fig-trees have taken root, and threaten it with premature destruction. This memorial bears the name of Nahar Rao, the last of the Parihars.[2] As I looked up to the stupendous walls,

> Where time hath leant his hand, but broke his scythe,

I felt the full force of the sentiment of our heart-stricken Byron:

> there is a power
> And magic in the ruined battlement,
> For which the palace of the present hour
> Must yield its pomp, and wait till ages are its dower.

---

[1] [*Ficus glomerata.*]

[2] [Near the cave an inscription of Kakka Parihār, probably tenth century A.D., has recently been found (Erskine iii. A. 196.]

Ages have rolled away since these were raised, and ages will yet roll on, and find [727] them immovable, unchanged. The immense blocks are piled upon, and closely fitted to, each other without any cement, the characteristic of all the Etruscan cities termed Cyclopean. We might indeed smuggle a section of Mandor into the pages of Micali,[1] amongst those of Todi or Volterra, without fear of detection. The walls, following the direction of the crest of the ridge, are irregular ; and having been constructed long before artillery was thought of, the Parihar or Pali engineer was satisfied with placing the palace on the most commanding eminence, about the centre of the fortress. The bastions or towers are singularly massive, and like all the most antique, their form is square. Having both fever and ague upon me, I was incapable of tracing the direction of the walls, so as to form any correct judgement of the space they enclose ; but satisfied with gaining the summit, I surveyed the ruin from the site of the palace of the Parihars. The remains, though scanty, are yet visible ; but the materials have been used in the construction of the new capital Jodhpur, and in the cenotaphs described. A small range of the domestic temples of the palace, and some of the apartments, are yet distinctly to be traced ; the sculptured ornaments of their portals prove them to have been the work of a Takshak or Buddhist architect. Symbolical figures are frequently seen carved on the large blocks of the walls, though probably intended merely as guides to the mason. These were chiefly Buddhist or Jain : as the quatre-feuille, the cross ; though the mystic triangle, and triangle within a triangle ✡ [2] (a sign of the Saivites, only, I believe), was also to be seen. The chief memorials of the Parihara are a gateway and magnificent Toran, or triumphal arch, placed towards the south-east angle of the castle. It is one mass of sculpture ; but the pencil was wanting,

[1] *L'Italie avant la domination des Romains.*

[2] Amongst ancient coins and medals, excavated from the ruins of Ujjain and other ancient cities, I possess a perfect series with all the symbolic emblems of the twenty-four Jain apostles. The compound equilateral triangle is amongst them : perhaps there were masons in those days amongst the Pali. It is hardly necessary to state that this Trinitarian symbol (the double triangle) occurs on our (so-called) Gothic edifices, *e.g.* the beautiful abbey gate of Bury St. Edmunds, Suffolk, erected about A.D. 1377. [See Count Goblet D'Alviella, *The Migration of Symbols*, 185 ff.]

and I had not leisure even to bring away a rude resemblance of this memento of some victory of the ancient lords of Mandor.

Thāna Pir.—A little distance to the northward of my position is the Than or 'station' of a Muhammadan saint, a disciple of the celebrated Khwaja Kutab, whose shrine at Ajmer is celebrated. This of Thana Pir,[1] as they call him, was a place of great resort to the unsanctified Kafirs, the mercenary Sindis and Afghans, who long prowled about these regions in quest of [728] prey, or plunder, or both. Nearly in the same direction, beyond the walls, are the cenotaphs of the early Rathors and the Satis already mentioned; but tradition's voice is mute as to the spot which contains the ashes of the Parihars. To the east and north-east, nature has formed at once a barrier to this antique castle, and a place of recreation for its inhabitants; a lengthened chasm in the whole face, appearing like a dark line, were it not for the superb foliage of gular, mango, and the sacred bar and pipal, which rise above the cleft, planted about the fountain and perpendicular cliffs of the Nagda, and which must have proved a luxurious retreat to the princes of Mandor from the reverberation of the sun's rays on the rock-built palace; for there is but a scanty brushwood scattered over the surface, which is otherwise destitute of all vegetation.

Let us now descend by the same causeway to the glen of Panchkunda, where there is much to gratify both the lover of the picturesque and the architectural antiquary. At the foot of the causeway, terminated by a reservoir of good water, are two gateways, one conducting to the gardens and their palaces erected by the Rathors; the other, to the statues of the Paladins of the desert. Leaving both for a moment, I pursued the 'serpentine' rivulet to its fountain, where

> Couched among fallen columns, in the shade
> Of ruined walls that had survived the names
> Of those who reared them,

I reposed in meditative indolence, overwhelmed with the recollections such scenes inspire. In a recess or cave is a rude altar sanctified by the name of Nahar Rao, the famed king of Mandor, who met in equal combat the chivalrous Chauhan in the pass of

[1] [Erskine (iii. A. 197) calls him Tanna Pīr; the shrine was built in the time of Mahārāja Mān Singh, and is held in high estimation.]

the Aravalli.[1] A Nai, or barber, performs worship to the manes of this illustrious Rajput, in whose praise Chand is most eloquent. Whence the choice of a barber as a priest I know not; but as he has the universal care of the material portion of the Rajput, being always chosen as the cook, so there may be reasons for his having had an interest in the immaterial part in olden days, the tradition of which may have been lost. There is a piece of sculpture containing nine figures, said to represent Ravaṇa, who came from "th'utmost isle Taprobane,"[2] to marry the daughter of the sovereign of Mandor. There was a lengthened legend to account for the name of Nagda, or, 'serpentine,' being applied to the [729] rivulet, but it is too long to relate. We must therefore quit the fountain, where the gallant Prithiraj and his fair bride, the cause of strife between the Chauhans and Pariharas, may have reposed, and visit the most remarkable relic within the precincts of this singular place.

Images of Heroes.—A short distance from the foot of the causeway, an archway opens into an enclosed court or area, in the retired part of which, and touching the mountain, is an extensive saloon; the roof is supported by a triple row of columns, of that light form peculiar to the Jains. Here are displayed, in all "the pomp and circumstance of war," the statues of the knights-errant of the desert, armed cap-à-pie, bestriding steeds whose names are deathless as their riders', all in the costume of the times in which they lived. They are cut out of the rock, but entirely detached from it, and larger than life. Though more conspicuous for strength than symmetry, the grim visages of these worthies, apparently frowning defiance, each attended by his pandu or squire, have a singularly pleasing effect. Each chieftain is armed with lance, sword, and buckler, with quiver and arrows, and poniard in his girdle. All are painted; but whether in the colours they were attached to, or according to the fancy of the architect, I know not. Before, however, entering this saloon, we pass a huge statue of Ganesa, placed as the guardian of the portal, having on each side the two Bhairavas, sons of the god of war. Then appears the statue of Chamunda

[1] See p. 793.

[2] *Tapu Ravana*, 'the isle of Ravana,' wherever that may be. [Taprobane represents the river Tāmraparni, 'the copper-coloured leaf' (*IGI*, xxiii. 215).]

CHĀMUNDA. KANKĀLI.

Rock Sculptures at Mandor.

To face page 842.

(the goddess of destruction), and that of the terrific mother, Kankali, treading on the black demon Bhainsasur, in whose flank her tiger-courser has buried his bloodthirsty tongue : in each of her eight arms she holds a weapon of destruction. The black Bhairon (son of Time), with a sable flag, bearing argent a horse courant, marshals the way through the field of blood to his mother. Between her and the heroes whose lives passed " in devotion to the sword," is a statue of the Nathji, or 'spiritual guide' of the Rathors : in one hand he holds his *mala* or 'chaplet'; in the other his *chhari* or 'patriarchal rod,' for the guidance of his flock. Mallinath [1] heads the procession, mounted on a white charger, with a lance over his shoulder, to which is attached a flag ; his quiver resting on his horse's right flank, and his mistress, Padmavati, with a platter of food welcoming him from the raid, and who accompanied him when slain to Suryaloka, or 'the mansion of the sun.'

Then follows Pabuji,[2] mounted on his famous charger 'Black Caesar' (Kesar [730] Kali), whose exploits are the theme of the itinerant bard and showman, who annually goes his round, exhibiting in pictorial delineations, while he recites in rhyme, the deeds of this warrior to the gossiping villagers of the desert.

Next comes Ramdeo [3] Rathor, a name famed in Marudesa, and in whose honour altars are raised in every Rajput village in the country.

Then we have the brave Harbuji Sankhla,[4] to whom Jodha was indebted for protection in his exile, and for the redemption of Mandor when seized by the Rana of Chitor.

Guga,[5] the Chauhan, who with his forty-seven sons fell defending the passage of the Sutlej on Mahmud's invasion. Mehaji Mangalia brings up the rear, a famous chieftain of the Guhilot

[1] [Eldest son of Rāo Salkha, one of the early traditional ancestors of the Jodhpur chiefs, after whom the Mallāni district is named.]

[2] [A Rāthor chief, who first brought the camel into use, and was noted for protecting cows.]

[3] [A Tonwar or Tuar Rājput, of the family of Anangpāl of Delhi, now worshipped under the name of Rāmsāh Pīr.]

[4] [A Panwār Rājput, of Bengti, near Phalodi, where his cart is still worshipped.]

[5] [Gūgaji or Guggaji, already mentioned (p. 807 above), said to have been killed in battle with Fīroz Shāh of Delhi, at the end of the thirteenth century A.D.]

race. It would be tedious to relate any of the exploits of these worthies.

Taintīs Kula Devata Ra Thān.—Another saloon, of similar architecture and still greater dimensions, adjoins that just described; it is termed Taintis kula [1] devata ra than, or 'abode of the (tutelary) divinities of the thirty-three races': in short, the Pantheon of the Rajputs. The statues are of gypsum, or stone covered with that substance; they are of large proportions. First, is the creator, Brahma; then Surya, 'the sun-god,' with his seven-headed steed; then the monkey-faced deity, Hanuman; Rama, and his beloved Sita; Kanhaiya, in the woods of Vraj, surrounded by the Gopis; and a most grave figure of Mahadeva, with a bull in his hand. These six, with the goddesses of life and death, and of wisdom, constitute the eight chief divinities of the Hindus; whose qualities and attributes, personified, form an assemblage for which St. Peter's and the Vatican to boot would be a confined dwelling.

Palace and Gardens.—I now retired to the palace and gardens built by Raja Ajit; of which, however superb, it is impossible for the pen to give a definite idea. Suites of colonnaded halls, covered with sculpture of easy and even graceful execution, some with screens of lattice-work to secure the ladies from the public gaze, are on the lower range; while staircases lead to smaller apartments intended for repose. The gardens, though not extensive, as may be supposed, being confined within the adamantine walls reared by the hand of Nature, must be delightfully cool even in summer. Fountains, reservoirs, and water-courses, are everywhere interspersed; and though [731] the thermometer in the open air was 86°,[2] the cold within doors (if this be not a solecism, considering that there were no doors) was excessive. Some attention was paid to its culture; besides many indigenous shrubs, it boasted of some exotics. There was the golden champa,[3] whose

[1] I imagine the word *kula*, or 'race,' of which, as often remarked, there are not thirty-three but thirty-six, has given rise to the assertion respecting the thirty-three crore or millions of gods of Hindustan [more probably only an indefinite number].

[2] Thermometer 55°, 72°, 86°, 80° at daybreak, ten, two, and at sunset; on the 3rd November, the day of our arrival, the variations were 50°, 72°, 80°, and 75° at those hours.

[3] [*Michelia champaka.*]

MALLINĀTH. NĀTHJI.

Rock Sculptures at Mandor.

To face page 844.

aroma is overpowering, and if laid upon the pillow will produce headache ; the pomegranate, at once " rich in flower and fruit " ; the apple of Sita, or Sitaphala, which, from similitude of taste, we call the custard-apple ; a delicious species of the plantain, whose broad, verdant, glossy leaf alone inspires the mind with the sensation of coolness ; the mogra ;[1] the chameli, or jessamine ; and the queen of flowers, the barahmasha,[2] literally the 'twelve-month,' because it flowers throughout the year. It is a delightful spot, and I felt a peculiar interest in it. Let the reader imagine the picture of a solitary Englishman scribbling amidst the ruins of Mandor: in front a group of venerable mango-trees; a little further an enormous isolated tamarind, " planted by the hand of a juggler in the time of Nahar Rao, the last of the Pariharas, before whom he exhibited this proof of legerdemain," and, as the legend goes, from whose branches the juggler met his death :[3] amidst its boughs the long-armed tribe, the allies of Rama, were skipping and chattering unmolested ; while beneath, two Rathor Rajputs were stretched in sleep, their horses dozing beside them, standing as sedately as the statue of 'Black Caesar' : a grenadier Sepoy of my escort parading by a camp-basket, containing the provender of the morning, completes the calm and quiet scene.

An Atīt Hermit.—On the summit of the rock, across the narrow valley, several *guphas*, or caves, the abode of the hermit Atit,[4] were in sight. How the brains of these ascetics can stand the heat and confined air is a wonder, though, if they possessed any

[1] [The double jasmine, *Jasminum zambak*.]

[2] [Sir D. Prain, who has kindly investigated this flower, identifies it with a species of *Bauhinia*. He remarks that " *B. acuminata*, which differs from *B. purpurea* and *B. variegata*, both in being a smaller plant and in beginning to flower when *B. variegata* does, goes on flowering all through the rains, and still continues to flower when *B. purpurea* is in blossom. It does not flower all the year round in Bengal, and I doubt if it does so in Rājputāna, though Balfour in his *Cyclopaedia* suggests that it does so. My idea is that the term *bārah-māsha* in Upper India should not be taken too literally, and that it is only a figurative way of saying that the particular *Bauhinia* is in flower alongside of both the others when flowering seasons are separated by half the year."]

[3] See the Autobiography of Jahangir, translated by that able Oriental scholar, Major Price [p. 96 f.], for the astonishing feats these jugglers perform in creating not only the tree but the fruit.

[4] [The Atīt is a mendicant follower of Siva, and the term is usually equivalent to Sannyāsi.]

portion of that which is supposed to be necessary to the guidance of the machine, they would scarcely occupy such a position, nor consequently, the world's attention. *Mais tout est vanité*, a cause which has produced ten times the number of saints that piety has, and ten times of ten these troglodyte philosophers. Having walked out on the terrace or house-top of the palace, to catch a sunbeam and scare away an ague which tormented me, I discovered one of these animals coiled up on a heap of bat's dung [732], in a corner of an apartment of the palace. He was dreadfully emaciated, and but for the rolling of a pair of eyes in a visage covered with hair, there was nothing which betokened animation, much less humanity. There was none but the bat to dispute his reign, or "the spider which weaves its web in this palace of the Caesars." I had no inclination to disturb the process of ratiocination, or to ask to which sect of philosophers belonged this Diogenes of Mandor, who might, if he had utterance, have desired me to walk downstairs, and not intercept the sunbeam for whose warmth we were competitors. The day was now nearly departed, and it was time for me to return to my friends in camp. I finished the evening by another visit to the knights of the desert; and inscribing my name on the foot of 'Black Caesar,' bade adieu to the ancient Mandor.

November 13.—The Raja having invited us to a dinner at the palace, we sallied forth, belted and padded, to partake of Rajput hospitality. He had made a request which will appear somewhat strange—that we would send our cuisine, as the fare of the desert might prove unpalatable; but this I had often seen done at Sindhia's camp, when joints of mutton, fowls, and fricassees would diversify the provender of the Mahratta. I intimated that we had no apprehension that we should not do justice to the gastronomy of Jodhpur; however, we sent our tables, and some claret to drink long life to the king of Marudes. Having paid our respects to our host, he dismissed us with the complimentary wish that appetite might wait upon us, and, preceded by a host of gold and silver sticks, we were ushered into a hall, where we found the table literally covered with curries, pillaus, and ragouts of every kind, in which was not forgotten the *haria mung Mandor ra*, the 'green pulse of Mandor,' the favourite dish, next to *rabri* or maize-porridge, of the simple Rathor. Here, however, we saw displayed the dishes of both the Hindu and Musulman, and nearly all were

RĀMDEO RĀTHOR. PĀBUJI, MOUNTED ON KESAR KĀLI.

Rock Sculptures at Mandor.

To face page 846.

served in silver. The curries were excellent, especially those of the vegetable tribes made of the pulses, the kakris or cucumbers, and of a miniature melon not larger than an egg, which grows spontaneously in these regions, and is transported by kasids, or runners, as presents, for many hundreds of miles around. The hall was an entire new building, and scarcely finished; it is erected on the northern projection of the rock, where the escarpment is most abrupt, and looks down upon the site of the batteries of the league of 1806. It is called the Man mahall [733], and, like the hall of audience, its flat roof is supported by numerous massive hewn columns. The view from it to the east is extensive, and we were told that the pinnacle of Kumbhalmer, though eighty miles distant, has been seen, in those clear days of the monsoon when the atmosphere is purified, after heavy showers, from the sand which is held suspended. Great care was taken that our meal should be uninterrupted, and that we should not be the lions to an hour's amusement of the court. There was but one trivial occurrence to interrupt the decorum and attention of all present, and that was so slight that we only knew it after the entertainment was over. One of the menials of the court, either from ignorance or design, was inclined to evince contumely or bad breeding. It will be considered perhaps a singular circumstance that the Hindu should place before a European the vessels from which he himself eats: but a little fire purifies any metallic vessels from all such contamination; and on this point the high-blooded Rajput is less scrupulous than the bigoted Muhammadan, whom I have seen throw on the ground with contempt a cup from which his officer had drunk water on a march. But of earthenware there can be no purification. Now there was a handsome china bowl, for which some old dowager fancier of such articles would have almost become a supplicant, which having been filled with curds to the Sudra Farangis could no longer be used by the prince, and it was brought by this menial, perhaps with those words, to my native butler. Kali Khan, or, as we familiarly called him, 'the black lord,' was of a temper not to be trifled with; and as the domestic held it in his hand, saying, "Take it, it is no longer of any use to us," he gave it a tap with his hand which sent it over the battlements, and coolly resuming his work, observed, "That is the way in which all useless things should be served"; a hint which, if reported to Raja Man, he seems to have acted on: for not many months after, the minister, Akhai Chand, who dreaded lest European influence should release his master from his faction and thraldom, was treated by him in the same manner as the china bowl by Kali Khan.

The Rāja visits the Author.—*November* 16.[1]—This day had been fixed for the Raja's visits to the envoy. In order to display his grandeur, he sent his own suite of tents, which were erected near mine [734]. They were very extensive, modelled in every way after those of the Emperors of Delhi, and lined throughout with the royal colour, crimson: but this is an innovation, as will appear from the formulas yet preserved of his despatches, "from the foot of the throne, Jodhpur." The tent, in fact, was a palace in miniature, the whole surrounded by walls of cloth, to keep at a distance the profane vulgar. The *gaddi*, or royal cushion and canopy, was placed in the central apartment. At three, all was noise and bustle in the castle and town; nakkaras were reverberating, trumpets sounding the alarm, that the King of Maru was about to visit the Farangi Wakil. As soon as the flags and pennant were observed winding down 'the hill of strife' (Jodhagir), I mounted, and with the gentlemen of my suite proceeded through the town to meet the Raja. Having complimented him *en route*, we returned and received him at the tents. The escort drawn up at the entrance of the tent presented arms, the officers saluting; a mark of attention which gratified him, as did the soldier-like appearance of the men. Hitherto, what he had seen of regulars belonging to the native powers was not calculated to give him a favourable impression of foot-soldiers, who are little esteemed by the equestrian order of Rajputana. His visit continued about an hour, when the shields were brought in, with jewels, brocades, shawls, and other finery, in all nineteen trays, being two less than I presented to the Rana of Udaipur. I likewise presented him with some arms of English manufacture, a telescope, and smaller things much valued by the Rajputs. After the final ceremony of perfumes, and itr-pan (which are admirable hints when you wish to get rid of a tiresome guest, though not so in this instance), the exterior wall was removed, and showed the caparisoned elephant and horses, which were part of the khilat. At the door of the tent we made our salaam, when the Raja gave me his hand, which, by the by, was his first salutation on receiving

[1] Thermometer 59°, 82°, 85°, 79°.

GŪGA THE CHAUHĀN. HARBUJI SĀNKHLA.

Rock Sculptures at Mandor.

To face page 848.

me. It is an ancient Rajput custom, and their bards continually allude to extending the right hand—" dextra extenta."

Taking Leave of the Rāja.—*November* 17.[1]—I went to take leave of the Raja: I had a long and interesting conversation on this our last interview. I left him in the full expectation that his energy of character would surmount the difficulties by which he was surrounded, though not without a struggle, and condign punishment to some of the miscreants, the misleaders of his son, the assassins of his minister and high priest, and consequently the authors of his humiliating and protracted incarceration [735]. Whether the first gratification of vengeance provoked his appetite, or whether the torrent of his rage, once impelled into motion, became too impetuous to be checked, so that his reason was actually disturbed by the sufferings he had undergone, it is certain he grew a demoniac; nor could any one, who had conversed with the bland, the gentlemanly, I might say gentle, Raja Man, have imagined that he concealed under this exterior a heart so malignant as his subsequent acts evinced. But the day of retribution must arrive; the men who wrote that dignified remonstrance, which is given in another place,[2] will not tamely bear their wrongs, and as they dare not levy war against their prince, who reposes under British protection, the dagger will doubtless find a way to reach him even in " the thousand-columned hall " of Jodhpur.

Besides the usual gifts at parting, which are matter of etiquette, and remain untouched by the individual, I accepted as a personal token of his favour, a sword, dagger, and buckler, which had belonged to one of his illustrious ancestors. The weight of the sword, which had often been " the angel of death," would convince any one that it must have been a nervous arm which carried it through a day. With mutual good wishes, and a request for a literary correspondence, which was commenced but soon closed, I bade adieu to Raja Man and the capital of Marwar [736].

[1] Thermometer 59°, 73°, 89°, 82°; at six, ten, two, and sunset.

[2] See Vol. I. p. 228.

CHAPTER 28

Nāndla.—*November* 19.—We broke ground for Nandla, distant six miles. The first two miles from the capital was through deep sand; for the remainder of the journey the red sandstone protruded, which gives some relief to the footing of the traveller. About half-way we passed a small sheet of water, called after the mother of the pretender, Dhonkal Singh, the Shaikhawat Talao. This lady has constructed a dharmsala, or 'hall for travellers,' on its bank, where she has erected a statue of Hanuman, and a pillar to commemorate her own good works. Not a shrub of any magnitude occurs, for even the stunted khair [1] is rare in this plain of sand; which does not, however, appear unfavourable to the moth,[2] a vetch on which they feed the cattle. Near the village we crossed the Jogini, the same stream which we passed between Jhalamand and the capital, and which, joined by the Nagda from Mandor, falls into the Luni. The only supply of water for Nandla is procured from two wells dug on the margin of the stream. The water is abundant, and only four feet from the surface, but brackish. There are a hundred and twenty-five houses in Nandla, which is in the fief of the chieftain of Ahor. A few cenotaphs are on the banks of a tank, now dry. I went to look at them, but they contained names "unknown to fame."

Bīsalpur.—Bisalpur, the next place, is distant six estimated coss of the country, and [737] thirteen miles one furlong by the perambulator: heavy sand the whole way. Nevertheless we saw traces of the last autumnal crop of bajra and juar, two species of millet, which form the chief food of the people of the desert; and the vetch was still in heaps. Bisalpur is situated on a rising ground; the houses are uniform in height and regularly built, and coated with a compost of mud and chaff, so that its appearance is picturesque. It is protected by a circumvallation of thorns, the *kanta-ka-kot* and the stacks of chaff, as described at Indara. They are pleasing to the eye, as is everything in such a place which shows the hand of industry. There was an ancient city here in former days, which was engulfed by an earthquake,

[1] [*Acacia catechu.*]

[2] [The aconite-leaved kidney-bean, *Phaseolus aconitifolius.*]

MEHAJI MANGALIA.

Rock Sculptures at Mandor.

To face page 850.

though part of a gateway and the fragment of a wall still mark its site. No inscriptions were observed. The water is obtained from a lake.

Pachkalia, Bīchkalia.—*November* 21.—Pachkalia, or Bichkalia, five coss (11 miles 5 furlongs): crossed and encamped on the Jojri. The soil improving, of a brown sandy texture. Wheat and barley of excellent quality are grown on the banks of the river. It was a relief to meet once more a babul or a nim tree; even our Godwar cypress reared its head on the margin of the Jojri. Although now only containing a hundred houses, this was once a place of some importance. I found a defaced inscription, in which "the son of Sonang, S. 1224," was still legible; but the mercenary Pathans have ruined the harvest of the antiquary. The village is a grant in fee to a Bhatti chieftain. Water is obtained from wells excavated on the margin of the river.

Pīpār.—*November* 22.—Pipar, four coss (8 miles 2 furlongs). Pursued the course of the river, the most extended arm of the Luni, coming from the hills near Parbatsar, on the frontiers of Jaipur. Its course is marked by the trees already mentioned. The soil, a mixture of black earth and sand, is termed *dhamani*. Pipar is a town of 1500 houses, one-third of which are inhabited by the Oswals of the Jain faith, the chief merchants of all their country. There are also about two hundred families of Mahesris, or merchants of the Saiva caste. Pipar carries on a considerable traffic, and has a chintz manufactory, which employs thirty families. It is in the grant of the feudal chief of Nimaj, whose death has been already related. A cenotaph, dedicated to one of his ancestors, has been half destroyed by the Goths of India. Pipar is celebrated in the traditions of the desert as one of the cities [738] founded by Gandharvasen, the Pramara monarch of Avanti, prior to the Christian era.[1] The only inscription I discovered was in a temple of the sea-goddess Lakshmi. It bore the names of Bijai Singh and Delanji, Rajputs of the Guhilot race, with the ancient title of Rawal. It was a happy confirmation of the most ancient chronicle of Mewar, which divides the Guhilots into twenty-four *sakha* or branches, of which one is called 'Piparia,' doubtless from their having conquered this tract from the Takshak Pramara.

[1] [See p. 913, below.]

There is an abundance of wells, from sixty to eighty feet in depth. Of one recently excavated, I obtained the following details of the strata, which may be gratifying to the geologist. The first twenty feet are composed entirely of that kind of earth called *dhamani*, chiefly decomposed sandstone with a mixture of black earth, in which occurs a stratum of bluish clay mixed with particles of quartz: this earth is called *morar* in Marwar, and *morand* in Jaipur. It was then necessary to cut through a rock of red granite [1] for thirty feet; then several feet of an almost milk-white steatite, succeeded by stalactitic concretions of sandstone and quartz.

Legend of the Sâmpu Lake.—Good water is also obtained from a lake called the Sampu, which is connected with the tradition of the foundation of Pipar. A Brahman of the Pali tribe, whose name was Pipa, was in the habit of carrying milk to a deity of the Serpent (Takshak) race, whose retreat was on the banks of this lake, and who deposited two pieces of gold in return for the Paliwal's offering. Being compelled to go to Nagor, he gave instructions to his son to perform his charitable office; but the youth, deeming it a good opportunity to become master of the treasure, took a stick with him, and when the serpent issued forth for his accustomed fare, he struck him violently; but the snake being "scotched, not killed," retreated to his hole. The young Brahman related his adventure to his mother; when the good woman, dreading the vengeance of the serpentine deity, prepared a servant and bullock to convey her son to his father at Nagor. But what was her horror in the morning, when she went to call the youth, to find, instead of him, the huge serpent coiled up in his bed! Pipa, on his return, was inconsolable; but stifling his revenge, he propitiated the serpent with copious libations of milk. The scaly monster was conciliated, and revealed the stores he guarded to Pipa, commanding him to raise a monument which would transmit a knowledge of the event to future ages [739]. Hence Pipar arose from Pipa the Pali, and the name of the lake Sampu, from his benefactor the 'serpent' (sampa). All these allegorical tales regard the Takshak races, the followers of the religion of Buddha or Jaina, and their feuds with the Brahmanical sects. It is evident that Pipa the Pali worshipped both; and the very name

[1] Specimens of all these I brought home.

induces a belief that the whole Paliwal caste are converts from Buddhism.[1]

Lākha Phulāni.—There is a kund or fountain, called after Lakha Phulani, who ruled in ancient times at Phulra, in the farther corner of the desert, but carried his arms even to the ocean. Wherever I have travelled, tradition is loud in praise of Phulani, from the source of the Luni to its embouchure in the Delta of the Indus.[2]

Mādreo.—*November* 23.—Madreo, five coss (10 miles 2 furlongs). Roads good; soil as yesterday, but the country very desolate; only stunted shrubs since we removed from the margin of the river. This is a moderate-sized village, with a tank of good water.

Bharūnda.—*November* 24.—Bharunda, four coss, or eight miles. The face of the country now changes materially; our route was over a low undulating ridge of sandstone, in which the stunted shrubs of this region find a bed. At one time the elevation was sufficiently great to allow the chasm through which the road passed to be dignified with the name of the Ghasuria Pass, in which a party of the Raja's men is posted for defence, and the levy of transit duties. Bharunda is in the fief of Gopal Singh, the chief of Kuchaman, one of the most conspicuous of the Mertia clan. It consists of one hundred and fifty houses; the cultivators are Jats, as are those of all the preceding villages.

I paid a visit to the humble cenotaphs of Bharunda; one of

[1] [This seems to be merely an instance of serpent-worship.]

[2] The traditional stanzas are invaluable for obtaining a knowledge both of ancient history and geography:

> " Kasyapgarh, Surajpura,
> Basakgarh, Tako,
> Udhanigarh, Jagrupura,
> Jo Phulgarh, i Lakho."

In this stanza we have the names of six ancient cities in the desert, which belonged to Lakha, the Tako, Tak, or Takshak, *i.e.* of the race figuratively called the 'serpent.' [Many tales are told of Lākha Phulāni, who by one account was a Rāo of Cutch, slain fighting in Kāthiāwār (*BG*, v. 133, viii. 111 note). Others identify him with Lakha, son of Phulada, who defeated the Chaulukya king, Mūlarāja, in the eleventh century (*ibid.* i. Part i. 160). By another account, he was father-in-law of the great Siddharāja (Tod, *WI*, 179). He is mentioned twice later on. He was probably a powerful king of the desert, round whom many legends have collected.]

them bore the name of Badan Singh, a sub-vassal of Kuchaman, who was slain in the heroic charge against De Boigne's brigades, in the patriot field of Merta. His name claims the admiration of all who esteem loyalty and patriotism, the inherent virtues of the chivalrous Rajput. Raja Bijai Singh had resumed Bharunda, when the Thakur [740] retired to the adjacent court of Jaipur, where he was well received according to the hospitable customs of the Rajput, and had risen to favour at the period when the Mahrattas invaded his *bapota*, 'the land of his fathers.' Resentment was instantly sacrificed at the altar of patriotism; he put himself at the head of one hundred and fifty horse, and flew to his sovereign's and his country's defence. Unhappily, the whole Mahratta army interposed between him and his countrymen. To cut their way through all impediments was the instant resolve of Badan and his brave companions. They fell sword in hand upon a multitude; and, with the exception of a few, who forced their way (amongst whom was the chief whose monument is referred to), they were cut to pieces. Badan Singh lived to reach his ancient estate, which was restored to his family in token of his sovereign's gratitude for the gallant deed. It is valued at seven thousand rupees annual rent, and has attached to it, as a condition, the service of defending this post. There was another small altar erected to the manes of Partap, who was killed in the defence of this pass against the army of Aurangzeb.

Indāwar.—*November* 25.—Indawar, five coss (10 miles 2 furlongs). This place consists of two hundred houses; the cultivators are Jats. I have said little of these proprietors of the soil, a sturdy, independent, industrious race, who "venerate the plough," and care little about the votaries of Mars or their concerns, so that they do not impose excessive taxes on them. They are a stout, well-built, though rather murky race. The village is assigned to the ex-prince of Sind, who derives his sole support from the liberality of the princes of Marwar. He is of the tribe called Kalhora,[1] and claims descent from the Abbassides of Persia. His family has been supplanted by the Talpuris, a branch of the

[1] [The Kalhoras, closely allied to the Dāūdputras, rose to power in the Lower Indus valley at the end of the seventeenth century A.D. They trace their origin to Abbās, uncle of the Prophet. They were expelled by Fateh Ali of Tālpur, and the last of the Kalhoras fled to Jodhpur, where his descendants now hold distinguished rank (*IGI*, xxii. 397 ff.).]

Numris (the foxes) of Baluchistan, who now style themselves Afghans, but who are in fact one of the most numerous of the Getae or Jat colonies from Central Asia. But let us not wander from our subject.

I will beg the reader to descend seventy or eighty feet with me to view the stratification of Indawar. First, three feet of good soil; five feet of red sandy earth, mixed with particles of quartz; six feet of an unctuous indurated clay;[1] [741]—then follows a sand-rock, through which it was necessary to penetrate about sixty feet; this was succeeded by twenty feet of almost loose sand, with particles of pure quartz embedded; nodules and stalactitic concretions of sandstone, quartz, and mica, agglutinated together by a calcareous cement. The interior of the well throughout this last stratum is faced with masonry: the whole depth is more than sixty-five cubits, or forty yards. At this depth a spring of excellent water broke in upon the excavators, which supplies Indawar.

Merta.—*November* 26.—Merta, four coss (9 miles 1 furlong). The whole march was one extended plain; the Aravalli towering about twenty-five miles to our right. To the west a wide waste, consisting of plains gently undulating, and covered with grass and underwood. Natural sterility is not the cause of this desert aspect, for the soil is rich; but the water is far beneath the surface, and they cannot depend upon the heavens. Juar, moth, and sesamum were cultivated to a considerable extent in the immediate vicinity of the villages, but the product had this season been scanty. The appearanee of the town is imposing, its site being on a rising ground. The spires of the mosque which was erected on the ruins of a Hindu temple by the tyrant Aurangzeb overtop the more ponderous and unaspiring mandirs which surround it. Notwithstanding, this monarch was the object of universal execration to the whole Hindu race, more especially to the Rathors (whose sovereign, the brave Jaswant, together with his elder son, he put to death by poison, and kept Ajit twenty long years from his birthright, besides deluging their fields with the richest blood of his nobles); still, such is Hindu toleration, that a marble is placed, inscribed both in Hindi and Persian, to protect the mosque from violence. This mark of liberality proceeded from the pretender Dhonkal Singh, as if with a view

[1] Mr. Stokes, of the Royal Asiatic Society, pronounces it to be a steatite.

of catching golden opinions from the demoralized Pathans, by whose aid he hoped to regain his rights. But how was he deceived! His advances were met by the foul assassination, at one fell swoop, of all his party, by the chief of these mercenaries, Amir Khan.

Merta was founded by Rao Duda of Mandor, whose son, the celebrated Maldeo, erected the castle, which he called Malkot.[1] Merta, with its three hundred and sixty townships, became the appanage of his son Jaimall, and gave its name of Mertia to the bravest of the brave clans of the Rathors. Jaimall [742] was destined to immortalize his name beyond the limits of Maru. Distrusted by his father, and likely to be deserving of suspicion, from the very ruse to which Sher Shah acknowledged he owed his safety, he was banished from Marwar. He was hospitably received by the Rana, who assigned to the heir of Mandor the rich district of Badnor, equalling his own in extent, and far richer in soil than the plains he had abandoned. How he testified his gratitude for this reception, nobler pens than mine have related. The great Akbar claimed the honour of having with his own hand sealed his fate: he immortalized the matchlock with which he effected it, and which was also the theme of Jahangir's praise, who raised a statue in honour of this defender of Chitor and the rights of its infant prince.[2] Abu-l-fazl, Herbert, the chaplain to Sir T. Roe, Bernier, all honoured the name of Jaimall; and the chivalrous Lord Hastings, than whom none was better able to appreciate Rajput valour, manifested his respect by his desire to conciliate his descendant, the present brave baron of Badnor.[3]

The town of Merta covers a large space of ground, and is enclosed with a strong wall and bastions, composed of earth to the westward, but of freestone to the east. All, however, are in a state of decay, as well as the town itself, which is said to contain twenty thousand houses. Like most Hindu towns, there is a mixture of magnificence and poverty; a straw or mud hut adjoins a superb house of freestone, which "shames the meanness" of its neighbour. The castle is about a gun-shot to the south-west of the

[1] Rao Duda had three sons, besides Maldeo; namely: First, Raemall; second, Birsingh, who founded Amjera in Malwa, still held by his descendants; third, Ratan Singh, father of Mira Bai, the celebrated wife of Kumbha Rana.

[2] [See Vol. I. p. 382, above.]

[3] See Vol. I. p. 567.

town, and encloses an area of a mile and a half. Some small sheets of water are on the eastern and western faces. There are plenty of wells about the town, but the water has an unpleasant taste, from filtering through a stiff clay. There are but two strata before water is found, which is about twenty-five feet from the surface: the first a black mould, succeeded by the clay, incumbent on a loose sand, filled with quartzose pebbles of all hues, and those stalactitic concretions which mark, throughout the entire line from Jodhpur to Ajmer, the stratum in which the springs find a current. There are many small lakes around the town, as the Dudasar, or 'lake (*sar*) of Duda'; the Bejpa, the Durani, the Dangolia, etc.

The Battlefield.—The plain of Merta is one continuous sepulchre, covered with altars to the manes of the warriors who, either in the civil wars which have distracted this State [743], or in the more patriotic strife with the southron Goths, have drenched it with their blood. It is impossible to pass over this memorable field without a reference to these acts; but they would be unintelligible without going to the very root of dissension, which not only introduced the Mahratta to decide the intestine broils of the Rajput States, but has entailed a perpetuity of discord on that of Marwar. I have already succinctly related the parricidal murder of Raja Ajit, which arose out of the politics of the imperial court, when the Sayyids of Barha [1]—the Warwicks of the East—deposed the Emperor Farrukhsiyar, and set up a puppet of their own. With his daughter (whose marriage with the emperor originated, as already recorded, the first grant of land to the East-India Company), he retired to his dominions, leaving his son Abhai Singh at court, and refusing his sanction to the nefarious schemes of the Sayyids. They threatened destruction to Marwar, declaring to the son of Ajit that the only mode of averting its ruin was his own elevation, and his subservience to their views, which object could only be obtained by his father's deposal and death. Even the reasoning resorted to, as well as the dire purpose of the miscreants, is preserved, and may serve as an illustration of Rajput feeling. When Abhai Singh refused or hesitated, he was asked, "*Ma bap ka sakha, ya zamin ka sakha?*" which, though difficult to render with accuracy, may be translated: "Are you a branch (*sakha*) of the land or

[1] [See Vol. I. p. 467, above.]

of your parents ?" As before said, land is all in all to the Rajput; it is preferred to everything: Abhai's reply may therefore be inferred. Immediate installation was to be the reward of his revenging the Sayyids. That nature could produce from the same stock two such monsters as the brothers who effected the deed, is, perhaps, hardly conceivable, and would, probably, not be credited, were not the fact proved beyond doubt. I should desire, for the honour of the Rajput race, whose advocate and apologist I candidly avow myself, to suppress the atrocious record: but truth is dearer even than Rajput character. Of the twelve sons of Ajit, Abhai Singh and Bakhta Singh were the two elder; both were by the same mother, a princess of Bundi. To Bakhta Singh, who was with his father, the eldest brother wrote, promising him the independent sovereignty of Nagor (where they then were), with its five hundred and fifty-five townships, as the price of murdering their common sire. Not only was the wretch unstartled by the proposition, but he executed the deed with his own hands, under circumstances of unparalleled atrocity. His [744] mother always dreaded the temperament and disposition of Bakhta, who was bold, haughty, impetuous, with a perpetual thirst for action; and she cautioned her husband never to admit him into his presence after dusk, or when unattended. But the Raja, whose physical strength was equal to his bravery, ridiculed her fears, observing, "Is he not my child? Besides, a slap on the face from me would annihilate the stripling." Upon receiving the note from his brother, Bakhta, after taking leave of his father, concealed himself in a chamber adjoining that where his parents reposed. When all was still the murderer stole to the bed in which lay the authors of his existence, and from a pallet, on which were placed the arms of Ajit, he seized his sword, and coolly proceeded to exhaust those veins which contained the same blood that flowed in his own. In order that nothing might be wanting to complete the deed of horror, the mother was awakened by the blood of her lord moistening her bosom. Her cries awoke the faithful Rajputs who lay in the adjacent apartments, and who, bursting into the chamber, discovered their prince and father dead: "Treason had done its worst." The assassin fled to the roof of the palace, barring the gates behind him, which resisted all attempts to force them until morning, when he threw into the court below the letter of his brother, exclaiming, "This put the Maharaja to death, not I." Abhai Singh was now their sovereign; and it is the actual occupant of the throne whom the Rajput deems entitled to his devotion. Eighty-four Satis took place on this dire occasion, the parent of these unnatural regicidal and parricidal sons leading the funeral procession. So much was Ajit beloved, that even men devoted themselves on his pyre. Such was the tragical end of the great Ajit, lamented by his chiefs, and consecrated by the bard, in stanzas in honour of him and in execration of the assassins; which afford proof of the virtuous independence of the poetic chronicler of Rajasthan.

Bakhta, Bakhta, bāhira,
Kyūn māryo Ajmāl[1]
Hindwāni ro sevro
Turkāni ka sāl?

"Oh Bakhta, in evil hour
Why slew you Ajmāl,
The pillar of the Hindu,
The lance of the Turk?" [745][2]

The Sons of Ajīt Singh.—Bakhta Singh obtained Nagor; and Abhai Singh was rewarded with the viceroyalty of Gujarat, which gift he repaid by aiding in its partition, and annexing the rich districts of Bhinmal, Sanchor, and others, to Marwar; on which occasion he added Jalor to the domain of his brother Bakhta, or, as the bard styles him, *bad-bakhta*, 'the unfortunate.' This additional reward of parricide has been the cause of all the civil wars of Marwar.

We may slightly notice the other sons of Ajit, whose issue affected the political society of Rajputana. Of these,

Devi Singh was given for adoption to Maha Singh, head of the Champawat clan, he having no heirs. Devi Singh then held Bhinmal, but which he could not retain against the Koli tribes around him, and Pokaran was given in exchange. Sabal Singh, Sawai Singh, and Salim Singh (whose escape from the fate of the chieftain of Nimaj has been noticed) are the lineal issue of this adoption.

[1] The bards give adjuncts to names in order to suit their rhymes: Ajit is the 'invincible'; Ajmāl, a contraction of Ajayamāl, 'wealth invincible.'

[2] [Major Luard's Pandit gives the word in the third line as *sihura* or *sihra*, the veil worn by the bridegroom to avert the Evil Eye.]

Anand Singh, another son of Ajit, was in like manner adopted into the independent State of Idar, and his issue are heirs-presumptive to the throne of Marwar.

Effects of Adoption.—From these races we derive the knowledge of a curious fact, namely, that the issue of the younger brother maintains a claim, though adopted into a foreign and independent State; while all such claims are totally extinguished by adoption into a home clan. Under no circumstances could the issue of Devi Singh sit on the *gaddi* of Marwar; when adopted into the Champawat clan, he surrendered all claims derived from his birth, which were merged into his vassal rank. Still the recollection must give weight and influence; and it is evident from the boast of the haughty Devi Singh, when his head was on the block, that there is danger in these adoptions.

Abhai Singh died, leaving a memorial of his prowess in the splendid additions he made to his territories from the tottering empire of Delhi. He was succeeded by his son Ram Singh, on whose accession his uncle Bakhta sent his aged foster-mother, an important personage in Rajwara, with the *tika* and gifts, and gifts, and other symbols of congratulation. Ram Singh, who had all the impetuosity of his race, received the lady-ambassador with no friendly terms, asking her if his uncle had no better messenger to salute his new sovereign. He refused the gifts, and commanded her to tell his uncle to surrender Jalor. The offended dame [746] extenuated nothing of the insolence of the message. The reply was, however, courteous, implying that both Jalor and Nagor were at his disposal. The same sarcastic spirit soon precipitated matters between them in the following manner.

Kusal Singh of Awa, the premier noble of Marwar, and of all the clans of Champawat, more brave than courtly, was short in stature, sturdy, boorish, and blunt; he became the object of his young sovereign's derision, who used to style him the *gurji gandhak*, or 'turnspit dog,' and who had once the audacity to say, "Come, gurji"; when he received the laconic reproof: "Yes; the gurji that dare bite the lion."

Brooding over this merited retort, he was guilty of another sarcasm, which closed the breach against all reconciliation. Seated one day in the garden of Mandor, he asked the same chief

PAIKS OF MĀRWĀR

To face page 860.

the name of a tree. "The champa," was the reply, "and the pride of the garden, as I am of your Rajputs." "Cut it down instantly," said the prince; "root it out; nothing which bears the name of champa shall exist in Marwar."

Kaniram of Asop, the chief of the next most powerful clan, the Kumpawat, was alike the object of this prince's ridicule. His countenance, which was not "cast in nature's finest mould," became a butt for his wit, and he would familiarly say to him, '*ao budha bandar*,' "Come along, old monkey." Boiling with rage, the chief observed, "When the monkey begins to dance, you will have some mirth." Leaving the court, with his brother chieftain of Awa, they collected their retainers and families, and marched to Nagor. Bakhta Singh was absent, but being advised by his locum tenens of his visitors, and of their quarrel with his nephew, he lost no time in joining them. It is said he expostulated with them, and offered himself as mediator; but they swore never again to look in the face of Ram Singh as their sovereign. They offered to place Bakhta Singh on the *gaddi* of Jodha; and threatened, if he refused, to abandon Marwar. He played the part of our Richard for a short time; but the habitual arrogance of his nephew soon brought matters to a crisis. As soon as he heard that the two leaders of all his vassals were received by his uncle, he addressed him, demanding the instant surrender of Jalor. Again he had the courtly reply: "He dare not contend against his sovereign; and if he came to visit him, he would meet him with a vessel of water."[1] War, a [747] horrid civil war, was now decided on; the challenge was given and accepted, and the plains of Merta were fixed upon to determine this mortal strife, in which brother was to meet brother, and all the ties of kin were to be severed by the sword. The Mertia clans, the bravest, as they are the most loyal and devoted, of all the brave clans of Maru, united to a man under the sovereign's standard; the chiefs of Rian, Budsa, Mihtri, Kholar, Bhorawar, Kuchaman, Alniawas, Jusari, Bokri, Bharunda, Irwa, Chandarun, collected around them every vassal who could wield a brand. Most of the clans of Jodha, attracted by the name of

[1] This reply refers to a custom analogous to the Scythic investiture, by offering "water and soil." [The Kols and other forest tribes deliver a handful of soil to a purchaser of a piece of land (Macpherson, *Memorials of Service*, 64).]

swamidharma, 'fidelity to their lord,' united themselves to the Mertias; though a few, as Ladnun, Nimbi, were on the adverse side; but the principal leaders, as Khairwa, Govindgarh, and Bhadrajun, were faithful to their salt. Of the services of others, Ram Singh's insolence deprived him. Few remained neuter. But these defections were nothing to the loss of a body of five thousand Jareja auxiliaries, whom his connexion with a daughter of the prince of Bhuj brought to his aid. When the tents were moved outside the capital, an incident occurred which, while it illustrates the singular character of the Rajput, may be regarded as the real cause of the loss of sovereignty to Ram Singh. An inauspicious raven had perched upon the *kanat*, or wall of the tent in which was the Jareja queen, who, skilled in the art of the *suguni* [1] (augur), determined to avert it. Like all Rajputnis, who can use firearms on occasion, she seized a matchlock at hand, and, ere he "thrice croaked," she shot him dead. The impetuous Raja, enraged at this instance of audacity and disrespect, without inquiry ordered the culprit to be dragged before him; nor was his anger assuaged when the name of the Rani was given. He reviled her in the grossest terms: "Tell the Rani," he said, "to depart my dominions, and to return from whence she came." She entreated and conjured him, by a regard to his own safety, to revoke the decree; but all in vain; and with difficulty could she obtain a short interview, but without effecting any change in her obdurate lord. Her last words were, "With my exile from your presence, you will lose the crown of Marwar." She marched that instant, carrying with her the five thousand auxiliaries whose presence must have ensured his victory.

The Udawat clans, led by their chiefs of Nimaj, Raepur, and Raus, with all [748] the Karansots under the Thakur of Khinwasar, united their retainers with the Champawats and Kumpawats under the banners of Bakhta Singh.

Battle between Bakhta Singh and Rāja Rām Singh, A.D. **1752.**— Ram Singh's array fell far short of his rival's since the defection of the Jarejas; yet, trusting to the name of sovereign as "a tower of strength," he boldly marched to the encounter, and when he reached the hostile field encamped near the Ajmer gate of Merta. His rival was not long behind, and marshalled his

[1] *Sugun pherna* means to avert the omen of evil.

clans within three miles of the northern portal, called the gate of Nagor. The spot he chose had a sacred character, and was called Mataji ka Than, where there was a shrine of the Hindu Hecate, with a fountain said to have been constructed by the Pandavas.

Bakhta Singh commenced the battle. Leaving his camp standing, he advanced against his nephew and sovereign, whom he saluted with a general discharge of his artillery. A vigorous cannonade was continued on both sides throughout the day, without a single man seeking a closer encounter. It is no wonder they paused ere the sword was literally drawn. Here was no foreign foe to attack; brother met brother, friend encountered friend, and the blood which flowed in the veins of all the combatants was derived from one common fountain. The reluctance proceeded from the στοργή, the innate principle of natural affection. Evening advanced amidst peals of cannon, when an incident, which could only occur in an army of Rajputs, stopped the combat. On the banks of the Bejpa lake, the scene of strife, there is a monastery of Dadupanti ascetics, built by Raja Sur Singh. It was nearly midway between the rival armies, and the shot fell so thick amidst these recluses that they fled in a body, leaving only the old patriarch. Baba (father) Kishandeo disdained to follow his disciples, and to the repeated remonstrances from either party to withdraw, he replied, that if it was his fate to die by a shot he could not avert it; if not, the balls were innoxious: but although he feared not for himself, yet his gardens and monastery were not "charmed," and he commanded them to fight no longer on that ground. The approach of night, and the sacred character of the old abbot Dadupanti, conspired to make both parties obey his commands, and they withdrew to their respective encampments.

The dawn found the armies in battle-array, each animated with a deadly determination. It was Raja Ram's turn to open this day's combat, and he led the van against his uncle. Burning with the recollection of the indignities he had [749] suffered, the chief of Awa, determined to show that "the cur could bite," led his Champawats to the charge against his sovereign. Incited by loyalty and devotion "to the gaddi of Marwar," reckless who was its occupant, the brave Mertias met his onset steel in hand. The ties of kin were forgotten, or if remembered, the sense of the unnatural strife added a kind of frenzy to their valour, and confirmed their resolution to conquer or die. Here the Mertia, fighting under the eye of this valiant though intemperate prince, had to maintain his ancient fame, as "the first sword of Maru." There his antagonist, the Champawat, jealous of this reputation, had the like incentive, besides the obligation to revenge the insults offered to his chief. The conflict was awful: the chieftains of each valiant clan met hand to hand, singling out each other by name. Sher Singh, chief of all the Mertias, was the first who sealed his devotion by his death. His place was soon filled by his brother, burning for vengeance. Again he cheered on his Mertias to avenge the death of their lord, as he propelled his steed against the chief of the Champawats. They were the sons of two sisters of the Jaipur house, and had hitherto lived in amity and brotherly love, now exchanged for deadly hate. They encountered, when the "cur" bit the dust, and was borne from the field. The loss of their leaders only inflamed the vassals on both sides, and it was long before either yielded a foot of ground. But numbers, and the repeated charges of Bakhta Singh who led wherever his nephew could be found, at length prevailed; though not until the extinction of the clan of Mertia, who, despising all odds, fought unto the death. Besides their head of Rian, there fell the sub-vassals of Irwa, Sewara, Jusari, and Mithri, with his three gallant sons, and almost all their retainers.

The Death of the Mithri Chief.—There is nothing more chivalrous in the days of Edward and Cressy than the death of the heir of Mithri, who, with his father and brothers, sealed his fealty with his blood on this fatal field. He had long engaged the hand of a daughter of a chief of the Narukas, and was occupied with the marriage rites, when tidings reached him of the approach of the rebels to Merta. The knot had just been tied, their hands had been joined—but he was a Mertia—he unlocked his hand from that of the fair Naruki, to court the Apsaras in the field of battle. In the bridal vestments, with the nuptial coronet (*maur*) encircling his forehead, he took his station with his clan in the second day's fight, and "obtained a bride in Indra's [750] abode." [1] The

[1] [The authority quoted by Compton (*Military Adventurers*, 61) speaks of the "serd kopperah wallas" (*zard kaprawāla*, 'those wearing yellow wedding garments'), as the forlorn hope in the battle.]

bards of Maru dwell with delight on the romantic glory of the youthful heir of Mithri, as they repeat in their Doric verse,

> Kānān moti bulbula
> Gal sonē ki māla
> Assi kos khariya āya
> Kunwar Mīthriwala.[1]

The paraphernalia here enumerated are very foreign to the cavalier of the west: "with pearls shining in his ears, and a golden chaplet round his neck, a space of eighty coss came the heir of Mithri."

The virgin bride followed her lord from Jaipur, but instead of being met with the tabor and lute, and other signs of festivity, wail and lamentation awaited her within the lands of Mithri, where tidings came of the calamity which at once deprived this branch of the Mertias of all its supporters. Her part was soon taken; she commanded the pyre to be erected; and with the turban and *tora*[2] which adorned her lord on this fatal day, she followed his shade to the mansions of the sun. I sought out the cenotaph of this son of honour in the blood-stained field; but the only *couronne immortelle* I could wreathe on the sandy plain was supplied by the Bardai, whose song is full of martial fire as he recounts the gallantry of Kunwar Mithriwala.

The Mertias, and their compeers on the side of the prince, made sad havoc amongst their opponents; and they still maintain that it was owing to the artillery alone that they were defeated. Their brave and loyal leader, Sher Singh of Rian, had fruitlessly endeavoured to recall his brother-in-law from the path of treason, but ineffectually; he spoke with sarcasm of his means to supplant Ram Singh by his uncle. The reply of the old baron of Awa is characteristic: "At least I will turn the land upside down"; to which Sher Singh rejoined, angrily, he would do his best to prevent him. Thus they parted; nor did they meet again till in arms at Merta.

In surveying this field of slaughter, the eye discerns no *point d'appui*, no village or key of position, to be the object of a struggle: nothing to obstruct the doubly-gorged falconet, which has no

[1] [Major Luard's Pandit reads in the first line *bhalbhala*, 'a lustre,' and in the third *kharoho*, 'rode hard.']

[2] [A neck ornament.]

terrors for the uncontrollable valour of the Rathor; it perceives but a level plain, extended to the horizon, and now covered with the memorials of this day's strife. Here appears the colonnaded mausoleum, with its airy cupola; there the humble altar, with its simple record of the name, clan, and *sakha* of him whose ashes repose beneath, with the date of the event [751], inscribed in rude characters. Of these monumental records I had copies made of about a score; they furnish fresh evidence of the singular character of the Rajput.

Ram Singh retired within the walls of the city, which he barricaded; but it being too extensive to afford the chance of defence against the enemy, he formed the fatal resolution of calling to his aid the Mahrattas, who were then rising into notice. At midnight he fled to the south; and at Ujjain found the Mahratta leader, Jai Apa Sindhia, with whom he concerted measures for the invasion of his country. Meantime his uncle being master of the field, repaired, without loss of time, to the capital, where he was formally enthroned; and his *an* was proclaimed throughout Marwar. As skilful as he was resolute, he determined to meet on his frontier the threatened invasion, and accordingly advanced to Ajmer, in order to interpose between the Mahrattas and Jaipur, whose prince, Isari Singh,[1] was father-in law to his rival. He wrote him a laconic epistle, requiring him either instantly to unite with him in attacking the Mahrattas, or declare himself his foe. The Jaipur prince had many powerful reasons for not supporting Raja Bakhta, but he at the same time dreaded his enmity. In this extremity, he had recourse to an expedient too common in cases of difficulty. Concerting with his wife, a princess of Idar (then ruled by one of the sons of Ajit), the best mode of extrication from his difficulties, he required her aid to revenge the foul murder of Ajit, and to recover his son's right. "In either case," said he, "the sword must decide, for he leaves me no alternative: against him I have no hopes of success; and if I march to the aid of an assassin and usurper, I lose the good opinion of mankind." In short, he made it appear that she alone could rescue him from his perils. It was therefore resolved to punish one crime by the commission of another. Isari Singh signified his assent; and to lull all suspicion, the Rathorni was to visit her uncle in his camp on the

[1] [Isari Singh, Mahārāja of Jaipur, A.D. 1742–60.]

(1) DURGA DAS. (2) MAHARAJA SHER SINGH OF RIAN.

To face page 866.

joint frontier of the three States of Mewar, Marwar, and Amber. A poisoned robe was the medium of revenge. Raja Bakhta, soon after the arrival of his niece, was declared in a fever; the physician was summoned: but the man of secrets, the Vaidya, declared he was beyond the reach of medicine, and bade him prepare for other scenes. The intrepid Rathor, yet undismayed, received the tidings even with a jest: "What, Suja," said he, "no cure? Why do you take my lands and eat their produce, if you cannot combat my maladies? What is your art good for?" The Vaidya excavated a [752] small trench in the tent, which he filled with water; throwing into it some ingredient, the water became gelid. "This," said he, "can be effected by human skill; but your case is beyond it: haste, perform the offices which religion demands." With perfect composure he ordered the chiefs to assemble in his tent; and having recommended to their protection, and received their promise of defending the rights of his son, he summoned the ministers of religion into his presence. The last gifts to the church, and these her organs, were prepared; but with all his firmness, the anathema of the Satis, as they ascended the funeral pyre on which his hand had stretched his father, came into his mind; and as he repeated the ejaculation, "May your corpse be consumed in foreign land!" he remembered he was then on the border. The images which crossed his mental vision it is vain to surmise: he expired as he uttered these words; and over his remains, which were burnt on the spot, a cenotaph was erected, and is still called Bura Dewal, the 'Shrine of Evil.'

But for that foul stain, Raja Bakhta would have been one of the first princes of his race. It never gave birth to a bolder; and his wisdom was equal to his valour. Before the commission of that act, he was adored by his Rajputs. He was chiefly instrumental in the conquests made from Gujarat; and afterwards, in conjunction with his brother, in defeating the imperial viceroy, Sarbuland.[1] His elevation could not be called a usurpation, since Ram Singh was totally incapacitated, through his

[1] [Nawāb Mubārizu-l-mulk, Governor of Gujarāt under Muhammad Shāh, from which office he was removed because he consented to pay blackmail (*chauth*) to the Marāthas. He refused to give up his post, and fell into disgrace. He was afterwards Governor of Allāhābād, and died A.D. 1745 (Beale, *Dict. Oriental Biog.* *s.v.*; *BG*, i. Part i. 304 ff.).]

ungovernable passions, for sovereign sway; and the brave barons of Marwar, "all sons of the same father with their prince," have always exercised the right of election, when physical incapacity rendered such a measure requisite. It is a right which their own customary laws, as well as the rules of justice, have rendered sacred. According to this principle, nearly all the feudality of Maru willingly recognized, and swore to maintain, the claims of his successor, Bijai Singh. The Rajas of Bikaner and Kishangarh, both independent branches of this house, gave in their assent. Bijai Singh was accordingly proclaimed and installed at Marot, and forthwith conducted to Merta.

The ex-prince, Ram Singh, accompanied Jai Apa to the siege of Kotah, and subsequently through Mewar, levying contributions as they passed to Ajmer. Here a dispute occurred between the brave Rathor and Sindhia, whose rapacious spirit for plunder received a severe reproof: nevertheless they crossed the frontier [753], and entered Marwar. Bijai Singh, with all the hereditary valour of his race, marched to meet the invaders, at the head of nearly all the chivalry of Maru, amounting to 200,000 men.

Battle of Merta, about A.D. 1756.—The first day both armies encountered, they limited their hostility to a severe cannonade and partial actions, the inhabitants of Merta supplying the combatants with food, in which service many were killed; even the recluse Dadupantis ran the risk in this patriotic struggle, and several of the old patriarch's disciples suffered. The second day passed in the same manner, with many desperate charges of cavalry, in which the Mahrattas invariably suffered, especially from a select body of 5000 select horse, all cased in armour, which nothing could withstand. The superior numerical strength of Ram Singh and his allies compelled Bijai Singh not to neglect the means of retreat. Throughout the first and second days' combat, the cattle of the train had been kept yoked; on the third, they had carried them to a small rivulet in the rear to water. It was at the precise moment of time when the legion of cuirassiers were returning from a charge which had broken to pieces the Mahratta line, as they approached their friends, the word '*daga*' spread like wildfire; they were mistaken for Ram Singh's adherents, and a murderous shower of grape opened upon the flower of their own army, who were torn to pieces ere the fatal error was discovered. But such was the impression which this band of heroes had just made on the Mahrattas, that they feared to take advantage of this disaster. A feeling of horror pervaded the army of Bijai Singh, as the choice of their chivalry conveyed the slain and the wounded to the camp. A council of war was summoned, and the aid of superstition came to cool that valour which the Mahrattas, in spite of their numbers, could never subdue. The Raja was young—only twenty years of age ; and being prudent as well as brave, he allowed experience to guide him. The Raja of Bikaner, of the same kin and clan, took the lead, and advised a retreat. In the accident related, he saw the hand of Providence, which had sent it to serve as a signal to desist. The Raja had a great stake to lose, and doubtless deemed it wise to preserve his auxiliaries for the defence of his own dominions. It was a case which required the energy of Bakhta : but the wavering opinion of the council soon spread throughout the camp, and was not unobserved by the enemy ; nor was it till Bikaner marched off with his aid, towards the close of the day, that any advantage was taken of it [754]. Then Ram Singh at the head of a body of Rajputs and Mahrattas poured down upon them, and '*sauve qui peut*' became the order of the day. To gain Merta was the main object of the discomfited and panic-struck Rathors; but many chiefs with their vassals marched direct for their estates. The guns were abandoned to their fate, and became the first proud trophy the Mahrattas gained over the dreaded Rajputs. The Raja of Kishangarh, also a Rathor, followed the example of his brother prince of Bikaner, and carried off his bands. Thus deserted by his dispirited and now dispersed barons, the young prince had no alternative but flight, and at midnight he took the route of Nagor. In the darkness he mistook the road, or was misled into that of Rain, whose chieftain was the companion of his flight. Calling him by name, Lal Singh, he desired him to regain the right path ; but the orders of a sovereign at the head of a victorious army, and those of a fugitive prince, are occasionally received, even amongst Rajputs, with some shades of distinction. The chief begged permission, as he was near home, to visit his family and bring them with him. Too dignified to reply, the young prince remained silent and the Thakur of Rain[1] loitered in the rear. The Raja

[1] Or *Rahin* in the map, on the road to Jahil from Merta.

reached Kajwana, with only five of his cuirassiers (*silahposh*) as an escort. Here he could not halt with safety; but as he left the opposite barrier, his horse dropped down dead. He mounted another belonging to one of his attendants, and gained Deswal, three miles farther. Here the steeds, which had been labouring throughout the day under the weight of heavy armour, in addition to the usual burden of their riders, were too jaded to proceed; and Nagor was still sixteen miles distant. Leaving his worn-out escort, and concealing his rank, he bargained with a Jat to convey him before break of day to the gate of Nagor for the sum of five rupees. The peasant, after stipulating that the coin should be bijaishahis,[1] 'the new currency,' which still remains the standard, the common car of husbandry was brought forth, on which the king of Maru ascended, and was drawn by a pair of Nagori oxen. The royal fugitive was but little satisfied with their exertions, though their pace was good, and kept continually urging them, with the customary cry of "*hank! hank!*" The honest Jat, conscious that his cattle did their best, at length lost all temper. Repeating the sounds "*hank! hank!*" "Who are you," asked he, "that are hurrying on at this rate? It were more becoming [755] that such a sturdy carl should be in the field with Bijai Singh at Merta, than posting in this manner to Nagor. One would suppose you had the southrons (*dakkhinis*) at your heels. Therefore be quiet, for not a jot faster shall I drive." Morning broke, and Nagor was yet two miles distant: the Jat, turning round to view more attentively his impatient traveller, was overwhelmed with consternation when he recognized his prince. He leaped from the vehicle, horror-struck that he should have been sitting 'on the same level' with his sovereign, and absolutely refused to sin any longer against etiquette. "I pardon the occasion," said the prince mildly; "obey." The Jat resumed his seat, nor ceased exclaiming *hank! hank!* until he reached the gate of Nagor. Here the prince alighted, paid his price of conveyance, and dismissed the Jat of Deswal, with a promise of further recompense hereafter. On that day the enemy invested Nagor, but not before Bijai Singh had dispatched the chief of Harsor to defend the capital, and issued his proclamations to summon the ban of Marwar.

[1] [Coins made in the reign of Bijai Singh (A.D. 1753–93), (Webb, *Currencies of the Hindu States of Rājputāna*, 40).]

Resistance of Bijai Singh.—During six months he defended himself gallantly in Nagor, against which the desultory Mahrattas, little accustomed to the operations of a siege, made no impression, while they suffered from the sallies of their alert antagonist. Encouraged by their inactivity, the young prince, imbued with all the native valour of his race, and impelled by that decisive energy of mind which characterized his father, determined upon a step which has immortalized his memory. He resolved to cut his way through the enemy, and solicit succours in person. He had a dromedary corps five hundred strong. Placing on these a devoted band of one thousand Rajputs, in the dead of night he passed the Mahratta lines unobserved, and made direct for Bikaner. Twenty-four hours sufficed to seat him on the same *gaddi* with its prince, and to reveal to him the melancholy fact, that here he had no hopes of succour. Denied by a branch of his own house, he resorted to a daring experiment upon the supporter of his antagonist. The next morning he was on his way, at the head of his dromedary escort, to the capital of the Kachhwahas, Jaipur. The "ships of the desert" soon conveyed him to that city. He halted under the walls, and sent a messenger to say that in person he had come to solicit his assistance.

Isari Singh, the son and successor of the great Sawai Jai Singh, had neither the talents of his father, nor even the firmness which was the common inheritance [756] of his race. He dreaded the rival Rathor; and the pusillanimity which made him become the assassin of the father, prompted him to a breach of the sacred laws of hospitality (which, with courage, is a virtue almost inseparable from a Rajput soul), and make a captive of the son. But the base design was defeated by an instance of devotion and resolution, which will serve to relieve the Rajput character from the dark shades which the faithful historian is sometimes forced to throw into the picture. Civil war is the parent of every crime, and severs all ties, moral and political; nor must it be expected that Rajputana should furnish the exception to a rule, which applies to all mankind in similar circumstances. The civil wars of England and France, during the conflicts of the White and Red Roses, and those of the League, will disclose scenes which would suffice to dye with the deepest hues an entire dynasty of the Rajputs. Let such deeds as the following be placed on the virtuous side of the account, and the crimes on the opposite side be ascribed to the peculiarities of their condition.

Devotion of the Mertias.—The devoted sacrifice of Sher Singh, the chief of the Mertia clan, has already been recorded. When victory declared against the side he espoused, the victorious Bakhta Singh resumed the estates of Rian from his line, and conferred them on a younger branch of the family. Jawan Singh was the name of the individual, and he was now with the chosen band of the son of his benefactor, soliciting succour from the king of the Kachhwahas. He had married the daughter of the chief of Achrol, one of the great vassals of Jaipur, who was deep in the confidence of his sovereign, to whom he imparted his design to seize the person of his guest and suppliant at the interview he had granted. Aware that such a scheme could not be effected without bloodshed, the Achrol chieftain, desirous to save his son-in-law from danger, under an oath of secrecy revealed the plot, in order that he might secure himself. The Jaipur prince came to the 'Travellers' hall' (*dharmsala*), where the Rathor had alighted; they embraced with cordiality, and seated themselves on the same *gaddi* together. While compliments were yet passing, the faithful Mertia, who, true to his pledge, had not even hinted to his master the danger that threatened him, placed himself immediately behind the Jaipur prince, sitting, as if accidentally, on the flowing skirt of his robe. The Raja, turning round to the leader of "the first of the swords of Maru," remarked "Why, Thakur, have you taken a seat in the background to-day?" "The day requires it, Maharaja" [757], was the laconic reply: for the post of the Mertias was the sovereign's right hand. Turning to his prince, he said, "Arise, depart, or your life or liberty is endangered." Bijai Singh arose, and his treacherous host made an attempt to follow, but felt his design impeded by the position the loyal chief had taken on his garment, whose drawn dagger was already pointed to his heart, where he threatened to sheathe it if any hindrance was offered to the safe departure of his sovereign, to whom he coolly said, as the prince left the astonished assembly, "Send me word when you are mounted." The brave Bijai Singh showed himself worthy of his servant, and soon sent to say, "He now only waited for him": a message, the import of which was not understood by the treacherous Kachhwaha. The leader of the Mertias sheathed his dagger—arose—and coming in front of the Raja, made him a respectful obeisance. The Jaipur prince could not resist the impulse which such devotion was calculated to produce; he arose, returned the salutation, and giving vent to his feelings, observed aloud to his chiefs, "Behold a picture of fidelity! It is in vain to hope for success against such men as these."

Bijai Singh returns to Nāgor.—Foiled in all his endeavours, Bijai Singh had no resource but to regain Nagor, which he effected with the same celerity as he quitted it. Six months more passed away in the attempt to reduce Nagor; but though the siege was fruitless, not so were the efforts of his rival Ram Singh in other quarters, to whom almost all the country had submitted: Marot, Parbatsar, Pali, Sojat had received his flag; and besides the capital and the town he held in person, Jalor, Siwana, and Phalodi were the only places which had not been reduced. In this extremity, Bijai Singh listened to an offer to relieve him from these multiplied difficulties, which, in its consequences, alienated for ever the brightest gem in the crown of Marwar.

The Assassination of Jai Āpa Sindhia, A.D. 1759.—A Rajput and an Afghan, both foot-soldiers on a small monthly pay, offered, if their families were provided for, to sacrifice themselves for his safety by the assassination of the Mahratta commander. Assuming the garb of camp-settlers, they approached the head-quarters, feigning a violent quarrel. The simple Mahratta chief was performing his ablutions at the door of his tent, and as they approached they became more vociferous, and throwing a bundle of statements of account on the ground, begged he would decide between them. In this manner they came nearer and nearer, and as he listened to their story, one plunged his dagger in his side, exclaiming, "This for Nagor!" and "This for Jodhpur!" said his companion [758], as he repeated the mortal blow. The alarm was given; the Afghan was slain; but the Rajput called out "Thief!" and mingling with the throng, escaped by a drain into the town of Nagor.[1] Though the crime was rewarded, the

[1] [According to Grant Duff (*Hist. Mahrattas*, 310), Bijai Singh, following the infamous example of his father in regard to Pīlaji Gāēkwār, engaged two persons who, on the promise of a rent-free estate (*jāgīr*), went to Jai Āpa as accredited envoys, and assassinated him. Hari Charan Dās (Elliot-Dowson viii. 210) says that the Rājput leader warned Jai Āpa to leave

Rathor refused to see the criminal. The siege continued, but in spite of every precaution, reinforcements both of men and provisions continued to be supplied. It ill suited the restless Mahratta to waste his time in these desert regions, which could be employed so much more profitably on richer lands: a compromise ensued, in which the cause of Ram Singh was abandoned, on stipulating for a fixed triennial tribute, and the surrender of the important fortress and district of Ajmer in full sovereignty to the Mahratta, in *mundkati*, or compensation for the blood of Jai Apa. The monsoon was then approaching; they broke up, and took possession of this important conquest, which, placed in the very heart of these regions, may be called the key of Rajputana.

The cross of St. George now waves over the battlements of Ajmer,[1] planted, if there is any truth in political declarations, not for the purpose of conquest, or to swell the revenues of British India, but to guard the liberties and the laws of these ancient principalities from rapine and disorder. It is to be hoped that this banner will never be otherwise employed, and that it may never be execrated by the brave Rajput.

The deserted Ram Singh continued to assert his rights with the same obstinacy by which he lost them; and for which he staked his life in no less than eighteen encounters against his uncle and cousin. At length, on the death of Isari Singh of Jaipur. having lost his main support, he accepted the Marwar share of the Salt Lake of Sambhar, and Jaipur relinquishing the other half, he resided there until his death [759].

Mārwār. Jai Āpa abused him, and the Rājput killed him by a blow with his dagger. Three of the Rājput party were killed, and three, in spite of their wounds, escaped.]

[1] [Surrendered to the British by Daulat Rāo Sindhia by treaty of June 25, 1818, and occupied by the Agent, Mr. Wilder, on July 28 of the same year.]

CHAPTER 29

Mahādaji Sindhia, A.D. 1759-94. Battle of Lālsot, A.D. 1787.— Mahadaji Sindhia succeeded to the command of the horde led by his relation, Jai Apa. He had the genius to discover that his southron horse would never compete with the Rajputs, and he set about improving that arm to which the Mahrattas finally owed success. This sagacious chief soon perceived that the political position of the great States of Rajasthan was most favourable to his views of establishing his power in this quarter. They were not only at variance with each other, but, as it has already appeared, were individually distracted with civil dissensions. The interference of the Rana of Udaipur had obtained for his nephew, Madho Singh, the *gaddi* of Jaipur; but this advantage was gained only through the introduction of the Mahrattas, and the establishment of a tribute, as in Marwar. This brave people felt the irksomeness of their chains, and wished to shake them off. Madho Singh's reign was short; he was succeeded by Partap, who determined to free himself from this badge of dependence.[1] Accordingly, when Mahadaji Sindhia invaded his country, at the head of a powerful army, he called on the Rathors for aid. The cause was their own; and they jointly determined to redeem what had been lost. As the bard of the Rathors observes, they [760] forgot all their just grounds of offence [2] against the Jaipur court, and sent the flower of their chivalry under the chieftain of Rian, whose fidelity has been so recently recorded. At Tonga (the battle is also termed that of Lalsot), the rival armies encountered. The celebrated Mogul chiefs, Ismail Beg and Hamdani, added their forces to those of the combined Rajputs, and gained an entire victory, in which

[1] [Mādho Singh, A.D. 1760–78: Prithi Singh II. was succeeded within a year by Partāp Singh, 1778–1803.]

[2] *Pat rakhi Partāp ki*
No koti ka nāth.
Gunha agla bagasnē
Abē pakriyo hāth.

"The lord of the nine castles preserved the honour of Partāp. He forgave former offences, and again took him by the hand." [In the third line Major Luard's Pandit reads *bakhas di*, 'forgave.']

the Rathors had their full share of glory. The noble chief of Rian formed his Rathor horse into a dense mass, with which he charged and overwhelmed the flower of Sindhia's army, composed of the regulars under the celebrated De Boigne.[1] Sindhia was driven from the field, and retired to Mathura; for years he did not recover the severity of this day. The Rathors sent a force under the Dhaibhai, which redeemed Ajmer, and annulled their tributary engagement.

Battle of Pātan, June 20, 1790.—The genius of General Comte de Boigne ably seconded the energetic Sindhia. A regular force was equipped, far superior to any hitherto known, and was led into Rajputana to redeem the disgrace of Tonga. The warlike Rathors determined not to await the attack within their own limits, but marched their whole force to the northern frontier of Jaipur, and formed a junction with the Kachhwahas at the town of Patan (*Tuarvati*).[2] The words of the war-song, which the inspiring bards repeated as they advanced, are still current in Marwar; but an unlucky stanza, which a juvenile Charan had composed after the battle of Tonga, had completely alienated the Kachhwahas from their supporters, to whom they could not but acknowledge their inferiority:

Ūdhalti Amber né rākhi Rāthorān.

"The Rathors guarded the petticoats of Amber."[3]

---

[1] "A la gauche la cavalerie rhatore, au nombre de dix mille hommes, fondit sur les bataillons de M. de Boigne malgré le feu des batteries placées en avant de la ligne. Les pièces bien servies opéraient avec succès; mais les Rhatores, avec le courage opiniâtre qui les caractérise, s'acharnaient à poursuivre l'action, et venaient tuer les artilleurs jusques sur leurs pièces. Alors, les bataillons s'avancèrent, et les Rhatores, qui avaient perdu beaucoup de monde, commencèrent à s'ébranler. M. de Boigne, les voyant se retirer en désordre, réclama l'aide du centre; mais les prières et les menaces furent également inutiles: les vingt-cinq bataillons mogols, restés inactifs pendant toute la journée, et simples spectateurs du combat, demeurèrent encore immobiles dans ce moment décisif. Les deux armées se retirèrent après cette action sanglante, qui n'eut aucun résultat."

[2] [There is some doubt about the exact date. Grant Duff (*Hist. Mahrattas*, 497) fixes it on June 20, 1790. See Erskine's note (iii. A. 68), which is followed in the margin. For the battle see Compton, *Military Adventurers*, 51 ff.]

[3] [The translation in the text seems to be wrong. The best authorities translate: "But for the Rāthors Amber would have run away."]

This stanza was retained in recollection at the battle of Patan; and if universal [761] affirmation may be received as proof, it was the cause of its loss, and with it that of Rajput independence. National pride was humbled: a private agreement was entered into between the Mahrattas and Jaipurians, whereby the latter, on condition of keeping aloof during the fight, were to have their country secured from devastation. As usual, the Rathors charged up to the muzzles of De Boigne's cannon, sweeping all before them: but receiving no support, they were torn piecemeal by showers of grape and compelled to abandon the field. Then, it is recorded, the brave Rathor showed the difference between fighting on *parbhum*, or 'foreign land,' and on his own native soil. Even the women, it is averred, plundered them of their horses on this disastrous day; so heart-broken had the traitorous conduct of their allies rendered them. The Jaipurians paid dearly for their revenge, and for the couplet which recorded it:

Ghoro, joro, pagri,
Mūcham Khag Mārwār,
Pānch rakam mel lidha
Pātan men Rāthor.[1]

Verbatim:

"Horse, shoes, turban,
Mustachio, sword [of] Marwar,
Five things surrendered were
At Patan by the Rathor."

Both these "ribald strains" are still the taunt of either race: by such base agencies are thrones overturned, and heroism rendered abortive!

When the fatal result of the battle of Patan was communicated to Raja Bijai Singh, he called a council of all his nobles, at which the independent branches of his family, the Rajas of Bikaner, Kishangarh, and Rupnagarh, assisted, for the cause was a common one. The Raja gave it as his own opinion, that it was better to

[1] [In this version the first and third lines do not scan. According to Dr. Tessitori, a better text runs:

Ghoro, joro, pāgri,
Mūcham tāni maror,
Yān pānchām gun agli,
Rājpūti Rāthor.]

fulfil the terms of the former treaty, on the murder of Jai Apa, acknowledge the cancelled tribute, and restore Ajmer, which they had recovered by a *coup de main*. His valorous chieftains opposed the degrading suggestion, and unanimously recommended that they should again try the chances of war ere they signed their humiliation. Their resolution swayed the prince, who issued his summons to every Rathor in his dominions to assemble under their Raja's banner, once more planted on the ensanguined plains of Merta. A fine army was embodied; not a Rathor who could wield a sword but brought it for service in the cause of his country; and full thirty thousand men assembled on the 10th September 1790, determined to efface the recollections of Patan [762].

Battle of Merta, September 1790 A.D.—There was one miscreant of Rathor race, who aided on this occasion to rivet his country's chains, and his name shall be held up to execration—Bahadur Singh, the chief of Kishangarh. This traitor to his suzerain and race held, jointly with his brother of Rupnagarh, a domain of two hundred and ten townships: not a fief emanating from Marwar, but all by grant from the kings; still they received the *tika*, and acknowledged the supremacy of the head of Jodhpur. The brothers had quarrelled; Bahadur despoiled his brother of his share, and being deaf to all offers of mediation, Bijai Singh marched and re-inducted the oppressed chief into his capital, Rupnagarh. The fatal day of Patan occurred immediately after; and Bahadur, burning with revenge, repaired to De Boigne, and conducted him against his native land. Rupnagarh, it may be supposed, was his first object, and it will afford a good proof of the efficiency of the artillery of De Boigne, that he reduced it in twenty-four hours. Thence he proceeded to Ajmer, which he invested: and here the proposal was made by the Raja for its surrender, and for the fulfilment of the former treaty. Mahadaji in person remained at Ajmer, while his army, led by Lakwa, Jiwa-dada, Sudasheo Bhao, and other Mahratta leaders of horse, with the brigades of De Boigne and eighty pieces of cannon, advanced against the Rathors. The Mahrattas, preceding by one day's march the regulars under De Boigne, encamped at Natria. The Rathor army was drawn out on the plains of Merta, one flank resting on the village of Dangiwas. Five miles separated the Rathors from the Mahrattas; De Boigne was yet in the rear, his guns being deep sunk in the sandy bed of the Luni. Here a golden opportunity was lost, which could never be regained, of deciding 'horse to horse' the claims of supremacy; but the evil genius of the Rathor again intervened: and as he was the victim at Patan to the jealousy of the Kachhwaha, so here he became the martyr to a meaner cause, the household jealousies of the civil ministers of his prince. It is customary in all the Rajput States, when the sovereign does not command in person, to send one of the civil ministers as his representative. Him the feudal chiefs will obey, but not one of their own body, at least without some hazard of dissension. Khub Chand Singwi, the first minister, was present with the Raja at the capital: Gangaram Bhandari and Bhimraj Singwi were with the army. Eager to efface the disgrace of Patan, the two great Rathor leaders, Sheo Singh of Awa, and Mahidas of Asop, who had sworn to free their country or die in the [763] attempt, demanded a general movement against the Mahrattas. This gallant impatience was seconded by all the other nobles, as well as by a successful attack on the foragers of the enemy, in which the Mahrattas lost all their cattle. But it was in vain they urged the raging ardour of their clans, the policy of taking advantage of it, and the absence of De Boigne, owing to whose admirable corps and well-appointed park the day at Patan was lost; Bhimraj silenced their clamour for the combat by producing a paper from the minister Khub Chand commanding them on their allegiance not to engage until the junction of Ismail Beg, already at Nagor. They fatally yielded obedience. De Boigne extricated his guns from the sands of Alniawas, and joined the main body. That night the Bikaner contingent, perceiving the state of things, and desirous to husband their resources to defend their own altars, withdrew. About an hour before day-break, De Boigne led his brigade to the attack, and completely surprised the unguarded Rajputs.[1] They were awoke by showers of grape-shot, which soon broke their position: all was confusion; the resistance was feeble. It was the camp of the irregular infantry and guns which broke, and endeavoured to gain Merta; and the civil commanders took to flight. The alarm reached the more distant quarters of the brothers-in-arms, the chiefs of Awa and Asop. The latter was famed for the immense quantity of opium he consumed; and with difficulty could his companion awake him, with the appalling tidings, "The camp has fled, and

[1] [See the graphic account in Keene, *Fall of the Mogul Empire*, 205 f.]

we are left alone!" "Well, brother, let us to horse." Soon the gallant band of both was ready, and twenty-two chiefs of note drank opium together for the last time. They were joined by the leaders of other clans; and first and foremost the brave Mertias of Rian, of Alniawas, Irwa, Chanod, Govindgarh; in all four thousand Rathors. When mounted and formed in one dense mass, the Awa chieftain shortly addressed them: "Where can we fly, brothers? But can there be a Rathor who has ties stronger than shame (*laj*)? If any one exist who prefers his wife and children to honour, let him retire." Deep silence was the only reply to this heroic appeal; and as the hand of each warrior was raised to his forehead, the Awa chief gave the word "Forward!" They soon came up with De Boigne's brigade, well posted, and defended by eighty pieces of cannon. "Remember Patan!" was the cry, as, regardless of showers of grape, this heroic band charged up to the cannon's mouth, driving everything before them, cutting [764] down the line which defended the guns, and passing on to assault the Mahrattas, who were flying in all directions to avoid their impetuous valour. Had there been a reserve at this moment, the day of Merta would have surpassed that of Tonga. But here the skill of De Boigne, and the discipline of his troops, were an overmatch for valour unsustained by discipline and discretion. The Rathor band had no infantry to secure their victory; the guns were wheeled round, the line was re-formed, and ready to receive them on their return. Fresh showers of shot and grape met their thinned ranks; scarcely one of the four thousand left the field. The chiefs of Asop, Irwa, Chanod, Govindgarh, Alniawas, Morira, and others of lesser note, were among the slain; and upon the heaps of wounded, surrounded by his gallant clan, lay the chief of Awa, pierced with seven-and-twenty wounds. He had lain insensible twenty-four hours, when an old servant, during the night, searched for and found him on the field. A heavy shower had fallen, which increased the miseries of the wounded. Blind and faint, the Thakur was dragged out from the bodies of the slain. A little opiate revived him; and they were carrying him off, when they were encountered by Lakwa's harkaras in search of chiefs of note; the wounded Thakur was conveyed to the headquarters at Merta. Lakwa sent a surgeon to sew up his wounds; but he disdained the courtesy, and refused all aid, until the meanest of his wounded vassals was attended to. This brave man, when sufficiently recovered, refused all solicitation from his sympathizing foes that the usual rejoicing might be permitted, and that he would shave and perform the ablutions after sickness, till he could see his sovereign. The Raja advanced from his capital to meet him, and lavished encomiums on his conduct. He now took the bath, preparatory to putting on the honorary dress; but in bathing his wounds opened afresh, and he expired.

Bhimraj Singwi received at Nagor, whither he had fled, a letter of accusation from his sovereign, on which he swallowed poison; but although he was indirectly the cause of the defeat, by his supineness, and subsequent disgraceful flight, it was the minister at the capital whose treason prevented the destruction of the Mahrattas: Khub Chand was jealous of Bhimraj; he dreaded being supplanted by him if he returned from Merta crowned with success; and he therefore penned the dispatch which paralysed their energies, enjoining them to await the junction of Ismail Beg [765].

Thus, owing to a scurrilous couplet of a bard, and to the jealousy of a contemptible court-faction, did the valiant Rathors lose their independence—if it can be called lost—since each of these brave men still deems himself a host, when "his hour should come" to play the hero. Their spirit is not one jot diminished since the days of Tonga and Merta.[1]

[1] Three years ago I passed two delightful days with the conqueror of the Rajputs, in his native vale of Chambéry. It was against the *croix blanche* of Savoy, not the *orange flag* of the Southron, that four thousand Rajputs fell martyrs to liberty; and although I wish the Comte long life, I may regret he had lived to bring his talents and his courage to their subjugation. He did them ample justice, and when I talked of the field of Merta, the remembrance of past days flitted before him, as he said "all appeared as a dream." Distinguished by his prince, beloved by a numerous and amiable family, and honoured by his fellow-citizens, the years of the veteran, now numbering more than fourscore, glide in agreeable tranquillity in his native city, which, with oriental magnificence, he is beautifying by an entire new street and a handsome dwelling for himself. By a singular coincidence, just as I am writing this portion of my narrative I am put in possession of a *Mémoire* of his life, lately published, written under the eye of his son, the Comte Charles de Boigne. From this I extract his account of the battle of Merta. It is not to be supposed that he could then have been acquainted with the secret intrigues which were arrayed in favour of the "white cross" on this fatal day.

"Les forces des Rajepoutes se composaient de trente mille cavaliers, de

British Policy towards the Rajputs.—By a careful investigation of the circumstances which placed those brave races in their present political position, the paramount protecting power may be enabled to appreciate them, either as allies or as foes; and it will demonstrate more effectually than mere opinions, from whatever source, how admirably qualified they are, if divested of control, to harmonize, in a very important respect, with the British system of government in the East. We have nothing to dread from them, individually or collectively; and we may engage their very hearts' blood in our cause against whatever foes may threaten us, foreign or domestic, if we only exert our interference when mediation will be of advantage to them, without offence to [766] their prejudices. Nor is there any difficulty in the task; all honour the peacemaker, and they would court even arbitration if once assured that we had no ulterior views. But our strides have been rapid from Calcutta to Rajputana, and it

---

vingt mille hommes d'infanterie régulière, et de vingt-cinq pièces de canon. Les Marhattes avaient une cavalerie égale en nombre à celle de l'ennemi, mais leur infanterie se bornait aux bataillons de M. de Boigne, soutenus, il est vrai, par quatre-vingts pièces d'artillerie. Le général examina la position de l'ennemi, il étudia le terrain et arrêta son plan de bataille.

"Le dix, avant le jour, la brigade reçut l'ordre de marcher en avant, et elle surprit les Rajepoutes pendant qu'ils faisoient leurs ablutions du matin. Les premiers bataillons, avec cinquante pièces de canon tirant à mitraille, enfoncèrent les lignes de l'ennemi et enlevèrent ses positions. Rohan, qui commandait l'aile droite, à la vue de ce premier avantage, sans avoir reçu aucun ordre, eut l'imprudence de s'avancer hors de la ligne du combat, à la tête de trois bataillons. La cavalerie Rathore profitant de cette faute, fondit à l'instant sur lui et faillit lui couper sa retraite sur le gros de l'armée, qu'il ne parvint à rejoindre qu'avec les plus grandes difficultés. Toute la cavalerie ennemie se mit alors en mouvement, et se jetant avec impétuosité sur la brigade, l'attaqua sur tous les côtés à la fois. Elle eût été infailliblement exterminée sans la présence d'esprit de son chef. M. de Boigne, s'étant aperçu de l'erreur commise par son aile droite et prévoyant les suites qu'elle pouvait entraîner, avait disposé sur-le-champ son infanterie en carré vide (hollow square); et par cette disposition, présentant partout un front à l'ennemi, elle opposa une résistance invincible aux charges furieuses des Rathores, qui furent enfin forcés de lâcher prise. Aussitôt l'infanterie reprit ses positions, et s'avançant avec son artillerie, elle fit une attaque générale sur toute la ligne des Rajepoutes. Déjà sur les neuf heures, l'ennemi était complètement battu; une heure après, les Marhattes prirent possession de son camp avec tous ses canons et bagages; et pour couronner cette journée, à trois heures après midi la ville de Mirtah fut prise d'assaut" (*Mémoire sur la carrière militaire et politique de M. le Général Comte De Boigne, Chambéry*, 1829).

were well if they credit what the old Nestor of India (Zalim Singh of Kotah) would not, who, in reply to all my asseverations that we wished for no more territory, said, "I believe you think so; but the time will come when there will be but one *sikka* [1] throughout India. You stepped in, Maharaj, at a lucky time, the *phut* [2] was ripe and ready to be eaten, and you had only to take it bit by bit. It was not your power, so much as our disunion, which made you sovereigns, and will keep you so." His reasoning is not unworthy of attention, though I trust his prophecy may never be fulfilled.

Jharāu.—*November* 28.—Camp at Jharau, five coss (11 miles). On leaving Merta, we passed over the ground sacred to "the four thousand," whose heroic deeds, demonstrating at once the Rajput's love of freedom and his claim to it, we have just related. We this day altered our course from the N.N.E., which would have carried us, had we pursued it, to the Imperial city, for a direction to the southward of east, in order to cross our own Aravalli and gain Ajmer. The road was excellent, the soil very fair; but though there were symptoms of cultivation near the villages, the wastes were frightfully predominant; yet they are not void of vegetation: there is no want of herbage or stunted shrubs. The Aravalli towered majestically in the distant horizon, fading from our view towards the south-east, and intercepted by rising grounds.

The Mirage.—We had a magnificent mirage this morning: nor do I ever recollect observing this singularly grand phenomenon on a more extensive scale, or with greater variety of form. The morning was desperately cold; the thermometer, as I mounted my horse, a little after sunrise, stood at 32°, the freezing-point, with a sharp biting wind from the north-east. The ground was blanched with frost, and the water-skins, or *bihishtis mashaks*, were covered with ice at the mouth. The slender shrubs, especially the milky *ak*, were completely burnt up; and as the weather had been hitherto mild, the transition was severely felt, by things animate and inanimate [767].

[1] ['Seal,' 'coinage.']

[2] *Phūt* is a species of pumpkin, or melon, which bursts and flies into pieces when ripe. [*Cucumis mormodica*, Watt, *Comm. Prod.* 438 f.] It also means *disunion*; and Zalim Singh, who always spoke in parables, compared the States of India to this fruit.

It is only in the cold season that the mirage is visible; the sojourners of Maru call it the *siya-kot*, or 'castles in the air.'[1] In the deep desert to the westward, the herdsmen and travellers through these regions style it *chitram*, 'the picture'; while about the plains of the Chambal and Jumna they term it *disasul*, 'the omen of the quarter.' This optical deception has been noticed from the remotest times. The prophet Isaiah alludes to it when he says, "and the parched ground shall become a pool";[2] which the critic has justly rendered, "and the *shārābh*[3] shall become real water." Quintus Curtius, describing the mirage in the Sogdian desert, says that "for the space of four hundred furlongs not a drop of water is to be found, and the sun's heat, being very vehement in summer, kindles such a fire in the sands, that everything is burnt up. There also arises such an exhalation, that the plains wear the appearance of a vast and deep sea"; which is an exact description of the *chitram* of the Indian desert. But the *shārābh* and *chitram*, the true mirage of Isaiah, differ from that illusion called the *siya-kot*; and though the traveller will hasten to it, in order to obtain a night's lodging, I do not think he would expect to slake his thirst there.

When we witnessed this phenomenon at first, the eye was attracted by a lofty opaque wall of lurid smoke, which seemed to be bounded by, or to rise from, the very verge of the horizon. By slow degrees the dense mass became more transparent, and assumed a reflecting or refracting power: shrubs were magnified into trees; the dwarf *khair* appeared ten times larger than the gigantic *amli* of the forest. A ray of light suddenly broke the

[1] Literally, 'the cold-weather castles.'

[2] Isaiah xxxv. 7.

[3] *Sahra* is 'desert'; Arabic *sarāb*, Hebrew *shārābh*, 'the water of the desert,' a term which the inhabitants of the Arabian and Persian deserts apply to this optical phenomenon. The 18th verse, chap. xli. of Isaiah is closer to the critic's version: "I will make the wilderness (*sahra*) a pool of water." Doubtless the translators of Holy Writ, ignorant that this phenomenon was called *shārābh*, 'water of the waste,' deemed it a tautological error; for translated literally, "and the water of the desert shall become real water," would be nonsense: they therefore lopped off the *āb*, water, and read *sahra* instead of *shārābh*, whereby the whole force and beauty of the prophecy is not merely diminished, but lost. [The Author is mistaken, the words *shārābh* and *sahra* having no connexion. See *Encyclopaedia Biblica*, i. 1077. The mirage in Sanskrit is called *mrigatrish*, 'deer's thirst.' Another name is *Gandharvapura*, 'city of the heavenly choristers.]

line of continuity of this yet smoky barrier; and, as if touched by the enchanter's wand, castles, towers, and trees were seen in an aggregated cluster, partly obscured by magnificent foliage. Every accession of light produced a change in the *chitram*, which from the dense wall that it first exhibited had now faded into a thin transparent film, broken into a thousand masses, each mass being a huge lens; until at length the [768] too vivid power of the sun dissolved the vision: castles, towers, and foliage melted, like the enchantment of Prospero, into "thin air."

I had long imagined that the nature of the soil had some effect in producing this illusory phenomenon; especially as the *chitram* of the desert is seen chiefly on those extensive plains productive of the *sajji*, or alkaline plant, whence by incineration the natives produce soda,[1] and whose base is now known to be metallic. But I have since observed it on every kind of soil. That these lands, covered with saline incrustations, tend to increase the effect of the illusion, may be concluded.[2] But the difference between the *sarāb* or *chitram*, and the *siya-kot* or *disasul* is, that the latter is never visible but in the cold season, when the gross vapours cannot rise; and that the rarefaction, which gives existence to the other, destroys this, whenever the sun has attained 20° of elevation. A high wind is alike adverse to the phenomenon, and it will mostly be observed that it covets shelter, and its general appearance is a long line which is sure to be sustained by some height, such as a grove or village, as if it required support. The first time I observed it was in the Jaipur country; none of the party had ever witnessed it in the British provinces. It appeared like an immense walled town with bastions, nor could we give credit to our guides, when they talked of the *siya-kot*, and assured us that the objects were merely "castles in the air." I have since seen, though but once, this panoramic scene in motion, and nothing can be imagined more beautiful.

It was at Kotah, just as the sun rose, whilst walking on the terraced roof of the garden-house, my residence. As I looked towards the low range which bounds the sight to the south-east, the hills appeared in motion, sweeping with an undulating or rotatory movement along the horizon. Trees and buildings were

[1] Properly a carbonate of soda [barilla, Watt, *Econ. Prod.* 112 f.].

[2] [Mirage is due to variations in the refractive index of the atmosphere, caused by sporadic variations of temperature (*EB*, 11th ed. xviii. 573).]

magnified, and all seemed a kind of enchantment. Some minutes elapsed before I could account for this wonder; until I determined that it must be the masses of a floating mirage, which had attained its most attenuated form, and being carried by a gentle current of air past the tops and sides of the hills, while it was itself imperceptible, made them appear in motion.

But although this was novel and pleasing, it wanted the splendour of the scene of this morning, which I never saw equalled but once. This occurred at Hissar, where I went to visit a beloved friend—gone, alas! to a better world [769],—whose ardent and honourable mind urged me to the task I have undertaken. It was on the terrace of James Lumsdaine's house, built amidst the ruins of the castle of Firoz, in the centre of one extended waste, where the lion was the sole inhabitant, that I saw the most perfect specimen of this phenomenon: it was really sublime. Let the reader fancy himself in the midst of a desert plain, with nothing to impede the wide scope of vision, his horizon bounded by a lofty black wall encompassing him on all sides. Let him watch the first sunbeam break upon this barrier, and at once, as by a touch of magic, shiver it into a thousand fantastic forms, leaving a splintered pinnacle in one place, a tower in another, an arch in a third; these in turn undergoing more than kaleidoscopic changes, until the "fairy fabric" vanishes. Here it was emphatically called Harchand Raja ki puri, or 'the city of Raja Harchand,' a celebrated prince of the brazen age of India.[1] The power of reflection shown by this phenomenon cannot be better described than by stating that it brought the very ancient Agroha,[2] which is thirteen miles distant, with its fort and bastions, close to my view.

The difference then between the mirage and the *siya-kot* is,

[1] [For the tale of the sufferings of the righteous Harischandra see J. Muir, *Original Sanskrit Texts*, i. 88 ff.; Dowson, *Classical Dict. s.v.* For the mirage city compare "The City of Brass" (Burton, *Arabian Nights*, iii. 295).]

[2] This is in the ancient province of Hariana, and the cradle of the Agarwal race, now mercantile, and all followers of Hari or Vishnu. It might have been the capital of Aggrames, whose immense army threatened Alexander; with Agra it may divide the honour, or both may have been founded by this prince, who was also a Porus, being of Puru's race. [For Xandrames or Aggrames see Smith, *EHI*, 40; McCrindle, *Alexander*, 409. His capital is supposed to have been Pātaliputra, the modern Patna.]

that the former exhibits a horizontal, the latter a columnar or vertical stratification; and in the latter case, likewise, a contrast to the other, its maximum of translucency is the last stage of its existence. In this stage, it is only an eye accustomed to the phenomenon that can perceive it at all. I have passed over the plains of Meerut with a friend who had been thirty years in India, and he did not observe a *siya-kot* then before our eyes: in fact so complete was the illusion, that we only saw the town and fort considerably nearer. Monge gives a philosophical account of this phenomenon in Napoleon's campaign in Egypt; and Dr. Clarke perfectly describes it in his journey to Rosetta, when "domes, turrets, and groves were seen reflected on the glowing surface of the plain, which appeared like a vast lake extending itself between the city and travellers." It is on reviewing this account that a critic has corrected the erroneous translation of the Septuagint; and further dilated upon it in a review of Lichtenstein's travels in Southern Africa,[1] who exactly describes our *siya-kot*, of the magnifying and reflecting powers of which he gives a [770] singular instance. Indeed, whoever notices, while at sea, the atmospheric phenomena of these southern latitudes, will be struck by the deformity of objects as they pass through this medium: what the sailors term a fog-bank is the first stage of our *siya-kot*. I observed it on my voyage home; but more especially in the passage out. About six o'clock on a dark evening, while we were dancing on the waste, I perceived a ship bearing down with full sail upon us so distinctly, that I gave the alarm, in expectation of a collision; so far as I recollect, the helm was instantly up, and in a second no ship was to be seen. The laugh was against me—I had seen the "flying Dutchman,"[2] according to the opinion of the experienced officer on deck; and I believed it was really a vision of the mind: but I now feel convinced it was either the reflection of our own ship in a passing cloud of this vapour, or a more distant object therein refracted. But enough of this subject: I will only add, whoever has a desire to see one of the grandest phenomena in nature, let him repair to the plains of Merta or Hissar, and watch before the sun rises

[1] See *Edinburgh Review*, vol. xxi. pp. 66 and 138.

[2] This phenomenon is not uncommon; and the superstitious sailor believes it to be the spectre of a Dutch pirate, doomed, as a warning and punishment, to migrate about these seas.

the fairy palace of Harchand, infinitely grander and more imposing than a sunrise upon the alpine Helvetia, which alone may compete with the *chitram* of the desert.

Cenotaph of a Thākur.—Jharau is a thriving village appertaining to a sub-vassal of the Mertia chief of Rian. There was a small sheet of water within a musket-shot to the left of the village, on whose margin, peeping through a few nims and the evergreen jhal,[1] was erected an elegant, though small *chhatri*, or cenotaph, of an ancestor of the possessor. The Thakur is sculptured on his charger, armed at all points; and close beside him, with folded hands, upon the same stone, his faithful partner, who accompanied the warrior to Indra's abode. It bore the following epitaph: "On the 2d Margsir, S. 1689 (A.D. 1633), Maharaja Jaswant Singh attacked the enemy's (Aurangzeb's) army, in which battle Thakur Harankarna Das, of the Mertia clan, was slain. To him was erected this shrine, in the month of Margsir, S. 1697."

Water from wells is about thirty-five cubits from the surface; the strata as follows: four cubits of mixed sand and black earth; five of kankar, or calcareous concretions; twenty of stiff clay and sand; six of indurated clay, with particles of quartz and mica [771].

Alniawās.—*November* 29.—Alniawas, five coss. Half-way, passed the town of Rian, so often mentioned as the abode of the chief of the Mertia clan. It is large and populous, and surrounded by a well-constructed wall of the calcareous concrete already described, here called *morar*, and which resists the action of the monsoon. The works have a most judicious slope. The Thakur's name is Badan Singh, one of the eight great barons of Maru. The town still bears the name of *Sher Singh ka Rian*, who so gallantly defended to the death the rights of his young sovereign Ram Singh against his uncle. A beautiful landscape is seen from the high ground on which the town stands, in the direction of the mountains; the intermediate space being filled with large villages, relieved by foliage, so unusual in these regions. Here I had a proof of the audacity of the mountaineers of the Aravalli, in an inscription on a cenotaph, which I copied: "On Monday the 3d Magh, S. 1835 (A.D. 1779), Thakur Bhopal Singh fell at the foot of his walls, defending them against the Mers, having first, with

[1] [*Jhāl, Salvadora persica.*]

his own hand, in order to save her honour, put his wife to death."[1] Such were the Mers half a century ago, and they had been increasing in boldness ever since. There was scarcely a family on either side the range, whose estates lay at its foot, whose cenotaphs do not bear similar inscriptions, recording the desperate raids of these mountaineers; and it may be asserted that one of the greatest benefits we conferred on Rajputana was the conversion of this numerous banditti, occupying some hundred towns, into peaceful, tax-paying subjects. We can say, with the great Chauhan king, Bisiladeva, whose monument still stands in Firoz's palace at Delhi, that we made them "carry water in the streets of Ajmer"; and, still more, deposit their arms on the Rana's terrace at Udaipur. We have, moreover, metamorphosed a corps of them from breakers, into keepers, of the public peace.

Between Rian and Alniawas we crossed a stream, to which the name of the Luni[2] is also given, as well as to that we passed subsequently. It was here that De Boigne's guns are said to have stuck fast.

The soundings of the wells at Rian and Alniawas presented the same results as [772] at Jharau, with the important exception that the substratum was steatite, which was so universal in the first part of my journey from Jodhpur.

Alniawas is also a fief of a Mertia vassal. It is a considerable town, populous, and apparently in easy circumstances. Here again I observed a trait of devotion, recorded on an altar "to the memory of Suni Mall," who fell when his clan was exterminated in the charge against the rival Champawats, at Merta, in the civil wars.

Govindgarh.—*November* 30.—Govindgarh, distance three coss, or six miles. The roads generally good, though sometimes heavy; the soil of a lighter texture than yesterday. The castle and town of Govinda belong to a feudatory of the Jodha clan; its founder,

[1] A second inscription recorded a similar end of Sewa, the Baori, who fell in another inroad of the Mers, in S. 1831.

[2] I must deprecate criticism in respect to many of my geographical details. I find I have omitted this branch; but my health totally incapacitated me from reconstructing my map, which has been composed by the engraver from my disjointed materials. It is well known to all practical surveyors and geographers that none can do this properly but their author, who knows the precise value of each portion. [It is the main stream of the Lūni river.]

Govind, was grandson to Udai *le gros*; or, as Akbar dubbed him, the "Mota Raja," from his great bulk. Of this clan is the chief of Khairwa, having sixteen townships in his fief: Banai, and Masuda, with its "fifty-two townships," both now in Ajmer; having for their present suzerain the "Sarkar Company Bahadur"; though in lapses they will still go to Jodhpur, to be made "belted knights." These places are beyond the range; but Pisangan, with its twelve villages; Bijathal, and other fiefs west of it, also in Ajmer, might at all events be restored to their ancient princes, which would be considered as a great boon. There would be local prepossessions to contend with, on the part of the British officers in charge of the district; but such objections must give way to views of general good.

Fox-hunting: Hyaenas.—This was another desperately cold morning; being unprovided with a great-coat, I turned the *dagla*, or 'quilted brocade tunic,' sent me by the high priest of Kanhaiya, to account. We had some capital runs this morning with the foxes of Maru, which are beautiful little animals, and larger than those of the provinces. I had a desperate chase after a hyaena on the banks of the Luni, and had fully the speed of him; but his topographical knowledge was too much for me, and he at length led me through a little forest of reeds or rushes, with which the banks of the river are covered for a great depth. Just as I was about giving him a spear, in spite of these obstacles, we came upon a blind nullah or 'dry rivulet,' concealed by the reeds; and Bajraj (the royal steed) was thrown out, with a wrench in the shoulder, in the attempt to clear it: the *jhirak* laughed at us.

We crossed a stream half a mile west of Govindgarh, called the Sagarmati [773], which, with another, the Sarasvati, joining it, issues from the Pushkar lake. The Sagarmati is also called the Luni; its bed is full of micaceous quartzose rock. The banks are low, and little above the level of the country. Though water is found at a depth of twelve cubits from the surface, the wells are all excavated to the depth of forty, as a precautionary measure against dry seasons. The stratification here was—one cubit sand; three of sand and soil mixed; fifteen to twenty of yellow clayish sand; four of morar, and fifteen of steatite and calcareous concretions, with loose sand, mixed with particles of quartz.

Pushkar Lake.—*December* 1.—Lake of Pushkar, four coss: the thermometer stood at the freezing-point this morning:—heavy sands the whole way. Crossed the Sarasvati near Nand; its banks were covered with bulrushes, at least ten feet in height—many vehicles were lading with them for the interior, to be used for the purposes of thatching—elephants make a feast among them. We again crossed the Sarasvati, at the entrance of the valley of Pushkar, which comes from Old (*burha*) Pushkar, four miles east of the present lake, which was excavated by the last of the Pariharas of Mandor. The sand drifted from the plains by the currents of air has formed a complete bar at the mouth of the valley, which is about one mile in breadth; occasionally the *tibas*, or sand-hills, are of considerable elevation. The summits of the mountains to the left were sparkling with a deep rose-coloured quartz, amidst which, on the peak of Nand, arose a shrine to 'the Mother.' The hills preserve the same character: bold pinnacles, abrupt sides, and surface thinly covered. The stratification inclines to the west; the dip of the strata is about twenty degrees. There is, however, a considerable difference in the colour of the mountains: those on the left have a rose tint; those on the right are of greyish granite, with masses of white quartz about their summits.

Pushkar is the most sacred lake in India; that of Mansarovar in Tibet may alone compete with it in this respect. It is placed in the centre of the valley, which here becomes wider, and affords abundant space for the numerous shrines and cenotaphs with which the hopes and fears of the virtuous and the wicked amongst the magnates of India have studded its margin. It is surrounded by sand-hills of considerable magnitude, excepting on the east, where a swamp extends to the very base of the mountains. The form of the lake may be called an irregular ellipse. Around its margin, except towards the marshy outlet, is a display of [774] varied architecture. Every Hindu family of rank has its niche here, for the purposes of devotional pursuits when they could abstract themselves from mundane affairs. The most conspicuous are those erected by Raja Man of Jaipur, Ahalya Bai, the Holkar queen, Jawahir Mall of Bharatpur, and Bijai Singh of Marwar. The cenotaphs are also numerous. The ashes of Jai Apa, who was assassinated at Nagor, are superbly covered; as are those of his brother Santaji, who was killed during the siege of that place.

The Brahma Temple.—By far the most conspicuous edifice is the shrine of the creator Brahma, erected, about four years ago, by a private individual, if we may so designate Gokul Parik, the minister of Sindhia; it cost the sum of 130,000 rupees (about £15,000), though all the materials were at hand, and labour could be had for almost nothing. This is the sole tabernacle dedicated to the ONE GOD which I ever saw or have heard of in India.[1] The statue is quadrifrons; and what struck me as not a little curious was that the *sikhar*, or pinnacle of the temple, is surmounted by a cross. Tradition was here again at work. Before creation began, Brahma assembled all the celestials on this very spot, and performed the *Yajna*; around the hallowed spot walls were raised, and sentinels placed to guard it from the intrusion of the evil spirits. In testimony of the fact, the natives point out the four isolated mountains, placed towards the cardinal points, beyond the lake, on which, they assert, rested the *kanats*, or cloth-walls of inclosure. That to the south is called Ratnagir, or 'the hill of gems,' on the summit of which is the shrine of Savitri. That to the north is Nilagir, or 'the blue mountain.' East, and guarding the valley, is the Kuchhaturgir; and to the west, Sonachaura, or 'the golden.' Nandi, the bull-steed of Mahadeva, was placed at the mouth of the valley, to keep away the spirits of the desert; while Kanhaiya himself performed this office to the north. The sacred fire was kindled: but Savitri, the wife of Brahma, was nowhere to be found, and as without a female the rites could not proceed, a young Gujari took the place of Savitri; who, on her return, was so enraged at the indignity, that she retired to the mountain of gems, where she disappeared. On this spot a fountain gushed up, still called by her name; close to which is her shrine, not the least attractive in the precincts of Pushkar. During these rites, Mahadeva, or, as he is called, Bholanath, represented always in a state of stupefaction from the use of intoxicating [775] herbs, omitted to put out the sacred fire, which spread, and was likely to involve the world in combustion; when Brahma extinguished it with the sand, and hence the *tibas* of the valley. Such is the origin of the sanctity of

[1] [At least three other temples of Brahma are known: at Khed Brahma in Mahikāntha (*BG*, v. 437 f.); Cebrolu and Māla in S. India (Oppert, *Original Inhabitants of Bharatavarsa*, 288 ff.). The Author mentions one at Chitor (Vol. I. p. 322).]

THE SACRED LAKE OF PUSHKAR IN MARWĀR.

To face page 892.

Pushkar. In after ages, one of the sovereigns of Mandor, in the eagerness of the chase, was led to the spot, and washing his hands in the fountain, was cured of some disorder. That he might know the place again, he tore his turban into shreds, and suspended the fragments to the trees, to serve him as guides to the spot—there he made the excavation. The Brahmans pretend to have a copper-plate grant from the Parihara prince of the lands about Pushkar; but I was able to obtain only a Persian translation of it, which I was heretical enough to disbelieve. I had many grants brought me, written by various princes and chiefs, making provision for the prayers of these recluses at their shrines.

The name of Bisaladeva, the famed Chauhan king of Ajmer, is the most conspicuous here; and they still point out the residence of his great ancestor, Ajaipal, on the Nagpahar, or 'serpent-rock,' directly south of the lake, where the remains of the fortress of the Pali or Shepherd-king are yet visible. Ajaipal was, as his name implies, a goatherd, whose piety, in supplying one of the saints of Pushkar with daily libations of goats' milk, procured him a territory. Satisfied, however, with the scene of his early days, he commenced his castle on the serpent-mount; but his evil genius knocking down in the night what he erected in the day, he sought out another site on the opposite side of the range: hence arose the far-famed Ajamer.[1] Manika Rae is the most conspicuous connecting link of the Chauhan Pali kings, from the goatherd founder to the famed Bisaladeva.[2] Manika was slain in the first century of the Hijra, when "the arms of Walid conquered to the Ganges"; and Bisaladeva headed a confederacy

[1] ["The name probably suggested the myth [that he was a goatherd, Ajapāla = 'goatherd'], and it is more reasonable to suppose that the appellation was given to him when, at the close of his life, he became a hermit, and ended his days at the gorge in the hills about ten miles from Ajmer, which is still venerated as the shrine of Ajaipāl. It has been shown, however, by more recent research that Aja or Ajāya flourished about A.D. 1000, and that the foundation of Ajmer must be attributed to this period" (Watson, *Gazetteer*, i. A. 9).]

[2] Classically, Visaladeva. [Cunningham remarks that the date of Manik Rāē is fixed by a memorial verse in Sambat 741 or 747, but of what era is uncertain. Tod adopts the Vikrama era, and fixes his date twenty years before the invasion of Muhammad bin Kāsim, A.D. 712. He seems to have reigned in the beginning of the ninth century (*ASR*, ii. 253). Vīsaladeva lived in the middle of the twelfth century (Smith, *EHI*, 386). Tej Singh is mentioned in inscriptions A.D. 1260–67 (Erskine ii. B. 10).]

of the Hindu kings, and chased the descendants of Mahmud from Hindustan, the origin of the recording column at Delhi. Bisaladeva, it appears from inscriptions, was the contemporary of Rawal Tejsi, the monarch of Chitor, and grandfather of the Ulysses of Rajasthan, the brave Samarsi, who fell with 13,000 of his kindred in aid of the last Chauhan Prithiraj, who, according to the genealogies of this race, is the fourth in descent from Bisaladeva. If this is not sufficient proof of the era of this king, be it known that Udayaditya, the prince of the Pramaras (the period of [776] whose death, or A.D. 1096, has now become a datum),[1] is enumerated amongst the sovereigns who serve under the banners of the Chauhan of Ajmer.

Bhartrihari.—The 'serpent-rock' is also famed as being one of the places where the wandering Bhartrihari, prince of Ujjain, lived for years in penitential devotion ; and the slab which served as a seat to this royal saint has become one of the objects of veneration. If all the places assigned to this brother of Vikrama were really visited by him, he must have been one of the greatest tourists of antiquity, and must have lived to an antediluvian old age. Witness his castle at Sehwan, on the Indus; his cave at Alwar; his *thans* at Abu, and at Benares. We must, in fact, give credit to the couplet of the bards, "the world is the Pramara's." There are many beautiful spots about the serpent-mount, which, as it abounds in springs, has from the earliest times been the resort of the Hindu sages, whose caves and hermitages are yet pointed out, now embellished with gardens and fountains. One of the latter issuing from a fissure in the rock is sacred to the Muni Agastya, who performed the very credible exploit of drinking up the ocean.

St. George's banner waved on a sand-hill in front of the cross on Brahma's temple, from which my camp was separated by the lake ; but though there was no defect of legendary lore to amuse us, we longed to quit "the region of death," and hie back to our own lakes, our cutter, and our gardens.

Ajmer.—*December* 2.—Ajmer, three coss. Proceeded up the valley, where lofty barriers on either side, covered with the milky thor (*cactus*),[2] and the "yellow anwla of the border," showed they

[1] See *Transactions of the Royal Asiatic Society*, vol. i. p. 223.
[2] [*Euphorbia neriifolia.*]

were but the prolongation of our own Aravalli. Granite appeared of every hue, but of a stratification so irregular as to bid defiance to the geologist. The higher we ascended the valley, the loftier became the sand-hills, which appeared to aspire to the altitude of their granitic neighbours. A small rill poured down the valley ; there came also a cold blast from the north, which made our fingers tingle. Suddenly we changed our direction from north to east, and ascending the mountain, surveyed through a gap in the range the far-famed Daru-l-Khair. The view which thus suddenly burst upon us was magnificent. A noble plain, with trees, and the expansive lake of Bisaladeva, lay at our feet, while 'the fortress of the goatherd' crowned the crest of a majestic isolated hill. The point of descent affords a fine field for the mineralogist ; on [777] each side, high over the pass, rise peaks of reddish granite, which are discovered half-way down the descent to be reposing on a blue micaceous slate, whose inclination is westward, at an angle of about 25° with the horizon. The formation is the same to the southward, but the slate there is more compact, and freer from mica and quartz. I picked up a fragment of black marble ; its crystals were large and brilliant.

Passed through the city of Ajmer, which, though long a regal abode, does not display that magnificence we might have expected, and, like all other towns of India, exhibits poverty and ease in juxtaposition. It was gratifying to find that the finest part was rising, under the auspices of the British Government and the superintendent of the province, Mr. Wilder. The main street, when finished, will well answer the purpose intended—a place of traffic for the sons of commerce of Rajasthan, who, in a body, did me the honour of a visit : they were contented and happy at the protection they enjoyed in their commercial pursuits. With the prosperity of Bhilwara, that of Ajmer is materially connected ; and having no interests which can clash, each town views the welfare of the other as its own : a sentiment which we do not fail to encourage

Breakfasted with Mr. Wilder,[1] and consulted how we could best promote our favourite objects—the prosperity of Ajmer and Bhilwara [778].

[1] [Mr. Wilder was in charge of Ajmer, 1818-24.]

CHAPTER 30

Ajmer.—Ajmer has been too long the haunt of Moguls and Pathans, the Goths and Vandals of Rajasthan, to afford much scope to the researches of the antiquary. Whatever time had spared of the hallowed relics of old, bigotry has destroyed, or raised to herself altars of materials, whose sculptured fragments serve now as disjointed memorials of two distinct and distant eras: that of the independent Hindu, and that of the conquering Muhammadan, whose idgahs and mosques, mausoleums and country-seats, constructed from the wrecks of aboriginal art, are fast mouldering to decay. The associations they call forth afford the only motive to wish their preservation; except one "relic of nobler days and noblest arts," which, though impressed with this double character, every spectator must desire to rescue from the sweeping sentence—the edifice before the reader, a visit to which excited these reflections. Let us rather bless than execrate the hand, though it be that of a Turk, which has spared, from whatever motive, one of the most perfect, as well as the most ancient, monuments of Hindu architecture. It is built on the western declivity of the fortress, and called Arhai din ka jhonpra, or, 'the shed of two and a half days,' from its having occupied (as tradition tells) its magical builders only this short period. The skill of the Pali or Takshak architect, the three sacred mounts of these countries abundantly attest: nor had he occasion for any mysterious arts, besides those of masonry, to accomplish them. In discussing the cosmogony of the Hindus, we have had occasion to convert their years into days; here we must reverse the method, and understand (as in [779] interpreting the sacred prophecies of Scripture) their days as meaning years. Had it, indeed, been of more humble pretensions, we might have supposed the monotheistic Jain had borrowed from the Athenian legislator Cecrops, who ordained that no tomb should consist of more work than ten men could finish in three days; to which Demetrius, the Phalerian, sanctioned the addition of a little vessel to contain the ghost's victuals.[1]

[1] See Archbishop Potter's *Archaeologia*, vol. i. p. 192. [Cicero, *De Legibus*, ii. 25, 26; Grote, *Hist. of Greece*, ed. 1869, xii. 184.]

ANCIENT JAIN TEMPLE AT AJMER.

To face page 896.

Arhāi din ka jhonpra Mosque.—The temple is surrounded by a superb screen of Saracenic architecture, having the main front and gateway to the north. From its simplicity, as well as its appearance of antiquity, I am inclined to assign the screen to the first dynasty, the Ghorian sultans, who evidently made use of native architects. The entrance arch is of that wavy kind, characteristic of what is termed the Saracenic, whether the term be applied to the Alhambra of Spain, or the mosques of Delhi; and I am disposed, on close examination, to pronounce it Hindu.[1] The entire façade of this noble entrance, which I regret I cannot have engraved, is covered with Arabic inscriptions. But, unless my eyes much deceived me, the small frieze over the apex of the arch contained an inscription in Sanskrit,[2] with which Arabic has been commingled, both being unintelligible. The remains of a minaret still maintain their position on the right flank of the gate, with a door and steps leading to it for the muazzin to call the faithful to prayers. A line of smaller arches of similar form composes the front of the screen. The design is chaste and beautiful, and the material, which is a compact limestone of a yellow colour, admitting almost of as high a polish as the *jaune antique*, gave abundant scope to the sculptor. After confessing and admiring the taste of the Vandal architect, we passed under the arch to examine the more noble production of the Hindu. Its plan is simple, and consonant with all the more ancient temples of the Jains. It is an extensive saloon, the ceiling supported by a quadruple range of columns, those of the centre being surmounted by a range of vaulted coverings; while the lateral portion, which is flat, is divided into compartments of the most elaborate sculpture. But the columns are most worthy of attention; they are unique in design, and with the exception of the cave-temples, probably amongst the oldest now existing in India. On examining them, ideas entirely novel, even in Hindu [780]

[1] [Fergusson (*Hist. Indian Arch.* ii. 210 f.) says it was begun in A.D. 1200, and completed during the reign of Iyaltimish (1211–36). The temple may have been originally Jain, but it had been altered by Hindus.]

[2] [Cunningham searched in vain for the Sanskrit inscription. "I am inclined to believe that Tod may have mistaken some of the square Cufic writing for ancient Sanskrit. It is, indeed, possible that the square Cufic inscription which records the building of the mosque in A.H. 596 (A.D. 1200) may once have occupied the position described by Tod over the apex of the central arch" (*ASR*, ii. 262 f.).]

art, are developed. Like all these portions of Hindu architecture, their ornaments are very complex, and the observer will not fail to be struck with their dissimilarity; it was evidently a rule in the art to make the ornaments of every part unlike the other, and which I have seen carried to great extent. There may be forty columns but no two are alike. The ornaments of the base are peculiar, both as to form and execution; the lozenges, with the rich tracery surmounting them, might be transferred, not inappropriately, to the Gothic cathedrals of Europe. The projections from various parts of the shaft (which on a small scale may be compared to the corresponding projections of the columns in the Duomo at Milan), with the small niches still containing the statues, though occasionally mutilated, of the Pontiffs of the Jains, give them a character which strengthens the comparison, and which would be yet more apparent if we could afford to engrave the details.[1] The elegant Kamakumbha, the emblem of the Hindu Ceres, with its pendent palmyra-branches, is here lost, as are many emblematical ornaments, curious in design and elegant in their execution. Here and there occurs a righly carved corbeille, which still further sustains the analogy between the two systems of architecture; and the capitals are at once strong and delicate. The central vault, which is the largest, is constructed after the same fashion as that described at Nadol; but the concentric annulets, which in that are plain, in this are one blaze of ornaments, which with the whole of the ceiling is too elaborate and complicated for description. Under the most retired of the compartments, and nearly about the centre, is raised the mimbar, or pulpit, whence the Mulla enunciates the dogma of Muhammad, "there is but one God": and for which he dispossessed the Jain, whose creed was like his own, the unity of the Godhead. But this is in unison with the feeling which dictated the external metamorphosis. The whole is of the same materials as already described, from the quarries of the Aravalli close at hand, which are rich in every mineral as well as metallic production:—

> I ask'd of *Time* for whom *those* temples rose,
> That prostrate by his hand in silence lie;

---

[1] ["It is certain that they are not Jain pillars, as I found many four-armed figures sculptured on them, besides a single figure of the skeleton goddess, Kāli" (*ibid.* 259).]

His lips disdain'd the myst'ry to disclose,
And borne on swifter wing, he hurried by!
The broken columns *whose*? I ask'd of *Fame*:
(Her kindling breath gives life to works sublime;)
With downcast looks of mingled grief and shame,
She heaved the uncertain sigh, and follow'd *Time* [781].
Wrapt in amazement o'er the mouldering pile,
I saw *Oblivion* pass with giant stride;
And while his visage wore *Pride's* scornful smile,
Haply *thou know'st*, then tell me, *whose* I cried,
Whose these vast domes that ev'n in ruin shine?
I *reck not whose*, he said: they *now are mine*.

Shall we abandon them to cold 'oblivion'; or restore them to a name already mentioned, Samprati, or Swampriti, the Shah Jahan [1] of a period two centuries before the Christian era, and to whom the shrine in Kumbhalmer is ascribed? Of one thing there is no doubt, which is, that both are Jain, and of the most ancient models: and thus advertised, the antiquary will be able to discriminate between the architectural systems of the Saivas and the Jains, which are as distinct as their religions.

Having alluded to the analogy between the details in the columns and those in our Gothic buildings (as they are called), and surmised that the Saracenic arch is of Hindu origin; I may further, with this temple and screen before us, speculate on the possibility of its having furnished some hints to the architects of Europe. It is well known that the Saracenic arch has crept into many of those structures called Gothic, erected in the twelfth and thirteenth centuries, when a more florid style succeeded to the severity of the Saxon or Romans; but I believe it has been doubted whence the Saracens obtained their model; certainly it was neither from Egypt nor Persia. The early caliphs of Baghdad, who were as enlightened as they were powerful, kept alive the light of science when Europe was in darkness; and the most accomplished noble who accompanied our Cœur de Lion, though "brave as his sword," was a clown compared to the infidel Saladin, in mind as well as manners. The influence of these polished foes on European society it would be superfluous to descant upon. The lieutenants of these caliphs, who pene-

[1] Both epithets imply 'Lord of the Universe,' [?] and of which the name of Prithiraj, that of the last Chauhan emperor, is another version.

trated from the Delta of the Indus to the Ganges from four to five centuries prior to this event, when Walid's arms triumphed simultaneously on the Indus and the Ebro, produced no trifling results to the arts. This very spot, Ajmer, according to traditional couplets and the poetic legends of its ancient princes, the Chauhans, was visited by the first hostile force which Islam sent across the Indus, and to which Manika Rae fell a sacrifice. What ideas might not this Jain temple have afforded to [782] "the Light of Ali," for Roshan Ali is the name preserved of him who, "in ships landing at Anjar," marched through the very heart of India, and took Garh Bitli, the citadel of Ajmer, by assault. The period is one of total darkness in the history of India, save for the scattered and flickering rays which emanate from the chronicles of the Chauhans and Guhilots. But let us leave the temple, and slightly describe the castle of Manika Rae, on whose battlements an infidel's arrow of Roshan's army reached the heir of the Chauhan; since which Lot, for such was his name, has been adopted amongst the lares and penates of this celebrated race. This was the first Rajput blood which the arms of conversion shed, and the impression must have been strong to be thus handed down to posterity.

The mind, after all, retires dissatisfied: with me it might be from association. Even the gateway, however elegant, is unsuitable to the genius of the place. Separately considered, they are each magnificent; together, it is as if a modern sculptor were (like our actors of the last age) to adorn the head of Cato with a peruke. I left this precious relic, with a malediction upon all the spoilers of art—whether the Thane who pillaged Minerva's portico at Athens, or the Turk who dilapidated the Jain temple at Ajmer.[1]

Ajmer Fort.—The reader will see as much of this far-famed fortress as I did: for there was nothing to induce me to climb the steep, where the only temple visible was a modern-looking whitewashed mosque, lifting its dazzling minarets over the dingy antique towers of the Chauhan: "he who seven times captured the sultan, and seven times released him." The hill rises majestically from its base to the height of about eight hundred feet; its crest encircled by the ancient wall and towers raised by Ajaipal—

[1] Chance obtained me the drawing of this temple; I wish it had also given me the name of its author to grace the page.

FORTRESS AND TOWN OF AJMER.

To face page 900.

> There was a day when they were young and proud,
> Banners on high, and battles passed below;
> But they who fought are in a bloody shroud,
> And those which waved are shredless dust ere now,
> And the bleak battlements shall bear no future blow; [1]

unless the Cossack should follow the track of Roshan Ali or Mahmud, and try to tear the British flag from the *kunguras* of Ajmer. On the north side a party of the superintendent's were unlocking the latent treasures in the bowels of the mountain. The vein is of lead; a sulphuret, or galena [783].[2]

The Bisal Tālāb.—I have already mentioned the lake, called after the excavator, the Bisal Talab. It is about eight miles in circumference, and besides the beauty it adds to the vale of Ajmer, it has a source of interest in being the fountain of the Luni, which pursues its silent course until it unites with the eastern arm of the Delta of the Indus: the point of outlet is at the northern angle of the Daulat Bagh, 'the gardens of wealth,' built by Jahangir for his residence when he undertook to conquer the Rajputs. The water is not unwholesome, and there are three outlets at this fountainhead for the escape of the water fitting its periodical altitudes. The stream at its parent source is thence called the Sagarmati. It takes a sweep northward by Bhaonta and Pisangan, and close to where we crossed it, at Govindgarh, it is joined by the Sarasvati from Pushkar; when the united waters (at whose *sangam*, or confluence, there is a small temple to the manes) are called the Luni.

The gardens erected on the embankment of the lake must have been a pleasant abode for "the king of the world," while his lieutenants were carrying on the war against the Rana: but the imperial residence of marble, in which he received the submissions of that prince, through his grandson, and the first ambassador sent by England to the Mogul, are now going fast to decay. The walks on which his majesty last paraded, in the state-coach sent by our James the First, are now overgrown with shrubs.

The stratification of the rock, at the point of outlet, would

[1] *Childe Harold*, Canto iii. [47].

[2] [The Tāragarh hill is rich in lead, and iron and copper mines have been worked, but did not pay expenses. The lead is purer than European pig lead, but lack of fuel and cheap transport have driven it from the market. (Watson i. A. 60 f.)]

interest the geologist, especially an extensive vein of mica, adjoining another of almost transparent quartz.

Anasāgar Lake.—Eastward of this lake about a mile is another named the Anasagar, after the grandson of Bisaldeo, who has left the reputation of great liberality, and a contrast with Visala. The vestiges of an island are yet seen in the lake, and upon its margin; but the materials have been carried away by the Goths. There are two small buildings on the adjacent heights, called "the annulets of Khwaja Kutb," and some other saint.

Such are the wonders in the environs of Daru-l-Khair, "celebrated in the history of the Moguls, as well as of the Hindus." But my search for inscriptions to corroborate the legends of the Chauhans proved fruitless. I was, however, fortunate enough to add to my numismatic treasures some of the currency of these ancient kings, which give interest to a series of the same description, all appertaining [784] to the Buddhists or Jains. The inscription occupying one side is in a most antique character, the knowledge of which is still a desideratum: the reverse bears the effigies of a horse, the object of worship to the Indo-Scythic Rajput.[1] It is not improbable that the Agnikula Chauhan may have brought these letters with him from higher Asia. Researches in these countries for such monuments may yet discover how far this conjecture is correct. At Pushkar I also found some very ancient coins. Had the antiquary travelled these regions prior to the reign of Aurangzeb he would have had a noble field to explore: many coins were destroyed by this bigot, but many were buried underground, which time or accident may disclose. He was the great foe of Rajput fame; and well might the bard, in the words of the Cambrian minstrel, bid

> Ruin seize thee, ruthless king.

They did repay his cruelties by the destruction of his race. In one short century from this tyrant, who grasped each shore of the peninsula, the Mogul power was extinct; while the oppressed Rajputs are again on the ascendant. But the illiterate and mercenary Afghan, "the descendant of the lost tribes of Israel,"[2] if we credit their traditions, may share the iniquity with Aurangzeb:

[1] [Probably the "Bull and Horseman" type, see p. 809, above. The inscription is in Hindi characters.]

[2] They claim Ishmael as their common ancestor.

for they fulfilled literally a duty which their supposed forefathers pertinaciously refused, and made war against every graven image. Had they even spared us a few of the monsters, the joint conceptions of the poet and the sculptor, I might have presented some specimens of griffins (*gras*)[1] and demons almost of a classical taste: but the love of mischief was too strong even to let these escape: the shoe was applied to the prominent features of everything which represented animation.

By a medium of several meridian observations, I made the latitude of Ajmer 26° 19′ north; its longitude, by time and measurement from my fixed meridian, Udaipur, 74° 40′, nearly the position assigned to it by the father of Indian geography, the justly celebrated Rennell.[2]

Return March to Udaipur.—*December* 5.—At daybreak we left the towers of Manika Rae, enveloped in mist, and turned our horses' heads to the southward, on our return to Udaipur. While at Ajmer, I received accounts of the death of the prince of Kotah, and did intend to proceed direct to that capital, by Shahpura and Bundi; but my presence was desired by the Rana to repair the dilapidations which only two months' absence had [785] occasioned in the political fabric which I had helped to reconstruct. Other interesting objects intervened: one, a visit to the new castle of Bhimgarh, erecting in Merwara to overawe the Mers; the other to compose the feuds which raged between the sectarian merchants of the new mart, Bhilwara, and which threatened to destroy all my labour. We made two marches to Bhinai, in which there was nothing to record. Bhinai is the residence of a Rathor chieftain, whose position is rather peculiar. Being placed within the district of Ajmer, and paying an annual quit-rent to the British, he may consider the Company as his sovereign; but although this position precludes all political subordination to the chief of the race, the tie would be felt and acknowledged, on a lapse, in the anxiety for the usual *tika* of recognition to his successor, from the Raja of Marwar. I argue on knowledge of character and customs; though it is possible this individual case might be against me.

[1] [The *grāsda* or *sārdūla*, a figure of a horned lion or panther (Fergusson-Burgess, *Cave Temples of India*, 439).]

[2] [He was nearly right—Ajmer, 26° 27′ N. lat., 74° 37′ E. long.; Udaipur, 24° 35′ N. lat., 73° 42′ E. long.]

The castle of Bhinai is a picturesque object in these level plains; it is covered with the cactus, or prickly pear, so abundant on the east side of the Aravalli. This was anciently the residence of a branch of the Parihara princes of Mandor, when held as a fief of the Chauhans of Ajmer; and from it originated a numerous mixed class, called the Parihara Minas, a mixture of Rajput and aboriginal blood.

Deolia.—*December* 6.—Deolia, near the northern bank of the Khari, the present boundary of Ajmer and Mewar. From Ajmer to Deolia the direction of the road is S.S.E., and the distance forty miles. This important district in the political geography of Rajputana, which, with the posts of Nimach and Mhow, is the connecting link between the British dominions on the Jumna and in the Deccan, was obtained by cession from Sindhia in 1818. A glance at the map is sufficient to show its importance in our existing connexion with Rajputana. The greatest breadth of the district is between the Aravalli west and the Banas east, and measures about eight miles. The greatest length is between the city of Ajmer and Jhak, a post in Merwara, measuring about forty miles. The narrowest portion is that where we now are, Deolia, whence the Kishangarh frontier can be seen over a neck of land of about twelve miles in extent. Within these bounds a great portion of the land is held by feudal chieftains paying a quit-rent, which I believe is fixed. I had to settle a frontier dispute at Deolia, regarding the right of cultivating in the bed of the Khari, which produces very good melons. The soil of Ajmer cannot [786] be called rich, and is better adapted for the lighter than the richer grains. Marks of war and rapine were visible throughout.

Dābla.—*December* 7.—This town was a sub-fee of Banera; but the vassal, a Rathor, had learned habits of insubordination during Mahratta influence, which he could not or would not throw aside. In these he was further encouraged by his connexion by marriage with the old ruler of Kotah, who had exemplified his hostility to the Dabla vassal's liege lord by besieging his castle of Banera. Having so long disobeyed him, his Rajput blood refused to change with the times; and though he condescended, at the head of his twenty retainers, to perform homage on stated days, and take his allotted position in the Banera darbar, he refused to pay the quit-rent, to which numerous deeds proved

CASTLE OF BHINAI.

To face page 904.

his suzerain had a right. Months passed away in ineffectual remonstrances; it was even proposed that he should hold the inferior dependencies free of quit-rent, but pay those of Dabla. All being in vain, the demand was increased to the complete surrender of Dabla; which elicited a truly Rajput reply: "His head and Dabla were together." This obstinacy could not be tolerated; and he was told that though one would suffice, if longer withheld both might be required. Like a brave Rathor, he had defended it for months against a large Mahratta force, and hence Dabla was vauntingly called "the little Bharatpur." Too late he saw his error, but there was no receding; and though he at length offered a nazarana, through the mediation of the Kotah wakil, of 20,000 rupees, to obtain the Rana's investiture, it was refused and a surrender was insisted on. Being an important frontier-post, it was retained by the Rana, and compensation was made to Banera. Every interest was made for him through the Nestor of Kotah, but in vain; his obstinacy offered an example too pernicious to admit of the least retrocession, and Dabla was forthwith incorporated with the appanage of the heir-apparent, Jawan Singh.

Almost the whole of this, the Badnor division, of 360 townships, is occupied by Rathors, the descendants of those who accompanied Jaimall to Mewar: the proportion of feudal to fiscal land therein is as three to one. It is a rich and fertile tract, and it is to be hoped will maintain in ease and independence the brave men who inhabit it, and who have a long time been the sport of rapine.

I received a visit from the chief vassal of the Badnor chief, then at the capital; and as I found it impossible to visit Merwara, I subsequently deputed Captain [787] Waugh who was hospitably received and entertained at Badnor. He hunted, and played the Holi with the old baron, who shows at all times the frankness of his race: but it being the period of the Saturnalia, he was especially unreserved; though he was the greatest stickler for etiquette amongst my many friends, and was always expatiating on the necessity of attending to the gradations of rank.

Banera.—*December* 8.—The castle of Banera is one of the most imposing feudal edifices of Mewar, and its lord one of the greatest of its chieftains. He not only bears the title of Raja, but has all the state-insignia attached thereto. His name happens to be the same as that of his sovereign—his being Raja Bhim, the prince's Rana Bhim,—to whom he is nearly related, and but for blind chance might have been lord of all the Sesodias. It may be recollected that the chivalrous antagonist of Aurangzeb, the heroic Rana Raj, had two sons, twins, if we may so term sons simultaneously born, though by different mothers. The incident which decided the preference of Jai Singh to Bhim has been related;[1] the circumstance of the latter's abandoning his country to court fortune under the Imperial standard—his leading his Rajput contingent amongst the mountains of Kandahar—and his death by dislocation of the spine, through urging his horse at speed amongst the boughs of a tree. The present incumbent of Banera is the descendant of that Raja Bhim, who was succeeded in the honours of his family by his son Suraj, killed whilst heading his contingent at the storm of Bijapur. The infant son of Suraj had four districts assigned to him, all taken from his suzerain, the Rana. In such esteem did the emperor hold the family, that the son of Suraj was baptized Sultan. He was succeeded by Sardar Singh, who, on the breaking up of the empire, came under the allegiance of his rightful sovereign the Rana. Rae Singh and Hamir Singh complete the chain to my friend Raja Bhim, who did me the honour to advance two miles from Banera to welcome and conduct me to his castle. Here I had a good opportunity of observing the feudal state and manners of these chiefs within their own domains during a visit of three hours at Banera. I was, moreover, much attached to Raja Bhim, who was a perfectly well-bred and courteous gentleman, and who was quite unreserved with me. From his propinquity to the reigning family, and from his honours and insignia being the gift of the king's, he had been an object of jealousy to the court, which tended much to retard the restoration [788] of his authority over his sub-vassals of Banera; the chief of Dabla is one instance of this. I found little difficulty in banishing the discord between him and his sovereign, who chiefly complained of the Banera kettle-drums beating, not only as he entered the city, but as far as the Porte—the sacred Tripolia; and the use of Chamar[2] in his presence. It was arranged that these emblems of honour, emanating from the great foes of Mewar, should never be obtruded

[1] See Vol. I. p. 456.

[2] [The yak tail, one of the insignia of royalty.]

on the eye or ear of the Rana; though within his own domain the Banera chieftain might do as he pleased. This was just; and Raja Bhim had too much good sense not to conciliate his "brother and cousin," Rana Bhim, by such a concession, which otherwise might have been insisted upon. The estate of Banera is in value 80,000 rupees of annual rent, one-half of which is in subinfeudations, his vassals being chiefly Rathors. The only service performed by Raja Bhim is the contributing a quota for the commercial mart of Bhilwara, with the usual marks of subordination, personal duty and homage to the Rana. His estate is much impoverished from its lying in the very track of the freebooters; but the soil is excellent, and time will bring hands to cultivate it, if we exercise a long and patient indulgence.

The 'velvet cushion' was spread in a balcony projecting from the main hall of Banera; here the Raja's vassals were mustered, and he placed me by his side on the *gaddi*. There was not a point of his rural or domestic economy upon which he did not descant, and ask my advice, as his "adopted brother." I was also made umpire between him and my old friend the baron of Badnor, regarding a marriage settlement, the granddaughter of the latter being married to the heir of Banera. I had, besides, to wade through old grants and deeds to settle the claims between the Raja and several of his sub-vassals; a long course of disorder having separated them so much from each other as to obliterate their respective rights. All these arbitrations were made without reference to my official situation, but were forced upon me merely by the claims of friendship; but it was a matter of exultation to be enabled to make use of my influence for the adjustment of such disputes, and for restoring individual as well as general prosperity. My friend prepared his gifts at parting; I went through the forms of receiving, but waived accepting them: which may be done without any offence to delicacy. I have been highly gratified to read the kind reception he gave to the respected Bishop Heber, in his tour through Mewar. I wonder, however, that this discerning and elegant-minded man did not [789] notice the peculiar circumstance of the Raja's teeth being fixed in with gold wire, which produces rather an unpleasant articulation.[1]

[1] [Bishop Heber writes: "He was an elderly man, and had lost many teeth, which made it very difficult for me to understand him" (*Narrative of a Journey*, ed. 1861, ii. 55).]

Banera adjoins the estates of the Rathors, and is no great distance from those of the Sangawats and Jagawats, which lie at the base of the Aravalli. All require a long period of toleration and unmolested tranquillity to emerge from their impoverished condition. My friend accompanied me to my tents, when I presented to him a pair of pistols, and a telescope with which he might view his neighbours on the mountains: we parted with mutual satisfaction, and I believe, mutual regret.

Bhīlwāra.—*December* 9.—I encamped about half-a-mile from *our* good town of Bhilwara, which was making rapid strides to prosperity, notwithstanding drawbacks from sectarian feuds; with which, however, I was so dissatisfied, that I refused every request to visit the town until such causes of retardation were removed. I received a deputation from both parties at my tents, and read them a lecture for their benefit, in which I lamented the privation of the pleasure of witnessing their unalloyed prosperity. Although I reconciled them to each other, I would not confide in their promises until months of improvement should elapse. They abided by their promise, and I fulfilled mine when the death of the Bundi prince afforded an opportunity, *en route* to that capital, to visit them. My reception was far too flattering to describe, even if this were the proper place. The sentiments they entertained for me had suffered no diminution when Bishop Heber visited the town. But his informant (one of the merchants), when he said it ought to have been called Tod-ganj, meant that it was so intended, and actually received this appellation: but it was changed, at my request, and on pain of withdrawing my entire support from it. The Rana, who used to call it himself in conversation "*Tod Sahib ki basti*," would have been gratified; but it would have been wrong to avail myself of his partiality. In all I was enabled to do, from my friendship, not from my official character, I always feared the dangers to his independence from such precedent for interference.[1]

Māndalgarh.—*December* 10.—I deviated from the direct course *homewards* (to Udaipur) to visit this beautiful spot, formerly the head of a flourishing district; but all was dilapidated. The first revenue derived from Mandal was expended on the repairs of the dam of its lake, which irrigates a great extent of rice-land. The Goths had felled [790] most of the fine trees which had ornamented

[1] See Vol. I. p. 562.

its dam and margin ; and several garden-houses, as well as that on the island in the lake, were in ruins. Not many years ago a column of victory, said to have been raised by Bisaladeva of Ajmer, in consequence of a victory over the Guhilots, graced this little isle. Mandal is now rising from its ruins, and one of the exiles was so fortunate as to find a vessel containing several pieces of gold and ornaments, in excavating the ruins of his ancient abode, though not buried by him. It involved the question of manorial rights, of which the Rana waived the enforcement, though he asserted them. To-day I passed between Pansal and Arja, the former still held by a Saktawat, the latter now united to the fisc. I have already related the feud between the Saktawats and the Purawats in the struggle for Arja, which is one of the most compact castles in Mewar, with a domain of 52,000 bighas, or 12,000 acres, attached to it, rendering it well worth a contest ; but the Saktawat had no right there, say the Purawats ; and in fact it is in the very heart of their lands.

Pur.—*December* 11.—This is one of the oldest towns of Mewar, and if we credit tradition, anterior in date to Vikrama. We crossed the Kotasari to and from Mandal, passing by the tin and copper mines of Dariba, and the Purawat estate of Pitawas. Pur means, *par eminence*, 'the city,' and anciently the title was admissible ; even now it is one of the chief fiscal towns. It is in the very heart of the canton, inhabited by the Babas, or 'infants' of Mewar, embracing a circle of about twenty-five miles diameter. The broken chain of mountains, having Banera on the northern point and Gurla to the south, passes transversely through this domain, leaving the estate of Bagor, the residence of Sheodan Singh, west, and extending to the S.E. to Mangrop, across the Berach. The policy which dictated the establishment of an isolated portion of the blood-royal of Mewar in the very centre of the country was wise ; for the Babas rarely or ever mix with the politics of the feudatory chieftains, home or foreign. They are accordingly entrusted with the command of all garrisons, and head the feudal quotas as the representative of their sovereign. They have a particular seat at court, the Baba ka Ol being distinct from the chieftains', and in front. Though they inhabit the lands about Pur, it is not from these they derive their name, but as descendants from Puru, one of the twenty-five sons of Rana Udai Singh, that blot in the scutcheon of Mewar [791].

Garnets.—About a mile east of Pur there is an isolated hill of blue slate, in which I found garnets embedded. I have no doubt persevering adventurers would be rewarded; but though I tried them with the hammer, I obtained none of any value. They are also to be obtained on the southern frontier of Kishangarh and Ajmer, about Sarwar. I received the visits of the 'infants' of Gurla and Gadarmala, both most respectable men, and enjoying good estates, with strong castles, which I passed the next day.

Rāsmi, on the Banās River.—*December* 12.—We had a long march through the most fertile lands of Mewar, all belonging to the Rana's personal domain. The progress towards prosperity is great; of which Rasmi, the head of a tappa or subdivision of a district, affords evidence, as well as every village. On our way we were continually met by peasants with songs of joy, and our entrance into each village was one of triumph. The Patels and other rustic officers, surrounded by the ryots, came out of the villages; while the females collected in groups, with brass vessels filled with water gracefully resting on their heads, stood at the entrance, their scarfs half-covering their faces, chaunting the *suhela*; a very ancient custom of the Hindu cultivator on receiving the superior, and tantamount to an acknowledgment of supremacy. Whether vanity was flattered, or whether a better sentiment was awakened, on receiving such tokens of gratitude, it is not for me to determine: the sight was pleasing, and the custom was general while I travelled in Mewar. The females bearing the *kalas* on their heads, were everywhere met with. These were chiefly the wives and daughters of the cultivators, though not unfrequently those of the Rajput sub-vassals. The former were seldom very fair, though they had generally fine eyes and good persons. We met many fragments of antiquity at Rasmi. Captain Waugh and the doctor were gratified with angling in the Banas for trout; but as the fish would not rise to the fly, I set the net, and obtained several dozens: the largest measured seventeen inches, and weighed seventy rupees, or nearly two pounds.

Merta.—*December* 16.—After an absence of two months we terminated our circuitous journey, and encamped on the ground whence we started, all rejoiced at the prospect of again entering "the happy valley." We made four marches across the *duab*, watered by the Berach and Banas rivers; the land naturally rich,

SOURCE OF THE BERACH RIVER, AND HUNTING SEAT OF THE RĀNA.

To face page 910.

and formerly boasting some large towns, but as yet only disclosing the germs of [792] prosperity. There is not a more fertile tract in India than this, which would alone defray the expenses of the court if its resources were properly husbanded. But years must first roll on, and the peasant must meet with encouragement, and a reduction of taxation to the lowest rate; and the lord-paramount must alike be indulgent in the exaction of his tribute. Our camels were the greatest sufferers in the march through the desert, and one-half were rendered useless. I received a deputation conveying the Rana's congratulation on my return 'home,' with a letter full of friendship and importunities to see me; but the register of the heavens—an oracle consulted by the Rajput as faithfully as Moore's Almanack by the British yeoman—showed an unlucky aspect, and I must needs halt at Merta, or in the valley, until the signs were more favourable to a re-entry into Udaipur. Here we amused ourselves in chalking out the site of our projected residence on the heights of Tus, and in fishing at the source of the Berach. Of this scene I present the reader with a view; and if he allows his imagination to ascend the dam which confines the waters of the lake, he may view the Udaisagar, with its islets; and directing his eye across its expanse, he may gain a bird's-eye view of the palace of the Kaisar of the Sesodias. The dam thrown across a gorge of the mountains is of enormous magnitude and strength, as is necessary, indeed, to shut in a volume of water twelve miles in circumference. At its base, the point of outlet, is a small hunting-seat of the Rana's, going to decay for want of funds to repair it, like all those on the Tiger Mount and in the valley. Nor is there any hope that the revenues, burthened as they are with the payment of a clear fourth in tribute, can supply the means of preventing further dilapidation.

December 19.—Tired of two days' idleness, we passed through the portals of Debari on our way to Ar, to which place the Rana signified his intention of advancing in person, to receive and conduct me 'home': an honour as unlooked-for and unsolicited as it was gratifying. Udaipur presents a most imposing appearance when approached from the east. The palace of the Rana, and that of the heir-apparent, the great temple, and the houses of the nobles, with their turrets and cupolas rising in airy elegance, afford a pleasing contrast with the heavy wall and pierced battlements of the city beneath. This wall is more extensive than solid. To remedy this want of strength, a chain of fortresses has [793] been constructed, about gunshot from it, commanding every road leading thereto, which adds greatly to the effect of the landscape. These castellated heights contain places of recreation, one of which belongs to Salumbar; but all wear the same aspect of decay.

Ahār.—Ar, or Ahar,[1] near which we encamped, is sacred to the manes of the princes of Udaipur, and contains the cenotaphs of all her kings since the valley became their residence; but as they do not disdain association, either in life or death, with their vassals, Ar presents the appearance of a thickly crowded cemetery, in which the mausoleums of the Ranas stand pre-eminent in "the place of great faith."[2] The renowned Amra Singh's is the most conspicuous; but the cenotaphs of all the princes, down to the father of Rana Bhim, are very elegant, and exactly what such structures ought to be; namely, vaulted roofs, supported by handsome columns raised on lofty terraces, the architraves of enormous single blocks, all of white marble, from the quarries of Kankroli. There are some smaller tombs of a singularly elaborate character, and of an antiquity which decides the claims of Ar to be considered as the remains of a very ancient city. The ground is strewed with the wrecks of monuments and old temples, which have been used in erecting the sepulchres of the Ranas. The great city was the residence of their ancestors, and is said to have been founded by Asaditya upon the site of the still more ancient capital of Tambavatinagari, where dwelt the Tuar ancestors of Vikramaditya, before he obtained Avinti, or Ujjain. From Tambavatinagari its name was changed to Anandpur, 'the happy city,' and at length to Ahar, which gave the patronymic to the Guhilot race, namely, Aharya. The vestiges of immense mounds still remain to the eastward, called the Dhul-kot, or 'fort,' destroyed by 'ashes' (*dhul*) of a volcanic eruption. Whether the lakes of the valley owe their origin to the same cause which is said to have destroyed the ancient Ahar, a more skilful geologist must determine. The chief road from the city is cut through this mound; and as I had observed fragments of sculpture and pottery on the excavated sides, I commenced a regular opening of the mound in search of medals, and obtained a few with the

[1] [See p. 924.] [2] [The Mahāsati.]

effigies of an animal, which I fancied to be a lion, but others the *gadha*, or ass, attributed to Gandharvasen, the brother of Vikrama, who placed this impress on his coins, the reason of which is given in a long legend.[1] My impious intentions were soon checked by some designing knaves about the Rana, and I would not offend [794] superstition. But the most superficial observer will pronounce Ar to have been an ancient and extensive city, the walls which enclose this sepulchral abode being evidently built with the sculptured fragments of temples. Some shrines, chiefly Jain, are still standing, though in the last stage of dilapidation, and they have been erected from the ruins of shrines still older, as appears from the motley decorations, where statues and images are inserted with their heads reversed, and Mahavira and Mahadeva come into actual contact: all are in white marble. Two inscriptions were obtained; one very long and complete, in the nail-headed character of the Jains; but their interpretation is yet a desideratum. A topographical map of this curious valley would prove interesting, and for this I have sufficient materials. The Teli-ki-Sarai would not be omitted in such a map, as adding another to the many instances I have met with, among this industrious class, to benefit their fellow-citizens. The 'Oilman's Caravanserai' is not conspicuous for magnitude; but it is remarkable, not merely for its utility, but even for its elegance of design. It is equi-distant from each of the lakes. The Teli-ka-Pul, or 'Oilman's Bridge,' at Nurabad, is, however, a magnificent memorial of the trade, and deserves preservation; and as I shall not be able now to describe the region (Gwalior) where it stands, across the Asan, I will substitute it for the Sarai, of which I have no memorial.[2] These Telis (oilmen) perambulate the country

[1] [These rude Indo-Sassanian coins, also known as Tātariya dirhams, are popularly called Gadhiya paisa, or "ass copper money," because the worn-down representation of a fire temple was believed to be the head of an ass (Cunningham, *Ancient Geography*, 313; Elliot-Dowson i. 3, note; *BG*, i. Part i. 469, note). Gandharvasen, as a punishment for offending Indra, was condemned to assume the form of an ass during the day: he consorted with a princess, and their offspring was Vikramāditya (*Asiatic Researches*, vi. 35 f.; W. Ward, *The Hindoos*, 2nd ed. i. 22).]

[2] [Nūrābād is on the old road from Agra to Gwalior, 63 miles S. of the former, and 15 miles N. of the latter. "There is a fair sketch of the bridge in Tod's 'Rajasthan,' which, however, scarcely does justice to it, as it is deficient in those architectural details which form the most pleasing part of the structure" (*ASR*, ii. 397).]

with skins of oil on a bullock, and from hard-earned pence erect the structures which bear their name. India owes much to individual munificence.

The planets were adverse to my happy conjunction with the Sun of the Hindus: and it was determined that I should pass another day amongst the tombs of Ahar; but I invoked upon my own devoted head all the evil consequences, as in this case I was the only person who was threatened. To render this opposition to the decree less noxious, it was agreed that I should make my *entrée* by the southern, not by the eastern portc, that of the sun. The Rana came, attended by his son, his chiefs, his ministers, and, in fact, all the capital in his train. The most hearty welcomes were lavished upon us all. "*Rama! Rama! Tod Sahib!*" (the Hindu greeting) resounded from a thousand throats, while I addressed each chief by name. It was not a meeting of formality, but of well-cemented friendship. My companions, Captain Waugh and Dr. Duncan, were busy interchanging smiles and cordial greetings, when the Rana, requesting our presence at the palace next day [795], bade us adieu. He took the direct road to his palace, while we, to avoid evil spirits, made a detour by the southern portal, to gain our residence, the garden of Rampiyari.

APPENDIX

Translations of Inscriptions, chiefly in the Nail-headed character of the Takshak Races and Jains, fixing eras in Rajput history.[1]

No. I

Memorial of a Gete or Jit prince of the fifth century, discovered 1820, in a temple at Kunswa, near the Chumbul river, south of Kotah.

May the Jit'ha be thy protector! What does this Jit'h resemble? which is the vessel of conveyance across the waters

[1] [The Inscriptions quoted in this appendix have been reprinted as they stand in the original text: partly, because it would have been necessary

BRIDGE OF NŪRĀBĀD.

To face page 914.

of life, which is partly white, partly red? Again, what does it resemble, where the hissing-angered serpents dwell? What may this Jit'ha be compared to, from whose root the roaring flood descends? Such is the Jit'h; by it may thou be preserved (1).

The fame of RAJA JIT I now shall tell, by whose valour the lands of SALPOORA (2) are preserved. The fortunes of Raja Jit are as flames of fire devouring his foe. The mighty warrior JIT SALINDRA (2) is beautiful in person, and from the strength of his arm esteemed the first amongst the tribes of the mighty; make resplendent, as does the moon the earth, the dominions of SALPOORI. The whole world praises the JIT prince, who enlarges the renown of his race, sitting in the midst of haughty warriors, like the lotos in the waters, the moon of the sons of men. The foreheads of the princes of the earth worship the toe of his foot. Beams of light irradiate his countenance, issuing from the gems of his arms of strength. Radiant is his array; his riches abundant; his mind generous and profound as the ocean. Such is he of SARYA (3) race, a tribe renowned amongst the tribes of the mighty, whose princes were ever foes to treachery, to whom the earth surrendered her fruits, and who added the lands of their foes to their own. By sacrifice, the mind of this lord of men has been purified; fair are his territories, and fair is the FORTRESS OF TAK'HYA (4). The string of whose bow is dreaded, whose wrath is the reaper of the field of combat; but to his dependents he is as the pearl on the neck; who makes no account of the battle, though streams of blood run through the field. As does the silver lotos bend its head before the fierce rays of the sun, so does his foe stoop to him, while the cowards abandon the field [796].

From this lord of men (*Narpati*) SÁLINDRA sprung DEVANGLI, whose deeds are known even at *this remote period*.

From him was born SUMBOOKA, and from him DEGALI, who married two wives of YADU race (5), and by one a son named VIRA NARINDRA, pure as a flower from the fountain.

Amidst groves of *amba*, on whose clustering blossoms hang myriads of bees, that the wearied traveller might repose, was this edifice erected. May it, and the fame of its founder, continue while ocean rolls, or while the moon, the sun, and hills endure. Samvat 597.—On the extremity of MALWA, this minster (MINDRA) was erected, on the banks of the river TAVELI, by SALICHANDRA (6), son of VIRACHANDRA.

Whoever will commit this writing to memory, his sins will be obliterated. Carved by the sculptor SEVANARYA, son of DWARASIVA, and composed by BUTENA, chief of the bards.

---

to discard the Author's versions, and to replace them by the translations of recent scholars; partly, as an example of the Author's methods of translation and annotation. With the help of Mr. Vincent A. Smith and Pandit Gaurishankar Ojha of the Rājputāna Museum, Ajmer, references have been added to modern translations of the Inscriptions.]

(*Note* 1).—In the prologue to this valuable relic, which superficially viewed would appear a string of puerilities, we have conveyed in mystic allegory the mythological origin of the Jit or Gete race. From the members of the chief of the gods ISWARA or Mahadeva, *the god of battle*, many races claim birth: the warrior from his arms; the Charun from his spine; the prophetic Bhat (*Vates*) from his tongue; and the Gete or Jit derive theirs from his tiara, which, formed of his own hair, is called *Jit'ha*. In this tiara, serpents, emblematic of TIME (kal) and DESTRUCTION, are wreathed; also implicative that the *Jits*, who are of *Takshac*, or the serpent race, are thereby protected. The "roaring flood" which descends from this *Jit'ha* is the river goddess, Ganga, daughter of Mena, wife of Iswara. The mixed colour of his hair, which is partly white, partly of reddish (*panduranga*) hue, arises from his character of ARD'HNARI, or Hermaphroditus. All these characteristics of the god of war must have been brought by the Scythic Gete from the Jaxartes, where they worshipped him as the Sun (*Balnat'h*) and as XAMOLSCIS (*Yama*, vulg. *Jama*) the infernal divinity.

The 12th chapter of the Edda, in describing BALDER the second son of Odin, particularly dwells on the beauty of his hair, whence "the *whitest of all vegetables is called the eyebrow of Balder, on the columns of whose temples there are verses engraved, capable of recalling the dead to life*."

How perfectly in unison is all this of the Jits of Jutland and the Jits of Rajast'han. In each case the hair is the chief object of admiration; of Balnath as Balder, and the magical effect of the Runes is not more powerful than that attached by the chief of the Scalds of our Gete prince at the end of this inscription, fresh evidences in support of my hypothesis, that many of the Rajpoot races and Scandinavians have a common origin—that origin, Central Asia.

(*Note* 2).—Salpoora is the name of the capital of this Jit prince, and his epithet of Sal-indra is merely titular, as the Indra, or lord of Sal-poori, 'the city of Sal,' which the fortunate discovery of an inscription raised by Komarpal, king of Anhulwarra (*Nehrwalla* of D'Anville), dated S. 1207, has enabled me to place "at the base of the Sewaluk Mountains." In order to elucidate this point, and to give the full value to this record of the Jit princes of the Punjab, I append (No. V.) a translation of the Nehrwalla conqueror's inscription, which will prove beyond a doubt that these JIT princes of SALPOORI in the *Punjab* were the leaders of that very colony of the Yuti from the Jaxartes, who in the fifth century, as recorded by De Guignes, crossed the Indus and possessed themselves of the Punjab; and strange to say, have again risen to power, for the Sikhs (*disciples*) of Nanuk are almost all of Jit origin.

(*Note* 3).—Here this Jit is called of SARYA SAC'HA, *branch* or *ramification* of the *Saryas*: a very ancient race which is noticed by the genealogists synonymously with the SARIASPA, one of the thirty-six royal races, and very probably the same as the SARWYA of the Komarpal Charitra, with the distinguished epithet "the flower of the martial races" (*Sarwya c'shatrya tyn Sar*).

(*Note* 4).—"The fortress of Takshac." Whether this TAKSHACNAGARI, or castle of the Tâk, is the [797] stronghold of SALPOORI, or the name given to a conquest in the environs of the place, whence this inscription, we can only surmise, and refer the reader to what has been said of Takitpoora. As I have repeatedly said, the Tâks and Jits are one race.

(*Note* 5).—As the Jits intermarried with the Yadus at this early period, it is evident they had forced their way amongst the thirty-six royal races, though they have again lost this rank. No Rajpoot would give a daughter to a Jit, or take one from them to wife.

(*Note* 6).—Salichandra is the sixth in descent from the first-named prince, JIT SALINDRA, allowing twenty-two years to each descent = 132—S. 597, date of ins. = S. 465 - 56 = A.D. 409; the period of the colonization of the Punjab by the Getes, Yuti, or Jits, from the Jaxartes.[1]

No. II

Translation of an inscription in the Nail-headed character relative to the Jit race, discovered at Ram Chundrapoora, six miles east of Boondee, in digging a well. It was thence conveyed, and deposited by me in the Museum of the Royal Asiatic Society.

To my foe, salutation! This foe of the race of JIT, CATHIDA (1), how shall I describe, who is resplendent by the favour of the round bosom of ROODRANI (2), and whose ancestor, the warrior TUKHYA (3), formed the garland on the neck of Mahadeva. Better than this foe on the earth's surface, there is none; therefore to him I offer salutation. The sparkling gems on the coronets of kings irradiate the nail of his foot.

Of the race of BOTENA (4) RAJA T'HOT was born; his fame expanded through the universe.

[1] [This Inscription is on a stone built into a wall of a temple of Mahādeva, at Kanaswa, near Kotah. The Author's "Jit prince" of Sālpur is due to a misunderstanding, and in all probability owes its origin to the words *Sambhor-jjatā*, 'the matted hair of Sambhu,' a title of Siva, in line 2 of the Inscription. The Inscription begins with verses in honour of Siva as Sambhu and Sthānu, and glorifies the Maurya race, and a king of that race named Dhavala. Dhavala had as his friend a prince of the Brāhman caste, named Sankuka, whose wife, Degini, bore to him the prince Sivagana, who built a temple to Siva, and endowed it with the revenues of two villages. The date is A.D. 738-9 (*IA*, xix. 55 ff.).]

Pure in mind, strong in arm, and beloved by mankind, such was CHANDRASEN (5). How shall he be described, who broke the strength of his foe, on whom when his sword swims in fight, he appears like a magician. With his subjects he interchanged the merchandise of liberality, of which he reaped the fruits. From him whose history is fair, was born KRITIKA, the deeds of whose arm were buds of renown, forming a necklace of praise in the eyes of mankind. His queen was dear to him as his own existence—how can she be described ? As the flame is inseparable from the fire, so was she from her lord—she was the light issuing from the sun—her name GOON-NEWASA (6), and her actions corresponded with her name. By her he had two sons, like gems set in bracelets, born to please mankind. The eldest was named SOOKUNDA, the younger DERUKA. Their fortunes consumed their foes: but their dependents enjoyed happiness. As the flowers of Calp-vricsha are beloved by the gods, so are these brothers by their subjects, granting their requests, and increasing the glory of the race, whence they sprung.—[A useless descriptive stanza left out (7).]

DERUKA had a son, KUHLA, and his was DHUNIKA, whose deeds ascended high—who could fathom the intentions of mankind—whose mind was deep as the ocean—whose ever-hungry faulchion expelled from their mountains and forests the MEENA tribes, leaving them no refuge in the three wolds, levelling their retreats to the ground. His quiver was filled with crescent-formed arrows—his sword the climber (*vela*) (8), of which pearls are the fruit. With his younger brother Dewaka he reverences gods and Brahmins—and with his own wealth perfumed a sacrifice to the sun [798].

For the much-beloved's (his wife) pleasure this was undertaken. Now the river of ease, life and death, is crossed over, for this abode will devour the body of the foe, into which the west wind wafts the fragrant perfume from the sandal-covered bosom of Lacshmi (9) ; while from innumerable lotos the gale from the east comes laden with aroma, the hum of the bees as they hang clustering on the flowers of the *padhul* is pleasing to the ear.

So long as Soomeru stands on its base of golden sands, so long may this dwelling endure. So long as the wind blows on the *koonjeris* (10), supporters of the globe, while the firmament endures, or while Lacshmi (11) causes the palm to be extended, so long may his praise and this edifice be stable.

KUHLA (12) formed this abode of virtue, and east thereof a temple to Iswara. By ACHIL, son of the mighty prince YASOOVERMA (13), has its renown been composed in various forms of speech.

(*Note* 1).—*Qu.* if this Jit is from (*da*, the mark of the genitive case) Cathay ? the land of the *Cat'hae* foes of Alexander, and probably of the Cathi of the Saurashtra peninsula, alike Scythic as the Jit, and probably the same race originally ?

(*Note* 2).—Roodrani, an epithet of the martial spouse of Harar-Siva, the god of war, whom the Jit in the preceding inscription invokes.

(*Note* 3).—Here we have another proof of the Jit being of Takshac race ; this at the same time has a mythological reference to the serpent (*takhya*), which forms the garland of the warlike divinities.

(*Note* 4).—Of this race I have no other notice, unless it should mean the race (*cula*) was from *Butan*.

(*Note* 5).—Chandrasen is celebrated in the history of the Pramaras as the founder of several cities, from two of which, *Chandrabhaga*, at the foot of the central plateau of India, in Northern Malwa, and CHANDRAVATI, the ruins of which I discovered at the foot of the Aravulli near Aboo, I possess several valuable memoria, which will, ere long, confirm the opinions I have given of the *Takshac* architect.

(*Note* 6).—The habitation of virtues.

(*Note* 7).—This shows these foresters always had the same character.

(*Note* 8).—Vela is the climber or ivy, sacred to Mahadeva.

(*Note* 9).—Lacshmi, the *apsara* or sea-nymph, is feigned residing amongst the waters of the lotos-covered lake. In the hot weather the Rajpoot ladies dip their corsets into an infusion of sandal-wood, hence the metaphor.

(*Note* 10).—Koonjiris are the elephants who support the eight corners of the globe.

(*Note* 11).—Lacshmi is also dame Fortune, or the goddess of riches, whence this image.

(*Note* 12).—Kuhl is the fifth in descent from the *opponent* of the Jit.

(*Note* 13).—Without this name this inscription would have been but of half its value. Fortunately various inscriptions on stone and copper, procured by me from Oojein, settled the era of the death of this prince in S. 1191, which will alike answer for Achil, his son, who was most likely one of the chieftains of KUHLA, who appears to have been of the elder branch of the Pramaras, the foe of the Jit invaders [799].

No. III

Inscription in the Nail-headed character of the Mori Princes of Cheetore, taken from a column on the banks of the lake Mansurwur, near that city.

By the lord of waters may thou be protected ! What is there

which resembles the ocean? on whose margin the red buds of honey-yielding trees are eclipsed by swarms of bees, whose beauty expands with the junction of numerous streams. What is like the ocean, inhaling the perfume of the Paryata (1), who was compelled to yield as tribute, wine, wealth, and ambrosia (2)? Such is the ocean!—may he protect thee.

Of a mighty gift, this is the memorial. This lake enslaves the minds of beholders, over whose expanse the varied feathered tribe skim with delight, and whose banks are studded with every kind of tree. Falling from the lofty-peaked mountain, enhancing the beauty of the scene, the torrent rushes to the lake. The mighty sea-serpent (3), o'erspent with toil in the churning of the ocean, repaired to this lake for repose.

On this earth's surface was Maheswara (4), a mighty prince, during whose sway the name of foe was never heard; whose fortune was known to the eight quarters (5); on whose arm victory reclined for support. He was the light of the land. The praises of the race of TWAST'HA (6) were determined by Brahma's own mouth.

Fair, filled with pride, sporting amidst the shoals of the lotos, is the swan fed by his hand, from whose countenance issue rays of glory: such was RAJA BHEEM (7), a skilful swimmer in the ocean of battle, even to where the Ganges pours in her flood (8) did he go, whose abode is *Avanti* (9). With faces resplendent as the moon, on whose lips yet marked with the wound of their husband's teeth, the captive wives of his foes, even in their hearts does Raja Bheem dwell. By his arm he removed the apprehensions of his enemies; he considered them as errors to be expunged. He appeared as if created of fire. He could instruct even the navigator (10) of the ocean.

From him was descended Raja BHOJ (11). How shall he be described; he, who in the field of battle divided with his sword the elephant's head, the pearl from whose brain (12) now adorns his breast; who devours his foe as does RAHOO (13) the sun or moon, who to the verge of space erected edifices in token of victory?

From him was a son whose name was MAUN, who was surcharged with good qualities, and with whom fortune took up her abode. One day he met an aged man: his appearance made him reflect that his frame was as a shadow, evanescent; that the spirit which did inhabit it was like the seed of the scented *Kadama* (14); that the riches of royalty were brittle as a blade of grass; and that man was like a lamp exposed in the light of day. Thus ruminating, for the sake of his race who had gone before him, and for the sake of good works, he made this lake, whose waters are expansive and depth unfathomable. When I look on this ocean-like lake, I ask myself, if it may not be this which is destined to cause the final doom (15).

The warriors and chiefs of RAJA MAUN (16) are men of skill and valour—pure in their lives and faithful. RAJA MAUN is a heap of virtues—the chief who enjoys his favour may court all the gifts of fortune. When the head is inclined on his lotos foot, the grain of sand which adheres becomes an ornament thereto. Such is the lake, shaded with trees, frequented by birds, which the man of fortune, SRIMAN RAJA MAUN, with great labour formed. By the name of its lord (*Maun*), that of the lake (*surwur*) is known to the world. By him versed in the *alankara*, PUSHHA, the son of NAGA BHUT, these stanzas have been framed. *Seventy had elapsed beyond seven hundred years* (*Samvatisir*), when the lord of men, the KING OF MALWA (17) formed this lake. By SEVADIT, grandson of KHETRI KARUG, were these lines cut [800].

(*Note* 1).—The Paryata is also called the Har-singar, or '*ornament of the neck*,' its flowers being made into collars and bracelets. Its aroma is very delicate, and the blossom dies in a few hours.

(*Note* 2).—*Imrita*, the food of the immortals, obtained at the churning of the ocean. The contest for this amongst the gods and demons is well known. *Vrishpati*, or Sookra, regent of the planet Venus, on this occasion lost an eye; and hence this Polyphemus has left the nickname of *Sookracharya* to all who have but one eye.

(*Note* 3).—His name *Matolae*.

(*Note* 4).—A celebrated name in the genealogies of the TAKSHAC *Pramara*, of which the *Mori* is a conspicuous *Sac'ha* or branch. He was the founder of the city of *Maheswar*, on the southern bank of the Nehrbudda, which commands the ford leading from *Awinti* and *Dhar* (the chief cities of the Mori Pramaras) to the Dekhan.

(*Note* 5).—The ancient Hindu divided his planisphere into eight quarters, on which he placed the Koonjerries or elephants, for its support.

(*Note* 6).—TWASTHA, or Takshac, is the celebrated *Nagvansa* of antiquity. All are *Agniculas*. Cheetore, if erected by the Takshac artist, has a right to the appellation Herbert has so singularly assigned it, namely, *Tacsila*, built by the Tâk; it would be the *Tâk-sillâ-nagar*, the 'stone fort of the Takshac,' alluded to in No. I.

(*Note* 7).—Raja Bheem, the lord of *Avanti* or Oojein, the king of Malwa, is especially celebrated in the Jain annals. A son of his led a numerous colony into Marwar, and founded many cities between the Looni river and the Aravulli mountains. *All became proselytes to the Jain faith*, and their descendants, who are amongst the wealthiest and most numerous of these mercantile sectarians, are proud of their Rajpoot descent; and it tells when they are called to responsible offices, when they handle the sword as well as the pen.

(*Note* 8).—*Ganga-Sagur*, or the Island at the mouth of the Ganges, is specified by name as the limit of Bheem's conquests. His memoria may yet exist even there.

(*Note* 9).—*Avanti-Nat'h*, Lord of Avanti or Oojein.

(*Note* 10).—*Paryataca*, a navigator.

(*Note* 11).—Raja Bhoj. There is no more celebrated name than this in the annals and literature of the Rajpoots; but there were three princes of the Pramara race who bore it. The period of the last Raja Bhoj, father of Udyadit, is now fixed, by various inscriptions discovered by me, A.D. 1035, and the dates of the two others I had from a leaf of a very ancient Jain MS., obtained at the temple of Nadole, namely, S. 631 and 721, or A.D. 575 and 665. Abulfazil gives the period of the first Bhoj as S. 545; but, as we find that valuable MS. of the period of the last Bhoj confirmed by the date of this inscription of his son Maun, namely, S. 770, we may put perfect confidence in it, and now consider the periods of the three, namely, S. 631, 721, and 1091—A.D. 567, 665, and 1035—as fixed points in Rajpoot chronology.

(*Note* 12).—In the head of that class of elephants called Bhadra, the Hindoo says, there is always a large pearl.

(*Note* 13).—The monster Rahoo of the Rajpoot, who swallows the sun and moon, *causing eclipses*, is *Fenris*, the wolf of the Scandinavians. The *Asi* carried the same ideas West, which they taught within the Indus.

(*Note* 14).—Kadama is a very delicate flower, that decays almost instantaneously.

(*Note* 15).—*Maha-pralaya!*

(*Note* 16).—The MS. annals of the Rana's family state that their founder, Bappa, conquered Cheetore from Maun Mori. This inscription is therefore invaluable as establishing the era of the conquest of [801] Cheetore by the Gehlotes, and which was immediately following the first irruption of the arms of Islam, as rendered in the annals of Mewar.

(*Note* 17).—As Raja Maun is called *King of Malwa*, it is evident that Cheetore had superseded both Dhar and Awinti as the seat of power. A palace of *Maun Mori* is still shown as one of the antiquities in Cheetore.[1]

No. IV

Inscription in the Devanagari character, discovered in January 1822 in Puttun Somnat'h, on the coast of the Saurashtra peninsula, fixing the era of the sovereigns of Balabhi, the '*Balhara kings of Nehrwalla*.'

Adoration to the Lord of all, to *the light of the universe* (1). Adoration to the form indescribable; Him! at whose feet all kneel.

In the year of Mohummud 662, and in that of Vicrama 1320,

[1] [For this Inscription see *ASR*, Progress Report West Circle, 1903–4 p. 56.]

and that of Srimad Balabhi 945, and the Siva-Singa Samvat 151, Sunday, the 13th (*badi*) of the month Asar (2).

The chiefs of Anhulpoor Patun obeyed by numerous princes (here a string of titles), Bhataric Srimad Arjuna Deva (3), of Chauluc race, his minister Sri Maldeva, with all the officers of government, together with *Hormuz of Belacool*, of the government of *Ameer Rookn-oo-Din*, and of *Khwaja Ibrahim* of *Hormuz*, son of the Admiral (*Nakhoda*) *Noor-oo-Din Feeroz*, together with the Chaura chieftains Palookdeva, Ranik Sri Someswadeva, Ramdeva, Bheemsing, and all the Chauras and other tribes of rank being assembled (4);

Nansi Raja, of the Chaura race, inhabiting *Deo Puttun* (5), assembling all the merchants, established ordinances for the repairs and the support of the temples, in order that flowers, oil, and water should be regularly supplied to *Rutna-iswara* (6), *Choul-iswara* (7), and the shrine of *Pulinda Devi* (8), and the rest, and for the purpose of erecting a wall round the temple of Somnat'h, with a gateway to the north. Keelndeo, son of Modula, and Loonsi, son of Johan, both of the Chaura race, together with the two merchants, Balji and Kurna, bestowed the weekly profits of the market for this purpose. While sun and moon endure, let it not be resumed. Feeroz is commanded to see this order obeyed, and that the customary offerings on festivals are continued, and that all surplus offerings and gifts be placed in the treasury for the purposes afore-named. The Chaura chiefs present, and the Admiral Noor-oo-Din, are commanded to see these orders executed on all classes. Heaven will be the lot of the obedient; hell to the breaker of this ordinance.[1]

(*Note* 1).—The invocation, which was long, has been omitted by me. But this is sufficient to show that Bal-nat'h, the deity worshipped in Puttun Somnat'h, 'the city of the lord of the Moon,' was the sun-god *Bal*. Hence the title of the dynasties which ruled this region, Bal-ca-Rae, 'the princes of Bal,' and hence the capital Balicapoor, 'the city of the sun,' familiarly written *Balabhi*, whose ruins, as well as this inscription, rewarded a long journey. The Rana's ancestors, the *Suryas*, or 'sun-worshippers,' gave their name to the peninsula Saurashtra, or Syria, and the dynasties of Chaura, and Chauluc, or Solanki, who succeeded them on their expulsion by the Parthians, retained the title of Balicaraes, corrupted by Renaudot's Arabian travellers into Balhara [802].

(*Note* 2).—The importance of the discovery of these *new eras* has already been descanted on in the annals, S. 1320 – 945, the date of this inscription = 375 of Vicrama for the first of the Balabhi era; and 1320 – 151 gives S. 1169 for the establishment of the *Sevasinga* era—established by the Gohils of the island of Deo,

[1] [See *IA*, xi. 242 f.]

of whom I have another memorial, dated 927 Balabhi Samvat. The Gohils, Chauras, and Gehlotes are all of one stock.

(*Note* 3).—Arjuna-Deva, *Chaluc*, was prince of Anhulpoor or Anhulwarra, founded by Vanraj Chaura in S. 802—henceforth the capital of the Balica-raes after the destruction of Balabhi.

(*Note* 4).—This evinces that Anhulwarra was still the emporium of commerce which the travellers of Renaudot and Edrisi describe.

(*Note* 5).—From this it is evident that the Islandic Deo was a dependent fief of Anhulwarra.

(*Note* 6).—The great temple of Somnath.

(*Note* 7).—The tutelary divinity of the Chauluc race.

(*Note* 8).—The goddess of the Bhil tribes.

No. V

Inscription from the ruins of Aitpoor.[1]

In Samvatsir 1034, the 16th of the month Bysak, was erected this dwelling[2] of Nanukswami.

From Anundpoor came he of Brahmin[3] race (may he flourish), Muhee Deva Sri Goha Dit, from whom became famous on the earth the Gohil tribe:

2. Bhoj.
3. Mahindra.
4. Naga.
5. Syeela.
6. Aprajit.
7. Mahindra, no equal as a warrior did then exist on the earth's surface.
8. Kalbhoj was resplendent as the sun.[4]
9. Khoman, an unequalled warrior; from him
10. Bhirtrpad, the Tiluk of the three worlds; and from whom was
11. Singji; whose Ranee Maha Lakmee, of the warlike race of Rashtra (Rahtore), and from her was born:
12. Sri Ullut. To him who subdued the earth and became its lord, was born Haria Devi: her praise was known in Hurspoora; and from her was born a mighty warrior in whose arm victory reposed; the Khetri of the field of battle, who broke the confederacy of his foes, and from the tree of whose fortune riches were the fruit: an altar of learning; from him was
13. Nirvahana. By the daughter of Sri Jaijah, of Chauhana race, was born
14. Salvahana.

[1] [This name is wrongly transliterated. It is Ātapura, now Ād, Āhad or Āhar, 2 miles E. of Udaipur (*IA*. xxxix., 1910, p. 186 ff.).]

[2] Aitun. [3] Vipra cula. [4] Ark.

Such were their (the princes whose names are given) fortunes which I have related. From him was born [803].

15. Secti Koomar. How can he be described?—He who conquered and made his own the three qualifications (*sacti*);[1] whose fortunes equalled those of Bhirtrpad. In the abode of wealth Sri Aitpoor, which he had made his dwelling, surrounded by a crowd of princes; the *kulpdroom* to his people; whose foot-soldiers are many; with vaults of treasure—whose fortunes have ascended to heaven—whose city derives its beauty from the intercourse of merchants; and in which there is but one single evil, the killing darts from the bright eyes of beauty, carrying destruction to the vassals of the prince.[2]

No. VI

Inscription of Kumar Pal Solanki, in the Mindra of Brimha, in Cheetore, recording his conquest of Salpoori, in the Punjab.

To him who takes delight in the abode of waters; from whose braided locks ambrosial drops continually descend; even this Mahadeva, may he protect thee!

He of Chaulac tribe, having innumerable gems of ancestry, flowing from a sea of splendour, was Moolraj, sovereign of the earth.

What did he resemble, whose renown was bright as a fair sparkling gem, diffusing happiness and ease to the sons of the earth? Many mighty princes there were of his line; but none before had made the great sacrifice.

Generations after him, in the lapse of many years, was Sid Raj, a name known to the world; whose frame was encased in the riches of victory, and whose deeds were sounded over the curtain of the earth; and who, by the fire of his own frame and fortune, heaped up unconsumable wealth.

After him was Kumar Pal Deo. What was he like, who by the strength of his invincible mind crushed all his foes; whose commands the other sovereigns of the earth placed on their foreheads; who compelled the lord of Sacambhari to bow at his feet:

---

[1] 1. Pribhoo.
2. Ootchha.
3. Muntri. } Three Sactis.

[2] [Erskine, who obtained a correct copy of this Inscription from Pandit Gaurishankar H. Ojha, writes: "In his translation Tod left out several names, namely, Mattat, Khumān II., Mahāyak, Khumān III., and Bhartari Bhat II.; but with the help of a copy recently discovered at Māndal in the house of a descendant of the Pandit whom Tod employed, it has been possible to supply the omissions, and it may be added that these names are confirmed by other inscriptions" (ii. A. 14). Erskine gives a corrected list of the Chiefs of Mewār in ii. B. 8 ff.]

who in person carried his arms to Sewaluk, making the mountain lords to bow before him, even in the city of Salpoori ?

On the mountain Chutterkote . . . ar, the lord of men, in sport placed this [writing] amidst the abode of the gods : even on its pinnacle did he place it. Why ? That it might be beyond the reach of the hands of fools !

As Nissa-Nath, the lord who rules the night, looking on the faces of the fair Kamunis below, feels envious of their fairness, and ashamed of the dark spots on his own countenance, even so does Chutterkote blush at seeing this (Prasishta) on her pinnacle.

Samvat 1207 (month and day broken off) [804].[1]

No. VII

Inscriptions on copper-plates found at Nadole relative to the Chohan princes.

The treasury of knowledge of the Almighty (JINA) cuts the knots and intentions of mankind. Pride, conceit, desire, anger, avarice. It is a partition to the three [2] worlds. Such is MAHAVIRA : [3] may he grant thee happiness !

In ancient times the exalted race of Chohan had sovereignty to the bounds of ocean ; and in NADOLE swayed Lacshman, Raja. He had a son named LOHIA ; and his BULRAJ, his VIGRAHA PAL ; from him sprung MAHINDRA DEVA ; his son was SRI ANHULA, the chief amongst the princes of his time, whose fortunes were known to all. His son was SRI BAL PRESAD ; but having no issue, his younger brother, JAITR RAJ, succeeded. His son was PRITHWI PAL, endued with strength and fiery qualities ; but he having no issue, was succeeded by his younger brother JUL ; he by his brother MAUN RAJA, the abode of fortune. His son was ALANDEVA.[4] When he mounted the throne, he reflected this world was a fable : that this frame, composed of unclean elements, of flesh, blood, and dust, was brought to existence in pain. Versed in the books of faith, he reflected on the evanescence of youth, resembling the scintillation of the fire-fly ; [5] that riches were as the dew-drop on the lotos-leaf, for a moment resembling the pearl, but soon to disappear. Thus meditating, he commanded

[1] [See *Epigraphia Indica*, ii. 422 ff.]

[2] Tribhawun-loca ; or Patala, Mirtha, Swerga.

[3] *Mahavira*, to whom the temple was thus endowed by the Chohan prince, follower of Siva, was the last of the twenty-four Jinas, or apostles of the Jains.

[4] The prince being the twelfth from Lacshman, allowing twenty-two years to a reign, 264—1218 ; date of inscription, S. 954, or A.D. 898, the period of Lacshman.

[5] *Kudheata.*

his servants, and sent them forth to his chieftains, to desire them to bestow happiness on others, and to walk in the paths of faith.

In Samvat 1218, in the month of Sawun the 29th,[1] performing the sacrifice to fire, and pouring forth libations to the dispeller of darkness, he bathed the image of the omniscient, the lord of things which move and are immovable, Sudasiva, with the *panch-amrit*,[2] and made the gifts of gold, grain, and clothes to his spiritual teacher, preceptor, and the Brahmins to their hearts' desire. Taking *til* in his hand, with rings on his finger of the *cusa* (grass), holding water and rice in the palm of his hand, he made a gift of five *moodras* monthly in perpetuity to the *Sandera Gatcha*[3] for saffron, sandal-wood, and ghee for the service of the temple of MAHAVIRA in the white market (*mandra*) of the town. Hence this copper-plate. This charity which I have bestowed will continue as long as the SANDERA GATCHA exist to receive, and my issue to grant it.

To whoever may rule hereafter I touch their hands, that it may be perpetual. Whoever bestows charity will live sixty thousand years in heaven; whoever resumes it, the like in hell!

Of Pragvavansa,[4] his name Dhurnidhur, his son Kurmchund being minister, and the *sastri* Munorut Ram, with his sons Visala and Sridhara, by writing this inscription made his name resplendent. By SRI ALAN'S own hand was this copper-plate bestowed. Samvat 1218 [805].[5]

TREATY between the Honourable the English East-India Company and Maharana Bheem Sing, Rana of Oudeepoor, concluded by Mr. Charles Theophilus Metcalfe on the part of the Honourable Company, in virtue of full powers granted by his Excellency the Most Noble the Marquis of Hastings, K.G., Governor-General, and by Thakoor Ajeet Sing on the part of the Maharana, in virtue of full powers conferred by the Maharana aforesaid.

First Article.—There shall be perpetual friendship, alliance, and unity of interests between the two states, from generation to generation, and the friends and enemies of one shall be the friends and enemies of both.

Second Article.—The British Government engages to protect the principality and territory of Oudeepoor.

Third Article.—The Maharana of Oudeepoor will always act in subordinate co-operation with the British Government, and acknowledge its supremacy, and will not have any connection with other chiefs or states.

[1] *Sudi choudus.*

[2] Milk, curds, clarified butter, honey, butter, and sugar.

[3] One of eighty-four divisions of Jain tribes.

[4] Poorval, a branch of the Oswal race of Jain laity.

[5] [See *Epigraphia Indica* ii. 422 ff.]

Fourth Article.—The Maharana of Oudeepoor will not enter into any negotiation with any chief or state without the knowledge and sanction of the British Government; but his usual amicable correspondence with friends and relations shall continue.

Fifth Article.—The Maharana of Oudeepoor will not commit aggressions upon any one; and if by accident a dispute arise with any one, it shall be submitted to the arbitration and award of the British Government.

Sixth Article.—One-fourth of the revenue of the actual territory of Oudeepoor shall be paid annually to the British Government as tribute for five years; and after that term three-eighths in perpetuity. The Maharana will not have connection with any other power on account of tribute, and if any one advance claims of that nature, the British Government engages to reply to them.

Seventh Article.—Whereas the Maharana represents that portions of the dominions of Oudeepoor have fallen, by improper means, into the possession of others, and solicits the restitution of those places: the British Government from a want of accurate information is not able to enter into any positive engagement on this subject; but will always keep in view the renovation of the prosperity of the state of Oudeepoor, and after ascertaining the nature of each case, will use its best exertions for the accomplishment of the object, on every occasion on which it may be proper to do so. Whatever places may thus be restored to the state of Oudeepoor by the aid of the British Government, three-eighths of their revenues shall be paid in perpetuity to the British Government.

Eighth Article.—The troops of the state of Oudeepoor shall be furnished according to its means, at the requisition of the British Government.

Ninth Article.—The Maharana of Oudeepoor shall always be absolute ruler of his own country, and the British jurisdiction shall not be introduced into that principality.

Tenth Article.—The present treaty of ten articles having been concluded at Dihlee, and signed and sealed by Mr. Charles Theophilus Metcalfe and Thakoor Ajeet Sing Buhadoor [806], the ratifications of the same, by his Excellency the Most Noble the Governor-General, and Maharana Bheem Sing, shall be mutually delivered within a month from this date.

Done at Dihlee, this thirteenth day of January, A.D. 1818.

(*Signed*) C. T. METCALFE (L.S.).
THAKOOR AJEET SING (L.S.)

THE LATE MAHĀRĀJA SIR SUMER SINGH, OF JODHPUR (*b.* 1901; *d.* 1918), AND HIS BROTHER, THE PRESENT MAHĀRĀJA UMMED SINGH (*b.* 1903).

To face page 928.

BOOK V

ANNALS OF MĀRWĀR

CHAPTER 1

Etymology of Mārwār.—Marwar is a corruption of Maruwar, classically Marusthali or Marusthan, 'the region of death.' It is also called Marudesa, whence the unintelligible Mardes of the early Muhammadan writers. The bards frequently style it Mordhar, which is synonymous with Marudesa, or, when it suits their rhyme, simply Maru. Though now restricted to the country subject to the Rathor race, its ancient and appropriate application comprehended the entire 'desert,' from the Sutlej to the ocean.

The Rāthors.—A concise genealogical sketch of the Rathor rulers of Marwar has already been given;[1] we shall therefore briefly pass over those times "when a genealogical tree would strike root in any soil"; when the ambition of the Rathors, whose branches (*sakha*) spread rapidly over 'the region of death,' was easily gratified with a solar [2] pedigree. As it is desirable, however, to record their own opinions regarding their origin, we shall make extracts from the chronicles (hereafter enumerated), instead of fusing the whole into one mass, as in the Annals of Mewar. The reader will occasionally be presented with simple translations of whatever is most interesting in the Rathor records.

Authorities.—Let us begin with a statement of the author's authorities; first, a genealogical roll of the Rathors, furnished by a Yati, or Jain priest, from the temple of Narlai.[2] This roll

[1] See Vol. I. p. 105.

[2] An ancient town in Marwar [about 80 miles S.E. of Jodhpur city].

is about fifty feet in length, commencing, as usual, with a theogony, followed by the production of the 'first Rathor from the spine (*rahat*) of Indra,' [1] the nominal father being 'Yavanaswa, prince of Parlipur.' Of the topography of Parlipur, the Rathors have no other notion than that it was in the north; but in the declared race of their progenitor, a Yavan prince, of the Aswa or Asi tribe,[2] we have a proof of the Scythic origin of this Rajput family.

The chronicle proceeds with the foundation of Kanyakubja,[3] or Kanauj, and the origin of Kama-dhwaja [4] (*vulgo* Kamdhuj), the titular appellation of its princes, and concludes with the thirteen great Sakha, or ramifications of the Rathors, and their Gotracharya, or genealogical creed.[5]

Another roll, of considerable antiquity, commences in the fabulous age, with a long string of names, without facts; its sole value consists in the esteem in which the tribe holds it. We may omit all that precedes Nain Pal, who, in the year S. 526 (A.D. 470 [6]), conquered Kanauj, slaying its monarch Ajaipal; from which period the race was termed Kanaujia Rathor. The genealogy proceeds to Jaichand, the last monarch of Kanauj; relates the emigration of his nephew Sialiji, or Sivaji, and his establishment

[1] [A folk etymology, the name being derived from Rāshtrakūta, which may mean the chief, as opposed to the rank and file of the Ratta dynasty; but it has also been connected with Reddi, a Dravidian caste in S. India (*BG*, i. Part i. 119, Part ii. 22 note, 178, 383 ff.).]

[2] One of the four tribes which overturned the Greek kingdom of Bactria. The ancient Hindu cosmographers claim the Aswa as a grand branch of their early family, and doubtless the Indo-Scythic people, from the Oxus to the Ganges, were one race.

[3] From *kubja* (the spine) of the virgin (*kanya*) [referring to the legend of the hundred daughters of Kusanābha rendered crooked by Vāyu].

[4] Kama-dhwaja, 'the banner of Cupid.'

[5] Gotama Gotra, Mardwandani Sakha, Sukracharya Guru, Garapatya Agni, Pankhani Devi.

[6] It is a singular fact, that there is no available date beyond the fourth century for any of the great Rajput families, all of whom are brought from the north. This was the period of one of the grand irruptions of the Getic races from Central Asia, who established kingdoms in the Panjab and on the Indus. Pal or Pali, the universal adjunct to every proper name, indicates the pastoral race of these invaders [?]. [The reason why the Rājput genealogies do not go back to an early date is that many of them were recruited from Gurjara and other foreign tribes. The tale of the origin of the Rāthors from Kanauj is a myth, as the dynasty of that place belonged to the Gahadvāla or Gaharwār clan. The object of the story was to affiliate the tribe to the heroic Jaichand (Smith, *EHI*, 385).]

in the desert (Maruwar), with a handful of his brethren (a wreck of the mighty kingdom of Kanauj); and terminates with the death of Raja Jaswant Singh in S. 1735 (A.D. 1679), describing every branch and scion, until we see them spreading over Maru [3].

Genealogy ceases to be an uninteresting pursuit when it enables us to mark the progress of animal vegetation, from the germ to the complete development of the tree, until the land is overshadowed with its branches; and bare as is the chronicle to the moralist or historian, it exhibits to the observer of the powers of the animal economy, data which the annals of no other people on earth can furnish. In A.D. 1193 we see the throne of Jaichand overturned; his nephew, with a handful of retainers, taking service with a petty chieftain in the Indian desert. In less than four centuries we find the descendants of these exiles of the Ganges occupying nearly the whole of the desert; having founded three capitals, studded the land with the castles of its feudality, and bringing into the field fifty thousand men, *ek bap ka beta*, 'the sons of one father,' to combat the emperor of Delhi. What a contrast does their unnoticed growth present to that of the Islamite conquerors of Kanauj, of whom five dynasties passed away in ignorance of the renovated existence of the Rathor, until the ambition of Sher Shah brought him into contact with the descendants of Siahji, whose valour caused him to exclaim "he had nearly lost the crown of India for a handful of barley," in allusion to the poverty of their land! [1]

What a sensation does it not excite when we know that a sentiment of kindred pervades every individual of this immense affiliated body, who can point out, in the great tree, the branch of his origin, whilst not one is too remote from the main stem to forget its pristine connexion with it! The moral sympathies created by such a system pass unheeded by the chronicler, who must deem it futile to describe what all sensibly feel, and which renders his page, albeit little more than a string of names, one of paramount interest to the 'sons of Siahji.'

The third authority is the Suraj Prakas (Surya Prakasa), composed by the bard Karnidhan, during the reign and by command of Raja Abhai Singh. This poetic history, comprised in 7500 stanzas, was copied from the original manuscript, and

[1] [See p. 835.]

sent to me by Raja Man, in the year 1820.[1] As usual, the Kavya (bard) commences with the origin of all things, tracing the Rathors from the creation down to Sumitra; from whence is a blank until he recommences with the name of Kamdhuj, which appears to have been the title assumed by Nain Pal, on his conquest of Kanauj. Although Karnidhan must have taken his facts from the [4] royal records, they correspond very well with the roll from Narlai. The bard is, however, in a great hurry to bring the founder of the Rathors into Marwar, and slurs over the defeat and death of Jaichand. Nor does he dwell long on his descendants, though he enumerates them all, and points out the leading events until he reaches the reign of Jaswant Singh, grandfather of Abhai Singh, who "commanded the bard to write the Suraj Prakas."

The next authority is the Raj Rupak Akhyat, or 'the royal relations.' This work commences with a short account of the Suryavansa, from their cradle at Ajodhya; then takes up Siahji's migration, and in the same strain as the preceding work, rapidly passes over all events until the death of Raja Jaswant; but it becomes a perfect chronicle of events during the minority of his successor Ajit, his eventful reign, and that of Abhai Singh, to the conclusion of the war against Sarbuland Khan, viceroy of Gujarat. Throwing aside the meagre historical introduction, it is professedly a chronicle of the events from S. 1735 (A.D. 1679) to S. 1787 (A.D. 1734), the period to which the Suraj Prakas is brought down.

A portion of the Bijai Vilas, a poem of 100,000 couplets, also fell into my hands: it chiefly relates to the reign of the prince whose name it bears, Bijai Singh, the son of Bakhta Singh. It details the civil wars waged by Bijai Singh and his cousin Ram Singh (son of Abhai Singh), and the consequent introduction of the Mahrattas into Marwar.

From a biographical work named simply Khyat, or 'Story,' I obtained that portion which relates to the lives of Raja Udai Singh, the friend of Akbar; his son Raja Gaj, and grandson Jaswant Singh. These sketches exhibit in true colours the character of the Rathors.

Besides these, I caused to be drawn up by an intelligent man, who had passed his life in office at Jodhpur, a memoir of transactions from the death of Ajit Singh, in A.D. 1629, down to the treaty

[1] This manuscript is deposited in the library of the Royal Asiatic Society.

with the English Government in A.D. 1818. The ancestors of the narrator had filled offices of trust in the State, and he was a living chronicle both of the past and present.

From these sources, from conversations with the reigning sovereign, his nobles, his ambassadors, and subjects, materials were collected for this sketch of the Rathors—barren, indeed, of events at first, but redundant of them as we advance.

A genealogical table of the Rathors is added, showing the grand offsets, whose [5] descendants constitute the feudal frèrage of the present day. A glance at this table will show the claims of each house; and in its present distracted condition, owing to civil broils, will enable the paramount power to mediate, when necessary, with impartiality, in the conflicting claims of the prince and his feudatories.

Rāthor Origins.—We shall not attempt to solve the question, whether the Rathors are, or are not, Ravi-vansa, 'Children of the Sun'; nor shall we dispute either the birth or etymon of the first Rathor (from the *rahat* or spine of Indra), or search in the north for the kingdom of the nominal father; but be content to conclude that this celestial interference in the household concerns of the Parlipur prince was invented to cover some disgrace. The name of Yavana, with the adjunct Aswa or Asi, clearly indicates the Indo-Scythic 'barbarian' from beyond the Indus. In the genealogy of the Lunar races descended of Budha and Ila (Mercury and the Earth—see Table I. Vol. I.), the five sons of Bajaswa are made to people the countries on and beyond the Indus; and in the scanty records of Alexander's invasion mention is made of many races, as the Assasenac and Assakenoi, still dwelling in these regions.

This period was fruitful in change to the old-established dynastics of the Hindu continent, when numerous races of barbarians, namely, Huns, Parthians, and Getae, had fixed colonies on her western and northern frontiers.[1]

"In S. 526 (A.D. 470) Nain Pal obtained Kanauj, from which period the Rathors assumed the title of Kamdhuj. His son was Padarath,[2] his Punja, from whom sprung the thirteen great families, bearing the patronymic Kamdhuj, namely:

[1] Cosmas. Annals of Mewār. Getae or Jat Inscription, Appendix, Vol. I.

[2] Called Bharat in the Yati's roll; an error of one or other of the authorities in transcribing from the more ancient records.

"1st. Dharma Bambo: · ·his descendants styled Danesra Kamdhuj.

"2nd. Banuda, who fought the Afghans at Kangra, and founded Abhaipur: hence the Abhaipura Kamdhuj.

"3rd. Virachandra, who married the daughter of Hamira Chauhan, of Anhilpur Patan; he had fourteen sons, who emigrated to the Deccan: his descendants called Kapolia Kamdhuj.

"4th. Amrabijai, who married the daughter of the Pramara prince of Koragarh [1] on the Ganges;—slew 16,000 Pramaras, and took possession of Kora, whence the Kora Kamdhuj [2] [6].

"5th. Sujan Binod: his descendants Jarkhera Kamdhuj.

"6th. Padma, who conquered Orissa, and also Bogilana,[3] from Raja Tejman Yadu.

"7th. Aihar, who took Bengal from the Yadus: hence Aihara Kamdhuj.

"8th. Bardeo; his elder brother offered him in appanage Benares, and eighty-four townships; but he preferred founding a city, which he called Parakhpur:[4] his descendants Parakh Kamdhuj.

"9th. Ugraprabhu, who made a pilgrimage to the shrine of Hinglaj Chandel,[5] who, pleased with the severity of his penance, caused a sword to ascend from the fountain, with which he conquered the southern countries touching the ocean:[6] his descendants Chandela Kamdhuj.

"10th. Muktaman, who conquered possessions in the north from Bhan Tuar: his descendants Bira Kamdhuj.

"11th. Bharat, at the age of sixty-one, conquered Kanaksar, under the northern hills, from Rudrasen of the Bargujar tribe: his descendants styled Bhariau Kamdhuj.

"12th. Alankal founded Khairoda; fought the Asuras (Muslims) on the banks of the Attock: his descendants Kherodia Kamdhuj.

[1] [In the Fatehpur District (*IGI*, xv. 398.]

[2] An inscription given in the *Transactions of the Royal Asiatic Society* (vol. ix. p. 440), found at Kora, relates to a branch of the Kanauj family.

[3] [? Bāglān in Nāsik District, Bombay (*IGI*, vi. 190).]

[4] *Qu.* Parkar, towards the Indus?

[5] On the coast of Mekran.

[6] If we can credit these legends, we see the Rathor Rajputs spreading over all India. I give these bare facts *verbatim*, as some traces may yet remain of the races in those countries. [These are pure legends, see Smith, *EHI*, 377 ff.]

"13th. Chand obtained Tarapur in the north. He married a daughter of the Chauhan of Tahera,[1] a city well known to the world: with her he came to Benares.

"And thus the race of Surya multiplied.

"Bambo,[2] or Dharma-Bambo, sovereign of Kanauj, had a son, Ajaichand.[3] For twenty-one generations they bore the titles of Rao; afterwards that of Raja. Udaichand, Narpati, Kanaksen, Sahassal, Meghsen, Birabhadra, Deosen, Bimalsen, Dansen, Mukund, Budha, Rajsen, Tirpal, Sripunja, Bijaichand,[4] his son Jaichand, who became the Naik of Kanauj, with the surname Dal Pangla."

Jaichand.—Nothing is related of the actions of these princes, from the conquest of Kanauj [7] by Nain Pal, in A.D. 470, and the establishment of his thirteen grandsons in divers countries, until we reach Jaichand, in whose person (A.D. 1193) terminated the Rathor sovereignty on the Ganges; and we have only twenty-one names to fill up the space of seven centuries, although the testimony on which it is given[5] asserts there were twenty-one princes bearing the title of Rao prior to the assumption of that of Raja. But the important information is omitted as to who was the first to assume this title. There are names in the Yati's roll that are not in the Suraj Prakas, which we have followed; and one of these, Rangatdhwaj, is said to have overcome Jasraj Tuar, king of Delhi, for whose period we have correct data: yet we cannot incorporate the names in the Yati's roll with that just given without vitiating each; and as we have no facts, it is useless to perplex ourselves with a barren genealogy. But we can assert that it must have been a splendid dynasty, and that their actions, from the conqueror Nain Pal to the last prince, Jaichand, were well deserving of commemoration. That they were commemorated in written records there cannot be a doubt; for the trade of the bardic chroniclers in India has flourished in all ages.

[1] [Bahra] a city often mentioned by Ferishta [i. Introd. lxxii.] in the early times of the Muhammadans.

[2] Nain Pal must have preceded Dharma-Bambo by five or six generations.

[3] Called Abhaichand, in the Suraj Prakas.

[4] Also styled Bijaipal; classically Vijayapala, 'Fosterer of Victory.

[5] The Suraj Prakas.

The City of Kanauj.—Although we have abundant authority to assert the grandeur of the kingdom of Kanauj [1] at the period of its extinction, both from the bard Chand and the concurrent testimony of Muhammadan authors, yet are we astonished at the description of the capital, attested not only by the annals of the Rathors, but by those of their antagonists, the Chauhans.

The circumvallation of Kanauj covered a space of more than thirty miles; and its numerous forces obtained for its prince the epithet of 'Dal Pangla,' meaning that the mighty host (*Dal*) was lame or had a halt in its movements owing to its numbers, of which Chand observes that in the march "the van had reached their ground ere the rear had moved off." The Suraj Prakas gives the amount of this army, which in numbers might compete with the most potent which, in ancient or modern times, was ever sent into the field. "Eighty thousand men in armour; thirty thousand horse covered with *pakhar*, or quilted mail; three hundred thousand Paiks or infantry; and of bow-men and battle-axes two hundred thousand; besides a cloud of elephants bearing warriors" [8].

This immense army was to oppose the Yavana beyond the Indus; for, as the chronicle says, "The king of Gor and Irak crossed the Attock. There Jai Singh met the conflict, when the Nilab changed its name to Surkhab.[2] There was the Ethiopic (*Habshi*) king, and the skilful Frank learned in all arts,[3] overcome by the lord of Kanauj."

The chronicles of the Chauhans, the sworn foe of the Rathors, repeat the greatness of the monarch of Kanauj, and give him the title of "Mandalika."[4] They affirm that he overcame the king of the north,[5] making eight tributary kings prisoners; that he twice defeated Siddhraj, king of Anhilwara, and extended his dominions south of the Nerbudda, and that at length, in the fulness of his pride, he had divine honours paid him in the rite Swayam-

[1] See Inscriptions of Jaichand, Vijayachand, and Kora, in the 9th and 14th vols. of the *Asiatic Researches*.

[2] The Nilab, or 'blue water,' the Indus, changed its name to the 'Red-stream' (Surkhab), or 'ensanguined.'

[3] It is singular that Chand likewise mentions the Frank as being in the army of Shihabu-d-din, in the conquest of his sovereign Prithiraj. If this be true, it must have been a desultory or fugitive band of crusaders.

[4] [Ruler of a district (*mandal*).]

[5] They thus style the kings west of the Indus.

vara.[1] This distinction, which involves the most august ceremony, and is held as a virtual assumption of universal supremacy, had in all ages been attended with disaster. In the rite of Swayamvara every office, down to the scullion of the Rasora, or banquet-hall, must be performed by royal personages; nor had it been attempted by any of the dynasties which ruled India since the Pandu: not even Vikrama, though he introduced his own era, had the audacity to attempt what the Rathor determined to execute. All India was agitated by the accounts of the magnificence of the preparations, and circular invitations were despatched to every prince, inviting him to assist at the pompous ceremony, which was to conclude with the nuptials of the raja's only daughter, who, according to the customs of those days, would select her future lord from the assembled chivalry of India. The Chauhan bard describes the revelry and magnificence of the scene: the splendour of the Yajnasala, or 'hall of sacrifice,' surpassing all powers of description; in which were assembled all the princes of India, "save the lord of the Chauhans, and Samara of Mewar," who, scorning this assumption of supremacy, Jaichand made their effigies in gold, assigning to them the most servile posts; that of the king of the Chauhans being Poliya, or 'porter of the hall.' Prithiraj, whose life was one succession of feats of arms and gallantry, had a double motive for action—love and revenge. He determined to enjoy both, or perish in the attempt; "to spoil the sacrifice and bear away the fair of Kanauj from its halls, though beset [9] by all the heroes of Hind." The details of this exploit form the most spirited of the sixty-nine books of the bard. The Chauhan executed his purpose, and, with the élite of the warriors of Delhi, bore off the princess in open day from Kanauj. A desperate running-fight of five days took place. To use the words of the bard, "he preserved his prize; he gained immortal renown, but he lost the sinews of Delhi." So did Jaichand those of Kanauj; and each, who had singly repelled all attacks of the kings, fell in turn a prey to the Ghori Sultan,[2] who skilfully availed himself of these international feuds, to make a permanent conquest of India.

The Great States of North India.—We may here briefly describe

[1] [The "Seonair" of the text seems to represent *swayamvara*, the rite of selection of her husband by a maiden.]

[2] [Shihābu-d-dīn, A.D. 1175–1206.]

the state of Hindustan at this epoch, and for centuries previous to the invasions of Mahmud.

There were four great kingdoms, namely—

1. Delhi, under the Tuars and Chauhans.
2. Kanauj, under the Rathors.
3. Mewar, under the Guhilots.
4. Anhilwara, under the Chauras and Solankis.

To one or other of these States the numerous petty princes of India paid homage and feudal service. The boundary between Delhi and Kanauj was the Kalinadi, or 'black stream'; the Kalindi of the Greek geographers.[1] Delhi claimed supremacy over all the countries westward to the Indus, embracing the lands watered by its arms, from the foot of the Himalaya,—the desert —to the Aravalli chain. The Chauhan king, successor to the Tuars, enumerated one hundred and eight great vassals, many of whom were subordinate princes.

The power of Kanauj extended north to the foot of the Snowy mountains; eastward to Kasi (Benares); and across the Chambal to the lands of the Chandel (now Bundelkhand); on the south its possessions came in contact with Mewar.

Mewar, or Madhyawar, the 'central region,'[2] was bounded to the north by the Aravalli, to the south by the Pramaras of Dhar (dependent on Kanauj), and westward by Anhilwara, which State was bounded by the ocean to the south, the Indus on the west, and the desert to the north.

There are records of great wars amongst all these princes. The Chauhans and Guhilots, whose dominions were contiguous, were generally allies, and the Rathors and Tuars (predecessors of the Chauhans), who were only divided by the Kalinadi, often dyed it with their blood. Yet this warfare was never of an [10] exterminating kind; a marriage quenched a feud, and they remained friends until some new cause of strife arose.

If, at the period preceding Mahmud, the traveller had journeyed

[1] [The Kālindi River, the name of which was corrupted into Kālinadi, rises in the Muzaffarnagar District, and joins the Ganges near Kanauj, 310 miles from its source (*IGI*, xiv. 309).]

[2] [The word Mewār represents the original Medapāta, "land of the Med tribe." The bulk of the army of Chashtana, the Western Satrap, appears to have consisted of Mevas or Medas, from whose settlement in Central Rājputāna the province seems to have received its present name, Mewāda (*BG*, i. Part i. 33).]

through the courts of Europe, and taken the line of route, in subsequent ages pursued by Timur, by Byzantium, through Ghazni (adorned with the spoils of India), to Delhi, Kanauj, and Anhilwara, how superior in all that constitutes civilization would the Rajput princes have appeared to him !—in arts immeasurably so ; in arms by no means inferior. At that epoch, in the west, as in the east, every State was governed on feudal principles. Happily for Europe, the democratical principle gained admittance, and imparted a new character to her institutions ; while the third estate of India, indeed of Asia, remained permanently excluded from all share in the government which was supported by its labour, every pursuit but that of arms being deemed ignoble. To this cause, and the endless wars which feudality engendered, Rajput nationality fell a victim when attacked by the means at command of the despotic kings of the north.

The Invasion of Shihābu-d-dīn.—Shihabu-d-din, king of Ghor, taking advantage of these dissensions, invaded India. He first encountered Prithiraj, the Chauhan king of Delhi, the outwork and bulwark of India, which fell. Shihabu-d-din then attacked Jaichand, who was weakened by the previous struggle. Kanauj put forth all her strength, but in vain ; and her monarch was the last son of " the Yavana of Parlipur " who ruled on the banks of the Ganges. He met a death congenial to the Hindu, being drowned in the sacred stream in attempting to escape.[1]

This event happened in S. 1249 (A.D. 1193), from which period the overgrown, gorgeous Kanauj ceased to be a Hindu city, when the " thirty-six races " of vassal princes, from the Himalaya to the Vindhya, who served under the banners of Bardai Sena,[2] retired to their patrimonial estates. But though the Rathor name ceased to exist on the shores of the Ganges, destiny decreed that a scion should be preserved, to produce in a less favoured land a long line of kings ; that in thirty-one generations his descendant, Raja Man, " Raj, Rajeswara," 'the king, the lord of kings,' should be as vainglorious of the sceptre of Maru as either Jaichand when he commanded divine honours, or his still more

[1] [His corpse was recognized by his false teeth, " a circumstance which throws some light on the state of manners " (Elphinstone 365).]

[2] Another title of the monarch of Kanauj, " the bard of the host," from which we are led to understand he was as well versed in the poetic art as his rival, the Chauhan prince of Delhi.

remote ancestor Nain Pal fourteen [11] centuries before, when he erected his throne in Kanauj. The Rathor may well boast of his pedigree, when he can trace it through a period of 1360 years, in lineal descent from male to male; and contented with this, may leave to the mystic page of the bard, or the interpolated pages of the Puranas, the period preceding Nain Pal.

CHAPTER 2

Migration of the Rāthors into Rājputāna.—In S. 1268 (A.D. 1212), eighteen years subsequent to the overthrow of Kanauj, Siahji and Setram, grandsons of its last monarch, abandoned the land of their birth, and with two hundred retainers, the wreck of their vassalage, journeyed westward to the desert, with the intent, according to some of the chronicles, of making a pilgrimage to the shrine of Dwarka;[1] but according to others, and with more probability, to carve their fortunes in fresh fields, unscathed by the luxuries in which they had been tried, and proud in their poverty and sole heritage, the glory of Kanauj [12].

The Tribes of Rājputāna.—Let us rapidly sketch the geography of the tribes over whom it was destined these emigrants of the Ganges should obtain the mastery, from the Jumna to the Indus, and the Gara River to the Aravalli hills. First, on the east, the Kachhwahas, under Malesi, whose father, Rao Pajun, was killed in the war of Kanauj. Ajmer, Sambhar, and the best lands of the Chauhans fell rapidly to the Islamite—though the strongholds of the Aravalli yet sheltered some, and Nadol continued for a century more to be governed by a descendant of Bisaldeo. Mansi, Rana of the Indha[2] tribe, a branch of the Parihars, still held

[1] [The date of Siha or Siāhji, the traditional founder of the Mārwār dynasty, was until recently uncertain. An inscription on a memorial stone gives the date as Vikrama Sambat 1330, A.D. 1387, and for his grandson, Dhūhada V.S. 1336, A.D. 1393. He is called the eldest son of Asvatthāma mentioned in the text (*IA*, xi. 301). The tradition is vitiated by the fact that this was not the first appearance of Rāthors in Rājputāna. An inscription at Bījapur states that five of this clan ruled at Hathūndi (Hastikūndi) in the tenth century (Erskine iii. A. 54; *IGI*, vi. 247 f.).]

[2] [The Īndhas occupy the W. tract of Mārwār; will not eat the flesh of the boar; believe that no member of the clan can be struck by lightning, owing to the prediction of Khākhaji, one of their ancestors; no epidemic ever breaks out in their territory as it is under the protection of their goddess, Chāwanda Māta (*Census Report*, *Mārwār*, 1891, ii. 31).]

Mandor, and the various Bhumias around paid him a feudal subjection as the first chief of the desert. Northward, about Nagor, lived the community of the Mohils (a name now extinct), whose chief place was Aurint, on which depended 1440 villages. The whole of the tracts now occupied by Bikaner to Bhatner were partitioned into petty republics of Getae or Jats, whose history will hereafter be related. Thence to the Gara River, the Johyas, Dahyas, Kathis, Langahas, and other tribes whose names are now obliterated, partly by the sword, partly by conversion to Islamism. The Bhattis had for centuries been established within the bounds they still inhabit, and little expected that this handful of Rathors was destined to contract them. The Sodha princes adjoined the Bhattis south, and the Jarejas occupied the valley of the Indus and Cutch. The Solankis intervened between them and the Pramaras of Abu and Chandravati, which completed the chain by junction with Nadol. Various chieftains of the more ancient races, leading a life of fearless independence, acknowledging an occasional submission to their more powerful neighbours, were scattered throughout this space; such as the Dabhis of Idar and Mewa; the Gohils of Kherdhar; the Deoras of Sanchor; and Sonigiras of Jalor; the Mohils of Aurint; the Sankhlas of Sandli, etc.; all of whom have either had their birthright seized by the Rathor, or the few who have survived and yet retain them are enrolled amongst their allodial vassals.

The Exploits of Siāhji.—The first exploit of Siahji was at Kulumad (twenty miles west of the city of Bikaner, not then in existence), the residence of a chieftain of the Solanki tribe. He received the royal emigrants with kindness, and the latter repaid it by the offer of their services to combat his enemy, the Jareja chieftain of Phulra, well known in all the annals of the period, from the Sutlej to the ocean, as Lakha Phulani, the most celebrated riever of Maru, whose castle of Phulra stood amidst the almost inaccessible [13] sandhills of the desert. By this timely succour the Solanki gained a victory over Lakha, but with the loss of Setram and several of his band. In gratitude for this service, the Solanki bestowed upon Siahji his sister in marriage, with an ample dower; and he continued his route by Anhilwara Patan, where he was hospitably entertained by its prince, to the shrine of Dwarka. It was the good fortune of Siahji again to encounter Lakha, whose wandering habits had brought him on a foray into the territory of Anhilwara. Besides the love of glory and the ambition of maintaining the reputation of his race, he had the stimulus of revenge, and that of a brother's blood. He was successful, though he lost a nephew, slaying Lakha in single combat, which magnified his fame in all these regions, of which Phulani was the scourge.

Flushed with success, we hear nothing of the completion of Siahji's pilgrimage; but obedient to the axiom of the Rajput, "get land," we find him on the banks of the Luni, exterminating, at a feast, the Dabhis of Mewa,[1] and soon after the Gohils of Kherdhar,[2] whose chief, Maheshdas, fell by the sword of the grandson of Jaichand. Here, in the "land of Kher," amidst the sandhills of the Luni (the salt-river of the desert), from which the Gohils were expelled, Siahji planted the standard of the Rathors.

At this period a community of Brahmans held the city and extensive lands about Pali, from which they were termed Paliwal;[3] and being greatly harassed by the incursions of the mountaineers, the Mers and Minas, they called in the aid of Siahji's band, which readily undertook and executed the task of rescuing the Brahmans from their depredations. Aware that they would be renewed, they offered Siahji lands to settle amongst them, which were readily accepted; and here he had a son by the Solankani, to whom he gave the name of Asvatthama. With her, it is recorded, the suggestion originated to make himself lord of Pali; and it affords another example of the disregard of the early Rajputs for the sacred order, that on the Holi, or Saturnalia, he found an opportunity to "obtain land," putting to death the heads of this

[1] The Dabhi was one of the thirty-six royal races; and this is almost the last mention of their holding independent possessions. See Vol. I. p. 138, and the map for the position of Mewa at the bend of the Luni. [Kher is now a ruined village near Jasol, about 60 miles S.W. of Jodhpur city, on the left bank of the Lūni.]

[2] In my last journey through these regions, I visited the chief of the Gohils at Bhavnagar, in the Gulf of Cambay. I transcribed their defective annals, which trace their migration from 'Kherdhar,' but in absolute ignorance where it is! See Vol. I. p. 137.

[3] [Pāli, 45 miles S.S.E. of Jodhpur city. The Pāliwāls have some remarkable customs; they do not observe the Rākhi festival because of a tradition that on the day the town was sacked by Shihābu-d-dīn, the sacred cords of the men slain and the bangles of those women who immolated themselves weighed respectively 9 and 84 maunds. Compare the story of Chitor (Vol. I. p. 383) (*Census Report*, *Mārwār*, 1891, ii. 79).]

community, and adding the district to his conquests [14]. Siahji outlived his treachery only twelve months, leaving his acquisitions as a nucleus for further additions to his children. He had three sons, Asvatthama, Soning, and Ajmall.

Asvatthāma.—One of the chronicles asserts that it was Asvatthama, the successor of Siahji, who conquered " the land of Kher " from the Gohils. By the same species of treachery by which his father attained Pali, he lent his aid to establish his brother Soning in Idar. This small principality, on the frontiers of Gujarat, then appertained, as did Mewa, to the Dabhi race ; and it was during the *matam*, or period of mourning for one of its princes, that the young Rathor chose to obtain a new settlement. His descendants are distinguished as the Hathundia[1] Rathors. The third brother, Aja, carried his forays as far as the extremity of the Saurashtra peninsula, where he decapitated Bikamsi, the Chawara chieftain of Okhamandala,[2] and established himself. From this act his branch became known as the 'Vadhel';[3] and the Vadhels are still in considerable number in that furthest track of ancient Hinduism called the " World's End."

Asvatthama died, leaving eight sons, who became the heads of clans, namely, Duhar, Jopsi, Khampsao, Bhopsu, Dhandhal, Jethmall, Bandar, and Uhar ; of which, four, Duhar, Dhandhal, Jethmall, and Uhar, are yet known.

Duhar or Dhūhada.—Duhar succeeded Asvatthama. He made an unsuccessful effort to recover Kanauj ; and then attempted to wrest Mandor from the Parihars, but " watered their lands with his blood." He left seven sons, namely, Raepal, Kiratpal, Behar, Pital, Jugel, Dalu, and Begar.

Rāēpāl, Chhada, Thīda, Salkha, Biramdeo, Chonda.—Raepal succeeded, and revenged the death of his father, slaying the Parihar of Mandor, of which he even obtained temporary possession. He had a progeny of thirteen sons, who rapidly spread their issue over these regions. He was succeeded by his son Kanhal [or Kānpāl], whose successor was his son Jalhan ; he was

[1] [Who take their name from their capital, Hathūndi, now ruined, near Bījapur in S.E. Mārwār.]

[2] On the western coast of the Saurashtra peninsula. [The Okhamandal legend calls the Rāthor leaders Virāval and Bījal, who overcame the Chāwaras, and abandoning the name Rāthor, called themselves Vādhel, 'slayers' (*BG*, v. 590 f.).]

[3] From *badh*, *vadh*, 'to slay.'

succeeded by his son Chhada, whose successor was his son Thida. All these carried on a desperate warfare with, and made conquests from, their neighbours. Chhada and Thida are mentioned as very troublesome neighbours in the annals of the Bhattis of Jaisalmer, who were compelled to carry the war against them into the "land of Kher." Rao Thida took the rich district of Bhinmal from the Sonigira, and made other additions to his territory from the Deoras and Balechas [15]. He was succeeded by Salakh or Salkha. His issue, the Salkhawats, now Bhumias, are yet numerous both in Mewa and Rardara. Salkha was succeeded by his son Biramdeo, who attacked the Johyas of the north, and fell in battle. His descendants, styled Biramot and Bijawat, from another son Bija, are numerous at Setru, Siwana, and Dechu. Biramdeo was succeeded by his son Chonda, an important name in the annals of the Rathors. Hitherto they had attracted notice by their valour and their raids, whenever there was a prospect of success; but they had so multiplied in eleven generations that they now essayed a higher flight. Collecting all the branches bearing the name of Rathor, Chonda assaulted Mandor, slew the Parihar prince, and planted the banners of Kanauj on the ancient capital of Maru.

So fluctuating are the fortunes of the daring Rajput, ever courting distinction and coveting *bhum*, 'land,' that but a short time before this success, Chonda had been expelled from all the lands acquired by his ancestors, and was indebted to the hospitality of a bard of the Charan tribe, at Kalu; and they yet circulate the *kabit*, or quatrain, made by him when, in the days of his greatness, he came and was refused admittance to "the lord of Mandor"; he took post under the balcony, and improvized a stanza, reminding him of the Charan of Kalu: "*Chonda nahīn āwē chit, Khichar Kalu tanna? Bhup bhaya bhay-bhit, Mandawar ra mālya?*" "Does not Chonda remember the porridge of Kalu, now that the lord of the land looks so terrific from his balcony of Mandawar?" Once established in Mandor, he ventured to assault the imperial garrison of Nagor. Here he was also successful. Thence he carried his arms south, and placed his garrison in Nadol, the capital of the province of Godwar. He married a daughter of the Parihar prince,[1] who had the

[1] He was of the Indha branch of the Parihars, and his daughter is called the Indhavatni.

satisfaction to see his grandson succeed to the throne of Mandor. Chonda was blessed with a progeny of fourteen sons, growing up to manhood around him. Their names were Ranmall,[1] Satta, Randhir, Aranyakanwal,[2] Punja, Bhim, Kana, Ajo, Ramdeo, Bija, Sahasmall, Bagh, Lumba, Seoraj.

Chonda had also one daughter named Hansa, married to Lakha Rana of Mewar [16], whose son was the celebrated Kumbha. It was this marriage which caused that interference in the affairs of Mewar, which had such fatal results to both States.[3]

The feud between his fourth son, Aranyakanwal, and the Bhatti prince of Pugal, being deemed singularly illustrative of the Rajput character, has been extracted from the annals of Jaisalmer, in another part of this work.[4] The Rathor chronicler does not enter into details, but merely states the result, as ultimately involving the death of Chonda—simply that "he was slain at Nagor with one thousand Rajputs"; and it is to the chronicles of Jaisalmer we are indebted for our knowledge of the manner. Chonda acceded in S. 1438 (A.D. 1382), and was slain in S. 1465 [A.D. 1408-9].

Ranmall killed A.D. 1444.—Ranmall succeeded. His mother was of the Gohil tribe. In stature he was almost gigantic, and was the most athletic of all the athletes of his nation. With the death of Chonda, Nagor was again lost to the Rathors. Rana Lakha presented Ranmall with the township of Darla and forty villages upon his sister's marriage, when he almost resided at Chitor, and was considered by the Rana as the first of his chiefs. With the forces of Mewar added to his own, under pretence of conveying a daughter to the viceroy of Ajmer, he introduced his adherents into that renowned fortress, the ancient capital of the Chauhans, putting the garrison to the sword, and thus restored it to Mewar. Khemsi Pancholi, the adviser of this measure, was rewarded with a grant of the township of Kata, then lately captured from the Kaimkhanis.[5] Ranmall went on a pilgrimage

[1] The descendants of those numbering 1, 2, 4, 7 still exist.

[2] This is the prince mentioned in the extraordinary feud related (p. 731) from the annals of Jaisalmer. Incidentally, we have frequent synchronisms in the annals of these States, which, however slight, are of high import.

[3] See Vol. I. p. 323.

[4] See p. 730.

[5] [The Kāim or Qāimkhānis were originally Chauhāns, converted to

to Gaya, and paid the tax exacted for all the pilgrims then assembled.

The bard seldom intrudes the relation of civil affairs into his page, and when he does, it is incidentally. It would be folly to suppose that the princes of Maru had no legislative recorders; but with these the poet had no bond of union. He, however, condescends to inform us of an important measure of Rao Ranmall, namely, that he equalized the weights and measures throughout his dominions, which he divided as at present. The last act of Ranmall, in treacherously attempting to usurp the throne of the infant Rana of Mewar, was deservedly punished. and he was slain by the faithful Chonda, as related in the annals of that State.[1] This feud originated the line of demarcation of the two States,[2] and which remained [17] unaltered until recent times, when Marwar at length touched the Aravalli. Rao Ranmall left twenty-four sons, whose issue, and that of his eldest son, Jodha, form the great vassalage of Marwar. For this reason, however barren is a mere catalogue of names, it is of the utmost value to those who desire to see the growth of the frèrage of such a community.[3]

Names.	Clans.	Chieftainships or Fiefs.
1. Jodha (succeeded)	Jodha.	
2. Kandal . .	Kandalot, conquered lands in . .	Bikaner.
3. Champa . .	Champawat .	Awa, Kata, Palri, Harsola, Rohat, Jawala, Satlana, Singari.
4. Akhairaj . . had seven sons: 1st Kumpa .	Kumpawat .	Asop, Kantalia, Chandawal, Siryari, Kharla, Harsor, Balu, Bajoria, Surpura, Dewaria.
5. Mandla . .	Mandlot . .	Sarunda.

Islām in the time of Fīroz Shāh. They are said to derive their name from the first famous convert. It is a rule with them not to use wooden planks in their doorways (*Census Report*, *Mārwār*, 1891, ii. 37 f.; Rose, *Glossary*, iii. 257).]

[1] See Vol. I. p. 327. [2] See Vol. I. p. 328.

[3] It is only by the possession of such knowledge that we can exercise with justice our right of universal arbitration.

Names.	Clans.	Chieftainships or Fiefs.
6. Patta	Pattawat	Kurnichari, Bara, and Desnokh.[1]
7. Lakha	Lakhawat	———
8. Bala	Balawat	Dunara.
9. Jethmall	Jethmallot	Palasni.
10. Karna	Karnot	Lunawas.
11. Rupa	Rupawat	Chutila.
12. Nathu	Nathawat	Bikaner.
13. Dungra	Dungrot	Estates not mentioned; their descendants have become dependent on the greater clanships.
14. Sanda	Sandawat	
15. Manda	Mandot	
16. Biru	Birot	
17. Jagmall	Jagmallot	
18. Hampa [18]	Hampawat	
19. Sakta	Saktawat	
20. Karimchand	———	
21. Arival	Arivalot	
22. Ketsi	Ketsiot	
23. Satrasal	Satrasalot	
24. Tejmall	Tejmallot	

CHAPTER 3

Jodha, A.D. 1444–88. The Foundation of Jodhpur.—Jodha was born at Danla, the appanage of his father in Mewar, in the month Baisakh, S. 1484. In 1511 he obtained Sojat, and in the month Jeth, 1515 (A.D. 1459) laid the foundation of Jodhpur, to which he transferred the seat of government from Mandor. With the superstitious Rajput, as with the ancient Roman [19], every event being decided by the omen or the augur, it would be contrary to rule if so important an occasion as the change of capital, and that of an infant State, were not marked by some propitious prestige, that would justify the abandonment of a city won by the sword, and which had been for ages the capital of Maru. The intervention, in this instance, was of a simple

[1] Brave soldiers, but, safe in the deep sands, they refuse to serve except on emergencies.

nature; neither the flight of birds, the lion's lair, or celestial manifestation; but the ordinance of an anchorite, whose abode, apart from mankind, was a cleft of the mountains of Bakharchiriya. But the behests of such ascetics are secondary only to those of the divinity, whose organs they are deemed. Like the Druids of the Celts, the Vanaprastha Jogi,[1] from the glades of the forest (*vana*) or recess in the rocks (*gupha*), issue their oracles to those whom chance or design may conduct to their solitary dwellings. It is not surprising that the mandates of such beings prove compulsory on the superstitious Rajput: we do not mean those squalid ascetics, who wander about India, and are objects disgusting to the eye; but the genuine Jogi, he who, as the term imports, mortifies the flesh, till the wants of humanity are restricted merely to what suffices to unite matter with spirit; who has studied and comprehended the mystic works, and pored over the systems of philosophy, until the full influence of Maya (illusion) has perhaps unsettled his understanding; or whom the rules of his sect have condemned to penance and solitude; a penance so severe, that we remain astonished at the perversity of reason which can submit to it.[2] To these, the Druids of India, the prince and the chieftain would resort for instruction. They requested neither lands nor gold: to them "the boasted wealth of Bokhara" was as a particle of dust. Such was the ascetic who recommended Jodha to erect his castle on 'the Hill of Strife' (Jodhagir), hitherto known as Bakharchiriya, or 'the bird's nest,' a projecting elevation of the same range on which

[1] [The Vanaprastha or anchorite stage (*āsrama*) of a Brāhman's life (Manu, *Laws*, vi. 1 ff.).]

[2] We have seen one of these objects, self-condemned never to lie down during forty years, and there remained but three to complete the term. He had travelled much, was intelligent and learned; but far from having contracted the moroseness of the recluse, there was a benignity of mien, and a suavity and simplicity of manner in him, quite enchanting. He talked of his penance with no vainglory, and of its approaching term without any sensation. The resting position of this Druid (*vanaprastha*) was by means of a rope suspended from the bough of a tree, in the manner of a swing, having a cross-bar, on which he reclined. The first years of this penance, he says, were dreadfully painful; swollen limbs affected him to that degree, that he expected death; but this impression had long since worn off. 'Even in this, is there much vanity," and it would be a nice point to determine whether the homage of man or the approbation of the Divinity most sustains the energies under such appalling discipline.

Mandor was placed, and about four miles south of it. Doubtless its inaccessible position seconded the recommendation of the hermit, for its scarped summit renders it almost impregnable [20], while its superior elevation permits the sons of Jodha to command, from the windows of their palace, a range of vision almost comprehending the limits of their sway. In clear weather they can view the summits of their southern barrier, the gigantic Aravalli; but in every other direction it fades away in the boundless expanse of sandy plains. Neither the founder, nor his monitor, the ascetic, however, were engineers, and they laid the foundation of this stronghold without considering what an indispensable adjunct to successful defence was good water; but to prevent any slur on the memory of Jodha, they throw the blame of this defect on the hermit. Jodha's engineer, in tracing the line of circumvallation, found it necessary to include the spot chosen as his hermitage, and his remonstrance for undisturbed possession was treated with neglect; whether by the prince as well as the chief architect, the legend says not. The incensed Jogi pronounced an imprecation, that the new castle should possess only brackish water, and all the efforts made by succeeding princes to obtain a better quality, by blasting the rock, have failed. The memory of the Jogi is sanctified, though his anger compelled them to construct an apparatus, whereby water for the supply of the garrison is elevated from a small lake at the foot of the rock, which, being entirely commanded from the walls, an assailant would find difficult to cut off. This was the third grand event in the fortunes of the Rathors, from the settlement of Siahji.[1]

Such was the abundant progeny of these princes, that the limits of their conquests soon became too contracted. The issue of the three last princes, namely, the fourteen sons of Chonda, the twenty-four of Ranmall, and fourteen of Jodha, had already apportioned amongst them the best lands of the country, and it became necessary to conquer "fresh fields in which to sow the Rathor seed."

[1] Pali did not remain to Siahji's descendants, when they went westward and settled on the Luni: the Sesodias took it with other lands from the Parihar of Mandor. It was the feud already adverted to with Mewar which obtained for him the fertile districts of Pali and Sojat, by which his territories at length touched the Aravalli, and the fears of the assassin of Rana Kumbha made his parricidal son relinquish the provinces of Sambhar and Ajmer (see Vol. I. p. 339).

Jodha had fourteen sons, namely—

Names of Chiefs.	Clans.	Fiefs or Chieftainships.	Remarks.
1. Santal, or Satal	——	Satalmer .	Three coss from Pokaran.
2. Suja (Suraj)	——	——	Succeeded Jodha.
3. Gama [21] .	——	——	No issue.
4. Duda . . [Dhuhada]	Mertia .	Merta .	Duda took Sambhar from the Chauhans. He had one son, Biram, whose two sons Jaimall and Jagmall founded the clans Jaimallot and Jagmallot.
5. Birsingh .	Birsinghgot	Nolai .	In Malwa.
6. Bika . .	Bikayat .	Bikaner .	Independent State.
7. Baharmall .	Baharmallot	Bai Bhilara	——
8. Sheoraj .	Sheorajot .	Dunara .	On the Luni.
9. Karamsi .	Karamsot .	Khinwasar	——
10. Raemall .	Raemallot .	——	——
11. Savantsi .	Savantsiot .	Dawara	——
12. Bida . .	Bidawat .	Bidavati .	In Nagor district.
13. Banhar .	——	——	Clans and fiefs not mentioned.
14. Nimba .	——	——	

Sāntal, Sātal, 1488–91.—The eldest son, Santal, born of a female of Bundi, established himself in the north-west corner, on the lands of the Bhattis, and built a fort, which he called Satalmer, about five miles from Pokaran.[1] He was killed in action by a Khan of the Sahariyas (the Saracens of the Indian desert), whom he also slew. His ashes were burnt at Kasma, and an altar was raised over them, where seven of his wives became satis.

The fourth son, Duda [or Dhūhada], established himself on the plains of Merta, and his clan, the Mertia, is numerous, and

[1] [Now in ruins, about 85 miles N.W. of Jodhpur city, containing a large Jain temple and monuments of the Chief's family.]

has always sustained the reputation of being the "first swords" of Maru. His daughter was the celebrated Mira Bai, wife of Rana Kumbha,[1] and he was the grandsire of the heroic Jaimall, who defended Chitor against Akbar, and whose descendant, Jeth Singh of Badnor, is still one of the sixteen chief vassals of the Udaipur court.

The sixth son, Bika, followed the path already trod by his uncle Kandal, with whom he united, and conquered the tracts possessed by the six Jat communities. He erected a city, which he called after himself, Bikaner, or Bīkaner.

Death of Rāo Jodha, A.D. **1488.**—Jodha outlived the foundation of his new capital thirty years, and beheld his [22] sons and grandsons rapidly peopling and subjugating the regions of Maru. In S. 1545, aged sixty-one, he departed this life, and his ashes were housed with those of his fathers, in the ancestral abode of Mandor. This prince, the second founder of his race in these regions, was mainly indebted to the adversities of early life for the prosperity his later years enjoyed; they led him to the discovery of worth in the more ancient, but neglected, allodial proprietors displaced by his ancestors, and driven into the least accessible regions of the desert. It was by their aid he was enabled to redeem Mandor, when expelled by the Guhilots, and he nobly preserved the remembrance thereof in the day of his prosperity. The warriors whose forms are sculptured from the living rock at Mandor owe the perpetuity of their fame to the gratitude of Jodha; through them he not only recovered, but enlarged his dominions.[2] In less than three centuries after their migration from Kanauj, the Rathors, the issue of Siahji, spread over a surface of four degrees of longitude and the same extent of latitude, or nearly 80,000 miles square, and they amount at this day, in spite of the havoc occasioned, by perpetual wars and famine, to 500,000 souls.[3] While we thus contemplate the renovation of the Rathor race, from a single scion of that magnificent tree, whose branches once overshadowed the plains of Ganga, let us withdraw from oblivion some of the many noble names they displaced, which now live only in the poet's page. Well may the Rajput repeat the ever-recurring simile, "All is unstable;

[1] See Vol. I. p. 337.

[2] See p. 842.

[3] [The present area of Mārwār is 34,963 square miles; population 2,057,776, of which Rājputs form 27·0 per cent.]

life is like the scintillation of the fire-fly; house and land will depart, but a good name will last for ever!" What a list of noble tribes could we enumerate now erased from independent existence by the successes of 'the children of Siva' (*Siva-putra*)![1] Pariharas, Indhas, Sankhlas, Chauhans, Gohils, Dabhis, Sandhals, Mohils, Sonigiras, Kathis, Jats, Huls, etc., and the few who still exist only as retainers of the Rathor.

Sūja or Surajmall, A.D. 1491–1516.—Suja[2] (Surajmall) succeeded, and occupied the *gaddi* of Jodha during twenty-seven years, and had at least the merit of adding to the stock of Siahji.

The Rape of the Virgins.—The contentions for empire, during the vacillating dynasty of the Lodi kings of Delhi, preserved the sterile lands of Maru from their cupidity; and a second dynasty, the Shershahi, intervened ere "the sons of Jodha" were summoned to measure swords with the Imperialists. But in S. 1572 (A.D. 1516), a desultory [23] band of Pathans made an incursion during the fair of the Tij,[3] held at the town of Pipar, and carried off one hundred and forty of the maidens of Maru. The tidings of the rape of the virgin Rajputnis were conveyed to Suja, who put himself at the head of such vassals as were in attendance, and pursued, overtook, and redeemed them, with the loss of his own life, but not without a full measure of vengeance against the "northern barbarian." The subject is one chosen by the itinerant minstrel of Maru, who, at the fair of the Tij, still sings the rape of the one hundred and forty virgins of Pipar, and their rescue by their cavalier prince at the price of his own blood.

Suja had five sons, namely: 1. Bhaga, who died in non-age: his son Ganga succeeded to the throne. 2. Uda, who had eleven sons: they formed the clan Udawat, whose chief fiefs are Nimaj, Jaitaran, Gundoj, Baratia, Raepur, etc., besides places in Mewar. 3. Saga, from whom descended the clan Sagawat; located at Barwa. 4. Prayag, who originated the Prayaggot clan. 5. Biramdeo, whose son, Naru, receives divine honours as the Putra of Maru, and whose statue is worshipped at Sojat. His descendants

[1] Siahji is the Bhakha for Siva;—the *ji* is merely an adjunct of respect.

[2] One of the chronicles makes Satal occupy the *gaddi* after Jodha, during three years; but this appears a mistake — he was killed in defending Satalmer.

[3] For a description of this festival see p. 675.

are styled Narawat Jodha, of whom a branch is established at Pachpahar, in Haraoti.

Rāo Ganga, A.D. 1516–32.—Ganga, grandson of Suja, succeeded his grandfather in S. 1572 (A.D. 1516); but his uncle, Saga, determined to contest his right to the *gaddi*, invited the aid of Daulat Khan Lodi, who had recently expelled the Rathors from Nagor. With this auxiliary a civil strife commenced, and the sons of Jodha were marshalled against each other. Ganga, confiding in the rectitude of his cause, and reckoning upon the support of the best swords of Maru, spurned the offer of compromise made by the Pathan, of a partition of its lands between the claimants, and gave battle, in which his uncle Saga was slain, and his auxiliary, Daulat Khan, ignominiously defeated.

Rāthors join Mewār against Bābur, A.D. 1527.—Twelve years after the accession of Ganga, the sons of Jodha were called on to unite their forces to Mewar to oppose the invasion of the Moguls from Turkistan. Sanga Rana, who had resumed the station of his ancestors amongst the princes of Hind, led the war, and the king of Maru deemed it no degradation to acknowledge his supremacy, and send his quotas to fight under the standard of Mewar, whose chronicles do more justice to the Rathors than those of their own bards. This, which was the last confederation made by the Rajputs for national independence [24], was defeated, as already related, in the fatal field of Bayana, where, had treachery not aided the intrepid Babur, the Rathor sword would have had its full share in rescuing the nation from the Muhammadan yoke. It is sufficient to state that a Rathor was in the battle, to know that he would bear its brunt; and although we are ignorant of the actual position of the Rana, we may assume that their post was in the van. The young prince Racmall (grandson of Ganga), with the Mertia chieftains Kharto and Ratna, and many others of note, fell against the Chagatai on this eventful day.

Ganga died [1] four years after this event, and was succeeded by

Rāo Māldeo, A.D. 1532–62, or 1568–69.—Maldeo in S. 1588 (A.D. 1532),[2] a name as distinguished as any of the noble princes

[1] The Yati's roll says Ganga was poisoned; but this is not confirmed by any other authority.

[2] [The dates are doubtful. See the legend of the marriage of Rāo Māldeo to Uma, daughter of the Bhatti Chief of Jaisalmer (*IA*, iii. 96 ff.).]

in the chronicles of Maru. The position of Marwar at this period was eminently excellent for the increase and consolidation of its resources. The emperor Babur found no temptation in her sterile lands to divert him from the rich plains of the Ganges, where he had abundant occupation ; and the districts and strongholds on the emperor's frontier of Maru, still held by the officers of the preceding dynasty, were rapidly acquired by Maldeo, who planted his garrisons in the very heart of Dhundhar. The death of Sanga Rana, and the misfortunes of the house of Mewar, cursed with a succession of minor princes, and at once beset by the Moguls from the north, and the kings of Gujarat, left Maldeo to the uncontrolled exercise of his power, which, like a true Rajput, he employed against friend and foe, and became beyond a doubt the first prince of Rajwara, or, in fact, as styled by the Muhammadan historian Ferishta, " the most potent prince in Hindustan." [1]

The year of Maldeo's installation he redeemed the two most important possessions of his house, Nagor and Ajmer. In S. 1596 he captured Jalor, Siwana, and Bhadrajan from the Sandhals ; and two years later dispossessed the sons of Bika of supreme power in Bikaner. Mewa, and the tracts on the Luni, the earliest possessions of his house, which had thrown off all dependence, he once more subjugated, and compelled the ancient allodial tenantry to hold of him in chief, and serve with their quotas. He engaged in war with the Bhattis, and conquered Bikampur, where a branch of his family remained, and are now incorporated with the Jaisalmer State, and, under the name of Maldots,[2] have the credit of being the most daring robbers of the desert. He even established branches of [25] his family in Mewar and Dhundhar, took, and fortified Chatsu, not twenty miles south of the capital of the Kachhwahas. He captured and restored Sirohi from the Deoras, from which house was his mother. But Maldeo not only acquired, but determined to retain, his conquests, and erected numerous fortifications throughout the country. He enclosed the city of Jodhpur with a strong wall, besides erecting a palace, and adding other works to the fortress. The circumvallations of Merta and its fort, which he called Malkot, cost him £24,000.

[1] [" The most powerful of the Hindu princes who still retained their independence," trans. Briggs, ii. 121.]

[2] Mr. Elphinstone apprehended an attack from the Maldots on his way to Kabul.

He dismantled Satalmer, and with the materials fortified Pokaran, which he took from the Bhattis, transplanting the entire population, which comprehended the richest merchants of Rajasthan. He erected forts at Bhadrajan, on the hill of Bhimlod, near Siwana, at Gundoj, at Rian, Pipar, and Dunara. He made the Kundalkot at Siwana, and greatly added to that of Phalodi, first made by Hamira Nirawat. He also erected that bastion in Garh Bitli (the citadel of Ajmer) called the Kotburj, and showed his skill in hydraulics by the construction of a wheel to bring water into the fort. The chronicler adds, that "by the wealth of Sambhar," meaning the resources of this salt lake, he was enabled to accomplish these works, and furnishes a list of the possessions of Jodhpur at this period, which we cannot exclude: Sojat, Sambhar, Merta, Khata, Badnor, Ladnun, Raepur, Bhadrajan, Nagor, Siwana, Lohagarh, Jaikalgarh, Bikaner, Bhinmal, Pokaran, Barmer, Kasoli, Riwaso, Jajawar, Jalor, Baoli, Malar, Nadol, Phalodi, Sanchor, Didwana, Chatsu, Lawen, Malarna, Deora, Fatehpur, Amarsar, Khawar, Baniapur, Tonk, Toda, Ajmer, Jahazpur, and Pramar-ka-Udaipur (in Shaikhavati); in all thirty-eight districts, several of which, as Jalor, Ajmer, Tonk, Toda, and Badnor, comprehended each three hundred and sixty townships, and there were none which did not number eighty. But of those enumerated in Dhundhar, as Chatsu, Lawen, Tonk, Toda, and Jahazpur in Mewar, the possession was but transient; and although Badnor, and its three hundred and sixty townships, were peopled by Rathors, they were the descendants of the Mertias under Jaimall, who became one of the great vassals of Mewar, and would, in its defence, at all times draw their swords against the land which gave them birth.[1] This branch of the house of Jodha had for some time been too powerful [26] for subjects, and Merta was resumed. To this act Mewar was indebted for the services of this heroic chief. At the same time the growing power of others of the great vassalage of Marwar was checked by resumptions, when Jaitaran from the Udawats, and several other fiefs, were added to the fisc. The feudal allotments had never been regulated, but went on increasing with the energies of the State, and the progeny of its princes, each having on his birth an appanage assigned to him, until the whole

[1] Such is the Rajput's notion of *swamidharma*, or "fidelity to him whose salt they eat," their immediate lord, even against their king.

land of Maru was split into innumerable portions. Maldeo saw the necessity for checking this subdivision, and he created a gradation of ranks, and established its perpetuity in certain branches of the sons of Ranmall and Jodha, which has never been altered.

Inhospitable Conduct of Rāo Māldeo to Humāyūn, A.D. 1542.—Ten years of undisturbed possession were granted Maldeo to perfect his designs, ere his cares were diverted from these to his own defence. Babur, the founder of the Mogul dynasty, was dead, and his son and successor had been driven from his newly conquered throne by his provincial lieutenant, Sher Shah: so rapidly do revolutions crowd upon each other where the sword is the universal arbitrator. We have elsewhere related that the fugitive monarch sought the protection of Maldeo, and we stigmatized his conduct as unnational; but we omitted to state that Maldeo, then heir-apparent, lost his eldest, perhaps then only son Raemall in the battle of Bayana, who led the aid of Marwar on that memorable day, and consequently the name of Chagatai, whether in fortune or in flight, had no great claims to his regard. But little did Maldeo dream how closely the fortunes of his house would be linked with those of the fugitive Humayun, and that the infant Akbar, born in this emergency, was destined to revenge this breach of hospitality. Still less could the proud Rathor, who traced his ancestry on the throne of Kanauj one thousand years before the birth of the "barbarian" of Ferghana, deem it within the range of probability, that he should receive honours at such hands, or that the first title of Raja, Rajeswar, or 'raja, lord of rajas,' would be conferred on his own son by this infant, then rearing amidst the sandhills at the extremity of his desert dominion! It is curious to indulge in the speculative inquiry, whether, when the great Akbar girded Udai Singh with the sword of honour, and marked his forehead with the unguent of Raja-shah, he brought to mind the conduct of Maldeo, which doomed his birth to take place in the dismal castle of Umarkot, instead of in the splendid halls of Delhi [27].

Attack on Mārwār by Sher Shāh, A.D. 1544.—Maldeo derived no advantage from his inhospitality; for whether the usurper deemed his exertions insufficient to secure the royal fugitive, or felt his own power insecure with so potent a neighbour, he led an army of eighty thousand men into Marwar. Maldeo allowed them to advance, and formed an army of fifty thousand Rajputs to oppose him. The judgment and caution he exercised were so great, that Sher Shah, well versed in the art of war, was obliged to fortify his camp at every step. Instead of an easy conquest, he soon repented of his rashness when the admirable dispositions of the Rajputs made him dread an action, and from a position whence he found it impossible to retreat. For a month the armies lay in sight of each other, every day the king's situation becoming more critical, and from which he saw not the slightest chance of extrication. In this exigence he had recourse to one of those stratagems which have often operated successfully on the Rajput, by sowing distrust in his mind as to the fidelity of his vassals. He penned a letter, as if in correspondence with them, which he contrived to have dropped, as by accident, by a messenger sent to negotiate. Perhaps the severity of the resumptions of estates seconded this scheme of Sher Shah; for when the stipulated period for the attack had arrived, the raja countermanded it. The reasons for this conduct, when success was apparent, were soon propagated; when one or two of the great leaders, in order to demonstrate their groundlessness, gave an instance of that devotion with which the annals of these States abound. At the head of twelve thousand, they attacked and forced the imperial entrenched camp, carrying destruction even to the quarters of the emperor; but multitudes prevailed, and the patriotic clans were almost annihilated. Maldeo, when too late, saw through the stratagem which had made him doubt the loyalty of his vassals. Superstition and the reproaches of his chieftains for his unworthy suspicions, did the rest; and this first *levée en masse* of the descendants of Siahji, arrayed in defence of their national liberties, was defeated. With justice did the usurper pay homage to their gallantry, when he exclaimed, on his deliverance from this peril, "he had nearly lost the empire of Hindustan for a handful of barley."[1]

Attack by Akbar, A.D. **1558-62.**—Maldeo was destined to outlive the Shershahi dynasty, and to see the imperial crown of India once more encircle the brows of the fugitive Humayun.[2] It had

[1] In allusion to the poverty of the soil, as unfitted to produce richer grains [Ferishta ii. 123; see pp. 835, 931 above].

[2] There is a biographical account of this monarch, during his exile in Persia, written by his Abdar, or 'cup-bearer,' in the library of Major W. Yule, of Edinburgh, and which, when translated, will complete the series

[28] been well for the Rathors had his years been lengthened; for his mild disposition and natural indolence of character gave them some chance that these qualities would be their best advocate. But he did not long survive the restoration. Whether the mother of his successor, prince Akbar, not yet fifteen, stimulated by the recollection of her misfortunes, nursed his young animosity against Maldeo for the miseries of Umarkot, or, whether it was merely an act of cautionary policy to curb the Rajput power, which was inconsistent with his own, in S. 1617 (A.D. 1561) he invaded Marwar, and laid siege to Malakot or Merta, which he took after an obstinate and sanguinary defence, part of the garrison cutting their way through his host, and making good their retreat to their prince.[1] The important castle of Nagor was also captured; and both these strongholds and their lands were conferred by Akbar on the younger branch of the family, Rae Singh, prince of Bikaner, now established in independence of the parent State, Jodhpur.

In 1625 (A.D. 1569), Maldeo succumbed to necessity; and in conformity with the times, sent his second son, Chandarsen,[2] with gifts to Akbar, then at Ajmer, which had become an integral part of the monarchy; but Akbar was so dissatisfied with the disdainful bearing of the desert king, who refused personally to pay his court, that he not only guaranteed the free possession of Bikaner to Rae Singh, but presented him with the farman for Jodhpur itself, with supremacy over his race. Chandarsen appears to have possessed all the native pride of the Rathor, and to have been prepared to contest his country's independence, in spite of Akbar and the claims of his elder brother, Udai Singh, who eventually was more supple in ingratiating himself into the monarch's favour. At the close of life the old Rao had to stand a siege in his capital, and after a brave but fruitless resistance,[3] was obliged to yield homage, and pay it in the person of his son

---

of biography of the members of the house of Timur. [The *Tazkirātu-l-wāki'āt* of Jauhar, extracts from which are translated in Elliot-Dowson v. 136 ff.]

[1] [The capture of Merta in 1562 by Sharafu-dīn Husain Mirza is described in *Akbarnāma*, trans. H. Beveridge, ii. 247 f.; Smith, *Akbar*, 59.]

[2] [The statement that Chandarsen was second son of Māldeo rests on the Author's account, and is not mentioned in the *Akbarnāma*.]

[3] [For the capture of Jodhpur, "the strongest fort in that country," by Husain Kuli Khān see *Akbarnāma*, ii. 305.]

Udai Singh, who, attending with a contingent, was enrolled amongst the commanders of 'one thousand'; and shortly after was invested with the title of Mota Raja, or 'the fat Raja,' by which epithet alone he is designated in the annals of that period.[1]

Chandarsen, with a considerable number of the brave vassals of Maru, determined to cling to independence and the rude fare of the desert, rather than servilely follow in the train of the despot. When driven from Jodhpur, they took post in Siwana, in the western extremity of the State, and there held out to the death. For seventeen years he maintained his title to the *gaddi*, and divided the allegiance of [29] the Rathors with his elder brother Udai Singh (though supported by the king), and stood the storm in which he nobly fell, leaving three sons, Ugarsen, Askaran, and Rao Singh, who fought a duel with Rao Surthan, of Sirohi, and was slain, with twenty-four of his chiefs,[2] near the town of Datani.

Maldeo, though he submitted to acknowledge the supremacy of the emperor, was at least spared the degradation of seeing a daughter of his blood bestowed upon the opponent of his faith; he died soon after the title was conferred on his son, which sealed the dependence of Maru. His latter days were a dismal contrast to those which witnessed his conquests in almost every part o Rajputana, but he departed from this world in time to preserve his own honour untarnished, with the character of the most valiant and energetic Rajput of his time. Could he have added to his years and maintained their ancient vigour, he might, by a junction with Partap of Mewar, who single-handed commenced his career just as Maldeo's closed, have maintained Rajput independence against the rising power of the Moguls.[3]

Maldeo, who died S. 1625 (A.D. 1569), had twelve sons:

1. Ram Singh, who was banished, and found refuge with the Rana of Mewar; he had seven sons, the fifth of whom, Keshodas, fixed at Chuli Maheshwar.
2. Raemall, who was killed in the battle of Bayana.

[1] [See *Āīn*, i. 429 f. Erskine (iii. A. 587) suggests that Mota means 'good, potent'.]

[2] It was fought with a certain number on each side, Rathors against Deoras, a branch of the Chauhans, the two bravest of all the Rajput races. It reminds us of some of the duels related by Froissart.

[3] See Vol. I. 385 ff.

3. Udai Singh, Raja of Marwar.
4. Chandarsen, by a wife of the Jhala tribe; had three sons, the eldest, Ugarsen, got Binai; he had three sons, Karan, Kanji, and Kahan.
5. Askaran; descendants at Junia.
6. Gopaldas; killed at Idar.
7. Prithiraj; descendants at Jalor.
8. Ratansi; descendants at Bhadrajun.
9. Bheraj; descendants at Abari.
10. Bikramajit }
11. Bhan } No notice of them [30].
12. —— }

CHAPTER 4

Vassalage of Mārwār to the Mughals.—The death of Maldeo formed an important epoch in the annals of the Rathors. Up to this period the will had waited upon the wish of the gallant descendants of Siva; but now the vassals of Maru acknowledged one mightier than they. The banner of the empire floated pre-eminent over the *panchranga*, the five-coloured flag, which had led the Rathors from victory to victory, and waved from the sandhills of Umarkot to the salt-lake of Sambhar; from the desert bordering the Gara to the peaks of the Aravalli. Henceforward, the Rathor princes had, by their actions or subservience, to ascend by degrees the steps to royal favour. They were required to maintain a contingent of their proud vassals, headed by the heir, to serve at the Mogul's pleasure. Their deeds won them, not ignobly, the grace of the imperial court; but had slavish submission been the sole path to elevation, the Rathor princes would never have attained a grade beyond the first mansab,[1] conferred on Udai Singh. Yet though streams of wealth enriched the barren plains of Maru; although a portion of the spoils of Golkonda and Bijapur augmented its treasures, decorated its palaces, and embellished its edifices and mausoleums; although the desert kings took the 'right hand' of all the feudality of

[1] [Rank, prescribing precedence and gradation of pay (Irvine, *Army of the Indian Moghuls*, 3 ff.).]

Hind, whether indigenous or foreign—a feudal assemblage of no less than seventy-six petty kingdoms—yet the Rathor felt the sense of his now degraded condition, and it often burst forth even in the presenee of the suzerain.

Rāo Udai Singh, A.D. **1581-95.**—Maldeo's death occurred in S. 1625;[1] but the chronicles do not admit of Udai [31] Singh's elevation until the death of his brother Chandarsen, from which period we may reckon that he was, though junior, the choice both of his father and the nobles, who did not approve of Udai Singh's submission to Akbar. In fact, the Raja led the royal forces against the most powerful of his vassals, and resumed almost all the possessions of the Mertias, and weakened the others.

Before we proceed to trace the course pursued by Udai Singh, who was seated upon the cushion of Maldeo in S. 1640 (A.D. 1584), let us cast a short retrospect over the annals of Maru, since the migration of the grandson of the potentate of Kanauj, which, compared with the ample page of western history, present little more than a chronicle of hard names, though not destitute of facts interesting to political science.

Retrospect of Mārwār History.—In the table before the reader, aided by the explanations in the text, he will see the whole process of the conquest, peopling, and settlement of an extensive region, with its partition or allotments amongst an innumerable frèrage (*bhayyad*), whose children continue to hold them as vassals of their king and brother, the descendant of their mutual ancestor Siahji.

We may divide the annals of Marwar, from the migration of Siahji from Kanauj to the accession of Udai Singh, into three distinet epochs:

1. From the settlement of Siahji in the land of Kher, in A.D. 1212, to the conquest of Mandor by Chonda, in A.D. 1381.

2. From the conquest of Mandor to the founding of Jodhpur, in A.D. 1459; and

3. From the founding of Jodhpur to the accession of Udai Singh in A.D. 1584, when the Rathors acknowledged the supremacy of the empire.

The two first epochs were occupied in the subjugation of the western portion of the desert from the ancient allodiality; nor

[1] [The dates are uncertain; those in the margin follow Erskine (iii. B. 25).]

was it until Chonda conquered Mandor, on the decline of the Chauhans of the east, that the fertile lands on either side of the Luni were formed into fiefs for the children of Ranmall and Jodha. A change of capital with the Rajput is always productive of change in the internal organisation of the State; and not unfrequently the race changes its appellation with its capital. The foundation of Jodhpur was a new era, and henceforth the throne of Maru could only be occupied by the tribe of Jodha, and from branches not constituting the vassals of the crown, who were cut off from succession. This is a peculiar [32] feature in Rajput policy, and is common to the whole race, as will be hereafter more distinctly pointed out in the annals of Ajmer.

Feudalism in Mārwār.—Jodha, with all the ambition of the founder of a State, gave a new form to the feudal institutions of his country. Necessity, combined with pride, led him to promulgate a statute of limitation of the sub-infeudations of Maru. The immense progeny of his father Ranmall, twenty-four sons, and his own, of fourteen, almost all of whom had numerous issue, rendered it requisite to fix the number and extent of the fiefs; and amongst them, henceforward constituting permanently the frèrage of Maru, the lands were partitioned, Kandhal having emigrated and established his own numerous issue, the Kandhalots, in Bikaner. The two brothers next to Jodha, namely, Champa and Kumpa, with his two sons, Duda and Karamsi, and his grandson, Uda, were declared the heads of the feudal association under their names, the Champawats, Kumpawats, Mertias (sons of Duda), Karamsots, and Udawats, and continue to be "the pillars of Maru." Eight great estates, called the *ath thakurat*, or 'eight lordships' of Marwar, each of the nominal annual value of fifty thousand rupees (£5000), were settled on these persons, and their immense influence has obtained many others for younger branches of their clans. The title of the first noble of Maru was given to Champa and his issue, who have often made its princes tremble on their thrones. Besides these, inferior appanages were settled on the junior branches, brothers, sons, and grandsons of Jodha, which were also deemed hereditary and irresumable; to use their own phrase, their *bat*,[1] or 'allotment,' to which they consider their title as sacred as that of their prince

[1] From *batna*, 'to divide, to partition.'

to his throne, of whom they say, "When our services are acceptable, then is he our lord; when not, we are again his brothers and kin, claimants, and laying claim to the land." [1]

Rao Maldeo confirmed this division of Jodha, though he increased the secondary fiefs, and as the boundaries of Marwar were completed in his reign, it was essentially necessary to confirm the limitation. The feudal States of Marwar are, therefore, perpetuated in the offspring of the princes from Jodha to Maldeo, and a distinction exists between them and those subsequently conferred; the first, being [33] obtained by conquest, are deemed irrevocable, and must be perpetuated by adoption on the failure of lineal issue; whereas the other may, on lapses, be resumed and added to the fisc whence it emanated. The fiscal domain of the Rajput princes cannot, says their traditionary lore, be alienated for more than a life-interest; but this wise rule, though visible in anecdotes of past days, has been infringed with their general disorganization. These instances, it may be asserted, afford the distinctions of allodial and feudal lands. Of the numerous clans, the issue of Siahji to Jodha, which are spread over the northern and western parts of the State, some, partly from the difficulty of their position, partly from a feeling of respect to their remote ancestry, enjoy almost entire independence. Yet they recognize the prince of Maru as their liege lord when his crown is endangered, and render homage on his accession or any great family event. These clans hold without grant or fine, and may properly be called the allodial chieftains. Of this number we may enumerate the lordships of Barmer, Kotra, Sheo, Phulsund, etc. Others there are who, though less independent, may also be styled the allodiality of Marwar, who are to furnish their quotas when demanded, and perform personal homage on all great days of rejoicing; of these are Mewa, Sindari, etc. The ancient clans scattered over the land, or serving the more modern chieftains, are recognized by their patronymic distinctions, by those versed in the chronicles; though many hear the names of Duhariya, Mangalia, Uhar, and Dhandal, without knowing them to be Rathor. The mystic page of the bard is always consulted previous to any marriage, in order to prevent a violation of the matrimonial canons of the Rajputs, which are stricter than the Mosaic, and this keeps up the know-

[1] See the remonstrance of the vassal descendants of these chiefs, expelled their patrimony by their prince, to the English enemy, Vol. I. p. 230.

ledge of the various branches of their own and other races, which would otherwise perish

Whatever term may be applied to these institutions of a martial race, and which for the sake of being more readily understood we have elsewhere called, and shall continue to designate, "feudal," we have not a shadow of doubt that they were common to the Rajput races from the remotest ages, and that Siahji conveyed them from the seat of his ancestors, Kanauj. A finer picture does not exist of the splendour of a feudal array than the camp of its last monarch, Jaichand, in the contest with the Chauhan. The annals of each and every State bear evidence to a system strictly parallel to that of Europe; more especially Mewar, where, thirteen hundred years ago, we see the entire feudatories of the State throwing up their grants, giving their liege lord defiance, and threatening him with their [34] vengeance. Yet, having "eaten his salt," they forbore to proceed to hostilities till a whole year had elapsed, at the expiration of which they deposed him.[1] Akbar, who was partial to Hindu institutions, borrowed much from them, in all that concerned his own regulations.

In contrasting these customs with analogous ones in the West, the reader should never lose sight of one point, which must influence the analogy, namely, the patriarchal form which characterizes the feudal system in all countries; and as, amongst the Rajputs, all their vassalage is of their own kin and blood (save a slight mixture of foreign nobles as a counterpoise), the paternity of the sovereign is no fiction, as in Europe; so that from the son of Champa, who takes the right hand of his prince, to the meanest vassal, who serves merely for his *peti*[2] (rations), all are linked by the tie of consanguinity, of which it is difficult to say whether it is most productive of evil or good, since it has afforded examples as brilliant and as dark as any in the history of mankind. The devotion which made twelve thousand, out of the fifty thousand, "sons of Jodha" prove their fidelity to Maldeo has often been emulated even to the present day.

The chronicles, as before stated, are at variance with regard to the accession of Udai Singh: some date it from the death of Maldeo, in S. 1625 (A.D. 1569); others from that of his elder brother Chandarsen, slain in the storm of Siwana. The name of

[1] See Vol. I. p. 266.

[2] Literally, 'a bellyful.'

Udai appears one of evil portent in the annals of Rajasthan.[1] While "Udai, the fat," was inhaling the breeze of imperial power, which spread a haze of prosperity over Maru, Partap of Mewar, the idol of the Rajputs, was enduring every hardship in the attempt to work out his country's independence, which had been sacrificed by his father, Udai Singh. In this he failed, but he left a name hallowed in the hearts of his countrymen, and immortalized in the imperishable verse of the bard.

On the union of the imperial house with that of Jodhpur, by the marriage of Jodh Bai to Akbar,[2] the emperor not only restored all the possessions he had wrested from Marwar, with the exception of Ajmer, but several rich districts in Malwa, whose revenues doubled the resources of his own fiscal domain. With the aid of his imperial brother-in-law, he greatly diminished the power of the feudal aristocracy [35], and clipped the wings of almost all the greater vassals, while he made numerous sequestrations of the lands of the ancient allodiality and lesser vassals; so that it is stated, that, either by new settlement or confiscation, he added fourteen hundred villages to the fisc. He resumed almost all the lands of the sons of Duda, who, from their abode, were termed Mertia; took Jaitaran from the Udawats, and other towns of less note from the sons of Champa and Kumpa.

Udai Singh was not ungrateful for the favours heaped upon him by the emperor, for whom his Rathors performed many signal services: for the raja was latterly too unwieldy for any steed to bear him to battle. The "king of the Desert" (the familiar epithet applied to him by Akbar) had a numerous progeny; no less than thirty-four legitimate sons and daughters, who added new clans and new estates to the feudal association of Maru: of these the most conspicuous are Govindgarh and Pisangan; while some obtained settlements beyond its limits which became independent and bear the name of the founders. Of these are Kishangarh and Ratlam in Malwa.

Death of Rāo Udai Singh.—Udai Singh died thirteen years after his inauguration on the cushion of Jodha, and thirty-three

[1] Instead of being, as it imports, the 'ascending,' (Skt. *udaya*), it should for ever, in both the houses of Maru and Mewar, signify 'setting'; the pusillanimity of the one sunk Mewar, that of the other Marwar.

[2] [There has been some controversy about Jodh Bāī, but it is clear that she was wife of Jahāngīr, not of Akbar (*Āīn*, i. 619).]

after the death of Maldeo. The manner of his death, as related in the biographical sketches termed Khyat, affords such a specimen of superstition and of Rajput manners that it would be improper to omit it. The narrative is preceded by some reflections on the moral education of the Rathor princes, and the wise restraints imposed upon them under the vigilant control of chiefs of approved worth and fidelity; so that, to use the words of the text, "they often passed their twentieth year, ignorant of woman." If the "fat raja" had ever known this moral restraint, in his riper years he forgot it; for although he had no less than twenty-seven queens, he cast the eye of desire on the virgin-daughter of a subject, and that subject a Brahman.

Brāhman sacrifices his Daughter.—It was on the raja's return from court to his native land that he beheld the damsel, and he determined, notwithstanding the sacred character of her father and his own obligations as the dispenser of law and justice, to enjoy the object of his admiration. The Brahman was an Ayapanthi,[1] or votary of Ayamata, whose shrine is at Bhavi-Bhilara. These sectarians of Maru, very different from the abstinent Brahmans of Bengal, eat flesh, drink wine, and share in all the common enjoyments of life with the martial spirits around them. Whether the scruples of the [36] daughter were likely to be easily overcome by her royal tempter, or whether the raja threatened force, the Khyat does not inform us; but as there was no other course by which the father could save her from pollution but by her death, he resolved to make it one of vengeance and horror. He dug a sacrificial pit, and having slain his daughter, cut her into fragments, and mingling therewith pieces of flesh from his own person, made the Homa, or burnt sacrifice to Ayamata, and as the smoke and flames ascended he pronounced an imprecation on the raja: "Let peace be a stranger to him! and in three pahars,[2] three days, and three years, let me have revenge!" Then exclaiming, "My future dwelling is the Dabhi Baori!" sprung into the flaming pit. The horrid tale was related to the raja, whose imagination was haunted by the shade of the Brahman;

[1] [This is one of the Jogi orders (Rose, *Glossary*, ii. 9). The Author (*Western India*, 136) says that Ayāmāta is tutelary goddess of the Koli tribe. One branch of the Lohānas specially worship her (*Census Report, Mārwār*, 1891, ii. 139).]

[2] A pahar is a watch of the day, about three hours.

and he expired at the assigned period, a prey to unceasing remorse.

Superstition is sometimes made available for moral ends; and the shade of the Ayapanthi Brahman of Bhilara has been evoked, in subsequent ages, to restrain and lead unto virtue libidinous princes, when all other control has been unavailing. The celebrated Jaswant Singh, the great-grandson of Udai, had an amour with the daughter of one of his civil officers, and which he carried on at the Dabhi Baori.[1] But the avenging ghost of the Brahman interposed between him and his wishes. A dreadful struggle ensued, in which Jaswant lost his senses, and no effort could banish the impression from his mind. The ghost persecuted his fancy, and he was generally believed to be possessed with a wicked spirit, which, when exorcised, was made to say he would only depart on the self-sacrifice of a chief equal in dignity to Jaswant. Nahar Khan, "the tiger lord," chief of the Kumpawat clan, who led the van in all his battles, immediately offered his head in expiation for his prince; and he had no sooner expressed this loyal determination, than the holy men who exorcised the spirit caused it to descend into a vessel of water, and having waved it thrice round his head, they presented it to Nahar Khan, who drank it off, and Jaswant's senses were instantly restored. This miraculous transfer of the ghost is implicitly believed by every chief of Rajasthan, by whom Nahar was called "the faithful of the faithful." Previous to dying, he called his son, and imposed on him and his descendants, by the solemnity of an oath, the abjuration of the office of Pardhan, or hereditary premier of Marwar, whose dignity involved such a sacrifice [37]; and from that day the Champawats of Awa succeeded the Kumpawats of Asop, who renounced the first seat on the right for that on the left of their princes.

We shall conclude the reign of Udai Singh with the register of his issue from "the Book of Kings." It is by no means an unimportant document to such as are interested in these singular communities, and essentially useful to those who are called upon

[1] A reservoir excavated by one of the Dabhi tribe. [This is a mistake. The proper name is Tāpi Bāori or 'pit of fire' (*Census Report, Mārwār*, 1891, ii. 65). For similar ghost stories see Crooke, *Popular Religion and Folklore of N. India*, i. 193 ff. The original name of Nāhar Khān, before his conversion to Islām, was Mukunddās.]

to interfere in their national concerns. Here we see the affinities of the branch (*sakha*) to the parent tree, which in one short century has shaded the whole land; and to which the independents of Kishangarh, Rupnagarh, and Ratlam, as well as the feudal chiefs of Govindgarh, Khairwa, and Pisangan, all issues from Udai Singh, look for protection.

Issue of Raja Udai Singh:—

1. Sur Singh, succeeded.
2. Akhairaj.
3. Bhagwandas; had issue Bala, Gopaldas, Govinddas, who founded Govindgarh.
4. Narardas } had no issue attaining eminence.
5. Sakat Singh }
6. Bhopat }
7. Dalpat had four sons: 1. Maheshdas, whose son, Ratna, founded Ratlam;[1] 2. Jaswant Singh; 3. Partap Singh; 4. Kaniram.
8. Jeth had four sons: 1. Har Singh; 2. Amra; 3. Kaniram; 4. Premraj, whose descendants held lands in the tract called Balati and Khairwa.
9. Kishan, in S. 1669 (A.D. 1613), founded Kishangarh; he had three sons, Sahasmall, Jagmall, Biharmall, who had Hari Singh, who had Rup Singh, who founded Rupnagarh.
10. Jaswant, his son Man founded Manpura, his issue called Manpura Jodha.
11. Kesho founded Pisangan.
12. Ramdas. } No mention of them.
13. Puranmall. }
14. Madhodas. }
15. Mohandas. }
16. Kirat Singh. }
17. —— }

And seventeen daughters not registered in the chronicle [38].

[1] Ratlam, Kishangarh, and Rupnagarh are independent, and all under the separate protection of the British Government.

CHAPTER 5

Rāja Sūr Singh, A.D. 1595-1620.—Sur Singh succeeded in S. 1651 (A.D. 1595). He was serving with the Imperial forces at Lahore, where he had commanded since S. 1648, when intelligence reached him of his father's death. His exploits and services were of the most brilliant nature, and had obtained for him, even during his father's life, the title of "Sawai Raja,"[1] and a high grade amongst the dignitaries of the empire. He was commanded by Akbar to reduce the arrogant prince of Sirohi, who, trusting to the natural strength of his mountainous country, still refused to acknowledge a liege lord. This service well accorded with his private views, for he had a feud (*wair*) with Rao Surthan, which, according to the chronicle, he completely revenged. "He avenged his feud with Surthan and plundered Sirohi. The Rao had not a pallet left to sleep upon, but was obliged to make a bed for his wives upon the earth." This appears to have humbled the Deora, "who, in his pride, shot his arrows at the sun for daring to shine upon him."

Campaign in Gujarāt.—Surthan accepted the imperial [39] farman in token of submission, and agreed to serve with a contingent of his hardy clansmen in the war then entrusted to Raja Sur against the king of Gujarat, whose success we shall relate in the simple language of the chronicle: "The Raja took the *pan* against the king Muzaffar, with the title of viceroy of Gujarat. The armies met at Dhandhuka,[2] where a terrible conflict ensued. The Rathors lost many valiant men, but the Shah was defeated, and lost all the insignia of his greatness. He sent the spoil of seventeen thousand towns to the king, but kept a crore of *drabs*[3] for himself, which he sent to Jodhpur, and therewith he enlarged the town and fort. For this service Akbar increased his *mansab*, and sent him a sword, with a khilat, and a grant of fresh lands."

[1] [Sawāi means 'a quarter better than any one else.']

[2] [Dhandhuka about 40 miles W. of Cambay; the account in the text is possibly a confused reference to the insurrection of Muzaffar Husain Mīrza, which began in 1577 and ended in the suicide of the rebel in 1591-92 (*BG*, i. Part i. 268 ff.).]

[3] [Coins, perhaps gold mohurs (Skt. *dravya*, 'wealth')].

Raja Sur, it appears in the sequel, provided liberally for the bards; for no less than "six lords of verse," whose names are given, had in gift £10,000 each of the spoils of Gujarat, as incentives to song.

On the conquest of Gujarat, Raja Sur was ordered to the Deccan. "He obeyed, and with thirteen thousand horse, ten large guns, and twenty elephants, he fought three grand battles. On the Rewa (Nerbudda) he attacked Amra Balecha,[1] who had five thousand horse, whom he slew, and reduced all his country. For this service the king sent him a *naubat* (kettle-drum), and conferred on him Dhar and its domain."

On Akbar's death and the accession of Jahangir, Sur Singh attended at court with his son and heir, Gaj Singh, whom the king with his own hands invested with the sword, for his bravery in the escalade of Jalor, which had been conquered by the monarch of Gujarat and added to his domain. The poet thus relates the event: "Gaj[2] was commanded against Bihari Pathan; his war-trump sounded; Arbuda [Abu] heard and trembled. What took Alau-d-din years, Gaj accomplished in three months; he escaladed Jalandhara[3] sword in hand; many a Rathor of fame was killed, but he put to the sword seven thousand Pathans, whose spoils were sent to the king."

Raja Sur, it would appear, after the overthrow of the dynasty of Gujarat, remained at the capital, while his son and heir, Gaj Singh, attended the king's [40] commands, and, soon after the taking of Jalor, was ordered with the Marwar contingent against Rana Amra of Mewar: it was at the very moment of its expiring liberties,[4] for the chronicle merely adds, "Karan agreed to serve the king, and Gaj Singh returned to Taragarh.[5] The king increased both his own *mansab* (dignity) and that of his father, Raja Sur."

Thus the Rajput chronicler, solicitous only to record the fame of his own princes, does not deem it necessary to concern himself

[1] Balecha is one of the Chauhan tribes. [It does not appear in recent lists.]

[2] *Gaj*, 'the elephant.'

[3] Classical appellation of Jalor.

[4] The chronicle says, "In S. 1669 (A.D. 1613), the king formed an army against the Rana"; which accords exactly with the date in the emperor's own memoirs.

[5] Ajmer, of which the citadel is styled Taragarh.

with the agents conjoined with them, so that a stranger to the events of the period would imagine, from the high relief given to their actions, that the Rathor princes commanded in all the great events described; for instance, that just mentioned, involving the submission of the Rana, when Raja Gaj was merely one of the great leaders who accompanied the Mogul heir-apparent, Prince Khurram, on this memorable occasion. In the Diary of Jahangir, the emperor, recording this event, does not even mention the Rathor prince, though he does those of Kotah and Datia, as the instruments by which Prince Khurram carried on the negotiation;[1] from which we conclude that Raja Gaj merely acted a military part in the grand army which then invaded Mewar.

Death of Rāja Sūr Singh, A.D. 1620: his Character.—Raja Sur died in the Deccan, in S. 1676 (A.D. 1620). He added greatly to the lustre of the Rathor name, was esteemed by the emperor, and, as the bard expresses it, "His spear was frightful to the Southron." Whether Raja Sur disapproved of the exterminating warfare carried on in these regions, or was exasperated at the unlimited service he was doomed to, which detained him from his native land, he, in his last moments, commanded a pillar to be erected with a curse engraven thereon, imprecated upon any of his race who should once cross the Nerbudda. From his boyhood he had been almost an alien to his native land: he had accompanied his father wherever he led the aid of Maru, was serving at Lahore at the period of his accession, and died far from the monuments of his fathers, in the heart of the peninsula. Although the emperor was not ungrateful in his estimate of these services,—for Raja Sur held by patent no less than "sixteen [41] grand fiefs"[2] of the empire, and with the title of Sawai raised above all the princes, his associates at court,—it was deemed no compensation for perpetual absence from the hereditary domain, thus abandoned to the management of servants. The great

[1] See Annals of Mewār, Vol. I. p. 418.

[2] Of these, nine were the subdivisions of his native dominions, styled "The Nine Castles of Maru"; for on becoming one of the great feudatories of the empire, he made a formal surrender of these, receiving them again by grant, renewed on every lapse, with all the ceremonies of investiture and relief. Five were in Gujarat, one in Malwa, and one in the Deccan. We see that thirteen thousand horse was the contingent of Marwar for the lands thus held.

vassals, his clansmen, participated in this dissatisfaction, separated from their wives, families, and estates; for to them the pomp of imperial greatness, or the sunshine of court-favour, was as nothing when weighed against the exercise of their influence within their own cherished patrimony. The simple fare of the desert was dearer to the Rathor than all the luxuries of the imperial banquet, which he turned from with disgust to the recollection of "the green pulse of Mandawar," or his favourite *rabri*, or 'maize porridge,' the prime dish with the Rathor. These minor associations conjoined with greater evils to increase the *mal de pays*, of whose influence no human being is more susceptible than the brave Rajput.

Raja Sur greatly added to the beauty of his capital, and left several works which bear his name; amongst them, not the least useful in that arid region, is the lake called the Sur Sagar, or 'Warrior's Sea,' which irrigates the gardens on its margin. He left six sons and seven daughters, of whose issue we have no account, namely, Gaj Singh, his successor; Sabal Singh, Biramdeo, Bijai Singh, Partap Singh, and Jaswant Singh.

Rāja Gaj Singh, A.D. **1620–38.**—Raja Gaj, who succeeded his father in A.D. 1620, was born at Lahore, and the *tika* of investiture found him in the royal camp at Burhanpur. The bearer of it was Darab Khan, the son of the Khankhanan,[1] or premier noble of the emperor's court, who, as the imperial proxy, girt Raja Gaj with the sword. Besides the "nine castles" (*Naukoti Marwar*), his patrimony, his patent contained a grant of "seven divisions" of Gujarat, of the district of Jhalai in Dhundhar; and what was of more consequence to him, though of less intrinsic value, that of Masuda in Ajmer, the heirloom of his house. Besides these marks of distinction, he received the highest proof of confidence in the elevated post of viceroy of the Deccan; and, as a special testimony of imperial favour, the Rathor cavaliers composing his contingent were exempted from the *dagh*,[2] that is, having their steeds branded with the imperial signet. His elder son, Amra Singh, served with [42] his father in all his various battles, to the success of which his conspicuous gallantry on every occasion contributed. In the sieges and battles of Kirkigarh, Golkonda,

[1] [Mirza Abdu-r-rahīm, son of Bairām Khān (*Āīn*, i. 334 ff.).]

[2] [For this branding system see *Āīn*, i. 139 f.; Irvine, *Army of the Indian Moghuls*, 45 ff.]

Khelna, Parnala, Gajangarh, Asir and Satara, the Rathors had their full share of glory, which obtained for their leader the title of Dalthaman, or 'barrier of the host.' We have already[1] remarked the direct influence which the Rajput princes had in the succession to the imperial dignity, consequent upon the intermarriage of their daughters with the crown, and the various interests arising therefrom. Sultan Parvez, the elder son and heir of Jahangir, was the issue of a princess of Marwar,[2] while the second son, Khurram, as his name imports, was the son of a Kachhwaha[3] princess of Amber. Being the offspring of polygamy and variously educated, these princes were little disposed to consider consanguinity as a bond of natural union; and their respective mothers, with all the ambition of their race, thought of nothing but obtaining the diadem for the head of their children. With either of these rival queens, the royal children who were not her own had no affinity with her or hers, and these feelings were imparted from the birth to their issue, and thus it too often happened that the heir of the throne was looked upon with an envious eye, as a bar to be removed at all hazards. This evil almost neutralized the great advantages derived from intermarriage with the indigenous races of India; but it was one which would have ceased with polygamy.

Death of Parvez, A.D. 1626.—Khurram felt his superiority over his elder brother, Parvez, in all but the accidental circumstance of birth. He was in every respect a better man, and a braver and more successful soldier; and, having his ambition thus early nurtured by the stimulants administered by Bhim of Mewar, and the intrepid Mahabat,[4] he determined to remove this barrier

[1] See Vol. I. p. 435.

[2] [Parvez or Parvīz was son of Sāhib Jamāl, daughter of Khwāja Hasan, uncle of Zain Khān Koka; but this is not quite certain (*Āīn*, i. 310; *Tuzuk-i-Jahāngīri*, trans. Rogers-Beveridge, 19; Beale, *Oriental Biographical Dict.* s.v.).]

[3] Kachhua and Khurram are synonymous terms for the race which rules Amber—the Tortoises of Rajasthan. [This is an extraordinary misapprehension. *Khurram* is a Persian word, meaning 'pleased, glad'; the Author confuses it with Skt. *Kūrma*, 'a tortoise.' The mother of Khurram, Balmati or Jagat Gosāīn, was daughter of Udai Singh of Mārwār; see *Tuzuk*, 19; Beale, s.v. *Shāh Jahān*.]

[4] A Rajput of the Rana's house, converted to *the faith*. [Mahābat Khān, Khānkhānān, Sipāhsālār Zamāna Beg, was not a Rājput, but son of Ghiyās Beg, Kābuli (Manucci i. 167; Elliot-Dowson vi. 288).]

between him and the crown. His views were first developed whilst leading the armies in the Deccan, and he communicated them to Raja Gaj of Marwar, who held the post of honour next the prince, and solicited his aid to place him on the throne. Gratitude for the favours heaped upon him by the king, as well as the natural bias to Parvez, made the Raja turn a deaf ear to his application. The prince tried to gain his point through Govinddas, a Rajput of the Bhatti tribe, one of the foreign nobles of Maru, and confidential adviser of his prince ; but, as the annals say, "Govinddas reckoned no one but his master and the [43] king." Frustrated in this, Khurram saw no hopes of success but by disgusting the Rathors, and he caused the faithful Govinddas to be assassinated by Kishan Singh ;[1] on which Raja Gaj, in disgust, threw up his post, and marched to his native land. From the assassination of Parvez, which soon followed,[2] the deposal of his father appeared but a step ; and Khurram had collected means, which he deemed adequate to the design, when Jahangir appealed to the fidelity of the Rajputs, to support him against filial ingratitude and domestic treason ; and, in their general obedience to the call, they afforded a distinguished proof of the operation of the first principle, Gaddi-ka-an, allegiance to the throne, often obeyed without reference to the worth of its occupant. The princes of Marwar, Amber, Kotah, and Bundi put themselves at the head of their household retainers on this occasion, which furnishes a confirmation of a remark already made, that the respective annals of the States of Rajasthan so rarely embrace the contemporaneous events of the rest, as to lead to the conclusion that by the single force of each State this rebellion was put down. This remark will be further exemplified from the annals of Bundi.

Offence given to the Rāthors.—Jahangir was so pleased with the zeal of the Rathor prince—alarmed as he was at the advance

[1] This was the founder of Kishangarh ; for this iniquitous service he was made an independent Raja in the town which he erected. His descendant is now an ally by treaty with the British Government. [Kishan Singh, born A.D. 1575, founded Kishangarh, a State in the centre of Rājputāna, in 1611, died 1615 (*IGI*, xv. 311).]

[2] [Parvez died at Burhānpur in 1626. "He was first attacked with colic, then he became insensible, and after medical treatment fell into a heavy sleep. . . . His illness was attributed to excessive drinking" (Elliot-Dowson vi. 429).]

of the rebels—that he not only took him by the hand, but what is most unusual, kissed it. When the assembled princes came in sight of the rebels, near Benares, the emperor gave the *harawal*, or vanguard, to the Kachhwaha prince, the Mirza raja of Amber. Whether this was a point of policy, to secure his acting against prince Khurram, who was born of this race, or merely, as the Marwar annals state, because he brought the greater number into the field, is immaterial; but it was very nearly fatal in its consequences: for the proud Rathor, indignant at the insult offered to him in thus bestowing the post of honour, which was his right, upon the rival race of Amber, furled his banners, separated from the royal army, and determined to be a quiet spectator of the result. But for the impetuous Bhim of Mewar, the adviser of Khurram, he might that day have been emperor of India. He sent a taunting message to Raja Gaj, either to join their cause or "draw their swords." The Rathors overlooked the neglect of the king in the sarcasm of one of their own tribe; and Bhim was slain, Govinddas avenged, the rebellion quelled, and Khurram put to flight, chiefly by the Rathors and Haras [44].

Death of Rāja Gaj Singh, A.D. **1638.**—In S. 1694 (A.D. 1638), Raja Gaj was slain in an expedition into Gujarat;[1] but whether in the fulfilment of the king's commands, or in the chastisement of freebooters on his own southern frontier, the chronicles do not inform us. He left a distinguished name in the annals of his country, and two valiant sons, Amra and Jaswant, to maintain it: another son, Achal, died in infancy.

Rāja Jaswant Singh, A.D. **1638-78.**—The second son, Jaswant, succeeded, and furnishes another of many instances in the annals of Rajputana, of the rights of primogeniture being set aside. This proceeded from a variety of motives, sometimes merely paternal affection, sometimes incapacity in the child "to head fifty thousand Rathors," and sometimes, as in the present instance, a dangerous turbulence and ever-boiling impetuosity in the individual, which despised all restraints. While there was an enemy against whom to exert it, Amra was conspicuous for his gallantry, and in all his father's wars in the south was ever foremost in the battle. His daring spirit collected around him those of his own race, alike in mind, as connected by blood, whose actions, in periods of peace, were the subjects of eternal complaint to his father,

[1] [By another account he died at Agra (Erskine iii. A, 59).]

who was ultimately compelled to exclude Amra from his inheritance.

Amra, Amar Singh excluded from the Succession.—In the month of Baisakh, S. 1690 (A.D. 1634), five years before the death of Raja Gaj, in a convocation of all the feudality of Maru, sentence of exclusion from the succession was pronounced upon Amra, accompanied by the solemn and seldom practised rite of Desvata or exile. This ceremony, which is marked as a day of mourning in the calendar, was attended with all the circumstances of funereal pomp. As soon as the sentence was pronounced, that his birthright was forfeited and assigned to his junior brother, and that he ceased to be a subject of Maru, the khilat of banishment was brought forth, consisting of sable vestments, in which he was clad ; a sable shield was hung upon his back, and a sword of the same hue girded round him ; a black horse was then led out, being mounted on which, he was commanded, though not in anger, to depart whither he listed beyond the limits of Maru.

Amra went not alone ; numbers of each clan, who had always regarded him as their future lord, voluntarily partook of his exile. He repaired to the imperial court ; and although the emperor approved and sanctioned his banishment, he employed him. His gallantry soon won him the title of Rao and the mansab of a leader of three thousand, with the grant of Nagor as an independent domain, to be held directly from the crown. But the same arrogant and uncontrollable spirit [45] which lost him his birthright, brought his days to a tragical conclusion. He absented himself for a fortnight from court, hunting the boar or the tiger, his only recreation. The emperor (Shah Jahan) reprimanded him for neglecting his duties, and threatened him with a fine. Amra proudly replied that he had only gone to hunt, and as for a fine, he observed, putting his hand upon his sword, that was his sole wealth.

Amra, Amar assassinates Salābat Khān.—The little contrition which this reply evinced determined the king to enforce the fine, and the paymaster-general, Salabat Khan,[1] was sent to Amra's

[1] Salabat Khan Bakhshi, he is called. The office of Bakhshi is not only one of paymaster (as it implies), but of inspection and audit. We can readily imagine, with such levies as he had to muster and pay, his post was more honourable than secure, especially with such a band as was headed by Amra, ready to take offence if the wind but displaced their moustache.

quarters to demand its payment. It was refused, and the observations made by the Sayyid not suiting the temper of Amra, he unceremoniously desired him to depart. The emperor, thus insulted in the person of his officer, issued a mandate for Amra's instant appearance. He obeyed, and having reached the Amm-khass, or grand divan, beheld the king, "whose eyes were red with anger," with Salabat in the act of addressing him. Inflamed with passion at the recollection of the injurious language he had just received, perhaps at the king's confirmation of his exclusion from Marwar, he unceremoniously passed the Omrahs of five and seven thousand, as if to address the king; when, with a dagger concealed in his sleeve, he stabbed Salabat to the heart. Drawing his sword, he made a blow at the king, which descending on the pillar, shivered the weapon in pieces. The king abandoned his throne and fled to the interior apartments. All was uproar and confusion. Amra continued the work of death, indifferent upon whom his blows fell, and five Mogul chiefs of eminence had fallen, when his brother-in-law, Arjun Gaur, under pretence of cajoling him, inflicted a mortal wound, though he continued to ply his dagger until he expired. To avenge his death, his retainers, headed by Balu Champawat and Bhao Kumpawat, put on their saffron garments, and a fresh carnage ensued within the Lal kila.[1] To use the words of their native bard, "The pillars of Agra bear testimony to their deeds, nor shall they ever be obliterated from the record of time: they made their obeisance to

---

The annals declare that Amra had a feud (*vair*) with Salabat; doubtless for no better reason than that he fulfilled the trust reposed in him by the emperor. [The title Khān implies that Salābat Khān was a Pathān, not a Sayyid, whose title would be Mīr.]

[1] The palace within the citadel (*kila*), built of red (*lal*) freestone. [This tragedy occurred on August 5, 1644 (Beale, *Oriental Biographical Dict.* sv. "Salābat Khān," gives July 25, 1644). European writers of the period give varying accounts of what seems to have been the same event. Tavernier (ed. Ball, ii. 219) says that the victim was "the Grand Master of the King's house," and that it occurred in 1642. Manucci states that the officer who was assassinated was the Wazīr, Wazīr Khān (i. 207 f.). It forms the subject of a popular song, still sung by the bards (Temple, *Legends of the Panjāb*, ii. 242 ff.). Though the assassination occurred at Agra, a mark is still shown on a pillar in the Dīwān-i-'Āmm at Delhi, possibly marking the same occurrence, where a prince of Chitor is said to have stabbed one of the ministers (Sleeman, *Rambles*, 515). The tomb of Bakhshi Salābat Khān stands between Agra and Sikandra (Syad Muhammad Latif, *Agra*, 77, 105).]

Amra in the mansions of the sun." The faithful band was cut to pieces; and his wife, the princess of Bundi, came in person and [46] carried away the dead body of Amra, with which she committed herself to the flames. The Bokhara gate by which they gained admission was built up, and henceforward known only as "Amra Singh's gate"; and in proof of the strong impression made by this event,[1] it remained closed through centuries, until opened in 1809 by Capt. Geo. Steell, of the Bengal engineers.[2]

[1] It may be useful to record such facts, by the way of contrast with the state policy of the west, and for the sake of observing that which would actuate the present paramount power of India should any of its tributary princes defy them as Amra did that of the universal potentate of that country. Even these despots borrowed a lesson of mercy from the Rajput system, which does not deem treason hereditary, nor attaints a whole line for the fault of one unworthy link. Shah Jahan, instead of visiting the sins of the father on the son, installed him in his fief of Nagor. This son was Rae Singh; and it devolved to his children and grandchildren,* until Indar Singh the fourth in descent, was expelled by the head of the Rathors, who, in the weakness of the empire, reannexed Nagor to Jodhpur. But perhaps we have not hitherto dared to imitate the examples set us by the Mogul and even by the Mahratta; not having sufficient hold of the affections of the subjected to venture to be merciful; and thence our vengeance, like the bolt of heaven, sears the very heart of our enemies. Witness the many chieftains ejected from their possessions; from the unhallowed league against the Rohillas, to that last act of destruction at Bharatpur, where, as arbitrators, we acted the part of the lion in the fable. Our present attitude, however, is so commanding, that we can afford to display the attribute of mercy; and should, unfortunately, its action be required in Rajputana, let it be ample, for there its grateful influence is understood, and it will return, like the dews of heaven, upon ourselves. But if we are only to regulate our political actions by the apprehension of danger, it must one day recoil upon us in awful retribution. Our system is filled with evil to the governed, where a fit of bile in ephemeral political agents, may engender a quarrel leading to the overthrow of a dominion of ages.

[2] Since these remarks were written, Captain Steell related to the author a singular anecdote connected with the above circumstance. While the work of demolition was proceeding, Captain Steell was urgently warned by the natives of the danger he incurred in the operation, from a denunciation on the closing of the gate, that it should thenceforward be guarded by a huge serpent—when suddenly, the destruction of the gate being nearly

* Namely, Hathi Singh, his son Anup Singh, his son Indar Singh, his son Mokham Singh. This lineal descendant of Raja Gaj, and the rightful heir to the "cushion of Jodha," has dwindled into one of the petty Thakurs, or lords of Marwar. The system is one of eternal vicissitudes, amidst which the germ of reproduction [47] never perishes.

CHAPTER 6

Rāja Jaswant Singh, A.D. 1638–78.—Raja Jaswant, who obtained, by the banishment of Amra, the "cushion" of Marwar, was born of a princess of Mewar; and although this circumstance is not reported to have influenced the change of succession, it will be borne in mind that, throughout Rajputana, its princes regarded a connexion with the Rana's family as a primary honour.

"Jaswant (says the Bardai) was unequalled amongst the princes of his time. Stupidity and ignorance were banished; and science flourished where he ruled: many were the books composed under his auspices."[1]

The south continued to be the arena in which the martial Rajput sought renown, and the emperor had only rightly to understand his character to turn the national emulation to account. Shah Jahan, in the language of the chronicler, "became a slave to the seraglio," and sent his sons, as viceroys, to govern the grand divisions of the empire. The first service of Jaswant was in the war of Gondwana, when he led a body composed of "twenty-two different contingents" in the army under Aurangzeb.[2] In this and various other services (to enumerate which would be to go [48] over the ground already passed),[3] the Rathors were conspicuous. Jaswant played a comparatively subordinate part, until the illness of the emperor, in A.D. 1658, when his elder son Dara was invested with the powers of regent.[4] Prince Dara increased the mansab of Jaswant to a leader of "five thousand," and nominated him his viceroy in Malwa.

---

completed, a large cobra-de-capello rushed between his legs, as if in fulfilment of the anathema. Captain Steell fortunately escaped without injury. [The south gate of the Agra Fort is known as that of Amar Singh.]

[1] [See Grierson, *Vernacular Literature of Hindustān*, Index sv. "Jaswant Singh."]

[2] [The Bundela Campaign of 1635 against Jujhār Singh (Jadunāth Sarkar, *Life of Aurangzib*, i. 14 ff.).]

[3] The new translation of Ferishta's *History*, by Lieut.-Col. Briggs, a work much wanted, may be referred to by those who wish to see the opinion of the Muhammadan princes of their Rajput vassalage.

[4] [It is a mistake to call him Dāra, his name being Dāra Shukoh, 'majesty like that of Darius.' He was appointed regent in 1657, when Shāh Jahān fell ill (*ibid.* i. 304 ff.).]

The War of Succession.—In the struggle for empire amongst the sons of Shah Jahan, consequent upon this illness, the importance of the Rajput princes and the fidelity we have often had occasion to depict, were exhibited in the strongest light. While Raja Jai Singh was commanded to oppose prince Shuja, who advanced from his viceroyalty of Bengal, Jaswant was entrusted with means to quash the designs of Aurangzeb, then commanding in the south, who had long cloaked, under the garb of hypocrisy and religion, views upon the empire.

Campaign against Aurangzeb, A.D. **1657-58—The Battle of Dharmātpur.**—The Rathor prince was declared generalissimo of the army destined to oppose Aurangzeb, and he marched from Agra at the head of the united contingents of Rajputana, besides the imperial guards, a force which, to use the hyperbole of the bard, "made Shesnag [1] writhe in agony." Jaswant marched towards the Nerbudda, and had encamped his army in a position fifteen miles south of Ujjain, when tidings reached him of his opponent's approach. In that field on which the emperor erected a town subsequently designated Fatehabad, or 'abode of victory,' Jaswant awaited his foes.[2] The battle which ensued, witnessed and so circumstantially related by Bernier, as has been already noticed in this work,[3] was lost by the temerity of the Rathor commander-in-chief, who might have crushed the rebellious hopes of Aurangzeb, to whom he purposely gave time to effect a junction with his brother Murad, from the vainglorious desire "to conquer two princes at once." Dearly did he pay for his presumption; for he had given time to the wily prince to sow intrigues in his camp, which were disclosed as soon as the battle joined, when the Mogul horse deserted and left him at the head of his thirty thousand Rajputs, deemed, however, by their leader and themselves, sufficient against any odds. "Jaswant, spear in hand, mounted his steed Mahbub, and charged the imperial brothers; ten thousand Muslims fell in the onset, which cost seventeen hundred Rathors [49], besides Guhilots, Haras, Gaurs,

[1] [The serpent which upholds the world.]

[2] [The battle fought at Dharmātpur, 14 miles S.W. of Ujjain, April 15 or 25, 1658. See a full account by Jadunāth Sarkar, ii. 3 ff., who remarks that the description in Bernier (p. 36 ff.) is untrustworthy, while Tod "merely records the wild fictions of the Rajput bards" (ii. 13 note). Fatehābād was the name given to Samūgarh, fought June 8, following.]

[3] P. 724.

and some of every clan of Rajwara. Aurang and Murad only escaped because their days were not yet numbered. Mahbub and his rider were covered with blood ; Jasa looked like a famished lion, and like one he relinquished his prey." The bard is fully confirmed in his relation of the day, both by the Mogul historian and by Bernier, who says, that notwithstanding the immense superiority of the imperial princes, aided by a numerous artillery served by Frenchmen, night alone put a stop to the contest of science, numbers, and artillery, against Rajput courage. Both armies remained on the field of battle, and though we have no notice of the anecdote related by the first translator of Ferishta, who makes Jaswant " in bravado drive his car round the field," [1] it is certain that Aurangzeb was too politic to renew the combat, or molest the retreat which took place next day towards his native dominions. Although, for the sake of alliteration, the bard especially singles out the Guhilots and Gaurs, the tribes of Mewar and Sheopur, all and every tribe was engaged ; and if the Rajput ever dared to mourn the fall of kindred in battle, this day should have covered every house with the emblems of grief ; for it is stated by the Mogul historian that fifteen thousand fell, chiefly Rajputs. This was one of the events glorious to the Rajput, showing his devotion to whom fidelity (*swamidharma*) had been pledged—the aged and enfeebled emperor Shah Jahan, whose " salt they ate "—against all the temptations offered by youthful ambition. It is forcibly contrasted with the conduct of the immediate household troops of the emperor, who, even in the moment of battle, worshipped the rising sun, whilst the Rajput sealed his faith in his blood ; and none more liberally than the brave Haras of Kotah and Bundi. The annals of no nation on earth can furnish such an example, as an entire family, six royal brothers, stretched on the field, and all but one in death.[2]

Of all the deeds of heroism performed on this day, those of Ratna of Ratlam, by universal consent, are pre-eminent, and " are wreathed into immortal rhyme by the bard " in the Raesa Rao Ratna.[3] He also was a Rathor, the great-grandson of Udai

[1] [Dow, 2nd ed. iii. 206.]

[2] See Kotah annals, which state that that prince and five brothers all fell in this field of carnage.

[3] Amongst the MSS. presented by the author to the Royal Asiatic Society, is this work, the Raesa Rao Ratna. [" To Ratan Singh of Ratlam a noble

Singh, the first raja of Maru; and nobly did he show that the Rathor blood had not degenerated on the fertile plains of Malwa. If aught were wanting to complete the fame of this memorable day, which gave empire to the scourge of Rajputana [50], it is found in the conduct of Jaswant's queen, who, as elsewhere related,[1] shut the gates of his capital on her fugitive lord, though he "brought back his shield" and his honour.

Battle of Jâjau.—Aurangzeb, on Jaswant's retreat, entered the capital of Malwa in triumph, whence, with all the celerity requisite to success, he pursued his march on the capital. At the village of Jajau, thirty miles south of Agra, the fidelity of the Rajputs again formed a barrier between the aged king and the treason of his son; but it served no other purpose than to illustrate this fidelity. The Rajputs were overpowered, Dara was driven from the regency, and the aged emperor deposed.[2]

Battle of Khajwa.—Aurangzeb, soon after usurping the throne, sent, through the prince of Amber, his assurances of pardon to Jaswant, and a summons to the presence, preparatory to joining the army forming against his brother Shuja, advancing to vindicate his claims to empire. The Rathor, deeming it a glorious occasion for revenge, obeyed, and communicated to Shuja his intentions. The hostile armies met at Khajwa, thirty miles north of Allahabad.[3] On the first onset, Jaswant, wheeling about with his Rathor cavaliers, attacked the rearward of the army under prince Muhammad, which he cut to pieces, and plundering the imperial camp (left unprotected), he deliberately loaded his camels with the most valuable effects, which he despatched under part of the force, and leaving the brothers to a contest, which he heartily wished might involve the destruction of both, he followed

---

monument was raised by his descendants on the spot where his corpse was burnt. Time overwhelmed it, but in 1909 its place was taken by a lofty structure of white marble, decorated with relief-work of a bold but conventional type, and surmounted with a stone horse" (Jadunāth Sarkar ii. 27).]

[1] See p. 724.

[2] [The battle of Samūgarh, nine miles E. of Agra, fought June 8, 1658, or, according to Jadunāth Sarkar (ii. 32) on May 29, 1658.]

[3] [The battle of Khajwa or Khajuha, in the Fatehpur District, nearly 100 miles N.W. of Allāhābād, on January 14, 1659, or, according to Jadunāth Sarkar, on January 4-5, 1659. The dates fixed by Irvine (*IA*, xl. 69 ff.) are probably correct, and have been followed in the notes.]

the cortège to Agra. Such was the panic on his appearance at that capital, joined to the rumours of Aurangzeb's defeat, which had nearly happened, that the wavering garrison required only a summons to have surrendered, when he might have released Shah Jahan from confinement, and with this " tower of strength " have rallied an opposition fatal to the prince.

Policy of Jaswant Singh.—That this plan suggested itself to Jaswant's sagacity we cannot doubt; but besides the manifest danger of locking up his army within the precincts of a capital, if victory was given to Aurangzeb, he had other reasons for not halting at Agra. All his designs were in concert with prince Dara, the rightful heir to the throne, whom he had instructed to hasten to the scene of action; but while Jaswant remained hovering in the rear of Aurangzeb, momentarily expecting the junction of the prince, the latter loitered on the southern frontier of Marwar, and thus lost, for [51] ever, the crown within his grasp. Jaswant continued his route to his native dominions, and had at least the gratification of housing the spoils, even to the regal tents, in the castle of Jodha. Dara tardily formed a junction at Merta; but the critical moment was lost, and Aurangzeb, who had crushed Shuja's force, rapidly advanced, now joined by many of the Rajput princes, to overwhelm this last remnant of opposition. The crafty Aurangzeb, however, who always preferred stratagem to the precarious issue of arms, addressed a letter to Jaswant, not only assuring him of his entire forgiveness, but offering the viceroyalty of Gujarat, if he would withdraw his support from Dara, and remain neuter in the contest. Jaswant accepted the conditions, and agreed to lead the Rajput contingents, under prince Muazzam, in the war against Sivaji, bent on reviving the independence of Maharashtra. From the conduct again pursued by the Rathor, we have a right to infer that he only abandoned Dara because, though possessed of many qualities which endeared him to the Rajput, besides his title to the throne, he wanted those virtues necessary to ensure success against his energetic brother. Scarcely had Jaswant reached the Deccan when he opened a communication with Sivaji, planned the death of the king's lieutenant, Shaista Khan, on which he hoped to have the guidance of the army, and the young viceroy. Aurangzeb received authentic intelligence of this plot, and the share Jaswant had in it; but he temporized, and even sent letters of congratulation on his succeeding to the command in chief. But he soon superseded him by Raja Jai Singh of Amber, who brought the war to a conclusion by the capture of Sivaji.[1] The honour attending this exploit was, however, soon exchanged for disgrace; for when the Amber prince found that the tyrant had designs upon the life of his prisoner, for whose safety he had pledged himself, he connived at his escape.[2] Upon this, Jaswant was once more declared the emperor's lieutenant, and soon inspired prince Muazzam with designs, which again compelled the king to supersede him, and Diler Khan was declared general-in-chief. He reached Aurangabad, and the night of his arrival would have been his last, but he received intimation and rapidly retreated, pursued by the prince and Jaswant to the Nerbudda. The emperor saw the necessity of removing Jaswant from this dangerous post, and he sent him the farman as viceroy of Gujarat, to which he commanded him to repair without delay. He obeyed, reached Ahmadabad, and found the king had outwitted him and his [52] successor in command; he therefore continued his course to his native dominions, where he arrived in S. 1726 (A.D. 1670).

The wily tyrant had, in all these changes, used every endeavour to circumvent Jaswant, and, if the annals are correct, was little scrupulous as to the means. But the Raja was protected by the fidelity of his kindred vassalage. In the words of the bardic chronicler, "The Aswapati,[3] Aurang, finding treachery in vain, put the collar of simulated friendship round his neck, and sent him beyond the Attock to die."

The emperor saw that the only chance of counteracting Jaswant's inveterate hostility was to employ him where he would be least dangerous. He gladly availed himself of a rebellion amongst the Afghans of Kabul; and with many promises of favour to himself and his family, appointed him to the chief command,[4] to lead his turbulent Rajputs against the equally turbulent and almost savage Afghans. Leaving his elder son, Prithi Singh, in charge of his ancestral domains, with his wives,

[1] [June 23, 1665.]

[2] [Jai Singh seems to have had no direct part in the escape of Sivaji from Delhi, August 29, 1666 (Grant Duff, *Hist. Mahrattas*, 96).]

[3] The common epithet of the Islamite emperors, in the dialect of the bard, is *Aspat*, classically *Aswapati*, 'lord of horses.'

[4] [He was appointed Faujdār of Jamrūd at the mouth of the Khaibar Pass.]

family, and the chosen bands of Maru, Jaswant departed for the land of the "barbarian," from which he was destined never to return.

Treatment of Prithi Singh by Aurangzeb.—It is related, in the chronicles of Maru, that Aurangzeb having commanded the attendance at court of Jaswant's heir, he obeyed, and was received not only with the distinctions which were his due, but with the most specious courtesy; that one day, with unusual familiarity, the king desired him to advance, and grasping firmly his folded hands (the usual attitude of deference) in one of his own, said, "Well, Rathor, it is told me you possess as nervous an arm as your father; what can you do now?" "God preserve your majesty!" replied the Rajput prince, "when the sovereign of mankind lays the hand of protection on the meanest of his subjects, all his hopes are realized; but when he condescends to take both of mine, I feel as if I could conquer the world." His vehement and animated gesture gave full force to his words, and Aurangzeb quickly exclaimed, "Ah! here is another Khatan"[1] (the term he always applied to Jaswant); yet, affecting to be pleased with the frank boldness of his speech, he ordered him a splendid dress, which, as customary, he put on, and, having made his obeisance, left the presence in the certain assurance of exaltation.

That day was his last!—he was taken ill soon after reaching his quarters, and [53] expired in great torture, and to this hour his death is attributed to the poisoned robe of honour presented by the king.[2]

Prithi Singh was the staff of his father's age, and endowed with all the qualities required to lead the swords of Maru. His death,

[1] [A near relation by marriage.]

[2] This mode of being rid of enemies is firmly believed by the Rajputs, and several other instances of it are recorded in this work. Of course, it must be by porous absorption; and in a hot climate, where only a thin tunic is worn next the skin, much mischief might be done, though it is difficult to understand how death could be accomplished. [See p. 728.] That the belief is of ancient date we have only to recall the story of Hercules put into doggerel by Pope:

—"He, whom Dejanire
Wrapp'd in th' envenom'd shirt, and set on fire."

["The Wife of Bath," 380-1. The tragical death of Prithi Singh is still the subject for songs of the bards (Temple, *Legends of the Panjāb*, iii. 252 ff.).]

thus reported, cast a blight on the remaining days of Jaswant, who, in this cruel stroke, saw that his mortal foe had gone beyond him in revenge. The sacrifice of Prithi Singh was followed by the death of his only remaining sons, Jagat Singh and Dalthamman, from the ungenial climate of Kabul, and grief soon closed the existence of the veteran Rathor. He expired amidst the mountains of the north, without an heir to his revenge, in S. 1737 (A.D. 1681), having ruled the tribes of Maru for two-and-forty years. In this year, death released Aurangzeb from the greatest terrors of his life; for the illustrious Sivaji and Jaswant paid the debt to nature within a few months of each other.[1] Of the Rathor, we may use the words of the biographer of his contemporary, Rana Raj Singh of Mewar: "Sighs never ceased flowing from Aurang's heart while Jaswant lived."

Character of Jaswant Singh.—The life of Jaswant Singh is one of the most extraordinary in the annals of Rajputana, and a full narrative of it would afford a perfect and deeply interesting picture of the history and manners of the period. Had his abilities, which were far above mediocrity, been commensurate with his power, credit, and courage, he might, with the concurrent aid of the many powerful enemies of Aurangzeb, have overturned the Mogul throne. Throughout the long period of two-and-forty years, events of magnitude crowded upon each other, from the period of his first contest with Aurangzeb, in the battle of the Nerbudda, to his conflicts with the Afghans amidst the snows of Caucasus. Although the Rathor had a preference amongst the sons of Shah Jahan, esteeming the frank Dara above the crafty Aurangzeb, yet he detested the whole race as inimical to the religion and the independence of his own; and he only fed the hopes of any of the brothers, in their struggles for empire, expecting that they would end in the ruin of all. His blind [54] arrogance lost him the battle of the Nerbudda, and the supineness of Dara prevented his reaping the fruit of his treachery at Khajwa. The former event, as it reduced the means and lessened the fame of Jaswant, redoubled his hatred to the conqueror. Jaswant neglected no opportunity which gave a chance of revenge. Im-

[1] [This is an error. Jaswant Singh died December 18, 1678 (Irvine's note on Manucci ii. 233, *IA*, xl. 77). Sivaji died probably on April 17, 1680 (Fryer, *New Account of East India and Persia*, ed. Hakluyt Society, iii. 167).]

pelled by this motive, more than by ambition, he never declined situations of trust, and in each he disclosed the ruling passion of his mind. His overture to Sivaji (like himself the implacable foe of the Mogul), against whom he was sent to act; his daring attempt to remove the imperial lieutenants, one by assassination, the other by open force; his inciting Muazzam, whose inexperience he was sent to guide, to revolt against his father, are some among the many signal instances of Jaswant's thirst for vengeance. The emperor, fully aware of this hatred, yet compelled from the force of circumstances to dissemble, was always on the watch to counteract it, and the artifices this mighty king had recourse to in order to conciliate Jaswant, perhaps to throw him off his guard, best attest the dread in which he held him. Alternately he held the viceroyalty of Gujarat, of the Deccan, of Malwa, Ajmer, and Kabul (where he died), either directly of the king, or as the king's lieutenant, and second in command under one of the princes. But he used all these favours merely as stepping-stones to the sole object of his life. Accordingly, if Jaswant's character had been drawn by a biographer of the court, viewed merely in the light of a great vassal of the empire, it would have reached us marked with the stigma of treachery in every trust reposed in him; but, on the other hand, when we reflect on the character of the king, the avowed enemy of the Hindu faith, we only see in Jaswant a prince putting all to hazard in its support. He had to deal with one who placed him in these offices, not from personal regard, but because he deemed a hollow submission better than avowed hostility, and the raja, therefore, only opposed fraud to hypocrisy, and treachery to superior strength. Doubtless the Rathor was sometimes dazzled by the baits which the politic king administered to his vanity; and when all his brother princes eagerly contended for royal favour, it was something to be singled out as the first amongst his peers in Rajputana. By such conflicting impulses were both parties actuated in their mutual conduct throughout a period in duration nearly equal to the life of man; and it is no slight testimony to Aurangzeb's skill in managing such a subject, that he was able to neutralize the hatred and the power of Jaswant throughout this lengthened [55] period. But it was this vanity, and the immense power wielded by the kings who could reward service by the addition of a vice-royalty to their hereditary domains, that made the Rajput princes slaves;

for, had all the princely contemporaries of Jaswant—Jai Singh of Amber, the Rana Raj of Mewar, and Sivaji—coalesced against their national foe, the Mogul power must have been extinct. Could Jaswant, however, have been satisfied with the mental wounds he inflicted upon the tyrant, he would have had ample revenge; for the image of the Rathor crossed all his visions of aggrandizement. The cruel sacrifice of his heir, and the still more barbarous and unrelenting ferocity with which he pursued Jaswant's innocent family, are the surest proofs of the dread which the Rathor prince inspired while alive.

The Tale of Nāhar Khān.—Previous, however, to entering on this and the eventful period which followed Jaswant's death, we may record a few anecdotes illustrative of the character and manners of the vassal chieftains, by whose aid he was thus enabled to brave Aurangzeb. Nor can we do better than allow Nahar Khan, chief of the Kumpawats and premier noble, to be the representative portrait of the clans of Maru. It was by the vigilance of this chief, and his daring intrepidity, that the many plots laid for Jaswant's life were defeated; and in the anecdote already given, when in order to restore his prince from a fit of mental delusion,[1] he braved the superstitions of his race, his devotion was put to a severer test than any which could result from personal peril. The anecdote connected with his *nom de guerre* of Nahar (*tiger*) Khan, exemplifies his personal, as the other does his mental, intrepidity. The real name of this individual, the head of the Kumpawat clan, was Mukunddas. He had personally incurred the displeasure of the emperor, by a reply which was deemed disrespectful to a message sent by the royal Ahadi,[2] for which the tyrant condemned him to enter a tiger's den, and contend for his life unarmed. Without a sign of fear he entered the arena, where the savage beast was pacing, and thus contemptuously accosted him: "Oh, tiger of the Miyan,[3] face the tiger of Jaswant"; exhibiting to the king of the forest a pair of eyes, which anger and opium had rendered little less inflamed than his own. The animal, startled by so unaccustomed a salutation, for a moment looked at his visitor, put down his

[1] See p. 967. [2] [See p. 784.]

[3] *Miyān* is a term used by the Hindu to a Muslim, who himself generally applies it to a pedagogue: the village schoolmaster has always the honourable epithet of *Miyān-ji*!

head, turned round and [56] stalked from him. "You see," exclaimed the Rathor, "that he dare not face me, and it is contrary to the creed of a true Rajput to attack an enemy who dares not confront him." Even the tyrant, who beheld the scene, was surprised into admiration, presented him with gifts, and asked if he had any children to inherit his prowess. His reply, "How can we get children, when you keep us from our wives beyond the Attock?" fully shows that the Rathor and fear were strangers to each other. From this singular encounter he bore the name of Nahar Khan, 'the tiger lord.'

On another occasion, from the same freedom of speech, he incurred the displeasure of the Shahzada, or prince-royal, who, with youthful levity, commanded the 'tiger lord' to attempt a feat which he deemed inconsistent with his dignity, namely, gallop at speed under a horizontal branch of a tree and cling to it while the steed passed on. This feat, requiring both agility and strength, appears to have been a common amusement, and it is related in the Annals of Mewar that the chief of Banera broke his spine in the attempt; and there were few who did not come off with bruises and falls, in which consisted the sport. When Nahar heard the command, he indignantly replied, he "was not a monkey"; that "if the prince wished to see his feats, it must be where his sword had play"; on which he was ordered against Surthan, the Deora prince of Sirohi, for which service he had the whole Rathor contingent at his disposal. The Deora prince, who could not attempt to cope against it in the field, took to his native hills; but while he deemed himself secure, Mukund, with a chosen band, in the dead of night, entered the glen where the Sirohi prince reposed, stabbed the solitary sentinel, bound the prince with his own turban to his pallet, while, environing him with his clansmen, he gave the alarm. The Deoras starting from their rocky beds, collected round their prince, and were preparing for the rescue, when Nahar called aloud, "You see his life is in my hands; be assured it is safe if you are wise; but he dies on the least opposition to my determination to convey him to my prince. My sole object in giving the alarm was that you might behold me carry off my prize." He conveyed Surthan to Jaswant, who said he must introduce him to the king. The Deora prince was carried to court, and being led between the proper officers to the palace, he was instructed to perform that profound obeisance, from which none were exempted. But the haughty Deora replied, "His life was in the king's hands, his [57] honour in his own; he had never bowed the head to mortal man, and never would." As Jaswant had pledged himself for his honourable treatment, the officers of the ceremonies endeavoured by stratagem to obtain a constrained obeisance, and instead of introducing him as usual, they showed him a wicket, knee high, and very low overhead, by which to enter, but putting his feet foremost, his head was the last part to appear.[1] This stubborn ingenuity, his noble bearing, and his long-protracted resistance, added to Jaswant's pledge, won the king's favour; and he not only proffered him pardon, but whatever lands he might desire. Though the king did not name the return, Surthan was well aware of the terms, but he boldly and quickly replied, "What can your majesty bestow equal to Achalgarh? let me return to it is all I ask." The king had the magnanimity to comply with his request; Surthan was allowed to retire to the castle of Abu,[2] nor did he or any of the Deoras ever rank themselves amongst the vassals of the empire; but they have continued to the present hour a life of almost savage independence.

From such anecdotes we learn the character of the tiger lord of Asop; and his brother Rathors of Marwar; men reckless of life when put in competition with distinction and fidelity to their prince, as will be abundantly illustrated in the reign we are about to describe.

CHAPTER 7

Fate of the Family of Jaswant Singh.—"When Jaswant died beyond the Attock, his wife, the (future) mother of Ajit, determined to burn with her lord, but being in the seventh month of her pregnancy, she was forcibly prevented by Uda Kumpawat.

[1] [This is a common legend, told of the Nikumbh Rājputs of the United Provinces (Crooke, *Tribes and Castes*, iv. 87); by Bernier of Shāh Jahān and the Persian ambassador (p. 151 f.); of the Hatkars of the Deccan (*BG*, xvi. 56 note; Russell, *Tribes and Castes of Central Provinces*, i. 37 f.).]

[2] Achalgarh, or 'the immovable castle,' is the name of the fortress of the Deora princes of Abu and Sirohi, of which wonderful spot I purpose in another work to give a detailed account [58].

His other queen and seven Patras (concubines) mounted the pyre; and as soon as the tidings reached Jodhpur, the Chandravati queen, taking a turban of her late lord, ascended the pile at Mandor. The Hindu race was in despair at the loss of the support of their faith. The bells of the temple were mute; the sacred shell no longer sounded at sunrise; the Brahmans vitiated their doctrines and learned the Muslim creed."[1]

Birth of Ajīt Singh.—The queen was delivered of a boy, who received the name of Ajit. As soon as she was able to travel, the Rathor contingent, with their infant prince, his mother, the daughters, and establishment of their late sovereign, prepared to return to their native land. But the unrelenting tyrant, carrying his vengeance towards Jaswant even beyond the grave, as soon they reached Delhi, commanded that the infant should be surrendered to his custody. "Aurang offered to divide Maru amongst [59] them if they would surrender their prince; but they replied, 'Our country is with our sinews, and these can defend both it and our Lord.' With eyes red with rage, they left the Amm-khass. Their abode was surrounded by the host of the Shah. In a basket of sweetmeats they sent away the young prince, and prepared to defend their honour; they made oblations to the gods, took a double portion of opium, and mounted their steeds. Then spoke Ranchhor, and Govind the son of Jodha, and Chandarbhan the Darawat, and the son of Raghu, on whose shoulders the sword had been married at Ujjain, with the fearless Baharmall the Udawat, and the Sujawat, Raghunath. 'Let us swim,' they exclaimed, 'in the ocean of fight. Let us root up these Asuras, and be carried by the Apsaras to the mansions of the sun.' As thus each spoke, Suja the bard took the word: 'For a day like this,' said he, 'you enjoy your fiefs (*pattas*), to give in your lord's cause your bodies to the sword, and in one mass to gain *swarga* (heaven). As for me, who enjoyed his friendship and his gifts, this day will I make his salt resplendent. My father's fame will I uphold, and lead the death in this day's fight, that future bards may hymn my praise.' Then spake Durga, son of Asa: 'The teeth of the Yavans are whetted, but by the lightning emitted from our swords, Delhi shall witness our deeds; and the flame of our anger shall consume the troops of the Shah.'

[1] [Erskine (iii. A, 62) gives the story from local sources; also see Elliot-Dowson vii. 297 f.]

As thus the chiefs communed, and the troops of the king approached, the Rajloka[1] of their late lord was sent to inhabit Swarga. Lance in hand, with faces resembling Yama,[2] the Rathors rushed upon the foe. Then the music of swords and shields commenced. Wave followed wave in the field of blood. Sankara[3] completed his chaplet in the battle fought by the children of Duhar in the streets of Delhi. Ratna contended with nine thousand of the foe; but his sword failed, and as he fell, Rambha[4] carried him away. Dila the Darawat made a gift of his life;[5] the salt of his lord he mixed with the water of the field.[6] Chandarbhan was conveyed by the [60] Apsaras to Chandrapur.[7] The Bhatti was cut piecemeal and lay on the field beside the son of Surthan. The faithful Udawat appeared like the crimson lotus; he journeyed to Swarga to visit Jaswant. Sanda the bard, with a sword in either hand, was in the front of the battle, and gained the mansion of the moon.[8] Every tribe and every clan performed its duty in this day's pilgrimage to the stream of the sword, in which Durgadas ground the foe and saved his honour."[9]

The Johar.—When these brave men saw that nothing short of the surrender of all that was dear to a Rajput was intended

[1] A delicate mode of naming the female part of Jaswant's family; the 'royal abode' included his young daughters, sent to inhabit heaven (*swarga*).

[2] Pluto.

[3] 'The lord of the shell,' an epithet of Siva, as the god of war; his war-trump being a shell (*sankh*); his chaplet (*mala*), which the Rathor bard says was incomplete until this fight, being of human skulls. [Sankara, a title of Siva, means 'causing happiness,' and has no connexion with *sankh*, 'a shell.']

[4] Queen of the Apsaras, or celestial nymphs.

[5] Pope makes Sarpedon say:

> "The life that others pay, let us bestow,
> And give to fame what we to nature owe."

[6] *I.e.* blood.

[7] "The city of the moon."

[8] The lunar abode seems that allotted for all bards, who never mention Bhanloka, or the 'mansion of the sun,' as a place of reward for them. Doubtless they could assign a reason for such a distinction.

[9] This is but a short transcript of the poetic account of this battle, in which the deeds, name, and tribe of every warrior who fell are related. The heroes of Thermopylae had not a more brilliant theme for the bard. [Compare the more matter-of-fact accounts of Khāfi Khān, Elliot-Dowson (vii. 296 f.), and of Manucci (ii. 233 f.).]

by the fiend-like spirit of the king, their first thought was the preservation of their prince; the next to secure their own honour and that of their late master. The means by which they accomplished this were terrific. The females of the deceased, together with their own wives and daughters, were placed in an apartment filled with gunpowder, and the torch applied—all was soon over. This sacrifice accomplished, their sole thought was to secure a niche in that immortal temple, which the Rajput bard, as well as the great minstrel of the west, peoples with "youths who died, to be by poets sung." For this, the Rajput's anxiety has in all ages been so great, as often to defeat even the purpose of revenge, his object being to die gloriously rather than to inflict death; assured that his name would never perish, but, preserved in "immortal rhyme" by the bard, would serve as the incentive to similar deeds. Accordingly, "the battle fought by the sons of Duharia [1] in the streets of Delhi" is one of the many themes of everlasting eulogy to the Rathors; and the seventh of Sravan, S. 1736 (the second month of the Monsoon of A.D. 1680), is a sacred day in the calendar of Maru.

In the midst of this furious contest, the infant prince was saved. To avoid suspicion the heir of Maru, concealed in a basket of sweetmeats, was entrusted to a Muslim, who religiously executed his trust and conveyed him to the appointed spot, where he was joined by the gallant Durgadas with the survivors who had cut their way through all opposition, and who were doomed often to bleed for the prince thus miraculously preserved. It is pleasing to find that if to "the leader [61] of the faithful," the bigoted Aurangzeb, they owed so much misery, to one (and he of humble life), of the same faith, they owed the preservation of their line. The preserver of Ajit lived to witness his manhood and the redemption of his birthright, and to find that princes are not always ungrateful; for he was distinguished at court, was never addressed but as *Kaka*, or uncle, by the prince; and to the honour of his successors be it told, the lands then settled upon him are still enjoyed by his descendants.

The Youth of Ajīt Singh. Campaign of Aurangzeb in Mārwār.—With the sole surviving scion of Jaswant, the faithful Durga

[1] Here is another instance of the ancient patronymic being brought in by the bards, and it is thus they preserve the names and deeds of the worthies of past days. Rao Duhar was one of the earliest Rathor kings of Marwar.

and a few chosen friends repaired to the isolated rock of Abu, and placed him in a monastery of recluses. There the heir of Maru was reared in entire ignorance of his birth. Still rumours prevailed, that a son of Jaswant lived; that Durga and a few associates were his guardians; and this was enough for the loyal Rajput, who, confiding in the chieftain of Dunara, allowed the mere name of Dhani (lord) to be his rallying-word in the defence of his rights. These were soon threatened by a host of enemies, amongst whom were the Indhas, the ancient sovereigns of Maru, who saw an opening for the redemption of their birth-right, and for a short time displayed the flag of the Parihars on the walls of Mandor. While the Indhas were rejoicing at the recovery of their ancient capital, endeared to them by tradition, an attempt was made by Ratna,[1] the son of Amra Singh (whose tragical death has been related), to obtain the seat of power, Jodhpur. This attempt, instigated by the king, proved futile; and the clans, faithful to the memory of Jaswant and the name of Ajit, soon expelled the Indhas from Mandor, and drove the son of Amra to his castle of Nagor. It was then that Aurangzeb, in person, led his army into Maru; the capital was invested; it fell and was pillaged, and all the great towns in the plains, as Merta, Didwana, and Rohat, shared a similar fate. The emblems of religion were trampled under foot, the temples thrown down, mosques were erected on their site, and nothing short of the compulsory conversion to the tenets of Islam of every Rajput in Marwar would satisfy his revenge.[2] The consequences of this fanatical and impolitic conduct recoiled not only upon the emperor but his whole race, for it roused an opposition to this iron yoke, which ultimately broke it in pieces. The emperor promulgated that famous edict, the Jizya, against the whole Hindu race, which cemented into one compact union all who cherished either patriotism or religion. It was at this period of time, when the Rathors and Sesodias united [62] against the tyrant, that Rana

[1] [According to Musalmān authorities, the name of the son of Amar Singh was Indar Singh, not Ratan Singh (Jadunath Sarkar, *Life of Aurangzib*, iii. 369).]

[2] [In 1679 Khān Jahān arrived from Jodhpur, bringing several cart-loads of idols pillaged from Hindu temples. It was ordered that some should be cast away into the out-offices, and the remainder to be placed beneath the steps of the Great Mosque, there to be trampled under foot (Elliot-Dowson vii. 187; Jadunath Sarkar iii. 323).]

Raj Singh indited that celebrated epistle, which is given in a preceding part of this work.[1]

"Seventy thousand men," says the bard,[2] "under Tahawwur Khan, were commanded to destroy the Rajputs, and Aurang followed in person to Ajmer. The Mertia clan assembled, and advanced to Pushkar to oppose him. The battle was in front of the temple of Varaha, where the swords of the Mertias, always first in the fight, played the game of destruction on the heads of the Asuras. Here the Mertias were all slain on the 11th Bhadon, S. 1736.

"Tahawwur continued to advance. The inhabitants of Murdhar fled to the mountains. At Gura the brothers Rupa and Kumbha took post with their clan to oppose him; but they fell with twenty-five of their brethren. As the cloud pours water

[1] Vol. I. p. 442.

[2] It may be well to exhibit the manner in which the poetic annalist of Rajputana narrates such events, and to give them in his own language rather than in an epitome, by which not only the pith of the original would be lost, but the events themselves deprived of half their interest. The character of historic fidelity will thus be preserved from suspicion, which could scarcely be withheld if the narrative were exhibited in any but its native garb. This will also serve to sustain the Annals of Marwar, formed from a combination of such materials, and dispose the reader to acknowledge the impossibility of reducing such animated chronicles to the severe style of history. But more than all, it is with the design to prove what, in the preface of this work, the reader was compelled to take on credit; that the Rajput kingdoms were in no ages without such chronicles: and if we may not compare them with Froissart, or with Monstrelet, they may be allowed to compete with the Anglo-Saxon chronicles, and they certainly surpass those of Ulster. But we have stronger motives than even legitimate curiosity, in allowing the bard to tell his own tale of the thirty years' war of Rajputana; the desire which has animated this task from its commencement, to give a correct idea of the importance of these events, and to hold them up as a beacon to the present governors of these brave men. How well that elegant historian, Orme, appreciates their importance, as bearing on our own conduct in power, the reader will perceive by reference to his *Fragments* [ed. 1782, note i.], where he says, "There are no states or powers on the continent of India, with whom our nation has either connexion or concern, which do not owe the origin of their present condition to the reign of Aurangzebe, or to its influence on the reigns of his successors." It behoves us, therefore, to make ourselves acquainted with the causes as well as the characters of those who occasioned the downfall of our predecessors in the sovereignty of India. With this object in view, the bard shall tell his own tale from the birth of Ajit, in S. 1737, to 1767, when he had vanquished all opposition to Aurangzeb, and regained the throne of Maru.

upon the earth, so did Aurang pour his barbarians over the land. He remained but five days at Ajaidurg (Ajmer), and marched against Chitor. It fell: it appeared as if the heavens had fallen. Ajit was protected by the Rana, and the Rathors led the van in the host of the Sesodias. Seeing the strength of the Yavans, they shut up the young prince, like a flame confined in a vessel. Delhipat (the king of Delhi) came to Debari,[1] at whose pass he was opposed by Kumbha, Ugarsen, and Uda, all Rathors. While Aurangzeb attacked Udaipur, Azam was left at Chitor. Then the king learned that Durgadas had invaded Jalor; he abandoned his conquest, and returned to Ajmer, sending Mukarrab Khan to aid Bihari at Jalor; but Durga had raised contributions [63] (*dand*), and passed to Jodhpur, alike forced to contribute; for the son of Indar Singh, on the part of the king, now commanded in Trikuta (triple-peaked mount). Aurang Shah measured the heavens; he determined to have but one faith in the land. Prince Akbar was sent to join Tahawwur Khan. Rapine and conflagration spread over the land. The country became a waste; fear stalked triumphant. Providence had willed this affliction. The Indhas were put in possession of Jodhpur; but were encountered at Ketapur and put to the sword by the Champawats. Once more they lost the title of Raos of Murdardes, and thus the king's intentions of bestowing sovereignty on the Parihars were frustrated on the 13th day of Jeth, S. 1736.

Retreat of the Rathors.—"The Aravalli gave shelter to the Rathors. From its fastnesses they issued, and mowed down entire harvests of the Muslim, piling them in *khallas*.[2] Aurang had no repose. Jalor was invaded by one body, Siwana by another of the faithful chiefs of Ajit, whose *an*[3] daily increased, while Aurang's was seldom invoked. The king gave up the war against the Rana to send all his troops into Maru; but the Rana, who provoked the rage of Aurang from granting refuge to Ajit, sent his troops under his own son, Bhim, who joined the Rathors, led by Indarbhan and Durgadas in Godwar. Prince Akbar and Tahawwur Khan advanced upon them, and a battle took place

[1] The cenotaph of these warriors still marks the spot where they fell, on the right on entering the portals.

[2] The heaps of grain thrashed in the open field, preparatory to being divided and housed, are termed *khallas*.

[3] Oath of allegiance.

at Nadol. The Sesodias had the right. The combat was long and bloody. Prince Bhim fell at the head of the Mewaris: he was a noble bulwark to the Rathors.[1] Indarbhan was slain, with Jeth the Udawat, performing noble deeds; and Soning Durga did wonders on that day, the 14th Asoj, S. 1737" (the winter of A.D. 1681).

The Rebellion of Prince Akbar, A.D. **1681.**—The gallant bearing of the Rajputs in this unequal combat, their desperate devotion to their country and prince, touched the soul of Prince Akbar, who had the magnanimity to commiserate the sufferings he was compelled to inflict, and to question the policy of his father towards these gallant vassals. Ambition came to the aid of compassion for the sufferings of the Rathors, and the persecution of the minor son of Jaswant. He opened his mind to Tahawwur Khan, and exposed the [64] disgrace of bearing arms in so unholy a warfare, and in severing from the crown such devoted and brave vassals as the Rathors. Tahawwur was gained over, and an embassy sent to Durgadas offering peace, and expressing a wish for a conference. Durga convened the chiefs, and disclosed the overture; but some suspected treachery in the prince, others selfish views on the part of Durga. To prevent the injurious operation of such suspicions, Durga observed, that if assent were not given to the meeting, it would be attributed to the base motive of fear. "Let us proceed in a body," said he, "to this conference; who ever heard of a cloud being caught?" They met; mutual views were developed; a treaty was concluded, and the meeting ended by Akbar waving the umbrella of regality over his head.[2] He coined in his own name; he established his own weights and measures. The poisoned intelligence was

[1] The Mewar chronicle claims a victory for the combined Rajput army, and relates a singular stratagem by which they gained it; but either I have overlooked it, or the Raj Vilas does not specify that Prince Bhim, son of the heroic Rana Raj, fell on this day, so glorious in the annals of both States. See Vol. I. p. 448. [According to Manucci (ii. 234) the Rāja "was obliged to cede to Aurangzeb a province and the town of Mairtha." According to another story, Aurangzeb offered the succession to Ajīt Singh on condition that he was converted to Islām. The Emperor kept a counterfeit Ajīt Singh in ward, and brought him up as a Musalmān, called him Muhammadi Rāj, and on his death he was buried as a Musalmān (Jadunath Sarkar iii. 374).]

[2] [On Akbar's rebellion see Jadunath Sarkar iii. 402 ff.]

poured into Aurang's ear at Ajmer; his soul was troubled; he had no rest; he plucked his beard in grief when he heard that Durga and Akbar had united. Every Rathor in the land flocked to Akbar's standard. The house of Delhi was divided, and Govind [1] again supported the Hindu faith.

The dethronement of the tyrant appeared inevitable. The scourge of the Rajputs was in their power, for he was almost alone and without the hope of succour. But his energies never forsook him; he knew the character of his foes, and that on an emergency his grand auxiliary, stratagem, was equal to an army. As there is some variation both in the Mogul historian's account of this momentous transaction and in the annals of Mewar and Marwar,[2] we present the latter *verbatim* from the chronicle.

"Akbar, with multitudes of Rajputs, advanced upon Ajmer. But while Aurang prepared for the storm, the prince gave himself up to women and the song, placing everything in the hands of Tahawwur Khan. We are the slaves of fate; puppets that dance as it pulls the strings. Tahawwur allowed himself to dream of treason; it was whispered in his ear that if he could deliver Akbar to his father, high rewards would follow. At night he went privily to Aurangzeb, and thence wrote to the Rathors: 'I was the bond of union betwixt you and Akbar, but the dam which separated the waters has broken down. Father and son again are one. Consider the pledges, given and received, as restored, and depart for your own lands.' Having sealed this with his signet, and dispatched a messenger to the Rathors, he appeared before Aurangzeb to receive the fruit of his service. But his treason met its [65] reward, and before he could say, the imperial orders were obeyed, a blow of the mace from the hand of the monarch sent his soul to hell. At midnight the Dervesh messenger reached the Rathor camp; he put the letter into their hand, which stated father and son were united; and added from himself that Tahawwur Khan was slain. All was confusion; the Rathors saddled and mounted, and moved a coss from Akbar's camp. The panic spread to his troops, who fled like the dried leaves of the sugar-cane when carried up in a whirlwind, while the prince was attending to the song and the wiles of the wanton."

[1] Krishna.

[2] [Orme, *Fragments*, ed. 1782, 142 ff.; Khāfi Khān in Elliot-Dowson vii. 298 ff.]

The Rāthors abandon Akbar.—This narrative exemplifies most strongly the hasty unreflecting character of the Rajput, who always acts from the impulse of the moment. They did not even send to Akbar's camp, although close to their own, to inquire the truth or falsehood of the report, but saddled and did not halt until they were twenty miles asunder. It is true, that in these times of peril they did not know in whom to confide; and being headed by one of their own body, they could not tell how far he might be implicated in the treachery.

The next day they were undeceived by the junction of the prince, who, when made acquainted with the departure of his allies, and the treason and death of Tahawwur Khan, could scarcely collect a thousand men to abide by his fortunes. With these he followed his panic-struck allies, and threw himself and his family upon their hospitality and protection—an appeal never made in vain to the Rajput. The poetic account, by the bard Karnidhan, of the reception of the prince by the chivalry of Maru, is remarkably minute and spirited:—the warriors and senators enter into a solemn debate as to the conduct to be pursued to the prince now claiming *saran* (sanctuary), when the bard takes occasion to relate the pedigree and renown of the chiefs of every clan. Each chief delivers his sentiments in a speech full of information respecting their national customs and manners. It also displays a good picture of "the power of the swans, and the necessity of feeding them with pearls," to enable them to sing with advantage. The council breaks up with the declaration of its determination to protect Akbar at all hazards, and Jetha, the brother of the head of the Champawats, is nominated to the charge of protector of Akbar's family. The gallant Durga, the Ulysses of the Rathors, is the manager of this dramatic convention, the details of which are wound up with an eulogy in true oriental hyperbole, in the Doric accents of Maru: [66]—

Māi chā pūt jin,
Jehā Durgādās,
Band Murdhara rakhiyo
Vin thāmbhā ākās.[1]

[1] [The reading in the text is that of Dr. Tessitori. Major Luard's Pandit, questioning the Author's translation, says that the words *Band Murdharā ra rakhyo* mean 'governed Mārwār well,' and that *bin thāmbh ākās*, 'the heavens without a prop,' refers to the ruler who was a minor.]

" O mother ! produce such sons as Durgadas, who first supported the dam of Murdhara, and then propped the heavens."

Character of Durgadās.—This model of a Rajput, as wise as he was brave, was the saviour of his country. To his suggestion it owed the preservation of its prince, and to a series of heroic deeds, his subsequent and more difficult salvation. Many anecdotes are extant recording the dread Aurangzeb had of this leader of the Rathors, one of which is amusing. The tyrant had commanded pictures to be drawn of two of the most mortal foes to his repose, Sivaji and Durga: " Siva was drawn seated on a couch ; Durga in his ordinary position, on horseback, toasting *bātis,* or barley-cakes, with the point of his lance, on a fire of maize-stalks. Aurangzeb, at the first glance, exclaimed, ' I may entrap that fellow (meaning Sivaji), but this dog is born to be my bane.' "

Durga at the head of his bands, together with young Akbar, moved towards the western extremity of the State, in hopes that they might lead the emperor in pursuit amongst the sandhills of the Luni ; but the wily monarch tried other arts, and first attempted to corrupt Durga. He sent him eight thousand gold mohurs,[1] which the Rajput instantly applied to the necessities of Akbar, who was deeply affected at this proof of devotion, and distributed a portion of it amongst Durga's retainers. Aurangzeb, seeing the futility of this plan, sent a force in pursuit of his son, who, knowing he had no hope of mercy if he fell into his father's hands, was anxious to place distance between them. Durga pledged himself for his safety, and relinquished all to ensure it. Making over the guardianship of young Ajit to his elder brother, Soning, and placing himself at the head of one thousand chosen men, he turned towards the south. The bard enumerates the names and families of all the chieftains of note who formed the bodyguard of prince Akbar in this desperate undertaking. The Champawats were the most numerous, but he specifies several of the home clans, as the Jodha and Mertia, and amongst the foreign Rajputs, the Jadon, Chauhan, Bhatti, Deora, Sonigira, and Mangalia [67].

Escape of Prince Akbar.—" The king followed their retreat : his troops surrounded the Rathors ; but Durga with one thousand chosen men left the north on their backs, and with the speed of

[1] The Mewar chronicle says forty thousand.

the winged quitted the camp. Aurang continued the pursuit to Jalor, when he found he had been led on a wrong scent, and that Durga, with the prince, keeping Gujarat on his right, and Chappan [1] on his left, had made good his retreat to the Nerbudda. Rage so far got the better of his religion, that he threw the Koran at the head of the Almighty. In wrath, he commanded Azam to exterminate the Rathors, but to leave Udaipur on one side,[2] and every other design, and first secure his brother. The deeds of Kamunda [3] removed the troubles of Mewar, as the wind disperses the clouds which shade the brightness of the moon. In ten days after Azam marched, the emperor himself moved, leaving his garrisons in Jodhpur and Ajmer. Durga's name was the charm which made the hosts of locusts quit their ground.[4] Durga was the sea-serpent; Akbar the mountain with which they churned the ocean Aurang, and made him yield the fourteen gems, one of which our religion regained, which is Lakshmi, and our faith, which is Dhanwantari [5] the sage.

"In fidelity who excelled the Khichis Sheo Singh and Mukund, who never left the person of Ajit, when his infancy was concealed in the mountains of Arbud? to them alone, and the faithful Sonigira, did Durga confide the secret of his retreat. The vassals of the Nine Castles of Maru knew that he was concealed; but where or in whose custody all were ignorant. Some thought he was at Jaisalmer; others at Bikampur; others at Sirohi. The eight divisions nobly supported the days of their exile; their sinews sustained the land of Murdhar. Raos, Rajas, and Ranas applauded their deeds, for all were alike enveloped in the net of destruction. In all the nine thousand [towns] of Murdhar, and the ten thousand of Mewar,[6] inhabitants there were none. Inayat Khan was left with ten thousand men to preserve Jodhpur; but the Champawat is the Sumer [7] of Maru, and without fear was Durga's brother, Soning. With Khemkaran the Karanot, and

[1] [The hill tract about Siwāna, in S. Mewār.]

[2] That is, dropped all schemes against it at that moment.

[3] The Kamdhuj; epithet of the Rathors.

[4] Charms and incantations, with music, are had recourse to, in order to cause the flight of these destructive insects from the fields they light on.

[5] [The physician of the gods, born at the churning of the ocean.]

[6] The number of towns and villages formerly constituting the arrondissement of each State.

[7] [Meru, the sacred mountain.]

Sabhal the Jodha, Bijmall the Mahecha, Jethmall Sujot, Kesari Karanot, and the Jodha brethren Sheodan and Bhim, and many more collected their clans and kin, and as soon as they heard that the king was within four coss of Ajmer they blockaded the Khan [68] in the city of Jodha; but twenty thousand Moguls came to the rescue. Another dreadful conflict ensued at the gates of Jodhpur, in which the Jadon Kishor, who led the battle, and many other chiefs were slain, yet not without many hundreds of the foe; the 9th Asarh, S. 1737.

"Soning carried the sword and the flame into every quarter. Aurang could neither advance nor retreat. He was like the serpent seizing the musk-rat, which, if liberated, caused blindness; but if swallowed, was like poison. Harnath and Kana Singh took the road to Sojat. They surrounded and drove away the cattle, which brought the Asurs to the rescue. A dreadful strife ensued; the chief of the Asurs was slain, but the brothers and all their kin bedewed the land with their blood. This, the *sakha* of Sojat, was when 1737 ended and 1738 commenced, when the sword and the pestilence (*mari* [1]) united to clear the land.

[1] *Mari*, or 'death' personified, is the name for that fearful scourge the spasmodic cholera morbus, which has caused the loss of so many lives for the last thirteen years throughout India. It appears to have visited India often, of which we have given a frightful record in the Annals of Mewar in the reign of Rana Raj Singh (see Vol. I. p. 454), in S. 1717 or A.D. 1661 (twenty years prior to the period we treat of); and Orme [*Fragments*, ed. 1782, p. 200] describes it as raging in the Deccan in A.D. 1684. They had likewise a visitation of it within the memory of many individuals now living.

Regarding the nature of this disease, whether endemic, epidemic, or contagious, and its cure, we are as ignorant now as the first day of our experience. There have been hundreds of conflicting opinions and hypotheses, but none satisfactory. In India, nine medical men out of ten, as well as those not professional, deny its being contagious. At Udaipur, the Rana's only son, hermetically sealed in the palace against contact, was the first seized with the disorder; a pretty strong proof that it was from atmospheric communication. He was also the last man in his father's dominions likely, from predisposition, to be attacked, being one of the most athletic and prudent of his subjects. I saw him through the disorder. We were afraid to administer remedies to the last heir of Bappa Rawal, but I hinted to Amarji, who was both bard and doctor, that strong doses of musk (12 grs. each) might be beneficial. These he had, and I prevented his having cold water to drink, and also checking the insensible perspiration by throwing off the bedclothes. Nothing but his robust frame and youth made him resist this tremendous assailant.

"Soning was the Rudra of the field; Agra and Delhi trembled at his deeds; he looked on Aurang as the waning moon. The king sent an embassy to Soning; it was peace he desired. He offered the mansab of Sat Hazari for Ajit,[1] and what dignities he might demand for his brethren—the restoration of Ajmer, and to make Soning its governor. To the engagement was added, 'the panja is affixed in ratification of this treaty, witnessed by God Almighty.'[2] The Diwan, Asad Khan, was the negotiator, and the Aremdi,[3] who was with him, solemnly swore to its maintenance. The treaty concluded, the king, whose thoughts could not be diverted from Akbar, departed for the Deccan. Asad Khan was left at Ajmer, and Soning at Merta [69]. But Soning was a thorn in the side of Aurangzeb; he bribed the Brahmans, who threw pepper into the Homa (burnt sacrifice) and secured for Soning a place in Suraj Mandala (the mansion of the sun). The day following the treaty, by the incantations of Auranga, Soning was no more.[4] Asoj the 6th, S. 1738.

"Asad sent the news to the king. This terror being removed, the king withdrew his *panja* from his treaty, and in joy departed for the Deccan. The death of Soning shed gloom and grief over the land. Then Mukund Singh Mertia, son of Kalyan, abandoned his mansab and joined his country's cause. A desperate encounter soon followed with the troops of Asad Khan near Merta, in which Ajit, the son of Bitaldas, who led the fight, was slain, with many of each clan, which gave joy to the Asurs, but grief to the faithful Rajput; on the second day of the bright half of the moon of Kartik, S. 1738.

"Prince Azam was left with Asad Khan; Inayat at Jodhpur; and their garrisons were scattered over the land, as their tombs (*gor*) everywhere attest. The lord of Chandawal, Shambhu Kumpawat, now led the Rathors with Udang Singh Bakhshi, and Tejsi, the young son of Durga, the bracelet on the arm of Mahadeva, with Fateh Singh and Ram Singh, just returned from

[1] [A command of 7000 troops.]

[2] See Vol. I. p. 419, for an explanation of the *panja*—and the treaty which preceded this, made by Rana Raj Singh, the fourth article of which stipulates for terms to the minor son of Jaswant.

[3] I know not what officer is meant by the Aremdi, sent to swear to the good faith of the king.

[4] His death was said to be effected by incantations, most probably poison.

placing Akbar safely in the Deccan, and many other valiant Rathors.[1] They spread over the country even to Mewar, sacked Pur-Mandal, and slew the governor Kasim Khan."

These desultory and bloody affrays, though they kept the king's troops in perpetual alarm and lost them myriads of men, thinned the ranks of the defenders of Maru, who again took refuge in the Aravalli. From thence, watching every opportunity, they darted on their prey. On one occasion they fell upon the garrison of Jaitaran, which they routed and expelled, or as the chronicle quaintly says, "with the year 1739 they also fled." At the same time, the post of Sojat was carried by Bija Champawat, while the Jodhawats, under Ram Singh, kept their foes in play to the northward, and led by Udaibhan attacked the Mirza Nur Ali at Charai: "the contest lasted for three hours; the dead bodies of the Yavans lay in heaps in the Akhara; who even abandoned their Nakkaras."[2]

"After the affair of Jaitaran, when Udai Singh Champawat and Mohkam Singh Mertia were the leaders, they made a push for Gujarat, and had penetrated to [70] Kheralu,[3] when they were attacked, pursued, and surrounded in the hills at Renpur, by Sayyid Muhammad, the Hakim of Gujarat. All night they stood to their arms. In the morning the sword rained and filled the ears of the Apsaras. Karan and Kesari were slain, with Gokuldas Bhatti, with all their civil officers, and Ram Singh himself renounced life on this day.[4] But the Asurs pulled up the reins, having lost many men. Pali was also attacked in the month of Bhadon this year 1739; then the game of destruction was played with Nur Ali, three hundred Rathors against five hundred of the king's troops, which were routed, losing their leader, Afzal Khan, after a desperate struggle.

"Bala was the hero who drove the Yavan from this post. Udaya attacked the Sidi at Sojat. Jaitaran was again reinforced. In Baisakh, Mohkam Singh Mertia attacked the royal post at Merta, slew Sayyid Ali, and drove out the king's troops."

[1] Many were enumerated by the bardic chronicler, who would deem it sacrilege to omit a single name in the page of fame.

[2] [*Akhāra*, 'a place of wrestling,' rhyming with *nakkāra*, 'a kettle-drum.']

[3] [In Baroda State, about 63 miles N. of Ahmadābād.]

[4] He was one of the gallant chiefs who, with Durga, conveyed prince Akbar to the sanctuary with the Mahrattas.

Assistance given by the Bhattis.—The year 1739 was one of perpetual conflict, of captures and recaptures, in which many parties of twenty and thirty on each side fell. They afford numerous examples of heroic patriotism, in which Rathor blood was lavishly shed ; but while to them each warrior was a loss not to be replaced, the despot continued to feed the war with fresh troops. The Bhattis of Jaisalmer came forward this year, and nobly shed their blood in seconding the efforts of the Rathors in this patriotic warfare.

"In S. 1740, Azam and Asad Khan joined the emperor in the Deccan, and Inayat Khan was left in command at Ajmer—being enjoined not to relax the war in Marwar, even with the setting in of the rains. Merwara afforded a place of rendezvous for the Rathors, and security for their families. Here eleven thousand of the best troops of Inayat invaded the hills to attack the united Jodhas and Champawats, who retaliated on Pali, Sojat, and Godwar. The ancient Mandor, which was occupied by a garrison under Khwaja Salah, was attacked by the Mandecha Bhatti and driven out. At Bagri, a desperate encounter took place in the month of Baisakh, when Ram Singh and Samant Singh, both Bhatti chiefs, fell, with two hundred of their vassals, slaying one thousand of the Moguls. The Karamsots and Kumpawats, under Anup Singh, scoured the banks of the Luni, and put to the sword the garrisons of Ustara and Gangani. Mohkam, with his Mertias, made a descent on his patrimonial lands, and drew upon him the whole force of its [71] governor, Muhammad Ali. The Mertias met him on their own native plains. The Yavan proposed a truce, and at the interview assassinated the head of the Mertias, tidings of whose death rejoiced the Shah in the Deccan.

"At the beginning of 1741, neither strife nor fear had abated. Sujan Singh led the Rathors in the south, while Lakha Champawat and Kesar Kumpawat, aided by the Bhattis and Chauhans, kept the garrison of Jodhpur in alarm. When Sujan was slain, the bard was sent to Sangram, who held a mansab and lands from the king ; he was implored to join his brethren ; he obeyed, and all collected around Sangram.[1] Siwancha[2] was attacked, and with Bhalotra and Panchbhadra were plundered ; while the

[1] We are not informed of what clan he was, or his rank, which must have been high.

[2] The tract so called, of which Siwana is the capital [in S. Mewār].

blockaded garrisons were unable to aid. An hour before sunset every gate of Maru was shut. The Asurs had the strongholds in their power; but the plains resounded with the An[1] of Ajit. Udaibhan, with his Jodhawats, appeared before Bhadrajun; he assaulted the foe and captured his guns and treasure. An attempt from Jodhpur made to recapture the trophies, added to the triumph of the Jodha.

Abduction of the Asāni Girls.—" Purdil Khan[2] held Siwana; and Nahar Khan Mewati, Kunari. To attack them, the Champawats convened at Mokalsar. Their thirst for vengeance redoubled at the tidings that Nur Ali had abducted two young women of the tribe of Asani. Ratna led the Rathors; they reached Kunari and engaged Purdil Khan, who was put to the sword with six hundred of his men. The Rathors left one hundred in the field that day, the ninth of Chait. The Mirza[3] no sooner heard of this defeat than he fled towards Toda, with the Asani damsels, gazing on the mangoes as they ripened, and having reached Kuchal, he encamped. Subhal Singh, the son of Askaran, heard it; he took his opium, and though the Mirza was surrounded by pillars, the dagger of Askaran's son reached his heart; but the Bhatti[4] was cut in pieces. The roads were now impassable; the Thanas[5] of the Yavans were reduced to great straits [72].

" The year 1742 commenced with the slaughter of the king's garrison at Sambhar by the Lakhawats and Asawats;[6] while from Godwar the chiefs made incursions to the gates of Ajmer. A battle took place at Merta, where the Rathors were defeated and dispersed; but in revenge Sangram burned the suburbs of Jodhpur, and then came to Dunara, where once more the clans assembled. They marched, invested Jalor, when Bihari, left without succour, was compelled to capitulate, and the gate of honour (*dharmadwara*) was left open to him. And thus ended 1742."

[1] Oath of allegiance.

[2] It is almost superfluous to remark, even to the mere English reader, that whenever he meets the title Khan, it indicates a Muhammadan [and a Pathān]; and that of Singh (lion) a Rajput.

[3] Nur Ali. Mirza is a title only applied to a Mogul.

[4] As a Bhatti revenged this disgrace, it is probable the Asani damsels, thus abducted by the Mirza, were of his own race.

[5] Garrisons and military posts.

[6] These are of the most ancient vassalage of Maru.

CHAPTER 8

Ajit Singh produced to the Rāthors, A.D. **1686.**—" In the year 1743, the Champawats, Kumpawats, Udawats, Mertias, Jodhas, Karamsots, and all the assembled clans of Maru, became impatient to see their sovereign. They sent for the Khichi Mukund, and prayed that they might but [73] behold him ; but the faithful to his trust replied : ' He,[1] who confided him to me, is yet in the Deccan.'—' Without the sight of our Lord, bread and water have no flavour.' Mukund could not withstand their suit. The Hara prince Durjan Sal, having come to their aid with one thousand horse from Kotah,[2] they repaired to the hill of Abu, when on the last day of Chait 1743 they saw their prince. As the lotus expands at the sunbeam, so did the heart of each Rathor at the sight of their infant sovereign ; they drank his looks, even as the papiha in the month Asoj sips drops of amrita (ambrosia) from the Champa.[3] There were present, Udai Singh, Sangram Singh, Bijaipal, Tej Singh, Mukund Singh, and Nahar son of Hari, all Champawats; Raj Singh, Jagat Singh, Jeth Singh, Samant Singh, of the Udawats ; Ram Singh, Fateh Singh, and Kesari, Kumpawats. There was also the Uhar chief of pure descent,[4] besides the Khichi Mukund, the Purohit, the Parihar, and the Jain priest, Yati Gyan, Bijai. In a fortunate hour, Ajit became known to the world. The Hara Rao first made his salutation ; he was followed by all Marwar with offerings of gold, pearls, and horses.

Inayat conveyed the tidings to Aurang Shah; the Asur chief said to the king, ' If without a head so long they had combated him, what could now be expected ? ' He demanded reinforcements.

[1] Meaning Durgadas.

[2] His principal object was to marry the daughter of Shujāwan Singh Champawat, the sister of the brave Mukund Singh, often mentioned in the chronicle. The Kotah prince dared not, according to every Rajput maxim of gallantry, refuse his aid on such occasion ; but the natural bravery and high mind of Durjan Sal required no stimulus.

[3] The Hindu poet says the Papiha bird [the cuckoo] becomes intoxicated with the flowers [of the Champa (*Michelia champaka*)].

[4] A name now lost.

Ajīt Singh installed.—" In triumph they conveyed the young Raja to Awa, whose chief made the *badhava*[1] with pearls, and presented him with horses; here he was entertained, and here they prepared the *tika daur*.[2] Thence, taking Raepur, Bilara, and Barunda in his way, and receiving the homage and nazars of their chiefs, he repaired to Asop, where he was entertained by the head of the Kumpawats. From Asop he went to the Bhatti fief of Lawera; thence to Rian, the chief abode of the Mertias; thence to Khinwasar, of the Karamsots. Each chief entertained their young lord, around whom all the clans gathered. Then he repaired to Kalu, the abode of Pabhu Rao Dhandal,[3] who came forth with all his bands; and at length [74] he reached Pokaran, where he was joined by Durgadas from the Deccan, the 10th of Bhadon 1744.

" Inayat Khan was alarmed. He assembled a numerous array to quell this fresh tumult, but death pounced upon him. The king was afflicted thereat. He tried another stratagem, and set up a pretended son of Jaswant, styled Muhammad Shah, and offered Ajit the mansab of five thousand to submit to his authority.[4] The pretender also died as he set out for Jodhpur, and Shujaat Khan[5] was made the governor of Marwar in place of Inayat. Now the Rathors and Haras united, having cleared Maru of their foes, attacked them in a foreign land. The garrisons of Malpura and Pur Mandal were put to the sword, and here the Hara prince was killed by a cannon shot in leading the storm. Here they levied eight thousand mohurs in contribution and returned to Marwar, while the civil officers and Purohits made collections in his country; and thus passed 1744.

" The year 1745 commenced with proposals from Shujaat Khan to hold Marwar in farm; he promised one-fourth of all transit duties if the Rathors would respect foreign commerce: to this they agreed. The son of Inayat left Jodhpur for Delhi; he had reached Renwal, but was overtaken by the Jodha Harnath.

[1] Waving a brass vessel, filled with pearls, round his head.

[2] [The inauguration foray. See Vol. I. p. 315.]

[3] Pabhu Rao Rathor is immortalized by the aid of his lance on this occasion; he was of the ancient chivalry of Maru, and still held his allodial domain.

[4] [See p. 997 above.]

[5] [His original name was Kārtalab Khān, and he served as viceroy of Surat and Gujarāt (Manucci ii. 259, iv. 247).]

who released him both of wives and wealth. The Khan fled to the Kachhwahas for shelter. Suja Beg, who left Ajmer to release him, fared no better: he was attacked, defeated, and plundered by Mukunddas Champawat.

War with the Mughals.—" In 1747, Safi Khan was Hakim of Ajmer: Durga determined to attack him. The Hakim took post in the pass which defends the road; there Durga assailed him, and made him fly to Ajmer. The tidings reached the king; he wrote to the Khan, if he discomfited Durgadas, he would raise him over all the Khans of the empire; if he failed, he should send him bracelets,[1] and order Shujaat from Jodhpur to supersede him. Safi, before abandoning his trust, tried to retain his honours by the circumvention of Ajit. He addressed a letter to him, saying he held the imperial sanad for the restoration of his paternal domains, but that, as the king's representative, he must come and receive it. Ajit marched at the head of twenty thousand Rathors, sending in advance Mukund Champawat to observe whether any treachery was contemplated. The snare was discovered and reported to Ajit, as he arrived at the foot of the pass beyond the mountains. 'Let us, however, have [75] a sight of Ajaidurg as we are so near,' said the young prince, 'and receive the compliments of the Khan.' They moved on towards the city, and Safi Khan had no alternative but to pay his obeisance to Ajit. To enjoy his distress, one said, 'Let us fire the city.' The Hakim sat trembling for its safety and his own; he brought forth jewels and horses which he presented to Ajit.

" In 1748, the troubles recommenced in Mewar. Prince Amra rebelled against his father, Rana Jai Singh, and was joined by all his chiefs. The Rana fled to Godwar, and at Ghanerao collected a force, which Amra prepared to attack. The Rana demanded succour of the Rathors, and all the Mertias hastened to relieve him; and soon after Ajit sent Durgadas and Bhagwan, with Ranmall Jodha, and 'the eight ranks of Rathors,' to espouse the father's cause. But the Chondawats and Saktawats, the Jhalas and Chauhans, rather than admit foreign interference in their quarrel, thought it better to effect a reconciliation between father and son; and thus the Rana was indebted to Marwar for the support of his throne.

Aurangzeb negotiates about Akbar's Daughter.—" The year

[1] A mark of contempt.

1749 passed in negotiation to obtain the daughter of prince Akbar, left in charge of Durgadas, for whose honour Aurangzeb was alarmed, as Ajit was reaching manhood; Narayandas Kulumbi was the medium of negotiation, and Safi Khan caused all hostilities to cease while it lasted.

"In 1750, the Muslim governors of Jodhpur, Jalor, and Siwana combined their forces against Ajit, who was again compelled to retreat to the mountains. Akha, the Bala, received their attack, but was defeated in the month of Magh. Another combat was hastened by the wanton slaughter of a *sand*,[1] when the Hakim of Chank, with all his train, were made prisoners at Mokalsar by the Champawat Mukanddas.

"To such straits were the Muslims put in 1751, that many districts paid chauth, others tribute, and many, tired of this incessant warfare, and unable to conquer their bread, took service with the Rathors. This year, Kasim Khan and Lashkar Khan marched against Ajit, who took post at Bijaipur. Durga's son led the onset, and the Khan was defeated. With each year of Ajit grew the hopes of the Rathors; while Aurangzeb was afflicted at each month's growth of his granddaughter. He wrote to Shujaat, the Hakim of Jodhpur, to secure his honour at whatever cost; his applications for Akbar's daughter were unwearied [76].

Ajīt Singh marries a Princess of Mewār.—"This year the coconut studded with gems,[2] two elephants and ten steeds, all richly caparisoned, were sent by the Rana to affiance the daughter of his younger brother, Gaj Singh, to Ajit. The present was accepted, and in the month of Jeth, the prince of the Rathors repaired to Udaipur, where the nuptials were solemnized. In Asarh he again married at Deolia.[3]

"In 1753, negotiations were renewed through Durgadas, and the protracted restoration of the Sultani obtained the seat of his ancestors for the Jodhani. Durga was offered for himself the mansab of five thousand, which he refused; he preferred that Jalor, Siwanchi, Sanchor, and Tharad[4] should revert to his

[1] One of those pampered bulls, allowed to wander at liberty and fed by every one.

[2] The coco, the symbol of a marriage offer.

[3] Partabgarh Deolia, a small principality grown out of Mewar [*IGI*, xx. 14].

[4] [In the Pālanpur Agency, Bombay Presidency (*IGI*, xix. 346).]

country. Even Aurang admired the honourable and distinguished treatment of his granddaughter.

"In Pus 1757,[1] Ajit regained possession of his ancestral abode: on his reaching Jodhpur he slew a buffalo at each of its five gates.[2] The Shahzada Sultan led the way, Shujaat being dead.[3]

"In 1759, Azam Shah again seized on Jodhpur, and Ajit made Jalor his abode. Some of his chiefs now served the foe, some the Rana whose hopes were on Eklinga alone; while the lord of Amber served the king in the Deccan. The enormities of the Asurs had reached their height; the sacred kine were sacrificed even at Mathura, Prayag, and Okhamandal; the Jogis and Bairagis invoked heaven for protection, but iniquity prevailed as the Hindu strength decayed. Prayers were everywhere offered up to heaven to cleanse the land from the iniquities of the barbarians.[4] In this year, the month of Magh 1759, the Mithun Lagan (the 'sun in Gemini'), a son was born of the Chauhani, who was called Abhai Singh. (See end of this chapter, p. 1019, for the Horoscope of Abhai Singh.)

"In 1761, Yusuf was superseded by Murshid Kuli as Hakim of Jodhpur. On his arrival he presented the royal sanad for the restoration of Merta to Ajit. Kusal Singh, the Mertia Sarmor, with the Dhandhal Govinddas, were ordered to [77] take the charge, which incensed the son of Indar (Mohkam Singh), who deemed his faithful service during his minority overlooked by this preference. He wrote to the king to nominate him to the command of Marwar, and that he would fulfil his charge to the satisfaction both of Hindu and Muslim.

"In 1761 the star of the foe began to decline. Murshid Kuli, the Mogul, was relieved by Jaafar Khan. Mohkam's letter was intercepted. He had turned traitor to his prince, and joined

[1] I cannot now call to mind whether this break of four years in the chronicle of the bard Karnidhan occurs in the original, or that in translating I left the hiatus from there being nothing interesting therein. The tyrant was now fully occupied in the Deccan wars, and the Rajputs had time to breathe.

[2] [To propitiate the gate spirit.]

[3] This Shahzada must have been prince Azam, who was nominated viceroy of Gujarat and Marwar.

[4] This record of the manifold injuries, civil and religious, under which the Hindu nation groaned is quite akin to the sentiments of the letter of remonstrance addressed by Rana Raj Singh to Aurangzeb. See Vol. I. p. 442.

the king's troops. Ajit marched against them; he fought them at Dunara; the king's troops were defeated, and the rebel Indhawat was slain. This was in 1762.

Death of Aurangzeb, March 3, 1707.—" In 1763, Ibrahim Khan, the king's lieutenant [1] at Lahore, passed through Marwar to relieve Azam in the vice-royalty of Gujarat. On the second day of Chait, the obscure half of the moon, the joyful tidings arrived of the death of the king.[2] On the fifth, Ajit took to horse; he reached the town of Jodha, and sacrificed to the gates, but the Asurs feared to face him. Some hid their faces in fear, while others fled. The Mirza came down, and Ajit ascended to the halls of his ancestors. The wretched Yavans, now abandoned to the infuriated Rajputs smarting under twenty-six years of misery, found no mercy. In hopeless despair they fled, and the wealth which they had amassed by extortion and oppression returned to enrich the proprietor. The barbarians, in turn, were made captive; they fought, were slaughtered and dispersed. Some sought *saran* (sanctuary), and found it; even the barbarian leader himself threw fear to the winds in the unconcealed sanctuary of the Kumpawat. But the triumph of the Hindu was complete, when, to escape from perdition, their flying foes invoked Sitaram and Hargovind, begging their bread in the day, and taking to their heels at night. The chaplet of the Mulla served to count the name of Rama, and a handful of gold was given to have their beards removed.[3] Nothing but the despair and flight of the Mlechchha was heard throughout Murdhar. Merta was evacuated, and the wounded Mohkam fled to Nagor. Sojat and Pali were regained, and the land returned to the Jodhani. Jodhgarh was purified from the contaminations of the barbarian with the water of the Ganges and the sacred Tulasi, and Ajit received the tilak of sovereignty.

"Then Azam marched from the south and Muazzam from the north. At Agra a [78] mighty battle for empire took place

[1] He is called the samdhi, or 'son-in-law of the king.' [There is no record of his marriage to a daughter of Aurangzeb (*IA*, xl. 83). It is the fathers of a bride and bridegroom who stand in the relation of *samdhi* to each other.]

[2] 5th Chait S. 1763. The 28th Zu-lqa'ada [March 3, 1707].

[3] The Rajputs gave up beards the better to distinguish them from the Muslims.

between the two Asurs, but Alam [1] prevailed and got the throne. The tidings soon reached the king, that Ajit had plundered his armies in Maru and taken possession of the 'cushion' of his fathers.

Campaign of Bahādur Shāh.—"The rainy season of 1764 had vanished, the king had no repose; he formed an army and came to Ajmer. Then Haridas, the son of Bhagwan, with the Uhar and Mangalia chiefs,[2] and Ratna the leader of the Udawats, with eight hundred of their clan, entered the castle and swore to Ajit, that whatever might be his intentions, they were resolved to maintain the castle to the death. The royal army encamped at Bhavi Bilara, and Ajit prepared for the storm; but the king was advised to try peaceful arts, and an overture was made, and the messenger was sent back to the king accompanied by Nahar Khan. The embassy returned bearing the royal farman to Ajit; but before he would accept it, he said he would view the royal army, and on the first day of Phalgun he left the hill of Jodha and reached Bisalpur. Here he was received by a deputation from the king, headed by Shujaat Khan, son of the Khankhanan accompanied by the Raja of the Bhadaurias and Rao Budh Singh of Bundi—the place of meeting was Pipar. That night passed in adjusting the terms of the treaty.[3] The ensuing morn he marched forward at the head of all the men of Maru; and at Anandpur the eyes of the king of the barbarians (Mlechchha) fell on those of the lord of the earth. He gave him the title of Tegh Bahadur.[4] But fate decreed that the city of Jodha was coveted by the king; by stealth he sent Mahrab Khan to take possession, accompanied by the traitor Mohkam. Ajit burned with rage when he heard of this treachery, but he was compelled to dissimulate and accompany Alam to the Deccan, and to serve

[1] Shah Alam, who assumed the title of Bahadur Shah on mounting the throne. [The battle in which Azam was defeated was fought on June 7, 1707.]

[2] The Mangalia is a branch of the Guhilots, severed from the original stem in the reign of Bappa Rawal eleven centuries ago.

[3] [According to Khāfi Khān, the submission of Ajīt Singh was complete; he even asked that the mosque at Jodhpur should be rebuilt, temples destroyed, and the law about the summons to prayer and the killing of cows enforced—concessions he would not have been likely to make unless he was reduced to extremities (Elliot-Dowson vii. 405).]

[4] 'The warrior's sword.'

under Kambakhsh. Jai Singh of Amber [1] was also with the king, and had a like cause for discontent, a royal garrison being placed in Amber, and the *gaddi* of the Raja bestowed on his younger brother, Bijai Singh. Now the army rolled on like a sea overflowing its bounds. As soon as the king crossed the Nerbudda,[2] the Rajas executed their designs, and, without saying a word, at the head of their vassals retrograded to Rajwara. They repaired to Udaipur, and were received by Rana Amra with rejoicing and distinction [79], who advanced to conduct them to his capital. Seated together, the *chaunri* waving over their heads, they appeared like the Trianga,[3] Brahma, Vishnu and Mahesa. From this hour the fortunes of the Asurs sunk, and virtue again began to show herself.[4] From Udaipur the two Rajas passed to Marwar. They reached Awa, and here the Champawat Sangram, son of Udaibhan, spread the foot-carpet (*pagmanda*) for his lord.

"The month of Sawan 1765 set in, and the hopes of the Asur expired. Mahrab was in consternation when he heard that Ajit had returned to his native land. On the 7th the hall of Jodha was surrounded by thirty thousand Rathors. On the 12th the gate of honour was thrown open to Mahrab; he had to thank the son of Askaran [5] for his life. He was allowed an honourable retreat, and Ajit once more entered the capital of Maru.

"Jai Singh encamped upon the banks of the Sur Sagar; but a prince without a country, he was unhappy. But as soon as the rains were passed, Ajmall, the sanctuary of the Kachhwaha, proposed to reinstate him in Amber. When conjoined they had reached Merta, Agra and Delhi trembled. When they arrived at Ajmer its governor sought *saran* with the saint,[6] and paid the contributions demanded. Then, like the falcon, Ajit darted upon

[1] This is the Mirza Raja, Jai Singh—the posterior Jai Singh had the epithet *Sawai* [see Vol. II. p. 969].

[2] The Muslim historian mentions in Vol. I. p. 464, that Bahadur was then *en route* to Lahore.

[3] Trianga, the triple-bodied, or *trimurti*.

[4] The bard of Maru passes over the important fact of the intermarriage which took place on this occasion of the Rajput triple alliance. See Vol. I. p. 465.

[5] Durgadas, who recommended the acceptance of the proffered capitulation.

[6] The shrine of Khwaja Kutb.

Sambhar; and here the vassals of Amber repaired from all quarters to the standard of their lord. With twelve thousand men, the Sayyid advanced along the edge of the salt lake, to encounter Ajmall. The Kumpawat led the charge; a desperate battle ensued; Husain, with six thousand men, lay on the field, while the rest took to flight and sought refuge in the castle.[1] His lieutenant, the Parihar, chief Pandu,[2] here fell into the hands of Ajit; he then felt he had recovered Mandor. On intelligence of this history, the Asurs abandoned Amber, and having placed a garrison in Sambhar, in the month of Margsir, Ajit restored Jai Singh to Amber, and prepared to attack Bikaner. Ajit committed the administration of all civil affairs to the faithful Raghunath Bhandari, with the [80] title of Diwan. He was well qualified, both from his experience in civil affairs and from his valour as a soldier.

Death of Prince Kāmbakhsh.—" In Bhadon of the year 1766, Aurangzeb put to death Kambakhsh,[3] and Jai Singh entered into negotiations with the king. Ajit now went against Nagor; but Indar Singh being without resource, came forth and embraced Ajit's feet, who bestowed Ladnun upon him as a heritage. But this satisfied not him who had been the lord of Nagor, and Indar carried his complaints to Delhi.[4] The king was enraged—his threats reached the Rajas, who deemed it safe again to reunite. They met at Kolia near Didwana, and the king soon after reached Ajmer. Thence he sent his firmans and the panja as terms of friendship to the Rajas: Nahar Khan, Chela of the king, was the bearer. They were accepted, and on the 1st Asarh both the Rajas repaired to Ajmer. Here the king received them

[1] Although the Marwar chronicler takes all the credit of this action, it was fought by the combined Rajputs of the alliance. Vol. I. p. 466.

[2] Pandu is the squire, the shield-bearer, of the Rajputs.

[3] Kambakhsh was the child of the old age of the tyrant Aurangzeb, by a Rajput princess. He appears to have held him in more affection than any of his other sons, as his letter on his death-bed to him testifies. See Vol. I. p. 439. [Kāmbakhsh was son of Bāi Udaipuri, who was probably a dancing girl, but one account states that she was a Georgian Christian, formerly in Dāra Shukoh's harem; she died in June 1707. Kāmbakhsh, born March 6, 1667, died from wounds received in battle with his brother Muazzam, fought near Haidarābād, Deccan, January 13, 1709.]

[4] Indar Singh was the son of Amra, the eldest brother of Jaswant, and the father of Mohkam, who, being disappointed of the government of Merta, deserted to the king.

graciously, in the face of the world; to Ajit he presented the sanad of the Nine Castles of Maru, and to Jai Singh that of Amber. Having taken leave of the king, the two Rajas went on the *parab*[1] to the sacred lake of Pushkar. Here they separated for their respective domains, and Ajit reached Jodhpur in Sawan 1767. In this year he married a Gaur Rani, and thus quenched the feud caused by Arjun, who slew Amra Singh in the Ammkhass.[2] Then he went on a pilgrimage to Kurukshetra, the field of battle of the Mahabharata, and made his ablutions in the fountain of Bhishma.[3] Thus 1767 passed away" [81].

[1] [The day on which the sun enters a new sign of the zodiac.]

[2] This is another of the numerous instances of contradictory feelings in the Rajput character. Amra, elder brother of Jaswant, was banished Marwar, lost his birthright, and was afterwards slain at court, as already related. His son, Indar Singh and grandson Mohkam, from Nagor, which they held in separate grants from the king, never forgot their title as elder branch of the family, and eternally contested their claim against Ajit. Still, as a Rathor, he was bound to avenge the injuries of a Rathor, even though his personal foe.—Singular inconsistency!

[3] There is an anecdote regarding the fountain of this classic field of strife, the Troad of Rajasthan, which well exemplifies the superstitious belief of the warlike Rajput. The emperor Bahadur Shah was desirous to visit this scene of the exploits of the heroes of antiquity, stimulated, no doubt, by his Rajputni queen, or his mother, also of this race. He was seated under a tree which shaded the sacred fount, named after the great leader of the Kauravas, his queen by his side, surrounded by *kanats* to hide them from profane eyes, when a vulture perched upon the tree with a bone in its beak, which falling in the fountain, the bird set up a scream of laughter. The king looked up in astonishment, which was greatly increased when the vulture addressed him in human accents, saying "that in a former birth she was a Jogini, and was in the field of slaughter of the Great War, whence she flew away with the dissevered arm of one of its mighty warriors, with which she alighted on that very tree, that the arm was encumbered with a ponderous golden bracelet, in which, as an amulet, were set thirteen brilliant symbols of Siva, and that after devouring the flesh, she dropped the bracelet, which fell into the fountain, and it was this awakened coincidence which had caused the scream of laughter." We must suppose that this, the *palada* of the field of slaughter, spoke Sanskrit or its dialect, interpreted by his Rajput queen. Instantly the pioneers were commanded to clear the fountain, and behold the relic of the Mahabharata, with the symbolic emblems of the god all-perfect! and so large were they, that the emperor remarked they would answer excellently well for "slaves of the carpet." * The Hindu princes then present, among whom were the Rajas Ajit and Jai Singh, were shocked at this levity, and each entreated of the king one of

* [The weights which keep it down.]

Eulogy of Durgadās.—Here let us, for a while, suspend the narrative of the chronicler, and take a retrospective glance at the transactions of the Rathors, from the year 1737 [A.D. 1680], the period of Raja Jaswant's death at Kabul, to the restoration of Ajit, presenting a continuous conflict of thirty years' duration. In vain might we search the annals of any other nation for such inflexible devotion as marked the Rathor character through this period of strife, during which, to use their own phrase, "hardly a chieftain died on his pallet." Let those who deem the Hindu warrior void of patriotism read the rude chronicle of this thirty years' war; let them compare it with that of any other country, and do justice to the magnanimous Rajput. This narrative, the simplicity of which is the best voucher for its authenticity, presents an uninterrupted record of patriotism and disinterested loyalty. It was a period when the sacrifice of these principles was rewarded by the tyrant king with the highest honours of the state; nor are we without instances of the temptation being too strong to be withstood; but they are rare, and serve only to exhibit, in more pleasing colours, the virtues of the tribe which spurned the attempts at seduction. What a splendid example is the heroic Durgadas of all that constitutes the glory of the Rajput! Valour, loyalty, integrity, combined with prudence in all the difficulties which surrounded him, are qualities which entitle him to the admiration which his memory continues to enjoy. The temptations held out to him were almost irresistible: not merely the

---

the phallic symbols. The Mirza Raja obtained two, and both are yet at Jaipur, one in the Temple of Silah Devi,* the other in that of Govinda. Ajit had one, still preserved and worshipped at the shrine of Girdhari at Jodhpur. My old tutor and friend, the Yati Gyanchandra, who told the story while he read the chronicles as I translated them, has often seen and made homage to all the three relics. There is one, he believed, at Bundi or Kotah, and the Rana by some means obtained another. They are of pure rock crystal, and as each weighs some pounds, there must have been giants in the days of the Bharat, to have supported thirteen in one armlet. Homer's heroes were pigmies to the Kauravas, whose bracelet we may doubt if Ajax could have lifted. My venerable tutor, though liberal in his opinions, did not choose to dissent from the general belief, for man, he said, had beyond a doubt greatly degenerated since the heroic ages, and was rapidly approximating to the period, the immediate forerunner of a universal renovation, when only dwarfs would creep over the land.

---

* The goddess of arms, their Pallas.

gold, which he and thousands of his brethren would alike have spurned, but the splendid offer of power in the proffered mansab of five thousand, which would at once have lifted him from his vassal condition to an equality with the [82] princes and chief nobles of the land. Durga had, indeed, but to name his reward; but, as the bard justly says, he was *amol*, beyond all price, *anokha*, unique. Not even revenge, so dear to the Rajput, turned him aside from the dictates of true honour. The foul assassination of his brother, the brave Soning, effected through his enemies, made no alteration in his humanity whenever the chance of war placed his foe in his power; and in this, his policy seconded his virtue. His chivalrous conduct, in the extrication of prince Akbar from inevitable destruction had he fallen into his father's hands, was only surpassed by his generous and delicate behaviour towards the prince's family, which was left in his care, forming a marked contrast to that of the enemies of his faith on similar occasions. The virtue of the granddaughter of Aurangzeb, in the sanctuary (*saran*) of Dunara,[1] was in far better keeping than in the trebly-walled harem of Agra. Of his energetic mind, and the control he exerted over those of his confiding brethren, what a proof is given, in his preserving the secret of the abode of his prince throughout the six first years of his infancy! But, to conclude our eulogy in the words of their bard: he has reaped the immortality destined for good deeds; his memory is cherished, his actions are the theme of constant praise, and his picture on his white horse, old, yet in vigour, is familiar amongst the collections of portraits of Rajputana.[2]

But there was not a clan, or family, that did not produce men of worth in this protracted warfare, which incited constant emulation; and the bards of each had abundant materials to emblazon the pages of their chronicles. To the recollection of these, their expatriated descendants allude in the memorial[3] of their hardships from the cruel policy of the reigning chief, the last lineal descendant of the prince, whose history has just been narrated. We now resume the narrative in the language of the chronicle [83].

[1] Durga's fief on the Luni.

[2] See Vol. I. p. 451.

[3] See Vol. I. p. 228.

HOROSCOPE OF RAJA ABHAI SINGH

In the Janampatri, or horoscope of Abhai Singh (referred to in p. 1011), the 4th, 7th, 8th, 10th, 11th, and 12th houses denote the destinies of the heir of Ajit. In the 4th we have the monster Rahu, the author of eclipses. Of the 7th, or house of heirs, the Moon and Venus have taken possession; of the 8th, or house of strife, the Sun and Mercury. In the 10th is Ketu, brother of Rahu, both signs of evil portent. Mars rides in the house of fate, while Saturn and Jupiter are together in the abode of sovereignty. Like that of every man living, the horoscope of the heir of Maru is filled with good and evil: could the Jotishi or astrological seer have put the parricidal sign in the house of destiny, he might have claimed some merit for superior intelligence. Those who have ever consulted any works on this foolish pursuit will observe that the diagrams of the European astrologers are exact copies of the Hindu, in proof of which I have inserted this; to trace darkness as well as light from the East!

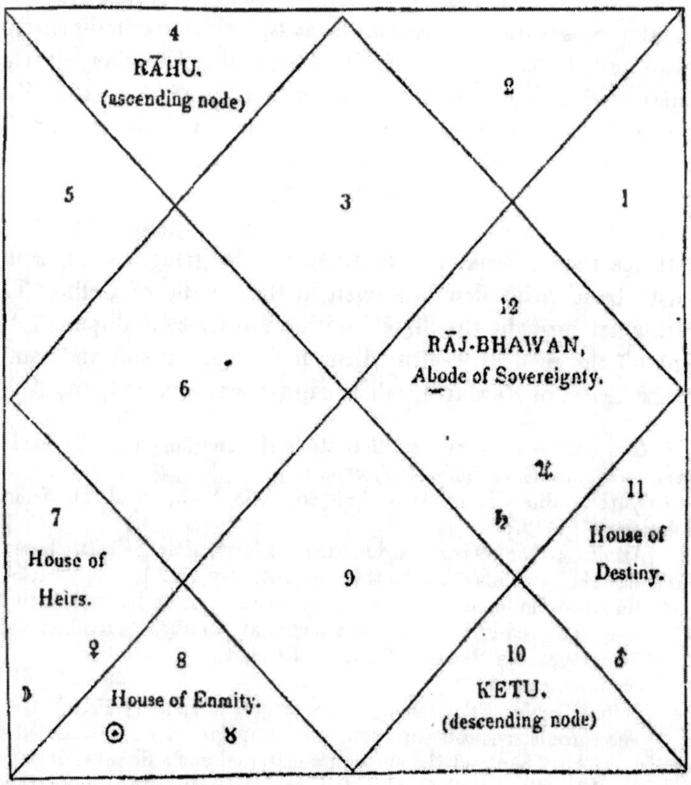

CHAPTER 9

Ajīt Singh attacks Nāhan.—" In 1768 Ajit was sent against Nahan [1] and the chiefs of the snowy mountains, whom he reduced to obedience. Thence he went to the Ganges, where he performed his ablutions, and in the spring he returned to Jodhpur.

" In 1769 Shah Alam [2] went to heaven. The torch of discord was lighted by his sons, with which they fired their own dwelling. Azim-ush-shan was slain,[3] and the umbrella of royalty waved over the head of Muizzu-d-din.[4] Ajit sent the Bhandari Kaimsi to the presence, who returned with the sanad of the vice-royalty of Gujarat. In the month of Margsir 1769, he prepared an army to take possession of the *Sattra-sahas*,[5] when fresh dissensions broke out in the house of the Chagatai. The Sayyids slew Muizzu-d-din, and Farrukhsiyar became king.[6] Zulfikar Khan was [85] put to death,[7] and with him departed the strength of the Moguls. Then the Sayyids became headstrong. Ajit was commanded to send his son, Abhai Singh, now seventeen years of age, with his contingent, to court; but Ajit having learned that the traitor Mukund was there and in great favour, sent a trusty band, who slew him even in the middle of Delhi. This daring act brought the Sayyid with an army to Jodhpur.[8] Ajit sent off the men of wealth to Siwanah, and his son and family to the desert of Rardarra.[9] The capital was invested, and Abhai

[1] [Now known as Sirmūr, a Hill State in the Panjāb, on the W. bank of the Jumna, and E. of Simla (*IGI*, xxiii. 3).]

[2] [Kutbu-d-dīn Shāh 'Alam, Bahādur Shah I., died at Lahore, February 17, 1712.]

[3] [Azīmu-sh-shān was drowned in the river Rāvi, after the battle between Jahāndār Shāh and his other brothers, in February 1712.]

[4] [Muizzu-d-dīn Jahāndār Shāh, crowned Emperor at Lahore, April 10, 1712, was murdered in 1713, and was buried at Humāyūn's tomb, Delhi.]

[5] The " seventeen thousand " towns of Gujarat.

[6] [On January 9, 1713.]

[7] [Zulfikār Khān, Nasrat Jang, was strangled in January 1713.]

[8] [The chronicler is reticent about this campaign which was carried out by Husain Ali Khān and the emperor's maternal uncle Shāista Khān. It was caused by the expulsion of Mughals from Mārwār by Ajīt Singh (Khāfi Khān in Elliot-Dowson vii. 446 f.).]

[9] The tract west of the Luni.

Singh demanded as a hostage for the conduct of Ajit, who was also commanded to court. To neither was the Raja inclined, but the advice of the Diwan and still more of Kesar the bard, who gave as a precedent the instance of Rao Ganga when invaded by the Lodi, Daulat Khan, who entrusted his affairs to his son Maldeo, was unanimously approved.[1] Abhai Singh was recalled from Rardarra, and marched with Husain Ali to Delhi, the end of Asarh 1770. The heir of Maru received the mansab of five thousand from the king.

"Ajit followed his son to the court, then held at Delhi. There the sight of the altars raised over the ashes of chiefs who had perished to preserve him in his infancy, kindled all his wrath, and he meditated revenge on the whole house of Timur. Four distinct causes for displeasure had Ajmall :—

"1. The Nauroza.[2]

"2. The compulsory marriage of their daughters with the king.

"3. The killing of kine.

"4. The Jizya, or capitation tax." [3]

Ajit Singh marries his Daughter to Farrukhsiyar, A.D. **1716.**— Here we must interrupt the narrative, in order to supply an important omission of the bard, who slurs over the hardest of the conditions demanded of Ajit on the invasion of the Sayyid, namely, the giving a daughter to Farrukhsiyar, the important political results of which are already related in the first part of this work.[4] This compulsory marriage only aggravated Ajit's desire of vengeance, and he entered into the views of the Sayyids with the true spirit of his father ; obtaining meanwhile, as the price of coalition, the compliance with the specified demands, besides others of less moment, such as "that the bell for prayer should be allowed to toll in the [86] quarters of the city allotted to the Rajputs, and that their temples should be held sacred ; and last, but not least, the aggrandisement of his hereditary dominions." Let us again recur to the chronicle.

"In Jeth 1771, having secured all his wishes, Ajit left the court, and with the renewed patent as viceroy of Gujarat, returned to

[1] They slur over the most important demand—a daughter to wife to the king—it is at this Ajit hesitates, and for which the precedent is given.

[2] See Vol. I. p. 400. [3] Described Vol. I. p. 441. [4] Vol. I. p. 468.

Jodhpur. Through Kaimsi, his minister, the jizya was repealed. The Hindu race owed eternal obligation to the Mor (crown) of Murdhar, the sanctuary of princes in distress.

Ajit Singh, Viceroy of Gujarāt, A.D. 1715–16.—" In 1772, Ajit prepared to visit this government: Abhai Singh accompanied his father. He first proceeded to Jalor, where he passed the rainy season. Thence he attacked the Mewasa:[1] first Nimaj, which he took, when the Deoras paid him tribute. Firoz Khan advanced from Palanpur to meet him. The Rao of Tharad paid a lakh of rupees. Cambay was invested and paid; and the Koli chief, Kemkaran, was reduced. From Patan, Sakta the Champawat, with Bija Bhandari, sent the year preceding to manage the province, came forth to meet him.

" In 1773, Ajit reduced the Jhala of Halwad, and Jam of Nawanagar, who paid as tribute three lacs of rupees, with twenty-five choice steeds;[2] and having settled the province, he worshipped at Dwarka, and bathed in the Gomati.[3] Thence he returned to Jodhpur, where he learned that Indar Singh had regained Nagor; but he stood not before Ajit.

Ajit Singh visits Delhi.—" The year 1774 had now arrived. The Sayyids and their opponents were engaged in civil strife. Husain Ali was in the Deccan, and the mind of Abdulla was alienated from the king. Paper on paper came, inviting Ajit. He marched by Nagor, Merta, Pushkar, Marot, and Sambhar, whose garrisons he strengthened, to Delhi. From Marot he sent Abhai Singh back to take care of Jodhpur. The Sayyid advanced from Delhi to meet the Dhani (lord) of Marwar, who alighted at

[1] Mewasa is a term given to the fastnesses in the mountains, which the aboriginal tribes, Kolis, Minas, and Mers, and not unfrequently the Rajputs, make their retreats; and in the present instance the bard alludes to the Mewasa of the Deoras of Sirohi and Abu, which has annoyed the descendants of Ajit to this hour, and has served to maintain the independence of this Chauhan tribe.

[2] [Tharād in Pālanpur Agency, Bombay (*IGI*, xix. 346); Halwad in Kāthiāwār (*ibid.* viii. 13); Nawanagar in Kāthiāwār, the ruler, known as the Jām (Yule, *Hobson-Jobson*, 447), being a Jādeja Rājput (*IGI*, xviii. 419 ff.).]

[3] This is all in the district of Okha (Okhamandala), where the Vadhels fixed themselves on the migration of Siahji from Kanauj. It would have been instructive had the bard deigned to have given us any account of the recognition which this visit occasioned, and which beyond a doubt caused the " books of Chronicles and Kings " to be opened and referred to.

Allahwirdi's sarai. Here the Sayyid and Ajit formed a league to oppose Jai Singh and the Moguls, while the king remained like a snake coiled up in a closed vessel. To get rid of their chief opponent, Zu-l-faqar Khan, was first determined [87].

"When the king heard that Ajit had reached Delhi, he sent the Hara Rao Bhim of Kotah, and Khandauran Khan to introduce him to the presence. Ajit obeyed. Besides his own Rathors, he was accompanied by Rao Bishan Singh of Jaisalmer, and Padam Singh of Derawar, with Fateh Singh, a noble of Mewar, Man Singh, Rathor, chief of Sita Mhau, and the Chandarawat, Gopal of Rampura, besides Udai Singh of Kandela, Sakat Singh of Manoharpur, Kishan of Kalchipur, and many others.[1] The meeting took place at the Moti Bagh. The king bestowed the mansab of Haft Hazari (seven thousand horse) on Ajit, and added a crore of dams to his rent-roll. He presented him with the insignia of the Mahi Muratib,[2] with elephants and horses, a sword and dagger, a diamond aigrette (*sarpech*) and plume, and a double string of pearls. Having left the presence, Ajit went to visit Abdulla Khan. The Sayyid advanced to meet him, and his reception, with his attendants, was distinguished. They renewed their determination to stand or fall together. Their conference caused dismay to the Moguls, who lay in ambush to put Ajit to death.

"On the second day of the bright moon of Pus, 1775 [A.D. 1718], the king honoured Ajit with a visit. Ajit seated the king on a throne formed of bags of rupees to the amount of one lakh,[3] and presented elephants, horses, and all that was precious. In the month of Phalgun, Ajit and the Sayyid went to visit the king; and after the conference wrote to Husain Ali revealing their plans, and desiring his rapid march to unite with them from the Deccan. Now the heavens assumed portentous appearances; the Disasul[4] was red and fiery; jackasses brayed un-

[1] This list well exemplifies the tone now assumed by the Rathors; but this grand feudal assemblage was in virtue of his office of viceroy of Gujarat. Each and all of these chieftainships the author is as familiar with as with the pen he now holds.

[2] [The fish symbol, for which see Sleeman, *Rambles*, 137 f. James Skinner, who recovered Mahādāji Sindhia's order in a fight with the Rājputs, speaks of it as "a brass fish with two chources (*chaunri*, horse-hair or yak tails) hanging to it like mustachios" (Irvine, *Army of the Indian Moghuls*, 33).]

[3] £10,000 to £12,000.

[4] Omen of the quarter.

usually; dogs barked; thunder rolled without a cloud; the court, late so gay, was now sad and gloomy; all were forebodings of change at Delhi. In twenty days, Husain reached Delhi; his countenance was terrific; his drum, which now beat close to the palace, was the knell of falling greatness. He was accompanied by myriads of horse. Delhi was enveloped in the dust raised by his hostile steeds. They encamped in the north of the city, and Husain joined Ajit and his brother. The trembling king sent congratulations and gifts; the Mogul chiefs kept aloof in their abodes; even as the quail cowers in the grass when the falcon hovers over it, so did the Moguls when Husain reached Delhi.[1] The lord of Amber was like a lamp left without oil [88].

The Revolution at Delhi.—"On the second day, all convened at Ajit's tents, on the banks of the Jumna, to execute the plans now determined upon. Ajit mounted his steed; at the head of his Rathors he marched direct to the palace, and at every post he placed his own men: he looked like the fire destined to cause *pralaya*.[2] When the sun appears darkness flies; when the oil fails the lamp goes out: so is it with crowns and kings, when good faith and justice, the oil that feeds their power, is wanting. The crash which shivered the umbrella of Delhi reverberated throughout the land. The royal treasures were plundered. None amidst the Moguls came forward to rescue their king (Farrukhsiyar), and Jai Singh fled from the scene of destruction. Another king was set up, but in four months he was seized with a distemper and died. Then Daula[3] was placed on the throne. But the Moguls at Delhi set up Neko Shah[4] at Agra, and Husain marched against them, leaving Ajit and Abdulla with the king.[5]

[1] [For an account of these transactions see Keene, *Sketch of the History of Hindustan*, 287 ff.]

[2] The final doom.

[3] [Farrukhsīyar was murdered in prison, and two sickly youths were placed in succession on the throne by the Sayyids—Rafiu-d-darajāt and Rafiu-d-daula—the first of whom died on May 31, the second on September 6, 1719.]

[4] [Nekosīyar, son of Muhammad Akbar, youngest son of Aurangzeb, who was defeated and taken prisoner by the Sayyids (Keene, *op. cit.* 299).]

[5] This is both minutely and faithfully related, and fully as much so as the Muhammadan record of this black deed. We have already (Vol. I. p. 475) described it, and given a translation of an autograph letter of the prince of Amber, written on this memorable day. The importance of the transaction, as well as the desire to show the Bardic version, will justify its repetition.

Muhammad Shah, Emperor, A.D. **1719–48.**—" In 1776, Ajit and the Sayyid moved from Delhi ; but the Moguls surrendered Neko Shah, who was confined in Salimgarh. At this time the king died, and Ajit and the Sayyids made another, and placed Muhammad Shah on the throne. Many countries were destroyed, and many were made to flourish, during the dethronement of kings by Ajit. With the death of Farrukhsiyar Jai Singh's views were crushed, and the Sayyids determined to punish him. The lord of Amber was like water carried in a platter.[1] The king reached the Dargah at Sikri, in progress to Amber, and here the chieftains sought the *saran* (sanctuary) of Ajit. They said the Kurma [2] was lost if he protected them not against the Sayyids. Even as Krishna saved Arjun in the Bharat, so did Ajit take Jai Singh under his protection. He sent the chiefs of the Champawats and his minister to dispel his fears ; they returned with the lord of Amber, who felt like one who had escaped the doom (*pralaya*). Ajit placed one monarch on the throne, and saved another from destruction. The king bestowed upon him the grant of Ahmadabad, and gave him permission to visit his home. With Jai Singh of Amber, and Budh Singh Hara of Bundi, he marched for Jodhpur, and in the way contracted a marriage with the daughter of the Shaikhavat [89] chief of Manoharpur. In the month of Asin he reached Jodhagir, when the lord of Amber encamped at Sur Sagar, and the Hara Rao north of the town.

Ajīt Singh marries his Daughter to Jai Singh.—" The cold season had fled ; the spring (*basant*) approached. The peacock was intoxicated with the nectar-drops distilled from the sweet-blossomed *amba* (mango) ; the rich sap exuded ; the humming-bees clustered round the flowers ; new leaves budded forth ; songs of joy resounded ; the hearts of gods, men, and women expanded with mirth. It was then the lord of Amber was bedecked in saffron robes, to espouse the ' virgin of the sun ' (Surya Kumari), the child of Ajit. On this he had consulted the Champawats, and according to ancient usage, the Ad-Pardhan, or chief minister, the Kumpawat : likewise the Bhandari Diwan, and the Guru. But were I to dwell on these festivities, this book would become too large ; I therefore say but little !

[1] In allusion to his vacillation, for which the Mirza Rāja was notorious.

[2] [That is to say, the Kachhwāha Rāja.]

The Assassination of the Sayyids. Ajit Singh asserts his Independence.—" The rains of 1777 set in, and Jai Singh and Budh Singh remained with Ajit, when a messenger arrived with tidings that the Moguls had assassinated the Sayyids, and were now on the watch for Ajit.[1] He drew his sword, and swore he would possess himself of Ajmer. He dismissed the lord of Amber. In twelve days after Ajit reached Merta. In the face of day he drove the Muslim from Ajmer and made it his own. He slew the king's governor and seized on Taragarh.[2] Once more the bell of prayers was heard in the temple, while the *bang*[3] of the Masjid was silent. Where the Koran was read, the Puran was now heard, and the Mandir took the place of the Mosque. The Kazi made way for the Brahman, and the pit of burnt sacrifice (*homa*) was dug, where the sacred kine were slain. He took possession of the salt lakes of Sambhar and Didwana, and the records were always moist with inserting fresh conquests. Ajit ascended his own throne; the umbrella of supremacy he waved over his head. He coined in his own name, established his own *gaz* (measure), and *ser* (weight), his own courts of justice, and a new scale of rank for his chiefs, with nalkis and mace-bearers, naubats and standards, and every emblem of sovereign rule. Ajmall in Ajmer was equal to Aspati in Delhi.[4] The intelligence spread over the land; it reached even Mecca [90] and Iran, that Ajit had exalted his own faith, while the rites of Islam were prohibited throughout the land of Maru.

Imperialist Attack on Ajmer.—" In 1778 the king determined to regain Ajmer. He gave the command to Muzaffar, who in the rains advanced towards Marwar. Ajit entrusted the conduct of this war to his son, the 'shield of Maru,' the 'fearless' (Abhai), with the eight great vassals, and thirty thousand horse; the

[1] [For this revolution see Elliot-Dowson vii. 474 ff.]

[2] The *Star Fort*, the castle of Ajmer.

[3] The call to prayer of the Muslim.

[4] This exact imitation of the manners of the imperial court is still strictly maintained at Jodhpur. The account of the measures which followed the possession of Ajmer is taken from the chronicle Surya Prakas; the only part not entirely translated from the Raj Rupak Akhyat. Ajmall is a licence of the poet, where it suits his rhyme, for Ajit. Aspati, 'lord of steeds,' is the common epithet applied to the emperors of Delhi. It is, however, but the second degree of paramount power—Gajpati, 'lord of elephants,' is the first.

Champawats on the right, the Kumpawats on the left, while the Karamsots, Mertias, Jodhas, Indhas, Bhattis, Sonigiras, Deoras, Khichis, Dhondals and Gogawats,[1] composed the main body. At Amber, the Rathors and imperialists came in sight; but Muzaffar disgraced himself, and retired within that city without risking an encounter. Abhai Singh, exasperated at this display of pusillanimous bravado, determined to punish the king. He attacked Shahjahanpur, sacked Narnol, levied contributions on Patan (Tuarvati) and Rewari.[2] He gave the villages to the flames, and spread conflagration and consternation even to Allahwirdi's Sarai. Delhi and Agra trembled with affright; the Asurs fled without their shoes at the deeds of Abhai, whom they styled Dhonkal, 'the exterminator.' He returned by Sambhar and Ludhana, and here he married the daughter of the chief of the Narukas.[3]

Muhammad Shah attacks Ajīt Singh.—"In 1779, Abhai Singh remained at Sambhar, which he strengthened, and hither his father Ajit came from Ajmer. The meeting was like that between 'Kasyapa and Surya';[4] for he had broken the bow of Muzaffar and made the Hindu happy. The king sent his Chela, Nahar Khan, to expostulate with Ajit; but his language was offensive, and the field of Sambhar devoured the tiger lord (Nahar Khan) and his four thousand followers. The son of Churaṃan the Jat[5] now claimed sanctuary with Ajit. Sick of these dissensions, the unhappy Muhammad Shah determined to abandon his crown and retire to Mecca. But, determined to revenge the death of Nahar Khan, he prepared a formidable army. He collected [the contingents of] the twenty-two Satraps[6] of the empire, and placed at their head Jai Singh of Amber, Haidar Kuli, Iradat

[1] The two latter tribes are amongst the most ancient of the allodial chieftains of the desert: the Dhondals being descendants of Rao Gango; the Gogawats, of the famous Goga [or Gūga] the Chauhan, who defended the Sutlej in the earliest Muslim invasion recorded. Both Goga and his steed Jawadia are immortal in Rajasthan. The Author had a chestnut Kathiawar, called Jawadia; he was perfection, and a piece of living fire when mounted, scorning every pace but the antelope's bounds and curvets.

[2] [Pātan in Jaipur State; Narnol in Patiāla; Rewāri in Gurgaon District, Panjāb.]

[3] One of the great clans of Amber; of whom more hereafter.

[4] [The tortoise (Kachhwāha) and the sun (the sun-born tribes).]

[5] Founder of the Bharatpur State.

[6] The Bāīsa, or 'twenty-two' viceroys of India.

Khan Bangash, etc. In the month of Sawan (July), Taragarh was invested; Abhai Singh marched out and left its defence to [91] Amra Singh. It had held out four months, when through the prince of Amber (Jai Singh), Ajit listened to terms, which were sworn to on the Koran by the nobles of the king; and he agreed to surrender Ajmer.[1] Abhai Singh then accompanied Jai Singh to the camp. It was proposed that in testimony of his obedience he should repair to the presence. The prince of Amber pledged himself; but the Fearless (Abhai) placed his hand on his sword, saying, 'This is my surety!'"

Ajīt Singh's Heir received at the Imperial Court.—The heir of Marwar was received by the king with the utmost honour; but being possessed of a double portion of that arrogance which forms the chief characteristic of his race (more especially of the Rathor and Chauhan, from which he sprang), his reception nearly produced at Delhi a repetition of the scene recorded in the history of his ancestor Amra at Agra. Knowing that his father held the first place on the king's right hand, he considered himself, as his representative, entitled to the same honour; and little heeding the unbending etiquette of the proudest court in the world, he unceremoniously hustled past all the dignitaries of the State, and had even ascended a step of the throne, when, checked by one of the nobles, Abhai's hand was on his dagger, and but for the presence of mind of the monarch, "who threw his own chaplet round his neck" to restrain him, the Divan would have been deluged with blood.

The Murder of Ajīt Singh, A.D. 1724.—We shall now drop the chronicles, and in recording the murder of Ajit, the foulest crime in the annals of Rajasthan, exemplify the mode in which their poetic historians gloss over such events. It was against Ajit's will that his son went to court, as if he had a presentiment of the fate which awaited him, and which has been already circumstantially related.[2] The authors from whose records this narrative is chiefly compiled, were too polite to suffer such a stigma to appear in their chronicles, "written by desire" and under the eye of the parricide, Ajit's successor. The Surya Prakas merely says, "at this time Ajit went to heaven"; but affords no indication of the person who sent him there. The Raj Rupaka, how-

[1] [This was in 1723. The chronicler disguises the defeat of Ajīt Singh.]

[2] See p. 857.

ever, not bold enough to avow the mysterious death of his prince, yet too honest altogether to pass it over, has left an expressive blank leaf at this part of his chronicle, certainly not accidental, as it intervenes between Abhai Singh's reception at court, and the incidents following his father's death, which I translate verbatim, as they present an excellent picture of the results of a Rajput potentate's demise [92].

"Abhai, a second Ajit, was introduced to the Aspati; his father heard the news and rejoiced. But this world is a fable—a lie. Time will sooner or later prey on all things. What king, what raja can avoid the path leading to extinction? The time allotted for our sojourn here is predetermined; prolong it we cannot. The decree penned by the hand of the Creator is engraven upon each forehead at the hour of birth. Neither addition nor subtraction can be made. Fate (honhar) must be fulfilled. It was the command of Govinda [1] that Ajit (the Avatar of Indra) should obtain immortality, and leave his renown in the world beneath. Ajit, so long a thorn in the side of his foe, was removed to Parloka.[2] He kept afloat the faith of the Hindu, and sunk the Muslim in shame. In the face of day, the lord of Maru took the road which leads to Paradise (*Vaikuntha*). Then dismay seized the city; each looked with dread in his neighbour's face as he said, 'Our sun has set!' But when the day of Yamaraj [3] arrives, who can retard it? Were not the five Pandus enclosed in the mansion of Himala? [4] Harchand escaped not the universal decree; nor will gods, men, or reptiles avoid it, not even Vikrama or Karna; all fall before Yama. How then could Ajit hope to escape?

"On Asarh, the 13th, the dark half of the moon of 1780, seventeen hundred warriors of the eight ranks of Maru, for the last time marched before their lord.[5] They placed his body in a boat,[6] and carried him to the pyre,[7] made of sandal-wood and

[1] The sovereign judge of mankind [Krishna].

[2] 'The other world'; lit. 'another place.'

[3] 'Lord of hell.'

[4] *Hima*, 'ice,' and *ālaya*, 'an abode.'

[5] Both head and feet are uncovered in funeral processions.

[6] *Id est*, a vehicle formed like a boat, perhaps figurative of the sail crossing the Vaitarani, or Styx of the Hindu.

[7] For the mode of conveying princes to their final abode, I refer the reader to a description at vol. i. p. 152, *Trans. Royal Asiatic Society*.

perfumes, with heaps of cotton, oil, and camphor. But this is a subject of grief: how can the bard enlarge on such a theme? The Nazir went to the Rawala [1] and as he pronounced the words 'Rao siddhi āyē,' the Chauhani queen, with sixteen damsels in her suite, came forth: 'This day,' said she, 'is one of joy; my race shall be illustrated; our lives have passed together, how then can I leave him?' [2]

The Sati.—"Of noble race was the Bhattiani queen, a scion (*sakha*) of Jaisal, and daughter of Birjang. She put up a prayer to the Lord who wields the discus.[3] 'With joy [93] I accompany my lord; that my fealty (*sati*) may be accepted, rests with thee.' In like manner did the Gazelle (Mrigavati) of Derawal,[4] and the Tuar queen of pure blood,[5] the Chawara Rani,[6] and her of Shaikhavati, invoke the name of Hari, as they determined to join their lord. For these six queens death had no terrors; but they were the affianced wives of their lord: the curtain wives of affection, to the number of fifty-eight, determined to offer themselves a sacrifice to Agni.[7] 'Such another opportunity,' said they, 'can never occur, if we survive our lord; disease will seize and make us a prey in our apartments. Why then quit the society of our lord, when at all events we must fall into the hands of Yama, for whom the human race is but a mouthful? Let us leave the iron age (*Kaliyuga*) behind us.' 'Without our lord, even life is death,' said the Bhattiani, as she bound the beads of Tulsi[8] round her neck, and made the *tilak* with earth from the Ganges. While thus each spoke, Nathu, the Nazir,[9] thus addressed them: 'This is no amusement; the sandal-wood you now anoint with is cool: but will your resolution abide, when you remove it with the flames of Agni? When this scorches your tender frames, your hearts may fail, and the desire to recede will disgrace your lord's memory. Reflect, and remain where you are. You have

[1] The queen's palace.

[2] This is the lady whom Ajit married in his non-age, the mother of the parricide.

[3] Krishna [Chakrāyudha, Krishna, or Vishnu].

[4] Ancient capital of the Bhattis.

[5] Descended from the ancient dynasty of the Hindu kings of Delhi.

[6] Tribe of the first dynasty of Anhilwara Patan.

[7] The fire.

[8] [The sacred basil, *Ocymum sanctum*.]

[9] The Nazir (a Muslim epithet) has the charge of the harem.

lived like Indrani,[1] nursed in softness amidst flowers and perfumes; the winds of heaven never offended you, far less the flames of fire.' But to all his arguments they replied: 'The world we will abandon, but never our lord.' They performed their ablutions, decked themselves in their gayest attire, and for the last time made obeisance to their lord in his car. The ministers, the bards, the family priests (*Purohits*), in turn, expostulated with them. The chief queen (*Patrani*) the Chauhani, they told to indulge her affection for her sons, Abhai and Bakhta; to feed the poor, the needy, the holy, and lead a life of religious devotion. The queen replied: 'Kunti, the wife of Pandu, did not follow her lord; she lived to see the greatness of the five brothers, her sons; but were her expectations realized?[2] This life is a vain shadow; this dwelling one of sorrow; let us accompany our lord to that of fire, and there close it.'

"The drum sounded; the funeral train moved on; all invoked the name of [94] Hari.[3] Charity was dispensed like falling rain, while the countenances of the queens were radiant as the sun. From heaven Uma[4] looked down; in recompense of such devotion she promised they should enjoy the society of Ajit in each successive transmigration. As the smoke, emitted from the house of flame, ascended to the sky, the assembled multitudes shouted Kaman! Kaman! 'Well done! Well done!' The pile flamed like a volcano; the faithful queens laved their bodies in the flames, as do the celestials in the lake of Manasarovar.[5] They sacrificed their bodies to their lord, and illustrated the

[1] The queen of heaven.

[2] [Kunti escaped the fire and protected the children of Mādri, the other wife of Pāndu, who was burnt with him.]

[3] Hari Krishna is the mediator and preserver of the Hindu Triad; his name alone is invoked in funeral rites (see p. 621). The following extract from Dr. Wilkins' translation of the *Gīta* will best disclose his attributes:—Krishna speaks: "I am the journey of the good; the comforter; the creator; the witness; the resting-place; the asylum; and the friend. I am generation and dissolution; the place where all things are deposited, and the inexhaustible soul of all nature. I am death and immortality; I am never-failing time; the preserver, whose face is turned on all sides. I am all grasping death; and I am the resurrection of those who are about to die."

[4] A name of Durga, the Hindu Juno.

[5] The sacred lake in Tibet. [See C. A. Sherring, *Western Tibet and the British Borderlands*, 259 ff.]

races whence they sprung. The gods above exclaimed, 'Dhan Dhan[1] Ajit! who maintained the faith, and overwhelmed the Asuras.' Savitri, Gauri, Sarasvati, Ganga, and Gomati[2] united in doing honour to these faithful queens. Forty-five years, three months, and twenty-two days, was the space of Ajit's existence, when he went to inhabit Amarapura, an immortal abode!"

Character of Ajīt Singh.—Thus closed the career of one of the most distinguished princes who ever pressed the 'cushion' of Maru; a career as full of incident as any life of equal duration. Born amidst the snows of Kabul, deprived at his birth of both parents, one from grief, the other by suicidal custom; saved from the Herodian cruelty of the king by the heroism of his chiefs, nursed amidst the rocks of Abu or the intricacies of the Aravalli until the day of danger passed, he issued forth, still an infant, at the head of his brave clans, to redeem the inheritance so iniquitously wrested from him. In the history of mankind there is nothing to be found presenting a more brilliant picture of fidelity than that afforded by the Rathor clans in their devotion to their prince, from his birth until he worked out his own and his country's deliverance. It is one of those events which throw a gleam of splendour upon the dark picture of feudalism, more prolific perhaps in crime than in virtue. That of the Rajputs, indeed, in which consanguinity is superadded to the other reciprocal [95] ties which bind a feudal body, wears the more engaging aspect of a vast family. How affecting is the simple language of these brave men, while daily shedding their blood for a prince whom, until he had attained his seventh year, they had never beheld! "Without the sight of our lord, bread and water have no flavour." And how successfully does the bard portray the joy of these stern warriors, when he says, "As the lotus expands at the sunbeam, so did the heart of each Rathor at the sight of their infant sovereign; they drank his looks even as the *papiha* in the month of Asoj sips the drops of *amrita* (ambrosia) from the *Champa*."

[1] *Dhan* is 'riches,' but is here used in the sense of glory; so that riches and glory are synonymous in term with the Hindu, as in practice in the west; the one may always command the other, at least that species of it for which nine-tenths of mankind contend, and are satisfied with obtaining.

[2] Celestial queens.

The prodigality with which every clan lavished its blood, through a space of six-and-twenty years, may in part be learned from the chronicle; and in yet more forcible language from the cenotaphs scattered over the country, erected to the manes of those who fell in this religious warfare. Were other testimony required, it is to be found in the annals of their neighbours and their conquerors; while the traditional couplets of the bards, familiar to every Rajput, embalm the memory of the exploits of their forefathers.

Ajit was a prince of great vigour of mind as well as of frame. Valour was his inheritance; he displayed this hereditary quality at the early age of eleven, when he visited his enemy in his capital, displaying a courtesy which can only be comprehended by a Rajput. Amongst the numerous desultory actions, of which many occurred every year, there were several in which the whole strength of the Rathors was led by their prince. The battle of Sambhar, in S. 1765, fought against the Sayyids, which ended in a union of interests, was one of these; and, for the rest of Ajit's life, kept him in close contact with the court, where he might have taken the lead had his talent for intrigue been commensurate with his boldness. From this period until his death, Ajit's agency was recognized in all the intrigues and changes amongst the occupants of Timur's throne, from Farrukhsiyar to Muhammad. He inherited an invincible hatred to the very name of Muslim, and was not scrupulous regarding the means by which he was likely to secure the extirpation of a race so inimical to his own. Viewing the manifold reasons for this hatred, we must not scrutinize with severity his actions when leagued with the Sayyids, even in the dreadful catastrophe which overwhelmed Farrukhsiyar, to whom he owed the twofold duty of fealty and consanguinity.

His Conduct to Durgadās.—There is one stain on the memory of Ajit which, though unnoticed in the chronicle [96], is too well ascertained to be omitted in a summary of his character, more especially as it illustrates that of the nation and of the times, and shows the loose system which holds such governments together. The heroic Durgadas, the preserver of his infancy, the instructor of his youth, the guide of his manhood, lived to confirm the proverb, "Put not thy faith in princes." He, who, by repeated instances of exalted self-denial, had refused wealth and honours that might have raised himself from his vassal condition to an equality with his sovereign, was banished from the land which his integrity, wisdom, and valour had preserved. Why, or when, Ajit loaded himself with this indelible infamy was not known; the fact was incidentally discovered in searching a collection of original newspapers written from the camp of Bahadur Shah,[1] in one of which it was stated, that "Durgadas was encamped with his household retainers on the banks of the Pichola Lake at Udaipur, and receiving daily five hundred rupees for his support from the Rana; who when called on by the king (Bahadur Shah) to surrender him, magnanimously refused." Imagining that Ajit had been compelled to this painful sacrifice, which is not noticed in the annals, the compiler mentioned it to a Yati deeply versed in all the events and transactions of this State. Aware of the circumstance, which is not overlooked by the bards, he immediately repeated the couplet composed on the occasion—

Durgo desām kādhiyo
Golām Gāmgāni!

Durga was exiled, and Gamgani given to a slave.[2]

Gamgani, on the north bank of the Luni, was the chief town of the Karanot fief, of which clan Durga was the head. It is now attached to the Khalisa, or fisc, but whether recently, or ever since Durga, we know not. The Karanots still pay the last rites to their dead at Gamgani, where they have their cenotaphs (*chhatris*). Whether that of the noble Durga stands there to serve as a memorial of princely ingratitude, the writer cannot say; a portrait of the hero, in the autumn of his days, was given to him by the last lineal descendant of Ajit, as the reader is already

[1] Discovered by the author amongst the Rana's archives.

[2] [Dr. Tessitori writes that the correct version is:

"Mahārāja Ajmāl ri
Jad parkha jāni.
Durgo Saphara dāgajē,
Golām Gāmgāni."

"The mind of Mahārāja Ajit Singh then became known (when he saw) Durgadās burned on the banks of the Sipra River and Gāmgāni bestowed on slaves." According to tradition, the exiled Durgadās died at Ujjain, near which the Sipra flows.]

aware.[1] Well may we repeat, that the system of feudality is the parent of the most brilliant virtues and the darkest crimes. Here, a long life of uninterrupted fidelity could not preserve Durga from the envenomed breath of slander, or the serpent-tooth [97] of ingratitude: and whilst the mind revolts at the crime which left a blank leaf in the chronicle, it is involuntarily carried back to an act less atrocious, indeed, than one which violates the laws of nature, but which in diminishing none of our horror for Abhai Singh, yet lessens our sympathy for the persecutor of Durgadas

CHAPTER 10

Mahārāja Abhai Singh, A.D. **1724–50.**—The parricidal murder of Ajit is accounted the germ of destruction, which, taking root in the social edifice of Marwar, ultimately rent it asunder. Bitter has been the fruit of this crime, " even unto the third and fourth generation " of his unnatural sons, whose issue, but for this crime, would in all human probability have been the most potent princes in India, able single-handed to have stopped Mahratta aggrandisement.

" It was in 1781 (says the bard) Ajit went to heaven. With his own hand did the emperor Muhammad Shah put the *tika* on the forehead of Abhai Singh, girded him with the sword, bound the *turah*[2] on his head, placed a dagger set with gems [98] in his girdle, and with Chaunris, Naubats, and Nakkaras,[3] and many valuable gifts, invested the young prince in all the dignities of his father. Even Nagor was resumed from the son of Amra and included in his sanad. With these marks of royal favour, he took leave of the court, and returned to his paternal dominions. From village to village, as he journeyed homeward, the *kalas* was raised on the head.[4] When he reached Jodhpur, he dis-

[1] Vol. I. p. 451.

[2] [A plumed crest worn on the turban.]

[3] [Fly-flappers, bands of music, kettledrums.]

[4] The *kalas* is a brazen vessel, of household use. A female of each family, filling one of these with water, repairs to the house of the head of the village, when, being all convened, they proceed in a body to meet the person to

tributed gifts to all his chiefs, and to the Bardais (bards and Charans), and lands to the family priests (*Purohits*)."

A day at the court of the desert king, related in the phraseology of the chronicle, would be deemed interesting as a picture of manners. It would also make the reader more familiar with Karna, the most celebrated bard in the latter days of Rajput independence : but this must be reserved for an equally appropriate vehicle,[1] and we shall at present rest satisfied with a slight sketch of the historian of Maru.

Karan, the Bard.—Karna-Kavya, or simply Karna, who traced his descent from the last household bard of the last emperor of Kanauj, was at once a politician, a warrior, and a scholar, and in each capacity has left ample proofs of his abilities. In the first he took a distinguished part in all the events of the civil wars ; in the second, he was one of the few who survived a combat almost without parallel in the annals even of Rajput chivalry ; and as a scholar, he has left us, in the introduction to his work,[2] the most instructive proof, not only of his inheriting the poetic mantle of his fathers, but of the course he pursued for the maintenance of its lustre. The bare enumeration of the works he had studied evinces that there was no royal road to Parnassus for the Rajput Kaviswar,[3] but that, on the contrary, it was beset with difficulties not a little appalling. The mere nomenclature of works on grammar and historical epics, which were to be mastered ere he could hope for fame, must have often made Karna exclaim, "How hard it is to climb the steeps" on which from afar he viewed her temple. Those who desire to see, under a new aspect, an imperfectly known but interesting family of the human race, will be made acquainted with the qualifications of our bardic historians, and the particular course of studies which [99] fitted

---

whom they render honour, singing the *suhaila*, or 'song of joy.' The presenting water is a token of homage and regard, and one which the author has often had paid to him, especially in Mewar, where every village met him in this way.

[1] I hope some day to present a few of the works of the great bard Chand, with a dissertation on the Bardais, and all the 'sons of song.' [Karan flourished about A.D. 1730 : see Grierson, *Modern Vernacular Literature of Hindustan*, 98.]

[2] Entitled the *Surya Prakas*, of 7500 stanzas.

[3] *Kāvīswar*, or *kāvya-īswara*, 'lord of verse,' from *kāvya*, 'poesy,' and *īswara*, 'lord.'

Karna "to sit in the gate [1] of Jodhagir," and add a new book to the chronicles of its kings.

These festivities of the new reign were not of long duration, and were succeeded by warlike preparations against Nagor, which, during the contentions between Ajit and the emperor, had been assigned to the descendant of the ancient princes of Mandor.

"When Ajmer was invested by the collective force of the empire,[2] Iradat Khan (Bangash), collector of the Jizya,[3] took the Indha by the arm, and seated him in Nagor.[4] But as soon as the Holi [5] was past, the 'Avatars of Jawalamukhi' [6] were consecrated: goats were sacrificed, and the blood, with oil and vermilion, was sprinkled upon them. The tents were moved out. Hearing this, Rao Indra produced the imperial patent, with the personal guarantee of Jai Singh of Amber. Abhai heeded not, and invested Nagor; but Indra left his honour and his castle to the Fearless,[7] who bestowed it on Bakhta his brother. He received the congratulations of Mewar, Jaisalmer, Bikaner, and Amber, and returned to his capital amidst the rejoicings of his subjects. This was in S. 1781.

"In S. 1782 he was employed in restraining the turbulent Bhumias on the western frontiers of his dominions; when the

[1] The portal of the palace appears to have been the bard's post. Pope gives the same position to his historic bards in 'the Temple of Fame':

"Full in the passage of each spacious gate,
The sage Historians in white garments wait;
Grav'd o'er their seats the form of Time was found,
His scythe revers'd, and both his pinions bound." [l. 145-8.]

[2] In the original, "by the *bāīsa*," the 'twenty-two,' meaning the collective force of the twenty-two *subahdars*, 'or satraps of the provinces.'

[3] Capitation tax.

[4] The poet calls it by its classic appellation, *Nāgadurga*, the 'castle of the serpent' [rather Nāgapura, capital of the Nāga sept of Rājputs].

[5] For this festival see p. 661.

[6] Jawalamukhi, the 'mouth of flame,' the cannon, which are thus consecrated before action. They are called *avatars*, or 'incarnations' of Jawalamukhi, the Etna of India, at the edge of whose crater the Hindu poet very properly places the temple of Jawali Rani, 'the terrific' Kali Ma, the Hindu Hecate. [Jawālamukhi in the Kāngra District, Panjāb (*IGI*, xiv. 86 f.).]

[7] *Abhai*, the name of the prince, means 'fearless,' from *bhai*, 'fear,' and privative prefix.

Sindhals, the Deoras, the Balas, the Boras, the Balechas, and the Sodhas were compelled to servitude.

Abhai Singh summoned to Delhi, A.D. 1726.—" In S. 1783 a farman of summons arrived, calling the prince to attend the Presence at Delhi. He put it to his head, assembled all his chiefs, and on his passage to court made a tour of his dominions, examining his garrisons, redressing [100] wrongs, and adjusting whatever was in disorder. At Parbatsar [1] he was attacked by the small-pox: the nation called on Jagrani [2] to shield him from evil.

" In 1784 the prince reached Delhi. Khandauran, the chief noble of the empire, was deputed by the emperor to conduct him to the capital; and when he reached the Presence, his majesty called him close to his person, exclaiming, ' Welcome, *Khushbakht*,[3] *Maharaja Rajeswar*,[4] it is long since we met; this day makes me happy; the splendour of the Ammkhass is redoubled.' When he took leave, the king sent to his quarters, at Abhaipur, choice fruits of the north, fragrant oils, and rose-water."

The prince of Maru was placed at the head of all the nobility. About the end of S. 1784, Sarbuland Khan's rebellion broke out,[5] which gave ample scope for the valour of the Rathors and materials for the bard, who thus circumstantially relates it:

" The troubles in the Deccan increased. The Shahzada Jangali [6] rebelled, and forming an army of sixty thousand men, attacked the provincial governors of Malwa, Surat, and Ahmadpur,

[1] [On the Kishangarh border, N.E. of Jodhpur State.]

[2] *Jagrani* (I write all these phrases exactly as pronounced in the western dialect), ' Queen of the world.' Sitala Mata is the common name for the goddess who presides over this scourge of infancy.

[3] ' Of happy fortune.'

[4] Mahārāja-Rājeswar, the pompous title of the kings of Maru; ' great Raja, lord of Rajas.'

[5] [Sarbuland Khān was Governor of Gujarāt, A.D. 1724, and was removed from office in 1730 because he consented to pay *Chauth* or blackmail to the Marāthas. He opposed the installation of Abhai as his successor, and defeated him at Adālaj (Beale, *Dict. Oriental Biography*, s.v.; Grant Duff 217).]

[6] In none of the Muhammadan histories of this period is it mentioned, that there was an imperial prince at the head of the first Mahratta irruption; probably he was a mere tool for the purposes of others. [The ' Boorish Prince,' as the name implies, was a nickname of Hāmid Khān Bahādur, uncle of Nizāmu-l-mulk, Āsaf Jāh (Grant Duff 217; *BG*, i. Part i. 303 ff.).]

slaying the king's lieutenants, Girdhar Bahadur, Ibrahim Kuli,[1] Rustam Ali, and the Mogul Shujaat.

Rebellion of Sarbuland Khan. Scene at the Imperial Court.—" Hearing this, the king appointed Sarbuland Khan to quash the rebellion. He marched at the head of fifty thousand men, having a crore of rupees for their subsistence; but his advanced army of ten thousand men being defeated in the first encounter, he entered into terms with the rebels, and agreed to a partition of the country."

It was at this time the prince of Marwar begged permission to retire to his hereditary dominions. The bard's description of the court, and of the emperor's distress on this occasion, though prolix, deserves insertion:

" The king was seated on his throne, attended by the seventy-two grand Omras of the empire, when tidings reached him of the revolt of Sarbuland. There was the wazir Kamaru-din Khan, Itimadu-Daula, Khandauran, commander-in-chief [101] (Mir Bakhshi), Samsamu-d-daula, the Amiru-Umara, Mansur Ali, Roshanu-d-daula, Tura Baz Khan, the Lord Marcher (*Sim ka Bakhshi*); Rustam Jang, Afghan Khan, Khwaja Sayyidu-d-din, commandant of artillery (*Mir Atish*); Saadat Khan,[2] grand chamberlain (*Darogha Khawass*), Burhanu-l-Mulk, Abdul Samad Khan, Dalil Khan, Zafariyab Khan, governor of Lahore, Dalel Khan, Mir Jumla, Khankhanan; Zafar Jang, Iradat Khan, Murshid Kuli Khan, Ja'far Khan, Allahwirdi Khan,[3] Muzaffar Khan, governor of Ajmer. Such and many more were assembled in the Presence.

" It was read aloud that Sarbuland had reduced Gujarat, and proclaimed his own *an*; that he had ground the Kolis to dust; that he had vanquished the Mandalas, the Jhalas, the Chudasamas, the Baghels, and the Gohils, and had nearly exterminated the Balas; that Halar had agreed to pay tribute, and that such was the fire of this Yavan, that the Bhumias of themselves abandoned their strongholds to seek sanctuary with him

[1] [Girdhar Bahādur was a Nāgar Brāhman; Ibrāhīm Kuli, son of Shujā'at Khān.]

[2] Afterwards Wazir of Oudh, a State founded and maintained by consummate treason.

[3] Nawab of Bengal, another traitor.

whom the 'seventeen thousand'[1] now called sovereign; that he had set himself up a king in Ahmadabad, and made a league with the 'Southron.'

"The emperor saw that if this defection was not quelled, all the viceroys would declare themselves independent. Already had Jagaria Khan in the north, Saadat Khan in the east, and the Mlechchha Nizamu-l-mulk in the south, shown the blackness of their designs. The *tap* (verve) of the empire had fled.

"The *bira* was placed on a golden salver, which the Mir Tajik bore in his extended arms, slowly passing in front of the nobles ranged on either side of the throne, mighty men, at the sight of whose faces the rustic would tremble: but in vain he passed both lines; no hand was stretched forth; some looked awry; some trembled; but none cast an eye upon the *bira*.

"The 'almighty monarch' (*Parameswar Padshah*), who could make the beggar an Omra of twelve thousand, and the noble of twelve thousand a beggar, was without resource. 'Who,' said one, 'would grasp the forked lightning, let him engage Sarbuland!' Another exclaimed, 'Who would seize the vessel, and plunge with her in the whirlpool, he may contend with Sarbuland.' And a third, 'Whoever [102] dare seize the forked tongue of the serpent, let him engage Sarbuland.' The king was troubled; he gave a sign to the Mir Tajik to return the *bira* to him.

"The Rathor prince saw the monarch's distress, and as he was about to leave the Ammkhass, he stretched forth his hand, and placed the *bira* in his turban, as he said, 'Be not cast down, O king of the world; I will pluck down this Sarbuland:[2] leafless shall be the boughs of his ambition, and his head (*sar*) the forfeit of his arrogant exaltation (*buland*).'

"When Abhai Singh grasped the *bira*, the breasts of the mighty were ready to burst with the fulness of envy, even like the ripe pomegranate, as the king placed the grant of Gujarat into the hands of the Rathor. The Shah's heart was rejoiced, as he said, 'Thus acted your ancestors in support of the throne; thus was quelled the revolt of Khurram and Bhim in the time of Jahangir; that of the Deccan settled; and in like manner do

[1] This number of cities, towns, and villages constituted the kingdom of Gujarat under its ancient sovereigns.

[2] *Sar*, 'the head,' *buland*, 'exalted, high, arrogant.' I write the name *Sirbullund*, being the orthography long known.

I trust that by you the honour and the throne of Muhammad Shah will be upheld.'

" Rich gifts, including seven gems of great price, were bestowed upon the Rathor; the treasury was unlocked and thirty-one lakhs of coin were assigned for the troops. The guns were taken from the arsenals, and with the patent of the vice-royalties of Ahmadabad and Ajmer, in the month of Asarh (1786), Abhai took leave of the king." [1]

Abhai Singh starts for Gujarāt, A.D. 1730.—The political arrondissement of Marwar dates from this period; for the rebellion of Sarbuland was the forerunner of the disintegration of the empire. It was in June A.D. 1730 that the prince of Marwar left the court of Delhi. He had a double motive in proceeding direct to Ajmer, of which province he was viceroy; first, to take possession of his stronghold (the key not only of Marwar but of every State in Rajputana); and second, to consult with the prince of Amber on the affairs of that critical conjuncture. What was the cause of Jai Singh's presence at Ajmer the chronicle says not; but from circumstances elsewhere related, it may be conjectured that it was for the purpose of celebrating "the rites of the Pitrideva" (manes of his ancestors) at Pushkar. The bard gives a most prolix account of the meeting, even to the *pagtar*, 'or foot-clothes' spread for "the kings of the Hindus" to walk on, "who feasted together, and together plotted the destruction of the [103] empire": from which we perceive that Karna, the bard, had a peep behind the curtain.

Having installed his officers in Ajmer, Abhai Singh proceeded to Merta, when he was met by his brother, Bakhta Singh, on which occasion the grant of Nagor was bestowed upon the latter. The brothers continued their route to the capital, when all the chiefs were dismissed to their homes with injunctions to assemble their vassals for the ensuing campaign against Sarbuland. At the appointed time, the Kher (feudal array) of Marwar assembled under the walls of Jodhpur. The occasion is a delightful one to the bard, who revels in all "the pomp and circumstance of war": from the initiatory ceremony, the moving out the tents, to the consecration of the 'mighty tubes' (*bahwannal*), the 'volcanos of the field,' or, as he terms them, the 'crocodile-mouths' (*magar-*

[1] In the original, the emperor is called the *Aspati*, 'lord of swords,' or perhaps *Aswapati*, 'lord of steeds.'

mukhan), 'emblems of Yama,' which were sprinkled abundantly with the blood of goats slain under their muzzles. He describes each clan as it arrives, their steeds, and caparisons.

Abhai Singh attacks Sirohi.—Instead, however, of proceeding direct to the main object of the war, Abhai Singh took advantage of the immense army thus placed under his command, as viceroy of Gujarat, to wreak his own vengeance upon his neighbour, the gallant prince of Sirohi, who, trusting to his native strength, had spurned every compromise which involved his independence. This resolution he maintained by his natural position, strengthened by alliances with the aboriginal races who hemmed his little State on all sides, excepting that towards Marwar.

These Minas, the mountaineers of the Aravalli, had given offence to Abhai Singh; for while the prince, between his arrival at Jodhpur and the assemblage of the Kher, gave himself up to indolence and opium, they carried off the whole cattle of the train to the mountains. When this was reported to Abhai Singh, he coolly said, "Let them go, they knew we were short of forage, and have only taken them to their own pastures in the mountains." Strange to say, they did return them, and in excellent condition, as soon as he prepared to march. When he heard of this, he observed, "Did I not tell you these Minas were faithful subjects?"

The order to march was now given, when the bard enumerates the names and strength of the different Rajput princes, whose contingents formed this array, in which there were only two Muhammadan leaders of distinction: "The Haras of Kotah and Bundi; the Khichis of Gagraun; the Gaurs of Sheopur; the Kachhwahas of [104] Amber, and [even] the Sodhas of the desert, under their respective princes or chiefs, were under the command of the Marwar prince. His native retainers, the united clans of Marwar, formed the right wing of the whole army, headed by his brother Bakhta.

"On the 10th Chait (Sudi) S. 1786, Abhai marched from Jodhpur, by Bhadrajun and Malgarh, Siwana and Jalor. Rewara was assaulted; the swords of the enemy showered, and the Champawat fell amidst heaps of slain. The Deoras abandoned the hill and fled. The trees were levelled to the summit; a garrison was posted, and the array moved on to Pusalia. Then Abu shook with affright. Affliction seized Sirohi; its prince was in despair when he heard Rewara and Pusalia were destroyed.[1] The Chauhan preferred decking his daughter in the bridal vestments to arraying his army to oppose Abhaimall."

Submission of Sirohi to Abhai Singh.—Rao Narayan Das, through the intervention of a Rajput chieftain, named Mayaram, of the Chawara tribe, made overtures to the Rathor, proposing his niece (daughter of Man Singh his predecessor) in marriage.[2] "In the midst of strife 'the coco-nut,' with eight choice steeds and the price of four elephants, were sent and accepted. The drum of battle ceased; the nuptials were solemnized, and in the tenth month Ram Singh was born at Jodhpur." The bard, however, lets us into the secret, and shows that the Rajputs had 'secret articles,' as well as the more polished diplomacy of Europe; for besides the fair Chauhani, the Rao consented to pay Peshachchanni a 'concealed tribute.'

The Deora chiefs united their contingents to the royal army, for the subjugation of Sarbuland, and the march recommenced by Palanpur and Siddhpur, or the Sarasvati. Here they halted, and "an envoy was dispatched to Sarbuland, summoning him to surrender the imperial equipments, cannons, and stores; to account for the revenues, and to withdraw his garrisons from Ahmadabad and all the strongholds of the province." The reply was laconic and dignified; "that he himself was king, and his head was with Ahmadabad" [105].

A grand council of war was convened in the Rajput camp,

[1] Both these places are famous in the Mewasa, or fastnesses of Sirohi, and gave the Author, who was intrusted with its political affairs, much trouble. Fortunately for the Deora prince, descendant of Rao Narayan Das, the Author knew their history, and was enabled to discriminate the claims which Jodhpur asserted over her in virtue of such attacks as this; in short, between the claims of 'the princes of Marwar,' and the king's lieutenants of Gujarat. In these negotiations wherein Jodhpur advanced its pretensions to *suzeraineté* over Sirohi, which as stoutly denied the right, he clearly distinguished the claims of the princes of Jodhpur, in their capacities of viceroys of the empire, and argued that claims conceded by Sirohi in that character guaranteed none to them, in their individual capacity, as chiefs of Marwar, a distinction which they affected not to comprehend, but which was at length fully recognized and acted on by the paramount power. Sirohi is maintained in its ancient independence, which but for this previous knowledge must have been inevitably lost.

[2] [It was Rāo Mān Singh III. (A.D. 1705–49) who gave his daughter in marriage to Abhai Singh. The Sirohi records contain no mention of a Rāo named Nārāyan Dās (Erskine iii. A. 213).]

which is described *con amore* by the bard. The overture and its reception were communicated, and the debates and speeches which ensued thereon, as to the future course of proceeding, are detailed. The bard is, however, satisfied with recording the speeches of 'the chiefs of the eight grades of Maru.'

"First spoke the chief of the children of Champa, Kusal, son of Harnath of Awa, whose seat is on the right of the throne. Then Kanairam of Asop, leader of the Kumpawats, whose place is on the left: 'let us, like the Kilkila,[1] dive into the waters of battle.' He was followed by Kesari, the Mertia Sarmor—then by the veteran who led the Udawats: old and brave, many a battle had he seen. Then the chief of Khanua, who led the clan of Jodha, protested he would be the first to claim the immortal garland from the hand of the Apsaras:[2] 'Let us stain our garments with saffron, and our lances with crimson, and play at ball with this Sarbuland.'[3] Fateh the Jethawat, and Karnavat Abhaimall, re-echoed his words. All shouted 'battle!' 'battle!' while some put on the coloured garments, determined to conquer Bhanuloka. Karna, the Champawat, said aloud, 'With sparkling cup the Apsaras will serve us in the mansion of the sun.'[4] Every clan, every chief, and every bard re-echoed 'battle!'

[1] The *kilkila* is the bird we call the kingfisher.

[2] The maids of war, the Valkyries of Rajput mythology.

[3] Another *jeu-de-mots* on the name Sarbuland, with whose head (*sar*) the Jodha chief proposes to play at ball.

[4] The young chieftain of Salumbar, the first of the nobles of Mewar, was sitting with me, attentively listening as I was translating the war against Sarbuland, read by my old tutor. His family possess an hereditary aversion to 'the cup,' which is under solemn prohibition from some cause which I forget, and so far did his grandfather carry his antipathy, that a drop falling upon him at an entertainment, he cut out the contaminated part with his dagger. Aware of this, I turned round to the young chief and said: "Well, Rawatji, would you accept the cup from the hand of the Apsaras or would you refuse the *munawwar* (pledge)?" "Certainly I would take it; these are very different cups from ours," was his reply. "Then you believe that the heavenly fair carry the souls of those who fall in battle to the Mandal of Surya?" "Who dare doubt it? When my time comes, I will take *that* cup!" a glorious creed for a soldier! He sat for hours listening to my old tutor and friend; for none of their bards expounded like him the *bhujanga* (serpentine verse) of the poet. I have rated the Rawat for being unable to repeat the genealogy of his house from Chonda to himself; but the family bard was dead and left no progeny to inherit his mantle. This young chief is yet (A.D. 1820) but twenty-two, and promises to be better prepared.

"Then Bakhta stood up to claim the onset, to lead the van in battle against Sarbuland, while his brother and prince should await the result in his tents. A jar of saffron-water was placed before the prince, with which he sprinkled each chief, who shouted, 'They would people Amarapur.'"[1]

The bard then describes the steeds of the Rajput chivalry, in which the Bhimthadi [106][2] of the Deccan takes precedence; he is followed by the horses of Dhat and Rardara in Marwar, and the Kathiawar of Saurashtra.

The Battle with Sarbuland.—Sarbuland's plans of defence are minutely detailed. At each gate he posted two thousand men and five guns, "manned by Europeans," of whom he had a body of musketeers round his person. The cannonade had been kept up three days on both sides, in which the son of Sarbuland was killed. At length, Bakhta led the storm, when all the *ots* and *awats* performed prodigies of valour. The Champawat Kusal was the first to be carried to the "immortal abode"; but though "the sun stood still to see the deeds of the son of Harnath" we cannot particularize the bard's catalogue of heroes transferred to Suryaloka[3] on this day, when the best blood of Rajputana was shed on the walls of Ahmadabad. Both the princely brothers had their share in "the play of swords," and each slew more than one leader of note. Amra, who had so often defended Ajmer, slew five chiefs of the grades of two and three thousand horse.

"Eight gharis of the day remained, when Sarbuland fled; but Aliyar, the leader of his vanguard, made a desperate resistance, until he fell by the hand of Bakhta Singh. The drum of victory sounded. The Nawab left his *pani* in the Rankund.[4] The 'would-be-king' was wounded; his elephant showed the speed of the deer. Four thousand four hundred and ninety-three were

[1] 'The city of immortality.'

[2] [The Bhimthadi or Bhivarthadi horses, which take their name from a division of the Poona District in the valley of the Bhima River, were highly esteemed by the Marāthas, being middle-sized, strong, good-looking, generally dark bay with black legs (*BG*, xviii. Part i. 61). It was on a horse of this breed that Mahādāji Sindhia escaped after the battle of Pānipat (Elliot-Dowson viii. 156).]

[3] The abode of heroes, the Valhalla of the Rajput mythology.

[4] Rankund is the 'fountain of battle,' and *pāni* is applied, as we use the word water, to the temper or spirit of a sword: a play on words.

slain, of whom one hundred were Palkinishins, eight Hathinishins,[1] and three hundred entitled to the Tazim on entering the Diwan-i-amm.[2]

"One hundred and twenty of Abhai Singh's chieftains of note, with five hundred horse, were slain, and seven hundred wounded.

"The next morning, Sarbuland surrendered with all his effects. He was escorted towards Agra, his wounded Moguls dying at every stage; but the soul of the 'Fearless' was sad at the loss of his kin.[3] Abhaimall ruled over the seventeen [107] thousand towns of Gujarat, and the nine thousand of Marwar, besides one thousand elsewhere. The princes of Idar, of Bhuj, of Parkar, of Sind, and of Sirohi, the Chalukya Ran of Fatehpur, Jhunjunu, Jaisalmer, Nagor, Dungarpur, Banswara, Lunawara, Halwad, every morning bowed the head to Abhaimall.

"Thus, in the enlightened half of the moon, on the victorious tenth[4] (S. 1787, A.D. 1731), the day on which Ramachandra captured Lanka, the war against Sarbuland, an Omrah (lord) of twelve thousand, was concluded."[5]

[1] Chiefs entitled to ride in palkis and on elephants.

[2] A long list of names is given, which would only fatigue the reader; but amongst them we select a singular one, Nolakh Khan Anglez, 'Nolakh the Englishman.'

[3] The bard enumerates with the meed of praise each vassal who fell, whether Rathor or of the contingents of the other principalities serving under the prince of Marwar. The Champawats bore the brunt, and lost Karan of Pali, Kishan Singh of Sandri, Gordhan of Jalor, and Kalyan. The Kumpawats lost also several leaders of clans, as Narsingh, Surthan Singh, Padma, son of Durjan. The Jodha tribe lost three leaders, namely, Hayatmall, Guman, and Jogidas. The brave Mertias also lost three: Bhum Singh, Kusal Singh, and Gulab, son of Hathi. The allodial chieftains, the Jadons, the Sonigiras, the Dhondals, and Khichis, had many brave men "carried to Bhanuloka," and even bards and purohits were amongst the slain.

[4] *Vijaya daswin.*

[5] With this battle the *Raj Rupaka* and *Surya Prakas* terminate. [All the rhetoric of the bard cannot disguise what was really a Rājput defeat. Their force advanced to Adālaj, about eight miles from Ahmadābād, and was defeated. Abhai Singh took up a new position, and a still more bloody engagement followed, in which each side tried to kill the opposing commander; but as both Mubārizu-l-mulk, who was known as Sarbuland Khān, and Abhai Singh fought in disguise, neither party succeeded. The Rāthors were finally pursued as far as Sarkhej, and it was only on Mubārizu-l-mulk receiving a lakh of rupees (£6666) that he was induced to go to Agra. See Khāfi Khan's account in Elliot-Dowson vii. 530, and *BG*, i. Part i. 310 f.]

Having left a garrison of seventeen thousand men for the duties of the capital and province, Abhai Singh returned to Jodhpur with the spoils of Gujarat, and there he deposited four crores of rupees, and one thousand four hundred guns of all calibres, besides military stores of every description. With these, in the declining state of the empire, the desert king strengthened his forts and garrisons, and determined, in the general scramble for dominion, not to neglect his own interests [108].

CHAPTER 11

Jealousy of Abhai Singh to Bakht Singh.—The tranquillity which for a while followed the campaign in Gujarat was of no long duration. The love of ease and opium, which increased with the years of Abhai Singh, was disturbed by a perpetual apprehension of the active courage and military genius of his brother, whose appanage of Nagor was too restricted a field for his talents and ambition. Bakhta was also aware that his daring nature, which obtained him the suffrages, as it would the swords, of his turbulent and easily excited countrymen, rendered him an object of distrust, and that without great circumspection, he would be unable to maintain himself in his *imperium in imperio*, the castle and three hundred and sixty townships of Nagor. He was too discreet to support himself by foreign aid, or by fomenting domestic strife; but with the aid of the bard he adopted a line of policy, the relation of which will develop new traits in the Rajput character, and exemplify its peculiarities. Karna, after finishing his historical chronicle, concluding with the war against Sarbuland, abandoned "the gate of Jodhpur for that of Nagor." Like all his tribe, the bard was an adept in intrigue, and his sacred character forwarded the secret means of executing it. His advice was to embroil their common sovereign with the prince of Amber, and an opportunity was not long wanting [109].

Abhai Singh attacks Bikaner.—The prince of Bikaner,[1] a junior but independent branch of Marwar, had offended his yet nominal suzerain Abhai Singh, who, taking advantage of the weakness of their common liege lord the emperor, determined

[1] [Sujān Singh (A.D. 1700–35) served in the Deccan from 1707 to 1719.]

to resent the affront, and accordingly invested Bikaner, which had sustained a siege of some weeks, when Bakhta determined to make its release subserve his designs ; nor could he have chosen a better expedient. Although the prince of Marwar had led his united vassalage against Bikaner, they were not only lukewarm as to the success of their own arms, but, anomalous as it must appear in the annals even of feudal warfare, they furnished the besieged with the means of defence, who, but for the supplies of opium, salt, and ammunition, would soon have been compelled to surrender. We can account for this : Bikaner was of their own kin, a branch of the great tree of which Siahji was the root, and to which they could cling in emergency ; in short, Bikaner balanced the power between themselves and their head.

The scheme being approved, its execution and mode of development to Jai Singh were next canvassed. " Touch his pride," said Karna ; " tell him the insult to Amber, which your ancestor invested, has never been balanced, and that he will never find a time like the present to fling a few shot at Jodhpur."

Bakht Singh intrigues to cause War with Jaipur.—Bakhta addressed a letter to Jai Singh, and at the same time sent instructions to the envoy of Bikaner at his court how to act.

The prince of Amber, towards the close of his career, became partial to ' the cup ' ; but, aware of the follies it involved him in, an edict prohibited all official intercourse with him while he was under its influence. The direct overture of Bakhta was canvassed, and all interference between the kindred belligerents was rejected in a full council of the chiefs of Amber. But the envoy had a friend in the famous Vidyadhar,[1] the chief civil minister of the State, through whose means he obtained permission to make 'a verbal report, standing.' " Bikaner," he said, " was in peril, and without his aid must fall, and that his master did not consider the sovereign of Marwar, but of Amber, as his suzerain." Vanity and wine did the rest. The prince took up the pen and wrote to Abhai Singh, " That they all formed one great family ; to forgive Bikaner and raise his batteries " : and as he took another cup, and [110] curled his moustache, he gave the letter

[1] Vidyadhar was a Brahman of Bengal, a scholar and man of science. The plan of the modern city of Amber, named Jaipur, was his : a city as regular as Darmstadt. He was also the joint compiler of the celebrated genealogical tables which appear in the first volume of this work.

to be folded. "Maharaja," said the envoy, "put in two more words: 'or, my name is Jai Singh.'" They were added. The overjoyed envoy retired, and in a few minutes the letter was on transit to its destination by the swiftest camel of the desert. Scarcely had the envoy retired, when the chief of Bansko,[1] the Mentor of Jai Singh, entered. He was told of the letter, which "would vex his Saga."[2] The old chief remonstrated; he said, "Unless you intend to extinguish the Kachhwahas, recall this letter." Messenger after messenger was sent, but the envoy knew his duty. At the dinner hour all the chiefs had assembled at the (*Rasora*) banquet-hall, when the spokesman of the vassalage, old Dip Singh, in reply to the communication of his sovereign, told him he had done a cruel and wanton act, and that they must all suffer for his imprudence.

The reply, a laconic defiance, was brought back with like celerity; it was opened and read by Jai Singh to his chiefs: "By what right do you dictate to me, or interfere between me and my servants? If your name is 'Lion of Victory' (Jai Singh), mine is 'the Lion without Fear' (Abhai Singh)."[3]

The ancient chief, Dip Singh, said: "I told you how it would be; but there is no retreat, and our business is to collect our friends." The Kher, or 'levy *en masse*,' was proclaimed: Every Kachhwaha was commanded to repair to the great standard planted outside the capital. The home-clans came pouring in, and aid was obtained from the Haras of Bundi, the Jadons of Karauli, the Sesodias of Shahpura, the Khichis, and the Jats, until one hundred thousand men were formed beneath the castle of Amber. This formidable array proceeded, march after march, until they reached Gangwana, a village on the frontier of Marwar.[4] Here they encamped, and, with all due courtesy, awaited the arrival of the 'Fearless Lion.'

Battle of Gangwāna.—They were not long in suspense. Mortally offended at such wanton interference, which compelled him to relinquish his object on the very eve of attainment, Abhai

[1] [One of the twelve kothris or houses of Jaipur, the Kumbhāni.]

[2] *Saga* is a term denoting a connexion by marriage [more generally a blood relation].

[3] I write the names as pronounced, and as familiar to the readers of Indian history. *Jaya*, in Sanskrit, is 'victory,' *Abhai*, 'fearless.'

[4] [Now in Ajmer District, about 8 miles N.N.W. of Ajmer city.]

Singh raised his batteries from besieging Bikaner and rapidly advanced to the encounter.

Bakhta now took alarm. He had not calculated the length to which his intrigues would involve his country; he had sought but to embroil the border princes, but [111] had kindled a national warfare. Still his fears were less for the discovery of his plot than for the honour of Marwar, about to be assailed by such odds. He repaired to his brother and liege lord, and implored him not to raise the siege; declaring that he alone, with the vassals of Nagor, would receive the Bhagatia's[1] battle, and, by God's blessing, would give a good account of him. Abhai Singh, not averse to see his brother punished for his conduct, though determined to leave him to the brunt of the battle, rejected with scorn the intriguing proposition.

The Nakkara sounded the assembly for the chivalry of Nagor. Bakhta took post on the balcony over the Delhi gate, with two brazen vessels; in the one was an infusion of opium, in the other saffron-water. To each Rajput as he entered he presented opium, and made the impress of his right hand on his heart with the saffron-water. Having in this manner enrolled eight thousand Rajputs, sworn to die with him, he determined to select the most resolute; and marching to the edge of an extensive field of luxuriant Indian corn[2] (*bajra*), he halted his band, and thus addressed them: "Let none follow me who is not prepared for victory or death: if there be any amongst you who desire to return, let them do so in God's name." As he spoke, he resumed the march through the luxuriant fields, that it might not be seen who retired. More than five thousand remained, and with these he moved on to the combat.

The Amber prince awaited them at Gangwana: soon as the hostile lines approached, Bakhta gave the word, and, in one dense mass, his gallant legion charged with lance and sword the deepened lines of Amber, carrying destruction at every pass. He passed through and through this host; but when he pulled up in the rear, only sixty of his band remained round his person. At this moment the chief of Gajsinghpura, head of all his vassals, hinted there was a jungle in the rear: "And what is there in front," said

[1] *Bhagatia* is 'a devotee': the term is here applied reproachfully to Jai Singh, on account of his very religious habits.

[2] [Rather millet, *Pennisetum typhoideum.*]

the intrepid Rathor, "that we should not try the road we came?" and as he espied the Panchranga, or five-coloured flag, which denoted the headquarters of Amber, the word again was given. The cautious Kumbhani [1] advised his prince to avoid the charge: with some difficulty he was made to leave the field, and as a salvo to his honour, by a flank movement towards Kandela north, that it might not be said he turned his back on his foe. As he [112] retreated, he exclaimed, "Seventeen battles have I witnessed, but till this day never one decided by the sword." Thus, after a life of success, the wisest, or at least the most learned and most powerful prince of Rajwara, incurred the disgrace of leaving the field in the face of a handful of men, strengthening the adage "that one Rathor equalled ten Kachhwahas."

Jai Singh's own bards could not refrain from awarding the meed of valour to their foes, and composed the following stanzas on the occasion: "Is it the battle cry of Kali, or the war-shout of Hanumanta, or the hissing of Seshnag, or the denunciation of Kapaliswar? Is it the incarnation of Narsingh, or the darting beam of Surya? or the death-glance of the Dakini? [2] or that from the central orb of Trinetra? [3] Who could support the flames from this volcano of steel, when Bakhta's sword became the sickle of Time?"

But for Karna the bard, one of the few remaining about his person, Bakhta would a third time have plunged into the ranks of the foe; nor was it till the host of Amber had left the field that he was aware of the extent of his loss.[4] Then, strange inconsistency! the man, who but a few minutes before had affronted death in every shape, when he beheld the paucity of survivors, sat down and wept like an infant. Still it was more the weakness of ambition than humanity; for, never imagining that his brother would fail to support him, he thought destruction had overtaken Marwar; nor was it until his brother joined and assured him he had left him all the honour of the day, that he recovered his port. Then "he curled his whiskers and swore an oath, that he would yet drag the 'Bhagat' from his castle of Amber."

[1] The clan of the Bansko chief.

[2] The witch of India is termed *Dakini*.

[3] A title of Siva, god of destruction, the 'three-eyed.'

[4] Though the bard does not state, it is to be supposed that the main body came up and caused this movement.

Jai Singh, though he paid dear for his message, gained his point, the relief of Bikaner; and the Rana of Udaipur mediated to prevent the quarrel going further, which was the less difficult since both parties had gained their ends, though Jai Singh obtained his by the loss of a battle.

Marriage of a God.—It is related that the tutelary deity of Bakhta Singh fell into the hands of the Amber prince, who carried home the sole trophy he could boast, married the Rathor deity to a female divinity of Amber, and returned him with his compliments to Bakhta. Such were the courteous usages of Rajput chivalry. The triple alliance [113] of the chief Rajput princes followed this battle, cemented by the union of the rival houses to daughters of Mewar. There they met, attended by their vassalage, and, in the nuptial festivities and the 'cup,' forgot this bitter strife, while enmity and even national jealousy were banished by general courtesy. Such is the Rajput, who can be judged after no known standard: he stands alone in the moral history of man.[1]

Death and Character of Abhai Singh.—This is the last conspicuous act of Abhai Singh's life on record. He died in S. 1806 (A.D. 1750) at Jodhpur. His courage, which may be termed ferocious, was tempered only by his excessive indolence, regarding which they have preserved many amusing anecdotes; one of these will display the exact character of the man. The chronicle says: "When Ajit went to marry the Chauhani, he found two lions in his path—the one asleep, the other awake. The interpretation of the Saguni (augur) was, that the Chauhani would bear him two sons; that one would be a *soti kan* (sluggard), the other an active soldier." Could the augur have revealed that they would imbrue their hands in a father's blood, he might have averted the ruin of his country, which dates from this black deed.

The Rathors profess a great contempt for the Kachhwahas as soldiers; and Abhai Singh's was not lessened for their prince, because he happened to be father-in-law to the prince of Amber, whom he used to mortify, even in the 'Presence,' with such sarcasm as, "You are called a Kachhua, or properly Kuswa, from the Kusa; and your sword will cut as deep as one of its

[1] This singular piece of Rajput history, in the Annals of Mārwār, is confirmed by every particular in the "one hundred and nine acts" of the Great Jai Singh of Amber. The foe does ample justice to Rathor valour.

blades":[1] alluding to the grass thus called. Irritated, yet fearing to reply, he formed a plan to humble his arrogance in his only vulnerable point, the depreciation of his personal strength. While it was the boast of Jai Singh to mingle the exact sciences of Europe with the more ancient of India, Abhai's ambition was to be deemed the first swordsman of Rajwara. The scientific prince of Amber gave his cue to Kirparam, the paymaster-general, a favourite with the king, from his skill at chess, and who had often the honour of playing with him while all the nobles were standing. Kirparam praised the Rathor prince's dexterity in smiting off a buffalo's head ; on which the king called out, "Rajeswar, I have heard much of your skill with the sword." "Yes, Hazrat, I can use it on an occasion." A huge animal [114] was brought into the area, fed in the luxuriant pastures of Hariana. The court crowded out to see the Rathor exhibit ; but when he beheld the enormous bulk, he turned to the king and begged permission to retire to his post, the imperial guardroom, to refresh himself. Taking a double dose of opium, he returned, his eyes glaring with rage at the trick played upon him, and as he approached the buffalo they fell upon Jai Singh who had procured this monster with a view to foil him. The Amber chief saw that mischief was brewing, and whispered his majesty not to approach too near his son-in-law. Grasping his sword in both hands, Abhai gave the blow with such force that the buffalo's head "dropped upon his knees," and the raja was thrown upon his back. All was well ; but, as the chronicle says, "the king never asked the raja to decollate another buffalo."

Invasion of Nādir Shāh.—It was during the reign of Abhai Singh that Nadir Shah[2] invaded India ; but the summons to the Rajput princes, to put forth their strength in support of the tottering throne of Timur, was received with indifference. Not a chief of note led his myrmidons to the plains of Karnal ; and Delhi was invested, plundered, and its monarch dethroned, without exciting a sigh. Such was their apathy in the cause, when the

[1] [A pun on Kachhwāha, *Kachhua*, 'a tortoise,' and the sacred *Kusa*, grass, *poa cynosuroides*.]

[2] [Nādir Shāh, King of Persia, invaded India and defeated the forces of the Emperor, Muhammad Shāh, at Karnāl, near the historic field of Pānīpat on February 13, 1739 ; entered Delhi, which was sacked and a terrible massacre perpetrated, and returned home with the Peacock Throne and immense treasures.]

imbecility of Muhammad Shah succeeded to the inheritance of Aurangzeb, that with their own hands these puppets of despotism sapped the foundations of the empire.

Unfortunately for Rajputana, the demoralization of her princes prevented their turning to advantage this depression of the empire, in whose follies and crimes they participated.

With the foul and monstrous murder of the Raja Ajit (A.D. 1750) commenced those bloody scenes which disgrace the annals of Marwar; yet even in the history of her crimes there are acts of redeeming virtue, which raise a sentiment of regret that the lustre of the one should be tarnished by the presence of the other. They serve, however, to illustrate that great moral truth, that in every stage of civilization crime will work out its own punishment; and grievously has the parricidal murder of Ajit been visited on his race and country. We shall see it acting as a blight on that magnificent tree, which, transplanted from the native soil of the Ganges, took root and flourished amidst the arid sands of the desert, affording a goodly shade for a daring race, who acquired fresh victories with poverty—we shall see its luxuriance checked, and its numerous and widely spread branches, as if [115] scorched by the lightnings of heaven, wither and decay; and they must utterly perish, unless a scion, from the uncontaminated stem of Idar,[1] be grafted upon it: then it may revive, and be yet made to yield more vigorous fruit.

CHAPTER 12

Rāja Rām Singh, A.D. 1750-52.—Ram Singh succeeded at that dangerous age when parental control is most required to restrain the turbulence of passion. Exactly twenty years had elapsed since the nuptials at Sirohi, when Hymen extinguished the torch of discord, and his mother was the bearer of the olive branch to Abhai Singh, to save her house from destruction. The Rajput, who attaches everything to pedigree, has a right to lay an interdict on the union of the race of Agni,[2] with the already too

[1] The heir of Idar is heir presumptive to the *gaddi* of Marwar.

[2] The Deora of Sirohi is a branch of the Chauhans, one of the four Agnikulas, a race sprung from fire. See Vol. I. p. 112.

fiery blood of the Rathor. Ram Singh inherited the arrogance of his father, with all the impetuosity of the Chauhans; and the exhibition of these qualities was simultaneous with his coronation. We are not told why his uncle, Bakhta Singh, absented himself from the ceremony of his prince's and nephew's installation, when the whole kin and clans of Maru assembled to ratify their allegiance by their presence. As the first in blood and rank, it was his duty to make the first mark of inauguration on the [116] forehead of his prince. The proxy he chose on the occasion was his Dhai, or 'nurse,' a personage of no small importance in those countries. Whether by such a representative the haughty warrior meant to insinuate that his nephew should yet be in leading strings, the chronicle affords us no hint; but it reprehends Ram Singh's conduct to this venerable personage, whom, instead of treating, according to usage, with the same respect as his mother, he asked, "if his uncle took him for an ape, that he sent an old hag to present him with the *tika*?" and instantly dispatched an express desiring the surrender of Jalor. Ere his passion had time to cool, he commanded his tents to be moved out, that he might chastise the insult to his dignity. Despising the sober wisdom of the counsellors of the state, he had given his confidence to one of the lowest grade of these hereditary officers, by name Anna, the Nakkarchi,[1] a man headstrong like himself. The old chief of the Champawats, on hearing of this act of madness, repaired to the castle to remonstrate; but scarcely had he taken his seat before the prince assailed him with ridicule, desiring "to see his frightful face as seldom as possible." "Young man," exclaimed the indignant chief, as with violence he dashed his shield reversed upon the carpet, "you have given mortal offence to a Rathor, who can turn Marwar upside down as easily as that shield." With eyes darting defiance, he arose and left the Presence, and collecting his retainers, marched to Mundiavar.[2] This was the residence of the Pat-Bardai, or 'chief bard,' the lineal descendant of the Bardai Roera, who left Kanauj with Siahji. The esteem in which his sacred office was held may be appreciated by his estate, which equalled that of the first noble, being one lakh of rupees (£10,000) of revenue.

[1] The person who summons the nobles by beat of the state *nakkara*, or 'great kettledrum.'

[2] [Mūndwa, about 90 miles N.E. of Jodhpur city.]

The politic Bakhta, hearing of the advance of the chief noble of Maru on the border of his territory, left Nagor, and though it was midnight, advanced to welcome him. The old chief was asleep; Bakhta forbade his being disturbed, and placed himself quietly beside his pallet. As he opened his eyes, he called as usual for his pipe (*hukka*), when the attendant pointing to the prince, the old chief scrambled up. Sleep had cooled his rage, and the full force of his position rushed upon him; but seeing there was now no retreat, that the Rubicon was crossed, "Well, there is my head," said he; "now it is yours." The bard, who was present at the interview, was sounded by being requested to bring the chief's wife and family from [117] Awa to Nagor; and he gave his assent in a manner characteristic of his profession: "farewell to the gate of Jodhpur," alluding to the station of the bard. The prince immediately replied, "there was no difference between the gate of Jodhpur and Nagor; and that while he had a cake of *bajra* he would divide it with the bard."

Civil War between Rām Singh and Bakht Singh.—Ram Singh did not allow his uncle much time to collect a force; and the first encounter was at Kherli. Six actions rapidly followed; the last was at Lunawas, on the plains of Merta, with immense loss of life on both sides. This sanguinary battle has been already related,[1] in which Ram Singh was defeated, and forced to seek safety in flight; when Jodhpur was surrendered, and Bakhta invested with the Rajtilak and sword by the hands of the Jethawat chief of Bagri, whose descendants continue to enjoy this distinction, with the title of Marwar ka bar Kewar, 'the bar to the portal of Marwar.'

Accession of Bakht Singh, A.D. 1752-53.—With the possession of the seat of government, and the support of a great majority of the clans, Bakhta Singh felt secure against all attempts of his nephew to regain his lost power. But although his popularity with his warlike kindred secured their suffrages for his maintenance of the throne which the sword had gained him, there were other opinions which Bakhta Singh was too politic to overlook. The adhesion of the hereditary officers of the State, especially those personal to the sovereign, is requisite to cloak the crime of usurpation, in which light only, whatever the extent of provocation, Bakhta's conduct could be regarded. The military

[1] See p. 862.

premier, as well as the higher civil authorities, were won to his cause, and of those whose sacred office might seem to sanctify the crime, the chief bard had already changed his post "for the gate of Nagor." But there was one faithful servant, who, in the general defection, overlooked the follies of his prince, in his adherence to the abstract rules of fidelity; and who, while his master found refuge at Jaipur, repaired to the Deccan to obtain the aid of the Mahrattas, the mercenaries of Rajputana. Jaga was the name of this person; his office, that of Purohit, the ghostly adviser of his prince and tutor to his children. Bakhta, at once desirous to obtain his suffrage, and to arrest the calamity of foreign invasion, sent a couplet in his own hand to the Purohit:

"The flower, O bee, whose aroma regaled you, has been assailed by the blast; not a leaf of the rose-tree is left; why longer cling to the thorns?" [118]

The reply was in character: "In this hope does the bee cling to the denuded rose-tree; that spring may return, and fresh flowers bud forth." [1]

Bakhta, to his honour, approved the fidelity which rejected his overtures.

Intervention of Mahādaji Sindhia.—There was a joyousness of soul about Bakhta which, united to an intrepidity and a liberality alike unbounded, made him the very model of a Rajput. To these qualifications were superadded a majestic mien and Herculean frame, with a mind versed in all the literature of his country, besides poetic talent of no mean order; and but for that one damning crime, he would have been handed down to posterity as one of the noblest princes Rajwara ever knew. These qualities not only riveted the attachment of the household clans, but secured the respect of all his exterior relations, so that when the envoy of the expatriated prince obtained Sindhia's aid for the restoration of Ram Singh, the popularity of Bakhta formed an army which appalled the "Southron," who found arrayed against him all the choice swords of Rajwara. The whole allodial power of the desert, "the sons of Siahji" of every rank, rose to oppose

[1] That beautiful simile of Ossian, or of Macpherson, borrowed from the canticles of the Royal Bard of Jerusalem, will be brought to mind in the reply of the Purohit—"I was a lovely tree in thy presence, Oscar, with all my branches around me," etc.

this first attempt of the Mahrattas to interfere in their national quarrels, and led by Bakhta in person, advanced to meet Mahadaji, the Patel.[1] But the Mahratta, whose object was plunder rather than glory, satisfied that he had little chance of either, refused to measure his lance (*barchhi*) with the *sang* and *sirohi*[2] of the Rajput.

Bakht Singh Poisoned.—Poison effected what the sword could not accomplish. Bakhta determined to remain encamped in that vulnerable point of access to his dominions, the passes near Ajmer. Hither, the Rathor queen of Madho Singh, prince of Amber, repaired to compliment her relative, and to her was entrusted the task of removing the enemy of her nephew, Ram Singh. The mode in which the deed was effected, as well as the last moments of the heroic but criminal Bakhta, have been already related.[3] He died in S. 1809 (A.D. 1753), leaving a disputed succession, and all the horrors of impending civil strife, to his son, Bijai Singh.

Repression of Islām.—During his three years of sovereignty, Bakhta had found both time and resources to strengthen and embellish the strongholds of Marwar. He completed the fortifications [119] of the capital, and greatly added to the palace of Jodha, from the spoils of Ahmadabad. He retaliated the injuries on the intolerant Islamite, and threw down his shrines and his mosques in his own fief of Nagor, and with the wrecks restored the edifices of ancient days. It was Bakhta also who prohibited, under pain of death, the Islamite's call to prayer throughout his dominions, and the order remains to this day unrevoked in Marwar. Had he been spared a few years to direct the storm then accumulating, which transferred power from the haughty Tatar of Delhi to the peasant soldier of the Kistna, the probability was eminently in favour of the Rajputs resuming their ancient rights throughout India. Every principality had the same motive for union in one common cause, the destruction of a power inimical to their welfare: but crimes, moral and political, rendered an opportunity,

[1] [Mahādāji Sindhia used the title of Patel or village headman to mark his assumed deference to the Peshwa (Grant Duff 212).]

[2] *Sang* is a lance about ten feet long, covered with plates of iron about four feet above the spike. The *sirohi* is the sword made at the city, whence its name, and famous for its temper.

[3] See p. 867.

such as never occurred in their history, unavailing for their emancipation from temporal and spiritual oppression.

Rājput Morals compared with those of Europe in the Middle Ages.—We will here pause, and anticipating the just horror of the reader, at finding crime follow crime—one murder punished by another—prevent his consigning all the Rajput dynasties to infamy, because such foul stains appear in one part of their annals. Let him cast his eyes over the page of western history; and commencing with the period of Siahji's emigration in the eleventh century, when the curtain of darkness was withdrawn from Europe, as it was simultaneously closing upon the Rajput, contrast their respective moral characteristics. The Rajput chieftain was imbued with all the kindred virtues of the western cavalier, and far his superior in mental attainments. There is no period on record when these Hindu princes could not have signed their names to a charter; many of them could have drawn it up, and even invested it, if required, in a poetic garb; and although this consideration perhaps enhances, rather than palliates, crime, what are the instances in these States, we may ask, compared to the wholesale atrocities of the 'Middle Ages' of Europe?

The reader would also be wrong if he leaped to the conclusion that the bardic chronicler passed no judgment on the princely criminal. His "empoisoned stanzas" (*vishwa sloka*), transmitted to posterity by the mouth of the peasant and the prince, attest the reverse. One couplet has been recorded, stigmatizing Bakhta for the murder of his father; there is another of the chief bard, improvised while his prince Abhai Singh and Jai Singh of Amber were passing the period devoted [120] to religious rites at the sacred lake of Pushkar. These ceremonies never stood in the way of festivity; and one evening, while these princes and their vassals were in the height of merriment, the bard was desired to contribute to it by some extemporaneous effusion. He rose, and vociferated in the ears of the horror-struck assembly the following quatrain:—

Jodhāno Āmber ē
Donon thāp uthāp;
Kuram māryo dikro,
Kāmdhaj māryo bāp.

"[The princes of] Jodhpur and Amber can dethrone the

enthroned. But the Kurma[1] slew his son; the Kamdhaj[2] murdered his father."

The words of the poetic seer sank into the minds of his hearers, and passed from mouth to mouth. They were probably the severest vengeance either prince experienced in this world, and will continue to circulate down to the latest posterity. It was the effusion of the same undaunted Karna, who led the charge with his prince against the troops of Amber.

The Curse of a Sati.—We have also the anathema of the prophetic Sati, wife of Ajit, who, as she mounted the pyre with her murdered lord, pronounced that terrific sentence to the ears of the patriotic Rajput: "May the bones of the murderer be consumed out of Maru:"[3] In the value they attach to the fulfilment of the prophecy, we have a commentary on the supernatural power attached to these self-devoted victims. The record of the last moments of Bakhta, in the dialogue with his doctor,[4] is a scene of the highest dramatic and moral interest; and, if further comment were required, demonstrates the operations of the hell within, as well as the abhorrenee the Rajput entertains for such crimes [121].

CHAPTER 13

Rāja Bijai Singh, A.D. **1753-93.**—Bijai Singh, then in his twentieth year, succeeded his father, Bakhta. His accession was acknowledged not only by the emperor, but by all the princes around him, and he was inaugurated at the frontier town of Marot,[5] when proceeding to Merta, where he passed the period of *matam* or mourning. Hither the independent branches of his family, of Bikaner, Kishangarh, and Rupnagarh, came simultaneously with their condolence and congratulations. Thence he advanced to the capital, and concluded the rites on death and accession with gifts and charities which gratified all expectations.

[1] Kurma or Kachhua (the tribe of the princes of Amber) slew his son, Sheo Singh.

[2] Kamdhaj, it must be remembered, is a titular appellation of the Rathor kings, which they brought from Kanauj.

[3] See p. 867.

[4] *Ibid.*

[5] [On the N. frontier of Jodhpur.]

Rām Singh invites Marātha Aid.—The death of his uncle afforded the ex-prince, Ram Singh, the chance of redeeming his birthright; and in conjunction with the prince of Amber, he concluded a treaty [1] with the Mahrattas, the stipulations of which were sworn to by their leaders. The "Southrons" advanced by Kotah and Jaipur, where Ram Singh [122], with his personal adherents and a strong auxiliary band of Amber, united their forces, and they proceeded to the object in view, the dethronement of Bijai Singh.

The Battle of Merta.—Bijai Singh was prepared for the storm, and led his native chivalry to the plains of Merta, where, animated with one impulse, a determination to repel foreign interference, they awaited the Mahrattas, to decide the rival claims to the throne of the desert.[2] The bard delights to enumerate the clans who mustered all their strength; and makes particular allusion to the allodial Pattawats, who were foremost on this occasion. From Pushkar, where the combined army halted, a summons was sent to Bijai Singh "to surrender the gaddi of Maru." It was read in full convention and answered with shouts of "Battle! Battle!" "Who is this Hapa,[3] thus to scare us, when, were the firmament to fall, our heads would be pillars of support to preserve you?" Such is the hyperbole of the Rajput when excited, nor does his action fall far short of it. The numerical odds were immense against the Rathors; but they little esteemed the Kachhwahas, and their courage had very different aliment to sustain it, from the mercenary Southron. The encounter was of the most desperate description, and the bard deals out a full measure of justice to all.

Two accidents occurred during the battle, each sufficient to turn victory from the standard of Bijai Singh, on the very point of fruition. One has elsewhere been related,[4] namely, the destruc-

[1] This treaty is termed *haldi*, or *balpatra*, 'a strong deed' [*haldi* means 'turmeric,' with which the hand-marks on the treaty were made]. The names of the chiefs who signed it were Jankoji Sindhia, Santoji Bolia, Danto Patel, Rana Bhurtiya, Ato Jaswant Rae, Kano, and Jiwa, Jadons; Jiwa Punwar, Piluji and Satwa, Sindhia Malji, Tantia Chitu, Raghu Pagia, Ghusalia Jadon, Mulla Yar Ali, Firoz Khan; all great leaders amongst the 'Southrons' of that day.

[2] [The date of the battle is uncertain. According to Erskine (iii. A. 66) it was fought "about 1756".]

[3] The *A*, to the Rajput of the north-west, is as great a Shibboleth as to the Cockney—thus *Apa* becomes *Hapa*.

[4] See p. 868.

tion of the "Silahposhians," or cuirassiers, the chosen cohort of the Rathors, when returning from a successful charge, who were mistaken for the foe, and mowed down with discharges of grape-shot. This error, at a moment when the courage of the Mahrattas was wavering, might have been retrieved, notwithstanding the superstitious converted the disaster into an omen of evil. Sindhia had actually prepared to quit the field, when another turn of the wheel decided the event in his favour: the circumstance exhibits forcibly the versatile character of the Rajput.

Treachery of Sardār Singh of Kishangarh.—The Raja of Kishangarh had deprived his relative of Rupnagar of his estates; both were junior branches of Marwar, but held direct from the emperor. Sawant Singh, chieftain of Rupnagar, either from constitutional indifference or [123] old age, retired to the sanctuary of Brindaban on the Jumna, and, before the shrine of the Hindu Apollo, poured forth his gratitude for "his escape from hell," in the loss of his little kingdom. But it was in vain he attempted to inspire young Sardar with the like contempt of mundane glory; to his exhortations the youth replied, "It is well for you, Sire,[1] who have enjoyed life, to resign its sweets so tranquilly; but I am yet a stranger to them." Taking advantage of the times, he determined to seek a stronger auxiliary for the recovery of his rights than the poetic homilies of Jayadeva. Accordingly, he joined the envoy of Ram Singh, and returned with the Mahratta army, on whose successful operations his hope of reconquering his patrimony rested. It was at that moment of doubt that Apa, the Mahratta commander, thus addressed young Sardar: "Your star, young man, is united to Ram Singh's, which fortune does not favour; what more is to be done before we move off?" Inexperienced as he was, Sardar knew his countrymen, and their vacillation when touched by superstition; and he obtained permission to try a ruse, as a last resort. He dispatched a horse-man of his own clan to the division which pressed them most, who, coming up to the Mainot minister, as if of his own party, asked "what they were fighting for, as Bijai Singh lay dead, killed by a cannon-shot in another part of the field?" Like the ephemeral tribe of diplomacy, the Mainot saw his sun was set. He left the field, followed by the panic-struck clans, amongst whom the report circulated like wildfire. Though accustomed to these stratagems,

[1] *Bapji.*

with which their annals teem, the Rajputs are never on their guard against them; not a man inquired into the truth of the report, and Bijai Singh,—who, deeming himself in the very career of victory, was coolly performing his devotions amidst the clash of swords,—was left almost alone, even without attendants or horses. The lord of Marwar, who, on that morning, commanded the lives of one hundred thousand Rajputs, was indebted for his safety to the mean conveyance of a cart and pair of oxen.[1]

Every clan had to erect tablets for the loss of their best warriors; and as in their civil wars each strove to be foremost in devotion, most of the chieftains of note [124] were amongst the slain.[2] The bard metes out a fair measure of justice to their auxiliaries, especially the Saktawats of Mewar, whose swords were unsheathed in the cause of the son-in-law of their prince. Nor is the lance of the Southron passed over without eulogy, to praise which, indeed, is to extol themselves.

Results of Rāthor Defeat.—With the loss of this battle and the dispersion of the Rathors, the strongholds rapidly fell. The cause of Ram Singh was triumphing, and the Mahrattas were spreading over the land of Maru, when foul assassination checked their progress.[3] But the death of Jai Apa, which converted his hordes from auxiliaries to principals in the contest, called aloud for vengeance, that was only to be appeased by the cession of Ajmer, and a fixed triennial tribute on all the lands of Maru, both feudal and fiscal. This arrangement being made, the

[1] The anecdote is related, p. 870. The Bijai Vilas states that the prince rewarded the peasant with five hundred bighas of land in perpetuity, which his descendants enjoy, saddled with the petite serjanterie of "curds and bajra cakes," in remembrance of the fare the Jat provided for his prince on that emergency.

[2] Rae Singh, chief of the Kumpawats, the second noble in rank of Marwar; Lal Singh, head of the Sisawats, with the leader of the Kutawats, are especially singled out as sealing their fidelity with their blood; but all the *ots* and *awats* of the country come in for a share of glory.

[3] This occurrence has been related in the Personal Narrative, p. 873, but it is more amply narrated in the chronicle, the Bijai Vilas, from which I am now compiling. In this it is said that Jai Apa, during the siege, having fallen sick, the Rathor prince sent his own physician, Surajmall, to attend him; that the doctor at first refused the mission, saying, "You may tell me to poison him, and I will not obey." "On the contrary," said his prince, "let your skill cure in two days what would take you four, and I shall favour you"; but what was far more strange, Apa objected not, took the medicines of the *baid*, and recovered.

Mahrattas displayed the virtue common to such mercenary allies: they abandoned Ram Singh to his 'evil star,' and took possession of this stronghold, which, placed in the very heart of Rajasthan, perpetuated their influence over its princes.

With this gem, thus rudely torn from her diadem, the independence of Marwar from that hour has been insecure. She has struggled on, indeed, through a century of invasions, rebellions, and crimes, all originating, like the blank leaf on her annals, from the murder of Ajit. In the words of the Doric stanza of the hostile bards on this memorable chastisement:

Yād ghana din āvasi,
Āpawāla hel;
Bhāga tinon bhupati,
Māl khajāna mel.[1]

"For many a day will they remember the time (*hel*) of Apa, when the three sovereigns fled, abandoning their goods and treasures": alluding to the princes of Marwar, Bikaner, and Kishangarh, who partook in the disasters and disgrace of that day [125].

The youthful heir of Rupnagar claimed, as he justly might, the victory to himself; and going up to Apa to congratulate him, said, in the metaphorical language of his country, "You see I sowed mustard-seed in my hand as I stood": comparing the prompt success of his stratagem to the rapid vegetation of the seed. But Sardar was a young man of no ordinary promise; for when Sindhia, in gratitude, offered immediately to put him in possession of Rupnagar, he answered, "No; that would be a retrograde movement," and told him to act for his master Ram Singh, "whose success would best insure his own." But when treachery had done its worst on Jai Apa, suspicion, which fell on every Rajput in the Mahratta camp, spared not Sardar: swords were drawn in every quarter, and even the messengers of peace, the envoys, were everywhere assailed, and amongst those who fell ere the tumult could be appeased, was Rawat Kabir Singh, the premier noble of Mewar, then ambassador from the Rana with the Mahrattas.[2] With his last breath, Jai Apa pro-

[1] [*Hel, halla*, 'onset,' the Marātha invasion.]

[2] I have many original autograph letters of this distinguished Rajput on the transactions of this period; for it was he who negotiated the treaty

tected and exonerated Sardar, and enjoined that his pledge of restoration to his patrimony should be redeemed. The body of this distinguished commander was burned at the Taussar, or 'Peacock pool,' where a cenotaph was erected, and in the care which the descendants even of his enemies pay to it, we have a test of the merits of both victor and vanquished.

Death of Rām Singh.—This was the last of twenty-two battles, in which Ram Singh was prodigal of his life for the recovery of his honours. The adversity of his later days had softened the asperity of his temper, and made his early faults be forgotten, though too late for his benefit. He died in exile at Jaipur in A.D. 1773. His person was gigantic; his demeanour affable and courteous; and he was generous to a fault. His understanding was excellent and well cultivated, but his capricious temperament, to which he gave vent with an unbridled vehemence, disgusted the high-minded nobles of Maru, and involved him in exile and misery till his death. It is universally admitted that, both in exterior and accomplishments, not even the great Ajit could compare with Ram Singh, and witchcraft, at the instigation of the chieftain of Asop, is assigned to account for his fits of insanity, which might be better attributed to the early and immoderate use of opium. But in spite of his errors, the fearless courage he displayed, against all odds, kept some of the [126] most valiant of the clans constant to his fortunes, especially the brave Mertias, under the heroic Sher Singh of Rian, whose deeds can never be obliterated from the recollections of the Rathor. Not the least ardent of his adherents was the allodial chief Rup Singh, of the almost forgotten clan, Pattawat; who held out in Phalodi against all attempts, and who, when provisions failed, with his noble associates, slew and ate their camels. The theme is a favourite one for the Kamarya[1] minstrel of Maru, who sings the fidelity of Rupa and his band to the notes of his rabab,[2] to their ever attentive descendants.

The Character of Rāja Rām Singh.—We may sum up the

between Raja Madho Singh, of Jaipur, the 'nephew of Mewar,' and the Mahrattas. At this time, his object was to induce Jai Apa to raise the siege of Nagor.

[1] [A class of minstrels and buffoons (*Census Report, Mārwār*, 1891, ii. 178).]

[2] [*Rabāb*, 'a viol'.]

character of Ram Singh in the words of the bard, as he contrasts him with his rival. "Fortune never attended the stirrup of Bijai Singh, who never gained a battle, though at the head of a hundred thousand men; but Ram Singh, by his valour and conduct, gained victories with a handful."

The death of Ram Singh was no panacea to the griefs of Marwar or of its prince. The Mahrattas, who had now obtained a *point-d'appui* in Rajwara, continued to foster disputes which tended to their advantage, or when opportunity offered, to scour the country in search of pay or plunder. Bijai Singh, young and inexperienced, was left without resources; ruinous wars and yet more ruinous negotiations had dissipated the hoards of wealth accumulated by his predecessors. The crown-lands were uncultivated, the tenantry dispersed; and commerce had diminished, owing to insecurity and the licentious habits of the nobles, who everywhere established their own imposts, and occasionally despoiled entire caravans. While the competitor for the throne was yet living, the Raja was compelled to shut his eyes on these inroads upon his proper power, which reduced him to insignificance even in his own palace.

Power of the Aristocracy of Mārwār.—The aristocracy in Marwar has always possessed more power than in any of the sister principalities around. The cause may be traced to their first settlement in the desert; and it has been kept in action by the peculiarities of their condition, especially in that protracted struggle for the rights of the minor Ajit, against the despotism of the empire. There was another cause, which, at the present juncture, had a very unfortunate influence on the increase of this preponderance, and which arose out of the laws of adoption.

The Pokaran Fief.—The fief of Pokaran, the most powerful (although a junior) branch of the Champawat clan, adopted a son of Raja Ajit as their chief; his name was Devi Singh [127]. The right of adoption, as has been already explained, rests with the widow of the deceased and the elders of the clan. Why they exercised it as they did on this occasion does not appear; but not improbably at the suggestion of the dying chief, who wished to see his sovereign's large family provided for, having no sons of his own: or, the immediate claimants may not have possessed the qualities necessary to lead a clan of Maru. Although the moment such adoption takes place, when "the turban of the late incumbent encircled the new lord of Pokaran," he ought to forget he had any other father than him he succeeded, yet we can easily imagine that, in the present case, his propinquity to the throne, which under other circumstances he might soon have forgotten, was continually forced upon his recollection by the contentions of his parricidal brothers and their offspring for the 'cushion' of Marwar. It exemplifies another feature in Rajput institutions, which cut off this son (guiltless of all participation in the treason) from succession, because he was identified with the feudality; while the issue of another, and junior brother, at the same period adopted into the independent house of Idar,[1] were heirs presumptive to Marwar; nay, must supply it with a ruler on failure of heirs, though they should have but one son and be compelled to adopt in his room.[2]

Mercenaries enrolled.—The Champawats determined to maintain their influence over the sovereign and the country; and Devi Singh leagued with Awa and the other branches of this clan to the exclusion of all competitors. They formed of their own body a guard of honour for the person of the prince, one half remaining on duty in the castle, the other half being in the town below. While the Raja would lament the distracted state of his country, the inroads of the hill tribes, and the depredations of his own chiefs, Devi Singh of Pokaran would reply, "Why trouble yourself about Marwar? it is in the sheath of my dagger." The young prince used to unburthen his griefs to his foster-brother Jaga, a man of caution and experience, which qualities he instilled into his sovereign. By dissimulation, and an apparent acquiescence in their plans, he not only eluded suspicion, but, availing himself of their natural indolence of character, at length obtained leave not only to entertain some men of Sind as guards for the town, but to provide supplies for their subsistence: the first approximation towards a standing mercenary force, till then unknown in their annals [128]. We do not mean that the Rajput princes never employed any other than their own feudal clans; they had foreign Rajputs in their pay, but still on the same tenure, holding lands for service; but never till this period had they

[1] It will be remembered that Idar was conquered by a brother of Siahji's.

[2] We shall explain this by a cutting of the genealogical tree: it may be found useful should we be called on to arbitrate in these matters.

soldiers entertained on monthly stipend. These hired bands were entirely composed of infantry, having a slight knowledge of European tactics, the superiority of which, even over their high-minded cavaliers, they had so severely experienced in their encounters with the Mahrattas. The same causes had operated on the courts of Udaipur and Jaipur to induce them to adopt the like expedient; to which, more than to the universal demoralization which followed the breaking up of the empire, may be attributed the rapid decay of feudal principles throughout Rajputana. These guards were composed either of Purbia [1] Rajputs, Sindis, Arabs, or Rohillas. They received their orders direct from the prince, through the civil officers of the State, by whom they were entrusted with the execution of all duties of importance or dispatch. Thus they soon formed a complete barrier between the prince and his vassals, and consequently became objects of jealousy and of strife. In like manner did all the other States make approaches towards a standing army; and though the motive in all cases was the same, to curb, or even to extinguish, the strength of the feudal chiefs, it has failed throughout, except in the solitary instance of Kotah, where twenty well-disciplined battalions, and a hundred pieces of artillery, are maintained chiefly from the feudal sequestrations.

To return: the Dhabhai, having thus secured a band of seven hundred men, and obtained an aid (which we may term scutage) from the chiefs for their maintenance, gradually transferred them from their duties above to the gates of the castle. Somewhat released from the thraldom of faction, the Raja concerted with his foster-brother and the Diwan, Fateh Chand, the means of restoring prosperity and order. So destitute was the prince of resources, that the Dhabhai had recourse to threats of suicide to obtain 50,000 rupees from his mother, acquired as the nurse (*dhai*) of his sovereign; and so drained was the country of horses, that he was compelled to transport his cavaliers (who were too proud to walk) on cars to Nagor. There, under the pretence of curbing the hill tribes, he formed an army, and dismounting the guns from the walls of the town, marched an ill-equipped force against the border-mountaineers, and being successful he attacked on his return [129] the castle of Silbakri. This was deemed a sufficient indication of his views; the whole feudality of Maru

[1] Purbias, 'men of the east,' as the Maghrabis are 'of the west.'

took alarm, and united for mutual safety at Bisalpur, twenty miles east of the capital.

Gordhan Singh negotiates with the Chiefs.—There was a foreign Rajput, whose valour, fidelity, and conduct had excited the notice and regard of Bakhta Singh, who, in his dying hour, recommended him to the service of his son. To Gordhan, the Khichi, a name of no small note in the subsequent history of this reign, did the young Raja apply in order to restrain his chiefs from revolt. In the true spirit of Rajput sentiment, he advised his prince to confide in their honour, and, unattended, to seek and remonstrate with them, while he went before to secure him a good reception. At daybreak, Gordhan was in the camp of the confederates; he told them that their prince, confiding in their loyalty, was advancing to join them, and besought them to march out to receive him. Deaf, however, to entreaty and to remonstrance, not a man would stir, and the prince reached the camp uninvited and unwelcomed. Decision and confidence are essential in all transactions with a Rajput. Gordhan remained not a moment in deliberation, but instantly carried his master direct to the tent of the Awa chief, the premier noble of Marwar. Here the whole body congregated, and silence was broken by the prince, who demanded why his chiefs had abandoned him?

"Maharaja," replied the Champawat, "our bodies have but one pinnacle; were there a second, it should be at your disposal." A tedious discussion ensued; doubts of the future, recriminations respecting the past; till wearied and exhausted, the prince demanded to know the conditions on which they would return to their allegiance, when the following articles were submitted:

1. To break up the force of the Dhabhai;
2. To surrender to their keeping the records of fiefs (*pattabahi*);
3. That the court should be transferred from the citadel to the town.

There was no alternative but the renewal of civil strife or compliance; and the first article, which was a *sine qua non*, the disbanding of the obnoxious guards, that anomalous appendage to a Rajput prince's person, was carried into immediate execution. Neither in the first nor last stipulation could the prince feel surprise or displeasure; but the second sapped the very foundation of his rule, by depriving the crown of its dearest prerogative, the power of dispensing favour. This shallow reconciliation being effected, the malcontent nobles dispersed, some to their estates [130], and the Chondawat oligarchy to the capital with their prince, in the hope of resuming their former influence over him and the country.

Massacre of the Chiefs.—Thus things remained, when Atmaram, the Guru or 'ghostly comforter' of Bijai Singh, fell sick, and as he sedulously attended him, the dying priest would tell him to be of good cheer, for when he departed, he "would take all his troubles with him." He soon died, and his words, which were deemed prophetic, were interpreted by the Dhabhai. The Raja feigned immoderate grief for the loss of his spiritual friend, and in order to testify his veneration, an ordinance was issued commanding that the Kiryakarma, or 'rites for the dead,' should be performed in the castle, while the queens, on pretence of paying their last duty to his remains, descended, carrying with them the guards and retainers as their escort. It was an occasion on which suspicion, even if awake, could not act, and the chiefs ascended to join in the funeral rites to the saint. As they mounted the steps cut out of the rock which wound round the hill of Jodha, the mind of Devi Singh suddenly misgave him, and he exclaimed that "the day was unlucky"; but it passed off with the flattering remark, "you are the pillar of Maru; who dare even look at you?" They paced slowly through the various barriers, until they reached the Alarum Gate.[1] It was shut! "Treachery!" exclaimed the chief of Awa, as he drew his sword, and the work of death commenced. Several were slain; the rest were overpowered. Their captivity was a sufficient presage of their fate; but, like true Rajputs, when the Dhabhai told them they were to die, their last request was, "that their souls might be set at liberty by the sword, not by the unsanctified ball of the mercenary." The chronicle does not say whether this wish was gratified, when the three great leaders of the Champawats, with Jeth Singh of Awa; Devi Singh of Pokaran; the lord of Harsola; Chhattar Singh, chief of the Kumpawats; Kesari Singh of Chandren; the heir of Nimaj; and the chief of Ras,[2] then the

[1] The Nakkara Darwaza, where the grand kettledrum is stationed, to give the alarm or summons to the chieftains to repair to the Presence. To this gate Raja Man advanced to meet the Author, then the representative of the Governor-General of India.

[2] [Rās, 70 miles E. of Jodhpur city.]

principal fief of the Udawats, met their fate. The last hour of Devi Singh was marked with a distinguished peculiarity. Being of the royal line of Maru, they would not spill his blood, but sent him his death-warrant in a jar of opium. On receiving it, and his prince's command to make his own departure from life, "What!" said the noble spirit, as they presented the jar, "shall Devi [131] Singh take his *amal* (opiate) out of an earthen vessel? Let his gold cup be brought, and it shall be welcome." This last vain distinction being denied, he dashed out his brains against the walls of his prison. Before he thus enfranchised his proud spirit, some ungenerous mind, repeating his own vaunt, demanded, "where was then the sheath of the dagger which held the fortunes of Marwar?" "In Subhala's girdle at Pokaran," was the laconic reply of the undaunted Chondawat.

This was a tremendous sacrifice for the maintenance of authority, of men who had often emptied their veins in defence of their country. But even ultra patriotism, when opposed to foreign aggression, can prove no palliative to treason or mitigate its award, when, availing themselves of the diminished power of the prince, an arrogant and imperious oligarchy presumes to enthral their sovereign. It is the mode in which vengeance was executed at which the mind recoils, and which with other instances appears to justify the imputation of perfidy amongst the traits of Rajput character. But if we look deeply into it, we shall find reason to distrust such conclusion. The Rajput abhors, in the abstract, both perfidy and treason; but the elements of the society in which he lives and acts, unfortunately too often prompt the necessity of sacrificing principles to preservation: but this proceeds from their faulty political constitution; it is neither inculcated in their moral code, nor congenial to their moral habits.

Right of Primogeniture.—The perpetual struggle between the aristocracy and the sovereign, which is an evil inherent in all feudal associations, was greatly aggravated in Marwar, as well as in Mewar, by the sacrifice of that corner-stone even of constitutional monarchy, the rights of primogeniture. But in each case the deviation from custom was a voluntary sacrifice of the respective heirs-apparent to the caprices of parental dotage. In no other country in the world could that article of the Christian decalogue, "Honour thy father and thy mother," be better illustrated than in Rajputana, where, if we have had to record two horrid examples of deviation from, we have also exhibited splendid proofs of, filial devotion, in Chonda of Mewar, and Champa of Marwar, who resigned the "rods" they were born to wield; and served, when they should have swayed, to gratify their father's love for the fruit of their old age. These are instances of self-denial hardly to be credited; from such disinterested acts, their successors claimed an importance which, though natural, was totally unforeseen, and which the extent of compensation contributed [132] to foster. They asserted the right, as hereditary premiers of the State, to be the advisers, or rather the tutors, of their sovereigns, more especially in non-age, and in allusion to this surrender of their birthright, arrogantly applied the well-known adage, *Pat ka malik main ho, Raj ka malik uha,* 'He is sovereign of the State, but I am the master of the Throne'; and insisted on the privilege of being consulted on every gift of land, and putting their autograph symbol to the deed or grant.[1] These pretensions demanded the constant exertions of the sovereign to resist them; for this purpose, he excited the rivalry of the less powerful members of the federated vassalage, and thus formed a kind of balance of power, which the monarch, if skilful, could always turn to account. But not even the jealousies thus introduced would have so depreciated the regal influence in Marwar, nor even the more recent adoption of a son of the crown into the powerful fief of Pokaran, had not the parricidal sons of Ajit degraded the throne in the eyes of their haughty and always overreaching vassals, who, in the civil strife which followed, were alternately in favour or disgrace, as they adhered to or opposed the successful claimant for power. To this foul blot, every evil which has since overtaken this high-minded race may be traced, as well as the extirpation of that principle of devoted obedience which, in the anterior portion of these annals, has been so signally recorded. To this hour it has perpetuated dissensions between the crown and the oligarchy, leading to deposal and violence to the princes, or sequestration, banishment, and death to the nobles. To break the bonds of this tutelage, Ram Singh's intemperance lost him the crown, which sat uneasy on the head of his successor, who had no other mode of escape but by the severity which has been related. But though it freed him for a time, the words of the dying chief of Pokaran continued to ring in his ears;

[1] See Vol. I. p. 235.

and "the dagger left in the girdle of his son" disturbed the dreams of his rest throughout a long life of vicissitudes, poisoning the source of enjoyment until death itself was a relief.

The nuncupatory testament of the Champawat was transmitted across the desert to his son at Pokaran, and the rapidity of its transmission was only equalled by the alacrity of Sabhala, who at the head of his vassals issued forth to execute the vengeance thus bequeathed. First, he attempted to burn and pillage the mercantile town of Pali; foiled in which, he proceeded to another wealthy city of the fisc [133], Bhilwara on the Luni; but here terminated both his life and his revenge. As he led the escalade, he received two balls, which hurled him back amongst his kinsmen, and his ashes next morning blanched the sandy bed of the Luni.

Suppression of Aristocratic Influence.—For a time the feudal interest was restrained, anarchy was allayed, commerce again flourished, and general prosperity revived: to use the words of the chronicle, "the subject enjoyed tranquillity, and the tiger and the lamb drank from the same fountain." Bijai Singh took the best means to secure the fidelity of his chiefs, by finding them occupation. He carried his arms against the desultory hordes of the desert, the Khosas and Sahariyas, which involved him in contests with the nominal sovereign of Sind, and ended in the conquest of Umarkot, the key to the valley of the Indus, and which is now the most remote possession of Marwar. He also curtailed the territories of Jaisalmer, on his north-west frontier. But more important than all was the addition of the rich province of Godwar, from the Rana of Mewar. This tract, which nearly equals in value the whole fiscal domain of Maru, was wrested from the ancient princes of Mandor, prior to the Rathors, and had been in the possession of the Sesodias for nearly five centuries, when civil dissension made the Rana place it for security under the protection of Raja Bijai Singh; since which it has been lost to Mewar.

Rājput Confederation against the Marāthas. Battle of Tonga A.D. 1787. Battles of Pātan and Merta, 20th June, 10th, 12th September 1790.—Marwar had enjoyed several years of peace, when the rapid strides made by the Mahrattas towards universal rapine, if not conquest, compelled the Rajputs once more to form an union for the defence of their political existence. Partap

Singh, a prince of energy and enterprise, was now on the *gaddi* of Amber. In S. 1843 (A.D. 1787), he sent an ambassador to Bijai Singh, proposing a league against the common foe, and volunteering to lead in person their conjoined forces against them. The battle of Tonga ensued, in which Rathor valour shone forth in all its glory. Despising discipline, they charged through the dense battalions of De Boigne, sabring his artillery-men at their guns, and compelling Sindhia to abandon not only the field, but all his conquests for a time.[1] Bijai Singh, by this victory, redeemed the castle of Ajmer, and declared his tributary alliance null and void. But the genius of Sindhia, and the talents of De Boigne, soon recovered this loss; and in four years the Mahratta marched with a force such as Indian warfare was stranger to, to redeem that day's disgrace. In S. 1847 (A.D. 1791), the murderous [134] battles of Patan and Merta took place, in which Rajput courage was heroically but fruitlessly displayed against European tactics and unlimited resources, and where neither intrigue nor treason was wanting. The result was the imposition of a contribution of sixty lakhs of rupees, or £600,000; and as so much could not be drained from the country, goods and chattels were everywhere distrained, and hostages given for the balance.

Ajmer lost to Mārwār.—Ajmer, which had revolted on the short-lived triumph of Tonga, was once more surrendered, and lost for ever to Marwar. When invested by De Boigne, the faithful governor, Damraj, placed in the dilemma of a disgraceful surrender, or disobedience to his prince's summons, swallowed diamond-powder.[2] "Tell the raja," said this faithful servant, "thus only could I testify my obedience; and over my dead body alone could a Southron enter Ajmer."[3]

[1] See p. 875 for the details of this battle.

[2] [It is commonly believed in India that diamond dust is poisonous (Chevers, *Manual of Medical Jurisprudence in India*, 289 ff.). Powdered glass is used in the same way, as in a recent case at Agra (*The Times*, 19th December 1912; Labanés, *Les Curiosities de la Medicine*, 146 ff.).]

[3] Damraj was not a Rajput, but of the Singhi tribe, one of the civil officers; though it is a curious and little-known fact, that almost all the mercantile tribes of Western India are of Rajput origin, and sank the name and profession of arms when they became proselytes to Jainism, in the reign of Raja Bhim Pramar. The Chitor inscription (see p. 919 and note 7, p. 921) records the name of this prince. He was ancestor of Raja

Influence of Court Morals.—The paramount influence which the morals and manners of a court exert upon a nation, is everywhere admitted. In constitutional governments, there is a barrier even to court influence and corruption, in the vast portion of wealth and worth which cannot be engulphed in their vortex. But in these petty sovereignties no such check is found, and the tone of virtue and action is given from the throne. The laws of semi-barbarous nations, which admit of licentious concubinage, have ever been peculiar to orientals, from the days of the wise king of the Jews to those of Bijai Singh of Marwar; and their political consequence has been the same, the sacrifice of the rights of lawful inheritance to the heirs of illicit affection. The last years of the king of Maru were engrossed by sentimental folly with a young beauty of the Oswal tribe, on whom he lavished all the honours due only to his legitimate queens. Scandal affirms that she frequently returned his passion in a manner little becoming royal dignity, driving him from her presence with the basest of missiles—her shoes. As the effects of this unworthy attachment completed the anarchy of Marwar, and as its consequences on deviating from the established rules of succession have entailed a perpetuity of crime and civil war, under which this unfortunate State yet writhes, we shall be minute, even to dullness, in the elucidation [135] of this portion of their annals, to enable those who have now to arbitrate these differences to bring back a current of uncontaminated blood to sway the destinies of this still noble race.

Raja Ajit had fourteen sons:

- Abhai Singh.
  - Ram Singh.
- Bakht Singh.
  - Bijai Singh.
    - Fateh Singh, died of small-pox in infancy.
    - Zalim Singh, by a princess of Mewar, the rightful heir of Bijai Singh.
    - Sawant Singh.
      - Sur Singh.
    - Sher Singh.
      - adopted Man Singh.
    - Bhum Singh.
      - Bhim Singh.
        - Dhonkal Singh (Pretender).
    - Guman Singh.
      - Man Singh.
    - Sardar Singh, killed by Bhim.
- Anand Singh, adopted into the Idar house.
- Rasa, adopted into Jhabua (in Malwa).
- Devi Singh, adopted into Pokaran.

Man, whose date S. 770 (A.D. 714) allows us to place this grand conversion prior to A.D. 650. [The Singhis were originally Brāhmans converted to Jainism (*Census Report, Mārwār*, 1891, ii. 116).]

Influence of his Concubine on Bijai Singh.—So infatuated was Bijai Singh with the Pasbani [1] concubine, that on losing the only pledge of their amours, he 'put into her lap' (adopted) his own legitimate grandchild, Man Singh. To legalize this adoption, the chieftains were ordained to present their *nazars* and congratulations to the declared heir of Marwar; but the haughty noblesse refused 'to acknowledge the son of a slave' as their lord, and the Raja was compelled to a fresh adoption to ensure such token of sanction. Content at having by this method succeeded in her wishes, the Pasbani sent off young Man to the castle of Jalor; but fearing lest the experience of Sher Singh, his adopted father, might prove a hindrance to her control, he was recalled, and her own creatures left to guide the future sovereign of Marwar. The dotage of Bijai Singh, and the insolence of his concubine, produced fresh discord, and the clans assembled at Malkosni [2] to concert his deposal.

Rebellion of the Clansmen against Bijai Singh.—Recollecting the success of his former measures to recall them to their duty, Bijai Singh proceeded to their camp; but while he was negotiating, and as he supposed successfully, the confederates wrote to the chieftain of Ras, whose tour of duty was in the castle, to descend with Bhim Singh. The chief acquainted the Pasbani that her presence was required at the camp by the Raja, and that a guard of honour was ready to attend her. She was thrown off her guard, and at the moment she entered her litter, a blow from an unseen hand ended her existence. Her effects were instantly confiscated, and the chief of Ras descended with Bhim, whose tents were pitched at the Nagor barrier of the city. If, instead of encamping there, they had proceeded to the camp of the confederates, his arrival and the dethronement of Bijai Singh would have been simultaneous: but the Raja received the intelligence as soon as the chiefs. Hastening back, he obtained the person of the young aspirant, to whom, to reconcile him to his disappointment, he gave in appanage the districts of Sojat and Siwana, and sent him off to the latter stronghold; while to restrain the resent-

[1] [Pāsbāni, meaning 'guarding, protecting,' is a synonym for Gola, the hereditary slave class, illegitimate offspring by Rājputs of women attendants in the Zanāna; they are also known as Dārogha, Khawāss, or Chela (*Census Report, Mārwār*, 1891, ii. 181).]

[2] [In the Bhīlāra Hakūmat, in the centre of Jodhpur State.]

ment of his eldest son, Zalim Singh, whose birthright he had so unworthily sacrificed, he enfeoffed him with the rich district of Godwar, giving him private orders to attack his brother Bhim, who, though apprised of the design in time to make head against his uncle, was yet defeated and compelled to fly. He found refuge at Pokaran, whence he went to Jaisalmer.

Death of Rāja Bijai Singh.—In the midst of this conflict, his dominions curtailed, his chiefs in rebellion, his sons and grandsons mutually opposed to each other, and the only object which attached him to life thus violently torn from him, Bijai Singh died, in the month Asarh S. 1850, after a reign of thirty-one years [136].

CHAPTER 14

Rāja Bhīm Singh, A.D. 1793-1803.—The intelligence of Bijai Singh's death was conveyed by express to his grandson Bhim, at Jaisalmer. In "twenty-two hours" he was at Jodhpur, and ascending directly to the citadel, seated himself upon the *gaddi*, while his rival, Zalim Singh, the rightful heir, little expecting this celerity, was encamped at the Merta gate, awaiting the "lucky hour" to take possession. That hour never arrived; and the first intelligence of Bhim being on "the cushion of Jodha," was conveyed to the inhabitants by the nakkaras of his rival on his retreat from the city, who was pursued to Bhilara, attacked, defeated, and forced to seek shelter at Udaipur, where, with an ample domain from the Rana, he passed the rest of his days in literary pursuits. He died in the prime of life: attempting to open a vein with his own hand, he cut an artery and bled to death. He was a man of great personal and mental qualifications; a gallant soldier, and no mean poet.[1] [137]

Rāja Bhīm disposes of his Rivals.—Thus far successful, Raja Bhim determined to dismiss "compunctious visitings," and be a king *de facto* if not *de jure*. Death had carried off three of his uncles, as well as his father, previous to this event; but there

[1] My own venerable tutor, Yati Gyanchandra, who was with me for ten years, said he owed all his knowledge, especially his skill in reciting poetry (in which he surpassed all the bards at Udaipur), to Zalim Singh. [He died at Kāchbali in the British District of Merwāra in 1799 (Erskine iii. A. 70).]

were still two others, Sher Singh, his adopted father, and Sardar Singh, who stood in his way: the last was put to death; the former had his eyes put out; and, soon after, the unfortunate prince released himself from life by dashing out his brains. Sur Singh, the favourite of all Bijai Singh's descendants, remained. His superior claims were fatal to him and his life fell a sacrifice with the others.

A single claimant alone remained of all the blood royal of Maru to disturb the repose of Bhim. This was young Man, the adopted son of the concubine, placed beyond his reach within the walls of Jalor. Could Bhim's dagger have reached him, he would have stood alone, the last surviving scion of the parricide,

> With none to bless him,
> None whom he could bless:

an instrument, in the hand of divine power, to rid the land of an accursed stock. Then the issue of Abhai Singh would have utterly perished, and their ashes might have been given to the winds, and no memorial of them left. Idar must then have supplied an heir,[1] and the doubtful pretensions of Dhonkal,[2] the

[1] [138] Amongst the numerous autograph correspondence of the princes of Rajputana with the princes of Mewar, of which I had the free use, I selected one letter of S. 1784, A.D. 1728, written conjointly by Jai Singh of Amber and Abhai Singh of Jodhpur, regarding Idar, and which is so curious, that I give a verbatim translation in the Appendix (No. I.). [See end of Vol. III.] I little thought at the time how completely it would prove Abhai Singh's determination to cut off all but his own parricidal issue from the succession. An inspection of the genealogy (p. 1075) will show that Anand Singh, of Idar, who was not to be allowed "to escape alive," was his younger brother, adopted into that house.

[2] Dhonkal Singh, the posthumous issue of Bhim, the last of the parricidal line, whether real or supposititious, must be set aside, and the pure current of Rathor blood, derived from Siahji, Jodha, Jaswant, and Ajit, be brought from Idar, and installed on "the gaddi of Jodha." This course of proceeding would meet universal approbation, with the exception of some selfish miscreants about the person of this pretended son of Bhim, or the chieftain of Pokaran, in furtherance of his and his grandfather's yet unavenged feud. A sketch of the events, drawn from their own chronicles, and accompanied by reflections, exposing the miseries springing from an act of turpitude, would come home to all, and they would shower blessings on the power which, while it fulfilled the duties of protector, destroyed the germ of internal dissension, and gave them a prince of their own pure blood, whom all parties could honour and obey. If a doubt remained of the probable

posthumous and reputed son of the wholesale assassin Bhim, to sit upon the *gaddi* of Ajit, would never have been brought forward to excite another murderous contest amongst the sons of Jodha.

Escape of Mān Singh.—Having sacrificed all those within his reach who stood between him and the [139] throne, Bhim tried to secure the last sole claimant in Jalor. But the siege of such a stronghold with his feudal levies, or loose mercenary bands, was a tedious operation, and soon became an imperfect blockade, through which young Man not unfrequently broke, and by signal formed a junction with his adherents, and plundered the fiscal lands for support. One of these excursions, however, an attempt to plunder Pali, had nearly proved fatal to him; they were attacked on their return, and young Man, whose secluded education had confined him more to mental than to personal accomplishments, was unhorsed, and would have been captured, but for the prowess of the chief of Ahor, who took him up behind him and bore him off in safety. Nothing but the turbulence of the chiefs who supported Raja Bhim saved young Man's life. A disputed succession has always produced an odious faction; and Bhim, who was not disposed to bend to this oligarchy, appears to have had all the imprudence of the dethroned RamSingh: he threatened those entrusted with the siege to give them "oxen to ride instead of horses." The chiefs fired at the insult, and retired to Ghanerao, the principal fief in Godwar; but, disgusted with both parties, instead of obeying the invitation of young Man, they abandoned their country altogether, and sought an asylum in the neighbouring States. Many fiefs were sequestrated, and Nimaj, the chief seat of the Udawats, was attacked, and after a twelve months' defence, taken; its battlements were ignominiously destroyed, and the victors, chiefly foreign mercenaries, reinforced the blockade of Jalor.

Siege of Jālor. Death of Rāja Bhīm Singh.—With the exile of his partisans and daily diminishing resources, when the lower town was taken, there appeared no hope for young Man. A small supply of millet-flour was all the provision left to his half-famished garrison, whose surrender was now calculated upon,

unanimity of such policy, let it be previously submitted to a *panchayat*, composed of the princes of the land, namely, of Mewar, Amber, Kotah, Bundi, Jaisalmer, etc., leaving out whichever may be influenced by marriage connexions with Dhonkal Singh.

when an invitation came from the hostile commander for Man to repair to his camp, and adding "he was now the master; it was his duty to serve." On that day (the 2nd Kartik S. 1860, Dec. 1804), after eleven years of defence, his means exhausted, his friends banished, and death from starvation or the sword inevitable, intelligence came of Raja Bhim's demise! This event, as unlooked-for as it was welcome, could scarcely at first be credited; and the tender of the homage of the commander to Man as his sovereign, though accompanied by a letter from the prime minister Induraj, was disregarded till the Guru Deonath returned from the camp with confirmation of the happy news, that "not a moustache [140] was to be seen in the camp."[1] Thither the prince repaired, and was hailed as the head of the Rathors.

It is said that the successor of the Guru Atmaram, "who carried all the troubles of Bijai Singh with him to heaven," had predicted of young Man Singh, when at the very zero of adversity, that "his fortunes would ascend." What were the means whereby the ghostly comforter of Raja Bhim influenced his political barometer, we know not; but prophetic Gurus, bards, astrologers, physicians, and all the Vaidyas or 'cunning-men,'[2] who beset the persons of princes, prove dangerous companions when, in addition to the office of compounders of drugs and expounders of dreams, they are invested with the power of realizing their own prognostications.

Rāja Mān Singh, A.D. 1803-43.—On the 5th of Margsir, 1860 (A.D. 1804), Raja Man, released from his perils, succeeded to the honours and the feuds of Bijai Singh. He had occupied the 'cushion of Maru' but a very short period, when the Pokaran chief "took offence," and put himself in hostility to his sovereign. The name of this proud vassal, the first in power though only of secondary rank amongst the Champawats, was Sawai Singh, with whom now remained "the sheath of the dagger which held the fortunes of Maru." If the fulfilment of vengeance be a virtue, Sawai was the most virtuous son on earth. The dagger of Devi Singh, bequeathed to Sabhala, was no imaginary weapon in the

[1] This mark of mourning is common to all India. Where this evidence of manhood is not yet visible, the hair is cut off; often both.

[2] *Vaidya*, or 'learned man'; the term *veda* is also used to denote cunning, magic, or knowledge of whatever kind.

hands of his grandson Sawai, who held it suspended over the head of Raja Man from his enthronement to his death-hour. Soon after Raja Man's accession, Sawai retired with his partisans to Chopasni, a spot about five miles from the capital, where the conspiracy was prepared. He told the chiefs that the wife of Raja Bhim was pregnant, and prevailed on them to sign a declaration, that if a son was born, he should be installed on the *gaddi* of Jodha. They returned in a body to the capital, took the pregnant queen from the castle, and placed her in a palace in the city, under their own protection. Moreover, they held a council, at which the Raja was present, who agreed to recognise the infant, if a male, as the heir-apparent of Maru, and to enfeoff him in the appanage of Nagor and Siwana; and that if a female, she should be betrothed to a prince of Dhundhar [141].

Dangers from Posthumous Births.—Posthumous births are never-failing germs of discord in these States; and the issue is inevitably branded by one party with the title of 'supposititious.' It is likewise a common saying, almost amounting to a proverb, that a male child is the uniform result of such a position. In due course, a male infant was born; but, alarmed for its safety, the mother concealed both its birth and sex, and placing it in a basket, conveyed it by a faithful servant from the city, whence it soon reached Sawai Singh at Pokaran. He bestowed upon it the inauspicious name of Dhonkal, that is, one born to tumult and strife. It is said that during two years he kept the birth a profound secret, and it is even added, that it might have remained so, had Raja Man forgot the history of the past, and dispensed even-handed justice. Wanting, however, the magnanimity of the Fourth Henry of France, who scorned "to revenge the wrongs of the prince of Navarre," he reserved his favours and confidence for those who supported him in Jalor, whilst he evinced his dislike to others who, in obedience to their sovereign, served against him. Of these adherents, only two chiefs of note were of his kin and clan; the others were Bhatti Rajputs, and a body of those religious militants called Bishanswamis, under their Mahant, or leader, Kaimdas.[1]

[1] They follow the doctrines of Vishnu (Bishan). They are termed Gosains, as well as the more numerous class of church militants, devoted to Siva. Both are *célibataires*, as Gosain imports, from mastery (*sain*) over the sense (*go*). They occasionally come in contact, when their sectarian principles

Sawāi Singh supports Dhonkal Singh.—At the expiration of two years, Sawai communicated the event to the chiefs of his party, who called upon Raja Man to redeem his promise and issue the grant for Nagor and Siwana. He promised compliance if, upon investigation, the infant proved to be the legitimate offspring of his predecessor. Personal fear overcame maternal affection, and the queen, who remained at Jodhpur, disclaimed the child. Her reply being communicated to the chiefs, it was for a time conclusive, and the subject ceased to interest them, the more especially as her concealed accouchement had never been properly accounted for.

Though Sawai, with his party, apparently acquiesced, his determination was taken ; but instead of an immediate appeal to arms, he adopted a deeper scheme of policy, the effects of which he could not have contemplated, and which involved his own destruction, and with it the independence of his country, which was transferred to [142] strangers, their very antipodes in manners, religion, and every moral quality. His first act was to procure a more powerful protection than Pokaran afforded ; and under the guarantee of Chhattar Singh Bhatti, he was sent to the saran (sanctuary) of Abhai Singh of Khetri.[1] Having so far succeeded, he contrived an underplot, in which his genius for intrigue appears not below his reputation as a soldier.

Krishna Kunwāri.—The late prince Bhim had made overtures to the Rana of Mewar for the hand of his daughter, but he died before the preliminaries were adjusted. This simple circumstance was deemed sufficient by the Champawat for the groundwork of his plot. He contrived to induce the voluptuous Jagat Singh, the prince of Jaipur, to put himself in the place of Raja

---

end in furious combats. At the celebrated place of pilgrimage, Haridwar (Hardwar), on the Ganges, we are obliged to have soldiers to keep the peace, since a battle occurred, in which they fought almost to extirpation, about twenty years ago. They are the Templars of Rajasthan. [Gosāīn, Skt. *gosvāmin*, 'master of cows : one who is master of his organs of sense.' The Bishan or Vishnuswāmis are a group of Bairāgi ascetics, who are said to have come to Mārwār about A.D. 1779, in the reign of Bijai Singh. Some of them are now employed as State sepoys (*Census Report, Mārwār*, 1891, ii. 86). In 1760 the rival mobs of Gosāīns and Bairāgis fought a battle, in which 1800 are said to have perished (*IGI*, xiii. 53).]

[1] One of the principal chiefs of the Shaikhawat confederation. [Khetri is about 80 miles N. of Jaipur city (*IGI*, xv. 276).]

Bhim, and to propose for the fair hand of Krishna. This being accomplished, and nuptial presents, under a guard of four thousand men, being dispatched to Udaipur, Sawai intimated to Raja Man that he would be eternally disgraced if he allowed the prince of Amber to carry off "the betrothed"; that "it was to the throne of Maru, not its occupant, she was promised." The bait was greedily swallowed, and the summons for the Kher (or levy *en masse*) of the Rathors was immediately proclaimed. Man instantly assembled three thousand horse, and joining to them the mercenary bands of Hira Singh then on the frontier of Mewar, he intercepted the nuptial gifts of Amber. Indignant at this outrage, Jagat Singh took to arms, and the muster-book was declared open to all who would serve in the war which was formally declared against Maru.

Attack by Rāja Jagat Singh of Jaipur on Mārwār. Treachery of Jaswant Rāo Holkar.—Having thus opened the drama, Sawai threw off the mask, and repaired to Khetri, whence he conveyed the pretender, Dhonkal, to the court of Jagat Singh at Jaipur. Here his legitimacy was established by being admitted 'to eat from the same platter' with its prince; and his claims, as the heir of Marwar, were publicly acknowledged and advocated, by his 'placing him in the lap of his aunt,'[1] one of the wives of the deceased Raja Bhim. His cause thus espoused, and being declared the nephew of Amber, the nobles of Marwar, who deemed the claims of the pretender superior to those of Raja Man, speedily collected around his standard. Amongst these was the prince of Bikaner, whose example (he being the most powerful of the independents of this house) at once sanctioned the justice of Dhonkal's cause, and left that of Raja Man almost without support. Nevertheless, with the hereditary [143] valour of his race, he advanced to the frontiers to meet his foes, whose numbers, led by the Jaipur prince and the pretender, exceeded one hundred thousand men! This contest, the ostensible object of which was the princess of Mewar, like the crusades of ancient chivalry, brought allies from the most remote parts of India. Even the cautious Mahratta felt an unusual impulse in this rivalry, beyond the stimulants of pay and plunder which ordinarily rouse him, and corps after corps left their hordes to support either cause.

[1] [*Godlenā*, 'to take on the lap,' the technical form of adoption, or of recognition of legitimacy.]

The weightier purse of Jaipur was the best argument for the justice of his cause and that of the pretender; while Raja Man had only the gratitude of Holkar to reckon upon for aid, to whose wife and family he had given sanctuary when pursued by Lord Lake to the Attock. But here Sawai again foiled him; and the Mahratta, then only eighteen miles from Man, and who had promised to join him next day, made a sudden movement to the south. A bribe of £100,000, in bills upon Kotah, to be paid on Holkar's reaching that city, effected this desertion; which being secured, Jagat Singh and the pretender advanced to overwhelm their antagonist, who was posted at Gingoli. As the armies approached each other, Raja Man's chiefs rode up to salute him, preparatory, as he thought, to head their clans for the combat; but it was their farewell obeisance. The cannonade opened, they rallied under the standard of the pretender, and on Sawai advancing on the right of the allied line, so entire was the defection, that even the Mertia clan, whose virtue and boast it is "to adhere to the throne, whoever is the occupant," deserted, with the Champawats, Jethawats, and minor chiefs. Four chieftains alone abided the evil hour of Raja Man, namely, Kuchaman, Ahor, Jalor, and Nimaj; and with their quotas alone, and the auxiliary bands of Bundi, he would have rushed into the battle. Hindered from this, he attempted his own life: but the design was frustrated by Sheonath of Kuchaman, who dismounted him from his elephant, and advised his trusting to the fleetness of his steed, while they covered his flight. The Raja remarked, he was the first of his race who ever disgraced the name of Rathor by showing his back to a Kachhwaha. The position he had taken that morning was favourable to retreat, being a mile in advance of the pass of Parbatsar:[1] this was speedily gained, and nobly defended by the battalions of Bundi, and those of Hindal Khan, in the pay of Raja Man, which retarded the pursuit, headed by the Rao of Uniara. Raja Man reached Merta in safety; but deeming it incapable of long [144] resistance, he continued his flight by Pipar to the capital, which he reached with a slender retinue, including the four chiefs, who still shared his fortunes. The camp of Raja Man was pillaged. Eighteen guns were taken by Bala Rao Inglia, one of Sindhia's commanders, and the lighter effects, the tents, elephants, and baggage, were captured by

[1] [About 110 miles N.E. of Jodhpur city, S.W. of the Sāmbhar Lake.]

Amir Khan ; while Parbatsar, and the villages in the neighbourhood, were plundered.

Rāja Mān Singh defends Jodhpur.—Thus far, the scheme of Sawai and the pretender advanced with rapid success. When the allied army reached Merta, the prince of Jaipur, whose object was the princess of Mewar, proposed to Sawai to follow up their good fortune, while he repaired to Udaipur, and solemnized the nuptials. But even in the midst of his revenge, Sawai could distinguish " between the cause of Man Singh and the *gaddi* of Marwar " ; and to promote the success of Jaipur, though he had originated the scheme to serve his own views, was no part of his plan. He was only helped out of this dilemma by another, which he could not anticipate. Not dreaming that Raja Man would hold out in the capital, which had no means of defence, but supposing he would fly to Jalor, and leave Jodhpur to its fate and to the pretender, Sawai, desirous to avoid the further advance of the allies into the country, halted the army for three days at Merta. His foresight was correct: the Raja had reached Bisalpur in full flight to Jalor, when, at the suggestion of Gyanmall Singhi, a civil officer in his train, he changed his intention. "There," said the Singhi, "lies Jodhpur only nine coss to the right, while Jalor is sixteen further ; it is as easy to gain the one as the other, and if you cannot hold out in the capital, what chance have you elsewhere ? while you defend your throne your cause is not lost." Raja Man followed the advice, reached Jodhpur in a few hours, and prepared for his defence. This unexpected change, and the halt of the allied army, which permitted the dispersed bands to gain the capital, defeated the schemes of Sawai.

The Siege of Jodhpur.—With a body of three thousand men, selected from Hindal Khan's brigade, the corps of Bishanswamis, under Kaimdas, and one thousand foreign Rajputs, consisting of Chauhans, Bhattis, and Indhas (the ancient lords of Mandor), Raja Man formed a garrison of five thousand men, on whom he could depend. So ample did he deem this number, that he dispatched strong garrisons from Hindal's brigade, with some Deora Rajputs, to garrison Jalor, and preserve the distant castle of Umarkot from surprise by the Sindis. Having thus provided against the storm [145] he fearlessly awaited the result. But so alienated was his mind from his kindred, that he would not even admit to the honour of defending his throne the four faithful chieftains who, in the general desertion, had abided by his fortunes. To all their entreaties to be received into the castle, that "they might defend the *kunguras* (battlements) of Jodha," he replied, they might defend the city if they pleased; and disgusted with such a return for their fidelity, they increased the train of his opponents, who soon encompassed Jodhpur.

The town, little capable of defence, was taken and given up to unlicensed plunder; and with the exception of Phalodi, which was gallantly defended for three months, and given to Bikaner as the reward of its alliance, the *an* of the pretender was proclaimed throughout Marwar, and his allies only awaited the fall of the capital, which appeared inevitable, to proclaim him king. But a circumstance occurred, which, awakening the patriotism of the Rathors, thwarted these fair prospects, relieved Raja Man from his peril, and involved his adversaries in the net of destruction which they had woven for him.

The siege had lasted five months without any diminution of the ardour of the defenders; and although the defences of the north-east angle were destroyed, the besiegers, having a perpendicular rock of eighty feet to ascend before they could get to the breach, were not nearer their object, and, in fact, without shells, the castle of Jodha would laugh a siege to scorn. The numerous and motley force under the banners of Jaipur and the pretender, became clamorous for pay; the forage was exhausted, and the partisan horse were obliged to bivouac in the distant districts to the south. Availing himself of their separation from the main body, Amir Khan, an apt pupil of the Mahratta school, began to raise contributions on the fiscal lands, and Pali, Pipar, Bhilara, with many others, were compelled to accede to his demands. The estates of the nobles who espoused the cause of the pretender, fared no better, and they complained to the Xerxes of this host of the conduct of this unprincipled commander.

Amir Khān supports Mān Singh. Defeat of the Jaipur Army A.D. 1806.—The protracted defence having emptied the treasury of Amber, the arch-intriguer of Pokaran was called upon to contribute towards satisfying the clamour of the troops. Having exhausted the means of his own party, he applied to the four chieftains who had been induced to join the cause of the pretender by the suspicions of Raja Man, to advance a sum of money.

This appeal proved a test of [146] their zeal. They abandoned the pretender, and proceeded direct to the camp of Amir Khan. It required no powerful rhetoric to detach him from the cause and prevail upon him to advocate that of Raja Man ; nor could they have given him better counsel towards this end, than the proposal to carry the war into the enemy's country : to attack and plunder Jaipur, now left unguarded. At this critical moment, the Jaipur prince, in consequence of the representation of the Marwar chiefs, had directed his commander-in-chief, Sheolal, to chastise Amir Khan for his lawless conduct. Sheolal put a stop to their deliberations, attacked and drove them across the Luni, surprised them at Govindgarh, again in a night attack at Harsuri, and pursued the Khan to Phaggi,[1] at the very frontier of Jaipur. Astonished at his own success, and little aware that the chase was in the direction projected by his enemy, Sheolal deemed he had accomplished his orders in driving him out of Marwar ; halted, and leaving his camp, repaired to Jaipur to partake of its festivities. The Khan, who with his allies had reached Pipla near Tonk, no sooner heard of this, than he called to his aid the heavy brigades of Muhammad Shah Khan and Raja Bahadur (then besieging Isarda[2]), and availed himself of the imprudent absence of his foe to gain over the Haidarabad Rasala, a legion well known in the predatory wars of that period. Having effected this object, he assailed the Jaipur force, which, notwithstanding this defection and the absence of its commander, fought with great valour, the battalions of Hira Singh being nearly cut to pieces. The action ended in the entire defeat of the Jaipurians, and the capture of their camp, guns, and equipage. Prompted by the Rathor chieftains, whose valour led to this result, Amir Khan rapidly followed up his success, and Jaipur was dismayed by the presence of the victor at her gates. The generalship of the Khan was the salvation of Raja Man ; it dissolved the confederacy, and fixed the doom of Sawai, its projector.

The Confederacy against Jodhpur dissolved.—The tempest had been some time gathering ; the Rajas of Bikaner and Shahpura had already withdrawn from the confederacy and marched home, when, like a clap of thunder, the effeminate Kachhwaha, who had in the outset of this crusade looked to a full harvest both of glory

[1] [About 32 miles S. of Jaipur city.]

[2] [About 60 miles S.S.W. of Jaipur city.]

and of love, learned that his army was annihilated, and his capital invested by the Khan and a handful of Rathors. Duped by the representations of Sawai, Rae Chand, Diwan or prime minister of Jaipur, concealed for some days these disasters from his sovereign, who received the intelligence by a special messenger sent by the queen-mother. Enraged, perplexed, and alarmed [147] for his personal safety, he broke up the siege, and sending on in advance the spoils of Jodhpur (including forty pieces of cannon), with his own chieftains, he sent for the Mahratta leaders,[1] and offered them £120,000 to escort him in safety to his capital; nay, he secretly bribed, with a bond of £90,000 more, the author of his disgrace, Amir Khan, not to intercept his retreat, which was signally ignominious, burning his tents and equipage at every stage, and at length with his own hand destroying his favourite elephant, which "wanted speed for the rapidity of his flight."

Jodhpur Booty recovered.—But the indignities he had to suffer were not over. The chieftains whose sagacity and valour had thus diverted the storm from Raja Man, determined that no trophies of Rathor disgrace should enter Jaipur, united their clans about twenty miles east of Merta, on the line of retreat, appointing Induraj Singhi their leader. This person, who had held the office of Diwan under two predecessors of Raja Man, was driven to a temporary defection from the same suspicions which made the chiefs join the pretender. But they resolved to wash away the stain of this brief alienation from Raja Man with the blood of his enemies, and to present as a token of returning fidelity the recaptured trophies. The encounter took place on the joint frontier. It was short, but furious; and the Kachhwahas, who could not withstand the Rathors, were defeated and dispersed, and the spoils of the spoiler, including the forty cannon, were safely lodged in Kuchaman. Flushed with success, the victors addressed the Raja of Kishangarh, who, though a Rathor,

[1] Bapu Sindhia, Bala Rao Inglia, with the brigade of Jean Baptiste, all Sindhia's dependents. This was early in 1806. The author was then in Sindhia's camp and saw these troops marched off; and in 1807, in a geographical tour, he penetrated to Jaipur, and witnessed the wrecks of the Jaipur army. The sands round the capital were white with the bones of horses, and the ashes of their riders, who had died in the vain expectation of getting their arrears of pay.

had kept aloof, to advance funds to secure the continuanee of Amir Khan's aid. Two lakhs of rupees (£20,000) effected this object ; and the Khan, pledging himself to continue his support to Raja Man, repaired to Jodhpur. The four chiefs who had thus signalized themselves, preceded him, and were received with open arms : their offences were forgiven, and their estates restored, while Induraj was appointed Bakhshi or commander of the forces [148].

CHAPTER 15

Amīr Khān received at Jodhpur.—Amir Khan was received by Raja Man with distinguished honours ; a palace in the castle was assigned as his residence ; valuable gifts were presented to him and great rewards held in perspective, if, through his agency, the rebellion should be completely subdued. He swore to extirpate Sawai's faction, and in token of identity of views with Raja Man, he was admitted to the honour of that last proof of devotion to his cause, "an interchange of turbans," with an advance of three lakhs, or £30,000, for the immediate payment of his bonds.

On the raising of the siege of Jodhpur, Sawai conducted the pretender to the appanage of the heirs of Marwar, the city of Nagor. There they were deliberating as to their future plans, when a message was brought from Amir Khan from [149] Mundiawar,[1] ten miles distant, begging permission to perform his devotions at the shrine of the Muslim saint, Pir Tarkin, the sole relic of the Islamite, which Bakhta Singh had spared. His request being complied with, he with a slight cavalcade left his camp, and having gone through the mummeries of devotion, paid his respects to Sawai. When about to take leave, he threw out hints of Raja Man's ungrateful return for his services, and that his legions might have been better employed. Sawai greedily caught at the bait ; he desired the Khan to name his terms, and offered £200,000 on the day that Dhonkal should possess the *gaddi* of Jodhpur. The Khan accepted the conditions and ratified the engagement on the Koran, and to add to the solemnity

[1] [Mūndwa.]

of the pledge, he exchanged turbans with Sawai. This being done, he was introduced to the pretender, rèceived the usual gifts, pledged his life in his cause, took leave, and returned to his camp, whither he invited the prince and his chiefs on the following day to accept of an entertainment.

Amīr Khān massacres the Chiefs.—On the morning of the 19th of Chait, S. 1864 (A.D. 1808), Sawai, attended by the chief adherents of the pretender and about five hundred followers, repaired to the camp of the Khan, who had made every preparation for the more effectual perpetration of the bloody and perfidious deed he meditated. A spacious tent was pitched in the centre of his camp for the reception of his guests, and cannon were loaded with grape ready to be turned against them. The visitors were received with the most distinguished courtesy; turbans were again exchanged; the dancing-girls were introduced, and nothing but festivity was apparent. The Khan arose, and making an excuse to his guests for a momentary absence, retired. The dancing continued, when at the word '*dhaga*,' pronounced by the musicians, down sunk the tent upon the unsuspicious Rajputs, who fell an easy prey to the ferocious Pathans. Forty-two chieftains were thus butchered in the very sanctuary of hospitality, and the heads of the most distinguished were sent to Raja Man. Their adherents, taken by surprise, were slaughtered by the soldiery, or by cannon charged with grape, as they fled. The pretender escaped from Nagor, which was plundered by the Khan, when not only all the property of the party, but the immense stores left by Bakhta Singh, including three hundred pieces of cannon, were taken, and sent to Sambhar and other strongholds held by the Khan. Having thus fulfilled his instructions, he repaired to Jodhpur, and received ten lakhs or £100,000, and [150] two large towns, Mundiawar and Kuchilawas, of thirty thousand rupees annual rent, besides one hundred rupees daily for table-allowance, as the reward of his signal infamy.

Thus, by the murder of Sawai and his powerful partisans, the confederacy against Raja Man was extinguished; but though the Raja had thus, miraculously as it were, defeated the gigantic schemes formed against him, the mode by which it was effected entailed upon him and upon his country unexampled miseries. The destruction of the party of the pretender was followed by retaliation on the various members of the league. The Jaipur territory was laid waste by the troops of Amir Khan, and an expedition was planned against Bikaner. An army consisting of twelve thousand of Raja Man's feudal levies, under the command of Induraj, with a brigade of Amir Khan, and that of Hindal Khan with thirty-five guns, marched against the chief of the independent Rathors. The Bikaner Raja formed an army little inferior in numbers, and gave his suzerain the meeting at Bapri; but after a partial encounter, in which the former lost two hundred men, he fell back upon his capital, pursued by the victors, who halted at Gajner.[1] Here terms were offered; two lakhs as the expenses of the war, and the surrender of the bone of contention, the town of Phalodi, which had been assigned to Bikaner as the price of joining the confederacy.

Amīr Khān rules Mārwār.—The Khan was now the arbiter of Marwar. He stationed Ghafur Khan with a garrison in Nagor, and partitioned the lands of Merta amongst his followers. He likewise placed his garrison in the castle of Nawa, which gave him the command of the salt-lakes of Nawa and Sambhar. Induraj and the high-priest Deonath were the only counsellors of Raja Man, and all the oppressions which the chieftains suffered through this predominant foreign interference, were attributed to their advice. To cut them off the chiefs in their turn applied to Amir Khan, who for seven lakhs (£70,000), readily consented to rid them of their enemies. A plot was laid, in which some of his Pathans, under pretence of quarrelling with Induraj for their arrears, put this minister and the high-priest to death.

Insanity of Mān Singh.—The loss of Deonath appeared to affect the reason of Raja Man. He shut himself up in his apartments, refused to communicate with any one, and soon omitted every duty, whether political or religious, until at length he was recommended to name his only son Chhattar Singh as his successor. To this he acceded [151], and with his own hand made the mark of inauguration on his forehead. But youth and base panders to his pleasure seduced him from his duties, and he died, some say the victim of illicit pursuits, others from a wound given by the hand of one of the chieftains, whose daughter he attempted to seduce.

The premature death of his only son, before he had attained the years of majority, still more alienated the mind of Raja Man

[1] [Nineteen miles S.W. of Bikaner city.

from all State affairs, and his suspicions of treacherous attempts on his person extended even to his wife. He refused all food, except that which was brought by one faithful menial. He neglected his ablutions, allowed his face to be covered with hair, and at length either was, or affected to be insane. He spoke to no one, and listened with the apathy of an idiot to the communications of the ministers, who were compelled to carry on the government. By many it is firmly believed that the part he thus acted was feigned, to escape the snares laid for his life; while others think that it was a melancholy mania, arising from remorse at having consented to the murder of Induraj, which incidentally involved that of the Guru.[1] In short, his alliance with the atrocious Khan exposed him to the suspicion of a participation in his crimes, which the bent of his policy too much favoured. In this condition—the government being managed by an oligarchy headed by Salim Singh (son of Sawai)—did Raja Man remain, until the tide of events carried the arms of Britain even to the desert of Maru.

British Intervention. Restoration of Mān Singh.—When, in 1817, we invited the Rajputs to disunite from the predatory powers, and to join us in establishing order throughout India, the young son of Raja Man, or rather his ministers, sent envoys to Delhi. But ere the treaty was ratified, this dissipated youth was no more. On this event, the Pokaran faction, dreading Raja Man's resumption of the government, made an application to Idar for a son to adopt as their sovereign. But splendid as was the offer, the Raja, who had but one son, rejected it, unless the demand were sustained by the unanimous suffrages of the nobles. Unanimity being unattainable, the faction had no alternative save the restoration of Raja Man; but it was in vain they explained the new position of Marwar, the alliance with the English, which awaited his sanction, and the necessity that he, as the last prop of the royal family, should resume the reins of power. He listened to all with the most apathetic indifference [152]. But although he saw in this new crisis of the political condition of his country, motives for effecting his escape from bondage, his mind was so tutored by bitter experience that he never for an instant betrayed its workings. When at length he allowed himself to comprehend the full nature of the changes which made even the

[1] For the character of this priest, see p. 825.

faction desire his egress from solitude, so far from expressing any joy, he even disapproved of part of the treaty, and especially the article relating to the armed contingent of his vassals to be at the disposal of the protecting power, in which he wisely saw the germ of discord, from the certainty of interference it would lead to.

Treaty with the British.—It was in December 1817 that the treaty [1] was negotiated at Delhi by a Brahman named Byas Bishan Ram, on the part of the regent prince, and in December 1818, an officer of the British government [2] was deputed to report on its actual condition. Notwithstanding the total disorganization of the government, from the combination of causes already described, the court had lost nothing of its splendour or regularity; the honour of all was concerned in preserving the dignity of the *gaddi*, though its incumbent was an object of distrust and even detestation. The ministry at this period was conducted by Akhai Chand (Diwan), and Salim Singh of Pokaran, as the representative of the aristocracy, with the title of Bhanjghar. All the garrisons and offices of trust throughout the country were held by the creatures of a junto, of which these were the heads. There was, however, already the nucleus of an opposition in the brother of the murdered minister, named Fateh Raj, who was entrusted with the care of the city. The instructions of the agent were to offer the aid of the British government towards the settlement of Raja Man's affairs; and at a private interview, three days after the agent's arrival, troops were offered to be placed at his disposal. But the wariness of his character will be seen in the use he made of this offer. He felt that the lever was at hand to crush faction to the dust; and with a Machiavellian caution, he determined that the existence of this engine should suffice; that its power should be felt, but never seen; that he should enjoy all the advantages this influence would give, without risking any of its dangers if called into action. Thus, while he rejected, though with thanks, the essential benefit tendered, qualifying his refusal with a sufficient reason—"reliance on himself to restore his State to order"—he failed not to [153] disseminate the impression amongst his chiefs, which was enough for his purpose, and which besides checked the dictation and interference that uniformly result from such unequal alliances.

[1] See treaty, Appendix No. II. [See end of Vol. III.]

[2] Mr. Wilder, superintendent of the district of Ajmer.

Energetic counsels and rapid decision are unknown to Asiatic governments, whose subjects are ever prone to suspicion whenever unusual activity is visible; and Raja Man had been schooled into circumspection from his infancy. He appeared anxious to bury the past in oblivion, by choosing men of both parties for the inferior duties of the ministry; and the blandness of his manners and his conciliatory address lulled the most suspicious into security. After a short residence, the Agent returned to Ajmer, having in vain tried to convince Raja Man that his affairs were irretrievable without the direct aid of the paramount power, which he persisted in repudiating, assigning as his reason that he felt convinced, from "the measures then in train," he should accomplish the task himself: of these measures conciliation appeared to be the basis,

The Author appointed Envoy to Jodhpur.—At this period [1] an envoy was appointed, with powers direct from the Governor-General to Raja Man, but he was for some months prevented from proceeding to his court, from various causes.[2]

[1] In February 1819, the Author had the political duties of Marwar added to those of the States of Udaipur, Kotah, Bundi, and Sirohi.

[2] One of these was an unpleasant altercation, which took place between the townspeople of the Commercial Mart of Pali and an English gentleman, sent unofficially to feel his way as to the extension of commercial enterprise, carrying specimens of the staple commodities of our trade. This interference with the very fountain-head of their trade alarmed the monopolists of Pali, who, dreading such competition, created or took advantage of an incident to rid themselves of the intruder. The commercial men of these regions almost all profess the Jain religion, whose first rule of faith is the preservation of life, in beast as in man. By them, therefore, the piece-goods, the broad-cloths and metals of the Christian trader, were only less abhorred than his flesh-pots, and the blood of the goats sworn to have been shed by his servants within the bounds of Pali, rose in judgment against their master, of whom a formal complaint was laid before Raja Man. It lost none of its acrimony in coming through the channel of his internuncio at Udaipur, the Brahman, Bishan Ram. Mr. Rutherford rebutted the charge, and an investigation took place at the capital on oath, upon which, as the merchants and the governor of Pali (a nephew of the minister) could not substantiate their charge, the latter was severely reprimanded for his incivility. But whether the story was true or false, it was quite enough for their purpose. The interdict between Mr. Rutherford and the inhabitants of Pali was more effectual than the sanitary cordon of any prince in Christendom. The feeling of resentment against him reached the Agent of government, who was obliged to support what appeared the cause of truth, even according to the deposition made before their own judgment-seat, and he was consequently deemed inimical to the prince and the faction

Demoralization at Jodhpur.—The Agent, who reached Jodhpur early in the month of November, found matters [154] in nearly the same state as on his predecessor's departure in February. The same faction kept the prince and all the officers of government at their disposal. The Raja interfered but little with their measures, except to acquiesce in or confirm them. The mercenary bands of Sindis or Pathans were in miserable plight and clamorous for their pay, not having been accounted with for three years; and they were to be seen begging in the streets of the capital, or hawking bundles of forage on their heads to preserve them from starvation. On the approach of the Agent of the British Government, the forms of accounts were gone through, and they gave in acquittances in full of demands, on condition of receiving 30 per cent of their arrears; but this was only a form, and with his departure (in about three weeks), they despaired even of that.

The name of justice was unknown:—though, in allusion to the religion of the men in power, it was common to hear it said, "You may commit murder and no one will notice it; but woe to him who beats or maims a brute, for dogs are publicly fed while the soldier starves." In short, the sole object of the faction was to keep at a distance all interposition that might lead the prince to emancipate himself from their control. During the Agent's stay of nearly three weeks, he had several private interviews with Raja Man. The knowledge he had of the history of his ancestry and his own situation, and of the causes which had produced it, failed not to beget a corresponding confidence; and these interviews were passed in discussions on the ancient history of the country as well as on his own immediate affairs. The Agent took leave with these words: "I know all the perils through which you have passed; I am aware how you surmounted them.

which then guided his councils. Mr. Rutherford proceeded afterwards to Kotah, to exhibit the same wares; but he was there equally an object of jealousy, though from letters of recommendation from the Agent, it was less strongly manifested. It furnished evidence that such interference would never succeed. It is well his mission did not appear to be sanctioned by the government. What evil might not be effected by permitting unrestricted and incautious intercourse with such people, who can, and do obtain all they require of our produce without the presence of the producers, who, whether within or without the pale of the Company's service, will not, I trust, be prematurely forced on Rajputana, or it will assuredly hasten the day of inevitable separation!

By your resolution, your external enemies are now gone: you have the British Government as a friend; rely upon it with the same fortitude, and, in a very short time, all will be as you could desire."

Raja Man listened eagerly to these observations. His fine features, though trained to bear no testimony to the workings within, relaxed with delight as he rapidly replied, "In one twelvemonths, my affairs will be as friendship could wish." To which the Agent rejoined, "In half the time, Maharaja, if you are determined": though the points to which he had to direct his mind were neither few nor slight, for they involved every branch of government; as

Reforms in Mārwār.—1. Forming an efficient administration [155].

2. Consideration of the finances; the condition of the crown lands; the feudal confiscations, which, often unjust, had caused great discontent.

3. The reorganization and settlement of the foreign troops, on whose service the Raja chiefly depended.

4. An effective police on all the frontiers, to put down the wholesale pillage of the Mers in the south, the Larkhanis in the north, and the desert Sahariyas and Khosas in the west; reformation of the tariff, or scale of duties on commerce, which were so heavy as almost to amount to prohibition; and at the same time to provide for its security.

Scarcely had the Agent left Jodhpur, before the faction, rejoiced at the removal of the only restraint on their narrow-minded views, proceeded in the career of disorder. Whether the object were to raise funds, or to gratify ancient animosities, the course pursued by the Diwan and his junto was the same. Ghanerao, the chief fief of Godwar, was put under sequestration, and only released by a fine of more than a year's revenue. All the minor chiefs of this rich tract suffered in the same manner, besides the indignity of having their lands placed under the control of a brother of the minister. Chandawal[1] was put under sequestration, and only released on a very heavy fine. At length the Diwan had the audacity to put his hand on Awa, the chief fief of Marwar; but the descendant of Champa replied, "My estate is not of to-day, nor thus to be relinquished." Gloom, mistrust, and resent-

[1] [Fifty-five miles S.W. of Jodhpur city.]

ment pervaded the whole feudal body. They saw a contemptible faction sporting with their honour and possessions, from an idea they industriously propagated, that an unseen but mighty power was at hand to support their acts, given out as those of the prince. If the Raja did dictate them, he took especial care it should not be seen; for in the absence of the British Agent, he once more resumed his sequestered habits, and appeared to take no interest in the government further than to promote a coalition between Akhai Chand and Fateh Raj, who was supported by a strong party of the chiefs, and the influence of the favourite queen. But Akhai Chand, who commanded, through his creatures, all the resources of the country, and its strongholds, even to the castle of Jodhpur, rejected these overtures, and feigning that there were plots against his personal safety, left the city; and the better to exclude his adversaries from the prince, resided entirely in the citadel.

Cruelty of Rāja Mān Singh.—Six months had thus fled. The fiat of Akhai Chand was supreme; he alone was [156] visible; his orders alone were obeyed. Raja Man was only heard of as an automaton, moving as the Diwan pleased. But while the latter was thus basking in the full sunshine of prosperity, enriching himself and his dependents, execrated by the nobles and envied by his fellow-citizens, they heard of his fall! Then, the insanity of his master proved to be but a cloak to the intensity of his resentment. But a blind revenge would not have satisfied Raja Man. The victims of his deep dissimulation, now in manacles, were indulged with hopes of life, which, with the application of torture, made them reveal the plunder of prince and subject. A schedule of forty lakhs, or £400,000, was given in by the Diwan and his dependents, and their accounts being settled in this world, they were summarily dismissed to the other, with every mark of ignominy which could add to the horrors of death. Nagji, the Kiladar,[1] and misleader of the late regent prince, with Mulji Dandal, one of the old allodial stock, had each a cup of poison, and their bodies were thrown over the 'Gate of Victory' (Fateh Pol). Jivaraj, a brother of the Dandal, with Biharidas Khichi, and the tailor, had their heads shaved, and their bodies were flung into the cascade beneath. Even the sacred character of "expounder of the Vedas," and that of

[1] [Commander of the fort.]

"revealer of the secrets of heaven," yielded no protection; and Byas Sheodas, with Srikishan, Jotishi, the astrologer, were in the long list of proscriptions. Nagji, commandant of the citadel, and Mulji, had retired on the death of the regent-prince; and with the wealth they had accumulated, while administering to his follies, had erected places of strength. On the restoration of Raja Man, and the general amnesty which prevailed, they returned to their ancient offices in the castle, rose into favour, and forgot they had been traitors. Having obtained their persons, Man secured the ancient jewels of the crown, bestowed on these favourites during the ephemeral sway of his son. Their condemnation was then passed, and they were hurled over the battlements of the rock which it was their duty to guard. With such consummate skill was the plot contrived, that the creatures of the minister, in the most remote districts, were imprisoned simultaneously with himself. Of the many subordinate agents thus confined, many were liberated on the disclosure of their wealth; and by these sequestrations, Raja Man obtained abundant supplies. The enormous sum of a crore, or near one million sterling, was stated; but if they yielded one-half (and this was not unlikely), they gave the means, which he was not slow to use, for the prosecution of what he termed a just punishment, though it [157] better deserves the name of a savage revenge. Had he been satisfied with inflicting the last penalty of the law on the nefarious Akhai Chand, and some of the household officers whose fidelity ought ever to be firm, and with the sequestration of the estates of some two or three of the vassals whose power had become dangerous, or their treason too manifest to be overlooked, he would have commanded the services of the rest, and the admiration of all conversant with these events. But this first success added fuel to his revenge, and he sought out more noble victims to glut it. His circumspection and dissimulation were strengthened, not relaxed, by his success. Several of the chiefs, who were marked out for death, had received, only a few days before, the highest proof of favour in additional lands to their rent-roll, and accident alone prevented a group of the most conspicuous from falling into the snare which had inveigled Akhai Chand. Salim Singh of Pokaran, and his constant associate Surthan of Nimaj, with Anar Singh of Ahor, and the minors of their clans, whose duty daily carried them to the court, as the chief advisers of the prince, formed a part of the administration of the Diwan, and they naturally took alarm upon his confinement. To obviate this, a deputation was sent by the prince to tranquillize them by the assurance that, in the confinement of the minister, whose rapacity and misconduct deserved punishment, the Raja had attained all his ends. Thus, in order to encompass the destruction of the Pokaran chief, he would not have scrupled to involve all the rest. The prince, with his own mouth, desired the confidential servant of Anar Singh, who was his personal friend, to attend with the others. Their distrust saved him. The same night, the mercenary bands, to the number of eight thousand men, with guns, attacked Surthan Singh in his dwelling. With one hundred and eighty of his clan, he defended himself against great guns and small arms, as long as the house was tenable, and then sallied out sword in hand, and, with his brother and eighty of his kin, fell nobly in the midst of his foes. The remainder retreated with their arms to defend Nimaj and their infant chief. This gallant defence, in which many of the townspeople were slain, prevented a repetition of the attempt against the Pokaran chief, who remained on the defensive ; until, seeing an opportunity, he fled to his asylum in the desert, or he would that day have renounced " the sheath of the dagger which held the fortunes of Marwar," and which now contained the accumulated revenge of four generations : of Deo Singh, of Sabhala, of Sawai, and his own. His death would have terminated this branch of Ajit's issue, adopted into the house of [158] Pokaran, in the history of which we have a tolerable picture of the precariousness of existence in Marwar.[1]

What better commentary can be made on Raja Man's character, than the few recorded words addressed to Fateh Raj,

[1] In a letter addressed to the Government on these events, dated July 7, 1820, I observed, " The danger is, that success may tempt him to go beyond the line of necessity, either for the ends of justice or security. If he stops with the Pokaran chief, and one or two inferior, concerned in the coalition of 1806 and the usurpation of his son, with the condign punishment of a few of the civil officers, it will afford a high opinion of his character ; but if he involves Awa, and the other principal chiefs, in these proscriptions, he may provoke a strife which will yet overwhelm him. He has done enough for justice, and even for revenge, which has been carried too far as regards Surthan Singh, whose death (which I sincerely regret) was a prodigal sacrifice."

whom he sent for to the Presence, on the day succeeding these events? "Now you may perceive the reasons why I did not sooner give you office." This individual, the brother of the late Induraj, was forthwith installed in the post of Diwan; and with the sinews of war provided by the late sequestrations, the troops were satisfied, while by the impression so sedulously propagated and believed, that he had only to call on the British power for what aid he required, the whole feudal body was appalled: and the men, who would have hurled the tyrant from his throne, now only sought to avoid his insidious snares, more dangerous than open force.

Nimaj was besieged and nobly defended; but at length the son of Surthan capitulated, on receiving the sign-manual of his prince promising pardon and restoration, guaranteed by the commander of the mercenary bands. To the eternal disgrace of the Raja, he broke this pledge, and the boy had scarcely appeared in the besieging camp, when the civil officer produced the Raja's mandate for his captivity and transmission to the Presence. If it is painful to record this fact, it is pleasing to add, that even the mercenary commander spurned the infamous injunction. "No," said he; "on the faith of my pledge (*bachan*) he surrendered; and if the Raja breaks his word, I will maintain mine, and at least place him in security." He kept his promise, and conveyed him to the Aravalli mountains, whence he passed over to, and received protection in Mewar.

Estrangement of the Chiefs.—This and similar acts of treachery and cold-blooded tyranny completely estranged all the chiefs. Isolated as they were, they could make no resistance against the mercenary battalions, amounting to ten thousand men, exclusive of the quotas; and they dared not league for defence, from the dreaded threat held over them, of calling in the British troops; and in a few months the whole feudal association of [159] Marwar abandoned their homes and their country, seeking shelter in the neighbouring States from the Raja's cruel and capricious tyranny. To his connexion with the British Government alone he was indebted for his being able thus to put forth the resources of his policy, which otherwise he never could have developed either with safety or effect; nor at any former period of the history of Marwar could the most daring of its princes have undertaken, with any prospect of success, what Raja Man accomplished under this alliance.

These brave men found asyla in the neighbouring States of Kotah, Mewar, Bikaner, and Jaipur. Even the faithful Anar Singh, whose fidelity no gratitude could ever repay, was obliged to seek refuge in exile. He had stood Man's chief shield against the proscription of Raja Bhim, when cooped up in Jalor, and sold his wife's ornaments, "even to her nose-ring," to procure him the means of subsistenee and defenee. It was Anar Singh who saved him when, in the attempt upon Pali, he was unhorsed and nearly made prisoner. He was among the four ehiefs who remained by his fortunes when the rest deserted to the standard of the pretender; and he was one of the same body, who reseued the trophies of their disgrace from the hands of their enemies when on the road to Jaipur. Last of all, he was mainly instrumental in the Raja's emancipation and in his resumption of the reins of government. Well might the fury of his revenge deserve the term of madness! In A.D. 1821, the greater chieftains of Marwar, thus driven into exile, were endeavouring to obtain the mediation of the British authorities; but another year had elapsed without the slightest advance to accommodation. Their conduct has been exemplary, but their degrading position, dependent on the scanty resources of others, must of itself work a cure. Their manly remonstrance addressed to the British functionary is already before the reader.[1] He did not hesitate to tell them, that if in due time no mediation was held out, they must depend on themselves for redress!

Such was the political condition of Marwar until the year 1823. Had a demoniacal spirit of revenge not blinded Raja Man, he had a fine opportunity to lay the principles of order on a permanent basis, and to introduce those reforms neeessary for his individual welfare as well as for that of the State. He had it in his power to modify the institutions, to curb without destroying the feudal chiefs, and [160] to make the whole subservient to the altered condition of affairs. Instead of having the glory of fixing the constitution of his country, he has (reposing on external protection) broken up the entire feudal association, and rendered the paramount power an object of hatred instead of reverence.

Retrospect of Mārwār History.—Having thus rapidly sketched the history of this interesting branch of the Rajput race, from

[1] Vol. I. p. 228.

the destruction of their ancient seat of empire, Kanauj, and their settlement in the Indian desert more than six centuries ago, to the present day, it is impossible to quit the subject without a reflection on the anomalous condition of their alliance with the British Government, which can sanction the existence of such a state of things as we have just described. It illustrates the assertions made in an early part of this work,[1] of the ill-defined principles which guide all our treaties with the Rajputs, and which, if not early remedied, will rapidly progress to a state of things full of misery to them, and of inevitable danger to ourselves. These "men of the soil," as they emphatically designate themselves, cling to it, and their ancient and well-defined privileges, with an unconquerable pertinacity; in their endeavours to preserve them, whole generations have been swept away, yet has their strength increased in the very ratio of oppression. Where are now the oppressors? the dynasties of Ghazni, of Ghor, the Khiljis, the Lodis, the Pathans, the Timurs, and the demoralizing Mahratta? The native Rajput has flourished amidst these revolutions, and survived their fall; and but for the vices of their internal sway, chiefly contracted from such association, would have risen to power upon the ruin of their tyrants. But internal dissension invited the spoiler; and herds of avaricious Mahrattas and ferocious Pathans have reaped the harvest of their folly. Yet all these faults were to be redeemed in their alliances with a people whose peculiar boast was, that wisdom, justice, and clemency were the corner-stones of their power: seeking nothing from them beyond the means for their defence, and an adherence to the virtues of order. How far the protecting power has redeemed its pledge, in allowing years to pass away without some attempt to remedy the anarchy we have described, the reader is in a condition to judge. If it be said that we have tied up our hands by leaving them free agents in their internal administration, then let no offer of support be given to the head, for the oppression of the vassal and his rights, co-equal with those of the sovereign [161]; and if our mediation cannot be exerted, let us withdraw altogether the checks upon the operation of their own system of government, and leave them free agents in reality. A wiser, more humane, and liberal policy would be, to impose upon ourselves the task of understanding their political condition,

[1] Vol. I. p. 146.

and to use our just influence for the restoration of their internal prosperity, and with it the peace, present as well as prospective, of an important part of our empire. The policy which such views would suggest, is to support the opinion of the vast majority of the Rathors, and to seize the first opportunity to lend at least our sanction to an adoption, from the Idar branch, of Rathor blood, not only uncontaminated, but heirs-presumptive to Jodha, and exclude the parricidal line which will continue to bring misery on the country. If, however, we apply only our own monarchical, nay, despotic principles to this feudal society, and interfere but to uphold a blind tyranny, which must drive these brave chiefs to despair, it will be well to reflect and consider, from the acts we have related, of what they are capable. Very different, indeed, would be the deeds of proscribed Rajputs from those of vagabond Pindaris, or desultory Mahrattas ; and what a field for aggression and retreat ! Rumour asserts that they have already done themselves justice ; and that, driven to desperation, and with no power to mediate, the dagger has reached the heart of Raja Man ! If this be true, it is a retribution which might have been expected ; it was the only alternative left to the oppressed chiefs to do themselves justice. It is also said, that the 'pretended' son of Raja Bhim is now on the *gaddi* of Jodha. This is deeply to be lamented. Raja Dhonkal will see only the party who espoused his pretensions, and the Pokaran chief and faction will hold that place in the councils of his sovereign, which of right belongs to the head of his clan, the Champawat chief of Awa, an exile in Mewar.[1] Jealousy, feuds, and bloodshed will be the consequence, which would at once be averted by an adoption from Idar. Were a grand council of Rajputs to be convened, in order to adjust the question, nine-tenths would decide as proposed ; the danger of

[1] He was so when the author left India in 1823. [In 1827 Dhonkal Singh raised forces in Jaipur for the invasion of Mārwār. Mān Singh demanded aid from the British Government, which was refused. "At the same time, the Jaipur State was considered to have acted in breach of its engagements with Government by having allowed an armed confederacy to form against Jodhpur within its territory, and strong remonstrances were addressed to the Darbār ; lastly, Dhonkal Singh was required to withdraw from the confederacy, and the nobles settled their differences among themselves" (Erskine iii. A. 72). In 1839 the misgovernment of Mān Singh led to British military intervention. He died on 5th September 1843.]

interference would be neutralized, and peace and tranquillity would be the boon bestowed upon thousands, and, what is of some consequence, future danger to ourselves would be avoided [162].

CHAPTER 16

Extent of Mārwār.—The extreme breadth of Marwar lies between two points in the parallel of the capital, namely, Girab, west, and Shamgarh, on the Aravalli range, east. This line measures two hundred and seventy British miles. The greatest length, from the Sirohi frontier to the northern boundary, is about two hundred and twenty miles.[1] From the remote angle, N.N.E., in the Didwana district, to the extremity of Sanchor, S.W., the diagonal measurement is three hundred and fifty miles. The limits of Marwar are, however, so very irregular, and present so many salient angles and abutments into other States, that without a trigonometrical proeess we cannot arrive at a correct estimate of its superficial extent: a nicety not, indeed, required.

Physical Features, Population.—The most marked feature that diversifies the face of Maru is the river Luni, which, rising on her eastern frontier at Pushkar, and pursuing a westerly course, nearly bisects the country, and forms the boundary between the fertile and sterile lands of Maru. But although the tracts south of this stream, between it and the Aravalli, are by far the richest part of Marwar, it would be erroneous to describe all the northern part as sterile. An ideal line, passing through Nagor and Jodhpur, to Balotra, will mark the just distinetion. South of this line will lie the districts of Didwana, Nagor, Merta, Jodhpur, Pali, Sojat, Godwar, Siwana, Jalor, Bhinmal, and Sanchor, most of which are fertile and populous; and we may [163] assign a population of eighty souls to the square mile. The space north of this line is of a very different character, but this requires a subdivision; for while the north-east portion, which includes a portion of Nagor, the large towns of Phalodi, Pokaran, etc., may be calculated at thirty, the remaining space to the south-west, as Gugadeo-ka-thal, or 'desert of Guga,' Sheo, Barmer, Kotra, and Chhotan, can

[1] [At present greatest length about 320 miles, greatest breadth 170 miles.]

scarcely be allowed ten. In round numbers, the population of Marwar may be estimated at two millions of souls.[1]

Classes of Inhabitants.—Of this amount, the following is the classification of the tribes. The Jats constitute five-eighths, the Rajputs two-eighths,[2] while the remaining classes, sacerdotal,[3] commercial, and servile, make up the integral number. If this calculation be near the truth, the Rajputs, men, women, and children, will amount to five hundred thousand souls, which would admit of fifty thousand men capable of bearing arms, especially when we recollect that the Jats or Jāts are the industrious class.

The Rāthors.—It is superfluous to expatiate on the peculiarities of the Rathor character, which we have endeavoured to extract from their own actions. It stands deservedly high in the scale of the "Thirty-six Tribes," and although debased by one besetting sin (the use of opium), the Rathor is yet a noble animal, and requires only some exciting cause to show that the spirit, which set at defiance the resources of the empire in the zenith of its prosperity, is dormant only, not extinct. The reign of the present prince has done more, however, than even the arms of Aurangzeb, to deteriorate the Rathors. Peace would recruit their thinned ranks, but the mistrust sown in every house by unheard-of duplicity, has greatly demoralized the national character, which until lately stood higher than that of any of the circumjacent tribes. A popular prince, until within these very few years, could easily have collected a magnificent army, *ek bap ke bete*, 'the sons of one father,' round the '*gaddi* of Jodha': in fact, the *panchas hazar tarwar Rathoran*, meaning the 'fifty thousand Rathor swords,' is the proverbial phrase to denote the muster of Maru, of which they estimated five thousand cavalry. This was exclusive of the household and foreign troops supported on the fiscal lands. The Rathor cavalry was the best in India. There were several horse-fairs, especially those of Balotra and Pushkar where the horses of [164] Cutch and Kathiawar, the Jungle, and Multan, were brought in great numbers. Valuable horses were also bred on the western frontier, on the Luni, those of Rardara being in high estimation. But the events of the last twenty

[1] [In 1911 the population was 2,057,553.]

[2] [In 1911 respectively 125 and 279 per mille.]

[3] The district of Sanchor is almost entirely Brahman, forming a distinct tribe, called the Sanchora Brahmans.

years appear to have dried up every source of supply. The breeding studs of Rardara, Cutch, and the Jungle are almost extinct, and supplies from the west of the Indus are intercepted by the Sikhs.[1] The destruction of the predatory system, which created a constant demand, appears to have lessened the supply. So much for the general peace which the successes of Britain have produced.

In periods of civil commotion, or when the safety of the State was perilled, we hear of one clan (the Champawat) mustering four thousand horse. But if ever so many of "the sons of Champa" were congregated at one time, it is an extraordinary occurrence, and far beyond the demand which the State has upon their loyalty. To estimate what may be demanded of them, we have only to divide the rent-roll by five hundred rupees, the qualification for a cavalier in Maru, and to add, for each horse, two foot-soldiers. A schedule of the greater feudal estates shall be appended.

Soil, Agriculture, Products.—The following is the classification of the different heads of soil in Marwar: Bekal, Chikni, Pīla, and Safed. The first (whose etymology I know not) pervades the greater part of the country, being a light sand, having little or no earthy admixture, and only fit to produce *bajra* (millet), *mung*, *moth* (pulse), *til* (sesamum), melons and *gawar*.[2] Chikni (fat), a black earth, pervades the district of Didwana, Merta, Pali, and several of the feudal lands in Godwar. Wheat and grain are its products. The Pīla (yellow) is a sandy clay, chiefly about Khinwasar [3] and the capital, also Jalor and Balotra, and portions of other districts. It is best adapted for barley, and that kind of wheat called *pattagehun* (the other is *kathagehun*); [4] also tobacco, onions, and other vegetables: the staple millets are seldom grown in this. The Safed (white) is almost pure silex, and grows little or nothing, but after heavy falls of rain.[5]

[1] [At present the horses of Mallāni are most esteemed. By the "Jungle," the Lākhi Jangal is meant.]

[2] [Gawār, the horse bean, *Dolichus biflorus*.]

[3] [In Nāgor district, N.W. of Jodhpur city.]

[4] [This variety is grown without irrigation (Erskine iii. A. 103).]

[5] [The varieties of soil now recognized are: *matiyāli*, clayey loam; *bhūri*, brown-coloured, and with less clay than *matiyāli*; *retla*, fine sand without clay; *magra* or *tharra*, on the slopes of hills, hard and containing pebbles (*ibid.* iii. A. 99).]

The districts south of the Luni, as Pali, Sojat, and Godwar, fertilized by the numerous petty streams flowing from the Aravalli, produce abundantly every species of grain with the exception of *bajra*, which thrives best in a sandy soil; and in Nagor and Merta considerable quantities of the richer grains are raised by irrigation from wells. The extensive western divisions of Jalor, Sanchor, and Bhinmal, containing [165] five hundred and ten towns and villages, which are Khalisa, or 'fiscal land,' possess an excellent soil, with the advantage of the rills from Abu, and the great southern barrier; but the demoralized government of Raja Man never obtains from them one-third of their intrinsic capability, while the encroachment of the Sahariyas, and other robbers from the Sindi desert, encroach upon them often with impunity. Wheat, barley, rice, *juar* (millet), *mung* (pulse), *til* (sesamum), are the chief products of the richer lands; while amidst the sandy tracts they are confined to *bajra*, *mung*, and *til*. With good government, Marwar possesses abundance of means to collect stores against the visitations which afflict these northern regions: but prejudice steps in to aid the ravages of famine, and although water is near the surface in all the southern districts, the number of wells bears no proportion to those in Mewar. The great district of Nagor, of five hundred and sixty towns and villages, the appanage of the heirs-apparent of Maru, in spite of physical difficulties, is, or has been made, an exception; and the immense sheet of sandstone, on which a humid soil is embedded, has been pierced throughout by the energies of ancient days, and contains greater aids to agriculture than many more fertile tracts in the country.

Natural Productions.—Marwar can boast of some valuable productions of her sterile plains, which make her an object of no little importance in the most distant and more favoured regions of India. The salt lakes of Pachbhadra, Didwana, and Sambhar, are mines of wealth, and their produce is exported over the greater part of Hindustan; while to the marble quarries of Makrana (which gives its name to the mineral), on her eastern frontier, all the splendid edifices of the imperial cities owe their grandeur. The materials used in the palaces of Delhi, Agra, their mosques, and tombs, have been conveyed from Marwar.[1] The quarries, until of late years, yielded a considerable

[1] [Makrāna is 12 miles W. of Sāmbhar Lake. For its marbles see

revenue; but the age for palace-building in these regions is no more, and posterity will ask with surprise the sources of such luxury. There are also limestone quarries near Jodhpur and Nagor; and the concrete called *kankar* is abundant in many of the districts, and chiefly used for mortar. Tin and lead are found at Sojat; alum about Pali, and iron is obtained from Bhinmal and the districts adjoining Gujarat.

Manufactures.—The manufactures of Marwar are of no great importance in a commercial point of view. Abundance of coarse cotton cloths, and blankets, are [166] manufactured from the cotton and wool produced in the country, but they are chiefly used there. Matchlocks, swords, and other warlike implements are fabricated at the capital and at Pali; and at the latter place they make boxes of iron, tinned, so as to resemble the tin boxes of Europe. Iron platters for culinary purposes are in such great demand as to keep the forges constantly going.

Commercial Marts.—None of these States are without traffic; each has her mart, or entrepôt; and while Mewar boasts of Bhilwara, Bikaner of Churu, and Amber of Malpura (the city of wealth), the Rathors claim Pali, which is not only the rival of the places just mentioned, but may make pretensions to the title of emporium of Rajputana. These pretensions we may the more readily admit, when we recollect that nine-tenths of the bankers and commercial men of India are natives of Marudes, and these chiefly of the Jain faith. The laity of the Khadatara sect send forth thousands to all parts of India, and the Oswals, so termed from the town of Osian, near the Luni, estimate one hundred thousand families whose occupation is commerce. All these claim a Rajput descent, a fact entirely unknown to the European enquirer into the peculiarities of Hindu manners. The wealth acquired in foreign lands, from the Sutlej to the ocean, returns chiefly to their native soil; but as neither primogeniture nor *majorats* are sanctioned by the Jain lawgivers, an equal distribution takes place amongst all the sons, though the youngest (as amongst the Getae of Asia, and the Jutes of Kent), receives often a double portion. This arises when the division takes place while the parent is living, being the portion set apart for his own

Sleeman, *Rambles*, 318; Hervey, *Some Records of Crime*, i. 100. The best marbles in Rājputāna are found at Makrāna, Tonkra in Kishangarh, Kharwar in Ajmer, and Raiālu in Jaipur; see Watt, *Comm. Prod.* 715.]

support, which ultimately falls to the youngest, with whom he probably resides. It would be erroneous to say this practice is extensive; though sufficient instances exist to suppose it once was a principle.[1] The bare enumeration of the tribes following commerce would fill a short chapter. A priest of the Jains [167] (my own teacher), who had for a series of years devoted his attention to form a catalogue, which then amounted to nearly eighteen hundred classes, renounced the pursuit, on obtaining from a brother priest, from a distant region, one hundred and fifty new names to add to his list.

Pali was the entrepôt for the eastern and western regions, where the productions of India, Kashmir, and China, were interchanged for those of Europe, Africa, Persia, and Arabia. Caravans (*kitars*), from the ports of Cutch and Gujarat, imported elephants' teeth, copper, dates, gum-arabic, borax, coco-nuts, broadcloths, silks, sandal-wood, camphor, dyes, drugs, oxide and sulphuret of arsenic, spices, coffee, etc. In exchange, they exported chintzes, dried fruits, *jira*,[2] asafoetida from Multan, sugar, opium (Kotah and Malwa), silks and fine cloths, potash, shawls, dyed blankets, arms, and salt of home manufacture.

Caravans.—The route of the caravans was by Suigam,[3] Sanchor, Bhinmal, Jalor to Pali, and the guardians of the merchandise

[1] There is nothing which so much employs the assessors of justice, in those tribunals of arbitration, the Panchayats, as the adjudication of questions of property. The highest compliment ever paid to the Author was by the litigants of property amounting to half a million sterling, which had been going the rounds of various Panchayats and appeals to native princes, alike unsatisfactory in their results. They agreed to admit as final the decision of a court of his nomination. It was not without hesitation I accepted the mediation propounded through the British superintendent of Ajmer (Mr. Wilder); but knowing two men, whose integrity as well as powers of investigation were above all encomium, I could not refuse. One of these had given a striking instance of independence in support of the award his penetration had led him to pronounce, and which award being set aside on appeal, through favouritism, he abjured every future call as an arbitrator. He was not a wealthy man, but such was the homage paid to his integrity and talents, that the greatest despot in India found it politic to reassemble the court, have the case reconsidered, and permit justice to take its course. In like manner, his demand was, that, before he agreed to devote his time to unravelling all the intricacies of the case, both litigants should sign a *muchalka*, or 'bond,' to abide by the award. I have no recollection how it terminated.

[2] [Cumin, *Cuminum cyminum* (Watt, *Comm. Prod.* 442).]

[3] [Suigām in Pālanpur State, near the Ran of Cutch (*BG*, v. 348).]

were almost invariably Charans, a character held sacred by the Rajput. The most desperate outlaw seldom dared to commit any outrage on caravans under the safeguard of these men, the bards of the Rajputs. If not strong enough to defend their convoy with sword and shield, they would threaten the robbers with the *chandni*, or 'self-immolation';[1] and proceed by degrees from a gash in the flesh to a death-wound, or if one victim was insufficient a whole body of women and children was sacrificed (as in the case of the Bamaniya Bhats), for whose blood the marauder is declared responsible hereafter.

Decay of Commerce. The Opium Trade.—Commerce has been almost extinguished within these last twenty years; and paradoxical as it may appear, there was tenfold more activity and enterprise in the midst of that predatory warfare, which rendered India one wide arena of conflict, than in these days of universal pacification. The torpedo touch of monopoly has had more effect on the Kitars than the spear of the desert Sahariya, or Barwatia (outlaw) Rajput—against its benumbing qualities the Charan's dagger would fall innocuous; it sheds no blood, but it dries up its channels. If the products of the salt-lakes of Rajputana were preferred, even at Benares, to the sea-salt of Bengal, high impost duties excluded it from the market. If the opium of Malwa and Haraoti competed in the China market with our Patna monopoly, again we intervened, not with high export duties, which we were competent to impose, but by laying our shackles upon it at the fountain-head. "*Aut Caesar, aut nullus,*" is our maxim [168] in these regions; and in a country where our Agents are established only to preserve political relations and the faith of treaties, the basis of which is non-interference in the internal arrangement of their affairs—albeit we have not a single foot of land in sovereignty—we set forth our *parwanas*, as peremptory as any Russian ukase, and command that no opium shall leave these countries for the accustomed outlets, under pain of confiscation. Some, relying on their skill in eluding our vigilance, or tempted by the high price which these measures produce, or perhaps reckoning upon our justice, and upon impunity if discovered, tried new routes, until confiscation brought them to submission.

[1] [See p. 815.]

We then put an arbitrary value upon the drug, and forced the grower to come to us, and even take credit to ourselves for consulting his interests. Even admitting that such price was a remunerating one, founded upon an average of past years, still it is not the less arbitrary. No allowance is made for plentiful or bad seasons, when the drug, owing to a scarcity, will bear a double price. Our legislation is for "all seasons and their change." But this virtual infraction of the faith of treaties is not confined to the grower or retailer; it affects others in a variety of ways; it injures our reputation and the welfare of those upon whom, for benevolent purposes, we have forced our protection. The transit duties levied on opium formed an item in the revenues of the princes of Rajputana; but confiscation guards the passes of the Aravalli and Gujarat, and unless the smuggler wrap up his cargo in ample folds of deceit, the Rajput may go without his *amal-pani*, the infusion of this poison, dearer to him than life. It is in vain to urge that sufficient is allowed for home consumption. Who is to be the judge of this? or who is so blind as not to see that any latitude of this kind would defeat the monopoly, which, impolitic in its origin, gave rise in its progress to fraud, gambling, and neglect of more important agricultural economy. But this policy must defeat itself: the excess of quantity produced will diminish the value of the original (Patna) monopoly, if its now deteriorated quality should fail to open the eyes of the quick-sighted Chinese, and exclude it from the market altogether.[1]

Fairs.—There were two annual fairs in his country, Mundwa and Balotra; the first chiefly for cattle. The merchandise of various countries was exposed [169] and purchased by the merchants of the adjoining States. It commenced with the month of Magh, and lasted during six weeks. The other was also for cattle of all kinds, horses, oxen, camels, and the merchandise enumerated amongst the imports and exports of Pali. Persons from all parts

[1] The Author learns that important modifications of this system have been made by the legislative authorities at home: of their extent he is ignorant, except that remuneration to chiefs for the loss of transit duties has not been omitted. This is as it should be! [The opium question is still in a state of transition. Exports to China were closed in 1913, and, owing to the loss of revenue, compensation has been awarded to the Native States by the Government of India. For the trade up to 1911 see *IGI*, iv. 242 ff.; Watt, *Comm. Prod.* (1908), 845 ff.]

of India frequented them; but all these signs of prosperity are vanishing.[1]

Administration of Justice.—The administration of justice is now very lax in these communities; but at no time were the customary criminal laws of Rajputana sanguinary, except in respect to political crimes, which were very summarily dealt with when practicable. In these feudal associations, however, such crimes are esteemed individual offences, and the whole power of the government is concentrated to punish them; but when they are committed against the community, justice is tempered with mercy, if not benumbed by apathy. In cases even of murder, it is satisfied with fine, corporal punishment, imprisonment, confiscation, or banishment. Inferior crimes, such as larcenies, were punished by fine and imprisonment, and, when practicable, restitution; or, in case of inability to pay, corporal punishment and confinement. But under the present lax system, when this impoverished government has to feed criminals, it may be supposed that their prisons are not overstocked. Since Raja Bijai Singh's death, the judgment-seat has been vacant. His memory is held in high esteem for the administration of justice, though he carried clemency to excess. He never confirmed a sentence of death; and there is a saying of the criminals, yet extant, more demonstrative of his humanity than of good policy: "When at large we cannot even get *rabri* (porridge), but in prison we eat *laddu* (sweetmeat)." Here, as at Jaipur, confined criminals are maintained by individual charity; and it is a well-known fact, that at the latter place, but for the humanity of the mercantile classes, especially those of the Jain persuasion, they might starve. Perhaps it is the knowledge of this circumstance, which holds back the hand of the government, or its agents, who may apply to their own uses the prison-fare. When once confined, the criminals are little thought of, and neglect answers all the ends of cruelty. They have, however, a source of consolation unknown to those who have passed "the bridge of sighs," or become inmates of the oubliettes of more civilized regions. That fortitude and resignation which religion alone can bestow on the one is obtained through superstition by the other; and the prayers of the prison are poured forth for one of those visitations of Providence [170], which, in humbling

[1] [For these fairs see Erskine iii. A. 206, 208.]

the proud, prompts acts of mercy to others in order to ensure it to themselves.[1] The celestial phenomena of eclipses, whether of the sun or moon, although predicted by the Pandits, who for ages have possessed the most approved theory for calculation, are yet looked upon with religious awe by the mass, and as "foreboding change to princes." Accordingly, when darkness dims the beams of Surya or Chandra, the face of the prisoner of Maru is lighted up with smiles; his deliverance is at hand, and he may join the crowd to hoot and yell, and frighten the monster Rahu[2] from his hold of the "silver-moon."[3] The birth of a son to the prince, and a new reign, are events likewise joyful to him.

Trial by Ordeal.—The trial by *sagun*, literally 'oath of purgation,' or ordeal, still exists, and is occasionally had recourse to in Maru, as in other parts of Rajputana; and, if fallen into desuetude, it is not that these judgments of God (as they were styled in the days of European barbarism) are less relied on, but that society is so unhinged that even these appeals to chance find no subjects for practice, excepting by Zalim Singh; and he to the last carried on his antipathy to the Dakins (witches) of Haraoti, who were always submitted to the process by 'water.' Trial by ordeal is of very ancient date in India: it was by 'fire' that Rama proved the purity of Sita, after her abduction by Ravana, and in the same manner as practised by one of our Saxon kings, by making her walk over a red-hot ploughshare.[4] Besides the two most common tests, by fire and water, there is a third, that of washing the hands in boiling oil. It should be stated, that, in all cases, not only the selection but the appeal to any of these ordeals is the voluntary act of the litigants, and chiefly after the Panchayats, or courts or arbitration, have failed. Where justice is denied, or bribery shuts the door, the sufferer will dare his adversary to the *sagun*, or submission to the

[1] [The State jails have been reorganized, and humane treatment of prisoners is enforced (Erskine iii. A. 163 ff.).]

[2] The Rajputs and Hindus in general hold precisely the same idea, of the cause of eclipses, as the Getae of Scandinavia. [This is a form of sympathetic magic: as prisoners are released, so will the sun and moon be freed from the demon.]

[3] Chandrama. The moon is represented by silver, which is called after her (or him) *chandi*.

[4] [According to the more common story, she walked through a pile of burning wood.]

judgment of God; and the solemnity of the appeal carries such weight, that it brings redress of itself, though cases do occur where the challenge is accepted, and the author has conversed with individuals who have witnessed the operation of each of the ordeals.[1]

Panchayats.—The Panchayats arbitrate in civil cases. From these courts of equity, there is an appeal to the Raja; but as unanimity is required in the judges, and a fee or fine must be paid by the appellant, ere his case can come before the prince [171], litigation is checked. The constitution of this court is simple. The plaintiff lays his case before the Hakim of the district, or the Patel of the village where he resides. The plaintiff and defendant have the right of naming the villages (two, each), from whence the members of the Panchayat are to be drawn. Information is accordingly sent to the Patels of the villages specified, who, with their respective Patwaris (Registers), meet at the Atai or 'village-court.' Witnesses are summoned and examined on oath, the most common of which is the *gaddi-ki-an*, 'allegiance to the throne,' resembling the ancient adjuration of the Scythians as recorded by Herodotus.[2] This oath is, however, more restricted to Rajputs; the other classes have various forms based upon their religious notions. When the proceedings are finished, and judgment is given, the Hakim puts his seal thereto, and carries it into effect, or prepares it for appeal. It is affirmed that, in the good times of Rajputana, these simple tribunals answered every purpose.

Fiscal Revenues.—The fiscal revenues of Marwar are derived from various sources; the principal are—

1. The Khalisa, or 'crown-lands.'
2. The salt lakes.
3. Transit and impost duties.
4. Miscellaneous taxes, termed Hasil.

The entire amount of personal revenue of the princes of Marwar

[1] [Since the reorganization of the Courts of Justice and the introduction of criminal codes, trial by ordeal has been prohibited (Erskine iii. A. 132 ff.). In 1854 Sir H. Lawrence made a treaty with Mewār which provided that "no person be seized on the plea of sorcery, witchcraft, or incantations" (Lee Warner, *Native States of India*, ed. 1910, p. 305).]

[2] [The most solemn oath among the Scythians was by the royal hearth (Herodotus iv. 68).]

does not at present exceed ten lakhs of rupees (£100,000 sterling), though in the reign of Bijai Singh half a century ago, they yielded full sixteen lakhs, one-half of which arose from the salt lakes alone. The aggregate revenue of the feudal lands is estimated as high as fifty lakhs, or £500,000. It may be doubted whether at present they yield half this sum.[1] The feudal contingents are estimated at five thousand horse, besides foot, the qualification being one cavalier and two foot-soldiers for every thousand rupees of income.[2] This low estimate is to keep up the nominal value of estates, notwithstanding their great deterioration ; for a 'knight's fee' of Marwar was formerly estimated at five hundred rupees.

The sum of ten lakhs, mentioned as the gross income of the prince, is what is actually realized by the treasury, for there are many public servants provided for out of the crown-lands, whose estates are not included.

Methods of Revenue Collection.—The revenues are collected from the ryots in kind. A corn-rent, the only one recognized in ancient India, and termed Batai, or 'division,' is apportioned equally [172] between the prince and the husbandman : a deviation from the more lenient practice of former times, which gave one-fourth, or one-sixth to the sovereign. Besides this, the cultivator has to pay the expense of guarding the crops, and also those who attend the process of division. An assessment of two rupees is made on every ten maunds,[3] which more than covers the salaries paid to the Shahnas (watchmen), and Kanwaris,[4] and leaves a surplus divided by the Patel and village register (Patwari). A cart-load of *karbi* (the stalks of *juar* and *bajra*) is exacted from every cultivator as fodder for the prince's cattle ; but this is commuted for a rupee, except in seasons of scarcity, when it is stored up. The other officers, as the Patwaris and Patels, are paid out of the respective shares of the farmer and the crown, namely, one-fourth of a ser each, from every maund of produce, or an eightieth part of the gross amount. The cultivators of

[1] [The normal revenue of the State at the present time is about 56, and the expenditure 42 lakhs of rupees (Erskine iii. A. 140 ff.).]

[2] [The State now maintains two regiments of Imperial Service Lancers, 1210 men, the whole force, including local troops, being about 2700 (*ibid.* iii. A. 158 ff.).]

[3] The maund is about seventy-five lbs. weight.

[4] *Kan*, 'corn.'

the Pattawats or feudal chiefs are much better off than those of the Khalisa: from them only two-fifths are exacted; and in lieu of all other taxes and charges, a land-tax of twelve rupees is levied on every hundred bighas of land cultivated. The cultivators repay this mild assessment by attachment to the chiefs.

Poll Tax.—Anga is a poll-tax (from *anga*, 'the body') of one rupee, levied on adults of either sex throughout Marwar.

Cattle Tax.—Ghasmali is a graduated tax on cattle, or, as the term imports, the right of pasture. A sheep or goat is estimated at one anna (one-sixteenth of a rupee); a buffalo eight annas, or half a rupee; and each camel, three rupees.

Door Tax.—Kewari is a tax on doors (*kewar*), and is considered peculiarly oppressive. It was first imposed by Bijai Singh, when, towards the latter end of his reign, his chiefs rebelled, and retired in a body to Pali to concert schemes for deposing him. Thither he fruitlessly followed in order to pacify them, and on his return found the gates (*kewar*) of his capital shut in his face, and Bhim Singh placed upon the *gaddi*. To supply the pecuniary exigencies consequent upon this embarrassing situation, he appealed to his subjects, and proposed a 'benevolence,' in aid of his necessities, of three rupees for each house, giving it a denomination from the cause whence it originated. Whether employed as a punishment of those who aided his antagonist, or as a convenient expedient of finance, he converted this temporary contribution into a permanent tax, which continued until the necessities of the confederacy against the [173] present prince, Raja Man, and the usurpation of the fiscal lands by the Pathans, made him raise it to ten rupees on each house. It is, however, not equally levied; the number of houses in each township being calculated, it is laid on according to the means of the occupants, and the poor man may pay two rupees, while the wealthy pays twenty. The feudal lands are not exempted, except in cases of special favour.

Sāir.—In estimating the amount of the sair, or imposts of Marwar, it must be borne in mind that the schedule appended represents what they have been, and perhaps might again be, rather than what they now are. These duties are subject to fluctuation in all countries, but how much more in those exposed to so many visitations from predatory foes, civil strife, and famine! There is no reason to doubt that, in the "good old times " of Maru, the amount, as taken from old records, may have been realized :—

Jodhpur	Rs. 76,000
Nagor	75,000
Didwana	10,000
Parbatsar	44,000
Merta	11,000
Kolia	5,000
Jalor	25,000
Pali	75,000
Jasol and Balotra fairs	41,000
Bhinmal	21,000
Sanchor	6,000
Phalodi	41,000
TOTAL	430,000

The Danis, or collectors of the customs, have monthly salaries at the large towns, while the numerous petty agents are paid by a percentage on the sums collected. The sair, or imposts, include all those on grain, whether of foreign importation, or the home-grown, in transit from one district to another.

The revenue arising from the produce of the salt lakes has deteriorated with the land and commercial revenues; and, though affected by political causes, is yet the most certain branch of income. The following schedule exhibits what has been derived from this lucrative source of wealth [174] :—

Pachbhadra	Rs. 200,000
Phalodi	100,000
Didwana	115,000
Sambhar	200,000
Nawa	100,000
TOTAL	715,000

Banjāras: Salt Trade.—This productive branch of industry still employs thousands of hands, and hundreds of thousands of oxen, and is almost entirely in the hands of that singular race of beings called Banjaras, some of whose *tandas*, or caravans, amount to 40,000 head of oxen. The salt is exported to every region of Hindustan, from the Indus to the Ganges, and is universally known and sold under the title of Sambhar Lun, or 'salt of Sambhar,' notwithstanding the quality of the different lakes varies, that of Pachbhadra, beyond the Luni, being most esteemed.[1] It is produced by natural evaporation, expedited by dividing the surface into pans by means of mats of the Sarkanda grass,[2] which lessens the superficial agitation. It is then gathered and heaped up into immense masses, on whose summit they burn a variety of alkaline plants, such as the *sajji*,[3] by which it becomes impervious to the weather.

We may recapitulate what the old archives state of the aggregate fiscal revenues in past times, amounting to nearly thirty lakhs of rupees. It would be hazardous to say to what extent the amount was overrated:

1. Khalisa, or fiscal land, from 1484 towns and villages	Rs. 1,500,000
2. Sair or imposts	430,000
3. Salt lakes	715,000
4. Hasil, or miscellaneous taxes; fluctuating and uncertain; not less than . .	300,000
Total . .	2,945,000
Feudal and ministerial estates . .	5,000,000
GRAND TOTAL .	7,945,000

Thus the united fiscal and feudal revenues of Marwar are said to have amounted almost to eighty lakhs of rupees (£800,000). If they ever did reach this sum [175], which may be doubted, we do not err in affirming that they would not be overrated at half that amount. Large fortunes are said to centre in the families of the ex-ministers, especially the Singhi family, reported to be immensely rich. Their wealth is deposited in foreign capitals. But much bullion is lost to the currency of these countries by the

[1] The average selling price at Jodhpur is two rupees the maund; four at Sambhar and Didwana, and five at Pachbhadra, Phalodi, and Nawa. Why the price at the capital is 50 per cent lower than elsewhere, I know not, even if this statement is correct. [On the Rājputāna salt trade see Watt, *Comm. Prod.* 968 f. The present State income is now about 15 lakhs of rupees *per annum* (Erskine iii. A. 150 f.).]

[2] [*Saccharum sara.*]

[3] [On the production of barilla (*sajji khar*) see Watt, *op. cit.* 112 ff.).]

habits of secreting money. A very large treasure was discovered in Nagor by Bijai Singh, when demolishing some old buildings.

Military Forces.—It only remains to state the military resources of the Rathors, which fluctuate with their revenues. The Rajas maintain a foreign mercenary force upon their fiscal revenues to overawe their own turbulent vassalage. These are chiefly Rohilla and Afghan infantry, armed with muskets and matchlocks; and having cannon and sufficient discipline to act in a body, they are formidable to the Rajput cavaliers. Some years ago, Raja Man had a corps of three thousand five hundred foot, and fifteen hundred horse, with twenty-five guns, commanded by Hindal Khan, a native of Panipat. He has been attached to the family ever since the reign of Bijai Singh, and is (or was) familiarly addressed *kaka*, or 'uncle,' by the prince. There was also a brigade of those monastic militants, the Bishanswamis, under their leader, Kaimdas, consisting of seven hundred foot, three hundred horse, and an establishment of rockets (*bhan*), a very ancient instrument of Indian warfare, and mentioned long before gunpowder was used in Europe. At one period, the Raja maintained a foreign force amounting to, or at least mustered as, eleven thousand men, of which number two thousand five hundred were cavalry, with fifty-five guns, and a rocket establishment. Besides a monthly pay, lands to a considerable amount were granted to the commanders of the different legions. By these overgrown establishments, to maintain a superiority over the feudal lords which has been undermined by the causes related, the demoralization and ruin of this country have been accelerated. The existence of such a species of force, opposed in moral and religious sentiment to the retainers of the State, has only tended to widen the breach between them and their head, and to destroy every feeling of confidence.

In Mewar there are sixteen great chiefs; in Amber, twelve; in Marwar, eight. The following table exhibits their names, clans, residences, and rated revenue. The contingent required by their princes may be estimated by the qualification of a cavalier, namely, one for every five hundred rupees of rent [176].

[TABLE

Names of Chiefs.	Clans.	Places of Abode.	Revenue.	Remarks.
		FIRST CLASS.		
1. Kesari Singh	Champawat	Awa	100,000	Premier noble of Marwar. Of this sum, half is the original grant: the rest is by usurpation of the inferior branches of his clan.
2. Bakhtawar Singh	Kumpawat	Asop	50,000	
3. Salim Singh	Champawat	Pokaran	100,000	The Pokaran chief is by far the most powerful in Marwar.
4. Surthan Singh	Udawat	Nimaj	50,000	The fief of Nimaj is now under sequestration, since the last incumbent was put to death by the Raja.
5. ..	Mertia	Rian	25,000	The Mertia is deemed the bravest of all the Rathor clans.
6. Ajit Singh	Mertia	Ghanerao	50,000	This feoff formed one of the sixteen great feoffs of Mewar.
7. ..	Karamsot	Khinwasar	40,000	The town, which is large, has been dismantled, and several villages sequestrated.
8. ..	Bhatti	Khejarla	25,000	The only foreign chief in the first grade of the nobles of Marwar.
		SECOND CLASS		
1. Sheonath Singh	Udawat	Kuchaman	50,000	A chief of considerable power.
2. Surthan Singh	Jodha	Khari-ka-dewa	25,000	
3. Prithi Singh	Udawat	Chandawal	25,000	
4. Tej Singh	Do.	Khada	25,000	
5. Anar Singh	Bhatti	Ahor	11,000	In exile.
6. Jeth Singh	Kumpawat	Bagori	40,000	
7. Padam Singh	Do.	Gajsinghpura	25,000	
8. ..	Mertia	Mehtri	40,000	
9. Kartan Singh	Udawat	Marot	15,000	
10. Zalim Singh	Kumpawat	Rohat	15,000	
11. Sawai Singh	Jodha	Chaupar	15,000	
12. ..	..	Budsu	20,000	
13. Sheodan Singh	Champawat	Kaota (great)	40,000	
14. Zalim Singh	Do.	Harsola	10,000	
15. Sawal Singh	Do.	Degod	10,000	
16. Hukm Singh	Do.	Kaota (little)	11,000	

These are the principal chieftains of Marwar, holding lands on the tenure of service. There are many who owe allegiance and service on emergencies, the allodial vassals of Marwar, not enumerated in this list; such as Barmer, Kotra, Jasol, Phulsund,

Birgauw, Bankaria, Kalindri, Barunda, who could muster a strong numerical force if their goodwill were conciliated, and the prince could enforce his requisition. The specified census of the estates may not be exactly correct. The foregoing is from an old record, which is in all probability the best they have ; for so rapid are the changes in these countries, amidst the anarchy and rebellion we have been describing, that the civil officers would deem it time thrown away, to form, as in past times, an exact *pattabahi*, or 'register' of feoffs. The ancient qualification was one horseman and two foot soldiers, "when required," for each five hundred rupees in the rental; but as the estates have been curtailed in extent and diminished in value, in order to keep up their nominal amount, one thousand is now the qualification [178].[1]

[1] [At the present time the estates and septs of the Rāthor clan to which the twelve nobles belong are: Pokaran, Awa—Champāwat; Rian, Alnia-wās—Mertia; Rāēpur, Rās, Nīmāj, Agewa—Udāwat; Kharwa, Bhadrājan—Jodha. At a Darbār the Champāwats and Kūmpāwats sit to the right and the Jodhas, Mertias, and Udāwats to the left of the Mahārāja (Erskine iii. B. 40).]

BOOK VI

ANNALS OF BĪKANER

CHAPTER 1

BIKANER holds a secondary rank amongst the principalities of Rajputana. It is an offset of Marwar, its princes being scions of the house of Jodha, who established themselves by conquest on the northern frontier of the parent State; and its position, in the heart of the desert, has contributed to the maintenance of their independence.

Rāo Bīka, A.D. 1465-1504.—It was in S. 1515 (A.D. 1459), the year in which Jodha transferred the seat of government from Mandor to Jodhpur, that his son Bika,[1] under the guidance of his uncle Kandhal, led three hundred of the sons of Siahji to enlarge the boundaries of Rathor dominion amidst the sands of Maru. Bika was stimulated to the attempt by the success of his brother Bida, who had recently subjugated the territory inhabited by the Mohils for ages.

Such expeditions as that of Bika, undertaken expressly for conquest, were almost [179] uniformly successful. The invaders set out with a determination to slay or be slain; and these forays had the additional stimulus of being on "fated days," when the warlike creed of the Rajputs made the abstraction of territory from foe or friend a matter of religious duty.

Bika, with his band of three hundred, fell upon the Sankhlas[2]

[1] [According to Erskine (iii. B. 85) Bika was born in 1439; left Jodhpur, 1465; founded Bikaner city, 1488.]

[2] [The Sānkhlas are said to be a Panwār clan, but this is not certain (*Census Report, Rājputāna*, 1911, i. 256). Jānglu is about 20 miles S. of Bikaner city.]

of Janglu, whom they massacred. This exploit brought them in contact with the Bhattis of Pugal,[1] the chief of which gave his daughter in marriage to Bika, who fixed his headquarters at Kuramdesar, where he erected a castle, and gradually augmented his conquests from the neighbourhood.

The Conquest of the Jats.—Bika now approximated to the settlements of the Jats or Getae, who had for ages been established in these arid abodes; and as the lands they held form a considerable portion of the State of Bikaner, it may not be uninteresting to give a sketch of the condition of this singular people prior to the son of Jodha establishing the feudal system of Rajwara amongst their pastoral commonwealths.

Of this celebrated and widely spread race we have already given a succinct account.[2] It appears to have been the most numerous as well as the most conspicuous of the tribes of ancient Asia, from the days of Tomyris and Cyrus to those of the present Jat prince of Lahore, whose successor, if he be endued with similar energy, may, on the reflux of population, find himself seated in their original haunts of Central Asia, to which they have already considerably advanced.[3] In the fourth century we find a Yuti or Jat kingdom established in the Panjab;[4] but how much earlier this people colonized those regions we are ignorant. At every step made by Muhammadan power in India it encountered the Jats. On their memorable defence of the passage of the Indus against Mahmud, and on the war of extirpation waged against them by Timur, both in their primeval seats in Mawaru-l-nahr,[5] as well as east of the Sutlej, we have already enlarged; while Babur, in his Commentaries, informs us that, in all his irruptions into India, he was assailed by multitudes of Jats[6] during his progress through the Panjab, the peasantry of

[1] [About 120 miles N. of Bikaner city: the ruler at present is one of the leading nobles of the State.]

[2] Vol. I. p. 127, History of the Rajput Tribes—*Article*, Jats or Getae.

[3] Ranjit has long been in possession of Peshawar, and entertained views on Kabul, the disorganized condition of which kingdom affords him a favourable opportunity of realizing them.

[4] See Inscription, p. 914.

[5] [The land beyond the Oxus.]

[6] "On Friday the 14th (Dec. 29, A.D. 1525), of the first Rabi, we arrived at Sialkot. Every time that I have entered Hindustan, the Jats and Gujars have regularly poured down in prodigious numbers from their hills and

which region, now proselytes to Islam, are chiefly of this tribe; as well as the [180] military retainers, who, as sectarian followers of Nanak, merge the name of Jat, or Jāt, into that of Sikh or 'disciple.'[1]

In short, whether as Yuti, Getae, Jats, Juts, or Jāts, this race far surpassed in numbers, three centuries ago, any other tribe or race in India; and it is a fact that they now constitute a vast majority of the peasantry of western Rajwara, and perhaps of northern India.

At what period these Jats established themselves in the Indian desert, we are, as has been already observed, entirely ignorant; but even at the time of the Rathor invasion of these communities their habits confirmed the tradition of their Scythic origin. They led chiefly a pastoral life, were guided, but not governed by the elders, and with the exception of adoration to the 'universal mother' (Bhavani), incarnate in the person of a youthful Jatni, they were utter aliens to the Hindu theocracy. In fact, the doctrines of the great Islamite saint, Shaikh Farid,[2] appear to have overturned the pagan rites brought from the Jaxartes; and without any settled ideas on religion, the Jats of the desert jumbled all their tenets together. They considered themselves, in short, as a distinct class, and, as a Punia Jat informed me, "their *watan* was far beyond the Five Rivers." Even in the name of one of the six communities (the Asaich), on whose submission Bika founded his new State, we have nearly the Asi, the chief of the four tribes from the Oxus and Jaxartes, who overturned the Greek kingdom of Bactria.[3]

wilds, in order to carry off oxen and buffaloes" [Elliot-Dowson iv. 24]. The learned commentator draws a distinction between the Jat inhabitants of the Panjab and of India, which is not maintainable.

[1] "It is worthy of remark," says Colonel Pitman (who accompanied Mr. Elphinstone to Kabul), "that in the two first Doabehs (return of the embassy) we saw very few Sikhs, the Jat cultivators of the soil being in general Moosulmauns, and in complete subjugation to the Sikhs."

[2] [Shaikh Farid, known as Shakkarganj, 'sugar-store,' on account of his supposed miraculous power of transmuting dust or salt into sugar, was disciple of the famous Saint, Kutbu-d-din Bakhtyār Kāki. His life is supposed to have extended from A.D. 1173 to 1265. His tomb at Ajūdhan in the Montgomery District is a scene of pilgrimage.]

[3] [He perhaps refers to the Asioi of Strabo (xi. 8. 2), who cannot be identified (Smith, *EHI*, 226). They have no connexion, except resemblance of name, with the Asaich.]

The period of Rathor domination over these patriarchal communities was intermediate between Timur's and Babur's invasion of India. The former, who was the founder of the Chagatai dynasty, boasts of the myriads of Jat souls he "consigned to perdition" on the desert plains of India, as well as in Transoxiana; so we may conclude that successive migrations of this people from the great "storehouse of nations" went to the lands east of the Indus, and that the communities who elected Bika as their sovereign had been established therein for ages. The extent of their possessions justifies this conclusion; for nearly the whole of the territory forming the boundaries of Bikaner was possessed by the six Jat cantons, namely—

1. Punia.	4. Asaich.
2. Godara.	5. Beniwal [or Bhanniwal].
3. Saharan.	6. Johya, or Joiya [181].

though this last is by some termed a ramification of the Yadu-Bhatti: an affiliation by no means invalidating their claims to be considered of Jat or Yuti origin.[1]

Each canton bore the name of the community, and was subdivided into districts. Besides the six Jat cantons, there were three more simultaneously wrested from Rajput proprietors; namely, Bagor, the Kharipatta, and Mohila. The six Jat cantons constituted the central and northern, while those of the Rajputs formed the western and southern frontiers.

Disposition of the Cantons at that period.

Cantons.	No. of Villages.	Districts.
1. Punia . . .	300	Bahaduran, Ajitpur, Sidmukh, Rajgarh, Dadrewa, Sanku, etc.
2. Beniwal [or Bhanniwāl] . . .	150	Bhukarka, Sondari, Manoharpur, Kui, Bai, etc.
3. Johya . . .	600	Jethpur, Kumbhana, Mahajan, Pipasar, Udaipur, etc.
4. Asaich . . .	150	Rawatsar, Barmsar, Dandusar, Gandeli.

[1] The Jats of the Agra province consider themselves illegitimate descendants of the Yadus of Bayana, and have a tradition that their *watan* [home] is Kandahar.

Cantons.	No. of Villages.	Districts.
5. Saran . . .	300	Kejar, Phog, Buchawas, Sawai, Badinu, Sirsila, etc.
6. Godara . . .	700	Pundrasar, Gosainsar (great), Shaikhsar Garsisar, Gharibdesar, Rangesar, Kalu, etc.
Total in the six Jat cantons . .	2200	
7. Bagor . . .	300	Bikaner, Nal, Kela, Rajasar, Satasar, Chhattargarh, Randasar, Bitnokh, Bhavanipur, Jaimallsar, etc.
8. Mohila . . .	140	Chaupar (capital of Mohila), Sonda, Hirasar, Gopalpur, Charwas, Bidasar, Ladnun, Malsasar, Kharbuza-ra-kot.
9. Kharipatta, or salt district . .	30	
GRAND TOTAL .	2670	

With such rapidity were States formed in those times, that in a few years after Bika left his paternal roof at Mandor he was lord over 2670 villages, and by a title far stronger and more legitimate than that of conquest—the spontaneous election of the cantons. But although three centuries have scarcely passed since their amalgamation [182] into a sovereignty, one-half of the villages cease to exist; nor are there now 1300 forming the *raj* of Surat Singh, the present occupant and lineal descendant of Bika.[1]

The Jats and Johyas of these regions, who extended over all the northern desert even to the Gara, led a pastoral life, their wealth consisting in their cattle, which they reared in great numbers, disposing of the superfluity, and of the *ghi* (butter clarified) and wool, through the medium of Sarsot (Sarasvati) Brahmans (who, in these regions, devote themselves to traffic), receiving in return grain and other conveniences or necessaries of life.

Bīda conquers the Mohil Clan.—A variety of causes conspired

[1] [Mahārāja Sūrat Singh reigned A.D. 1788–1828.]

to facilitate the formation of the State of Bikaner, and the reduction of the ancient Scythic simplicity of the Jat communities to Rajput feudal sway; and although the success of his brother Bida over the Mohils in some degree paved the way, his bloodless conquest could never have happened but for the presence of a vice which has dissolved all the republics of the world. The jealousy of the Johyas and Godaras, the two most powerful of the six Jat cantons, was the immediate motive to the propitiation of the "son of Jodha"; besides which, the communities found the band of Bida, which had extirpated the ancient Mohils when living with them in amity, most troublesome neighbours. Further, they were desirous to place between them and the Bhattis of Jaisalmer a more powerful barrier; and last, not least, they dreaded the hot valour and "thirst for land" which characterized Bika's retainers, now contiguous to them at Janglu. For these weighty reasons, at a meeting of the "elders" of the Godaras, it was resolved to conciliate the Rathor.

Pandu was the patriarchal head of the Godaras; his residence was at Shaikhsar.[1] The 'elder' of Ronia was next in rank and estimation to Pandu, in communities where equality was as absolute as the proprietary right to the lands which each individually held: that of pasture being common.

The elders of Shaikhsar and Ronia were deputed to enter into terms with the Rajput prince, and to invest him with supremacy over their community, on the following conditions:—

First. To make common cause with them, against the Johyas and other cantons, with whom they were then at variance.

Second. To guard the western frontier against the irruption of the Bhattis [183].

Third. To hold the rights and privileges of the community inviolable.

On the fulfilment of these conditions they relinquished to Bika and his descendants the supreme power over the Godaras; assigning to him, in perpetuity, the power to levy *dhuan*, or a

[1] This town is named after the Islamite saint, Shaikh Farid of Pakpattan, who has a *dargah* here. He was greatly esteemed by the Jats, before the Bona Dea assumed the shape of a Jatni, to whom, under the title of Kirani Mata, 'a ray of the mother,' all bend the head. [Her shrine is at Deshnok, about 25 miles S. of Bikaner city, and is a sanctuary (Hervey, *Some Records of Crime*, i. 139).]

'hearth tax,' of one rupee on each house in the canton, and a land tax of two rupees on each hundred bighas of cultivated land within their limits.

Apprehensive, however, that Bika or his descendants might encroach upon their rights, they asked what security he could offer against such a contingency? The Rajput chief replied that, in order to dissipate their fears on this head, as well as to perpetuate the remembrance of the supremacy thus voluntarily conferred, he would solemnly bind himself and his successors to receive the *tika* of inauguration from the hands of the descendants of the elders of Shaikhsar and Ronia, and that the *gaddi* should be deemed vacant until such rite was administered.

In this simple transfer of the allegiance of this pastoral people we mark that instinctive love of liberty which accompanied the Getae in all places and all conditions of society, whether on the banks of the Oxus and the Jaxartes, or in the sandy desert of India; and although his political independence is now annihilated, he is still ready even to shed his blood if his Rajput master dare to infringe his inalienable right to his *bapota*, his paternal acres.

Former Owners conferring Titles on their Successors.—It is seldom that so incontestable a title to supremacy can be asserted as that which the weakness and jealousies of the Godaras conferred upon Bika, and it is a pleasing incident to find almost throughout India, in the observance of certain rites, the remembrance of the original compact which transferred the sovereign power from the lords of the soil to their Rajput conquerors. Thus, in Mewar, the fact of the power conferred upon the Guhilot founder by the Bhil aborigines is commemorated by a custom brought down to the present times. (See Vol. I. p. 262.) At Amber the same is recorded in the important offices retained by the Minas, the primitive inhabitants of that land. Both Kotah and Bundi retain in their names the remembrance of the ancient lords of Haraoti; and Bika's descendants preserve, in a twofold manner, the recollection of their bloodless conquest of the Jats. To this day the descendant of Pandu applies the unguent of royalty to the forehead of the successors of Bika; on which occasion the prince places 'the fine of relief,' consisting of twenty-five pieces of gold, in the hand of the Jat. Moreover, the spot which he selected for his capital was the birthright of a Jat, who would only concede it for this purpose on the condition that his name should be linked in perpetuity with its surrender. Naira, or Nera [184], was the name of the proprietor, which Bika added to his own, thus composing that of the future capital, Bikaner.[1]

Besides this periodical recognition of the transfer of power, on all lapses of the crown, there are annual memorials of the rights of the Godaras, acknowledged not only by the prince, but by all his Rajput vassal-kin, quartered on the lands of the Jat; and although 'the sons of Bika,' now multiplied over the country, do not much respect the ancient compact, they at least recognize, in the maintenance of these formulae, the origin of their power.

On the spring and autumnal [2] festivals of the Holi and Diwali, the heirs of the patriarchs of Shaikhsar and Ronia give the *tika* to the prince and all his feudality. The Jat of Ronia bears the silver cup and platter which holds the ampoule of the desert, while his compeer applies it to the prince's forehead. The Raja in return deposits a *nazarana* of a gold mohur, and five pieces of silver; the chieftains, according to their rank, following his example. The gold is taken by the Shaikhsar Jat, the silver by the elder of Ronia.

Conquest of the Johya Tribe.—To resume our narrative: when the preliminaries were adjusted, by Bika's swearing to maintain the rights of the community which thus surrendered their liberties to his keeping, they united their arms, and invaded the Johyas. This populous community, which extended over the northern region of the desert, even to the Sutlej, reckoned eleven hundred villages in their canton; yet now, after the lapse of little more than three centuries, the very name of Johya is extinct. They appear to be the Janjuha of Babur, who, in his irruption into India, found them congregated with the Juds, about the cluster of hills in the first *duaba* of the Panjab, called 'the mountains of Jud'; a position claimed by the Yadus or Jadons in the very dawn of their history, and called Jadu ka dang, 'the Jadu hills.'[3] This supports the assertion that the Johya is of Yadu race, while it does not invalidate its claims to Yuti or Jat descent,

[1] [This is a folk etymology. The name is derived from Hindi *ner*, Skt. *nagara*, 'city'—the 'city of Bīka.']

[2] *Vide* pp. 661, 695 for an account of these festivals.

[3] [Elliot-Dowson iv. 232; the connexion of the mountains of Jūd, to which the Author constantly refers, with the Yādavas is incorrect.

as will be further shown in the early portion of the annals of the Yadu-Bhattis.[1]

The patriarchal head of the Johyas resided at Bharopal;[2] his name was Sher Singh [185]. He mustered the strength of the canton, and for a long time withstood the continued efforts of the Rajputs and the Godaras; nor was it until "treason had done its worst," by the murder of their elder, and the consequent possession of Bharopal, that the Johyas succumbed to Rathor domination.

Foundation of Bīkaner, A.D. 1455-88.—With this accession of power, Bika carried his arms westward and conquered Bagor from the Bhattis. It was in this district, originally wrested by the Bhattis from the Jats, that Bika founded his capital, Bikaner, on the 15th Baisakh, S. 1545 (A.D. 1489), thirty years after his departure from the parental roof at Mandor.

When Bika was thus firmly established, his uncle Kandhal, to whose spirit of enterprise he was mainly indebted for success, departed with his immediate kin to the northward, with a view of settling in fresh conquests. He successively subjugated the communities of Asaich, Beniwal, and Saran, which cantons are mostly occupied by his descendants, styled Kandhalot Rathors, at this day, and although they form an integral portion of the Bikaner State, they evince, in their independent bearing to its chief, that their estates were "the gift of their own swords, not of his patents"; and they pay but a reluctant and nominal obedience to his authority. When necessity or avarice imposes a demand for tribute, it is often met by a flat refusal, accompanied with such a comment as this: "Who made this Raja? Was it not our common ancestor, Kandhal? Who is he, who presumes

[1] I presented a work on this race, entitled *The Book of the Johyas* (sent me by the prime minister of Jaisalmer) to the Royal Asiatic Society. Having obtained it just before leaving Rajputana, I never had leisure to examine it, or to pronounce on its value as an historical document; but any work having reference to so singular a community can scarcely fail to furnish matter of interest. [The Joiya or Johya tribe represent the ancient Yaudheya or 'warlike' peoples. It is incorrect to say that the name is extinct, because they are found on the banks of the Sutlej down to its confluence with the Indus; in Bīkaner in the old bed of the Ghaggar River below Bhatner, their ancient seat; in Lahore, Fīrozpur, the Dorajāt, Multān, and the Salt Range (Cunningham, *Ancient Geography*, i. 65; Rose, *Glossary*, ii. 410 ff.).]

[2] [One hundred and ten miles N.N.E. of Bīkaner city.]

to levy tribute from us?" Kandhal's career of conquest was cut short by the emperor's lieutenant in Hissar; he was slain in attempting this important fortress.

Death of Bīka. Nūnkaran or Lūnkaran, A.D. **1504-26.**—Bika died in S. 1551 (A.D. 1495), leaving two sons by the daughter of the Bhatti chief of Pugal, namely, Nunkaran, who succeeded, and Garsi, who founded Garsisar and Arsisar. The stock of the latter is numerous, and is distinguished by the epithet Garsot Bika, whose principal fiefs are those of Garsisar and Gharibdesar, each having twenty-four villages depending on them.[1]

Jeth Singh, A.D. **1526-41.**—Nunkaran made several conquests from the Bhattis, on the western frontier. He had four sons; his eldest desiring a separate establishment in his lifetime, for the fief of Mahajan and one hundred and forty villages, renounced his right of primogeniture in favour of his brother Jeth, who succeeded in S. 1569. His brothers had each appanages assigned to them. He had three sons: (1) Kalyan Singh, (2) Siahji, and (3) Aishpal [186]. Jethsi reduced the district of Narnot from some independent Girasia chiefs, and settled it as the appanage of his second son, Siahji. It was Jethsi also who compelled 'the sons of Bida,' the first Rathor colonists of this region, to acknowledge his supremacy by an annual tribute, besides certain taxes.

Kalyān Singh, A.D. **1541-71.**—Kalyan Singh succeeded in S. 1603. He had three sons: (1) Rae Singh, (2) Ram Singh, and (3) Prithi Singh.

Rāē Singh, A.D. **1571-1611. Bīkaner subject to the Mughals. Akbar's Marriage.**—Rae Singh succeeded in S. 1630 (A.D. 1573). Until this reign the Jats had, in a great degree, preserved their ancient privileges. Their maintenance was, however, found rather inconvenient by the now superabundant Rajput popula-

[1] To the few who will peruse these annals of the desert tribes it will be interesting to observe the development of families, and the maintenance, by such distinctive patronymics, of their origin. In the annals of this remote State I shall not enter at any length into the history of their wars, which are, with a change of names and scene, all pretty much alike; but confine myself, after a succinct and connected genealogical relation, to the manners of the people, the aspect, productions, and government of the country. [Abu-l Fazl (*Akbarnāma*, i. 375) calls him Rāē Lonkaran. According to Erskine (iii. A. 316) the second chief of Bīkaner was Naro or Naruji, son of Bīka, who succeeded A.D. 1504, and died childless after a reign of four months.]

tion, and they were consequently dispossessed of all political authority. With the loss of independence their military spirit decayed, and they sunk into mere tillers of the earth. In this reign also Bikaner rose to importance amongst the principalities of the empire, and if the Jats parted with their liberties to the Rajput, the latter, in like manner, bartered his freedom to become a Satrap of Delhi. On his father's death, Rae Singh in person undertook the sacred duty of conveying his ashes to the Ganges. The illustrious Akbar was then emperor of India. Rae Singh and the emperor had married sisters, princesses of Jaisalmer.[1] This connexion obtained for him, on his introduction to court by Raja Man of Amber, the dignity of a leader of four thousand horse, the title of Raja, and the government of Hissar. Moreover, when Maldeo of Jodhpur incurred the displeasure of the king, and was dispossessed of the rich district of Nagor, it was given to Rae Singh. With these honours, and increased power as one of the king's lieutenants, he returned to his dominions, and sent his brother Ram Singh against Bhatner,[2] of which he made a conquest. This town was the chief place of a district belonging to the Bhattis, originally Jats[3] of Yadu descent, but who assumed this name on becoming proselytes to the faith of Islam.

Subjugation of the Johyas.—Ram Singh at the same time completely subjugated the Johyas, who, always troublesome, had recently attempted to regain their ancient independence. The Rajputs carried fire and sword into this country, of which they made a desert. Ever since it has remained desolate: the very name of Johya is lost, though the vestiges of considerable towns bear testimony to a remote antiquity.

Traditions of Greek Settlements.—Amidst these ruins of the

[1] [For Rāē Singh see Rogers-Beveridge, *Memoirs of Jahāngīr*, 130 f. According to the *Akbarnāma* (ii. 518) Akbar's wife was the daughter of Kahān, brother of Kalyānmall, Rāē of Jaisalmer. The *Tuzuk* (*Āīn*, i. 477) says that her father was Rāwal Bhīm, elder brother of Kalyān. Ferishta (ii. 234) says that Kalyānmall was her father, and this statement is accepted by Erskine (iii. A. 316) see Elliot-Dowson v. 336.]

[2] [Now known as Hanumāngarh, 144 miles N.E. of Bīkaner city (*IGI*, xiii. 38).]

[3] In the Annals of Jaisalmer the number of offsets from the Yadu-Bhatti tribe, which assumed the name of Jat, will be seen; an additional ground for asserting that the Scythic Yadu is in fact the Yuti.

Johyas, the name of Sikandar Rumi (Alexander the Great) [187] has fixed itself, and the desert retains the tradition that the ruin called Rangmahall, the 'painted palace,' near Dandusar, was the capital of a prince of this region punished by a visitation of the Macedonian conqueror. History affords no evidence of Alexander's passage of the Gara, though the scene of his severest conflict was in that nook of the Panjab not remote from the lands of the Johyas. But though the chronicler of Alexander does not sanction our indulging in this speculation, the total darkness in which we appear doomed to remain with regard to Bactria and the petty Grecian kingdoms on the Indus, established by him, does not forbid our surmise, that by some of these, perhaps the descendants of Python, such a visitation might have happened.[1] The same traditions assert that these regions were not always either arid or desolate, and the living chronicle alluded to in the note repeated the stanza elsewhere given, which dated its deterioration from the drying up of the Hakra river, which came from the Panjab, and flowing through the heart of this country, emptied itself into the Indus between Rohri Bhakkar and Uchh.

The affinity that this word (Hakra) has both to the Ghaggar, and Sankra,[2] would lead to the conclusion of either being the stream referred to. The former we know as being engulphed in the sands about the Hariana confines, while the Sankra is a stream which, though now dry, was used as a line of demarcation even in the time of Nadir Shah. It ran eastward, parallel with the Indus, and by making it his boundary, Nadir added all the fertile valley of the Indus to his Persian kingdom. (See map.)

[1] My informant of this tradition was an old inhabitant of Dandusar, and although seventy years of age, had never left the little district of his nativity until he was brought to me, as one of the most intelligent living records of the past. [General Hervey (*Some Records of Crime*, i. 209) says that a trace of Greek art may be found in the Grecian ram's head on the hilt of weapons in Bikaner. For traditions of descent from Alexander based on the Graeco-Bactrian kingdom see Sykes, *Hist. of Persia*, i. 257).]

[2] The natives of these regions cannot pronounce the sibilant; so that, as I have already stated, the *s* is converted into *h*. I gave as an example the name Jahilmer, which becomes 'the hill of fools' instead of 'the hill of Jaisal.' Sankra, in like manner, becomes Hankra. [Uchh in the Bahāwalpur State (*IGI*, xxiv. 82). For the Hakra depression see Malik Muhammad Din (*Bahāwalpur State Gazetteer*, i. 3 ff.). The Ghaggar, once an affluent of the Indus, is lost in the sands near Hanumāngarh or Bhatner (*IGI*, xii. 212 f.).]

The only date this legendary stanza assigns for the catastrophe is the reign of the Sodha prince, Hamir.

Rām Singh, having thus destroyed the power of future resistance in the Johyas, turned his arms against the Punia Jats, the last who preserved their ancient liberty. They were vanquished, and the Rajputs were inducted into their most valuable possessions. But the conqueror paid the penalty of his life for the glory of colonizing the lands of the Punias. He was slain in their expiring effort to shake off the yoke of the stranger ; and though the Ramsinghgots add to the numerical strength, and enlarge the territory of the heirs of Bika, they, like the Kandhalots, little increase the power [188]. of the State, to which their obedience is nominal. Sidmukh and Sanku are the two chief places of the Ramsinghgots.

Thus, with the subjugation of the Punias, the political annihilation of the six Jat cantons of the desert was accomplished : they are now occupied in agriculture and their old pastoral pursuits, and are an industrious tax-paying race under their indolent Rajput masters.

Rāē Singh in Akbar's Service.—Raja Rae Singh led a gallant band of his Rathors in all the wars of Akbar. He was distinguished in the assault of Ahmadabad, slaying in single combat the governor, Mirza Muhammad Husain.[1] The emperor, who knew the value of such valorous subjects, strengthened the connexion which already subsisted between the crown and the Rathors, by obtaining for prince Salim (afterwards Jahangir) Rae Singh's daughter to wife. The unfortunate Parvez was the fruit of this marriage.

Karan Singh, A.D. **1631-69.**—Rae Singh was succeeded by his only son, Karan, in S. 1688 (A.D. 1632).[2]

Karan held the 'mansab of two thousand,' and the govern-

[1] [His services are described in *Āīn*, i. 357 ff. Ferishta (ii. 243) says that Rāē Singh killed Muhammad Husain after he was captured. According to another account, Akbar spoke kindly to his captive, and gave him into Rāē Singh's custody (Elliot-Dowson v. 367).]

[2] [According to Erskine (iii. A. 319, iii. B. 83) Dalpat Singh and Sūr Singh were Rāos between Rāē Singh and Karan Singh. For these Chiefs see *Āīn*, i. 359. Karan Singh, according to Musalmān authorities, died in 1666–7 (Manucci ii. 22). In 1660 Aurangzeb sent a force under Amīr Khān to bring him to reason for his insolence in refusing to attend the Emperor's Court (Jadunath Sarkar, *Life of Aurangzib*, iii. 29 f.).]

ment of Daulatabad, in his father's lifetime. Being a supporter of the just claims of Dara Shukoh, a plot was laid by the general of his antagonist, with whom he served, to destroy him, but which he was enabled to defeat by the timely intelligence of the Hara prince of Bundi. He died at Bikaner, leaving four sons: (1) Padma Singh, (2) Kesari Singh, (3) Mohan Singh, and (4) Anup Singh.

This family furnishes another example of the prodigal sacrifice of Rajput blood in the imperial service. The two elder princes were slain in the storm of Bijapur, and the tragical death of the third, Mohan Singh, in the imperial camp, forms an episode in *Ferishta's History of the Dekhan* [189].[1]

Anūp Singh, A.D. 1669-98.—Anup Singh succeeded in S. 1730 (A.D. 1674). For the services of his family he had the castle and lands of Adoni[2] conferred upon him, with 'the mansab of five

[1] [J. Scott, *Ferishta's History of the Dekkan*, ii. 30.] The young desert chieftain, like all his tribe, would find matter for quarrel in the wind blowing in his face. Having received what he deemed an insult from the brother-in-law of the Shahzada, in a dispute regarding a fawn, he appealed to his sword, and a duel ensued even in the presence-chamber, in which young Mohan fell. The fracas was reported to his brother Padma, at no distance from the scene. With the few retainers at hand, he rushed to the spot, and found his brother bathed in his blood. His antagonist, still hanging over his victim, when he saw the infuriated Rathor enter, with sword and shield, prepared for dreadful vengeance, retreated behind one of the columns of the Āmm Khass (*Divan*). But Padma's sword reached him, and avenged his brother's death; as the record says, "he felled him to the earth, cleaving at the same place the pillar in twain." Taking up the dead body of his brother, and surrounded by his vassals, he repaired to his quarters, where he assembled all the Rajput princes serving with their contingents, as Jaipur, Jodhpur, Haraoti, and harangued them on the insult to their race in the murder of his brother. They all agreed to abandon the king's army, and retire to their own homes. A noble was sent to expostulate by Prince Muazzam; but in vain. He urged that the prince not only forgave, but approved the summary vengeance taken by the Rathor; they refused to listen, and in a body had retired more than twenty miles, when the prince in person joined them, and concessions and expostulations overcoming them, they returned to the camp. It was subsequent to this that the two elder brothers were slain. It is recorded of the surviving brother, that he slew an enormous lion in single combat. For this exploit, which thoroughly entitled him to the name he bore (Kesari), 'the Lion,' he received an estate of twenty-five villages from the king. He also obtained great renown for slaying a Habshi or Abyssinian chief, who commanded for one of the southern princes.

[2] [Adoni in the Bellary District, Madras (*IGI*, v. 24 ff.).]

thousand,' and the governments of Bijapur and Aurangabad. Anup Singh led his clans with the head of his race, the prince of Jodhpur, to quell a rebellion amongst the Afghans of Kabul, which having effected, he returned to the peninsula. Ferishta and the native annals are at variance on his death; the former asserting that he died in the Deccan, while the latter say that he left that country, disgusted with the imperial commander's interference about his ground of encampment, and that he died at Bikaner.[1] He left two sons, Sarup Singh and Sujan Singh.

Sarūp Singh, A.D. 1698-1700.—Sarup, who succeeded in S. 1765 (A.D. 1709), did not long enjoy his honours, being killed in attempting to recover Adoni, which the emperor had resumed on his father's leaving the army.[2]

Sujān Singh, A.D. 1700-1735.—Sujan Singh, his successor, did nothing.

Zorāwar Singh, A.D. 1735-45.—Zorawar Singh became raja in S. 1793 (A.D. 1737). The domestic incidents of this, as of the preceding reigns, are without interest.

Gaj Singh, A.D. 1745-88.—Gaj Singh succeeded in S. 1802 (A.D. 1746). Throughout a long reign of forty-one years, this prince carried on border strife with the Bhattis and the Khan of Bahawalpur. From the former he took Rajasar, Kela, Raner, Satasar, Banipura, Mutalai, and other villages of inferior note; and from the Khan he recovered the important frontier castle of Anupgarh.

He laid waste, filling up the wells, a considerable tract of country west of the frontier post of Anupgarh, to prevent the incursions of the Daudputras.[3]

Raja Gaj had some celebrity from the number of his offspring, having had sixty-one children, though all but six were the 'sons of love.' The legitimates were, Chhattar Singh, who died in infancy; Raj Singh, who was poisoned by the mother of Surat Singh, the reigning prince; Surthan Singh and Ajib Singh, both of whom fled the paternal roof to escape the fate of their elder

[1] [He died at Adoni in 1698 (Erskine iii. A. 322).]

[2] [According to Erskine (iii. B. 86) he died of smallpox in the Deccan.]

[3] 'The children of David,' the designation of the tract and inhabitants subject to the State of Bahawalpur, from its founder, Daud Khan, a native of Seistan. [For the Dāūdputra clan see Rose, *Glossary*, ii. 224 f. Their history is fully given by Malik Muhammad Din, *Bahāwalpur State Gazetteer*, i. 47 ff.]

brother, and are now at Jaipur; Surat Singh, Raja of Bikaner; and Shyam Singh, who enjoys a small appanage in Bikaner.

Rāj Singh, A.D. 1788.—Raj Singh succeeded his father, S. 1843 (A.D. 1787), but he enjoyed the dignity only thirteen days, being removed by a dose of poison by the mother [1] of Surat Singh, the fifth son of Raja Gaj. The crown thus nefariously obtained, this worthy son [190] of such a parent determined to maintain his authority by like means, and to leave no competitor to contest his claims. He has accordingly removed by death or exile all who stood between him and the '*gaddi* of Bika.'

Partāp Singh, A.D. 1788. Usurpation of Sūrat Singh.—Raj Singh left two sons, Partap Singh and Jai Singh. On the death of Raj Singh, the office of regent, a word of ominous import in these regions, was assumed by Surat Singh, who, during eighteen months, conducted himself with great circumspection, and by condescension and gifts impressed the chiefs in his favour. At length he broke his plans to the chiefs of Mahajan and Bahaduran, whose acquiescence in his usurpation he secured by additions to their estates. The faithful Bakhtawar Singh, whose family during four generations had filled the office of Diwan, discovered the scheme, though too late to counteract it, and the attempt was punished by imprisonment. Prepared for the last step, the regent collected foreign troops from Bhatinda [2] and other parts, sufficient to overcome all opposition. The infant prince was kept secluded, and at length the regent issued the warrant in his own name for the nobles to assemble at the capital. Except the two traitors enumerated, they to a man refused; but instead of combining to oppose him, they indolently remained at their castles. Collecting all his troops, the usurper passed to Nohar, where he enticed the chief of Bhukarka to an interview, and lodged him in the fortress of Nohar.[3] Thence he passed to Ajitpura, which he plundered; and advancing to Sankhu, he attacked it in form. Durjan Singh defended himself with valour, and when reduced to extremity, committed suicide. His heir was put in fetters, and a fine of twelve thousand rupees was levied from the vassals of Sankhu. The commercial town of

[1] She was the sister of the Jhalai chief, heir presumptive to the *gaddi* of Jaipur, on failure of lineal issue.

[2] [In the Patiāla State, Panjāb.]

[3] [Nohar and Bhukārka are about 120 miles N.E. of Bikaner city.]

Churu was next attacked; it held out six months, when the confined chief of Bhukarka, as the price of his own freedom, treacherously offered to put the tyrant in possession. He effected this, and a fine of nearly two lakhs of rupees (£20,000) was offered to spare the town from plunder.

By this act of severity, and the means it furnished, Surat returned to Bikaner, determined to remove the only bar between him and the crown, his prince and nephew. In this he found some difficulty, from the virtue and vigilance of his sister, who never lost sight of the infant. Frustrated in all attempts to circumvent her, and not daring to blazon the murder by open violence, he invited the needy Raja of Narwar to make proposals for his sister's hand. In vain she urged her advanced period of life; and in order to deter the suitor, that she had already been affianced to Rana Arsi of Mewar. All his scruples vanished at the dower of three lakhs, which the regent offered [191] the impoverished scion of the famous Raja Nala.[1] Her objections were overruled and she was forced to submit; though she not only saw through her brother's anxiety for her removal, but boldly charged him with his nefarious intentions. He was not content with disavowing them, but at her desire gave her the most solemn assurances of the child's safety. Her departure was the signal of his death; for not long after he was found strangled, and it is said by the regent's own hands, having in vain endeavoured to obtain the offices of the Mahajan chieftain as the executioner of his sovereign.

Sūrat Singh, A.D. 1788-1828.—Thus, in one short year after the death of Raja Raj, the *gaddi* of Bika was dishonoured by being possessed by an assassin of his prince. In S. 1857 (A.D. 1801), the elder brothers of the usurper, Surthan Singh and Ajib Singh, who had found refuge in Jaipur, repaired to Bhatner and assembled the vassals of the disaffected nobles and Bhattis in order to dethrone the tyrant. But the recollection of his severities deterred some, while bribes kept back others, and the usurper did not hesitate to advance to meet his foes. The encounter,

[1] The story of Nala and Damayanti (or Nal Daman, as it is familiarly called in these regions) is well known in oriental literature. From Nal the famed castle of Narwar is named, of which this suitor for the hand of the Bikaner princess was deprived by Sindhia. [The famous tale of Nala and Damayanti from the *Mahābhārata* is perhaps best known from Dean Milman's version. Narwar is now in Gwalior State.]

which took place at Bigor, was obstinate and bloody, and three thousand Bhattis alone fell. This signal victory confirmed Surat's usurpation. He erected a castle on the field of battle, which he called Fatehgarh, 'the fort of victory.'

Flushed with this brilliant success, Surat Singh determined to make his authority respected both at home and abroad. He invaded his turbulent countrymen, the Bidawats, and levied fifty thousand rupees from their lands. Churu,[1] which had promised aid to the late confederacy, was once more invested and mulcted, and various other places were attacked ere they could join. But one solitary castle was successfully defended, that of Chhani, near Bahaduran. Here the usurper was foiled, and, after six months' fruitless siege, compelled to return to his capital.

Shortly after, he eagerly availed himself of an opportunity to punish the excesses of the Daudputras, and to withdraw attention from himself, by kindling a popular war against these powerful and turbulent neighbours. The occasion was the Kirani chief of Tirhara demanding his aid against his liege lord, Bahawal Khan. As these border feuds are not extinguished even in these days of universal peace, it may not be uninteresting to see the feudal muster-roll of the desert chiefs on such occurrences, as well as the mode in which they carry on hostilities. It was very shortly before that victory had preponderated on the side of the Rathors by a gallant *coup-de-main* of [192] the lord marcher of Bikaner, who carried the castle of Mozgarh[2] in a midnight assault. The hero on this occasion was not a Rathor, but a Bhatti chief, in the service of Bikaner, named Hindu Singh, who gained 'immortality' by the style in which he scaled the walls, put Muhammad Maaruf Kirani, the governor, and the garrison to the sword, and brought away captive to Bikaner the governor's wife, who was afterwards ransomed for five thousand rupees and four hundred camels.

The outlaw who sought *saran* at Bikaner, on this occasion, was of the same tribe, Kirani, his name Khudabakhsh (' gift of God '), chief of Tirhara, one of the principal fiefs of the Daudputras. With all his retainers, to the amount of three hundred horse and five hundred foot, he threw himself on the protection of Surat Singh, who assigned him twenty villages, and one hundred rupees daily for his support. The Kiranis were the most powerful vassals

[1] [Churu, about 100 miles N.E.E. of Bikaner city.]

[2] [Possibly Mojarh, about 40 miles S.E. of Bahāwalpur city.]

of Bahawal Khan, who might have paid dear for the resumption of Tirhara, whose chief promised the Rajput nothing less than to extend his conquests to the Indus. Allured by this bait, the Kher was proclaimed and the sons of Bika assembled from all quarters.

			Horse.	Foot.	Guns.
	Abhai Singh, chief of	Bhukarka	300	2000	
	Rao Ram Singh, of	Pugal	100	400	
	Hathi Singh, of	Raner	8	150	
	Karan Singh, of	Satasar	9	150	
	Anup Singh	Jasara	40	250	
	Khet Singh	Jamansar	60	350	
	Beni Singh, of	Janglu	9	250	
	Bhum Singh, of	Bithnok	2	61	
	Feudal retainers		528	3611	
	Park under Maji Parihar		—		21
Foreign Brigade in the Raja's service.	Khas Paiga, or household troop		200	—	
	Camp of Ganga Singh		200	1500	4
	Do. of Durjan Singh		60	600	4
Auxiliary Levies.	Anoka Singh	Sikh chieftains	300	—	
	Lahori Singh		250	—	
	Budh Singh		250	—	
	Sultan Khan, Ahmad Khan	Afghans	400	—	
	TOTAL		2188	5711	29

[193].

Attack on Bahāwalpur.—The command-in-chief of this brilliant array was conferred on Jethra Mahto, son of the Diwan. On the 13th of Magh 1856 (spring of 1800) he broke ground, and the feudal levies fell in on the march by Kanasar, Rajasar, Keli, Raner, and Anupgarh, the last point of rendezvous. Thence he proceeded by Sheogarh,[1] Mozgarh, and Phulra, all of which were taken after a few weeks' siege, and from the last they levied a lakh and a quarter of rupees, with other valuables, and nine guns. They advanced to Khairpur,[2] within three miles of the

[1] Its former name was Balar, one of the most ancient cities of the desert, as is Phulra, a Johya possession.

[2] [Not the Khairpur in Sind; 38 miles N.E. of Bahāwalpur city.]

Indus, when being joined by other refractory chiefs, Jethra marched direct on the capital, Bahawalpur, within a short distance of which he encamped preparatory to the attack. The Khan, however, by this delay, was enabled to detach the most considerable of his nobles from the Rajput standard: on which the Bikaner Diwan, satisfied with the honour of having insulted Bahawalpur, retreated with the spoils he had acquired. He was received by the usurper with contempt, and degraded for not fighting.

Bhatti Invasion of Bikaner.—The Bhattis, smarting with the recollection of their degradation, two years after the battle of Bigor attempted the invasion of Bikaner, but were again repulsed with loss; and these skirmishes continued until S. 1861 (A.D. 1805), when Raja Surat attacked the Khan of the Bhattis in his capital, Bhatner. It capitulated after a siege of six months, when Zabita Khan, with his garrison and effects, was permitted to retire to Rania, since which this place has remained an appanage of Bikaner.

Attack on Jodhpur.—The coalition against Jodhpur was ruinous to Surat, who supported the cause of the pretender, on which the usurper expended twenty-four lakhs of rupees, nearly five years' revenue of this desert region. On this occasion, he led all his troops in person against Jodhpur, and united in the siege, which they were however compelled to abandon with dishonour, and retrograde to their several abodes. In consequence of this, the usurper fell sick, and was at the last extremity; nay, the ceremonies for the dead were actually commenced; but he recovered, to the grief and misery of his subjects. To supply an exhausted treasury, his extortions know no bounds; and having cherished the idea that he might compound his past sins by rites and gifts to the priests, he is surrounded by a group of avaricious Brahmans, who are maintained in luxury at the expense of his subjects. His cruelty keeps pace with his avarice and his fears. The chief of Bhukarka he put to death, notwithstanding his numerous services. Nahar Singh of Sidmukh, Gyan Singh and Guman Singh of Gandeli, amongst the chief [194] feudatories of the State, shared the same fate. Churu was invested a third time, and with its chief, fell into the tyrant's hands.

With this system of terror, his increasing superstition, and diminished attention to public duties, the country is annually deteriorating in population and wealth; and as if they had not misery enough within, they have not had a single good season for years.[1] Owing to the disobedience of the northern chiefs, and the continual incursions of the Ṛahats, or 'Bhatti robbers,' who sweep the land of cattle, and often cut and carry off entire crops, the peasant Jat, the ancient lord of the soil, is often left to the alternative of starvation or emigration. Many have consequently sought shelter in the British frontier territories, in Hansi and Hariana, where they are kindly received. Since the English have occupied Sirsa and the lands belonging to the Bhatti Bahadur Khan, the misfortunes of the cultivators of the northern parts of Bikaner have been doubled by the inroads of a band left without resource. In some parts, the Jats combine to protect themselves against these inroads: every hamlet has its post of defence, a tower of earth, on which is perched a watchman and kettledrum, to beat the alarm, which is taken up from village to village, and when an enemy is discovered, all are in arms to defend their property. The unfortunate Jat is obliged to plough his fields under the load of shield and *sang*, or heavy iron lance; so that, at no distant period, the whole of this region must become as desolate as the tracts once possessed by the Johyas.[2]

Such, at the end of three hundred and twenty-three years, is the change which a Rajput usurper has effected in the once comparatively populous communities of the Jats. From the founder, Bika, to the present tyrannical governor, there have been only eleven descents though thirteen reigns, giving an average of thirty years for the one, and twenty-five for the other: a fact which speaks forcibly for the general morality of the descendants of Bika.

Bīdāvati.—Before we enter on the physical aspect of the country, we must make mention of Bidavati, the lands of 'the sons of Bida,' now an integral portion of Bikaner.[3] It will be

[1] This account was drawn up in 1814.

[2] While putting this to the press, rumour says that the chiefs of Bikaner are in open rebellion against the Raja, who has applied, but without success, to the British Government for support. This, if true, is as it should be. [This rebellion occurred in 1815, and the Mahārāja invoked British aid. A treaty was signed on March 9, 1818, by which Sūrat Singh and his successors became subordinate to the British Government. A force under Brigadier-General Arnold restored order (Erskine iii. A. 326).]

[3] [Bīdāvati, now Sūjangarh, bounded on S. by Jodhpur, and E. by Shaikhāwaṭi (*ibid.* iii. A. 390 f.).]

borne in mind that Bida, the brother of Bika, led the first Rajput colony from Mandor, in search of a fresh establishment. His first attempt was in the province of Godwar, then belonging to the Rana: but his reception there was so warm, that [195] he moved northward, and was glad to take service with the chief of the Mohils. This ancient tribe is by some termed a branch of the Yadus, but is by others considered a separate race, and one of the 'Thirty-six Royal Races': all are agreed as to its antiquity. The residence of the Mohil chief was Chhapar,[1] where, with the title of Thakur, he ruled over one hundred and forty townships. Bida deemed circumvention better than open force to effect his purposes; and as, according to the Rajput maxim, in all attempts 'to obtain land,' success hallows the means, he put in train a scheme which, as it affords the least cause for suspicion, has often been used for this object. Bida became the medium of a matrimonial arrangement between the Mohil chief and the prince of Marwar; and as the relation and natural guardian of the bride, he conveyed the nuptial train unsuspected into the castle of the Mohils, whose chiefs were assembled to honour the festivities. But instead of the Rathor fair and her band of maidens, the valorous sons of Jodha rushed sword in hand from the litters and covered vehicles, and treacherously cut off the best men of Mohila. They kept possession of the inner fortress until tidings of their success brought reinforcements from Jodhpur. For this aid, Bida assigned to his father Ladnun and its twelve villages, now incorporated with Jodhpur. The son of Bida, Tej Singh, laid the foundation of a new capital, which he called after his father, Bidesar.[2] The community of the Bidawats is the most powerful in Bikaner, whose prince is obliged to be satisfied with almost nominal marks of supremacy, and to restrict his demands, which are elsewhere unlimited. The little region of the Mohilas, around the ancient capital Chhapar, is an extensive flat, flooded in the periodical rains from the surrounding *tibas* or 'sandhills,' the soil of which is excellent, even wheat being abundantly produced. This Oasis, as it is entitled to be termed, may be twenty-five miles (twelve cos) in extreme length, by about six in breadth. We cannot affirm that the entire Bidawat district of one hundred and forty villages, and to which is assigned a population of forty

[1] [On S. frontier of the State.]

[2] [Bidesar or Bidāsar is 64 miles S.S.W. of Bīkaner city.]

thousand to fifty thousand souls, one-third being Rathors, 'the sons of Bida,' is within this flat. It is subdivided into twelve fiefs, of which five are pre-eminent. Of the ancient possessors, the indigenous Mohils, there are not more than twenty families throughout the land of Mohila; the rest are chiefly Jat agriculturists and the mercantile castes.

We do the sons of Bida no injustice when we style them a community of plunderers. Like the sons of Esau, "their hand is against every man": and they are too powerful to fear retaliation. In former times they used to unite with the Larkhanis [196], another horde of robbers, and carry their raids into the most populous parts of Jaipur. In these habits, however, they only partake of the character common to all who inhabit desert regions. What nature has denied them, they wrest from those to whom she has been more bountiful. But it is to the absence of good government more than to natural sterility that we must attribute the moral obliquity of the Rajaputras, 'the offspring of regality,' spread over these extensive regions, who little discriminate between *meum* and *tuum*, in all that refers to their neighbours.

CHAPTER 2

Geography of Bikaner.—This region is but little known to Europeans, by whom it has hitherto been supposed to be a perfect desert, unworthy of examination. Its present condition bears little comparison with what tradition reports it to have been in ancient times; and its deterioration, within three centuries since the Rajputs supplanted the Jats, almost warrants our belief of the assertion, that these deserts were once fertile and populous; nay, that they are still capable (notwithstanding the reported continual increase of the sand) to maintain an abundant population, there is little room to doubt. The princes of Bikaner used to take the field at the head of ten thousand of their kindred retainers; and although they held extraordinary grants from the empire for the maintenance of these contingents, their ability to do so from their proper resources was undoubted. To other causes than positive sterility must be attributed the wretched condition of this State. Exposed to the continual attacks of organized bands of robbers from without, subjected internally to the never-ending demands of a rapacious government, for which they have not a shadow of advantage in return, it would be strange if aught but progressive decay and wretchedness were the consequence. In three centuries [197], more than one-half of the villages, which either voluntarily or by force submitted to the rule of the founder, Bika, are now without memorial of their existence, and the rest are gradually approximating to the same condition. Commercial caravans, which passed through this State and enriched its treasury with the transit duties, have almost ceased to frequent it from the increasing insecurity of its territory. Besides the personal loss to the prince the country suffers from the deterioration of the commercial towns of Churu, Rajgarh, and Rani, which, as entrepôts, supplied the country with the productions of Sind and the provinces to the westward, or those of Gangetic India. Nor is this confined to Bikaner; the same cause affects Jaisalmer, and the more eastern principalities, whose misgovernment, equally with Bikaner, fosters the spirit of rapine: the Maldots of Jaisalmer and the Larkhanis of Jaipur are as notorious as the Bidawats of Bikaner; and to these may be added the Sahariyas, Khosas, and Rajars, in the more western desert, who, in their habits and principles, are as demoralized as the Bedouins of Arabia.

Extent, Population, Soil, Tibas or Sandhills.—The line of greatest breadth of this State extends from Pugal to Rajgarh, and measures about one hundred and eighty miles; while the length from north to south, between Bhatner and Mahajan, is about one hundred and sixty miles: the area may not exceed twenty-two thousand miles.[1] Formerly they reckoned two thousand seven hundred towns, villages, and hamlets scattered over this space, one-half of which are no longer in existence.

Population.—An estimate of the population of this arid region, without presenting some data, would be very unsatisfactory. The tract to the north-west of Jethpur is now perfectly desolate, and nearly so from that point to Bhatner: to the north-east the population is but scanty, which observation also applies to the parts from the meridian of Bikaner to the Jaisalmer frontier;

[1] [Bikaner is bounded on N. and W. by Bahāwalpur; S.W. by Jaisalmer; S. by Mārwār; S.E. by Shaikhāwati of Jaipur; E. by Lohāru and Hissār; total area 23,311 square miles (*IGI*, viii. 202).]

while internally, from these points, it is more uniform, and equals the northern parts of Marwar. From a census of the twelve principal towns, with an estimate, furnished by well-informed inhabitants, of the remainder, we may obtain a tolerably accurate approximation on this point :

Chief Towns.	Number of Houses.
Bikaner	12,000
Nohar	2,500
Bahaduran	2,500
Reni	1,500
Rajgarh	3.000
Churu	3,000 [198]
Mahajan	800
Jethpur	1,000
Bidesar	500
Ratangarh	1,000
Desmukh	1,000
Senthal	50
	28,850
100 villages, each having 200 houses	20,000
100 ,, ,, 150 ,,	15,000
200 ,, ,, 100 ,,	20,000
800 hamlets ,, 30 each	24,000
Total number of houses	107,850

Allowing five souls to each house, we have a total of 539,250 souls, giving an average of twenty-five to the square mile, which I cannot think exaggerated, and making the desert regions depending on Bikaner equal, in the density of population, the highlands of Scotland.[1]

Of this population, full three-fourths are the aboriginal Jats; the rest are their conquerors, descendants of Bika, including the Saraswat Brahmans,[2] Charans, Bards, and a few of the debased classes, whose numbers, conjointly, are not one-tenth of the Rajputs.

[1] [In 1911 the population was 573,501, 4·79 souls per house.]

[2] [For the Saraswat or Sarsūt Brāhmans see Rose, *Glossary*, ii. 122 ff.]

Jats.—The Jats are the most wealthy as well as the most numerous portion of the community. Many of the old Bhumia landlords, representatives of their ancient communal heads, are men of substance; but their riches are of no use to them, and to avoid the rapacity of their government, they cover themselves with the cloak of poverty, which is thrown aside only on nuptial festivities. On these occasions they disinter their hoards, which are lavished with unbounded extravagance. They even block up the highways to collect visitors, whose numbers form the measure of the liberality and munificence of the donor of the fête.

Sarsūt, Saraswat Brāhman. — Sarsut (properly Sarasvati) Brahmans are found in considerable numbers throughout this tract. They aver that they were masters of the country prior to the Jat colonists. They are a peaceable, industrious race, and without a single prejudice of 'the order'; they eat meat, smoke tobacco, cultivate the soil, and trade even in the sacred kine, notwithstanding their descent from Sringi Rishi, son of Brahma.

Charans.—The Charans are the sacred order of these regions; the warlike tribes esteem [199] the heroic lays of the bard more than the homily of the Brahman. The Charans are throughout reverenced by the Rathors, and hold lands, literally, on the tenure of 'an old song.' More will be said of them in the Annals of Jaisalmer.

Mālis, Nāis.—Malis, Nais, gardeners and barbers, are important members of every Rajput family, and to be found in all the villages, of which they are invariably the cooks.

Chuhras, Thoris.—Chuhras, Thoris, are actually castes of robbers:[1] the former, from the Lakhi Jungle; the latter, from Mewar. Most of the chieftains have a few in their pay, entertained for the most desperate services. The Bahaduran chief has expelled all his Rajputs, and retains only Chuhras and Thoris. The Chuhras are highly esteemed for fidelity, and the barriers and portals throughout this tract are in their custody. They enjoy a very singular perquisite, which would go far to prove their being the aborigines of the country; namely, a fee of four

[1] [The Chuhras are the criminal branch of the Panjāb sweepers (Rose, *Glossary*, ii. 182 ff.). The Thoris are said to be connected with the Aheris, a well-known criminal tribe (*Census Report, Mārwār*, 1891, ii. 194). In Bahāwalpur they resemble the Dhedh outcastes, who eat the flesh of dead animals (Malik Muhammad Din, *Gazetteer*, i. 155).]

copper coins on every dead subject, when the funeral ceremonies are over.

Rājputs.—The Rathors of Bikaner are unchanged in their martial qualifications, bearing as high a reputation as any other class in India ; and whilst their brethren of Marwar, Amber, and Mewar have been for years groaning under the rapacious visitations of Mahrattas and Pathans, their distance and the difficulties of the country have saved them from such afflictions ; though, in truth, they have had enough to endure at home, in the tyranny of their own lord. The Rathors of the desert have fewer prejudices than their more eastern brethren ; they will eat food, without enquiring by whom it was dressed, and will drink either wine or water, without asking to whom the cup belonged. They would make the best soldiers in the world if they would submit to discipline, as they are brave, hardy, easily satisfied, and very patient ; though, on the other hand, they have imbibed some qualities, since their migration to these regions, which could only be eradicated in the rising generation : especially the inordinate use of opium, and smoking intoxicating herbs, in both which accomplishments 'the sons of Bika' are said to bear the palm from the rest of the Chhattis rajkula, the Thirty-six Royal Tribes of India. The *piyala*, or 'cup,' is a favourite with every Rajput who can afford it, and is, as well as opium, a panacea for ennui, arising from the absence of all mental stimulants, in which they are more deficient, from the nature of the country, than most of their warlike countrymen.

Face of the Country.—The whole of this principality, with the exception of a few isolated spots, or oases, scattered here and there, consists more or less of sand. From the eastern to the western boundary, in the line of greatest breadth, it is one continuous [200] plain of sand, though the *tibas*, or sandhills, commence in the centre of the country, the principal chain running in the direction of Jaisalmer, and shooting forth subordinate branches in every direction ; or it might be more correct to designate this main ridge, originating in the tracts bordering the eastern valley of the Indus, as terminating its elevations about the heart of Bikaner. On the north-east quarter, from Rajgarh to Nohar and Rawatsar, the soil is good, being black earth, slightly mixed with sand, and having water near enough to the surface for irrigation ; it produces wheat, gram, and even rice, in considerable quantities. The same soil exists from Bhatner to the banks of the Gara. The whole of the Mohila tract is a fertile oasis, the *tibas* just terminating their extreme offsets on its northern limit: being flooded in the periodical rains, wheat is abundantly produced.

Products of the Desert.—But exclusive of such spots, which are "few and far between," we cannot describe the desert as a waste where "no salutary plant takes root, no verdure quickens"; for though the poverty of the soil refuses to aid the germination of the more luxuriant grains, Providence has provided a countervailing good, in giving to those it can rear a richness and superiority unknown to more favoured regions. The bajra of the desert is far superior to any grown in the rich loam of Malwa, and its inhabitant retains an instinctive partiality, even when admitted to revel in the luxurious repasts of Mewar or Amber, for the *vatis* or *batis* or 'bajra cakes,' of his native sandhills, and not more from association than from their intrinsic excellence. In a plentiful season they save enough for two years' consumption. The grain requires not much water, though it is of the last importance that this little should be timely.

Besides bajra we may mention moth and til;[1] the former a useful pulse both for men and cattle; the other the oil-plant, used both for culinary purposes and burning. Wheat, gram, and barley are produced in the favoured spots described, but in these are enumerated the staple products of Bikaner.

Cotton is grown in the tracts favourable for wheat.[2] The plant is said to be septennial, even decennial, in these regions. As soon as the cotton is gathered, the shoots are all cut off, and the root alone left. Each succeeding year, the plant increases in strength, and at length attains a size unknown where it is more abundantly cultivated.

Nature has bountifully supplied many spontaneous vegetable products for the use of man, and excellent pasture for cattle. Guar, Kachri, Kakri, all of the cucurbitaceous family, and water-melons of a gigantic size, are produced in great plenty.[3] The latter is most valuable; for being cut in slices and dried in the

[1] [*Moth, phaseolus aconitifolius*; *til, sesamum indicum*.]

[2] [Only a few acres of cotton are now grown.]

[3] [*Guār, dolichos biflorus*; water-melons are known as *matira*; *kakri*, a coarse variety of melon.]

sun, it is stored up [201] for future use when vegetables are scarce, or in times of famine, on which they always calculate. It is also an article of commerce, and much admired even where vegetables are more abundant. The copious mucilage of the dried melon is extremely nourishing; and deeming it valuable as an anti-scorbutic in sea voyages, the Author sent some of it to Calcutta many years ago for experiment.[1] Our Indian ships would find no difficulty in obtaining a plentiful supply of this article, as it can be cultivated to any extent, and thus be made to confer a double benefit on our seamen and the inhabitants of those desert regions. The superior magnitude of the water-melons of the desert over those of interior India gives rise to much exaggeration, and it has been gravely asserted by travellers in the sand *tibas*,[2] where they are most abundant, that the mucilage of one is sufficient to allay the thirst both of a horse and his rider.

In these arid regions, where they depend entirely on the heavens for water, and where they calculate on a famine every seventh year, nothing that can administer to the wants of man is lost. The seeds of the wild grasses, as the *bharut*, *baru*, *harara*, *sawan*, are collected, and, mixed with bajra-flour, enter much into the food of the poorer classes. They also store up great quantities of the wild *ber*, *khair*, and *karel* berries; and the long pods of the *khejra*, astringent and bitter as they are, are dried and formed into a flour. Nothing is lost in these regions which can be converted into food.

Trees.—Trees they have none indigenous (mangoes and tamarind are planted about the capital), but abundant shrubs, as the *babul*, and ever-green *pilu*, the *jhal*, and others yielding berries. The Bidawats, indeed, apply the term 'tree' to the *rohira*, which sometimes attains the height of twenty feet, and is transported to all parts for house-building; as likewise is the *nima*, so well known throughout India. The *phog* is the most useful of all these, as with its twigs they frame a wicker-work to line their wells, and prevent the sand from falling in.

The *ak*, a species of euphorbia, known in Hindustan as the

[1] I sent specimens to Mr. Moorcroft so far back as 1813, but never learned the result.—See Article "On the Preservation of Food," *Edin. Review*, No. 45, p. 115.

[2] Mr. Barrow, in his valuable work on Southern Africa, describes the water-melon as self-sown and abundant.

madar, grows to an immense height and strength in the desert; from its fibres they make the ropes in general use throughout these regions, and they are reckoned superior, both in substance and durability, to those formed of *munj* (hemp), which is however cultivated in the lands of the Bidawats.

Their agricultural implements are simple and suited to the soil. The plough is one [202] of single yoke, either for the camel or ox: that with double yoke being seldom required, or chiefly by the Malis (gardeners), when the soil is of some consistence. The drill is invariably used, and the grains are dropped singly into the ground, at some distance from each other, and each sends forth a dozen to twenty stalks. A bundle of bushes forms their harrow. The grain is trodden out by oxen; and the moth (pulse), which is even more productive than the bajra, by camels.

Water.—This indispensable element is at an immense distance from the surface throughout the Indian desert, which, in this respect, as well as many others, differs very materially from that portion of the great African Desert in the same latitudes. Water at twenty feet, as found at Mourzook by Captain Lyon, is here unheard of, and the degree of cold experienced by him at Zuela, on the winter solstice, would have "burnt up" every natural and cultivated production of our Hindu Sahara. Captain Lyon describes the thermometer in lat. 26°, within 2° of zero of Reaumur. Majors Denham and Clapperton never mark it under 40° of Fahrenheit, and mention ice, which I never saw but once, the thermometer being 28°; and then not only the mouths of our *mashaks*, or 'water-skins,' were frozen, but a small pond, protected from the wind (I heard, for I saw it not), exhibited a very thin pellicle of ice. When at 30° the cold was deemed intense by the inhabitants of Maru in the tracts limiting the desert, and the useful *ak*, and other shrubs, were scorched and withered; and in north lat. 25°, the thermometer being 28°, desolation and woe spread throughout the land. To use their own phrase, the crops of gram and other pulses were completely "burnt up, as if scorched by the lightnings of heaven"; while the sun's meridian heat would raise it 50° more, or up to 80°, a degree of variability at least not recorded by Captain Lyon.

At Deshnokh,[1] near the capital, the wells are more than two

[1] [Twenty miles S. of Bīkaner city, containing a temple of Karniji, the guardian deity of the Mahārāja's family.]

hundred cubits, or three hundred feet, in depth; and it is rare that water fit for man is found at a less distance from the surface than sixty, in the tracts decidedly termed *thal*, or 'desert': though some of the flats, or oases, such as that of Mohila, are exceptions, and abundance of brackish water, fit for cattle, is found throughout at half this depth, or about thirty feet. All the wells are lined with basket-work made of *phog* twigs, and the water is generally drawn up by hand-lines [203].[1]

Sar, or 'Salt Lakes.'—There are a few salt lakes, which, throughout the whole of the Indian desert, are termed *sar*, though none are of the same consequence as those of Marwar. The largest is at the town of Sar,[2] so named after the lake, which is about six miles in circumference. There is another at Chhapar about two miles in length, and although each of them frequently contains a depth of four feet of water, this entirely evaporates in the hot winds, leaving a thick sheet of saline incrustation. The salt of both is deemed of inferior quality to that of the more southerly lakes.

Physiography of the Country.—There is little to vary the physiography of this region, and small occasion to boast either of its physical or moral beauties; yet, strange to say, I have met with many whose love of country was stronger than their perceptions of abstract veracity, who would dwell on its perfections, and prefer a mess of *rabri*, or porridge made of bajra, to the greater delicacies of more civilized regions. To such, the *tibas*, or 'sand-ridges,' might be more important than the Himalaya, and their diminutive and scanty brushwood might eclipse the gigantic foliage of this huge barrier. Verdure itself may be abhorrent to eyes accustomed to behold only arid sands; and a region without *tufans* or 'whirlwinds'; or armies of locusts rustling like a

[1] Water is sold, in all the large towns, by the Malis, or 'gardeners,' who have the monopoly of this article. Most families have large cisterns or resorvoirs, called *tankas*, which are filled in the rainy season. They are of masonry, with a small trap-door at the top, made to exclude the external air, and having a lock and key affixed. Some large *tankas* are established for the community, and I understand this water keeps sweet for eight and twelve months' consumption. [The proper form of the word seems to be *tānkh*, *tānkha* (Yule, *Hobson-Jobson*, 2nd ed. 898 f.; H. Beveridge, *The Academy*, xlvi. 174).]

[2] [About 40 miles N.W. of Bīkaner city. The chief salt lakes are at Chhāpar and Lūnkaransar (Erskine iii. A. 350).]

tempest, and casting long shadows on the lands, might be deemed by the prejudiced, deficient in the true sublime. Occasionally the sandstone formation rises above the surface, resembling a few low isolated hills; and those who dwell on the boundaries of Nagor, if they have a love of more decided elevations than their native sandhills afford, may indulge in a distant view of the terminations of the Aravalli.

Mineral Productions.—The mineral productions of this country are scanty. They have excellent quarries of freestone in several parts, especially at Hasera, thirteen coss to the north-east of the capital, which yield a small revenue estimated at two thousand rupees annually. There are also copper mines at Biramsar and Bidesar; but the former does not repay the expense of working, and the latter, having been worked for thirty years, is nearly exhausted.

An unctuous clay is excavated from a pit, near Kolait, in large quantities, and exported as an article of commerce, besides adding fifteen hundred rupees annually to the treasury. It is used chiefly to free the skin and hair from impurities, and the Cutchi ladies are said to eat it to improve their complexions.[1]

Animal Productions.—The kine of the desert are highly esteemed; as are the camels, especially those used for expedition and the saddle, which bear a high price,[2] and are [204] considered superior to any in India. They are beautifully formed, and the head possesses much blood and symmetry. Sheep are reared in great abundance, and find no want of food in the excellent grasses and shrubs which abound. The *phog*, *jawas*,[3] and other prickly shrubs, which are here indigenous, form the dainties of the camel in other regions. The Nilgae, or elk, and deer of every kind, are plentiful; and the fox of the desert is a beautiful little animal. Jackals and hyaenas are not scarce, and even lions are by no means unknown in Bikaner.

Commerce and Manufactures.—Rajgarh[4] was the great commercial mart of this country, and the point of rendezvous for caravans from all parts. The produce of the Panjab and Kashmir

[1] [Multāni mitti, fuller's earth, found near Madh in the S. of the State, and sometimes eaten (Erskine iii. A. 251; Watt, *Econ. Prod.* 329 f.).]

[2] One thousand rupees have been given for one; one hundred is the average value.

[3] [The camel thorn, *Alhagi maurorum.*]

[4] [N.W. of Bīkaner city, near the Panjâb frontier.]

came formerly direct by Hansi-Hisar—that of the eastern countries by Delhi, Rewari, Dadri, etc., consisting of silks, fine cloths, indigo, sugar, iron, tobacco, etc.; from Haraoti and Malwa came opium, which supplied all the Rajput States; from Sind, via Jaisalmer, and by caravans from Multan and Shikarpur, dates, wheat, rice, *lungis* (silk vestments for women), fruits, etc.; from Pali, the imports from maritime countries, as spices, tin, drugs, coco-nuts, elephants' teeth, etc. Much of this was for internal consumption, but the greater part a mere transit trade, which yielded considerable revenue.

Woollens.—The wool of the sheep pastured in the desert is, however, the staple commodity both of manufacture and trade in this region. It is worked into every article of dress, both male and female, and worn by all, rich and poor. It is produced from the loom, of every texture and quality, from the coarse *loi* or 'blanket,' at three rupees per pair (six shillings), to thirty rupees. The quality of these last is very fine, of an intermediate texture between the shawl and camlet, and without any nap; it is always bordered with a stripe of chocolate brown or red. Of this quality are the *dopattas* or 'scarfs' for the ladies. Turbans are also manufactured of it, and though frequently from forty to sixty-one feet in length, such is the fineness of the web, that they are not bulky on the head.

From the milk of the sheep and goats as well as kine, *ghi* or 'clarified butter' is made, and forms an important article of trade.

Manufactures in Iron.—The Bikaneris work well in iron, and have shops at the capital and all the large towns for the manufacture of sword blades, matchlocks, daggers, iron lances, etc. The sword-handles, which are often inlaid with variegated steel, or burnished, are in high request, and exported to various parts of India. They have also expert artists in ivory, though the articles are chiefly such as are worn by females, as *churis*, or 'bracelets' [205].

Coarse cotton cloths, for internal consumption, are made in considerable quantities.

Fairs.—Annual fairs were held, in the months of Karttik and Phalgun, at the towns of Kolait and Gajner,[1] and frequented by

[1] [These towns are respectively 25 miles S.W. and 19 miles S.W. of Bikaner city.]

the merchants of the adjacent countries. They were celebrated for cattle, chiefly the produce of the desert, camels, kine, and horses from Multan and the Lakhi Jungle,[1] a breed now almost extinct. These fairs have lost all their celebrity; in fact, commerce in these regions is extinct.

Government Revenues.—The personal revenues of the Raja were derived from a variety of sources: from the Khalisa, or 'crown-lands' imposts, taxes on agriculture, and that compendious item which makes up the deficiencies in all oriental budgets, *dand*, or 'contribution.' But with all these "appliances and means to boot," the civil list of this desert king seldom exceeded five lakhs of rupees, or about £50,000 per annum.[2] The lands of the feudality are more extensive proportionally in this region than in any other in Rajputana, arising out of the original settlement, when the Bidawats and Kandhalots, whose joint acquisitions exceeded those of Bika, would not admit him to hold lands in their territory, and made but a slight pecuniary acknowledgment of his supremacy. The districts in which the crown-lands lie are Rajgarh, Reni, Nohar, Gharib, Ratangarh, Rania, and more recently Churu.

The following are the items of the revenue: (1) Khalisa, or fiscal revenue; (2) Dhuan; (3) Anga; (4) Town and transit duties; (5) Paseti, or 'plough-tax'; (6) Malba.

Khālisa Lands.—1. The fisc. Formerly this branch of revenue yielded two lakhs of rupees; but with progressive superstition and prodigality, the raja has alienated almost two-thirds of the villages from which the revenue was drawn. These amounted to two hundred; now they do not exceed eighty, and their revenue is not more than one lakh of rupees. Surat Singh is guided only by caprice; his rewards are uniform, no matter what the service or the object, whether a Brahman or a camel-driver. The Khalisa is the only source which he considers he has merely a life-interest in. To supply the deficiencies, he has direct recourse to the pockets of his subjects.

[1] [The tract S. of the Sutlej, having its E. limits at Ludhiāna and Sunām; to the S. of it lay the Bhāti desert (Manucci i. 320, iv. 426). Its importance is shown by Aurangzeb appointing Muhammad Muizzu-d-dīn, eldest son of Sultān Muazzam, Faujdār of the Lākhi Jungle, in A.D. 1706 (Bilimoria, *Letters of Aurangzeb*, 75.]

[2] [At present the normal revenue of the State is about 32 lakhs of rupees, or £213,000.]

Hearth-Tax.—2. Dhuan may be rendered hearth-tax, though literally it is a smoke (*dhuan*) tax. All must eat; food must be dressed; and as they have neither chimneys nor glass windows on which to lay the tax, Surat Singh's chancellor of the exchequer makes the smoke pay a transit duty ere it gets vent from the various orifices of the edifice. It only amounts to one rupee on each house or family, but would form an important item if not evaded by the powerful chiefs; still it yields a lakh of rupees. The town [206] of Mahajan, which was settled on Ratan Singh, son of Raja Nunkaran, on the resignation of his right of primogeniture and succession, enjoys exemption from this tax. It is less liable to fluctuation than other taxes, for if a village becomes half-deserted, those who remain are saddled with the whole. Dhuan is only known to the two western States, Bikaner and Jaisalmer.

Poll-Tax.—3. *Anga.* This is not a capitation but a body tax (from *anga*, the body), and was established by Raja Anup Singh. It might almost be termed a property-tax, since it embraced quadrupeds as well as bipeds of every sex and age, and was graduated according to age and sex in the human species, and according to utility in the brute. Each male adult was assessed one *anga*, fixed at four annas (about sixpence), and cows, oxen, buffaloes, were placed upon a level with the lord of the creation. Ten goats or sheep were estimated as one *anga*; but a camel was equivalent to four *angas*, or one rupee, which Raja Gaj Singh doubled. This tax, which is by far the most certain in a country perhaps still more pastoral than agricultural, is most providently watched, and though it has undergone many changes since it was originally imposed, it yet yields annually two lakhs of rupees.

4. *Sāīr*, or 'imposts.' This branch is subject to much fluctuation, and has diminished greatly since the reign of Surat Singh. The duties levied in the capital alone formerly exceeded what is collected throughout the whole of his dominions; being once estimated at above two lakhs, and now under one. Of this amount, half is collected at Rajgarh, the chief commercial mart of Bikaner. The dread of the Rahats, who have cut off the communications with the Panjab, and the want of principle within, deter merchants from visiting this State, and the caravans from Multan, Bahawalpur, and Shikarpur, which passed through

Bikaner to the eastern States, have nearly abandoned the route. The only duties of which he is certain are those on grain, of four rupees on every hundred maunds sold or exported, and which, according to the average sale price of these regions, may be about two per cent.

Paseti.—5. Paseti is a tax of five[1] rupees on every plough used in agriculture. It was introduced by Raja Rae Singh, in commutation of the corn-tax, or levy in kind, which had long been established at one-fourth of the gross produce. The Jats were glad to compound, and get rid of the agents of corruption, by the substitution of the plough-tax. It formerly yielded two lakhs of rupees, but with decreasing agriculture has fallen, like every other source, to a little more than one-half, but still yields a lakh and a quarter.

Malba.—6. Malba[2] is the name of the original tax which the Jat communities imposed [207] upon themselves, when they submitted to the sway in perpetuity of Bika and his successors. It is the land-tax[3] of two rupees on each hundred bighas of land cultivated in Bikaner. It is now unproductive, not realizing fifty thousand rupees, and it is said that a composition has been effected, by which it has been, or will be, relinquished: if so, Surat Singh gives up the sole legitimate source of revenue he possesses.

Recapitulation

1. Khalisa, or fisc[4]	Rs.	100,000
2. Dhuan		100,000
3. Anga		200,000

---

[1] [*Pānch*, from which the tax derives its name.]

[2] [Malba properly means 'sweepings, rubbish,' then miscellaneous revenue.]

[3] *Mal* is the term for land which has no irrigation but from the heavens.

[4]

Nohar district .	84 villages	Revenue . .	Rs. 100,000
Reni . . .	24 „	„ . .	10,000
Rania . . .	44 „	„ . .	20,000
Jaloli . . .	1 „	„ . .	5,000
		Total original Fiscal Lands .	135,000

since Rajgarh, Churu, and other places recovered.

4. Sair, imposts [1]	Rs. 75,000
5. Paseti, plough-tax	125,000
6. Malba, land-tax	50,000
TOTAL	650,000

Besides this, the fullest amount arising to the prince from annual taxation, there are other items which occasionally replenish the treasure of Surat Singh.

Datoi.—Datoi is a triennial tax of five rupees levied on each plough.[2] It was instituted by Raja Zorawar Singh. The whole country is liable to it, with the exception of fifty villages in Asaichwati, and seventy of the Beniwals, conditionally exempted, to guard the borders. It is now frequently evaded by the feudal chieftains, and seldom yields a lakh of rupees.

In addition to these specific expedients, there are many arbitrary methods of increasing the "ways and means" to satisfy the necessities or avarice of the present ruler, and [208] a train of dependent harpies, who prey upon the cultivating peasantry, or industrious trader. By such shifts, Surat Singh has been known to double his fixed revenue.

Dand, Khushhali.—The terms Dand and Khushhali, though etymologically the antipodes of each other—the first meaning a 'compulsory contribution,' the other a 'benevolence, or voluntary,' [3]—have a similar interpretation in these regions, and make the subjects of those parts devoutly pray that their prince's house may be one rather of mourning than rejoicing, and that defeat rather than victory may be attendant on his arms.

The term dand is coeval with Hindu legislation. The bard Chand describes it, and the chronicler of the life of the great

[1] Impost Duties in old times, namely:

Town of Nunkaran	Rs. 2,000
Rajgarh	10,000
Shaikhsar	5,000
Capital—Bikaner	75,000
From Churu and other towns	45,000
	137,000

[2] [*Dānt, dānta,* 'a tooth,' then 'a ploughshare.']

[3] *Khush* means 'happiness, pleasure, volition'; *ap ki khushi,* 'at your pleasure.' [*hāl* = 'circumstances.']

Siddhraj of Anhilwara, "who expelled the seven Daddas," or 'great evils,' whose initial letter was *d*, enumerates dand as one of them, and places it with the Dholis and Dakins, or minstrels and witches, giving it precedence amongst the seven plagues which his ancestors and tyrant custom had inflicted on the subject. Unhappily, there is no Siddhraj to legislate for Rajputana; and were there fourteen Daddas by which Surat Singh could swell his budget, he would retain them all for the oppression of the impoverished Jats, who, if they could, would be happy to expel the letter *S* from amongst them. But it is from the chieftain, the merchant, and the banker that the chief sums are realized; though indirectly the poor peasant contributes his share. There are fourteen collectors of dand,[1] one to every *chira* or division, and these are furnished with arbitrary schedules according to the circumstances, actual or supposed, of each individual. So unlimited are these exactions, that the chief of Gandeli for two years offered the collector of his quarter ten thousand rupees if he would guarantee him against any further demand during even twelve months; and being refused, he turned the collector out, shut the gates of his castle, and boldly bid his master defiance.

One of his expedients to levy a khushhali, or 'benevolence,' is worth relating: it was on the termination of his expedition against Bhatner, which added this celebrated desert and castle to his territory, and in which he was attended by the entire feudal army of Bikaner. On his return, "flushed with conquest," he demanded from each house throughout his dominions the sum of ten rupees to cover the expenses of the war. If the tyrant-ridden subjects of Surat Singh thus rejoice in his successes, how must they feel for his defeats! To them both are alike ominous, when every [209] artifice is welcomed, every villainy practised, to impoverish them. Oppression is at its height, and must work out its own cure.

Feudal Levies.—The disposable force of all these feudal principalities must depend on the personal character of the Raja. If Surat Singh were popular, and the national emergencies demanded the assemblage of the Kher, or *levée en masse*, of the "sons of Bika," he might bring ten thousand Rajputs into the field, of whom twelve hundred might be good horse, besides the foreign troops and park; but under present circumstances, and the

[1] This was written in 1813.

rapid deterioration of every branch of society, it may be doubted whether one-half could be collected under his standard.

The household troops consist of a battalion of foreign infantry, of five hundred men with five guns, and three squadrons of horse, about two hundred and fifty in number; all under foreign leaders. This is independent of the garrison of the capital, whose commandant is a Rajput of the Parihar tribe, who has twenty-five villages assigned for the payment of his troops.[1]

[1] [The State now supports for Imperial service the well-known Camel Corps, called the Ganga Risāla.]

[Table

Schedule exhibiting the Fiefs of Bikanér.

Names of Chieftains.	Clans.	Places of Abode.	Revenue.	Retainers: Foot.	Retainers: Horse.	Remarks.
Behri Sal	Bika	Mahajan	40,000	5,000	100	One hundred and forty villages, attached to this fief, settled on the heir of Raja Nunkaran, who consequently forfeited the *gaddi*.
Abhai Singh	Benirot	Bhukarka	25,000	5,000	200	The first of the chiefs of Bikaner.
Anup Singh	Bika	Jasana	5,000	400	40	
Pem Singh	Do.	Bai	5,000	400	25	
Chain Singh	Benirot	Sawa	20,000	2,000	300	
Himmat Singh	Rawat	Rawatsar	20,000	2,000	300	
Sheo Singh	Benirot	Churu	25,000	2,000	200	
Ummed Singh, Jeth Singh	Bidawat	Bidesar, Sondwa	50,000	10,000	2,000	One hundred and forty *kothri* (families, lit. *chambers*) of this class.
Bahadur Singh, Suraj Mall, Guman Singh, Atai Singh	Narnot	Mainsar, Tendesar, Katar, Kachor	40,000	4,000	500	
Sher Singh	Narnot	Nimbaj	5,000	500	125	
Devi Singh, Ummed Singh, Surthan Singh, Karnidhan	Narnot	Sidmukh, Karipura, Ajitpura, Beasar	20,000	5,000	400	
Surthan Singh	Kachhwaha	Nainawas	4,000	150	30	These two fiefs are held by foreign nobles of the house of Amber, and the ancient Pramara (*vulg.* Panwar).
Padam Singh	Panwar	Jethsisar	5,000	200	100	
Kishan Singh	Bika	Hayadesar	5,000	200	50	
Rao Singh	Bhatti	Pugal [1]	6,000	1,500	40	The fief of Pugal was wrested from the Bhattis of Jaisalmer.
Sultan Singh	Do.	Rajasar	1,500	200	50	
Laktir Singh	Do.	Raner	2,000	400	75	
Karnai Singh	Do.	Satasar	1,100	200	9	
Bhum Singh	Do.	Chakara	1,500	60	4	
Four Chieftains,[2] viz.						
1. Bhoni Singh	Bhatti	Bichnok	1,500	60	6	
2. Zalim Singh	Do.	Gariala	1,100	40	4	
3. Sardar Singh	Do.	Surjara	800	30	2	
4. Khet Singh	Do.	Randisar	600	32	2	
Chand Singh	Karamsot	Nokha	11,000	1,500	500	Twenty-seven villages dependent on this family from Jodhpur, and settled here eleven years.
Satidan	Rupawat	Badila	5,000	200	25	
Bhum Singh	Bhatti	Janglu	2,500	400	9	
Ketsi	Do.	Jaminsar	15,000	500	150	Twenty-seven villages.
Isari Singh	Mandla	Sarunda	11,000	2,000	150	
Padam Singh	Bhatti	Kudsu	1,500	60	4	
Kalyan Singh	Do.	Nainea	1,000	40	2	
		TOTAL .	332,100	44,072	5,402	[210]

[1] Pugal Patta.

[2] These chiefs are called Sardars of Khari Patta, one of the original conquests of the founder, Bika.

If ever the whole feudal array of Bikaner amounted to this, it would assuredly be found difficult now, were the ban proclaimed, to assemble one-fourth of this number [211].

Foreign Troops

	Foot.	Horse.	Guns.
Sultan Khan	—	200	—
Anokha Singh, Sikh	—	250	—
Budh Singh Dewara	—	200	—
Durjan Singh's Battalion . .	700	4	4
Ganga Singh's Battalion . .	1000	25	6
Total Foreigners .	1700	679	10
Park.	—	—	21
	1700	679	31

CHAPTER 3

Bhatner.—Bhatner, which now forms an integral part of Bikaner, was anciently the chief abode of another Jat community, so powerful as at one time to provoke the vengeance of kings, and at others to succour them when in distress. It is asserted that its name is in nowise connected with the Bhattis, who colonized it, but derived from the Bardai, or Bhat, of a powerful prince, to whom the lands were granted, and who, desirous to be the founder of a poetic dynasty, gave his professional title to the abode. In the annals of Jaisalmer, it will be seen that there is another story accounting for the appellation, which recalls the founding of Carthage or Byrsa. Both legends are improbable; and the Bhatti annals confirm what might have been assumed without suspicion, that to a colony of this race Bhatner owes its name, though not its existence. The whole of the northern part is called Ner in the ancient geographical nomenclature of Marusthali; and when some of the Bhatti clans became proselytes to Islam, they changed the vowel *a* to *u*, to distinguish them from the parent stock, namely [212], Bhati for Bhatti.[1] We shall,

[1] [Bhatner, Bhatti-nagara, 'town of the Bhattis,' the Po-to-lu-lo or Bhatosthala of the Buddhist pilgrims (Cunningham, *Ancient Geography*, 147; *ASR*, xxiii. (1887), 4 f.).]

however, furnish evidence by and by, in the annals of the original race, that in all probability the Yadu-Bhatti is the original Yuti colony from Central Asia; and that "the Jat prince of Salpur," whose inscription is in the first volume of this work, was the predecessor of these very races.

Neither the tract depending on Bhatner, nor that north of it to the Gara River, presented formerly the scene of absolute desolation they now exhibit, and I shall append a list of towns, to which a high antiquity is assigned, whose vestiges still remain, and from which something might perhaps be gleaned to confirm or overturn these deductions.

Bhatner has attained great historical celebrity from its position, being in the route of invasion from Central Asia to India. It is more than probable that the Jats, who resisted the advance of Mahmud of Ghazni in a naval warfare on the Indus, had long before that period established themselves in the desert as well as in the Panjab; and as we find them occupying a place amongst the Thirty-six Royal Tribes, we may infer that they had political power many centuries before that conqueror. In A.D. 1205, only twelve years after the conquest of India by Shihabu-d-din, his successor, Kutb, was compelled to conduct the war in person against the Jats of the northern desert, to prevent their wresting the important post of Hansi from the empire;[1] and when the unfortunate and intrepid queen Raziyah, the worthy heiress of the great Firoz, was compelled to abandon her throne to a usurper, she sought and found protection amongst the Jats, who, with their Scythic brethren, the Gakkhars, assembled all their forces and marched, with their queen at their head, like Tomyris of old, to meet her foes.[2] She was not destined to enjoy the same revenge but gained a glorious death in the attempt to overturn the Salic law of India.[3] Again, in A.D. 1397, when Timur invaded India,

[1] [Kutbu-d-dīn Ībak (A.D. 1206–10). The leader of the Hindu revolt was Jatwān, who was defeated and slain on the borders of Bāgar ('the land of the Bāgri, or warriors,' or according to others, from *bāgar*, 'a thorn hedge'), a name still applied to a tract in the Sirsa and Hissār Districts of the Panjāb (Cunningham, *Ancient Geography*, 247; *IGI*, xiii. 149 f.). For the revolt see *Tabaqāt-i-Nasiri*, trans. Raverty, 516 f.; Elliot-Dowson ii. 217 ff.; Ferishta i. 191 f., who calls the leader Jīwan Rāī, general of the forces of Nahrwāla in Gujarāt.]

[2] [Sultān Razīyah (A.D. 1236–40) was supported in her attack on Delhi by a force of Gakkhars and Jats (Ferishta i. 221).]

[3] I presented to Mr. Marsden a unique coin of this ill-fated queen.

Bhatner was attacked for "having distressed him exceedingly on his invasion of Multan," when he "in person scoured the country, and cut off a tribe of banditti called Jats."[1] In short, the Bhattis and Jats were so intermingled that distinction was impossible. Leaving this point, therefore, to be adjusted in the annals of the Bhattis, we proceed to sketch the history of the colony which ruled Bhatner when subjugated by the Rathors.

The Bhatti Migration.—It was shortly after Timur's invasion that a colony of Bhattis migrated from Marot and Phulra, under their leader Bersi, and assaulted and captured Bhatner from a [213] Muhammadan chief; but whether one of Timur's officers, or a dependent of Delhi, remains unknown, though most probably the former. His name, Chaghat Khan, almost renders this certain, and they must have made a proper name out of his tribe, Chagatai, of which he was a noble. This Khan had conquered Bhatner from the Jats, and had acquired a considerable territory, which the Bhatti colony took advantage of his return to invade and conquer. Sixteen generations have intervened since this event, which, bringing it to the period of Timur's invasion, furnishes an additional reason for concluding the Khan of Bhatner to have been one of his nobles, whom he may have left entrusted with this important point of communication, should he meditate further intercourse with India.

Bersi ruled twenty-seven years, and was succeeded by his son Bhairon, when the sons of Chaghat Khan, obtaining aid from the Delhi monarch, invaded Bhatner, and were twice repulsed with great loss. A third army succeeded; Bhatner was invested and reduced to great straits, when Bhairon hung out a flag of truce, and offered to accept any conditions which would not compromise his castle. Two were named: to embrace Islamism, or seal his sincerity by giving his daughter to the king. He accepted the first alternative, and from that day, in order to distinguish these proselytes, they changed the name of Bhati to Bhatti. Six chiefs intervened between Bhairon and

Rao Dalich, surnamed Hayat Khan, from whom Rae Singh of Bikaner wrested Bhatner, and Fatehabad became the future residence of the Bhatti Khans. He was succeeded by

Husain Khan (the grandson of Hayat), who recaptured

[1] [For Timūr's attack on Bhatner and on the Jats see Elliot-Dowson iii. 420 ff., 487 ff., 428 f., 492 f.]

Bhatner from Raja Shujawan Singh, and it was maintained during the time of Husain Mahmud and Imam Mahmud, until Surat Singh made the final conquest of it from Bahadur Khan, father to the present titular head of the Bhattis,[1]

Zabita Khan, who resides at Reni, having about twenty-five villages dependent thereon.[2] Reni was founded by Rae Singh of Bikaner, and named after his queen (*Rani*), to whom it was assigned. It was taken by Imam Mahmud. The Bhatti Khan is now a robber by profession, and his revenues, which are said to have sometimes amounted to three lakhs of rupees, are extorted by the point of his lance. These [214] depredations are carried to a frightful extent, and the poor Jats are kept eternally on the alert to defend their property. The proximity of the British territory preventing all incursions to the eastward, they are thrown back upon their original haunts, and make the whole of this northern region their prey. To this circumstance is attributed the desertion of these lands, which once reared cattle in abundance, and were highly valued. It is asserted that from the northern boundary of Bhatner to the Gara there are many tracts susceptible of high cultivation, having water near the surface, and many large spaces entirely free from *thal*, or 'sandhills.' To the drying up of the Hakra, or Ghaggar, many centuries ago, in conjunction with moral evils, is ascribed the existing desolation. According to tradition, this stream took a westerly direction, by Phulra, where it is yet to be traced, and fell into the Indus below Uchh. The couplet recording its absorption by the sands of Ner has already been given, in the time of Rao Hamir, prince of Dhat. If the next European traveller who may pass through the Indian desert will seek out the representative of the ancient Sodha princes at Chor, near Umarkot, he may learn from their bard (if they retain such an appendage) the date of this prince, and that of so important an event in the physical and political history of their regions. The vestiges of large towns, now buried in the sands, confirm the truth of this tradition, and several of

[1] In S. 1857 (A.D. 1801) the celebrated George Thomas, for the sum of three lakhs, put the Bhattis into the temporary possession of Bhatner; but the succeeding year it was again taken from them by the Rathors.

[2] This memoir was written in 1813–14, and may contain many inaccuracies, from its very remote situation, and the difficulty of obtaining correct information. [Reni is 120 miles N.E. of Bīkaner city, and is said to take its name from a legendary Rāja Renpāl.]

them claim a high antiquity; such as the Rangmahall, already mentioned, west of Bhatner, having subterranean apartments still in good preservation. An aged native of Dandusar (twenty-five miles south of Bhatner) replied, to my inquiry as to the recollections attached to this place, that "it belonged to a Panwar prince who ruled once all these regions, when Sikandar Rumi attacked them."

An excursion from Hansi Hissar, our western frontier, into these regions, would soon put the truth of such traditions to the test, as far as these reported ruins are concerned; though what might appear the remains of palaces of the Pramaras, the Johyas, and the Jats of ancient days, to the humble occupant of a hut in the desert, may only prove the foundations of some castellated building. But the same traditions are circulated with regard to the more western desert, where the same kind of vestiges is said to exist, and the annals make mention of capitals, the sites of which are now utterly unknown. Considering the safety, and comparative ease, with which such a journey can be made, one cannot imagine a more agreeable pursuit than the prosecution of archaeological inquiries in the northern deserts of Rajputana, where traditions abound, and where the existing manners, amongst such a diversity of tribes, would furnish ample materials [215] for the portfolio, as well as for memoirs. Its productions, spontaneous or cultivated, though its botanical as well as zoological specimens may be limited, we know to be essentially different from those of Gangetic India, and more likely to find a parallel in the natural productions and phenomena of the great African desert. The Bhattis, the Khosas, the Rajars, the Sahariyas, the Mangalias, the Sodhas, and various other nomadic tribes, present a wide field for observation; and the physiologist, when tired of the habits of man, may descend from the nobler animal to the lion, the wild ass, every kind of deer, the flocks of sheep which, fed on the succulent grasses, touch not water for six weeks together, while the various herbs, esculent plants and shrubs, salt lakes, natron beds, etc., would give abundant scope for commentary and useful comparison. He will discover no luxuries, and few signs of civilization; the *jhonpra* (hut) constructed of poles and twigs, coated inside with mud and covered with grass, being little better than the African's dwelling.

Ancient Cities.—We shall conclude this imperfect sketch of

Bikaner and the desert with the names of several of their ancient towns, which may aid the search of the traveller in the regions on its northern border: Abohar; Banjara ka Nagar; Rangmahall; Sodal, or Soratgarh; Machotal; Ratibang; Kalibang; Kalyansar; Phulra; Marot; Tilwara; Gilwara; Bani; Manikkhar; Sursagar; Bamani; Koriwala; Kal-Dherani.[1]

Some names in this list may be unimportant, but if two, or even one, should be the means of eliciting some knowledge of the past, the record will not be useless.

Phulra and Marot have still some importance: the first is very ancient, and enumerated amongst the 'Nau-koti Maru-ki,' in the earliest periods of Pramara (vulg. Panwar) dominion. I have no doubt that inscriptions in the ornamental nail-headed character belonging to the Jains will be found here, having obtained one from Lodorva in the desert, which has been a ruin for nine centuries. Phulra was the residence of Lakha Phulani, a name well known to those versed in the old traditions of the desert. He was cotemporary with Siddh Rae of Anhilwara, and Udayaditya of Dhar [216].

[1] [Few of these names are traceable on modern maps.]

BOOK VII

ANNALS OF JAISALMER

CHAPTER 1

Limits of Jaisalmer.—Jaisalmer is the modern name of a tract of country comprehended, according to ancient geography, in Marusthali, the desert of India. It is termed Mer in the traditional nomenclature of this region, from being a rocky (mer) oasis in the heart of the sandy desert, interesting both from its physical features and its position as the Ultima Thule of independent Hinduism. Yet, however entitled to regard from its local peculiarities or its products, the history of the tribe which inhabits it presents a still more engrossing subject for investigation.

The Bhatti Tribe.—This tribe is the Bhatti, a branch of the Yadu or Jadon race, whose power was paramount in India three thousand years ago; and the prince now governing this distant [217] corner of India claims descent from those Yadu kings who ruled from the Yamuna to the 'world's end,' [1] at that remote period.

It were preposterous to expect to find, in the annals of a people so subject to the vicissitudes of fortune, an unbroken series of historical evidence in support of this ancestry; but they have preserved links of the chain which indicate original affinities. In tracing the Yadu-Bhatti history, two hypotheses alternately present themselves to our minds, each of which rests upon plausible

[1] Jagat Khunt, the point of land beyond Dwarka, the last stronghold of the Yadus when their power was extinguished.

grounds; the one supposing the Bhattis to be of Scythic, the other of Hindu origin. This incongruity may be reconciled by presuming the co-mixture of the two primitive races; by enlarging our views, and contemplating the barrier, which in remote ages separated Scythia and India, as ideal; and admitting that the various communities, from the Caspian to the Ganges, were members of one grand family, having a common language and common faith,[1] in that ancient central empire whose existence has been contended for and denied by the first names in science;[2] the Bharatavarsha of the Hindus, the Indo-Scythic empire of king Bharat, son of Budha, the ancestor of the Yadu-Bhattis, now confined to a nook of the desert.[3]

It would be vain to speculate upon the first colonization of India proper by the Rajkula, or 'royal tribes.' It appears to have possessed an indigenous population prior to the races of Surya, or Indu, though the genealogies which give the origin of these degraded races of Kabas,[4] Bhils, Meras, Gonds, etc., assert

[1] Manu says: "But in consequence of the omission of the sacred rites, and of their not consulting Brāhmanas, the following tribes of Kshatriyas have gradually sunk in the world to the condition of Sūdras: viz. the Paundrakas, the Kodas, the Dravidas, the Kāmbogas, the Yavanas, the Sākas, the Pāradas, the Pahlavas, the Kīnas, the Kirātas, and the Daradas" (*Laws*, x. 43-44, trans. G. Bühler, *Sacred Books of the East*, xxv. 412).

It is a great mistake to suppose the Bactrian Greeks are these Yavanas, who are descended from Yavan, fifth son of Yayati, third son of the patriarchal Nahustha, though the Ionians may be of this race. The Sakas are the Sakae, the races of Central Asia (the Sakha Rajput); the Pahlavas, the ancient Persians, or Guebres; the Chinas, the inhabitants of China; and the Chasas, inhabitants of the great snowy mountains (*koh*), whence Kohchasa (the Casia montes of Ptolemy), corrupted to Caucasus [?].

[2] The illustrious Cuvier questions the existence of an ancient central kingdom, because "ni Moïse, ni Homère, ne nous parlait d'un grand empire dans la Haute-Asie" (*Discours sur les révolutions de la surface du globe*, p. 206). Who, then, were "the sons of Togarmah" (mentioned by Ezekiel [xxvii. 14]) who conquered and long held Egypt? [Togarmah was N. Assyria (Hastings, *Dict. Bible*, iv. 789 f.).]

[3] [Bharata, from whom the Kauravas and Pāndavas, more especially the latter, were called Bhāratas, was a prince of the Puru branch of the Lunar race, son of Dushyanta and Sakuntala.]

[4] The Kaba race is almost extinct; it was famed, even in the days of Krishna, as the savage inhabitants of Saurashtra. When the forester Bhil, who mortally wounded Krishna, was expressing his contrition for the unintentional act, he was forgiven, with the remark that it was only retributive justice, as "in a former birth," as the godlike Rama, Krishna had slain him. Thus Rama appears as the subjugator and civilizer of these

that they were all from the same stem, and that their political debasement was the effect of moral causes. But as there is no proof of this, we must attribute the fable to the desire of the Brahman [218] archaeologist to account for the origin of all things. Modern inquiries into these matters have been cramped by an erroneous and contracted view of the power of this ancient people, and the direction of that power. It has been assumed that the prejudices originating in Muslim conquests, which prevented the Hindu chieftain from crossing the forbidden waters of the Attock, and still more from "going down to the sea in ships," had always existed. But were it not far more difficult to part with erroneous impressions than to receive new and correct views, it would be apparent that the first of these restrictions is of very recent origin, and on the other hand, that the Hindus of remote ages possessed great naval power, by which communication must have been maintained with the coasts of Africa,[1] Arabia, and Persia, as well as the Australian Archipelago.[2] It is ridiculous,

---

indigenous tribes, of whom the Kabas are described as plundering Krishna's family after his decease. [The Kābas, now extinct, were regarded as savage inhabitants of Saurāshtra in the Krishna tradition, and are said to be the ancestors of the modern Vāghers (*BG*, viii. 271, 587).]

[1] Whence the Hindu names of towns at the estuaries of the Gambia and Senegal Rivers, the Tambaconda and other *kondas*, already mentioned?

[2] Mr. Marsden, at an early period of his researches into Hindu literature, shares the merit of discovering with Sir W. Jones that the Malayan language, disseminated throughout the Archipelago, and extending from Madagascar to Easter Island, a space of 200 degs. of longitude, is indebted to the Sanskrit for a considerable number of its terms, and that the intercourse which effected this was many centuries previous to their conversion to the Muhammadan religion. He is inclined to think that the point of communication was from Gujarat. The legends of these islanders also abound with allusions to the Mahabharata and Ramayana. (See *Asiatic Researches*, vol. iv. p. 226, second edition.) [*EB*, xvii. 475 ff.]

Since Mr. M. wrote, the revelation of the architectural antiquities in these isles, consequent to British conquests, establishes the fact that they were colonized by the Suryas, whose mythological and heroic history is sculptured in their edifices and maintained in their writings. Nor should we despair that similar discoveries may yet disclose the link which of yore connected India with Egypt, and to which Ceylon was but the first stepping-stone. That Rama possessed great naval means is beyond doubt, inherited from his ancestor Sagara 'the sea-king,' twenty generations before the hero of Lanka, which place I have long imagined to be Ethiopia; whence ancient writers assert Egypt to have had her institutions, and that the Ethiopians were of Indian origin. Cuvier, quoting Syncellus, even assigns the reign

with all the knowledge now in our possession, to suppose that the Hindus always confined themselves within their gigantic barriers, the limits of modern India. The cosmography of the Puranas, imperfect and puerile as it is, and some of the texts of Manu, afford abundant evidence of an intimate intercourse between the countries from the Oxus to the Ganges; and even in their allegories, we trace fresh streams of knowledge flowing into India from that central region, stigmatized in latter days as the land of the Barbarian (Mlechchha). Manu corroborates the Puranas, from which we infer the fact that in distant ages one uniform faith extended from Sakadvipa, the continent of the Sakae, to the Ganges.[1] These observations [219] it is necessary to premise before we attempt, by following the tide of Yadu migration during the lapse of thirty centuries, to trace them from Indra-

---

of Amenophis as the epoch of the colonization of Ethiopia from India.—P. 180 of his '*Discours*,' etc. [For early Hindu voyages to Java and the neighbouring region see Smith, *HFA*, 259 ff.; *BG*, i. Part i. 489 ff.]

[1] The cosmography of the Agni Purana divides the world then known to the Hindus into seven *dwipas*, or continents: one of these is "Sakadvipa, whose inhabitants, descended from Bhavya, are termed Sakeswara (*i.e.* Sakae-lords)." His (Bhavya's) offspring or descendants were Jalad, Sukamara, Manivaka, Kusumada, Mandaki, Mahadruma, each of whom gave his name to a *khand*, or division (*qu.* Sukmarkhand?). The chief ranges of mountains were Jaldas, Raivat, Syama, Indak, Amki, Rim, and Kesari. "There were seven grand rivers, namely, Mag, Magad, Arvarna, etc. The inhabitants worship the sun."

Slight as this information is, we must believe that this Sakadvipa or Sakatai is the Scythia of the Ancients; and the Sakeswara (the Sakas of Manu), the Sakae so well known to western history, the progenitors of the Parthians, whose first (*adi*) king was Arsaka. The sun-worship indicates the adorer of Mithras, the Mitra or Surya of the Hindu; the Arvarna recalls the Araxes applied to the Jaxartes; while Jalad, the proper name of the son of the first king of Sakadvipa, appears to be the Yulduz of the Tatar historian Abulghazi, who uses the same term as does the Hindu, to designate a range of mountains. Whence this identity between Puranic and Tatar cosmography? [These speculations possess no value.]

"A chief of the twice-born tribe (*i.e.* Brahmans) was brought by Vishnu's eagle from Sakadvipa, and thus have Sakadvipa Brahmans become known in Jambudwipa" (India). Mr. Colebrooke on Indian Classes, *Asiatic Researches*, vol. v. p. 53. And Manu says that it was only on their ceasing to sanction Brahmans residing amongst them, that the inhabitants of these remote western regions became 'Mlechchha,' or barbarians: testimonies which must be held conclusive of perfect intercourse and reciprocity of sentiment between the nations of Central Asia and India at periods the most remote.

prastha, Suryapura, Mathura, Prayaga, Dwarka, Jadu-ka-dang (the mountains of Jud), Bahra, Gajni in Zabulistan ; and again refluent into India, at Salbahana or Salpura in the Panjab, Tanot, Derawar, Lodorva in the desert, and finally Jaisalmer, founded in S. 1212, or A.D. 1156.

Having elsewhere descanted at length on the early history of the Yadus,[1] we may refer those who are likely to take an interest in this discussion to that paper, and proceed at once to glean what we can from the native annals before us, from the death of their leader, Hari-Krishna, to the dispersion of the Yadus from India. The bare fact of their migration altogether out of India proper proves that the original intercourse, which conducted Budha, the patriarch of the Yadu race, into India [2] (where he espoused Ila, a princess of the Surya race, and by whom his issue was multiplied), was not forgotten, though fifty generations had elapsed from the patriarchal Budha to Hari—to whom and the chronicle we return.

Early Legends.—" Prayaga [3] is the cradle of the Yadus who are Somavansa (of the lunar race). Thence Mathura founded by Pururavas remained for ages the seat of power. The name of Jadon (Yadu), of whom there were fifty-six tribes,[4] became famous in the world, and of this race was the mighty Hari-Krishna, who founded Dwarka."

The grand international conflicts amongst the " fifty-six Yadu tribes," at Kurukshetra, and subsequently at Dwarka, are sufficiently known to the reader of Hindu history [220], and may

[1] *Vide* " Essay on the Hindu and Theban Hercules," *Transactions of the Royal Asiatic Society*, vol. iii.

[2] The Bhagavat says: " Budha (a wise man—a patriarch) came to Bharatkhand to perform penitential rites, and espoused Ila, by whom he had Pururavas (founder of Mathura), who had six sons, namely, Ayu, etc., who carried on the lunar (Indu) races in India." Now this Ayu is likewise the patriarch of the Tatars, and in that language signifies the moon, a male divinity both with Tatars and Rajputs. Throughout there are traces of an original identity, which justifies the application of the term Indo-Scythic to the Yadu race.—*Vide* Genealogical table, Vol. I.

[3] Prayaga is the modern Allahabad, at the confluence of the Jumna and Ganges, the capital of the Prasioi of Megasthenes. [Their capital was Pātaliputra, Patna.]

[4] This is alternately called Chhappan Kula and Chhappan Kror, " fifty-six tribes," and " fifty-six millions," of Yadus. As they were long supreme over India, this number is not inadmissible.

be referred to elsewhere.[1] These events are computed to have happened about 1100 years before Christ. On the dispersion of these races many abandoned India, and amongst these, two of the many sons of Krishna. This deified leader of the Yadus had eight wives, and the offspring of the first and seventh, by a singular fate, now occupy what may be termed the outposts of Hinduism.[2]

Rukmini was the senior of these wives; and the eldest of her sons was Pradyumna, who was married to a princess of Vidarbha; she bore him two sons, Aniruddha and Vajranabha, and from the latter the Bhattis claim descent. Vajra had two sons, Sankhanabha and Khira.[3]

"When the Jadons were exterminated in the conflict at Dwarka, and Hari had gone to heaven, Vajra was on his way from Mathura to see his father, but had only marched twenty coss (forty miles), when he received intelligence of that event, which had swept away his kindred. He died upon the spot, when Nabha was elected king and returned to Mathura, but Khira pursued his journey to Dwarka.

"The thirty-six tribes of Rajputs hitherto oppressed by the Yadus, who had long held universal dominion, now determined to be revenged. Nabha was compelled to fly the holy city [Dwarka]; he became prince of Marusthali in the west.

"Thus far from the Bhagavat" (says the Bhatti chronicler), and I continue the history of the Bhattis, by the Brahman Sukhdharma of Mathura.

"Nabha had issue Prithibahu.

"Khira had two sons, Jareja and Judhbhan.[4]

"Judhbhan was on a pilgrimage; the goddess heard his vows;

[1] *Transactions of the Royal Asiatic Society*, vol. iii. *Vide* paper entitled "Comparison of the Hindu and Theban Hercules."

[2] Jambuvati was the name of the seventh wife, whose eldest son was called Samba; he obtained possession of the tracts on both sides the Indus, and founded the Sind-Samma dynasty, from which the Jarejas are descended. There is every probability that Sambus, of Sambanagari (Minnagara), the opponent of Alexander, was a descendant of Samba, son of Krishna [?]. The Jareja chronicles, in ignorance of the origin of this titular appellation, say that their "ancestors came from Sham, or Syria." [These speculations possess no value.]

[3] [This name does not appear in the Vishnu Purāna list.]

[4] Jad, Jud, Jadon, are the various modes of pronouncing Yadu in the Bhakha, or spoken dialects of the west. Judh-bhan, 'the rocket of the Yadus,' would imply the knowledge of gunpowder at a very remote period [?].

she awoke him from his sleep, and promised whatever he desired. 'Give me land that I may inhabit,' said the youth; 'Rule in these hills,' replied the goddess, and disappeared. When Judhbhan awoke, and was yet pondering on the vision of the night, a confused noise assailed him; and looking out, he discovered that the prince of the country had just died without issue, and they were disputing who should succeed him. The prime minister said, 'he dreamed that a descendant of Krishna had arrived at Bahra,'[1] and proposed [221] to seek him out and invest him as their prince. All assented, and Judhbhan was elected king. He became a great prince, had a numerous progeny, and the place of their abode was henceforth styled Jadu-ka-dang, 'the mountains of Jadu.'

"Prithibahu ('the arm of the earth'), son of Nabha, prince

[1] The precise knowledge of the topography of these regions, displayed in the Bhatti annals, is the most satisfactory proof of their authenticity. In the present day, it would be in vain to ask any native of Jaisalmer the position of the "hill of Jud," or the site of Bahra; and but for the valuable translation of Babur's *Memoirs*, by Mr. Erskine, we should have been unable to adduce the following testimony. Babur crossed the Indus the 17th February 1519, and on the 19th, between that river and one of its great towns, the Behat, he reached the very tract where the descendant of Krishna established himself twenty-five centuries before. Babur says, "Seven kos from Behreh to the north there is a hill. This hill in the Zefer Nameh (History of Timoor), and other books, is called the Hill of Jud. At first I was ignorant of the origin of its name, but afterwards discovered that in this hill there were two races of men descended of the same father. One tribe is called Jud, the other Jenjuheh. From old times they have been the rulers and lords of the inhabitants of this hill, and of the Ils and Uluses (political divisions) between Nilab and Behreh. Their power is exerted in a friendly and brotherly way. They cannot take from them whatever they please. They take as their share a portion that has been fixed from very remote times. The Jud is divided into various branches or families, as well as the Jenjuheh. The chief man amongst them gets the name of Rae." —Erskine's *Baber*, p. 254.

Here is a decided confirmation that this Hindu colony preserved all their original manners and customs even to Babur's day. The tribe of Janjuhahs, beyond a doubt, is the tribe of Johya, so celebrated in the region skirting the Sutlej, and which will be noticed hereafter. I presented a small work entirely relating to their history to the Royal Asiatic Society. As Babur says they are of the same family as the Juds, they are probably the descendants of Janj, the brother of Bhatti, who changed the family patronymic from Jadu or Judu to Bhatti; and thus it appears that when the elder branch was driven from Gajni, they retreated amongst their relations of the hills of Jud. Babur was quite enamoured with the beauty of the hill of Jud, which, with its lake and valleys, he describes as a miniature Kashmir. —P. 255.

of Marusthali, inherited the insignia of Sri-Krishna with the regal umbrella (*chhatri*) made by Viswakarma. He had a son Bahubal ('strong arm'), who espoused Kamalavati, daughter of Vijaya Singh, prince of Malwa, who gave in dower (*daeja*) [1] one thousand horses of Khorasan, one hundred elephants, pearls, gems, and gold innumerable, and five hundred handmaids, with chariots and bedsteads of gold. The Puar (Pramar) Kamalavati became the chief queen and bore her lord one son,

"Bahu, killed by a fall from his horse; he left one son,

"Subahu, who was poisoned by his wife, a daughter of Mand Raja, Chauhan of Ajmer; he left a son,

"Rajh, who reigned twelve years. He was married to Subhag Sundari, daughter of Ber Singh, prince of Malwa. Having, when pregnant, dreamed that she was delivered of a white elephant, the astrologers, who interpreted this as an indication of greatness, desired he might be named Gaj: [2] as he approached manhood, the coco-nut came from Judhbhan, prince of Purabdes (the eastern), and was accepted. At the same time tidings arrived that from the shores of the ocean, the barbarians (Mlechchha), who had formerly attacked Subahu, [3] were again advancing,

[1] The Pramars were formerly the most powerful potentates of Central India. Handmaids, and bedsteads of gold, were always a part of the *daeja* or dower of Hindu princesses.

[2] Abulfazl [? Abulghazi] mentions Joga as prince of Gasmien and Kashmir, who was slain by Aghuz Khan, the Patriarch of the Tatar tribes.

[3] In this early portion of the annals there is a singular mixture of historical facts, and it appears that the Yadu scribes confound their connexions with the Syrian and Bactrian Greeks, and with the first Muslim conquerors. Imperfect as is this notice of Subahu, his son Rajh, and grandson Gaj, who were thus assailed by Farid of Khorasan (Bactria), and his auxiliary, the king of Rum (Syria), we have a powerful allusion to Antiochus the Great, who, two hundred and four years before Christ, invaded Bactria and India. Amongst the few facts left of this expedition is his treaty with Sophagasenas, the Indian monarch, in which the Syrian king stipulated for a tribute in elephants. There are, even in this medley of incidents, grounds for imagining that Sophagasenas is the Yadu prince of Gajni. Whether, out of Subahu and Gaj, the Greeks manufactured their Sophagasenas, or whether prince Gaj could have been entitled Subhagsen, in compliment to his mother, Subhag-Sundari, of Malwa, must be left for the speculative to decide. It is not unlikely that the nature of the tribute, said to have been elephants, which the Indian agreed to furnish to the Greek prince, may have originated with the name of *Gaj*, which means 'elephant.' [Sophagasenas, mentioned by Polybius (xi. 34) was probably an Indian king, Subhāgasena, who ruled in the Kâbul valley.]

having Farid Shah of Khorasan at [222] the head of four lakhs of horse, from whom the people fled in dismay. The Raja sent scouts to obtain accurate intelligence, and marched to Hariau to meet him; while the foe encamped two coss from Kunjshahr.[1] A battle ensued, in which the invader was defeated with the loss

---

There is at the same time much that refers to the early progress of Islam in these regions of Central Asia. Price, in his excellent history, extracting from the Khulasatu-l-Akhbar, says, "Hejauge was entrusted with the government of Khorasan, and Obaidoolah with Seistan, who had orders from Hejauge, his superior, to invade Caubul, whose prince was Reteil or Retpeil, whom the Author supposes either a Tatar or Hindoo prince. Artfully retiring, he drew the Mohamedan army into the defiles, and blocking up the rear, cut off their retreat, and Obaidoolah was compelled to purchase his liberation by the payment of seven hundred thousand dirhems." [See Elliot-Dowson ii. 417; "Retpeil" is possibly Ratnapāla.]

This was the seventy-eighth year of the Hegira, or A.D. 697. Conjoined to what follows, it appears to have reference to Rajh, father of Gaj. Again,

"Obaidoolah and Abdoorehman invaded Seistan with forty thousand men. The prince of Caubul tried the same manœuvre, but was outwitted by the Mohamedan, who conquered a great part of Caubul and acquired great booty, with which he returned to Seistan, to the great displeasure of Hejauge; and Abdoorehman entered into a confederacy with Retpeil to attack Hejauge, and absolve Caubul from tribute. Moghairah was the successor of Abdoorehman in Khorasan, while his father, Mohilel, was employed beyond the Jehoon, but died at Meru of a burning diarrhoea, bequeathing his government to Yezzid."

This account of Mughaira's (the governor of Khorasan) death, while carrying on war against the Hindu "Retpeil" of Kabul, has much analogy to the sudden death of Mamrez, the foe of Rajh of Zabulistan. One thing is now proved, that princes of the Hindu faith ruled over all these regions in the first ages of Islamism, and made frequent attempts, for centuries after, to reconquer them. Of this fact, Babur gives us a most striking instance in his description of Gajni, or, as he writes, Ghazni. He says, "I have seen, in another history, that when the Rai of Hind besieged Subaktegin in Ghazni, Subaktegin ordered dead flesh and other impurities to be thrown into the fountain, when there instantly arose a tempest and hurricane, with rain and snow, and by this device he drove away the enemy." Babur adds, "I made then inquiry in Ghazni for this well, but nobody could give me the slightest information regarding it" (p. 150). Doubtless, when Babur conquered India, and became better acquainted with the Hindu warriors, he would have got to the bottom of this anecdote, and have seen that the success of the ruse of Sabuktegin arose out of the religion of his foes, who could not use water thus contaminated by the flesh of the sacred kine. The celebrated Valabhi was reduced by the same stratagem.

[1] Neither of these towns appears in any map. "There is a Koonj Reshak in Khorasan, and a Penjher in Balk." Sir W. Ouseley's *Ebn Haukal*, pp. 213-223.

of thirty thousand men, and four thousand on the part of the Hindus. But the foeman rallied, and Raja Rajh, who again encountered him, was wounded and died just as prince Gaj returned with Hansavati, his bride, daughter of Judhbhan of the east. In two battles the king of Khorasan was vanquished, when he obtained an auxiliary in the king of Rum (Romi-pati), to establish the Koran and the law of the prophet in infidel lands. While the armies of the Asuras were thus preparing their strength, Raja Gaj called a council of ministers. There being no stronghold of importance, and it being impossible to stand against numbers, it was determined to erect a fortress amidst the mountains of the north. Having summoned his friends to his aid, he sought counsel of the guardian goddess of his race; who [223] foretold that the power of the Hindus was to cease, but commanded him to erect a fort and call it Gajni. While it was approaching completion, news came that the kings of Rum and Khorasan were near at hand :

> *Rūmī-pat, Khorāsān-pat, haya, gaya, pākhar, pāī,*
> *Chinta teri, chit lagi; sūna Jadpat Rāē.*[1]

The stick wounded the drum of the Jadon prince; the army was formed, gifts were distributed, and the astrologers were commanded to assign such a moment for marching as might secure the victory.

"Thursday (Brihaspati) the 13th of Magh, the enlightened half of the moon, when one ghari[2] of the day had fled, was the auspicious hour; and the drum of departure sounded. That day he marched eight coss, and encamped at Dulapar. The combined kings advanced, but in the night the Shah of Khorasan died of indigestion. When it was reported to the king of Rum (Shah Sikandar Rumi) that Shah Mamrez was dead, he became alarmed and said, 'while we mortals have grand schemes in hand, He above has other views for us.' Still his army advanced like waves of the ocean; caparisons and chains clank on the backs of elephants, while instruments of war resound through the host. Elephants move like walking mountains; the sky is black with

[1] "The king of Rum and the king of Khorasan, with horse (*haya*), elephants (*gaya* or *gaj*), caparisons (*pākhar*), and foot-soldiers (*pāē* or *pāyik*) [are at hand]. Beware, let it enter your mind, O Rāē, Lord of the Jadus!"

[2] [A *ghari* = 24 minutes.]

clouds of dust; bright helms reflect the rays of the sun. Four coss (eight miles) separated the hostile armies. Raja Gaj and his chieftains performed their ablutions, and keeping the Joginis [1] in their rear, advanced to the combat. Each host rushed on like famished tigers; the earth trembled; the heavens were overcast; nor was aught visible in the gloom but the radiant helm. War-bells resound; horses neigh; masses of men advance on each other, like the dark rolling clouds of Bhadon. Hissing speeds the feathered dart; the lion roar of the warriors is re-echoed; the edge of the sword deluges the ground with blood; on both sides the blows resound on the crackling bones. Here was Judhrae, there the Khans and Amirs, as if Time had encountered his fellow. Mighty warriors strew the earth; heroes fall in the cause of their lords. The army of the Shah fled; he left twenty-five thousand souls entangled in the net of destruction; he abandoned elephants and horses, and even his throne. Seven thousand Hindus lay dead on the field. The drum of victory resounded, and the Jadon returned triumphant to his capital [224].

"On Sunday, the 3rd of Baisakh, the spring season (Vasant), the Rohini Nakshatra, and Samvat Dharmaraja (Yudhishthira) 3008,[2] seated on the throne of Gajni, he maintained the Jadon race. With this victory his power became firm: he conquered all the countries to the west, and sent an ambassador to Kashmir to call its prince Kandrapkel [3] to his presence. But the prince refused the summons: he said the world would scoff at him if he attended the stirrup of another without being first worsted in fight. Raja Gaj invaded Kashmir; and married the daughter of its prince, by whom he had a son, called Salbahan.

"When this child had attained the age of twelve, tidings of another invasion came from Khorasan. Raja Gaj shut himself up for three entire days in the temple of Kuladevi: [4] on the fourth day the goddess appeared and revealed to him his destiny; the Gajni would pass from his hands, but that his posterity would

[1] The unclean spirits of Rajput martial mythology, who feed on the slain.

[2] This date is circumstantial, and might be fixed or disproved by calculation; if the heterogeneous mixture of such widely separated incidents as those in Syro-Macedonian and Muhammadan history did not deter us from the attempt.

[3] No such name appears in Wilson's *Raj Taringini.* [Nor in Stein's Index.]

[4] Tutelary goddess, or "of the race (*kula*)."

reinherit it, not as Hindus but as Muslims; and directed him to send his son Salbahan amongst the Hindus of the east, there to erect a city to be named after him. She said that he would have fifteen sons, whose issue would multiply; 'that he (Raja Gaj) would fall in the defence of Gajni, but would gain a glorious reward hereafter.'

"Having heard his fate revealed Raja Gaj convened his family and kin, and on pretence of a pilgrimage to Juala-mukhi,[1] he caused them to depart, with the prince Salbahan, for the east.

"Soon after the foe approached within five coss of Gajni. Leaving therein his uncle Sahideo for its defence, Raja Gaj marched to meet him. The king of Khorasan divided his army into five divisions; the Raja formed his into three: a desperate conflict ensued, in which both the king and the Raja were slain. The battle lasted five *pahars*,[2] and a hundred thousand Mirs and thirty thousand Hindus strewed the field. The king's son invested Gajni; for thirty days it was defended by Sahideo, when he performed the Sakha,[3] and nine thousand valiant men gave up their lives.

Sālivāhana.—"When tidings of this fatal event were conveyed to Salbahan, for twelve days the ground became his bed.[4] He at length reached the Panjab, where he fixed on a spot with abundance of water, and having collected his clansmen around him, he laid the foundation of a city which he named after himself, Salbahanpur. The surrounding [225] Bhumias attended, and acknowledged his supremacy. Seventy-two years of the era of Vikrama had elapsed when Salbahanpur was founded, upon Sunday, the 8th of the month of Bhadon.[5]

[1] This volcano [or rather jets of combustible gas] is a well-known place of pilgrimage in the Siwalik mountains [in the Kāngra District, Panjāb].

[2] A pahar is one-fourth of the day.

[3] For a description of this rite see Vol. I. pp. 85, 309.

[4] In conformity with the Hindu ordinances of *matam*, or mourning.

[5] Here is another circumstantial date, S. 72, or A.D. 16, for the foundation of Salbahana in the Panjab, by the fugitive Yadu prince from Gajni. Of its exact position we have no means of judging, but it could not have been remote from Lahore. It may be deemed a fortunate coincidence that I should discover that ancient inscription (p. 914) of this capital, styled Salpur, governed by a Gete or Jat in the fourth century; which suggested the idea (which many facts tend to prove), whether these Yadus (whose illegitimate issue, as will appear in the sequel, are called Jats) may not be the Yuti or Getes from Central Asia. The coincidence of the date of Sal-

"Salbahan conquered the whole region of the Panjab. He had fifteen sons, who all became Rajas: namely, Baland, Rasalu, Dharmangad, Vacha, Rupa, Sundar, Lekh, Jaskaran, Nema, Mat, Nipak, Gangau, Jagau; all of whom, by the strength of their own arms, established themselves in independence.

"The coco-nut from Raja Jaipal Tuar was sent from Delhi, and accepted.[1] Baland proceeded to Delhi, whose prince advanced to meet him. On his return with his bride, Salbahan determined to redeem Gajni from the foe and avenge his father's death. He crossed the Attock to encounter Jalal, who advanced at the head of twenty thousand men. Crowned with victory, he regained possession of Gajni, where he left Baland, and returned to his capital in the Panjab; he soon after died, having ruled thirty-three years and nine months.

Bāland.—"Baland succeeded. His brothers had now established themselves in all the mountainous tracts of the Panjab. But the Turks[2] began rapidly to increase, and to subjugate all beneath their sway, and the lands around Gajni were again in their power. Baland had no minister, but superintended in person all the details of his government. He had seven sons: Bhatti, Bhupati, Kalar, Janj,[3] Sarmor, Bhainsrekha, Mangreo. The second son Bhupati (*i.e.* lord of the earth) had a son, Chakito, from whom is descended the Chakito (Chagatai) tribe [226].[4]

---

bahan-Yadu with that of the Saka Salivahan, the Tak, will not fail to strike the inquirer into Hindu antiquities: and it is not the least curious circumstance, that these Yadus, or Yuti, displaced the Takshak, or Tak, from this region, as will appear immediately. In further corroboration, see notes 2 and 4, p. 916 f., and Inscriptions II. p. 917 and VI. p. 925.

[1] At every page of these annals, it is evident that they have been transcribed by some ignoramus, who has jumbled together events of ancient and modern date. The prince of Delhi might have been Jaipal, but if we are to place any faith in the chronology of the Tuar race, no prince of this family could be synchronous with the Yadu Salbahan. I am inclined to think that the emigration of Salbahan's ancestors from Gajni was at a much later period than S. 72, as I shall note as we proceed. [As will be seen later on, the whole story swarms with anachronisms.]

[2] Turk is the term in the dialects which the Hindus apply to the races from central Asia, the Turushka of the Puranas.

[3] Doubtless the ancestor of the Johya race, termed the Janjuha by Babur, and who dwelt with the Juds in the hills of Jud, the Jadu-ka-dang of the Bhatti MSS.

[4] However curious this assertion, of the Chagatais being descended from

"Chakito had eight sons, namely, Deosi, Bharu, Khemkhan, Nahar, Jaipal,[1] Dharsi, Bijli Khan, Shah Samand.

"Baland, who resided at Salbahanpur, left Gajni to the charge of his grandson Chakito; and as the power of the barbarian (Mlechchha) increased, he not only entertained troops of that race, but all his nobles were of the same body. They offered, if he would quit the religion of his fathers, to make him master of Balkh, Bokhara, where dwelt the Usbek race, whose king had no offspring but one daughter. Chakito married her, and became king of Balkh, Bokhara, and lord of twenty-eight thousand horse. Between Balkh and Bokhara runs a mighty river, and Chakito was king of all from the gate of Balakhshan to the face of Hindustan; and from him is descended the tribe of Chakito Mongols.[2]

"Kalar, third son of Baland, had eight sons, whose descendants are designated Kalar.[3] Their names were, Sheodas, Ramdas, Aso, Kistna, Sama, Ganga, Jassa, Bhaga; almost all of whom became Musalmans. They are a numerous race, inhabiting the mountainous countries west of the river,[4] and notorious robbers.

the Yadus, it ought not to surprise us: I repeat, that all these tribes, whether termed Indo-Scythic or Tatar, prior to Islamism professed a faith which may be termed Hinduism.

[1] As it is evident the period has reference to the very first years of Islamism, and it is stated that the sons of Gaj were to be proselytes, it is by no means improbable that this is Jaipal, the infidel prince of Khwarizm.—See Price's *Mahomedan History*.

[2] This is a most important admission of the proselytism of the ancient Indo-Scythic Yadu princes to the faith of Islam, though there can be no reasonable doubt of it. Temugin, better known by his *nomme de guerre*, Jangiz, the father of Chagatai, according to the Muhammadan historians, is termed an infidel, and so was Takash, the father of Muhammad of Khwarizm: the one was of the Getic or Yuti race; the other, as his name discloses, of the Tak or Takshak, the two grand races of Central Asia. The insertion of this pedigree in this place completely vitiates chronology; yet for what purpose it could have been interpolated, if not founded on some fact, we cannot surmise.

[3] We can, by means of the valuable translation of the Commentaries of Babur, trace many of these tribes.

[4] It has already been stated that the fifteen brothers of Baland established themselves in the mountainous parts of the Panjab, and that his sons inherited those west of the Indus, or Daman. The Afghan tribes, whose supposed genealogy from the Jews has excited so much curiosity, and who now inhabit the regions conquered by the sons of Salbahan, are possibly Yadus, who, on conversion, to give more éclat to their antiquity, converted Yadu into Yahudi or Jew, and added the rest of the story from the Koran.

"Janj, the fourth son, had seven sons: Champa, Gokul, Mehraj, Hansa, Bhadon, Rasa, Jaga, all whose issue bore the name of Janj;[1] and in like manner did the other sons become the patriarchs of tribes.

Bhatti.—"Bhatti succeeded his father Baland. He conquered fourteen princes, and added [227] their fortunes to his own. Among his effects he reckoned twenty-four thousand mules[2] laden with treasure, sixty thousand horse, and innumerable foot. As soon as he mounted the *gaddi*, he assembled all his forces at Lahore preparatory to the *tika-daur*[3] destined against Birbhan Baghel, lord of Kanakpur. Birbhan fell in the battle which ensued, at the head of forty thousand men.

"Bhatti had two sons, Mangal Rao and Masur Rao. With Bhatti, the patronymic was changed, and the tribe thenceforth was distinguished by his name.

Mangal.—"Mangal Rao succeeded, but his fortune was not equal to that of his fathers. Dhundi, king of Ghazni, with a mighty force, invaded Lahore;[4] nor did Mangal Rao oppose him, but with his eldest son fled into the wilds on the banks of

---

That grand division of Afghans called the Yusufzai, or 'Sons of Joseph,' whose original country was Kabul and Ghazni, yet retain the name of Jadon (vulgar of Yadu) as one of their principal subdivisions; and they still occupy a position in the hilly region east of the Indus, conquered by the sons of Baland. It would be a curious fact could we prove the Afghans not Yahudis but Yadus [?].

[1] Doubtless the junction of Janj with that of Johya, another numerous tribe, formed the Janjuha of Babur; the Johyas of the Bhatti annals, now known only by name, but whose history forms a volume. The sons of Janj have left numerous traces—Janjian on the Gara; Jinjiniali in the desert, etc.

[2] Even the mention of an animal unknown in the desert of India evinces the ancient source whence these annals are compiled. Had the Yadu colony at this period obtained a footing in the desert, south of the Sutlej, the computation would have been by camel-loads, not by mules.

[3] See Vol. I. p. 315, for an account of this military foray.

[4] This would almost imply that Lahore and Salbahana were one and the same place, but from what follows, the intervening distance could not have been great between the two cities. There is a Sangala, south of Lahore, near the altars of Alexander, and a Sialkot in our modern maps. Salbahana, Salbahanpur, or simply Salpura, may have been erected on the ruins of Kampilanagari. We may hope that researches in that yet untouched region, the Panjab, will afford much to the elucidation of ancient history. [Sālbahanpur is usually identified with Siālkot (Cunningham, *ASR*, ii. 21).]

the river. The foe then invested Salbahanpur, where resided the family of the Raja; but Masur Rao escaped and fled to the Lakhi Jungle.[1] There being only a cultivating peasantry in this tract, he overcame them, and became master of the country. Masur Rao had two sons, Abhai Rao and Saran Rao. The elder, Abhai Rao, brought the whole Lakhi Jungle under his control, and his issue, which multiplied, became famous as the Aboharia Bhattis.[2] Saran quarrelled with and separated from his brother, and his issue descended to the rank of cultivators, and are well known as the Saran Jats.[3]

"Mangal Rao, the son of Bhatti, and who abandoned his kingdom, had six sons: Majam Rao, Kalarsi, Mulraj, Sheoraj, Phul, Kewala.

"When Mangal Rao fled from the king, his children were secreted in the houses of his subjects. A Bhunia named Satidas, of the tribe of Tak,[4] whose ancestors had been reduced from

[1] The Lakhi Jungle is well known in India for its once celebrated breed of horses, extinct within the last twenty years.

[2] [They take their name from the old town of Abohar in the Firozpur District, Panjāb (*IGI*, v. 2). Compare the local legend with that from Hissār (Rose, *Glossary*, ii. 103 f.).]

[3] Thus it is that the most extensive agricultural races spread all over India, called Jāts or Jats, have a tradition that they are descended from the Yadu race (*qu.* Yuti ?), and that their original country is Kandahar. Such was stated to me as the origin of the Jats of Bayana and Bharatpur. Why the descendants of Saran assumed the name of Jats is not stated.

[4] This incidental mention of the race of Tak, and of its being in great consideration on the settlement of the Yadus in the Panjab, is very important. I have given a sketch of this tribe (Vol. I. p. 123), but since I wrote it I have discovered the capital of the Tak, and on the very spot where I should have expected the site of Taxila, the capital of Taxiles, the friend of Alexander. In that sketch I hesitated not to say that the name was not personal, but arose from his being the head of the Takshak or Naga tribe, which is confirmed. It is to Babur, or rather to his translator, that I am indebted for this discovery. In describing the limits of Banu, Babur thus mentions it: "And on the west is Dasht, which is also called Bazar and Tak"; to which the erudite translator adds, "Tak is said long to have been the capital of Daman." In Mr. Elphinstone's map, Bazar, which Babur makes identical with Tak, is a few miles north of the city of Attok. There is no question that both the river and city were named after the race of Tak or Takshak, the Nagas, Nagvansi, or snake race, who spread over India. Indeed, I would assume that the name of Omphis, which young Taxiles had on his father's death, is Ophis, the Greek version of Tak, the 'serpent.' The Taks appear to have been established in the same regions at the earliest period. The Mahabharata describes the wars between Janamejaya and the Takshaks,

power and wealth by the ancestors of the Bhatti prince, determined to avenge himself, and informed the king that some of the children were concealed in [228] the house of a banker (*sahukar*). The king sent the Tak with a party of troops, and surrounded the house of Sridhar, who was carried before the king, who swore he would put all his family to death if he did not produce the young princes of Salbahana. The alarmed banker protested he had no children of the Raja's, for that the infants who enjoyed his protection were the offspring of a Bhumia, who had fled, on the invasion, deeply in his debt. But the king ordered him to produce them; he demanded the name of the village, sent for the Bhumias belonging to it, and not only made the royal infants of Salbahana eat with them, but marry their daughters. The banker had no alternative to save their lives but to consent: they were brought forth in the peasant's garb, ate with the husbandmen (Jats), and were married to their daughters. Thus the offspring of Kalarrae became the Kalhora Jats; those of Mundraj and Sheoraj, the Mudna and Seora Jats; while the younger boys, Phul and Kewala, who were passed off as a barber (Nai) and a potter (Kumhar), fell into that class.[1]

"Mangal Rao, who found shelter in the wilds of the Gara, crossed that stream and subjugated a new territory. At this period, the tribe of Baraha[2] inhabited the banks of the river; beyond them were the Buta Rajputs of Butaban.[3] In Pugal dwelt the Pramara;[4] in Dhat the Sodha[5] race; and the Lodra[6] Rajputs in Lodorva. Here Mangal Rao found security, and

---

to revenge on their king the death of his father Parikshit, emperor of Indraprastha, or Delhi. [These theories have no foundation. Omphis is the Greek form of Skt. Āmbhi, and has no connexion with a snake cult (Smith, *EHI*, 60).]

[1] [This is a series of folk etymologies intended to explain the intermixture of these tribes. For the Kalhora tribe see Rose, *Glossary*, ii. 440 ff.]

[2] The names of these Rajput races, several of which are now blotted from the page of existence, prove the fidelity of the original manuscript. The Barahas are now Muhammadans.

[3] The Buta is amongst the extinct tribes.

[4] Pugal from the most remote times has been inhabited by the Pramar race. It is one of the Nau-koti Maru-ki, the nine castles of the desert.

[5] The Sodhas of Umarkot have inhabited the desert from time immemorial, and are in all probability the Sogdoi of Alexander. See Vol. I. p. 111.

[6] Lodorva will be described hereafter.

with the sanction of the Sodha prince, he fixed his future abode in the centre of the lands of the Lodras, the Barahas, and the Sodhas.[1] On the death of Mangal Rao, he was succeeded by

"Majam Rao, who escaped from Salbahanpur with his father. He was recognized by all the neighbouring princes, who sent the usual presents on his accession, and the [229] Sodha prince of Umarkot made an offer of his daughter in marriage, which was accepted, and the nuptials were solemnized at Umarkot. He had three sons, Kehar, Mulraj,[2] and Gogli.

Kehar Rāo.—"Kehar became renowned for his exploits. Hearing of a caravan (kafila) of five hundred horses going from Aror[3] to Multan, he pursued them with a chosen band disguised

[1] [The above series of legends of the Bhatti settlement in the desert is a mass of fiction. "We are told that Sālivāhan founded the city of Sālbāhanpur in Vikrama Sambat 72, or about A.D. 16; that the third in succession to him, Mangal Rāo, was driven southward into the desert, and that Mangal Rāo's grandson, Kehar, laid the foundations of a castle called Tanot (still in Jaisalmer territory), which was completed in A.D. 731; or, in other words, that Sālivāhan and his five immediate successors reigned for more than seven hundred years. Again, it is said that in Sālivāhan's time the coconut, an offer of marriage, came from Rāja Jaipāl Tonwar of Delhi, whereas the Tonwar dynasty ruled at Delhi for just a century from about A.D. 1050." This Sālivāhana cannot be the hero who is said to have conquered the Indo-Scythians, but some of the many legends connected with him may have suggested the fictions of the Bhatti bards (Erskine iii. A. 96).]

[2] Mulraj had three sons, Rajpal, Lohwa, and Chubar. The elder son had two sons, Rana and Giga; the first of whom had five sons, Dhukur, Pohor, Budh, Kulru, Jaipal, all of whom had issue, and became heads of clans. The descendants of Giga bore the name of Khengar (*qu.* chiefs of Girnar?). The annals of all these States abound with similar minute genealogical details, which to the Rajputs are of the highest importance in enabling them to trace the affinities of families, but which it is imperative to omit, as they possess no interest for the European reader. I have extracted the names of the issue of Mulraj to show this. The Khengars were famed in the peninsula of Surashtra—nine of them ruled in Junagarh Girnar; and but for this incidental relation, their origin must have ever remained concealed from the archaeologist, as the race has long been extinct. On some future day I hope to present a sketch of Khengar's palace, on the sacred mount Girnar, to the public. [The famous well, at least, is attributed to Rāo Khengār II. (A.D. 1098–1125) (*BG*, viii. 444).]

[3] The remains of this once famous town, the ancient capital of the upper valley of the Indus, I had the happiness to discover by means of one of my parties, in 1811. It is the Alor of Abu-l-fazl, the capital of Raja Siharas, whose kingdom extended north to Kashmir, and south to the ocean; and the Azour of D'Anville, who, on the authority of Ebn Haukal, says, "Azour est presque comparable à Multan pour la grandeur." He adds, that Azizi

as camel merchants, and came up with his prey across the Panjnad,[1] where he attacked and captured it, and returned to his abode. By such exploits he became known, and the coco-nut (*nariyal*) was sent to Majam Rao, and his two elder sons, by Alansi Deora, of Jalor.[2] The nuptials were celebrated with great splendour, and on their return Kehar laid the foundation of a castle, which he named Tanot in honour of Tana [or Tanuja] Devi. Ere it was completed, Rao Majam died.

Kehar Rāo.—" Kehar succeeded. On his accession, Tanot was attacked by Jasrath, chief of the Barahas,[3] because it was erected on the bounds of his tribe; but Mulraj defended it, and the Barahas were compelled to retire.

" On Mangalwar (Tuesday), the full-moon of Magh, S. 787[4] (A.D. 731), the fortress of Tanot was completed, and a temple erected to Tana-Mata. Shortly after a treaty of peace was formed

---

places it "trente parasanges de Mansora." If Mansura is the ancient Bakhar (capital of the Sogdoi), we should read three instead of thirty. See Map, Vol. I. [Mansūra was near Bāhmanābād.]

[1] Panjnad is the name which the Indus bears immediately below the point of confluence of the five streams (panj-nadi). The mere mention of such terms as the Panjnad, and the ancient Aror, stamps these annals with authenticity, however they may be deformed by the interpolations and anachronisms of ignorant copyists. Of Aror, or the Panjnad, excepting the regular kasids, or messengers, perhaps not an individual living in Jaisalmer could not speak.

[2] [This is another anachronism. The Deora sept of the Chauhāns, of which the Rāja of Sirohi is head, did not come into existence until the thirteenth century, and Jālor was then held by the Paramāras, who kept possession till they were ousted by the Chauhāns at the end of the twelfth century (Erskine iii. A. 10).]

[3] This shows that the Baraha tribe was of the same faith with the Yadu Bhatti; in fact 'the star of Islam' did not shine in these regions for some time after, although Umar, in the first century, had established a colony of the faithful at Bakhar, afterwards Mansura. The Barahas are mentioned by Pottinger in his travels in Balochistan.

[4] There are but six descents given from Salbahan, the leader of the Yadu colony from Zabulistan into the Panjab, and Kehar, the founder of their first settlement in the desert of India. The period of the first is S. 72, of the other S. 787. Either names are wanting, or the period of Salbahan is erroneous. Kehar's period, namely, S. 787, appears a landmark, and is borne out by numerous subsequent most valuable synchronisms. Were we to admit one hundred years to have elapsed between Salbahan and Kehar, it would make the period of expulsion from Zabulistan about S. 687, which is just about the era of Muhammad.

with the Barahas, which was concluded by the nuptials of their chief with the daughter of Mulraj [230]."

Having thus fairly fixed the Yadu Bhatti chieftain in the land of Maru, it seems a proper point at which to close this initiatory chapter with some observations on the diversified history of this tribe, crowded into so small a compass; though the notes of explanation, subjoined as we proceeded, will render fewer remarks requisite, since with their help the reader may draw his own conclusions as to the value of this portion of the Bhatti annals, which may be divided into four distinct epochs:

Recapitulation of Bhatti History.—1. That of Hari, the ancestor of the Yadu race.

2. Their expulsion, or the voluntary abandonment of India by his children, with their relations of the Harikula and Pandu races, for the countries west of the Indus; their settlements in Marusthali; the founding of Gajni, and combats with the kings of Rum and Khorasan.

3. Their expulsion from Zabulistan, colonization of the Panjab, and creation of the new capital of Salbahanpur.

4. Their expulsion from the Panjab, and settlement in Mer, the rocky oasis of Maru, to the erection of Tanot.

It is the more unnecessary to enter into greater details on these outlines of the early Yadu history, since the subject has been in part treated elsewhere.[1] A multiplicity of scattered facts and geographical distinctions fully warrants our assent to the general truth of these records, which prove that the Yadu race had dominion in central Asia, and were again, as Islamism advanced, repelled upon India. The obscure legend of their encounters with the allied Syrian and Bactrian kings would have seemed altogether illusory, did not evidence exist that Antiochus the Great was slain in these very regions by an Indo-Scythian prince, called by the Greek writers Sophagasenas: a name in all probability compounded from Subahu and his grandson Gaj (who might have used the common affix of *sena*), the Yadu princes of Gajni, who are both stated to have had conflicts with the Bactrian (Khorasan) kings.

Sistan (the region of cold, *siya*)[2] and both sides of the valley

[1] See "Essay on the Hindu and Theban Hercules," *Transactions of the Royal Asiatic Society*, vol. iii.

[2] [Sīstān is Sakastēnē, "The Saka country".]

were occupied in the earliest periods by another branch of the Yadus; for the Sind-Samma dynasty was descended from Samba (which like Yadu became a patronymic)—of which the Greeks made Sambos—and one of whose descendants opposed Alexander in his progress down the Indus. The capital of this dynasty was Samma-ka-kot, or Samanagari, yet existing on the lower Indus, and which was corrupted into Minnagara by the Greeks [231].[1]

Ancient Sites in Jaisalmer.—It is an interesting hypothesis, that would make the Chagatais descendants of the Yadus.[2] In like manner, Bappa, the ancestor of the Ranas of Mewar, abandoned Central India after establishing his line in Chitor, and retired to Khorasan. All this proves that Hinduism prevailed in these distant regions, and that the intercourse was unrestricted between Central Asia and India. We have undiscovered fields of inquiry in Transoxiana, and in the still more accessible region of the Panjab, where much exists to reward the archaeologist; Salbahanpur, Kampilanagari, Bahra, the hill of Jud, perhaps Bucephalia,[3] the seven towns of Uchh, but, above all, the capital of

[1] [The capital of Sambos was Sindimana, probably Sihwān (Smith, *EHI*, 101).]

[2] Mr. Wilson discovered the name of Pandu in Ptolemy's *Geography of Sogdiana*; and according to Ebn Haukal, the city of Herat is also called Hari. This adjoins Maru, or Merv, and to Marusthali the Pandu and Harikula races retired on their exile from India. If ever these remote regions are searched for ancient inscriptions, we may yet ascend the ladder of Time. What was that Hamiri language, inscribed on the gate of Samarkand? (Ouseley, *Ebn Haukal*, p. 254). The lamented death of that enterprising traveller, Mr. Brown, when he was about visiting Transoxiana, leaves a fine field to the adventurous. The Buddhist colossal sculptures and caves at Bamian, with such inscriptions as they may contain, are of the highest importance; and I have little doubt, will be found of the same character as those discovered in the cave temples of India, attributed to the Pandus. [The author depended on Wilford (*Asiatic Researches*, vi. 462 ff.). For Bamiān see *EB*, 11th ed. iii. 304 f.]

[3] In a portion of the essay "On the Theban and Hindu Hercules," which I suppressed as better suited to an intended dissertation "On the Sepulchral Monuments of the Rajpoots," where I trace a close analogy between their customs and those of the Scythic and Scandinavian Warriors, my particular attention was drawn to that singular monument discovered by Elphinstone, called the "Tope Manikiala." I had before (*Trans. R.A.S.* vol. i. p. 330) conjectured it to be one of the many mausoleums erected to Menander, but on observing the geography of St. Croix, in his *Examen Critique des Historiens d'Alexandre*, who places the city of Bucephalus on the very spot where the monument found by Mr. E. exists, I gave up Menander for Alexander's horse, and this, long anterior to its reported excavation by the

Taxiles. Let us hope that, in this age of enterprise, these suggestions may be followed up ; we can promise the adventurer a very different result from that which tempts the explorer of barbarous Africa, for here he would penetrate into the first haunts of civilization, and might solve one of the great problems which still distract mankind [232].

CHAPTER 2

Question of Dates.—The dates of the varied events related in the preceding chapter may be of doubtful accuracy, but we have at length arrived on the *terra firma* of Bhatti chronology. We may distrust the date, 3008 of Yudishthira's era, for the victory obtained by the Jadon prince of Gajni over the kings of Rum and Khorasan ;[1] as well as that of S. 72 assigned for the exode of Salbahan and his Yadus from Zabulistan, and their colonization of the Panjab ;[2] but their settlements in the desert, and the foundation of [233] Tanot, their first seat of power, in S. 787 (A.D. 731), are corroborated by incontrovertible synchronisms in almost every subsequent reign of these annals.

Rāo Kehar I.—Kehar, a name highly respected in the history of the Bhatti race, and whose exploit has been already recorded, must have been the cotemporary of the celebrated Caliph Al Walid,[3] the first whose arms extended to the plains of India, and one of whose earliest conquests and chief positions was Aror, the capital of Upper Sind.

Chev. Ventura, for whose subsequent observations we impatiently wait. [Mānikiāla, in the Rāwalpindi District ; the Stūpa marks the spot where Gautama Buddha offered his body to appease the hunger of seven tiger cubs (*IGI*, xvii. 182 f.). The site of Boukephala is practically identical with the modern Jihlam (Smith, *EHI*, 71).]

[1] The emperor Babur tells us, in his *Commentaries*, that the people of India apply the term Khorasan to all the regions west of the Indus.

[2] Notwithstanding the lapse of eleven hundred years since the expulsion of the Bhattis from the Panjab, and in spite of the revolutions in laws, language, and religion, since the descendants of Salbahan abandoned that region, yet, even to this day, there is abundant testimony in its geographical nomenclature that the Bhattis had dominion there. We have Pindi Bhattia-ka, Bhatti-ka-chak, in the very position where we should look for Salbahanpur.—See Elphinstone's Map. [Sālbāhanpur is generally identified with Siālkot (*ASR*, ii. 21).]

[3] [Walid I., seventh Caliph of the house of Ummaya (A.D. 705–14).]

Rāo Tano or Tanuji.—Kehar[1] had five sons; namely, Tano, Utirao, Chanar, Kaphrio, Them. All of them had offspring,[2] who became the heads of clans, retaining the patronymic. All were soldiers of fortune, and they conquered the lands of the Chana Rajputs;[3] but the latter revenged themselves upon Kehar, whom they attacked and slew as he was hunting.

Tano succeeded. He laid waste the lands of the Barahas,[4] and those of the Langaha of Multan. But Husain Shah advanced with the Langaha Pathans,[5] clothed in armour with iron helms, with the men of Dudi,[6] of Khichi[7] the Khokhar;[8] the Mogul, the Johya,[9] the Jud,[9] and Sayyid, all mounted on horses, to the

[1] Although I omit the inverted commas indicative of translation, the reader is to understand that what follows is a free interpretation of the original chronicle.

[2] Utirao had five sons, Sorna, Sahasi, Jiva, Chako, and Ajo; their issue had the generic term of Utirao. It is thus their clans and tribes are multiplied *ad infinitum*, and since the skill of the genealogist (Bhat) is required to keep them clear of incestuous marriages, even such uninteresting details have some value, as they stamp their annals with authenticity.

[3] The tribe of Chana is now extinct.

[4] These Indo-Scythic tribes were designated by the names of animals. The Barahas are the hogs; the Numris, the foxes; Takshaks, the snakes; Aswas or Asi, the horses, etc. [possibly an indication of totemism].

[5] These Langaha Pathans were proselytes from the Solanki Rajputs, one of the four Agnikula races. Probably they inhabited the district of Lamghan, west of the Indus. It is curious and interesting to find that the Solanki gotracharya, or 'genealogical creed,' claims Lohkot as their settlement. The use of the word Pathan by no means precludes their being Hindus. [The Langāhs, originally Afghāns, are now agriculturists (Rose, *Glossary*, iii. 30 f.).]

[6] Babur, in his valuable *Autobiography*, gives us the names of all the tribes he met in his passage into India, and this enumeration goes far to prove the authenticity of the early annals of the Bhattis. Babur does not mention "the men of Dudi."

[7] The introduction of the name of this tribe here is highly important, and very interesting to those who have studied, in the Rajput bards, their early history. The bards of the Khichis give them this northern origin, and state that all Sindsagar, one of the duabs of the Panjab, belonged to them.

[8] The Khokhar is most probably the Ghakkar. Babur writes the name Gakar, a singular race, and decidedly Scythic in their habits even in his day. [The Khokhar and Ghakkar tribes are often confused (Rose ii. 554).]

[9] Of the Judis and Johyas we have already spoken as inhabiting the range called in the native annals Jadu-ka-dang, and by Babur "the hill of Jud," skirting the Behat. The position of Bahara is laid down in that monument of genius and industry, the Memoir of Rennel (who calls it

number of ten thousand men, to attack the Jadon. They reached the territory of the Barahas, who [234] joined them, and there they encamped. Tano collected his brethren around him, and prepared for defence. During four days they defended the castle; and on the fifth the Rao ordered the gates to be thrown open, and with his son, Bijairae, sallied out sword in hand, and attacked the besiegers. The Barahas were the first to fly, and they were soon followed by the rest of the Asurs. The victors carried the spoils of the field into Tanot. As soon as the armies of Multan and Langaha were driven off, the coco-nut came from Jiju, chief of the Butas of Butaban,[1] and an alliance offensive and defensive was formed against the prince of Multan.

Tano had five sons, Bijairae, Makar, Jaitang, Alan, and Rakecha. The second son, Makar, had issue Maipa, who had two sons, Mohola and Dakao, the latter of whom excavated the lake known by his name. His issue became carpenters (Sutar), and are to this day known as the Makar Sutar.[2]

The third son, Jaitang, had two sons, Ratansi and Chohar. The first repaired the ruined city of Bikampur.[3] Chohar had two sons, Kola and Girraj, who founded the towns of Kolasar and Girrajsar.[3]

The fourth son, Alan, had four sons, Deosi, Tirpal, Bhaoni, and

---

Bheera), in 32° N. and 72° 10′ E.; and by Elphinstone in 32° 10′, but a whole degree further to the east, or 73° 15′. This city, so often mentioned in the Yadu-Bhatti annals as one of their intermediate places of repose, on their expulsion from India and migration to Central Asia, has its position minutely pointed out by the Emperor Babur (p. 259), who, in his attack on the hill tribes of Jats, Gujars, Ghakkars, etc., adjoining Kashmir, "expelled Hati Guker from Behreh, on the Behut River, near the cave temples of Gar-kotri at Bikrum," of which the able annotator remarks, that as well as those of But Bamian, they were probably Buddhist. Babur (p. 294) also found the Jats masters of Sialkot, most likely the Salpur of the Inscription (p. 916 above), conquered from a Jat prince in the twelfth century by the Patan prince, and presumed to be the Salbahanpur founded by the fugitive Yadu prince of Gajni [see p. 1183 above].

[1] Butaban, probably from *vana*, pronounced in the dialect *ban*, the 'wild' or 'forest' of Buta.

[2] Illegitimate children can never overcome this natural defect amongst the Rajputs. Thus we find among all classes of artisans in India, some of royal but spurious descent. [This is a good instance of high-caste blood in artisan castes; see Russell, *Tribes and Castes of Central Provinces*, ii. 200.]

[3] These towns and lakes are well known, but have been seized by Bikaner. See Map. [Bikampur, 95 miles N.E. of Jaisalmer city.]

Rakecha. The descendants of Deosi became Rabaris (who rear camels),[1] and the issue of Rakecha became merchants (Banias), and are now classed amongst the Oswal tribe.[2]

Tano having, by the interposition of the goddess Bijaiseni, discovered a hidden treasure, erected a fortress, which he named Bijnot;[3] and in this he placed a statue of the goddess, on the 13th, the enlightened part of the month Margsir, the Rohini Nakshatra, S. 813 (A.D. 757). He died after ruling eighty years.

Bijairāē.—Bijairae succeeded in S. 870 (A.D. 814). He commenced his reign with the *tika-daur* against his old enemies, the Barahas, whom he defeated and plundered. In S. 892, he had a son by the Buta queen, who was called Deoraj. The Barahas and Langahas once more united to attack the Bhatti prince; but they were defeated [235] and put to flight. Finding that they could not succeed by open warfare, they had recourse to treachery. Having, under pretence of terminating this long feud, invited young Deoraj to marry the daughter of the Baraha chief, the Bhattis attended, when Bijairae and eight hundred of his kin and clan were massacred. Deoraj escaped to the house of the Purohit (of the Barahas, it is presumed), whither he was pursued. There being no hope of escape, the Brahman threw the Brahmanical thread round the neck of the young prince, and in order to convince his pursuers that they were deceived as to the object of their search, he sat down to eat with him from the same dish.[4] Tanot was invested and taken, and nearly every soul in it put to the sword, so that the very name of Bhatti was for a while extinct.

[1] [The Rabāris say that they were created by Siva to take care of the first camel which Pārvati formed for her amusement (*Census Report, Mārwār*, 1891, ii. 157). Rose (*Glossary*, iii. 269) writes Rahbāri, probably Persian *rahwār*, 'active.']

[2] The Oswal is the richest and most numerous of the eighty-four mercantile tribes of India, and is said to amount to one hundred thousand families. They are called 'Oswal' from their first settlement, the town of Osian. They are all of pure Rajput birth, of no single tribe, but chiefly Puars, Solankis, and Bhattis. All profess the Jain tenets, and it is a curious fact, though little known, that the pontiffs of that faith must be selected from the youth of Osian. The wealthy bankers and merchants of these regions scattered throughout India, are all known under one denomination, Marwari, which is erroneously supposed to apply to the Jodhpur territory, whereas, in fact, it means belonging to the desert. It is singular that the wealth of India should centre in this region of comparative sterility.

[3] See Map.

[4] [Such tales are common, and generally imply a flaw in the pedigree.]

Rāo Deorāj.—Deoraj remained for a long time concealed in the territory of the Barahas; but at length he ventured to Buta, his maternal abode, where he had the happiness to find his mother, who had escaped the massacre at Tanot. She was rejoiced to behold her son's face, and " waved the salt over his head," then threw it into the water, exclaiming, " Thus may your enemies melt away!" Soon tired of a life of dependence, Deoraj asked for a single village, which was promised; but the kin of the Buta chief alarmed him, and he recalled it, and limited his grant to such a quantity of land as he could encompass by the thongs cut from a single buffalo's hide; and this, too, in the depth of the desert. For this expedient he was indebted to the architect Kaikeya, who had constructed the castle of Bhatner.[1] Deoraj

[1] This deception practised by the Bhatti chief to obtain land on which to erect a fortress is not unknown in other parts of India, and in more remote regions. Bhatner owes its name to this expedient, from the division (*bantna*) of the hide. The etymology of Calcutta is the same, but should be written Khalkata, from the cuttings of the hide (*khal*). Byrsa, the castle of Carthage, originates from the same story. If there existed any affinity between the ancient Pali languages of India and the Punic or Phoenician (as the names of its princes and their adjuncts of *bal* would indicate), and the letters B and Ch were as little dissimilar in Punic as in Sanskrit, then Byrsa would become charsa, 'hide' or 'skin,' which might have originated the capital of the African Mauritania, as of the Indian Maruthan. Thus Marocco may be from Maruka, of or belonging to Maru, the desert, also probably the origin of the Merv of Iran. The term Moor may likewise be corrupted from Mauri, an inhabitant of Maruka, while the Sahariya of our Indian desert is the brother in name and profession of the Saracen of Arabia, from Sahra, a desert, and zadan, to assault. The Nomadic princes of Mauritania might therefore be the Pali or shepherd kings of Maruthan, the great African desert. And who were these Philita or Pali kings of Barbary and Egypt? It is well known that the Berbers who inhabited Abyssinia and the south coast of the Red Sea, migrated to the northern coast, not only occupying it, as well as Mount Atlas, but pushing their tribes far into the grand *sahra*, or desert. To those colonists, that coast owes its name of Barbary. From the days of Solomon and his contemporary Shishak, an intimate communication subsisted between the eastern coast of Africa and India; and I have already hazarded the opinion, that we must look to this coast of Aethiopia and Abyssinia for the Lanka of the Rameses (Rameswar) of India; and from the former country the most skilful archaeologists assert that Egypt had her mythology, and more especially that mystery—the prominent feature of both systems—the Phallic rites, or worship of the lingam. Berber, according to Bruce, means a shepherd, and as *ber* is a sheep in the language of India, Berber is a shepherd in the most literal sense, and consequently the synonym of Pali. It has been asserted that this race colonized these coasts of Africa from India about the time of

immediately commenced erecting a [236] place of strength, which he called after himself Deogarh, or Derawar,[1] on Monday, the 5th of the month Magh (sudi), the Pushya Nakshatra, S. 909.

Soon as the Buta chief heard that his son-in-law was erecting, not a dwelling, but a castle, he sent a force to raze it. Deoraj despatched his mother with the keys to the assailants, and invited

---

Amenophis, and that they are the Hyksos, or 'shepherd-kings,' who subjugated Egypt. On this account a comparison of the ancient architectural remains of Abyssinia and Aethiopia with those of the ancient Hindus is most desirable. It is asserted, and with appearance of truth, that the architecture of the Pyramids is distinct from the Pharaonic, and that they are at once Astronomic and Phallic. In India, the symbolic pinnacle surmounting the temples of the sun-god are always pyramidal. If the forthcoming history of the Berbers should reveal the mystery of their first settlements in Abyssinia, a great object would be attained; and if search were made in the old cave-temples of that coast, some remains of the characters they used might aid in tracing their analogy to the ancient Pali of the East; an idea suggested by an examination of the few characters found in the grand desert inhabited by the Tuaregs, which have a certain resemblance to the Punic, and to the unknown characters attributed to the Indo-Scythic tribes of India, as on their coins and cave-temples. Wide asunder as are these regions, the mind that will strive to lessen the historical separation may one day be successful, when the connexion between Aethiopia (*qu.* from *aditya* and contracted *ait*, the Sun ?) and Surashtra, 'the land of the Sun,' or Syria of India, may become more tangible. Ferishta (*vide* Briggs' translation, vol. iv. p. 402), quoting original authorities, says, "the inhabitants of Selandip, or the island of Ceylon, were accustomed to send vessels to the coast of Africa, to the Red Sea, and Persian Gulf, from the earliest ages, and Hindu pilgrims resorted to Mecca and Egypt for the purpose of paying adoration to the idols. It is related also that this people trading from Ceylon became converts to the true faith at so early a period as the first caliphs"; all which confirms the fact of early intercourse between Egypt and India.—See Vol. II. p. 702. [It is unnecessary to criticize in detail the etymologies suggested in this note, a good instance of the Author's manner. The etymology of Calcutta is unknown, the most recent suggestion being that it is *Khālkata*, 'a place where a flood cut a creek' (Yule, *Hobson-Jobson*, 2nd ed. 146; Hoernle, *JASB*, 1898, p. 48 f.; K. Blechynden, *Calcutta Past and Present*, 1905, p. 5). Bhatner means 'city of the Bhattis.' Berber is either Greek βάρβαροι, or a tribal term, Barabara; that of Aethiopia is unknown (*EB*, 11th ed. iii. 764, ix. 845). The story of fixing the limits of a territory by riding round it or by encircling it with strips of hide, as in the story of Carthage, is common in India (Bradley-Birt, *Chota Nagpore*, 16 f.; Brett, *Chhattisgarh Gazetteer*, i. 192; *BG*, xiii. Part i. 160, and many others.]

[1] Deorawal is in the map; it was one of the points of halt in Elphinstone's mission to Kabul. This discloses to us the position of the Buta territory, and as astronomical data are given, those inclined to prove or disprove the Bhatti chronology have ample means afforded.

the leaders to receive the castle and his homage; when the chief men, to the number of a hundred and twenty, entered, they were inveigled, under pretence of consultation, ten at a time, and each party put to death and their bodies thrown over the wall. Deprived of their leaders, the rest took to flight.

Soon after, the prince was visited by his patron, the Jogi who had protected him amongst the Barahas, and who now gave him the title of Siddh.[1] This Jogi, who possessed the art of transmuting metals, lodged in the same house where Deoraj found protection on the massacre of his father and kindred. One day, the holy man had gone abroad, leaving his jarjarikakaṇtha, or 'tattered doublet,' in which was the Raskumbha, or 'elixir-vessel,' a drop of which having fallen on the dagger of Deoraj and changed it to gold, he decamped with both, and it was by the possession of this he was enabled to erect Derawar. The Jogi was well aware of the thief whom he now came to visit; and he confirmed him in the possession of the stolen property, on one condition, that he should become his chela and disciple, and, as a token of submission and fidelity, adopt the external symbols of the Jogi. Deoraj assented, and was invested with the Jogi robe of ochre.[2] He placed the mudra[3] in his ear, the little horn round his neck, and [237] the bandage (langota) about his loins; and with the gourd (khopra) in his hand, he perambulated the dwellings of his kin, exclaiming, Alakh! Alakh![4] The gourd was filled with gold and pearls; the title of Rao was abandoned for that of Rawal;[5] the tika was made on his forehead; and exacting a pledge that these rites of inauguration should be continued to the latest posterity, the Baba Rata (for such was the Jogi's name) disappeared.

Deoraj determined to wreak his revenge on the Barahas, and he enjoyed it even "to stripping the scarfs from the heads of their females." On his return to Derawar, he prepared for an attack on Langaha, the heir of which was then on a marriage expedition at Alipur. There, Deoraj attacked and slew a thousand

[1] ['One who has attained beatitude.']

[2] Called *geru*; garments coloured with this dye are worn by all classes of mendicants.

[3] The mudra is a round prickly seed worn by the ascetics as ear-rings.

[4] The Supreme Being; the universal and One God.

[5] Rawal [*rājakula*, 'of the royal house'] is still the title of the princes of Jaisalmer, as it once was that of the Mewar house.

of them, the rest henceforth acknowledged his supremacy. The Langahas were gallant Rajputs.

The Langāha Tribe.—As the tribe of Langaha, or Langa, will from this period go hand in hand, in all the international wars of the Yadu-Bhattis, from their expulsion from the Panjab to their final settlement in the Indian desert, it is of some interest to trace its origin and destiny. It is distinctly stated that, at this epoch, the Langahas were Rajputs; and they are in fact a subdivision of the Solanki or Chalukya race, one of the four Agnikula; and it is important to observe that in their gotracharya, or 'genealogical tree,' they claim Lohkot in the Panjab as their early location; in all probability prior to their regeneration on Mount Abu, when they adopted Brahmanical principles. From the year S. 787 (A.D. 731), when the castle of Tanot was erected by the leader of the Bhatti colony, down to S. 1530 (A.D. 1474), a period of seven hundred and forty-three years, perpetual border-strife appears to have occurred between the Bhattis and Langahas, which terminated in that singular combat, or duel, of tribe against tribe, during the reign of Rawal Chachak, in the last-mentioned period. Shortly after this, Babur conquered India, and Multan became a province of the empire, when the authority of tribes ceased. Ferishta, however, comes to our aid and gives us an account of an entire dynasty of this tribe as kings of Multan. The first of this line of five kings began his reign A.H. 847 (A.D. 1443), or thirty years anterior to the death of Rawal Chachak. The Muslim historian (see Briggs' Ferishta, vol. iv. p. 379) says that when Khizr Khan Sayyid [1] was emperor of Delhi, he sent Shaikh Yusuf as his lieutenant to Multan, who gained the esteem of the surrounding princes; amongst whom was Rae Sahra, chief of Sivi, head of the tribe of Langaha [238], who came to congratulate him, and to offer his services and a daughter in marriage. The offer was accepted; constant communication was kept up between Sivi and Multan, till at length Rae Sahra disclosed the object of all this solicitude; he threw aside the mask, confined the Shaikh, sent him off to Delhi, and crowned himself king of Multan, under the title of Kutbu-d-din.

Ferishta [2] calls Rae Sehra and his tribe of Langaha, Afghans;

[1] [Khizr Khān was left in charge of Delhi after the sack of that city by Timūr in A.D. 1398; possessed little power, and died in 1421.]

[2] [iv. 380, 383 f. Abu-l-fazl (*Āīn*, ii. 337) calls them Nohmardi; see *Census Report, Baluchistan*, 1911, i. 171.]

and Abu-l-fazl says, the inhabitants of Sivi were of the Numri (fox) tribe, which is assuredly one of the most numerous of the Jat or Gete race, though they have all, since their conversion, adopted the distinctive term of Baloch. The Bhatti chronicle calls the Langahas in one page Pathan, and in another Rajput, which are perfectly reconcilable, and by no means indicative that the Pathan or Afghan of that early period, or even in the time of Rae Sahra, was a Muhammadan. The title of Rae is sufficient proof that they were even then Hindus. Mr. Elphinstone scouts the idea of the descent of the Afghans from the Jews; and not a trace of the Hebrew is found in the Pushtu, or language of this tribe, although it has much affinity to the Zend and Sanskrit. I cannot refrain from repeating my conviction of the origin of the Afghans from the Yadu, converted into Yahudi, or 'Jew.' Whether these Yadus are or are not Yuti, or Getae, remains to be proved.[1]

To the south of Derawar dwelt the Lodra Rajputs; their capital was Lodorva,[2] an immense city, having twelve gates. The family Purohit, having been offended, took sanctuary (saran) with Deoraj, and stimulated him to dispossess his old masters of their territory. A marriage was proposed to Nripbhan, the chief of the Lodras, which being accepted, Deoraj, at the head of twelve hundred chosen horse, departed for Lodorva. The gates of the city were thrown open as the bridegroom approached; but no sooner had he entered with his suite, than swords were drawn, and Deoraj made himself master of Lodorva.[3] He married the

[1] [The theory of the Jewish descent of the Afghāns is not now accepted by any serious student. They are probably of Aryan origin, though the Yadu theory in the text is not supported by good evidence. They link India on the east with Persia on the west (Sykes, *Hist. of Persia*, ii. 306; Bellew, *Races of Afghanistan*, 15 ff.).]

[2] [Lodorwa, 10 miles N. of Jaisalmer. For its temples see Erskine iii. A. 17.]

[3] We are not told of what race (*kula*) was the Lodra Rajput; in all probability it was Pramara, or Puar, which at one time occupied the whole desert of India. Lodorva, as will be seen, became the capital of the Bhattis, until the founding of their last and present capital, Jaisalmer; it boasts a high antiquity, though now a ruin, occupied by a few families of shepherds. Many towns throughout the desert were formerly of celebrity, but are now desolate, through the conjoined causes of perpetual warfare and the shifting sands. I obtained a copper-plate inscription of the tenth century from Lodorva, of the period of Bijairaj, in the ornamental Jain character; also some clay signets, given to pilgrims, bearing Jain symbols. All these relics attest the prevailing religion to have been Jain.

chief's daughter, left a garrison in Lodorva, and returned to Derawar. Deoraj was now lord of fifty-six thousand horse, and a hundred thousand camels [239].[1]

At this period, a merchant of Derawar, named Jaskaran, having gone to Dharanagari, was imprisoned by its prince, Brajbhan Puar, and compelled to pay a ransom for his liberty. On his return to Derawar, he showed the mark of the iron-collar to his sovereign, who, indignant at the dishonour put upon his subject, swore he would not drink water until he had avenged the insult. But he had not calculated the distance between him and his foe; in order, however, to redeem his pledge, a *Dhar* of clay (*gar-ra-dhar*) was constructed, on which he was about to wreak his vengeance, but there were Pramars in his army, who were at their post ready to defend their mock capital; and, as their astonished prince advanced to destroy it, they exclaimed—

Jān Puār tān Dhār hai
Aur Dhār tān Puār
Dhār bina Puār nahīn
Aur nahīn Puār bina Dhār,

which may be thus translated:

"Wherever there is a Puar, there is a Dhar; and where there is a Dhar, there is a Puar. There is no Dhar without a Puar; neither is there a Puar without a Dhar."[2]

Under their leaders, Tejsi and Sarang, they protected the mock Dhar, and were cut to pieces to the number of one hundred and twenty.[3] Deoraj approved their valour, and provided for their children. Being thus released from his oath, he proceeded towards Dhar, reducing those who opposed his progress. Brajbhan defended Dhar during five days, and fell with eight hundred of his men; upon which Deoraj unfurled the flag of victory and returned to his late conquest, the city of Lodorva.

Deoraj had two sons, Mund and Chedu; the last, by a wife of the Baraha tribe, had five sons, whose descendants were styled Cheda Rajputs. Deoraj excavated several large lakes in the

[1] A gross exaggeration of the annalist, or a cypher in each added by the copyist.

[2] Dhar, or Dharanagari, was the most ancient capital of this tribe, the most numerous of the Agnikula races. See a sketch of the Puars, or Pramaras, Vol. I. p. 107. [The proverb is repeated by Forbes, *Rāsmāla*, 115.]

[3] [The story reads like a piece of sympathetic or imitative magic.]

territory of Khadal (in which Derawar is situated); one at Tanot is called Tanosar; another, after himself, Deosar. Having one day gone to hunt, slightly attended, he was attacked by an ambush of the Chana Rajputs, and slain with twenty-six of his attendants, after having reigned fifty-five years. His kin and clans shaved their locks and moustaches, excepting [1]

Mund, who succeeded, and performed all the ceremonies during the twelve days. Having made his ablutions with the water from sixty-eight different wells, in which [240] were immersed the leaves of one hundred and eight different shrubs and trees, a female of spotless virtue waved the burning frankincense over his head. Before him was placed the panjamrit, consisting of curds, milk, butter, sugar, and honey; likewise pearls, gems, the royal umbrella, the grass called dub, various flowers, a looking-glass, a young virgin, a chariot, a flag or banner, the *vela* flower, seven sorts of grain, two fish, a horse, a *nakhank* (unknown),[2] a bullock, a shell, a lotus, a vessel of water, the tail of the wild ox (*chaunri*), a sword, a female calf, a litter, yellow clay, and prepared food. Then, seated on the lion's hide—(on which were painted the seven dwipas or continents of Hindu cosmography, apparelled in the dress of the Jogi, and covered with ashes (*bhabut*), with the *mudra* in his ears)—the white *chaunri* (ox-tail) was waved over his head, and he was inaugurated on the *gaddi* of Deoraj, while the Purohit and chiefs presented their offerings. The *tika-daur* was against the assassins of his father, who had congregated for defence, eight hundred of whom were put to death. Rawal Mund had one son, who was called Bachera. When about fourteen years of age the coco-nut came from Balabhsen Solanki, Raja of Patan.[3] He forthwith proceeded to Patan,

[1] There is no interregnum in Rajwara; the king never dies.

[2] [? *Nikhang*, 'a quiver.']

[3] This affords a most important synchronism, corroborative of the correctness of these annals. Raja Valabhsen of Patan (Anhilwara) immediately followed Chamund Rae, who was dispossessed of the throne by Mahmud of Ghazni, in the year A.D. 1011, or S. 1067. [Valabhsen Durlabha, A.D. 1010–22.] Valabhsen died the year of his installation, and was succeeded by Durlabh, whose period has also been synchronically fixed by an inscription belonging to the Pramaras.—See *Transactions of the Royal Asiatic Society*, vol. i. p. 223. [The annalist seems to have confounded Anhilwāra Pātan in Gujarāt with Patan Munām, also called Fatan or Patanpur, five miles from Rahīmyār Railway Station, on E. bank of the Indus, locally called Sej (Malik Muhammad Dīn, *Bahāwalpur State Gazetteer*, A. 376 f.).]

where he married the Solanki princess, and died not long after his father.

Rāwal Bachera or Wachuji.—Bachera succeeded on Saturday the 12th Sravan, S. 1035.[1] The same rites of installation were performed; the Kanphara (split-eared) Jogi was the first to put the regal *tilak* on his forehead, and "his hand upon his back." Rawal Bachera had five sons, Dusaj, Singh, Bapi Rao, Ankho, and Malpasao; all of whom had issue, forming clans.

A merchant came to Lodorva with a caravan of horses, of which there was one of a race so superior that a lakh of rupees was fixed as his price; the breed belonged to a Pathan chief, west of the Indus. To obtain it, Dusaj and his son Ankho put themselves at the head of a band, crossed the Indus, slew Ghazi Khan, the Pathan chief, and carried off his stud [241].

Singh had a son, Sachharae; his son was Bala, who had two sons, Ratan and Jaga; they attacked the Parihar prince Jagannath of Mandor, and carried off five hundred camels: their descendants are styled Singhrao Rajputs.

Bapi Rao had two sons, Pahu and Mandan. Pahu had likewise two, Biram and Tular, whose numerous issue were styled the Pahu Rajputs. The Pahus issued from their abode of Bikampur, and conquered the lands of the Johyas, as far as Devijhal; and having made Pugal[2] their capital, they dug numerous wells in the *thal*, which still go by the name of the Pahu wells.

Near Khata, in the Nagor district of Marwar, there dwelt a warrior of the Khichi tribe, named Jadra, who often plundered even to the gates of Pugal, slaying many of the Jaitang Bhattis. Dusaj prepared a kafila ('caravan') under pretence of making a pilgrimage to the Ganges, invaded unawares the Khichi chief's territory, and slew him, with nine hundred of his men.

[1] This date, S. 1035, is evidently an error of the copyist. Bachera married Balabhsen's daughter in S. 1067, and he died in S. 1100; so that it should be either S. 1055 or 1065. It is important to clear this point, as Rawal Bachera was the opponent of Mahmud of Ghazni in his invasion of India, A.H. 393, A.D. 1000, =S. 1056 or S. 1066, the Samvat era being liable to a variation of ten years (Colebrooke). If we are right, a passage of Ferishta, which has puzzled the translators, should run thus: "Mahmud directed his march against the Bhatti, and passing Multan arrived at Bahra, a Bhatti city."—Compare Dow, vol. i. p. 39 (2nd ed.), and Briggs, vol. i. p. 38.

[2] See Map. This was one of the points touched at in Mr. Elphinstone's journey. [The town is about 48 miles N.W. of Bikaner city.]

Dusaj, with his three brothers, went to the land of Kher, where dwelt Partap Singh, chief of the Guhilots,[1] whose daughters they espoused. "In the land of Kher, the Jadon showered gold, enriching it." In the *daeja* (dower) with his daughter, the Guhilot gave fifteen Dewadharis, or 'virgin lamp-holders.' Soon after, the Balochs made an inroad into the territory of Khadal; a battle ensued, in which five hundred were killed, and the rest fled beyond the river. Bachera died, and was succeeded by

Rāwal Dusaj.—Dusaj, in the month of Asarh, S. 1100. Hamir, prince of the Sodhas,[2] made an incursion into his territories, which he plundered. Dusaj having unavailingly remonstrated, reminding him of ancient ties, he marched into Dhat, and gained a victory. Dusaj had two sons, Jaisal and Bijairaj, and in his old age a third son, by a Ranawat princess of the house of Mewar, called Lanja Bijairae, who, when Dusaj died, was placed on the throne by the nobles and civil officers of the State. Previous to his elevation, he had espoused a daughter of Siddhraj Jai Singh, Solanki. During the nuptial ceremonies, as the mother of the bride was marking the forehead of the bridegroom [242] with the *tilak*, or 'inauguration mark,' she exclaimed, "My son, do thou become the portal of the north—the barrier between us and the king, whose power is becoming strong."[3] By the princess of Patan he had a son,

[1] The chief of the Guhilots is now settled at Bhavnagar, at the estuary of the Mahi; where I visited him in 1823. The migration of the family from Kherdhar occurred about a century after that period, according to the documents in the Rao's family. And we have only to look at the opening of the Annals of Marwar to see that from its colonization by the Rathors the Gohil community of Kherdhar was finally extinguished. To the general historian these minute facts may be unimportant, but they cease to be so when they prove the character of these annals for fidelity.

[2] If this is the Hamira alluded to in the Annals of Bikaner, in whose time the Ghaggar River ceased to flow in these lands, we have another date assigned to a fact of great physical importance.

[3] Here we have another synchronism. In the Kumarpal Charitra, or history of the kings of Anhilwara Patan, the reign of Siddhraj was from S. 1150 to S. 1201, or A.D. 1094 to 1145 [1094–1143]; the point of time intermediate between the invasion of Mahmud of Ghazni and the final conquest of India by Shihabu-d-din, during which there were many irruptions into India by the lieutenants of the monarchs of Ghazni. There was one in the reign of Masud, in A.H. 492 (A.D. 1098), four years after the accession of Siddhraj; another in A.D. 1120, in the reign of Bairam Shah, during which, according to Ferishta, the Ghaznevide general, Balin, rebelled

who was named Bhojdeo, and who, by the death of his father when he attained the age of twenty-five, became lord of Lodorva. The other sons of Dusaj were at this time advanced in manhood, Jaisal being thirty-five, and Bijairaj thirty-two years of age.

Some years before the death of Dusaj, Raedhawal Puar, son (or descendant) of Udayaditya of Dhar, had three daughters, one of whom he betrothed to Jaipal (Ajaipal) Solanki, son of Siddhraj;[1] another to Bijairaj Bhatti, and the third to the Rana of Chitor. The Bhatti prince left Lodorva for Dhar at the head of seven hundred horse, and arrived at the same time with the Sesodia and Solanki princes. On his return to Lodorva, he erected a temple to Seshalinga, close to which he made a lake. By the Puar princess he had a son named Rahar, who had two sons, Netsi and Keksi.

Bhojdeo had not long occupied the *gaddi* of Lodorva, when his uncle Jaisal conspired against him; but being always surrounded by a guard of five hundred Solanki Rajputs, his person was unassailable. At this time the prince of Patan was often engaged with the king's troops from Tatta. Jaisal, in pursuance of his plan, determined to coalesce with the king, and cause an attack

---

and assailed the Hindu Rajas from Nagor, where he established himself. [His real name was Muhammad Bahlīm (Ferishta i. 151).] In all probability this is the event alluded to by the queen of Patan, when she nominated the Bhatti prince as her champion.

[1] [Siddharāja Jayasingha had no son, and he was succeeded by Kumārapāla; and Ajayapāla, who succeeded in A.D. 1174, was son of Mahipāla, brother of Kumārapāla (*BG*, i. Part i. 194).] The mention of these simultaneous intermarriages in three of the principal Rajput monarchies of that day, namely, Dhar, Patan, and Chitor, is important, not only as establishing fresh synchronisms, but as disclosing the intercourse between the Bhattis and the more ancient princely families of India. The period of Udayaditya Pramar has been established beyond cavil (see *Trans. R.A.S.* vol. i. p. 223), and that of Siddhraj, likewise, whose son and successor, Ajaipal, had but a short reign when he was deposed by Kumarpal, whose date is also found from inscriptions. It is a singular fact that all the Rajput dynasties of these regions were established about the same epoch, namely, Patan by the Chawaras, Chitor by the Guhilots, Delhi, refounded by the Tuars, and the Bhatti principality by the descendant of Salbahan. This was in the middle of the eighth century of Vikramaditya, when the older Hindu governments were broken up. The admission of the Bhatti to intermarry with their families proves one of two facts: either that they were considered Rajputs, notwithstanding their being inhabitants of the regions beyond the Indus; or, that the families mentioned, with which they intermarried, were Indo-Scythic like themselves.

on Patan (Anhilwara), by which alone he could hope for the departure of the Solanki body-guard. Jaisal, with his chief kin, escorted by two hundred horse, marched to the Panjnad, where he saw the king of Ghor, who had just overcome the king of Tatta,[1] and placed his own garrison there [243],[2] and he accompanied him to Aror, the ancient capital of Sind. There he unfolded his views, and having sworn allegiance to the king, he obtained a force to dispossess his nephew of his territory. Lodorva was encompassed, and Bhojdeo slain in its defence. In two days the inhabitants were to carry off their effects, and on the third the troops of Ghor were permitted the license of plunder. Lodorva was sacked, and Karim Khan departed for Bakhar with the spoils.

The Foundation of Jaisalmer, *c.* A.D. 1156.—Jaisal thus obtained the *gaddi* of Lodorva; but it being open to invasion, he sought a spot better adapted for defence, and he found one only five coss (ten miles) from Lodorva. Upon the summit of a rocky ridge, he discovered a Brahman, whose solitary hermitage adjoined the fountain of Brahmsar. Having paid homage, and disclosed the purport of his visit, the recluse related the history of the triple-peaked hill, which overlooked his hermitage. He said that in the Treta, or 'silver age,' a celebrated ascetic called Kak, or Kaga, resided at this fountain, after whom the rivulet which issued thence had its name of Kaga; that the Pandu Arjun, with Hari Krishna, came there to attend a great sacrifice, on which occasion Krishna foretold that, in some distant age, a descendant of his should erect a town on the margin of that rivulet, and should raise a castle on Trikuta, the triple-peaked mount.[3] While Krishna thus prophesied, it was observed to

[1] At every step we see, however meagre may be the outline, the correctness of this historical sketch. It was, according to Ferishta, in A.H. 555 (A.D. 1159 [1150], or S. 1215) that the prince of Ghor conquered Ghazni, and immediately after overran Multan and Sind (see Briggs, vol. i. p. 153); and doubtless it was on this occasion that the Bhatti prince swore allegiance to Shihabu-d-din, and obtained the force which drove his nephew from Lodorva, which being sacked by his auxiliaries, he founded Jaisalmer in S. 1212. The three years' discrepancy between the Muhammadan and Hindu dates is of little consequence; but even this could be remedied, when we recollect that the Samvat, according to Mr. Colebrooke, is liable to a variation of ten years.

[2] Tatta was not then in existence. It was founded about the middle of the fifteenth century.

[3] If there were no better support for the assumed descent of the Bhatti

him by Arjun that the water was bad, when Krishna smote the rock with his chakra (discus), whereupon a sweet spring bubbled up, and on its margin were inscribed the prophetic stanzas which the hermit Isal now pointed out to the Bhatti prince, who read as follows:

1.

"Oh prince of Jadu-vansa! come into this land, and on this mountain's top erect a triangular castle.

2.

"Lodorva is destroyed, but only five coss therefrom is Jasana, a site of twice its strength.

3.

"Prince, whose name is Jaisal, who will be of Yadu race, abandon Lodorpura; here erect thy dwelling."

The hermit Isal alone knew the existence of the fountain on whose margin these lines were engraved. All that he stipulated for himself was that the fields to the [244] westward of the castle should retain his name, "the fields of Isal." He foretold that the intended castle should twice and a half times be sacked; that rivers of blood would flow, and that for a time all would be lost to his descendants.

On Rabiwar, 'the day of the sun' (a favourite day for commencing any grand undertaking with all these tribes), the 12th of Sravan, the enlightened half of the moon, S. 1212 (A.D. 1156), the foundation of Jaisalmer was laid, and soon the inhabitants, with all that was valuable, abandoned Lodorva,[1] and began to erect new habitations. Jaisal had two sons, Kelan and Salbahan. He chose his chief ministers and advisers from the children of Sodal, of the Pahu tribe, who became too powerful. Their old enemies, the Chana Rajputs, again invaded the lands of Khadal; but they suffered for their audacity. Jaisal survived this event five years, when he died, and was succeeded by his youngest son, Salbahan the Second [245].

---

founder of Jaisalmer from the Yadus of the Bharat than this prophecy, we should be confirmed in our suspicion that they are a colony of the Yuti, and that the Brahmans took advantage of the nominal resemblance to incorporate them in the Chhattis Rajkula, or Thirty-six Royal Races.

[1] Lodorva remains in ruins; a journey thither might afford subject-matter for the antiquary, and enable him to throw light upon the origin of the Bhatti tribe. I omitted to place it in the Map; it is ten miles N.W. of the present capital.

CHAPTER 3

Having thus epitomized the Bhatti annals, from the expulsion of the tribe from the Panjab, and the establishment of Tanot in the Indian desert, in A.D. 731, to the foundation of the existing capital, Jaisalmer, in A.D. 1156, we shall continue the sketch to the present day, nearly in the language of the chronicle, adding explanatory notes as we proceed.

Retrospect of Bhatti History.—The interval between the erection of the castle of Tanot and the present time is exactly eleven hundred years; during which the historical narrative, whatever may be its value, is at least continuous, and the events recorded are corroborated, even in the darkest period, by numerous synchronisms in the annals of the other States; and viewed synoptically, it presents matter of deep interest to the explorer of Indian history. The period of four hundred and twenty-five years, embraced in the preceding chapter, is full of incidents. It is a record of a people who once deemed their consequence and their fame imperishable. And even were it less diversified by anecdotes descriptive of manners, it would still possess claims to interest as a simple relation of the gradual peopling of a great portion of the Indian desert. We see tribes and cities disappearing; new races and new capitals taking their place; and although not a syllable is written which [246] bears directly upon religion, we can see, incidentally, the analogy of these Indo-Scythic tribes, from Zabulistan and Salbahana, with the Hindu, confirming what Manu says, that the Sakas, Yavanas, Pahlavas, and the Khasas [1] of Central Asia, were all Chhattris or Rajputs. We now proceed with the chronicle.

Jaisal, the founder of Jaisalmer, survived the change of capital only twelve years. His elder son, Kailan, having given dis-

[1] [Manu, *Laws*, x. 44, which does not name the Khasas.] There is a race in the desert, now Muhammadan, and called Khosas. Elphinstone mentions the Khasa-Khel. Kashgar is 'the region of the Khasas,' the Casia Regia of Ptolemy [?]. [The Khosas are a Muhammadan tribe, driven from Sind in A.D. 1786, who lived beside the Rann of Cutch, and levied blackmail on their neighbours. They are believed to be a branch of the Rind, and it is improbable that they can be connected with the Khasas of Manu (*Laws*, x. 22).]

pleasure to the Pahu minister, was expelled, and his younger brother placed upon the *gaddi*.

Rāwal Sālivāhan I.—Salbahan, a name of celebrity in the annals, renewed in the son of Jaisal, succeeded in S. 1224 (A.D. 1168). His first expedition was against the Kathi tribe, who, under their leader, Jagbhan, dwelt between the city of Jalor and the Aravalli.[1] The Kathi Rao was killed, and his horses and camels were carried to Jaisalmer. The fame of this exploit exalted the reputation of Salbahan. He had three sons, Bijar, Banar, and Haso.

Embassy from Badarināth.—In the mountains of Badarinath, there was a State whose princes were of the Jadon (Yadu) race, descended from the first Salbahan at the period of the expulsion from Gajni.[2] At this time, the prince of this State dying without

[1] We can scarcely refuse our assent to the belief that the Kathi or Katti tribe, here mentioned, is the remnant of the nation which so manfully opposed Alexander. It was then located about Multan, at this period occupied by the Langahas. The colony attacked by the Bhatti was near the Aravalli, in all probability a predatory band from the region they peopled and gave their name to, Kathiawar, in the Surashtra peninsula. [The Kāthis were probably a nomadic Central Asian tribe, driven down the valley of the Indus by the tide of early Muhammadan invasions. Their appearance in Jaisalmer at the end of the twelfth century A.D. probably marks a stage in their southerly progress. Thence they seem to have moved into Mālwa, thence to Cutch, and finally to Kāthiāwār (*BG*, ix. Part i. 252 ff., viii. 128).]

[2] Mr. Elphinstone enumerates the Jadon as a subdivision of the Yusufzais, one of the great Afghan tribes, who were originally located about Kabul and Ghazni. I could not resist surmising the probability of the term Jadon, applied to a subdivision of the Afghan race, originating from the Hindu-Scythic Jadon, or Yadu; whence the boasted descent of the Afghans from Saul, king of the Jews (Yahudis). The customs of the Afghans would support this hypothesis: "The Afghans (says the Emperor Babur, p. 159), when reduced to extremities in war, come into the presence of their enemy with grass between their teeth, being as much as to say, 'I am your ox.'" This custom is entirely Rajput, and ever recurring in inscriptions recording victories. They have their bards or poets in like manner, of whom Mr. Elphinstone gives an interesting account. In features, also, they resemble the Northern Rajputs, who have generally aquiline noses, or, as Mr. Elphinstone expresses it in the account of his journey through the desert, "Jewish features"; though this might tempt one to adopt the converse of my deduction, and say that these Yadus of Gajni were, with the Afghans, also of Yahudi origin: from the lost tribes of Israel. [The Jadūn, as Rose writes their name, are not Yūsufzais, but live S. of them, and have no connexion with the Rājput Jādons (*Glossary*, ii. 272 f., iii. 251).]

issue, a deputation came to Jaisalmer to obtain a prince to fill the vacant *gaddi*. Haso was accordingly sent, but died just as he arrived. His wife, who was pregnant, was taken with the pains of labour on the journey, and was delivered of a son under the shade of a *palas* tree, whence the child was called Palasia. This infant succeeding, the *raj* (principality) was named after him Palasia.[1]

Proposals of marriage came from Mansi Deora of Sirohi.[2] The Rawal left Jaisalmer [247] to the care of his eldest son Bijal. Soon after his departure, the foster-brother (Dhabhai) of the young prince propagated the report of the Rawal's death in an encounter with a tiger, and prompted Bijal to assume the dignity. Salbahan, on his return, finding his seat usurped, and having in vain expostulated with his traitorous son, proceeded to Khadal, of which Derawar is the capital, where he was slain, with three hundred of his followers, in repelling an irruption of the Balochs. Bijal did not long enjoy the dignity; having in a fit of passion struck the Dhabhai, the blow was returned, upon which, stung with shame and resentment, he stabbed himself with his dagger.

Rāwal Kailan, c. A.D. 1200-19.—Kailan, the elder brother of Salbahan, who was expelled by the Pahus, was now (A.D. 1200) recalled, and installed at the age of fifty. He had six sons, Chachakdeo, Palhan, Jaichand, Pitamsi, Pitamchand, and Asrao. The second and third had numerous issue, who are styled Jaser and Sihana Rajputs.

Khizr Khan Baloch, with five thousand men, at this time again crossed the Mihran (Indus), and invaded the land of Khadal, which was the second irruption since he slew Salbahan. Kailan marched against him at the head of seven thousand Rajputs, and, after a severe engagement, slew the Baloch leader and fifteen hundred of his men. Kailan ruled nineteen years.

Rāwal Chāchakdeo I., c. A.D. 1219-41.—Chachakdeo succeeded, in S. 1275 (A.D. 1219). Soon after his accession, he carried on war against the Chana Rajputs (now extinct), of whom he slew

[1] See Mr. Elphinstone's map for the position of the Jadon branch of the Yusufzais at the foot of the Siwalik hills.

[2] [" If this is correct, the date of the foundation of Jaisalmer must be wrong, for Mān Singh's father is known to have been alive in 1249. Moreover the Deora sept did not exist, as it took the name from Mān Singh's son Deoraj " (Erskine iii. A. 11).]

two thousand, capturing fourteen thousand cows, and compelling the tribe to take refuge with the Johyas. Soon after, the Rawal invaded the lands of Rana Armsi, prince of the Sodhas, who, though taken by surprise, assembled four thousand horse; but was defeated, and forced to fly for shelter to the walls of his capital, Umarkot. The Puar was glad to obtain the absence of his foe by the offer of his daughter in marriage.[1]

The Rathors, recently established in the land of Kher, had become troublesome [248] neighbours; Chachak obtained the aid of the Sodha troops to chastise them, and he proceeded to Jasal and Bhalotra, where they were established; but Chhadu and his son Thida averted his wrath by giving him a daughter to wife.[2]

Rawal Chachak ruled thirty-two years. He had only one son,

[1] In this single passage we have revealed the tribe (*got*), race (*kula*), capital, and proper name of the prince of Dhat. The Sodha tribe, as before stated, is an important branch of the Pramara (Puar) race, and with the Umras and Sumras gave dynasties to the valley of Sind from the most remote period. The Sodhas, I have already observed, were probably the Sogdoi of Alexander, occupying Upper Sind when the Macedonian descended that stream. The Sumra dynasty is mentioned by Ferishta from ancient authorities, but the Muhammadan historians knew nothing, and cared nothing, about Rajput tribes. It is from such documents as these, scattered throughout the annals of these principalities, and from the ancient Hindu epic poems, that I have concentrated the "Sketches of the Rajput Tribes," introductory to the first volume, which, however slight they appear, cost more research than the rest of the book. I write this note chiefly for the information of the patriarch of oriental lore on the Continent, the learned and ingenious De Sacy. If this mentor ask, "Where are now the Sodhas?" I reply, the ex-prince of Umarkot, with whose ancestors Humayun took refuge—in whose capital in the desert the great Akbar was born—and who could on the spur of the moment oppose four thousand horse to invasion, has only one single town, that of Chor, left to him. The Rathors, who, in the time of Armsi Rana and Rawal Chachak, were hardly known in Marudes, have their flag waving on the battlements of the 'immortal castle' (Amarkuta), and the Amirs of Sind have incorporated the greater part of Dhat with their State of Haidarabad. [Umarkot is not the 'immortal castle,' but the fort of Umar, chief of the Sūmra tribe (*IGI*, xxiv. 118).]

[2] To those interested in the migration of these tribes, it must be gratifying to see these annals thus synchronically corroborating each other. About two centuries before this, in the reign of Dusaj, when the Bhatti capital was at Lodorva, an attack was made on the land of Kher, then occupied by the Guhilots, who were, as related in the Annals of Marwar, dispossessed by the Rathors. None but an inquirer into these annals of the desert tribes can conceive the satisfaction arising from such confirmation.

Tej Rao, who died at the age of forty-two, from the smallpox, leaving two sons, Jethsi and Karan. To the youngest the Rawal was much attached; and having convened the chiefs around his death-bed, he entreated they would accede to his last wish, that his youngest grandson might be his successor.

Rāwal Karan Singh I., A.D. **1241-71.**—Karan having succeeded, his elder brother, Jethsi, abandoned his country, and took service with the Muhammadans in Gujarat. About this time, Muzaffar Khan, who occupied Nagor with five thousand horse, committed great outrages. There was a Bhumia of the Baraha tribe, named Bhagawatidas, who resided fifteen coss from Nagor, and was master of one thousand five hundred horse. He had an only daughter, who was demanded by the Khan, and being unwilling to comply, and unable to resist, he resolved to abandon the country. For this purpose he prepared carriages, in which he placed his family and chattels, and at night proceeded towards Jaisalmer; but the Khan, gaining intelligence of his motions, intercepted the convoy. A battle ensued, in which four hundred of the Barahas were killed, and his daughter and other females were carried off. The afflicted Baraha continued his route to Jaisalmer, and related his distress to Rawal Karan, who immediately put himself at the head of his followers, attacked the Khan, whom he slew, with three thousand of his people, and re-inducted the Bhumia in his possessions. Karan ruled twenty-eight years, and was succeeded, in S. 1327, by his son,

Rāwal Lākhansen, A.D. **1271-75.**—He was so great a simpleton, that when the jackals howled at night, being told that it was from being cold, he ordered quilted dresses (*daglas*) to be prepared for them. As the howling still continued, although he was assured his orders had been fulfilled, he commanded houses to be built for the animals in the royal preserves (*ramna*), many of which yet remain. Lakhan was the contemporary of Kanirdeo Sonigira, whose life was saved by his (Lakhan's) wife's knowledge of omens. Lakhan was ruled by this Rani, who was of the Sodha tribe. She invited her brethren from Umarkot; but the madman, her husband, put [249] them to death, and threw their bodies over the walls. He was allowed to rule four years, and was then replaced by his son,

Rāwal Pūnpāl, A.D. **1275-76.**—This prince was of a temper so violent that the nobles dethroned him, and recalled the exiled

Jethsi from Gujarat. Punpal had a residence assigned him in a remote quarter of the State. He had a son, Lakamsi, who had a son called Rao Raningdeo, who by a stratagem pointed out by a Kharal [1] Rajput, took Marot from the Johyas, and Pugal from the Thoris, thieves by profession, whose chief, styled Rao, he made captive; and in Pugal he settled his family. Rao Raning had a son called Sadul, who alternately bathed in the sea of pleasure, and struggled in that of action: to their retreat the father and son conveyed the spoils seized from all around them.

Rāwal Jeth Singh I., A.D. **1276-94.**—Jethsi obtained the *gaddi* in S. 1332 (A.D. 1276). He had two sons, Mulraj and Ratansi. Deoraj, the son of Mulraj, espoused the daughter of the Sonigira chief of Jalor. Muhammad [Khuni] [2] Padshah invaded the dominions of Rana Rupsi, the Parihar prince of Mandor, [3] who, when defeated, fled with his twelve daughters, and found refuge with the Rawal, who gave him Baru [4] as a residence.

Alāu-d-din attacks Jaisalmer.—Deoraj, by his Sonigira wife, had three sons, Janghan, Sarwan, and Hamir. This Hamir was a mighty warrior, who attacked Kumpa Sen of Mewa, [5] and plundered his lands. He had issue three sons, Jetha, Lunkaran, and Mairu. At this period, Ghori Alau-d-din commenced the war against the castles of India. The tribute of Tatta and Multan, consisting of fifteen hundred horses and fifteen hundred mules laden with treasure and valuables, was at Bakhar in progress to the king at Delhi. The sons of Jethsi determined to lay an ambush and capture the tribute. Disguised as grain-merchants, with seven thousand horse and twelve hundred camels, they set out on their expedition, and on the banks of the Panjnad found the convoy, escorted by four hundred Mogul and the like number of Pathan horse. The Bhattis encamped near the convoy; and in the night they rose upon and slew the escort, carrying the treasure to Jaisalmer. The survivors carried

[1] This tribe is unknown to Central India. [They are a branch of the Parihārs.]

[2] [Alāu-d-dīn.]

[3] The title, tribe, and capital of this race show that the Bhattis were intimately connected with the neighbouring States.

[4] [About 100 miles N.N.E. of Jodhpur city.]

[5] [In Mallāni, the 'cradle of the Rāthors.']

the news to the king, who prepared to punish this insult. When tidings reached Rawal Jethsi that the king was encamped on the Anasagar at Ajmer, he prepared Jaisalmer for defence. He laid in immense stores of grain, and deposited all round the ramparts of the fort large round stones to hurl on the besiegers. All the aged, the infirm, and his female grandchildren were [250] removed into the interior of the desert, while the country around the capital for many miles was laid waste, and the towns made desolate. The Rawal, with his two elder sons and five thousand warriors, remained inside for the defence of the castle, while Deoraj and Hamir formed an army to act against the enemy from without. The sultan in person remained at Ajmer and sent forward an immense force of Khorasanis and Kuraishes, cased in steel armour, "who rolled on like the clouds in Bhadon." The fifty-six bastions were manned, and three thousand seven hundred heroes distributed amongst them for their defence, while two thousand remained in reserve to succour the points attacked. During the first week that the besiegers formed their entrenchments, seven thousand Musalmans were slain, and Mir Muhabbat and Ali Khan remained on the field of battle. For two years the invaders were confined to their camp by Deoraj and Hamir, who kept the field, after cutting off their supplies, which came from Mandor, while the garrison was abundantly furnished from Khadal, Barmer, and Dhat. Eight years [1] had the siege lasted, when Rawal Jethsi died, and his body was burnt inside the fort.

During this lengthened siege, Ratansi had formed a friendship with the Nawab Mahbub Khan, and they had daily friendly meetings under a khejra [2] tree, between the advanced posts, each attended by a few followers. They played at chess together, and interchanged expressions of mutual esteem. But when duty called them to oppose each other in arms, the whole world was enamoured with their heroic courtesy. Jethsi had ruled eighteen years when he died.

[1] This can mean nothing more than that desultory attacks were carried on against the Bhatti capital. It is certain that Ala never carried his arms in person against Jaisalmer. [It is impossible to reconcile the dates, and this siege is not mentioned by Muhammadan historians. It is said to have lasted from A.D. 1286 to 1295. Balban reigned 1266–1286-7, and Alāu-d-dīn did not ascend the throne till 1296. Much of the narrative is a fiction of the Bhatti bards.]

[2] [*Prosopis spicigera.*]

Rāwal Mūlrāj III., A.D. 1294-95.—Mulraj III., in S. 1350 (A.D. 1294), ascended the *gaddi* surrounded by foes. On this occasion, the customary rejoicings on installation took place at the moment when the two friends, Ratansi and Mahbub Khan, had met, as usual, under the khejra tree. The cause of rejoicing being explained to the Nawab, he observed that the Sultan had heard of, and was offended with, these meetings, to which he attributed the protracted defence of the castle, and acquainted Ratansi that next day a general assault was commanded, which he should lead in person. The attack took place; it was fierce, but the defence was obstinate, and the assailants were beaten back with the loss of nine thousand men. But the foe obtained reinforcements, and towards the conclusion of the year the garrison was reduced to the greatest privations, and the blockade being perfect, Mulraj assembled his kinsmen and thus addressed them: "For so many years [251] we have defended our dwellings; but our supplies are expended, and there is no passage for more. What is to be done?" The chiefs, Sahar and Bikamsi, replied, "A *sakha* must take place; we must sacrifice ourselves": but that same day the royal army, unaware of the distress of the besieged, retreated.

The Sati: Johar.—The friend of Ratansi had a younger brother, who, on the retreat of the royal forces, was carried inside the fort, when, seeing the real state of things, he escaped and conveyed intelligence of it, upon which the siege was renewed. Mulraj reproached his brother as the cause of this evil, and asked what was fit to be done? to which Ratansi replied, "There is but one path open: to immolate the females, to destroy by fire and water whatever is destructible, and to bury what is not; then open wide the gates, and sword in hand rush upon the foe, and thus attain Swarga." The chiefs were assembled; all were unanimous to make Jaisalnagar resplendent by their deeds, and preserve the honour of the Jadon race. Mulraj thus replied: "You are of a warlike race, and strong are your arms in the cause of your prince; what heroes excel you, who thus tread in the Chhatri's path? In battle, not even the elephant could stand before you. For the maintenance of my honour the sword is in your hands; let Jaisalmer be illumined by its blows upon the foe." Having thus inspired the chiefs and men, Mulraj and Ratan repaired to the palace of their queens. They told them to take the *sohag*,[1] and prepare to meet in heaven, while they gave up their lives in defence of their honour and their faith. Smiling, the Sodha Rani replied, "This night we shall prepare, and by the morning's light we shall be inhabitants of Swarga" (heaven); and thus it was with the chiefs and all their wives. The night was passed together for the last time in preparation for the awful morn. It came; ablutions and prayers were finished, and at the Rajdwara[2] were convened *bala*, *praurha*, and *briddhu*.[3] They bade a last farewell to all their kin; the Johar commenced, and twenty-four thousand females, from infancy to old age, surrendered their lives, some by the sword, others in the volcano of fire. Blood flowed in torrents, while the smoke of the pyre ascended to the heavens: not one feared to die, every valuable was consumed with them, not the worth of a straw was preserved for the foe. This work done, the brothers looked upon the spectacle with horror. Life was now a burden, and they prepared to quit it. They purified themselves with water, paid adoration to the divinity, made gifts [252] to the poor, placed a branch of the Tulsi[4] in their casques, the Salagram[4] round their neck; and having cased themselves in armour and put on the saffron robe, they bound the *mor*[5] (crown) around their heads, and embraced each other for the last time. Thus they awaited the hour of battle. Three thousand eight hundred warriors, with faces red with wrath, prepared to die with their chiefs.

Ratansi had two sons, named Gharsi and Kanar, the eldest only twelve years of age. He wished to save them from the impending havoc, and applied to his courteous foeman. The Muslim chief swore he would protect them, and sent two confidential servants to receive the trust; to whom, bidding them a last farewell, their father consigned them. When they reached the royal camp they were kindly welcomed by the Nawab, who,

1 Sohagan, one who becomes Sati previous to her lord's death; Duhagan, who follows him after death.

2 Literally, 'the royal gate'; an allusion to the female apartments, or Rajloka.

3 *Bala*, is under sixteen; *praurha*, middle-aged; *briddhu*, when forty.

4 The funereal qualities of the tulsi plant, and the emblematic Salagram, or stone found in the Gandak River, have been often described.

5 On two occasions the Rajput chieftain wears the *mor* [*maur*], or 'coronet': on his marriage, and when going to die in battle; symbolic of his nuptials with the Apsaras, or 'fair of heaven.'

putting his hand upon their heads, soothed them, and appointed two Brahmans to guard, feed, and instruct them.

On the morrow, the army of the Sultan advanced to the assault. The gates were thrown wide, and the fight began. Ratan was lost in the sea of battle; but one hundred and twenty Amirs fell before his sword ere he lay in the field. Mulraj plied his lance on the bodies of the barbarians: the field swam in blood. The unclean spirits were gorged with slaughter; but at length the Jadon chief fell, with seven hundred of the choice of his kin. With his death the battle closed; the victors ascended the castle, and Mahbub Khan caused the bodies of the brothers to be carried from the field and burned. The *sakha* took place in S. 1351, or A.D. 1295. Deoraj, who commanded the force in the field, was carried off by a fever. The royal garrison kept possession of the castle during two years, and at length blocked up the gateways, and dismantled and abandoned the place, which remained long deserted, for the Bhattis had neither means to repair the *kunguras* (battlements) nor men to defend them [253].

CHAPTER 4

Rāthor Settlement at Jaisalmer. Dūda Rāwal, A.D. 1295-1306. —Some years subsequent to this disastrous event in the Bhatti annals, Jagmall, son of Maloji Rathor, chief of Mewa, attempted a settlement amidst the ruins of Jaisalmer, and brought thither a large force, with seven hundred carts of provisions. On hearing this, the Bhatti chiefs, Dudu and Tilaksi, the sons of Jaisar, assembled their kinsmen, surprised the Rathors, drove them from the castle, and captured the supplies. Dudu, for this exploit, was elected Rawal, and commenced the repairs of Jaisalmer. He had five sons. Tilaksi, his brother, was renowned for his exploits. He despoiled the Baloch, the Mangalea, the Meawa, and the Deoras and Sonagiras of Abu and Jalor felt his power. He even extended his raids to Ajmer, and carried off the stud of Firoz Shah from the Anasagar (lake), where they were accustomed to be watered.[1] This indignity provoked another attack upon Jaisalmer, attended with the same disastrous results. Again the

[1] [If the dates are approximately correct, this was Jalālu-d-dīn Fīroz Shāh, Sultān of Delhi, A.D. 1290–96.]

sakha was performed, in which sixteen thousand [254] females [1] were destroyed; and Dudu, with Tilaksi and seventeen hundred of the clan, fell in battle, after he had occupied the *gaddi* ten years.

Gharsi Rāwal, A.D. 1306-35. Jaisalmer restored.—On the death of Rawal Dudu, in S. 1362 (A.D. 1306), the young princes, Gharsi and Kanar, by the death of their patron Mahbub, were left to the protection of his sons, Zulfikar and Ghazi Khan. Kanar went privately to Jaisalmer, and Gharsi obtained leave to proceed westward to the Mewa tract, where he married Bimaladevi, a widow, sister to the Rathor, who had been betrothed [2] to the Deora. While engaged in these nuptials, he was visited by his relation Soningdeo, a man of gigantic strength, who agreed to accompany him on his return to Delhi. The king made trial of his force, by giving him to string an iron bow sent by the king of Khorasan, which the nervous Bhatti not only bent but broke. The invasion of Delhi by Timur Shah [3] having occurred at this time, the services of Gharsi were so conspicuous that he obtained a grant of his hereditary dominions, with permission to re-establish Jaisalmer. With his own kindred, and the aid of the vassals of his friend Jagmall of Mewa, he soon restored order, and had an efficient force at command. Hamir and his clansmen gave their allegiance to Gharsi, but the sons of Jaisar were headstrong.

The Adoption of Kehar. Rāwal Gharsi assassinated.—Deoraj, who married the daughter of Rupra, Rana of Mandor, had a son named Kehar, who, when Jaisalmer was about to be invested by the troops of the Sultan, was conveyed to Mandor with his mother. When only twelve years of age, he used to accompany the cow-

[1] The Rajputs, by their exterminating *sakhas*, facilitated the views of the Muhammadans. In every State we read of these horrors.

[2] The mere act of being betrothed disqualifies from a second marriage; the affianced becomes a *rand* (widow), though a *kumari* (maid).

[3] Even these anachronisms are proofs of the fidelity of these Annals. Ignorant native scribes, aware but of one great Moghul invasion, consider the invader to be Timur; but there were numerous Moghul invasions during the reign of Alau-d-din. In all probability that for which the services of the Bhatti prince obtained him the restoration of his dominions was that of Ibak Khan, general of the king of Transoxiana, who invaded India in A.H. 705 (A.D. 1305), and was so signally defeated that only three thousand out of fifty-seven thousand horse escaped the sword, and these were made prisoners and trod to death by elephants, when pillars of skulls were erected to commemorate the victory.—See Briggs' Ferishta, vol. i. p. 363 f. [Elliot-Dowson iii. 199.]

herds of the old Rao's kine, and his favourite amusement was penning up the calves with twigs of the *ak*, to imitate the picketing of horses. One day, tired of this occupation, young Kehar fell asleep upon the hole of a serpent, and the reptile issuing therefrom, arose and spread its hood over him as he slept. A Charan (bard, or genealogist), passing that way, reported the fact and its import immediately to the Rana, who, proceeding to the spot, found it was his own grandson whom fate had thus pointed out for sovereignty.[1] Gharsi, having no offspring by Bimaladevi, proposed to her to adopt a son. All the Bhatti youth were assembled, but none equalled Kehar, who [255] was chosen. But the sons of Jaisar were displeased, and conspired to obtain the *gaddi*. At this time, Rawal Gharsi was in the daily habit of visiting a tank, which he was excavating, and they seized an occasion to assassinate him; whereupon, in order to defeat their design, Bimaladevi immediately had Kehar proclaimed. The widowed queen of Gharsi, with the view of securing the completion of an object which her lord had much at heart, namely, finishing the lake Gharsisar, as well as to ensure protection to her adopted son Kehar, determined to protract the period of self-immolation; but when six months had elapsed, and both these objects were attained, she finished her days on the pyre. Bimaladevi named the children of Hamir as the adopted sons and successors of Kehar. These sons were Jetha and Lunkaran.

The coco-nut was sent by Kumbha, Rana of Chitor, to Jetha. The Bhatti prince marched for Mewar, and when within twelve coss of the Aravalli hills, was joined by the famous Sankhla Miraj, chief of Salbahni. Next morning, when about to resume the march, a partridge began to call from the right; a bad omen, which was interpreted by the brother-in-law of the Sankhla, deeply versed in the science of the Suguni and the language of birds.[2] Jetha drew the rein of his horse, and to avert the evil, halted that day. Meanwhile, the partridge was caught and found to be blind of an eye, and its ovary quite filled. The next morning, as soon as they had taken horse, a tigress began to roar, and the Suguni chieftain was again called upon to expound the omen. He replied that the secrets of great houses should not be

[1] [Another version of a common folk-tale (Vol. I. 342).]

[2] It is scarcely necessary to repeat that this is a free translation of the chronicle.

divulged, but he desired them to dispatch a youth, disguised as a female Nai (barber class), to Kumbhalmer, who there would learn the cause. The youth gained admission to 'the ruby of Mewar' (Lala Mewari), who was anointing for the nuptials. He saw things were not right, and returning made his report; upon hearing which, the Bhatti prince married Marad, the daughter of the Sankhla chief. The Rana was indignant at this insult, but a sense of shame prevented his resenting it; and instead of proclaiming the slight, he offered his daughter's hand to the famous Khichi prince, Achaldas of Gagraun, and it was accepted.[1] Jetha met his death, together with his brother Lunkaran, and his brother-in-law, in an attempt to surprise Pugal: he fell with a hundred and twenty followers. When the old Rao, Raningdeo, discovered against whom he had thus successfully defended himself, he clad himself in black garments [256], and in atonement performed pilgrimage to all the shrines in India.[2] On his return, he was forgiven and condoled with by Kehar.

Lachhman Rāwal, c. A.D. **1402.**—Kehar had eight sons: (1) Somaji, who had a numerous offspring, called the Soma-Bhattis; (2) Lachhman;[3] (3) Kailan, who forcibly seized Bikampur, the appanage of his elder brother Soma, who departed with all his

[1] The Khichi prince, we may suppose, had no follower skilled in omens—they lived very happily, as appears by the Khichi chronicle, and she bore him a son, who was driven from Gagraun. The scandal propagated against the 'ruby of Mewar' was no doubt a ruse of the Sankhla chief, as the conclusion shows. However small the intrinsic worth of these anecdotes, they afford links of synchronisms, which constitute the value of the annals of all these States.

[2] Sadhu was the son and heir of Raningdeo, and it was from this portion of the Bhatti annals I extracted that singular story, related at p. 730, to illustrate the influence which the females of Rajputana have on national manners. The date of this tragical event was S. 1462, according to the Bhatti annals; and Rana Mokal, the contemporary of Rawal Jeth and Rao Raningdeo, was on the throne of Mewar from S. 1454 to S. 1475. The annals of this State (Vol. I. p. 331) notice the marriage of the 'Ruby' to Dhiraj, son of Achaldas, but say nothing on the other point. A vague recollection of some matrimonial insult being offered evidently yet prevails, for when a marriage was contracted in A.D. 1821, through the Author's intervention, between the Rana of Udaipur's daughter and the present Rawal Gaj Singh of Jaisalmer, it was given out that there was no memorial of any marriage-alliance between the two houses. After all, it may be a vainglorious invention of the Bhatti annalist.

[3] [The date of Lachhman Rāwal is uncertain. Inscriptions at Jaisalmer mention him as reigning in A.D. 1402 and 1416 (Erskine iii. B. 9).]

basai,[1] and settled at Girab; (4) Kilkaran; (5) Satal, who gave his name to an ancient town, and called it Satalmer. The names of the rest were Bija, Tana, and Tejsi.

When the sons of Raningdeo became converts to Islam, in order to avenge their father's feud with the Rathor prince of Nagor, they forfeited their inheritance of Pugal and Marot, and thenceforward mixed with the Aboharia Bhattis, and their descendants are termed Mumin Musalman Bhatti. On this event, Kailan, the third son of the Rawal, took possession of the forfeited lands, and besides Bikampur, regained Derawar, which had been conquered by their ancient foes, the Dahya Rajputs.

Kailan built a fort on the Bias, called, after his father, Kara, or Karor, which again brought the Bhattis into collision with the Johyas and Langahas, whose chief, Amir Khan Korai, attacked him, but was defeated. Kailan became the terror of the Chahils,[2] the Mohils,[2] and Johyas,[2] who lived in this quarter, and his authority extended as far as the Panjnad. Kailan married into the Samma family of Jam,[3] and [257] arbitrated their disputes

[1] The term *basai* has been explained in Vol. I. p. 206. The Basai is a slave in the mildest sense; one who in distress sells his liberty. His master cuts the *choti*, or lock of hair, from the centre of the head, as a mark of bondage. They are transferable, like cattle. This custom prevails more in the desert States than in central Rajwara; there every great man has his Basai. Shyam Singh Champawat of Pokaran had two hundred when he fled to Jaipur, and they all fell with him fighting against the Mahrattas. All castes, Brahmans and Rajputs, become Basais; they can redeem their liberty by purchase.

[2] These three tribes are either extinct, or were lost on becoming proselytes to Islam.

[3] The Sama or Samma tribe, which is well known in Muhammadan history, as having given a dynasty to Sind in modern times, is a great branch of the Yadus, and descended from Samba, son of Krishna; and while the other branch colonized Zabulistan, maintaining the original name of Yadus, the sons of Samba made his name the patronymic in Seistan and the lower valley of the Indus. Samma-ka-kot, or Sammanagari, was the capital, which yet exists, and doubtless originated the Minnagara of the Greeks. Sambos, the opponent of Alexander, it is fair to infer, was the chief of the Samma tribe. Samba, meaning 'of, or belonging to, Sham or Syama' (an epithet of Krishna, from his dark complexion), was son of Jambuvati, one of the eight wives of this deified Yadu. The Jarejas of Cutch and Jams of Sind and Saurashtra are of the same stock. The Sind-Samma dynasty, on the loss of their faith and coming into contact with Islam, to which they became proselytes, were eager to adopt a pedigree which might give them importance in the eyes of their conquerors; *Sam* was transformed into *Jam*, and the Persian king, Jamshīd, was adopted as

on succession, which had caused much bloodshed. Shujaat Jam, whom he supported, accompanied him to Marot, on whose death, two years after, Kailan possessed himself of all the Samma territory, when the Sind River became the boundary of his dominion. Kailan died at the age of seventy-two, and was succeeded by [1]

Chāchakdeo Rāwal, *c.* A.D. **1448.**—Chachakdeo made Marot his headquarters, to cover his territories from the attacks of Multan, which took umbrage at the return of the Bhattis across the Gara. The chief of Multan united in a league all the ancient foes of the Bhattis, the Langahas, the Johyas, the Khichis, and all the tribes of that region. Chachak formed an army of seventeen thousand horse and fourteen thousand foot, and crossed the Bias to meet his foes. The encounter was desperate; but the Bhattis were victorious, and returned with rich spoil to Marot. In the year following another battle took place, in which seven hundred and forty Bhattis were slain, and three thousand of the men of Multan. By this success, the conquests of Chachak were extended, and he left a garrison (*thana*) under his son in Asinikot, beyond the Bias, and returned to Pugal. He then attacked Maipal, chief of the Dhundis,[2] whom he defeated. After this victory he repaired to Jaisalmer, to visit his brother Lachhman, reserving the produce of the lands dependent on Asinikot [3] for his expenses at court. On his return home by Baru, he was accosted by a

---

the patriarch of the Sammas, in lieu of the legitimate Samba. Ferishta gives an account of this dynasty, but was ignorant of their origin. He says, "The Zemindars of Sinde were originally of two tribes or families, Somuna and Soomura; and the chief of the former was distinguished by the appellation of Jam."—Briggs' Ferishta, vol. iv. p. 424. The historian admits they were Hindus until A.H. 782 (A.D. 1380, S. 1436); a point of little doubt, as we see the Bhatti prince intermarrying with this family about twenty years subsequent even to the date assigned by Ferishta for their proselytism. I may here again state, once for all, that I append these notes in order not to interfere with the text, which is abridged from the original chronicle.

[1] It is said that Ranmall succeeded; but this was only to the northern portion, his appanage: he lived but two months.

[2] [Probably a branch of the Panwārs (Rose, *Glossary*, ii. 240).]

[3] Position unknown, unless it be the Tchin-kot of D'Anville at the confluence of the river of Kabul with the Indus. There is no doubt that this castle of the Bhatti prince was in the Panjab; and coupled with his alliance with the chief of Sehat or Swat, that it is the Tchin-kot, or Ashnagar of that celebrated geographer, whence the Acesines of the Greeks. [The Acesines or Chīnāb is the Vedik Asikni.]

Janjua Rajput,[1] pasturing an immense flock of goats, who presented the best of his flock, and demanded protection against the raids of Birjang Rathor. This chief had wrested the celebrated fortress of Satalmer,[2] the abode of wealthy merchants, from a Bhatti chief, and extended his forays far into the desert, and the Janjua was one of those who had suffered by his success [258]. Not long after Rao Chachak had passed by the pastures of the Janjua, he received a visit from him, to complain of another inroad, which had carried off the identical goat, his offering. Chachak assembled his kinsmen, and formed an alliance with Shumar Khan, chief of the Seta tribe,[3] who came with three thousand horse. It was the custom of the Rathors of Satalmer to encamp their horse at a tank some distance from the city, to watch, while the chief citizens used daily to go abroad. Chachak surprised and made prisoners of the whole. The bankers and men of wealth offered large sums for their ransom ; but he would not release them from bondage, except on condition of their settling in the territory of Jaisalmer. Three hundred and sixty-five heads of families embraced this alternative, and hence Jaisalmer dates the influx of her wealth. They were distributed over the principal cities, Derawar, Pugal, Marot, etc.[4] The three sons of the Rathor were also made prisoners ; the two youngest were released, but Mera, the eldest, was detained as a hostage for his father's good conduct. Chachak dismissed his ally, the Seta chief, whose granddaughter, Sonaldevi, he married. The father of the bride, Haibat Khan,[5] gave with her in *daeja* (dower)

[1] I may here repeat that the Janjūa or Janjūha and Johya were no doubt branches of the same race ; the Janjūha of Babur, who locates them about the mountains of Jud. [Rose, *Glossary*, ii. 353 f. ; *ASR*, ii. 17).]

[2] Now belonging to Marwar, and on its north-western frontier ; but I believe in ruins. [Near Pokaran, 85 miles N.W. of Jodhpur city. It is in ruins.]

[3] Most likely the Swatis, or people of Swat, described by Mr. Elphinstone (Vol. I. p. 506) as of Indian origin, and as possessing a kingdom from the Hydaspes to Jalalabad, the Souasteno of Ptolemy. [Souastēnē is the basin of the Souastos, the river of Swāt, the original form of the name being Subhavastu, which, by the usual mode of contraction, becomes Subhāstu or Suvāstu (McCrindle, *Ptolemy*, 106 f.). It seems hardly likely that this tribe interfered in the politics of the Indian desert.]

[4] It must not be forgotten that Satalmer was one of the Bhatti castles wrested from them by the Rathors, who have greatly curtailed their frontiers.

[5] From this and many other instances we come to the conclusion that

fifty horses, thirty-five slaves, four palkis, and two hundred female camels, and with her Chachak returned to Marot.

War with the Khokhars.—Two years after this, Chachak made war on Tharraj Khokhar, the chief of Pilibanga,[1] on account of a horse stolen from a Bhatti. The Khokhars were defeated and plundered; but his old enemies the Langahas, taking advantage of this occasion, made head against Chachak, and drove his garrison from the new possession of Dhuniapur.[2] Disease at length seized on Rawal Chachak, after a long course of victorious warfare, in which he subdued various tracts of country, even to the heart of the Panjab. In this state he determined to die as he had lived, with arms in his hands; but having [259] no foe near with whom to cope, he sent an embassy to the Langaha prince of Multan, to beg, as a last favour, the Juddhdan, or 'gift of battle,' that his soul might escape by the steel of his foeman, and not fall a sacrifice to slow disease.[3] The prince, suspecting treachery, hesitated; but the Bhatti messenger pledged his word that his master only wished an honourable death, and that he would only bring five hundred men to the combat. The challenge being accepted, the Rawal called his clansmen around him, and on recounting what he had done, seven hundred select Rajputs, who had shared in all his victories, volunteered to take the last field, and make Sankalp (oblation) of their lives with their leader. Previous to setting forth, he

---

the Tatar or Indo-Scythic title of Khan is by no means indicative of the Muhammadan faith. Here we see the daughter of the prince of Swat, or Suvat, with a genuine Hindi name.

[1] The position of Pilibanga is unknown; in all probability it has undergone a metamorphosis with the spread of 'the faith' over these regions. As before mentioned, I believe this race called Khokhar to be the Gakkhar, so well known to Babur, and described as his inveterate foes in all his irruptions into India. Their manners, especially that distinctive mark, polyandry, mentioned by Ferishta, mark the Ghakkars as Indo-Scythic. The names of their chiefs are decidedly Hindu. They were located with the Judis in the upper part of the Panjab, and, according to Elphinstone, they retain their old position, contiguous to the Yusufzai Jadons. [See Rose, *Glossary*, ii. 540. They have no connexion with the Rājput Jādons.]

[2] Dhuniapur is not located.

[3] In this chivalrous challenge, or demand of the Juddhdan, we recognize another strong trait of Scythic manners, as depicted by Herodotus. The ancient Getae of Transoxiana could not bear the idea of dying of disease; a feeling which his offspring carried with them to the shores of the Baltic, to Yeut-land, or Jutland! [?]

arranged his affairs. His son Gaj Singh, by the Seta Rani, he sent with her to her father's house. He had five other sons, namely, Kumbha, Barsal, Bhimdeo (by Lala Rani, of the Sodha tribe), Rata and Randhir, whose mother was Surajdevi, of Chauhan race. Barsal, his eldest son, he made heir to all his dominions, except the land of Khadal (whose chief town is Derawar), which he bestowed upon Randhir, and to both he gave the *tika*, making them separate States. Barsal marched to Kahror,[1] his capital, at the head of seventeen thousand men.

Heroic Death of Rāwal Chachakdeo.—Meanwhile, Rawal Chachak marched to Dhuniapur, "to part with life." There he heard that the prince of Multan was within two coss. His soul was rejoiced; he performed his ablutions, worshipped the sword[2] and the gods, bestowed charity, and withdrew his thoughts from this world.

The battle lasted four gharis (two hours), and the Jadon prince fell with all his kin after performing prodigies of valour. Two thousand Khans fell beneath their swords; rivers of blood flowed in the field; but the Bhatti gained the abode of Indra, who shared his throne with the hero. The king crossed the Bias, and returned to Multan.

While Randhir was performing at Derawar the rites of the twelve days of *matam*, or 'mourning,' his elder brother, Kumbha, afflicted with insanity, rushed into the assembly and swore to avenge his father's death. That day he departed, accompanied by a single slave, and reached the prince's camp. It was surrounded by a [260] ditch eleven yards wide, over which the Bhatti leaped his horse in the dead of night, reached the harem, and cut off the head of Kalu Shah, with which he rejoined his brethren at Derawar. Barsal re-established Dhuniapur, and then went to Kahror. His old foes, the Langahas, under Haibat Khan, again attacked him, but they were defeated with great slaughter. At the same time, Husain Khan Baloch invaded Bikampur.[3]

[1] This fortress, erected by Rao Kailan, is stated to be twenty-two coss, about forty miles, from Bahawalpur; but though the direction is not stated, there is little doubt of its being to the northward, most probably in that *duab* called Sind-Sagar. [Probably Kahror in Multān District, about 20 miles from Bahāwalpur.]

[2] Couple this martial rite with the demand of Juddhdan, and there is an additional reason for calling these Yadus Indo-Scythic. See p. 680 for an account of the worship of the sword, or Khadga-sthapna.

[3] The foregoing (from p. 1219), including the actions of Kailan, Chachak,

Rāwal Bersi, *c.* A.D. **1436-40.**—Rawal Bersi,[1] who at this time occupied the *gaddi* of Jaisalmer, went forth to meet Rao Barsal on his return from his expedition in the Panjab. In S. 1530 (A.D. 1474) he made the gates and palace of Bikampur.

We may, in this place, desert the literal narrative of the chronicle; what follows is a record of similar border-feuds and petty wars, between 'the sons of Kailan'[2] and the chiefs of the Panjab, alternately invaders and invaded, which is pregnant with mighty words and gallant deeds, but yielding no new facts of historical value. At length the numerous offspring of Kailan separated, and divided amongst them the lands on both sides of the Gara; and as Sultan Babur soon after this period made a final conquest of Multan from the Langahas, and placed therein his own governor, in all probability the Bhatti possessors of Kahrorkot and Dhuniapur, as well as Pugal and Marot (now Muhammadans), exchanged their faith (sanctioned even by Manu) for the preservation of their estates.[3] The bard is so much occupied with this Pugal branch that the chronicle appears almost devoted solely to them.

He passes from the main stem, Rawal Bersi, to Rawals Jeth, Nunkaran, Bhim, Manohardas, to Sabal Singh, five generations, with little further notice than the mere enumeration of their issue. With this last prince, Sabal Singh, an important change occurred in the political condition of the Bhattis [261].

---

and Barsal, must be considered as an episode, detailing the exploits of the Raos of Pugal, established by Kailan, third son of Rawal Kehar of Jaisalmer. It was too essential to the annals to be placed in a note.

[1] [Rāwal Bersi, son of Lachhman, son of Kehar, is mentioned in inscriptions as Chief of Jaisalmer, A.D. 1436, and 1440 (Erskine iii. B. 9).]

[2] Rao Kailan had established his authority over nine castles, heads of districts, namely, Asini, or Aswinikot, Bikampur, Marot, Pugal, Derawar, Kahror (twenty-two coss, or about forty miles, from Bahawalpur), Guman, Bahan, Nadno, and Matela, on the Indus.

[3] There never was anything so degrading to royalty as the selfish protection guaranteed to it by this Lycurgus of the Hindus, who says, "Against misfortune, let him preserve his wealth; at the expense of his wealth, let him preserve his wife; but let him at all events preserve himself, even at the hazard of his wife and riches."—Manu, *Laws*, vii. 213. The entire history of the Rajputs shows they do not pay much attention to such unmanly maxims.

CHAPTER 5

Jaisalmer a Mughal Fief.—We have now reached that period in the Bhatti annals when Shah Jahan was emperor of India. Elsewhere, we have minutely related the measure which the great Akbar adopted to attach his Rajput vassalage to the empire; a policy pursued by his successors. Sabal Singh, the first of the princes of Jaisalmer who held his dominions as a fief of the empire, was not the legitimate heir to the '*gaddi* of Jaisal [262].'[1] Manohardas had obtained the *gaddi* by the assassination of his nephew, Rawal Nathu, the son and heir of Bhim, who was returning from his nuptials at Bikaner, and had passed the day at Phalodi,[2] then a town of Jaisalmer, when poison was administered to him by the hands of a female. But it was destined that the line of the assassin should not rule, and the dignity fell to Sabal Singh, the third in descent from Maldeo, second son of Rawal Nunkaran.

Rāwal Sabal Singh, A.D. **1651-61.**—The good qualities of young Sabal, and the bad ones of Ramchand, son of the usurper, afforded another ground for the preference of the former. Moreover, Sabal was nephew to the prince of Amber, under whom he held a distinguished post in the government of Peshawar, where he saved the royal treasure from being captured by the Afghan

[1] Nunkaran had three sons, Harraj, Maldeo, and Kalyandas; each had issue. Harraj had Bhim (who succeeded his grandfather Nunkaran). Maldeo had Ketsi, who had Dayaldas, father of Sabal Singh, to whom was given in appanage the town of Mandila, near Pokaran. The third son, Kalyandas, had Manohardas, who succeeded Bhim. Ramchand was the son of Manohardas. A slip from the genealogical tree will set this in a clear light.

1. Nunkaran.
- Harraj.
  - 2. Bhim.
    - Nathu.
- Maldeo.
  - Ketsi.
    - Dayaldas.
      - 4. Sabal Singh.
- Kalyandas.
  - 3. Manohardas.
    - Ramchand.

[2] [About 75 miles N.W. of Jodhpur city.]

mountaineers. For this service, and being a favourite of the chiefs who served with their contingents, the king gave Jaswant Singh of Jodhpur command to place him on the *gaddi*. The celebrated Nahar Khan Kumpawat [1] was entrusted with this duty, for the performance of which he received the city and domain of Pokaran, ever since severed from Jaisalmer.

Pokaran lost to Jaisalmer.—This was the first considerable abstraction from the territories which had been progressively increased by Rawal Jaisal and his successors, but which have since been woefully curtailed. A short time before Babur's invasion, the dependencies of Jaisalmer extended on the north to the Gara River,[2] west to the Mihran or Indus; and on the east and south they were bounded by the Rathors of Bikaner and Marwar who had been gradually encroaching for two centuries, and continue to do so to this day. The entire *thal* of Barmer and Kotra,[3] in the south, were Bhatti chieftainships, and eastward to the site of Bikaner itself.

Rāwal Amār Singh, A.D. 1661-1702.—Amra Singh, son of Sabal, succeeded. He led the *tika-daur* against the Balochs, who had invaded the western tracts, and was installed on the field of victory. Soon after, he demanded aid from his subjects to portion his daughter, and being opposed by his Rajput minister, Raghunath, he put him to death. The Chana Rajputs, from the north-east, having renewed their old raids, he in person attacked and compelled them to give bonds, or written obligations, for their future good conduct.

Provoked by the daily encroachments of the Kandhalot Rathors, Sundardas and Dalpat, chiefs of Bikampur, determined to retaliate: "let us get a name in the [263] world," said Dalpat, "and attack the lands of the Rathors." Accordingly, they invaded, plundered, and fired the town of Jaju, on the Bikaner frontier. The Kandhalots retaliated on the towns of Jaisalmer, and an action took place, in which the Bhattis were victorious,

1 Another synchronism (see Annals of Marwar for an account of Nahar Khan) of some value, since it accounts for the first abstraction of territory by the Rathors from the Bhattis.

2 The Gara is invariably called the Bias in the chronicle. Gara, or Ghara, is so called, in all probability, from the mud (*gar*) suspended in its waters. The Gara is composed of the waters of the Bias and Sutlej. [See *IGI*, vii. 139, xxiii. 179.]

3 [About 60 miles S. of Jaisalmer city.]

slaying two hundred of the Rathors. The Rawal partook in the triumph of his vassals. Raja Anup Singh [1] of Bikaner was then serving with the imperial armies in the Deccan. On receiving this account, he commanded his minister to issue a summons to every Kandhalot capable of carrying arms to invade Jaisalmer, and take and raze Bikampur, or he would consider them traitors. The minister issued the summons; every Rathor obeyed it, and he added, as an auxiliary, a Pathan chief with his band from Hissar. Rawal Amra collected his Bhattis around him, and instead of awaiting the attack, advanced to meet it; he slew many of the chiefs, burnt the frontier towns, and recovered Pugal, forcing the Rathor chiefs of Barmer and Kotra to renew their engagements of fealty and service.

Amra had eight sons, and was succeeded by Jaswant, the eldest, in S. 1758 (A.D. 1702), whose daughter was married to the heir-apparent of Mewar.

Here ends the chronicle, of which the foregoing is an abstract: the concluding portion of the annals is from a MS. furnished by a living chronicler, corrected by other information. It is but a sad record of anarchy and crime.

Soon after the death of Rawal Amra, Pugal, Barmer, Phalodi, and various other towns and territories in Jaisalmer, were wrested from this State by the Rathors.[2]

The territory bordering the Gara was taken by Daud Khan, an Afghan chieftain from Shikarpur, and it became the nucleus of a State called after himself, Daudputra.[3]

Rāwal Jaswant Singh, A.D. 1702-22.—Jaswant Singh succeeded. He had five sons, Jagat Singh, who committed suicide, Isari Singh, Tej Singh, Sardar Singh, and Sultan Singh. Jagat Singh had three sons, Akhai Singh, Budh Singh, and Zorawar Singh.

[1] [A.D. 1669-95.]

[2] The most essential use to which my labours can be applied is that of enabling the British Government, when called upon to exercise its functions, as protector and arbitrator of the international quarrels of Rajputana, to understand the legitimate and original grounds of dispute. Here we perceive the germ of the border-feuds, which have led to so much bloodshed between Bikaner and Jaisalmer, in which the former was the first aggressor; but as the latter, for the purpose of redeeming her lost territory, most frequently appears as the agitator of public tranquillity, it is necessary to look for the remote cause in pronouncing our award.

[3] [Bahāwalpur.]

Rāwal Akhai Singh, A.D. 1722-62.—Akhai Singh succeeded. Budh Singh died of the smallpox; Tej Singh, uncle to the Rawal, usurped the government, and the princes fled to Delhi to save their lives. At this period, their grand-uncle, Hari Singh (brother of Rawal Jaswant), was serving the king, and he returned in order to displace the usurper. It is customary for the [264] prince of Jaisalmer to go annually in state to the lake Gharsisar, to perform the ceremony of *Las*, or clearing away the accumulation of mud and sand.[1] The Raja first takes out a handful, when rich and poor follow his example. Hari Singh chose the time when this ceremony was in progress to attack the usurper. The attempt did not altogether succeed; but Tej Singh was so severely wounded that he died, and was succeeded by his son,

Sawai Singh, an infant of three years of age. Akhai Singh collected the Bhattis from all quarters, stormed the castle, put the infant to death, and regained his rights.

Akhai Singh ruled forty years. During this reign, Bahawal Khan, son of Daud Khan, took Derawar, and all the tract of Khadal, the first Bhatti conquest, and added it to his new State of Bahawalpur, or Daudputra.

Rāwal Mūlrāj, A.D. 1762-1820. Conspiracy against Mūlrāj.—Mulraj succeeded in S. 1818 (A.D. 1762). He had three sons, Rae Singh, Jeth Singh, and Man Singh. The unhappy choice of a minister by Mulraj completed the demoralization of the Bhatti principality. This minister was named Sarup Singh, a Bania of the Jain faith and Mehta family, destined to be the exterminators of the laws and fortunes of the 'sons of Jaisal.' The cause of hatred and revenge of this son of commerce to the Bhatti aristocracy arose out of a disgraceful dispute regarding a Bakhtan, a fair frail one, a favourite of the Mehta, but who preferred the Rajput, Sardar Singh, of the tribe of Aef.[2] The Bhatti chief carried his complaint of the minister to the heir-apparent, Rae Singh, who had also cause of grievance in the reduction of his income. It was suggested to the prince to put this presumptuous minister to death; this was effected by the prince's own hand,

[1] [Lāsa, 'anything clammy,' like mud. This is a common pious act, performed at sacred tanks, and by some castes, like the Idaiyans of Madras, at marriages (*North Indian Notes and Queries*, ii. 111; Thurston, *Tribes and Castes of S. India*, i. 360 f.).]

[2] [This tribe has not been traced.]

in his father's presence; and as the Mehta, in falling, clung to Mulraj for protection, it was proposed to take off Mulraj at the same time. The proposition, however, was rejected with horror by the prince, whose vengeance was satisfied. The Rawal was allowed to escape to the female apartments; but the chieftains, well knowing they could not expect pardon from the Rawal, insisted on investing Rae Singh, and if he refused, on placing his brother on the *gaddi*. The *an* of Rae Singh was proclaimed; but no entreaty or threat would induce him to listen to the proposal of occupying the throne; in lieu of which he used a pallet (khat). Three months and five days had passed since the deposal and bondage of Mulraj, when a female resolved to emancipate him: this female was the wife of the chief conspirator, and confidential adviser of the regent prince. This noble dame, a Rathor Rajputni, of the Maleeha clan, was the wife of Anup Singh of Jinjiniali, the premier noble of Jaisalmer, and who, wearied with the tyranny of the minister and the weakness of his [265] prince, had proposed the death of the one and the deposal of the other. We are not made acquainted with any reason, save that of Swamidharma, or 'fealty,' which prompted the Rathorni to rescue her prince even at the risk of her husband's life; but her appeal to her son Zorawar, to perform his duty, is preserved, and we give it verbatim: "Should your father oppose you, sacrifice him to your duty, and I will mount the pyre with his corpse." The son yielded obedience to the injunction of his magnanimous parent, who had sufficient influence to gain over Arjun, the brother of her husband, as well as Megh Singh, chief of Baru. The three chieftains forced an entrance into the prison where their prince was confined, who refused to be released from his manacles, until he was told that the Mahechi had promoted the plot for his liberty. The sound of the grand nakkara, proclaiming Mulraj's repossession of the *gaddi*, awoke his son from sleep; and on the herald depositing at the side of his pallet the sable *saropa*,[1] and all the insignia of exile—the black steed and black vestments—the prince, obeying the command of the emancipated Rawal, clad himself therein, and accompanied by

[1] *Saropa* is the Rajput term for khilat, and is used by those who, like the Rana of Udaipur, prefer the vernacular dialect to the corrupt jargon of the Islamite. *Sar-o-pa* (from 'head,' *sar*, to 'foot,' *pa*) means a complete dress; in short, *cap-à-pied*. [See Yule, *Hobson-Jobson*, 2nd ed. 808.]

his party, bade adieu to Jaisalmer and took the road to Kotra. When he arrived at this town, on the southern frontier of the State, the chiefs proposed to "run the country"; but he replied, "the country was his mother, and every Rajput his foe who injured it." He repaired to Jodhpur, but the chieftains abided about Sheo Kotra and Barmer, and during the twelve years they remained outlaws, plundered even to the gates of Jaisalmer. In the first three years they devastated the country, their castles were dismantled, the wells therein filled up, and their estates sequestrated. At the end of the twelve, having made the *talak*, or oath against further plunder, their estates were restored, and they were readmitted into their country.

The banished prince remained two years and a half with Raja Bijai Singh, who treated him like a son. But he carried his arrogant demeanour with him to Jodhpur; for one day, as he was going out to hunt, a Bania, to whom he was indebted, seized his horse by the bridle, and invoking the *an* of Bijai Singh, demanded payment of his debt. The prince, in turn, required him, with the invocation "by Mulraj!" to unloose his hold. But the man of wealth, disregarding the appeal, insolently replied, "What is Mulraj to me?" It was the last word he spoke; the sword of Rae Singh was unsheathed, and the Bania's head rolled on the ground: then, turning his horse's [266] head to Jaisalmer, he exclaimed, "Better be a slave at once than live on the bounty of another." His unexpected arrival outside his native city brought out the entire population to see him. His father, the Rawal, sent to know what had occasioned his presence, and he replied that it was merely preparatory to pilgrimage. He was refused admittance; his followers were disarmed, and he was sent to reside at the fortress of Dewa, together with his sons Abhai Singh and Dhonkal Singh, and their families.

Sālim Singh, Prime Minister.—Salim Singh, who succeeded his father as prime minister of Jaisalmer, was but eleven years of age at the time of his murder. His young mind appears, even at that early age, to have been a hotbed for revenge; and the seeds which were sown soon quickened into a luxuriance rarely equalled even in those regions, where human life is held in little estimation. Without any of that daring valour which distinguishes the Rajput, he overcame, throughout a long course of years, all who opposed him, uniting the subtlety of the serpent to the ferocity of the tiger. In person he was effeminate, in speech bland; pliant and courteous in demeanour; promising, without hesitation, and with all the semblance of sincerity, what he never had the most remote intention to fulfil. Salim, or, as he was generally designated by his tribe, the Mehta, was a signal instance of a fact of which these annals exhibit too many examples, namely, the inadequacy of religious professions, though of a severe character, as a restraint on moral conduct; for though the tenets of his faith (the Jain) imperatively prescribe the necessity of "hurting no sentient being," and of sitting in the dark rather than, by luring a moth into the flame of a lamp, incur the penalty attached to the sin of insect-murder, this man has sent more of 'the sons of Jassa' to Yamaloka[1] than the sword of their external foes during his long administration. He had scarcely attained man's estate when the outlawed chiefs were restored to their estates by a singular intervention. Raja Bhim Singh had acceded to the *gaddi* of Marwar, and the Mehta was chosen by the prince of Jaisalmer, as his representative, to convey his congratulations, and the *tika* of acknowledgment on his succession, to Raja Bijai Singh. On his return from this mission, he was waylaid and captured by the outlawed chieftains, who instantly passed sentence of death upon the author of their miseries. The sword was uplifted, when, "placing his turban at the feet of Zorawar Singh," he implored his protection—and he found it! Such is the Rajput—an anomaly amongst his species; his character a compound of the opposite and antagonistical qualities which impel mankind to virtue and to crime. Let me recall to the mind of the reader that the protector of this vampire [267] was the virtuous son of the virtuous Rajputni who, with an elevation of mind equal to whatever is recorded of Greek or Roman heroines, devoted herself, and a husband whom she loved, to the one predominant sentiment of the Rajput, Swamidharma, or 'fealty to the sovereign.' Yet had the wily Mehta effected the disgrace of this brave chief, to whom the Rawal owed his release from bondage and restoration to his throne, and forced him to join the outlaws amidst the sand-hills of Barmer. Nothing can paint more strongly the influence of this first of the Bhatti chiefs over his brethren than the act of preserving the life of their mortal foe, thus cast into their hands; for not only did they

[1] Pluto's realm.

dissuade him from the act, but prophesied his repentance of such mistaken clemency. Only one condition was stipulated, their restoration to their homes. They were recalled, but not admitted to court: a distinction reserved for Zorawar alone.

Death of Rāe Singh.—When Rae Singh was incarcerated in Dewa, his eldest son, Abhai Singh, Rajkumar, 'heir-apparent,' with the second son, Dhonkal, were left at Barmer, with the outlawed chiefs. The Rawal, having in vain demanded his grandchildren, prepared an army and invested Barmer. It was defended during six months, when a capitulation was acceded to, and the children were given up to Mulraj on the bare pledge of Zorawar Singh, who guaranteed their safety; and they were sent to the castle of Dewa, where their father was confined. Soon after, the castle was fired, and Rae Singh and his wife were consumed in the flames. On escaping this danger, which was made to appear accidental, the young princes were confined in the fortress of Ramgarh, in the most remote corner of the desert, bordering the valley of Sind, for their security and that of the Rawal (according to the Mehta's account), and to prevent faction from having a nucleus around which to form. But Zorawar, who entertained doubts of the minister's motives, reminded the Rawal that the proper place for the heir-apparent was the court, and that his honour stood pledged for his safety. This was sufficient for the Mehta, whose mind was instantly intent upon the means to rid himself of so conscientious an adviser. Zorawar had a brother named Ketsi, whose wife, according to the courtesy of Rajwara, had adopted the minister as her brother. Salim sounded his adopted sister as to her wish to see her husband become lord of Jinjiniali. The tempter succeeded: he furnished her with poisoned comfits, which she administered to the gallant Zorawar; and her lord was inducted into the estates of Jinjiniali. Having thus disposed of the soul of the Bhatti nobility, he took off in detail the chiefs of Baru, Dangri, and many others, chiefly by the same means, though some by [268] the dagger. Ketsi, who, whether innocent or a guilty participant in his brother's death, had benefited thereby, was marked in the long list of proscription of this fiend, who determined to exterminate every Rajput of note. Ketsi knew too much, and those connected with him shared in this dangerous knowledge: wife, brother, son, were therefore destined to fall by the same blow. The immediate cause of enmity was as follows. The minister, who desired to set aside the claims of the children of Rae Singh to the *gaddi*, and to nominate the youngest son of Mulraj as heir-apparent, was opposed by Ketsi, as it could only be effected by the destruction of the former; and he replied, that "no co-operation of his should sanction the spilling of the blood of any of his master's family." Salim treasured up the remembrance of this opposition to his will, though without any immediate sign of displeasure. Soon after, Ketsi and his brother Sarup were returning from a nuptial ceremony at Kanera, in the district of Balotra. On reaching Bhikarai, on the Jaisalmer frontier, where the ministers of the Mehta's vengeance were posted, the gallant Zorawar and his brother were conducted into the castle, out of which their bodies were brought only to be burnt. Hearing of some intended evil to her lord, Ketsi's wife, with her infant son, Megha, sought protection in the minister's own abode, where she had a double claim, as his adopted sister, to sanctuary and protection. For five days, the farce was kept up of sending food for herself and child; but the slave who conveyed it remarking, in coarse, unfeeling language, that both her husband and her brother were with their fathers, she gave a loose to grief and determined on revenge. This being reported to the Mehta, he sent a dagger for her repose.

The princes, Abhai Singh and Dhonkal Singh, confined in the fortress of Ramgarh, soon after the murder of Ketsi were carried off, together with their wives and infants, by poison. The murderer then proclaimed Gaj Singh, the youngest but one of all the posterity of Mulraj, as heir-apparent. His brothers sought security in flight from this fiend-like spirit of the minister, and are now refugees in the Bikaner territory. The following slip from the genealogical tree will show the branches so unmercifully lopped off by this monster:

Mulraj.

Rae Singh, poisoned. — Jeth Singh (*kana*), living. — Man Singh, killed by a fall from his horse.

Rae Singh: …i Singh, …soned. — Dhonkal Singh, poisoned.

Jeth Singh: Maha Singh, blind.

Man Singh: Tej Singh, in exile. — Devi Singh, in exile. — Gaj Singh, reigning prince. — Fateh Singh, in exile.

[269.]

Maha Singh, being blind of one eye[1] (*kana*), could not succeed; and Man Singh being killed by a fall from his horse, the Mehta was saved the crime of adding one more "mortal murther to his crown."

Long Reigns of Rājput Princes.—It is a singular fact, that the longest reigns we know of in Rajwara occurred during ministerial usurpations. The late Maharao of Kotah occupied the *gaddi* upwards of half a century, and the Rawal Mulraj swayed the nominal sceptre of this *oasis* of the desert upwards of fifty-eight years. His father ruled forty years, and I doubt whether, in all history, we can find another instance of father and son reigning for a century.[2] This century was prolific in change to the dynasty, whose whole history is full of strange vicissitudes. If we go back to Jaswant Singh, the grandfather of Mulraj, we find the Bhatti principality touching the Gara on the north, which divided it from Multan; on the west it was bounded by the Panjnad, and thus included a narrow slip of the fertile valley of Sind; and we have seen it stretch, at no remote period, even to the ancient capital Mansura, better known to the Hindu as Rori-Bakhar,[3] the islandic capital of the Sogdoi (Sodha) of Alexander. To the south, it rested on Dhat, including the castles of Sheo, Kotra, and

[1] A person blind of one eye is incompetent to succeed, according to Hindu law. Kana is the nickname given to a person labouring under this personal defect, which term is merely an anagram of *ânka*, 'the eye.' [This is wrong. It is derived from Skt. *kāna*, 'one-eyed'.] The loss of an eye does not deprive an occupant of his rights—of which we had a curious example in the siege of the imperial city of Delhi, which gave rise to the remark, that the three greatest men therein had only the complement of one man amongst them: the emperor had been deprived of both eyes by the brutality of Ghulam Kadir; the besieging chief Holkar was kana, as was the defender, Sir D. Ochterlony. Holkar's name has become synonymous with kana, and many a horse, dog, and man, blind of an eye, is called after this celebrated Mahratta leader. The Hindus, by what induction I know not, attach a degree of moral obliquity to every individual kana, and appear to make no distinction between the natural and the acquired defect; though to all kanas they apply another and more dignified appellation, Sukracharya [the regent of the planet Venus], the Jupiter of their astro-mythology, which very grave personage came by his misfortune in no creditable way—for, although the Guru, or spiritual head of the Hindu gods, he set as bad a moral example to them as did the classical Jupiter to the tenants of the Greek and Roman Pantheon.

[2] [Ummed Singh of Kotah, A.D. 1771–1819; Mūlrāj of Jaisalmer, 1762–1820; Akhai Singh of Jaisalmer, 1722–62.]

[3] Mansura was many miles south of Bakhar.

Barmer, seized on by Marwar; and in the east embraced the districts of Phalodi, Pokaran, and other parts, also in the possession of Marwar or Bikaner. The whole of the State of Bahawalpur is formed out of the Bhatti dominion, and the Rathors have obtained therefrom not a small portion of their western frontier. This abstraction of territory will account for the heartburnings and border-feuds which continually break out between the Bhattis and Rathors, and 'the children of David (Daudputras).'

Could the same prophetic steel which carved upon the pillar of Brahmsar the destinies of the grandson of the deified Hari, eleven hundred years before Christ, have subjoined to that of Jaisal the fate which awaited his descendant Mulraj, he would doubtless have regarded the prophecy as conveying a falsehood too gross for belief. That the offspring of the deified prince of Dwarka, who founded Ghazni, and fought the [270] united kings of Syria and Bactria, should, at length, be driven back on India, and compelled to seek shelter under the sign of the cross, reared amidst their sand-hills by a handful of strangers, whose ancestors, when they were even in the maturity of their fame, were wandering in their native woods, with painted bodies, and offering human sacrifices to the sun-god—more resembling Balsiva than Balkrishna—these would have seemed prodigies too wild for faith.

CHAPTER 6

Treaty with the British.—It was in the Samvat (era) of Vikrama, 1818,[1] that Rawal Mulraj was inaugurated on the throne of Jaisal; and it was in the year of our Lord 1818, that a treaty of "perpetual friendship, alliance, and unity of interests" was concluded between the Honourable East-India Company and Maha Rawal Mulraj, the Raja of Jaisalmer, his heirs and successors, the latter agreeing "to act in subordinate co-operation with the British Government, and with submission to its supremacy."[2] This was almost the last act of Rawal Mulraj, who had always been a mere puppet in the hands of Mehta Salim Singh or his father. He died A.D. 1820, when his grandson, Gaj Singh, was proclaimed.

[1] [A.D. 1762.]

[2] See Appendix No. III. for a copy of this treaty. [See end of Vol. III.]

Maharāwal Gaj Singh, A.D. **1820-46.**—Rawal Gaj Singh was fitted, from his years, his past seclusion, and the examples which had occurred before his eyes, to be the submissive pageant Salim Singh required. Isolated, in every sense, from intercourse with the rest of mankind, by the [271] policy of the minister, he had no community of sympathy with them, and no claim upon their aid. Surrounded by the creatures of Salim Singh, who, even to their daily dole, ascribe everything to this man's favour, each word, each gesture, is watched and reported. The prince himself, his wives and family, are alike dependents on the minister's bounty, often capriciously exercised. If he requires a horse, he must solicit it; or if desirous of bestowing some recompense, he requests to be furnished with the means, and deems himself fortunate if he obtain a moiety of his suit.

It will be observed from the date of this treaty (Dec. 1818), that Jaisalmer was the last of the States of India received under the protection of the British Government. Its distance made it an object of little solicitude to us; and the minister, it is said, had many long and serious consultations with his oracles before he united his destiny with ours. He doubted the security of his power if the Rawal should become subordinate to the British Government; and he was only influenced by the greater risk of being the sole State in Rajwara without the pale of its protection, which would have left him to the mercy of those enemies whom his merciless policy had created around him. The third and most important article of the treaty [1] tranquillized his apprehensions as to external foes; with these apprehensions all fear as to the consequences arising from ministerial tyranny towards the princely exiles was banished, and we shall presently find that this alliance, instead of checking his rapacity and oppression, incited them. But it is necessary, in the first place, to bestow a few remarks on the policy of the alliance as regards the British Government.

The Treaty of Alliance.—Its inequality requires no demonstration; the objects to be attained by it to the respective parties

[1] Art. III. "In the event of any serious invasion directed towards the overthrow of the principality of Jessulmer, or other danger of great magnitude occurring to that principality, the British Government will exert its power for the protection of the principality, provided that the cause of the quarrel be not ascribable to the Raja of Jessulmer."

having no approximation to parity. The advantages to Jaisalmer were immediate; and to use the phraseology of the treaty, were not only of "great magnitude," but were vitally important. From the instant the treaties were exchanged, her existence as a permanent State, which was not worth half a century's purchase, was secured. Her power had been gradually declining, and reign after reign was narrowing her possessions to the vicinity of the capital. One State, Bahawalpur, had been formed from her northern territory; while those of Sind, Bikaner, and Jodhpur, had been greatly aggrandized at her expense; and all were inclined, as occasion arose, to encroach upon her feebleness. The faithless character of the minister, Salim Singh [272], afforded abundant pretexts for quarrel, and the anarchy of her neighbours proved her only safeguard during the later years of her independent existence. Now, the British Government having pledged itself to exert its power for the protection of the principality, in the event of any "serious invasion," her fears either of Sindis, Daudputras, or of Rathors, are at rest. The full extent of this pledge may not have been contemplated when it was given; like all former alliances, it is the base of another step in advance. Instead of restricting the vast circle of our political connexions, it at once carried us out of India, placing us in actual contact and possible collision with the rulers of Sind and the people beyond the Indus. Marwar and Bikaner being already admitted to our alliance, the power of settling their feuds with the Bhattis is comparatively simple; but with Daudputra we have no political connexions, and with Sind, only those of "perpetual friendship and mutual intercourse"; but no stipulation ensuring respect to our remonstrances in case of the aggression of their subjects on our Bhatti ally. Are we then to push our troops through the desert to repel such acts, or must we furnish pecuniary subsidies (the cheapest mode), that she may entertain mercenaries for that object? We must view it, in this light, as an event, not only not improbable, but of very likely occurrence. Our alliance with Cutch involved us in this perplexity in 1819. Our armies were formed and moved to the frontier, and a declaration of war was avoided only by accepting a tardy *amende* in no way commensurate with the insult of invading, massacring, and pillaging our allies.[1] In this instance, our means of chastisement

[1] The attitude assumed by the energetic governor of Bombay, Mr.

were facilitated by our maritime power of grappling with the enemy; but if the insult proceeds from the government of Upper Sind (only nominally dependent on Haidarabad), or from Bahawalpur, how are we to cope with these enemies of our ally? Such wars might lead us into a *terra incognita* beyond the Indus, or both the spirit and letter of the treaty will be null.

The Strategical Importance of Jaisalmer.—What, therefore, are the advantages we can hold out to ourselves for the volunteer of our amity and protection to this oasis of the desert? To have disregarded the appeal of Jaisalmer for protection, to have made her the sole exception in all Rajputana from our amicable relations, would have been to consign her to her numerous enemies, and to let loose the spirit of rapine and revenge, which it was the main object [273] of all these treaties to suppress; the Bhattis would have become a nation of robbers, the Bedouins of the Indian desert. Jaisalmer was the first link in a chain of free States, which formerly united the commerce of the Ganges with that of the Indus, but which interminable feuds had completely severed; the possibility of reunion depending upon a long continuance of tranquillity and confidence. This object alone would have warranted our alliance with Jaisalmer. But if we look to futurity, to the possible invasion of India, which can be best effected through the maritime provinces of Persia, the valley of the Indus will be the base of the invader's operations. The possession of Jaisalmer would then be of vital importance, by giving us the command of Upper Sind, and enabling us to act against the enemy simultaneously with our armies east of the Delta, the most practicable point of advance into India. We may look upon invasion by the ancient routes pursued by Alex-

Elphinstone, on that occasion, will for a long time remain a lesson to the triumvirate government of Sind. To the Author it still appears a subject of regret, that, with the adequate preparation, the season, and everything promising a certainty of success, the pacific tone of Lord Hastings' policy should have prevented the proper assertion of our dignity, by chastising an insult, aggravated in every shape. A treaty of amity and mutual intercourse was the result of this armament; but although twelve years have since elapsed, our intercourse has remained *in statu quo*; but this is no ground for quarrel. [Rāo Bharmall of Cutch, on account of his disloyalty to the British Government, was coerced by a force commanded by Captain MacMurdo, the Resident, which, on 25th March 1819, escaladed the fort of Bhuj, and compelled the Rāo to surrender (*BG*, v. 162).]

ander, Mahmud, and Timur, as utterly visionary, by an army encumbered with all the *matériel* necessary to success, and thus the valley of Sind presents the only practicable route. But it would be a grand error, both in a political and military point of view, to possess ourselves of this valley, even if an opportunity were again to occur. It is true, the resources of that fertile region, so analogous to Egypt, would soon, under our management, maintain an army sufficient to defend it; and this would bring us at once into contact with the power (Persia) which clings to us for support, and will be adverse to us only when rendered subservient to Russia. It were well to view the possible degradation and loss of power to Russia, in Europe, as likely to afford a fresh stimulant to her ancient schemes of oriental aggrandizement. By some these schemes are looked upon as Quixotic, and I confess myself to be of the number. The better Russia is acquainted with the regions she would have to pass, the less desire will she evince for an undertaking, which, even if successful in the outset, would be useless; for if she conquered, she could not maintain India.[1] But, to me, it still appears imperative that this power should formally renounce such designs; the state of perpetual preparation rendered necessary by her menacing position, being so injurious to our finances, is worse than the actual attempt, which would only entail upon her inevitable loss. We lost, through our unwise economy, a noble opportunity of maintaining an ascendancy at the court of Kabul, which would have been easily prevailed upon, for our pecuniary aid, to make over to us the sovereignty of Sind (were this desirable), which is still considered a grand division of Kabul.

But setting the political question aside, and considering our possession of the [274] valley of Sind only in a military point of view, our occupation of it would be prejudicial to us. We should have a long line to defend, and rivers are no barriers in modern warfare. Whilst an impassable desert is between us, and we have the power, by means of our allies, of assailing an enemy at several points, though we are liable to attack but from one, an invader could not maintain himself a single season. On this ground, the maintenance of friendship with this remote nook of Rajput civilization is defensible, and we have the additional incitement of rescuing the most industrious and wealthy commercial com-

[1] [This prediction has been fulfilled by recent events.]

munities in India from the fangs of a harpy; to whom, and the enormities of his government, we return.

Effect of the Treaty on the Policy of Sālim Singh.—No language can adequately represent the abuse of power with which the treaty has armed the rapacious minister of Jaisalmer, and it is one of the many instances of the inefficacy of our system of alliances to secure prosperity, or even tranquillity to these long-afflicted regions; which, although rescued from external assailants, are still the prey of discord and passion within. It will not be difficult, at the proper time and place, to make this appear.[1] The Mehta felt the advantages which the treaty gave him, in respect to neighbouring States; but he also felt that he had steeped himself too deeply in the blood of his master's family, and in that of his noblest chieftains, to hope that any repentance, real or affected, could restore to him the confidence of those he had so outraged. With commercial men, with the industrious husbandman or pastoral communities, he had so long forfeited all claim to credit, that his oath was not valued at a single grain of the sand of their own desert dominion.

The bardic annalist of Rajputana, when compelled to record the acts of a tyrant, first announces his moral death; then comes the metempsychosis—the animating his frame with the spirit of a demon. In this manner is delineated the famed Bisaldeo, the Chauhan king of Ajmer. Whether the Bhatti minister will obtain such a posthumous apology for his misdeeds, a future historian will learn; but assuredly he is never mentioned, either in poetry or prose, but as a vampire, draining the life-blood of a whole people. For a short time after the treaty was formed, he appeared to fall in with the march of universal reformation; but whether it was that his crimes had outlawed him from the sympathies of all around, or that he could feel no enjoyment but in his habitual crimes, he soon gave indulgence to his rapacious spirit. The cause of his temporary forbearance was attributed to his anxiety to have [275] an article added to the treaty, guaranteeing the office of prime minister in his family, perhaps with a view to legalize his plunder; but seeing no hope of fixing an hereditary

[1] It is my intention (if space is left) to give a concise statement of the effects of our alliances, individually and collectively, in the States of Rajwara, with a few hints towards amending the system, at the conclusion of this volume. [This was not done.]

race of vampires on the land, his outrages became past all endurance, and compelled the British agent, at length, to report to his government (on December 17, 1821), that he considered the alliance disgraceful to our reputation, by countenancing the idea that such acts can be tolerated under its protection. Representations to the minister were a nullity; he protested against their fidelity; asserted in specious language his love of justice and mercy; and recommenced his system of confiscations, contributions, and punishments, with redoubled severity.

Misgovernment of Sālim Singh.—All Rajwara felt an interest in these proceedings, as the bankers of Jaisalmer, supported by the capital of that singular class, the Paliwals, are spread all over India. But this rich community, amounting to five thousand families, are nearly all in voluntary exile, and the bankers fear to return to their native land with the fruits of their industry, which they would renounce for ever, but that he retains their families as hostages. Agriculture is almost unknown, and commerce, internal or external, has ceased through want of security. The sole revenue arises from confiscation. It is asserted that the minister has amassed no less than *two crores*, which wealth is distributed in the various cities of Hindustan, and has been obtained by pillage and the destruction of the most opulent families of his country during the last twenty years. He has also, it is said, possessed himself of all the crown-jewels and property of value, which he has sent out of the country. Applications were continually being made to the British agent for passports (*parwanas*), by commercial men, to withdraw their families from the country. But all have some ties which would be hazarded by their withdrawing, even if such a step were otherwise free from danger; for while the minister afforded passports, in obedience to the wish of the agent, he might cut them off in the desert. This makes many bear the ills they have.[1]

[1] [" Up to 1823 Sālim Singh constantly urged, in the name of his master, claims to the territories of other chiefs, but these were rejected as the investigation of them was inconsistent with the engagements subsisting between the British Government and other States. In 1824 Sālim Singh was wounded by a Rājput, and as there was some fear that the wound might heal, his wife gave him poison." [Some support was given for the succession of his eldest son as prime minister, but the British Government declined to interfere in the appointment or punishment of a minister, on which all parties returned to their allegiance, and Rāwal Gaj Singh assumed personal charge of the administration (Erskine iii. A. 15 f.).]

A Border Feud.—We shall terminate our historical sketch of Jaisalmer with the details of a border feud, which called into operation the main condition of the British alliance—the right of universal arbitration in the international quarrels of Rajputana. The predatory habits of the Maldots of Baru originated a rupture, which threatened to involve the two States in war, and produced an invasion of the Rathors, sufficiently serious to warrant British interference. It will hardly be credited that this aggression, which drew down upon the Maldots the vengeance of Bikaner, was covertly stimulated by the minister, for the express purpose of their extirpation, for reasons which will [276] appear presently; yet he was the first to complain of the retaliation. To understand this matter, a slight sketch of the Maldot tribe is requisite.

The Maldot Tribe.—The Maldots, the Kailans, the Birsangs, the Pohars, and Tejmalots, are all Bhatti tribes; but, from their lawless habits, these names have become, like those of Bedouin, Kazzak, or Pindari, synonymous with 'robber.' The first are descended from Rao Maldeo, and hold the fief (*patta*) of Baru, consisting of eighteen villages, adjoining the tract called Kharipatta, wrested from the Bhattis by the Rathors of Bikaner, who, to confess the truth, morally deserve the perpetual hostility of this Bhatti lord-marcher, inasmuch as they were the intruders, and have deprived them (the Bhattis) of much territory. But the Rathors, possessing the right of the strongest, about twenty-five years ago exercised it in the most savage manner; for, having invaded Baru, they put almost the entire community to the sword, without respect to age or sex, levelled the towns, filled up the wells, and carried off the herds and whatever was of value. The survivors took shelter in the recesses of the desert, and propagated a progeny, which, about the period of connexion with the British, reoccupied their deserted lands. The minister, it is asserted, beheld the revival of this infant colony with no more favourable eye than did their enemies of Bikaner, whom, it is alleged, he invited once more to their destruction. The lawless habits of this tribe would have been assigned by the minister as his motive for desiring their extermination; but if we look back (p. 1232), we shall discover the real cause in his having incurred the lasting enmity of this clan for the foul assassination of their chief, who had been a party to the views of the heir-apparent, Rae Singh, to get rid of this incubus on their freedom. The opportunity afforded to take vengeance on the Maldots arose out of a service indirectly done to the British Government. On the revolt of the Peshwa, he sent his agents to Jaisalmer to purchase camels. One herd, to the number of four hundred, had left the Bhatti frontiers, and whilst passing through the Bikaner territory, were set upon by the Maldots, who captured the whole and conveyed them to Baru. It is scarcely to be supposed that such an aggression on the independence of Bikaner would have prompted her extensive armament, or the rapidity with which her troops passed the Bhatti frontier to avenge the insult, without some private signal from the minister, who was loud in his call for British interference; though not until Nokh [1] and Baru, their principal towns, were levelled, the chief killed, the wells filled up, and the victorious army following up its success by a rapid march on Bikampur, in which the fiscal lands began to suffer. The minister then discovered he had overshot the mark, and claimed [277] our interference,[2] which was rapid and effectual; and the Bikaner commander the more willingly complied with the request to retire within his own frontier, having effected more than his object.

The tortuous policy, the never-ending and scarcely-to-be-comprehended border feuds of these regions, must, for a long while, generate such appeals. Since these associated bands attach no dishonour to their predatory profession, it will be some time before they acquire proper notions; but when they discover there is no retreat in which punishment may not reach them, they will learn the benefits of cultivating the arts of peace, of whose very name no trace exists in their history.

We have lost sight of the Rawal, the title of the prince of Jaisalmer, in the prominent acts of his minister. Gaj Singh, who occupies the *gaddi* of Jaisal, to the prejudice of his elder brothers, who are still in exile in Bikaner, appears very well suited to the minister's purpose, and to have little desire beyond his horses, and vegetating in quiet. The physiognomists of Jaisalmer,

[1] [Nokh, 96 miles N.E. of Jaisalmer city.]

[2] The Author has omitted to mention that he was political agent for Jaisalmer; so that his control extended uninterruptedly, almost from Sind to Sind; *i.e.* from the Indus, or great Sindh, to the Chhota-Sindh, or little river (see map). There are several streams designated Sindh, in Central India, a word purely Tatar, or Scythic. Abusin, 'the Father-river,' is one of the many names of the Indus. [Sindhu is a Sanskrit word, probably connected with the root *syand*, 'to flow.']

however, prognosticate the development of moral worth in due season; a consummation devoutly to be wished, and the first symptom of which must be the riddance of his minister by whatever process. The artful Salim deemed that it would redound to his credit, and bolster up his interest, to seek a matrimonial alliance with the Rana's family of Mewar. The overture was accepted, and the coco-symbol transmitted to the Rawal, who put himself at the head of the Bhatti chivalry to wed and escort his bride through the desert. The Rathor princes of Bikaner and Kishangarh, who were at the same time suitors for the hands of another daughter and a granddaughter of the Rana, simultaneously arrived at Udaipur with their respective cortèges; and this triple alliance threw a degree of splendour over the capital of the Sesodias, to which it had long been a stranger. Gaj Singh lives very happily with his wife, who has given him an heir to his desert domain. The influence of high rank is seen in the respect paid to the Ranawatji (the title by which she is designated), even by the minister, and she exerts this influence most humanely for the amelioration of her subjects [1] [278].

CHAPTER 7

Geography of Jaisalmer.—The country still dependent on the Rawal extends between 70° 30′ and 72° 30′ E. long., and between the parallels of 26° 20′ and 27° 50′ N. lat., though a small strip protrudes, in the N.-E. angle, as high as 28° 30′. This irregular surface may be roughly estimated to contain fifteen thousand square miles.[2] The number of towns, villages, and hamlets,

[1] I had the honour of receiving several letters from this queen of the desert, who looked to her father's house and his friends, as the best objects for support, whilst such a being as Sālim was the master of her own and her husband's destiny. [Gaj Singh earned the special thanks of the British Government for his services in supplying camel transport in the Afghān war of 1838-39; and in 1844, after the conquest of Sind, the forts of Shāhgarh, Gharsia, and Ghotāru, which had formerly belonged to Jaisalmer, were restored to that State. Gaj Singh died without issue in 1846, and his widow adopted his nephew, Ranjīt Singh, who died without an heir in 1864 (Erskine iii. A. 16).]

[2] [The State, according to later surveys, lies between 26° 4′ and 28° 23′ N. lat. and 69° 30′ and 72° 42′ E. long., with an area of 16,062 square miles.

scattered over this wide space, does not exceed two hundred and fifty; some estimate it at three hundred, and others depress it to two hundred; the mean cannot be wide of the truth. To enable the reader to arrive at a conclusion as to the population of this region, we subjoin a calculation, from data furnished by the best-informed natives, which was made in the year 1815; but we must add, that from the tyranny of the minister, the population of the capital (which is nearly half of the country), has been greatly diminished.

Towns.	Fiscal and Feudal.	Number of Houses.	Number of Inhabitants.	Remarks.
Jaisalmer	Capital	7,000	35,000	
Bikampur	Pattayat	500	2,000	The chief has the title of Rao, and twenty-four villages dependent, not included in this estimate.
Sirara	Do.	300	1,200	Kelan Bhatti: the Kelan tribe extends to Pugal.
Nachna	Do.	400	1,600	Rawalot chief.
Katori	Fiscal	300	1,200	
Kaba	Do.	300	1,200	
Kuldaro	Do.	200	800	
Satta	Pattayat	300	1,200 [279]	Rawalot: first noble of Jaisalmer.
Jinjiniali	Do.	300	1,200	
Devi-Kot	Fiscal	200	800	
Bhap	Do.	200	800	
Balana	Pattayat	150	600	
Satiasa	Do.	100	400	
Barn	Do.	200	800	Maldot: has eighteen villages attached, not included in this.
Chaun	Do.	200	800	
Loharki	Do.	150	600	
Noantala	Do.	150	600	All of the Rawalot clan.
Lahti	Do.	300	1,200	
Dangari	Do.	150	600	
Bijorai	Fiscal	200	800	
Mandal	Do.	200	800	
Ramgarh	Do.	200	800	
Birsalpur	Pattayat	200	800	
Girajsar	Do.	150	600	
			56,400	
Two hundred and twenty-five villages and hamlets, from four to fifty houses each; say, each average twenty, at four inhabitants to each			18,000	
TOTAL . . .			74,400	

According to this census, we have a population not superior

In 1911 the population amounted to 80,891, that of the capital, Jaisalmer, being 7420. There were 471 villages in the State, the average population of which was even lower than of those in Bikaner.]

to one of the secondary cities of Great Britain, scattered over fifteen thousand square miles; nearly one-half, too, belonging to the capital, which being omitted, the result would give from two to three souls only for each square mile.

Face of the Country.—The greater part of Jaisalmer is *thal*, or *rui*, both terms meaning 'a desert waste.' From Lohwar, on the Jodhpur frontier, to Khara, the remote angle touching Sind, the country may be described as a continuous tract of arid sand, frequently rising into lofty *tibas* (sand-hills), in some parts covered with low jungle. This line, which nearly bisects Jaisalmer, is also the line of demarcation of positive sterility and comparative cultivation. To the north is one uniform and naked waste; to the south are ridges of rock termed *magra*, *rui*, and light soil [280].

The ridge of hills is a most important feature in the geology of this desert region.[1] It is to be traced from Cutch Bhuj, strongly or faintly marked, according to the nature of the country. Sometimes it assumes, as at Chhotan, the character of a mountain; then dwindles into an insignificant ridge scarcely discernible, and often serves as a bulwark for the drifting sands, which cover and render it difficult to trace it at all. As it reaches the Jaisalmer country it is more developed; and at the capital, erected on a peak about two hundred and fifty feet high, its presence is more distinct, and its character defined. The capital of the Bhattis appears as the nucleus of a series of ridges, which diverge from it in all directions for the space of fifteen miles. One branch terminates at Ramgarh, thirty-five miles north-west of Jaisalmer; another branch extends easterly to Pokaran (in Jodhpur), and thence, in a north-east direction, to Phalodi; from whence, at intervals, it is traceable to Gariala, nearly fifty miles due north. It is a yellow-coloured sandstone, in which ochre is abundantly found, with which the people daub their houses.

These barren ridges, and the lofty undulating *tibas* of sand, are the only objects which diversify the almost uniform sterility of these regions. No trees interpose their verdant foliage to relieve the eye, or shelter the exhausted frame of the traveller. It is nearly a boundless waste, varied only by a few stunted shrubs of the acacia or mimosa family, some succulent plants, or prickly

[1] [Rocks of Jurassic age, such as sandstone, shales, and limestone, crop up beneath the sand, and a large area of Nummulitic rock occurs to the N.W. of the capital (*IGI*, xiv. 1).]

grasses, as the *bharut*[1] or burr, which clings to his garment and increases his miseries. Yet compared with the more northern portion, where "a sea of sand without a sign of vegetation"[2] forms the prospect, the vicinity of the capital is a paradise.

There is not a running stream throughout Jaisalmer; but there are many temporary lakes or salt-marshes, termed *sar*, formed by the collection of waters from the sand-hills, which are easily dammed in to prevent escape. They are ephemeral, seldom lasting but a few months; though after a very severe monsoon they have been known to remain throughout the year. One of these, called the Kanod Sar, extends from Kanod[3] to Mohangarh, covering a space of eighteen miles, and in which some water remains throughout the year. When it overflows, a small stream issues from the Sar, and pursues an easterly direction for thirty miles before it is absorbed; its existence [281] depends on the parent lake. The salt which it produces is the property of the crown, and adds something to the revenue.

Soil, Husbandry, and Products.—Notwithstanding the apparent poverty of this desert soil, nature has not denied it the powers of production; it is even favourable to some grains, especially the bajra, which prefers a light sand. In a favourable season they grow sufficient for the consumption of two and even three years, and then they import only wheat from Sind. When those parts favourable for bajra have been saturated with two or three heavy showers, they commence sowing, and the crops spring up rapidly. The great danger is that of too much rain when the crops are advanced, for, having little tenacity, they are often washed away. The *bajra* of the sand-hills is deemed far superior to that of Hindustan, and prejudice gives it a preference even to wheat, which does not bear a higher price, in times of scarcity. Bajra, in plentiful seasons, sells at one and a half maunds for a rupee;[4]

[1] [*Cenchrus catharticus.*]

[2] So Mr. Elphinstone describes the tract about Pugal, one of the earliest possessions of the Bhattis, and one of the Naukotī Maru-ki, or 'nine castles of the desert,' around whose sand-hills as brave a colony was reared and maintained as ever carried lance. Rao Raning was lord of Pugal, whose son originated that episode given on p. 733. Even these sand-hills which in November appeared to Mr. Elphinstone without a sign of vegetation, could be made to yield good crops of bajra.

[3] [About 20 miles N.W. of Jaisalmer city.]

[4] About a hundredweight for two shillings.

but this does not often occur, as they calculate five bad seasons for a good one. Juar is also grown, but only in the low flats. Cotton is produced in the same soil as the bajra. It is not generally known that this plant requires but a moderate supply of water ; it is deteriorated in the plains of India from over-irrigation; at least such is the idea of the desert-farmer, who perhaps does not make sufficient allowance for the cooler substratum of his sand-hills, compared with the black loam of Malwa. A variety of pulses grows on the sheltered sides of the *tibas*, as *mung*, *moth*, etc. ; also the oil-plant (*til*) and abundance of the *gawar*, a diminutive melon, not larger than a hen's egg, which is sent hundreds of miles, as a rarity. Around the capital, and between the ridges where soil is deposited or formed, and where they dam up the waters, are grown considerable quantities of wheat of very good quality, turmeric, and garden-stuffs. Barley and gram are, in good seasons, reared in small quantities, but rice is entirely an article of import from the valley of Sind.

Implements of Husbandry.—Where the soil is light, it will be concluded that the implements are simple. They have two kinds of plough, for one or two oxen, or for the camel, which animal is most in requisition. They tread out the grain with oxen, as in all parts of India, and not unfrequently they yoke the cattle to their hakerries,[1] or carts, and pass the whole over the grain.

Manufactures.—There is little scope for the ingenuity of the mechanic in this tract. They make coarse cotton cloths, but the raw material is almost all exported. Their grand article of manufacture is from the wool of the sheep pastured in the desert [282], which is fabricated into *lois*, or blankets, scarfs,[2] petticoats, turbans, of every quality. Cups and platters are made from a mineral called *abrak*, a calcareous substance, of a dark chocolate ground, with light brown vermiculated stripes ;[3] female ornaments of elephants' teeth, and arms of an inferior quality. These comprehend the artificial productions of this desert capital.

Commerce.—Whatever celebrity Jaisalmer possesses, as a commercial mart, arises from its position as a place of transit

[1] [Hindustāni *chhakra*, 'a cart' (Yule, *Hobson-Jobson*, 2nd ed. 407 f.).]

[2] I brought home several pairs of these, with crimson borders, sufficiently fine to be worn as a winter shawl in this country.

[3] [Commonly known as soapstone or potstone, a soft magnesian or talcose mineral (Watt, *Comm. Prod.* 1049 f.).]

between the eastern countries, the valley of the Indus, and those beyond that stream, the Kitars (the term for a caravan of camels) to and from Haidarabad, Rori-Bakhar, Shikarpur and Uchh, from the Gangetic provinces, and the Panjab, passing through it. The indigo of the Duab, the opium of Kotah and Malwa, the famed sugar-candy of Bikaner, iron implements from Jaipur, are exported to Shikarpur [1] and lower Sind; whence elephants' teeth (from Africa), dates, coco-nuts, drugs, and chandan,[2] are imported, with pistachios and dried fruits from Bahawalpur.

Revenues and Taxes.—The personal revenue of the princes of Jaisalmer [3] is, or rather was, estimated at upwards of four lakhs of rupees, of which more than one lakh was from the land.[4] The transit duties were formerly the most certain and most prolific branch of the fiscal income; but the bad faith of the minister, the predatory habits of the Bhatti chiefs proceeding mainly from thence, and the general decrease of commerce, have conspired nearly to annihilate this source of income, said at one time to reach three lakhs of rupees. These imposts are termed *dan*, and the collector *dani*, who was stationed at convenient points of all the principal routes which diverge from the capital.

Land-tax.—From one-fifth to one-seventh of the gross produce of the land is set aside as the tax of the crown, never exceeding the first nor falling short of the last.[5] It is paid in kind, which is purchased on the spot by the Paliwal Brahmans, or Banias, and the value remitted to the treasury [283].

[1] Shikarpur, the great commercial mart of the valley of Sind, west of the Indus.

[2] Chandan is a scented wood, for *malas*, or 'chaplets.' [Sandalwood, *Pterocarpus santalinus* (Watt, *Comm. Prod.* 909).]

[3] I have no correct data for estimating the revenues of the chieftains. They are generally almost double the land-revenue of the princes in the other States of Rajwara; perhaps about two lakhs, which ought to bring into the field seven hundred horse.

[4] [The normal revenue at present is about one lakh of rupees. The transit duties have been largely reduced.]

[5] This, if strictly true and followed, is according to ancient principles; Manu ordains the sixth. I could have wished Colonel Briggs to have known this fact, when he was occupied on his excellent work on *The Land-tax of India*; but it had entirely escaped my recollection. In this most remote corner of Hindustan, in spite of oppression, it is curious to observe the adherence to primitive custom. These notes on the sources of revenue in Jaisalmer were communicated to me so far back as 1811, and I laid them before the Bengal Government in 1814–15.

Dhuan.—The third and now the most certain branch of revenue is the *dhuan*, literally 'smoke,' and which we may render 'chimney or hearth-tax,' though they have neither the one nor the other in these regions. It is also termed *thali*, which is the brass or silver platter out of which they eat, and is tantamount to a table-allowance. It never realizes above twenty thousand rupees annually, which, however, would be abundant for the simple fare of Jaisalmer. No house is exempt from the payment of this tax.

Dand.—There is an arbitrary tax levied throughout these regions, universally known and detested under the name of *dand*, the make-weight of all their budgets of ways and means. It was first imposed in Jaisalmer in S. 1830 (A.D. 1774), under the less odious appellation of 'additional *dhuan* or *thali*,' and the amount was only two thousand seven hundred rupees, to be levied from the monied interest of the capital. The Mahesris [1] agreed to pay their share, but the Oswals (the two chief mercantile classes) holding out, were forcibly sent up to the castle, and suffered the ignominious punishment of the bastinado. They paid the demand, but immediately on their release entered into a compact on oath, never again to look on the Rawal's (Mulraj's) face, which was religiously kept during their mutual lives. When he passed through the streets of his capital, the Oswals abandoned their shops and banking-houses, retiring to the interior of their habitations in order to avoid the sight of him. This was strenuously persevered in for many years, and had such an effect upon the prince, that he visited the principal persons of this class, and 'spreading his scarf' (*pala pasarna*),[2] intreated forgiveness, giving a writing on oath never again to impose *dand*, if they would make the *dhuan* a permanent tax. The Oswals accepted the repentance of their prince, and agreed to his terms. In S. 1841 and 1852, his necessities compelling him to raise money, he obtained by loan, in the first period, twenty-seven thousand, and in the latter, forty thousand rupees, which he faithfully

[1] [The Mahesri trading class, which derive their name from that of their caste deity, Mahesh, 'the great lord,' a title of Siva or Mahādeo, claim descent from Chauhān, Parihār, or Solanki Rājputs (*Census Report, Mārwār*, 1891, ii. 131).]

[2] *Pala pasārna*, or 'to spread the cloth or scarf,' is the figurative language of entreaty, arising from the act of spreading the garment, preparatory to bowing the head thereon in token of perfect submission.

repaid. When the father of the present minister came into power, he endeavoured to get back the bond of his sovereign abrogating the obnoxious *dand*, and offered, as a bait, to renounce the *dhuan*. The Oswals placed more value on the virtue of this instrument than it merited, for in spite of the bond, he in S. 1857 levied sixty thousand, and in 1863, eighty thousand rupees. A visit of the Rawal to the Ganges was seized upon as a fit opportunity by his subjects to get this oppression redressed, and fresh oaths were made by the prince, and broken by the minister, who has bequeathed his rapacious spirit to his son [284].

Since the accession of Gaj Singh, only two years ago,[1] Salim Singh has extorted fourteen lakhs (£140,000). Bardhman, a merchant of great wealth and respectability, and whose ancestors are known and respected throughout Rajwara as Sahukars, has been at various times stripped of all his riches by the minister and his father, who, to use the phraseology of the sufferers, "will never be satisfied while a rupee remains in Jaisalmer."

Establishments, Expenditure.—We subjoin a rough estimate of the household establishment, etc., of this desert king:

	Rupees.
Bar[2]	20,000
Rozgar Sardar[3]	40,000
Sihbandis or Mercenaries[4]	75,000
Household horse, 10 elephants, 200 camels, and chariots	36,000
Carry forward . .	171,000

[1] This was written in 1821–22.

[2] The *Bar* includes the whole household or personal attendants, the guards, and slaves. They receive rations of food, and make up the rest of their subsistence by labour in the town. The *Bar* consists of about 1000 people, and is estimated to cost 20,000 rupees annually.

[3] Rozgar-Sardar is an allowance termed *kansa*, or 'dinner,' to the feudal chieftains who attend the Presence. Formerly they had an order upon the Danis, or collectors of the transit-duties; but being vexatious, Pansa Sah, minister to Rawal Chaitra, commuted it for a daily allowance, varying, with the rank of the person, from half a silver rupee to seven rupees each, daily. This disbursement is calculated at 40,000 rupees annually.

[4] Sihbandis are mercenary soldiers in the fort, of whom 1000 are estimated to cost 75,000 rupees annually. [The word seems to mean 'persons paid quarterly' (Yule, *Hobson-Jobson*, 2nd ed. 805).]

	Rupees.
Brought forward . .	171,000
500 Bargir[1] horse	60,000
Rani's or queen's establishment . . .	15,000
The wardrobe	5,000
Gifts	5,000
The kitchen	5,000
Guests, in hospitality	5,000
Feasts, entertainments	5,000
Annual purchase of horses, camels, oxen, etc.	20,000
TOTAL . .	Rs. 291,000

The ministers and officers of government receive assignments on the transit-duties, and some have lands. The whole of this State-expenditure was more than covered, in some years, by the transit-duties alone; which have, it is asserted, amounted to the almost incredible sum of three lakhs, or £30,000.

Tribes.—We shall conclude our account of Jaisalmer with a few remarks on the [285] tribes peculiar to it; though we reserve the general enumeration for a sketch of the desert.

Of its Rajput population, the Bhattis, we have already given an outline in the general essay on the tribes.[2] Those which occupy the present limits of Jaisalmer retain their Hindu notions, though with some degree of laxity from their intercourse with the Muhammadans on the northern and western frontiers; while those which long occupied the north-east tracts, towards Phulra and the Gara, on becoming proselytes to Islam ceased to have either interest in or connexion with the parent State. The Bhatti has not, at present, the same martial reputation as the Rathor, Chauhan, or Sesodia, but he is deemed at least to equal if not surpass the Kachhwaha, or any of its kindred branches, Naruka or Shaikhavat. There are occasional instances of Bhatti intrepidity as daring as may be found amongst any other tribe; witness the feud between the chiefs of Pugal and Mandor. But this changes not the national characteristic as conventionally established; though were we to go back to the days of chivalry

[1] [A man riding his own horse was called Silahdār, 'equipment-holder'; one riding a horse belonging to the State or to some one else was Bārgīr, 'burden-taker' (Irvine, *Army of the Indian Moghuls*, 37).]

[2] Vol. I. p. 102.

and Prithiraj, we should select Achalesa Bhatti, one of the bravest of his champions, for the portrait of his race. The Bhatti Rajput, as to physical power, is not perhaps so athletic as the Rathor, or so tall as the Kachhwaha, but generally fairer than either, and possessing those Jewish features which Mr. Elphinstone remarked as characteristic of the Bikaner Rajputs. The Bhatti intermarries with all the families of Rajwara, though seldom with the Ranas of Mewar. The late Jagat Singh of Jaipur had five wives of this stock, and his posthumous son, real or reputed, has a Bhattiani for his mother.[1]

Dress.—The dress of the Bhattis consists of a *jama*, or tunic of white cloth or chintz reaching to the knee ; the *kamarband*, or ceinture, tied so high as to present no appearance of waist ; trousers very loose, and in many folds, drawn tight at the ankle, and a turban, generally of a scarlet colour, rising conically full a foot from the head. A dagger is stuck in the waistband ; a shield is suspended by a thong of deer-skin from the left shoulder, and the sword is girt by a belt of the same material. The dress of the common people is the *dhoti*, or loin-robe, generally of woollen stuff, with a piece of the same material as a turban. The dress of the Bhattianis, which discriminates the sex, consists of a *ghaghra*, or petticoat, extending to thirty feet in width, made generally of the finer woollen, dyed a brilliant red, with a scarf of the same material. The grand ornament of rich and poor, though varying in the materials, is the *churi*, or rings of ivory or bone, with which they cover their arms from the shoulder to [286] the wrist.[2] They are in value from sixteen to thirty-five

[1] [Bhatti women have a reputation for strength and beauty. One of them was the mother of Fīroz Shāh Tughlak (Elliot-Dowson iii. 272).]

[2] The churi of ivory, bone, or shell is the most ancient ornament of the Indo-Scythic dames, and appears in old sculpture and painting. [For bangles made of conch-shell, see J. Hornell, *The Sacred Chank of India*, Madras, 1914.] I was much struck with some ancient sculptures in a very old Gothic church at Moissac, in Languedoc. The porch is the only part left of this most antique fane, attributed to the age of Dagobert. It represents the conversion of Clovis, and when the subject was still a matter of novelty. But interesting as this is, it is as nothing when compared to some sculptured figures below, of a totally distinct age ; in execution as far superior as they are dissimilar in character, which is decidedly Asiatic ; the scarf, the *champakali* or necklace, representing the buds of the jessamine (*champa*); and *churis*, such as I have been describing. To whom but the Visigoths can we ascribe them ?—and does not this supply the connecting

rupees a set, and imported from Maskat-Mandavi, though they also manufacture them at Jaisalmer. Silver *karis* (massive rings or anklets) are worn by all classes, who deny themselves the necessaries of life until they attain this ornament. The poorer Rajputnis are very masculine, and assist in all the details of husbandry.

Use of Opium.—The Bhatti is to the full as addicted as any of his brethren to the immoderate use of opium. To the *amalpani*, or 'infusion,' succeeds the pipe, and they continue inhaling mechanically the smoke long after they are insensible to all that is passing around them; nay, it is said, you may scratch or pinch them while in this condition without exciting sensation. The *hukka* is the dessert to the *amalpani*; the panacea for all the ills which can overtake a Rajput, and with which he can at any time enjoy a paradise of his own creation. To ask a Bhatti for a whiff of his pipe would be deemed a direct insult.

Pāliwāls.—Next to the lordly Rajputs, equalling them in numbers and far surpassing them in wealth, are the Paliwals. They are Brahmans, and denominated Paliwal from having been temporal proprietors of Pali, and all its lands, long before the Rathors colonized Marwar. Tradition is silent as to the manner in which they became possessed of this domain; but it is connected with the history of the Pali, or pastoral tribes, who from the town of Pali to Palitana, in Saurashtra, have left traces of their existence;[1] and I am much mistaken if it will not one day be demonstrated, that all the ramifications of the races figuratively denominated Agnikula, were Pali in origin; more especially the Chauhans, whose princes and chiefs for ages retained the distinctive affix of *pal*.

These Brahmans, the Paliwals, as appears by the Annals of Marwar, held the domain of Pali when Siahji, at the end of the twelfth century, invaded that land from Kanauj, and by an act of treachery first established his power.[2] It is evident, however, that he did not extirpate them, for the cause of their migration to

link of this Asiatic race, destined to change the moral aspect of Europe? [?] I recommend all travellers, who are interested in tracing such analogies, to visit the church at Moissac, though it is not known as an object of curiosity in the neighbourhood.

[1] [There is no evidence in support of this suggestion.]

[2] See p. 942.

the desert of Jaisalmer [287] is attributed to a period of a Muhammadan invasion of Marwar, when a general war-contribution (*dand*) being imposed on the inhabitants, the Paliwals pleaded caste, and refused. This exasperated the Raja; for as their habits were almost exclusively mercantile, their stake was greater than that of the rest of the community, and he threw their principal men into prison. In order to avenge this, they had recourse to a grand *chandni*, or 'act of suicide'; but instead of gaining their object, he issued a manifesto of banishment to every Paliwal in his dominions. The greater part took refuge in Jaisalmer, though many settled in Bikaner, Dhat, and the valley of Sind. At one time their number in Jaisalmer was calculated to equal that of the Rajputs. Almost all the internal trade of the country passes through their hands, and it is chiefly with their capital that its merchants trade in foreign parts. They are the Metayers of the desert, advancing money to the cultivators, taking the security of the crop; and they buy up all the wool and *ghi* (clarified butter), which they transport to foreign parts. They also rear and keep flocks. The minister, Salim Singh, has contrived to diminish their wealth, and consequently to lose the main support of the country's prosperity. They are also subject to the visits of the Maldots, Tejmallots, and other plunderers; but they find it difficult to leave the country owing to the restrictive cordon of the Mehta. The Paliwals never marry out of their own tribe; and, directly contrary to the laws of Manu,[1] the bridegroom gives a sum of money to the father of the bride. It will be deemed a curious incident in the history of superstition, that a tribe, Brahman by name, at least, should worship the bridle of a horse. When to this is added the fact that the most ancient coins discovered in these regions bear the Pali character and the effigies of the horse, it aids to prove the Scythic character of the early colonists of these regions, who, although nomadic (Pali), were equestrian. There is little doubt that the Paliwal Brahmans are the remains of the priests of the Pali race, who, in their pastoral and commercial pursuits, have lost their spiritual power.[2]

Pokharna Brāhmans.—Another singular tribe, also Brahmanical, is the Pokharna, of whom it is calculated there are fifteen

[1] [*Laws*, iii. 31.]

[2] [For the Pāliwāl Brāhmans see J. Wilson, *Indian Caste*, ii. 119; *Census Report, Mārwār*, 1891, ii. 79 f.]

hundred to two thousand families in Jaisalmer. They are also numerous in Marwar and Bikaner, and are scattered over the desert and valley of the Indus. They follow agricultural and pastoral pursuits chiefly, having little or no concern in trade. The tradition of their origin is singular; it is said that they were Beldars, and excavated the sacred lake of Pushkar or Pokhar, for which act they obtained the favour of the deity and the grade of Brahmans, with the title of Pokharna. Their chief object of emblematic worship, the *kudala*, a kind of pick-axe used in digging, seems to favour this tradition [288].[1]

Jats or Jāts.—The Jats here, as elsewhere, form a great part of the agricultural population; there are also various other tribes, which will be better described in a general account of the desert.

Castle of Jaisalmer.—The castle of this desert king is erected on an almost insulated peak, from two hundred to two hundred and fifty feet in height, a strong wall running round the crest of the hill. It has four gates, but very few cannon mounted. The city is to the north, and is surrounded by a *shahrpanah*, or circumvallation, encompassing a space of nearly three miles, having three gates and two wickets. In the city are some good houses belonging to rich merchants, but the greater part consists of huts. The Raja's palace is said to possess some pretension to grandeur, perhaps comparative.[2] Were he on good terms with his vassalage, he could collect for its defence five thousand infantry and one thousand horse, besides his camel-corps; but it may be doubted whether, under the oppressive system of the monster who has so long continued to desolate that region, one half of this force could be brought together [289].[3]

[1] [See *Census Report, Mārwār*, 1891, ii. 61 ff.]

[2] [The Mahārāvali palace, the top of which is 987 feet above sea-level, surmounts the main entrance of the fort, and is "an imposing pile crowned by a huge umbrella of metal, a solid emblem of dignity of which the Bhatti chiefs are justly proud; but the interior is ill-arranged, and space is frittered away in numberless small apartments" (Erskine iii. A. 38).]

[3] It has been reported that the dagger has since rid the land of its tyrant. The means matter little, if the end is accomplished. Even assassination loses much of its odious character when resorted to for such a purpose. [Gaj Singh died in his bed in 1846.]